✓ Nov 2012

CW00740508

Euston
Knettishall
Hopton
Coney Weston
Market Weston
Theinetham
Redgrave
Wortham
Palgrave
Stuston
Oakley
Fakenham Magna
Barningham
Hinderclay
Thrandeston
Brome
Saptston
Hepworth
Botesdale
Burgate
Mellis
Yaxley
Eye
Honington
Wattisfield
Rickinghall Inferior
Troston
Ixworth Thorpe
Bardwell
Stanton 2
Rickinghall Superior
Gislingham
Thornham Parva
Braiseworth
Great ivermere
Ixworth
Walsham le Willows
Finningham
Westhorpe
Thornham Magna
Stoke Ash
Occold
Redlingfield
Langham
Badwell Ash
Wickham Skeith
Thorndon
Rishangles
Pakenham
Stowlangtoft
Hunston
Great Ashfield
Wyverstone
Cotton
Thwaite
eat Barton
Norton
Bacton
Wetheringsett cum Brockford
Aspall
Thurston
Mendlesham
Rougham
Tostock
Elmswell
Wetherden
Haughley
Old Newton
Gipping
Beyton
Hessett
Woolpit
Harleston
Stowupland
Little melnetham
Bradfield St George
Drinkstone
Spelland
Onehouse
Stowmarket
Creeting St Peter
Bradfield St Clare
Gedding
Rattlesden
Buxhall
Great Finborough
Combs
Creeting All Saints
Bradfield Combust
Felsham
Cockfield
Thorpe Morieux
Brettenham
Little Finborough
heton
Hitcham
Wattisham
Lavenham
Preston
Kettlebaston
Bildeston
Brent Eleigh
Monks Eleigh 1
Chelsworth
Nedging
Naughton
Elmsett
Acton
Little Waldingfield
Milden
Semer
Whatfield
Great Waldingfield
Lindsey
Aldham
Chilton
Edwardstone
Groton
Kersey
Hadleigh 1
Great Cornard
Newton
Layham
Boxford
Little Cornard
Assington
Polstead
Stoke by Nayland
Bures St Mary
Nayland with Wissington

Wills of the County of Suffolk

WILLS OF THE ARCHDEACONRY
OF SUDBURY

1439–1474

WILLS FROM THE REGISTER 'BALDWYNE'

Part II: 1461–1474

SUFFOLK RECORDS SOCIETY

President
Norman Scarfe

Vice-Presidents
James Campbell
David Dymond
Joy Rowe
Bill Serjeant

Chairman
John Blatchly

Co-ordinating Editor
David Sherlock

Secretary
Claire Barker
Westhorpe Lodge, Westhorpe,
Stowmarket,
Suffolk IP14 4TA

website: www.suffolkrecordssociety.com

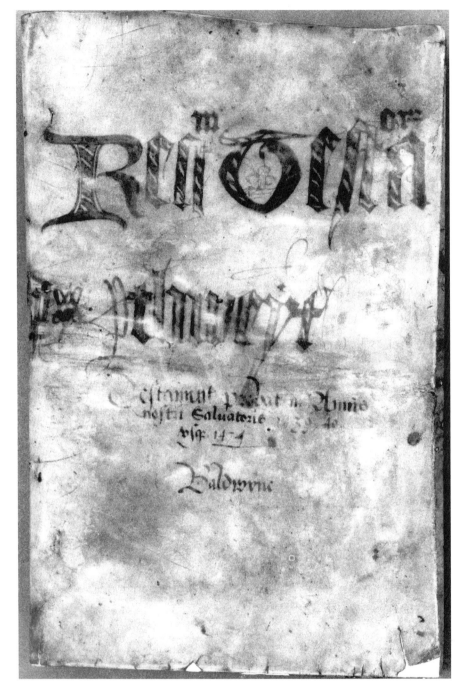

The original front cover of the Register 'Baldwyne'. Photo: Geoff Cordy.

WILLS OF
THE ARCHDEACONRY
OF SUDBURY

1439–1474

WILLS FROM THE REGISTER 'BALDWYNE'
Part II: 1461–1474

Edited by
PETER NORTHEAST and HEATHER FALVEY

General Editor
DAVID DYMOND

The Boydell Press

Suffolk Records Society
VOLUME LIII

© The Trustees of the Suffolk Records Society 2010

All Rights Reserved. Except as permitted under current legislation
no part of this work may be photocopied, stored in a retrieval system,
published, performed in public, adapted, broadcast,
transmitted, recorded or reproduced in any form or by any means,
without the prior permission of the copyright owner

A Suffolk Records Society publication
First published 2010
The Boydell Press, Woodbridge

ISBN 978–1–84383–532–5

Issued to subscribing members for the year 2009–2010

The Suffolk Records Society is grateful to the Marc Fitch Fund for
a generous grant towards the cost of the research for this publication

The Boydell Press is an imprint of Boydell & Brewer Ltd
PO Box 9, Woodbridge, Suffolk IP12 3DF, UK
and of Boydell & Brewer Inc.
668 Mt Hope Avenue, Rochester, NY 14620, USA
website: www.boydellandbrewer.com

A catalogue record for this book is available
from the British Library

This publication is printed on acid-free paper

Printed in Great Britain by
CPI Antony Rowe, Chippenham and Eastbourne

Contents

pages

List of illustrations   viii

Preface   ix

Peter Northeast, FSA, 1930–2009   x

Editorial Methods   xi

Abbreviations   xiv

Saints' Days and Festivals   xvi

Glossary   xviii

Introduction   xliii

THE REGISTER 'BALDWYNE': Part II   1

Bibliography   509

Index of Testators in Parts I and II   515

Index of Place of Residence of Testators in Parts I and II   538

Illustrations

Endpapers
The parishes of the archdeaconry of Sudbury

Frontispiece
The original front cover of the Register 'Baldwyne'

pages

Plate 1
The original cover and the two volumes into which the original has   xlvii
been rebound

Plate 2
Wills nos 352 and 353 (fol. 417), the wills of Agnes Bogays of Edwardstone   208
and Richard Howett of Edwardstone

Plate 3
Will no. 621 (fol. 511), the will of Thomas Deneys of Combs   362

Plate 4
Fol. 521, line drawing of Miles Crosby   380

Preface

My illness meant that I had to stop working on this volume in 2007. I am immensely grateful to Dr Heather Falvey for 'rescuing' 'Baldwyne' and to the Suffolk Records Society for finding the wherewithal to fund her work on it. Heather has been responsible for more than half the text and all the footnotes and indexes. This is a remarkable achievement considering that she came to the task as a stranger to Suffolk history. Without her work 'Baldwyne II' would not have seen the light of day.

Peter Northeast
Rattlesden, May 2009

In the Preface to Part I, written in June 2000, Peter outlined the background to his involvement with the Baldwyne Register which then extended back over more than thirty years. My own association has been far shorter but it is easy to see how the register could occupy such a large part of one's life. In all, 'Baldwyne' contains the wills or probate sentences of some 2,000 men and 300 women who lived in the archdeaconry of Sudbury during roughly the third quarter of the fifteenth century. These people, few of whom were particularly wealthy, live on in the register over 500 years later, even though the more tangible monuments that some of them requested were swept away in the religious upheavals of the following two centuries. As might be expected, the wills provide a great deal of information for local historians interested in the building, extension and ornamentation of parish churches, and in land and property in the various towns and villages. Perhaps unexpectedly, they also provide numerous personal details, such as favourite items of coloured clothing or discord within extended families.

Both Peter himself and David Dymond have read the whole text but any inaccuracies are mine alone, and I hope that I will be forgiven, since, as Peter has pointed out, I am not a native of Suffolk but, like his wife Judy, was brought up in the 'other' Sudbury, in Middlesex. However, perhaps I can be considered an honorary Suffolk local historian because between 1993 and 1999 I was taught by, amongst others, Mark Bailey, David Dymond, Nesta Evans and Clive Paine on various courses organised by the University of Cambridge's Institute of Continuing Education. Other relevant credentials for undertaking this task include working on the publication, by the Richard III Society, of *The Logge Register of PCC Wills, 1479–86*, not only as one of the team of transcribers and translators, but also as technical editor.

Peter and I would like to thank the unfailingly helpful staff of the Bury branch of the Suffolk Record Office, who have produced the incredibly heavy 'Baldwyne' on numerous occasions and offered much assistance and encouragement. Thanks are also due to Geoff Cordy who took the photographs for both Parts I and II, and to David Dymond, the general editor.

Heather Falvey
Croxley Green, July 2009

PETER NORTHEAST, F.S.A. (1930–2009)

Peter Northeast, co-editor of this volume, died peacefully at his home in Rattlesden on 29 August 2009. For over three years he had suffered from the progressive effects of motor neurone disease, and in 2007 was forced to stop work on this book. However, he was subsequently delighted to witness its completion by Heather Falvey, and was able to give his comments and to help in checking the final text. It is poignant that he and his wife Judy had quietly celebrated their Golden Wedding only four weeks before his death.

Peter was born in London, moved several times when his father changed jobs, but from the age of about 11 became settled at Spexhall in Suffolk. He won a scholarship to Bungay Grammar School, where in particular he learnt the Latin that served him so well in adult life. After military service in the RAF he trained as a primary school teacher at the college of SS Mark and John in Chelsea. He then taught in several Suffolk schools and in 1961 gained his first headship at Blewbury in Berkshire. There he caught the local history bug, simply because he was curious about the handsome Queen Anne house that went with his job. In 1964 he and Judy returned to Suffolk when he became head of Rattlesden Primary School, a post which he held for twenty-one years. During this time, he also became heavily involved in village and church life.

In autumn and winter evenings Peter lectured all over Suffolk for the Cambridge Extra-mural Board and the WEA, and famously did huge amounts of research in preparation for his classes. He also lectured to many voluntary societies and was a member and hard-working officer of county organisations such as the Suffolk Local History Council (which he steered through a particularly rocky period after 1985), the Suffolk Institute of Archaeology and History and the Suffolk Records Society. Of the latter he was secretary in 1987–93 and continued to distribute its books until *c*.2006. Among his publications three volumes of the SRS's General Series bear his name as editor.

Peter was friendly, generous and hugely energetic. Furthermore he was a natural scholar, blessed with a prodigious memory. He built up a huge collection of notes, transcripts, translations, photocopies, card-indexes and slides relating to Suffolk's history, which were all methodically stored. Everything he wrote was in a highly legible hand and scrupulously accurate. The last piece of work he was able to finish, his notes on Suffolk churches, is already being used in revising the Suffolk volume of Pevsner's *Buildings of England.* His most remarkable achievement was undoubtedly the translation of some 15,000 Suffolk wills from the fourteenth century to the 1540s. The 'Northeast Collection' has now been taken into the Suffolk Record Office, as Peter himself wished, and will be a boon for generations to come. In 1980, in recognition of his services to local history, he was elected a Fellow of the Society of Antiquaries of London.

Peter encouraged many beginners and corresponded with large numbers of people in Suffolk and further afield, including leading medieval scholars. Hearing of his death one academic from a Scottish university wrote, 'his loss is a national one'. Once he knew an individual's interests, Peter would send a handwritten note whenever he found a relevant reference or piece of information. Over the years hundreds of people must have benefited from his instinctive generosity.

It was due measure of Peter's achievements and reputation that his Memorial Service in Rattlesden church on 10 September 2009 was packed to capacity by family, neighbours, friends and colleagues.

David Dymond
21 October 2009

Editorial Methods

Although 'Baldwyne' Part II is presented here as English abstracts, most of the entries in the register were written in Latin, just thirty-nine items in Part II being written partly or wholly in English, although many more contain English words where the scribe could not translate various everyday items into Latin. Three documents (nos 38, 208 and 805) begin in Latin and then switch to English; in six (nos 266, 417, 483, 623, 720 and 733), the testament is written in Latin and the separate will proper is written in English; the other thirty are written only in English, six of which are from Soham (Cambs).[1]

The following editorial symbols have been used:

\   / for insertions by the scribe

[. . . . .] for illegible or unintelligible words or letters

[   ] for omitted words

deletions have been struck through ~~thus~~

All editorial insertions are given in italics within square brackets.

Words within round brackets are quotations from the original text, Latin in italics, English within quotation marks. Latin words have been left unextended when the scribe's intentions are unclear.

An italicised question mark before a word or number in the text indicates that its reading or meaning is in doubt; a question mark in the footnotes indicates a doubtful identification.

The use of capital letters has been standardised: proper names, that is, names of people, places, roads, fields etc., have been given initial capitals, where they were lacking in the original; lower-case initial letters have replaced capitals used to begin ordinary nouns in the original.

Dates have been converted into calendar form where liturgical feasts were used. In the case of dates falling between 1 January and 24 March, the double year has been indicated.

No attempt has been made to modernise money or measures:
Money:
1 pound (£) contained 20 shillings (s) or 240 pennies (d), equivalent to £1 today
1 shilling (s) contained 12 pennies (d), equivalent to 5p today
1 mark was a sum of money (not a coin), 13s 4d, approx. equivalent to 67p today

[1]   Wills in English: nos 21, 22, 102, 209, 222, 224, 262, 414, 449, 470, 515, 524, 525, 530, 532, 538, 579, 600, 614, 622, 624, 639, 654, 659, 723, 744, 748, 756, 758 and 786.

Weight:
    1 pound (lb) contained 16 ounces (oz), approx. equivalent to 0.45 kg
    1 stone contained 14 lb
    1 hundredweight (cwt) contained 112 lb, approx. equivalent to 50.8 kg
Length:
    1 foot (ft) contained 12 inches (in), approx. equivalent to 30 cm
    1 yard (yd) contained 3 ft, approx. equivalent to 0.9 m
    1 perch contained 5½ yards
Liquid measure:
    1 quart (qt) contained 2 pints, approx. equivalent to 1.14 litres
    1 gallon (gal) contained 8 pints (pt), approx. equivalent to 4.55 litres
Corn measure:
    1 bushel (bush) contained 4 pecks (pk), approx. equivalent to 27 kg
    1 quarter (qtr) contained 8 bushels, approx. equivalent to 217 kg
    1 coomb contained 4 bushels
Land area:
    1 acre (ac) contained 4 roods (r), approx. equivalent to 0.4 hectare

The abstracts

The abstracts retain all important matter, only dispensable words being omitted. Christian names are given in their modern form where possible, surnames exactly as written in the original, and so there may be variations in the spelling of the same surname within an abstract. Place-names are printed in their modern form, but the register spelling is quoted if it differs materially from today's; unless otherwise stated, all places mentioned are in Suffolk.

    Certain elements have been omitted from the abstracts but all of the elements are explained in the Introduction:

Invocation: Always omitted.

State of mind: This has not been printed, but any comment as to bodily health has been given.

Commendation: Where the commendation of the soul takes the usual form, that is, 'to Almighty God, the Blessed Virgin Mary and all the saints in heaven' (or similar), this has been omitted; exceptional wording has been noted, for example, no. 519, which includes St John the Evangelist; it has also been noted where the commendation is given in the form 'to God [Almighty] &c' as it is unclear whether this was a scribal convention or was written thus in the original will – there does not appear to be any consistency in the use of this abbreviated form; the absence of any form of commendation has always been recorded.

Residue: The general instructions to executors have usually been summarised, but are given in full where they contain unusual elements or specific names, such as souls to be prayed for.

Probate sentence: When this consists merely of the statement that the will had been proved before the official of the archdeacon, this has been given simply as 'proved'; where individuals are named they are quoted.

Foliation: Folio numbers from the original volume have been given; when a will runs over from one folio to another this has been shown at the appropriate point.

Footnotes: In references to wills/probates in Part I, the folio number in 'Baldwyne' is followed by the document number in the published edition, e.g.: SROB, Baldwyne 34; Pt I, no. 188.

Abbreviations

Sources

For further details, see the Bibliography at the end of the volume.

Blomefield	F. Blomefield, *History of Norfolk*
CAS	Cambridge Antiquarian Society
Cautley	H. M. Cautley, *Suffolk Churches and their Treasures* (5th edn)
Cheney	C. R. Cheney, *Handbook of Dates*
CPR	*Calendar of Patent Rolls*
CRO	Cambridgeshire Record Office
Cross	F. L. Cross, *Oxford Dictionary of the Christian Church*
DB	Domesday Book
Duffy	E. Duffy, *The Stripping of the Altars*
EETS	Early English Text Society
Emden, *BRUC*	A. B. Emden, *Biographical Register of the University of Cambridge*
Emden, *BRUO*	A. B. Emden, *Biographical Register of the University of Oxford*
Historical Atlas	*An Historical Atlas of Suffolk*, ed. D. Dymond and E. Martin
Knowles and Hadcock	D. Knowles and R. N. Hadcock, *Medieval Religious Houses*
Lambeth	Lambeth Palace Library
Logge Register	Boatwright *et al.*, *Logge Register of PCC Wills*
Morley	C. Morley, 'Suffolk Clergy'
NCC	Norwich Consistory Court
NRO	Norfolk Record Office, Norwich
PCAS	*Proceedings of the Cambridge Antiquarian Society*
PCC	Prerogative Court of Canterbury
PCHAS	*Proceedings of the Cambridgeshire and Huntingdonshire Archaeological Society*
PSIA	*Proceedings of the Suffolk Institute of Archaeology*
RCHM	Royal Commission on Historical Monuments
SIAH	Suffolk Institute of Archaeology & History
SROB	Suffolk Record Office, Bury St Edmunds branch
SROI	Suffolk Record Office, Ipswich branch
SRS	Suffolk Records Society
Tanner	Index to the registers of the bishops of Norwich, vol. 2 (NRO, DN/Reg/31; SROB, microfilm J510/2)
TEAS	*Transactions of the Essex Archaeological Society*
TNA	The National Archives
VCH	*Victoria County History*
Watkin	A. Watkin, *Inventory of Church Goods temp. Edward III*

Other miscellaneous abbreviations

A.M.	*Artium Magister* (Master of Arts)
admon	administration
BCnL	Bachelor of Canon Law ('decrees')
c.	*circa*, about (in time)
cal.	calendar: abbreviated abstract of a document
cf.	*confer*, compare
d	penny, pence (pre-decimalisation)
DCnL	Doctor of Canon Law ('decrees')
ed., eds	editor(s)
edn, edns	edition(s)
&c (in text)	*etcetera*, as written by scribe in the text
exec., execs	executor(s)
fol., fols	folio(s)
IPM	Inquisition post mortem
journ.	journal
£	pound(s) (money)
lb	pound(s) (weight)
MS	manuscript
n.d.	not dated, no date given
no., nos	number(s)
n.s.	new series
OW	original will
p., pp.	page(s)
Perp.	Perpendicular (architecture)
pr.	proved
Proc.	*Proceedings*
pt	part/pint(s)
pubs	publications
qv	*quod vide*, 'which see'
rev.	revised
s	shilling(s)
v	verso (of folio)

Saints' Days and Festivals
mentioned in 'Baldwyne' Part II

Agatha, virgin and martyr: 5 February
All Saints (or, Hallowmas): 1 November
All Souls: 2 November
Andrew: 30 November
Ascension (of Our Lord): Thursday after Rogation Sunday
Augustine, archbishop of Canterbury: 26 May
Barnabas: 11 June
Bartholomew: 24 August
Brice, bishop of Tours: 13 November
Corpus Christi: Thursday after Trinity Sunday
Dunstan: 19 May
Easter: Sunday after full moon on, or next after, 21 March
Edmund, king and martyr: 20 November
Edward, king and martyr: 18 March
Edward, king and martyr, first translation of: 18 February
Edward, king and martyr, second translation of: 20 June
Epiphany: 6 January
Etheldreda: 23 June
Faith, virgin and martyr: 6 October
Feast of Relics: *see* Relic Sunday
Francis, confessor: 4 October
Gregory: 12 March
Hallowmas: *see* All Saints
Hilary: 13 January
Holy Cross, exaltation of: 14 September
Holy Cross, invention of: 3 May
James: 25 July
Jerome: 30 September
John the Baptist, decollation of: 29 August
John the Baptist, nativity of: 24 June
John, before the Latin Gate: 6 May
Katherine (or, Catherine): 25 November
Lawrence, martyr: 10 August
Lent: 40 weekdays preceding Easter
Leonard: 6 November
Luke: 18 October
Martin: 11 November
Mary (Blessed Virgin), annunciation of: 25 March
Mary (Blessed Virgin), assumption of: 15 August

Mary (Blessed Virgin), nativity of: 8 September
Mary (Blessed Virgin), purification of: 2 February
Matthew: 21 September
Michael: 29 September
Mid-Lent Sunday: the fourth Sunday in Lent
Nativity (of Our Lord): 25 December
Nicholas: 6 December
Passion Sunday: 5th Sunday in Lent
Paul, conversion of: 25 January
Pentecost (Whit-Sunday): 7th Sunday after Easter
Peter and Paul: 29 June
Peter, *ad vincula*: 1 August
Peter, *in cathedra*: 22 February
Relic Sunday (or, Feast of Relics): 1st Sunday after 7 July
Rogation Sunday: 5th Sunday after Easter
Silvester: 31 December
Simon and Jude: 28 October
Stephen: 26 December
Thomas, apostle, translation of: 3 July
Thomas, archbishop and martyr: 29 December
Thomas, archbishop and martyr, translation of: 7 July
Trinity Sunday: 1st Sunday after Pentecost
Valentine: 14 February
Wulfstan: 19 January

Glossary

Sources

Bristow   Joy Bristow, *The Local Historian's Glossary of Words and Terms* (3rd edn, 2001)
Draper's   S. W. Beck, *The Draper's Dictionary* (n.d.)
Duffy   E. Duffy, *The Stripping of the Altars: Traditional Religion in England, c.1400–c.1580* (1992)
Halliwell   J. O. Halliwell, *A Dictionary of Archaic and Provincial Words* (2 vols, 1847)
Hey   D. Hey, *The Oxford Companion to Local and Family History* (1996)
Jacob   E. F. Jacob, *Register of Henry Chichele* (1938), ii, 847–65, 'Glossary'
MED   *Middle English Dictionary* (in progress, 1956–)
Milward   R. Milward, *A Glossary of Household, Farming and Trade Terms from Probate Inventories* (Derbyshire Record Society, 3rd edn, 1986)
OED   *Oxford English Dictionary* (2nd edn, online version)
Powell   J. L. Fisher, *Medieval Farming Glossary of Latin and English Words* (2nd edn, revised A. and R. Powell, Essex Record Office, 1997)
Purvis   J. S. Purvis, *Dictionary of Ecclesiastical Terms* (1962)
Watkin   A. Watkin (ed.), *Inventory of Church Goods temp. Edward III*, Part II (Norfolk Record Society, 1948)
Yaxley   D. Yaxley (ed.), *A Researcher's Glossary of Words found in Historical Documents of East Anglia* (2003)

abut: to adjoin, border on, referring to land.
accounts, executors': statement of expenses and receipts connected with the administration of testator's estate.
acquit: discharge executors from further action.
acre: measure of land area, 4840 square yards, approx. 0.4 hectare.
administration (admon): the management and disposal of the estate of a deceased person (*OED*).
advower: saint regarded by individual as a special protector (no. 731).
age of discretion: 14 years.
age, full: 21 years (boys), 14 years (girls).
age of inheritance: for lands, 21 years; for goods, 14 years; unless otherwise specified.
aid: tax or subsidy payable to the Crown.
aisle: part of church built alongside and parallel to nave or chancel, from which it is separated by pillars and arches.
alb: *see* **vestments**.
ale: *see* **churchale**.
allowance: the amount allowed out of income, in accounts, for the cost of certain goods or services, without actual payment.

almery: *see* **ambry**.

alms, free alms: charitable gift to poor or religious institution, without payment in return and without requirement of services other than spiritual.

altar: stone table at which mass was celebrated.

ambry, almery, aumbry: cupboard with a door, safe, locker, for food, books, etc. (Yaxley).

amice: *see* **vestments**.

andiron: fire-dog; bar of metal on feet in the fireplace, on which logs were placed.

anniversary: an obit; the commemoration of the deceased a year after death, and in subsequent years, taking the form of a re-enactment of the funeral ceremony, that is (at its fullest) the evening service of *placebo*, preceded by the ringing of bells, with the morning service of *dirige* followed by requiem mass the next day.

annual (noun): (1) the services of a priest saying requiem mass, etc., for a year; (2) **anniversary** (*qv*).

annulet: little ring (*OED*) (no. 38).

antiphon: musical composition based on scriptural text and sung (*MED*).

antiphonal, antiphoner: service book containing music for the antiphons and other parts of divine service (Watkin).

apparels: strips of coloured material attached to the amice and alb of the priest's vestments (Watkin).

appropriate (verb): take a benefice and its income (wholly or partly) to the use of a religious house or other institution; the religious house, etc. then became the rector of the benefice.

arable: tilled land, as distinct from meadow and pasture.

archdeacon: ordained ecclesiastical dignitary next under bishop in church hierarchy, responsible for part of diocese called archdeaconry; he exercised jurisdiction on the bishop's behalf in his archdeaconry. See Hamilton-Thompson, 'Diocesan Organization in the Middle Ages', pp.153–94.

ark: chest, box, coffer (*MED*).

ashes: the burning of underwood produced ashes, from which was obtained potash, used as a cleanser in the dyeing of cloth.

attorney: legal representative, not necessarily a lawyer.

axe: there were many different types of axe, some designed for a specific purpose, *see* **belt**, **chip-axe**, **hatchet**, **twibill**.

back-house, 'bachus': subsidiary house or building which lies behind the main house (*OED*); although possibly **bakehouse** (*qv*), here (no. 76) the building was to be used for malting and brewing as well as baking.

bail: the arched handle of a pot or the like (*MED*).

bailiff: manorial official; the agent or steward of landlord.

bakehouse: building or room in which baking is being, or has been, carried out (Latin *pistrinum*).

banker: covering, of tapestry or other fabric, for a bench, couch or chair (*MED*).

banks, 'bankes': here (no. 572) 4 'yerdys' of 'bankes' probably means 4 yards of cloth to make one or more **bankers** (*qv*).

banner cloth: a banner, as used in a procession; *cf.* **cross-cloth**.

bark: bark, especially oak-bark; used in tanning.

barker: a tanner, one who tans leather.

bark-house: shed, etc., for storing bark.

bark-vats: vats used in tanning (*MED*).

barrow-hog: a castrated boar; a swine: a pig called a 'barwe' (no. 354).

basilard: dagger (fashionable) (*MED*).

beadle: in the context of the parish, from the late sixteenth century onwards, the beadle was an 'inferior parish officer appointed by the vestry to keep order in church, punish petty offenders and act as the servitor or messenger of the parish generally' (*OED*). At Bures St Mary (for example, nos 310, 326, 460, 658, 781) the beadle may have carried out the sexton's duties, as the **bedesman** appears to have done at Lavenham.

beads: usually, especially when 'a pair of beads', a rosary; *see* **paternoster**.

beam: *see* **candlebeam**.

bearing sheet: bearing-cloth; cloth in which a child was wrapped, to go to church for baptism (Halliwell).

bed: usually denotes bedding, rather than a complete bed in the modern sense; a typical 'bed' consisted of a donge or mattress, a pair of sheets, a pair of blankets and a cover.

bede-roll: list of names of people to be specially prayed for in church, read out from the pulpit each Sunday.

bedesman: one who prays for another, sometimes for payment; but at Lavenham 'bedeman' seems to have implied the inclusion of sexton's duties.

belt: (1) belt or girdle (Latin *zona*); (2) large axe for splitting wood (Yaxley).

bifolium (plural **bifolia**): single sheet of paper or parchment, forming two attached folios when folded, as used in a manuscript book.

bill: financial document or schedule.

blanket: kind of woollen cloth, often white or undyed (*MED*).

boardcloth: table-cloth or altar-cloth (*MED*).

bona notabilia: (literally, notable goods), possessions worth a minimum sum which varied according to the custom of the diocese.

bond: of land, etc., implying feudal obligation, its holder being bound to certain duties and payments; later became **copyhold** (*qv*).

borough: used of towns like Framlingham and Lavenham, though not incorporated boroughs (Latin *burgus*).

bound: (1) strapped with metal, as in the case of domestic vessels; (2) obliged, either morally (e.g. to pray for souls or pay debts), or by written bond (to pay money or fulfil certain conditions).

bounds: boundary, limits; *see* **metes**.

bowgett, 'bowgy': leather bag, wallet, budget (French *bougette*); occurs in an East Anglian inventory made in 1463 (Yaxley). Here (no. 374) the sense seems to demand a household item, such as a bowl.

Braban cloth: a kind of linen made in Brabant, an historical region of the Low Countries (*MED*) (no. 662).

brass: alloy of copper with tin or zinc (*OED*) (Latin *eneus*).

broadcloth: woollen cloth woven on a broadloom; the measurements of a broad-cloth were later laid down by an Act of 1483–4 (1 Rich. III c.8: *Statutes of the Realm*, ii, 485): 2 yards (approx. 1.83 metres) wide and 24 yards (22 metres) long.

broadloom: *see* **broadcloth**.

buckler, 'bokelere': a small round shield.

built-up: *see* **messuage**.

bullimong: mixed crop for fodder (Powell); usually oats, peas and vetches (Halliwell) (no. 801).

bullock: bull-calf, steer (*MED*), but used of both sexes.

bure: coarse woollen stuff (*OED*).

burial, Christian: (1) the action of being buried with Christian rites; (2) the place where Christian burials are laid.

burnet: brown woollen cloth of fine quality (*MED*); of a dark brown colour (*OED*) (nos 247, 276, 677).

bushel: a unit of dry measure, for grain etc., 2 of which made a coomb, and 8 of which made a quarter (Latin *bussellus* or *modium*).

butts: artificial mounds behind archers' targets, usually constructed in pairs, one at each end of a range.

calion, 'calyon': a flint nodule; a boulder or pebble (often *collective*) (*OED*) (no. 252).

candle: generic term for all cylinders of wax incorporating wicks, but often used of the smallest type; *cf.* **taper** and **torch**.

candlebeam: literally, the beam, behind, on or over which stood the **rood** (*qv*), and on which candles and lights were placed in honour of the rood; often used for the whole **roodloft** (*qv*).

canon: a member of a religious order following the rule of St Augustine, whose priests might serve the cures of their priory's parishes, but who were not instituted as incumbents.

canonically: according to the rules, or canons, of the church.

canvas: coarse fabric made from flax or hemp (*MED*).

capital: chief, principal (dwelling etc).

card: kind of fabric (*MED*); material of rougher character, woven from coarse silk and sometimes from linen (Watkin); **cards, pair of cards:** implements similar to wire brushes for separating and combing out the fibres of wool, hemp etc. (Milward) (nos 256, 390).

cast: to dig, throw up with a spade; fye out, dredge (Yaxley). Here (no. 350) it relates to carrying out road repairs.

cauldron: kettle or pot for heating water or cooking (*MED*).

causey, causeway: a series of flagstones laid down on wet or soft terrain to prevent the formation of holloways; 'causey' is derived from a Norman French word meaning 'trodden', and is not a shortening of 'causeway', which comes from a similar root (Hey).

celebrate: perform a religious rite, especially celebrate mass.

cellarer: the monk responsible for the supply of food, drink and fuel for a religious community and its guests (no. 821).

celure, selure: canopy of bed or altar.

censer: a ceremonial container, suspended by chains and swung from the hand, in which incense was burned. Censers were made of silver, pewter or latten and were used at high mass, lauds and evensong, for processional use and at the burial of the dead (Watkin).

certain: denotes the inclusion of the name of a deceased person in weekly reading of the bede-roll, usually from the pulpit, for a whole year; in East Anglia frequently called a **sangred**; the payment for this was normally 4s 4d for a year, i.e. 1d per week (Latin *certitudo, certagium* etc.).

certain of masses: the weekly celebration of mass for a year; *see* **certain.**

chafing-dish, 'chafour': vessel containing burning charcoal, for keeping food hot.

chalice: a goblet of precious metal to contain the wine at mass; communion cup.

chamber: a room, on ground or upper floor, for private use and usually containing a bed or beds.

chapel: a building containing an altar, either within a church or other building, or free-standing, in some instances acting almost as a parish church, e.g. Sudbury St Peter.

chaplain: usually, an unbeneficed priest; **parish chaplain:** priest serving the cure on behalf of the incumbent, but not officially instituted.

charger: large serving-dish or plate.

charitable deeds: actions undertaken for the benefit of others, with no expectation of pecuniary or material benefit to the instigator (but usually with considerable expectation of spiritual benefit); *see* **alms.**

charter: a written deed; a grant.

chasuble: *see* **vestments.**

chattels: property of any kind, goods, treasure, money, land etc. (*MED*).

chaunlor, 'chawnlere': candlestick (Milward) (no. 252).

'chettle': *see* **kettle.**

'chephogge': *see* **sheephog.**

chest: large, strong box.

chief lord of the fee: major landlord in the feudal pyramid, holding his land (fee) directly of the crown.

chip-axe, 'chypex': small axe used with one hand for shaping timber (Yaxley) (no. 490).

chorus: a Hebrew dry measure (no. 664).

chrismatory: a small vessel used for keeping the three holy oils: oil of the catechumens, oil for extreme unction, and chrism (Purvis).

churchale: a money-raising social event for which quantities of ale were specially brewed (nos 580 and 764).

clepe: to call by the name of, call, name (*OED*).

clerk: cleric (used of a **priest**, as today); in reference to those in the choir implies a person in minor orders, i.e. below the rank of **subdeacon** (*qv*); *see also* **parish clerk.**

cloak: loose outer garment (*MED*) (Latin *armilausa, epitogium*).

close: piece of land appropriated to private use, such as meadow or field, usually hedged or fenced (*MED*).

close table: some kind of table or bench (*MED*); ?folding table.

clue, clew: ball of yarn or thread (Yaxley); 'iij le cluis yarne' means 'three clues of yarn' (no. 466).

coffer: trunk, chest or case of any size (*MED*).

cogware: coarse kind of cloth made of inferior wool (*MED*).

collar-maker: one who made collars, especially for horses and other draught animals (*OED*).

college: a community of secular clergy under a master or warden, performing worship in a (collegiate) church, as at Sudbury, where it was attached to the church of St Gregory.

commendation of soul: the commending, by the testator at the beginning of a will, of his or her soul to God, etc.

commissary: one who had a commission, either temporary or permanent, usually from a bishop or archdeacon, to carry out some particular duty or duties.

common (adj.)**:** for general and public use, e.g. way, well.

common, in: to be used jointly or shared (*MED*).

community: can refer to the members of local gilds (nos 471, 1462), or to all the inhabitants of a parish (nos 469, 802).

community/common hall: a building specially constructed for social and recreational purposes, owned by the parish, and not by an individual gild (nos 75, 109, 669); *cf.* **gildhall**.

coney, cony: rabbit (from Old French, *conil*, pl. *conis*). The rabbit was introduced into England in early Norman times; coney/cony was the usual medieval name for the animal; the fur was used for clothes and bedclothes; *see also* **pane**.

consecration: the setting apart, ceremonially, of a new church, etc., for the service of God.

consistory: general court of a bishop.

convent: a religious community (of either sex); **conventual:** belonging to, or being part of, a convent.

conversation: manner of living, conduct, behaviour (*MED*).

coomb: unit of dry measure, for corn etc; 4 bushels (half a quarter) made a coomb.

cope: a full-length, hooded cloak of rich fabric, fastened at breast, worn by clergy especially in processions and at choir services. As vestments not used specifically at mass, copes were not rejected at the Reformation.

copy (noun)**:** copy of court roll (no. 212); *see next entry*.

copy (adj.)**, copyhold:** of customary, or bond land, held by copy of court roll, whereby the tenant, a **copyholder**, has, as his title-deed, a copy of the entry in the court roll of his admittance to the property.

coral: the name belongs to the beautiful red coral, an arborescent species, found in the Red Sea and Mediterranean, prized from times of antiquity for ornamental purposes, and often classed among precious stones (*OED*).

cordwainer: shoemaker; originally, a worker in Cordovan leather from Spain (*OED*).

corporal: linen cloth spread in the middle of the altar on which were placed the **chalice** (*qv*) and **host** (*qv*) at mass.

corse: a ribbon or band of silk (or other material), serving as a ground for ornamentation with metalwork or embroidery, and used as a girdle, garter, etc. (*OED*).

cottage: holding consisting of a cottage and the land belonging to it (*MED*).

coulter: on a plough, the knife-like blade which cuts the vertical side of the furrow.

court of Rome: the Papal Curia; *see* **stations**.

court roll: the record of a manorial court, later in book-form, but still referred to as the court roll.

cover: usually refers to bed-cover, but also used for the covers of vessels, especially silver, and also fonts.

coverlet: bed-cover.

croft: small piece of ground used for farming purposes (usually enclosed; often adjoining a house) (*MED*).

'croppys': fur of some kind (?from the back of an animal) (*MED*); no. 38, 'my gown furred with "croppys"'.

cross cloth: pennon attached to processional cross (Watkin).

cruets: vessels to hold the wine and water for mass (Watkin).

curate: technically, any member of clergy who has the cure of souls, not necessarily an assistant as implied today; often used by testator of priest in whose special care he has been, or his confessor.

curtains: the hangings about a bed, *not* at windows.

curtilage: small court, yard or piece of ground attached to a house (*OED*).

custom: rules operating within a manor, built up over time, and often embodied in a written 'custumal'.

customary: subject to manorial custom, e.g. bond land.

cutting saw, 'kyttyng sawe': saw of medium size between the long saw and the handsaw, used for cutting across the grain (Yaxley).

daggarde: dagger.

dalmatic: *see* **vestments**.

Dame: title of woman of rank, and courtesy title of a nun.

Dan: used as title of monk (from Latin *dominus*); equivalent to modern 'Dom'.

deacon: (1) a cleric immediately below the rank of priest; (2) the chief assistant of the priest at high **mass** (*qv*).

dead stock: the inanimate items among agricultural and domestic stock.

Dec. Lic.: *in decretis licentiatus*, licentiate in canon law. A man who had received the licence enabling him to teach canon law. This was the stage before the mastership in the university *cursus honorum* (information from Dr Henry Summerson).

dedication: consecration (*qv*).

deeds of charity: see **charitable deeds**.

deeds (works) of mercy: traditionally divided into two groups of seven: corporal (feeding the hungry, giving drink to the thirsty, clothing the naked, harbouring strangers, visiting the sick, ministering to prisoners, burying the dead) and spiritual (converting the sinner, instructing the ignorant, counselling the doubtful, comforting the sorrowful, bearing wrongs patiently, forgiving injuries, praying for the living and dead).

default of heirs: lack of direct heirs of the person being referred to.

degree: status, position in society.

diaper: fabric having repeated patterns of figures or geometrical designs; garment or cloth of this fabric (*MED*).

dike: ditch.

dirige: origin of the English word 'dirge'; the matins of the office of the dead, said in church after the corpse had been brought in and before the requiem mass; so called from the antiphon with which it began, *Dirige domine deus* etc.

distrain: seize goods by way of **distress** (*qv*).

distress: the act of seizing goods or entering property in order to force the owner or tenant to honour some obligation.

divine service: literally, any religious service, but usually implying the celebration of mass.

dominical letter: To determine the date of Easter it is necessary to know the sequence of the days of the week following paschal full moon, and for this purpose special tables were devised in early Christian times. There are 7 possible relationships of the days of the week to the calendar of the year, and the letters A to G were used to indicate the cycle of 7 days beginning at 1 January. The dominical letter for the year is the letter allocated, according to this system, to the first Sunday of the year (Cheney, *Handbook of Dates*, pp.8, 9).

donge: mattress.

double feasts, double festivals: certain important feast days in the church's calendar, indicated in the breviary and missal. A simple feast commenced with the chapter (*capitulum*) of first vespers, and ended with none. It had three lessons and took the psalms of matins from the ferial office; the rest of the office was like the semi-double. A semi-double feast had two vespers, nine lessons in matins, and ended with compline. The antiphons before the psalms were only intoned. In the mass, the semi-double had always at least three prayers. On a double feast, the antiphons were sung in their entirety, before and after the psalms (*Catholic Encyclopedia*). Here (nos 678, 692) the testators made provision for the extra candles that were needed on such feasts.

doublet: man's tight-fitting garment, covering the body from the neck to the hips or thighs (*MED*).

dovecote: building, usually detached, in which were bred pigeons, so that the young could be taken for food; see McCann, *The Dovecotes of Suffolk*.

dower: the portion of a deceased's property in which his widow could claim a life-interest, normally a third of the total.

drain: channel in the Fens, for draining surface water.

draper: one who weaves and/or sells cloth; clothier (*MED*).

draught animals: animals for pulling (drawing) cart, plough, etc.

dropping pan: dripping pan, used to catch fat from roasting meat (no. 401).

dudde: a cloak or mantle, usually made of coarse woollen cloth; also a kind of coarse cloth (*MED*).

ear: small lug or handle, often unperforated (Yaxley).

easement: the right or privilege of using something not one's own (*MED*), e.g. well, domestic facilities, crossing land, etc.

Easter sepulchre: *see* **sepulchre**.

egress: going out, exit.

emend: repair or make good (*OED*); can be used of new, as well as old, work.

enfeoff: to put into the hands of **feoffee(s)** (*qv*).

eremitic: hermit-like; the Austin friars were described as eremitic friars.

esquire: originally a shield-bearer to a knight (Latin *armiger*, i.e. armour-bearer); a man belonging to the higher order of English gentry, immediately below a knight (*OED*).

estate: a legal interest in land.

estrich board: board imported from the Baltic or North Sea ports; the standard length was probably 10 feet (Yaxley) (see Salzman, *Building in England*, pp. 245–7). The 'throne of Eystrych boorde' before the *Pietà* requested for Thrandeston church (no. 252) was probably a special construction to hold candles before the image.

ewer: water-jug.

executor: one who is given the task of executing, or carrying into effect, the provisions of a will and/or testament; the feminine equivalent is **executrix**.

fabric: the construction and maintenance (of a church) (*OED*).

faggot: bundle of firewood.

falt table: folding table, usually a small portable table, either with X-legs or legs that fold inwards (Yaxley).

farm (verb): let out for rent; **farm** (noun): that which was let out for rent ('farmed'), or the rent itself.

feast: a saint's day, or a day celebrating events in the earthly life of Christ and the early church. Feasts were divided in various ways: (a) according to external celebration – *festa fori*, with a double obligation to rest from work and hear mass; *festa chori*, kept only in the liturgy; (b) according to extension – universal feasts, celebrated everywhere; particular feasts, celebrated only by certain religious orders, countries, dioceses etc.; (c) according to their position in the calendar – moveable feasts, which always fell on a certain day of the week; immoveable feasts, which always fell on a particular date; (d) according to the solemnity of the office or rite – simple, semi-double and **double feasts** (*qv*) – all three were regulated by the recitation of the divine office or breviary.

featherbed: bed, i.e. mattress, filled with feathers.

fee: land held of a superior lord (*OED*); *see* **chief lord of the fee**.

feedings: grazing ground (*OED*).

fee simple: freehold estate; the nearest possible, in England, to actual ownership under the crown.

fee tail: entailed estate; *see* **tail**.

felling belt: axe for felling trees.

feoffee: one to whom property was entrusted (enfeoffed), and who then held the estate or interest in the property on behalf of the original grantor or **feoffor**.

feoffment: the action of enfeoffing; *see* **enfeoff**.

festival: *see* **feast**.

field: usually referred to open-field land, divided into furlongs and strips; *cf.* **close**.

fifteenth: *see* **tax**.

fire and flet: 'fire and house-room'; an expression often occurring in wills (*OED*); here (no. 262) the testator's widow was to have houseroom with unlimited access to the fire; **flet** was literally 'the floor or ground under one's feet' (*OED*).

fishery: a fishing site; the right to fish in a particular place.

five wounds of Christ: a votive, or special, mass, commemorating the wounds to hands, feet and side of Christ at his crucifixion; it was very popular in the late Middle Ages, being regarded as having particular benefit for souls in purgatory (see Duffy, pp.243–6).

fold, foldage: *see* **liberty of fold**.

forcer: small chest, coffer, casket (*MED*) (no. 803).

fraternity: brotherhood, usually a gild, but sometimes a religious house.

free: of land, exempt from customary services or exactions (*MED*); *cf.* **bond**.

frende: a kind of cloak (Jacob) (nos 259, 307).

fuller: one who fulls, or scours and thickens, cloth.

furlong: originally the length (220 yards) of a furrow, but here refers to a block of land in the open field, of varied dimensions (Latin *quarentina*).

furnace: an oven, hearth or fireplace, kiln, furnace, etc. (*MED*) (Latin *fornax*).

furred: trimmed or lined with fur.

fustian: kind of cloth, made from cotton, flax or wool (*MED*).

gallon: liquid measure of 8 pints, approx. 4.55 litres.

garnish: set of dishes (usually twelve) (Halliwell).

gathering: quire or section of leaves, several of which were sewn together to make a book.

gaud, 'gawde': one of the large beads of the rosary, representing a *paternoster* (Jacob) (no. 388); *see* **beads**.

gild: a religious and social confraternity, brotherhood or association, formed for the mutual aid and protection of its members (*OED*).

gildhall: building where gild or gilds met.

girdle: (Latin *zona*), belt worn round waist, to secure or confine the garments (*OED*); *see* **vestments**.

good: property; could include land.

gown: an outer garment, robe (*MED*).

gradual: a grail (book) containing all the music sung by the choir during the celebration of mass (Watkin).

Gregorian mass: one of the masses of a Gregorian **trental** (*qv*).

grey: fur of badger (Halliwell) (nos 38 and 698).

gridiron, 'gredyll': an iron grid, like a grill, sometimes with legs and handle, for roasting, broiling or toasting in front of an open hearth (*MED*; Yaxley).

groundfast and nailfast: of **ostilments** (*qv*), furnishings etc. that are firmly fixed to the ground or nailed down (Latin *fixa in argilla et clavis*) (no. 374).

groundsill: horizontal timber used as a foundation for a wall.

grovet: a little grove (*OED*).

hake: adjustable hooks incorporating a ratchet on which pothooks or S-hooks hung above an open hearth, usually found in pairs (Yaxley); an iron instrument called 'a heke' (no. 256).

hale: a pot-hook used in the chimney (no. 374).

hall: the main, communal, room in a medieval house, open to the roof until the insertion of chimneys; the lower end was usually that against the 'screens passage', while at the upper end was normally a dais, used by the head of the household.

handsaw: a small-toothed saw that could be used with one hand (Yaxley).

hand-traces: *see* **traces**.

harnessed: decorated (girdle, basilard, etc.).

hatchet: small or light axe with a short handle, adapted for use with one hand (*OED*).

head: the end of a piece of land, meadow, etc. (*MED*).

headland, 'havydlonde', 'hevedlond': land where the plough-team turned at the end of furrows. In Mildenhall (no. 629), there seems to have been a field called 'Havydlonde'.

heifer: commonly used of a young cow that has not had a calf (*OED*) but, technically, a cow prior to having a second calf.

heriot: payment, usually the best beast, payable to the lord of the manor by the heir of a deceased **copyholder**.

herse: metal or wooden structure for supporting cloths, candles, statues, etc., placed over the corpse in church during a funeral.

high altar: the chief altar of a church, but used in wills before the Reformation to mean the incumbent or priest serving the cure, to whom were due offerings and tithes.

highway, often **king's highway:** a major road.

hog, hoggaster, hogget: castrated male sheep aged one year, i.e. between its first and second shearing (Bailey, 'Sheep Accounts', p.94).

holland: linen cloth, originally from Holland (Yaxley) (no. 276).

hollow: (of basin) deep (*MED*).

holy water carrier: priest's assistant, usually the **parish clerk**, who carried the holy (blessed) water at **mass** and other religious services and ceremonies, and also sprinkled parishioners' houses after mass; also called **holy water clerk** (no. 436).

homage: the body of tenants attending a manorial court (*MED*).

honest: (Latin *honestus*) (1) honourable, respectable; (2) suitable, competent (*MED*).

hood: hood, either attached to outer garment, or worn as a separate head-covering (*MED*).

hose: close-fitting garment resembling tights worn by men and boys; joined hose (*MED*); often termed a pair of hose.

host: round wafer consecrated at **mass** and believed to become the body of Christ.

housling towel: a long and narrow white linen cloth used at **mass**, which was spread before, or held up by, the communicants at the time of receiving the sacrament to prevent any dropping of the host (no. 360).

house: (1) dwelling; (2) portion of a building, an apartment, chamber, room; (3) structure for housing domestic animals or birds (*MED*).

'howyd': ?hued, coloured (nos 22, 96, 524, 729).

huke: outer garment, a cloak with a hood (*MED*) (nos 135, 228).

hundred: measure used for various commodities: (1) 5 score or 6 score; *see* **hundred, long**; (2) a hundredweight; (3) measure of quantity of varying number of units (*MED*); (4) subdivision of a county, used for administrative purposes.

hundred, long: a hundred of 6 score, used for measuring some items, e.g. masses; 'Six score to the hundred in women, walnuts and pins, And five score to the hundred in all other things' (Knowland (ed.), *Samuel Dove's Debenham*, p.131).

hutch, 'huche': a chest (*MED*).

image: representation of holy subject by statue or painted picture.

impeachment: bringing charge or accusation against someone for committing a misdeed; *see* **waste**.

indented: in the form of an indenture, i.e. a deed between parties; two or more copies were written on the same sheet, and then separated by being indented or serrated for identification and security.

indulgence: pardon, a remission of certain penalties for sin; in medieval times usually expressed as a reduction of the expected time of the soul in purgatory and earned by visiting or contributing to specified holy places.

in extremis: abbreviated form of *languens in extremis* (*qv*).

ingress: entrance.

inheritance, lands of: property inherited as part of the family possessions, as distinct from that purchased during the individual's lifetime.

inquisition post mortem (IPM): enquiry held after the death of a tenant-in-chief to ascertain what property was held by the deceased, and the lawful heir.

inventory: list of goods, chattels and possessions, especially those of the deceased, as required by ecclesiastical courts of executors and administrators.

iron plate: *see* **plate, iron**.

iron-shod: in the case of carts, furnished with iron tyres or projecting studs on the tyres (*MED*).

issue: children or lineal descendants.

issues: the product of any source of income; proceeds from livestock, land, rents, services, fines, etc. (*MED*).

iuger: *see* **juger**

jack, 'jake', 'jakke': short, close-fitting, sleeveless jacket, often of quilted leather, sometimes plated; a coat of mail; in bequests often paired with a **sallet** (*qv*), thus providing the beneficiary with some very basic armour.

jet: a coal-like substance (lignite) which can be carved and polished, much used in the past for jewellery; the chief centre of production in Britain was Whitby (Yorks); Latin: *gagates*, from Gages, a town in Asia Minor, an early source of the material. See Kendall, *The Story of Whitby Jet*.

juger: an ancient Roman measure of land, containing 28,800 (Roman) square feet, or 240 by 120 (Roman) feet, i.e. about three-fifths of an acre (*OED*) (no. 374).

kendal: cloth originally made at Kendal (Cumbria), a coarse fabric (*Draper's*).

kercher, kerchief: properly a cloth to cover the head ('coverchief'); cloth to cover some part of person (*Draper's*).

kettle: vessel, usually metal, for boiling water and cooking; until the eighteenth century it was a pot or cauldron, sometimes covered, and without a spout (Yaxley).

kirtle: garment for men or boys varying as to length, shape and materials, usually worn as outer garment (no. 27); garment for women or girls, often outer garment, sometimes worn over smock (*MED*).

lake: shallow open piece of water, of variable size and well stocked with fish, a feature of the undrained Fens.

languens in extremis: 'sick unto death'.

latten: alloy of tin and other metals (*MED*); **counterfeit latten:** imitation latten.

laver: water-pitcher, ewer (*MED*).

lawn: fine linen (*MED*).

lead: the medieval noun 'lead' (Latin *plumbum*) had at least 6 definitions: (1) a tank or cistern; (2) a milklead or cooler; (3) a vat for steeping barley before malting; (4) a large cooking-pot or cauldron; (5) a form of washhouse 'copper'; (6) a lid. See Yaxley, *The Prior's Manor-Houses*, pp.53–4, for a full discussion of these meanings. Here (no. 587) a 'brewing lead' must be as no. (3).

leap: the sudden fall of a river to a lower level; a **salmon leap** is a precipitous fall in a river (either natural or contrived artificially) over which salmon leap in ascending the river for breeding (*OED*). Here (no. 354) the 'lepes' belonging to the **fishery** (*qv*) were probably particular sections of a watercourse that had been artificially modified to facilitate fishing.

leasow: pasture; pasturage; meadow-land (no. 361).

legal age: *see* **age**.

legend: lesson-book, containing lessons of Bible-readings, ancient homilies and sermons, and lives of the saints.

Lent: 40 days from Ash Wednesday to Easter eve (but not counting the Sundays).

lessee: one to whom something is let or leased.

let (noun)**:** hindrance, obstacle; **let** (verb)**:** to hinder, obstruct.

liberty of fold: the right of erecting a sheepfold over certain ground, so that the animals manure the soil overnight.

lights: various forms of lighting in church, including candles, tapers, torches, basins, etc.

liripipe: the long tail of a graduate's hood (*OED*) but here (no. 350) simply a long hood.

litany: a form of prayer consisting of a series of petitions; **litany of the saints:** service of intercession addressed to individual saints.

livery: clothes, insignia, etc. provided by a master for his retainers and servants; a kind of uniform.

living: ecclesiastical benefice.

long hundred: *see* **hundred**.

loom: loom for weaving; *see also* **pair**.

lower: (1) relating to part of **hall** (*qv*); (2) describing chamber on ground floor.

malt: barley or other grain prepared for brewing by steeping, germinating and kiln-drying (*OED*).

maniple: *see* **vestments**.

manor: an administrative unit held by a landlord – 'the lord' – who himself held it of a superior lord, often the king; only rarely did the term refer to the actual manor house.

manour, 'menowr': to hold, occupy, take charge or possession of (land or property); to have the tenure of; to administer, control, or manage (*OED*) (no. 659).

manual: a priest's portable prayer book, used in the administration of the sacraments.

marblestone: stone used for paving the floors of churches and for grave-slabs (nos 89, 381); rarely actually marble, more usually limestone, and, later, slate.

mark: a unit of account (not a coin) equal to two thirds of a pound, 13s 4d.

mash-fat, mashing fat: vessel (vat) used in brewing, in which to prepare the wort of malt and boiling water.

maslin, mixtlin, 'mystlon': mixed grain, especially rye with wheat.

mass: the service of holy eucharist, the chief service of the medieval church, which could be said or sung; **high mass:** mass celebrated with full ceremony by the celebrant, assisted by deacon and subdeacon, with music, whereas **low mass** had no music and less ceremony.

maison dieu, 'massendewe': hospital, hospice; a home for the poor (Anglo-Norman) (no. 558).

mass-penny, -pence: the offering made by those attending mass, especially requiem mass at a funeral, when it was placed on the bier (e.g. nos 193, 258, 317, 515, 724); often referred to the mass-pence given by fellow gild-members, when its disposal was according to the will of the deceased, but not to be confused with the mortuary or the priest's fee.

Master: correctly, title used of a man who was an MA or had gained a higher university degree; often used of a man of higher social standing, e.g. Master John Clopton of Long Melford.

mazer: originally a drinking bowl of maple-wood, but often used of similar bowls made of metal.

mediety: a half-part, especially one portion of a benefice whose revenues were divided between two incumbents.

medley, 'medly': cloth woven with wools of different colours (nos 83, 698) (*OED*).

mendicant: literally, begging; used of the friars who, not being allowed by their rule to hold property, relied on alms.

mercer: a merchant, a dealer in textiles (*MED*); perhaps implying membership of the Mercers' Company of London.

mercy, deeds of: *see* **deeds of mercy**.

mere: a boundary between fields, etc. (*MED*); often in the form of an unploughed grass baulk.

mese: a **messuage** (*qv*).

messuage: a house-site and the land belonging to it; although a building is implied, a 'built-up messuage' emphasises the presence of a building or buildings, whereas 'lately built-up' (Latin *nuper edificatum*), in a period when the population had declined, would indicate ruinous or totally disappeared buildings; *cf.* **tenement**.

metes and bounds: tautological expression for a marked boundary.

mickle, muckle, 'mekyll': (1) much, great (adj.); (2) a great quantity (noun); (3) much (adv.).

mill, horse: a mill in which the stone is turned by horse-power.

missal: mass-book, containing everything necessary for the priest at the altar when saying or singing mass (Watkin).

moiety: half-part; *cf.* **mediety**.

morrow: (1) the early part of the day, e.g. morrow mass; (2) the day after, as in dates; *cf.* **vigil**.

mortar: bowl used for grinding and mixing ingredients (*MED*).

mortise wimble, 'morteys wymbyll': specialist tool for boring a mortise (*OED*) (no. 723).

mortuary: also called **principal**: the traditional death-gift or burial payment due to the incumbent on behalf of a deceased parishioner, usually the second-best animal (after the heriot had been claimed by the manorial lord) which was sometimes made to precede the corpse to the church at the burial; by the late Middle Ages the enforcement of the mortuary was maintained in only a minority of East Anglian parishes.

moryeve, 'morngefte': in the context of no. 41, **dower**, dowry (*qv*); (see *OED*).

motley: diversified in colour, variegated, particoloured (*OED*); *cf.* **medley**.

murrey: dark red or purple-red colour (*MED*).

musterdevillers, 'musterdelere': kind of woollen cloth, originally from Montivilliers in Normandy, usually of a mixed grey colour (*MED*).

napery: linen, sheets, table cloths, napkins, etc. (*MED*).

neat-house, 'nethus': cattle-shed (no. 76).

noble: gold coin, usually equivalent of 6s 8d. (*MED*).

nonage: the condition of being under age, the period of legal infancy (*OED*).

notary: person legally authorised to record an action or attest the accuracy of a copied document; in the Middle Ages notaries were appointed either by the pope or the emperor, and so were termed papal or imperial; **notarial instrument:** legal document drawn up and attested by a notary; **notarial sign:** the personal mark of attestation placed on a document by a notary; notaries developed their own individual signs, in the form of an elaborately decorated cross, sometimes so elaborate that the basic cross is difficult to make out. See Purvis, *Notarial Signs.*

nuncupative: of wills, given orally on the death-bed, and later written in the third person.

obit: *see* **anniversary.**

obsequies: funeral rites.

octave: (1) the eighth day after a feast-day, counting the feast-day itself; (2) the period of eight days consisting of a feast-day and the next seven days.

offerings: payments due, by tradition and law, from parishioners to incumbent or priest having the cure of souls; *see also* **mass-penny.**

official, archdeacon's: officer appointed by archdeacon and empowered, among other duties, to prove wills within the archdeaconry.

oil: oil obtained from a variety of animal and vegetable sources, widely used in lamps.

ordinary: an ecclesiastical officer who, by his office, has jurisdiction over others; usually, according to circumstances, archbishop, bishop or archdeacon; *see* **peculiar.**

ornaments: the accessories or furnishings of the church and its worship (*OED*).

ostilments: utensils, equipment, furnishings, household goods (*MED*); later becomes 'hustlement'.

overseer: supervisor (*qv*).

pack (of wool): a pack of wool weighed about 240 pounds (Bristow) (no. 309); in 1845, a large bag, known as a wool pack, was capable of containing about 250 pounds of wool, or about 100 average fleeces (*OED*), suggesting that a medieval pack also contained about 100 fleeces.

pack-cloth: cloth placed under a **pack-saddle** (*qv*), or one to wrap up the goods carried by a pack horse (Milward).

pack-saddle: saddle on which packs or burdens were carried (Milward).

painter, 'peyntour': usually likely to have been a painter-stainer, who produced stained cloths; but the 'kerver et peyntour' to be employed to make a tabernacle of the Blessed Virgin Mary at Barningham (no. 338) may well have painted wooden items.

pair: often means a set, rather than just two, e.g. of beads, a string of beads (rosary); of organs, a complete organ.

palm cross: a churchyard cross, usually near the north-east corner of the church, which played a significant part in the Palm Sunday procession. See Duffy, pp.23–4.

pan: a cooking vessel, shallower than a kettle, but often of considerable size (Latin *patella*).

pane, panne: Latin *pannus*, cloth; **(counter)pane:** bedcovering; 'pane' of coney skins (no. 259), a bedcovering of rabbit fur.

panel: painted or carved **table** (*qv*), often of alabaster, placed above or behind an altar as part of a reredos (Latin *tabula*).

pantry: storeroom, especially for bread.

parcelmeal, 'parcel-mele', parsonell: by parcels, parts or portions; bit by bit, piecemeal (*OED*).

parclose: a screen or railing in a church enclosing an altar, a tomb, etc., or separating a chapel, etc., from the main body of the church (*OED*) (nos 96, 669).

pardon: indulgence (*qv*).

parents: often means, as well as actual parents, forebears, ancestors and kinsmen.

parish clerk: the pre-Reformation parish clerk was more an assistant to the parish priest than his post-Reformation equivalent. See Platt, *Parish Churches of Medieval England*, pp.61–3.

parlour: room off main hall affording some privacy and suitable for conversation; separate chamber or apartment (*MED*).

parson: in the Middle Ages an alternative title for a rector, but not used of other clergy.

particoloured: partly of one colour, and partly of another (*OED*).

paternoster: the large bead in a rosary, usually occurring every eleventh bead; so called from the practice of saying a *Paternoster* ('Our Father') at each large bead, and an *Ave* ('Hail Mary') at each small one (nos 421, 698).

peck: unit of dry measure, for grain, etc., a quarter of a **bushel** (*qv*) (Latin *pecca*).

peculiar: parish, church or district exempt from the jurisdiction of the **ordinary** (*qv*) but subject to the jurisdiction of one who thereby becomes its ordinary (Purvis). See Barber, 'What is a Peculiar?'.

peel: a long-handled shovel with which bread etc. is thrust into a hot oven, or taken out (Halliwell).

pelisse: cloak.

pelwe: pillow (no. 259).

pence: *see* **mass-penny**.

perk, perch: used as a colloquial term for **roodloft** (*qv*) (Latin *pertica, perceta,* literally 'perch') (no. 488).

perpetual vicar: *see* **vicar**.

perpetuity, in: for ever.

pewter: alloy of tin with various other ingredients, chiefly copper and lead.

piece: an item of silverware; **standing piece:** piece of silver incorporating stem and foot.

pightle: small enclosed piece of land; term used in east of England (Latin *pictellum*).

pious: devout, godly, religious (*OED*); referring to uses, deeds, etc.

Pity, Our Lady of: the *Pietà*, an image showing Mary grieving over the dead Christ, a popular subject for both statues and stained glass in late medieval churches, with indulgences granted to those offering their prayers and devotion before it (no. 252).

place: (1) house, property; (2) religious house.

placebo: the vespers of the office of the dead, said in church or the deceased's house in the evening before the burial; so called from the antiphon with which it began, *Placebo domino,* etc.

plain-work: plain needlework or sewing, as distinct from fancy-work or embroidery (*OED*).

plaincloth, 'pleynclothe': cloth without embroidery or embellishment.

plate, iron: metal plate used in connection with a hearth or fireplace (*MED*); form of fireback.

platter: flat dish.

pledge: one who becomes a surety for another.

porringer: small basin or similar vessel of metal, earthenware or wood (*OED*).

portasse: a breviary, a prayer book containing the daily offices, or services, in one volume.

posnet: small cooking-pot with a handle and three feet.

postern: side door or gate, small entrance-way.

pot: cooking-pot, with legs, to stand over fire.

potash: *see* **ashes**.

pottle: measure of liquid containing two pints.

powder box: box for powdered spice (*MED*).

power reserved: Part of the probate sentence was the grant of **administration** ('admon') (*qv*) where the executors present in court were named and 'power reserved' to those not present, that is, power was reserved to the court to make grant of administration to the other executor(s) when they came to 'take it up'.

priest: cleric ordained to celebrate mass, hear confessions and administer all other sacraments except confirmation and ordination.

primer: book of prayers and devotions, popular with the more educated laity in the later Middle Ages (Purvis).

principal: mortuary (*qv*).

prior: head of a priory or friary, or deputy to the abbot in an abbey.

probate: the approval, in an ecclesiastical court by an official appointed for the purpose, of will and/or testament submitted to him by executors; **probate sentence:** the certificate of that approval entered on the will by the clerk to the proving authority, usually including the **administration** (*qv*).

procession: processions round the church were usual on Sundays and **feasts** (*qv*) in the Middle Ages; processions at Rogation-tide followed the parish boundary which therefore became known as the 'processional way'.

processional: book containing the music for the responsories and anthems sung in processions.

professed: of a member of a religious community who has taken the necessary vows for full membership.

psalter: book of psalms for singing or reading in church; in no. 247 the psalter was owned by the testator.

purgatory: in the teaching of the medieval church, the place of 'purging' or cleansing, after death, of souls on their passage to heaven. See Burgess, ' "A Fond Thing Vainly Invented": an Essay on Purgatory', but the definitive study is Le Goff, *The Birth of Purgatory*.

pyx: small container of metal, ivory or wood to hold the consecrated host, suspended over the altar and covered with a pyx-cloth; occasionally the pyx had an ornate wooden canopy (no. 803).

quart: unit of liquid measure, containing 2 pints.

quarter: dry measure for grain, etc., of 8 bushels; unit of weight, a quarter of a hundredweight, or 28 pounds.

quern: small (hand) mill for grinding; a quern-stone (*MED*).

quindene: the fifteenth day after any feast, including the actual day of the feast in the reckoning.

quilt: bed-covering stuffed with down, wool, etc. often stitched through to retain an even thickness.

quittance: acquittance; *see* **acquit**.

rack: support for the spit, usually made of iron.

rector: incumbent of a parish who was entitled to the whole income of the living, unless a vicarage had been established.

rectory: the benefice of a rector (not the house, though a house is usually included).

re-enter: take over property when another party had been holding it.

reeve: officer or official, of church (i.e. churchwarden), or town or manor.

regular: (of priest) one who lives under a 'rule' in a religious order; *cf.* **secular**.

remainder: (as in expression 'with remainder to …') the route specified by a testator for the eventual descent of estate or interest.

renounce: decline (to act as executor).

renter: small, subsidiary dwelling attached to a house (?and rented out).

repairing: can sometimes refer to new work, not merely repairing old.

requiem, mass of: mass said or sung for the repose of the dead, from the opening words: *Requiem eternam dona eis, Domine* (Purvis).

reredos: carving, tapestry, etc. at back of altar.

residue: remainder of testator's possessions not hitherto disposed of.

retable: panel or **reredos** (*qv*) standing behind or above altar.

reversion: return of estate or property to its ultimate owner(s) after certain speci-fied conditions.

rochet: a vestment (*qv*) of linen, of the nature of a surplice, usually worn by bishops and abbots, but here (no. 767) linen was to be purchased to make vestments for the parish priest of Kersey.

rod, by the: expression used in connection with bond or copyhold tenure, referring to the ceremony to seal the transference of land, the handing over of a 'rod' or baton to signify the land itself.

rood: (1) literally, cross; the carved crucifix, with figures of Mary and John, one on each side, which stood on the **roodloft** (*qv*); (2) unit of land measure, quarter of an **acre** (*qv*).

roodloft: literally meaning the loft or walkway on top of the roodscreen, on which the rood stood, but frequently used of the whole structure; *see* **candlebeam**.

rood solar: loft or passage running along the top of the roodscreen (no. 419); *see also* **solar**.

russet: coarse woollen cloth of reddish-brown, grey or neutral colour, formerly used for the dress of peasants and country-folk (*OED*).

sacrament of the altar: the consecrated **host** (*qv*); also used to refer to the holy eucharist in general.

sacrist, sacristan: (1) official in a parish church responsible for the contents of the church, especially those used in divine service, and acting as sexton; (2) official in an abbey responsible for the fabric of the church, the altars, the sacred vessels, the services and the shrine.

sallet: a form of basinet, a fifteenth-century helmet.

salt: saltcellar (usually silver).

salting-trough: see **trough**.

sanctuary: a consecrated place, usually, in wills of this period, referring to the churchyard.

sangred: the East Anglian name for a **certain** (*qv*).

sanguine: blood-coloured.

sarcenet: very fine soft silk cloth, used for clothes and linings and as a furnishing fabric in the fifteenth to seventeenth centuries (Yaxley). Here (no. 697), a tapestry made of sarcenet.

saw: saws with differentiating names are found in several wills, in particular nos. 490 and 723, but not all are identifiable; *see* **cutting saw**, **handsaw**, **splitting saw**.

say: cloth of fine texture, originally of linen (by sixteenth century, of wool or wool mixture).

Scala Celi: indulgence for the souls of the departed earned by the saying of masses, originally in the chapel of Scala Celi, on the outskirts of Rome; named because of a reputed vision of St Bernard there, in which he saw souls ascending to heaven on *scala celi* (steps, or ladder, of heaven); later the privilege was extended to Westminster and other named churches, and, by the time of the Reformation, to all churches. See Duffy, pp.375–6.

schedule: bill or document; not necessarily a list.

school, schooling: although in Part I of 'Baldwyne' this usually referred to university education, the three references to school in Part II refer explicitly or implicitly to grammar school (nos 482, 579 and 720). See Orme, *Education and Society in Medieval and Renaissance England*.

seal: wax imprint, formed by metal (etc.) stamp, with which a document was sealed, often on a pendant seal-tag.

seam, 'seem', 'sem': a dry measure, originally a pack-horse load but standardised from the thirteenth century as a **quarter** (*qv*) (Yaxley) (nos 290, 651).

secular: of a priest who was not of a religious order or community; *cf.* **regular**.

selure: *see* **celure**.

sepulchre: the Easter sepulchre, sepulchre of Our Lord, etc., a structure, either temporary or permanent, on the north side of the chancel. On Good Friday a host (consecrated wafer) was placed in the sepulchre and there remained, with 'watchers' in attendance and decorated with lights and hangings; on Easter Sunday morning the host was removed with great ceremony; the lights, burning night and day, attracted gifts from the devout. See Duffy, pp.29–34.

service: (1) employment, e.g. of priest; (2) duty, in the feudal system, consisting of either money or labour, required of a tenant by his lord; (3) *see also* **divine service**.

seven-day, seventh-day: the seventh day after death or burial, similar to **thirty-day** and **anniversary** (*qv*).

several: of land held by an individual, not in common.

sexton: parish officer who looked after the church, dug graves, rang bells, etc.

share, ploughshare: on a plough, the pointed metal blade, attached to the plough-head, which cuts the earth at the bottom of the furrow.

shearman's shears: large shears, used in cloth manufacture to trim the nap of cloth after fulling.

sheephog, 'shepe hog', 'chephogge': sheep before its first shearing (Bristow) (nos 414, 636).

sheriff's aid: *see* **aid**.

shod: of cart, *see* **iron-shod**.

shop: usually implies 'workshop' in the Middle Ages.

shrine: place to which pilgrims came, to pray to and venerate a saint or other holy person, often incorporating an elaborate tomb.

sickle: tool used for cutting corn.

Sir: courtesy title (Latin *dominus*) given to priests not having a master's degree from a university (*see* **Master**); not to be confused with the same title given to a knight, the name of the latter usually being followed by 'knight' (Latin *miles*).

skepmaker: basket-maker.

slough: a muddy place or large pothole in a road.

smock, 'smoke': a woman's undergarment, a shift or chemise (*OED*) (Latin *camisia*).

solar: a private upper room; perhaps derived from Latin *sol* = sun, and thus a room open to the sun, but a more convincing derivation is from Old French, *sol*, floor, and *solive*, beam, that is, a room on a beam, the upper floor (Yaxley).

solder: used in the Middle Ages to join strips of lead in stained-glass windows and on roofs.

sorrel: reddish-brown coloured horse.

soul priest: priest employed specifically to celebrate masses for the souls of the departed.

spar: length of timber used, e.g., for rafters; also used as **studs** (*qv*) for timber-framed buildings (Yaxley).

spit: long iron rod on which meat was roasted over the fire.

spital, 'spetyll': (i.e. *ho*spital) house for the reception of the indigent or diseased (*OED*) (no. 2).

splitting saw: a saw for cleaving timber along the grain.

Spruce, spruce: the country of Prussia, and so, by extension, brought or obtained from Prussia; in some instances the adjective implies 'made of spruce fir', or pine, is the case here: a 'spruce huche' (no. 697).

square, 'sqwyer': an L-shaped tool of wood or metal, or a combination of both, used by carpenters for measuring and setting a right-angle (Yaxley) (no. 23).

squint: an aperture in wall or pier of a church, through which a priest celebrating at a side-altar could see the priest at the high altar; also known as a hagioscope.

stainer: *see* **painter**.

stall: a temporary standing for a market trader.

standard: (1) upright timber or pole (*MED*); (**2**) tall candlestick standing on the ground; (**3**) chest, trunk, box (*MED*).

standing piece: *see* **piece**.

starred, 'sterryd': of a horse or cow: having a (white) star on the forehead (*OED*) (no. 659).

station: position or rank in life.

stations: the churches, shrines, etc., accustomed to be visited by the medieval pilgrim to Rome, all conveying certain indulgences to those praying at them; going round the stations (not necessarily all) referred to as the circuit or circle (no. 544). (See *Indulgences* in the Introduction.)

steeple: a tall tower; a building of great altitude in proportion to its length and breadth (*OED*). In connection with Suffolk churches, a 'steeple' *always* means a 'tower' (e.g. no. 266).

'stelyd': fitted with a 'stele' or handle, referring to tools, vessels, etc. (*MED*).

stert: handle of cooking vessel (*MED*), hence a 'stertepane' (no. 745) is a pan with a handle.

stirk, 'sterkyn': young bullock or heifer, usually between one and two years old (Yaxley) (no. 524).

stock: the assets, both possessions and money, of a gild etc.

stoddle: loom, or framework of loom (*MED*).

stole: *see* **vestments**.

stond: a stand, often for (barrels of) ale (Yaxley) (no. 256).

stone: unit of weight equivalent to 14 pounds, an eighth of a hundredweight and half a quarter.

stool: a bench or seat at the hall-table or in church.

stot: horse, especially one used for ploughing (*MED*).

strip: spoliation of land, destruction of parts of a tenement, etc. (*MED*) *cf.* **waste**.

stud, 'stode': upright post in timber-framed buildings; substantial sawn building timber (Yaxley).

stuff: foodstuffs, grain, etc. (*MED*); also household stuff.

subdeacon: a cleric immediately below the rank of deacon; *see also* high **mass**.

summerland: land left fallow for a season to rest the soil (before the days of break-crops); it would be ploughed three times in order to turn in the previous year's stubble and subsequent weeds.

supervisor: one appointed by a testator to oversee the proper carrying out of the terms of a will by the executors; also called the **overseer** (Purvis).

surety: a person (guarantor) or money, land, etc.; provided as a security by a person entering into an agreement, for the proper fulfilment of the terms specified.

surplice: a loose linen clerical garment, reaching right down to the feet, with very large sleeves cut so that the openings hung down vertically, and ample material gathered in at the neck (Watkin).

surrender: in feudal tenure, the giving up of his right to hold a bond tenement by a tenant; the surrender was made to the lord, either in the manorial court, or into the hands of other tenants of the manor.

tabard: overgarment, usually sleeveless, worn primarily by member of the lower classes or by monks (*MED*).

tabernacle: (1) canopied recess or niche of stone or wood, built to receive the image of a saint (e.g. nos 19, 745); (2) receptacle for the sacrament on or over an altar, as in Roman Catholic churches today, or for carrying the host in procession.

table: panel or retable, often of carved alabaster (Latin *tabula*); the alabaster 'Adoration of the Magi', now set in the wall in Long Melford church, was part of a medieval 'table'.

tail: entail of estate, which was required to descend strictly in order, e.g. general entail: to the heirs of the body of the holder; tail male: to the male heirs of the body of the holder.

talshide, 'talsshyde': a hide or piece of wood of prescribed length, either round, or split in two or four, according to thickness, for cutting into billets for firewood (*OED*) (no. 803).

taper: type of candle used at religious ceremonies; usually smaller than a torch.

tapestry-work: tapestry, needle-work.

tapet: piece of figured cloth used as a hanging, table-cover, carpet, or the like (*OED*); in no. 697 it may mean a decorated cover for a bow (information from Dr Ralph Moffat).

tax: in the period covered by 'Baldwyne', taxes were usually granted by parliament to the crown at the rate of a tenth (of movable property) in towns and of a fifteenth in the country; often called 'the king's tax' or subsidy. See Jurkowski, Smith and Crook, *Lay Taxes in England and Wales 1188–1688*; Jurkowski, 'Income Tax Assessments of Norwich, 1472 and 1489'.

tenant-in-chief: in the feudal system, one who held land directly from the king and who, after death, was the subject of an inquisition post mortem.

tenement: property held in tenure (*MED*); literally, a holding, often, but not always, implying the inclusion of a dwelling.

tenter: wooden frame on which fulled cloth was dried and stretched (no. 504); set in a tenteryard; the L-shaped hooks used to hold the cloth in place led to the expression 'on tenterhooks'.

'terment': burial, interment; also commemoration as at **seventh-day** and **anniversary** (*qv*).

testament: the section of a will, normally appearing first, dealing with items other than land.

tester: bed-head, often of tapestry matching the curtains of the bed.

thirty-day: the thirtieth day after death or burial, similar to **seventh-day** and **anniversary** (*qv*); often called 'month-mind'.

thurible: censer, a metal vessel with a lid, perforated and carried on chains, for the burning of incense ceremonially during church services (Purvis).

tippet, 'typett': a long narrow slip of cloth or hanging part of dress, formerly worn either attached to and forming part of the hood, head-dress or sleeve, or loose, as a scarf or the like (*OED*) (no. 350).

tithes: the tenth of a parishioner's produce or wages for the year, due to the rector and/or vicar of a parish.

title: the right to ownership of property.

toft: the plot of land on which a house stands; a vacant plot of land usable for a homestead (*MED*).

torch: the largest of the **lights** (*qv*) of a church, used for illuminating the church and at funerals.

'tovere', toyere, tuyere: the nozzle through which the blast is forced in a forge (*OED*) (no. 815; see note to that will).

town: formerly referred to any parish or community, in the sense of township, without any reference to size; the more distant part of a village was therefore 'townsend'.

traces, hand-traces: pair of ropes, chains or leather straps by which the collar of a draught-animal was connected with the splinter-bar or swingletree (*OED*) (no. 1); 'shaktrays', a particular type of traces (no. 240).

trammel: (1) a long narrow fishing net (*OED*, 1440); (2) the hopper of a mill (*OED*, 1440); (3) a horse-hobble; device for teaching a horse to move the legs on the same side together (Yaxley: *OED*, 1550); (4) chimney iron to hang pots on (Yaxley: *OED*, 1557). Here (no. 375) the context of the bequest ('a brass pot with a plate and a trammel') suggests the fourth definition despite the late date of the *OED* example.

translation: used in dates, with reference to saints, meaning the anniversary of the removal of remains (relics) from one shrine to another, or from grave to shrine.

transom: bolster on a bed. Tymms noted that 'the transome is usually considered to be that part of the bedstead which is between the two head-posts, and is frequently elaborately carved; but the general association of the word with feather beds would lead us to think the bolster was meant' (Tymms, *Bury Wills*, p.242).

trendle wheel: wheel-shaped chandelier hung in a church, often before the rood.

trental: set of 30 masses, which could be celebrated over a period of time or all on one day; in a **trental of St Gregory**, the masses had to be celebrated at certain specified festivals. See Duffy, pp.293–4.

trestle: wooden support, used in pairs, for table-top.

tripartite: of deed, made in three corresponding parts or copies; *see* **indented**.

trivet: three-legged iron stand on which to heat plate, dish, etc., by fire.

trough: wooden box-like tub, for kneading, brewing, salting, etc.

tumbrel: a two-wheeled cart, designed to tip backwards to empty its load (*MED*).

tunic: body-garment or coat, over which a loose mantle or cloak was worn (*OED*).

turf: slab of peat dug with spade in Fenland and dried as fuel.

twibill, 'twbyll': axe with two cutting edges, often used for cutting mortises (Yaxley) (no. 490).

tye: term for green or common occurring only in north Essex and south Suffolk.

underwood: low shrubs, undergrowth; cuttings, brushwood (*MED*); the product of periodic coppicing in woodland.

use: purpose, end; benefit, profit, advantage (*MED*).

usufruct: legal term meaning the right of temporary possession, use, or enjoyment of the advantages of property belonging to another, so far as may be had without causing damage or prejudice to this (*OED*) (no. 824).

utensils: equipment, especially within the house.

vespers: the evening office, or service, of the church.

vestments, mass: special garments worn by the **priest** when celebrating mass, as follows (in the order in which they are put on): **amice:** white linen garment worn in the manner of a hood and secured by tapes or strings passing round the shoulders; **alb:** white linen garment with sleeves, covering the whole figure; **stole:** long narrow strip of coloured fabric, hung from the neck and reaching nearly down to the feet; **girdle:** twisted cord or narrow sash which gathered the folds of the alb round the waist; **maniple:** narrow strip of coloured material worn on the left arm and reaching to the knees; **chasuble:** large conical garment, covering the whole figure from the neck to below the knees. The **deacon** wore a **dalmatic** (a tunic with wide sleeves, reaching to below the knees) instead of a chasuble, while the

subdeacon wore a tunic (similar to the dalmatic) instead of the chasuble and stole (Watkin).

vestry: room in or adjoining a church in which the vestments and equipment for divine worship were kept (Purvis).

vicar: incumbent of a church appropriated to a religious house, etc., and therefore entitled to only part of the income of the benefice, usually including the small tithes; *cf.* **rector**; **perpetual vicar:** a form of tautology, since every canonically instituted vicar had security of tenure; frequently used in such documents as bishops' registers, presumably to emphasise the regularity of the appointment.

vice: a spiral staircase.

vigil: the evening, or day, before a feast-day; *cf.* **morrow**.

visitation: inspection of an ecclesiastical district, parish or religious house by a superior official (e.g. bishop or archdeacon) or his deputy.

wantel, 'wantayll', 'wangtayll': bundle, burden, pack (*OED*), but here (no. 544) may be **wantow:** rope or band used to fasten the pack on a pack-saddle or a load on the back of a horse (*OED*).

warden: one who has something in safe keeping, e.g. churchwarden.

waste: (1) the illegal consumption or using up of material, resources, etc.; *see* **strip, impeachment**; **(2)** the consumption of candles, etc. at a funeral or obit (*OED*).

watering: pond or ford where animals could drink.

way: road or track; *see* **procession**.

webster: weaver.

wether, 'wederschepe', 'wedyrhog': a castrated male sheep (Latin *aries, multo aries*) (nos 471, 636).

wheel, 'whele': spinning wheel (no. 256).

will: (1) correctly, the part of the 'testament and last will' which was concerned with real estate; **(2)** wish, e.g. 'at the will of the lord'.

wimble, 'wymbyll': gimlet, auger (Anglo-French *wimble*, variant of *guimble*); a brace to hold bits, often of considerable size (Yaxley) (no. 723).

woad: the processed leaves of the woad plant, used to produce a blue dye; the leaves were crushed, dried and formed into balls to supply dyers.

wood-ash: *see* **ashes**.

wounds: *see* **five wounds**.

yard: (1) unit of linear measure containing 3 feet, 0.9144 metres; **(2)** enclosed area by a house (Latin *ortus*).

yarn: spun wool, ready for use in weaving.

Introduction[1]

Historians have for long recognised the value of wills as original sources,[2] and many collections have been printed. Among the first to be published were such pioneering volumes as Nicolas's *Testamenta Vetusta* (1826)[3] and Raine's *Testamenta Eboracensia* Part I (1836).[4] Soon afterwards came the selection relating to the western part of Suffolk made by Samuel Tymms in 1850,[5] which was much quoted in the *Oxford English Dictionary*. The editors of these early volumes chose to treat their material differently. Nicolas provided only extracts of selected wills, in keeping with his sub-title, 'being illustrations from wills, of manners, customs, &c'. The wills in Raine's volume were also selected, but appear to be entire.[6] Tymms printed his selection *in extenso*, with no omissions, even using special type for Latin contractions. All three of these volumes, however, consisted of selections of wills, chosen because they were in some way outstanding, and tending, therefore, to represent the wealthier sections of society.

In 1987 the Suffolk Records Society published the first volume of a new series, containing abstracts of wills from a lower court.[7] All surviving wills in that court, for a particular period, are printed. They are therefore more representative, insomuch as wills can be, when one remembers that only about a third of the population made them. The wills are presented as 'full abstracts', that is, including all items of substance and all personal and place names, and omitting only words considered dispensable. Part I and the present volume are part of that series, in the same form, but dealing with the oldest surviving wills of the archdeaconry, beginning nearly two hundred years earlier than those in Mrs Evans's volume.

The administrative system of probate

Before 1858, when the Principal Probate Registry was set up and England was divided into Probate Districts,[8] probate jurisdiction had been, with a few exceptions such as certain corporations and the two ancient universities, in the hands of the church. It was therefore ecclesiastical boundaries, rather than civil, which governed the proving of wills. Medieval England was, for ecclesiastical purposes, divided into seventeen dioceses, each administered by a bishop and his officers. The dioceses were divided into archdeaconries, supervised by archdeacons, and the archdeacon-

---

[1]   In outline this Introduction is substantially the same as that to Part I but, of course, where applicable, references have been given to documents in Part II. Also some of the sections have been expanded.

[2]   See, for example, Zell, 'Fifteenth- and Sixteenth-century Wills', pp.67–74.

[3]   N. H. Nicolas, 2 vols.

[4]   J. Raine (ed.), Surtees Society, iv.

[5]   *Wills and Inventories* (Camden Society, xlix).

[6]   Although later volumes in the same series omitted many minor bequests.

[7]   N. Evans (ed.), *Wills of the Archdeaconry of Sudbury 1630–1635* (SRS, xxix).

[8]   Under the Act 'to amend the Law relating to Probates and Letters of Administration in England' (20 & 21 Vict. c.77), dated 25 August 1857 and effective from 12 January 1858.

ries were subdivided into deaneries. It is said that rural deans, the clerics responsible for deaneries, once had probate jurisdiction, but in practice and in recorded time, the archdeacon's court was the lowest level at which wills were proved.

The great majority of testators had their wills proved in the archdeacon's court. Knights, clergy and those having substantial possessions (*bona notabilia*: usually over £10 for this purpose) had to have their wills proved in the bishop's, or consistory, court. Possession of *bona notabilia* of more than £5 in more than one archdeaconry of the same diocese also required wills to be proved in the consistory court. Where property was held in more than one diocese, wills had to be proved in the archbishop's court, in southern England that of the archbishop of Canterbury, which later became known as the Prerogative Court of Canterbury (PCC). The exceptions to this general rule were mainly the wills of those living in any parish known as a 'peculiar', for whom the court of the person holding the peculiar jurisdiction had to be used. It has been estimated that, before the 1857 Act, at least 300 different courts had probate jurisdiction in England.[9] A vacancy in a see, when there was no bishop or archbishop, resulted in wills having to be proved in a higher court. If the vacancy were in a diocese, the archbishop's court had to be resorted to. If there were no archbishop of Canterbury, wills had to be proved in the priory of Christ Church, Canterbury, becoming known as *sede vacante* wills.[10] Higher courts than those required by law seem often to have been used by executors, possibly because they were regarded as having greater validity. Wills of the nobility, and of the wealthy such as merchants and manorial lords, were often taken to the archbishop's court even when there were no territorial requirements for this.

The probate system in Suffolk

Suffolk, until the reorganisation of 1837 was carried out by the Ecclesiastical Commissioners, had been part of the diocese of Norwich and, since the twelfth century, had consisted of two archdeaconries, known as 'Sudbury' and 'Suffolk', each having separate probate jurisdiction.[11] The archdeaconry of Suffolk was administered from Ipswich, while the administration of the archdeaconry of Sudbury, despite its name, was centred on Bury St Edmunds.[12]

The archdeaconry of Sudbury was the western part of the county of Suffolk, having almost the same boundaries as the old county of West Suffolk, before the amalgamation of East and West Suffolk in 1974.[13] The medieval archdeaconry

---

[9] Camp, *Wills and their Whereabouts*, p.iii.

[10] For example, following the death in March 1486 of Thomas Bourgchier, Archbishop of Canterbury, the final 77 wills in the PCC Register Logge (fols 173–212) were proved *sede vacante* before Master David William, as representative of the prior and convent of Christchurch, Canterbury. (*Logge Register*, I, pp.32–4.)

[11] By an Order in Council (*London Gazette*, 30 May 1837, p.1368) the archdeaconry of Sudbury became part of the diocese of Ely, with the exception of the deaneries of Hartismere and Stow which were transferred to the archdeaconry of Suffolk.

[12] Its name suggests that, at its original formation, the archdeaconry had been administered from Sudbury, the 'south borough' (as compared with Bury St Edmunds to the north?), but from a time before records began it had been centred on Bury. See Martin, 'Ecclesiastical Jurisdictions'.

[13] The county of West Suffolk, formed in 1889, had the same boundaries as the ancient liberty of St Edmund, the 'eight and a half hundreds', which were under the control of Bury abbey until its dissolution.

differed from the later county of West Suffolk in having the two extra deaneries of Hartismere and Stow at its eastern edge,[14] while on its western fringe the deanery of Fordham anciently included several Cambridgeshire parishes.[15] The archdeaconry contained several 'peculiars', which were jurisdictions belonging to someone other than the archdeacon of Sudbury. Isleham (Cambs) and Freckenham were in the jurisdiction of the bishop of Rochester,[16] while Hadleigh, Monks Eleigh and Moulton were part of the archbishop of Canterbury's deanery of Bocking (Essex).[17]

By far the most important of the 'peculiars' was that of the town of Bury St Edmunds, which was regarded as a separate archdeaconry under the jurisdiction of the abbey. The sacrist of the abbey then in office was the archdeacon, and wills of the inhabitants of the town, or anyone dying in it, had to be proved in the sacrist's court. The abbey was exempt from all superior jurisdiction in this country and was subject only to Rome. Consequently, neither the bishop's court nor the archbishop's was recognised by the abbey authorities, and the wills of all inhabitants of the town, regardless of status, had to be proved by the sacrist. Wills of a few Bury residents can, nevertheless, be found in the registers of the consistory court of Norwich and of the archbishop's court, but in each case the deceased had property elsewhere, as well as in Bury, and it was in respect of that property that the other court had been used.[18] Sometimes similar wills were proved in both the sacrist's court and the bishop's or archbishop's, and were registered in both. Each court, though, made it clear that the subsequent grant of administration related only to the goods in its own jurisdiction.[19] On the dissolution of the abbey in 1539 Bury became a royal peculiar and archdeacons were nominated by the crown. By the end of 1556 the jurisdiction had passed to the bishop of Norwich who appointed a commissary to act on his behalf.[20] Wills in the commissary's court continued to be registered separately until 1566/7,[21] after which they and the wills proved in the court of the archdeacon of Sudbury were combined into one series.[22]

There have always been instances where civil and ecclesiastical boundaries,

---

[14] See Martin, 'Ecclesiastical Jurisdictions', and Thomas, 'Local Government since 1872'.

[15] These became the Fordham deanery of the diocese of Ely at the formation of the diocese of St Edmundsbury and Ipswich in 1914, with the exception of Newmarket All Saints which remained in the archdeaconry of Sudbury for ecclesiastical purposes.

[16] Registers of the consistory court of Rochester contain wills from 1440 and include a few medieval ones for Freckenham, but none for Isleham. See Duncan, *Index of Wills Proved in the Rochester Consistory Court*.

[17] No medieval wills survive for the deanery of Bocking. See *PSIA*, xiv (1915), p.19.

[18] The will of widow Joan Rowland, proved in July 1485 (NRO, NCC 248 A. Caston), seems to have been the solitary exception to this rule. She mentioned no property or interest outside Bury, and it is difficult to see why the will was allowed to be taken to the consistory court.

[19] For wills being proved in two courts simultaneously see Jacob (ed.), *Chichele Register*, ii, xiii–xiv. This situation could lead to 'selective registering'. For example, the will of Simon Burgon, rector of Elveden and master of the hospital of St Nicholas in Bury, who died in 1504, was proved both at Norwich (NRO, NCC 550 Popy) and at Bury (SROB, Pye 157), but the version entered in the sacrist's register made no mention of his being rector of Elveden. Conversely, the PCC version of the 1478 will of Nicholas Mors *alias* Mos (PCC 35 Wattys) omitted quite a large section relating to a tenement in Bury, which is present in the version in the sacrist's register (SROB, Hawlee 260).

[20] See the probate sentences in the register Sunday for this period, SROB.

[21] In the register Sunday, the last of a series of seven which had been started by the sacrist in 1354.

[22] Technically, though, the commissary's court continued in existence until it was combined with the archdeacon's by Order in Council in 1844. See Tymms, *Bury Wills*, p.vii.

though close, have not coincided. This has led to anomalies of jurisdiction. Reference has already been made to the Cambridgeshire parishes on the western boundary which were in the archdeaconry of Sudbury. In the south, Bures and Haverhill each had a 'hamlet' on the other side of the river in Essex which was, nevertheless, regarded ecclesiastically as part of its Suffolk parish. This was partly regularised towards the end of the nineteenth century when the Essex portion of Haverhill was taken into Suffolk. Bures hamlet, however, has remained in Essex, although in the Sudbury archdeaconry as part of the ecclesiastical parish of Bures St Mary. One further boundary anomaly existed in the north of the archdeaconry, at Thetford. Part of Thetford, consisting mainly of the parish of St Mary the Less, was in Suffolk, but had for long been regarded as being in the archdeaconry of Norwich. Even the ecclesiastical authorities seem to have had doubts, for the wills of some inhabitants of St Mary's parish, though proved before officials of the archdeaconry of Norwich, were registered with those of the archdeaconry of Sudbury.[23]

Registers surviving for the archdeaconry of Sudbury

The records of the archdeaconry held by the Suffolk Record Office at Bury St Edmunds (SROB) contain just over a hundred volumes of registered wills. They date from 1439 to 1858, when civil probate registries were set up.[24] In addition there are many hundreds of separate wills, mostly the originals or copies of those entered in the registers.[25] The separate wills are mainly from the years after 1550, but about two hundred are of the fifteenth century.

Many medieval probate registries named their will registers for ease of reference. The names usually referred to the first testator's surname, or sometimes the first testator of significance, in each volume.[26] Register 'Baldwyne' is the first in the archdeaconry of Sudbury series.[27] It was originally a very large volume of nearly 600 folios, bound within large parchment covers: when V. B. Redstone was preparing his *Calendar* (published in 1907), he estimated that the original single volume was five inches thick.[28] No will of a person named Baldwyne occurs near the beginning of the register, so it has to be assumed that some folios had been lost before the original binding took place.[29] About fifty years ago the register was completely rebound

---

[23] For example, the will of Thomas Gelyon, of Thetford St Mary, was proved before the commissary of the bishop of Norwich during a visitation of the deanery of Thetford in October 1520, but was entered in the register of the archdeacon of Suffolk (SROB, Johnson 80).

[24] The last will in the archdeacon's court was proved on 21 December 1857, although there is a subsequent note of 5 January 1858 (SROB, IC500/2/114/331–4).

[25] When a will was proved, an 'office copy' was made as well as its being registered. Sometimes the copy and sometimes the original was the one retained in the registry, but all are referred to as 'original wills' for archival purposes. The truly original wills sometimes retain their seal-tags, but only rarely their seals.

[26] The archdeaconry of Sudbury used surnames and so did the consistory court of Norwich, but the archdeaconry of Suffolk merely numbered its registers in date sequence.

[27] For archival convenience the registers have been given modern call-numbers. For example, register 'Baldwyne' is now IC500/2/9–10, register 'Hervye' is IC500/2/11 and register 'Fuller' IC500/2/12. Similarly, the prefix for original wills is IC500/1/-. In this volume registers will be referred to by their original names.

[28] *PSIA*, xii, p.vii [*2nd set*].

[29] The succeeding registers, 'Hervye' and 'Fuller', begin with wills of their respective names.

Plate 1. The original cover and the two volumes into which the original has been rebound. *Photo: Geoff Cordy.*

into two separate parts. The second part, folios 308 to 591, is printed in this present volume; also included are 17 wills that had 'strayed' into register Fuller.[30]

Register 'Baldwyne'

The complete register called 'Baldwyne' contains well over 2,000 items for the period 1439–1474[31] and was compiled under the supervision of William Thweytes, a notary. This we learn from the original parchment covers: a large portion of the inner cover has been sewn into the first part of the rebound volume; on the front of this inner cover is written *Registrum testamentorum archidiaconatus Sudburie, per Thweytes*,[32] accompanied by a small notarial sign. This title, preceded by the date, *AD 1439*, appears again on the inside of the old cover, where it is part of a long statement in Latin telling of the beginning of the register by Thweytes[33] in the time of Clement Denston, archdeacon, and his official. The succession of archdeacons and their officials is then spelt out, as in the following table:

Archdeacons of Sudbury and their Officials, 1439–1470

Archdeacon (all described as 'Master')	*Official* (all described as 'Master')
Clement Denston, BCnL[34]	Henry Sythyng[35]
John Wygenhale[36]	Robert Spylman[37]
John Selot, DCnL[38]	William Woode[39]
	John Crofftes, BCnL[40]
	John Ramsey, BCnL[41]
	William Duffeld, BCnL[42]

[30] See the final section of the Introduction, *The assembling of register 'Baldwyne'*.

[31] Wills relating to 1478–79 occur on fols 586–9, but these are entered on two bifolia which have been mistakenly bound into 'Baldwyne'. Numbers at the tops of these folios match those in the following volume, 'Hervye', showing where they truly belong.

[32] That is, 'The register of testaments of the archdeaconry of Sudbury, by Thweytes'.

[33] Thweytes is styled 'commissary', but was almost certainly acting as registrar. See O'Day, 'The Role of the Registrar in Diocesan Administration', pp.77–94.

[34] Appointed archdeacon in 1429 (Emden, *BRUC*, p.182); during his time as archdeacon he briefly held the living of Hardingham, Norfolk, where a Thweytes family were lords of a manor (Blomefield, x, 225; Rye, *Norfolk Families*, pp.906–7).

[35] Warden of the college of St Gregory, Sudbury, and rector of both medieties of Wortham; will proved December 1464 (NRO, NCC 335 Brosyard). Not in Emden, *BRUC* or *BRUO*; see Blomefield, iii, 660.

[36] John Wygenhale *alias* Saresson, appointed in 1452 (Emden, *BRUC*, p.655); had been dean of college of St Mary in the Fields, Norwich, where he wished to be buried; will dated January 1460/61 (no probate) (NRO, NCC 9 Betyns).

[37] Warden of Sudbury college after Sythyng's death (Emden, *BRUC*, p.547); will pr. October 1467 (NRO, NCC 82 Jekkys); to be buried in the church of St Gregory, Sudbury.

[38] Archdeacon by 1462; held many livings in Norwich diocese at his death, including mastership of St Giles's hospital, Norwich (Emden, *BRUC*, pp.517–18; Rawcliffe, *Medicine for the Soul*, pp.256–7).

[39] Rector of Fornham All Saints and warden of the college at Sudbury; will pr. June 1493 (NRO, NCC 76 Typpes); he left property in Sudbury for the founding of a grammar school (Emden, *BRUC*, p.650).

[40] Will pr. March 1478/79 (SROB, Hawlee 264); to be buried by cross of St Thomas in churchyard of Bury abbey; seems to have been living in hospital of St Nicholas, Bury, at writing of will (bed, boards and 'other stuff' there) (Emden, *BRUC*, pp.167–8).

[41] Rector of Thelnetham from June 1469; dead by May 1473 (Emden, *BRUC*, p.471).

[42] 'Now' (*nunc*), presumably when Thweytes was preparing 'Baldwyne' for binding, *c*.1474; held many livings in Suffolk and elsewhere and was made archdeacon of Stafford in 1497 (Emden, *BRUC*, p.197).

Beneath the statement is written, in Latin, 'On the souls of the above-written may God have mercy, and on those for whom they are bound. Amen'.[43] Added to this is a larger version of the notarial sign, followed by the words, *per Thweytes*. Underneath the whole, as though it were an after-thought, appears, *et omnium fidelium defunctorum* ('and of all the faithful departed').

In addition to the inner cover, the original outer cover has also been preserved and separately boxed. This is made of very stout parchment and has the stitch-marks of two straps which fastened what was originally a very large volume. Across this outer cover is written, in large letters, *Reg^m Testa^orum per Thweytes*, with a notarial sign between *per* and *Thweytes*, and beneath that, *Testament' probat' in Anno nostri salvatoris 1439, 40 usque 1474*, followed by *Baldwyne*. (See frontispiece.)

Very little is known of William Thweytes himself.[44] His sign identifies him as a notary and as such he must have been a man of some consequence in Bury. He acted as executor of the wills of two of the archdeacon's officials of his time, Sythyng in 1464 and Crofftes in 1479, and also for the wealthy cleric, William Coote, who first set up a college of priests in Bury.[45] He was one of the feoffees of the properties of both John (Jankyn) Smyth and Margaret Odeham, the two great benefactors of medieval Bury.[46] Thweytes seems to have had a son with the same Christian name, for both Smyth and Margaret Odeham referred to William Thweytes the elder and William Thweytes the younger as feoffees.[47]

The form of a medieval will

A medieval will contained three elements: testament, will proper[48] and probate sentence. Although the expression 'last will and testament' nowadays implies one and the same item, the two were originally separate documents. This arose because under feudal law in England, real estate could not be bequeathed by a testator and church courts could not deal with land matters.[49] Consequently the practice developed of using the testament (Latin *testamentum*) for stating bequests of goods and chattels, and giving religious instructions, especially for the good of the testator's soul (all concerns of the church, the proving body), while directions concerning the disposal of land were contained in the will (Latin *voluntas* or *ultima voluntas*). Strictly speaking the church was not concerned with the testator's real estate, and had no power over it, but more often than not the probate sentence appears to relate to the will as well as to the testament, where both are present. Because the will proper was not really the concern of the church, it was frequently not presented for probate and so the testament only was proved and registered. In such cases, unless

---

[43] By the phrase, 'for whom they are bound' was understood, 'for whom they are bound to pray'.
[44] See Emden, *BRUC*, p.600.
[45] Will pr. May 1475 (SROB, Hawlee 196); he was rector of Fornham All Saints and Barningham.
[46] In 1481 and 1492 respectively; the properties they left formed the basis of the Guildhall Feoffment, which still continues today.
[47] Their two wills were printed by Tymms in *Bury Wills*, pp.55–81.
[48] For the purpose of this introduction the term 'will proper' will be used when referring to the actual will, the *voluntas*, as distinct from the testament, whereas 'will' is used as a broad generic term covering both aspects.
[49] See Jacob, *Chichele Register*, ii, p.xix.

they survive elsewhere, one cannot tell whether wills proper were ever associated with the testaments. By the time of register 'Baldwyne', testators were not always observing the distinction between testaments and wills proper. Consequently many wills of the time incorporated elements of both: some described as testament included instructions relating to land, others termed will (*voluntas*) contained testamentary directions, and many compilers used the composite term 'testament and will'.[50]

Probate sentences (for convenience called 'probates' in this volume) were added to wills by the registry clerk. Occasionally the probate was omitted from the registered version of the will, which makes it difficult to tell whether the will was actually proved or not. The will(s) of Thomas Deneys/Deynes of Combs (nos 621 and 694) are especially interesting in this regard: no. 621 seems to be an earlier version of no. 694; the former, although entered in the register, does not have a probate clause, whereas the latter does, suggesting that although both versions were presented to the court, the latter was the one that was proved. In many instances only the probate was registered, without the relevant will.[51] What the criteria were for entering or not entering the will we have no means of telling, but the existence of a probate shows that there had been a will to prove.

The shape of a medieval testament

By the fifteenth century will-writers had developed a fairly standard sequence in shaping a testament. This pattern was not sacrosanct, nor did every testament include all the elements, but, generally speaking, what follows is a summary of the contents of a pre-Reformation testament.

Invocation: The majority of testaments began with the words, 'In the name of God, Amen', although the Trinity was also included on occasion, sometimes all three persons being spelt out.[52]

Date of writing: Usually expressed as day, month and year, but quite frequently by reference to liturgical feast-days.[53] Use of the regnal year was normally reserved for dating wills proper;[54] but within 'Baldwyne' Part II it was employed nine times in testaments[55] and eight times in composite testaments and wills.[56] The will of Simon Galte of Worlington (no. 426) demonstrates contemporary awareness of the crown

---

[50] See Jacob, *Chichele Register*, ii, pp.xix–xxi. Of approximately 760 wills in Part II of 'Baldwyne', excluding those repeated or deleted in the register, about 260 contain testaments only, about 440 are mixtures of testaments and wills proper, and about 50 consist of separate testaments and wills proper. In addition a handful are wills proper only.

[51] There are fifty probates registered in the second part of 'Baldwyne'. The probate of John Goore of Barnham was registered on 21 September 1458 (Pt I, no. 1303) and then on 13 March 1468/69 a codicil to his will was proved, twice (nos 292 and 293 in this volume).

[52] For example, no. 229.

[53] The feast-days used in Part II of 'Baldwyne', with their equivalent dates, are given above, p. xvi.

[54] Charts for converting regnal years can be found in such books as Cheney, *Handbook of Dates*, and Richardson, *Local Historian's Encyclopedia*.

[55] Nos 77, 173, 245, 246, 260, 267, 312, 421 and 426.

[56] Nos 67, 239, 378, 483, 628, 668, 683 and 731.

changing hands during what is now known as the Wars of the Roses: it is dated '49 Henry VI from the first beginning of his reign and [in] the first year of his majesty's readeption'.[57] The Roman calendar, based on the Kalends, Nones and Ides of the months, was used just three times to date testaments.[58]

The testator: After giving his/her name the testator usually, but by no means always, gave their place of abode, only rarely their occupation. When an occupation was given, it was usually a means of identification, to distinguish two or more individuals of the same name. This was a situation more likely to occur in, for instance, urban Bury St Edmunds than in the rural archdeaconry.[59] In Part II only fourteen testators stated their occupation: three fullers, three husbandmen, two barkers, two 'bochers' (butchers), a clerk, a glover, a smith and a turner.[60] A further twelve men had an *alias*, of which ten had an occupational *alias* and one had a place-related surname.[61] Where appropriate, descriptions of status and condition such as esquire (one), gentleman (three) and widow (more than thirty) were more likely to be stated.[62] Three of the women explicitly stated that they were 'the wife of ...', which might indicate that they owned goods or property in their own right, usually inherited either from their father or a former husband, or that they were executrix to a former husband, whose bequests had not yet been fully implemented.[63] The

---

[57] See note to that will regarding this phrasing.

[58] Nos 326, 612 and 789; Margaret Wetherard (no. 669) stated that the anniversaries of her husband and herself were both to be observed on 5 Kalends September. The *Handbook of Dates* has the relevant conversion tables.

[59] Apart from fathers and sons with the same name, in Part II there are no instances where such a distinction is obviously needed, unlike the two men named John Wareyn in Part I (nos 108, 301) where John Wareyn the barker of Nayland was to be distinguished from his namesake the fuller at nearby Stoke.

[60] John Pondere of Sudbury, fuller (no. 306); John Syday of Great Waldingfield, fuller (no. 225); John Flegge of Sudbury, the elder, fuller (no. 727); John Duke of Little Saxham, husbandman (no. 373); John Osmond of Assington, husbandman (no. 459); Stephen Byrd of Kersey, husbandman (no. 595); Thomas Puttok of Mildenhall, barker (no. 147); Robert Judy of Tostock, barker (no. 771); Andrew Att Herne of Icklingham St James, 'bocher' (nos 72 and 403); John Breon of Little Waldingfield, 'bocher' (no. 349); Robert Webbe of Woolpit, clerk (no. 624); John Roodese of Ixworth, glover (no. 37); John Bakoun of Brent Eleigh, smith (no. 300); John Caldewell of Thelnetham, the elder, turner (no. 703).

[61] Those with occupational *aliases* are: Stephen Hecham *alias* Bochere (no. 180); Ralph Penteney *alias* Sporyere (no. 220); William Hawkedon *alias* Glovere (no. 284); Richard Worliche *alias* Flecchere (no. 345); Richard Lotkyn *alias* Roper (no. 347); John Salle *alias* Cooke (no. 484); Nicholas Stroude *alias* Taylour (no. 637); Walter Nicoll *alias* Clerk (no. 642); John Clerk *alias* Webbe (no. 646); John Sawyer *alias* Gylly (no. 663). The place-related name is Robert Spryng *alias* Wederdeyn (no. 810); although arguably William Hawkedon *alias* Glovere could also fit in this category. William At Lee *alias* Hurlebate (no. 370) is the twelfth *alias*. It is, of course, possible that the *aliases* relate to predecessors. There is one woman with an *alias*, Isabel Cake *alias* Reve (nos 172 and 177).

[62] Robert Hunte of Rushbrooke, esquire (no. 191); Roger Drury of Hepworth, gentleman (no. 402); Baldwin Coksedge of Felsham, gentleman (no. 417); John Turnour of Great Thurlow, gentleman (no. 608). Of the widows, some identified themselves as 'the relict of', some as 'the widow of' and others 'late the wife of'.

[63] From the text of their wills, it is clear that some others were wives, rather than widows. Margery Hunte of Barnardiston, wife of John (no. 677), required her husband to implement both her will and that of her late husband, John Burgeyn; Elizabeth Cake of Stowmarket, wife of Robert (no. 689), required her husband to recover 20 marks bequeathed to her by her father, Robert Gavell; Isabel Grome of Melford, wife of John, the elder (no. 728) required her messuage, formerly John Bakere's (her late husband), to be sold to pay her legacies, which included prayers for the soul of John Bakere and also of John Bullyngton,

most interesting status self-description is that of John Russell the elder of Great Waldingfield (no. 424), who proudly declared that he was a churchwarden and that he had made his will in the presence of many of the great of the parish.[64] Although the majority of men had common Christian names such as John, Thomas or William, some unusual names do occur, such as Gerard Fodryngay of Brockley (no. 35), Baldwin Coksedge of Felsham (no. 417), Patrick Kedlowe of Newton (no. 597) and Benedict Othoo of Bradfield St George (no. 772). Similarly, although many of the women were called Agnes or Margaret, some had less common names, such as the two named Mariota – Mariota Baldwyn of Assington (no. 458) and Mariota Sprunte of Clare (no. 662) – as well as Amfritha Waryn of Sudbury (no. 32), and Britana Hummys of Kersey (no. 701).

State of mind: Testators were careful to emphasise their mental competence and so began by declaring themselves to be sound of mind and of good memory, although, they might add, being sick of body, in peril of death or 'sick unto death' (*in extremis*).[65] If the testator was near to death the will could be nuncupative, that is, spoken, it being left to witnesses to have it written down later; it would then be in the third person, as reported speech, although occasionally they were written in the first person.[66]

Commendation: Almost always the first effective words of the testament were, 'I commend my soul unto Almighty God, the Blessed Virgin Mary and all the saints in heaven', or something very similar.[67] If the testator had a favourite saint, the name might be included before 'all the saints in heaven' but this occurs rarely in Part II.[68] Amfritha Wareyn of Sudbury (no. 32) included St Katherine. These personal saints were sometimes referred to as 'advowers'. John Flemyng of Elveden (no. 731), one of the few testators who did name a saint in his commendation, included 'Blessed Andrew the Apostle, my advower'.

---

who seems to have been another former husband. Marion Hethe of Rattlesden (no. 57) stated that she made her will 'by licence and will of my husband', Thomas Hethe.

[64] Russell seems to anticipate the sentiments of churchwardens in the following century who, following the expansion of their role into civil matters, became the 'chief inhabitants' of the community. See, for example, Hindle, *State and Social Change in Early Modern England*, pp.204–25. The will itself is quite short and uninformative, giving little indication of Russell's wealth or possessions, although admittedly there is only a testament and no will proper.

[65] It seems likely that Joan Swanton of Depden, widow (no. 685) and John Swanton of Rede (no. 686) (mother and son, or mother and stepson) were suffering from the same mortal illness. Both testators, declaring themselves 'sick in body and seeing the peril of death approaching', in the presence of their acquaintances and friends, made their wills within a day of each other; and the wills were both proved six weeks later on 2 March 1471/72.

[66] There are 41 nuncupative wills in Part II; nos 79 and 490 have been written in the first person. Indeed, no. 490 is so long and detailed that it was perhaps 'dictated' rather than 'nuncupative' in the strict sense of the word.

[67] A number of testators from Mildenhall used the commendation 'to Almighty God my Creator and Saviour, the Blessed Virgin Mary his mother and all the saints'. See, for example, no. 378.

[68] In 1446 Marion Fenkele of Gipping had included in her commendation St Peter and St Paul, the joint patron saints of the mother church of Stowmarket, as well as St Nicholas, to whom Gipping chapel was dedicated (SROB, Baldwyne 72; Pt I, no. 346).

Place of burial: Linked to the commendation were almost invariably directions for burial. The great majority of testators had to be satisfied with burial somewhere in the parish churchyard (*cimiterium*), the 'Christian burial' of the church. The powerful and the wealthy could request burial inside the church, and the very powerful and the very wealthy could specify an actual spot within the building. Only incumbents and patrons, though, were able to be buried in the chancel, the most desirable part of the church. Because few very wealthy or important testators had their wills proved in the archdeacon's court, requests for these privileged places of burial are relatively uncommon in this volume: Robert Hunte, esquire (no. 191) expected to be buried in the Lady Chapel of Rushbrooke parish church; John Turnour, gentleman (no. 608) requested burial in the chancel of All Saints, Great Thurlow. Several others requested burial inside their church but this would depend on the agreement of the community concerned.[69] Richard Wryghte of Bures St Mary (no. 67) obviously had this in mind when he specified burial inside the church 'if the parishioners of that town agree to it'. He was aware that agreement was more likely to be forthcoming if he gave generously to the church, so he bequeathed 'to the reparation of the church 13s 4d in money and a quarter of malt; but if the parishioners will not allow me to be buried in the church, but [*only*] in the churchyard, then to the reparation of the church half that gift'. Burial in areas within the church to which parishioners paid particular attention meant that the person buried there was more likely to be remembered, so, for example, Robert Cosyn (no. 750) requested burial within the church of SS Peter and Paul, Stowmarket, 'in the aisle beyond the font near the position of the torches', a place where people would linger to pray. John Dunche (no. 657) even asked to be buried before the great cross, perhaps the rood, in Wordwell church. Walter Oldhalle (no. 702) asked to buried inside Sudbury church opposite the window that he had had made, in the hope that people looking at it would remember to pray for its donor.

Whether they were requesting burial inside or outside the church, testators often mentioned the dedications of their churches. This practice has proved of great value to historians, for a substantial proportion of churches 'lost' their dedications after the Reformation or adopted new ones in the eighteenth century.[70] Sometimes the registry clerk omitted the commendation and burial directions when copying testaments into the register.

Unpaid debts: In an age in which the church taught that, immediately after death, the soul began a long and painful passage through purgatory, it was inevitable that the 'health' of their souls should greatly concern those approaching death. Consequently a substantial portion of most testaments related directly or indirectly to the health of the soul.[71] And so, to avoid any penalties for dying in debt, and before considering funeral arrangements, testators emphasised that their debts and dues should be paid before all else. These included various payments to the church; tithes,

---

[69] For example, Thomas Cros of Edwardstone (no. 96) asked to be buried in the new aisle, before the altar.

[70] For an examination of this subject see Orme, *English Church Dedications*, especially Chapter 4, 'From the Reformation to 1800', pp.42–51.

[71] The word used is 'health' (Latin *salus*), only very rarely 'salvation' (Latin *salvatio*).

offerings and mortuaries were the most frequent, and all were obligatory. Money for forgotten tithes and offerings were always given to the 'high altar', usually implying the incumbent, of the appropriate parish church. Gifts for tithes to churches other than the testator's parish church usually indicate that land and/or property were held elsewhere. The amount given to the high altar can be a rough guide to the wealth of the testator: under 12d, fairly poor; 3s 4d and 6s 8d, fairly wealthy, equivalent to the yeoman farmer of later centuries; 10s and £1, wealthy and very wealthy.[72]

Offerings included in the tithe-payments were chiefly those expected to be paid by parishioners to the priest at major festivals,[73] but could refer to any other incidental payments omitted by the testator. The mortuary, also known as the 'principal', could be demanded by the incumbent after the death of any parishioner. It was not a burial fee and it was not related to tithe. By the period covered by 'Baldwyne', the practice of paying a mortuary had apparently ceased over most of the area: in Part II, only twelve testators from eight different parishes made provision for a mortuary, some leaving a particular animal, others 'whatever is right'.[74]

The burial: One important aspect of the doctrine of purgatory was the belief that the soul's progress could be helped by the prayers of the living. The burial presented an opportunity for gathering together large numbers of people who would add their prayers in this way, and various attractions and rewards were offered to achieve this. Refreshments were provided, occasionally for the whole parish; priests and clerks were paid; money was given to the poor and sometimes food – and all this, in many cases, was repeated seven days later and again after a month. Of the few wills in Part II that give details of the requirements for a fifteenth-century funeral, that of Richard Barbore of Clare (no. 46) is the most informative. He gave 6d to the vicar of Clare church being present at his obsequies and at the mass on the day of his burial; 4d to each other priest saying divine service and ministering; 2d each to the two parish clerks; 1d to each of the other clerks; and 1d to each of the needy poor at his burial mass, praying for his soul. He also gave 12lbs of wax, with all the other stuff (*stuffur'*) necessary for making three small torches to be held about his body on the day of his burial, at his seven-day and thirty-day. Others took care to provide food and drink at their funeral, for example, John Botwryght of Lakenheath (no. 399) wanted all his neighbours and the poor at his obsequies to have sufficient bread, cheese and ale, to pray for his soul. As in Part I, the extremely lavish funerals of the wealthy do not feature in this volume because the testators were all of fairly low 'degree'.

The medieval funeral began with the saying of *placebo*, the vespers of the service for the dead, on the evening before the burial. On the day of burial the body, sewn

---

[72] Care, of course, should be taken when interpreting this very rough and ready guide. Examples can always be found of quite wealthy testators making comparatively small tithe-payments.

[73] See Walcott, 'Parish Churches before the Reformation', pp.79–120, especially pp.104–5, 'Alms and Offerings'.

[74] The parishes with two testators leaving mortuaries were Barnardiston (nos 598, 655), Honington (nos 157, 474), Soham (Cambs) (nos 204, 397) and Thorpe Morieux (nos 131, 351); those with one were Burgate (no. 718), Occold (no. 443), Thorndon (no. 146) and West Stow (no. 304). In Bedfordshire, on the other hand, only a handful of places were *not* paying a mortuary. See Bell (ed.), *Bedfordshire Wills*. Tate, *The Parish Chest*, pp.69–70, records payment of mortuaries in the eighteenth century.

into a sheet or shroud, but with no coffin,[75] was carried into the church on a bier made of boards.[76] Over the bier was placed a herse, a wooden or metal frame, triangular in section, designed to hold candles.[77] The bier would also be surrounded by large torches, either on tall holders or 'standards', or carried by men.[78] Then would follow *dirige*, the matins of the funeral service, and after that requiem mass. During mass, mourners made offerings of money (presumably for the deceased's soul), the 'mass-pence' mentioned in various wills.[79] The burial or interment then took place.[80]

A re-enactment of the funeral, with an empty bier, but complete with herse and candles, took place on the seven-day and thirty-day with the same prayers and ceremonial as for the funeral proper, and also provision of refreshments and money for the poor.[81] If the grave were inside the church, paving, or covering the grave with stone, would often not be done until after the thirty-day.[82] Only five testators actually mentioned gravestones.[83] Robert Nooke of Kersey (no. 153), who described himself as executor to Robert Pury, made provision for the purchase of a marble gravestone to lie on Pury's grave. Similarly, Agnes Dyke of Stoke by Clare (no. 803) asked her executors to provide and purchase a marble stone to place over the bodies of her and her late husband John.[84] Yet another re-enactment of the funeral service, together with the distribution of alms and food, took place at the anniversary or obit. Depending on how well they were endowed, anniversaries could be continued for many years, some being intended to last for ever.[85] For example, William Metewyn of Wattisfield (no. 240) bequeathed 11 acres of pasture to the parish church for various purposes, including the celebration of the anniversaries of him, his wife and parents by the parish priest for ever. Since he included the condition 'if it can be done', perhaps John Mellere of Stanton (no. 463) realised that he was being rather hopeful when he bequeathed 20s to buy two cows for the church and requested in return that his anniversary be kept annually, for ever, by ringing bells and offering 1d at mass. The longest definite period of time for which anniversary celebrations were requested was eighty years – for the soul of John Taylour of Thorndon (no. 126) – four times longer than the longest requests in Part I.[86]

The various officers of the church were, naturally, involved in these successive services, and they frequently appear in testaments as beneficiaries. Apart from

---

[75] Only the wealthy were 'chested' as it was later called.

[76] John Smyth of Stansfield (no. 121) bequeathed 13s 4d for a cover to cover the bier.

[77] See Peacock, *English Church Furniture*, p.128n.

[78] John Smyth of Clare (no. 815), for example, bequeathed 4d to four needy poor folk holding four torches around his body at mass on the day of his burial.

[79] For example, see no. 43, and also 'mass-penny' in Glossary.

[80] For a very detailed account of the medieval funeral, see Rock, *Church of Our Fathers*, ii, pp.377–419.

[81] Thomas Alston of Sudbury (no. 290) left instructions for the distribution of 100s to the poor 'in greatest need' on both his seven-day and his thirty-day.

[82] Will of Edward Bettes of Ipswich, clothier, pr. Jan. 1536/37 (PCC 4 Crumwell): 'the ground to be paved within three days of my thirty-day at my cost and charge'.

[83] Nos 89, 153, 266, 381 and 803.

[84] See 'marblestone' in Glossary.

[85] Those testators requesting anniversaries for ever include nos 240, 463, 519, 626, 646, 669, 678, 801 and 823.

[86] Even the wealthy clothier Thomas Spring II of Lavenham only asked for his anniversary to be kept for twenty years (*Logge Register*, no. 352).

the officiant, usually the incumbent, parish priest or parish chaplain, the two most important officers were the parish clerk, who usually also acted as the holy-water carrier, and the sacrist who was also the sexton.[87] At Bures St Mary the beadle may have carried out the sexton's duties.[88] Members of the choir, clerks (lesser and greater) and boys, were often given small payments, also. In his testament, Robert Sparrow of Melford (no. 436, repeated at 779) made bequests to all such people officiating at his funeral. He gave 12d to each chaplain serving in the church on the day of his death and being at his first obsequies and at the mass of Requiem on the day of his burial; 8d to each 'outside' priest present at the same time; 8d to each of the two holy water clerks of Melford present; 2s to the sacrist ringing the bells, making his grave and performing other duties; 4d to each adult clerk there to say *dirige* and mass; 2d to each surpliced boy clerk singing and reading; and, also, 1d to each of the needy poor coming to the church on his burial day, taking alms and praying for his soul.

Bequests to churches: The period covered by 'Baldwyne' was one of tremendous activity in the building, rebuilding, extension and beautifying of parish churches, and wills provide more information about this than any other source. The great majority of testators left something towards the upkeep ('emendation') of the fabric of their parish churches, and many gave towards special projects in their own and neighbouring churches. It is from wills that we know of about sixty church towers being constructed in Suffolk in this period, and about half of them are mentioned in this volume or in Part I.[89] Some of these bequests were monetary, others were eminently practical, such as the twelve 'cartsfull of calyon' bequeathed to Eye tower by Margaret Folkes (no. 252). Bells needed constant attention and numerous bequests were made to them.[90] Sometimes gifts to bells indicate the stage which tower-building had reached. Many porches were also being built at this time.[91] The beginning of the dramatic rebuilding of Melford church is marked in October 1467 by the bequest of John Brokhole (no. 363) of 6s 8d 'to the new fabric of the church, now begun'.[92] Similarly, work on roodlofts, roofs and aisles is mentioned, which helps to date those features.[93]

---

[87] John Cowper of Boxford (no. 247) mentioned two 'officials' (*officiariis*) by name, Thomas Cote and Thomas Nott, but it is not clear whether they were clerics or lay officers of the parish.

[88] For example, nos 310, 326, 460, 658 and 781. At Lavenham, the 'bedesman' appears to have carried out the sexton's duties.

[89] For example, a bequest to 'the making of the steeple of [Great] Barton' (no. 266).

[90] For example, in 1474, the parishioners of St Andrew's, Burwell, were considering changing the bells. If the churchwardens, with the consent of the parishioners, wished to sell the small bell in the tower and buy a larger one, that would be the biggest and tenor to the other two bells, then William Wylkyn would give 40s for the new bell; if they decided not to buy it, the 40s would be disposed elsewhere in the church (no. 626).

[91] For example, Thomas Forthe of Cockfield (no. 350) offered to pay for the building of the porch: he would cover the cost of the stone and 'menys' (presumably workmen), on condition that the parishioners provided the 'tymber' for the work. Several testators made provision for the new porch at Boxford (nos 247, 331, 332 and 440).

[92] See Paine, 'Building of Long Melford Church', p.10. Robert Sparrow made two substantial bequests to the rebuilding (nos 436 and 779).

[93] Nicholas Rodys of Combs (no. 478) bequeathed 12d 'to the making of the steps by which to get onto the beam of the candleloft', that is, for inserting twisting rood-stair at the east end of the nave. At Exning

Church interior: Frequent bequests were made to fittings and the decoration of churches. Among the most beautiful decorative features of medieval churches were stained glass windows, of which few, for various reasons, have survived intact. In Part II, thirteen testators made bequests for or towards windows in their parish church, of which eight specifically mentioned the glazing of those windows; the other five referred to 'windows', which might mean glass but which might also mean the masonry of the windows.[94] Whereas John Bakoun (no. 300) simply bequeathed 40s to a window in Brent Eleigh church, two other men provided whole windows. As already noted, during his lifetime, Walter Oldhalle (no. 702) had had a window made in St Gregory's, Sudbury, opposite which he wished to be buried, and consequently remembered by the parish. John Huberd (no. 543) wanted a new window in the chapel of St Mary in All Saints', Redgrave, to be made at his expense, following the form of the adjacent window; he also wanted to have the old material of the window in the chapel, presumably meaning that his executors should have it in part-payment for the new window. Work on the magnificent windows in the east end of the south aisle at St Mary's, Combs, some of which still remains, is recorded in two wills: both Nicholas Rodys (no. 478) and Simon Turnour (no. 594) made bequests to 'the east window of the south side' of that church.[95]

The details provided by those eight testators who made bequests for glazing vary greatly. William Goodewyn of Burwell (no. 12) and Ed' Man of Rattlesden (no. 797) simply bequeathed money for the glazing of a window in their respective parish churches. Others were more specific about the windows to be glazed: Stephen Heacham (no. 180), the new glass window in the Lady Chapel of Haughley parish church; William Chatysle (no. 219), a window of glass (*de glasse*) at the end of the altar of St James in Ixworth; and John Swyftt (no. 258), the glass of a clerestory window at Walsham le Willows.[96] Two widows made bequests to the windows of the splendid porch at Felsham: Rose Goddrych (no. 533) 'for the glass and work of a window' in the 'porche'; and Isabel Machon (no. 557) 'for the glass of a window' of the 'porche'.[97] The most detailed bequest for glazing was that of Richard Barbore of Clare (no. 46).

In his will proper Barbore allocated '5 marks towards glazing a window in the chapel of the Blessed Mary, on the north side of the church, called "le Babylwyndowe" of the story of the Assumption of the Blessed Mary'. His description of the window is very specific, if somewhat confusing, mixing Old Testament imagery with a scene from the life and death of the Virgin; perhaps a 'Babylwyndowe' of the

---

there were plans to re-roof the nave but by the time Henry Mason made his will (no. 450), in February 1469/70, the type of roofing material had not been chosen, so he bequeathed quantities of lead or reeds depending on the final decision. Thomas Wareyn of Haughley (no. 547) bequeathed the trunk of an oak to the church, probably to replace a roof truss.

[94] In her study of the deanery of Dunwich from 1370 to 1547, Judith Middleton-Stewart found only seven wills that specified glazing. See Middleton-Stewart, *Inward Purity and Outward Splendour*, Chapter 11, 'Divine Lights'. In a rare bequest to the abbey of Bury St Edmunds, William Hert of Elmswell (no. 519) bequeathed 13s 4d for 'the glasyng' to be done in the refectory there.

[95] See illustration in Cautley, p.211.

[96] For a discussion of the clerestory, see Blatchly and Northeast, *Decoding Flint Flushwork*, Walsham le Willows St Mary.

[97] Cautley (p.284) notes that 'the stone and flint panelled north porch is a fine and lofty structure with exceptional windows for a porch'.

story of the Assumption would have depicted the Virgin ascending into Heaven with people reaching up to her from the top of the Tower of Babel.[98] Medieval stained glass windows rarely depicted Old Testament stories, and even then the subjects were usually the stories of the Creation, Adam and Eve or Noah's Ark.[99] On the other hand, representations of the Virgin Mary were frequently shown as part of a cycle of her life which, in its entirety, was sometimes called 'The Joys and Sorrows of the Virgin'.[100] Some depictions of the Assumption have survived, the nearest to Suffolk being that at East Harling (Norfolk). As is well known, the ornamentation of Clare church was subject to destruction by William Dowsing. According to his diary: 'At Clare, 6 January 1643 [1643/44]. We brake down a 1000 pictures super-stitious; and brake down 200, 3 of God the Father, and 3 of Christ, and the Holy Lamb, and 3 of the Holy Ghost like a dove with wings; and the 12 Apostles were carved in wood, on the top of the roof, which we gave order to have taken down; and 20 cherubims to be taken down. And the sun and moon in the east window, by the King's Arms, to be taken down'.[101] However, surviving evidence shows that Dowsing did not destroy as much of the ornamentation there as his diary suggests.[102] Barbore's description of 'his' window is striking, not to say exceedingly unusual, but it is not known whether it was ever constructed; certainly nothing of it remains.

Apart from the provision of windows and the renewal of roodlofts referred to above, many other ecclesiastical fixtures, fittings and accoutrements were supplied for church interiors. For example, new tabernacles (and images to put in them) and altar-pieces were being made, new equipment provided for use on or at altars, and new books (or repairing of old ones) for use in services.[103] John Cowper of Boxford (no. 247) bequeathed his own psalter to the parish church and specified that it should be fixed with a chain to the stool or chest before the image of the Blessed Mary, that is, for use in the Lady Chapel. The purpose of such donations was usually 'to the glory of God and the health of my soul'.

Several people made bequests of textiles, or money for them, to their parish church, some for making vestments or copes, others for altar cloths or other napery. Most of these testators were very specific in their bequests, indicating close attention to detail. For example, Alice Huntt of Withersfield (no. 171) left 10 marks 'to assemble a complete vestment of one suit to serve in Withersfield church on prin-

---

[98] The Tower of Babel is recorded in Genesis 11, v.4.
[99] Cowen, *Guide to Stained Glass*, pp.29–39, 'The Iconographic Programme'. There are no surviving English medieval windows showing the Tower of Babel although there are some more modern windows that depict it, such as that at Ely Cathedral (1851). The Victoria and Albert Museum (London) has a sixteenth-century German example.
[100] Cowen, *Guide to Stained Glass*, pp.30–2.
[101] Cooper (ed.), *Journal of William Dowsing*, pp.214–15.
[102] As Cooper has noted: '[Dowsing's] "1000 pictures" has always seemed like exaggeration, and an estimate of the numbers of subjects (two in a tall light, even four in the east window) which could have been accommodated is worth making. Including the clerestory (assuming it was fully glazed, as at Melford) the total is about 186 and cannot exceed 200, the more believable number "brake down".' (*Journal of William Dowsing*, p.215).
[103] There were fewer gifts towards service books in this volume than in Part I but see, for example, gifts of or towards a missal (nos 314, 541), an antiphoner (nos 621, 771 and 805) and a 'book' for the church (nos 802, 820). John Pery of Great Whelnetham (no. 66) bequeathed a cow to the 'reparation of the book of sacraments' of his parish church.

cipal days and greater feasts'. Henry Monnynge of Norton by Woolpit (no. 362) bequeathed 6s 8d for a cope worn during the celebration of obsequies for the dead. The colour of the fabric used for a cope was not determined by the parish, but by the Church: liturgical colours fell into four groups, which were worn on particular days or during specified seasons.[104] The silk cope of 'sateyn cremesyn' that Richard Wederton (no. 181) wanted for Hitcham church could have been worn only at Pentecost and on the feasts of the Apostles and male martyrs. Wederton had bequeathed money to purchase and make that particular cope. Other parishioners gave their own cloths, some of which were quite sumptuous: Margaret Sketh of Stanton (no. 711) bequeathed to the adornment of the high altar of All Saints' church a 'sanguine-coloured cover with white and blue roses interwoven (*or*, embroidered)'; Henry Bothe (no. 697) bequeathed to Shelland church his tapestry of 'Sarcenet' to 'the honour of the sacrament of the altar'. Other bequests were more humble, such as the cloth for a housling towel, given by Agnes Browster (no. 359).

Like the bells in the tower, lights, that is, candles, tapers or torches, in the church needed constant attention and frequent replenishment. The common light (before the rood), the sepulchre light(s) and the lights before the high altar received most contributions, some in the form of land and cows which provided a continuous income.[105] Individual images all had their lights and many bequests were left to them, the most popular being those of Our Lady.[106]

Priests' services: As it was believed that the soul's passage through purgatory could be eased by prayers of the living, who better to provide them than the professionals?[107] Throughout the Middle Ages many unbeneficed chaplains were pleased to have employment, and so too were convents of the religious. Almost all testaments of the period contained bequests to members of the clergy and/or to convents of friars and nuns, specifically requesting their prayers or implying such a request by their donations.[108] The most popular form of priest's service was the Requiem mass. Priests were paid to celebrate mass for a stated number of years or fractions of a year. Wealthier testators often requested large numbers of masses to be celebrated immediately after death, creating problems for executors, who had to arrange the requisite number of priests.

In addition, the contents of the mass were often varied, partly in association with the 'new feasts' being introduced,[109] and partly to emphasize different aspects

---

[104] See Middleton-Stewart, *Inward Purity*, Chapter 9, 'The Riches of Apparel', especially p.198.

[105] Alice Huntt of Withersfield (no. 171) bequeathed a cow to the sepulchre light there and was very explicit about the management of this bequest: 'the wardens and their successors for the time being shall see that the farmers of the cow shall produce and wean a calf from [it], so that there is always a cow to support the light for ever'.

[106] For example: Isabel Machon (no. 557) bequeathed a cow to the finding of two lights in Felsham church, one before the image of Corpus Christi and the other before the image of St Katherine; Margaret Page of Kirtling (no. 609) bequeathed a cow to the lights of the Blessed Mary in the chapel and in the church.

[107] Thomas Colman of Thorndon (no. 337) explicitly stated that prayers that he requested were for the souls of his friends and benefactors 'now in purgatory'.

[108] Some of the clergy or religious so appointed were members of the testator's family, for example, nos 127, 205 and 820.

[109] See Pfaff, *New Liturgical Feasts*.

of devotion ('votive masses'), like 'the Name of Jesus'.[110] A popular request was for the trental, composed of thirty masses, sometimes required to be said all on the same day. A trental of St Gregory, on the other hand, was a more complex devotion that required the saying of thirty masses spread out over a year, friars often being commissioned as celebrants in preference to parish clergy.[111] The standard fee for a trental was 10s. A set of prayers, as distinct from masses, popular with testators was the 'certain', called a 'sangred' in East Anglia: the name of the deceased was added to the parish bede-roll, to be read out from the pulpit each week and thereby included in the prayers of those attending Sunday worship. The priest was paid 4s 4d for providing a certain for a year, that is, a penny per week.[112]

Religious houses: The numerous religious houses of medieval England offered ready reservoirs of prayer-providers, and many testators mentioned at least one.[113] Few bequests to monks appear in this volume,[114] but nuns seem to have been more highly regarded, especially those at Thetford.[115] It was chiefly the friars to whom bequests were made and who were asked to say masses, for they would have been more widely known in the district from their preaching and hearing of confession. There were four main orders of friars: the Friars Minor or Franciscans, the Friars Preachers or Dominicans, the Carmelite Friars and the Augustinian, or Austin, Friars. Several testators took care to leave bequests to each of the four orders, giving to the houses in each order geographically most convenient to them. Within the archdeaconry there were houses of Minors (Babwell, outside the north gate of Bury), Preachers (Sudbury) and Augustinians (Clare), but for Carmelites testators had to look to Cambridge, Norwich or Ipswich.[116] Being placed so centrally in the archdeaconry, Babwell received far more bequests from local testators than any of the other friaries in the area; but several bequests were left to friaries further afield,

---

[110] For example, no. 45.

[111] For details of St Gregory's trental see Duffy, *Stripping of the Altars*, pp.293–4 and Pfaff, 'The English Devotion of St Gregory's Trental', pp.75–90. The devotion was accompanied by a legend in which Pope Gregory's deceased mother appeared to him, disfigured by her torments in purgatory, and asked him to celebrate the trental of thirty masses for her. This story was versified in Middle English, one version of which has been reprinted in Furnivall (ed.), *Political, Religious and Love Poems*, pp.114–22.

[112] For example, John Roodese of Ixworth (no. 37), Isabel Boole of Little Livermere (no. 129), Adam Northaghe of Thorndon (no. 146); William Hert of Elmswell (no. 519); Rose Goddrych of Felsham (no. 533). Richard Buntyng of Tostock (no. 821) left land to provide money for a sangred to be celebrated every week for ever.

[113] The standard guide is Knowles and Hadcock, *Medieval Religious Houses: England and Wales*. For Suffolk see Northeast, 'Religious Houses'; for Norfolk see Rickett and Rose, 'Monastic Houses', pp.64–5; for Essex see Edwards, *Essex Monasteries*. See also the appropriate volumes of the *Victoria County History* of Suffolk, Norfolk, Essex and Cambridgeshire.

[114] Richard Barbore of Clare (no. 46) bequeathed 20s to the monks of the monastery of St Edmund at Bury; Thomas Puttok of Mildenhall (no. 147) bequeathed 5s to Dan John Lynne, monk in that monastery, to celebrate a trental for his soul; John Cotelere of Barnham (no. 282) bequeathed 4d to John Chambyr, monk.

[115] Bequests to the nuns at Thetford include nos 68, 294, 453, 590, 634, 792 and 820. Other bequests to nuns include Bruisyard (no. 89), Hedingham (no. 698) and Redlingfield (nos 83, 89, 126, 337, 417 and 726).

[116] In 'Baldwyne' II, testators giving to the 'four orders' or 'four houses' of friars usually gave to the Carmelites at Cambridge: see nos 133, 142, 152, 160, 244, 286, 436, 508, 528, 628, 779 and 785. Nos 38, 78 and 79 include bequests to all four orders but do not explicitly say 'to the four orders'.

including Walsingham (no. 45). Three bequests were made to the Trinitarian Friars of Mottenden (Kent).[117] The mention of the 'fraternity' of friars' orders refers to members of the laity paying in their lifetime for a form of 'associate member-ship' whereby they were to receive certain benefits.[118] Not least among these was the circulation among houses of the order of lists of deceased members, a form of mortuary-roll, so that those named on them should be prayed for throughout the order.[119] It appears that those who had not subscribed to this 'fraternity' in their lifetime but bequeathed a posthumous payment hoped, nevertheless, to enjoy similar benefits. For example, Thomas Smyth of Stansfield (no. 121) bequeathed 13s 4d to the friars of Clare for his confraternity and that of his wife.

Gilds: Another body of prayer-providers was the gild. Most parishes in the arch-deaconry had at least one religious gild, and a large proportion of the population of each parish appear to have been members.[120] Although Bainbridge has produced a detailed study of gilds in Cambridgeshire, she did not discuss the gilds in those Cambridgeshire parishes that were within the archdeaconry of Sudbury, and so it is worth indicating here the references in Part II to gilds in those parishes.[121] The notes to the relevant wills provide what scant details there are regarding the various gilds. The parishes and gilds concerned are: Cheveley, two gilds (St John the Baptist, St Mary);[122] Chippenham, four gilds (the Holy Trinity, Corpus Christi, St John, St Margaret);[123] Kennett, one gild (the Holy Trinity);[124] Kirtling, one gild (St Mary);[125] Soham, four gilds (Corpus Christi, St Mary, St Peter, St John the Baptist);[126] Wicken, one gild (All Saints);[127] Woodditton, one gild (the Holy Trinity).[128]

One of the obligations of gild membership was to attend funerals of fellow members and make offerings of mass-pence for the souls of the deceased.[129] The deceased would have made known his or her wishes for the disposal of the mass-pence 'for the good of my soul', either verbally or by will, and so membership

---

[117] Nos 295, 634 and 636.
[118] John Bakere of Glemsford (no. 751) bequeathed 5s to the houses of the Friars Preachers of Sudbury, the Friars Minor of Babwell and the Friars Carmelite of Cambridge, his 'brethren' (*confratribus*).
[119] See Thurston, 'Mediaeval Mortuary-Card'.
[120] For Suffolk gilds see Northeast, 'Parish Gilds'. For a general discussion of gilds in Cambridgeshire see Bainbridge, *Gilds in the Medieval Countryside*.
[121] Although an older and less comprehensive work for Cambridgeshire as a whole, Palmer's discus-sion of village gilds does include (some of) those in the archdeaconry of Sudbury (Palmer, 'Village Gilds of Cambridgeshire'). The index to 'Baldwyne' Part I gives references to Cambridgeshire gilds in that volume. Individual parish sections in the *VCH Cambs* also give some details of gilds under 'Parish Church'.
[122] John Sawndyr the younger (no. 623); John Gateward (no. 649).
[123] Isabel Rawlyn (no. 199); Joan Norman of Badlingham in Chippenham (no. 438).
[124] William Lardynere (no. 585).
[125] John Tylbrok (no. 499).
[126] John Parys (no. 204); John Smyth (no. 397).
[127] Nicholas Qwycherch (no. 427); William Say (no. 747). Qwycherch also mentioned a gild of St Mary but it is possible that that gild was in Cambridge. See note to his will.
[128] John Avbre (no. 630); John Clerk alias Webbe (no. 646); Agnes Glovere (no. 762).
[129] The surviving statutes of the gild of St James at Dullingham (Cambs), dated 1517, indicate the benefits and obligations of gild membership (CUL, Baker MSS, Mm1.47, pp.161–2). These statutes appear to be typical of a small rural parish gild. Reference supplied by David Dymond.

had earned the prayers of the attending members *and* the benefits arising from the disposal of mass-pence.[130] As in the case of fraternal membership of an order of friars, a testator might well expect to be admitted member of a gild posthumously.

Bequests to gilds might also be of a practical nature. In many places gilds met in the parish church, but in some towns and villages gilds had their own meeting place or gildhall, and in others various gilds shared a hall. Roger Charite of Hitcham (no. 75) referred to the gildhall there as the 'community hall' implying that the hall was used for a range of public and private purposes, rather than by one group or gild. Such buildings, some of which still survive today, would have been in need of maintenance from time to time.[131] The gildhall at Stowmarket received several bequests to help with repair costs: in 1458, Margaret Wetherard of Stowmarket (no. 669) bequeathed a pasture for, amongst other things, the reparation of the common hall called the 'Gyldehalle'; and in 1462, William Schelton (no. 109) bequeathed 6s 8d to the emendation of 'le gyldehall' there.

As well as attendance at the funerals of fellow-members, gild members were also expected to attend the annual gild dinner, the scale of which depended on the wealth of the gild in question. Many gilds owned their own dining and cooking equipment and some testators made bequests for the provision or repair of such items. Walter Noble (no. 432) bequeathed 12d to the gilds of Great Horringer for the repair of the vessels belonging to the gildhall. Margaret Sketh (no. 711) bequeathed to the 'emendation' of the gild of All Saints, in the parish of All Saints, Stanton, 6 wooden dishes, 6 wooden platters, 6 wooden vessels called 'sawseres', 6 goblets, a pewter salt and 6 trenchers. John Russhford (no. 189) bequeathed the gild of St George, Sudbury, his best iron spit and Thomas Alston (no. 290) bequeathed the same gild a brass pot. Such items could be either sold for the benefit of the gild or used at communal celebrations.

In addition to saying prayers for the souls of deceased members, gilds were often responsible for providing candles for processions, for funerals and before images or altars.[132] Frequently membership dues or fines were payable in wax. In some parishes groups of people belonged to a minor gild or 'light' that maintained a particular light or 'taper' in the church; members of these lights might be of a particular status within the parish such as 'maidens', bachelors or wives.[133] John Wepsted of Brettenham (no. 298), who appears to have been unmarried, bequeathed 12d to the light of the 'Bachelers tapers', the only such bequest in Part II.

Charitable giving: Giving to good works, to the poor, sick and needy, to poor prisoners, to the repair of roads and bridges, etc., as corporal deeds of mercy, were believed to be for the 'health of the soul'. Many of the testators in 'Baldwyne' Part II

---

[130] Those testators leaving instructions for the disposal of gild mass-pence include: Richard Person of the gild of St Peter, Ampton (nos 515, 538); Stephen Blome of the gild of the Trinity, Cockfield (no. 540); John Derman (no. 724) and William Wyburgh (no. 785) of the gild of St John the Baptist, Denston; Thomas Roote of the gild of St Thomas, Glemsford (no. 508); and Adam Rodyng of both the gild of St John the Baptist and of the Trinity, Great Horringer (no. 654).
[131] The gildhall at Dullingham survives as a private house.
[132] See Hanawalt, 'Keepers of the Lights'
[133] Duffy, *Stripping of the Altars*, pp.147–51.

made such charitable bequests; for example, William Godfrey of Great Horringer (no. 773) gave 4 marks to the blind, lame and imprisoned, and especially to the repair of 'Clenewall strete'. William Wyburgh of Denston (no. 785) specifically named the poor folk to whom he wished to give practical support in the form of grain in return for prayers for his soul: John Flechere of Denston, 'needy poor man', Robert Pyngyll of Denston, John Preston, Agnes Chapman of Stanningfield and William Bradbrook of Stradishall. Simon Gardener of Mildenhall (no. 636) targeted a very particular group of prisoners: he bequeathed money 'for the redemption of the captives of the Holy Land who are imprisoned for the faith of our Lord Jesus Christ by the pagans'.[134] John Taylour of Thorndon (no. 126) was the only person to leave money to leper-hospitals: he left 40d to the leper-hospital of Norwich, 40d to that of Eye, 20d to that of Bury and 20d to that of Ipswich.[135] Two testators, in particular, made substantial practical bequests of materials for the repair of roads in their local communities. Robert Hardyng of Eye (no. 457) left 30 cartloads of clay for repairing each of four roads in the town: 'Lamset' way, 'Spetyll' way, 'Kynggesstrete' way and Priory way. Walter Nicoll (no. 642) bequeathed 40 loads of stone for the repair of 'Mellestrete' in Great Bradley.

Five testators, three of whom were parishioners of Lavenham, made provision for the foundation of almshouses, the inhabitants of which were expected to pray for the soul of the founder in return for their accommodation.[136] Four of these almshouses were modest affairs, such as that to be founded for William Orderych of Hitcham (no. 587), who wished his smallest house, which stood next to the 'manor' (?manor house) there, to remain to the use and accommodation of the poor. William Schedde, on the other hand, required the gild of the Holy Trinity of Lavenham to establish six houses for the poor in the town. In general, the understanding was that the almsmen (and/or women) who dwelt in such properties were some of the 'deserving' poor of the parish, that is, parishioners of long-standing who, through age or ill-health, were no longer able to support themselves.[137] John Eryswell (no. 342) made a different kind of provision for the poor, one that would not have been popular with the 'better sort' of Eriswell, for he wanted to offer hospitality to some of the vagrant poor, that is, people wandering about the countryside without work or master.[138]

---

[134] The bequest was made to the Trinitarian Friars of Mottenden (Kent) (strictly speaking, canons rather than friars), a third of whose income was devoted to freeing captive Christians. One wonders what prompted this particular bequest; perhaps an itinerant member of the order visited Suffolk. For Christian slaves in the following centuries see Davis, *Christian Slaves, Muslim Masters*.

[135] For lepers and leper-hospitals in general see Rawcliffe, *Leprosy in Medieval England*; for these particular hospitals see the notes to this will.

[136] Andrew Grygges (no. 11), John Newman the elder (no. 87) and William Schedde (no. 339), all of Lavenham, William Orderych of Hitcham (no. 587) and John Kendale the elder of Sudbury (no. 607). Perhaps the large number of cloth-workers in Lavenham meant that there was a greater need for accommodation for elderly inhabitants who were no longer able to work and who had little or no income from agriculture.

[137] The concept of the deserving and undeserving poor was fully developed in the Poor Law legislation of the Tudor period; see Slack, *Poverty and Policy*, passim, and especially pp.61–90, 'The Respectable Poor'.

[138] His son Thomas was to have John's tenement and household utensils on condition that he kept two beds in the house to provide hospitality for the vagrant poor, for the good of the souls of his (Thomas's) parents. For the vagrant or 'dangerous' poor see Slack, *Poverty and Policy*, pp.91–112.

In the same category of charitable giving came helping parishioners to pay the 'king's tax', that is, lay subsidies, or 'tenths' (in urban centres) and 'fifteenths' (in the countryside); a cause for which three testators in Part II made provision. Chris Dyer has noted that such bequests can be seen as an early form of community poor-relief, aimed at ensuring that the poor did not have to contribute to taxation but at the same time ensuring that the community's taxation 'quota' was met.[139] In 1456 John Foot of Buxhall (no. 383) bequeathed a piece of land called 'Aldewerk', containing about half an acre, 'to the aid and relief of the poor of the town of Buxhall from the tax of the lord king when it falls'. Similarly, in 1465, William Metewyn of Wattisfield (no. 240) bequeathed 'to God and the church of St Margaret of Wattisfield' an enclosure lying at 'Dawis-at-Grene' containing about 11 acres of pasture, the rent from which was to go towards 'paying the fifteenths of the lord king, a half or a quarter each time', whenever they were levied in Wattisfield, provided that the anniversaries of William, his wife and parents were kept.[140] In 1472 John Nunne the elder of Rougham (no. 634) bequeathed three pieces of land, amounting to 3½ acres, 'to the acquittance of the poor and most needy of the town of the fifteenths or taxes of the king imposed on them'.[141]

Indulgences: Another means of shortening the soul's time in purgatory, it was believed, was to take advantage of some of the many indulgences, or pardons, which had been granted by bishops and popes over the years. These usually involved visiting the building or shrine for which the indulgence had been granted, but in some cases, such as at the hospital of St Thomas of Acre (or Acon) in London and the Knights Hospitallers at Clerkenwell (no. 319), donations from afar would earn the benefit of the pardon. Many pilgrimage sites had also been granted indulgences, and pilgrimage itself was regarded as beneficial to the soul. Several testators asked for pilgrimages to be done for them, these pilgrimages varying enormously in distance, some as near as Woolpit, others as far away as Rome or Compostella. Robert Agas of Thurston (no. 414) asked his son to go on, or have done, various pilgrimages within East Anglia: to the image of the Holy Trinity in Norwich cathedral, to the image of St Leonard in Norwich, to the chapel of St Nicholas at Tibenham [*Norfolk*], to Our Lady of Woolpit, to Our Lady of Sudbury, and to the chapel of St Theobald at Newmarket.[142] Only a handful of testators requested pilgrimages to the major English shrines of Our Lady of Walsingham and St Thomas at Canterbury;[143] whereas nineteen requested pilgrimages to Rome or bequeathed money to the Holy City.[144]

---

[139] Dyer, 'English Medieval Village Community'; Dyer, 'Taxation and Communities'.

[140] In 1458, John Mettewynd of Wattisfield (?a relative) had bequeathed 20s to the fifteenths of the town of Wattisfield (SROB, Baldwyne 194; Pt I, no. 945).

[141] This bequest might have been drawn on almost immediately: on 30 November 1472, the Commons granted the king a subsidy to pay the wages of 13,000 archers for one year, at the rate of 6d per day. This hefty sum (£118,625) was to be raised by means of a tax of one-tenth of the income of owners or occupiers of lands (Jurkowski, 'Income Tax Assessments of Norwich', p.103).

[142] Agas actually asked for seven pilgrimages to be done but only these six were specified. See the notes to his will for details of the various pilgrimage sites.

[143] For example, Thomas Roote of Glemsford (no. 508) and Nicholas Robertson of Stradishall (no. 640) requested pilgrimages to both Walsingham and Canterbury.

[144] Nos 16, 89, 184, 244, 251, 294, 319, 323, 338, 348, 401, 454, 467, 490, 495, 511, 522, 544 and 579.

Some of the requests for pilgrimages to Rome were very detailed, specifying the completion of one or more 'circles' of Rome or visits to various stations on the pilgrimage circuit of the Holy City.[145] For example, William Grene of Creeting St Peter (no. 89) required a priest to go to Rome immediately after his death, and to stay there until he had completed the stations and to pray for his soul and those of his parents.[146] John Deynys of Woolpit (no. 579) left £10 to a priest to go to Rome and to sing there or to have sung three masses at *Scala Celi* and two masses at SS Fabian and Sebastian.[147] On his return, the priest was to sing 'the residue of the year' in Woolpit church for Deynys, his wife and benefactors. Three testators (nos 89, 280 and 294) requested pilgrimages to the shrine of St James in Compostella, northern Spain. The logistics of having such a request fulfilled were complicated but by the late fifteenth century pilgrimage routes and modes of transport to that shrine were well established.[148]

Household: While houses, as real estate, should have been dealt with in the will proper, household articles, as chattels, were the subject of the testament. Probate inventories rarely survive from this period so that testators' descriptions of their household articles are important for the historian.[149] Tables were still, in the main, table-tops on trestles, although some people now owned a folding table (no. 523). Forms provided seating and chairs were few, though Joan Deynys (no. 259) had enough to call one her 'best chair'. In fact, this widow's will provides much information about household items of the period. Perhaps the nearest thing to the modern concept of furniture was the chest, present in most houses at that time; also called 'forcer', 'hutch' and 'coffer', it was frequently made of pine ('spruce'; no. 697), often painted and sometimes bound with iron.

Pots and pans were the normal cooking vessels, but far larger than the modern equivalents: pots were the large cooking pots as illustrated in the *Luttrell Psalter*, some might hold as much as 16 gallons (Part I, no. 933) but those in Part II seem to have held no more than four gallons; pans were of the large fish-kettle variety (one in no. 571 held 10 gallons). The basin and ewer seemed to be stock household items, the ewer sometimes 'hanging'. Candlesticks were essential. The equipment for the open hearth or chimney – spit, andiron, trivet, etc. – was sometimes specifically bequeathed.[150] Given their absence from the wills, presumably 'treen' or wooden

---

[145] A 'station' may be defined as 'the appointed visitation of some church, altar, shrine or other the like ecclesiastic locale, for pious purposes, and with certain spiritual graces annexed'. According to Francino, an Italian writing in the late sixteenth century, there were some 389 stations celebrated throughout the city of Rome on set days (Rossetti, 'Stacyons of Rome', pp.xxi, xxii).

[146] Grene's father, Thomas, had also requested a pilgrimage to Rome (Pt I, no. 20).

[147] The chapel of *Scala Celi* ('Ladder of Heaven') was built over the cemetery of St Zeno in Rome. It derives its name from a vision of St Bernard's, who, while celebrating a funeral mass, saw the souls for whom he was praying going up to heaven by a ladder (Rossetti, 'Stacyons of Rome', p.xxvi). The Basilica of SS Fabian and Sebastian marked the site of early Christian catacombs just outside Rome. The church stood about two miles beyond the gate of St Sebastian on the Appian Way (Rossetti, 'Stacyons of Rome', p.xxviii).

[148] See Storrs, *Jacobean Pilgrims*, especially Chapter 3, 'The Journey by Land and Sea'.

[149] See below, *The probate sentence*, for a brief discussion of early probate inventories.

[150] For example, nos 32, 228 and 613.

items were not considered worth bequeathing separately. The table-ware mentioned in the wills usually consisted of pewter, although several testators possessed silver spoons.[151] Agnes Dyke of Stoke by Clare (no. 803) had at least eleven silver spoons, of which five had lions and crowns, decorated with gold. Several testators bequeathed mazers or drinking-bowls, some of which were silver. William Cobbe of Wetheringsett (no. 778) even had a clock.

The household item most frequently mentioned was bedding. Sometimes a 'complete bed' was given (as in no. 333) which typically consisted of a 'donge' or mattress, a pair of sheets, a pair of blankets and a coverlet, with, occasionally, a 'transom' or bolster. Bedsteads were never mentioned until some years later, although the Flemish illustrations for Boccaccio's *Decameron*,[152] painted *c*.1430– 40, show that they were in use in Flanders then.[153] In this country, either the 'donge' lay directly on the floor, or perhaps there was a simple wooden frame that was not mentioned in bequests.[154] Wealthier testators at this time often referred to 'hanging' beds, that is, a bed with hangings. For example, although not described as a hanging bed, Amfritha Waryn (no. 32) bequeathed her daughter Joan her 'best bed', that comprised: a white coverlet with the tester, two blankets, two pairs of sheets, a mattress, a celure with the tester and three curtains of blue 'card'. Similarly, in addition to the usual components noted above, the 'whole bed' bequeathed to her brother by Joan Deynys (no. 259) had a covering of coney skins, a celure, a tester and three curtains. Bed-covers might even be multi-coloured or patterned: Alice Webbe (no. 251) bequeathed a bed-cover of 'three divers colours, that is, yellow, blue and white'; Agnes Hukton (no. 276) had a green bed-cover with yellow birds and also an old red bed-cover with roses. Such items were evidently fairly durable, since another bed-cover bequeathed by Alice Webbe was to be passed on at the death of three successive legatees, finally being distributed to the poor.

It is not surprising that bequests of clothing by both men and women were very common as they were among the few possessions that everyone owned; what is perhaps surprising is that the clothing of ordinary people might be of one (or more) of a wide array of colours.[155] The basic item of clothing was the gown, lined, unlined or furred, with or without a hood.[156] Also bequeathed were doublet, tunic, smock and petticoat, and over-garments such as tabard, cloak, kirtle and huke. The belt, or girdle, kerchief, hose and shoes were among accessories mentioned. Two of the most detailed lists of clothing are in the wills of Agnes Hukton of Clare (no. 276)

---

[151] For example, nos 436, 728 and 779.

[152] Pognon, *Boccaccio's Decameron* (trans. J. P. Tallon, 1978).

[153] See also Evans (ed.), *Flowering of the Middle Ages*, p.197.

[154] Robert Sparowe of Melford (no. 436, repeated at no. 779) bequeathed his servant Helen 'a bed, that is, a blue-coloured cover next the best, 2 blankets and 2 linen sheets and a felted cover (*fultru'*) of the best'. The word *fultru[m]* might conceivably be a derivative of *fulcimen* (*fultura*) (bed [tenth century] or buttress (support) [after 1550]) but a derivative of *filtrum* (piece of felt, cover, cloak, horse-cloth) seems more likely (Latham, pp.191, 203).

[155] Although medieval textiles and clothing might be passed on to successive generations, few of these material artefacts have survived to the present day. Together with evidence in paintings and manuscript illustrations, it is the (brief) written records of such items in wills that tell us most about the dress and household furnishings of the times. See the useful summary in Burkholder, 'Threads Bared'.

[156] See Glossary for definitions of the various items of clothing, some of which have familiar names but then had different forms or uses.

and John Barkere of Cowlinge (no. 490).[157] Agnes's clothing included a blue tunic furred with rabbit skin, a violet kirtle, a blue tabard, a blue hood, a burnet-coloured hood and a sanguine and scarlet hood. John bequeathed four gowns, including a russet-coloured one and another of 'musterdevelys', and two doublets, one of which was of black fustian. Whilst these two were fairly wealthy individuals, many of their bequests were to friends and relatives and so these colourful items would be dispersed amongst the local community. Even the more humble Edith Bullebrook (no. 135) had a small tunic, a russet tunic, a veil, a red hood, a blue hood and a huke. John Walsham (no. 295) bequeathed his wife Katherine all her own linen and woollen clothing.[158] John Man (no. 712) was concerned that his daughter Margaret should have a wedding dress (*vestem nupsialem*) 'decently prepared' for her. At least two people, John Kendale the elder of Sudbury (no. 607) and Joan Mynton of Stowmarket (no. 648), bequeathed items of their clothing to the needy poor. A few of the men possessed basic armour comprising a jack (a close-fitting padded sleeve-less jacket) and a sallet (a helmet).[159] Although this was a period during which all able-bodied men were supposed to carry out military drill from time to time, only a few wills mention weapons of any kind: for example, William Metewyn (no. 240) had a sword and shield, and a bow and arrows; Henry Boothe (no. 697) had a sword, an axe, a bow and a buckler, as well as a protective tunic and helmet.[160]

Several testators possessed jewellery made of precious metals and/or semi-precious materials such as jet, amber or coral. Many such items comprised 'a pair of beads', that is, a set of rosary beads. Some of these objects might be sold to raise money, or bequeathed to friends and family, or given as religious offerings. Alice Markaunte (no. 644) wanted her pair of coral beads sold 'to implement her will', and Alice Turnour (no. 698) bequeathed her daughter-in-law Joan a pair of silver beads with gilt paternosters. Bequests to churches or chapels, especially by women, might comprise jewellery that would be used to adorn a particular image.[161] Alice Thystelden of Stowmarket (no. 421) had several sets of rosary beads, including pair of jet beads with silver paternosters that she gave to the image of the Virgin in the Lady Chapel of St Peter's. Agnes Dyke of Stoke by Clare (no. 803) wanted her best pair of beads and her wedding ring to be offered to the Blessed Mary of Walsingham. Isabel Smyth of Great Finborough (no. 142) left a pair of amber beads, with two rings and a silver brooch to the image of Our Lady of Woolpit. But it was

---

[157]   See also, for example, William Metewyn (no. 240), Alice Peddere (no. 228), Joan Deynys (no. 259), John Cok (no. 313).

[158]   In recognition of the legal status of a wife's goods, that is, the property of her husband; however, there are only a few such bequests in this volume. But see, for example, the inventory of Roger Baldwyn of Rickmansworth (Herts) (11 March 1559/60) which valued separately 'all suche goodes wich were [his wife's] before there marraige & was in the possessyon of the sayd Roger at the tyme of hys deathe wich he bequethed to her agayne as by his last Wyll dothe appere' (Hertfordshire Archives and Local Studies, A25/384).

[159]   For example, nos 240, 456 and 547.

[160]   Included in this list of arms and armour was also a tapet, which, unless it has a meaning other than 'carpet, or hanging', is out of place here.

[161]   For donations of jewellery to shrines see Swanson, *Catholic England*, Chapter 7, 'Saints, Shrines, Miracles and Pilgrimages', especially pp.179–81, which lists the jewellery and precious objects left at the shrines in York Minster in 1509–10.

not only women who made such bequests: William Godman of Thorpe Morieux (no. 351) gave to the Lady Chapel there a pair of beads with a silver ring.

Outside the dwelling-house: farming: As one would expect of a time when, whatever his chief occupation, almost every man was involved in farming to some extent, farm animals, equipment and crops feature prominently in most late fifteenth-century wills. It is, of course, impossible to judge how many animals an individual owned in total from the number bequeathed but that number indicates the minimum.[162] Horses were frequently identified by their names or their markings: John Wryht of Wickham Skeith (no. 210)[163] gave to Alice his wife three horses, one called 'Brokke', the second 'Bayard' and the third 'Hobbe'; John Schildyrston the elder of Mildenhall (no. 629) bequeathed variously a foal, a grey-coloured horse, a bay horse and a red horse.[164] As in Part I, the number of cows bequeathed does not suggest the presence of large herds: William Derysle of Kirtling (no. 461) seems to have bequeathed the most (eighteen): eight to his wife and two each to five of his daughters. It appears that in Part II sheep occurred in significant numbers only in Mildenhall and Wickhambrook: William Chapman the elder of Mildenhall (no. 230) gave his wife a hundred of his best sheep;[165] Simon Gardener of Mildenhall (no. 636) bequeathed sheep of various kinds (ewes, 'sheephoges', sheep, lambs, 'wedyrhogges') to various people amounting to at least 206 animals; and Thomas Motte of Wickhambrook (no. 286) mentioned five hundred sheep.[166] A few testators mentioned pigs, oxen or bullocks.[167] Once again John Barkere of Cowlinge (no. 490) is particularly informative for he gave detailed bequests of his livestock in all its shapes and sizes: eight (of the best) cows, nine bullocks, six calves, two bulls, four horses and 'all the sheep, pigs and piglets, geese, cocks and hens'.[168] The only horse-drawn implements on medieval farms were ploughs, carts and harrows. Ploughs and carts (either 'shod' or 'unshod') were frequently bequeathed but this volume contains only two mentions of harrows: John Reve of Hepworth (no. 392) left his wife the cart, plough and harrows and their harness; and Robert Page of Great Saxham (no. 534) gave his wife all his cows and horses and all his carts, ploughs and harrows, with all the harness. Wheat and barley were the chief corn crops over the whole archdeaconry but rye and oats were also grown in many places.[169] Peas and beans were mentioned in several wills. Perhaps this brief section on farming in

---

[162] Time has not permitted me to undertake an analysis of the number of animals mentioned in the wills in Part II, so it is not possible to say whether the figures that Peter calculated for Part I are borne out here. He found that less than 10 per cent of testators in Part I bequeathed horses, and of those the largest number bequeathed by any one person was six (no. 1416); more than three times as many testators left cows but the wills give no indication of large dairy herds anywhere in the archdeaconry, the largest number in Part I actually bequeathed being nine. The proportions may well be similar in Part II.

[163] This will was also registered in SROB, Baldwyne 239 (Pt I, no. 1200).

[164] John Tyso (no. 205) bequeathed his son Sir George his riding boots and a pair of spurs, suggesting the possession of a horse, but none is mentioned in the will.

[165] That is, a long hundred, 120 in our reckoning – and he obviously had others, as these were 'of the best'.

[166] That is, 600 in our reckoning.

[167] For example, nos 89 and 343.

[168] These bequests are in Barkere's will rather than his testament.

[169] Again, it has not been possible to analyse the crops mentioned in the wills.

the archdeaconry is best summarised by the bequests made by William Metewyn of Wattisfield (no. 240) to his wife Elizabeth: 'a horse of her choice, the two best cows, two pigs with two piglets, a cart with a pair of traces, a saddle belonging to the same cart, with two horse-collars and with a pair of traces, a plough with the traces, plough-beam [*and*] shackles, with the coulter [*and*] share; three coombs of wheat, three coombs two bushels of rye, six coombs of barley, a coomb of beans, a bushel of green peas and a coomb of oats; … sufficient straw, hay, fodder and chaff for her animals for a year'.[170]

Outside the dwelling-house: crafts and trades: Workshops, whether within the house or in outbuildings, would have been included in the will proper, but the equipment in them was regarded as chattels and so would usually be included in the testament.[171] Of the wills of those testators who stated their occupation, not one specifically mentioned the various tools of their trade. Indeed, only Robert Judy, a barker (no. 771) even mentioned his craft and then only to say that the moveables and unmoveables pertaining to his craft were excepted from his bequest to his wife. Only a few other wills give any indication of any occupation other than farming. These exceptions include William Metewyn of Wattisfield (no. 240), who left instructions for the completion of his apprentice's training as wheelwright; Richard Wryghte of Bures St Mary (no. 67), who left his looms and their equipment; William Eve of Little Waldingfield (no. 83), perhaps a dyer, who left all his white wool and 96lbs of coloured wool, blue and madder-red; William Wethere of Stanton All Saints (no. 256), who left his wife a 'whele' with the 'cardes'; John Petywate of Glemsford (no. 504), who gave instructions for his sons to be allowed access to his wide tenter for 'the hanging and working of their cloths'; and several testators who bequeathed lengths of cloth, suggesting that they were weavers.[172]

Appointment of executors: Usually towards the end of their testaments, testators named their executors, sometimes termed 'attorneys'. They frequently appointed their spouse and/or other family members, or else business or social acquaintances in the locality. A supervisor of the executors, who was frequently of higher social standing, might be named as well.[173] Occasionally the court might appoint a supervisor if the named executor(s) were not considered sufficiently competent, perhaps if they were relatively young.[174] Executors and supervisors might also be members

---

[170]   This long list of bequests is actually included in Metewyn's will proper but technically they should have been in his testament.

[171]   Although it should be said that some of the information that follows comes from the will proper rather than the testament.

[172]   For example, nos 374, 430, 456, 681, 711 and 786.

[173]   Sometimes more than one supervisor was appointed.

[174]   For example, Ralph Trapett of Hepworth (no. 68) had appointed as executors his son John, Walter Cowpere and Stephen Dey. When his will was proved, administration was granted to John Trapett, 'with the supervision and advice of John Smyth of Bury, whom we have constituted supervisor for this purpose'. Power was reserved to the other executors, who had not appeared in court. The probate sentence of John Botwryght of Lakenheath (no. 399) recorded that administration had been granted to the named executors, 'with the supervision and advice of John Myllere and William Lacy, whom we, the Official, for various good reasons ordained and assigned as supervisors'.

of the clergy, some of whom were not named in any other records. In general, testators anticipated that their appointed executors would fulfil their task competently, not least because they knew that they would be answerable for the same before 'the High Judge' on Judgement Day. However, some foresaw that trouble might be caused for, if not by, their executors. Thomas Forthe of Cockfield (no. 350) stated that his goods were not be administered without the agreement of all three of his executors, Joan his wife, Thomas Forthe (his nephew) and John Brown; and if any of them contravened his will, he was to be dismissed, especially if it adversely affected his wife. Similarly, John Sawyer *alias* Gilly of Bradfield St George (no. 663) appointed as his executors his wife Isabel and his three sons, but he stated that Isabel was not answerable to the other three, only to God, Holy Church and its ministers, but the others were to be answerable to her, and if any of them violated or obstructed his will, he would forgo his legacies. On the other hand, Robert Dunch the elder of Mendlesham (no. 374) bequeathed his (?second) wife Margery half of the residue of his goods, nineteen animals, various quantities of grain, blankets and wool on condition that she did not vex or impede his executors in the execution of his will, nor claim any right in his lands or tenements; if she caused or produced any dissension then she would receive none of those bequests.

Bequests were usually made to executors in recompense for their labour or 'pains' about the execution of a will. The amount given varied greatly, not only according to the wealth of the testator but perhaps also according to amount of work envisaged for the executors. For example, Alexander Cook, chaplain, and John Kendale the younger, executors of Richard Mody of Newton (no. 311), were to be given 20s each for their labours, whereas Matilda Stace of Sudbury (no. 307) gave her executors, John Pondere and Edmund Sponere, only 20d each, but 'if this appears small, it to be augmented according to their conscience'. Executors frequently incurred expenses in the execution of their task: those of Thomas Cook of Cotton (no. 700) were not only to have 6s 8d for their labour, but also as much for their expenses 'as right and conscience require'. The role of an executor might be quite onerous, with bequests being continued for a long period of time; the role might also be wracked by dissent. Peter Kyng of Sapiston (no. 544) appreciated that it would take his executors some time to realise his assets but knew that his older children might not be patient: if any of them 'ungratefully worry my executors by importuning and impetuously claiming their legacies or gifts, or obstruct my testament or this will, then it shall be at the disposition and will of my executors to limit and reduce the legacies and gifts, and if in their view the demand is made maliciously, to withhold and deny them totally'. Again the executors were allowed to use their discretion. Occasionally one or more of the executors renounced their appointment, leaving the execution to the other(s).[175] Reasons for this are not recorded so it is impossible to determine whether the one left to administer the will was considered perfectly competent, or impossible to work with, or neither.

The residue: After all the specific gifts and legacies and provision for religious services, etc., the testator usually bequeathed the residue of all goods and chattels, not previously mentioned, to his executors, often desiring them to 'have God before

---

[175] For example, no. 224.

their eyes' when fulfilling their duties. These duties were sometimes spelled out in detail, as in the testament of John Tylere of Westley (no. 128): he left the residue to his executor Henry Banyard 'to sell, receive, and dispose for my soul and the souls of my parents and benefactors, and all the faithful departed, in celebrating masses and other deeds of charity, as he sees best to please God and profit the aforesaid souls'. The duties required of executors might be onerous and long running, so much so that testators sometimes anticipated that their bequests might involve another generation of executors: certain items would have to be sold by the 'executors of my executors', not least because the items in question had been bequeathed for the legatee's lifetime and they were also the original executor.[176]

Sealing: After the testament had been written by a scrivener and read out to the testator and gathered witnesses ('specially summoned' it was sometimes stated), a seal was applied to the document.[177] Some of the 'original wills' relating to 'Bald-wyne' retain their seal-tags, formed by partially cutting a strip of parchment along the bottom of the will. The wax seals themselves have not survived, but a few of the tags have pieces of wax adhering to them. The names of witnesses were sometimes, but by no means always, added.

The form of the will proper

The will, more correctly, the last will (*ultima voluntas*), was a legal document, whereas the testament was an ecclesiastical one and hence was proved in an ecclesiastical court. As a legal document the will could exist separately from the testament and therefore sometimes it was not proved at the same time as the testament. Again because of its legal status, the last will often used the regnal year instead of the calendar year, and it could have been made at a different time and bear quite a different date from the testament. Sometimes the will was presented as an indented deed (no. 125), or even as a notarial instrument, and was often written in the third person. The main purpose of the last will was to convey instructions or requests to the testator's feoffees with respect to real estate.

Feoffees: Because testators were not allowed by law to bequeath real estate, a practice called 'enfeoffment to use' had been developed, whereby the holder of property enfeoffed (that is, conveyed the property to) feoffees or trustees, to his or her 'use'.[178] In other words, the feoffees held the property on behalf of the original holder and since they held it to his or her 'use', the feoffees could, subsequently, be told what to do with it. This was the purpose of the last will. In it the testator would request the feoffees to hand over the 'estate' or title in the property, or certain parts of it, to other named beneficiaries. A straightforward example of the use of feoffees can be seen in no. 225, while a much more complex situation existed in no. 89.

---

[176] For example, no. 164.
[177] See Owen, 'A Scrivener's Notebook'.
[178] For a succinct description of the use of feoffees in this way, see Virgoe, 'The Will of Hugh atte Fenne', esp. pp.34–5; for a more detailed account, see Bean, *Decline of English Feudalism*, Chapter 3, 'The Origins and Development of Uses'.

Houses and buildings: Directions to feoffees in wills often contain information of great interest to today's students of social history and domestic architecture. The fragility of medieval houses is concisely conveyed in the brief set of instructions from Thomas Howton of Hawkedon (no. 676) to his wife Margaret concerning the maintenance of his 'principal house' and bakehouse: she was see to the repairs of the houses with straw and clay. Detailed descriptions of houses and rooms are rare in the 'Baldwyne' wills but occasionally we get a glimpse indoors. Thomas Blowere of Bildeston (no. 285) bequeathed to his wife Rose all the moveables belonging to his house, that is, 'of the hall and chamber, pantry or buttery, and kitchen'. Provision made for the housing of a widow can be even more informative; for example, William Wethere (no. 256) gave to Katherine his wife 'a chamber at the east end of the hall, with free entrance and exit as often as she pleases; Katherine to have her fire in the hall at this time, until William my son newly makes [*her*] a chamber with a chimney in my messuage, with free entrance and exit to the same'. From this we see that the concept of a 'granny-flat' is no modern invention. Legally the widow could claim a third of her deceased husband's estate as dower, but testators often made arrangements for their widows conditional upon their *not* claiming dower.[179] Special provision was often made also in case the widow subsequently re-married.[180]

When the will of Richard Howett of Edwardstone (no. 353) was proved, his son and executor John made the court record in the register an agreement that had been reached with his brother Thomas concerning one of their father's properties. Thomas was then living in 'Howettes', a cottage with a garden, that, from its name, obviously belonged to the family. The brothers had agreed that Thomas would remain there during John's lifetime, after which, presumably, its disposal would be directed by John in his will.

Some testators also bequeathed their shop, or workshop, in their will proper. Again, like details of tools in their testament, this is sometimes the only indication of their occupation. Robert Burwe of Hundon (no. 79) seems to have been, at the very least, a herbalist: he bequeathed to his son William 'half of all the things and medicines (*medicinis*) at present in my shop, with all the volumes (*copiis*) of my books'. John Femnale of Ashley in the parish of Silverley (Cambs) (no. 80) owned four shops, or market stalls: one in Fordham (Cambs) and three in Newmarket, one in the 'Old Bocherye', one in the 'Oolde Mersery' and the other rented out to Richard Badwyck.[181]

Lands: Testators' descriptions of their lands varied enormously, from the simple 'all my lands and tenements, both free and bond, that I have in Gislingham, Finningham and Westhorpe' (no. 622), to the descriptions of individual small pieces of land in the open fields of Mildenhall (no. 230), Rougham (no. 634) and Soham (no. 232), and various closes in Tostock (no. 821). Many testators made the statement that lands were held 'of the chief lords of the fee by rents and services and due

---

[179] For example, nos 246, 256 and 266.
[180] For example, no. 195.
[181] For the 'Bocherye' and 'Oolde Mersery' in Newmarket see May, *Newmarket: Medieval and Tudor*, p.45. Richard Abell of Stowmarket (no. 103) had two shops near the church gate and John Browster of Bildeston (no. 359) had a shop in the market there, but neither gave any indication of their trade or craft.

custom'. This formula emphasised the fact that, although the lands were freehold (feoffees were not necessary for copyhold land since that was controlled by the relevant manor court), nevertheless they were held of superior lords to whom were due certain payments 'by custom'. All land was held of superior lords, the most superior being the 'tenant in chief' who held directly of the king.[182]

Although most of the testators were quite specific regarding the person to whom their lands were to pass, some were not so sure. Robert Chylderston the elder of Mildenhall (no. 644) apparently had no preference concerning which of his five sons would inherit his messuage after his wife's death: he left the decision to his executor John Sygo. Similarly, after the death of his wife, William Coppyng of Somerton (no. 125) wanted his lands and tenements to pass to one of his five sons, 'that is, to him of them that is of the best bearing, behaviour and conduct, by the discretion of my executors' and the son so inheriting would make cash payments to his brothers.

Sometimes it appears that problems were anticipated when a second wife was allowed to live in the family home. For example, Nicholas Barkere of Ickworth (no. 138) wanted his wife Alice to have his messuage and lands for term of her life, and then they would pass to his eldest son John 'on condition that he does not trouble or worry Alice my wife about my gift of the house and land during her lifetime'; if he did, it would pass to Nicholas's son Thomas.

Witnesses: Sometimes the names of witnesses are recorded in last wills, not necessarily the same as in the testament, especially if the will bore a different date.

Testaments and wills

As has been mentioned above, testators rarely observed the strict division between testament and will. Of the near 760 'wills' in Part II of 'Baldwyne' (excluding those repeated or deleted in the register), only about 50 consist of separate testaments and wills proper, and in many of those the testaments contain some will material and *vice versa*. Of the remainder, about 440 are mixtures of testament and will proper, while about 260 have only testamentary bequests; in addition a handful are wills proper only.

The probate sentence

The probate sentence (in this volume often referred to as 'the probate') was a certificate of approval added to the original will (whether that consisted of testament only, or testament and will proper) by the clerk of the proving officer. In the archdeaconry of Sudbury this was almost always the archdeacon's official, who was empowered to prove wills. The first part of the probate usually stated that the will had been proved 'before' (Latin *coram*) the official, who was only rarely named, and gave place and date. The places and dates of successive probates sometimes show the moving of the official from place to place, possibly while conducting the archdeacon's visitation in a particular deanery. In occasional cases, a member of the clergy was commis-

---

[182] Only the king had no superior since he was regarded (as the crown technically still is) as owning all the land of the country.

sioned to act on behalf of the official, when he was termed a 'commissary'.[183] No. 804 was proved before William Duffeld, Commissary General in the archdeaconry of Sudbury to Bishop James of Norwich, on his ordinary visitation. Very rarely the archdeacon himself proved a will, probably, again, during a visitation. It was the responsibility of the executors named in the will to obtain probate. They had to decide which court the will should go to (or which they wanted to take it to) and where the appropriate official was to be found. In the circumstances it is surprising how soon after the making of wills some of them were proved, suggesting that some prior discussion and planning had taken place.

In general, it was necessary for an inventory to be taken of the personal possessions of the deceased, properly valued by competent persons, and for it to be exhibited in the probate court before probate could be granted. Some historians have assumed that this practice only began following an act of 1529.[184] However, the survival of earlier inventories clearly suggests otherwise: the earliest surviving inventory from Exeter (Devon) was drawn up in 1324 and the earliest from Cornwall was made in 1342.[185] Furthermore, even where early inventories have not survived, as in Suffolk, references to them in other documents, such as probate sentences, again indicate that they had existed.[186] In the 'Baldwyne' register, the first mention of an inventory was in July 1443.[187] In Part II, the only executors explicitly required to exhibit an inventory were those of Margaret Cole, widow of John, of Stoke by Nayland (no. 150). Executors might also be required to produce an account of the winding up and distribution of the estate, as were Margaret Cole's.[188] Once this had been done, and verified by the court, their duties would be complete. John Coldham of Barningham (no. 338) had instructed his three executors not to do anything, nor to administer any of his goods, without the agreement of the others or without the authority of his supervisor. However, it appears that they completed their task competently: all three were granted administration on 12 December 1469 and they were acquitted and dismissed just 6 months later, on 18 June 1470.

One of the purposes of an inventory was to determine whether the value of the possessions of the deceased would meet the value of the bequests made in their

---

[183] For example, no. 55.

[184] 21 Hen. VIII, c.5. Cox and Cox have pointed out that the primary purpose of this act was to prevent the ecclesiastical authorities overcharging for probate ('Probate 1500–1800', p.26). They have also drawn attention to earlier regulations concerning inventories in 'Probate Inventories: the Legal Background', p.133.

[185] The Exeter inventory has been published in Lepine and Orme (eds), *Death and Memory in Medieval Exeter*; the Cornwall inventory has been published in Orme (ed.), *Cornish Wills*.

[186] Rather more unusually, on 11 December 1329, together with a probate account, the detailed inventory of the goods of William Lene of Walsham le Willows was recorded in the Walsham manor court roll (Lock (ed.), *Court Rolls of Walsham le Willows*, pp.133–5).

[187] In the probate sentence to the will of John Heylok of Barnardiston, will pr. 1 July 1443 (SROB, Baldwyne 47; Pt I, no. 249). For references to inventories in Part I see William atte Fen of Glemsford, probate only, October 1451 (Pt I, no. 644); John Herward of Sudbury, probate only, November 1451 (Pt I, no. 645); Richard Fenn of Kersey, administration only, dated September 1452 (Pt I, no. 720); Roger Tyllot of Rougham, will proved July 1459 (Pt I, no. 1240). The earliest inventory cited by Cox and Cox is from Southampton and is dated 1447 (Cox and Cox, 'Probate 1500–1800', p.26, citing Roberts and Parker, *Southampton Probate Inventories*, pp.2–13).

[188] Cox and Cox, 'Probate 1500–1800', p.25.

will. Peter Kyng of Sapiston (no. 544) recognised that he might have been over-generous: 'if my goods are not sufficient for the legacies, then the executors, with the supervisor, to moderate them and dispose according to the extent of the goods'. Occasionally the court did not grant probate to a will because there was an 'insufficiency' or 'deficiency' of goods, that is, the goods of deceased were insufficient to fulfil the various bequests and so the executors would be unable to complete their appointed task. Again, the fact that the court was able to determine an 'insufficiency' suggests that an inventory had been drawn up. At least seven testators in Part II were deemed to have insufficient goods.[189] In general, in such cases the executors were excused from rendering further accounts and were acquitted, signifying that they had no further responsibilities in that regard; however, the executors of John Cotelere (no. 282) were apparently concerned about provision for the testator's son, provision that was not mentioned in the registered will. The probate clerk recorded that 'because the executors, being sworn, deposed that, besides what was contained in the testament, the testator willed that out of the residue of all his goods his son should have his provision and sustentation, they were charged accordingly'. These two men exceeded their legal obligation in favour of their moral obligation.

Part of the probate sentence was the grant of administration ('admon') where the executors present were named and 'power reserved' to those not present.[190] The whole probate sentence should have been copied by the registry clerk when he registered the will, but this did not always happen.

Physical aspects of register 'Baldwyne'[191]

The writing in register 'Baldwyne': Most of the folios of 'Baldwyne' II are written in what appears to be the same fairly neat, regular, legible hand, suggesting that many of the entries were made by the same man, or, perhaps more likely, by clerks who had been trained to write in the same way. The Latin is abbreviated, but not drastically so, as can be seen in various illustrations in this volume. Occasionally the writing is very different, when clerks who wrote in other hands made the entries, some of them very hurriedly, in highly abbreviated Latin, or with a poor pen (for example, nos 435, 656 and 792), others with great care and painstaking writing (for example, nos 412 and 628). In general, the probate sentence was written in the same hand as the text of the will, but sometimes it was added (?later) in a different hand, usually less legibly (such as no. 634) but occasionally more neatly (no. 628).

There are very few scribal flourishes in the register: on occasion, the initial 'I' at the beginning of a will (*In dei nomine Amen*) might extend down the side of the page to the third or fourth line, but none of the register clerks produced any intricate capitals. It comes as some surprise, therefore, to find on folio 521, in the space after the will of Alice Markaunte of Badwell (no. 644), a contemporary line-drawing of a curly-haired man wearing a hat, a (very) short doublet and hose. The inscription,

---

[189]   John Noble of Nayland (no. 141), Robert Shukford of Langham (no. 207), John Cotelere of Barnham (no. 282), Joan Facon of Edwardston (no. 328), Margaret Warde of Haverhill (no. 341), James Drewe of Mellis (no. 391) and Thomas Vyell of Ixworth (no. 804).

[190]   That is, power reserved to the court to make grant of administration to the other executor(s) when they came to 'take it up'.

[191]   A description of the physical appearance of the actual register has been given above.

perhaps in a later sixteenth-century hand, reads [*?*]*M' Crosby Mylys at the*.[192] (See illustration.)

The assembling of register 'Baldwyne': Many church records – perhaps most – seem to have begun life as separate quires of paper which were subsequently collected into gatherings and eventually, or not as the case may be, bound into books.[193] Since it was often some years later that binding took place, the loose leaves were constantly in danger of being misplaced or even lost. The proving dates of successive items in the 'Baldwyne' register show that this is exactly what happened, and this accounts for the absence of a testator called Baldwyne in the first few folios. The misplacing of leaves or whole gatherings has resulted in blocks of wills being out of their proper sequence. For example, folios 353 to 372 (nos 144 to 211) have been bound into the bifolium containing folios 352 and 373, and so a run of wills proved in 1464 (old style) occurs among those proved in 1462. Similarly, folios 584 to 591 (nos 799 to 808) are not consecutive: the bifolia containing folios 584 and 591, 585 and 590 are two similar sheets, containing wills of approximately the same dates; the biofolia containing folios 586 and 589, 587 and 588 are two dissimilar sheets, which have been sewn one into the other, and which together have been sewn into the two previously mentioned sheets. Consequently nos 799 to 808 are not in any logical date sequence.

The 'Baldwyne' register has twelve 'parts', or gatherings and the last will in the register is number 810 on folio 591. However, folios 586 to 589 (wills 803 to 807) do not actually belong in 'Baldwyne': these five wills, dated between December 1477 and October 1479, and proved between October 1478 and November 1479, have 'strayed' into 'Baldwyne' from the next register, 'Hervye'.[194] Furthermore, seventeen wills that do belong to 'Baldwyne' have 'strayed' into a later register, known as 'Fuller'.[195] The first 26 folios of 'Fuller' are not part of 'Fuller' proper, but are leaves gathered together and sewn in before the current folio 27. Six of these folios (three bifolia) should be in 'Baldwyne': folios 11 and 22, 12 and 21, 15 and 18. The wills on these folios were proved in 1462 and 1463. In this volume they are presented as nos 811 to 827. No attempt has been made to put them in date order; they are presented in the order in which they now appear in 'Fuller'. At the begin-

---

[192] The *M'* at the beginning might be a symbol, or it might be an abbreviated form of 'Master'; there is no word after '*at the*'. It is unclear to whom this drawing and caption refer: in the sixteenth century there were two, if not three, men named Miles (or, Myles) Crosby of Bury St Edmunds. In 1522, Miles Crosby, gentleman, was general collector of the 'loan' for the archdeaconry of Sudbury that had been 'granted by the general clergy' in all dioceses of England (*Letters & Papers of Henry VIII, Addenda*, no. 358, p.111). Miles Crosby was supervisor of the will of Thomas Hall of Mildenhall, dated 10 January 1524/25 (TNA, PCC 19 Porch) and of the will of William Bushy, vicar of Great Barton, dated 3 December 1527 (NRO, NCC 235 Briggs). In 1528 Miles Crosby deputised for the abbot of Leiston in proving a will (SROB, Fuller 26). The notary Miles Crosby of Bury St Edmunds witnessed the will of William Wyborowe of Bury, dated 2 April 1535 (TNA, PCC 1 Crumwell). The will of Miles Crosby, dated 15 February 1528/29, was proved on 22 April 1539 (SROB, Holland, fol. 53v). In 1541, the notary's son, also named Miles Crosby, styled 'gentleman of London', sold all his lands in Stanton, Bardwell, Hepworth, Weston and Wattisfield to Thomas Bacon, salter of London (SROB, HD 1591/1/145). Finally, written in the old outer cover of 'Baldwyne' is the note: 'Miles Crosby jun[io]r, poet laureate of Bury St Edmunds'.

[193] See Northeast (ed.), *Boxford Churchwardens' Accounts*, p.xi.

[194] SROB, IC500/2/11.

[195] SROB, IC500/2/12. 'Fuller' is not even the next register in date sequence; that is 'Hervye'.

ning of each of these wills the folio number in 'Fuller' has been indicated after the will's number in this volume. The survival of these stray folios in 'Fuller' suggests that some of the folios of 'Baldwyne' have been lost completely. As Peter Northeast commented at the end of the Introduction to Part I, 'In spite of these blemishes, it is remarkable that a document such as 'Baldwyne' should have survived at all, and for that we must be grateful.'[196]

---

[196]   Part I, Introduction, p.lv.

WILLS FROM THE REGISTER 'BALDWYNE'
1439–1474

Part II: 1461–1474

Suffolk Record Office (Bury St Edmunds)
IC500/2/10

[*Sewn in before fol. 308*]
1. JOHN PARMENTER of GREAT FINBOROUGH ('Fymburugh Magna'), 16 May 1422

[*Will only*]

Dated the Sabbath day before the feast of St Dunstan the bishop, 1422, at Finborough. To Alice my wife all my lands and tenements in the town of Great Finborough, with a piece of meadow lying at 'Hunteburugh' in Buxhall, except a piece of meadow lying at 'Tylyers', she to have them until the feast of St Michael next after the day when Joan my daughter shall be married, and then, after that, Alice to have all the tenement which Robert Edward formerly held, to her and her heirs, and Joan to have all my other lands and tenements in the said town, and out of these lands and tenements, Alice to have 6s 8d annually during her lifetime.

To the said Joan the excepted piece of meadow, or 10 marks in money from its sale, at her marriage.

To Alice my wife £10, to be received of William Dec' for a tenement sold to him in Rattlesden ('Ratyllysden'), that is, in the next 15 years, by equal portions; also to her all my ostilments and utensils, and also an ambling (*ambil'*) horse, 4 cows, 12 ewes and all my wool and all the crop (*vestur'*) of two crofts sown with wheat, of which one is called 'Longlond' and the other 'Schotelond', 4 ?acres [*damaged*] of land sown with barley, a piece of land called 'Netherwent' sown with peas, and 3 acres of land sown with oats.

I wish a suitable and honest chaplain to be found to celebrate divine service for my soul and for the souls of my parents and benefactors, and all those at rest in Christ, in the church of the said Finborough, for 2 whole years.

To the convent of friars of Babwell, for a trental of St Gregory to be celebrated there for the health of my soul,[1] 10s; [*similarly*] to the convent of Carmelite Friars of Ipswich (*Gippiwc'*) 10s[2] to the convent of Friars Minor of the same town 10s[3] and to the convent of Austin Friars of Clare 10s.[4]

To the fabric of the porch of the said church 26s 8d.

To Margaret my daughter 10 marks in money; to John the son of the said Margaret 13s 4d and to William [*son*] of the said Margaret 6s 8d.

To the oldest son of John Whederarde 3s 4d and to the oldest daughter of the said John 3s 4d.

To Mariota Perye 33s 4d, to be received from the above tenement sold to William Dec'.

To Peter Parmenter a horse with an old 'paksadyll', a green-coloured gown with a black hood and a silvered 'daggarde', and to his wife a quarter of wheat.

To Katherine my servant 40s and a bed.

To Margaret the wife of Simon Well 6s 8d, and to the daughter of the same Simon 6s 8d.

To John Hardeman and his son a striped (*stragulat' talor'*) gown and a doublet of green worsted with a hood, and to John's wife a bullock.

To Robert Fuller a tunic of 'dudde' and a pelisse (*pellic'*) with a black hood.

To He . . . [*damaged*] Charles a gown of russet and to Richard Gasseleye a gown of 'dudde'.

To each chaplain coming to my obsequies 4d, to each clerk 2d and to each of the poor 1d.

Alice my wife and Joan my daughter to repair and keep up all the buildings (*domos*) and walls of all my said tenements in all necessary ways until the day when my daughter shall be married and then, after that, Joan faithfully to bear all the dues (*onera*) and costs of the repairs and upkeep of the said buildings and walls during the lifetime of the said Alice.

To Margaret and Joan my daughters a piece of land with the wood at the lower head, called 'Lesquens', in Little Finborough ('Fynburgh Parva'), after the death of Alice my wife.

To John Coppynge 6s 8d, Simon Well 6s 8d and John Geddynge 6s 8d, execs, for their labour; to Sir William Coppynge, clerk, supervisor, 6s 8d, and ?he to have 'stodes' and 'sparrys' sufficient for making a barn out of them, and 13s 4d for its making.

To the daughter of that Adam a bullock.

Alice my wife to have all my stock, both live and dead, until the feast of St Michael next and then the stock to be faithfully disposed by my execs.

To Adam my son, aforesaid, a cart with 2 horse collars, a pair of old hand-traces (*tract' manual'*) and another pair of traces; to Alice my wife a new cart with a tumbrel, with all the harness (*apparat'*) for 3 horses and also a saddle and a 'paksadyll' with the fittings (*apparat'*) belonging to the saddles.

Seal appended.

[*No probate recorded*]

[*After the end of the will appears the beginning of another version of the same will*] This is the will of John P. of F. made &c [*sic*].

To Alice my wife all my lands and tenements in the towns of F.[*sic*] and Buxhall, except a piece of meadow lying at 'Tylers', she to have [*them*] until the feast of St Michael next after the day when Joan my daughter shall be married and then, after that, I assign to the said Alice all that tenement at 'Churchestritte', formerly Robert Edward's, together with a piece of meadow lying at 'Hunborugh', to her and her heirs for ever, and all my other lands and tenements I assign to Joan my daughter, to her and her heirs for ever. To the said Joan that piece of meadow aforesaid, or 10 marks in money from its sale, at her marriage.

[*Nothing further*]

[*On the dorse of the will is what appears to be the draft of a brief letter, in a later hand and in English, to an unnamed 'ryght worschipfull syr' asking him to be a good master to 'the berer off this lytill letter' in 'such cause as he schall move to your mastership off at this tym'. No indication of identity of sender.*]

[*At foot of dorse is written*]
Testament examined (*scrutat' testa'*) ?*per* Thomas Parman de Wykhambroke iii[xx] [*60*] yers agoo.

---

1   When the Franciscans (Grey Friars or Friars Minor) tried to establish a house at Bury St Edmunds there was a great deal of opposition from the great monastery of Bury. Reconciliation was eventually achieved and in 1262 the monks granted the friars a site beyond the north gate, just outside the town's jurisdiction, called Babwell, and here they continued till the Dissolution. The popularity of the Babwell friars is proved by the frequency of bequests to them (*VCH Suffolk*, ii, pp.124–5).

2   The Carmelite Friars (White Friars) were probably established at Ipswich in 1278. Their land eventually extended from St Stephen's Lane to Queen Street, on the south side of the Butter Market (*VCH Suffolk*, ii, pp.130–1).

3   Early in the reign of Edward I a convent of Franciscans (Friars Minor) was founded on the west side of Ipswich, in the parish of St Nicholas. Very few records relating to this house have survived (*VCH Suffolk*, ii, pp.126–7).

4   Richard de Clare, earl of Gloucester, was the first to introduce the Austin Friars into England, and it is generally assumed that their first establishment was at Clare, in 1248. They were not permitted by their rule to hold any property except the site of their house, but here the rule was interpreted liberally and the Clare house possessed numerous plots of land, which are recorded in a surviving cartulary. The high position of the founder and his posterity, coupled with the fact that Clare was the parent house of the order in England, placed this friary in an exceptional position. It was a favourite residence for royalty in the thirteenth and fourteenth centuries (*VCH Suffolk*, ii, pp.127–9).

[fol. 308]
2. WILLIAM GOLDYNG of EYE ('Eya'),[1] 7 September 1463

[*Commendation*: to God, the Blessed Mary &c]; to be buried in the churchyard of Eye parish church; to the high altar for tithes negligently forgotten 3s 4d; to each priest present at my obsequies 4d and to each surpliced clerk 1d; to the reparation of the tower 6s 8d.

To the gild of the Blessed Mary 2s;[2] to the gild of St Peter 2s;[3] to each poor person living in 'le Spytell' 1d.[4]

My wife to care well for my mother and my 5 children, and as long as she does so lovingly, she to have my tenement in the borough (*burg'*) of the said town for her lifetime. After her death one of my children who is best placed (*aptissim' mundo*) is to have it and find a priest for 2 years to celebrate for the souls of his parents and for the souls of all their benefactors. My wife to have a close with the garden, containing 3½ acres by estimation, at 'Lamsetbrigge',[5] for her lifetime, on condition that she do not marry again. If she does, the close to be sold and the money distributed among my children then living, according to the discretion of my execs. Residue of my goods to Sir Thomas Hervy, vicar of the said church,[6] and Robert Saxcy, execs.

Seal appended.

Proved at Eye 18 January 1463/64. Admon to execs.

1   Executor of Sybil Deye of Eye, probate September 1457 (SROB, Baldwyne 183; Pt I, no. 886).

2   Agnes Jenews (no. 94), John Carwent (no. 395), Robert Turnour (no. 405) and Robert Hardyng (no. 457) also made bequests to the gild of the Blessed Mary, or of St Mary, at Eye, as did Roger Ropkyn of Thrandeston (SROB, Baldwyne 108; Pt I, no. 492).

3   Agnes Jenews, Robert Turnour and Robert Hardyng (see note above) also made bequests to the gild of St Peter at Eye; from the will of Agnes's husband, John Jenews, it appears that this gild was sometimes known as the gild of SS Peter and Paul (SROB, Baldwyne 133; Pt I, no. 624).

4   The hospital of St Mary Magdalene, known to be in existence from at least 1329 to 1521 (*PSIA*, xix, p.184). Agnes Jenews also made a bequest to the poor living in the hospital; Robert Hardyng made a bequest of 30 cartloads of clay for the repair of 'Spetyll way' in Eye.

5   Agnes Jenews made a bequest to repairs of Lambseth bridge, which is to the north-west of the town of Eye, in Lambseth Street, the road leading out of the town to the north; Robert Hardyng bequeathed 30 cartloads of clay to the repairs of 'Lamset way'.

6   Thomas Hervy was vicar of Eye from 1452 to 1488 (Tanner, p.1300); see also nos 222, 395, 442 and 457.

3. ROBERT CHIRCHE of EYE ('Eya'), 18 January 1463/64 [*probate only*]

Proved. Admon to Nicholas Hardyng and Thomas Hervy, execs.

4. MARGARET HYLLE of WESTHORPE ('Westthorp'), 3 August 1463

Dated at Westhorpe; [*commendation*: to God &c]; to be buried in the churchyard of the parish church of Westhorpe; to the altar of Westhorpe St Mary[*sic*] a diaper cloth; to the altar of St James another diaper cloth, of second quality (*secundaria'*). To Robert Leve *alias* Fletcher a basin with the ewer.

Residue of goods to disposition of my execs: William Fysche of Westhorpe and John Savage of Winfarthing [*Norfolk*].

Proved at Eye 18 January 1463/64. Admon to execs.

5. WILLIAM NOREYS[1] of BROCKFORD ['Brokford'] [in WETHERINGSETT],[2] 14 December 1463

Of Brockford in the diocese of Nowich; at the point of death (*in extremis*); [*commendation*: to God the Father &c]; my body to Christian burial; to the high altar of Wetheringsett church 3s 4d; for a trental to be celebrated for my soul 10s; for a suitable priest to celebrate in Wetheringsett church for a whole year for my soul and for the souls of all my friends and benefactors, 8 marks 6s 8d; to the said church a lead (*unu' plumbu'*), now with my father, to the covering of the south side of the church; to each priest present at my obsequies 4d; to each clerk there 1d; to each of the poor there 1d.

[fol. 308v] To each of my godsons 4d; to Joan my wife all my household (*domicilia*) and utensils; to John my son £10 or a close called 'Pellynges Feld'; if John dies before reaching legal age I wish to have a priest to celebrate in Wetheringsett church for a year and the residue of the £10 to be disposed by my execs in deeds of mercy. Residue of all my goods to my execs: Sir John Tought, chaplain,[3] and Thomas Knyght of Brockford, to each of whom for their labour 6s 8d.

Proved at Eye, 18 January 1463/64. Admon to execs.

1   Executor of Henry Taylour of Brockford, will pr. October 1461 (SROB, Baldwyne 296; Pt I, no. 1453).
2   Brockford was one of those Domesday vills that never achieved autonomy as a parish and has remained within Wetheringsett, the combined parish often being known as Wetheringsett-*cum*-Brockford. Jocelin referred to a church there in the late twelfth century (*Chronicle of Jocelin of Brakelond*, ed. Butler, p.63).
3   Will (as of Stonham Aspal) pr. October 1469 (NRO, NCC 152 Jekkys).

6. WILLIAM OSBERN of COTTON, 26 September 1463

Dated Monday before the feast of St Michael the Archangel 1463 at Cotton; [*commendation*: to God the Father, the Blessed Mary &c]; my body to Christian burial; to the high altar of Cotton church for my tithes and offerings forgotten 40d; to the high altar of Finningham for tithes forgotten 12d; to the church of Cotton 6s 8d.

To the convent of friars of Orford ('Offord') 10s to pray for my soul.[1]

All my goods, that is, lands and tenements, meadows, pastures, feedings, in both Cotton and Finningham, to Margaret my wife for term of her life and after her death, to remain to Simon my son and his heirs; if Margaret should take another husband after my death my son Simon to have and take possession of all my goods except such lands and tenements as Margaret and I have purchased, and those Margaret to have for her lifetime, and after her death to remain to Simon and his heirs. If Margaret and Simon should both die without heirs all [*my*] goods, that is, lands and tenements, to be sold by Margaret's execs or my son's and [*disposed*] as they see best.

Execs: Margaret my wife and my son Simon.

Proved at Eye, 18 January 1463/64. Admon to execs.

1   A priory of Austin Friars was founded at Orford in the reign of Edward I: in 1295 Robert de Hewell gave them a plot of ground in Orford to build on (*VCH Suffolk*, ii, p.130). Four testators in Part II made bequests to the house: this testator William Osbern and Thomas Cook (no. 700) of Cotton, Geoffrey Bussch (no. 202) of Mendlesham, and William Kendale (no. 726) of Occold. Kendale had a particular interest as his sons John and William were friars there.

7. KATHERINE METEWYN of WATTISFIELD ('Watlesfeld'),[1] 28 February 1463/64 [*probate only*]

Proved at Wattisfield, on the penultimate day of February 1463/64. Admon to John Metewyn and Robert Frawnces, execs.

1   Wife of John Mettewynd of Wattisfield, will pr. January 1458/59 (SROB, Baldwyne 194; Pt I, no. 945).

[fol. 309]

8. THOMAS FYSCHE of SOHAM ('Saham') [*Cambs*], 2 June 1462 [*probate only*]

Proved at Soham. Admon to John Fysche his son, exec.

9. RICHARD SKYNALL of SNAILWELL ('Snaylwell') [*Cambs*], 16 May 1462

['Skynale' *in margin*] [*Commendation*: to God &c; *no burial directions*]

To Margaret my wife my best cow [*and*] the residue of all my goods after my debts have been paid; to John Skynall the younger [*my*] green gown with the cap (*pilio*) of felt.

To Thomas Mayhow my black tabard; the same Thomas Mayhow to dispose all my goods and justly pay my debts with the help of John Wellys, and them I make execs.

Witnesses: William Bregeman, Thomas Lake, Richard Brygeman and others.

Proved at Fornham [*St Martin*], 9 May 1462[*sic*]. Admon to execs.

10. WILLIAM WELHAM of GREAT HORRINGER ('Hornyngysherth Magna'), 6 & 26 September 1461

Dated 6 September 1461; [*commendation*: to God &c; *no burial directions*]; to the high altar of the parish church of the aforesaid Horringer, for tithes and offerings underpaid, 6s 8d; to the reparation of the said church 6s 8d; to the high altar of the parish church of [*place-name omitted*] 20d.

To the Friars Minor of Babwell 10s.[1]

To Isabel my wife all my ostilments and utensils and jewels belonging to my house; also to Isabel 2 cows and 6 ewes.

To John my son the elder a horse and my best gown, and after the death of Isabel he to have my best brass pot.

To John my son the younger 2 horses and my second-best gown, and after the death of Isabel he to have the second brass pot.

To Margaret my daughter 40s, a cow and half a quarter of wheat; to Katherine my daughter 5 marks; to Joan my daughter a mark; to Margery the wife of John my son a quarter of barley; to each of the children of Joan my daughter half a quarter of barley.

To William Clerk my godson half a quarter of barley.

Residue of all my goods and chattels, after my burial [*costs*] and debts have been paid and my testament fulfilled, to disposition of my execs, Isabel my wife, Thomas Redere of Bury St Edmunds and Robert Noble of the said Horringer; supervisor, John Brycete of Horringer, the elder; to each of them, for their labour, 3s 4d.

[fol. 309v]

[*Will; dated 26 September 1461*]

All my debts to be fully paid.

Isabel my wife and John my son the younger to have and to hold together my tenement in which I live, with a croft opposite the gate of the tenement and a piece of land there lying between the said croft and the new garden [*and*] another piece of land called 'Penylond', with 2 pieces of land at 'Hurrelebattes Hetche', for the term of Isabel's life, John paying Isabel each year half the farm of the said tenement and land as long as she chooses to live there; but if she chooses to live with John my son the elder, or elsewhere, then John my son the younger to pay Isabel the whole farm of the tenement and land each year for her lifetime. After the death of Isabel the tenement and land to remain to John my son the younger and his heirs for ever, on condition that he pay my execs named in my testament 4 marks in 4 years after the death of his mother.

Isabel and John my son the elder to have and hold together my tenement called 'le Newplace' with the garden adjacent, and all my land lying opposite the tenement and garden on the east, with 2 crofts lying under the wood called 'Herdwyk', another piece of land called 'Potteris alfeacre', with another piece of land at 'le grendyll',[2] for the lifetime of the said Isabel, John paying Isabel and my execs in the same way as above.

After the death of Isabel a suitable chaplain to celebrate divine service for a whole year in the parish church of the aforesaid Horringer for my soul and for the souls of Margaret and Isabel my wives and all the faithful departed, and the residue of all the money from my land and tenements I give to my execs to dispose in deeds of charity. Proved at Fornham St Martin, 10 June 1462. Admon to execs.

---

[1] See note to no. 1.

[2] From the Old English 'grendel', meaning a gravelly hollow or stream bed; occurs today as 'grindle' or 'grundle' in several parts of Suffolk, such as Stanton and Wattisfield.

[fol. 310]

11. ANDREW GRYGGES of LAVENHAM, 4 May 1462

Dated at Lavenham; [*commendation*: to God the Father Almighty, the Blessed Virgin Mary &c]; my body to Christian burial; to the high altar of the church of the town, for my tithes and offerings forgotten or underpaid, 3s 4d; to each chaplain present at my obsequies 8d; to each officially-appointed (*officiario*) clerk of the town present at my obsequies 4d, and to each boy singing or reading at my obsequies 1d.

To the friars of Sudbury 13s 4d;[1] to the friars of Clare 10s; to the friars of Babwell 10s; to the Friars Minor of Ipswich (*Gippewico*) 13s 4d;[2] to each of the poor coming on my burial-day 1d.

For the celebration of four hundred masses on one day, immediately after my death, for my soul and the souls for whom I am bound, 40s.

To the reparation of Lavenham church 10 marks, to be paid out of my debts.

A suitable chaplain to celebrate in Lavenham church for my soul and the souls for whom I am bound, at the altar of the Blessed Virgin Mary, for 3 years following my death, taking for his salary 8 marks per annum; 52s to be distributed, in one year after my death, to 12 of the poor each week, on a Thursday, 1d each.

To Alice my wife all my tenement in which I live, with the other messuages adjoining it, in Lavenham, in the streets called 'Heighstrete' and 'Maisterjonestrete',[3] to her and her heirs for ever, on condition that she have an almshouse (*elemosinar'*) built in the street called 'Maisterjonestrete', the poor people of which to pray for my soul and the souls of my parents and all my benefactors. To the same Alice all my ostilments and jewels and all my utensils belonging to my house, and also all my goods and chattels in the manor and town of Kettlebaston, she paying £17 which the stock there is valued at (*appreciat'*) by the tenants of that town. Also to Alice my two tenements in the town of Preston, one of which is called 'Hoodys' and the other 'Scottis', to her and her heirs for ever.

To Joan Forwele, Alice's sister, my messuage in Lavenham, in the street called 'Heighstrete', set between the messuage of Robert Ditton on one side and the messuage of Thomas Groos on the other, to her and her heirs, and 40s in money when she comes to marriage.

All my lands and tenements, both free and bond (*virgat'*), with the meadows, pastures, feedings, woods, rents and services, in the towns of Monks Eleigh ('Illeigh Monachorum') and Hadleigh, to be sold by my execs and the money from them to be disposed by them for the souls of Andrew Kyng my uncle (*avi*) and Joan his wife,[4] and the souls of John Griggys[5] and Agnes his wife,[6] my parents, and for my soul and the souls of Agnes Careles and all the faithful departed.

All my other lands and tenements, both free and bond, with the meadows, pastures, woods, rents and services, in the towns of Great Waldingfield ('Magna Waldyngfeld') and Preston, to my execs to sell, receive [*the money*] and dispose [*it*] in paying all my debts and faithfully fulfilling this my testament.

Residue of all my goods to execs to sell, receive and dispose for the health of my soul and all my benefactors and all the faithful departed in the celebration of masses and giving of alms and other deeds of charity, as they see best to please God and profit my soul.

Execs: Alice my wife, John Wryte, clerk,[7] Roger Cryketott and John Newman of Lavenham,[8] to each of whom, for their labour, 6s 8d.

Seal appended.

Proved at Lavenham, 1 July 1462. Admon to Alice, executrix. Power reserved to John Wryte, clerk, Roger Cryketoot and John Newman, the other execs, when they come and if they wish to take up admon. Seal of the official appended.

---

[1] The Dominican Friars (Friars Preachers) were established in Sudbury before 1247. The site of their house was enlarged several times over the years (*VCH Suffolk*, ii, pp.123–4). Some scanty remains of the friary can still be seen in Friars Street.

[2] For the friars of Clare and Babwell and the Friars Minor of Ipswich see notes to no. 1.

[3] Master John Street, Lavenham, is probably the road now called Lady Street. Master John Street is mentioned in the will of Thomas Spring I (SROB, Baldwyne 19; Pt I, no. 102). See Betterton and Dymond, *Lavenham: Industrial Town*, p.10.

4　The testator's father, John, also requested prayers for Andrew Kyng and Joan his wife (see note below).

5　John Grygge of Lavenham, will pr. October 1446 (SROB, Baldwyne 74; Pt I, no. 350).

6　Agnes had predeceased John; when he made his will he requested prayers for her soul and his then wife's name was Rose.

7　John Wryte, or Wryth, was a chaplain at Lavenham prior to becoming rector of Bradfield St Clare in 1445, where he remained until 1470; however he seems to have continued as chaplain at Lavenham during this time. On leaving Bradfield, he remained at Lavenham as chaplain until death; will pr. June 1477 (NRO, NCC 163 Gelour). See Pt I, nos 126, 130, 298, 350 and 1058.

8　Will of John Newman the elder of Lavenham, no. 87 below; he had been executor to John Grygge (SROB, Baldwyne 74; Pt I, no. 350).

[fol. 310v]

12. WILLIAM GOODEWYN of BURWELL [*Cambs*],[1] 18 November 1463

[*Commendation*: to God the Father Almighty &c]; to be buried in the churchyard of St Mary of the same [*town*]; to the high altar of the same, in satisfaction of all my tithes not well and faithfully paid, 20d; to the glazing (*vitriacionem*) of a window of the same church 6s 8d; to the rood-loft (*solar' crucis*) of the same church, when it is made, 5s.[2]

To Olive my wife all the utensils of my house; also to Olive my tenement for term of her life, on condition that Thomas my son have easement in the solar and in the barn when necessary.

To Margaret my niece a tenement in 'le Newnham strete'[3] when she comes to the time of marriage, to her and her heirs.

Residue of all my goods to the disposition of Olive my wife and Thomas my son, execs, to dispose for the health of my soul as they see best to please God and profit my soul.

Proved at Newmarket (*Nov'mercat'*), 9 March 1463/64. Admon to exec. Power reserved to Olive Goodewyn, co-executrix, when she comes.

1　?Related to William Goodwyn of Burwell, no. 550 below.

2　The panelled wall above the chancel arch of St Mary's, Burwell, is dated 1464: Goodewyn's bequest towards the new rood-loft was for planned work that was to be carried out shortly.

3　The road leading north from the High Town to the hamlet of Newnham (RCHM, *Cambs* II, pp.16–25).

13. JOHN DUCHEMAN of HAVERHILL ('Haverhyll'), 22 March 1463/64 [*probate only*]

Proved in the parish church of Haverhill.[1] Admon to Alice his wife, executrix. Seal of official appended.

1　Does not specify which parish church of Haverhill. See note to no. 14 below.

14. JOHN ADAM of HAVERHILL ('Haverhyll'), 11 November 1420

Dated 3 Ides November; [*commendation*: &c *only*]; to be buried in the churchyard of St Mary the upper (*superiore*);[1] to the high altar for my tithes forgotten 2s 6d; I give enough ?panels (*tot' tabulas*) for the reparation of the selure (*cellur'*) of the holy cross in the said church.

To each priest coming to my obsequies 4d; to our parish clerk 2d.

To the making of a cross before the gate of William Wasshpok 6s 8d.

To my wife a tenement lying between William Wasshpok on one side and John

Segryn on the other, one head of which abuts on the tenement of the said William and the other on the highway, with an acre of land in the field called 'le Dene'.

Residue of all my goods to William Wasshpok and Robert Revell, execs, to dispose for the health of my soul, as seems best to please God.

Seal appended.

Proved 2 July 1421. Admon to execs. Seal of official appended.

[1] Haverhill had two parish churches, the upper and the lower, both dedicated to St Mary; the upper, sometimes known as the Button church (from 'abovetown') and later misconstrued to 'St Botulph', was the mother church, while the lower began as a chapel in the market-place; the upper church was dissolved in 1551 (*CPR, 1550–1553*, pp.93–4).

15. MARGARET BOWNE, 18 June 1464 [*probate only*]

Proved in the chapel of Botesdale.[1] Admon to John Wareyn, exec. Seal of official appended.

[1] Although Botesdale became a civil parish in 1866, it never achieved ecclesiastical independence and has remained a chapelry of Redgrave. See Dymond, 'Chapels-of-Ease and the Case of Botesdale'. Anne Riches (Cautley, p.386) stated that the chapel of St Botolph was built *c*.1500, but it was mentioned by name in the will of Robert Fletcher, dated 1446 (SROB, Baldwyne 66; Pt I, no. 325) and alluded to by John Sclawe in April 1442 (SROB, Baldwyne 48; Pt I, no. 252).

[fol. 311]

16. WILLIAM WELLYS of BARDWELL ('Berdwelle'),[1] 12 June 1463

[*No burial directions*]; [*commendation*: to God &c]; to the high altar of Bardwell church for tithes forgotten 2s; to the fabric of the same church 6s 8d; to the fabric and emendation of Barningham ('Bernyngham') church 6s 8d.

To Julian my wife all my place in 'Brake . . .'[*damaged*], with all the lands, except 10 acres, for term of her life, and except 7½ acres of land; to Julian all my ostilments and utensils of my house.

To John my son 10 acres of arable land, formerly called 'Campsones', with the foldage.

Robert my son to have 7 acres of arable land, of which 3 acres lie in the furlong (*quarent'*) called 'Grenehowe', and 4 acres in 'Sondeweywent'.

After the death of Julian my wife all my place, with all the lands and commodities, to remain to John my son and his heirs for ever, he paying my execs 20 marks, that is, 10 marks now and 10 marks after the death of Julian my wife.

A suitable chaplain to be found out of my goods and chattels to celebrate for me and my friends at Rome.[2]

My execs to demand and obtain from Richard Sheve . . .[*damaged*] of Stoke Ash £3 5s, from Hugh Dryvere of Wattisfield 2 marks 2s 8d, from John Jude of Badwell 4s 4d, from Thomas Bonde of Walsham 6d, from John Perkyn 6s 8d and from John Bete of Sapiston 22d.

Residue of all my goods to my execs, to see to my funeral, pay my debts and do other good things as they see best to please God and profit my soul.

Execs: Juliana my wife, Robert Well my brother[3] and John Walter of Hepworth, to each of whom 3s 4d for their labour.

Supervisor: Sir Stephen Purdy.[4]

Proved at Fornham [*St*] Martin, 20 June 1463. Admon to execs.

1   Executor of Matilda Wellis, probate November 1452 (SROB, Baldwyne 100; Pt I, no. 451).
2   The first of many testators in Part II to request a commemoration in Rome. See Introduction under *Indulgences*.
3   Executor (as 'Wellis') of Matilda Wellis (see note above); perhaps Robert and William were the sons of Matilda.
4   According to no. 489 below Stephen Purdy was rector of Honington in 1472 (not mentioned in Tanner); will pr. 1485 (NRO, NCC 254 A. Caston).

[fol. 311v]

17. JOHN HEYNES, late of THORPE MORIEUX ('Thorpmor"), 21 June 1463 [*nuncupative*]

Struggling at the point of death (*in extremis laborans*); [*commendation*: to God &c; *no burial directions*]; to a suitable chaplain to celebrate for his soul and for the souls for whom he is bound, for half a year after his death, £3.

Residue of all his goods to Eleanor his wife, she to pay his debts and bury his body, and anything over to remain to Eleanor for her sustentation, and she to be executrix.

Witnesses: discreet men William Qweynt, Thomas Brundysche and other trustworthy [*persons*] present there.

Proved at Fornham St Martin, 26 June 1463. Admon to executrix.

18. JOHN GLAMVYLE of DRINKSTONE ('Drenkston'), 10 December 1462

To be buried in holy burial in the churchyard of All Saints of Drinkstone; to the high altar of the same church for my tithes forgotten 12d; to the tabernacle of St Peter 6s 8d which Simon Joly owes me.

To Cecily my daughter 2 pots of 'bras', 6s 8d and all my clothing.

To Alice my daughter 6s 8d and 2 'possenettes'.

Residue of all my goods to the disposition of my execs, to dispose for the health of my soul as seems to them best to please God and profit the health of my soul.

Execs: Sir John Ragge, chaplain, and Alexander Neve.[1]

Proved 7 October 1463. Admon to execs.

1   The same executors as for the will of John Seman the elder of Drinkstone (no. 19).

19. JOHN SEMAN the elder of DRINKSTONE ('Drenkston'), 12 January 1460/61

[*Commendation*: to God &c; *no burial directions*]; to the high altar of Drinkstone 12d; to the brethren of the gild of the Holy Trinity[1] 12d; to the tabernacle of St Mary 13s 4d; to the emendation or reparation of the bell (*campan'*) 6s 8d.

To be distributed among the poor 10s; to the reparation of the ways 20s; to each of my execs 40d.

To Thomas my son a bed, a gown and a doublet.

To [*name omitted*] my daughter a bed, a pot.

To Henry Caldenell a tunic and a doublet; to Agnes Kaldenell a tunic.

Residue of all my goods to my execs, to dispose, etc.[*sic*]

Execs: Sir John Rage, chaplain, and Alexander Neve.[2]

Proved at Drinkstone, 7 October 1463. Admon to execs.

1   For other bequests to the gild of the Holy Trinity of Drinkstone see the wills of John Paton (no. 95) and John Tyso (no. 205). John Paton's will reveals that the parish also had a gild of St John.
2   The same executors as for the will of John Glamvyle of Drinkstone (no. 18).

[fol. 312]

20. ROBERT THURGORE of ACTON ('Aketon'),[1] 25 November 1462

Dated the feast of St Katherine the Virgin, 1462; [*commendation*: to God &c; *no burial directions*]; to the high altar of Acton 20d; to the reparation of the same church 2s.

To each of my goddaughters 2 bushels of barley; 6d to be distributed among the needy poor in the town of Acton.

James my son[2] to have my tenement in Acton, called 'Chaundelere', to him for ever. Residue of all my goods, utensils, ostilments and chattels to my wife and William my son, execs, to see to my funeral and pay my debts and do other deeds of mercy for my soul, as seems to them best to profit the health of my soul.

Proved at Sudbury, 15 December 1462. Admon to William, exec. Power reserved to the wife of the deceased when she comes, if she wishes to take up admon.

> [1]   Executor of John Longe of Acton, smith, will pr. September 1445 (SROB, Baldwyne 88; Pt I, no. 404).
> [2]   Will (as 'Thurgor'), no. 651 below.

21. JOHN TYLKYS of GLEMSFORD, 8 May 1462 [*English*]

[*Commendation*: to Almighty God &c; *no burial directions*]; a trental of masses to be said for my soul in the church of Glemsford by a friar of the order of the house of Clare,[1] he having 10s.

Robert Jerveys, the son of Thomas Jerveys of Pentlowe [*Essex*], to have 40d; Margaret Jerveys, the daughter of the said Thomas, to have 40d.

Alice my wife to have, for term of her life, my house and land, both free and copy, in the town of Glemsford, if she keep herself a widow; if she be married again, the house and lands to be sold and Alice to have half of the money for which it is sold and 20s of my part.

A light to be found before the image of Our Lady in the chancel of Glemsford, as long as 20s lasts, if it may be spared; 20s to be given to poor men if it may be spared and the residue [*of the money for the house*] to be done in ways where there is most need; the parson to have at my *dirige* 4d and every priest of the same town 2d, and every clerk 1d; I will have burning 4 torches of the town, they having 12d to[*wards*] the same torches.

Alice my wife to have all my ostilments and my beasts and cattle ('catell').

Execs: Alice my wife and John Merk, he to have 6s 8d for his labour.

Seal appended.

Proved at Glemsford, 15 December 1462. Admon to execs.

> [1]   See note to no. 1.

[fol. 312v]

22. JOHN PAGE of STANSTEAD ('Stansted'),[1] 8 October 1462 [*English*]

[*Commendation*: to Almighty God &c; *no burial directions*]; to the high altar of Stanstead 40d.

Alice my wife to have all my ostilments within my place; she to have my tenement at 'Cherche' and 2 acres of free land for the term of her life if she keep herself a widow; after her death it to be sold and done for her and for me and for all my friends' souls; if she be in need and in poverty, she to sell it and live thereby.

John my son to have my horse and my cart and my beasts, my corns ('cornys') in the barn and my sheep; he to till all my land while Alice remains a widow and sow it the first year.

Alice my daughter to have 40s when she comes to marriage, the day that she is married, and 4 sheep and a red 'howyd' bullock.

A trentall of masses to be done by all four orders of friars on a day, if it may be done, 10s [*each*].

Friar Richard Morall to have 40d.[2]

Execs: John my son and Alice my wife, to dispose my goods to the worship of God and helping of my soul.

Seal appended; will written 'by my hand'.

Proved at Glemsford, 16 December 1462. Admon to John, exec. Power reserved to Alice, executrix, when she comes, if she wishes to take it up.

[1]   Executor of John Moore of Stanstead, will pr. June 1440 (SROB, Baldwyne 26; Pt I, no. 132).
[2]   In February 1459/60 John Hedgeman the elder of Glemsford requested Friar Richard Morall of the order of Friars Minor to celebrate for the souls of him and his wife (SROB, Baldwyne 249; Pt I, no. 1246) and in 1461 Roger Copcy of Brockley requested Friar Richard Morell to celebrate for his soul (SROB, Baldwyne 283; Pt I, no. 1390).

[fol. 313]

23. WILLIAM ROWHEY of LITTLE THURLOW ('Thyrlowe Parva'), 10 March 1461/62 [*nuncupative*]

[*Commendation*: to God Almighty &c; *no burial directions*]; to the parish church of Little Thurlow 40s; to the parish church of Great Thurlow ('Magna Thyrlowe') 40s; to the church of Brinkley [*Cambs*] 13s 4d; to the church of Great Bradley ('Bradley Magna') 6s 8d; to the parish church of Little Bradley ('Bradley Parva') 6s 8d.

He wished all his lands and tenements in Little Thurlow formerly John Lord's, chaplain, to be sold and disposed by his execs for the fulfilling of his will.

Residue of all his goods to his execs to dispose for his soul and the souls of Roger Lorde and John Lorde, chaplain.

Execs: John Rowhey and Nicholas Bedford.

Witnesses: Ed' Lakyngheth, chaplain, Roger Herri, chaplain, William Folkys and others.

Proved at Haverhill, 21 May 1462. Admon to execs.

24. JOHN DERLYNG of SNAILWELL ('Snaylwell') [*Cambs*], 12 May 1462

[*Commendation*: to God Almighty &c; *no burial directions.*]

To my son Thomas the crop (*fruct'*) growing on 5 acres less 1 rood; to Thomas 5 roods of land, sown with barley, together with the toft called 'Foresleves', he, and whoever succeeds him in the 5 roods and toft in the future (*sempitern'*), finding at each feast of the Blessed Mary, before her image in the said church, for ever, 5 candles of wax to burn at divine service, in the way that I have been doing; to Thomas 2 horses with the plough and its equipment. Also to him all that part of the messuage which I hold by copy, with the third part in free tenure, 2 cupboards with the largest chest and the second gown; also the brass pot with the brass cauldron, on condition that he keeps my anniversary and my wives' as long as he lives.

To Nicholas Hoode the crop of 3 roods sown with rye, the best gown and 2 cupboards.
A priest to celebrate for a year for the health of my soul, my father's and mother's
[*souls*] and the rest of my friends, in the university or in my parish, according to the
discretion of the rector.[1]

Residue of all my goods to my execs, Thomas my son and Nicholas Hoode, faithfully to perform my will and pray for me most devoutly.

Proved at Icklingham, 22 May 1462. Admon to execs.

---

[1]   The rectory of Snailwell belonged to the bishops of Ely and was a valuable living. During the
medieval period the rectory was frequently held in plurality by absentees, although John Warde,
rector 1491–1526, was resident in the parish. At the time of this will, there was no direct connection between the parish and the university (*VCH Cambs*, x, pp.85–8).

[fol. 313v]
25. THOMAS WHYTE of HAUGHLEY ('Haughle'), 26 March 1462

To be buried in the churchyard of Haughley church; to the high altar of the same
church for my tithes underpaid 6d.

To Joan my wife my whole tenement on Haughley Green ('Haughle Grene') for
term of her life, and after her decease it to be sold by my execs or theirs and the
money from it to be disposed for our souls; also to Joan all my utensils.

Residue of all my goods and chattels I leave to Joan my wife and Henry Cok, execs,
they, having God before their eyes, to dispose [*them*] in the best way to please God
and profit my soul.

Seal appended.

Proved at Stowe, ?23 (*xxijiiij*) June 1462. Admon to execs.

26. JOHN PELTYR of CLARE, [*1462*]

[*No date*; *commendation*: to God &c]; my body to Christian burial; to the high altar
of Clare parish church 12d.

My tenement in which I live in the market-place (*mercat'*) of Clare to be sold by
my exec, and the money arising to be disposed for my soul, according to the discretion of my execs; my garden lying in 'le Bay' to be disposed for my soul, similarly.

Residue of my goods to John Hyncheman, to dispose for my soul, as he knows best
to please God and profit my soul.

Exec: John Hyncheman.

Proved at Clare, 3 July 1462. Admon to exec.

[fol. 314]
27. JOHN RUS of WOOLPIT ('Wolpet'), 18 November 1453 and 10 November 1454

Dated the Saturday after the feast of St Martin, bishop and confessor, 1453, at
Woolpit; to be buried in the churchyard of the church of the Blessed Mary of
Woolpit; to the high altar of the same church for my tithes forgotten and not well
paid, 6d.

To James Pusk 2d; to the same James my white kirtle (*kirtellu'*).

To John Marlere my godson my cow.

Residue of all my goods to Agnes my wife.

Execs: Geoffrey Wysman of Woolpit and Richard Fen.

Seal appended.

[*Will; dated 10 November 1454*]

Dated the Saturday before the feast of St Martin, bishop and confessor, 33 Henry VI. Agnes my wife to have my messuage for term of her life; and after her decease, Joan my daughter to have it for term of her life for 40s, to be paid for my funeral expenses [*incurred*] on the day of my burial; if there is any residue from the 40s it to be disposed by Joan among the poor townsfolk of Woolpit in deeds of charity, as seems to her best and most healthy [*for my soul*] and best to please God. After the decease of Joan my daughter my tenement to remain to John Marlere and his heirs, for ever.

Seal appended.

Proved at Fornham [*St Martin*], 5 October 1461. Admon to execs.

28. RICHARD COWDON of DALHAM, 26 September 1461

Dated the Sabbath day after the feast of the dedication of the church of Norwich,[1] 1461; at the point of death; to be buried in the churchyard of Dalham church; to the high altar of the said church for tithes forgotten and withheld 12d; to the making of the tower 20d.

To Richard the son of John Clerk a sheep; to Nicholas the son of the same a sheep; to Isabel the daughter of the same a sheep.

To the high altar of Saxham church 12d.

Residue of all [*my*] goods, after my obsequies have been done and all my debts paid, to Isabel my wife and John Clerk, execs, to dispose for the health of my soul and my benefactors, as seems to them most expedient.

Seal appended.

Proved before the commissary [*no date given*]. Admon to execs.

1   That is, the feast on 24 September commemorating the dedication of the cathedral-priory of the Holy Trinity at Norwich, the mother church of Norfolk and Suffolk.

29. WILLIAM CURTEYS of TOSTOCK ('Tostoke'), 16 April 1461

[*Will only*]

My debts to be paid before all else.

To Margaret my wife all my lands and tenements for term of her life and after her decease, they to remain to Robert my son and his heirs; if Robert dies without heirs the said lands and tenements to be sold and the money from them to be disposed in pious uses for the health of the souls of my parents and all my benefactors.

All my feoffees in my said lands and tenements to transfer possession of them to Margaret my wife and others by the advice of my supervisor, when so required for the fulfilling of my will.

Executrix: Margaret my wife.

Supervisor: Master William [*recte* Robert] Wolman, rector of Tostock church.[1]

Proved 5 October [*year omitted*]. Admon to executrix.

1   Will pr. May 1464 (NRO, NCC 318 Brosyard); Master Nicholas Irby, rector of Norton from 1435 to 1467, was Wolman's executor; see also no. 435 below.

[fol. 314v]
30. SIMON CALLE of LITTLE WALDINGFIELD ('Waldyngfeld Parva'),[1] 15 July 1461 [*nuncupative*]

Dated at Preston in the diocese of Norwich, Simon then being there;[2] [*commendation*: to God Almighty &c; *no burial directions*].
To John Calle his son, and his heirs, all his lands and tenements, rents and services, meadows, pastures and feedings, with the ways, paths, fences, ditches and [*rights of*] common (*co 'is*), etc, in the towns of Great Waldingfield, Little Waldingfield and Milden ('Meldyng') in Suffolk, apart from all his entailed lands and tenements, etc, in those towns.
Residue of his goods to his exec, to pay [*his*] debts and dispose in deeds of charity for the health of his soul and his benefactors as he sees best to please God.
Exec: John Calle his son, to whom for his labour about the execution of the said will he gave the above legacy.
Witnesses: John Smyth of Bury St Edmunds, 'gentylman', Richard Alisandyr, Thomas Hagown, Thomas Brown and Thomas Hegge.
Proved at Fornham St Martin, 31 July 1462. Admon to exec.

[1]   Executor of John Sheldrake of Little Waldingfield, will pr. October 1458 (SROB, Baldwyne 238; Pt I, no. 1193).
[2]   Only about five miles from home, but presuambly not able to make the journey.

[fol. 315]
31. WILLIAM SYNTON of SUDBURY,[1] 31 May 1463

Dated at Sudbury; sick in body; to be buried in the churchyard of the church of St Gregory of Sudbury; to the high altar of the chapel of St Peter of Sudbury 20d.
To Isabel my wife 10 marks in money, to be paid as quickly as possible after my decease; to the same Isabel all the utensils of my house, nothing being excepted, other than jewels and the apparel for my body. All my grain at the time of the making of this will, that is, wheat and malt, bought by me from divers persons, to remain, after my decease, to Isabel my wife, provided that payment for the grain has been fully made by my execs to those who should be paid, before all else.
To Alice the wife of Thomas Gooch 5 marks.
To Friar Stephen my son 10 marks to celebrate, for a whole year after my decease, especially for my soul and the soul of Agnes my wife and for the souls of all the faithful departed.
The said Isabel to have my capital messuage after my decease, in which to live for two years running (*continuos*) and no more; after those two years my capital messuage to revert to my execs to sell for £40, to pay my debts, and if Isabel wishes to buy it, she to have it at a better price than any other person by 40s.
Any other lands and tenements of mine in Sudbury to be sold by my execs to implement this testament.
Residue of all [*my goods*], together with my debts, to my execs, they to see to my funeral, pay my debts and do other (*cetera*) deeds of mercy for my soul, as they see best to please God and profit my soul.
Execs: John Hoo of 'Foxherdhalle'[2] and Thomas Gooch of Sudbury, they to dispose for my soul as above-written and as they will answer before God on the Day of Judgement.

All my feoffees to deliver full seisin of all my lands and tenements when so required by my execs.

Seal appended.

To Joan Lokyere my servant 13s 4d; to Roger Same my apprentice 40d.

Proved at Sudbury, 27 September 1463. Admon to execs.

1   Executor of Thomas Goday of Sudbury, 'karpenter', will pr. May 1448 (*recte* 1449) (SROB, Baldwyne 63; Pt I, no. 310); witness to the will of Thomas Lavenham of Sudbury, cutler, pr. December 1459 (SROB, Baldwyne 258; Pt I, no. 1274).
2   Foxearth Hall, Essex.

[fol. 315v]
32. AMFRITHA WARYN of SUDBURY,[1] 28 July 1463

Dated at Sudbury in the diocese of Norwich; [*commendation*: to God Almighty, the Blessed Mary Glorious Virgin, St Katherine and all the saints]; to be buried in the churchyard of the church of St Gregory of Sudbury; to the high altar of the chapel of St Peter of the same town 3s 4d; to the college of Sudbury 20s.[2]

To Joan my daughter my best bed, that is, a white coverlet ('coverlyght') with the 'tester' of the same suit, 2 'blanketts', 2 pairs of sheets, a mattress, a celure with the 'tester' and 3 curtains ('cortins') of blue 'card';[3] to the same Joan the best basin of latten with the best ewer and my best furred gown and my best 'kirtill' and my best cloak, my best silvered belt, 6 silver spoons, the best brass pot and the best brass pan, with a chafer and 20 pieces of pewter, that is, 2 chargers, 6 platters, 6 dishes and 6 saucers ('sawceres'), an iron spit with an iron andiron ('awnderne') and 2 latten candlesticks; to the same Joan my 'forcer' with my kerchiefs and 40s in money.

To Sir John Wryght my son my small mazer and my silver piece.[4]

To Thomas Gooch my son a blue coverlet with the tester of the same suit, 2 blankets, a pair of sheets, the second basin with the ewer, 6 silver spoons, the second brass pot with a brass pan, a charger of pewter, 4 platters, 4 dishes and 4 saucers and a latten candlestick.

To Agnes, the daughter of the said Thomas Gooch, a small basin of latten and my other silvered belt and 3s 4d in money; to each of the sons of the same Thomas 12d.

To John Gooch my son a basin with the ewer, a brass pot with a pan, a charger, 4 platters, 4 dishes, 4 saucers of pewter, a sanguine-coloured coverlet and a pair of sheets; to Joan the wife of the same John a blue gown lined with blue 'bokeram' and my sanguine kirtle and my second cloak; to each of the sons and daughters of the said John Gooch 12d.

To Robert Gooch my son a latten basin, a candlestick, a brass pot, 4 platters, 4 dishes and 4 saucers of pewter; to John the son of the same Robert 12d.

To Margaret Bover my servant 3s 4d and a brass pot holding a gallon, a small chest with the lock and key, a latten candlestick, and a coverlet, price 4s, to be bought for the same Margaret.

To the fraternity of the gild of St Mary of Melford 6s 8d.[5]

To Friar John Burton of Sudbury 12d.[6]

To Joan Aldhous the elder my sanguine gown; to Alice Lalford, the daughter of the same Joan, a tunic of 'musterdelere'.

My execs to provide (*exhibeant*) a secular chaplain to celebrate divine service for my soul and the souls of my deceased husbands and of all my benefactors for whom I am bound, in the church of St Peter of Sudbury.

Residue of all my goods, together with my debts, I leave to my execs, they to see to my funeral and pay my debts, and do other works of mercy for my soul, as they see best to please God and most to profit to the health of my soul.

Execs: Sir John Wryght and Thomas Gooch, my sons.

Seal appended.

Proved at Lavenham, 20 December 1463. Admon to execs.

1   Her name is given as 'Amflote' in the will of her husband, John Waryn of Long Melford, pr. September 1451 (SROB, Baldwyne 106; Pt I, no. 474).

2   In 1375 Archbishop Simon Sudbury and his brother, John, founded the college of St Gregory, Sudbury, on a plot of land that had been the site of their father's house, next to the old church of St Gregory. In the previous year the brothers had obtained the advowson of that church. The college comprised a warden, five secular canons and three chaplains; they kept the canonical hours and celebrated in the adjoining church of St Gregory (*VCH Suffolk*, ii, pp.150–2). See no. 782 for another bequest to the college.

3   See Glossary.

4   Witness of the will of Thomas Lavenham of Sudbury (SROB, Baldwyne 258; Pt I, no. 1273); see also nos 434 and 596 below.

5   Her husband, John, also made a bequest to the gild of St Mary in Melford (SROB, Baldwyne 106; Pt I, no. 474). Husband and wife had evidently been members of that gild and Amfritha maintained her interest even though she was now living in Sudbury. Their son, Richard Wareyn, was a member of the gild of Jesus in Long Melford (SROB, Baldwyne 271; Pt I, no. 1329). Henry Turnour *alias* Dyer bequeathed 6s 8d to the gild of St Mary (SROB, Baldwyne 279; Pt I, no. 1369).

6   Her husband had bequeathed Friar John Burton of Sudbury 13s 4d. Both John Hoket the elder of Long Melford (SROB, Baldwyne 22; Pt 1, no. 122) and Matilda Hyne of Sudbury (SROB, Baldwyne 93; Pt I, no. 421) had left bequests to the friar to celebrate a trental of St Gregory for their souls.

[fol. 316]

33. RICHARD KRENCHE of POLSTEAD ('Polsted'), 29 June 1463

Seeing the day of death approaching; [*commendation*: to God &c; *no burial directions*].

To my wife Margaret my capital messuage in which I live, and all the lands and tenements in the town of Polstead, for term of her life; after her death they to go to Adam my son and his heirs for ever.

Margaret my wife to pay my daughter Joan 13s 4d when she is 15 and 13s 4d at the age of 20; if Margaret should die before Joan reaches 15, the said Adam my son to pay the whole 26s 8d to the said Joan at the times stated for Margaret; if Adam dies before Joan reaches 15, or before she is 20, the tenements and lands to be sold by my execs and they to pay the said Joan the 26s 8d at the stated times, if she be then alive.

Margaret my wife to have all my goods and pay all my debts.

Execs: Margaret my wife and Robert Huite; Robert having 2s for his labours.

Proved at Bildeston ('Bylston'), 5 July 1463. Admon to execs.

34. AGNES ODELYN of WORTHAM ('Wurtham'), widow, 3 March 1462/63

Dated 3 March 1463; [*commendation*: to God &c; *no burial directions*].

I wish Friar John Dysse to have a service, to celebrate divine obsequies for a whole year for my soul and all my benefactors' [*souls*].

Residue of all [*my*] goods to disposition of John Brown of ?Deopham [*Norfolk*] ('Depham') and John Colman of Wortham, whom I make execs, to dispose for my soul and all my benefactors' [*souls*] as they see best to please God &c[*sic*].

Proved at Eye, 27 September 1463. Admon to John Brown, exec. Power reserved to John Colman when he comes, if he wish to take up admon.

[fol. 316v]
35. GERARD FODRYNGAY [of BROCKLEY], 13 May 1463

Sick of body; [*commendation*: to God Almighty &c; *no burial directions*]; to the high altar of the church of Brockley ('Brokleye') 13s 4d; to the rector for tithe of woods (*dec' silvarum*) 6s 8d; for a priest to celebrate for my soul and for the souls of all the faithful departed in Brockley church, for the whole year, 8 marks.

Sybil my wife to have of my manor what the law specifies.[1]

To Gerard my son 20s; to John my son the elder 20s; to John my son the younger 20s, if he be alive, and if not, to my execs to dispose for my soul; to my daughter Cecily 13s 4d; to Isabel my daughter 40s.

All my grain on the ground to be used to fulfil my legacies.

Execs: Sybil my wife, Sir Thomas Goslyn of Hartest ('Herthest'),[2] Gerard my son, John Taylore, rector of Brockley, and Richard Faryngton, rector of Rede;[3] the priests to have 3s 4d each for their labour.

To the Friars Minor of Babwell 6s 8d.[4]

Residue of my goods to my execs, to dispose for the health of my soul.

Proved at Fornham [*St*] Martin, 18 July 1463. Admon to execs.

1   That is, whatever a widow was permitted to inherit.
2   Will pr. October 1467 (NRO, NCC 79 Jekkys); he wanted to be buried in the churchyard chapel of St Mary in Hartest, for which he bequeathed a white vestment; his brother was Master William Goselyn, the archdeacon of Suffolk's official. See Pt I, nos 158, 365 and 687.
3   Richard Faryngton was rector of Rede from 1462 to 1467 (Tanner, p.1419).
4   See note to no. 1.

36. SIMON PERKEN of HOPTON,[1] 20 June 1463

[*Commendation*: to God &c; *no burial directions*]; to the high altar of the same church for my tithes forgotten 12d; to the fabric of Hopton church 6s 8d; to Robert See, to celebrate for a year for my soul and the souls of my benefactors in Hopton church [*amount omitted*].

To John Hamelyn 6s 8d.

Margaret my wife to have all my goods for term of her life, and after her death all of them to be sold and disposed as seems best to please God and to profit the health of my soul.

Execs: Margaret Perkyn my wife and John Hamelyn.

Supervisor: Sir John Brown, rector of Hopton.[2]

Seal appended.

Proved at Ixworth, 22 September 1463. Admon to execs.

[*Whole will and probate struck through; marginal note refers to amended and expanded form later in register; see no. 555.*]

1   As Simon 'Perkyn', possibly son of John Perkyn the elder of Barningham, will pr. September 1457 (SROB, Baldwyne 195; Pt I, no. 954).

2   In 1460 John Brown succeeded John Worlych as rector of Hopton (Tanner, p.1201); see also nos 393 and 555 below.

37. JOHN ROODESE of IXWORTH, glover, 24 June 1463

Dated on the feast of the nativity of St John the Baptist, 1463; [*commendation*: to God Almighty &c; *no burial directions*]; to the high altar of the said church, for tithes forgotten, 12d.

Katherine my wife to have my messuage called 'Grongeres' for term of her life; after her decease the messuage, together with the messuage formerly John Fraas's and the close lately Robert Peddere's,[1] to be sold by my execs, and of the money from them, 20s to go to the use of the parish church of Ixworth, 10s to the friars of Babwell[2] and 4s 4d to the parish chaplain of Ixworth for a sangred.

Residue of all my goods to Robert Berchere and William Byrd, execs, to dispose as they see best to please God.

Proved at Ixworth, 22 September 1463. Admon to [*no names given*].

1   Will (as 'Robert Hamond *alias* Pedder') pr. January 1458/59 (SROB, Baldwyne 207; Pt I, no. 1033).
2   See note to no. 1.

[fol. 317]

38. ALICE HYLL of STOKE BY NAYLAND ('Stokeneylond'), 12 August 1461

Dated at Stoke by Nayland; my body to Christian burial.

[*English from here*]

To the altar where my body shall be buried 40d; to the vicar ('vykery') of Stoke by Nayland my featherbed; to the church of Stoke by Nayland 40s; to a priest to sing for my soul, my lady Margaret's ('Marget's') soul[1] and my benefactors' [*souls*], by a whole year, 9 marks.

To the convent of Babwell, to Colchester, Sudbury and Clare, to each house, 10s for a trental.[2]

To 4 persons having most need in the town of Stoke by Nayland 6s 8d, parted by even portions.

To my master, Sir John Howard, knight,[3] a ring with a diamond ('dyamant'); to my lady, his wife,[4] a goblet of silver and 2 annulets of gold; to my goddaughter, my master's daughter,[5] 5 marks and my best girdle; to my mistress Margaret, his daughter,[6] the next best girdle; to my mistress Jane[7] the third girdle.

To Agnes Banyard my best gown and 'mustyrdelyre' gown furred with grey,[8] my furred cloak, my best kirtle, 2 pairs of sheets, a pillow and a cushion.

To Reynold my brother a boardcloth, 2 towels and a sheet of ...all [*damaged*] fine cloth; to his wife my gown furred with 'croppys'.

To Sir Thomas Hyll, my brother, a pair of sheets, a pillow and a cross of gold, all being in his own hands.[9]

To Thomas Hyll, my nephew, a pair of sheets and 6s 8d in money.

To Master Osbern 20s.

To Katherine Sampson 40s, my black gown, lined, and my furred kirtle.

To Sir John Brown, Sir Thomas Kyrkeby, Friar Moryell, John Brame, Thomas

Matsale, John Capell, John Notebeam, Thomas Wollet and John Mersche of the 'botery', each of them, 6s 8d.

To Wullette's wife a gown furred with black.

To Joan Fullere a gown, the collar furred with black; to Anne Fullere a gown lined with green at the collar and a kirtle; to Rose a kirtle of 'fusteyn'.

[*Here reverts to Latin*]

Residue of all my goods and chattels to Dame Katherine Howard, the wife of John Howard, knight,[10] and Agnes Banyard of Stoke by Nayland, execs, to sell, receive and dispose for my soul and the souls of my parents and benefactors, and all the faithful departed, in the celebration of masses and other deeds of charity, as they see best to please God and profit the souls aforesaid.

Proved at Fornham St Martin, 24 January 1462/63. Admon to Agnes Banyard, executrix. Power reserved to Dame Katherine Howard, the other executrix, when she comes and if she wishes to take up admon.

1   Lady Margaret Howard, née Mowbray, the mother of Sir John Howard; Margaret Howard had died in 1459. This and subsequent notes on John Howard and his family from Anne Crawford, 'Howard, John, first duke of Norfolk (d.1485)', *ODNB*, online edition, January 2008.

2   Houses of friars. A house of Franciscans (Grey Friars or Friars Minor) had been established at Colchester before 1279, not far from the town wall (*VCH Essex*, ii, pp.180–1). For the other friars see notes to nos 1 (Babwell and Clare) and 11 (Sudbury).

3   The future duke of Norfolk. In 1437, on the death of his grandfather, Sir John Howard, this Sir John inherited a small estate at Stoke by Nayland that had been the inheritance of his grandmother, Alice Tendring. This was to be his home until he was created duke in 1483. By 1468 Howard had built up an estate around Stoke by Nayland that consisted of some 16 manors. From his own memoranda and other surviving accounts it is clear that he took a considerable interest in the day-to-day management of his estates and was a careful and efficient administrator. His household books have been published in Crawford (ed.), *The Household Books of John Howard*.

4   Sir John's first wife, Lady Catherine Howard, daughter of William, styled Lord Moleyns, and Margaret Whalesborough. Catherine died on 3 November 1465, leaving six children: Thomas, earl of Surrey, Nicholas (died *c*.1468), Isabel, Anne, Margaret and Jane.

5   Either Isabel, who married Sir Robert Mortimer, or Anne, who married Sir Edmund Gorges.

6   Margaret Howard married Sir John Wyndham.

7   Jane Howard married John Tymperley.

8   See Glossary.

9   Perhaps the Master Thomas Hyll to whom 'in gratitude for his devotion to me', Robert Ferour, vicar of St Mary, Stowmarket, bequeathed 13s 4d in his will, pr. June 1478 (NRO, NCC 195 Gelour). Master Thomas Hyll witnessed the will of William Schelton of Stowmarket (no. 109 below).

10 From her various bequests to the Howard family and the appointment of Lady Catherine as one of her executrixes, it is clear that Alice Hyll had close connections with the family. The items of clothing that she bequeathed to various friends were quite sumptuous garments.

[fol. 317v]

39. ALAN LEGAT of HAWSTEAD ('Hawsted'),[1] 16 January 1462/63

Dated at Hawstead; [*commendation*: to God Almighty &c; *no burial directions*]; to the high altar in the parish church of Hawstead for my tithes and offerings forgotten or underpaid 12d.

To Rose my wife and John Legat the elder, my son, for term of Rose's life, all my goods and chattels, and after her decease they to be equally divided between the aforesaid John Legat the elder and John Legat the younger, chaplain.[2] To Rose all my lands and tenements in the towns and fields of Hawstead and Whepstead

('Qwhepsted'), for term of her life, and after her decease they to remain to John Legat the elder and his heirs for ever; if the said John die without heirs, all the lands and tenements to remain to John Legat the younger, chaplain, for his lifetime, and after his decease to be sold by his execs and the money received to be disposed for the health of my soul and the souls of Rose, John and John, and the souls of all my deceased friends, in the celebration of masses and almsgiving.

To John Legat the younger, chaplain, 7s per annum in money, for term of his life, to be paid out of the said lands and tenements, to pray for my soul.

To William Malveys 40s, when he is 20 years old.

To the friars of Babwell, for a trental to be celebrated there for my soul, 10s.[3]

Residue of all my goods to my execs, to sell and dispose for my soul and the souls for whom I am bound, in the celebration of masses and almsgiving, as they see best to please God and profit my soul.

Execs: Rose my wife, John Legat the younger, chaplain, and John Legat the elder. Proved at Fornham St Martin, 31 January 1462/63. Admon to execs.

[1] Executor of John Rewe of Whepstead, will pr. November 1446 (SROB, Baldwyne 74; Pt I, no. 351); executor of John Tuffeld the elder of Whepstead, no. 179 below (pr. 3 January 1462/63).
[2] ?The man of that name who was rector of Tuddenham from 1448 to 1492 (Tanner, p.1288).
[3] See note to no. 1.

40. JOHN SKEPPERE the elder of WOOLPIT ('Wolpyt'), 28 December 1462

[*Commendation*: to God &c; *no burial directions*]; to the high altar of the parish church of Woolpit 12d; to the emendation of the same church on the north side 13s 4d; to Shelland ('Schellond') church 12d; to Tostock church 12d.

To Edmund my son my violet gown and a small brass pot; to Rose my daughter a pan of 2 gallons and a small posnet; to Alice my daughter 6s 8d.

To John Skeppere, Joan Skeppere, Katherine Skeppere, John Hyll, Agnes Hyll, Richard Lenys, William ?Cirrirray and John Nedom, my godchildren, 4d each.

Residue of all my goods to William Skeppere my son and John Lenys, execs, to dispose for my soul as they see best to please God and profit the health of my soul. Proved 4 January 1462/63. Admon to execs.

[fol. 318]
[*The wills on folios 318 and 319 were proved in 1463; those on folios 321 and 322 were proved in July 1462.*]

41. THOMAS METSCHERPE of MENDLESHAM ('Mendlysham'),[1] 13 September 1463

Dated Tuesday after the feast of the Nativity of the Blessed Mary 1463; [*commendation*: to God &c; *no burial directions*]; to the high altar of Mendlesham church 3s 4d.

Margaret my daughter to have 26s 8d; Isabel my daughter to have 26s 8d; if Margaret dies the money wholly to remain to my execs to dispose for my soul; if Isabel dies the money to remain to my execs to dispose for my soul.

Olive my wife to have all my tenement in Mendlesham and all my other goods, except those excepted, to keep as long as she is a widow, and with them to pay all my debts; if Olive dies the tenement to remain to my exec, John [*Taylore*], to sell and find a priest to celebrate in the said church, immediately, for a whole year; if

Olive should marry again she to have 12 marks and [*then*] the tenement to remain to my exec, John Taylore, to sell and to find a priest to celebrate in the said church, as above, for my soul and the souls of my father and mother; if Olive makes any disruption or claims dower ('morngefte') the 12 marks to remain to my exec to find a priest to celebrate in the said church for the aforesaid souls. Olive to have the third part of all the bedding (*lectire*) and all the utensils and the household stuff (*domicil'*).

To Margaret and Isabel, my daughters, all the other part of the bedding, and all the utensils and household stuff in equal portions [*after the death of Olive*].

Residue of all my goods to the administration of my execs, they to levy, receive and dispose [*them*] for my soul and the souls of my father and mother, and for the souls of my benefactors.

Execs: Olive my wife and John Taylore; to John 3s 4d.

Proved at Mendlesham, 21 October 1463. Admon to execs.

1   ?Related to Roger Metessharpp of Mendlesham, will pr. October 1457 (SROB, Baldwyne 191; Pt I, no. 932).

[fol. 318v]

42. PETER BAXSTERE of HUNDON ('Honden'), 12 August 1462

[*Commendation*: to God &c; *no burial directions*.]

To the friars of Clare 3s 4d,[1] to pray for my soul and the souls of my parents; to the Carmelite Friars of Cambridge 20d;[2] to each priest present at my obsequies 4d and to each clerk of man's age 2d and to other clerks 1d.

To John Rydere my silver knives and my pair of jet beads.

To Margaret Norfolke 6s 8d.

My wife to have all my lands and tenements as long as she lives, and after her decease all to remain to Katherine my daughter and her heirs; if Katherine dies while her mother is still alive, all the said lands and tenements to be sold and the money from them to be spent in pious uses for my soul and for those by whom I have benefited in any way (*a quibus aliquod bonum habui*).

To each of my godsons 12d.

To Joan my wife all my goods and chattels, wherever they are, and with them to fulfil all my legacies in this testament.

To each of the poor at my obsequies and mass on the day of my burial 1d.

Execs: Joan my wife and John Rydere.

Proved at Clare, 26 October 1463. Admon to execs.

1   See note to no. 1.
2   A group of Carmelite Friars (White Friars) first arrived at Chesterton in 1249 and in 1256 moved to land in Newnham. Initially a contemplative order, they soon began preaching and hearing confession, so they moved to a more convenient location within Cambridge. They constructed a new church, in the parish of St John in Milne Street. The land acquired by the Carmelites in Milne Street ran from the highway to the river, and was extended over time until it eventually reached from the original court of Queens' College, which was built almost adjoining the convent wall, to the neighbourhood of King's College Chapel (*VCH Cambs*, ii, pp.282–6).

43. PETER QWYNTYN of HITCHAM ('Hetcham'), 4 May 1462

[*Commendation*: to God &c; *no burial directions*]; to the high altar of Hitcham 16d.

To the friars of Sudbury, to celebrate a trental for my soul and the souls of all my friends, 10s;[1] my mass-pence from the gild of All Saints of Hitcham to go to the said friars;[2] to the reparation of Hitcham church 20d; to the emendation of the way by my gate 3s; to the stipend of a chaplain to celebrate in Hitcham church for half a year £3.

To Katherine my wife all the utensils of my house, with 4 cows and the grain growing on my tenement.

My debts to be paid first and then my legacies executed if my goods will go that far. Residue of all my goods to the disposition of my execs, they to do for my soul deeds of charity as they see [best] to please God and profit my soul.

Execs: Katherine my wife, Thomas Wulward and Henry Bowle; to Thomas and Henry for their labour 20d each.

Proved at Bildeston ('Bylston'), 15 November 1463. Admon to execs.

[1]   See note to no. 11.
[2]   John Welham of Hitcham referred to the gildhall there as the community hall (*aule communit'*) implying that the hall was used for a range of public and private purposes, rather than by one group or gild (SROB, Baldwyne 160; Pt I, no. 772). Roger Charite used the same expression when he bequeathed 6s 8d to the reparation of the community hall of Hitcham (no. 75 below). The gildhall at Hitcham was by the churchyard (*PSIA*, xix, p.189). Margaret Wetherard referred to the common hall (*co'e aule*) called the 'Gyldehalle' at Stowmarket (no. 669).

[fol. 319]
44. [WILLIAM GRENE of CREETING ST PETER, 8 November 1462]

[*The ending and probate sentence of a will (at the head of fol. 319), all struck through. It proves to belong to no. 89 (below) which was written on the other leaf of the same bifolium. In assembling the Baldwyne register the bifolium was reversed and other material sewn into the fold, so separating the last few lines from the remainder of the will. These were then rewritten at the foot of the main will (now fol. 336v) and the original ending was struck through (now fol. 319).*]

45. THOMAS BROKHOOLE of LONG MELFORD ('Melford'),[1] 9 June 1463

['Brokhole' *in margin*] [*Commendation*: to God &c; *no burial directions*]; to the tower of Melford church 40d; to the Mass of Jesu (*Misse Jhu*) celebrated in Melford church 40d.[2]

To the friars of Walsingham [*Norfolk*] to celebrate a trental there 10s.[3]

To Agnes my wife 13s 4d.

To John Smyth and Robert Talbon, my execs, 6s 8d each.

Residue of all my goods to Agnes my wife.

Execs: John Smyth and Robert Talboon[*sic*].

Proved at Melford, 1 December 1463. Admon to execs.

[1]   ?Related to John Brokhole of Long Melford (no. 363). Both men had an executor named John Smyth. In his will John Hoket the elder of Long Melford surrendered lands and tenements into the hands of Thomas Brokhole; Hoket's will pr. October 1441 (SROB, Baldwyne 22; Pt I, no. 122).
[2]   The Jesus Mass, or Mass of Jesu, was one of the new forms of devotion that became popular in the fifteenth century. See Pfaff, *New Liturgical Feasts in Later Medieval England*, esp. pp.62ff. See also nos 52, 206, 363 and 722. Gilds of Jesus were also founded, at, for example, Melford (no. 436) and Wetherden (no. 451).
[3]   In 1347, licence was granted by Edward III to Elizabeth de Burgh, countess of Clare, to found a house of Friars Minor (Franciscans) in Walsingham (*VCH Norfolk*, ii, p.435).

46. RICHARD BARBORE of CLARE,[1] 5 August 1463

Of Clare in the diocese of Norwich; [*commendation*: to God &c]; to be buried in the churchyard of the parish church of Clare, against the stone cross, next to the graves of my parents. My execs to pay all my debts that I owe. To the high altar of Clare church for my tithes and offerings detained 6s 8d; to the vicar of Clare church, being present at my obsequies and at the mass on the day of my burial, 6d; to each other [*priest*] there at the same time, saying divine service and ministering, 4d; to the two parish clerks of the same church, at the same time, 2d each; to each other clerk there at the same time 1d; to each of the needy poor at my mass on the day of my burial, praying for my soul, 1d.

12 lb of wax, with all the other stuff (*stuffur'*) necessary for making 3 small torches to be held about my body on the day of my burial, at my seven-day and my thirty-day, and [*afterwards*] those 3 torches to go to the 3 altars in that church, to burn at the time of the elevation of the host (*corporis Christi*) as long as they last.

To John Colyn of Colchester (*Colcestria*) [*Essex*], [fol. 319v] lately my servant, to pray for my soul, my best violet gown, hooded with my best hood.

To Alice, now the wife of John Stalon, lately my servant, to pray for my soul, 20s in money and other necessaries.

Residue of all my goods to the disposition of my execs, they to pay my debts and fulfil my will and testament, as they will answer before the High Judge on the Day of Judgement.

Execs: Christian (*Christiana*) my wife, Henry Barkere of Clare and Richard Norman of the same,[2] they to execute and fulfil everything written above, in the best way they can to please God and profit my soul; to the same Henry, for his diligent labour about these premises, 13s 4d and to Richard Norman, similarly, 6s 8d.

Seal appended.

Witnesses: Master Thomas Ast', vicar of Clare,[3] Sir James Bakere, Henry Barkere, Robert Panell, Thomas Clerk, Richard Norman and Richard Clerk, and others specially called here.

[*Will, of same date*]

Made in my dwelling house at Clare; everything in my testament to be well and truly implemented.

Christian my wife to have and enjoy my whole tenement in which I now live, in the town of Clare, opposite (*ex opposit'*) the market there, lying between the messuage of Thomas Clerk on the east side and the messuage of Thomas Stoke on the west, and my newly-built barn in the same town, lying next to the outer bridge of the castle, and an enclosed croft of arable land in the same town, at 'Pesonbredge', lately William Wurlyche's, she to have and to hold them, to her and her heirs, of the chief lords of the fee for ever, by due service; my feoffees of and in the said barn and croft to deliver all right and estate in them to Christian or other persons named by her, when duly required after my death.

Christian also to have a piece of arable land called 'Stonyland' in the parish of Ashen [*Essex*], for a whole year after my death and from the day of my death to the feast of St Michael the Archangel next following, if God disposes that I die before that feast; and after that year, together with the days and weeks before St Michael, Robert [fol. 320] Panell to have and enjoy the piece of land, according to the agreement made between myself and him, that is, that he will pay my execs 20 marks 6s 8d in this manner: on the first day of his entering the land 10 marks, and in 1½ years following [*that*] 10 marks 6s 8d; my feoffees, Sir James Bakere, chaplain, Thomas Prentys and Thomas Clerk to deliver full estate and possession in the piece of land on the day of Robert's first payment, he providing sufficient surety to my execs, at the same time, for fully paying the remaining 10 marks 6s 8d at the time stated.

Out of the money received from Robert Panell, my execs to have Friar John Elmham to celebrate for my soul and the souls of my father and mother and for the souls of all my parents, friends and benefactors, for whom I am most bound, in Clare church, and not elsewhere, for a whole year immediately after my death, paying him £6 for his stipend for that time.

From the same money my execs to pay 5 marks towards glazing a window in the chapel of the Blessed Mary on the north side of the same church called 'le Babyl-wyndowe' of (*de*) the story of the Assumption of the Blessed Mary.[4]

The monks of the monastery of St Edmund of Bury to have, between them, 20s to pray for my soul; the convent of Friars Austin of Clare to have 13s 4d to pray for my soul;[5] the Friars Dominican, or Preachers, of London [*to have*] between them 6s 8d, to pray for my soul.

Christian to have all my ostilments and utensils, such as linen, woollen, pots, pans, cups, spoons and all the other necessaries belonging to my house, and all my other chattels and all the debts owing to me, on condition that she pay all my debts that I owe and the expenses on the day of my burial, seven-day and thirty-day, and pay and distribute 5 marks for my soul, in Clare church, in this way: each week on Friday, 3d among 6 needy poor, by her discretion, until the 5 marks have been distributed, and to fulfil my will with the 20 marks 6s 8d from [fol. 320v] the sale of the land. Seal appended.

Witnesses: Henry Barkere, Robert Panell, Thomas Clerk, Richard Norman, Richard Clerk and others.

Proved at Clare, 2 December 1463. Admon to execs.

1   Executor of William Smyth the elder of Clare, will pr. November 1454 (SROB, Baldwyne 174; Pt I, no. 832).
2   Henry Barkere and Richard Norman were also executors to William Smyth.
3   Thomas Asty was appointed vicar of Clare in 1462 (Tanner, p.1228); he also witnessed the will of Agnes Hukton (no. 276).
4   Richard Barbore was very definite in his description of the new window to be set into the Lady Chapel at Clare. Perhaps a 'Babylwyndowe' of the story of the Assumption would have depicted the Virgin ascending into Heaven with people reaching up to her from the top of the Tower of Babel (Genesis 11, v.4). See the Introduction, under *Church interior*, for a longer discussion of this window.
5   See note to no. 1.

47. ROBERT SANTON of WANGFORD, 12 September 1463

At the point of death; [*commendation*: to God Almighty &c]; to be buried in the churchyard of St Denis of Wangford; to the high altar for my tithes and offerings forgotten 4d; to the emendation of the said church 6d.

To John Santon 2d.

Residue of all my goods to Richard Roose, my attorney and exec,[1] he to pay my debts and distribute in other deeds of charity for my soul, as he sees best to please God and profit the health of my soul.

Seal appended.

Proved 20 February 1463/64. Admon to exec.

¹ Executor (as 'Rose') of William Santon of Wangford, probate September 1460 (SROB, Baldwyne 252; Pt I, no. 1254). The family relationship between Robert and William Santon is unclear.

[fol. 321]
48. JOHN FRYTHE of NAYLAND ('Neylond *iuxta* Stoke'), 3 July 1462

[*Commendation*: to God &c; *no burial directions*]; to the high altar of Nayland for tithes forgotten 12d; to the fabric of the said church 4d; to the making (*fabricacionem*) of the tower of Stoke by Nayland church 12d.¹

To the Friars Minor of Colchester (*Colcestria*) [*Essex*] for a trental for my soul.²

My wife to have my messuage as it lies, in length and breadth, for term of her life, whether she be unmarried or married; if she becomes in need such that she has to sell the messuage, she to dispose the money thus: one part for my soul, another part to be divided among [*my*] sons and daughters, if any be then alive, and the residue for herself; if she remarries and [*then*] dies the messuage to be sold by my execs and divided by equal portions, one being disposed for my soul and hers in the celebration of masses in Nayland church and the other to be divided by equal portions *pro rata* among my sons and daughters then alive, but if none is alive then all the money from the messuage to be disposed in Nayland church in masses and other pious deeds.

Residue of all my goods to the disposition of Agnes my wife, and Thomas Chaterys of the said Stoke, execs, they to dispose everything to the profit of my soul, as they will answer before God.

Witnesses: Henry Whytterat, clerk, John Hyde and John Lane.

Proved at Fornham [*St Martin*], 12 July [*1462*]. Admon to execs.

[*Whole will struck through and marginal note added,* registered below. *See no. 86.*]

¹ Money was left for building the tower at Stoke by Nayland between 1439 and 1462 (Pevsner, *sub nomine*).
² See note to no. 38.

49. RICHARD KEMPE of COCKFIELD ('Cokefeld'), 20 July 1462 [*probate only*]

Proved at Cockfield. Admon to Thomas Forthe and Henry Chenery, execs.

[*Whole probate struck through and marginal note added,* quer' infra. *See no. 85 for will and probate, which are, in fact, entered on the same bifolium as no. 49, though not adjacent.*]

[fol. 321v]
50. SIMON KENDALE of CHELSWORTH,¹ 2 July 1462

Sick of body; [*commendation*: to God &c; *no burial instructions*]; to the high altar of Chelsworth parish church 2s; to the fabric of the same church 20 marks.

To Lindsey ('Lellesey') church 13s 4d; to the fabric of Semer church 13s 4d; to the fabric of Nedging ('Neddyng') church 13s 4d; to the fabric of Naughton ('Nawton') church 13s 4d; to Wattisham ('Wachesham') church 13s 4d; to the reparation of Nedging chapel 3s 4d.²

To the Friars Minor of Ipswich (*Gybewic'*) 5 marks; to the friars of Clare 5 marks;³

27

to the Friars Preachers of Ipswich 5 marks;[4] to the Carmelite Friars of the same 5 marks;[5] to the friars of Sudbury 5 marks;[6] to the friars of Babwell 5 marks.[7]

To be distributed to the poor of Chelsworth, for a year, that is, 20d weekly.

A suitable priest to be hired to celebrate divine service in Chelsworth church for 4 years.

Agnes my wife to have the messuage with the adjacent croft, to her and her heirs in perpetuity, except a house with the attached garden; Agnes to have the household goods belonging to the house; to the same Agnes £40.

To Agnes my servant 40s together with her wages; to Joan Heyvard my servant 33s 4d, with her wages; to Margaret Clovere my sister 20s; to Joan, Margaret's daughter, 6s 8d; to Alice Fynn 6s 8d; to each of my godsons 12d; to John Markeday of Bildeston ('Bylston') [no sum].

Residue of all my goods to the disposition of my execs, Agnes my wife, John Hell of Chelsworth and James Grene of Lindsey, they to implement my will and testament. Supervisor: John Lyown of Hadleigh.

Seal appended.

John Kendale my brother to be 'found' out of my goods as long as he lives.

Proved at Cockfield, 20 July 1462. Admon to execs.

1   Executor of John Clerk of Chelsworth, will pr. February 1451/52 (SROB, Baldwyne 133; Pt I, no. 629).
2   Nedging chapel, dedicated to the Blessed Mary, was situated by 'Semer bridge'; see no. 721 below.
3   For the Friars Minor Ipswich and the Austin Friars of Clare see notes to no. 1.
4   The Dominican Friars (Black Friars, or Friars Preachers) were established at Ipswich by Henry III in 1263. Their church and house were dedicated to St Mary. By the 1350s, following various grants of land, they had a large site in the parish of St Mary at Quay, reaching in length from north to south, from St Margaret's Church to the church of St Mary at Quay (Star Lane), and in width from east to west, from Foundation Street to the town wall, parallel with the Lower Wash (*VCH Suffolk*, ii, pp.122–3).
5   See note to no. 1.
6   See note to no. 11.
7   See note to no. 1.

[fol. 322]
51. THOMAS GYBLOUE of BURES ST MARY, 29 April 1462

[*Commendation*: to God &c; *no burial directions*]; to the high altar of the parish church of the aforesaid Bures 12d; to the gild of St Mary 12d;[1] to the reparation of the same church 12d.

To Margaret my wife, for her lifetime, my tenement lately called 'Heriotes', as I had it, with others, of the gift and feoffment of John Dorward, esquire, as appears by the evidence raised then (*inde*), she to keep it in repair and meet (*defend'*) all spiritual and temporal dues; after her death the feoffees of the property to sell it and dispose half of the money for the stipend of a priest to celebrate in the parish church of Bures for my soul and the soul of Margaret and for [*the souls*] of all the faithful; the other two parts [*sic*] of the money to be divided by my feoffees between Christine and Margaret my daughters; if one of them should die before Margaret Gebelowe, late the wife of Thomas Gebelowe, then my feoffees are empowered, according to my will, to dispose both parts of the money on the reparation of Bures church for the souls of Thomas, Margaret, Christine and Margaret and all the faithful departed.

Residue of all my goods to Margaret Geblou, executrix, to dispose as seems best for the health of my soul.

Supervisor: John Geblou.

Proved at Sudbury, 21 July 1462. Admon to exec.

¹   The gild of the Assumption of the Blessed Mary at Bures St Mary received a bequest from William Smyth (no. 658 below). The gild is mentioned in a will of 1471 (*PSIA*, xxiii, p.53).

52. JOHN BRYGTH of LONG MELFORD, 4 June 1462

['Bryght' *in margin*] [*Commendation*: to God &c; *no burial directions*]; to the high altar 12d; to the tower of the said church 6s 8d.

To Margaret my wife my tenement in 'Fotysfordstrete', to give and to sell, and all my household necessaries (*omnia ostiliament' mea necessaria*), she to pay all my debts after my decease.

My tenement in Alpheton to be sold.

To the Mass of Jesu (*misse nomine Jhu*) 5 marks.¹

To each of my children 60s (*lx s*), that is, to John my son 40s (*xl s*), Elizabeth 40s (*xl s*) and Rose 40s (*xl s*), and Robert my son only 10s; if any of them die, each to be the other's heir.

To Margaret my wife 26s; to Agnes Hamond 20d; to John Wareyn at the sign of the Cock ('le Coke') 6s 8d.

Residue of my goods to my execs, Margaret my wife and John Wareyn, to dispose for my soul and the souls for whom I am bound, as seems to them best.

Proved at Sudbury, 21 July 1462. Admon to execs.

¹   See note to no. 45.

[fol. 322v]

53. JOHN TORNORE of DEPDEN,¹ 22 June 1462

Sick in body; [*commendation*: to God &c; *no burial directions*]; to the high altar of Depden for tithes forgotten 6s 4d; to the reparation of the same church 2 marks. To the high altar of Chevington 16d; to the high altar of Rede 3d; to the high altar of Hargrave 3d; to the reparation of Chedburgh ('Chetber') church 6s 4d.

My messuage in Brockley called 'Stolis' to be sold to pay my debts and fulfil my will as far as it can, and if it will not fulfil it, my wife to do so if she can, from her own goods; Marion my daughter to have 5 marks out of the mesuage; my execs to sell the said messuage to pay my debts, as above, and to collect 8s 8d from William Joc' of the same messuage, for the farm of the place.

Matilda my wife to have all my lands and tenements during the term of her life, except my tenement in Brockley; after the decease of Matilda, John my son to have a tenement called 'Vaunces', he providing a suitable chaplain to celebrate in Depden church for me, my wife and my benefactors for a whole year.

Also after the decease of Matilda my wife, William my son to have my tenement in which I live, with the tenement called 'Kentes' and the tenement called 'Copeland's Hostelry' (*Osteleris de* 'Copeland'), he providing a suitable chaplain to celebrate for a whole year, as specified above for his brother.

Thomas my son to have two crofts called 'Pylgrymys Croftes' after the decease of Matilda.

To Marion my daughter, the elder, 2 marks; to Margaret my daughter, the elder, 2 marks, provided that she be willing to marry according to the wishes of me and my wife.

To Margaret my daughter, the younger, 2 marks; to my four married daughters 6s 8d each.

For the celebration of masses for my father and mother, 6s 8d.

John and William my sons, each of them, to pay their mother 5 marks for her relief. My feoffees in the tenement in Brockley to deliver estate to my execs or their assigns without delay.

Execs: John Turnore and William Turnore my sons, of Depden, and John Sparue and William Sparue of Chedburgh, to each of whom, for their labour, 6s 8d; Matilda my wife to be supervisor; they to execute my testament and last will faithfully.

Note: the 5 marks which Marion shall have are of the legacy of William Scoyle, her uncle (*av'*).[2]

Matilda my wife to have a meadow in 'Suteres medewe', containing half an acre, to dispose according to her wish.

Proved at Stradishall, 24 July 1462. Admon to execs.

[1] Executor of John Skoyle of Brockley, will pr. September 1451 (SROB, Baldwyne 105; Pt I, no. 472).

[2] William Scoyle was not mentioned in the will of John Skoyle (see note above) but they must have been related.

[fol. 323]
54. JOHN GRENHELL of LAYHAM ('Leyham'), 8 December 1463

Having God before my eyes and not wishing to die intestate; [*commendation*: to God &c]; to be buried in the churchyard of Layham parish church; to the high altar of the same church, for my tithes and offerings forgotten and underpaid, 3s 4d; to the making of the new bells of the said church 13s 4d.

To Thomas Grenhell my son 20s; to Joan my daughter a quarter of barley; to Alice my daughter a quarter of barley.

To Margaret my wife my tenement in which I now live, for term of her life; and after her decease the tenement to remain to Richard Grenhell my son and his heirs for ever; if Richard should die during the lifetime of my wife, then after her decease the tenement to be sold as soon as possible by the discretion of her execs and [*the money*] disposed for the health of our souls and [*the souls*] of all the faithful departed, in what seems to them to be the best manner; all my other goods and chattels to the said Margaret, to be at her will.

Execs: Margaret my wife and Richard Grenhell my son, they to see everything implemented and my testament and will correctly executed.

Seal appended.

Witnesses: Thomas Rowyngton, Robert Watyre, William Towne and others.

To the order of the friars of St Francis in Ipswich (*Gipwico*) 20s.[1]

Proved in the parish church of Boxford ('Boxforthe'), 17 April 1464. Admon to execs.

[1] See note to no. 1.

55. ROBERT PODENEY of BURES ST MARY, 8 November 1463

Dated the Tuesday after the feast of St Leonard the abbot, 1463; sick in body; [*commendation*: to God &c]; to be buried in the churchyard of Bures church; to the high altar of the same church for tithes forgotten 3s 4d; to the emendation of the said church 6s 8d; to the gild of St John the Baptist there 3s 4d.[1]

To the Friars Minor of Colchester [*Essex*] 2s 6d;[2] to the Friars Preachers of Sudbury 2s 6d;[3] to the church of Mount Bures ('Bures ad montem') [*Essex*] 2s.

To each chaplain present on my burial day 4d; to each sufficient (*suffic'*) clerk 2d; to 60 of the poor on my burial day 1d each.

Residue of all my goods to my execs: Phyllis (*Feliciam*) my wife and John Strutt of Wickham ('Wykham') [*Essex*].

[*Will, undated*]

As to my lands and tenements:

Immediately after my death my execs to sell a croft of land called 'Tameres' for the stipend of a priest to celebrate in Bures St Mary church for a year, for my soul and my parents' and friends' [*souls*].

If Thomas Upchar is willing to pay my execs 30s which he promised me for 1½ acres of meadow in 'Tunmanholme',[4] my feoffees [fol. 323v] to transfer estate and possession in it to him; but if he is not willing to have the meadow for that sum or is not willing to compound with my execs, then my execs to sell it immediately after my death and dispose [*the proceeds*] in alms and deeds of charity according to their discretion.

My wife to have all the residue of all my lands and tenements for her lifetime; and after her death John Podeney my son to have them to him and his heirs, on condition that he pays my execs 20 marks to dispose in deeds of charity, as in the emendation of rutted (*perversarum*) ways and alms to the poor, according to their discretion; if John my son or his heirs are not willing to pay the 20 marks, my execs to sell all the said lands and tenements as they please, and out of the money from them John my son or his heirs to have 20 marks and the remainder of the money to be disposed for my soul etc[*sic*], as above-stated.

Witnessess: Alexander, rector of Mount Bures, Thomas Strut and John Resshey and others.

Proved in Boxford ('Boxforth') church, 17 April 1464. Admon to execs *via* Sir William Warner, vicar of Bures,[5] our commissary deputed for the purpose; seal of official appended.

1 The gild of St John the Baptist at Bures St Mary also received bequests from John Potyer (no. 326) and William Smyth (no. 658).
2 See note to no. 38.
3 See note to no. 11.
4 'Tunmanholme' means 'Townman's Meadow'.
5 William Warner (or, Waryner) was vicar of Bures St Mary from 1444 to 1473 (Tanner, p.1352); he witnessed the will of John Colyere (no. 283).

56. JOHN HALE of GREAT BRADLEY ('Bradley Magna'), 26 April 1464

[*Commendation*: to God &c]; to be buried in the churchyard of the church of the said Bradley; to the high altar of the said church 20d.

To Thomas my son a black horse and an acre of land in the croft called 'Pycotes', by the lane called 'Pycotes Lane'.

To Alice my wife all my utensils of the house; Alice to have, for term of her life, my crofts lately purchased of John Lennard, and after her decease all the said crofts to remain to Thomas my son and his heirs in perpetuity.

Residue of all my goods to Alice my wife, she to pay my debts and legacies and fulfil my will and dispose for my soul as seems to her most expedient, and she to be executrix.

Seal appended.

Proved in Great Bradley church, 11 June 1464. Admon to executrix.

[fol. 324]
57. MARION HETHE of RATTLESDEN ('Ratlesden'), 10 September 1459

By licence and will of my husband; [*commendation*: to God &c; *no burial directions*]; to Sir Robert Bernard, rector of the same church,[1] for my tithes forgotten or underpaid, 20d; to the high altar there a sheet; to the painting of the image of the Blessed Mary there 3s 4d.

To Thomas Hethe my husband all my tenement in Rattlesden ('Ratylesden') called 'Cowperis', with all the lands, pastures and feedings, for the term of his life, and after his decease my execs to sell it and dispose it according to the form and effect of the testament and will of John Cowper, formerly my husband.

All my part of the tenement called 'Halydays' to be sold by my execs and out of the proceeds a sangred to be celebrated in the same church for 4 years, for my soul and for the souls of the said John Cowpere and Katherine his wife, John Makemere[2] and Emme his wife and for the souls of all our benefactors and all the Christian departed.

Residue of my goods to the disposition of my exec and the execution of my will.

Exec: Peter Redenale, to dispose for me and my soul where he sees most expedient to please God.

Supervisors: Robert Legat[3] and Thomas Hethe my husband.

Proved at Rattlesden, 15 February 1462/63. Admon to exec.

[1] In 1454 Friar Robert Bernard, canon of the order of St Augustine, was appointed rector of Rattlesden; he was succeeded by Master Henry Strother in 1460 (Tanner, p.1440).
[2] Probate of John Makemere, dated May 1440 (SROB, Baldwyne 27; Pt I, no. 148); one of his executors was Marion Cowpere, that is, this testatrix as wife (or widow) of John Cowpere.
[3] The other executor of John Makemere. See note above.

58. JOHN ANGOLD of FORNHAM ALL SAINTS, 26 August 1462

Dated at Fornham; [*commendation*: to God &c; *no burial directions*]; to the high altar of the parish church of the aforesaid Fornham 12d.

To Agnes my wife all my utensils in my house; to Agnes my whole tenement, with all my lands in any way belonging to it; and after her decease, the tenement with all the free and bond lands to remain to Thomas my son and his assigns.

To each of my daughters, after the decease of Agnes my wife, 20s, if it can be raised from my goods and chattels after (*ultra*) the payment of my debts and the support (*exibic'*) of the said Agnes have been met.

Residue of all my goods to be distributed by my execs for my soul and the souls of all my benefactors, as they know best to please God.

Execs: Agnes my wife and Thomas Angold my son.

Seal appended.

Proved the last day of February [28th] 1462/63. Admon to Thomas Angold, exec. Power reserved to Agnes the other exec when she comes &c[*sic*].

[fol. 324v]

59. JOHN ROKELL of MELFORD TYE ('Melforth Tyie'), 18 February 1462/63 [*nuncupative*]

To be buried in the churchyard of Melford parish church.

To Alice his wife all his lands and tenements in the town of Melford, for term of her life, and after her decease they to remain to John Rokell of Borley ('Borle') in Essex and Geoffrey Smyth of Melford Tye, execs, to pay his debts and dispose for his soul as seems most expedient and profit to the health of his soul.

Witnesses: Roger Fullere, John Neele and John Fullere.

Proved at Melford, 3 March 1462/63. Admon to execs.

[fol. 325]

60. RICHARD CAVENHAM of FORDHAM [*Cambs*], 5 March 1461/62

[*Commendation*: to God &c; *no burial directions*]

To Margaret my wife my tenement in 'le Hygh Strete' for term of her life, and after her decease the tenement to remain to William our son, if he then be alive; if William should die while his mother is [*still*] alive, then the tenement to remain to Thomas our son, the younger, for term of his life; after the death of the longest liver of them the tenement to be sold and with the money a suitable chaplain to be found to celebrate for a whole year in Fordham parish church, for our souls and the souls of John and Agnes my father and mother, Richard and Agnes my grandfather and grandmother (*avi et avie*), and William Cavenham, chaplain, and all our parents and benefactors; what remains of the money from the tenement to be divided into three parts: one part to be disposed in the upkeep (*sustentacione*) of the said parish church of the Blessed Mary; another to be distributed among the poor of the said town in greatest need; and the third part to be disposed in the common ways of the said town, where most need is.

To the same William, when he comes to the age of 12, an acre of land lying at 'Rogeres Walle', with 5 ewes and as many lambs.

To John my son, at the same age, 5 roods of land, of which 3 roods abut upon the way leading to Freckenham, and half an acre of land in the same field abutting on the same way, and 5 ewes and as many lambs.

To Thomas my son, at the same age, 1 acre ½ rood of land, of which 3 roods are in the same field, which I purchased of Richard Hykedon, and 1½ roods are in the same furlong, which I purchased of John Lowke, with 5 ewes and as many lambs.

If William, John and Thomas die in their mother's lifetime, the aforesaid land to remain with Margaret my wife for term of her life; and after her decease the land to be sold and the money disposed in pious deeds of mercy, that is, in the celebration of masses for our souls and in the reparation of the church and in alms.

To Margaret my wife my household utensils, a cart, 4 horses, all the cows and 3 score ewes.

To John my son, the elder, 3 acres 1½ roods of land, of which 1½ acres and half a rood lie together at '?Toftetyestown-ende' and 1 acre 3 roods in 'le Cherchefelde undyr downe'; to the same John 5 coombs of rye or maslin, with as many coombs of barley.

To Andrew Cheswryte, chaplain,[1] 6s 8d; to Richard Cavenham, son of the said John, 2 ewe-hoggs; to Christian Clerk 2 ewe-hoggs; to Robert my servant 2 ewe-hoggs; to Agnes Cowell 2 ewes with 2 lambs; to Agnes Fowlere a ewe-hogg.

Residue of my goods to the disposition of Margaret my wife, she to dispose them, with the supervision of John Tebaud, as she sees best to please God and profit my soul and the souls of [my] parents and benefactors.

Proved at Fornham [St Martin], 23 April 1462. Admon to executrix.

[1] Sir Andrew Chesewrygh (or, Cheswryte) was chaplain of the chantry of Our Lady at Fordham; will pr. March 1474/75 (NRO, NCC 89 Gelour). See also nos 187 and 602 below.

[fol. 325v]
61. WILLIAM WARNERE of BRADFIELD ST GEORGE ('Bradfeld Monachorum'), 3 April 1462

[Commendation: to God &c; no burial directions]; to the [high] altar of the said Bradfield 3s 4d; to the reparation of the ornaments of the same church 6s 8d; to a suitable chaplain to celebrate in the same church for the souls of my father and my mother and for the souls of all my deceased benefactors, for a whole year, 8 marks.

Residue of all my goods, lands and tenements, which at present I have in the town of the said Bradfield, or elsewhere, to my execs, to sell and dispose for the health of my soul and the souls of all my friends deceased, in the celebration of masses and giving of alms, as they see best to please God and profit my soul.

Execs: Benedict Fordham and Walter Brown of the said Bradfield.

Supervisors: John Coket of Ampton[1] and John Andrew of Bury St Edmunds.

To each of my execs for their labour a coomb of wheat.

Proved at Fornham [St Martin], 10 May 1462. Admon to Benedict Fordham, exec. Power reserved to Walter the other exec when he comes, if he wishes to take up admon.

[1] Will pr. 2 October 1483 (TNA, PCC, 22 Logge; published in Logge Register, no. 301).

62. RICHARD HAMOND of BARROW ('Barwe'), 21 February 1461/62

[Commendation: to God &c; no burial directions]; to the high altar of Barrow 12d; to the fabric of the said church 3s 4d.

All my chattels and vessels and utensils to Agnes my wife.

Residue of all my goods to Agnes my wife and Thomas Fryot,[1] execs, to dispose for my soul as they see best to please God and profit the health of my soul.

My tenement and lands to Agnes my wife for term of her life; and if she wishes to sell the lands, Thomas Freot my godson to have them before [any] other.

Isabel my daughter to have my place after my wife's death only if she cannot recover the place in Tuddenham ('Tode'ham').

Proved at Fornham [St Martin], 10 May 1462. Admon to execs.

[1] Will, no. 600 below.

63. JOHN KENMAN of BARNINGHAM ('Bernyngham'), 26 April 1462
[*probate only*]

Proved at Fornham St Martin, the Monday after the first Sunday after Easter (*Dominica in Albis*) 1462. Admon to Stephen Bull and John Kenman, execs.

[fol. 326]
64. JOHN YESTAS of THORNDON, 12 January 1462/63 [*probate only*]

Proved at Finningham ('Fynyngham'). Admon to Robert Saham and William Anneys of Wetheringsett, execs.

65. ROBERT HUBBERD of FINNINGHAM ('Fenyngham'), 10 November 1462

Dated Wednesday before the feast of St Martin, bishop and confessor, 1462; [*commendation*: to God &c; *no burial directions*]. My execs to pay my debts as quickly as possible, before fulfilling [*my*] legacies and bequests. Then, after my debts have been paid: to the high altar of Finningham church 2s; to the emendation of the same church 6s 8d.
To the friars of Dunwich 10s;[1] to the friars of Babwell 4 bushels of barley.[2]
To Matilda my wife all my household equipment, that is, vessels, utensils and bedding, with all the other necessaries relating or belonging to both house and chamber.
To John my son 26s 8d; to Robert my son 40s.
Matilda my wife to have my tenement for the whole term of her life on this condition, that she be of good and honest disposition (*condicionis*) towards Thomas my son and his wife, if God wills him to marry, and then this bequest to stand; but if Matilda behaves (*duxerit mores suos*) contrary to this and is of bad, rude (*proterve*) and ill disposition (and it can be proved so by three or four trustworthy persons), then she is to be excluded from my tenement and Thomas my son shall then pay Matilda 33s 4d annually as a pension for the duration of her life.
If Matilda dies while Thomas is alive, my tenement to remain to him and his heirs; if he dies without heirs, the tenement to go to Robert my son and his heirs; if Robert dies without heirs, my execs and feoffees to sell the tenement and dispose the money in deeds of charity for my soul and the soul of Matilda my wife and for the souls of [*my*] parents, friends and those to whom I stand indebted in any way.
Robert my son to have his dwelling in my said tenement until he marries, if he behaves in an honest manner towards his mother and brother Thomas.
To each of my execs 3s 4d.
Residue of all my goods [fol. 326v] to my execs, to pay my debts and legacies and do other good works (*opera pietatis*) and alms-giving for my soul; none of my execs to dispose my goods on his own authority, but the major part of all my execs to act [*together*] in disposing of them.
Execs: Matilda my wife, Thomas my son, John Cook of Cotton, James Hawyse of Walsham and Robert my son; supervisor: the rector of Finningham; they to dispose for my soul and for the souls for whom I am most bound, in the best way to please God and profit my soul.
Proved 22 January 1462/63. Admon to execs.

1   There were two houses of friars at Dunwich. A house of Dominicans (Black Friars or Friars
     Preachers) was founded there in the middle of the thirteenth century. It was situated in the old
     parish of St John, not far from the house of the Franciscans (Grey Friars or Friars Minor). In
     1289, following a gift of the burgesses of the town, the house of the Franciscans was given a new
     site and was moved further inland (where the ruins and precinct walls still remain). Both friaries
     were suppressed at the same time in 1538 (*VCH Suffolk*, ii, pp.121–6).
2   See note to no. 1.

66. JOHN PERY of GREAT WHELNETHAM, 21 July 1462

[*Commendation*: to &c *only*; *no burial directions*]; to the high altar of the aforesaid
Whelnetham 3s 4d; to the high altar of Bradfield St Clare ('Senclere Bradfeld') 12d;
to the reparation of the book of the sacraments (*libri sacramentorum*) of the church
of the Blessed Mary of Whelnetham, a cow.

As soon as possible after my decease, my execs to provide a suitable chaplain to
celebrate for the health of my soul and my mother's soul, and for the health of my
friends' [*souls*], for a whole year, or for 2 years if my goods will allow it, in the
church of the aforesaid Whelnetham, and the chaplain to have for his stipend each
year 8 marks, and his vestments (*vestura*).

My part of certain lands of mine called 'Templeris Wodbrige' and 'Herrys Akere' to
be sold for the use of my execs.

To each of my godsons 4d; to Thomas Sawere my godson 12d.

Residue of all my goods to the disposition of my execs, Geoffrey Dyx of Ampton
and John Bend of the aforesaid Whelnetham; supervisor, John Appylby of Bury St
Edmunds; they to implement my will in the best way they can for the health of my
soul and of my friends' [*souls*], as they will answer before the High Judge on the
last day.

Proved at Fornham [*St*] Martin, 2 December 1462. Admon to execs.

[fol. 327]
67. RICHARD WRYGHTE of BURES ST MARY, 30 November 1462

['Wrythe' *in margin*] Dated Tuesday, the feast of St Andrew the Apostle 1462, 2
Edward IV; sick of body; to be buried in the church of the aforesaid Bures, if the
parishioners of that town agree to it; then, to the reparation of the church 13s 4d in
money and a quarter of malt; but if the parishioners will not allow me to be buried
in the church, but [*only*] in the churchyard, then to the reparation of the church half
that gift;[1] to the high altar of the same church for tithes forgotten and withheld 40d.
To the friars of Colchester (*Colcestrie*) 20d;[2] to the friars of the Sudbury house 20d.[3]
To John my son 40s in money and 2 good cows, and also my looms ('lomes'), with
the equipment (*instrumentis*) belonging to them, and 2 short gowns (*togis collobis*)
and my hoods (*capicis*).

To Joan my daughter 20s.

To Isabel my daughter a quarter of malt, to be delivered to her immediately after
my decease.

To the same Isabel 6s 8d and to Alice my daughter 6s 8d, to be delivered to them
within two years after my decease; if one of my daughters, Isabel and Alice, should
die in those two years, and the other live, the money bequeathed to the deceased
[*daughter*] to remain to the other one; if both should die, the 13s 4d to remain to
my wife.

To my wife the 14 marks which John Wyderelde of Colchester and his cofeoffees owe me for the sale of a tenement in the street called 'le Wyrestrete' in the town of Colchester, according to the form and effect of the indenture made at the time.

I will that Arnold Dunsteven, gentleman, living in the house (*hospic'*) of the earl of Essex,[4] deliver a legal estate to Joan my wife in all the lands and tenements called 'Bisshoppes' in the town of Bures, she to hold them to her and her heirs and carry out the covenants and payments agreed between Arnold and me.

My execs to keep my anniversary with due solemnity for 3 years following my decease, each priest present there having 4d and each clerk 2d.

Residue of all my goods to Joan my wife, she to pay my debts and faithfully implement my will.

Execs: Joan my wife and William Hoy the elder, of Wormingford ('Wethermoundesford') [*Essex*].

Seal appended.

Witnesses: the rector of Mount Bures ('Bures *ad Montem*') [*Essex*], Robert Wenden, John Resshey, John Waryn, Thomas Boryball, Robert Podeney, Thomas Garlond and others.

Proved at Sudbury, 15 December 1462. Admon to execs.

[*Folios 327 and 328 comprise one bifolium but folio 327 begins with this will proved in 1462 and is then completed with the following will proved in 1464.*]

¹   A rare example of an individual overtly exerting financial pressure to secure burial within the church, rather than in the churchyard.
²   See note to no. 38.
³   See note to no. 11.
⁴   It is not known where Dunsteven was living but Henry Bouchier, earl of Essex, owned various properties in the area; indeed, a few years later, in 1467, he and his wife Isabel, and their heirs, were granted the manor called 'Silvesteres Halle' in Bures St Mary, with the mills there and all the lands, rents, reversions and services in 'Saynt mary burys' (Patent Rolls, 7 Edward IV, pt ii.16, quoted in Copinger, *Manors of Suffolk*, i, p.51).

68. RALPH TRAPETT of HEPWORTH ('Heppeworth'),[1] 3 December 1463

[*Commendation*: to God &c]; to be buried in the churchyard of the parish church of St Peter of Hepworth.

The debts that I owe to be well and truly paid as quickly as possible and in the best manner.

To the high altar of the same town 20d; to the reparation of the same church 5 bushels (*mod'*) of wheat and a quarter of barley.

To Friar Laurence Wykyngham of Norwich, for a trental, 10s; to the friars of Babwell half a quarter of barley;[2] to the Friars Preachers of Thetford half a quarter of barley;[3] to the nuns of the same, 2 bushels of wheat.[4]

My execs to provide a suitable priest to celebrate for a whole year within the 8 years following my decease, for my soul and for the souls of all my benefactors.

A close called 'Lugmannes' and 3½ acres of land by 'le Northgrene' to be sold for 10 marks; if John my son wants to buy it, with the 3½ acres, for that price, he to have them before anyone else; if he refuses and does not want to have them at that price, then one of my execs to buy it for the same price and my feoffees to deliver estate and transfer possession of and in the said land to my execs or to those to whom they may assign it.

Thomas Scowle, chaplain, to deliver to John my son and my execs sufficient estate and possession of and in all the lands and tenements in which he stands enfeoffed, for the implementation and fulfilment of my last will.

To Lettice my wife a close called 'Buskesyerd', to hold to her and her heirs, to give and to sell or assign as she wishes; Lettice [fol. 327v] to have 2 cows, of her own choice, after my decease.

All the utensils of my house to be disposed and divided between Lettice my wife and John my son immediately after my decease; Lettice my wife and John my son to live together as long as they wish, but if any discord arises between them so that they cannot agree, then John shall provide Lettice [with] an honest chamber that is adequate and satisfactory for her, as long as she remains unmarried; John also to find Lettice sufficient fuel and the keeping (custodia') of 2 cows, both winter and summer, term of her life, if she remains unmarried, otherwise not, unless John pleases [to do so]; if Lettice and John do not live together in one place, then John to pay Lettice 10s annually, during her life.

My execs to have and hold, to them and their assigns, all my lands and tenements for the term of 10 years next following, so that the profits from them, together with the 10 marks from the close called 'Lugmannes' and the 3½ acres of land, may be sufficient for them to pay my debts and fulfil my last will.

After the end of the 10 years, to Thomas my son a close called 'Longdyche'.

To William my son a piece of land, with a parcel of meadow, containing altogether 3½ acres, at 'Netherbreche at the Wylugg'.

To Robert my son a pightle called 'Collesyerde' with the adjacent croft and a piece of meadow adjacent, together with an acre of land in 'Hykkescrofftt'.

To Walter my son 3 acres of land and meadow at 'Breche', next to the land of 'Reveshale' hall (aule) on both sides.

To Isaac my son 3½ acres of land in the furlong called 'Overheche', next to the land of John Man of [Market] Weston on the west.

To Alice my daughter 3½ acres of land in the furlong 'le Breche', next to land of 'Reveshale' hall on the west.

To Katherine my daughter 1 acre 3 roods of land in the furlong called 'le Breche', next to land of 'Reveshale' hall on the west.

Each of my above-named children, to whom I have bequeathed the said land, to be of 20 completed years before they enter and possess the land, and then my execs to deliver to them estate and possession in all the said lands bequeathed to them (after the said term of 10 years); if any of them should die before the age of 20, then the part of the deceased to be sold and disposed by my execs for the profit and benefit (merit') of the deceased's soul and our souls and all our benefactors' [souls]; if any of them decease after the term[sic] of 20 years, then each one to dispose his part according to his own disposition, as seems best to them (illis) in the future.

Residue of all my goods to John my son, Walter Cowper and Stephen Dey, whom I make execs and feoffees, to dispose for my soul and my benefactors' [souls] as seems to them best to please God in the future.

Proved at Ixworth, 7 February 1463/64. Admon to John the son of the deceased, exec, with the supervision and advice of John Smyth of Bury, whom we have constituted (constituimus) supervisor for this purpose (in ea parte). Power reserved to

Walter Cowpere and Stephen Dey, the other execs, when they come and if they wish to take up admon. Seal of official appended.

1   Thomas Trapet of Hepworth had both a brother and son called Ralph; Thomas's will pr. July 1460 (SROB, Baldwyne 254; Pt I, no. 1257). It seems likely that this testator was Thomas's brother since this will was proved less than four years later. See also the will of Ralph Trapet, probably the testator's son, pr. September 1485 (SROB, Hervye 347).

2   See note to no. 1.

3   The Dominican Friars (Friars Preachers) were not established at Thetford until 1335, when they were given the deserted site of the church of St Mary the Great. In 1347 Henry earl of Lancaster, son of the founder, granted them the site of the *Domus Dei*, which stood between their cloister and the High Street, which they were to maintain, and hence this friars' house was often termed the priory of the Maison-Dieu or God's House, or else the priory of the Old House (*VCH Norfolk*, ii, pp.433–5).

4   The Benedictine nunnery of St George, Thetford, was established in about 1160. It was aided by the abbey at Bury and from the beginning weekly supplies were sent from Bury St Edmunds not only of bread and beer but even of cooked meat. In 1369 it was agreed that instead the abbey should grant annually fixed quantities of grain and money (*VCH Norfolk*, ii, pp.354–6).

[fol. 328]

69. THOMAS GYLBERTT of IXWORTH THORPE ('Ixworthorpp'), 31 December 1463

Dated the day of St Silvester, 1463, at Ixworth Thorpe; [*commendation*: to &c *only*]; my body to the burial at the aforesaid Thorpe; to Sir Hugh Bury my various (*omnimodos*) missals of the gild of St John the Baptist of the same [*place*].[1]

To the prior of Ixworth 12d; to Sir Hugh, sub-prior, 8d, and to each of the canons there 6d;[2] to the church of the aforesaid Thorpe 2 bushels[*sic*] of wheat and 3 of malt.

To each of [*my*] stepchildren (*filiastr'*) under the age of 12 a bushel of barley.

To the Austin Friars of Thetford 40d.[3]

To each of the sons of John Gylbert my son 4 bushels (*mod'*) of barley; to John Page, servant of the said John my son, 4 bushels (*mod'*) of barley; to my niece Margaret 4 bushels (*mod'*) of barley.

To the regular church of Ixworth and the parish church of Thorpe 37 marks out of the goods of John de Pakenham, owed to me by Robert Berdewell, esquire, as exec of the said John de Pakenham, deceased,[4] at 20s each year, to be distributed equally to the said churches until the sum of 37 marks is fully paid; for the collection and recovering of the said 37 marks allotted to the churches above, my attorneys to be John Coket of Ampton,[5] Master William Thweyt of Bury[6] and John my son.

Residue of all [*my*] goods to Agnes my wife, to provide victuals and support for herself out of them.

Execs: Agnes my wife and John my son.

Proved at Ixworth, [?7] February 1463/64. Admon to Agnes, executrix. Power reserved to John, son of the deceased, when he comes, if he wish to take up admon.

1   Gylbertt's bequest implies that there was a gild of St John the Baptist in Ixworth Thorpe but as the wills of Anne Catour *alias* Neve (SROB, Baldwyne 66; Pt I, no. 321) and Ralph Pentney *alias* Sporyere (no. 220 below) mention a gild of St John the Baptist in Ixworth, it is probable that Gylbertt's bequest was to that gild. His ownership of various missals of the gild suggests that he was one of its officials.

2   The priory of St Mary, Ixworth, was first founded for Austin canons about the year 1100, by

Gilbert Blundus or Blunt. The buildings and chapel, which were erected near the parish church, were soon destroyed during the civil war; William, son of the founder, then rebuilt the priory on a different site. Reginald Tylney was appointed prior in 1439 and William Dense in 1467 (*VCH Suffolk*, ii, pp.105–7).

3   The Austin Friars (Eremetic Friars) were established at Thetford in about 1387 by John of Gaunt, duke of Lancaster, a great patron of the order. He built for them, on Castle Hill, a church with conventual buildings on the south side. He also gave them the old church or chapel of St John on the western side of the town, which they repaired and used as a chapel for the leper hospital there, under the rule of one of their brethren. The house of the Austin Friars was often known as the 'New House' of Thetford (*VCH Norfolk*, ii, pp.433–5).

4   The de Pakenham and Berdewell families were connected, although the exact links are difficult to follow. Between them they owned the manors of Bardwell (Copinger, *Manors of Suffolk*, i, pp.262–4), Norton (i, pp.349–50) and Thorpe by Ixworth (i, pp.380–1).

5   See note to no. 61 above.

6   See Introduction, under *Register 'Baldwyne'*.

70. THOMAS CLERK of BOXFORD, 17 December 1463

[*Commendation*: to God *only*]; to be buried in the churchyard of Boxford parish church; to the high altar of the same church, for tithes forgotten a quarter of barley; to each priest present at my obsequies 4d; to each greater clerk 2d; to each [*clerk*] 1d.

To Agnes my wife all my utensils, with all the other goods and chattels belonging to me, both inside and out of the house, freely to her own use; Agnes to have my tenement in Boxford for her lifetime, if she remains a widow after my death; and after her death, or if she remarries, John Clerk my son, the elder, to enter and enjoy the tenement, to him and his heirs for ever, on condition that he pays the legacies to my four daughters that I have assigned them, after first paying Robert Clerk my son 40s in money and Roger Clerk my son 40s in money, before he is granted possession in the tenement by my co-feoffees; if Robert or Roger should die before my wife, the survivor to have the other's legacy; if both die before that, then the £4 left to them to be disposed by John my son and my execs in the church and town of Boxford, for the health of my soul and all my benefactors' [*souls*].

The same John to pay Alice Clerk my eldest daughter 20s in money, Isabel Clerk my daughter 20s, Margery my daughter 20s in money and Joan my youngest daughter 20s in money; if any of my four daughters die before Agnes my wife, the legacies of the deceased to be equally disposed among the survivors of those daughters; if all die before Agnes the legacies to be disposed in Boxford church for the health of [*my soul*] and all my benefactors' [*souls*].

Residue of all my goods to the disposition of my execs, they to order them for the health of my soul as seems to them most expedient.

Execs: Agnes my wife and John Clerk my son.

Seal appended.

Proved at Lavenham, 10 February 14[*63/64*]. Admon to execs.

[fol. 328v]

71. MARGARET BRABY of ELMSETT ('Elmesset'), 10 February 1463/64

[*probate only*]

Proved. Admon to John Braby and John Braby the younger, execs.

72. ANDREW ATT HERNE of ICKLINGHAM ('Ikelyngham') [ST JAMES], 'bocher', 12 January 1462/63

[*Commendation*: to God Almighty, the Blessed Mary &c]; to be buried in the churchyard of the church of St James the Apostle in Icklingham ('Ykelyngham'); to the high altar of the same church, for tithes forgotten and negligently detained, 3s 4d; to the use of the same church 20s; to the church of All Saints in Icklingham 3s 4d; to the parish church of Ixworth 3s 4d.

To the Austin Friars in Thetford 3s 4d; to the Friars Preachers there 40d; to the friars of Babwell 3s 4d.[1]

A suitable priest to celebrate for my soul and the souls of all my benefactors in the parish church of St James of Icklingham, for two whole years.

To each of my godsons and goddaughters a ewe; to each child of my 3 daughters a ewe; to Alice Northfolk, my servant, a brass pot and a brass pan, and 20s in money. To Isolde my wife all my goods and chattels, both live and dead, and all my utensils; Isolde to have a messuage with the garden called 'Masouns', in Icklingham, to her and her assigns, for her lifetime; all my other lands and tenements to be sold by my execs and out of the money from them, 26s 8d each to be distributed to Margaret, Katherine and Agnes my daughters.

After the death of Isolde my wife the messuage with the garden called 'Masowns', to be sold by my execs, with all my other above-mentioned lands and tenements.

Residue of all my goods to my execs, Isolde my wife, William Heryng and Thomas Symond, to pay my debts and legacies, as seems to them most expedient and profitable to my soul in the future.

Seal appended.

Proved 5 March 1463/64. Admon to execs. Seal of official appended.

[*A shorter version of this testament is given below, no. 403.*]

[1]   For the friars see notes to nos 1 (Babwell), 68 (Friars Preachers of Thetford) and 69 (Austin Friars there).

73. WILLIAM RAWLYN of BARNHAM ('Bernham') [ST] GREGORY, 14 May 1464 [*probate only*]

Proved in the parish church of Fornham St Martin. Admon to Katherine, the daughter of the deceased, and Thomas Bosard, execs. Seal of official appended.

[fol. 329]

74. ADAM HYNDEBEST of THURSTON, 26 September 1461

Of Thurston in the diocese of Norwich; to be buried in the churchyard of St Peter's church, Thurston; to the high altar of the same church, for my tithes and offerings forgotten or underpaid, 20d; to the high altar of the same church, to a new alabaster panel (*tabula*) of the life of St Peter to be made there, 40s; to another alabaster panel to be made, to be put on (*ad*) the altar of the Blessed Virgin Mary in the same church, 13s 4d.

To the friars of the house of Preachers of Thetford 10s; to the friars of the house of Babwell 10s.[1]

To the fabric of the church of St Andrew of Tostock 6s 8d; to the fabric of the church

41

of the Blessed Mary of Beyton ('Beketon') 6s 8d; to the tower of the church of St John of Rougham ('Rowgham') 20s.

To William Hyndebest my son 42s.

Residue of all my goods and chattels to my execs, to dispose for my soul and the souls for whom I am bound, [*but*] firstly in the paying of my debts and executing this testament.

Execs: Alice my wife and Roger Agas; to the same Roger 2s for his labour.

[*Will, of same date*]

In addition to my testament.

To Alice my wife all my linen and woollen, and utensils and vessels of pewter, earthenware (*terrea*) and wood, and everything else belonging to my house, of whatever nature, to her own use and to dispose at her will; to Alice a lower chamber (*camera' bassa'*) in the south end of my messuage in Thurston, in which I live at present, for term of her life, and after her death, for a week, for her goods to be kept safe and carried out by her execs at reasonable times and without any gainsaying of any man. All the feoffees who are enfeoffed in all my lands and tenements in the town and fields of Thurston to deliver estate and possession of and in all of them to John Brygth of Thurston, to hold to him and his heirs of the chief lords of the fee, by due service and custom (except in one piece of land in Thurston Field called 'Whetecrofte', which I have sold to Nicholas Sergawnte), on condition that the said John Brygth pay, with sufficient security, my exec Adam[*sic*] Hyndebest £21 6s 8d in money, in the following manner, that is, at the feast of the Purification of the Blessed Virgin Mary next, 13s 4d of it, and at Easter next after that 40s, and at the feast of St Michael [fol. 329v] the Archangel following that 16 marks and at the feast of the Nativity of Our Lord after that 12 marks, without any default, and to provide Alice my wife, during her lifetime, with good and sufficient food and drink, or to pay her 6d a week, as it pleases her, during her lifetime.

To a suitable chaplain, to celebrate for my soul and all my benefactors' [*souls*], for a whole year, 8 marks.

Proved at Fornham St Martin, 5 April 1462. Admon to execs.

[*Earlier in the register the testament of Adam Hyndebest and the probate sentence were entered and then struck through; the will was not recorded there. See fol. 294 (Pt I, no. 1440).*]

---

1   For the friars see notes to nos 1 (Babwell) and 68 (Friars Preachers of Thetford).

75. ROGER CHARITE of HITCHAM ('Hecham'), 6 July 1461

['Charyte' *in margin*] [*Commendation*: to God Almighty &c; *no burial directions*]; to the high altar of the parish church of Hitcham, for tithes forgotten, 3s 4d; to the stipend of a chaplain, to celebrate in Hitcham church for a whole year, 10 marks; to the reparation of Hitcham church 6s 8d; to the reparation of the community hall (*aule communitatis*) of Hitcham 6s 8d.[1]

My debts, first and foremost, to be paid and then my legacies fulfilled, if the payment of my debts [*owing to me*] will come to that much.

Residue of all my goods to the disposition of my execs, to be done for my soul in deeds of charity, as they see best to please God and most profit my soul.

Execs: Roger Pryk, chaplain and vicar of Graveney ('Gravemyng') in Kent (*Cancia*),[2] and Richard Fen of Hitcham, to each of whom for his labour, 3s 4d.

Proved at Fornham [*St*] Martin, 17 January 1462/63. Admon to Richard Fen, exec. Power reserved to Roger Pryk, the other exec, when he comes and if he wish to take up admon.

1   In 1452 John Welham referred to the gildhall at Hitcham as 'the community hall' (SROB, Baldwyne 160; Pt I, no. 772). This hall was situated by the churchyard (*PSIA*, xix, p.189). Peter Qwyntyn (no. 43 above) bequeathed his mass-pence from the gild of All Saints, Hitcham, to the friars of Sudbury.

2   In 1441, Sir Roger Pryk, chaplain, was a beneficiary of the will of John Copenger of Buxhall (SROB, Baldwyne 15; Pt I, no. 90); in 1444, he was executor of Agnes Elyne of Hitcham (SROB, Baldwyne 50; Pt I, no. 265). Graveney is a low-lying parish, north of Faversham; prior to the Dissolution, its church, with the advowson of the vicarage, belonged to the Augustinian priory of St Mary Overy, Southwark. See Hasted, *History and Topographical Survey of the County of Kent*, vii (1798), pp.28–38.

[fol. 330]
76. JOHN COWPER of BROCKLEY ('Brokley'), [*1462*]

[Cowpere *in margin*] [*No date given*; *commendation*: to God &c]; my body to Christian burial; to the high altar of Brockley church, for my tithes and offerings underpaid 20d; to the reparation of the same church 6s 8d; to the reparation of dangerous ways (*viarum nocivarum*) in the town of Brockley 6s 8d.

To William my son 6s 8d; to Walter my son 6s 8d; to Ada my daughter 13s 4d; to Elizabeth my daughter 6s 8d; to Amye my daughter 6s 8d.

To John Gridge[1] 6s 8d; to Cecily Cowper 3s 4d; to Margaret the daughter of the same Cecily 3s 4d; to Margery Stonham 20d.

To Margaret my wife all the ostilments and all my chattels belonging to my dwelling (*hospicio*); to Margaret all my lands and tenements in the town of Brockley, for the term of her life, without any impeachment of waste done to them.

After Margaret's decease my two messuages in which I live, with an adjoining pightle, now divided thus: one of the messuages with half the said pightle and half a barn, which is situated more (*magis*) to the north, that Walter my son is to have to him and his heirs, together with easement to a building called 'le Nethus' on the other messuage, with room for two cows, and to another building there called 'le Bachows',[2] for doing his baking in (*ad pastam sua' ibid' pastand'*) and for making his malt in the maltkiln there (*ad brasiu' suu' super ustrin' ibid' ustrinand'*) and brewing it there, making only as much malt as he needs to use in his household (*hospicio*), and at the best and most suitable (*congruis et optimis*) times, without committing any waste, for the term of the life of the said Walter, on condition that he pays Margaret my wife, John Tuffeld the son of Alice Tuffeld and William Galte of Brockley, my execs, 46s 8d in 3 years after my death; the other messuage, with the other half of the barn, the other half of the pightle, situated more to the south, and my piece of arable land in Brockley, in the field called 'Heyfeld', William my son to have to him and his heirs, on condition that he pays the said Margaret, John Tuffeld and William Galte, my execs, 6 marks 6s 8d in 4 years after my death.

Residue of all my goods and chattels to my execs, to sell, receive and dispose for my soul and the souls of all the faithful deceased, in good works, as they see best to please God and profit my soul.

Proved at Fornham St Martin, 19 July 1462. Admon to execs.

1   Executor (as 'Grygge') of William Flechere of Brockley (no. 473). John Gridge/Grygge may
    have been the 'IG' commemorated on the exterior of the tower of Brockley church (Blatchly and
    Northeast, *Decoding Flint Flushwork*, Brockley St Andrew).
2   See Glossary for 'nethus' and 'bachows'.

[fol. 330v]

77. JOHN COSYN the elder of CAVENHAM, 19 January 1461/62

Dated at Cavenham, 1 Edward IV; [*commendation*: to God Almighty my Creator and Saviour, and the Blessed Mary his mother]; to be buried in the churchyard of Cavenham church; to the sustentation of the common light of the said town, 2 bushels of malt; to the sustentation of the sepulchre light of the said town, 2 bushels (*modios*) of malt.

To each of the children of Thomas Cosyn my son, to each for themselves, a ewe.

To each of the children of Anne Page my daughter, to each for themselves, a ewe.

A bushel of malt to the gild of St John the Baptist of the said town.[1]

Residue of all [*my*] goods and chattels to my execs, Agnes Cosyn my wife and John Cosyn my son the elder, to dispose for my soul as seems to them [*best*] to please God and profit my soul.

Seal appended.

Proved at Kentford, 24 July 1462. Admon to John Cosyn, exec. Power reserved to Agnes, co-executrix, when she comes and if she wishes to take up admon.

1   The gild of St John the Baptist also received a bequest from William at the Mere of Cavenham
    (SROB, Baldwyne 83; Pt I, no. 387) which shows that there was also a gild of St Mary at
    Cavenham. In the fourteenth century gilds of the Trinity and St Andrew flourished in the parish
    church (*PSIA*, xix, p.178).

78. JOHN QWHELMERE of HUNDON ('Honyden'), 30 June 1462

[*Commendation*: to God &c; *no burial directions*]; to the high altar of Hundon church for my tithes forgotten 3s 4d; to each priest present at my obsequies 4d and to each clerk 2d; to each of the poor of Hundon 1d.

To the reparation of the highway before my gate 3s 4d; to the footway (*vie pedestre*) between my house and Hundon church 3s 4d; to the reparation of the same church, where most need is, 6s 8d.

To the friars of Clare 6s 8d; to the friars of Sudbury 3s 4d; to the friars of Babwell 3s 4d; to the Carmelite Friars of Cambridge (*Cant'*) 3s 4d.[1]

Residue of all [*my*] goods to my execs, to dispose as seems to them most pleasing to God and profit to my soul.

Execs: Thomas Smyth the younger and William Whelere of Hundon, to each of whom for their labour 3s 4d.

Proved at Fornham St Martin, 26 July 1462. Admon to Thomas Smyth, exec. Power reserved to William Whelere the other co-exec when he comes, if he wishes to take up admon.

1   For the friars see notes to nos 1 (Babwell and Clare), 11 (Sudbury) and 42 (Carmelites of
    Cambridge). See also note to no. 133.

[fol. 331]

79. ROBERT BURWE of HUNDON ('Honden'), 29 September 1462

[*nuncupative*]

[*Commendation*: to God &c; *no burial directions*]; to the high altar of Hundon for tithes forgotten or underpaid 6s 8d; to each priest present at my obsequies and on my burial day 4d; to each clerk present there 2d; to the poor, to pray for the health of my soul, my father's and mother's and all my benefactors' [*souls*], 3s 4d.

Residue of all my goods to Christine (*Cristine*) my wife and John my son, my execs, to dispose for the health of my soul, my father's and mother's and all my benefactors' [*souls*], as seems to them most expedient.

[*Will, of same date; name spelled* 'Borwe']

Christine (*Cristiana*) my wife to have her dwelling in my tenement, with the use and easement of all my utensils during her lifetime, that is, if she remains unmarried.

John my son to have all my tenement in Hundon, to him and his heirs, and also all the profit of the said tenement, after my decease, except as previously assigned to Christine my wife, he providing her with all her necessaries, such as food, clothing, linen and woollen, footwear and shoes (*calciatur'*, *sotulari'*), with everything else for her (*sibi spectantibus*) during her lifetime, if she remains unmarried.

John my son to have all my movable goods after Christine's decease; William my son to have half of all the things and medicines (*medicinis*) at present in my shop, with all the volumes (*copiis*) of my books;[1] to Christine my daughter 20s; to Thomas my son 20s.

The said John my son to pay a priest a competent salary to celebrate for a whole year for the health of my soul, [*my*] father's and mother's and all my benefactors' [*souls*]. To the friars of Clare 6s 8d; to the friars of Babwell 6s 8d; to the friars of Cambridge (*Cantabr'*) 3s 4d; to the friars of Sudbury 3s 4d;[2] to the gild of the Holy Trinity of Hundon 3s 4d;[3] to the gild of St John the Baptist in Chilton by Clare ('Chylton') 3s 4d.[4]

Proved at Hundon, 3 March 1462/63. Admon to execs.

---

1   Perhaps the testator was a herbalist.
2   For the friars, see notes to nos 1 (Babwell and Clare), 11 (Sudbury) and 42 (Carmelites of Cambridge). See also note to no. 133.
3   John Coggeshall the elder also made a bequest to the gild of the Holy Trinity at Hundon (SROB, Baldwyne 242; Pt I, no. 1216).
4   John Currary of Chilton (no. 380) also made a bequest to the gild of St John the Baptist at Chilton, as did John Coggeshall the elder of Hundon (see note above). According to the chantry certificate of 1548, the Norman chapel at Chilton, to the north of Clare, had been granted to the master or warden of the gild of St John the Baptist there in 1444 (*PSIA*, xii, p.35).

80. JOHN FEMNALE of Ashley ('Aschele') [*in*] the parish of SILVERLEY ('Sylvyrle') [*Cambs*],[1] 31 July 1462 and 5 February 1462/63

[*Testament*]

Dated 31 July 1462; [*commendation*: to God Almighty &c]; to be buried in the churchyard at Silverley; to the high altar of the same church 3s 4d; to the same church a vestment for a priest, with a cope of the same suit; to the high altar of Ashley 3s 4d; to the fabric of the same church 3s 4d; to the fabric of Exning ('Ixnyng') church 3s 4d; to the fabric of Lidgate church 20d.

To the fraternity of the house of Babwell 6s 8d;[2] to the Friars Preachers of Cambridge (*Cantabr'*) 3s 4d;[3] to the Carmelite Friars of the same 3s 4d.[4]

To a priest to celebrate for my soul and my parents' [*souls*] for a year, a competent stipend.

To the emendation of the ways of Ashley 40 cartloads of stone (*carrect' lapid'*).

To Joan Tryll, my goddaughter and my servant, 2 bushels of wheat and 2 bushels of barley; to my godsons and goddaughters, each of the rest of them, a bushel of wheat and a bushel of barley.

Residue [fol. 331v] of all my goods to Agnes my wife and John Femnale my son, execs, to have God before their eyes and faithfully execute and fulfil this testament, with the supervision of Thomas Aschele whom I make supervisor and advisor (*gubernator'*), he to receive for his labour in this matter 6s 8d.

[*Will*]

Dated Saturday, 5 February 1462/63.

Rose[5] my daughter to have, to her and her heirs for ever, a piece of arable land containing 2 acres, in the field called 'Volwencroft', near the cross, and ½ rood of land there, and 3 roods of land in the croft behind Ashley rectory.

John my son to have, to him and his heirs, 2 shops in Newmarket (*Novomercat'*), in 'the Bocherye' and 'Oolde Mersery',[6] and a shop in Fordham [*Cambs*], to his own use.

The shop that Richard Badwyk has in farm of me, in Newmarket, to be sold by my execs and the money from it to be disposed for my soul.

Agnes my wife to have, to her and her assigns, a piece of land in the field called 'Wolvencroft', between the lands of John Kykeby, to her own use for ever, and also all my household utensils; Agnes to have, to her and her assigns for her lifetime, all my principal tenement, with all the buildings [*but*] without the duty of repairing or sustaining them, and my tenement called 'Goystones', with all the lands, pastures and feedings belonging to it, and a piece of land lying by 'Chevele Path'[7] and 2 acres of land by 'Roundell Pytell'.

The rest of my lands, not specified above, Agnes my wife and John my son to have to their joint profit during the lifetime of Agnes; and, after her decease, John my son to have them and my principal tenement, with all the buildings, and my tenement called 'Goystones', with all the lands, pastures and feedings belonging to it, and that piece of land by 'Chevele Path' and the 2 acres of land by 'Roundell Pytell', to him and his heirs for ever; my feoffees to put him in possession when they are so required.

To the church of Cheveley [*Cambs*] 20d; to the fabric of the chapel of the Blessed Mary of Newmarket 3s 4d.[8]

To John, William and Thomas, the sons of Rose my daughter 6s 8d each and a sheep (*bident'*); to Margaret the daughter of Rose 6s 8d.

To Edward, son of Thomas Aschele, my godson, 2 ewes.

Proved at Newmarket, 4 March 1462/63. Admon to execs.

1 Witness to the will of Richard Prath of Ashley, pr. 25 March 1444 (SROB, Baldwyne 46; Pt I, no. 247).

2 See note to no. 1.

3 The Dominicans (Black Friars, or Friars Preachers) were probably established in Cambridge in the 1230s. The exact site of their house is unknown but it lay in the parish of St Andrew, just outside Barnwell gate. Within 20 years of the Black Friars' first appearance in Cambridge, that

university had become one of the very few in Europe to possess a Faculty of Theology. Soon after the arrival of the Dominicans in England the province was divided into four Visitations or Vicaries, Cambridge being the head of one. Its exact limits are unknown, but it included the seven houses of Black Friars in Norwich diocese and certain others (*VCH Cambs*, ii, pp.269–76).

4   See note to no. 42.

5   Richard Prath made bequests to 'the two daughters of John Femnale the elder'. As Rose was the only daughter mentioned in John's will, and as she received a substantial bequest, it seems likely that the other daughter had predeceased their father.

6   For the 'Bocherye' and 'Oolde Mersery' in Newmarket see May, *Newmarket: Medieval and Tudor*, p.45.

7   Presumably the path from Ashley to Cheveley, the neighbouring village.

8   As Newmarket had grown up at the edges of two parishes, chapels of ease had been built in both, St Mary in Exning, on the north, and All Saints in Woodditton (Cambs), on the south. They only became churches in their own right in the sixteenth century (St Mary's) and the nineteenth century (All Saints). See May, *Newmarket: Medieval and Tudor*, pp.13, 35.

[fol. 332]

81. JOHN NEWHAWE of GREAT HORRINGER ('Magna Hornyngserth'),[1]
16 December 1463

Dated at the said Horringer; [*commendation*: to God Almighty &c]; my body to Christian burial; to the high altar of the aforesaid church of Horringer, for my tithes and offerings underpaid 3s 4d; to the reparation of the same church 3s 4d.

To the friars of Babwell,[2] to celebrate soon after my death (*prox' sequen' obit' meum*) 3 trentals for my soul and for the souls of my parents, [*my*] friends and all my benefactors, 30s, and for another trental for the soul of Agnes my wife, immediately after her decease, 10s.

To Adam my son a heifer and 4 sheep; to Margery my daughter a heifer and 4 sheep; to Thomas my son a heifer and 4 sheep; to John my son a heifer and 4 sheep.

To Agnes my wife all my other goods and chattels in the town of the aforesaid Horringer for her support, provided she see me buried and fulfil my testament; to Agnes my tenement in which I live, together with all my arable lands and pasture in the aforesaid Horringer, for her lifetime, she keeping up repairs of the tenement sufficiently during that time.

After the decease of Agnes, the tenement, lands and pasture to remain to Adam my son at his legal age, to hold to him and his heirs for ever, he paying the said Margery, and Thomas and John his brothers, 40s each in three years after he takes possession, that is, 13s 4d to each of them each year; if Adam should die before coming of age, or while in possession, the tenement, lands and pasture to remain wholly to Thomas my son at his legal age, to hold to him and his heirs for ever, he paying Margery his sister and John his brother 40s each in two years after he enters into possession of the lands and tenement and pasture, that is, 20s to each of them each year, and in the year following those two years, 40s to my execs, to be disposed for my soul and the soul of Agnes my wife in deeds of piety.

If Thomas should die before coming of age or being in possession, the tenement, lands and pasture to remain wholly to John my son at his legal age, to hold to him and his heirs for ever, he paying £6 in money in three years after being in possession of the tenement, lands and pasture, that is, 40s to Margery in the first year and £4 to my execs in the other two years, to be disposed for the health of my soul and the souls of my parents, children and friends deceased.

If John dies before coming of age or being in possession, then, after the decease of

Agnes my wife, the tenement, lands and pasture to remain to my execs, or theirs, to receive and dispose thus: to Margery my daughter 40s and the residue to be disposed for the health of my soul and for the souls aforesaid, in the celebration of masses and other deeds of charity, as they see best to please God and profit the said souls. Execs: Agnes my wife, Thomas Newhawe my brother and Adam Rodyng[3] of the aforesaid Horringer; to each of Thomas and Adam for their labour 3s 4d.
Seal appended.
Proved in the church of Fornham [*St Martin*], 14 May 1464. Admon to execs. Seal of official appended.

[1] As John 'Neuhawe', executor of the will of John Wykham of Great Horringer, pr. December 1453 (SROB, Baldwyne 46; Pt I, no. 247); executor of John Edward of Great Horringer, pr. July 1455 (SROB, Baldwyne 172; Pt I, no. 826).
[2] See note to no. 1.
[3] Will, no. 654 below.

[fol. 332v]
82. JOHN BRAY of GAZELEY ('Gaysle'), 5 April 1464

Dated at Gazeley; [*commendation*: to God Almighty &c]; my body to Christian burial; to the high altar of the parish church of Gazeley for my tithes and offerings forgotten 12d; to the reparation of the same church 6s 8d.
The feoffees of my lands and tenements to make feoffment, after my death, to John Bray my son of Needham, of and in all my lands and tenements, which John holds of me at farm in Needham, Gazeley and Kentford, to hold them to him and his heirs for ever, except those lands called 'Sparkes Londys', and to enfeoff Joan my wife of and in all my other lands and tenements called 'Sparkes', to hold for her lifetime; after Joan's death all those lands and tenements to remain to William my son, to hold to him and his heirs; if William should die without heirs, then all the lands and tenements to remain to Katherine and Margaret our daughters; if Katherine and Margaret should die without heirs the lands and tenements to remain to the feoffees to be distributed according to the discretion of my execs.
To Thomas my son £10 in money; to Agnes my daughter 6s 8d.
Residue of all my goods to Joan my wife for her support, she to pay all my debts and see me buried and to keep my anniversary day as long as it can conveniently be done.
Execs: Joan my wife, Thomas Frere and Robert Freman of Gazeley; they to see this testament well and truly fulfilled.
Seal appended.
Proved in the parish church of Fornham St Martin, 23 June 1464. Admon to execs. Seal of official appended.

[fol. 333]
83. WILLIAM EVE of LITTLE WALDINGFIELD ('Parva Waldyngfeld'), 27 June 1462

['Ive' *in margin*] [*Commendation*: to God &c; *no burial directions*]; to the buying of a new small bell, for ringing in the tower, sufficient from my goods; to the sustentation of the gild of St Lawrence in the same town[1] 20s.
To the fabric of the church of Brent Eleigh ('Illeygth Combust') 6s 8d; to the fabric

of Milden ('Meldynge') church 6s 8d; to the fabric of Great Waldingfield church 6s 8d; to the fabric of Great Cornard ('Cornerthe Magna') church 6s 8d; to the fabric of Acton ('Aketon') church 6s 8d; to the fabric of the parish church of Eye 20s; to the fabric of the church of Occold ('Hokholt') by Eye 6s 8d; to the fabric of Redlingfield parish church 6s 8d; to the fabric of Denham church 6s 8d; to the fabric of Wickham Market church 6s 8d.[2]

To the reparation of the highway running (*extend'*) from my dwelling house to 'Holbrok' 13s 4d.

To the Friars Minor of Babwell for a trental 10s; to the Austin Friars of Clare for a trental 10s; to the Dominican Friars of Sudbury for a trental 10s; to the Carmelite Friars of Ipswich for a trental 10s.[3]

To a suitable chaplain to celebrate and pray for my soul and the souls of [*my*] parents [*and*] friends in the said church, that is, at the altar of St Mary, for 3 years, a competent stipend.

To William Eve my son an iron plate (*plate' de ferro fact'*)[4] and 2 meal-tables (*tabl' mensal'*) with a chair and a hanging ewer of latten, my chest (*arch'*) called 'le long hutche', with 6 silver spoons, a mazer bound with silver-gilt (*una' murra' cu' argento ligata' de aur'*), a best brass pot with the pan.

To Margaret my wife all the utensils of my house except those before excepted; also to my wife all my white wool now in my dwelling house, with 4 score and 16 lbs of coloured wool, blue and madder-red ('madered'), and also £40 in money.

To the prioress of Redlingfield 6s 8d to distribute among the sisters of that place.[5]

To John Apylton the elder 6s 8d.

My tenement in Newton to be kept and maintained by my execs, and out of the profits arising from it my anniversary to be kept, and the anniversaries of Margaret and Margaret[*sic*] my wives and all my benefactors, in Little Waldingfield church, in perpetuity.

To the fabric of Monks Eleigh ('Illey Monachorum') church 6s 8d.

To John Fenn my servant 3 pieces of woollen cloth, that is, one of 'mustyrdelere', another of blue colour and the other 'medly'.

[fol. 333v] Residue of all my goods to the disposition of my execs, William Eve my son and John Sake the elder of Great Waldingfield, they faithfully to pay my debts and dispose for the health of my soul, as they will answer before the High Judge on the Day of Judgement (*in die examinationis*).

Seal appended.

Proved at Sudbury, 21 July 1462. Admon to execs.

[1] John Breon also bequeathed 20s to the gild of St Lawrence in Little Waldingfield (no. 349 below).
[2] The parish churches to which these bequests were made are widely dispersed within Suffolk.
[3] For the friars see notes to nos 1 (Babwell, Clare and Ipswich) and 11 (Sudbury).
[4] See Glossary.
[5] When the priory of Benedictine nuns at Redlingfield was founded in 1120 it was endowed with the manor of Redlingfield and all its members and also with the parish church. The foundation charter states that the house was dedicated to God and St Andrew, but the *Valor* of 1535 gave the joint dedication of the Blessed Virgin and St Andrew (*VCH Suffolk*, ii, pp.83–5). See also nos 89, 126, 337, 417 and 726.

84. RICHARD GYBELON of SUDBURY,[1] 1 April 1462

['Gebelown' *in margin*] [*Commendation*: to God &c; *no burial directions*]; to the high altar of the chapel of St Peter of the said town, for tithes and offerings forgotten, 3s 4d.

The money I owe for my messuage with the garden in Sudbury, lately purchased by me, to be paid out of my goods if they will stretch that far, and Isabel my wife to have that messuage with the garden, to her and her assigns, for the term of her life, she to bear (*supportet*) all the charges due for it in the meantime; and after her decease the messuage and garden to be sold and out of the money from it, to Richard my son[2] 5 marks, and to Joan my daughter, at her marriage, 40s, if she lives that long.

To Isabel my wife all the ustensils and ostilments of my house, and the residue of all my goods, she to pay my debts and dispose as seems best to please God and benefit my soul; which Isabel I make executrix.

Proved at Sudbury, 21 July 1462. Admon to executrix.

1   John Pondere of Sudbury, fuller (no. 306 below), made a bequest for prayers for the soul of this testator.
2   Legatee (as 'Gebelon') of John Pondere (no. 306 below).

[fol. 334]
85. RICHARD KEMPE of COCKFIELD ('Cokefeld'), 20 August 1461

[*Commendation*: to God &c; *no burial directions*]; to the high altar of the said church for tithes and offerings [*forgotten*] or underpaid 12d; to the emendation of the said church a quarter of malt.

To my wife 8 marks in money, and a chamber in the north end (*parte*) of my messuage and a cow kept sufficiently, for the term of her life; also to my wife all my ostilments; my wife to have the whole messuage, if she wishes to have it, before all others, on condition that she pays my execs 8 marks and also all my debts; otherwise Thomas my son to have it, he paying the said money and my debts, by the discretion of my execs.

My execs to pay first and foremost all the debts for which I am bound, before all other persons, as I am legally bound to do.

Residue of all my goods to my execs to sell and dispose in deeds of charity as they see best to please God and profit our souls.

Execs: Thomas Forthe and Henry Chynery.

To the friars of Babwell for a trental 10s.[1]

Seal appended.

Proved at Cockfield, 20 July 1462.

1   See note to no. 1.

[fol. 334v]
86. JOHN FRYTHE of NAYLAND ('Neylond *iuxta* Stoke'), 3 July 1462

[*Same will as no. 48 above, but does not include the names of witnesses and is stated to have been proved at* Sudbury, 21 July 1462.]

[fol. 335]

87. JOHN NEWMAN the elder of LAVENHAM,[1] 21 March 1463/64

[*Commendation*: to God &c]; to be buried in the churchyard of Lavenham church; to the high altar of the same church for my tithes and offerings unpaid 20s; to the parish chaplain of the same church, being present at my obsequies, 3s 4d; to each other chaplain of the said town of Lavenham present at my obsequies 20d; to each officiating clerk (*clerico offic'*) of the town of Lavenham present at my obsequies 12d.

A suitable chaplain to celebrate for my soul, and for the souls for whom I am bound, in Lavenham parish church, for a period of 7 years after my death, taking for his salary a reasonable stipend. To be distributed among the poor of Lavenham, for a period of 7 years, 12d weekly, to pray for my soul and for the souls of all the faithful departed.

To the emendation of the church of Great Cornard ('Cornerth Magna') 10 marks; to the emendation of the church of Little Cornard ('Cornerth Parva') 20s.

To the friars of the convent of Colchester 40s; to the friars of the convent of Sudbury 40s; to the friars of the convent of Clare 40s; to the friars of the convent of Babwell 40s;[2] to the three orders of friars of the conventual houses of Ipswich ('Epeswiche') 20s each.[3]

£40 to be disposed in emending the highways in and around the town of Lavenham, where greatest need is.

To each of my godsons and goddaughters 12d.

To John Newman my son £40; and to John my whole tenement in the town of Lavenham, to hold to him and his heirs for ever.

To Joan Sterne [*my*] servant a brass pot and a bed; and to Joan a 'shoppe' in the High Street (*alta strat'*) in (*inter*) the tenement called 'Pereshows', for her lifetime, if she remain a widow and unmarried; otherwise, the tenement called 'Pereshows' to be disposed by my exec for an almshouse[4] for my soul to be prayed for, and the souls of those for whom I am bound.

Residue of my goods to my exec, to dispose in deeds of charity for my soul and the souls for whom I am bound, as seems best to please God and profit my soul.

Exec: John Newman my son, of Lavenham, he to execute and faithfully perform this testament.

Seal appended.

Proved in the parish church of Fornham [*St Martin*], 9 April 1464. Admon to John Newman, exec.

[1] Executor of John Swayn of Lavenham, will pr. May 1441 (SROB, Baldwyne 30; Pt I, no. 164); executor of John Grygge of Lavenham, will pr. October 1446 (SROB, Baldwyne 74; Pt I, no. 350); supervisor of John Perle of Lavenham, will pr. 28 March 1458 (SROB, Baldwyne 215; Pt I, no. 1073); executor of Andrew Grygges of Lavenham (no. 11 above).

[2] For the friars see notes to nos 1 (Babwell and Clare), 11 (Sudbury) and 38 (Colchester).

[3] There were houses of Carmelite, Dominican and Franciscan friars at Ipswich; see notes to nos 1 and 50.

[4] A bequest to establish a small almshouse in Lavenham.

[fol. 335v]

88. SIMON CUSTE of GREAT HORRINGER ('Magna Horniygserthe'), 12 April 1464

Dated at Great Horringer; [*commendation*: to God Almighty &c]; my body to Christian burial; to the high altar of Great Horringer for my tithes and offerings forgotten or underpaid, and for the health of my soul, 3s 4d.

To the friars of Babwell, to celebrate a trental of St Gregory for my soul, 10s.[1]

To the lights burning about the sepulchre of Our Lord in the church of Great Horringer 3s 4d; to 'le porche' of the same church, to be newly made, 6s 8d.

To the lights burning about the sepulchre of Our Lord in the church of Little Horringer ('Parva Hornyngesherth') 3s 4d.

To the tower of the monastery of Bury St Edmunds, being newly built, 6s 8d;[2] to Simon Ryngsted, monk of the same monastery, 6s 8d; to the sustentation of the gild of the Holy Name of Jesu, held in the church of the Blessed Mary of Bury St Edmunds, 13s 4d.[3]

To Alice my daughter 2 heifers.

Residue of all my goods and chattels to my execs, to sell, receive and distribute for my soul and the souls for whom I am bound, and the souls of all the faithful departed, in the celebration of masses and other deeds of charity, as they see best to please God and profit my soul.

Execs: John Brycete and William Edward of Great Horringer; to John, for his labour, 3s 4d, and to William, for his labour, 2s.

Seal appended.

Proved at Fornham [*St Martin*], 14 May 1464. Admon to execs. Seal [*of official*] appended.

1   See note to no. 1.
2   The west tower of Bury abbey fell in 1430–31 and was rebuilt during the period 1435–65. See Whittingham, *Bury St Edmunds Abbey*, pp.10–11. Bequests to the Benedictine abbey of Bury St Edmunds are fairly uncommon at this period. William Hert of Elmswell (no. 519) made a bequest to the glazing of the refectory and Benedict Othoo (no. 772) to the 'new fabric of the monastery'.
3   Although there were many gilds in Bury St Edmunds this is the only bequest to any of them in Baldwyne Pt II. Other bequests to the gild of the Holy Name of Jesus in Bury are noted in *PSIA*, xii, p.75 and *PSIA*, xix, p.176.

[fol. 336; OW 24/145 (*testament only*); OW 24/Z/1 (*will only*)]

89. WILLIAM GRENE of CREETING ('Cretyng') ST PETER,[1] 8 November 1462

Dated Monday after the feast of All Saints; [*commendation*: to God &c]; to be buried in the church of Creeting St Peter; to the high altar of the church there, for tithes forgotten, 20s; to the emendation of the church there £10, at the discretion of my execs.[2]

To Elizabeth Crane, nun in Bruisyard ('Bresyerd'), 20s, and to the convent there 20s;[3] to the convent of Friars Minor of Ipswich (*Gippewic*) 20s; to the convent of Carmelite Friars there 13s 4d; to the convent of Friars Preachers 13s 4d;[4] to the convent of nuns of Redlingfield 13s 4d;[5] to the convent of Flixton 13s 4d;[6] to the convent of Friars Minor of Colchester 20s.[7]

To the emendation of the church of Earl Stonham ('Stonham Comitis') 20s; to the rector there for forgotten tithes 40d.

To Robert Bakere, John Rowte, John Lucas, Thomas Chychele, Thomas Maunger, Rose Dunche, and Anne Burgeys, my servants, a cow each.

To Marg' Hoxon 10s;[8] to Agnes Sparue 13s 4d.

To William Flegge and the son of John Coole, my godsons, 10s each.

To William Hotoft, the son of Thomas Hotoft, 6s 8d.

To William Draper and Thomas Gowty a coomb of wheat each.

To William Baldre, William Padnale, William Wynstede, John Webbere, William Dunche, Robert Cook and Thomas Tilere, my godsons, 40d each.

To the churches of Creeting St Mary, Creeting All Saints, Creeting St Olave and to the church of Badley, 6s 8d each; to the rector of St Olave 40d.

To William Cook, the son of William Cook of Creeting, 6s 8d; to Thomas Aleyn, clerk, 20s; to Edmund Bolton 20s; to William Hotoft 20s.

To the emendation and reparation of a bridge in Earl Stonham called 'Ladyesbredge' 10s, when it is carried out; to the emendation and reparation of a way leading from 'Cretyng Grene' towards 'Pulford', when it is carried out [no sum].

To each priest present at my obsequies 6d, to each clerk 2d and to each poor person 1d.

A suitable priest to go to Rome immediately after my death, and to stay there until he has well and truly completed the stations[9] and to pray there for my soul and my parents' [souls]; and a pilgrim to go to the tomb of St James in Compostella.[10]

To Anne my wife[11] all my household utensils to her own use.

My chattels, that is, sheep, oxen, horses, animals and grain, to be sold and my execs to have half of the money from them, and Anne my wife to have the other half, to dispose for my soul and the souls of my parents.

Residue of all my goods to my execs to dispose as above.

Execs: Anne my wife, if she remains unmarried, John Andrew of Baylham ('Beylham'), John Chapman of Shotley ('Schotley') and Thomas Aldows.

Supervisor: William Harlyston of Denham.

Seal appended.

[fol. 336v]

[*Will, of same date,* 2 Edward IV]

Immediately after my death, all my lands and tenements, apart from my tenement called 'Derboughtys', to be sold by my execs, as quickly as possible, and of the money from them, my execs to have one half and Anne my wife the other, to dispose for my soul and my parents' and my friends' [souls]; Anne my wife to have the tenement 'Derboughtys' for term of her life and the reversion of it to be sold by my execs and the money disposed by them in pious uses, alms and other deeds of charity.

My feoffees in my tenement called 'Newtones' in Gipping to enfeoff Robert Grene, my brother, of it, he to hold it to him and his heirs male; if he should die without male heirs, the tenement to be sold by my execs and disposed as above; provided always that, if Robert or any of his male heirs make feoffment or alienation of any of the said lands and tenements, it shall be lawful for my feoffees to re-enter those lands and tenements, and lands and tenements to be sold by my execs; and also provided that my feoffees shall not deliver any estate in lands and tenements to Robert until he provide sufficient security to my execs to make a lease to Nicholas Gernoun, now the farmer there, for a period of three years after the feast of St

Michael last past, and to permit Margaret Tyrell[12] and her heirs to have preference in the sale of the tenement when the time comes for it.

Richard Weston to have £20 [*and*] John Weston to have £20, provided that Richard Weston and his heirs [*are allowed to*] peacefully occupy a tenement in Colchester, in the parish of All Saints, without claim or obstruction by his brother John, as appears in the will of the father of John and Richard, and then John to have the £20 out of my goods when he reaches full age; otherwise, Richard to have the £20 assigned to John as well, when he comes to full age; also Anne Weston to have £20 at her marriage; these provided that the said children will be ruled by my execs.[13]

John Andrew of Baylham to have my tenement called 'Aldamys', with a meadow lately Richard Kebyll's and a little grove (*grovetto*) lately Master John's, provided that he does not occupy the tenement until the feast of St Michael the Archangel next; which tenement, meadow and little grove I have sold to the said John [*Andrew*] for 130 marks.

John Chapman of Shotley ('Schotle') to have preference in the sale of my tenement called 'Garneys and Lucas' in Wetheringsett and Brockford.

Lawrence Carleton, my servant, to have an annual pension of 13s 4d for his lifetime. I will have two stones of marble ('marbyll'),[14] one over my parents[15] and the other over me.

Thomas Aldhows to have his remuneration for his continuous service to me for many years, by the advice of my execs, as seems necessary to them, and with the agreement of the said Thomas.

Proved 25 June 1463. Admon to execs. Seal of official appended.

[*See also no. 44 above.*]

---

1   Supervisor of Robert Grene of Saxham Street, hamlet of Thorney, in Stowmarket, will pr. July 1457 (SROB, Baldwyne 183; Pt I, no. 882).

2   Grene must have been wealthy as this is a substantial bequest for repairs to the church.

3   In 1366 an earlier chantry or college at Bruisyard was surrendered for the use of an abbess and sisters belonging to the order of Nuns Minoresses or Sisters of St Clare. In 1390 the abbey acquired various plots of land in Bruisyard and adjacent parishes, and elsewhere (*VCH Suffolk*, ii, pp.131–2). Elizabeth Crane was still in the convent in 1481 (*VCH*, p.132, n.18).

4   For the friars of Ipswich see notes to nos 1 (Friars Minor and Carmelites) and 50 (Preachers).

5   See note to no. 83.

6   In 1258 an Austin nunnery was founded at Flixton in honour of the Blessed Virgin and St Katherine. The number of nuns was limited by the founders to 18, in addition to a prioress (*VCH Suffolk*, ii, pp.115–17).

7   See note to no. 38.

8   Could be Margaret or Margery Hoxon.

9   In this context, a 'station' was 'the appointed visitaton of some church, altar, shrine or other like ecclesiastic locale, for pious purposes, and with certain spiritual graces annexed'. According to Francino, an Italian writing in the late sixteenth century, there were some 389 stations celebrated throughout the city of Rome on set days (Rossetti, 'Stacyons of Rome', pp.xxi, xxii). See Introduction, under *Indulgences*. William Grene's father, Thomas, had also requested a pilgrimage to Rome (see note below).

10   The famous pilgrimage shrine of Santiago de Compostella, in north-western Spain. See Introduction, under *Indulgences*, and also Storrs, *Jacobean Pilgrims from England to St James of Compostella*.

11   'Anne Grene, wife of William Grene' was a legatee of Alice Swan of Creeting St Peter, widow, will pr. March 1458/59 (SROB, Baldwyne 211; Pt I, no. 1049).

12   A member of the Tyrrell family of Gipping. See Horrox, *Richard III: A Study in Service*, p.80.

13   The reference to the will of the father of John and Richard Weston, and the large bequests of

£20 each to John, Richard and Anne Weston suggest that they were the children of Anne Grene, current wife of the testator, by a former husband surnamed Weston.

14   See Glossary.
15   Thomas and Isabel Grene of Creeting St Peter. In his will, pr. November 1439, Thomas Grene appointed as executors his wife Isabel, his son William and John Lenge (SROB, Baldwyne 3; Pt I, no. 20).

[fol. 337]

90. ROBERT LEGAT of RATTLESDEN ('Ratlesden'),[1] 3 March 1461/62

[*Commendation*: to God &c; *no burial directions*].

To the Carmelite Friars of Ipswich (*Gipwic'*), to pray for my soul, 2s; to the friars of Clare, in the same way, 2s.[2]

To the emendation of the highway about 'Stonhamys' 6s 8d; to be distributed among the poor of the towns of Rattlesden, Buxhall and Drinkstone 40s.

To Joan[3] my wife my lands and tenements in the town of Rattlesden, as long as she remains unmarried; if she re-marries the lands and tenements to be sold for the best price possible and the money disposed in the celebration of masses, in alms for the poor and in other charitable deeds, for the health of my soul and the souls of my parents and benefactors and all the faithful at rest in Christ.

Joan my wife to have a meadow with an acre of land in Woolpit ('Wulpyt') until Alice my daughter is of the age of 18, and then the meadow and land to be sold, and out of the proceeds Alice to have £10 at her marriage; the rest of the money from them to be disposed in pious uses for the health of my soul; if Alice should die before that time, the meadow and acre of land to be sold without delay and disposed for the health of my soul in charitable deeds.

Any residue of all my goods to Joan my wife.

Execs: Joan my wife and Robert Gage, they, having God before their eyes, faithfully to execute and fulfil this testament; Robert having 6s 8d for his labour.

Proved at Fornham [*St Martin*], 20 August 1463. Admon to execs.

1   Executor and son-in-law of Joan Boleman of Rattlesden, will pr. April 1440 (SROB, Baldwyne 27; Pt I, no. 146).
2   For the Carmelite Friars of Ipswich and the friars of Clare see notes to no. 1.
3   The executors of Joan Boleman's will were named as 'Robert Legat and Alice my daughter, his wife', so presumably Alice had since died.

91. JOHN COPCY of COWLINGE ('Cowlynge'), 4 October 1463

['Copsy' *in margin*] [*Commendation*: to God &c; *no burial directions*]; to the making of the torches of Cowlinge 6s 8d.

'Sclechys Crofte' to be sold by my execs immediately after my decease and then my execs to provide a suitable and honest priest to celebrate in the said church for my soul and the souls of my parents, according to the amount (*ratu'*) of money received for the croft.

To my wife all my utensils and half my grain and chattels (*catalloru'*).

To each of my children 20s.

My wife to have, for term of her life if she remains unmarried, all my lands and tenements not otherwise bequeathed in this testament, she committing no waste and providing always that she repairs all the said lands and tenements well and suffi-ciently with all reparations for the whole term of her life; if she should marry at any time after my decease, John Copsy my son to have all the said lands and tenements, to him and his heirs, immediately after his mother marries, without any obstruction or deceit [*on the part*] of his mother or anyone in her name.

Residue of all my goods to Nicholas Bedford of Little Thurlow ('Parva Thyrlowe') and Thomas Mastyr of Little Bradley ('Bradle Parva'), my execs, to dispose as seems to them best to please God and profit my soul.

Proved at Stradishall ('Strad'), 13 October 1463. Admon to Thomas Mastyr, exec. Power reserved to Nicholas Bedford, the other exec, when he comes, if he wishes to take up admon.

[fol. 337v]

92. JOHN PUSKE of KERSEY,[1] 10 October 1463

[*Commendation*: to God &c; *no burial directions*]; to the high altar of Kersey church for my tithes and offerings forgotten 6s 8d.

To Alice my wife 20 marks in money; to Alice my house with my utensils, with a croft called 'Sere Robertys Crofte' and with a meadow in 'Levenhedge' belonging to the said house, for term of her life, if she remain sole, otherwise not so; similarly with the other lands in 'Levenhedche' and 'Wenysfeld', except [*certain*] lands in 'Levenhedche' and 'Wenysfeld' that are to be reserved and kept (*preservantur et custodiantur*) in order that there might be distributed every Sunday such alms as come to the value of the farm [*of the lands*], for ever; after the decease of Alice, the house to be sold and disposed by my execs, as best to profit the health of [*my*] soul and Alice's.

Sir Edmund Freman to celebrate divine service for me and all my benefactors and for the souls of all the faithful departed, for 4 years in the said church.

My tenement to be for the keeping of my obit and that of my father,[2] for ever.

To the painting of the candlebeam ('le candelbem') in the said church 15 marks.

Residue of all my goods to my execs, they faithfully to execute my testament and dispose for the health of my soul as seems most expedient by their discretion.

Execs: Alice my wife, Sir Edmund Freman and John Cook the elder.

Supervisor: John Wareyn the elder.

Proved at Bildeston ('Bylston'), 15 November 1463. Admon to Edmund Freman and John Cook the elder, execs.

1 Witness of the will of John Rodelond the elder of Kersey, dated October 1459 (SROB, Baldwyne 248; Pt I, no. 1245).
2 James Pusk of Kersey, will pr. July 1447 (SROB, Baldwyne 85; Pt I, no. 392); John Puske was his executor.

[fol. 338]

93. JOHN [*BUNNE*] of LITTLE WHELNETHAM,[1] 29 December 1462

['Bunne' *appears only in the margin.*] In peril of death (*videns mihi periculum mortis venire*); [*commendation*: to God &c; *no burial directions*]; to the high altar there 12d; to the altar of St Mary of Great Whelnetham 4d; to the altar of St Peter of Nowton 4d.

To Matilda my wife my messuage with 3 acres of land, purchased by me, for her whole lifetime; and after her decease the messuage and land to remain to John my son and his heirs; if John dies without children the messuage and 3 acres to be sold by the advice of my execs in the best manner possible.

My execs to provide a suitable priest to celebrate for a whole year in Little Whelnetham church, for my soul and for my parents' souls, and for those for whom I am bound to pray, he taking for his stipend 8 marks, to be paid out of my lands and tenements aforesaid.

To Isabel, Joan, Alice and Agnes, my daughters, 4 marks, to be paid to them by equal portions by my execs, if it pleases God so to dispose.

To John Mannyng of the aforesaid Whelnetham ('Qwelnetham') 3s 4d; to Thomas Ladyman 3s 4d;[2] to each of my godchildren 4d.

To the convent of St Francis of Babwell 5 bushels of barley.[3]

To Lucy Angold a ewe and to John Rawlyn a ewe.

To Matilda my wife all the necessaries and utensils belonging to my house.

All my goods not bequeathed in this testament to the disposition of my execs, Matilda my wife, John Mannyng and Thomas Ladyman, they to pay all my debts and implement this present testament in the best way they know to please God, as they will answer before the High Judge.

Proved at Fornham [*St*] Martin, 7 February 1462/63. Admon to execs.

1   Executor of Isabel Bunne of Little Whelnetham, probate March 1450/51 (SROB, Baldwyne 112; Pt I, no. 525); executor of Simon Balley of Little Whelnetham (no. 130 below).
2   Executor of Isabel Bunne (Pt I, no. 525); executor of Simon Balley (no. 130 below); his will no. 413 below.
3   See note to no. 1.

[fol. 338v]
94. AGNES JENEWS of EYE, 16 December 1463

Of Eye in the diocese of Norwich; [*commendation*: to God &c; *no burial directions*]; the will of John Jenews my late husband[1] to be properly fulfilled.

To the high altar of the same church for my tithes forgotten 3s 4d; to the fraternity of the gild of St Peter of Eye 3s 4d;[2] to the fraternity of the gild of St Mary of Eye 3s 4d.[3]

To each of my godsons 4 bushels of barley.

To Joan the daughter of Robert Jenews 4 bushels of barley; to Agnes the daughter of the said Robert my beads with the gold ring; to the said Agnes a heifer.[4]

To the emendation and reparation of Grundisburgh ('Growndysburgh') church 40s; to the emendation of Eye church 20s; to the emendation of 'Lamesheth' bridge 6s 8d;[5] to the poor of the 'Spetyll' 20d;[6] to each priest present at my obsequies 4d and to each clerk 1d; to the friars of Ipswich (*Gippywic'*), to celebrate a trental of St Gregory, 10s;[7] to the altar of St Mary of Eye a candlestick.

To Alice my daughter 6s 8d; to William the son of the said Alice 3s 4d; to Margaret and Alice the daughters of the said Alice 20d each.

To an honest priest to celebrate divine office in Eye church 8 marks.

Residue of all my goods to the disposition of Robert Jenews,[8] Alice Turnore my daughter, Robert Saxcy and John Saxci, my execs, to carry out the above for my soul and the souls for whom I am bound, as they see [*best*] to please God and profit the health of my soul.

Proved at Eye, 2 June 1463[*sic*]. Admon to execs.

1   Will pr. 26 January 1451/52 (SROB, Baldwyne 133; Pt I, no. 624).
2   For other bequests to the gild of St Peter at Eye see note to no. 2.

3   For other bequests to the gild of the Blessed Mary, or of St Mary, at Eye see note to no. 2.
4   Although referred to as the daughters of Robert Jenews, it is probable that Joan and Agnes were the daughters of Robert Turnour, Agnes Jenews's son by an earlier marriage (see his will, no. 405).
5   Her husband also made a bequest to repairs of Lambseth bridge, which is to the north-west of the town of Eye, in Lambseth Street, the road leading out of the town to the north. Robert Hardyng (no. 457) bequeathed 30 cartloads of clay to the repairs of 'Lamset way'. William Goldyng (no. 2) owned a close with a garden at Lambseth Bridge.
6   See note to no. 2.
7   There were three houses of friars at Ipswich: see notes to nos 1 (Franciscans and Carmelites) and 50 (Dominicans).
8   Probably Robert Turnour, her son (see note to his will, no. 405).

95. JOHN PATON of DRINKSTONE ('Drenkston'), 2 May 1463

[*Commendation*: to God &c; *no burial directions*]; to the high altar of Drinkstone a coomb of malt; to the gild of the Holy Trinity there 10s;[1] to the gild of St John there 10s.[2]

To each of my sons and daughters, when my debts have been paid, [*no sum*].

To Alice my wife[3] all my goods, she to pay all my debts and implement my testament.

To the friars of Babwell, to celebrate a trental of St Gregory for my soul, 10s.[4]

Residue of all my goods to my execs to dispose for the health of my soul, as seems to them best to please God and profit my soul.

Execs: Alice my wife, Robert Gerveys and Robert Kobold.

Proved at Drinkstone, 6 October 1463. Admon to execs.

1   For other bequests to the gild of the Holy Trinity of Drinkstone see nos 19 and 205.
2   Morley refers to a gild of St James at Drinkstone, known to be in existence in 1503 (*PSIA*, xix, p.181), but no other mention of the gild of St John at Drinkstone has been found.
3   Will, no. 336.
4   See note to no. 1.

[fol. 339]

96. THOMAS CROS of EDWARDSTONE ('Edwardeston'), 30 September 1462

['Crosse' *in margin*] [*Commendation*: to Almighty God and the Blessed Mary his mother]; dated the last day of September and the feast of St Jerome, priest, 1462; to be buried in the parish church, in the new aisle ('ylda'), before the altar made there; to the high altar of the same church, for my offerings and tithes forgotten and not well paid, 6s 8d; to the said church, for a parclose ('parclos') to be newly made there, £3 and more if necessary.

To each priest coming to my obsequies and being there 4d; to each greater clerk (*clerico maiori*) 2d; to each lesser clerk (*clerico minori*) 1d.

To the friars of Clare, to celebrate a trental of masses, 10s;[1] to the friars of Sudbury in the same way 10s;[2] to each poor man coming to my burial 1d.

To Thomas Cros my godson, the son of William Cros, a black 'howyd' cow.

I bequeath my two messuages, situated together in the said town, for keeping my anniversary annually for ever.

Residue of my goods to my execs to dispose in what seems to be the most expedient way for the health of my soul.

Execs: William Cros my son and John Portere.

Witnesses: William Bogeys, Alan Wrygthte[*sic*], John Englysche the elder and others.

Proved at Bildeston ('Bylston'), 28 September 1463. Admon to execs.

1   See note to no. 1.
2   See note to no. 11.

97. JOHN GAMELYN of POLSTEAD ('Polstede'), 5 May 1462

In fear of death (*timens mortis periculu'*); [*commendation*: to God &c; *no burial directions*]; to the high altar of the church of the Blessed Mary of Polstead 20d; to the painting of the image of St Mary the Virgin half a quarter of malt in ale (*in servicia*) [*and*] a bushel (*modium*) of wheat in bread (*in panibus*);[1] to the high altar of Layham ('Leyham') 20d; to the bells of Layham 20d.

To Matilda my wife my dwelling-house in Polstead for term of her life, with the utensils belonging [*thereto*].

To each of the children of Robert Gamelyn a lamb.

Residue of all my goods to Robert Gamelyn my son, exec, to dispose for me and [*my*] soul as he would I would do for him in like case.

Proved at Bildeston ('Bylston'), 28 September 1463. Admon to exec.

1   Perhaps the ale and bread were to be sold and the proceeds put towards the cost of painting the image.

98. JOHN JACOB of SUDBURY, 28 September 1463[1] [*probate only*]

Proved at Sudbury. Admon to William Jacob, exec.[2]

1   ?Related to William Jacob the elder of Sudbury, will pr. November 1450 (SROB, Baldwyne 124; Pt I, no. 578).
2   ?Will pr. September 1476 (SROB, Hervye 67); William Jacob the younger was executor to William Jacob the elder of Sudbury.

[fol. 339v]

99. ROBERT PERMAN of Aldersfield[1] ('Alvysfeld') in WICKHAMBROOK, 19 September 1463

[*Commendation*: to God &c; *no burial directions*]; to the high altar there 20d.

To Thomas Perman my son a cow.

Katherine Perman my wife to have and possess all my houses, lands and tenements for term of her life.

Residue of all my goods and chattels to the disposition of Simon Dalham of Hundon and Katherine Perman my wife for the paying of my debts and keeping my children and doing other deeds of charity for my soul, my parents', friends' and benefactors' souls, as best they can to please God and profit our souls.

Proved at Clare, 28 September 1463. Admon to Simon Dalham, exec. Power reserved to Katherine, the other co-exec, when she comes and if she wish to take up admon. [*The whole of the above struck through, and in margin*: Cancelled because written below at end of register, with witnesses examined (*cu' testibus examinatis*); *see no. 808*.]

1   Aldersfield was a hamlet of Wickhambrook; Aldersfield Hall lies 1½ miles north-east of Wickhambrook church.

100. JOAN HEGGEMAN of GLEMSFORD, 26 May 1461

['Hedgeman' *in margin*] Of Glemsford in the diocese of Norwich; [*commendation*: to God Almighty &c; *no burial directions*]; I beg my execs, in God's name, to pay all my debts that I owe.

For a trental of St Gregory to be said for my soul, with all possible haste after my death, 10s.

A suitable chaplain to celebrate for my soul and for the soul of John Hedgeman, my late husband,[1] and for the souls of all my parents, friends and benefactors, for whom I am most bound, for a whole year in Glemsford church, taking for his salary reasonably what he and my execs can agree.

To each priest present at my obsequies and at mass on my burial day 4d; to each clerk there, saying divine service on the same occasion, 2d.

Residue of all my goods to the disposition of my execs, they to dispose them in deeds of piety for the health of my soul and as they see most to the glory of God and best for my salvation (*mei salvacionem melius expedire*).

Execs: John Hedgeman[2] and Thomas Hedgeman[3] my sons, they to fulfil all the foregoing in the best way they can, to please God and profit my soul.

Proved at Fornham [*St*] Martin, 7 October 1463. Admon to John Hedgeman, exec. Power reserved to Thomas Heggeman, the other exec, when he comes and if he wishes to take up admon.

1. Will of John Hedgeman the elder of Glemsford pr. July 1460 (SROB, Baldwyne 249; Pt I, no. 1246); Joan had been executrix of her husband's will.
2. Legatee of his father John.
3. Legatee and executor of his father John.

[fol. 340]

101. WILLIAM HARE of PAKENHAM,[1] 28 July 1462

Dated at Pakenham; [*commendation*: to God Almighty &c]; to be buried in the churchyard of the church of the Blessed Mary of Pakenham, next to the grave of Elizabeth my late wife; to the high altar of the said church for tithes forgotten 2s; to the reparations of Pakenham church, at the disposition of my execs, 6s 8d.

For a trental to be celebrated for my soul, to the friars of Babwell, 10s;[2] to the friars of the two houses of Thetford, to be equally disposed, 5s.[3]

After my decease a suitable priest to celebrate in Pakenham church for a whole year, and he to have for his salary 8 marks and a gown.

Margaret my wife to have and enjoy my messuage in Pakenham, formerly Richard Hede's, with all the lands and tenements, rents and services [*belonging to it*], except a piece of meadow called 'le Pangyll', lately sold by me to Robert Clerk of Pakenham, to her and her heirs, to hold of the chief lords of the fee by due service and custom, for ever. My feoffees of and in the messuage and lands to transfer legal and peaceful possession of them to Margaret, and to fulfil my testament in all ways. Residue of all my goods to Margaret my wife, executrix.

Execs: Margaret my wife, John Fyssh of Stowlangtoft ('Stokelangtote') and Richard Brook of Pakenham, they to dispose for the health of my soul and the souls of my benefactors, as they will answer before the High Judge on the Day of Judgement; to the others of my execs, for their labour, 4s equally between them.

Seal appended.

Proved at Fornham [*St Martin*], 16 April 1464. Admon to Margaret Hare, executrix. Power reserved to John Fyssh of Stowlangtoft and Richard Brook, the other co-execs, when they come and if they wish to take up admon. Seal of official appended.

¹ Executor of William Glaswrygh of Pakenham, probate November 1457 (SROB, Baldwyne 183; Pt I, no. 887); executor of Thomas Fyston of Pakenham, probate November 1454 (SROB, Baldwyne 205; Pt I, no. 1017).
² See note to no. 1.
³ For the friars of Thetford see notes to nos 68 (Dominicans – the 'Old House') and 69 (Augustinians – the 'New House').

102. ED'D FYSHE of WESTHORPE, *?*1463 [*English*]

[*Date written*: Mᶦcccclxxx–xxxiij; *no day or month given*.] Of Westhorpe in the diocese of Norwich; to be buried in the churchyard at Westhorpe; to the high altar of the said church, for my tithes and offerings by me not paid or too little done, 20d; to an altar cloth 40d.

To Elizabeth ('Elsabt') my daughter 5 marks; to Eleanor 5 marks; to my two sons, William and Walter, all my land and tenements, [*they*] to see my two daughters discharged of their money.

[fol. 340v] To the reparation of the highways within the precincts of the town 6s 8d. If it chance one sister to die afore the other, she that lives to receive the other's part; if it chance one of my sons dies before the other, he that lives to have the other's part; if they both die, it shall remain to the next of my 'stock'.

I will and charge my childer, of my *?*soliciting ('silyssi…'), to see this my will and testament fulfilled.

Execs: Walter and William my sons.

Witnesses: William Clare, clerk, and John Lynke, with others.

[*No probate recorded.*]

[fol. 341]
103. RICHARD ABELL of STOWMARKET,¹ 11 January 1461 [*?new style*]

Dated Monday after the feast of the Epiphany; to be buried in the churchyard of the church of the Blessed Peter of Stowmarket ('Stowe'); to the high altar of the church 3s 4d; for a trental of St Gregory 10s; for a chaplain to celebrate for my soul and the souls of all my benefactors in the said church 8 marks.

My meadow at 'Dagworth Bregge' to be sold, with my land at 'Newmannys', to pay my debts [*and*] perform my will.

To Margaret my wife all my tenement and all the ostilments in the said tenement and all my chattels (*catall'*), to her and her assigns; to Margaret a pasture called 'le Teyntor Clos' in the same way, and my meadow at 'Sondyll'.

To the maintenance (*subsidium*) of the mass of the Blessed Mary in the said church 20d, to be received from the said meadow called 'Sondyll', for ever.

To John my son two shops near the church gate, to him and his assigns.

Execs: Margaret my wife, Edward Adgor and Robert Mylys.

Proved at Stowe, 18 September 1461. Admon to execs.

¹ *?*Executor of John Cook of Combs, probate April 1446 (SROB, Baldwyne 90; Pt I, no. 410).

104. JOHN ERNALD of POLSTEAD ('Polsted'), 13 July 1461

Seeing the peril of death drawing near to me (*videns m'mortis periculu' imminere*); to be buried in the sanctuary where God disposes me to die.

To Agnes my wife all my freehold holding (*libera'tenura'*), both built upon (*edificat'*) and not built upon, to possess and occupy all her lifetime, and after her decease it to revert to Joan my daughter and her heirs; if Joan should die without heirs, then my freehold holding to be sold and disposed for [*my*] soul and the souls of my friends. Agnes my wife to have all the utensils of my house.

Residue of all my goods to my execs, they to have God before their eyes and faithfully execute and fulfil this testament.

Execs: Agnes my wife and William Syward of Stoke by Nayland ('Stokeneylond'). Seal appended.

Proved at Bildeston ('Bilston'), 22 September 1461. Admon to execs.

105. JOHN STURDY of KEDINGTON ('Kedyton'),[1] 24 September 1461
[*probate only*]

Proved at Clare. Admon to Stephen Smethe, exec. Power reserved to Beatrice, wife of the deceased, and John Fole, execs, when they come.

[1] John Sturdy the elder was witness to the will of Herry Folky of Kedington, pr. September 1457 (SROB, Baldwyne 241; Pt I, no. 1213).

106. WILLIAM PEDDERE of STOKE [BY CLARE], 24 September 1461
[*probate only*]

Proved at Clare. Admon to John Peddere and Thomas Wever, execs.

[fol. 341v]
107. JOHN STALHAM the elder of MILDENHALL, 10 April 1459

Dated at Mildenhall, 37 Henry VI; to be buried in Mildenhall churchyard; to the high altar of the same church for my tithes and offerings forgotten and withheld, in exoneration of my soul, 6s 8d. My debts which I of right owe to anyone to be paid as soon as possible after my burial; my funeral expenses to be met according to the best direction and discretion of my execs, without worldly pomp and vain glory.

To the building (*fabricac'*) of the said church 6s 8d; to the gild of St Katherine of the said town 12d;[1] to the gild of St George of the same town 12d;[2] to the gild of St John the Baptist of the said town 12d.[3]

To the convent of Friars Minor of Babwell 3s 4d;[4] to the convent of nuns of Thetford 6s 8d; to the convent of Friars Preachers of Thetford 20d.[5]

To Chadenhalke[*sic*] the wife of William Chadenhalke of Mildenhall 13s 4d; to Joan the daughter of the said William, my goddaughter, 6s 8d.

To Christian Stalham, daughter of the late John Stalham my brother, of Mildenhall, 6s 8d;[6] to Joan Style 6s 8d; to John Stalham of Haverhill ('Haverylle') my son 20s; to William Stalham of the city of London 20s; to Joan, the relict of the late John Stalham my brother, 20s.[7]

To the wife of Holdeman (*uxori Holdeman*) of Chippenham [*Cambs*], my goddaughter, 20d; to John Halse my godson 12d; to John Chadenhalke my godson 3s 4d.

62

[*Will*]

A suitable priest to celebrate in the church of the glorious Virgin Mary of Mildenhall for a whole year, for my soul and the souls of Margery, Katherine, Alice and Katherine, my wives,[8] and the souls of my parents, friends and benefactors, and all the faithful departed, taking for his stipend 8 marks, and beginning as soon as my execs can receive the money from my debts and chattels; and afterwards 9 marks 6s 8d to be distributed among the poor of Mildenhall in greatest need, according to the discretion of my execs, as they see most expedient.

Residue of all my goods, debts and chattels, whatsoever and wherever they may be, after my debts have been paid and my burial done, and all my legacies fulfilled, wholly to my execs to dispose for my soul, as seems to them best to please God and profit the health of my soul, and as they would have me do for their souls in like case.

Execs: John Austyn, principal exec, John Stalham my son of Haverhill, tanner,[9] and Thomas Martyn, chaplain to the said John Austyn,[10] co-execs.

Seal appended.

Proved 26 September 1461. Admon to execs.

1   Testators in the Baldwyne register left bequests to six different gilds in the parish of Mildenhall: Corpus Christi, St George, Holy Trinity, St John the Baptist, St Katherine and St Mary the Virgin. For other bequests to the gild of St Katherine see wills of John Frere of Mildenhall (SROB, Baldwyne 144; Pt I, no. 683), John Staloun the younger of Mildenhall (SROB, Baldwyne 148; Pt I, no. 708) and Simon Chylderston of Mildenhall (SROB, Baldwyne 230; Pt I, no. 1156).

2   This testator, John Stalham, was the only Baldwyne testator to make a bequest to the gild of St George in Mildenhall; similarly John Frere (see note above) was the only one to make a bequest to the gild of Holy Trinity.

3   For other bequests to the gild of St John the Baptist, see wills of John Staloun the younger (see note above), John Bakhot of Mildenhall (no. 229 below) and Thomas Blake of Barton Mills (no. 717 below).

4   See note to no. 1.

5   For the nuns and Friars Preachers of Thetford see notes to no. 68.

6   Will, as 'John Staloun the younger', pr. February 1452/53 (see note above); when her father made his will in October 1452, Christian Stalham/Staloun was not yet 12 years old.

7   Joan Stalham/Staloun had been her husband's executrix.

8   The testator had apparently had four wives.

9   In the will of John Stalham/Staloun the younger, John Stalham of Haverhill was described as a barker, the term being interchangeable with tanner.

10   Elsewhere, and in his own will, Thomas Martyn was referred to as 'parish chaplain of Mildenhall'; he witnessed or supervised the wills of several parishioners (see Pt I, nos 489, 569, 708, 1009, 1117 and 1156); Martyn's own will pr. July 1469 (NRO, NCC 144 Jekkys).

108. THOMAS NORMAN of Badlingham ('Badlyngham') [in CHIPPENHAM] [*Cambs*],[1] 23 June 1462

[*Commendation*: to God Almighty &c; *no burial directions*]; to the high altar of Chippenham ('Chepynham') 6s 8d.

To Joan my wife[2] all the utensils of my house; to Joan the messuage with the adjacent croft, for her lifetime, and after her decease the messuage with the croft to go to Joan my daughter and her heirs.

Residue of all my goods, after the payment of my debts, to the disposition of my execs, Joan my wife, William Norman[3] and Thomas Bukkenam, to dispose for my soul and for the souls of all [*my*] benefactors, as they know best to please God &c[*sic*].

Proved at Fornham [*St Martin*], 21 June 1462[*sic*]. Admon to William Norman, exec. Power reserved to Joan, wife of the deceased, and Thomas Buknam, when they come.

1   Executor of his father, Thomas Norman of Badlingham, will pr. July 1448 (SROB, Baldwyne 97; Pt I, no. 440).
2   Will, no. 438.
3   Probably the testator's brother: Thomas Norman, this testator's father, made bequests to his sons Thomas and William (see note above).

[fol. 342]
109. WILLIAM SCHELTON of STOWMARKET ('Stowemarket'), 1 March 1461/62

[*Commendation*: to God Almighty &c; *no burial directions*]; to the high altar of the parish church of St Peter of the same [*place*], for my tithes forgotten or underpaid, 6s 8d; to the buying of a new basin for the lamp burning in the chancel there, 6s 8d; to the amending of the paving (*pavimentu'*) in the aisle of St John the Baptist 26s 8d; to the emendation of the hall called 'le gyldehalle' 6s 8d.[1]

To the Black Friars of Ipswich (*Gippewic'*), to pray for my soul, 6s 8d;[2] to Friar Thomas Darle, in the same way, 3s 4d; to Friar Lawshele of Babwell 3s 4d;[3] to the convent of friars of Babwell 3s 4d;[4] to Sir John Norwold, to pray for my soul, 3s 4d. To Joan Torp 6s 8d.

A suitable chaplain to celebrate divine service for my soul and the soul of Emme, my former wife, and for all my parents and benefactors and all those at rest in Christ, for two whole years, if my goods will stretch to it.

Any residue there might be of all my goods I leave to the disposition of my execs, they faithfully to execute this testament.

Execs: my beloved in Christ, Sir Robert Ferore, vicar of the church of the Blessed Mary of Stowe,[5] Master Thomas Hylle, clerk,[6] Richard Schelton my brother[7] and Robert Mylys, they having God before their eyes to fulfil everything as above; to the said Robert, Thomas and Robert, to each of them for their labour, 13s 4d; to the said Richard all that piece of pasture in Shelland ('Schellond') which I lately bought of John Hell of the same.

Proved at Stowe, 23 June 1462. Admon to execs.

1   In 1458, Margaret Wetherard of Stowmarket (no. 669 below) had bequeathed a pasture to the reparation of the common hall called the 'Gyldehalle'. Two years later John Gowle of Stowmarket bequeathed 6s 8d to the repairing of the community hall (*commune aule*) of Stow called 'the gylde halle' (SROB, Baldwyne 297; Pt I, no. 1462). The hall evidently served more than one gild and was in need of maintenance from time to time. Following the suppression of gilds and chantries in 1547 the gildhall in Stowmarket became a school. On 15 September 1619 charity commissioners made a decree concerning the house called the Guildhall, lately called 'The Schoolhouse' in Stowmarket: the western half was to be used for a schoolhouse for teaching the children of the inhabitants, the other half for the habitation of poor people (*PSIA*, xxiii, pp.72–3, quoting TNA, C93/8/10).
2   See note to no. 50.
3   The same man as Friar Thomas Lawshull of Babwell who is mentioned in the will of John Lee the elder of Stowmarket (no. 381).
4   See note to no. 1.
5   Vicar of the church of St Mary, Stowmarket, from 1461 to 1478 (Tanner, p.1341); will pr. June 1478 (NRO, NCC 195 Gelour); he witnessed the will of Margaret Wetherard (no. 669).
6   See note to the will of Alice Hyll of Stoke by Nayland (no. 38).
7   Beneficiary and witness of the will of Margaret Wetherard (no. 669).

110. MARGARET MONE of FORNHAM ST GENEVIEVE ('Genefefe'),[1] 31 March 1462

My body to Christian burial; to the high altar of the parish church of Fornham St Genevieve, for sangreds (*pro sangredis*) to be celebrated for my soul and the souls for whom I am bound, 20s; to the reparation of the chancel of the said church 6s 8d. To Katherine Moone[*sic*] 6s 8d; to John Mone 2 marks.

To the buying of a chalice, if it can conveniently be done (*si comede*[sic] *fieri poterit*) out of the goods of the deceased (*de bonis dict' defunct'*), 3 marks.

Residue of all my goods to John Lenge and John Wyseman,[2] execs, to dispose for my soul as seems best to please God and profit my soul.

Proved at Fornham St Martin, 12 July 1462. Admon to execs.

[1] Executrix of the will of her husband John Mone the elder, 'meller', pr. November 1457 (SROB, Baldwyne 189; Pt I, no. 924).
[2] 'John Wyseman the elder of Hengrave' was one of the executors of John Mone.

[fol. 342v]
111. ROBERT HEYVARD of WATTISHAM ('Watysham'), 15 January 1459/60

['Heyward' *in margin*] [*Commendation*: to God Almighty, the Blessed Virgin Mary &c; *no burial directions.*]

I assign a cow, from which to be provided two lights burning perpetually at the due times, that is, one before the image of the crucifix (*ymagine crucifixi*) in the said church, and the other before the image of St Petr[*onilla*] the Virgin there,[1] for the health of my soul and for the health of the souls of my wives, parents and benefactors and all those at rest in Christ, for ever.

To the Friars Minor of Ipswich (*Gybwic'*), to pray for my soul, 12d; to the Carmelite Friars there, in the same way, 12d; I wish to have, within 7 days after my decease if possible, 30 masses celebrated by the said friars of Ipswich.[2]

All the money remaining due to me after my decease from a tenement sold to John my son, to be disposed by my execs thus: during the time of the annual payments, annually on my anniversary day 12d to be spent appropriately (*debito modo*), and the rest of the money to go to the use and sustentation of the said (*prelibat'*) church.

To Collette my wife my messuage called 'Heyvardis', for a whole year after my decease; Collette to have all the land called 'Smethis' for a whole year after the day of my death (*post die' meu' extrem' complet'*) and after that year, it to go to the use and sustentation of the said church for ever. Collette to have all the toft, with the land, pasture and feedings belonging to it, called 'Andrews', to her and her heirs for ever.

Residue of all [*my*] goods to Collette my wife.

Execs: Collette my wife, Clement Mathelard and Thomas Meriell; they to have God before their eyes &c [*sic*].

Proved at Bildeston ('Bylston'), 1 July 1462. Admon to Collette, wife of the deceased, executrix. Power reserved to Clement Mathelard and Thomas Meriell, the other execs, when they come and if they wish to take up admon.

[1] Perhaps the only surviving reference to this image of St Petronilla: neither of the other two testators from Wattisham mentioned it (Geoffrey Artur, SROB, Baldwyne 274; Pt I, no. 1346; Richard Sherman, no. 433 below). There was also an image of that saint in a chapel of the same name in the church of All Saints, Stanton. See Dymond, *Parish Churches of Stanton*, pp.8–9.

2   For the Friars Minor and the Carmelite Friars of Ipswich see notes to no. 1.

[fol. 343]
112. WILLIAM LANGLEY of ICKWORTH ('Ikworth'), 25 November 1459

[*Commendation*: to God &c; *no burial directions*]; to the reparation of the orna-ments in Ickworth church, 13s 4d.

My execs to provide a suitable chaplain to celebrate in Ickworth church, at the altar of the Blessed Mary, for my soul and the souls of all my friends deceased, for a whole year.

To the convent of Babwell[1] for a trental to be celebrated for my soul and the souls of my friends 10s.

To Margaret Langley, the daughter of Joan Langley my wife, 40s.

To Katherine my daughter 5 marks in money; to Katherine a piece of land lying at 'le Medyll tenewall' in the town of Ickworth, which I lately purchased from Agnes Mellere, and reckoned at an acre of land, to her and her heirs for ever; to Katherine 25s from a piece of land at 'Bonyswode Ende'.

To Joan my wife all my movable goods; she to pay all my debts.

Residue of all my goods to my execs, to sell and dispose for my soul and the souls of all my deceased friends, in the celebration of masses and the distribution of alms, as they see best to please God and benefit my soul.

Execs: Joan my wife and Thomas Huske the elder, they faithfully to execute my testament. Supervisor: William Fege, clerk.[2]

Proved at Fornham St Martin, 10 December 1462. Admon to execs.

1   See note to no. 1.
2   William Fege (as 'Flegg') became the incumbent of neighbouring Whepstead in December 1460 (Tanner, p.1423); will of William Fegge, parson of 'Whepstade', pr. 1481 (NRO, NCC 87 A. Caston).

[fol. 343v]
113. RICHARD BOLDIROO of HESSETT ('Heggessete'), 14 April 1462

['Boldyro' *in margin*] [*Commendation*: to God &c; *no burial directions*]; to the high altar of Hessett church for my tithes and offerings forgotten or underpaid 20d; to the light of the Blessed Mary in the same church 4d; to the light of the Holy Trinity in the same church 4d.

My execs to provide a suitable chaplain to celebrate for my soul for half a year after my decease, if it can be done.

To Margaret my wife all my ostilments and utensils whatsoever belonging to my house; to John my son 20s after Margaret's decease, if it can be done; to my three daughters 20s, to be divided equally between them.

Residue of all my goods to my execs to sell and pay all my debts therewith; any surplus after my debts have been paid to remain to Margaret for maintaining my children.

Execs: Margaret my wife, John Bacun the elder and John Andrew of Hessett; to each of whom 12d for their labours, they faithfully to execute my testament.

Seal appended.

[*Will*]

To Margaret my wife my whole messuage in the town of Hessett called 'Prentysys' for term of her life; and after her decease the messuage to remain to John Boldyro my son and his heirs for ever; if John should die under legal age the messuage to remain to Margery, Joan and Margaret my daughters and their heirs for ever; if the said Margery, Joan and Margaret should die under age, the messuage to remain to my execs, to sell and dispose for my soul &c [*sic*].

Proved at Fornham [*St Martin*], 20 December 1462. Admon to execs.

114. JOHN CURRAY the elder of AMPTON, 23 May 1463 [*probate only*]

Proved at Fornham [*St Martin*]. Admon to John Curray the younger of Ampton and Robert Stanton of Bury, execs.

[fol. 344]
115. ELLEN CHENERY of COCKFIELD ('Cokefeld'), 3 June 1463

Dated Friday before the feast of Corpus Christi; [*commendation*: to God &c; *no burial directions*]; to the high altar of Cockfield church 12d; to the tabernacle of St Peter[1] my silvered silk belt (*zona' de cerico argent'*).

To John Cheneri my son all my grain and chattels (*catal'*), to pay all my debts and for that debt which he paid for me and his father.[2]

To the friars of Babwell,[3] to celebrate a trental for my soul and the souls for whom I am bound, 10s.

John my son to have all his legacies left to him by my husband.

Residue of all my goods to John my son, exec, to dispose for the health of my soul as seems to him best to please God and profit the health of my soul.

Witnesses: William Forthe, John Gent, Henry Hyll, William Assy and others.

Proved at Fornham [*St*] Martin, 7 November 1463. Admon to exec.

1   The dedication of the church.
2   John Chenery the elder of Cockfield, will dated March 1459/60 (SROB, Baldwyne 255; Pt I, no. 1260); he gave his wife's name as Helen.
3   See note to no. 1.

116. JOHN ELSEGOOD the elder of ELMSWELL,[1] 12 January 1462/63

To be buried in the churchyard of St John the Evangelist of Elmswell; to the high altar of the said church 12d.

To Thomas my son my tenement in Elmswell, with a close in the same town, next to my close called 'Mabyl Cloos', to him and his heirs for ever.

To my son John the close called 'Mabyl Cloos', to him and his heirs for ever.

To Agnes Talyfer a brass pot holding a gallon.

To my son Thomas a bed with the curtains.

To John Elsegood the younger a brass pot holding 4 gallons.

To John Creme a striped gown; to the wife of the said John a pair of the best sheets.

To the poor 20d.

To the sons of my sons a sheep each.

All my other utensils to my said sons Thomas and John.

To the Friars Preachers of Thetford ('Thetteforthe')[2] to celebrate a trental for my soul [*no sum*].

To Thomas my son a mattress and to John a mattress; to the said John Elsegood the younger a mattress with a sheet; to Joan my daughter a red cover and a blanket. Residue of all my goods to my execs, William Hertt, Thomas my son and John [*my son*], to dispose for my soul and for the souls of my benefactors as they see most expedient.

Proved at Fornham St Martin, 9 January 1463/64. Admon to execs.

1   Executor of John Woode of Elmswell, probate October 1452 (SROB, Baldwyne 109; Pt I, no. 496).
2   See note to no. 68.

[fol. 344v]

117. JOHN BROND the elder of GROTON, 10 December 1463 [*nuncupative*]

[*Commendation*: to God &c]; to be buried in the churchyard of Groton parish church; to the high altar of the same church, for his tithes forgotten and underpaid, 2s; to the high altar of Boxford parish church 12d.

To Matilda Brond his wife all the utensils of his house, and the rest of his goods and chattels, both inside the house and out.

To Joan Brond his daughter, after the decease of his wife, a tenement called 'le Brounes' in the town of Boxford, the parcels of which appear more fully in the deed made of it, to her and her heirs for ever.

To Matilda his wife his tenement in Boxford, in a street called 'Olywade', for term of her life; if she be reduced to such need or poverty that she cannot support herself as she would wish, then the tenement to be sold, with her agreement, and a third part of the money to go to providing for herself, and the other two parts to be equally disposed between John, his son, of Boxford, and Margaret Gybelown, his daughter, of Sudbury.

Residue of all his goods, both in Boxford and Groton, after his debts and dues have been fully met, to his wife Matilda, executrix.

Seal appended.

Witnesses: Thomas Pursere, clerk,[1] John Reve the younger, William Gybeloun and others.

Proved 25 January 1463/64.

1   Thomas Pursere, clerk, of Boxford was mentioned by many testators of Groton and Boxford. He appears to have acted at parish chaplain, John Wall even called him 'parish priest' (SROB, Baldwyne 131; Pt I, no. 612) and several gave him the courtesy title 'Sir'. See Pt I, nos 308, 316, 365, 380, 529, 586, 612 and 1089; and also nos 247 and 331 below.

118. THOMAS CLERE of LITTLE LIVERMERE ('Levermere Parva'), ?27 January 1463/64

[*Date written*: xvijx^mo]; my body to the Christian burial at the aforesaid Livermere. All the debts and agreed payments (*convenciones*) due to me from John my son,[1] which appear in an indented bill made between us, to be paid and made to my wife during her lifetime; to my wife all my movable goods and utensils, to her own use, except 2 scales (*scalis*), a quern and the vats ('fattes').

The residue of all my goods and debts to Peter Kyng of Sapiston[2] and John, my son, my execs, they to have priests celebrating for the souls of myself and my wife, after her decease, if those goods and debts will stretch to it, under the supervision of Sir William Boole.

Seal appended.

[*Will*]

As for my immovable goods:

To John my son all my lands and tenements in the town of the aforesaid Livermere, except 2 acres of arable land which were given to me in marriage and which I assign to Peter Kyng, to hold to him and his heirs of the chief lords of the fee by due service and custom, for ever, provided that John my son observe the agreement made between us by bill of indenture as to the said lands and tenements, except the 2 acres, to hold to him and his heirs of the chief lords of the fee by due service and custom, for ever, under the said conditions.

Proved at Fornham [*St Martin*], 26 February 1463/64. Admon to execs. Seal of official appended.

1   ?Will (as 'Clerys'), no. 653.
2   Will, no. 544.

[fol. 345]

119. JOHN HOY of ICKLINGHAM ('Ikelyngham') ST JAMES, 22 July 1463

[*nuncupative*]

Lately of Icklingham St James; dated Friday before the feast of St James; his body to Christian burial.

William Hoy his son to have 7 marks out of the tenement lately the said John Hoy's, deceased, now William Brown's, to pay all the debts of the said deceased and faithfully fulfil his will.

For a trental to be celebrated among the friars of Babwell 10s.[1]

Residue of all his goods to the said William Hoy *alias* Cowpere, exec, he to dispose all his goods for the health of his soul and to please God.

Witnesses: John Hardegrey, Robert Bagoote and John Hygge and many others.

Proved at Icklingham ('Ikelyngham'), 18 May 1464. Admon to exec. Seal of official appended.

1   See note to no. 1.

120. ROBERT TOLLERE of WANGFORD, 20 May 1464

Sick (*langues* [*sic*]); [*commendation*: to God Almighty &c]; to be buried in the churchyard of the church of St Denis in Wangford; to the high altar of the said church 20d; to the reparation and sustentation of the said church 40d.

To the Friars Preachers of Thetford 40d; to the nuns of the same [*place*] 12d;[1] to the church of St Laurence the Martyr [*in* ?*Eriswell*] 12d; to the Friars Minor of Babwell 12d.[2]

To each of my execs for their labour 16d.

Residue of all my goods to Joan my wife, John Man the younger of Lakenheath ('Lakynghethe') and Reginald Elyott of Wangford, execs, to dispose to the honour of God and health of my soul and [*of the souls*] of all the faithful departed, as seems most expedient.

Seal appended.

Proved in the parish church of Brandon, 19 June 1464. Admon to execs. Seal of official appended.

¹ For the Friars Preachers and the nuns of Thetford see notes to no. 68.
² See note to no. 1.

121. THOMAS SMYTH of STANSFIELD ('Stanysfeld'), 12 February 1462/63

Dated at Stansfield; sick in body and in peril of death; [*commendation*: to God &c]; my body to the Christian burial in Stansfield; to the high altar for [*my*] tithes forgotten and underpaid 3s 4d; for a cover to cover the bier (*feretru'*) 13s 4d.

A trental to the friars of Babwell, or otherwise (?*altern' vero*) to the friars of Clare;[1] to the friars of Clare for my confraternity (*fraternitat'*), and my wife's, 13s 4d.

To the reparation of the torches 20d; to the reparation of the light of the sepulchre of Our Lord 20d; to the painting of the roodloft ('rodelofftt') of Stansfield church 6s 8d.

To my four sons and daughters a cow [*worth*] 6s 8d.

To Thomas Grey my godson 12d.

To Robert my son 2 cows.

To each of my execs 6s 8d.

To Cecily Purdon 4s and a mattress.

John my son the elder to have my place and all the bedding (*supellectilibus*) of my house, on condition that he provides and orders everything necessary on my burial day, seven-day and thirty-day; if John has a wife but dies before her, his wife to have my place for her lifetime and after her decease it to be sold by my execs and done in alms for me and my benefactors and all faithful Christians; if John needs to sell the place, then he may, with the advice of my execs, for his benefit and mine and all Christians' [*benefit*].

To the two daughters of Thomas Cowlynge, Agnes and Margaret, 3s 4d each.

Residue of all my goods to my execs, to dispose for me according to my last will.

Execs: Robert Saverey, Robert Smyth and Thomas Collyng.

Seal appended.

Proved at Wratting, 4 July 1464. ~~Admon to Robert and Thomas Collyng, execs~~. Admon to execs.

¹ For the friars of Babwell and Clare see notes to no. 1.

[fol. 345v]

122. AGNES MEY of LAVENHAM,[1] 20 January 1462/63

Dated at Lavenham; [*commendation*: to God &c]; my body to Christian burial; to the making or maintenance (*fabricacionem sive sustentacionem*) of the parish church of Lavenham 3s 4d.

26s to be distributed among 12 of the poor in the said church, each week 6d, for the term of a year immediately after my death, that they may pray for me and for the souls for whom I am bound.

20s to the emendation or reparation of the highway next to the churchyard of Lavenham church, leading from the market of Lavenham towards Sudbury.

To John Mey my son 40s; to the same John[2] my best belt (*zonam*).

To the reparation of Great Waldingfield parish church 12d; to the reparation of Little Waldingfield church 12d; to the reparation of Milden ('Meldyng') church 12d; to the reparation of Brent Eleigh ('Illygh Combust') church 12d; to the reparation of Monks Eleigh ('Illigh Monachorum') parish church 12d; to the reparation of Preston parish church 12d; to the reparation of Thorpe Morieux ('Thorppmoryeux') church 12d.

Residue of my goods to my execs, to dispose in deeds of charity for my soul and the souls for whom I am bound, as they see best to please God and most benefit the health of my soul.

Seal appended.

Execs: John Mey my son, of Bury St Edmunds,[3] and Robert Dytton of Lavenham. Proved in Lavenham church, 3 July 1464. Admon to execs.

1   Wife and executrix of John Mey of Lavenham, will pr. December 1443 (SROB, Baldwyne 50; Pt I, no. 263).

2   When Agnes Mey's husband made his will, he made bequests to two sons named John but it appears that by the time she made her will the younger of the two had died (see note below).

3   This son was also executor of his father's will, where he was described by his father as 'John Mey the elder, of Bury St Edmunds, my son'.

123. THOMAS MELLERE of WITHERSFIELD (Wytheresfeld'), 21 April 1464

Of Withersfield in the diocese of Norwich; knowing the end of my life to be near (*sciens fine' mee presentis vite imminere*); [*commendation*: to God the Father Almighty, the Blessed Mary &c]; my body to the burial at Withersfield ('Wydresfeld'); to the high altar there for [*my*] tithes forgotten 3s 4d; to the buying of a new vestment in the said church 10 marks.

To William Mellere my father a croft called 'Dowehows Crofte' in the same town, and also a cow.

Residue of all my goods to Sir William Chauncerell, rector of Withersfield church, and John Mellere my brother of the same [*place*], execs, to dispose for the health of my soul, as seems to them best to please God.

Seal appended.

Proved in Great Wratting church, 4 July 1464. Admon to execs.

124. ROBERT RAWLYN of CHIPPENHAM ('Chypenham') [*Cambs*], 5 July 1464 [*probate only*]

Proved at Silverley [*Cambs*]. Admon to Isabel, wife[1] of the said Robert deceased, executrix. Seal of official appended.

1   Will, no. 199.

[fol. 346]

125. WILLIAM COPPYNG of SOMERTON, 11 March 1461/62

Of Somerton in the diocese of Norwich; [*commendation*: to God &c; *no burial directions*]; in God's name I beg my execs to pay all my debts which I owe, that is, those that can be truly proved. To the high altar of Somerton church, for my tithes forgotten, 6s 8d; to the reparation of the same church, where there is known to be most need, 20s.

To the fabric of Brockley ('Brokeley') church 3s 4d; to the fabric of Hawkedon church 3s 4d; to the fabric of Wickhambrook ('Wykhambrook') church 3s 4d.

To the convent of Austin Friars of Clare, for a trental of St Gregory to be said among them for my soul, with all possible haste after my decease, 10s; to the convent of friars of Babwell, similarly, 10s.[2]

To Thomas Coppyng my nephew, to pray for my soul, 6s 8d.

To the badly-worn and dangerous (*debil' et nocine'*) way between Brockley and Bury St Edmunds, where there is most need, according to the discretion of my execs, 6s 8d.

To be distributed among poor priests, clerks and the needy, and to be done in other necessary expenses about my burial, 40s.

Residue of all my goods to Katherine my wife.

Execs: Katherine my wife, William Scot of Glemsford and Richard Smyth *alias* Gardynere of Somerton; they to fulfil all my aforesaid legacies in the best way they can, to please God and benefit my soul; to each of my execs, for their diligent labour about these premises, 10s.

Witnesses: Roger Drury, esquire,[3] Walter Cook, canon, William Scot and others specially called here.

[*Will, indented; same date*]

Made in my own dwelling at Somerton.

Firstly, everything specified in my testament to be carried out.

Katherine my wife to have and enjoy, for the whole term of her life, all my lands and tenements which I have at this present time in the towns of Somerton, Hawkedon and Brockley, she keeping up repairs of all kinds and not committing any waste or strip; after her decease all my said lands and tenements to remain to one of my five sons named: Walter, Richard, Roger, John the elder and John the younger, that is, to him of them that is of the best bearing, behaviour and conduct, by the discretion of my execs, to have and to hold of the chief lords of the fee by due service and custom, to him and his heirs for ever.

My son who shall have all my lands and tenements in this way [fol. 346v] is to pay each of his other brothers named 10 marks at times (*dies*) set reasonably and indifferently by my execs; if any of my five sons dies during the lifetime of Katherine my wife, their mother, then their part or parts to remain to the brothers that survive, divided equally between them, from the first to the last; if God disposes that all my sons die during Katherine's lifetime, then, after her decease, all my lands and tenements to be sold by my execs or their execs, and the money from them to be disposed in deeds of charity, that is, in priests celebrating divine service, alms to the needy poor, the ornaments of churches, bad and dangerous muddy ways (*debil' et nocinis viis luteis*) and other deeds of piety in the town of Somerton and elsewhere where there is greatest need, as seems to them most expedient and to the glory of

God and my salvation and for the souls of my father and mother and all my parents and friends for whom I am most bound.

Thomas my son to have all my lands and tenements which I have at this time in the town of Wickhambrook in the said county, which I lately purchased of Roger Drury, esquire, when he comes to the age of 21, if he be of good behaviour, conduct and bearing, to hold to him and his heirs for ever, he paying Margaret my daughter, his sister, if she be married, 10 marks at the times reasonably set by my execs, and also paying another 10 marks to my execs at the times agreed between them, for the fulfilling of my legacies specified in my testament.

Katherine my wife to have all my chattels and stock, both live and dead, and all my grain, both sown and unsown, with all my jewels, ostilments and utensils, as linen, wool, pots, pans, cups (*ciphis*), spoons and all other necessaries and utensils belonging to me, for her sustentation and that of the children born to us, and for the satisfaction of all my debts and to receive all my debts owed to me.

Seal appended.

Witnesses of this bipartite will: Roger Drury, esquire, Walter Cook, canon, and others specially called for the purpose.

Proved at Hawstead, 9 June 1462. Admon to execs.

1 For the friars of Clare and Babwell see notes to no. 1.
2 Roger Drury of Hawstead, esquire, son of Nicholas Drury of Thurston, esquire; Roger's will pr. March 1500/01 (NRO, NCC 169 Cage); he was supervisor of John Hedgeman the elder of Glemsford (SROB, Baldwyne 249; Pt I, no. 1246) and Roger Copcy of Brockley (SROB, Baldwyne 283; Pt I, no. 1390); legatee and executor of Katherine Hunte of Rushbrooke (no. 470 below).

[fol. 347]
126. JOHN TAYLOUR of THORNDON,[1] 3 November 1463

[*Commendation*: to Almighty God, the Blessed Mary &c]; to be buried in the churchyard of Thorndon church; to the high altar there 6s 8d; to the rector of Thorndon 8s 4d[2] for a certain for two whole years.

To a chaplain £5 6s 8d to celebrate for my soul and the souls of my benefactors in Thorndon church for a whole year; to Thorndon church 53s 4d which William Kendale owes me, to buy a chalice for the same church; to the gild of the Holy Trinity 10s.[3]

To the Friars Minor of Ipswich (*Gipwic'*) 10s; to the Carmelite Friars 40d; to the Preachers 40d; to the Austin Friars 40d, if it can be done.[4]

To the leper-hospital of Norwich (*hospitali lep'sorum Norwic'*) 40d;[5] to the leper-hospital of Bury (*hospital' lepros' de* Bury) 20d;[6] to the leper-hospital of Ipswich (*hospitali lepero' Gipwic'*) 20d;[7] to the leper-hospital of Eye (*hospitali lepero' de* Eye) 40d.[8]

To my ten godsons and goddaughters 10s, to be distributed to them equally.

To the nuns of Redlingfield 10s.[9]

To Alice Starlyng 4 bushels (*mod'*) of malt; to John Starlyng 6s 8d, a heifer and 2 quarters of barley.

Residue of my goods to the disposition of my execs, Robert Wade, rector of Rishangles ('Rysanglys') church,[10] Robert Rolff and William Belton.

[*Will, of same date*]

All my debts to be fully paid.

73

Joan my wife to have the issues and profits of my tenements 'Horscroftes' and 'Gyes' in Thorndon, with all my free lands in the same town, except my tenement called 'Ebotes', until Rose my daughter comes to the age of 15, without making any waste, she providing both Rose and Margaret my daughters with all the necessaries they ought to have, and then Rose to have both the tenements to her and her heirs, and give Margaret her sister 10 marks when she comes to the age of marriage; if Rose should die without heirs, then Margaret to have the tenements with the other free lands above-mentioned, to her and her heirs; if Margaret should die without heirs then the tenements and the other free lands to be sold and the money from them to be disposed for my soul and the souls of all my benefactors by my attorneys. My above-mentioned tenement called 'Ebotes', with the other free lands, meadows and pastures in the towns of Wetheringsett ('Wetheryngsett'), Brockford ('Brokforth') Thweyt ('Theweyt') and Stoke Ash ('Stoke'), to be sold by the advice of Robert Anyell, and especially those lands, meadows and pastures which are furthest from (*longius distant'*) the tenements 'Horscroftes' and 'Gyes' and can best be dispensed with (*depelli seu deponi*).

My wife to have all my utensils with all my chattels, towards the keeping of my children until they come to the age of 15.

Joan my wife and Rose my daughter, and those who in the future shall have my tenements 'Horscroftes' and 'Gyes' and the above-mentioned free land, to provide and maintain a candle before the image of the crucifix in Thorndon and keep my anniversary for 80 years.

Robert Rolff and Joan his wife to have my tenement at [fol. 347v] 'Cherchegrene', paying £20 for it, out of which a suitable chaplain to have 8 marks to celebrate in Thorndon church for my soul and the souls of my benefactors; and also out of which my wife Joan to have 20 marks, by the advice of Robert Anyell, as she and the purchaser can best agree.

Execs: Robert Wade, rector of Rishangles ('Rysanglys') church, and Robert Rolff.
Supervisor: Robert Anyell of Eye.
Proved the last day of February [29] 1463/64. Admon to Robert Rolff, exec. Power reserved to Robert Wade, rector of Rishangles, the other exec, when he comes.

1 ?Son of John Talyour 'the younger' of Thorndon, will pr. February 1453/54 (SROB, Baldwyne 168; Pt I, no. 809); ?executor of Thomas Pyrty of Thorndon, will pr. July 1454 (SROB, Baldwyne 169; Pt I, no. 817). Pyrty had been executor of John Taylour 'the younger'.

2 A bequest for a certain for two years would usually be 8s 8d (104d), being the rate of 1d per week. See Glossary.

3 For other bequests to the gild of the Holy Trinity in Thorndon see John Mundeford of Rishangles (SROB, Baldwyne 137; Pt I, no. 648), William Loudon of Thorndon (SROB, Baldwyne 156; Pt I, no. 742), Thomas Pyrty of Thorndon (Pt I, no. 817) and Thomas Colman of Thorndon (no. 337 below).

4 For the friars of Ipswich, see notes to nos 1 (Friars Minor and Carmelites) and 50 (Friars Preachers). There was no house of Austin Friars at Ipswich but a house of Austin Canons, known as the Priory of the Holy Trinity, had been founded there during the reign of Henry II. Its lands and rents were mainly in the town and immediate neighbourhood of Ipswich. In the reign of Richard I, there were seven canons under a prior, but as endowments increased, the number was at one time rose to twenty (*VCH Suffolk*, ii, pp.103–5).

5 Giving to the sick was one of the corporal deeds of mercy but John Taylour was the only testator in Part II to leave money to any leper-hospitals. For lepers and leper-hospitals in general see Rawcliffe, *Leprosy in Medieval England*. At Norwich, a leper-hospital was founded in honour of St Mary Magdalen, before 1119. It was built nearly a mile to the north-east of the city out of the

Fybridge or Magdalen gate. There were five other smaller leper-houses, one at each of the chief gates of the city. In pre-Reformation wills, small bequests to the leper-houses at the five gates were frequent. The houses were: St Mary and St Clement, usually called St Clement's, without St Austin's gate; a leper-house, said to have been dedicated to St Benedict, outside Westwick and St Benet's gate; St Stephen's, outside Needham or St Stephen's Gate; the hospital of (probably) St Leonard, outside Fybridge or Magdalen gate, on the east side of the highway; the fifth on the outside of Newport or St Giles's Gate, on the north side of the highway (*VCH Norfolk*, ii, pp.442–50).

6   St Peter's Hospital stood outside the Risby gate of Bury, but within the abbey's jurisdiction. It was founded by Abbot Anselm, late in the reign of Henry I, for the maintenance of infirm, leprous, or invalided priests, or, in their absence, other aged and sick persons. Though not originally founded exclusively for lepers, this hospital was gradually confined to such cases (*VCH Suffolk*, ii, pp.134–5). The only testator in Part I who gave to lepers was William Calwe of Barrow, who, in 1439, bequeathed 4d to the lepers of Bury living in 'Rysbygatestrete' (SROB, Baldwyne 33; Pt I, no. 187).

7   In Ipswich, the two leper-hospitals of St Mary Magdalen and St James were united during the fourteenth century. Their joint mastership was usually annexed to the church of St Helen. In 1463, the master of the hospitals was Robert Markys. There was also the leper-hospital of St Leonard in Ipswich, in the parish of St Peter, near the old church of St Augustine (*VCH Suffolk*, ii, p.139).

8   Records of the leper hospital of St Mary Magdalen of Eye, situated outside the town, begin in the reign of Edward III. The hospital had no endowments and so was dependent on alms (*VCH Suffolk*, ii, p.138).

9   See note to no. 83.

10 Robert Wade was rector of Rishangles from September 1455; the date that he was succeeded is unknown (Tanner, p.1311).

127. ADAM GOOCHE of RUSHBROOKE ('Rosshebrok'), 23 March 1463/64

Fearful that the release of death draws near to me (*mortis liberatio' timens m' imminer'*); to be buried in the Christian burial of the church of St Nicholas of Rushbrooke; to the high altar of the same church for my tithes forgotten, for the health of my soul, 12d.

To the friars of the order of Minors of Babwell,[1] for celebrating a trental for the health of my soul, 10s; to Master William my son, to celebrate for the health of my soul, 10 marks.

To Joan my wife my tenement during her lifetime, and after her decease I beg those who are enfeoffed in it to allow my execs to sell it for the best price possible; to Joan my wife all the utensils of my house.

To John my son 6s 8d; to Alice my daughter 6s 8d.

Exec: my beloved in Christ, Master William my son, chaplain, to dispose for me and my soul where he sees most expedient and best to please God.

Seal appended.

Proved in the parish church of Fornham St Martin, 16 April 1464. Admon to Master William Gooche, exec.

1   See note to no. 1.

[fol. 348]

128. JOHN TYLERE of WESTLEY ('Westle'), 16 December 1461

[*Commendation*: to God &c; *no burial directions*]; to the high altar of Westley church, for my tithes and offerings underpaid, 12d; to the buying of the new bell for the said church 13s 4d.

To the hospitaller of the monastery of St Edmund, with his servants (*cu' servien's sui'*) in the hospital of St Saviour of Bury St Edmunds, 13s 4d.[1]

To the friars of Babwell,[2] to celebrate a trental of St Gregory for my soul and my wife's soul, 8 marks.

To John, Joan and Isabel, the children of Thomas Tylere my son,[3] when they come to legal age, 6s 8d each; to Hawise, the wife of the same Thomas,[4] after the abovesaid chaplain has been provided, 6s 8d.

Residue of all my goods and chattels and all my lands and tenements in the towns of Westley and Little Horringer ('Hornyngysherth Parva') to Henry Banyard of Bury, exec, to sell, receive, and dispose for my soul and the souls of my parents and benefactors, and all the faithful departed, in celebrating masses and other deeds of charity, as he sees best to please God and profit the aforesaid souls.

Proved at Fornham St Martin, 2 November 1462. Admon to exec.

1   The hospital of St Saviour, without the north gate, was begun by Abbot Samson about the year 1184 but it was not finished nor fully endowed until the time of King John. It was originally founded for a warden, twelve chaplain priests, six clerks, twelve poor men and twelve poor women. Surviving records indicate the terms on which inmates were admitted (*VCH Suffolk*, ii, pp.135–6).

2   See note to no. 1.

3   John's son Thomas had died by early 1462; probate only, February 1461/62 (SROB, Baldwyne 283; Pt I, no. 1391).

4   Executor of her husband Thomas (see note above).

129. ISABEL BOOLE of LITTLE LIVERMERE ('Lyveremere Parva'),[1]
20 October 1462 [*nuncupative*]

[*Commendation*: to God &c; *no burial directions*]; to the rector of the aforesaid Livermere 4s 4d, to celebrate a sangred for her soul; to the reparation of the same church 3s 4d.

To Joan Assy her sister a violet tunic and a pair of amber beads; to Agnes Westbroun a brass pot, with her cloak (*collobio*); to Katherine Greene of Great Livermere a violet tunic; to Margery Boole two kirtles.

Six ewes to be sold and the money from them to be disposed for her soul.

Residue of all her goods to Roger her son,[2] to dispose for her soul as he sees best to please God and profit her soul, and him she made exec.

Proved at Fornham [*St Martin*], 22 November 1462. Admon to exec.

1   Widow and executor of John Bole of Little Livermere, will pr. September 1449 (SROB, Baldwyne 144; Pt I, no. 684).

2   Will pr. April 1488 (SROB, Hervye 429).

[fol. 348v]

130. SIMON BALLEY of LITTLE WHELNETHAM ('Qhelwetham Parva'),
20 November 1462

['Bally' *in margin*]; seeing the danger of death approaching me (*videns m' periculu' mortis evenir'*); [*commendation*: to God Almighty &c; *no burial directions*]; to the high altar of Great Whelnetham ('Qwelwetham Magna') 6d; to the high altar of Nowton church 6d; to the reparation of Little Whelnetham church a quarter of barley. All my lands and tenements to remain to Katherine my wife for term of her life;

inasmuch as (*sicut*) those lands and tenements come to me by right as the heir of Thomas Balley my father, as more fully appears in a deed made of them, so I wish them all to remain to my eldest son and his heirs after the decease of Katherine; if he dies without heirs, then to remain to my next heirs, all other rights being reserved (*salvo iuris cuiuscumque*).

I beg Edmund Tylney, clerk,[1] my faithful and special attorney, to deliver estate and transfer possession to my attorneys, as empowered by my letter of attorney under my seal.

My execs to pay all my debts as quickly as possible and implement my will in the best way possible to please God, as they will answer before the Great Judge, to whose disposition I leave all my goods not previously bequeathed.

Execs: Katherine Balley my wife, Thomas Ladyman[2] and John Bunne[3] of the aforesaid Whelnetham; to the said Thomas Ladyman 20d, and to John Bunne 20d, for their labour.

Proved at Fornham [*St*] Martin, 13 December 1462. Admon to execs.

[1]   Edmund Tylney was rector of Bradfield St Clare from 1470 to 1479 (Tanner, p.1430); see also nos 184 and 772.
[2]   Will, no. 413.
[3]   Will, no. 93.

[fol. 349]

131. JOHN PYPERE of THORPE MORIEUX ('Thorpmor'), 20 April 1462

Dated at the aforesaid Thorpe; [*commendation*: to God &c; *no burial directions*]; to the high altar in the said church my best horse as my principal or mortuary; to the reparation of the said church 40s, to be disposed by my execs in paving and whitening the walls (*ut ?inpaviment' et ad albas pariet' faciend'*) of the said church. To the convent of friars of Babwell 6s 8d; to the convent of friars of Sudbury 6s 8d; to the convent of friars of Clare 6s 8d.[1]

To each of the sons of Thomas Pypere my son[2] 6s 8d.

To Emma my wife all the utensils belonging to my house; to Emma all my grain growing on the tenement and lands sometime Walter at the Tye's, and on the tenement and lands called 'Wedyrtonis', and all the grain growing on the land that I hold at farm of the lord. To Emma my wife all the goods and chattels on the said tenements and lands at the day of my death, after taking out the costs and expenses of my funeral, she providing, out of the said goods, an honest chaplain to celebrate divine service in Thorpe church for a whole year after my decease.

To Laurence my nephew 10s.

Residue of all my goods to the disposition of my execs, they to dispose for the health of my soul and the souls of my benefactors as they see best to please God and profit my soul.

Execs: Sir Robert Chapman, rector of Thorpe Morieux church,[3] and Thomas Pypere my son; to the rector for his labour 10s, and to Thomas 40s.

Proved at Lavenham, 1 December 1462. Admon to Thomas Pypere, exec. Power reserved to Robert Chapman, the other exec, when he comes, if he wishes to take up admon.

[1]   For the friars see notes to nos 1 (Babwell and Clare) and 11 (Sudbury).
[2]   Will, no. 238.

3   Robert Chapman was rector of Thorpe Morieux from 1452 to 1479 (Tanner, p.1393); he was also
     executor of Thomas Pypere (no. 238) and witness of the will of Marion Nune (no. 613).

132. JOHN CORDY of THELNETHAM ('Thelwetham'), 10 December 1462

[*probate only*]

Proved at Ixworth. Admon to Margaret Cordy, wife of the deceased, and John Boole
of Garboldisham [*Norfolk*], execs.

[fol. 349v]
133. JOHN GLOVYERE of CAVENDISH ('Cavendysche'), 9 June 1459

Of Cavendish in the diocese of Norwich; sick (*languens*); [*commendation*: to God
&c; *no burial directions*]; in God's name (*ex parte dei*) I request my execs to pay all
my debts; to the high altar of Cavendish church for tithes forgotten 6d.

To the four orders of friars, that is, Clare, Sudbury, Babwell and Cambridge
('Cambregge'), 13s 4d divided equally among them.[1]

To each priest present at my obsequies and at mass, at the time of my burial, 4d; to
each clerk present at the said obsequies 2d; to Sir Robert Dowes, chaplain, to pray
for my soul, 6d; to Friar James Exale, to celebrate a trental of St Gregory for my
soul, 10s.[2]

To the indigent poor of the town of Cavendish, for praying for my soul, 4 bushels
of wheat and 4 bushels of malt, divided equally among them.

To the fabric of Cavendish church 40s.

To Margaret my daughter 40s.

To a suitable priest, to celebrate, for a whole year, for my soul and the souls of my
parents and benefactors for whom I am most bound, in Cavendish church, in the
chapel of St John the Baptist there, 10 marks.

To Agnes my wife my messuage called 'Poleyns', on the west side of 'Kemsynge'
street (*strate de* 'Kemsynge') in Cavendish, to her and her heirs for ever.

Execs: Agnes my wife and John my son, they to implement all the foregoing in the
best way they can.

Residue of all my goods to Agnes my wife, that is, chattels and stock, both live and
dead, ostilments and utensils.

John Smyth of Cavendish to supervise the fulfilling of all the above.

Proved at Cavendish, 2 December 1462. Admon to John, exec. Power reserved to
Agnes, executrix, when she comes, if she wishes to take up admon.

1   For similar bequests to the four houses/orders of friars see nos 142, 152, 160, 244, 286, 436,
     508, 528, 628 and 763. For the Austin Friars of Clare and the Franciscan Friars of Babwell see
     notes to no. 1; for the Dominican Friars of Sudbury see note to no. 11; for the Carmelite Friars
     of Cambridge see note to no. 42.
2   Both Robert Belamy of Boxted (SROB, Baldwyne 204; Pt I, no. 1006) and Agnes Dyke of Stoke
     by Clare (no. 803 below) also requested Friar James Exsale to say a trental of St Gregory for their
     souls.

[fol. 350]
134. EDMUND BOOLE of GREAT LIVERMERE ('Magna Liveremere'), 16 July 1462

[*Commendation*: to God Almighty, the Blessed Virgin Mary &c; *no burial direc-*

tions]; to the high altar of the church of the aforesaid Livermere, for my tithes forgotten or underpaid, 2s; to the reparation of the same chuch 20s.

To the friars of Babwell, to celebrate a trental of St Gregory for my soul, 10s; to the Dominican Friars of Thetford [*for*] a Gregorian trental, 10s.[1]

To Sarah my wife all the ostilments and utensils of my dwelling house (*hospicii*) and half of all my grain, wherever it is, 2 cows and 20 marks in money from the sale of my lands and tenements which I lately sold to one John Jurdon.

To a suitable chaplain to celebrate for my soul and the souls for whom I am bound, in the aforesaid church, for a whole year after my death, 8 marks.

Residue of all my goods and chattels to my wife, to sell, receive and dispose for my soul and the souls of my benefactors and of all the faithful departed, in deeds of mercy, as she sees best to please God and profit my soul.

Execs: Sarah my wife, William Tofte of Bury St Edmunds, John Wynyeve of Troston, 'smyth'; to John and William for their labour 3s 4d each.

Supervisor: Sir Richard Port, chaplain.

Seal appended.

Proved 15 September 1462. Admon to Sarah and William, execs. Power reserved to John Wynyeve, the other exec, when he comes.

    [1]   For the friars see notes to nos 1 (Babwell) and 68 (Dominicans of Thetford).

135. EDITH BULLEBROOK of WHEPSTEAD ('Qwepsted'), 19 April 1462

[*Commendation*: to God &c; *no burial directions*]; to the high altar of Whepstead 8d; to the light of the Blessed Mary my best gown, with my hood.

To the friars of Babwell 10s.[1]

To William my son a brass pot; to John my son another brass pot; to William my son the best pan; to John my son another pan.

To the reparation of the bells of Whepstead 12d.

To Joan Bird ('Brrd') a small tunic; to Margaret Bird a russet tunic; to Margaret Lambard a best veil; to Joan Parysche the red hood; to Cecily Coddenham a huke ('le hewke') and the blue hood.

Residue of all my goods to Thomas Powle, exec, to dispose for my soul as he sees best to please God.

Supervisor: Sir William Feg.[2]

Seal appended.

Proved at Fornham [*St Martin*], 21 September 1462. Admon to exec.

    [1]   See note to no. 1.
    [2]   William Feg was the incumbent of Whepstead; see note to no. 112.

[fol. 350v]

136. MARGERY HUNTE of BARROW ('Barve'),[1] 1 August 1462

[*Commendation*: to God &c; *no burial directions*]; to the high altar of Barrow ('Barwe') 2s; to a priest to celebrate for the health of my soul and my friends' [*souls*], 8 marks; to the said church 10 marks, the 10 marks to be disposed, with the agreement of my execs, in Barrow church; to Stephen Baldevyn, priest, 20d.[2]

To the convent of friars of Babwell 6s 8d; to the convent of Friars Preachers of Thetford 6s 8d; to the convent of Friars Carmelite 6s 8d.[3]

To be distributed to the poor on the day of my burial 6s 8d.

To John Goldsmyth, clerk, 4d.

To Katherine Grene 6d.

To the church of Ousden ('Owesden') 3s.

Residue of all my goods to Simon Spark[4] and William Moriell of Barrow, execs, to dispose as they see best to please God and profit the health of my soul; to each of them for their labour 40d.

Proved at Fornham [*St Martin*], 3 October 1462. Admon to execs.

1   Wife and executrix of Roger Hunte of Barrow, will pr. July 1459 (SROB, Baldwyne 237; Pt I, no. 1191).

2   Stephen Baldewyn, priest, witnessed the will of Adam Chapman of Barrow (no. 152).

3   For the friars of Babwell see note to no. 1; for the Friars Preachers of Thetford see note to no. 68. The house of Carmelite friars is not specified: there was a house at Cambridge (see note to no. 42) and one at Ipswich (see note to no. 1).

4   Simon Spark of Barrow was also executor of her husband Roger.

137. JOHN CLERE of FELSHAM, 4 August 1462

[*Commendation*: to God Almighty &c]; to be buried in the churchyard of Felsham parish church; to the high altar of which 6s 8d; to the buying of a chalice there 6s 8d.

To Walter Clere and Thomas Clere my sons, in the seventh year after my death, 5 marks each.

Execs: Katherine my wife, Henry Lyly and John Attemore, they to dispose for the health of my soul, so as to please God and profit the health of my soul; to Henry Lyly and John Attemore 6s 8d each for their labour.

Proved at Fornham St Martin, 17 October 1462. Admon to execs.

[fol. 351]

138. NICHOLAS BARKERE of ICKWORTH ('Ikworth'), 15 September 1462

[*Commendation*: to God Almighty &c; *no burial directions*]; to the high altar of Ickworth parish church, for tithes forgotten, 20d.

To the convent of Friars Minor of Babwell 3s 4d.[1]

To my three sons 4 bushels of wheat each; to each of my daughters 4 bushels of wheat.

Alice my wife to have my messuage in which I live, with 4 acres of land in a close adjacent, in the town of Ickworth, for term of her life; after her death John my eldest son to have the messuage, with the 4 acres of land, to hold to him and his heirs born of him and his wife Margaret, on condition that he does not trouble or worry Alice my wife about my gift of the house and land during her lifetime; but if John does worry or trouble Alice about my bequest of the messuage and land in any way, then Thomas my son to have the messuage and 4 acres immediately after Alice's decease and John not to have [*them*], nor his heirs, but they to be excluded for ever.[2]

If John and Margaret should die without heirs, then Thomas my son to have the messuage and 4 acres, to him and his heirs; and if Thomas should die without heirs, Nicholas my son to have the messuage and land, to hold to him and his heirs; if Nicholas should die without heirs the messuage and 4 acres of land to remain to my feoffees, to sell and to dispose the money from them for the souls of me, my wife, [*my*] parents and all my benefactors.

Alice my wife to have my croft called 'Syre Robertes Crofte', with 2 acres of land and meadow, in the town of Ickworth, for term of her life, and after her decease Thomas my son to have the said croft and 2 acres, to hold to him and his heirs; if Thomas should die without heirs, Nicholas my son to have them, to hold to him and his heirs; if Nicholas die without heirs [fol. 351v] the croft with the 2 acres of land and meadow also to remain to my feoffees, to sell and dispose the money for the souls of me, the said John[*sic*; *recte* Nicholas] and Alice my wife, my parents and all my benefactors.

But, if John my eldest son and Margaret his wife should decease without heirs and Thomas my son survive, and he and his heirs enjoy the said messuage and 4 acres of land, then, immediately after he, Thomas my son, enters upon the said messuage and 4 acres, Nicholas my son shall have and enjoy the croft called 'Syre Robertys Crofte', with the 2 acres of land and meadow, to hold to him and his heirs as aforesaid, my gift to the said Thomas notwithstanding.

Residue of all my goods to Alice my wife, Thomas Brymmyng and William Langley, execs, to dispose for the health of my soul, as seems most expedient, and above all, to please Almighty God.

Seal appended.

Proved at Fornham St Martin, 20 October 1462. Admon to Alice, executrix. Power reserved to Thomas Brynnyng[*sic*] and William Langley, the other co-execs, when they come [*and*] if they wish to take up admon.

¹ See note to no. 1.
² The testator clearly anticipated discord between his wife Alice and his son and daughter-in-law; perhaps Alice was not John's mother.

[fol. 352]
139. JOHN COK of STOWMARKET, 5 July 1462

[*Commendation*: to God &c; *no burial directions*]; to the high altar of St Peter of Stowe 6d.

My mother and my wife to have their dwelling in my tenement for the term of their lives and after the decease of both of them, John my son to have the tenement to him and his assigns, on condition that he advises and supports the said women as far as he is able; if John dies without heirs, the tenement to be sold by my supervisors and disposed for the souls of my parents and benefactors.

Residue of my goods to John my son, exec.

Supervisors: John Waryn and Robert Mylys, to help him.

Proved at Stowe, 17 October [?*1462*]. Admon to exec.

140. JOHN MEKYLWOODE,¹ 13 October 1462 [*probate only*]

[*No place of residence given*]. Proved at Stowmarket. Admon to Isabel, wife of the deceased, executrix.

¹ Executor of William Knotyng, will pr. February 1441/42 (SROB, Baldwyne 19; Pt I, no. 103); executor and 'brother' of Henry Awnselme of Wyverstone, will pr. March 1461/62 (SROB, Baldwyne 286; Pt I, no. 1402).

141. JOHN NOBLE of NAYLAND ('Neylond'), 27 October 1462

Dated the vigil of the Apostles Simon and Jude, 1462; [*commendation*: to God &c; *no burial directions*]; to the high altar of Nayland for my tithes and offerings forgotten, if any there be, 3s 4d; to the altar of the Blessed Virgin Mary kept (*observat'*) in the said church 3s 4d.

To the church of Wormingford ('Wyrmyngford') in Essex, to the reparation of its fabric where most need is, 3s 4d.

To William Bonyng of Little Horkesley ('Horkysley') [*Essex*] my blue gown.

Residue of all my goods to my execs, that they pay my debts out of them, see to my funeral and dispose as best they can, to please God and profit my soul.

Execs: Geoffrey Brown and John Peryn of Nayland, to whom I give full power and special charge to execute my testament, and to each of them for their labour 3s 4d. Proved at Wetheringsett, 4 November 1462. Admon to Geoffrey Brown, exec. Power reserved to John Peryn, the other exec, when he comes and if he wishes to take up admon. And because of an insufficiency of goods of the deceased, Geoffrey Brown, exec, was excused exhibiting any further accounts and was acquitted.

[fol. 352v]
142. ISABEL SMYTH of GREAT FINBOROUGH ('Fynberth Magna'),
22 September 1462

Dated Wednesday after the feast of St Matthew, Apostle and Evangelist, 1462; [*commendation*: to God &c; *no burial directions*]; to the emendation of the same church 6s 8d.

To the image of St Mary in the chapel of Woolpit ('Wulpyt') a pair of amber beads, with two rings and a silver brooch.[1]

To the emendation of the highway before my cottage gate (*an' porta' cotagii mei*) 6s 8d.

For a trental of St Gregory to be celebrated for the health of my soul, 10s.

To the four houses of friars 3s 4d to each house, for saying and celebrating *placebo* and *dirige* with other prayers, for the health of my soul, my parents' and benefactors' [*souls*] and of all those at rest in Christ.[2]

To Robert Smyth of Stoke 6s 8d; to John Osbern 6s 8d; to Isabel Martyn 3s 4d; to Joan Armesby a brass pot holding a gallon, a brass pan holding 4 gallons, a gridiron and andiron (*andena'*), a spit, a 'fryingpanne', a pair of sheets, a blanket and 26s 8d to be received of the sale of my cottage called 'Cokerscote'.

To John Tymtone, Thomas Roggere, Richard Barkere, Isabel Smert and Isabel Roggere, my godchildren, a ewe each, and to John Martyn a ewe with a lamb.

To each chaplain coming to my obsequies 4d and to each clerk 2d, and to each poor beggar (*mendicant'*) 1d.

Residue of all my goods to Richard Schelton and John Talmage of Finborough, execs, to dipose them for the health of my soul as seems best to them, and to each of them for their labour 6s 8d.

Proved at Stowmarket, 13 October 1462. Admon to execs.

---

1   For Our Lady of Woolpit see Paine, 'The Chapel and Well of Our Lady of Woolpit', pp.8–11. For donations of jewellery to shrines see Swanson, *Catholic England*, Chapter 7, 'Saints, Shrines, Miracles and Pilgrimages', especially pp.179–81, which lists the jewellery and precious objects left at the shrines in York Minster in 1509–10. See also nos 351, 421 and 803.

² See note to no. 133.

143. JOHN OLDMAN of CHIPPENHAM ('Chypnam') [*Cambs*], 30 October 1462 [*probate only*]

Proved at Kennett. Admon to Katherine, wife of the deceased, and Richard Portere, execs.

[*Folios 353–72 (nos 144–211) have been bound into the bifolium containing folios 352 & 373; this accounts for the following run of wills proved in the year 1464 (old style) occurring here among those proved in 1462.*]

[fol. 353]
144. JOHN SIMOND of '?BERANS', 1 October 1464 [*probate only*]

Proved. Admon to William Simond, the father and John the eldest brother.

145. AGNES TYLLE of PRESTON, 5 January 1462/63 [*nuncupative*]

Sick unto death (*languens in extremis*); [*commendation*: to God &c]; her body to Christian burial.
To Friar Thomas Langham of Sudbury ('Sud'), to pray for her soul, 12d;[1] to the friars of Babwell, for celebrating a trental for the soul of her husband, 10s; to the friars of Sudbury, for celebrating another trental for *?*her (*sua'*) soul, 10s.[2]
To Margaret Roo her daughter 6s 8d; to Eleanor Hogon 6s 8d.
Residue of all her goods to John Tylle the elder, her son, exec, to dispose as seems [*best*] to please God and profit her soul.
Her feoffees to deliver estate and transfer possession to the said John Tylle in all her lands and tenements in which they are enfeoffed.
Witnesses: Thomas Machon, Thomas Damecell and John Jentte of Preston.
Proved at Fornham [*St*] Martin, 22 October 1464. Admon to exec. Seal of official appended.

> [1] Beatrice Turnour of Woolpit (SROB, Baldwyne 167; Pt I, no. 806) and Thomas Pypere of Thorpe Morieux (no. 238 below) also requested Friar Thomas Langham to celebrate for their souls.
> [2] For the friars see notes to nos 1 (Babwell) and 11 (Sudbury).

146. ADAM NORTHAGHE of THORNDON, 30 April 1442

[*Commendation*: to God &c]; to be buried in Thorndon churchyard; in the name of a mortuary, whatever is right (*iust'*); to the high altar of the same church 12d; to the fabric of the said church 12d.
To Julian my daughter 20s; Julian to have my messuage in Eye, for term of her life, and after her decease, John her son to have it, to him and his assigns for ever; if John should die before coming of age, the messuage to be sold by my execs and the money from it to be equally divided, so that Thomas Colman shall have half and the other half to be disposed by my execs for my soul and my benefactors' [*souls*].
I will have a certain in the said church, 4s 4d; to a chaplain to celebrate an annual for a year and a trental similarly, in the same church, 8 marks.
I will have a pilgrim [*go*] to Monyes.[1]
Execs: Julian my daughter and John Grey.

Proved at Finningham ('Fynyngham'), 6 May 1443. Admon to executrix.

¹ The pilgrimage site of 'Moynes' cannot be identified.

[fol. 353v]
147. THOMAS PUTTOK of MILDENHALL ('Myldenhale'), barker, 24 July 1464

Dated at Mildenhall ('Myld'); [*commendation*: to God &c]; my body to Christian burial; to the high altar of the church of the said town, for my tithes and offerings underpaid, 12d.

To Dan (*dompnus*) John Lynne, monk in the monastery of St Edmund [*at*] Bury, to celebrate a trental for my soul, 5s.

To Isabel my wife my messuage in which I live, she to see to my burial and the paying of my debts; to Isabel all my goods and chattels in the town of Mildenhall and elsewhere in the realm of England, to the sustentation of her and our children.

To my five sons 13s 4d each, when each reaches the age of 20; if any of them dies before that, his or their money to be divided among the surviving sons.

Residue of all my goods to my execs, to sell, receive and dispose for my soul and the souls for whom I am bound, and in charitable deeds, as they see best to please God and profit my soul.

Execs: Isabel my wife and John Wrygth, smith.

Seal appended.

Proved at Fornham [*St*] Martin, 5 November 1464. Admon to Isabel, wife of the deceased, executrix. Power reserved to John Wryth[*sic*], smith, the other exec, when he comes. Seal of official appended.

[fol. 354]
148. THOMAS MYLDE of CLARE,¹ 5 December 1463

Of Clare in the diocese of Norwich; [*commendation*: to God &c]; to be buried in the chapel of the Blessed Mary in Clare church, before the altar in the said chapel there; in God's name (*ex parte dei*) I beg my execs to pay all my debts which I owe, that is, those that can be genuinely proved; to the high altar of the said church, for my tithes forgotten and offerings withheld and underpaid, 13s 4d.

For 5 trentals of St Gregory to be said for my soul, with all possible haste after my decease, 10s for each of them; a good and honest secular chaplain to celebrate for my soul and the souls of my father and mother, in Clare church and nowhere else, for a whole year, he having for his stipend what can reasonably be agreed.

To Margaret my wife my tenement in which I live, in Clare, wholly as I now have it, to hold to her and her assigns for her lifetime; after her decease the tenement to be sold by my execs for the best price possible, and out of the money from it to be paid to Margaret, the daughter of the late Richard Skylman, to pray for my soul and the souls of my parents for whom I am most bound, £20; the residue of the money from the sale to be disposed by the discretion of my execs in deeds of charity for the health of my soul, as seems best to please God and profit my soul, as they will answer before the Great Judge at the Day of Judgement. But, if at any time in her lifetime Margaret wishes to sell the reversion of my said tenement, then it to be sold by her and my execs and then the £20 to be paid to Margaret Skylman, and the residue of the money from the sale to be disposed as above.

Margaret my wife to have, for her lifetime, a piece of wood of mine in Belchamp St Paul (*Bellocampo Sancti Pauli*) in Essex, called, of antiquity, 'Wylwenhegge', containing, by estimation [*blank*] acres more or less, for the purpose of finding annually three lights burning before the three images in Clare church, St Mary, St Peter and St Katherine, at all times when divine service is celebrated there;[2] after the decease of the said Margaret the three lights to be found as aforesaid, for ever, with the aforesaid piece of wood, if there is anyone else willing to provide the three lights as rent for the wood; if not it to be sold and the money from it to be used for the same purpose down to the last penny (*ad ultimu' den'*).

If Thomas Grene of Witham ('Wytham') [*Essex*], gentleman ('gentylman') and Joan his wife, my daughter, should die without heirs, then after their decease the reversion of my manor of Wentford ('Wanteford') in Poslingford ('Posselyngforde')[3] to be sold by my execs and the money arising from it to be disposed by them towards the fabric of Clare church and among needy poor priests, in foul and noxious (*debil' et noc'*) ways of the same town, and in other deeds of piety, for the health of my soul, as seems most expedient.

Residue of my goods to Margaret my wife, executrix, with Henry Barkere of Clare and Thomas Ede of the same, execs; to each of them for their diligent labour 20s. Seal appended.

[fol. 354v] Proved at Clare, 27 September 1464. Admon to Margaret, executrix. Power reserved to Henry Barkere and Thomas Ede, the other execs, when they come, if they wish to take up admon. Seal of official appended.

1   Supervisor of the will of William Baker of Clare, pr. May 1440 (SROB, Baldwyne 28; Pt I, no. 149).
2   None of the other 17 wills of parishioners of Clare in Parts I and II mention any of these images in Clare church.
3   Wentford is 1 mile south of Poslingford.

149. JOHN HESSETE of WETHERDEN,[1] 5 October 1464

[*Commendation*: to God &c]; to be buried in Wetherden churchyard; to the high altar of the same church for my tithes forgotten or underpaid, for the health of my soul, 12d; to the emendation of the same church 40d.

To the friars of Babwell, for a trental, 10s.[2]

To each of my children 40d; to Agnes Deye 40d; to Richard Thorpp 20d.

To Agnes my wife and her assigns all my lands and tenements in the said town.

Residue of all my goods to the disposition of my execs, Agnes my wife, Richard Hessett and John Fresshwater,[3] to dispose for the health of my soul where they see most expedient.

Proved at Wetherden, 16 November 1464. Admon to execs.

1   Executor (as 'Hesse') of Thomas Hesset of Wetherden (SROB, Baldwyne 236; Pt I, no. 1182).
2   See note to no. 1.
3   Probate, no. 315; executor (as 'Fresswater') of Thomas Hesset (see note above).

[fol. 355]

150. MARGARET COLE, widow of John Cole, of STOKE BY NAYLAND ('Stokeneylond'), 20 August 1464

Dated at Stoke in the diocese of Norwich; in extremity, sick of body, afflicted by a mortal illness by the hand of Almighty God (*languens in extremis, eger corpore, plaga mortis manu dei omnipotentis percussa*); to be buried in the churchyard of the parish church of the Blessed Virgin Mary of Stoke aforesaid; to the high altar of the said church, for [*my*] tithes forgotten, 40d.

To the reparation of Higham ('Hyham') church 40d.

To the convent of Friars Minor of Colchester (*Colcestria*) 40d.[1]

To Agnes Haddok my servant a brass pot holding 2 gallons ('galones') and a brass pan holding 4 gallons.

My tenement in the town of Nayland ('Neylond *iuxta* Stoke'), where my [?*husband's*] body lies buried (*ubi corpus meum requiescit et est humatu'*), to be put up for public sale by my execs and the money from it to be disposed in pious uses; my feoffees, when they are so required in the name of charity, to deliver possession of the tenement to my execs or their assigns, they, having God before their eyes, to dispose for my soul and the souls of my husbands (*maritorum*) and parents.

Execs: Richard Moor, William Purser of Stoke and John Brykeman of Hadleigh ('Hadley'), to the disposition of whom the residue of all my goods.

Witnesses: Master John Cranewise, perpetual vicar of the said church,[2] John Clampe of Nayland, Robert Hakon and Thomas Hakon of Higham.

Seal appended.

Proved at Fornham St Martin, 25 August 1464. Admon to Richard Moore, exec. Power reserved to William Pursere and John Brykeman when they come. Inventory to be exhibited, and the account, in the chapel of St Peter, Sudbury, on the Wednesday after the feast of St Matthew the Apostle next [*i.e. 26 September*].

---

1   See note to no. 38.
2   John Cranewyse (so spelled in his will) was vicar of Stoke from 1455 to 1483/84 (Tanner, p.1385); will pr. January 1483/84 (NRO, NCC 178 A. Caston); he left his newly built house to the parish to be used for gilds, ales, 'drinkings' etc. See Dymond, 'God's Disputed Acre', especially pp. 480–81. Cranewyse also witnessed nos 236, 409 and 556.

151. THOMAS HAMOND of LAWSHALL ('Lawshull'),[1] 3 July 1464

Dated at Lawshall; [*commendation*: to God the Father &c]; my body to Christian burial; to the high altar of the said church 12d.

My tenement called 'Pelomes', my tenement called 'Cherchestrete howse', in which John Lumkyn, carpenter, lives, my tenement next to the tenement of John Fanne and my tenement called 'Gaytones' I leave to the use of the said church.

To each of my godsons and goddaughters a coomb of malt; 10 coombs of wheat and 10 coombs of malt to be distributed among the poor where there is greatest need; to John Fanne a quarter of wheat and a coomb of malt.

[fol. 355v] To each of the sons and daughters of William my brother[2] 6s 8d; to John Hamond my godson a brass pot with a pan; to Agnes Hamond a brass pot and a pan.

My tenement called 'Kynges', in which I live, to remain to William my brother after my decease, to him and his heirs, for his lifetime, and after his decease to remain to

John his son for his lifetime; after John's decease it is to be sold and disposed for me and my soul and for the souls of my parents and friends and all the faithful departed. Residue of all my goods to my execs, William Hamond my brother and John Long of Alpheton ('Alfleton'), to dispose as they see best to please God and profit my soul. Seal appended.

Witnesses: John Byrd, carpenter, Elizabeth Fanne and others.

Proved at Fornham St Martin, 3 September 1464. Admon to William Hamond, exec. Power reserved to John Long of Alpheton, when he comes &c[*sic*]. Seal of official appended.

¹   'Thomas Hamaund of Lawshall' was executor of William Everard, will pr. June 1444 (SROB, Baldwyne 57; Pt I, no. 293). 'Joan the wife of Thomas Hamond' was executrix of John Hamond of Lawshall, probate only, December 1440 (SROB, Baldwyne 26; Pt I, no. 140) but this may not be the same Thomas since this testator did not refer to a wife, either living or dead.

²   Will pr. October 1489 (SROB, Hervye 380).

152. ADAM CHAPMAN of BARROW ('Barwe'),¹ 2 August 1462

Dated at Barrow; [*commendation*: to God Almighty &c]; to be buried in the churchyard of the parish church of All Saints of Barrow; to the high altar of the same church 40d; to the use of the church 40s.

To the emendation of the ways in the said town 20s; to each of the needy in the said town a bushel (*modium*) of malt.

To a suitable priest, to celebrate for a year for my soul and the souls of my benefactors, 8 marks.

To the house of Friars Minor of Babwell 20s; to the house of Austin Friars of Clare 40d; to the house of Carmelite Friars of Cambridge (*Cant'*) 40d; to the house of Friars Preachers of Thetford 40d.²

To each child that I have raised from the holy font³ a sheep.

To Margaret my daughter 20 marks; to William my son a messuage bought of John Welys, formerly called 'Aleyns'; to Thomas my son a messuage called 'Ketelys'.

Residue of my goods to Agnes my wife.

Execs: Agnes my wife and Simon Spark.

Supervisor: John my son, chaplain.⁴

To the said Simon, for his labour 6s 8d.

Witnesses: Stephen Baldewyn, clerk,⁵ Thomas Warner and others.

Proved at Fornham St Martin, 15 September 1464. Admon to execs. Seal of official appended.

¹   Executor of John Holm of Barrow, will pr. November 1443 (SROB, Baldwyne 57; Pt I, no. 290); executor of John Muriell of Barrow, will pr. September 1451 (SROB, Baldwyne 105; Pt I, no. 471); executor of Clarissa, widow of John Moriell of Barrow, will pr. March 1451/52 (SROB, Baldwyne 107; Pt I, no. 488).

²   See note to no. 133 regarding bequests to houses of the four different orders of friars.

³   That is, his godchildren.

⁴   'John Chapman, clerk', was a substantial beneficiary of the will of Clarissa Moriell: 20s a year, up to a period of 24 years. See note above.

⁵   'Stephen Baldevyn, priest', was a beneficiary of the will of Margery Hunt of Barrow (no. 136).

[fol. 356]

153. ROBERT NOOKE of KERSEY, executor of the testament of Robert Pury, deceased,[1] 17 August 1464

[*Will*]

Of Kersey in the diocese of Norwich.

Out of a messuage called 'Glovers' in Kersey, sold to Richard Gobett, 10 marks to be paid in twenty years, that is, 6s 8d annually at the obit of Robert Pury, for that 20 years, on the date on the calendar entitled the first day of Lent, for the soul of the said Robert Pury, in the church of the Blessed Mary of Kersey.

The tenement called 'Bondyners' to be sold to John Lorkyn for 14 marks of which 7 marks to go to the buying of a marble gravestone (*unu' graveston de marmorea*) to lie on Robert Pury's grave; of the other 7 marks, 20s to go to John Wale for an unpaid debt of the said Robert Pury and the remaining 5 marks 6s 8d, with the other debts owed to Robert Pury, to be disposed for the soul of the said Robert Pury and the souls of his benefactors, as seems [*best*] to please God and to profit the soul of the said Robert Pury.

Execs: Richard Gobett and Andrew Nyghynghale[*sic*].

Seal appended.

Proved at Bildeston ('Bylston'), 26 September 1464. Admon to execs.

1   Will (as 'Robert Perye') pr. March 1455/56 (SROB, Baldwyne 223; Pt I, no. 1115).

154. SIMON WEYNEYLD of CHELSWORTH ('Chelysworth'),[1] 23 August 1464

Sick of body due to the ?great number and extremity of my days (*eger corporis de superp' et extremitate dierum meorum*); [*commendation*: to God &c]; to be buried in the churchyard of the aforesaid church; to the high altar of the said church 10s; to the fabric (*fabricacionem*) and emendation of the same church 20s.

To the high altar of Shimpling ('Shymplyng') church 6s 8d; to the fabric and emendation of that church 20s; to Alpheton ('Alfleton') church 13s 4d.

To the Friars Minor of Babwell 10s; to the friars of Clare 10s; to the friars of Sudbury 10s;[2] to be distributed among the poor 10s.

To a suitable priest to celebrate for two years for the health of my soul, Christian my wife's and my parents' and benefactors' [*souls*], 18 marks.

To each of my godsons and goddaughters 12d.

To Katherine my sister 13s 4d.

To John Semere my servant 6s 8d; to Christian Powlyn my servant 6s 8d; to Joan Semere 6s 8d.

Residue of all my goods to my execs, that is, John Tylere the elder of Monks Eleigh ('Illigh Monachorum'), and Master Thomas Muryell,[3] to dispose for the health of my soul and Christian my wife's and the souls of our parents and friends, that our souls and the souls of my execs might best be conveyed (*consegnantur*) into the hands of God; everything bequeathed in this testament to be paid by my execs as quickly as it can be received of my debts.

Supervisor: John Clopton of Melford, esquire.[4]

Seal appended.

[fol. 356v]

[*Will, of same date*]

John Swalwe the elder to have my tenement in which I live, for his lifetime, and after his decease John Swalwe the younger, his son, to have it, to him and his heirs; if John Swalwe the younger should die without heirs, then it to remain to Joan Swalwe, John the younger's sister, to her and her heirs; if she should die without heirs, the tenement to be sold and disposed by my execs, or by theirs, in alms deeds (*piis elemosinis*) for the health of my soul, for Christian my wife's and for Joan's [*souls*].

Joan the daughter of John Swalwe the elder to have 20 marks at her marriage, out of the payments for a tenement sold to the said John Swalwe the elder, as appears more fully in the deed made of it to John Clopton, esquire, John Swalwe the elder, Master Thomas Muryell, John Tylere and John Havell.

John Swalwe the elder to have the field called 'Hacchysfeld' and 'Barkeres Croft'.

All my ostilments, with the livestock, as appear in an indenture made of them, to be divided between John Swalwe the younger and Joan his sister when they reach full age, by the discretion of their father.

Witnesses: John Howlott, John Hellys, Thomas Mows, Robert Prynchatt and many others.

Proved at Bildeston ('Bylston'), 26 September 1464. Admon to execs.

¹ Executor of Augustine Martyn of Semer, will pr. April 1440 (SROB, Baldwyne 27; Pt I, no. 143); executor of Henry Qwarry of Hitcham, will pr. July 1461 (SROB, Baldwyne 297; Pt I, no. 1459).

² For the friars see notes to nos 1 (Babwell and Clare) and 11 (Sudbury).

³ Thomas Muryell (Maryell) was rector of All Saints, Chelsworth *c.*1460–1495 (Tanner, p.1354); will pr. October 1495 (NRO, NCC 229 Wolman); in his will he required a canopy to be made, at his expense, over the high altar of Chelsworth. Not to be confused with Thomas Meryell (Muryell), rector of Market Weston (see no. 822 below).

⁴ The powerful benefactor of Long Melford church, who lived where Kentwell Hall now is, and died in 1497. See Hervy, *Visitation of Suffolk, 1561*, vol. I, pp.20–25; Dymond and Paine, *Spoil of Melford Church*, pp.4–5; and Paine, 'Building of Long Melford Church'. John Clopton was supervisor of, or mentioned in, the following wills in Pt I: 201, 375, 640, 929, 1064, 1246, 1280; also supervisor of nos 181, 436 and 779 below; and witness of no. 733 below.

155. RICHARD SPRONT of CLARE, 18 November 1462

Of Clare in the diocese of Norwich; sick (*languens*); [*commendation*: to God &c]; my body to Christian burial in Clare churchyard. I beg my execs in God's name (*ex parte dei*) to pay all my debts which I owe, that is, which can be truly proved. To the high altar of Clare church, for my tithes and offerings withheld, forgotten and underpaid, 3s 4d; to the vicar of Clare church to celebrate for my soul and the souls of all my parents and benefactors, one day each week for a whole year, with all possible haste after my decease, in Clare church, 4s 4d.

Residue of all my goods to my execs, to dispose in deeds of charity as they see best to please God and profit my soul.

Execs: Marion my wife¹ and Richard Norman of Clare, to implement all [*my*] foregoing bequests in the best way they know; to Richard Norman 3s 4d, for his diligent labour about these premises.

Seal appended.

Witnesses: John Melon, Thomas Clerk, John Horold, Richard Norman, William Nycoll and others, specially called.

Proved at Clare, 28 September 1464. Admon to execs.

1   Will (as 'Mariota Sprunte'), no. 622.

[fol. 357]
156. SEMAN SMYTH of GREAT FINBOROUGH ('Fynberth Magna'), 3 November 1464

[*Commendation*: to God &c]; my body to the Christian burial at the aforesaid Finborough; to the high altar of the same church, for my tithes forgotten &c[*sic*], 2s; to the emendation of the same church 2s.

To the use of the same church an enclosure in the aforesaid Finborough and Little Finborough ('Fynberth Parva'), reckoned (*computatur*) at 3 acres, of which 2 acres are arable land and 1 acre meadow, together with another piece of land containing 3 roods in Great Finborough, which enclosure and piece of land were formerly Augustine Joure's, of Great Finborough, for providing and sustaining a lamp perpetually in the chancel of the said church, burning at the due and best times (*debitis temporibus et optimis*), and what is left over from it (*inde superfuerit*) faithfully to be spent in other necessaries in the same church, for the health of my soul and for the health of the souls of my parents and benefactors and all those at rest in Christ.

John Smyth, my son and heir, to pay Thomas Smyth my son, 26s 8d, to Robert my son 20s and to Margaret Cros my daughter 26s 8d.

Whatever remains of my goods to the disposition of my execs, my beloved in Christ, Joan my wife, Thomas and Robert my sons.

Proved at Stowmarket ('Stowe'), 17 January 1464/65. Admon to Robert Smyth, exec. Power reserved to Joan Smyth and Thomas Smyth, the other execs, when they come.

157. MARGARET MARTYN of HONINGTON ('Honyngton'),[1] 16 January 1464/65

[*Commendation*: to God &c; *no burial directions*]; to the high altar of the same church, for my tithes forgotten, 6d; to the rector of the said church, for my mortuary, 2 sheep.

To the convent of Friars Minor of Babwell, 3s 4d, to be paid in two parts; to the convent of Friars Preachers of Thetford, 3s 4d, to be paid in the same way; to the convent of Eremitic Friars of Thetford, 20d, to be paid in the same way; to the convent of nuns of Thetford, 20d; to the convent of Carmelite Friars of Ipswich (*Gippewic'*), 2s, to be paid in the same way.[2]

Residue of all my goods to John Wedyr of Honington, and Thomas Candelere of the same town, my execs, to distribute my legacies and dispose for the health of my soul.

Seal appended.

Proved at Fornham [*St Martin*], 21 January 1464/65.

1   ?Executrix of Rose Wymere, probate November 1458 (SROB, Baldwyne 196; Pt I, no. 959).
2   For the Friars Minor of Babwell and Carmelite Friars of Ipswich see notes to no. 1; for the Friars Preachers and nuns of Thetford see notes to no. 68; for the Eremetic Friars of Thetford see note to no. 69.

158. WILLIAM THURGUR of [GREAT WALDINGFIELD],[1] 1464

[*No day or month given*]; in the presence of many of the faithful (*in presens pluriu' fid'*); [*commendation*: to God &c]; to be buried in the churchyard of Great Wald-ingfield ('Wald Magna') church; to the high altar of the said church, for tithes forgotten, 8d.

All my debts to be paid to my creditors by Joan my wife and Robert Smyth, execs.
To the fabric of the same church 20s.

To Joan my wife all my chattels and utensils, for her provision and that of my chil-dren, and my dwelling house, until my son reaches the age of 18, if he lives that long, and if not, until my daughter is that age; after that, or before, if my children do not live that long, my dwelling house to be sold and Joan my wife to have of the money, if she is then living, 5 marks, and the rest to be distributed between my son and daughter, if they live; if one of them dies, the one that lives to have the part of the deceased; if both die [fol. 357v] in the lifetime of Joan my wife, she to have half the price of my dwelling house and the other half to be given to the fabric of the said church and in other pious deeds; if my wife and all my children die before they are of the said age, then the whole price of my dwelling house to be given to the fabric of the aforesaid church and in other pious deeds.
Seal appended.

Proved at Lavenham; [*no date given*]. Admon to execs.

> [1] Executor of John Thugor of Waldingfield, probate October 1458 (SROB, Baldwyne 209; Pt I, no. 1038).

159. THOMAS TOFFAY of BARDWELL ('Berdewell'), 1 December 1464

[*Commendation*: to God &c]; my body to Christian burial; to the high altar of the said church, for my tithes and offerings forgotten, 12d.

To the monks of the house of Bromholm ('Bromholme') [*Norfolk*] 2s;[1] to the friars of Babwell 2s;[2] to the Austin Friars of Thetford 2s.[3]

To William Cowper 2 acres of arable land in Bardwell field, lying between two mill-mounds (*mont' molend'*),[4] to hold, to him and his heirs, of the chief lords of the fee by due service and custom.

Alice my wife to have all my lands and tenements, meadows, pasture and feedings, rents and services in the towns and fields of Bardwell and Stanton, in Suffolk, except the aforesaid 2 acres of land assigned to William Cowper, to hold to her and her heirs of the chief lords of the fee by due service &c[*sic*]; to Alice my wife all my utensils and necessaries, to her own use.

Residue of all my goods and chattels to Alice my wife and Robert Well, execs, to dispose as seems best to please God and profit my soul.

Proved at Ixworth, 29 January 1464/65. Admon to execs. Seal of official appended.

> [1] The Cluniac priory of Bromholm, dedicated to the honour of St Andrew, was founded in 1113 and was made subordinate to the priory of the same order at Castle Acre. On 29 May 1466, two years after Thomas Toffay made this will, John Paston, the son of Judge William Paston, was interred at Bromholm at very great expense. In 1477, his son Sir John requested burial there, near his father's tomb (*VCH Norfolk*, ii, pp.359–63).
> [2] See note to no. 1.
> [3] See note to no. 69.
> [4] Mill-mounds marked the sites of former post-mills, and were a common feature in Suffolk; a few survive today, as on Mellis Green.

160. JOHN AYNOTH of HUNDON ('Honedon'), 29 December 1464

Dated the feast of St Thomas the Martyr; sick in body (*eger cu' corpore*); [*commendation*: to God &c]; my body to Christian burial; to the high altar of Hundon, for tithes forgotten, 13s 4d.

To the Friars Preachers of the town of Sudbury, 6s 8d; to the Friars Minor of Babwell, 6s 8d; to the Carmelite Friars of Cambridge (*Cant'*), 6s 8d; to the Austin Friars of Clare, 40d.[1]

The rest of all my goods to my exec, to dispose in the best way for the health of my soul.

Exec: William Aynoth my son.

Seal appended.

[*Will, of same date*]

William my son to have my land and tenements in Newmarket (*Novo mercato*), Woodditton ('Dytton') and Exning ('Ixnynge'), to him and his heirs; to William all the necessaries belonging to my craft, wherever they are [*to be found*].

John my son to have my tenement in which I live, in 'Brokhoole' in the parish of Hundon.

To Richard my son £20.

Friar Thomas London to have 8 marks, to celebrate for my soul for a whole year.

To Alice my daughter, 10 marks; to Alice all her [. . . .], wherever they may be.

Witnesses: John Taylor, Simon Taylor.

Proved at Hundon, 7 February 1464/65. Admon to execs.

1   For bequests to the four orders of friars see note to no. 133.

[fol. 358]

161. THOMAS MELLE of POLSTEAD ('Polsted'), 6 November 1464

Mindful of my end and seeing the peril of death approaching (*cogitans de extremis meis, vidensque mortis periculu' imminer'*); [*commendation*: to God &c]; my body to Christian burial; to the high altar of the said church, for tithes and offerings forgotten, 20d; to the high altar of Stoke by Nayland ('Stoke') 20d; to each priest coming to my burial 4d; to each clerk 2d; my best gown and my best hood to the emendation of Polstead church.

To Alice my wife my tenement in Polstead, for her lifetime, and after her decease it is to be sold by my execs, and of the money I leave: 20s to Robert my son; 20s to John my son; 20s to Thomas my son; 20s to William my son.

Residue of all my goods to the disposition of my wife Alice and Hugh Smyth of Stoke by Nayland, execs, to dispose for my soul and the souls of my parents and benefactors, as seems to them best to please God &c[*sic*].

Proved at Glemsford, 19 December 1464. Admon to Hugh Smyth, exec. Power reserved to Alice, relict of the deceased.

162. JOHN MAKELL of LONG MELFORD ('Melford'), 18 June 1464

Dated at Melford; [*commendation*: to God &c]; to be buried in the churchyard of the Holy Trinity of Melford; I wish to have, on the day of my death, *placebo* and *dirige* celebrated by all the priests and clerks living in Melford, each priest having 4d and each clerk 2d; to the Mass of Jesu 12d.[1]

To Robert Hawkyn a round basin of latten; to John Hawkyn a large brass pan; the basin and pan to be delivered to Robert and John within a week after the decease of Clemence my wife.[2]

To the aforesaid Clemence all my ostilments except those excepted above, for the term of her life; all my other goods I leave to Clemence during her lifetime, for her own use, and after her decease to remain to John my son and his assigns, that he might pray diligently for the souls of his parents.

Execs: Clemence my wife and John my son, to see my testament executed and among other things, to see that my debts be paid.

Proved at Glemsford, 19 December 1464. Admon to execs. Seal of official appended.

[1]   See note to no. 45.
[2]   The 'wife of John Makell of Melford' was one of the witnesses to the nuncupative will of William Ketyll of Preston, dated November 1457 (SROB, Baldwyne 190; Pt I, no. 929).

[fol. 358v]
163. JAMES SWEYN of GLEMSFORD ('Glemesford'),[1] 5 February 1462/63

Dated on the feast of St Agatha the Virgin 1462; [*commendation*: to God &c]; my body to Christian burial; to the high altar, for my tithes forgotten, 20d; to the new crucifix 6s 8d; to the fabric of the *?parclose (clausur')* of the said church 6s 8d.

To James Sweyn of Belchamp ('Belcham') [*Essex*] 20d.

To Avice Rogyll a brass pan.

Residue of all my goods to the disposition of my execs, William Rogyll,[2] William Gamelyn and John Holdeyn, 'taylour', to dispose for my soul and the souls of my benefactors.

Proved at Glemsford, 19 December 1464. Admon to execs.

[1]   James Swayn was executor of Walter Pap' of Glemsford, probate May 1450 (SROB, Baldwyne 123; Pt I, no. 576).
[2]   Executor of Thomas Rogyll, no. 164 below.

164. THOMAS ROGYLL of GLEMSFORD ('Glemesford'),[1] 25 September 1464

My body to Christian burial; to the high altar there 3s 4d.

To Agnes my wife my tenement for her lifetime, and after her decease the messuage to be sold by the execs of my execs.[2]

To a suitable priest, to celebrate in the said church for a whole year, 9 marks.

To William Rogyll 3s 4d.

Thomas Rogyll my son to have a tenement in 'Wodestrete', he to pay Meliore Rogyll £7, as appears in agreements made between them; if Thomas should default in part or in whole, then the messuage in 'Wodestrete' to be sold by my execs.

Residue of all my goods to the disposition of my execs: William Rogyll[3] and Agnes Rogyll my wife, to dispose for my soul and for the souls of my friends, to please God with the most expedience.

Proved at Glemsford, 19 December 1464. Admon to execs.

[1]   In February 1459/60 Thomas Rogyll had recently sold land to John Hedgeman the elder of Glemsford, will pr. July 1460 (SROB, Baldwyne 249; Pt I, no. 1246).
[2]   On the assumption that his executors could, or would, be dead by then.

³ Executor of James Sweyn (no.163).

[fol. 359]

165. THOMAS WRYGTH of STUSTON, 13 February 1464/65 [*probate only*]

Proved at Thornham Magna. Admon to Roger Wrygth of Thrandeston and Henry Harald of Stuston.

166. MARGARET TYE of SUDBURY ALL SAINTS, 12 April 1464

Of Sudbury, in the parish of All Saints, in the diocese of Norwich; suffering serious infirmity (*gravi infirmitate laborante'*); last will, carefully remembered and after-wards put in writing (*ultima voluntas, diligent' memorata et postea in scriptis redacta*);¹ [*commendation*: to God &c]; to be buried in the churchyard of the church of All Saints.

William Smyth, the son of John Smyth, 'cowpere', to have, to him and his heirs for ever, my messuage with the solar, called 'le Garyte', lately John Clarew's and Joan his wife's, my mother, that is, on condition that the said William Smyth provide my body (*tradat corpus meum*) with Christian burial, as above, and pay my debts to those to whom I am in any way bound, and also pay and fulfil my legacies, as follows: to the high altar of the said church 20d; to the reparation of All Saints church 3s 4d; to William Tye my husband 6s 8d; to John Smyth, 'cowpere', 3s 4d; to Joan Cowpere my daughter 6s 8d; to Friar William Morehall of the convent of Sudbury 12d;² to John the son of the said John Coupere and Joan 13s 4d; to Joan their daughter 3s 4d.

My anniversary to be celebrated, for my soul and for the souls of my parents and friends, in All Saints church, annually for 7 years following my decease; there to be spent annually in the conducting of those obsequies 2s and more.

The said William,³ or someone else named by him, to go on pilgrimage for me (*laboret pro me peregrinando*), twice to Walsingham [*Norfolk*]⁴ and make offering there for me, in honour of the Blessed Mary, both times, as I should have done if I had been there in person (*prout ego ipse facerem si ib'm p'ter interessem*); he to go on pilgrimage once for me to Woolpit ('Wlpitt')⁵ with due offering being made there in my name; he to go on pilgrimage once for me to Manston [*Dorset*],⁶ to make offering there in my name, in oats, as much as a sleeve will hold (*quantum una manica capere possit*).⁷

In God's name, I beg all my cofeoffees in the said messuage to deliver their estate according to my will, when required to do so after my decease by the said William. Residue of all my goods and chattels, which by right or custom I can legally bequeath, to the said William, to do freely therewith as he wishes.

Witnesses: Thomas Tylere, vicar of the said church,⁸ John Smyth, 'cowpere', and others.

Proved at Lavenham, 18 February 1464/65. Admon to exec.

¹ But, from the text of the will, not strictly nuncupative.
² ?The same man as 'Friar William Morchall', godson of John Newman of Sudbury (SROB, Bald-wyne 170; Pt I, no. 818).
³ Presumably 'the said William' required to be pilgrim and executor was William Smyth, rather than her husband William Tye.
⁴ One of the major pilgrimage sites in medieval England.
⁵ See note to no. 142.

6   Manston (near Shaftesbury in Dorset); the church, dedicated to St Nicholas, contained an image
     known as 'the Maid of Manston' which attracted pilgrims. See Hutchins, *History and Antiquities
     of the County of Dorset*, pp.73–7. Isabel Man of Brettenham had requested a pilgrimage there
     (SROB, Baldwyne 299; Pt I, no. 1466), as had a testator in the deanery of Dunwich (Middleton-
     Stewart, *Inward Purity*, p.129).
7   This seems to be the testatrix's literal description of the quantity of oats to be offered: a 'sleeve'
     is not defined as a dry measure in any of the available glossaries or dictionaries.
8   Previously rector of Alby, Norfolk, Thomas Tyler was vicar of All Saints, Sudbury, from 1454 to
     1465 (Tanner, p.1390). See also no. 727.

167. ADAM BONSERGEAUNT of PAKENHAM, 4 March 1464/65 [*probate only*]

Proved at Fornham [*St*] Martin. Admon to Margaret, relict of the deceased, and
Thomas Smyth, execs. Seal of official appended.

[fol. 359v]
168. ALICE CLERK of BARDWELL ('Berdewell'),[1] [?*1464*]

[*No date given*]; in my pure widowhood (*in mea pura viduetate*); [*commendation*:
to God &c]; my body to Christian burial; to the high altar of Bardwell church 4d;
to Ixworth church 4d; to the emendation of the said church 6s 8d; to the reparation
of Haughley ('Hawgley') church 6s 8d.
To the friars of Babwell, for a trental, 10s.[2]
To Hervey Ingelond, the son of William Ingelond, 12d.[3]
Residue of all my goods to Hervey Clerk my son[4] and John Sillote, execs, to dispose
&c[*sic*].
Proved at Ixworth, 5 March 1464/65. Admon to execs.

1   Widow of James Clerk of Ixworth, probate December 1447 (SROB, Baldwyne 80; Pt I, no. 372).
2   See note to no. 1.
3   William Ingelond (as 'Inglond') was the brother of Alice Clerk; his will pr. June 1460 (SROB,
     Baldwyne 245; Pt I, no. 1231).
4   Hervey Clerk was one of the executors of his father James Clerk, together with his mother Alice
     and his uncle William Inglond. See note above.

169. JOHN RYGGE of COMBS ('Combes'), 11 January 1464/65

[*Commendation*: to God &c]; my body to Christian burial &c[*sic*]; to the high altar
of the same church 12d.
To Christian my wife 5 acres of land which I lately bought from John Russhebrook
to pay my debts and for my burial.
To Christian my wife and Thomas my son all my other lands and tenements, free and
bond, in the town of Combs ('Combys') for term of the life of Christian my wife;
and after her decease, I give all the said lands &c[*sic*] to Thomas my son and his
heirs; if Thomas should die before his mother, then after the decease of Christian, I
wish all the lands &c[*sic*] to be sold by my execs &c[*sic*].
To Isabel my daughter my one tenement in Needham Market ('Neddham Mareket'),
to her and her heirs.
Residue [*of my goods*] to my execs, Christian my wife, Richard Cowper and John
Hardy of the same.
Proved in the church of Buxhall ('Buxhale'), 12 March 1464/65. Admon to Christian,

relict of the deceased, executrix. Power reserved to Richard Cowper and John Hardy when they come &c[*sic*].

[fol. 360]

170. JOHN BROWN of WORTHAM, 6 March 1463/64

[*Commendation*: to &c]; to be buried in the churchyard of the church of the Blessed Mary of Wortham; to the high altar, for tithes forgotten, 12d; to John Chapman, parish chaplain of Wortham, 8d; for a trental 10s; to the reparation of the said church 4 bushels of wheat, 4 bushels of barley and 6s 8d; to the reparation of Burgate church 4 bushels of malt.

To the poor in greatest need 4 bushels of rye.

To each of my sons and daughters 4 bushels of barley.

Elizabeth my wife to have, for term of her life, all my lands and tenements, rents and services, in the towns of Wortham, Burgate and Redgrave, except a piece of land containing 5 roods in Redgrave, lying in a field called 'Menhaugh', on condition that she keeps herself unmarried (*custodiat se a thoro maritali*) and lives in pure widowhood for term of her life, and then she to have and to hold all the said lands and tenements, rents and services, for term of her life, of the chief lords of the fee, by due service.

After the decease of Elizabeth, William my son to have all the said lands and tenements, rents and services, to him and his heirs male; if William should die without heirs male, all the lands and tenements to remain to John my son and his heirs male; if John should die without heirs male, then the lands and tenements to remain to Walter my son, similarly; if Walter should die without male heirs then they to remain to Geoffrey my son and his heirs male, and if Geoffrey should die without male heirs then all the lands and tenements to be sold and the money from them to be disposed for the health of my soul and of all my friends' [*souls*].

To Elizabeth my wife half the utensils of the house and half of all my goods and chattels.

Residue of all my goods, after my debts have been paid, to my execs, to dispose for me and for the health of my soul.

Execs: Walter Smallebergh and Geoffrey Thorpp.

Proved at Cotton, 11 July 1464. Admon to execs.

171. ALICE HUNTT of WITHERSFIELD ('Wederysfeld'), 12 January 1463/64

['Huntte' *in margin*] [*Commendation*: to God &c]; my body to Christian burial; to the high altar of the same church, for my tithes forgotten and offerings underpaid, 3s 4d; to assemble (*comperand'*) a complete vestment of one suit (*unius secte*) to serve in Withersfield church on principal days and greater feasts, 10 marks, and this as soon as it can be done, to the honour of God, the Blessed Mary and all the saints, and for the health of my soul and the souls of my parents and husbands [*plural*].

To the fabric of the church of Great Thurlow ('Thyrlowe Magna') 40s, for the soul of Thomas Huntt my late husband, [fol. 360v] and for the health of my soul.

A cow, to the sustentation and augmentation of the sepulchre light in Withersfield [*church*], to be delivered by my execs, immediately after my decease, to the wardens (*custodibus*) of the said church, so that they can put it out to farm for the support of the said light, that my will may be fulfilled in this way, to the glory of God; and, in the name of charity, I ask that the parson of the church and his successors, and the wardens and their successors, will be supervisors, for ever, of the said cow, that my will may be well and truly executed in this way, to the honour of God; and I will that the said wardens and their successors for the time being shall see that the farmers of the said cow shall produce and wean (*emiterent et ablactabunt*) a calf from the said cow, so that there is always a cow (*quod una vacca semper habeatur*) to support the said light for ever.[1]

To each priest present at my obsequies 4d, and to each clerk 1d; to Friar John Hervy 26s 8d, to celebrate a complete trental (*trentale integrum*), with all the intercessions (*cu' omnibus suffragiis*) for my soul and the souls of my parents and husbands [*plural*].

Those 9 marks which William Umfrey owes me to be divided and disposed among my poor neighbours living in Withersfield and Great Thurlow, to be paid in 12 years by the same William as follows: each year of the 12 years, 10s to the maintenance and benefit of the said poor and needy, and this in malt or in any other grain, or in any other things most suitable for their maintenance; and I make my execs supervisors of this, to see my will well and truly preformed in this respect.

To Margaret my daughter 'Pollytes Croftt', and for this gift she is to acquit William her brother of 5 marks, part payment of the 10 marks which the same William is bound to pay the said Margaret, as is fully contained in a writing of obligation relating to it; and I require my feoffees to deliver full and peaceful possession of the croft called 'Pollites Croftt' to Margaret and her feoffees, without any delay, when so required by Margaret.

To my execs all the timber and crop (*vestur'*) of a copse called 'Gaytesberyes Grove', to sell, and the money from it to be disposed in the payment of my legacies and debts, and in other deeds of charity.

To Ed' my son all my tenement called 'Gatesberyes', apart from anything in it previously bequeathed, he to celebrate, for his father's soul and mine, and for the souls of all our benefactors, in Withersfield church, for the term of 3 years immediately following [*his coming into the tenement*], but one year in that term, he to celebrate solemnly in Hundon ('Honeyden') church for the soul of Richard Poperyk,[2] if he may serve the service there (*si poter' haber' servic' ibidem servend'*).

Residue of all my goods to John Sheldrak, Simon Sheldrak and Thomas Derman of Withersfield, execs, to dispose out of them for the health of my soul as seems most expedient and according to their discretion.

Supervisor: Ed' Hunte.

Seal appended.

Proved at Clare, 19 July 1464. Admon to execs. Seal of official appended.

[1]   This is a rare insight into the way in which the bequest of an animal would be administered in order to support the cost of a light.

[2]   Perhaps Richard Poperyk was a former husband of Alice Huntt: on two occasions in her will she refers to the souls of her parents and husbands.

[fol. 361]
172. ISABEL CAKE *alias* REVE of MILDENHALL ('Myldenhale'), 14 February 1464/65

[*Commendation*: to God &c; *no burial directions*]; to the high altar for tithes forgotten 12d; to the fabric of the same church 3s 4d.

To Robert my son my whole cart, with the horses and harness belonging to it; to Robert 3 cows.

To Margaret, the daughter of Thomas Woderes, a calf, a brass pot, a cauldron, a pair of sheets and a cover.

To Margery, the daughter of John Cake *alias* Reve, a calf.

To Robert my son all the utensils and ostilments belonging to my house.

Isabel, the wife of Robert Havet, to have 9 cows; Isabel also to have an acre of arable land for her lifetime, and after her decease Robert my son to have half the acre, and the other half to be sold by my execs; if Robert wishes to buy that half, he to have it before any other man.

To the said Robert my son another half acre of land, which his father bought from Draxes.

Residue of all my goods to my execs, John Dobyn and Robert Reve my son.

Proved at Mildenhall, 29 March 1465. Admon to execs.

[*This will is repeated on the reverse of the same folio, no. 177*]

173. THOMAS HOODE of FELSHAM,[1] 10 January 1464/65

Dated 10 January 4 Edward IV; [*commendation*: to God &c]; my body to Christian burial; to the high altar of the same church 3s 4d; to Felsham church 2 torches. To the friars of Clare 10s.[2]

To Agnes my daughter 7s; to Agnes Bekke 3s 4d; to Robert Bek 3s 4d; to Margery Hoode 3s 4d.

Execs: Joan Hoode my wife and George Hoode [*my*] son and Richard Stabelere the elder, of Rattlesden.

Proved at Fornham [*St*] Martin, 1 April 1465. Admon to execs. Power reserved to Richard Stabelere when he comes.

[1]   Executor (as 'Hod') of his father Thomas Hod of Felsham, will pr. June 1457 (SROB, Baldwyne 186; Pt I, no. 901).
[2]   See note to no. 1.

174. RICHARD BLOOME of IXWORTH ('Ixworthe'), 25 March 1465

Dated on the feast of the Annunciation of the Blessed Mary; [*commendation*: to God &c]; to buried in the churchyard of the church of the Blessed Mary of Ixworth; to the high altar of the said church, for tithes forgotten and others not duly paid, 13s 4d.

To Cecily my wife 6 marks in money.

To Marion my daughter 6s 8d.

To Robert my son 13s 4d, if so much can be raised from my goods beyond my legacies; to the same [?*Robert*] my primer.

To Cecily my wife 20s of the debt of Thomas Cok of Garboldisham ('Garboldysham') [*Norfolk*].

98

To the parish church of Ixworth 5 marks in money, to be received of my debts as appear in my papers (*papiris meis*).

To Cecily my wife all the utensils and bedding of my house.

Residue of all my goods to John Leman and Nicholas Dysneye, execs, firstly to pay all my debts and then dispose anything remaining in pious uses, as seems to them beneficial (*efficac'*) to my soul and profitable to the souls of all the faithful, according to the advice and conscience (*consciencia'*) of John Asshfeld of Stow-langtoft, esquire, supervisor;[1] to each of my execs for their diligence 3s 4d.

Seal appended.

Proved at Ixworth, 2 April 1465. Admon to execs.

> 1   John, only son of the first marriage of Robert Ashfield, inherited the manor of Stowlangtoft when his father died in 1459. John, who married Florentia, daughter of John Boteler of Meppershall (Beds), died in 1481 (IPM, 21 Edward IV, 32). See Copinger, *Manors of Suffolk*, i, pp.365–6.

[fol. 361v]

175. JOHN SPYCERE of WALSHAM LE WILLOWS ('Walsham'), 1 September 1450

Of Walsham in the diocese of Norwich; [*commendation*: to God &c; *no burial directions*]; to the high altar of the same church, for tithes forgotten, 12d; I wish to have two trentals if my goods be sufficient for them.

To William Potagere my godson 6s 8d; to Agnes, my wife's daughter, 3s 4d.

Avice my wife to have all my lands and tenements, to her and her assigns, for her lifetime, together with all the utensils and bedding in my house; my execs, if they see my wife to be in need of food and drink, and indigent, to sell now one parcel of land, now another, at their disposition, whereby she may be able to live, and, similarly, the utensils;[1] but if she be not in need, then all my lands and tenements remaining after the death of Avice to be sold, and the money to be distributed in pious uses, and especially to Walsham church, for the health of our souls and all our benefactors' [*souls*].

Residue of all my goods to the disposition of my execs, William Potagere, chaplain,[2] and William Fullere, to dispose [*sic*].

Witnesses: John Mellere and Thomas Page of Walsham.

Seal appended.

Proved at Ixworth, 2 April 1465. Admon to William Fullere, exec; William Potagere, co-exec, renouncing admon.

> 1   This will was made in 1450: the testator was referring to the mid-century recession.
> 2   Two wills of William Potagere survive, both pr. April 1482 (NRO, NCC 114 and 117 A. Caston); he requested burial in the chapel of St Katherine in Walsham church and bequeathed vestments to the churches of Walsham, Stanton St John and Langham.

176. JOHN SPARHAM of EYE, 3 April 1465 [*probate only*]

Proved. Admon to execs.

177. ISABEL CAKE *alias* REVE of MILDENHALL ('Myldenhale'), 14 February 1464/65

[*Same will as no. 172, qv*]

[fol. 362]
178. WALTER PAGE of EYE, [?*1462*]

[*Not dated; commendation*: to God &c; *no burial directions*]; to the high altar of Eye parish church, for tithes forgotten, 3s 4d; to the high altar of Eye abbey 3s 4d;[1] to the altar of St Thomas the Martyr, in Eye parish church, a towel;[2] to the reparation of the tower of the same church 6s 8d.

My wife to have a cow, a young pig (*porcell'*) [*and*] 6 hens with the cock going (*ambulant'*) on my tenement each year (*annuati'*) during her lifetime; she to have annually, from John my son, 10s and free entry to the chamber, to the fire, to the bakery and to the well, for her lifetime; she also to have 10s from my execs each year, for her lifetime, while the sum due to them from Sir John Chyrche, vicar of Cratfield ('Cratfeld'), lasts.

Residue of all my goods to Sir Richard Peyntore, chaplain, William Goldyng and Robert Saxi, execs, to dispose for my soul and the souls of all my friends, as they see best to please God and profit my soul.

Proved at Yaxley, 9 July 1462. Admon to Sir Richard Peyntore, exec. Power reserved to William Goldyng and Robert Saxi, the other execs, when they come and if they wish to take up admon.

1   The Benedictine priory of Eye, dedicated in honour of St Peter, was founded by Robert Malet, in the time of the Conqueror, as a cell to the abbey of Bernay. The very liberal foundation charter gave to the monks of Eye a portion of the founder's burgage in the town of Eye, together with the tithe of the market, and a large number of churches and vills. In 1537, following the formal suppression of the house the site of the priory and the whole of its possessions were granted to Charles, duke of Suffolk (*VCH Suffolk*, ii, pp.72–6).
2   The only reference in the whole register to an altar dedicated to St Thomas the Martyr in Eye church; the only gilds mentioned in the parish were the gild of the Blessed Mary and the gild of St Peter. Images of the Blessed Mary, St John and St Anne in Eye church are mentioned in no. 252 below.

179. JOHN TUFFELD the elder of WHEPSTEAD ('Qwepsted'),[1] 10 December 1462

Dated at Whepstead; [*commendation*: to God &c; *no burial directions*]; to the high altar in Whepstead church, for my tithes forgotten, 8d.

To the convent of Babwell, for a trental to be celebrated there for my soul, 10s.[2]

To Isodor my wife all my ostilments and utensils of any kind belonging to my house, for term of her life, and after her decease all the said ostilments and utensils to be divided equally between Thomas Tuffeld my son and Margaret, daughter of Isodor; but if it is necessary for Isodor to sell any part of the ostilments or utensils in her lifetime, then it to be sold to help her according to the advice and wishes of Alan Legat and the said Thomas Tuffeld.

Residue of all my goods to my execs, to sell and pay my debts, and dispose for my soul and the souls for whom I am bound.

Execs: Isodor my wife, Alan Legat of Hawstead[3] and Thomas Tuffeld my son; to each of them for their labour 12d.

Proved at Fornham [*St Martin*], 3 January 1462/63. Admon to Alan and Thomas, execs. Power reserved to Isodor, executrix, when she comes.

1   ?Son and executor of Alice Tuffeld of Whepstead, probate April 1444 (SROB, Baldwyne 50; Pt I, no. 267).

100

[fol. 362v]

180. STEPHEN HECHAM of HAUGHLEY ['Hawle'], 4 April 1462

[*In margin* 'Hecham *alias* Bochere'][1] [*Commendation*: to God &c; *no burial directions*]; to the high altar of Haughley parish church, for my tithes forgotten or underpaid, 20d; to the high altar of Old Newton ('Newton') church, in the same way, 20d. To Joan my wife all my lands and tenements, rents and services, in the towns of Haughley ('Hagle') and Wetherden, to hold of the chief lords of the fee, by due service, for term of her life; after her decease all the said lands and tenements, rents and services, to remain to John Saltere of Buxhall ('Buxale') and Margaret his wife, my daughter, to hold to them and their heirs of the chief lords of the fee by due service and custom, for ever, on condition that the said John Saltere pays 18 marks in money, in 10 years next following the decease of the said Joan, as follows: to the reparation of Haughley church 20s; to the new glass window in the chapel of St Mary there, 13s 4d; to the friars of Dunwich (*Donevic'*), for a trental of St Gregory to be celebrated there for my soul, 10s;[2] to the friars of Babwell, in the same way, 10s;[3] to the emendation of the way to 'Fliesgapp', where there is most need; to William Hecham my son 40s, and to his two sons 6s 8d; to the said Margaret my daughter, a chest, and to her 6 sons, 20s; Roger Hecham, the son of John Hecham, when he comes to legal age, to have 40s, but if he dies under that age, the 40s to remain to Haughley church; to our parish clerk 6d; the residue of the 18 marks to be spent faithfully in pious uses for the health of my soul, by my execs.

John Saltere and Margaret his wife to be responsible for (*sint onerati*) the reparation of the buildings (*domorum*) of the said tenements during the lifetime of Joan my wife.

Any residue of my goods to the disposition of my execs, my beloved in Christ, Joan my wife, and John Saltere, to dispose for me and my soul where they see most expedient to please God.

Supervisor: John Blowgate; he to have for his labour 3s 4d.

Seal appended.

Proved at Stowmarket, 10 July 1462. Admon to execs.

1 'Stephen Bocher' was executor of John Bocher of Haughley, will pr. March 1458/59 (SROB, Baldwyne 155; Pt I, no. 741). It is clear from John's will that his executor and the testator here were the same person; his will also suggests the likely origin of 'Hecham *alias* Bochere'. Evidently sometime after the death of her husband Bocher, the testator's mother Joan had married someone named Heacham; in his will Stephen identified his own surname as Heacham, but his brother John's will identified him as Bocher. The probate clerk's addition in the margin seems to be an attempt to clarify the matter.
2 See note to no. 65.
3 See note to no. 1.

[fol. 363]

181. RICHARD WEDERTON of HITCHAM ('Hecham'), 1 July 1461

Dated at Hitcham; [*commendation*: to God Almighty &c]; to be buried in the body (*in corpore*) of Hitcham parish church, before the image of the crucifix; to the high altar of the same church, for my tithes and offerings forgotten, 20s; to the necessary emendation of the said church 13s 4d; to the making of a silk cope, of the colour of 'sateyn cremesyn', for the use of the same church, 20s, and more as shall be needed for completing the cope.

My messuage in Bury St Edmunds, in 'Reyngatestrete', to be sold, and the money from it to be spent in the payment of my debts and in the performance of my legacies.

Joan my wife to have all my bedding and utensils of my house, and all my movable chattels; she also to have my messuage in Hitcham, and all my other lands and tenements in Hitcham, Brettenham, Preston and Bildeston ('Bylston'), to hold to her and her heirs for ever, on condition that she pays my debts which I rightfully owe, and fulfils my legacies, and also provides a suitable chaplain to celebrate divine service in Hitcham church, for my soul and for the souls of my parents and benefactors, deceased, for two whole years next after my death.

There to be 40s shared among my servants, by the discretion of John Clopton, esquire,[1] and the said Joan.

My grave to be made in all ways (*in omnibus*) according to the fashion (*forma'*) of the grave of William Cressenere, esquire,[2] in the church of the friars in Sudbury.[3]

My feoffees in my said lands and tenements to make and deliver estate in them according to this testament and last will, when they are so required.

Executrix: Joan my wife.

Supervisor: the said John Cloptone, he to have a complete [*suit of*] body armour, which used to be my own (*una' integra' armatur' que ad corpus meu' propriu' pertinere consue'*).

Seal appended.

Proved at Bildeston, 1 July 1462. Admon to executrix.

[1] See note to no. 154.
[2] William Cressener had died in 1454 (IPM, 32 Henry VI 16). The family's main manor was that of Cresseners in Hawkedon (Copinger, *Manors of Suffolk*, v, pp.249–50) but William also held Mores manor in Boxted (*Manors of Suffolk*, i, p.36) and Mortimer's manor in Preston (*Manors of Suffolk*, i, p.188). He had succeeded his father Robert de Cressener in 1410. He married Margaret, widow of Richard Lord Scrope of Bolton and daughter of Ralph Neville 1st earl of Westmorland.
[3] See note to no. 11.

[fol. 363v]
182. JOHN COWERDE of CHEVELEY ('Chevele') [*Cambs*], 4 April 1462

[*Commendation*: to God &c; *no burial directions*]; to the high altar of Cheveley 12d; to the same church 2 bushels (*modios*) of barley.

To the emendation of a way called 'Bredestrete lane' 20 cart[*load*]s of stones (*carect' lapidu'*).

Residue of all my goods to Agnes my wife and John my son, to dispose for the health of my soul, as seems to them best.

[*Will, of same date*]

Agnes my wife to have my messuage to live in for her whole lifetime, and 5 acres of arable land and the utensils of my house; after her decease John my son to have the messuage, with everything belonging to it, to him and his heirs for ever.

The same John to have, to him and his heirs for ever, a piece of arable land next to the pasture called 'Cowthey' in 'Parkfeld', and all my other lands except those excepted below.

My feoffees to deliver to Thomas my son a piece of land in 'Parkefeld', next to the land lately of John Horne; to Simon my son 'Chownescroft' with the toft there; to William my son of a piece of land called 'Dunnygges Appylton'; and to Amicia my daughter an acre of land where seems best to my execs.

My feoffees to deliver estate and possession to Thomas, Simon, William and Amicia, each for their part, when legally required; if any of these my children, that is, Thomas, Simon or William, die without heirs, or if all die without heirs, then the land to remain to John my son and his heirs for ever; if Thomas, Simon, William or Amicia wish to sell their part, John my son to have preference over all others if he so wish and can agree on a price.

Agnes my wife to have [*as*] the aforesaid 5 acres [*of arable land*] for term of her life: the first in the piece lying in 'Parkfeld', next to 'Cowthey'; the second in that piece in the same field next to the land lately John Horn's; the third in 'Dunnygges Apylton'; the fourth and fifth in other places where seems best to her; and my feoffees to deliver estate and possession to Agnes of the 5 acres of arable land, and of the said messuage, for term of her life, she making no strip or waste of the said messuage in any way.

Proved at Cheveley, 6 July 1462. Admon to execs.

[fol. 364]

183. HENRY HARLESTON [of STANTON], 1 May 1462

[*Commendation*: to God &c]; to be buried in the churchyard of the church of All Saints, Stanton.

Agnes my wife to have my tenement in Stanton called 'Amigeres' for 16 years of the life of Thomas my son, providing for him as he should be provided for; when he comes to the age of 16 all my feoffees to make him estate in the tenement, to hold to him and his heirs; if Thomas should decease without heirs the tenement to remain to John his brother and his heirs; if John should die without heirs, the tenement to be sold and the money from it to be disposed in pious uses.

Elizabeth my daughter to have my tenement called 'Gardeners' in Hartest ('Herthrust') when she comes to the age of 15; in the meantime Agnes my wife to have the said tenement in the same way; if Elizabeth should die before coming to the age of 15, the tenement called 'Gardeneres' to remain to Agnes my wife and her heirs.

Residue &c[*sic*] to Agnes my wife, Rose Bole of Hartest and John Bisshopp, execs. Seal appended.

Proved [*no more given*].

184. ROBERT HOGGE of ROUGHAM ('Rowgham'), 20 February 1464/65

[*Commendation*: to God &c]; my body to Christian burial; to the high altar there 3s 4d; to the fabric of the new tower £10, with the sum previously paid to it.[1]

My messuage, formerly the messuage of Alan de Rowgham, with all the lands belonging to it of ancient right, with all the timber (*silvis*), wood (*boscis*), and underwood, closes, meadows, feedings (*pascuis*) and rents, to remain to John Hogge my son and his heirs, on condition that Alice my wife have from John, out of the messuage, 40s in money annually, for the whole term of her life, at four times in the year, by equal portions.

My messuage called 'Collynes' to be sold after my decease, by the advice of my execs, for the best price possible, except that, if John my son wishes to buy the messuage with all the lands, then he to have it for 40s less than the realistic (*competens*) price.

To Alice my wife all the utensils belonging to my house.

To the friars of Babwell 10s, for celebrating a trental of St Gregory, for my soul and the souls for whom I am bound to pray, and a quarter of wheat; to the friars of St Augustine of Clare 5s; to the friars of Sudbury a quarter of wheat.[2]

To each of my godsons and goddaughters a bushel of wheat.

To Edmund Tylney, parish chaplain,[3] 12d, and from the alms collected from the brethren and sisters of the gild of St John the Baptist in Rougham, 12d, to be collected by the officers of the same gild, as is the custom.[4]

To Thomas ?Colmore, parish clerk, 6d.

To each of my execs, for their labour, 6s 8d.

All my feoffees to deliver estate and peaceful possession in my messuage called 'Collynys', with all the lands and rights, to my execs, as soon as they are required. A certain piece of my land called 'Margretes Lond' to remain to John Hogge my son, on condition that he and his successors provide, [fol. 364v] at his own cost, a candle burning before the sepulchre of Our Lord, in the accustomed manner, at Easter-time, and during the time of my anniversary and my parents', for ever, under the eye (*visu*) of my execs and their successors and execs.

If my aforesaid son, or any of my sons, oppose (*impedierint*) this will, or in any way challenge my execs as to my title in law, then he so doing shall forfeit the portion of my goods bequeathed to him.

To Alice, the servant of James Sampson, 4 bushels of wheat; to Alice Burnell, formerly my servant, 4 bushels of barley.

Residue of [*my*] goods &c[*sic*] to my execs, Alice my wife, John Bacon of Hessett ('Heggesset') and Nicholas Morse of Hengrave, they to fulfil my will in the best manner possible, as they will answer before the Judge, and pay all my debts to whomsoever they can.

My execs to provide a suitable chaplain to celebrate for my soul and to pray for those for whom I am bound to pray, for a whole year, and to go on pilgrimage for me to the Court of Rome, and to celebrate at the stations, as the custom is,[5] he having for his salary £10 in money, from my execs.

Witnesses: Philip Bokenham, Thomas Kervere, with many others.

Proved at Fornham [*St Martin*], 22 April 1465. Admon to executrix. Power reserved to John Bacon and Nicholas Morsse, execs, when they come.

---

[1] Substantial bequests to the building of the new tower were made over the 30-year period from 1458 to 1488, the first by Roger Tyllot, who left 50 marks and 'as much more [money] as is possible, according to the discretion of [my] supervisor' (SROB, Baldwyne 247; Pt I, no. 1240) and the last by John Bray (will pr. 1488: SROB, Hervye 398). See Blatchly and Northeast, *Decoding Flint Flushwork*, Rougham St John the Baptist. A photograph of the tower forms the frontispiece of Part I.

[2] For the friars see notes to nos 1 (Babwell and Clare) and 11 (Sudbury).

[3] See note to no. 130 and also no. 772.

[4] No other testator in Baldwyne mentioned this gild. Hogge's bequest to the parish chaplain provides an insight into the customs associated with gild membership.

185. REGINALD TOFTES of ELVEDEN,[1] 8 January 1464/65

To be buried in the churchyard of Eleveden parish church; to West Stow ('Westowe') church 40d; to Elveden church 40d.

Matilda my wife to have my tenement in Elvedon, lying next to 'Downynges', for term of her life; after her death the tenement to be sold and disposed for our souls. To each of my godsons a sheep.

Residue of all my goods to Matilda my wife to dispose for my soul, as she sees best to please God, and she to be executrix.

Proved [*no date or place*]. Admon to executrix.

1   ?Related to John Toftys of West Stow (no. 304).

[fol. 365]
186. JOHN MOYSE of HOPTON, 26 May 1464

Dated St Augustine's day in May; [*commendation*: to God Almighty, the Blessed Mary &c]; to be buried in the churchyard of the church of All Saints of Hopton; to the high altar of the said church, for tithes forgotten and not well paid, 12d; to a thurible to serve in Hopton church for ever, 4 marks.

To the gild of St John the Baptist of Thelnetham 12d;[1] to the nuns of Thetford 12d.[2] Isabel my wife to have all the utensils belonging to my house, with her dwelling there, in my tenement in Hopton, with 4 acres of arable land, for term of her life; after her decease the tenement to be sold and the money from it to be disposed for my soul and our benefactors' [*souls*].

The remainder of my lands to be sold by my execs to fulfil my legacies and pay my debts as quickly as conveniently can be done.

Residue of all my goods to my execs, to do (*fac'*) for the health of my soul, as seems to them most expedient and best to please God.

Execs: William Moyse my son and John Broun of Hopton;[3] to William 6s 8d and to John Broun 3s 4d.

Proved at Fornham St Martin, 21 July 1464. Admon to execs.

1   John Barker of Thelnetham also made a bequest to this gild (SROB, Baldwyne 255; Pt I, no. 1262). William Rewe of Thelnetham (SROB, Baldwyne 214; Pt I, no. 1063) and his brother, John Reve (no. 39 above), made bequests to the gild of St Peter in Thelnetham. Records also show that there was a gild of St Nicholas in the parish in 1524 (*PSIA*, xix, p.205).
2   See note to no. 68.
3   John Broun was rector of Hopton; see note to no. 36.

187. JOHN TEBAWDE of FORDHAM [*Cambs*],[1] 2 July 1464

Dated Monday after the feast of the Apostles Peter and Paul; [*commendation*: to God &c]; my body to Christian burial; to the high altar of the said church, for my tithes forgotten, 6s 8d.

To my mother 6s 8d.

To Joan my sister at Shouldham ('Shuldham') [*Norfolk*] 40d; to be distributed amongst the convent at Shouldham 40d, by the discretion of the same Joan.[2]

To Sir Andrew Chesewrygth, chaplain, 6s 8d;[3] to Friar Thomas Playforth 40d.

To each house of the four convents of Cambridge (*Cantabrig'*) 2s 6d.[4]

To William my son a cow and a bullock and 6 ewes; to each of my sons 6 ewes; to Margaret my daughter, 10 coombs of malt, a cow and 6 ewes.

To each of my godsons a sheep.

A suitable chaplain to celebrate for a whole year, for my soul and for the souls of [*my*] parents and all my benefactors, he taking for his salary 100s, and being a scholar of Cambridge (*Cant'*), coming to the town of Fordham for principal feasts, that is, Nativity of Our Lord, Easter, Pentecost and suchlike, and celebrating in the parish church there.[5]

Residue of all my goods, over and above my debts, to the disposition of Agnes my wife and John my son, the elder, execs, they, under the supervision of Thomas Lokton, esquire,[6] my master, and with the advice of Sir Robert, vicar of Fordham, to dispose as they see best to please God and profit my soul and the souls of all [*my*] parents and benefactors.

Proved in Fordham church, 20 July 1464. Admon to execs. Seal of official appended.

[1]   Executor (as 'Tebaude') of William Mardon of Fordham, will pr. March 1459/60 (SROB, Baldwyne 259; Pt I, no. 1277).

[2]   The priory at Shouldham, dedicated conjointly to the Holy Cross and the Blessed Virgin, was founded by Geoffrey FitzPiers, earl of Essex, in the reign of Richard I, for canons and nuns of the order of St Gilbert of Sempringham (*VCH Norfolk*, ii, pp.412–14).

[3]   See note to no. 60 and also no. 602 below.

[4]   Presumably meaning the four houses of friars at Cambridge. For the Carmelite Friars there, see note to no. 42; for the Dominican Friars see note to no. 80. The original house of Franciscans (Grey Friars) in Cambridge was founded on the cramped site but in 1238 it was enlarged by a grant from Henry III. In 1304 Edward I gave 25 marks to the Grey Friars, and this gift became a regular annual sum until the Dissolution. Their first humble chapel was enlarged during the 1350s and it then had several altars and an adjacent cloister and cemetery. Because of its convenient size, this church was used by the university for the ceremonies of Commencement (*VCH Cambs*, ii, pp.276–82). The Augustinian (or Austin) Friars were established in Cambridge in about 1290. By 1376 (until the Dissolution) the friary occupied the whole space lying between the modern thoroughfares of Peas Hill on the north, Pembroke Street on the south, Free School Lane on the west, and Corn Exchange Street on the east. In 1289 the pope had given the friars an indulgence of 100 days for those who visited their churches on certain feasts, and in 1302 the right of burial, as well as that of preaching and hearing confessions, was given them; thus these friars had spiritual advantages to offer to their benefactors (*VCH Cambs*, ii, pp.287–90).

[5]   Fordham church was incorporated with the Gilbertine priory at Fordham until the latter was suppressed in 1537; later, in 1558, Queen Mary granted the advowson of the church to Jesus College, Cambridge (*VCH Cambs*, x, pp.412–17). However, John Tebawde's bequest suggests that chaplains came to the parish from the university in the fifteenth century.

[6]   Supervisor of Thomas Paxman of Burwell, will pr. October 1457 (SROB, Baldwyne 187; Pt I, no. 911). In 1468 Thomas Lokton, esquire, was one of several men involved in the transfer of 'Burdeles' manor (Cambs) (Corpus Christi College, C09/17/2/51). He may have died before 1480, when a deed that recorded the transfer of some land in Thriplow (Cambs) in which he had a shared interest referred to 'Thomas Lokton, esquire, and Alexander Wode, gentleman, deceased' (Deed: C.6629, in 'Deeds C.6601 – C.6700', *Descriptive Catalogue of Ancient Deeds*, vi (1915), pp. 366–77).

[fol. 365v]

188. STEPHEN VYPOWND of LIDGATE ('Lydgate'), 26 December 1463

Of Lidgate in the diocese of Norwich; dated 26 December, on the feast of St Stephen the Martyr; [*commendation*: to God the Father Almighty &c]; my body to Christian burial; to the high altar there 3s 4d; to the fabric of the said church 6s 8d.

[*Will*]

Margaret Vipownd my wife to have and possess all my houses, lands and tenements in the town and fields of Lidgate and elsewhere, to hold to her and her heirs, of the chief lords of the fee by due service and custom, in perpetuity.

Residue of all my goods to Margaret Vipound my wife, and William Redyk, supervisor, to dispose for my soul, my parents', friends' and all my benefactors' [*souls*], in the best way seeming to please God and profit our souls.

Proved at Lidgate, 11 June 1464. Admon to executrix. Seal of official appended.

189. JOHN RUSSHFORD of SUDBURY, 9 July 1464

Dated at Sudbury; sick in body; [*commendation*: to God &c]; to be buried in the churchyard of St Gregory, by the grave of Matilda my wife; to the high altar of the chapel of St Peter of Sudbury, for my tithes forgotten, 3s 4d; to the reparation of the church of Middleton ('Myddelton') [*Essex*] 40d.

To the conventual church of the house of friars of Clare, to pray especially for my soul and the soul of Matilda my wife, 16s 8d.[1]

To Richard, the son of Thomas Russhford deceased, my nephew, 10 marks, to be paid to him when he comes to legal age, according to the discretion of my execs and the good disposition of the said Richard.

To the gild of St George of Sudbury my best iron ('eren') spit.[2]

A suitable secular priest and especially William Blak, chaplain, to celebrate in the chapel of St Peter, for the souls of me, John, and Matilda my wife, and the souls of all the faithful departed, for 2 whole years immediately following my decease, the said William being paid for his salary 8 marks 6s 8d annually.

My execs to keep annually, after my decease, an anniversary for my soul and the soul of Matilda my wife, in the chapel of St Peter, distributing to priests, clerks and the poor in greatest need, a total of 2 marks, as long as this can be done from my goods, after my debts and legacies have been paid.

Residue of all my goods, together with my debts, to my execs, George Prentys of Sudbury and William Martyn of the same place, to fulfil this testament and pay the debts that I owe, with the guidance of God (*a domino eterna' confer'*).

Seal appended.

To each of my execs for their labour 20s.

Proved at Fornham St Martin, 23 July 1464. Admon to execs.

[1] See note to no. 1.

[2] In 1469 Thomas Alston (no. 290 below) bequeathed a brass pot to this gild: the bequests of both Alston and Russhford were probably practical gifts for use during gild dinners rather than items to sell to raise money. There were several other gilds in the town: St Mary (will of Thomas Goday: Pt I, no. 310), St James in the parish of All Saints (will of John Broun: Pt 1, no. 1132), the Holy Ghost (*PSIA*, xix, p.204).

[fol. 366]

190. WILLIAM WYAT of PRESTON, 4 February 1464/65

['Wyott' *in margin*]; dated Monday after the feast of the Purification of the Blessed Mary; [*no commendation or burial directions*]; all my debts to be paid before everything else. To the high altar of Preston church a quarter of wheat; to the emendation of the said church a quarter of wheat; to a suitable chaplain to celebrate for my soul and for the souls of all my friends, in Preston church for half a year, 4 marks 6s 8d.

To Joan my wife my tenement in Preston situated in the street called 'Cherches-trete', called 'Munkes'; to Joan 2 cows and 12 sheep and a quarter of wheat and a quarter of malt, and all my ostilments and bedding.

To John my son 2 cows and a bullock and 6 sheep; to William my son 2 cows, a bullock and 6 sheep; to Isabel my daughter a bullock and 6 sheep; to Katherine my daughter a bullock and 6 sheep; to Agnes my daughter a bullock and 6 sheep; to Alice my daughter a bullock and 6 sheep; to Joan my daughter, in Romford [*Essex*], 6s 8d in money.

Residue of all [*my*] goods to my execs, John my son and Thomas Spryng of Lavenham.[1]

Supervisor: John Pakenham of Preston.

Proved at Bildeston ('Bylston'), 13 March 1464/65. Admon to John Wyott [*sic*], exec.

[1] Known as Thomas Spring II, the second of three important Lavenham clothiers bearing this name. See Betterton and Dymond, *Lavenham: Industrial Town*. Thomas I's will pr. February 1441/42 (SROB, Baldwyne 19; Pt I, no. 102); Thomas II's will pr. September 1486 (TNA, PCC 25 Logge; published in *Logge Register*, will no. 352). Thomas II was executor of John Place of Lavenham (SROB, Baldwyne 24; Pt I, no. 126); supervisor of Margaret Beere of Lavenham (no. 237 below); supervisor of William Schedde of Lavenham (no. 339 below).

191. ROBERT HUNTE of RUSHBROOKE ('Rosshbrok'), esquire,[1] 8 February 1464/65

[*Commendation*: to God &c]; to be buried in the chapel of the Blessed Mary of Rushbrooke; to the high altar of the same church, for tithes forgotten, 6s 8d; to the high altar of Little Whelnetham ('Parva Welnetham'), for tithes forgotten, 6s 8d.

To the friars of Babwell 6s 8d; to the Friars Preachers of Sudbury 6s 8d; to the Carmelite Friars of Cambridge (*Cantabrig'*) 6s 8d; to the Austin Friars of Thetford 6s 8d.[2]

To Thomas Lyncoln, friar of the order of the Holy Cross,[3] to celebrate divine service for my soul and for the souls for whom I am bound, for seven whole years immediately following my decease, 6 marks for each year of the seven, if Thomas lives that long, he to celebrate divine service each Friday during the term of seven years, in the chapel of the Blessed Mary [*of Rushbrooke*] aforesaid.

To be distributed to the poor on the day of my burial, 10 marks.

To Katherine my wife[4] a bowl with the cover, of silver-gilt, another bowl with cover, of silver, a bound mazer of silver-gilt, 12 silver spoons, a container (*pixidem*) of silver called a 'pouder boxe', a silver salt with cover and another silver salt, without a cover; the same Katherine to have all my larger ostilments (*grossa hostilimenta*) and utensils belonging to my house, for term of her life, and immediately after her decease all the larger ostilments and utensils to be sold and the money from them to be disposed for my soul and Katherine's soul, providing always that, after the decease of Katherine, John Grene, esquire,[5] shall have such of the said larger ostilments and utensils as he pleases, that is, of bedding, table-cloths, latten, brass, pewter, iron, tables, forms, benches and other things of the larger ostilments and utensils, he giving and paying for them to my execs as much as any other would give for those that he wants.

To Thomas Clerk my servant[6] 6s 8d and my third gown; to John Pepyre my servant my black gown, furred with white lamb.[7]

Residue of all my goods and chattels, after my legacies [fol. 366v] and debts have been paid, to my execs, to sell, receive &c[*sic*] and [*dispose*], especially (*maxime*) in the relief of the poor and the reparation of Rushbrooke church &c[*sic*].

Execs: Katherine my wife, Stephen Parkere, the parson of Little Whelnetham, John Stok, yeoman, and Simon Lyndesell, yeoman;[8] Stephen, for his labour, 6s 8d; to John Stok, for his labour, 6s 8d and my best gown; to Simon, for his labour 6s 8d and my second gown.

Seal appended.

Witnesses: William Barkere, clerk,[9] Giles Adam, Thomas Ladyman[10] and others.

[*Will, of same date,* 4 Edward IV]

My execs to sell two pieces of land called 'Geselislond', lying separately in the town of Rushbrooke, one piece being next to 'Rossebrok Hyll', and the other in a close called 'Le Longrowe', and, without delay, to dispose the money from them for my soul and for the souls for whom I am bound, in deeds of piety.

Thomas Wareyn of Rushbrooke to have my tenement called 'Glovers', in the town of Rushbrooke, to hold for term of his life, of the chief lords of the fee, he repairing the tenement in the meanwhile, as often as necessary; immediately after Thomas's death the tenement called 'Glovers' to be sold by my execs and the money from it to be disposed and distributed for my soul, the soul of Katherine my wife and for the souls of our parents and benefactors, in pious deeds, as they see best to please God and profit my soul and the aforesaid souls.

All my feoffees of and in the said lands and tenements to deliver the estate that they have in them according to the tenor of this will, when so required by my execs.

Witnesses: William Barkere, clerk, Giles Adams, Thomas Ladyman and others.

Proved at Fornham St Martin, 13 February 1464/65. Admon to Stephen Parkere, rector of Little Whelnetham church, John Stok and Simon Lyndesell, execs. Power reserved to Katherine Hunte, relict of the deceased, the other co-exec, when she comes, if she wishes to take up admon.

---

1 During the fifteenth century the manor of 'Rushbrook' in Rushbrooke was held by one Robert Hunt, although the dating of his tenure is unclear. According to Copinger: 'Sir William [de Russhebrok] by his will proved in 1383, gave the manor to his son, Thomas Rushbrook, whose sister Alice married Hugh Hunt, of Rushbrook, and the manor was inherited by their son and heir, Robert Hunt' (Copinger, *Manors of Suffolk*, vi, p.329).

2 For bequests to the four orders of friars see note to no. 133.

3 The Crutched Friars, or Brethren of the Holy Cross, had a house at Great Whelnetham; a prior and convent of Crutched Friars, dependent on London, had been placed in the chapel of St Thomas the Martyr there before 1308 (Knowles and Hadcock, *Medieval Religious Houses*, p.211).

4 Will no. 470 below.

5 Copinger noted a suit in Chancery, dated 1458, concerning the manor of 'Rushbrook' in which one of the parties was one John Green; perhaps this is the same man. See note above. 'Master John Grene', esquire, was supervisor of Thomas Schorthose of Sudbury, weaver, will pr. January 1459/60 (SROB, Baldwyne 235; Pt I, no. 1181).

6 Legatee of Katherine Hunte.

7 Presumably trimmed with lambs' fleece.

8 As 'Lynsell', executor of his wife Katherine.

9 Master William Barker *A.M.* was rector of Rushbrooke from 1439 to his death in 1470 (Tanner, p.1442); he was executor of his father, Thomas Barkere of Thelnetham (no. 820 below), and of his brother John, will pr. July 1460 (SROB, Baldwyne 255; Pt I, no. 1262).

10 Will, no. 413 below.

109

[fol. 367]

192. JOHN PONDERE of GREAT ASHFIELD ('Asshfeld'), 16 November 1464

[*Commendation*: to God &c]; my body to Christian burial; to the high altar of the same church, for my tithes forgotten or underpaid, for the health of my soul, 2s.
To Margaret Turnour of Norton a cow [*and*] 6s 8d.
To Ralph my son 6s 8d; to Marion my daughter 6s 8d; to Henry my son 6s 8d; to Agnes my daughter 6s 8d; to Ed' my son 6s 8d; to John my son 40d and 4 bushels (*mod'*) of wheat.
To Marion my wife, for the whole term of her life, the lower chamber (*inferior' camera'*) of [*my*] chief house (*domus capitalis*), below and above (*subtus et supra*), with free entrance and exit to the same, and easement to fire and water for that period, she to have access when her need becomes urgent (*semper qu' id' sua expostulat' utilitas*), without contradiction of John my son or anyone in his name. To the same Marion 5 marks; also to Marion two days-worth of arable land (*quantitate' duorum dierum terre arabil'*) each year,[1] on my tenement, for sowing wheat and barley, at the cost for ploughing (*per costag' in arur'*) of John my son, she having on the tenement, for the said term, a cow, a pig and 4 hens at the cost and maintenance of John, except the straw of the cow in winter. To the same Marion all my goods and chattels on my tenement or elsewhere, not [*otherwise*] bequeathed.
Execs: my beloved in Christ, Marion my wife, Thomas Wrygth and John my son, to dispose for the health of my soul as they see most expedient.
Proved at Norton, 15 January 1464/65. Admon to execs.

[1] Land being measured by time: perhaps that amount of land that could be ploughed in two days.

193. WILLIAM DORANT of THORNHAM MAGNA,[1] 1 December 1464

['Dorawnte' *in margin*] [*Commendation*: to God &c]; to be buried in the churchyard of the church of the Blessed Mary of the aforesaid Thornham; to the reparation of the mother church of Norwich 4d;[2] to the high altar of the church of the aforesaid Thornham 4d.
To the fabric of a new hall to be made, of the fraternity of the gild of St Mary of the aforesaid Thornham, 3s 4d;[3] to the gild of St John the Baptist of Wickham Skeith ('Wykham Skeyth') 4 bushels (*mod'*) of wheat.[4]
To Beatrice my wife all the utensils of my house and all my chattels, both live and dead; to Beatrice, now pregnant, all my lands and tenements for term of her life, on condition that she makes no strip or waste on the tenement, but repairs it sufficiently during her lifetime; and immediately after her death all those lands and tenements to remain wholly to the unborn child in her womb; if the child should die before Beatrice, then all the lands and tenements to be sold by my execs, or by the execs of my execs, and the money from them to be disposed for my soul and the souls of my friends.
Residue of all my goods, together with my debts, to the disposition of my execs, Beatrice my wife, John Torald[5] and Thomas Chambyrleyn, to dispose for the health of my soul &c[*sic*].
Proved at Finningham ('Fynyngham'), 16 January 1464/65. Admon to execs. Seal of official appended.

1   ?Executor (as 'Dorawnt') of John Beneyt of Thornham Magna, will pr. January 1434/35 (SROB, Baldwyne 1; Pt I, no. 1); executor (as 'Doraunt') of Richard Godewyne of Thornham Magna, will pr. May 1457 (SROB, Baldwyne 220; Pt I, no. 1096).
2   The cathedral-priory of the Holy Trinity at Norwich was the mother church of Norfolk and Suffolk.
3   There are no other bequests to this gild in the Baldwyne register but the building of a new hall suggests that the gild was flourishing at this time.
4   In 1456 Simon Dale bequeathed 40s to the fabric of the hall of the gilds of St John and St Peter at Wickham Skeith (SROB, Baldwyne 182; Pt I, no. 879); another example of a gildhall used by more than one gild.
5   ?Will of John Torold of Thornham Magna, dated September 1484 (no probate) (SROB, Hervye 330).

[fol. 367v]

194. EDMUND MASON the younger of RICKINGHALL ('Rykynghale') INFERIOR, 1463

[*No day or month given*; *commendation*: to God &c]; to be buried in the churchyard of the church of the Blessed Mary of Rickinghall Inferior; to the high altar for tithes forgotten 6d; to Sir Edmund Spark, chaplain, 6d; to the reparation of the said church 3s 4d; to the reparation of Rickinghall Superior church 12d.

To Ellen my wife my tenement called 'Runtynges and Berchere', with all the other lands, free and bond, to hold for term of her life; after her death the said tenement, with the lands, to Robert my son the younger, to hold to him and his heirs; if Robert should die without heirs in Ellen's lifetime, the tenement and other lands to be sold by my execs and disposed for the health of my soul.

To John my son the elder, after the decease of Ellen my wife, a garden (*ortologiu'*) lying next to his tenement.

To Ellen all my utensils and all my other necessities in my dwelling (*domicilio*).

Residue of all my goods to my execs, to dispose for the health of my soul, of all my benefactors and of all the faithful departed, as seems best to please God and profit my soul.

Execs: Ellen Mason my wife and Robert Mason my son.

Supervisor: Sir Edmund Spark, chaplain.[1]

Seal appended.

Proved at Finningham ('Fynyngham'), 16 January 1464/65. Admon to exec. Power reserved to Ellen, other exec, when she comes. Seal of official appended.

1   Edmund Spark was rector of Rickinghall Inferior from 1457 to 1486 (Tanner, p.1211); he was appointed supervisor by five parishioners in this volume (nos 194, 365, 376, 500 and 522).

195. JOHN SEMANCROFTH [?of REDGRAVE], 10 May 1462

[*No place of residence given*; *commendation to* God &c]; to be buried in the churchyard of Redgrave; to the high altar, for my tithes forgotten, 20d; to the said church 12d.

To Robert my son 6s 8d and a bed.

To Rose my wife, after my decease, all my goods, as long as she is a widow; if she be married again, the place (*locus*) to be sold and she to have half the price of it and the other half to be done for me and my friends.

Execs: Rose my wife and Thomas Ferdyng, they to pay all my debts and implement my last will, as seems best for my soul.
Proved at Finningham ('Fynyngham'), 16 January 1464/65. Admon to execs.

[fol. 368]
196. CECILY CROWE of HITCHAM ('Hecham'), widow, 16 August 1464

Formerly the wife of Thomas Crowe of the same [*place*];[1] [*commendation*: to God &c]; fearing the imminent danger of death (*timens cu' mortis periculum imminer'*); my body to the Christian burial of Hitcham; to the high altar of Hitcham, for my tithes and offerings forgotten or underpaid, 12d; to the reparation of Hitcham church 20d.
To Joan Bayle my daughter 6s 8d and 7 pieces of pewter.
To Rose Bayle my daughter, living at Dover ('Dowere'), 6s 8d.
To Agnes Carleman my daughter,[2] a cover of green colour, a gown and a blanket.
To Agnes Halle a bushel (*mod'*) of wheat and 2 cheeses.
To the needy poor of the same town, each of them, half a bushel of wheat and a cheese.
To Margaret Crowe my daughter a cow and 2s.
Residue of all my goods and chattels, and all my lands and tenements in the towns and fields of Hitcham and elsewhere, to my supervisor and execs, to sell, receive, and pay my debts quickly and dispose for my soul as seems best to them to please God and profit my soul; and if any part of the money remain from the sale of my tenement, then that part to be assigned to the support of a priest celebrating in Hitcham church, according to the extent (*exigenc'*) of that part of the money.
Supervisor: my beloved in Christ, Master William, chaplain.
Execs: John Love and Ralph Smyth,[3] to each of whom, for their labour, 40d.
Proved at Brent Eleigh ('Illigth Combust'), 5 February 1464/65. Admon to execs.
[*See no. 211 below for another testament of this testatrix.*]

1 Will pr. March 1455/56 (SROB, Baldwyne 223; Pt I, no. 1116).
2 As 'Carman', legatee of Thomas Crowe.
3 John Love and Ralph Smyth were co-executors, with Cecily, of her husband's will (see note above). In the later version of her testament, she appointed her daughter Margaret Crowe as her executrix (no. 211).

197. JOHN BERNERE of STOKE BY NAYLAND ('Stokeneylond'),[1] 12 January 1464/65

[*Commendation*: to God &c]; my body to the Christian burial of Stoke by Nayland; to the high altar of the same church 20d; to the church work (*opus ecclesiasticu'*) of the same, 6s 8d, provided that my goods are worth enough to stretch to it, and all my debts and legacies can be paid and implemented.
To Ellen my wife all the utensils of my house; to Ellen my tenement in which I now live, for the whole term of her life, so long as she can maintain and keep it well; after her decease, or before if she so wishes, the tenement to be sold by the discretion of my execs, and of the money from it, half to be distributed and given by my execs in the way of charity, for the health of my soul and Isabel my wife's, and the other half to go to Ellen my wife for her own benefit (*proficuu'*).

Residue of all my goods to my execs, to dispose as above.

Execs: Thomas Lynsey of Stoke by Nayland and John Ingrham of Langham [*Essex*]. Seal appended.

Proved at Brent Eleigh ('Illigh Combust'), 5 February 1464/65. Admon to execs. Seal of official appended.

1   ?Related to John Berner the elder of Stoke by Nayland, will pr. September 1458 (SROB, Bald-wyne 201; Pt I, no. 992).

[fol. 368v]

198. JOHN WADSELL of STRADISHALL ('Stradeshull'), 7 November 1464

[*Commendation*: to God &c]; my body to Christian burial; to the high altar of Strad-ishall, for tithes forgotten, 4s; to the fabric of the said church 6s 8d.

To Margaret my wife all the profit of my tenement for the whole term of her life; if my wife should not to be able to live on (*cu'*) the profit of the tenement during her lifetime, it to be sold and she to live on the money received for it; if enough money can be saved and kept after the decease of my wife, [*then*] to Robert my son 26s 8d, to John my son 26s 8d, to Katherine my daughter 20s and to Margaret my daughter, if she be alive after the decease of Margaret my wife, 20s.

With the residue of all my goods a chaplain to celebrate for my soul and my wife's for half a year, or for a whole year if it can be done, in Stradishall church.

Execs: William Baxtere of Hundon and Thomas Stok of Stradishall, together with Margaret my wife, to whom I leave 6s 8d, they to dispose for the health of my soul and all my benefactors' [*souls*].

Seal appended.

Proved at Hundon ('Honewden'), 7 February 1464/65. Admon to execs. Power reserved to Margaret, relict of the deceased, when she comes, &c[*sic*].

199. ISABEL RAWLYN of CHIPPENHAM ('Chipnham') [*Cambs*],[1]
15 December 1464

[*Commendation*: to God &c]; to be buried in the churchyard of the parish church of St Margaret of Chippenham; to the high altar of Chippenham for my [*tithes*] and offerings forgotten 2s and a coomb of barley; to the fabric of the said church a coomb of barley.

To the gild of the Holy Trinity 2 bushels (*mod'*) of barley; to the gild of Corpus Christi 2 bushels of barley; to the gild of St John 2 bushels of barley; to the gild of St Margaret 2 bushels of barley.[2]

To Thomas my son and William my son all my utensils.

My messuage to be sold and my debts to be paid therewith.

Residue of all my goods to the disposition of my execs, Robert Draweswerd and John Carle, to dispose for my soul and the souls of all my benefactors, as seems best to please God &c[*sic*].

Witnesses: Sir John Syngere,[3] John Persyvale, Luke Childe and others.

Proved at Cheveley [*Cambs*], 8 February 1464/65. Admon to execs.

1   Probate of husband, Robert, no. 124 above.
2   In her study of Cambridgeshire gilds Virginia Bainbridge did not consider gilds in the Cambridge-shire parishes within the Archdeaconry of Sudbury. (See Introduction to this volume, under *Gilds*.) Palmer's only source for the gilds of Corpus Christi, Holy Trinity, St John and St Margaret

in Chippenham was this will of Isabel Rawlyn (Palmer, 'Village Gilds of Cambridgeshire', p.387). Joan Norman of Badlingham in Chippenham also made a bequest to the gild of St Margaret (no. 438). During the reign of Elizabeth, the gildhall of Chippenham was sold to Yethwent and Brokesby (Palmer, p.387, citing Patent Roll, Elizabeth, part 10).

3   John Syngere was the incumbent at Chippenham from 1448 to 1478 (Tanner, p.1265).

200. KATHERINE SPERLYNGE of COMBS, 15 March 1464/65 [*probate only*]

Admon to John Drapere, exec.

[fol. 369]

201. JOHN BAKERE of STOWMARKET ST PETER ('Stowe Peter'), 10 October 1464 [*probate only*]

Proved at Old Newton ('Newton'). Admon to Joan Bakere, relict of the deceased, executrix; power reserved to John Tylere when he comes.

202. GEOFFREY BUSSH of MENDLESHAM ('Mendelesham'),[1] 15 April 1463

[*Commendation*: to God &c]; my body to Christian burial; to the high altar of Mendlesham church 12d; to the said church 6s 8d.

To Isabel my wife all my tenement in the said town, called 'Malyardes', for term of her life, and after her decease the tenement to be sold by my execs and then a suitable priest to be had to celebrate in the said church for a whole year, for my soul and the souls of all my friends and benefactors.

To each of my daughters 20s.

To the friars of Orford ('Orforthe') 3s 4d; to the friars of Babwell 3s 4d.[2]

To Isabel my wife all my movable goods.

Residue of all my goods to my execs, to dispose for my soul as seems best to please God and benefit my soul.

Execs: Robert Cake[3] and Isabel my wife; to Robert 3s 4d for his labour.

Proved at Mendlesham, 11 October 1464. Admon to execs.

1   Witness of the will of John Cake of Mendlesham, pr. April 1459 (SROB, Baldwyne 269; Pt I, no. 1315); executor of Richard Bussh, probate May 1461 (SROB, Baldwyne 303; Pt I, no. 1482).
2   For the friars see notes to nos 1 (Babwell) and 6 (Orford).
3   Son of John Cake (see note above).

203. THOMAS FRAWNCEYS of MENDLESHAM ('Mendelesham'), 20 April 1463

[*Commendation*: to God &c]; my body to Christian burial; to the high altar of the same church for tithes forgotten, 12d; for a trental to be celebrated for Joan Fraunceys my late wife, 10s.

For a church way (*una* 'chirche wey') from the 'ston crosse' to the 'churche style' on the south of the church,[1] in the best way my execs can do it (*sic ex' mei possint facer' optimo modo*); to the reparation of the said church, in leading the north side ('noth syde ledyng'), 20s; for a trental to be celebrated for my soul and the souls of all my friends and benefactors, 10s.

To John Fraunceys my son my whole tenement with all the land and with all my goods and chattels, to pay my debts and implement my last will.

Residue of all my goods to the administration of my execs, to sell, receive and dispose for the health of my soul as seems best to please God and profit my soul.

Execs: William Barett and John Fraunceys; to each of them 3s 4d for their labour.

Seal appended.

Proved at Mendlesham 11 October 1464. Admon to John Fraunceys, exec. Power reserved to William Barett, when he comes.

¹ A bequest apparently for making a new path in Mendlesham's churchyard from a cross to a stile, to the south of the church.

[fol. 369v]

204. JOHN PARYS of SOHAM ('Saham') [*Cambs*], 8 October 1464

[*Commendation*: to God &c]; to be buried in the churchyard of Soham church; my best animal in the name of a mortuary; to the priests present at my obsequies on the first day of my death (*prima die obitus mei*) 4d each and to each adult clerk 2d and to the rest of the boys according to the disposition of my execs.

To the three gilds of Soham, that is, Corpus Christi, St Mary and St Peter, each of them, 12d;¹ to the fabric of the said church 3s 4d.

To each order of friars in Cambridge, 5s.²

To Katherine my wife and Margaret Clerk my daughter all my household (*domiciliu'*) with appurtenances belonging to me, to be divided between them, except 2 large dishes (*perapsid'*) called chargers ('Chariours'), a basin and a ewer, which I wish to be sold and disposed for the health of my soul [*and*] my parents' [*souls*] by my execs.

To Katherine 1½ acres of arable land, lying scattered (*diversim*) in divers fields of Soham, as fully contained in the completed (*confectis*) deeds, for term of her life; and after her decease the 1½ acres of land to be sold and disposed for the health of my soul, my wives' (*uxorum*) and my parents' [*souls*]. Also, 6½ acres of arable land and meadow, lying in divers fields of Soham, as is fully contained in the completed deeds, to be sold and disposed in pious uses for my soul [*and*] my parents' similarly.

Residue of my goods to my execs to dispose in pious uses for the health of my soul and for the souls of my deceased friends.

Execs: Katherine my wife, John Smyth at Hyll³ and Edmund Clerk of Soham, they to have for their labour 3s 4d each, to do as they believe best for the health of my soul [*and*] to please God.

[*Will, of same date*]

Last will, closed and sealed (*claus' fact' et sigilat'*):

Katherine my wife to have 4 cows and 20 ewes with their lambs and she to have a cart with all the 'ploware and carteware'.

Margaret my daughter to have a ewe with its lamb.

To be divided and disposed to the needy and poor of the town of Soham, 10s; to the needy and poor of Fordham [*Cambs*], in the same way, 20d; and to the poor of Wicken ('Wylkyn') [*Cambs*], in the same way, 20d, for the health of my soul and all my friends' [*souls*].

Seal appended.

Proved at Fornham St Martin, 30 October 1464. Admon to execs. Seal of official appended.

¹ For the gilds of Cambridgeshire in general see Introduction, under *Gilds*, and note to no. 199.
The following wills in the Baldwyne register mention gilds in Soham: in 1442, John Wrygth
the younger of Barway in Soham, St John the Baptist (Pt I, no. 256); in 1457, Thomas Crowe
of Soham, Corpus Christi, St Mary and St Peter (Pt I, no. 903); in 1459, John Ode of Barway,
St John and St Mary (Pt I, no. 1319); in 1459, John Galey of Soham, Corpus Christi and St
Katherine (Pt I, no. 1327); in 1470, John Smyth of Soham, St John the Baptist (no. 397 below).
In 1503, the gild of Corpus Christi was still in existence; in 1525, there was a gild of Jesus in
Soham (Palmer, 'Village Gilds of Cambridgeshire', p.397). Interestingly both Thomas Crowe and
this testator referred to the gilds of Corpus Christi, St Mary and St Peter as 'the three gilds of
Soham'. In 1569 forfeited gild and chantry lands purchased by William James, gentleman, of the
city of London, and John Grey, gentleman, of Nettlestead, Suffolk, included 'all those lands lying
in Estfeld, Soham, near the lands of John Garsonne, given by Robert Rolynham for maintenance
of Corpus Christi Gild in Soham' (Palmer, p.370, quoting Patent Roll, 14 Elizabeth, part 7).

² See note to no. 187.

³ Executor (as 'John Smyth at Waleys Hyll') of Thomas Everard (no. 278).

[fol. 370]
205. JOHN TYSO of ?STOWMARKET,¹ 20 October 1463

Formerly (*quondam*) of Drinkstone ('Drenkston'); [*commendation*: to God &c]; to
be buried in the church of All Saints, Drinkstone, if this is allowable (*si hoc licite
fieri possit*); to the high altar of the same church for my tithes forgotten or underpaid, for the health of my soul, 3s 4d; to having a new bell there 40s, and beyond
this, if my goods will stretch to it, 40s at another time [*also*]; to the gild of the Holy
Trinity of the same town 6s 8d;² to the parish clerk 12d, and to the sacrist 8d.

To the high altar of Tostock church 2s 6d and to the emendation of the same church,
20s; to the emendation of Beyton ('Beketon') church 12d; to the high altar of the
church of St Mary, Stowmarket, 2s and to the emendation of the same church 3s 4d.
To each of my godsons 12d.

To the friars of Babwell, for a trental of St Gregory to be celebrated there, for my
soul and for the souls of Agnes my former wife, my parents and benefactors, and all
at rest in Christ, 10s; to the friars of Sudbury, for the same and in the same manner,
10s; to the Carmelite Friars of Ipswich (*Gippwic'*), similarly, for the same and in
the same manner, 10s.³

To Sir George my son a mazer, 6 silver spoons, a basin with a ewer, a charger, 4
platters, 4 dishes and 4 saucers of pewter, a brass pot holding 3 gallons, a kettle, a
posnet (*ollula'*), a 'stelyd' pan,⁴ a latten ladle, a best bedcover, a pair of sheets, a
pair of best blankets, a quilt, a best donge, a saddle with the bridle, a pair of riding
boots (*ocr'*), a pair of spurs (*calcar'*) and a wood-knife.

Residue of my goods to the disposition of the said Sir George, Roger Bereve and
John Cobold, execs, to dispose for the health of my soul in the manner which
seems best to them, they having God before their eyes and faithfully executing my
testament.

Supervisor: Master Robert Wollerman, rector of Tostock church.⁵

To each exec 3s 4d for their labour, and to the supervisor 6s 8d.

Seal appended.

[*Will, of same date*]

To Elizabeth my wife all my messuage in the town of Stowmarket, to hold, without
[*doing*] any intentional (*voluntar'*) waste, for the whole term of her life, she
repairing it sufficiently all that time, for which she shall be quit (*erga quoscumque
acquietab'*); and, after her decease, George my son to have the messuage, to hold to

him and his heirs for ever, if he be still alive and willing to celebrate divine service for my soul and for the souls of Elizabeth, John Wederard her former husband,[6] my parents and benefactors, and all the Christian faithful, in the church of the Blessed Mary in Stowmarket for a whole year; but if he be not [*so willing*] it is to be sold by my feoffees and all the money from it to be spent faithfully on chaplains celebrating divine service in the said church.

To the same George a close in Drinkstone, called 'Caldewellyerd', to hold to him and his heirs for ever, on condition that he pays £20 out of it to my execs, or celebrates divine service for my soul and for the souls of Agnes his mother, and of our parents and benefactors &c[*sic*], for 3 whole years; otherwise it to be sold and [*the money*] spent in the celebration of masses and in other deeds of charity, similarly.

To John Cobold and Anne his wife a messuage in Drinkstone, situated at 'le Halke' and called 'Hell', together with a half-acre of land called 'Amyeshalfakyr', to hold to him and his heirs for ever, on condition that they, John and Anne his wife, keep, during his lifetime (*vita sua*), as appropriate (*ut decet*), the anniversary day of Walter Tyso and Alice his wife, once a year, [fol. 370v] when it occurs, and also the anniversary day of me, John Tyso, and Agnes my wife, similarly, when it occurs.

My piece of land in 'Overdale', called 'le Langlond', to be sold, and out of it 10 marks to Alice my daughter.

My piece of land in 'le Nethirdale', at 'le Prabell', to be sold and distributed for the health of my soul.

Seal appended.

Proved at Fornham St Martin, 17 September 1464. Admon to execs. Seal of official appended.

1   'John Tyso of Drinkstone' was appointed as one of the executors of Nicholas Nunne of Hessett, but renounced the position: will pr. December 1447 (SROB, Baldwyne 80; Pt I, no. 370); supervisor of the will of Thomas Tyso of Drinkstone, pr. 15 May 1458 (SROB, Baldwyne 212; Pt I, no. 1054).
2   Presumably this refers to the gild of the Holy Trinity of Drinkstone. For other bequests to this gild see the wills of John Seman (no. 19) and John Paton (no. 95).
3   For the friars see notes to nos 1 (Babwell and Carmelites of Ipswich) and 11 (Sudbury).
4   See Glossary.
5   Master Robert Wolman. See note to no. 29.
6   Probate (as 'Wetherhard') 26 October 1457 (SROB, Baldwyne 191; Pt I, no. 934); Elizabeth had been her former husband's sole executrix.

206. ROGER CARTERE of LONG MELFORD ('Melford'), 26 August 1464

Dated at Melford; to be buried in the churchyard of Melford church; to the high altar of the same for tithes forgotten, 12d; to the said church 10s; to the Mass of Jesu (*misse Jhu*) 3s;[1] to the tower of Melford church 3s 4d.

To the chapel of the Blessed James in Melford, in the street called 'Halstrete', 6s 8d.[2]

To the friars 20s, to be disposed at the discretion of my execs.

Alice my wife to have her dwelling in my tenement during her life-time, and then it is to be sold by my execs at their will, for the greatest profit of my soul; after the sale of the tenement a suitable priest to be had for the space of a year, to celebrate for my soul and the souls of my friends for whom I am most bound. To Alice my wife all my ostilments and grain, of whatever kind, present in my tenement except that grain which is for my interment (*meo terement' pertinebunt*).[3]

Residue of all my goods to my execs, to dispose as seems best to please God, for my soul.

Execs: Richard Martyn and John Mylbourn; Richard Martyn to have 10s and John Melborn 6s 8d.

Proved 21 September 1464. Admon to execs.

1   See note to no. 45.
2   The chapel of St James served the southern end of Long Melford; it gave Chapel Green its name; the building itself survived until the seventeenth century. See Dymond and Paine, *Spoil of Melford Church*, p.8.
3   Presumably grain to be used for bread distributed at his funeral.

[fol. 371]

207. ROBERT SHUKFORD of LANGHAM, 20 September 1464

Dated the Thursday before the feast of St Matthew the Apostle and Evangelist, at Langham; [*commendation*: to God &c]; my body to Christian burial; to the high altar of Langham church, for tithes forgotten, 40d; to the emendation of the said church 6s 8d.

To the gild of St John the Baptist of Langham 20d.[1]

To the Friars Minor of Babwell 10s; to the Austin Friars of Thetford 10s.[2]

Joan my wife to have the residue of all my movable goods, after my debts have been paid and my testament fulfilled.

A secular priest to be had to celebrate for a whole year for my soul and the souls of all my benefactors in Langham church.

John my son[3] to have an acre of land in 'le Botome' on condition that he pays my execs 20s in the next three years following [*my death*].

Joan my wife to have my tenement called 'Munnygges' with the lands belonging to it, to her own use.

A cow to be got to provide a light in Langham church, on the candlebeam ('candylbeme').

To Robert Rokell 20d; to Robert Berdewell 20d; to Bartholomew Wymbyll 20s.

Execs: Joan my wife, Robert Rokell, Robert Berdewell and Bartholomew Wymbyll, they to dispose for my soul as seems best to please God and profit my soul.

Proved at Ixworth, 29 November 1464. Admon to execs. Because of an insufficiency of goods, execs excused from exhibiting any further accounts and [*so*] acquitted.

1   Richard Munnyng of Badwell Ash bequeathed his mass-pence from the gild of St John the Baptist of Langham to the Friars Preacher of Thetford, to celebrate for his soul (SROB, Baldwyne 175; Pt I, no. 842).
2   For the friars see notes to nos 1 (Babwell) and 69 (Austin Friars of Thetford).
3   ?Will (as of Thelnetham), no. 561 below.

208. WILLIAM FELTEWELL of CULFORD, 26 November 1464

[*Commendation*: to God &c]; my body to Christian burial; to the church of Culford 6 ewes; to the church of Santon Downham ('Downham') 4 ewes.

To each of my sons and daughters 10 ewes.

To my mother 6 ewes; to John Feltewell my brother 6 ewes; to Emme Barkere 3 ewes and 3 'hogewys'.

[*The last three bequests contain some English words in the original Latin; the remainder of the testament after this point is written in English.*]

To each of my godchildren a 'ewehog'; to Thomas Pursere 6 'ewehoggs'; to John Pursere 3 'ewehoggs'.

Residue of all my goods to Katherine my wife, she paying my debts 'be me dewe'.

Execs: Katherine my wife and John Feltewell.

Proved at Fornham [*St*] Martin, 3 December 1464. Admon to execs.

[fol. 371v]

209. JOHN GENTYLMAN of NORTON, 12 October 1464 [*English*]

Dated Friday after the feast of St Faith the Virgin at Norton; [*commendation*: to Almighty God &c]; to be buried in Norton churchyard; to the high altar of the said church of St Andrew, for tithes forgotten, 6s 8d.

To the Friars Preachers of Thetford 4 bushels of wheat and 4 bushels of barley; to the friars of Babwell a bushel of wheat and a bushel of barley.[1]

To Our Lady's light in Norton church 4 bushels of barley.

To every child of Thomas my son a bushel of barley; and to every child of Robert my son a bushel of barley; to every child of Marion my daughter a bushel of barley.

To Robert my son 6 marks, to be paid in six years, by even portions, by Thomas my son; to John my son 6 marks, to be paid to him in six years after Robert my son has been paid, by Thomas my son; to Robert my son my best gown and hood.

To John Scotte my man a cow, after the disposition of my execs.

To Thomas my son my land 'clepyd' 'Pouncys' and 'Clementes', customary land of the manor of 'Lytelhaughe', and an acre of meadow in 'Flemyng', customary meadow of the manor of 'Lytelhaughe' in the parish of Norton.[2]

Agnes my wife and Thomas my son, together, to have my lands, tenements, pasture, feedings, ways, closes, hedgerows, with all other commodities and 'fredoms' that I purchased of Richard Taylour, now dead, except an acre which John Walsham late bought of me, and 1 acre 3 roods lying in two pieces at 'Reysthegge', which 1 acre 3 roods Agnes my wife to have freely, to give and to sell; when the 1 acre 3 roods of land shall be sold or given, Thomas my son to buy it to the full value as another man will give therefor.

Agnes my wife to have all the foresaid lands and tenements for the term of her life; if she overlive Thomas my son, after her decease [*the lands and tenements*] to be done and disposed for my soul and for all my friends' souls; if Thomas overlive his mother then he to have them to him and his heirs. To Agnes my wife all chattels ('kateyll') not bequeathed, except plough, cart, horse, harness and other things pertaining ('teynyng') to the foresaid plough and cart, which I assign to Thomas my son.

Residue of all my goods to the disposition of my execs, that is, Thomas my son and Robert my son.

All other testaments and wills, written and unwritten, before this to stand in no effect or strength.

Seal appended.

Proved at Fornham [*St Martin*], 10 December 1464. Admon to execs. Seal of official appended.

¹   For the friars see notes to nos 1 (Babwell) and 68 (Friars Preachers of Thetford).
²   Little Haugh Hall, a manor within the parish of Norton; see also no. 362.

[fol. 372]
210. JOHN WRYHT of WICKHAM SKEITH ('Wykham Skeyth'),
20 November 1458

['Wrythe' *in margin*] Dated at Wickham; [*commendation*: to God &c]; to be buried in the churchyard of Wickham; to the high altar of Wickham 20d; to the reparation of the mother church of Norwich 12d;¹ to the reparation of Wickham church 4 bushels of wheat and 4 bushels of malt; to Thwaite ('Thweyte') church 4 bushels of wheat and 4 bushels of malt; to the reparation of Mendlesham ('Mendylsham') church 4 bushels of wheat and 4 bushels of malt.

To the friars of the convent of Babwell, to pray for my soul, 10s.²

To Alice my wife 3 horses, one called 'Brokke', the second 'Bayard' and the third 'Hobbe'; to Alice 7 cows and 2 ploughs, with all the traces, shares, coulters and other necessaries belonging to the ploughs; also 2 quarters of wheat and 4 bushels of barley, 2 pigs and all the corn and grain at present growing in the ground.

Alice to gather in all the debts owed to me from my debtors, and out of them to pay my debts; any residue remaining after the payment of my debts to be disposed by Alice for the health of my soul.

To Joan, wife of William Tripp, 2 bushels of wheat and 4 bushels of barley; to John, son of the same William, 4 bushels of barley.

To Edward, son of William Wryht [*my*] brother, 2 bushels of wheat and 4 bushels of barley.

To Henry, son of Robert Braxstrete, 2 bushels of barley.

To Isabel my mother 2 horses.

Those who have authority in my tenement called 'Reves' to release to Alice my wife all the lands and tenements according to my will; my feoffees to enfeoff Alice in all those lands and tenements, meadows, pastures and feedings, rents and services, purchased by me, the said John.

Residue of my goods to my execs, to sell, and the money from them to be disposed by Alice my wife for the health of my soul and the souls of my parents, friends and benefactors, in the celebration of masses and distribution of alms and other deeds of charity, as they see best to please God and profit my soul.

Executrix: Alice my wife; supervisor: John Grongere; to each of them 6s 8d for their labour.

Witnesses: Sir Thomas Wylkyn, clerk, Simon Bertlott, William Trypp, John Hadlay and others.

[*The above testament is another version of no. 1200 in Volume I; the associated will in this version is the same as that given in Volume I, except that this one is dated 27 November 1458 and is followed by a probate sentence. The will is not repeated here but the probate sentence is given.*]

Proved at Eye, 19 September 1464. Admon to executrix. Seal of official appended.

¹   See note to no. 193.
²   See note to no. 1.

[fol. 372v; OW 24/77]
211. CECILY CROWE of HITCHAM ('Hecham'),[1] 25 November 1464

['Krowe' *in margin and OW*]. Dated the day of St Katherine the Virgin, at Hitcham; to be buried in the churchyard of All Saints, Hitcham; to the high altar of the said church, for tithes forgotten, 12d; to the emendation of the same church 20d.

To Joan Rose my daughter,[2] 6s 8d and 7 pieces of pewter; to Agnes my daughter a gown of russet (colour [*OW*]).

John Jaye and his wife to have half a bushel of wheat; Foster and his wife the same; to Joan Bullok a peck ('pekke') of wheat; to Heldhalle and his wife half a bushel of wheat; to 'Lityll Elyne' a peck of wheat; to Margaret Balle a peck of wheat.

My tenement in Hitcham to be sold and out of the money from it a priest ([*OW* suitable chaplain) to celebrate for the soul of Thomas Crowe, my late husband,[3] and my soul, and the souls of our friends, for a whole year, in Hitcham church.

Residue of all my goods to Margaret Crowe my daughter, the same Margaret to be executrix.[4]

Witnesses: Hedhalle ([*OW*] Heldhall) and his wife, Richard Rerey ([*OW*]: Rarey) and his wife and others.

Proved at Fornham [*St Martin*], 5 January 1464/65. Admon to executrix. Seal of official appended.

[*For earlier testament of this testatrix, see no. 196 above.*]

[1] Widow of Thomas Crowe of Hitcham, will pr. March 1455/56 (SROB, Baldwyne 223; Pt I, no. 1116).
[2] The name and identity of this woman is somewhat unclear: in the registered copy, the scribe has written in Latin 'to Joan Rose my daughter'; in the original will the Latin seems to read 'to Joan daughter of Rose my daughter'; in his will Thomas Crowe made a bequest to Joan Josse, daughter of his wife Cecily. There is no doubt in the readings of 'Joan Rose' here (fol. 372) and 'Joan Josse' in fol. 223.
[3] See note above.
[4] In Cecily's earlier testament, she appointed John Love and Ralph Smyth her executors (no. 196 above).

[*This is the end of the sequence of wills proved in 1464 (old style) on folios 353–72 (nos 144–211) that have been bound into the bifolium containing folios 352 & 373.*]

[fol. 373]
212. JOHN CARLES of SUDBURY,[1] 26 August 1462

Dated at Sudbury in the diocese of Norwich; to be buried in the churchyard of St Gregory of the same town; to the high altar of the chapel of St Peter of Sudbury, for tithes and offerings forgotten, 40d.

To the convent of Friars Preacher of Sudbury 40d.[2]

To Avice my wife all the ostilments and utensils of my house; Avice to have my messuage in which I live, for term of her life, she to discharge and keep up all the dues (*incumbencia*) relating to it during that time; after her decease the messuage to be sold by my execs then alive, and out of the money from it there to be provided a secular chaplain, to celebrate divine service in the chapel of St Peter for a whole year, for my soul and the soul of Avice, and for all the others for whom I am bound.

To the use of the said chapel of St Peter, out of the money coming from the sale of the said messuage, 6s 8d; the residue of that money to be spent on the repair of ways and in other deeds of charity.

Avice my wife to have the lands and tenements called 'Smethes & Cracchedounhill' which I hold of the abbess of Malling ('Mallyng') [*Kent*] in Cornard ('Cornerde'),[3] by copy of court [*roll*], for a year next after my death, [*she*] paying the rent and farm for it to the abbess, as I used to pay.

My cofeoffees with me in my said messuage to deliver their estate in it to my execs when suitably (*congrue*) required so to do.

Residue of all my goods to my execs, they to pay my debts out of them and dispose for the health of my soul, as they see best to please God and most benefit me.

Execs: Avice my wife and James Rodeland of Sudbury; to James for his labour 10s. Seal appended.

Proved at Sudbury, 22 September 1462. Admon to execs.

1   Executor of William Pryor of Great Cornard, will dated February 1457/58 (SROB, Baldwyne 192; Pt I, no. 941).
2   See note to no. 11.
3   The abbess of Malling held Abbas Hall in Great Cornard.

213. THOMAS POUNCY of WICKHAMBROOK, 21 November 1458
[*nuncupative*]

Being at present in the city of London;[1] to be buried in the churchyard of St Denis Backchurch ('Bakchyrche'), in the city of London; to the parish chaplain of the same church 2s.

To Thomas Preston his horse being there (*ibidem exist'*).[2]

To Isabel his wife all his utensils and ostilments; to Isabel an annual pension of 5 marks, to be received for term of her life, out of his tenement in Aldersfield ('Alvesfeld') in Wickhambrook.

John his son to have his said tenement in Aldersfield when he comes to the age of 21, to him and his heirs, provided always that the pension of 5 marks be paid faithfully for term of Isabel's life.

His master, John Denston, esquire,[3] his execs and assigns, to have the governing of the said tenement in Aldersfield, and also of John his son, until he reaches the age of 21; if the said John should decease before reaching the said age, then the tenement in Aldersfield to be sold by his exec and disposed faithfully as he sees best to please God and benefit his soul and Isabel's soul. To his said master, John Denston, esquire, his heirs and assigns, his manor in Comberton, in Cambs.[4]

He required all his cofeoffees of and in the manor of Comberton to deliver estate [fol. 373v] and possession of and in the said manor to the same John Denston, his heirs and assigns, to hold to him and his heirs, when so requested by the said John Denston or his execs.

He wished all his debts to be faithfully paid by his said master, [*his*] exec.

Residue of all his goods to his master, John Denston, esquire, exec, to fulfil his testament and will.

Witnesses: Sir Michael, parish chaplain of the church of St Denis Backchurch, his confessor, Henry Turnour, gent, John Dentard, William Ofton [*and*] Agnes his wife, Thomas Preston, John Cartere, Thomas Combere and John Frend, clerk, called to hear [*these*] premises.

Proved at Denston, 2 December 1460 (Mcccclxij *altered to* Mcccclx^mo).

1   It has not been possible to discover anything about Pouncy's London connections; he was prob-
    ably not a member of one of the London gilds as he did not describe himself as 'citizen of
    London'.
2   Presumably Pouncy's horse, which was in London.
3   Son of William Denston of Denston, esquire, and executor of his will, pr. February 1433/34 (TNA,
    PCC 17 Luffenham). John Denston was supervisor of Thomas Bocher *alias* Grondysborgh of
    Stansfield (SROB, Baldwyne 110; Pt I, no. 507); and supervisor of William Comber of Stradishall
    (SROB, Baldwyne 228; Pt I, no. 1142). He was also one of several 'worthy men' named as feof-
    fees by John Hedgeman the elder of Glemsford (SROB, Baldwyne 249; Pt I, no. 1246). He died
    in 1462 (*VCH Cambs*, v, pp.175–89, n.218).
4   Pouncy held the manor of Burdeleys in Comberton (*VCH Cambs*, v, pp.175–89).

214. THOMAS LAKKE of SNAILWELL ('Snaywell') [*Cambs*], 12 September 1462

[*Commendation*: to God Almighty &c; *no burial directions*]; to the high altar of Snailwell 2 quarters of barley; to the reparation of the nave of the church a quarter of barley.

To Margaret my wife my messuage which I lately bought of William Porter; if he survives his mother, Henry my son to have the messuage to him and his heirs, to whom, for the reparation of the messuage, 2 quarters of barley.

To be distributed among poor parishioners, 2 quarters of maslin ('mestlyn'), or at least (*ad minus*) a quarter.

To Henry my son 3½ quarters of barley; to John my son, the elder, a coomb of maslin, with a blue gown; to John my son, the younger, a coomb of barley; to Agnes my daughter a coomb of barley.

To my five godsons 10 bushels (*modios*) of barley, to be equally divided.

To the parish church of Chippenham ('Chypnam') [*Cambs*], a quarter [*of barley*], if it can be done, and if not, a coomb only (*kumbam tantu'*).

Residue of all my goods to Margaret my wife and Henry my son, execs, to dispose as seems best for the health of my soul.

Supervisor: William Briggeman the elder.

Witnesses: Richard Brigeman, Thomas Undyrwood, John Padyll.

Proved at Kennett ('Kenet') [*Cambs*], 30 October 1462. Admon to execs.

[fol. 374]

215. WILLIAM FABBE of BURWELL [*Cambs*],[1] 4 November 1458

[*Commendation*: to God Almighty, the Blessed Virgin Mary &c; *no burial directions*]; to the high altar of St Andrew of Burwell, 4 bushels of barley; to the church of St Mary [*of Burwell*], 2 bushels of wheat.[2]

To Ellen Paxman[3] 3 bushels of barley and a sheep (*bident'*).

To Richard Fabbe[4] 4 bushels of barley.

To Margaret my wife all [*my*] lands and tenements, for term of her life, and after her decease the lands and tenements to be sold by my execs and [*the money*] distributed for the health of my soul and all my parents' [*souls*], in masses and other deeds of charity.

Residue of all my goods or chattels to Margaret my wife, John Fabbe[5] and Edmund Paxman,[6] execs.

Proved at Mildenhall, 27 September 1462. Admon to execs.

¹   Son and legatee of John Fabbe the elder of Burwell, will pr. 18 July 1460 (SROB, Baldwyne 256; Pt I, no. 1265); the will of John Fabbe the elder explains the relationships between various individuals mentioned in this will of William Fabbe.
²   See note to no. 234 regarding the two parish churches of Burwell.
³   William Fabbe's sister Margaret was married to Edmund Paxman; presumably Ellen was William's niece.
⁴   John Fabbe the elder had a son named Richard: this man may have been the testator's brother.
⁵   John Fabbe the elder had two sons named John: this man may have been one of the testator's brothers.
⁶   The testator's brother-in-law; will pr. May 1477 (SROB, Hervye 106).

216. THOMAS SWEYN of MILDENHALL ('Myldenhale'), 19 August 1462

[*Commendation*: to God Almighty &c; *no burial directions*]; to the high altar of Mildenhall 20d.

Residue of all my goods and chattels, and debts of whatever kind and wheresoever they be, after my debts have been paid and my burial seen to, and my legacies implemented, to Alice my wife, for ever, to dispose at her own free will, as if they were her own, without any gainsaying of anyone else, and to dispose out of them for my soul as she sees best to please God and profit the health of my soul.

Executrix: Alice my wife.

Seal appended.

Proved at Mildenhall, 26 September 1462. Admon to executrix.

217. WILLIAM TREYLYS of PALGRAVE, 1 October 1462 [*probate only*]

Proved at Finningham ('Fynyngham'). Admon to Christian his wife and John Treyl' his son, execs.

[fol. 374v]

218. JOHN BOLOWRE of THWAITE ('Thweyth'), 1 August 1462

[*Commendation*: to God &c; *no burial directions*]; to the high altar of Thwaite, for my tithes forgotten, 8d; to the reparation of the rectory (*rectorie*) of the same town 4d.

My tenement at Thorndon, and all my meadows lying in the meadow called 'Thweytes Medwe' to be sold by my execs and my debts paid out of the money received; if Edward Dale wishes to buy any or all of the parcels of meadow, he to have them before all others if he will give as much for them as others.

Margery my wife to have a competent (*compotente'*) part of my grain now growing on my land, and the remaining part to be sold by my execs and my farm and rent to be paid out of it; to Margery all the utensils of my house for the whole term of her life.

To the church, if it can be done after my debts have been paid, 2 torches, to be bought and ordered by the discretion of my execs, and also 6s 8d towards the buying of a new bell.

To each of my godsons 4d; on the same condition [*as above*], to Robert Baas 6s 8d. Margery my wife to have my tenement in which I live and my tenement called 'Margaretes' and my tenement called 'Garpys', for the whole term of her life; if, at a later time, she should be reduced to (*perveniet*) such need and poverty that she cannot support herself, then my tenement called 'Garypys' to be sold by my execs and Margery to have a competent annuity out of the money to keep her as long as it lasts; if she survives after the money received is spent, then my tenement called 'Margaretes' to be sold by my execs and the money from it to be used as above, if need be.

If Margaret, daughter of Katherine Glovere, is willing to live with Margery my wife to help and comfort her, and will stay there without any reluctance or obstruction on the part of her friends (*sive retractione aut impedimento suorum amicorum*), then the said Margaret to have 40s after the death of Margery my wife; otherwise she to have nothing of the 40s.

Execs: Sir Thomas Wylkyn, vicar of Wickham Skeith ('Wykham'),[1] and Edward Dale.

Any residue remaining of my goods, after the death of Margery my wife, to my execs, to dispose for my soul, the souls of Margery, our parents and friends, and all our benefactors, as seems best to please God and profit our souls.

Proved at Finningham, 1 October 1462. Admon to Sir Thomas, exec. Power reserved to Edward Dale, the other exec, when he comes, if he wishes to take up admon.

1   Thomas Wilkyn was vicar of Wickham Skeith from 1450 to 1479 (Tanner, p.1326); he was also executor of John Sporle (no. 715) and witnessed the will of Robert Dunch (no. 374).

[fol. 375]
219. WILLIAM CHATYSLE of IXWORTH, 20 April 1462

Dated Tuesday in Easter week; [*commendation*: to God Almighty &c; *no burial directions*]; to the high altar of Ixworth parish church 3s 4d; to the reparation of the same church 13s 4d.

To the friars of Babwell 10s; to the Austin Friars of Thetford 10s; to the Friars Preachers in Thetford 3s 4d.[1]

To the reparation of Ixworth bridge 2s.

To Agnes my wife 2 cows; to Robert my son a cow; to John my son a cow; to Matilda my daughter a cow; to Elizabeth my daughter a cow.

To Agnes my wife a horse with a saddle and bridle, together with a 'paksadyll'; to Sir Robert my brother one of the best horses (*unu' equ' optimu'*);[2] to Agnes my wife 16 ewes (*oves matric'*) and 8 wethers (*multon'*); to Sir Robert Chatysle my brother 12 ewes and wethers; to Elizabeth my daughter 12 ewes and wethers; to Robert Chatysle of Bury St Edmunds 4 ewes.

To the use of the gild of St Thomas of Canterbury (*Cantuar'*) in Ixworth, 4 ewes;[3] to the use of the light of the Blessed Mary in Ixworth church 2 ewes.

To Margery Redelysworth 2 ewes.

To Agnes my wife all my utensils and necessaries.

To Alice Baldevyn[*sic*], daughter of William Baldewyn, a ewe and a lamb.

Agnes my wife to have my tenement in which I live, in the town of Ixworth, immediately after my death and everything done (*post obitum meum et plenar' completori'*), for the term of 10 years, together with the tenement called 'Purchas' there; and after that term the two tenements to be sold by my execs, and out of the money arising from them Agnes my wife to have 20 marks, Robert my son 4 marks, Matilda my daughter 4 marks and Elizabeth my daughter 4 marks.

To John my son two pightles, with the adjacent land called 'Browsters', in Pakenham field, containing by estimation 3 acres, to hold to him and his heirs of the chief lords of the fee by due service and custom.

12 acres of land in the fields of Ixworth and Pakenham to be sold by my execs immediately after my death, and out of the money Sir Robert Chatysle my brother to have 5 marks to celebrate for my soul for half a year.

My execs to make a window of glass (*de glasse*) at the end of the altar of St James in Ixworth church,[4] and support Marion my mother during her life-time with food and drink and all other necessaries, as she ought to be, from my goods and chattels.

John Edmund my apprentice to be discharged from the obligation (*tant' convec'*) of his indenture of apprenticeship and to have 3s 4d.

Residue of all my goods to Sir Robert Chatysle my brother, Roger Bryon of Pakenham and John Vyell of Ixworth,[5] execs, to pay [*therewith*] all [*my*] debts and dispose as seems best to please God and profit my soul.

Proved at Ixworth, 26 July 1462. Admon to execs.

1   For the friars see notes to nos 1 (Babwell), 68 (Friars Preachers of Thetford) and 69 (Austin Friars of Thetford).
2   The testator was probably the brother of John Chattysley of Ixworth (no. 575) as both William and John stated that Sir Robert Chatysle/Chattysley was their brother and appointed him their executor.
3   In the second half of the fifteenth century there were several gilds in Ixworth, including those of Corpus Christi, St James, St John the Baptist, St Peter (and/or SS Peter and Paul) and St Thomas of Canterbury. See the following wills: Anne Catour *alias* Neve (Pt I, no. 321), John Freman (Pt I, no. 335), Robert Fraunceys (Pt I, no. 357), John Huchon (Pt I, no. 827), Ralph Pentney *alias* Sporyere (no. 220 below), Thomas Vyell (no. 723 below). In his will, pr. December 1476, John Purpyll left a tenement in Ixworth for the support of the gildhall there (SROB, Hervye 59).
4   See Introduction, under *church interior*.
5   Executor of no. 220 below.

[fol. 375v]
220. RALPH PENTENEY *alias* SPORYERE of IXWORTH, [*1462*]

Of Ixworth in the diocese of Norwich; [*no date given*; *commendation*: to God Almighty, the Blessed Mary &c; *no burial directions*]; to the high altar of Ixworth parish church, for my tithes forgotten, 2s; to the use of the said church 13s 4d; to the use of the gild of St John the Baptist in Ixworth 3s 4d.[1]

To Agnes my wife all my utensils which I lately had with her in marriage; to Agnes 6 plates (*plater'*), 6 dishes and 6 saucers of pewter, with half my utensils, except a large pan and a large pot, and the other half of my utensils to William my son.

Agnes my wife to have my tenement situated in the street called 'le Heygstrete', next to the tenement of John Byrd, to hold to her and her heirs, of the chief lords of the fee by due service and custom. She also to have a close containing 2½ acres of free land, in the field of Ixworth, to hold to her and her attorneys for term of her life; after her decease the close to remain to William my son, to hold to him and his heirs, of the chief lords of the fee by due service and custom, for ever.

My tenement in which I live to be sold by my execs and out of the money from it: to the prior and convent of Ixworth 6s 8d;[2] to Sir John Vauncy, canon, 6s 8d; to Margery, my wife's daughter, 6s 8d; to my servant called 'le Blaunche' 2s; and to Robert my son 20s.

My execs to have a chimney (*chamini'*) made in the aforesaid tenement and Agnes my wife to have, out of the money coming from the said tenement, [*no amount stated*], and she to have all the payment coming from the land and tenement in Wangford, to her own use; also to Agnes the barley grain (*gran' ord'*) growing on 2 acres of land in Ixworth field.

Residue of all my goods to John Elyngham and John Vyell,[3] execs, and John Herevord of Bardwell, supervisor; they to pay all my debts and dispose as they see best to please God and profit my soul.

Seal appended.

Proved at Ixworth ('Yxworth'), 27 July 1462. Admon to execs.

[1] See note to the will of William Chatysle (no. 219) regarding gilds in Ixworth.
[2] See note to no. 69.
[3] Executor of no. 219.

[fol. 376]
221. JOHN BOTELERE of PALGRAVE, 30 October 1462

[*Commendation*: to God &c; *no burial directions*]; to the high altar of Palgrave 6d; to the rector of the same town a certain, to be celebrated for me and Agnes my wife, for seven years [*no sum*]; a trental of St Gregory [*to be celebrated. No sum*]. Margaret my wife to have the house lately built on the west side of my tenement, with a portion of the land adjacent (*iuxta*) containing 1½ roods, more or less; to Margaret all my utensils, with my grain in the barn, on condition that if she makes any claim on my lands or tenements, or on any part of them, or makes any unjust prosecution or accusation (*aliquod occasu' aut calumpn'*) against my execs, the house with the land, and all my utensils and grain in the barn, to be sold and the money received to be spent for me and for the souls of my friends.

All my debts that can be legitimately proved are to be paid out of my goods.

Residue of all my goods, however little (*licet paucoru'*), to the disposition of my execs, John Catelyn and Thomas Cowper of Palgrave, to dispose as they see best to please God and profit my soul.

Proved at Eye, 18 November 1462. Admon to execs.

222. ?JOHN POPE of EYE, 10 October 1462 [*English*]

[*Christian name indistinctly written*] [*Commendation*: to God &c; *no burial directions*]; to the high altar of Eye 12d; to the reparation of the steeple of the same church 6s 8d.

To every priest being at my *dirige* 4d; to every clerk 1d; to the poor men at the 'Spetyll' 8d.[1]

To Sir Robert Salews 8 marks, for to sing and pray in Eye church, by the term of a whole year, for my soul and all my friends' souls.

The land that Sir Thomas Woode and I bought jointly together in Yaxley ('Yaxle'), to the sum of £10 13s 4d, to be sold and my priest to be paid with my part, which is 8 marks.

Thomas Pope of Yaxley, my son, owes me for farm of land and for a pension, 4 marks 3s, which I will my execs have to fulfil my testament withal.

Residue of my goods to be at the disposition of Robert Brond of Gyslyngham and Nicholas Hardyng of Eye, my execs.

Witnesses: Sir Thomas Hervy, vicar of Eye,[2] Thomas Hardyng and Sir Robert Salews.

Proved at Eye, 18 November 1462. Admon to execs.

¹   The hospital of St Mary Magdalene in Eye. In 1459 John Langlond of Eye bequeathed 2d to each of the poor living in the hospital and all his clothes to be divided amongst them (SROB, Baldwyne 264; Pt I, no. 1293).

²   Thomas Hervy was vicar of Eye from 1452 to 1488 (Tanner, p.1300); see also nos 2, 395, 442 and 457.

[fol. 376v]

223. THOMAS TAYLORE of LAVENHAM, 3 July 1462

Dated the feast of the translation of St Thomas; [*commendation*: to God &c; *no burial directions*]. All my debts to be paid before all else. To the high altar of Lavenham, for tithes and offerings in arrears and underpaid, 2s.

To a suitable priest 9 marks, to celebrate divine service in the aforesaid church immediately after my death, for a year, for my soul and my parents' souls.

20s to be distributed among the poor, immediately after my death, 6d a week until it is all distributed.

To Agnes Taylore my wife £10 in money and all my utensils belonging to my house.

To Agnes my tenement in which I live, for her lifetime; after her death the tenement to be sold by my execs and the money from it, together with the residue of all my goods, to be disposed by my execs in deeds of charity for my soul and my parents' souls, as they see best to please God and profit my soul, as they will answer before God and man on the Day of Judgement.

Execs: Agnes Taylore my wife, William Leveson of 'Hempeston'¹ and Robert Sawyere of Lavenham.

Proved at Lavenham, 1 December 1462. Admon to the executrix. Power reserved to William Leveson and Robert Sawyere, the other execs, when they come, if they wish to take up admon.

¹   'Hempeston' cannot be identified.

224. JOHN BAKERE of CAVENDISH ('Cavendysche'), [*1462*] [*English*]

[*No date given; no commendation of soul or burial directions.*]

Two trentals to be said for me and my good-doers, one at the friars of Clare and another at the friars of Babwell.¹

Alice my daughter to have 6s 8d after the decease of my wife, if it may be spared. Katherine my wife to have my tenement called 'Syotes' for her lifetime and if she may[*sic*] not live on the profit thereof, term of her life, then it to be sold by my execs and Katherine to live on the money from it, term of her life; if it must need be sold, then John my son 'the myddyll' to buy it before any other, if he will; if he will not, then he and John my son 'the younger' to buy it together, if they will; if they will not, then John Goldyng my exec to buy it.

My wife to have my ostilments and household.

My younger son to have 4 nobles after the decease of my wife, if it may be spared. There is to be bought a chalice for Cavendish church, after the decease of my wife, if it may be spared.

If my tenement 'Syotes' may be spared and not sold till after the decease of my wife, then the money to be disposed as above and the residue of the money to be disposed for me and my wives and my children and all my good-doers.

My middle son John to have a bushel [*of barley*] after the decease of my wife.

Execs: Katherine my wife, John my middle son and John Golding, barber; they to fulfil my last will.

Proved at Cavendish, 3 December 1462. Admon to Katherine the executrix; John Baker and John Goldyng, the other execs, renouncing.

1   For the friars of Babwell and Clare see notes to no. 1.

[fol. 377]

225. JOHN SYDAY of GREAT WALDINGFIELD ('Waldyngfeld Magna'), **fuller,** 20 April 1462 and 21 April 1462

Dated 20 April 1462; [*commendation*: to God Almighty; *no burial directions*]; to the high altar of the aforesaid Waldingfield, for tithes forgotten, 20d.

To Margaret my daughter, at her marriage, 20 marks; to Alice my daughter, at her marriage, 20 marks.

My execs, after my debts have been paid, to provide a secular priest to celebrate divine service for a whole year in the church of Great Waldingfield, for my soul and for the souls of my parents and my friends, and all the faithful departed, he having the usual stipend for his labour.

To Elizabeth my wife all my jewels, utensils and bedding of my house, to do with freely as she wishes.

Residue of all my goods and chattels, wherever they are, after my debts have been paid and my burial done, and my testament and last will implemented, to be disposed for my soul and the souls of my parents[1] and friends by the discretion of my execs, as seems to them best.

Execs: Elizabeth my wife, John Pellican and John Syday of Chilton; they faithfully to implement all the premises and each to have 20s for their labour.

[*Will; dated the next day*]

Dated 21 April 1462, 2 Edward IV; beyond what is specified in my testament, carefully remembered and afterwards reduced to writing by me (*diligent' memorata et postea in scriptis redact'*).

All my debts to be paid by my execs first and foremost, and all my legacies in my testament to be implemented as completely as possible.

Elizabeth my wife to have my principal tenement called 'Herietes' with a croft of 3 roods adjacent to it, and with another croft of land, with a pightle of pasture adjacent to it, against the lane called 'Grenecroft Lane', containing about 2 acres of land and pasture, in the aforesaid Waldingfield, for her lifetime, if she remains a widow that long; and after her death, or after her marrying again, in which case she is to have £20 in goods or money from my execs, from the said tenement, two crofts and pightle, the tenement, two crofts and pightle remaining wholly to my execs, [fol. 377v] until John my son shall be of legal age; my wife to have the said £20 piecemeal (*parcellat'*) from the issues and my other goods, as it can conveniently be paid. When John comes to legal age the tenement with the two crofts and pightle to remain to him, to hold them to him and his assigns for ever, of the chief lords of the fee by due service and custom; if John decease under legal age, the tenement with the two crofts to remain, after the decease of Elizabeth or after her re-marriage, to Margaret and Alice my daughters, to be divided equally between them if both live, or to the other at legal age if one dies, to hold them of the chief lords of the fee for ever; if both daughters die under legal age, as well as John my son, the tenement, two crofts and pightle to remain wholly to my execs, or their execs, to sell and the money to be expended for my soul and the souls of my parents and my friends.

Elizabeth my wife to have my tenement called 'Abbottes' in the aforesaid Walding-field and my crofts in Newton called 'Pondfeld' and 'Wodyshed' for all her lifetime, and after her decease to remain to the said John my son, after he is of legal age, for ever; if he decease before that, then after the decease of my wife the tenement called 'Abbottes' and the two crofts to remain, similarly, to my execs to sell and the money to be expended for my soul and for the souls of my parents and other friends in deeds of charity, and especially in masses.

Joan my sister to have, to her and her assigns, my tenement newly built in which William Perwe now lives, to hold it of the chief lords of the fee for ever.

Residue of all my goods, lands and tenements to my execs to sell, together with all my other goods and chattels as assigned in my testament, and out of the money my execs or theirs to pay my debts and legacies and do for the health of my soul &c[*sic*]. I beg and ask in God's name all my feoffees in the said lands and tenements, or in any other parcels, to deliver their estate for implementing my testament, when duly required by my execs or others of them.

Seal appended.

Witnesses: Robert Thurston, Richard Syday and others.

Proved at Sudbury, 22 September 1462. Admon to Elizabeth and John Syday, execs; John Pellican, the other exec, renouncing.

[1]   John was executor of his father, John Sydey of Great Waldingfield, 'wever', pr. July 1450 (SROB, Baldwyne 116; Pt I, no. 541).

[fol. 378]

226. HENRY FRERE of BURWELL [*Cambs*], 6 September 1465

[*Commendation*: to God &c]; to be buried in the churchyard of the church of the Blessed Mary of Burwell.

To Agnes my wife my messuage, for term of her life, and after her decease it to remain to William my son; if William should die without heirs the messuage to remain to Agnes my daughter and her heirs; if Agnes dies without heirs the messuage to remain to the child in her mother's womb, to it and its heirs;[1] if all my children die the messuage to be sold and disposed for the health of my soul.

There to be sold 10 of the best wethers (*biden' ariet'*), and the money to go to St Mary's church; the residue of all the sheep (*biden'*) to my wife, to her and our children.

To William my son 2 of the best ewes (*biden' matric'*); to William Sabbe 2 ewes; to Agnes my daughter 2 ewes; to John Frere my father 6 ewes and my best gown, [*my*] hose and a smock.

To William Redere and his wife a quarter of wheat and a quarter of malt.

Residue of all my goods, grain or animals (*catall'*) to Agnes my wife, executrix, to dispose for the health of my soul.

To the high altar of St Mary's church, for my tithes forgotten and not well paid, one of the best sheep (*biden'*).

To John Bray a wether.

Attorneys: Robert Wyott and William Wyott, to deliver their animals to everyone at the feast of St Michael.

Proved at Burwell, 17 October 1465. Admon to execs.

¹ That is, if his daughter Agnes died without heirs, the messuage was to pass to the child with which her mother Agnes, the testator's wife, was pregnant.

227. JOHN BARKERE of CULFORD, 6 October 1461

[*Commendation*: to God &c]; my body to Christian burial; to the high altar of Culford church, for tithes forgotten, 2s; to the reparation of the said church 40d; to the reparation of West Stow ('Westowe') church 20d; to the reparation of Wordwell church 20d.

To the friars of the convent of Babwell, to intercede for my soul, 40d.¹

To Emma my wife all the ostilments and utensils belonging to my house; Emma to have my tenement in which I live, to her and to her assigns for her lifetime; after her decease the tenement to be sold and the money from it to be distributed by my execs in deeds of charity for my soul and the soul of Emma and [*the souls*] of our parents.

Thomas Halle to have my tenement in Culford called 'Fystonys', with 8 acres of land belonging to it, to him and his assigns for ever.

Henry Fyncham to have my garden in Culford, with 3 roods of land adjoining it, to him and his assigns for ever.

To each of the children of the said Henry Fyncham 2 bushels of barley; to each of the children of William Feltewell 2 bushels of barley.

Residue of all my goods to my execs to dispose for my soul in the best way they can.

Execs: Emma my wife and Robert Burgeys of Bury St Edmunds; to Robert 6s 8d for his labour.

Proved at Fornham [*St Martin*], 14 October 1465. Admon to execs.

¹ See note to no. 1.

[fol. 378v]
228. ALICE PEDDERE of IXWORTH, widow, 3 September 1465

Lately the relict of Robert Peddere;¹ [*commendation*: to God &c]; to be buried in the priory church of Ixworth,² next to the grave of my aforesaid husband; to each canon of the same place, at my burial day, 2s; to Ixworth parish church, to the fabric, 10 marks, at the disposition of my exec; to Tostock ('Tostoke') parish church 13s 4d; to Ixworth Thorpe parish church 6s 8d.

To the Friars Preacher of Thetford 10s; to the Austin Friars of the same [*place*] 10s; to the Friars Minor of Babwell 10s.³

To the care and emendation of a certain common way in Barton Mills ('Berton') lately repaired by Robert Peddere my husband,⁴ at the disposition of my exec, 13s 4d.

To Alice Peddere my servant 40s; to Alice Meyr 6s 8d; to John Purpyll of Ixworth 40 marks; [*all*] to be received and paid out of my debts.

To the poor living in Ixworth 6d, one day a week, for a whole year after my death.

To Alice Peddere my daughter my best brass pot and the best cauldron, a spit, an andiron ('hawndeiryn'), 12 pieces of pewter, that is, 3 platters, 3 dishes, 3 bowls (*scutellas*) and 3 saucers, a pewter pot, a basin, a laver, a candlestick, a salt-cellar, a 'donge', a bed cover, 2 pairs of sheets, a pair of blankets, a 'gansape',[5] 2 towels (*manutergia anglice* 'towalys'), a green gown, a black 'harnessed' belt, a black gown, a black kirtle (*tunica' anglice* 'a kertyll') and a pair of jet beads.

To Alice Meyr a brass pot and 3 bowls; to Alice Meyr the elder a green kirtle, a sanguine-coloured kirtle and a 'huke'; to Marion Meyr a jug, a bowl, a dish and a salt-cellar of pewter.

To Agnes Cok a violet and green tabard.

To John Meyr, of his debt (*ex debito suo*), a coverlet, a pair of sheets and a pair of blankets.

To John Purpyll a hanging laver, a chafer, the best basin, the best laver and the round basin, a featherbed with its equipment (*appendic' suis*), a deep-green (*intenso virid'*) coverlet, a 'falt table'[6] and all the other tables and boards belonging to my house, and 2 candlesticks.

Exec: John Purpyll, to whom the residue of all my goods, to dispose for my soul as he sees best to please God and profit my soul and my husband's [*soul*].

Proved at Fornham [*St*] Martin, 14 October 1465. Admon to exec.

[1] Will (as 'Robert Hamond *alias* Pedder'), pr. January 1458/59 (SROB, Baldwyne 207; Pt I, no. 1033). In 1463 John Roodese of Ixworth, glover, had bequeathed his wife Katherine a close lately Robert Peddere's (no. 37 above).

[2] See note to no. 69.

[3] For the friars see notes to nos 1 (Babwell), 68 (Friars Preachers of Thetford) and 69 (Austin Friars of Thetford).

[4] Presumably the repairs to this road had been done during Robert Pedder's lifetime; he did not make such a bequest in his will.

[5] Meaning unknown.

[6] See Glossary.

[fol. 379]

229. JOHN BAKHOT of MILDENHALL ('Myldenhale'),[1] 20 December 1464

[*Testament begins with invocation to the Trinity*]; of Mildenhall in the diocese of Norwich; [*commendation*: to God &c]; to be buried in 'le South ele' of the church of St Mary of Mildenhall, next to my parents;[2] to the high altar of the said church a noble (*unu' nobile*); to the said church 40s, together with my best silver girdle (*singulo*), to the honour of the Trinity and SS Ed'[*sic*] and Nicholas, in the following manner: one of the parish clerks of Mildenhall to have the girdle on the vigils of the said SS Ed' and Nicholas each year, by the advice and discretion of the wardens of the said church for the time being, to the praise and honour of those saints.

To the Great Gild of the Trinity of Bishop's Lynn (*Lyne Episcopi*) a noble;[3] and a noble to the gild of Corpus Christi;[4] and 40d to the gild of St John of Mildenhall.[5]

A suitable chaplain to be chosen by the discretion of my execs to celebrate for my soul and the souls of my father and mother and all my parents, children and benefactors, for 4 years after my death.

To each of my godsons and goddaughters a ewe.

To Richard Busshe my nephew, and to each of the sons and daughters of John Bakhot my son, a ewe and a hogget (*hogest'*).

To Margaret Knygth my kinswoman my green silver girdle.

Richard my son to have the arrears of rent and service belonging to me, in whoso-ever's or whatsoever hands they be, together with all my rents and services as they are more clearly entered in the rent-rolls and other evidences made of them; to the same Richard my son a bowl (*cratere'*) with a gilt ?rim (*cu' summis deauratis*).

My household (*domiciliu'*) to be kept, together with my goods, up to the feast of St Michael the Archangel next, inclusively.

To John Bakhot my son my best striped (*stragulata'*) gown.

To Margaret my wife all the utensils and bedding belonging to my house, except what belongs to my body, together with my own 3 horses; to Margaret half of all my growing grain, at the harvest next after my death, and half my bovine animals and half of the two flocks pasturing and lying (*pascenc' et cubanc'*) in Herringswell ('Heryngewelle') and Mildenhall, after the feast of St Michael next after my death, the ewes previously bequeathed being first extracted, and except the oxen and cows, and all the ewes and wethers (*multon'*) necessary and sufficient for the upkeep of my house up to the feast of St Michael next, out of the two flocks.

Any obscurities, doubts, difficulties, contradictions [*etc*] (*obscur', dubietas, vari-atio', difficultas, diversitas, contradiccio', repugnat', seu ?gravietas*) in this my testament and last will to be clarified, amended and expounded by Richard my son, as seems necessary to him to prevent it causing disputes.

Residue of all my goods to the discretion and disposition of Margaret my wife and Richard my son, execs, providing always that my debts have been paid to my credi-tors out of my goods and debts.

Seal appended.

Proved at Fornham [*St*] Martin, 4 March 1464/65. Admon to Richard Bakhot, exec. Power reserved to Margaret the wife of the deceased when she comes.

1 ?Witness (as 'John Bakhot the elder') of the will of Simon Chylderston of Mildenhall, pr. November 1454 (SROB, Baldwyne 230; Pt I, no. 1156).

2 The Bakhot family were wealthy Mildenhall mercers, several of whom, like John, requested burial within the parish church; see, for example, the will of William Bakhote of Mildenhall, mercer, pr. May 1461 (SROB, Baldwyne 303; Pt I, no. 1481).

3 The Great Gild of the Trinity of Lynn was the Gild Merchant of the town.

4 The location of this gild was not indicated by the testator: there was a gild of Corpus Christi in Lynn, which had been founded in St Margaret's church *c*.1349; however, it is more likely that this bequest was made to the gild of that name at Mildenhall. John Bakhot had let one of his messuages in Mildenhall to the gild of Corpus Christi there for use as a gildhall. For further details of this gild and gildhall see note to no. 230 below.

5 For other bequests to the gild of St John the Baptist see note to no. 107.

230. WILLIAM CHAPMAN the elder of MILDENHALL ('Myldenhale'),[1]
26 November 1464

Dated at Mildenhall, 4 Edward IV; [*commendation*: to God &c]; to be buried in the church of the Blessed Mary of Mildenhall; to the high altar of the same church, for my tithes and offerings forgotten and withheld, in exoneration of my soul, 6s 8d; to the reparation of the great bell hanging in the tower of Mildenhall church 10 marks. To the gild of Corpus Christi of Mildenhall 6s 8d.[2]

To each of my godsons and goddaughters a ewe.

A suitable priest to celebrate as soon as possible in Mildenhall church for two years, for my soul and the souls of my father and mother and all my friends [*and*] benefactors, and all the faithful departed, taking for his salary 8 marks a year.

To Emma my wife all the utensils belonging to my house [fol. 379v] and all the stock on the tenement in which I live, of whatever kind, and all sorts of my grain, to do with them freely as she wishes, for ever, as if they were her own without any contradiction, and to dispose of them for my soul as seems to her best to please God and benefit the health of my soul, and as she would wish me to do for her in a similar situation. To Emma all my tenement in which I live, and two meadows, that is, 'Wyesmedewe' and 'Corryesmedewe', for term of her life; after her death all the said tenement and the two meadows to be sold by my execs, and the money from them to be given in pious uses, alms and deeds of charity, according to their discretion. To Emma 40 acres of land by the way called 'Grenewey', and of what I have in 'Mundysfurlong', 'Wamelfurlong' and 'Westyndiche', of the best land there (*et hoc de optimis terris*), for term of her life; after her lifetime the 40 acres to be sold by my execs for the best price they can, and the whole of the money from the sale to be faithfully disposed by my execs as they see most expedient. To Emma my wife a hundred of my best sheep.[3]

My execs, Thomas Gotche and William Childerston, to be preferred before [*any*] others in the buying of my land and chattels, at a satisfactory (*condigno*) price.

Residue of all my goods and chattels and my debts, whatsoever and wheresoever they be, to my execs, to dispose for the health of my soul as seems most expedient to them.

Execs: Emma my wife the principal exec, and Thomas Gotche and William Childerston of Mildenhall.[4]

Seal appended.

Proved at Fornham [*St Martin*], 8 April 1465. Admon to Thomas Gotche and William Childerston, execs. Power reserved to Emma the relict of the deceased when she comes. Afterwards admon granted by the chaplain.

1 ?Executor of Thomas Cake of Mildenhall, will pr. July 1454 (SROB, Baldwyne 205; Pt I, no. 1009). A messauge belonging to one William Chapman was situated in Beck Row, Mildenhall, adjacent that of John Frere (will of John Frere, pr. July 1448 (SROB, Baldwyne 144; Pt I, no. 683)).

2 For other bequests to the gild of Corpus Christi, see wills of: John Bygge of Mildenhall (Pt I, no. 569), John Staloun the younger of Mildenhall (Pt I, no. 708), Simon Chylderston of Mildenhall (Pt I, no. 1156), John Bakhot of Mildenhall (no. 229 above), Thomas Blake of Barton Mills (no. 717 below) and John Playford of Mildenhall (no. 754 below). The gild of Corpus Christi leased from John Bakhot a messuage which was known as the gildhall of Corpus Christi of Mildenhall. This gildhall abutted on one of the village's fields (will of Richard Colman, pr. March 1461/62 (SROB, Baldwyne 286; Pt I, no. 1403)).

3 A long hundred, i.e., 120 sheep. John Staloun of Mildenhall bequeathed his wife Joan a hundred sheep, comprising 60 wethers and 60 ewes (SROB, Baldwyne 148; Pt I, no. 708).

4 ?Son of Richard Childerston (SROB, Baldwyne 218; Pt I, no. 1084) and Matilda (no. 239 below); see also note to the latter will.

231. JOHN ROWT of RATTLESDEN ('Ratelesden'), 10 October 1464

[*Commendation*: to God &c; *no burial directions*]; to the high altar for tithes forgotten &c[*sic*] 12d; to the altar of St Mary of the same church 2s, for altar cloths to be bought for it.

To my sons and daughters 13s 4d each; to Mariota my daughter a brass pot now in the hands of John Rowte.

Any residue there may be of my goods I leave to my wife Christian.

Execs: Sir John Rowt my son, chaplain, and John Bacon; to each of whom 12d for their labour.

Proved at Fornham [*St Martin*], 16 September 1465. Admon to Sir John Rowt, exec. Power reserved to John Bacon when he comes.

[fol. 380]

232. WILLIAM WARNER of SOHAM ('Saham') [*Cambs*], 20 April 1465

[*Commendation*: to God Almighty &c]; to be buried in the churchyard of the church of St Andrew the Apostle of Soham; to the high altar of which, a coomb of barley. My chief messuage to be sold after my decease and the money from it disposed in three parts: one part to the church, another to ways and the third to the poor.

3½ acres of free arable land in 'Estfeld', John Peyton on both sides, and an acre of meadow lying at 'le Calow', and a piece of meadow in 'Longmedew' containing 8 perches, and 3 roods of 'Fenmedew' on the other side of the mere (*mar'*) by Thomas Kyng, all to be sold and disposed for my soul and the souls of all my benefactors.

19 acres of arable land and meadow in the north field[1] of Soham to be sold and with the money from them my debts to be paid and a priest provided, if it can be done, to celebrate for my soul and the souls of all my benefactors.

To Margery Warner my wife a messuage, formerly the messuage of Agnes Stephenes, with a garden on the other side of the street, to give, sell or dispose as she pleases; my wife to have an acre of arable land called '?Obschortes Akyr', for keeping the anniversary of William Warner [*and*] John Glemyford and Ellen his wife, as long as she lives, and after that, in the same way, whoever shall have [*it*], for ever. Also to my wife 3 roods of arable land in 'Berycroftes', by the common mere, and 2½ acres of arable land in 'Horscroft' and half an acre of arable land in 'Estfeld',[2] by the land of John Leyr, for term of her life; after her decease [*these*] to be sold and disposed for my soul and the souls of all my benefactors.

John Bochere to have the messuage, formerly Agnes Chapmanys, with the adjacent croft, containing 2 acres of land, with 3 acres of arable land, and 3 roods of meadow lying at 'Brokestretesende',[3] on condition that he pays 1 mark each year until 6 marks have been paid.

When all my debts have been paid, my wife to have 20 sheep, and the residue of all my animals (*catallorum*) not bequeathed to be divided between my wife and myself. To Joan Lowyn a heifer, two years old; to Alice my servant a ewe with [*a*] lamb and a heifer, two years old; to John ?Hacke a stirk (*stircu'*), two years old.

To my wife, in seed-corn (*granis seminatis*) 10 coombs of wheat and maslin (*mixtil'*) and 10 coombs of barley.

To the vicar 8d; to each of my execs 6s 8d.

Residue of all my goods, if any there be, to Margery Warner my wife, Henry Yakysle,[5] John Crople and John Northfolk the younger,[4] execs, to dispose for my soul and the souls of all my benefactors, as they see best to please God, the Blessed Mary and all the saints.

Seal appended.

Proved at Soham, 26 June 1465. Admon to execs. Seal of the official appended.

135

1   'Northfield' in Soham appears on a map of the manor drawn in 1656 (CRO, SOH65602 (Soham, 1656), tracing of an original map of Soham at Raynham Hall, Norfolk). Information on early-modern Soham supplied by Lynne Turner.
2   'Berrycroft Closes' and 'Horsecroft Common' appear on the same map but East Field ('Estfeld') seems to have been broken up before 1656.
3   'Brookstreete Closes' appear on the same map.
4   Executor (as 'Yakesley') of Richard Yakesley, probate only, May 1460 (SROB, Baldwyne 270; Pt I, no. 1326).
5   The Yaxley, Cropley and Norfolk families were prominent in Soham in the seventeenth century, several individuals being members of the parish élite.

[fol. 380v]

233. KATHERINE KEMPE of BURWELL [*Cambs*], 17 September 1435

Dated the Sabbath after the feast of the exaltation of the Holy Cross; [*commendation*: to God &c]; to be buried in the churchyard of the church of the Blessed Virgin Mary.

To John Kempe my husband[1] all my lands and tenements which I have in the town and fields of Burwell, for the whole of his life, and after his decease my tenement with the divers lands belonging to it to remain to Thomas Kempe my son; if Thomas should die without heirs, then the tenement with the lands belonging to it to remain to William Kempe my son; if William should die without heirs the tenement with the lands to remain to John Kempe my son, and so on, in order (*de gradu in gradum*); if all my sons should die without heirs, the tenement and lands to be sold and distributed by my feoffees for the health of my soul and my parents' [*souls*].

To William Kempe my son an acre of my land; to Margaret my daughter an acre of my land; to John Kempe my son an acre of my land; to John Kempe my son [*sic*] 3 acres of my land; to Alice my daughter an acre of my land; to John Kempe my son [*sic*] an acre of my land; to Nicholas Kempe my son an acre of my land; if any of my sons or daughters should die without heirs, their part of the land to be sold and distributed for the health of my soul and my parents' [*souls*] by my feoffees.

To Margaret the servant of John at the Hylle 1½ acres of my land in 'Northfeld', to her and her heirs.

3 acres of my land to be sold to pay my debts and perform my will, without delay. The residue of all my lands to be divided in two parts, one to be divided among my children then alive and the other to be sold and distributed by my feoffees for the health of my soul, and to the church of the Blessed Mary of Burwell and other deeds of charity.

[*Proved with the will of her husband: see next.*]

1   Will no. 234 below.

234. JOHN KEMPE of BURWELL [*Cambs*], 1 May 1465

[*Commendation*: to God &c]; my body to Christian burial; to the high altar for my tithes forgotten 8d; to the building (*edificac'*) of the church, for the health of my soul and that of Katherine my wife, 4 bushels of wheat and 4 bushels of barley, and a laver.[1]

To Isabel, the daughter of Thomas Calvysbane, a ewe with a lamb; to Thomas Calvysbane[2] a lamb.

To Alice my daughter 4 bushels of wheat; to Cecily my wife[3] the crop (*vestur'*) of an acre of wheat and the crop of an acre of barley.

Residue of all my goods, growing corn and other chattels or utensils to William Cuntforth, Thomas Calvysbane and Ed[mund] Paxman,[4] whom I make my attorneys, to sell and to pay all my debts and legacies and perform my will.

Proved at Soham ('Saham') [*Cambs*], together with the will of Katherine Kempe,[5] annexed, 26 June 1465. Admon to execs.

1   In the Middle Ages Burwell had two churches, St Mary's and St Andrew's. St Mary's was almost totally rebuilt in the second half of the fifteenth century and survives; St Andrew's was demolished in the eighteenth century. Some testators, such as John Kempe here, did not specify to which church their bequest was made but their executors would know which was their parish church. Regarding this particular testator, his wife (no. 233) requested burial in the churchyard of St Mary's.

2   Will, no. 512.

3   John Kempe's current wife.

4   Executor of William Fabbe of Burwell (no. 215); see note to that will.

5   Although written 30 years apart, these wills were proved together; in the meantime John Kempe had remarried.

[fol. 381]

235. JOHN HOROLD the elder of MELLIS ('Melles'), 26 September 1464

Dated Wednesday after the feast of St Matthew the Apostle; [*commendation*: to God &c]; my body to Christian burial. Firstly, all the debts that I owe to be well and truly paid as quickly as possible and in the best manner. To the high altar of Mellis church, for tithes forgotten &c[*sic*], 4d; to the use and emendation of Mellis church 12d.

To Roger Hawe my godson 4d; to Thomas Horold my son 13s 4d; to Clemence my daughter 20d; to Julian my daughter 20d; [*all*] to be paid out of the money which is owed to me if my debts can be gathered (*levar'*) by my execs.

To Margaret my wife all the bedclothes (*pannos lectorum*), such as sheets, covers, blankets and 'le undyrclothes'; to Margaret all my brass vessels, that is, pots, pans, cauldrons and [*all*] other brass vessels whatsoever, she to have and use them for term of her life, provided always that William Horold my son shall have access (*aisamentu'*) to all those vessels whenever he has need and Margaret not to take away any of the vessels from my tenement without the agreement of William and my execs; after Margaret's death all the said vessels to remain to William my son.

Margaret my wife and William my son jointly to have all my lands and tenements, meadows, pastures and feedings, with the adjacent curtilages, in the towns and fields of Mellis and Burgate, for the term of Margaret's life. If Margaret and William should not be able to agree, William and my execs to pay Margaret £5 6s 8d in money, by equal portions of 10s at the feasts of Easter and All Saints each year, without any delay, until the whole be paid to her and her execs, provided that Margaret have the choice of whether to live in my messuage and have the lands and tenements jointly with William for term of her life or to leave the tenement and have the £5 6s 8d at the said feasts, without any gainsaying. After the death of Margaret my wife all the said lands and tenements to remain to William my son, to hold them to him and his heirs of the chief lords of the fee for ever; if William should die without any sons or daughters alive, then Margaret my wife, if she be living with William in tenement, to

have all lands and tenements for term of her life; and after her death the lands and
tenements to remain to Thomas Horold my son, to hold to him and his heirs of the
chief lords &c[*sic*]. If Thomas should die before Margaret, then after her decease the
lands and tenements to be sold by my execs or feoffees, and the money from them
to be disposed in this way: a half part of it to be divided equally between Julian and
Clemence my daughters, if they be alive, otherwise among their sons and daughters
if any, or, if there be none, both that part and the other part to be disposed in the
celebration of masses, the relief of the poor and to the profit of Mellis church, for
the souls of me, the said John Horold, and my friends.

Residue of all my goods to be distributed in deeds of charity by my execs, John
Yeppeswych, gentleman, of Burgate,[1] William Horold my son and Roger Horold of
Mellis, as they &c[*sic*].

Seal appended.

Proved at Eye, 17 July 1465. Admon to execs. Power reserved to John Yepeswych
when he comes.

<blockquote>
1   The Yeppeswych family was one of consequence in Burgate. In 1440 Nicholas Yepisswich
     requested burial in the parish church of St Mary, will pr. October 1445 (SROB, Baldwyne 88;
     Pt I, no. 406). Nicholas's son John had a son named John. ?John senior's will, of which John
     'Yebyswych' was executor, probate only, January 1457/58 (SROB, Baldwyne 199; Pt I, no. 976).
     John Horold's executor here was probably the John Yeppeswych who died in 1481 (will, SROB,
     Hervye 226) and requested burial in the chancel of St Mary's, a position normally reserved for
     patrons and incumbents; his brother, another Nicholas, was rector of Stowlangtoft 1465–1506
     (Tanner, p.1213).
</blockquote>

[fol. 381v]

236. JOHN FYSHYVE of STOKE by NAYLAND ('Stokeneylond'),[1] 8 July 1465

My body to Christian burial; [*commendation*: to God &c]; to the high altar in the
said church for tithes forgotten 12d; to the [*?fabric*][2] of the said church 6s 8d.

To Isabel my wife two cottages in Stoke for term of her life, provided that she
repairs them sufficiently at her own cost; when Isabel considers it appropriate (*qu'
visu' fuerit prefate Isabelle*) Julian my daughter is to have the cottage called 'Jakes
Crofte', she paying Isabel 40s; to Isabel all my chattels and all my movable goods,
she seeing me honestly buried.

Execs: Isabel my wife and Robert Lunt of Stoke.

Witnesses: Master John Cranewyse, vicar there,[3] and John Spore.

Proved at Long Melford ('Melf'), 23 July 1465. Admon to Robert Lunte. Power
reserved to Isabel, executrix, when she comes.

<blockquote>
1   Executor of John Sperlyng of Stoke by Nayland, probate May 1458 (SROB, Baldwyne 262; Pt I,
     no. 1283). Perhaps the origin of this surname is 'fishwife'.
2   An ill-written word beginning with 'fa'.
3   See note to no. 150; Cranewyse also witnessed nos 150, 409 and 556.
</blockquote>

237. MARGARET BEERE of LAVENHAM, 28 August 1464

[*Commendation*: to God &c]; my body to Christian burial; to the ?candlebeam in
honour of the body of Christ (*candelabro in honor' corporis Christi*) 16s; to the high
altar of Lavenham church 20d.

To Katherine my daughter, the younger, my best chest and a mazer and the best pan, with a spit, and 40s, if it is possible after the payment of my debts; to Alice my daughter 40s, if it is possible after my decease and after my debts have been paid; to Matilda my daughter 20s [*similarly*]; to Agnes my daughter 20s [*similarly*]; to Denise my daughter 20s [*similarly*]; to Joan my daughter, the younger, 20s [*similarly*].

Execs: John Cooke, John Scarlett.

Supervisor: Thomas Spryng.[1]

Residue of all my goods to my execs.

Proved at Long Melford ('Melf'), 23 July 1465. Admon to John Cooke, exec. Power reserved to John Scarlet, the other co-exec, when he comes, with the supervision of Thomas Spryng.

[1] See note to no. 190.

[fol. 382]

238. THOMAS PYPERE of THORPE MORIEUX ('Thorppmorieux'),[1] 14 January 1465/66

[*Commendation*: to God &c]; my body to Christian burial; to the high altar in the church of the aforesaid Thorpe, for my tithes forgotten or underpaid, 6s 8d; to be distributed among priests, clerks and the poor on the day of my burial, 5s, that they may the more quickly (*celerius*) pray for my soul; to a suitable chaplain, secular or religious, to celebrate divine service in the said church after my death, 10 marks.

To the convent of friars of Sudbury, to celebrate a trental, 10s;[2] to Friar Thomas Langham 3s 4d;[3] to the convent of friars of Clare 3s 4d; to the convent of friars of Babwell ('Babbewell') 3s 4d.[4]

To Emma, the wife of John Chynory, 2 cows, and to her son, 8s 4d.

The debts that I owe[*d*] to John Pypere my father, for my lands and tenements, to be paid to Sir Robert Chapman[5] to dispose for the said John's soul, as in making a new ?candlebeam (*candelabro*) in the said church and in other deeds of charity.

To Emma my daughter, the younger, 40s; to Agnes my daughter 40s.

Alice my wife to have all my tenement, with the lands, for term of her life, and, after her decease or if she remarries, the lands and tenement to remain to John my son when he comes of age.

All my cofeoffees to surrender their estate and transfer possession of and in all my lands and tenements to John my son, when so required by him and my execs; the said John, when he is possessed of and in all the said lands and tenements, to pay a suitable priest or priests 5s annually, to celebrate masses until 10 marks have been completely disposed; if John should die before he comes of age, then, after his decease and after the decease of Alice my wife, all the aforesaid lands and tenements to be sold and disposed in deeds of charity.

Residue of all my goods, debts and chattels to Alice my wife.

Execs: Alice my wife and Sir Robert Chapman, rector of Thorpe church; they, having God before their eyes, to dispose for the health of my soul and the souls of my parents and benefactors as they see best to please God and profit my soul; to Sir Robert, for his labour, 6s 8d.

Proved at Lavenham, 11 February 1465/66. Admon to execs.

¹   One of the executors of his father, John Pypere (no. 131), dated 20 April 1462 and proved 1 December 1462.
²   See note to no. 11.
³   Beatrice Turnour of Woolpit (SROB, Baldwyne 167; Pt I, no. 806) and Agnes Tylle of Sudbury (no. 145 above) also requested Friar Thomas Langham to celebrate for their souls.
⁴   For the friars of Clare and Babwell see notes to no. 1
⁵   See note to no. 131. As the other executor of John Pypere, Sir Robert Chapman was jointly responsible with Thomas for collecting debts owed to John. Three years after his father's death Thomas still had not repaid money that he owed for land purchased from his father; now he wished to rectify his omission.

239. MATILDA CHYLDERSTON of MILDENHALL ('Myldenhale'), 20 May 1465

Lately the relict of Richard Childerston;¹ dated 5 Edward IV; [*commendation*: to God &c]; to be buried in the church of the Blessed Mary of Mildenhall, by the place where the body of Richard Childerston, my late husband, there lies buried;² to the high altar of the same church, for my tithes forgotten, 3s 4d; to the reparation of the said church 10s.

To the convent of Friars Minor of Babwell 10s; to the house and convent of friars of Thetford called 'le Oldehows' 10s; to the house and convent of friars of Thetford called 'le Newhows' 10s; that each house and convent of friars aforesaid celebrate among themselves (*per se*) a trental for my soul and for the soul of Richard [*my*] husband and for the souls of all my benefactors.³

[fol. 382v] A suitable priest to celebrate in Mildenhall church for my soul, the said Richard's and all my benefactors' [*souls*] for a whole year, taking 8 marks in money for his stipend.

To John Chylderston my son⁴ 3 acres of land lying in one piece, abutting on 'Fenhow Grene'; to the same John 3 roods of land abutting on 'Berehylle'.⁵

To Agnes Chylderston, daughter of the said John,⁶ 1 acre of land lying near 'Welmere' and a heifer of 2 years; to each of the children of the said John a ewe.

To William Chylderston my son⁷ 5 roods of land lying in 'Baggysholmefeld', abutting on 'Baggysholme'; to William 1½ acres of land at 'Thremhowehylle' and 3 roods of land at 'Lytyll Thremhowe'; William to have a pightle of meadow, lately purchased of the execs of John Tydde,⁸ on condition that he pays 33s 4d to the performing of my will.

To Matilda Chylderston, the daughter of the said William, 3 roods of land at 'Baggysholme havyddyn';⁹ to Richard Childerston, son of the said William, a cow, the best he can choose from my cows; to each of the children of the said William a ewe.

To each of the children of Thomas Tydde¹⁰ a ewe; to William Catelyn, the servant of William Childerston, a ewe; to Alice Wryte a ewe.

To each of my goddaughters and godsons a bushel of barley.

All my utensils to be divided equally between William Childerston and John Childerston my sons.

If my will and legacies cannot be fulfilled out of my goods and chattels, then an acre of land out of William's part and another acre of land out of John's part to be sold, from which to perform my legacies, if necessary.

Residue of all my goods and chattels, of whatever kind and wherever they are, after my debts have been paid and my funeral done and my legacies performed, I leave wholly to William and John Childerston, my sons, execs.

Proved at Fordham [*Cambs*], 14 February 1465/66. Admon to execs.

1 Will pr. September 1457 (SROB, Baldwyne 218; Pt I, no. 1084).
2 In his will Richard Childerston had not specified where he wished to be buried.
3 For the friars see notes to nos 1 (Babwell), 68 (the Old House, Thetford) and 69 (the New House).
4 Will (as 'John Schildyrston the elder'), no. 629 below; executor of his father Richard.
5 John subsequently bequeathed these 3 roods at 'Berehylle' to his daughter Joan.
6 Beneficiary of her father's will (no. 629).
7 ?Will pr. March 1470/80 (SROB, Hervye 186); executor of his father Richard.
8 Will (as 'Tyd') pr. April 1454 (SROB, Baldwyne 152; Pt I, no. 727).
9 'havyddyn' has not been found in any dictionary or glossary; 'heved' means 'head', as in 'heved-lond' for 'headland' (Powell).
10 Legatee and executor of no. 629 below, in which Thomas Tydde was identified as 'of Bury St Edmunds, tanner'.

[fol. 383]
240. WILLIAM METEWYN of WATTISFIELD ('Watlesfeld'), 27 & 28 September 1465

[*Testament, dated 28 September 1465*]

[*Commendation*: to God &c; *no burial directions*]; first, my debts that I owe to be well and truly paid; to the high altar of the same church [*of Wattisfield*] 40d; to the reparation of the said church 40d; to ?Market Weston ('Weston') church 13s 4d; to Hepworth church 40d; to the parish clerk of Wattisfield 6d.

To the friars of the Old House of Thetford 20d; to the friars of the New House of the same town 20d; to the friars of Babwell 20d.[1]

To John Margery my worst blue gown; to the same John my best doublet when he leaves his service (*cum recesserit a suo servicio*).

To John Wareyn a ?striped (*raet'*) gown.

Any residue that remains of my goods I leave to Roger Martyn, Robert Costyn[2] and Robert Banham, execs, that they &c[*sic*] in exoneration of their consciences towards God in this matter.

Seal appended.

[*Will, dated 27 September 1465*]

First I give to God and the church of St Margaret of Wattisfield an enclosure lying at 'Dawis-at-Grene' containing, by estimation, 11 acres of pasture, and I wish that, before all else, the money coming annually from it should go towards paying the fifteenths of the lord king,[3] a half or a quarter (*media' sive quart'*) each time when-ever they are levied in the township of Wattisfield,[4] provided always that whose-soever hands the money shall come to, the obit [*and*] anniversary of me, William Metewyn, [*my*] parents and my wife shall be kept annually, once in the year, with obsequies and mass on the morrow, in the said church; for the saying of which obsequies and mass, the rector of that place to have annually 5d offered at the mass by the churchwardens of the said church for ever (*perpetuis temporibus duratur'*).

My tenement called 'Leparys', with the adjacent croft, to go towards (*transeat*) the sustentation of the gild of St Margaret of Wattisfield,[5] except that the timber growing in the yard (*orto*) of the tenement is to be sold by my execs, and Elizabeth my wife shall have (*occupet*) the pasturage (*herbagiu'*) of the tenement and croft until the feast of St Michael the Archangel.

My wife to have my tenement called 'Metewynes', with 2 acres of land in the croft of the same tenement, 2 acres of land at 'Upstrete', 3 acres 3 roods of land at

'Derebowth' and an enclosure called 'Dellond', for the whole term of her life if she remains in pure widowhood; and then, after her decease, the land and tenement to be sold by my execs, or their attorneys if mine do not survive, and the money from them to be disposed charitably by my execs, or their attorneys, as above; if Elizabeth should marry another husband, then she to have 5 marks in money at the time of [*her*] marriage and the lands and tenement to be sold by my execs.

If Elizabeth should be pregnant by me (*cum semine de corpore meo*) the child, whether a son or daughter, to have the tenement with the lands after the decease of my wife, if she remains a widow, but, otherwise, the child to have and enter the lands and tenement at the time of Elizabeth's marriage.

All my other lands in Wattisfield to be sold by my execs and [*two illegible words*]. My tenement at ?Market Weston ('Weston'), with all the lands belonging to it, to be sold by my execs and the money from them to go to the finding of priests, that is, Sir Simon Dryvere[6] for a year, he to have that service as far away as (*usque*) Cambridge (*Cantabrig'*) and 8 marks in money for his stipend, and Friar Robert Brown,[7] to celebrate divine service for a year for the health of my soul, my friends' and benefactors' [*souls*], he having 5 marks in money for his stipend; the rest of the money from the tenement to be spent on the finding of priests as long as it lasts.

[fol. 383v] Elizabeth shall provide the repairs of the tenement called 'Metewynes' as long as she has it in [*her*] keeping.

My execs to sell the large brass pot, a pair of the best sheets, 2 cloths of red say (*rubeo sagio*), the red cover, a large lead, the spit with the andiron, all the boards (*asseres*, 'boordes') and planks (*plutea*, 'plankes'),[8] 6 yards of white cloth called 'blankkett', the basin, a pair of beads (*de precationu'*) called 'beedes', except the ring, my best blue gown, half the cheese, the other part to be reserved to my wife; also to be sold the sword with the shield (*parma*), the bow with the arrows, a 'jakke' with 'le salett'.[9]

My wife to have a horse of her choice, the 2 best cows, 2 pigs with 2 piglets, a cart with a pair of traces (*retinaculorum*) called 'bodytrays', a saddle belonging to the same cart, with 2 horse-collars and with a pair of ?traces (*straturarum*) called 'shak-trays', a plough with the traces, plough-beam (*temone*), [*and*] shackles (*torcill'*), with the coulter [*and*] share. She also to have 3 coombs of wheat, 3 coombs 2 bushels of rye, 6 coombs of barley, a coomb of beans, a bushel of green peas and a coomb of oats, with the ?bedding (*fulcimento*) of the house.

John Bettes to have a quarter of barley.

My wife to have sufficient straw, hay, fodder and chaff for her animals for a year.

William Flecchere to have a bed-cover, a pair of sheets, 2 augers (*terebra*) and the axe.

John Margery to have all the tools belonging to my trade, they to be delivered to him well and truly on the feast of St Michael the Archangel. The said John Margery to live in my tenement without any gainsaying, until the said feast of St Michael the Archangel and my execs to hire a man of my trade for a year and that craftsman and the aforesaid John to make wheels out of my timber at present in the house at 'Leperys' [*consisting*] of naves (*mediis*), spokes (*radiis*) and felloes (*cantis*);[10] and the said John to have such good instruction (*ita mere erudicionem*) in that year that he might fully master (*plenius habere*) the subtleties (*subtilitat'*) of his craft according to his ability (*secundum ingenii eius capacitat'*) and the money received for the work of the said craftsman and John in that time to be disposed by my execs, that is Roger Martyn, Robert Costyn and Robert Banham, as named in my testament.

There are other legacies there that are not recorded here (*aliqua sunt ibidem legat' que hic non intitulant'*).

Seal appended.

Proved at ?Market Weston ('Weston'), 22 October 1465. Admon to execs. Seal of official appended.

1   For the friars, see notes to nos 1 (Babwell), 68 (the Old House, Thetford) and 69 (the New House).
2   Executor of John Mettewynd of Wattisfield, will pr. January 1458/59 (SROB, Baldwyne 194; Pt I, no. 945).
3   'Fifteenths' were taxes levied intermittently by the Crown. See Glossary.
4   In 1458 John Mettewynd of Wattisfield (?a relative) had bequeathed 20s to the fifteenths of the town of Wattisfield (see note above). In 1445 William Herman of Rickinghall Superior bequeathed a rood of land called 'le Hevestech' to the 'general aid of the taxes of the townsmen', will pr. June 1445 (SROB, Baldwyne 35; Pt I, no. 194). In 1456 John Foot of Buxhall (no. 383 below) bequeathed half an acre for similar purposes and in 1472 John Nunne the elder of Rougham (no. 634 below) bequeathed three pieces of land, amounting to 3½ acres. See Introduction, under *Charitable giving*.
5   A substantial bequest to the gild. Thomas Walloure of Wattisfield (no. 741) made a more modest bequest of 4 bushels of barley and a tablecloth.
6   See note to no. 476.
7   In 1474 Thomas Walloure of Wattisfield (no. 741 below) requested that Friar Robert Brown of Babwell celebrate a trental for him; in 1462 Almeric Molows of the same parish (SROB, Baldwyne 287; Pt I, no. 1409) had bequeathed the friar his best bed.
8   The English words 'boordes' and 'plankes' are written above the Latin.
9   Some arms and armour that an individual might possess.
10 Testator must have been a wheelwright.

[fol. 384]

241. ALICE SKEETE of GREAT LIVERMERE ('Magna Lyvermere'), widow, 11 April 1465

['Skete' *in margin*] Alice Skeete, who was the wife of Robert Skeet, deceased, lately of Bardwell ('Berdewell'); [*commendation*: to God &c]; my body to Christian burial; to the high altar of the church of the said Livermere, for my tithes and offerings underpaid, 4d.[1]

To the friars of Babwell,[1] to celebrate a Gregorian trental (*j tricenale greg'*) for my soul and the soul of the said Robert, 5s; to the reparation of Stanton church 10s;[2] to the reparation of Bardwell church 2s.

To John Warnere of Great Livermere and Richard Redgrave of the same, my messuage formerly John Avenant's in the town of Stanton, to sell and dispose all the money arising from it for my soul and the soul of my aforesaid husband.

Residue of all my goods to my execs, to sell, receive and dispose for the health of my soul &c[*sic*].

Execs: John Warner and Richard Redgrave, to each of whom 3s 4d.

Supervisor: William Cokett, chaplain.[3]

Proved at Fornham [*St Martin*], 27 September 1465. Admon to execs.

1   See note to no. 1.
2   It is unclear to which church this bequest was given. Stanton was for long divided into two parishes: All Saints and St John the Baptist, each with its own church and rector; the two rectories were amalgamated in 1756 and after many years of insecurity, St John's church was finally abandoned in 1962. See Dymond, *Parish Churches of Stanton*.

3   William Cokett was succeeded as incumbent of Great Livermere by Master Christopher Calde-
cote in 1480 (Tanner, p.438); ?will of William Cokett, lately rector of Ingham, pr. 1492 (NRO,
NCC 59 Typpes).

242. JOHN GERVEYS of DENSTON ('Denardyston'), 12 October 1462

Of Denston in the diocese of Norwich; [*commendation*: to God &c]; to be buried in
Christian burial; to the high altar of the same church [*of Denston*] 2s.

Residue of all my goods to my execs, to dispose for my soul and the souls for whom
I am bound, as they see &c[*sic*]; to whom I give full power to collect (*levand'*) all
the debts owed to me and perform this testament.

Execs: Joan my wife and my two sons, Sir William Gerveys and John of the canons
(*canonicor'*).

Seal appended.

Proved at Clare, 26 September 1465. Admon to Joan, relict of the deceased, executrix. Power reserved to Sir William Gerveys and John of the canons.

243. WILLIAM BOYS of TUDDENHAM ('Tudenham'), 27 May 1465

[*Commendation*: to God &c; *no burial directions*]; to the high altar of the said
church for my tithes forgotten 6s 8d.

To each boy (*puero*) of Tuddenham, under the age of 20, a ewe when sheared (*cu'
tonse fuerint*).

To Robert Boys a cow which he has in his keeping.

To Cavenham church 3s 4d.

To Thomas Freborne a close called 'Hoodes yerde', on condition that he keep my
anniversary day on (*ad, ?*recte *et*) the anniversary day of Agnes my wife and all my
friends, as long as he lives, and he to distribute 12d among the poor each year on
my anniversary day and Agnes's; after the death of Thomas the close called 'Hoodes
yerde' to be sold and the money from it to be distributed for my soul and the souls
of all my benefactors.

My messuage in Tuddenham and all my lands and tenements in Tuddenham and
Cavendish to be sold by my execs, to fulfil my legacies and pay my debts.

To my priest Sir Urianus 8 marks 6s 8d; to the convent of Friars Minor of Babwell
20s.[1]

To Robert Boys 2 ewes; to John Boys the younger 20s; to Joan Boys 2 ewes.

To Thomas Hygham the elder, esquire, [fol. 384v] 6s 8d.

To Robert Lute, the rector of Barton Mills ('Berton Mylls') 6s 8d.[2]

Agnes my wife to have her food (*vict'*) honestly provided out of my goods not
bequeathed above, as long as she lives, and the residue to be disposed for me and
her and my friends.

Residue of all my goods to Robert Lute, rector of the aforesaid Barton, *alias* 'Berton
Toryng', and John Frebarn of Tuddenham, execs.

Supervisor: Thomas Heygham the elder, esquire.[3]

Seal appended.

Witnesses: John Draweswerd, Roger Mayner, Ed' Hedone, John Gadercold and
many others.

Proved at Fornham [*St Martin*], 26 September 1465. Admon to execs.

¹   See note to no. 1.
²   Robert Lute was appointed rector of Barton Mills *c.* April 1450 (Tanner, p.1261).
³   Probably the man named Thomas Higham who, in early 1481, acquired the manor of Denham
    near Barrow (Copinger, *Manors of Suffolk*, v, p.221; Hervy, *Visitation of Suffolk 1561*, i, pp.74–6
    and ii, pp.391–6). See also no. 297 below.

244. JOHN SHERMAN of YAXLEY, 20 August 1465

[*Commendation*: to God &c]; to be buried in the churchyard of Yaxley parish church. [*Will*]

My debts to be paid immediately after my death.

To Margaret my wife 10s annually during her lifetime and 1 acre of wheat and 1 acre of barley for a year (*dur' uno anno*).

To the high altar for tithes forgotten 12d.

Robert my son to have my whole tenement that was once Robert Sherman's, except 8 acres of land called 'Fyveacre' and 'ly herne'.

To the four orders of friars 4 bushels of barley.¹

Margaret my wife to have a garden called 'Bukkesyerde'.

A trental of St Gregory to be celebrated for me and for the souls of all my friends; a mass to be celebrated at *Scala Celi* [*Rome*];² I wish to have a church ale (*potac' ecclesiastic'*) in Yaxley church.³

Residue of all my goods to my execs, Robert Sherman my son and William his son, chaplain, that they &c[*sic*].

Proved at Thrandeston, 2 October 1465. Admon to execs.

¹   See note to no. 133.
²   The chapel of *Scala Celi* ('Ladder of Heaven') was built over the cemetery of St Zeno in Rome.
    It derives its name from a vision of St Bernard, who, while celebrating a funeral mass, saw the
    souls for whom he was praying going up to heaven by a ladder (Rossetti, 'Notes on the Stacyons
    of Rome', p.xxvi).
³   The testator expected the ale, or drinking, to be held within the church at Yaxley.

[fol. 385]

245. JOHN MAN the elder of LAKENHEATH ('Lakynghithe'),¹ 10 December 1465

Dated 5 Edward IV, at Lakenheath; [*commendation*: to God the Father Almighty, my Creator and Saviour, the Blessed Virgin Mary, mother of God, and all the saints]; to be buried in the churchyard of Lakenheath church; to the high altar of the said church, for my tithes and offerings forgotten and withheld, in exoneration of my soul, 3s 4d; to the reparation of the same church 6s 8d.

To John Man my son 6 silver spoons and a mazer, after the decease of Alice my wife.

Residue of all my goods and chattels and debts I leave wholly to Alice my wife and Thomas Man my son, to dispose, according to their discretion, for my soul and for the souls of [*my*] parents and friends and all the faithful departed, as seems to them best to please God and profit my soul.

Execs: Alice my wife, principal executrix, and Thomas Man, exec.

Seal appended.

Proved at Fornham St Martin ('For'), 17 February 1465/66. Admon to Thomas Man, exec. Power reserved to Alice, the other co-exec, when she comes.

¹   Executor of Gilbert Dowe of Lakenheath, will pr. February 1446/47 (SROB, Baldwyne 84; Pt I, no. 388).

[fol. 385v]
246. THOMAS JEGNERE of Undley ('Undeley') hamlet in LAKENHEATH ('Lakyng'), 6 July 1465

Dated 5 Edward IV, at Undley; [*commendation*: to God &c]; to be buried in the churchyard of Lakenheath church, next to the grave of Agnes, my late wife; to the high altar 6s 8d, for tithes forgotten or underpaid.

To the chapel of the Blessed Mary of the Sea (*de Mari*) in the parish of Leverington, in the county of Cambridge, 8 marks, with the intention that the priests and clerks serving God there might pray for the souls of me and of Agnes and Christian, my late wives, for ever.¹

To the Friars Minor of Babwell, 10s; to the Carmelite Friars of Cambridge (*Cant'*) 10s; to the Friars Preachers of Thetford 10s; to the Augustinian Friars of Thetford 3s 4d.²

On all the Sundays for a whole year next after my death 8d to be distributed among the poor townsfolk of Lakenheath.

To Christian my wife a blue-coloured belt 'harnessed' with silver and 26s 8d in money, in full recompense of 10 marks, [*and*] 2 cows, 2 heifers and 6s 8d in money, in full recompense for all the goods and chattels she should have by right of dower (*matrimo'iur'*), apart from 46 ewes, for which I assign her 40s; on condition that she, in her pure widowhood, delivers to my execs a sufficient sealed general acquittance for all kinds of personal actions (*accionibus personal'*); if she refuses to deliver, seal and make such a general acquittance, and be not willing to perform this my last will, then I will and command (*onero*) my execs that Christian have nothing, nor receive any of the chattels or money bequeathed to her above.

Residue of all my goods I leave to the distribution of Robert Wyse of Barton Mills ('Berton *iux'* Myldenhale') and Thomas Jegnere my son of Lakenheath, execs.
Seal appended.
Witnesses: William Lacy, John Man, Robert Jegnere, Thomas Clerk, William Tollare and others.
Proved at Tuddenham ('Todenham'), 17 December 1465. Admon to execs.

¹   The college or chantry of St Mary-on-the-Sea was actually in Newton, the parish adjacent to Leverington, at the northern most tip of Cambridgeshire, lying on the old estuary of the River Ouse. The chapel was rebuilt by Sir John Colville in the early fifteenth century. The college was endowed with lands in the neighbourhood and in nearby parishes in Norfolk. The endowments proved insufficient and in 1454 Bishop Bourchier modified the founder's statutes: the master was to be nominated by the Bishop of Ely and was to find three chaplains, of whom one was to serve the parish church of Newton; he should also maintain three clerks who could read and sing the service, one of them acting as parish clerk and the other two serving the chantry. These were the priests and clerks whom Thomas Jegnere required to pray for his and his wives' souls. There was also a fraternity associated with the college (*VCH Cambs*, ii, pp.312–14).
²   See notes to nos 1 (Babwell), 42 (Cambridge), 68 (Friars Preachers of Thetford) and 69 (Augustinians of Thetford).

[fol. 386]

247. JOHN COWPER at the Stone[1] at BOXFORD, 22 February 1465/66

To be buried in the new porch on the south side of Boxford church;[2] to the high altar of the same church, for my tithes forgotten and underpaid, 13s 4d; to the rector of the same church, if present at my public obsequies, 12d; to each other priest present at that time 8d; to Thomas Cote and Thomas Nott, officials (*officiariis*)[3] 4d [*each*]; to each greater clerk 2d; to each young clerk (*clericulo*) 1d; to each indigent and needy individual (*pacient'*) coming in person on my burial day 1d; to the reparation and sustentation of the greatest needs (*magis necessariorum*) of Boxford church 20s.

To Thomas Pursere, chaplain,[4] to celebrate for my soul and for the souls of all my parents in Boxford church, if he be willing and pleased to serve, for two years, £13 6s 8d.

To the convent of the Augustinian Friars of Clare, for celebrating a trental for my soul, 10s; to the convent of the order of Friars Preachers of Sudbury, for a trental, 10s; to the convent of the order of Friars Minor of Colchester, for a trental, 10s; to the convent of the Carmelite order of Ipswich (*Gipp'*), for a trental, 10s.[5]

To the building of the new porch in which I wish to be buried 20 marks,[6] as my execs can get it from my goods and debts.

To Groton church 13s 4d; to Edwardstone ('Edward') church 6s 8d; to Polstead church 6s 8d; to Assington church 6s 8d.

To a pinnacle or lantern (*pinnaculu' sive lanterna*) to be newly made on the top (*supra altitudine*) of the roof of Boxford tower, for the clock, otherwise called the 'clokbelle', £10, or more if the work requires more to be completed.[7]

My psalter to Boxford church, to be fixed there with a chain to the stool or chest (*ad scabellu' sive cistam*) before the image of the Blessed Mary on the north side of the church.

To Sir Thomas Pursere 13s 4d.

To John Cowper my brother my best hooded gown and my best 'harnessed' girdle and 6s 8d in money.

To William Cowper my brother my burnet gown and another 'harnessed' girdle and 6s 8d in money.

To Alice Bronde, the daughter of John Brond of 'Olywade',[8] 5 marks in money when she shall be married, which John Brond her father is then to pay; to the other three daughters of the same John, each of them, 6s 8d in money.

To Matilda Cowpere, the daughter of John Cowpere the elder, 6s 8d; to John Reve 3s 4d; to William Cowpere of 'Olywade' 3s 4d; to John Awbyn 3s 4d; to Margaret Awbyn 3s 4d.

To John Smyth of Kersey, my former servant, 20s; to John Gage my servant, when he completes the full term of his apprenticeship, 20s; to Alice Smyth my servant 3s 4d, over and above what is agreed to be due to her (*preter debit' conventus su'*); to Agnes Pryour of 'Cokkystrete' 3s 4d; to Stephen Boourne 18d; to each of my godsons and goddaughters 12d each (*per se*); to John Wygenale a green gown.

A shaft (*hasta*) of copper to be bought for the best cross; to Boxford church, for the feasts of St Nicholas, a mitre with a decent and convenient crozier.[9]

To Rose Bronde, my elder daughter,[10] 4 silver spoons; to Rose a tablecloth (*mappa'*) of diaper work, with a long towel (*tuell'*); to Rose my best brass pot and a brass pan, and 3 quarters of malt.

To Christian Tylere my daughter 4 silver spoons, and a tablecloth and a long towel of plain cloth (*plani panni*); to Christian a brass pot and a brass pan and 3 quarters of malt.

To Agnes Bogays my daughter 4 silver spoons, a tablecloth and a towel of plain cloth; to Agnes 3 quarters of malt, a brass pot and a brass pan.

To Alice Cowpere my daughter 4 silver spoons, a table-cloth and a towel of plain cloth; to Alice a basin, with the ewer belonging to it, a brass pot and the best brass pan; also to Alice my mazer, 3 quarters of malt and 3 quarters of barley.

The same Alice Cowpere my daughter to have, after [fol. 386v] my decease, my capital tenement in which I live, to her and her heirs for ever, with all the stock and necessaries being within the bounds of the tenement, such as salt, candle, soap, &c (*ut de sale, candel', smignal' &c*); Alice to have, to her and her heirs, according to the custom of the manor of Groton, a tenement lying opposite my aforesaid tenement, in Groton, with 'le forge', with the equipment that properly belongs to the forge (*cu' paritur' eidem* forge *convenient' spect' et pertin'*), to be delivered by my execs.

To Margaret Cowper my daughter, the younger, 4 spoons, a tablecloth and a towel of plain cloth; to Margaret a cauldron and a brass pan, a silver bowl and 3 quarters of malt.

My execs to distribute all my bedding, of whatever kind, equally between Alice Cowpere and Margaret, my daughters, with all the pewter vessels.

Margaret Cowper my daughter to have, when she comes to the age of 14, the value in money of a field lying in 'Byrchfeld', which shall be sold by my execs; also when she comes to the age of 14, my feoffees at the time, with the advice and agreement of my execs, to deliver to her their estate in a tenement formerly called 'Coye', with a renter adjoining it, to hold to her and her heirs for ever, provided, however, that my feoffees and execs receive from Margaret, or her assigns, 5 marks in money, and that sum to be delivered to Alice Cowper my daughter; if Margaret should die under that age, then the tenement with the renter to be sold by my execs or theirs, whichever it be at the time (*tunc tempore superstites*), and the money so raised to be distributed in deeds of piety in Boxford church and town, keeping the aforementioned 5 marks for Alice.

Residue of all my goods, after all my legacies and debts have been fully paid, to my execs, to dispose them for the health of my soul and all my parents' [*souls*], as seems to them most expedient, in deeds of piety (*operibus pietatis*).

Execs: John Bronde of Boxford, Thomas Tylere of Monks Eleigh ('Illigh Monachorum') and William Bogays of Edwardstone;[11] they to have God before their eyes in executing [*this testament*].

Supervisor: John Cowper the elder, my brother.

Seal appended.

Witnesses: Thomas Pursere, clerk, John Reve, William Cowpere the elder, Thomas Warry and others.

Furthermore, the fraternity of the gild of the Holy Trinity of Boxford, and their successors for ever, to have an acre of arable land, more or less, in the field called 'Sowthfeld' in Boxford.[12]

Proved at Boxford, 8 March 1465/66. Admon to execs.

[1]   John Cowper lived in what is now Stone Street. As Cowper (Couper) was such a common name in Boxford this description was added to distinguish the testator from several other Boxford

men of the same name. For example, Margaret Smyth of Boxford, widow, had two sons named John Couper; will pr. January 1444/45 (SROB, Baldwyne 62; Pt I, no. 308). Thomas Cowpere of Boxford had a brother and two sons named John; will pr. September 1451 (SROB, Baldwyne 103; Pt I, no. 458). Perhaps Thomas Cowpere was this testator's father as he (the testator) had a brother John Cowper, known as 'the elder', whom he appointed supervisor.

2   Bequests began to be made for building the south porch at Boxford in 1441 and continued to be made until 1480. From the will of John Cowpere of Boxford (apparently not directly related to this testator) it is clear that in 1445 work had not yet begun on the porch, will pr. March 1444/45 (SROB, Baldwyne 65; Pt I, no. 316). It is described as 'of stone and very beautiful, with rich panelling throughout and traceried and partly pierced parapet' (Cautley, pp.44, 61 and 226).

3   The exact role or function of these two men is unclear: given that they are mentioned after priests and before clerks, it seems likely that they were clerics officiating at Cowper's obsequies; alternatively, they may have been lay parish officers.

4   See note to no. 117 above and also no. 331 below.

5   For the various friars, see notes to nos 1 (Clare and Ipswich), 11 (Sudbury) and 38 (Colchester).

6   A substantial bequest to the porch; in 1444/45 his namesake had bequeathed 5 marks to it. See also nos 331, 332 and 440.

7   As the lantern, or spirelet, on the west tower was built to contain a clock in 1446, it seems likely that this bequest was for repairs to the lantern.

8   Olywade Street, now Stone Street. See Robinson, *Boxford: A Miscellany*, p.14. John Brond of 'Olywade' in Boxford was the son of John Brond the elder of Groton (no. 117 above).

9   The mitre and crozier were being provided for use of the parish's 'Boy Bishop', a child clad in episcopal vestments, who officiated to some degree in religious activities during December. The only surviving detailed description of a Boy Bishop's costume is in the accounts of King's College, Cambridge. See Hutton, *Rise and Fall of Merry England*, pp.10–12; Middleton-Stewart, *Inward Purity*, p.204.

10   Perhaps the wife of John Brond (see note above).

11   Son and executor of Agnes Bogays of Edwardstone (no. 352). Since John Cowper, the testator here, made bequests to daughters named Rose Bronde, Christian Tylere and Agnes Bogays, his executors John Bronde of Boxford, Thomas Tylere of Monks Eleigh and William Bogays of Edwardstone were probably his sons-in-law. He also had two younger, unmarried daughters but did not have any sons living when he made his will.

12   William Mawdyon also beqeathed land to the gild of the Holy Trinity, Boxford (no. 331 below). This gild and also those of St Peter, St John and St Christopher were still in existence at Boxford in 1522 (*PSIA*, xxiii, p.52).

[fol. 387]

248. WILLIAM MUMFORTE of POLSTEAD ('Polsted'), 18 June 1464

[*nuncupative*]

['Monfortt' *in margin*] [*Commendation*: to God &c; *no burial directions*]; to Polstead church 6s 8d.

To Agnes Aylemere a sheet and a blanket.

To Joan Osby a bed-cover (*supellectil'*).

To William Rewe all his movable ostilments in his dwelling.

Residue of all his goods to the disposition of his execs, William Rewe and William Scoyle of Polstead, that they &c[*sic*].

Witnesses: Master Robert Lynkfeld, rector there,[1] Robert Fownghale, John Heyward and John Greyve of Hadleigh ('Hadley').

Proved at Hitcham ('Hecham'), 5 November 1465. Admon to execs.

1   Robert Lynkfeld was rector of Polstead from 1463 to 1485 (Tanner, p.1383).

249. JOHN BOWYERE [*no place given*], 7 November 1465 [*probate only*]

Proved at Haverhill. Admon to William Bregge and Thomas Saare, execs.

250. JOHN CURPAYLE of HAVERHILL, 7 November 1465 [*probate only*]

Proved at Haverhill. Admon to Alice Spylman, executrix, with the supervision of John Spylman of Finchingfield ('Fynchefeld') [*Essex*] and John Foole of Sturmer [*Essex*].

251. ALICE WEBBE of PALGRAVE,[1] 15 June 1465

Dated at Palgrave; to be buried in the churchyard of the church of St Peter of Palgrave; to the high altar for tithes forgotten 12d; to the parish clerk 4d; to the emendation of the torches ('ly torchys').

To the reparation of 'ly castelweye' 40d.[2]

To a priest to celebrate in Palgrave church for me, and for the souls of Thomas Skulton, Nicholas Skulton and their friends, for a whole year, 8 marks; for a trental of St Gregory 10s; for a station at Rome[3] 40d.

To each of my execs for their labour, well and truly carried out, 40d.

To Alice, the daughter of John Crane, 1½ acres of land near 'Ponyscros' after my decease, she to have the profit from it if she is still alive; if she dies before being married, John her brother to be the next heir, to have it to him and his heirs; if he dies, Phyllis my daughter to enjoy it, to her and her heirs for ever.

To Phyllis Deynys a hive ('ly heve') with the bees; to Alice the wife of John Yystas a hive with the bees; to Alice, the daughter of John Yystas 2d.

To Phyllis my daughter my best cloak (*armilaus'*) and my best tunic; to Phyllis my sister and Joan Thruston my other cloak and another tunic, to be divided between them, Joan having the [*first*] choice.

To the other daughter of John Crane my best cooking pot and my small brass pot, with a pair of sheets.

To John, the son of John Crane, a bed-cover of three divers colours, that is yellow, blue and white, with a pair of sheets.

To Alice, the daughter of John Crane, my best bed-cover; and if she dies, John her brother to be the next possessor [*of it*]; if he dies Phyllis my daughter to enjoy it during her lifetime, and after her decease, it to be distributed to poor people.

To John Rande a cooking pot which was lately John Webbe's.

Residue of all my goods to my execs, John Chambere and Robert Deynys, to dispose as they see best to please God and profit my soul.

Seal appended.

Witnesses: John Strewen, clerk, John Cotelyn, John Valentyn, John Prenteys, Thomas Fulcher and others.

[fol. 387v] Proved at Eye, 13 November 1465. Admon to execs. Seal of official appended.

[1] ?Widow of John Webbe the elder of Palgrave, probate dated May 1460 (SROB, Baldwyne 271; Pt I, no. 1330); within her will Alice bequeathed a cooking pot 'lately John Webbe's'.

[2] Possibly a reference to the castle at Eye, about 3½ miles to the south-east.

[3] See note to no. 89.

252. MARGARET FOLKES of EYE ('Eya'), 1465

[*No day or month stated*]; to be buried in the churchyard of the parish church of the said town; to the high altar of the said church, for tithes negligently forgotten, 12d; to the said church a 'le torche'; to the reparation of the tower of the said church 12 'cartsfull of calyon'.[1]

To Sir John Teylyour my son a pair of sheets and a smock (*camisia*').

To Joan my daughter, of Thrandeston ('Thransston'), my best tunic, a salt-cellar ('saltsalere') and a 'chawnlere',[2] and a pair of beads of price 8d.

To John, the son of John Tweyth, my best chest.

A 'throne of Eystrych boorde'[3] to be hung in Thrandeston church, before the image of St Mary of Pity;[4] five lights to be lit on (*super*) the said throne and I bequeath 20d to the sustentation of those lights.

To Thwaite ('Thweyte') church 20d.

Five lights to burn before the images of the Blessed Mary, St John and St Anne in Eye church.[5]

To the church of Brockley ('Broccle') 3s 4d.

Residue of my goods to Robert my son and John Swytbrede, my execs, to dispose for the health of my soul as seems to them most expedient.

Proved at Eye, 13 November 1465. Admon to execs. Seal of official appended.

[1] Bequests indicate that the tower of Eye church was being built from 1453 to 1479; this bequest of 12 cartsful of 'calyon' is a particularly practical one.
[2] See Glossary.
[3] See Glossary.
[4] That is, the *Pietà*.
[5] There was also an altar of St Thomas the Martyr in Eye church (see no. 178).

253. REGINALD BROKE of RICKINGHALL ('Rykynghale') SUPERIOR, 25 October 1465

[*Probate sentence entered before will.*] Proved at Eye, 13 November 1465. Admon to John Blogate and Robert Wroo, execs.

[*Commendation*: to God &c]; my body to Christian burial; to the church of Rickinghall Superior 6s 8d; to the high altar of the same church 3s 4d.

To the friars of Babwell, for saying a trental, 10s.[1]

To Agnes my wife 3 perches of arable land.

Execs: John Blogate and Robert Wroo, to pay my debts out of my own goods and then the residue of my goods to remain wholly to Agnes my wife.

[1] See note to no. 1.

254. THOMAS NOTTE of GROTON, 22 November 1465 [*probate only*]

Proved at Lavenham, 22 November 1465. Admon to John Bokenham, exec.

[fol. 388]

255. JOHN SMYTH of STANSFIELD ('Stanysfeld'), 6 April 1465

My body to Christian burial in Stansfield.

Agnes my wife to have my messuage, with the cattle and beasts (*catall' ac bestijs*), together with the bedding (*supellectilibus*) of my house, for her lifetime, and after her decease John Caxstreet my godson to have the messuage; if John should die before Agnes, then after her decease the messuage to be disposed according to the wishes of John Caxstret.

Robert Caxstret my nephew to be my attorney, to dispose for me according to my will.

Seal appended.

Proved at Stradishall ('Stradeshull'), 26 November 1465. Admon to exec. Seal of official appended.

256. WILLIAM WETHERE of STANTON ALL SAINTS,[1] 10 November 1464

[*Commendation*: to God &c]; to be buried in the churchyard of the church of All Saints of Stanton; to the high altar of the said church, for tithes forgotten and not well paid, 12d.

To Katherine my wife a chamber at the east end of the hall, with free entrance and exit as often (*quocienscumque*) as she pleases; Katherine to have her fire in the hall at this time, until William my son newly makes [*her*] a chamber with a chimney in my messuage, with free entrance and exit to the same for term of her life, without the gainsaying of anyone.

To the same Katherine a cow, and that cow, or another in its place (*al' vacc' nomine dict' vacce*), to be kept with the animals of William my son at his cost, for term of her life; also 2 bushels of wheat, 2 bushels of rye and 4 bushels of malt annually, to be had of my son William, during her lifetime; and also a quarter of firewood (*focal'*), price 10d. To Katherine a brass pot holding a gallon, an old brass pan and another small brass pan called a 'peynte panne'; also 3 pieces of latten (*electri*), a candlestick of pewter (*stagno*), a trivet, a basin, an iron instrument called 'le heke',[2] 3 wooden vessels called 'le stondes', a wooden vessel called 'le bolle' holding 4 gallons, a bucket (*situla'*), a 'le whele' with 'le cardes', 3 whole sheets (*linthiam' integra*), 2 cloths called 'canvasis' and a green bed-cover.

Katherine to have all these bequests on condition that she does not claim (*petat*) dower; if she does claim dower, then, apart from the cow, she shall forgo (*privetur*) all the bequests made to her.[3]

To Alice my daughter 20d; to Margery my daughter 20d.

To the said William Wethere, my son and his heirs, all my lands and tenements in the town of Stanton.

Residue of all my goods I commit to the disposition of William my son, exec, that he &c[*sic*].

Proved at Fornham [*St Martin*], 9 December 1465. Admon to exec.

---

[1] In March 1450/51, William Wethyre was holding land at 'Oke' in Stanton adjacent to that of Simon Clerk, will dated March 1450/51 (SROB, Baldwyne 102; Pt I, no. 457).

[2] See Glossary for the following English words.

[3] It is not clear from the wording whether Katherine would also have had to forgo the chamber provided for her, or whether the condition applied only to the bequests that came after the cow.

[fol. 388v]

257. JOHN BYRLYNGHAM [of BOTESDALE in REDGRAVE], 19 October 1465

Lately of Wattisfield ('Wattlysfeld'); in peril of death (*in periculu' mortis imminer'*); [*commendation*: to God &c]; to be buried in the churchyard of Redgrave; to the high altar of Redgrave a cow.

Residue of all my goods to John Byrlyngham of Botesdale ('Botysdale'), my attorney, my exec, fully to pay my debts and legacies and faithfully dispose out of my goods &c[*sic*].

Proved at Finningham ('Fynyngham'), 4 December 1465. Admon to exec.

258. JOHN SWYFTT of WALSHAM LE WILLOWS ('Walsham'),[1] 15 August 1465

[*Commendation*: to God &c]; to be buried wheresoever God pleases to dispose for me; to the high altar for tithes forgotten &c[*sic*] 40d; to the carpentry work (*opus carpentarii*) of Walsham church 6s 8d; towards the glass (*propter vitriac'*) of a window in (*super*) 'le clerestory' of the same church [*no amount stated*].[2]

All the mass-pence coming from the gilds of the Holy Trinity, St John the Baptist and St Katherine[3] to [*go to*] the Friars Preachers and Augustinian of Thetford, to be disposed between them equally; to the Friars Minor of Babwell 2s 6d.[4]

To Katherine my wife a tenement called 'Osbernis' for term of her life, and after her decease and the passing of [*a further*] two years, John Hochown to have it if he be willing to give as much [*for it*] as another will give, and a little more (*et aliquantul' precio melior'*); if that tenement is insufficient to enable my wife to find her necessaries, then she to have money out of the price of another tenement sold to John Hochown, as my execs see most expedient; to my wife all the utensils of [*my*] house and 2 cows.

To Richard Molows 6s 8d; to William Toftes 4 wethers (*ariet'*); to Katherine and Margery, the daughters of Katherine Mellere, widow, each of them 4 ewes.

Execs: John Molows of Rickinghall ('Rykynghale') and James Hawys of Walsham; each of them to have 6s 8d for their labours.

Supervisor: Sir William Potager,[5] to whom 40d.

Residue of my goods to the aforesaid John and James, execs, to dispose for me and my friends &c[*sic*].

Proved at Wattisfield ('Wattysfeld'), 12 November 1465. Admon to execs.

[1] Executor of Thomas Well of Walsham, probate December 1452 (SROB, Baldwyne 121; Pt I, no. 562); executor of John Cowpere of Walsham le Willows, will pr. 25 February 1449/50 (SROB, Baldwyne 140; Pt I, no. 672); witness of the will of Robert Robhood of Walsham le Willows, pr. January 1453/54 (SROB, Baldwyne 159; Pt I, no. 767).

[2] For a discussion of the clerestory see Blatchly and Northeast, *Decoding Flint Flushwork*, Walsham le Willows St Mary.

[3] John Swyftt was apparently a member of all three gilds. Robert Fraunceys of Ixworth (SROB, Baldwyne 76; Pt I, no. 357) made bequests to the gilds of the Holy Trinity and St John the Baptist of Walsham; Nicholas Smyth of Walsham le Willows (SROB, Baldwyne 280; Pt I, no. 1370) gave 10s for a trental out of the money coming from the gilds of St John the Baptist and St Katherine.

[4] For the friars see notes to nos 1 (Babwell), 68 (Preachers of Thetford) and 69 (Augustinians of Thetford).

[5] See note to no. 175 and also no. 496.

[fol. 389]
259. JOAN DEYNYS of SUDBURY, widow, 6 June 1465

Of Sudbury in the diocese of Norwich; to be buried in the churchyard of the church of All Saints of the same town; to the high altar of the same church for my tithes and other dues negligently forgotten and not paid 3s 4d; to Henry Boorman, clerk, of the same church, to pray for my soul, 20d; to 'le arche', to be made between the church and the chapel on the north side of the same church, 20s.[1]

To the convent of the house of the order of Preachers of the same town,[2] to pray for my soul and all my parents' [souls], 20s and a quarter of wheat.

My execs to provide a suitable secular priest to celebrate for 4 years after my decease in the church of All Saints, Sudbury, to fulfil the last will of Robert Deynys my husband[3] and to pray for my soul and all my parents' [souls], giving him annually for his salary a competent stipend.

To Matilda my daughter[4] 10 marks in money, to be raised from the sale of my goods, a furred (penulat') gown of sanguine colour, a furred 'le frende'[5] of violet colour and my tunic of the same colour.

To John Cartere my brother, of Ballingdon ('Balyndon'), my whole bed in my chamber next to the parlour (parlura), that is, 'le fedyrbedde', 2 'le blanketes', a pair of sheets, 'le pane' of coney skins, 'le celere' and 'le testere' and 3 'le curteynes'.

To Isabel Kartere my sister my blue furred gown.

To Margaret, daughter of John Kartere, a green-coloured gown, 'lyned', and my red-coloured tunic; to Joan, daughter of the said John Kartere, my black gown.

To Margaret Reedehed my servant a bed-cover, a pair of sheets, a 'le pelwe', a brass pot, a pan, one of those holding 2 gallons, and 10s in money, to be received from her father, of the debt that he owes me for the farm of my tenement.

To John Deynes my son[6] £20 in money, out of my goods [which are] to be sold as quickly as possible by my execs; my best brass pot, the best pan, the best 'le cawdron', the best frying-pan (frixor'), the best spit, the best mortar and the second mortar, 2 'le gromys',[7] the best basin, 2 ewers, 2 candlesticks, a 'le gernysh' of my pewter, my largest mazer, 6 silver spoons, a silver 'le salt saler' with the cover, a 'le gredyll', a 'le fedyrbedd', 2 of the best bed-covers, the best pair of sheets and 2 [other] pairs of sheets, 2 pillows ('le pelwes') with the covers belonging to them, a 'le hangyn bedde' of 'le say' with 3 'le curteynes' and a bed-cover belonging to them, a meal table (tabula' mensal') with 2 leaves (foliis), a 'le bordecloth', a 'le borde towayle', an ark (archam), 'le flat', the best chair (cathedram), a 'le cowpebord', a 'le bankere' and 5 'le kusshonys'; on condition that he behaves himself peaceably and honestly towards my execs after my decease, in all ways (omnibus), and restores to Matilda his sister her tenement in 'Croosse Strete', lately John Jacob's, formerly the said Matilda's husband, and then he to have all those [goods] recited above, to him and his assigns, freely and peaceably for ever. If the said John Deynes in any way troubles or worries my execs, after my decease, about my testament, or the testament of Robert Deynes his father, or will not restore the said tenement to his sister, then I will he have nothing of the above-recited [goods], either in part or in whole.

To Robert, son of John Deynes, a silver bowl (cratere') of the smallest (de minimis) and a basin (pelvi'); to Margaret, daughter of John Deynes, a pair of sheets, a 'le pelwe' of the best, with the cover, and a basin; to Agnes, daughter of John Deynes, a pair of sheets and a 'le pelwe' with the cover.

To Matilda my daughter my second brass pot and a 'le kawdron'.

To John, son of [fol. 389v] John Meryell, a hollow basin (*pelvi' concava'*); to Thomas, son of John Meryell, a hollow basin.

To Rose, wife of William Wareyn, a green-coloured gown, furred.

All my lands and tenements to be sold and all my cofeoffees to deliver their estate [*in them*] when duly required by my execs, Henry Turnour of Haverhill, esquire, and William Scaldere of Sudbury;[8] they to pay my debts and fulfil my testament and the testament of Robert Deynys, my former husband.

Residue of all my goods [*my execs*] to dispose in deeds of charity in the best manner they know, to please God and profit my soul.

Seal appended.

Proved at Sudbury, 19 March 1465/66. Admon to execs.

1   This bequest for an arch into the north chapel is mentioned in Pevsner, *Buildings of England: Suffolk*, p.453.

2   See note to no. 11.

3   Will of Robert Deynes of Sudbury, dyer, pr. May 1453 (SROB, Baldwyne 154; Pt I, no. 740).

4   Legatee of her father Robert.

5   See the Glossary for the many English words in this will.

6   Legatee of his father Robert.

7   'gromys' cannot be identified.

8   In 1453, as well as Joan, her husband Robert had appointed 'Henry Turnour and William Scalder' as his executors; logic would suggest that her executors were the same men. A man named Henry Turnor of Haverhill, esquire, was recorded in the *Visitation of Suffolk* (Hervy, vol. I, pp.77–8); but according to Weever, he, together with his two wives and a son of his named John, lay buried in Haverhill church in 1464 (Hervy, p.78). Perhaps the executor here was that Henry's grandson, son of his (other) son John. See the will of John Turnour of Great Thurlow, gentleman (no. 608 below), of which 'Henry Turnour, esquire' was also executor.

260. WILLIAM DEYNIS of MILDENHALL ('Myldenhale'), 16 February 1465/66

Dated 5 Edward IV; [*commendation*: to God &c]; to be buried in the churchyard of Mildenhall church; to the high altar of the same church for my tithes and offerings forgotten and withheld, in exoneration of my soul, 12d; to the reparation of the said church 12d.

To the friars of Babwell,[1] faithfully to celebrate a trental for my soul, 10s.

Residue of all my goods to my execs, to dispose them according to their discretion, as seems to them best to please God and profit the health of my soul.

Execs: Walter Fostere, parish chaplain of Mildenhall, Roger Dextere and Robert Pynhorne of the same.

Seal appended.

Witnesses: John Brithwelle, William Cooke, Joan Browdyere, Constance Cooke and others.

Proved at Fornham [*St Martin*], 3 March 1465/66. Admon to execs.

1   See note to no. 1.

[OW 24/17; *at head of OW is written* 'Howes']
261. WILLIAM HOBBES of ACTON ('Aketon'), 16 March 1465/6

[*Commendation*: to God &c; *no burial directions*]; to the high altar of Acton 20d;
to the fabric of the same church 40d; to the high altar of Milden ('Meldyng') 20d;
to the fabric of the said church 6s 8d.
To the reparation of the way near my gate (*porta'*) 6s 8d.
Execs: Richard Wayte and John Pellican, [*they to have*] the residue &c[*sic*].
Proved at Fornham [*St*] Martin, 14 April 1466. Admon to execs.

[*As the 'original will' differs so much from the registered version, a full abstract is
given here*]
[*No place of domicile given*]; my body to Christian burial; to the high altar of
Milden ('Myldynge') parish church 20d; to the fabric of the said church 6s 8d.
To the reparation of the way near my gate (*porta'*) 6s 8d.
To the high altar of Acton ('Aketon') church 20d; to the fabric of the said church
40d.
I leave 3 trentals for my soul and the soul of Ellen my wife; I bequeath a trental for
the souls of my father and mother; I bequeath a trental for my soul and the souls of
all my benefactors and the faithful departed.
To John my son 40s; to Robert my son 40s; to be delivered to them after the age of
24; if John and Robert decease within that age, then the sum of 6 marks to remain
to my execs, Richard Wayte and John Pellycan.
To Agnes my daughter 6s 8d; to Margaret my daughter 6s 8d; to Alice my daughter
6s 8d; to Joan my daughter 6s 8d.
Execs: Richard Wayte and John Pellycan.
Residue of all my goods to my execs, to dispose for the health of my soul as seems
to them most expedient.
Witnesses: Thomas Welle and [*illeg.*].
Proved [*as above*].

[fol. 390]
262. JOHN FULLERE of GLEMSFORD ('Glemesford'), 17 November 1464
[*English*]

[*Commendation*: to God Almighty &c]; to be buried in Glemsford churchyard; to
the parson, to say ('seyn') a *dirige*, 4d, and the parson of Stanstead ('Stansted') 4d,
and the parish priest 4d, and every clerk that cometh to the *dirige* 1d; to the painting
of the rood ('rode') 6s 8d.
To Rose my wife all my ostilments within my place, 'excepte that longyth to the
plow and carte'; Rose to have of my goods 13s 4d a year for the term of her life;
if it so be that William my son will 'fyndyn' her, I will that he pays her no money,
if they may 'accordyn' together; if they may not 'accordyn', she to have the 13s
4d yearly term of her life. Rose to have the over-chamber with the solar thereover
'abovyn the benche',[1] with free ingoing and 'outecomyng' to the fire, 'no man her
to warne', and she to have 'fere and flett',[2] 'no man her to warne', as often as it
pleaseth her to come thereto; and she to have two 'hens-going' in the yard and an
apple tree 'that sche wylle chesyn'. If Rose have need to sell any ostilment, pot or
pan, or any other ostilment it pleases her to sell, she to sell [*it*] and 'lyve therby'; if

she removes and will not dwell there, she to have half a hundred wood every year, term of her life, but if 'sche wylle abydyn, none for to have'; she to have 8 bushels of wheat and 8 bushels of barley every year, term of her life, to 'fyndyn' herself with.³ Rose my wife to have a meadow containing 1 rood, by estimation, lying at '?Fedmelle', term of her life, and if she have need, to sell it and live thereby; if she may spare it, Thomas my son to have it, to give and to sell.

Execs: Rose my wife and Thomas my son, that they do truly for me as they would truly I did for them.

Sir John Weste, parson of Stanstead,⁴ to be 'overlooker'; he to have for his labour, 'for to seen that they dede wele', 6s 8d.

Witnesses: Hugh Weste, Herry Bolyngton, Robert Savage and John Wellys.

Seal appended 'with my hand'.

Proved at Melford, 11 December 1465. Admon to Thomas Fullere, exec. Power reserved to Rose, the other co-exec, when she comes.

¹ That is, 'above the dais'.
² See Glossary.
³ The testator has made very detailed provision for his widow, who was to live in the upper end of the house, behind the dais ('benche').
⁴ John Weste was rector of Stanstead from 1444 to 1483 (Tanner, p.1386); will pr. May 1483 (NRO, NCC 157 A. Caston); he had property in both Glemsford and Stanstead.

[fol. 390v]

263. ROBERT DENHAM of WICKHAMBROOK ('Wykhambroke'), 27 October 1465

Dated at Wickhambrook; [*commendation*: to God &c; *no burial directions*]; to the high altar of the said church for tithes forgotten 3s 4d.

To William my son 6s 8d; to Margaret my daughter 20s; to Anne my daughter 20s; to Katherine my daughter 6s 8d.

Residue of all my goods to my execs, Isabel my wife and John my son.

Proved at Hundon ('Honeden'), 16 January 1465/66. Admon to execs.

264. WILLIAM HACHE of STRADISHALL ('Stradhull'), 1 December 1465

Dated at Stradishall; to be buried in the churchyard of Stradishall; to the high altar for tithes forgotten 12d.

My horses and cart to be sold and out of the money from them my debts to be paid; a trental to be celebrated for my soul and for my benefactors.

Rest of my goods to Katherine my wife.

Execs: John Hache my father and Thomas Clerke the elder, together with Katherine my wife, to dispose as seems best.

Proved at Hundon ('Honeden'), 16 January 1465/66. Admon to execs. Power reserved to Thomas Clerke the elder when he comes, if he wishes to take up admon.

265. WILLIAM NOOTE of THURSTON ('Thruston'), ?6 December ?1456

Of Thurston in the diocese of Norwich; [*writing of date confused: day altered from* vij *to* vj; *year altered from* lxv *to* lvj *or* lxvj]; [*commendation*: to God &c]; to be buried in the churchyard of the church of St Peter, Thurston; to the high altar of the same church 12d; to the light of the Blessed Mary in the same church a ewe.

To the Friars Minor of Babwell 2 bushels of barley; to the Friars Preachers of Thetford 2 bushels of barley.[1]

To Agnes my wife all my lands and tenements, wherever they lie in the towns (*villis*) and fields of Thurston, for term of her life; and after her decease all the said lands and tenements to remain to John Noote my son,[2] to hold to him and his heirs of the chief lords &c[*sic*], on condition that he provides a suitable chaplain to celebrate in Thurston church for a year next after the death of Agnes my wife, for my soul and hers and all our benefactors' [*souls*].

To Agnes all my other goods and chattels wherever they may be found in the town and fields of Thurston.

Residue of all my goods and chattels to the disposition of my execs, Agnes my wife and John Noote my son, to ordain &c[*sic*].

Proved at Fornham [*St Martin*], 17 February 1465/66. Admon to execs.

[1]   For the friars see notes to nos 1 (Babwell) and 68 (Friars Preachers of Thetford).
[2]   Legatee (as 'John Note, son of William Note') of John Note of Thurston, will pr. September 1446 (SROB, Baldwyne 76; Pt I, no. 358).

[fol. 391]
266. ROBERT SEWALE of GREAT BARTON ('Berton Magna'),
16 September 1465

[*Commendation*: to God &c]; my body to Christian burial; to the high altar of Barton church, for tithes forgotten &c[*sic*], 3s 4d; to a suitable chaplain to celebrate for my soul and for the souls of my deceased friends in the said church, for a whole year, 8 marks.

To Joan my wife all my ostilments and utensils belonging to my house, and a cow; to Joan 20 marks in money, if possible, to the sustentation of my children, to be paid at [*the rate of*] 33s 4d a year; but if Joan, after my decease, makes any other demand or claim of any dower of my lands and tenements in the towns of Barton and Fornham St Martin, then she to have nothing of the said 20 marks. To Joan all my grain, wheat and rye, in my messuage in which I live; also to Joan 40 coombs of barley and rye, to be paid her in four years after my decease, to the support of my children and especially the four youngest, until they reach legal age.

To John my son, the elder, 20s; to Matthew my son 13s 4d; to William my son 13s 4d; to Alexander my son 13s 4d; to Thomas my son 13s 4d; to John my son, the younger, 13s 4d; to Robert my son, when he reaches legal age, 13s 4d; if any of my sons die under legal age, then his part of the money to remain to my execs, to dispose for my soul.

Residue of all my goods to my execs, to sell and dispose for my soul and the souls of all my deceased friends, in the celebration of masses and the distribution of alms, as they see best to please God &c[*sic*].

Execs: Robert Burgeys of Bury St Edmunds, 'barbour', and Thomas Sterne of Barton, faithfully to execute my testament; to each of them for their labour 16s 8d. [*Will; English*]

To the friars of the Old House of Thetford 6s 8d; to the New House of Thetford 3s 4d; to the house of Babwell 40d.[1]

To Robert Sherewyn my godson 3s 4d; to the same Robert my bow, my arrows ('harews') and a sallet.

To Katherine Sherwyn a coomb of barley.

To the making of the steeple[2] of Barton 20s.

To John Sevepens 2 bushels of maslin ('mystelyn') and 2 bushels of malt.

My execs to ordain a stone for my grave.

Proved at Fornham [*St*] Martin, 14 October 1465. Admon to execs.

1   For the friars see notes to nos 1 (Babwell), 68 (Old House of Thetford) and 69 (New House).
2   See Glossary.

267. NICHOLAS ABBOTT of CHELSWORTH ('Chellesworth'), 28 December 1464

Dated 4 Edward IV; my body to Christian burial; [*commendation*: to God &c]; to the high altar of Chelsworth church, for tithes &c[*sic*], 12d; to the fabric of the body of the same church 6s 8d.

The expenses of my burial day (*die obitus*), seven-day and thirty-day to be met (*fact'*) by the discretion of my execs; my execs, or one of them, to provide, within 4 years following my decease, a suitable priest to celebrate in the said church for a whole year, for my soul and for [*my*] parents' and friends' souls and for the souls of those for whom I am bound.

To Thomas my son and John [fol. 391v] my son 6s 8d each; to Katherine Cowper my daughter 6s 8d; to Alice Prynchett my daughter 13s 4d, or its value.

After the 4 years abovesaid, the remainder of my legacies to be paid in the next 3 years, without further delay, at a similar rate each year.

Residue of all my goods, chattels and debts, wherever they may be, after my debts have been paid, my burial completed and this [*testament*] fulfilled, to the disposition of my execs, as in the distribution of alms and other deeds of piety, as they see best [*to please*] God &c[*sic*].

Execs: John Abbott, Thomas Abbott and Walter Cowper; to each of whom 3s 4d.

Proved at Chelsworth, 7 October 1465. Admon to execs.

[fol. 392]
268. MARGERY TRAPETT of ?MARKET WESTON ('Weston'), 20 September 1462

Formerly wife of John Trapett, lately deceased, and executrix of his testament; dated Monday before the feast of St Matthew, Apostle and Evangelist.

I [*hereby*] make my testament of £20 coming from the reversion of a tenement or messuage, with all the lands, pastures, feedings, rents and services, in the town and fields of Hepworth ('Heppeworth'), which John Trapet, my late husband, gave and by his last will bequeathed to me, to hold for the term of my life, as is in that will and testament more plainly contained, dated Sunday after the feast of the Apostles Peter and Paul [*6 July*] 1427, and proved at Norton before the official of the lord archdeacon of Sudbury, 13 July 1427.[1]

[*Commendaton in full here*]; to be buried in the churchyard of the parish church of Weston. The debts that I owe to be well and truly paid, and that as quickly as possible and in the best manner.

On the day of my burial, or (*vel*) on the seventh day after my death, everyone coming then, both to obsequies and mass, to have white bread[2] and cheese, together

159

with ale and other food appropriate for the time (*pro tempore oportunos*[*sic*]); for the expenses of which my execs to receive 13s 4d of William Trapet of Hepworth,[3] which he owes me for 7 roods of land I sold to him. If William refuses to pay my execs the 13s 4d, they to sell the 7 roods of land and with the money implement my wishes above-written on my burial day. And if the 13s 4d be insufficient for those expenses, my execs to take whatever is [*required*] over 13s 4d out of the abovesaid sum of £20, which £20 the said William Trapet owes for the said tenement and lands and out of which £20 the said John Trapet left to Isabel, his and my daughter, who is married to John Man of Market Weston ('Weston Market'), 100s, which I wish to be paid as specified in the said testament.

And because John Trapet, my late husband, did not specifically assign the money coming from the tenement and lands, apart from the 100s to Isabel, I wish that whatever remainder there shall be unassigned of the £20 be disposed as follows: to the high altar of Weston 12d; to the high altar of Hepworth 12d; to a suitable priest, to celebrate mass in Hepworth parish church, 8 marks; to the friars of the Babwell house,[4] for a trental, 10s; to the friars of the Old House of Thetford,[5] for a trental, 10s; to the emendation of Hepworth parish church 20s; to the emendation of Weston church 20s; to the emendation of a way called 'Rawneslane' in Hepworth 6s 8d; to the emendation of the way called 'Slowgate' 3s 4d; to the emendation of the highway leading from 'Caldewellys Crosse' to 'Carbredge' 13s 4d.

To John Man and Isabel his wife, of Weston, 40s, because they have comforted and cared for me in my need, poverty and debility, at their own cost, both in food and clothing.[6]

On the day of my burial there to be distributed among the most needy poor, for the soul of John himself and me, and for the souls of all our benefactors, 12d, that is, 1d each.

To each of my execs 3s 4d as a reward, together with any expenses they have incurred about these premises.

Any residue there might be of my goods, and of the £20, my execs John Man of Weston, Ralph Trapet of Hepworth[7] and Stephen Muriell of Weston, to dispose for our souls, John Trapet's and Margery's, and our benefactors' [*souls*], in the celebration of masses and other deeds of piety most pleasing to God and in exoneration of their consciences before (*erga*) God in this matter.

Proved at Wattisfield ('Watlisfeld'), 12 November 1465. Admon to John Man, exec. Power reserved to Ralph Trapett[8] and Stephen Muryell, the other co-execs, when they come.

[1]   Wills of members of the Trapett family of Hepworth include: Thomas Trapet, will pr. July 1460 (SROB, Baldwyne 254; Pt I, no. 1257) and Ralph Trapet (no. 68 above). John's will has not survived.
[2]   Better quality bread to be provided for the mourners.
[3]   Will pr. May 1474 (SROB, Hervye 20).
[4]   See note to no. 1.
[5]   See note to no. 68.
[6]   Presumably the testatrix stated that she was 'of Weston' rather than 'of Hepworth' because her son-in-law and daughter had been caring for her in their home.
[7]   This executor may have been the testator of no. 68 above, since that will was made in December 1463, more than a year after this one; alternatively, the executor may have been the Ralph Trapet whose will was proved in September 1485 (SROB, Hervye 347).
[8]   If this executor was the testator of no. 68 above, the reason for his non-appearance is clear: he had died by February 1463/64.

[fol. 392v]

269. THOMAS CRANE of WORTHAM,[1] 5 August 1465

[*Commendation*: to God &c]; my body to Christian burial; to the high altar of the same church, for tithes forgotten, 2s; to the high altar of Palgrave church 12d; I wish to have a suitable chaplain for half a year, to celebrate for my soul and for those for whom I am bound, in Wortham church.[2]

To Katherine my servant 12d.

To the use of Wortham church 5 marks; to seven poor[*folk*] of the town of Wortham a bushel of wheat each.

Walter my son to have all my lands and tenements, rents and services, in the towns of Wortham and Palgrave, to hold to him and his heirs of the chief lords of the fee, &c[*sic*], he to provide Christine Lord with all the necessaries of life for the term of her life.

To the Augustinian Friars of Thetford 3s 4d;[3] to the Carmelite Friars of Norwich 3s 4d.[4]

Residue of all my goods I leave to my execs, to dispose for the health of my soul.

Execs: Walter my son and Richard Crane my brother.[5]

Proved at Palgrave, 23 October 1465.

[1] Thomas Crane 'the younger': executor of Ed' Odlyn of Wortham, probate January 1452/53 (SROB, Baldwyne 153; Pt I, no. 733); executor of Geoffrey Payn of Wortham, will pr. November 1455 (SROB, Baldwyne 181; Pt I, no. 873); executor of William Tubby of Wortham, will pr. November 1454 (SROB, Baldwyne 231; Pt I, no. 1164); executor of John Flemyng of Wortham, probate February 1459/60 (SROB, Baldwyne 246; Pt I, no. 1239). Thomas Crane: executor of Walter Crane of Wortham, will pr. October 1461 (SROB, Baldwyne 280; Pt I, no. 1372).

[2] The testator did not specify to which church in Wortham he was referring. There were two medieval churches there: Wortham Everard (St Mary) and Wortham Jervis (or Eastgate) (St Thomas); the identifying names Everard and Jervis were the surnames of the sitting rectors at the time of the *Valor Ecclesiasticus* in 1535. The livings were consolidated in 1769 and St Mary's became the parish church; the site of St Thomas's is thought to be on the south side of Long Green.

[3] See note to no. 69.

[4] In 1256 the Carmelite or White Friars settled in Norwich on a site between the river and St James's church, on the east side of a street called Cowgate; additional gifts enabled them to erect dwellings and a fine church dedicated to St Mary. A new, much larger church was built for the friars during the fourteenth century, the dimensions of which were recorded by William of Worcester (*VCH Norfolk*, ii, pp.428–33).

[5] The other executor of Walter Crane of Wortham, will pr. October 1461 (as above).

270. ANNE MALTYWARD of BRADFIELD ST GEORGE ('Bradfield Monachorum'), 20 November 1465

[*Commendation*: to God &c]; my body to Christian burial; to the high altar of the said church, for tithes forgotten, 12d; to the reparation of the said church 2s 6d; I wish to have an annual (*annuar'*) in the aforesaid Bradfield church for a whole year after my death.

Execs: John Maltyward of Thurston ('Thruston'), my son, and Walter Humfrey of Bradfield aforesaid.

Supervisor: Sir Walter Tylere, rector of the said church.[1]

Residue of all my goods to my execs, to sell, receive and dispose, for the health of my soul.

Seal appended.

Proved at Fornham (For') [*St Martin*], 17 February 1465/66. Admon to execs.

¹ Walter Tyler was rector of Bradfield St George from 1445 to 1469 (Tanner, p.1429, where he is erroneously called 'William'); will of Walter Tyler, rector of 'Bradfeld Monachors', pr. 1469 (NRO, NCC 137 Jekkys).

[fol. 393]
271. PHILIP PEERS of SUDBURY, 10 November 1465

Dated at Sudbury in the diocese of Norwich; to be buried in the burial place (*sepultura*) of the Friars Preachers of Sudbury;¹ to the high altar of the chapel of St Peter in Sudbury, for my tithes forgotten, 12d; to the Friars Preachers of Sudbury, to the reparation of their house, 20s.

To Emma my wife my messuage in which I live at 'Boromgate Ende', which I lately purchased of William Wryghte of Polstead ('Polstede'), to hold to her and her heirs, of the chief lords of the fee for ever.

To Joan my daughter my renter next to my messuage, formerly Henry Smyth's, to hold to her and her heirs for ever, or 40s for the same, at the discretion of my execs; to Joan my daughter, of my utensils, a red-painted chest and half a garnish of pewter vessels.

My execs to pay the said friars of Sudbury 10s in money, for a trental of St Gregory to be celebrated for my soul by the same friars as quickly as possible.

To Emma my wife all the other utensils, ostilments and bedding (*supellectil'*) of my house, to do with them freely as she wishes.

Execs: Emma my wife and James Rodelond, to whom the residue of my goods and chattels, to pay my debts with them and, furthermore, do for my soul with them as seems to my execs best to profit it.

I beg, in God's name, all my co-feoffees in all my lands and tenements, that they deliver estate of them in accordance with my testament, when duly required by my execs.

Seal appended.

Witnesses: Sir John Poteger, chaplain,² John Turnour, William Martyn and others.

Proved at Sudbury, 13 December 1465. Admon to Emma, executrix. Power reserved to James Rodeland, the other exec, when he comes, if he wishes to take up admon.

¹ See note to no. 11.
² (Sir) John Poteger/Potager, chaplain, witnessed, executed or oversaw several wills in the Baldwyne register, most of them made by testators from Sudbury (Pt I, nos 1274 and 1493; this volume, nos 271, 290, 306, 408, 425, 465, 607, 651 and 652).

272. WILLIAM SEGORE of STRADISHALL ('Stradeshul'), 5 December 1465

[*Commendation*: to God &c]; my body to Christian burial; to the high altar for tithes forgotten 40d.

To Alice my wife two crofts in the town of Cowlinge ('Cowlynge'), a copyhold tenement (*tenement'per copia'*) and another (*alter'*) copyhold one, to hold to her and her assigns for ever. Also to my wife, my messuage in the town of Stradishall during her life; and after her decease, John my son to have it if he survives his mother; and if not, it to be sold and out of the money from it there to be distributed for the health of our souls, our parents' and benefactors' [*souls*].

To John my son 6 sheep (*oves*); to Stephen my son 6 sheep; to Isabel my daughter 6 sheep; to Alice my daughter 6 sheep.

Remainder of my goods to Alice my wife.

Execs: John Bacon, Edmund Dobyn, together with my wife.

Sealed with my own hand.

Proved at Hundon ('Honeden'), 16 January 1465/66. Admon to execs.

273. ADAM HOBERD of WATTISFIELD ('Watlisfeld'),[1] 12 January 1465/66

[*Commendation*: to God &c]; my body to Christian burial; my debts to be fully paid; to the high altar of the said church 12d; to the parish clerk 6d.

To Margery my wife 6 marks.

To Robert my son, after the decease of Margery my wife, 3 roods of land in the field of Wattisfield called 'Gardeyneshende'.

To John my son 6s 8d; to Roger my son 6s 8d; to Hugh my son 6s 8d; to Alice my daughter 6s 8d.

All the ostilments of my house to Margery my wife.

Residue of all my goods [fol. 393v] to Margery my wife, Roger Martyn and Robert Banham of Wattisfield, my faithful execs; to each of whom, for their labour, 20d.

Proved at Westhorpe, 23 January 1465/66. Admon to execs.

> [1]   Feoffee of Almeric Molows of Wattisfield, will dated February 1461/62 (SROB, Baldwyne 287; Pt I, no. 1409).

274. ED' CLERK of EDWARDSTONE ('Edwardeston'), 6 October 1465

[*Commendation*: to God &c; *no burial directions*]; to the high altar of the same church, for tithes forgotten, 6d; to the fabric of the said church, to the making of the new arch (*archa'*), 6s 8d.[1]

To Agnes my wife all my goods, both small and large, and all my debts, in whosoever's hands they are, to pay my debts and provide for all my children.

Residue of all my goods to my executrix, Agnes my wife.

Proved at Bildeston ('Bilston'), 28 January 1465. Admon to executrix.

> [1]   In this context an 'arch' is a complete bay to an arcade.   *1465/6*

[fol. 394]
275. THOMAS NEVE of GREAT FINBOROUGH ('Fynberth Magna'),[1] 30 May 1465

Dated the penultimate (*pe'*) [*day*] of May; [*commendation*: to God &c]; my body to Christian burial; to the new bell to be newly bought [*for*] the said church 40s, to be paid in 3 years.

To Alice Smert my goddaughter 6s 8d; to Joan Roggere my maid 6s 8d.

To Marion my wife all my lands and tenements, rents and services in the towns of the aforesaid Finborough, Little Finborough ('Fynberth Parva'), Buxhall ('Buxale'), Combs, Battisford ('Batysford'), and Ringshall ('Ryngessell'), or elsewhere in Suffolk, to hold for the whole term of her life; and after her decease, all the said lands and tenements &c[*sic*] to remain to Margaret Cake my daughter, to hold to her and her heirs &c[*sic*].

Any residue there may be of all my goods I leave to Marion my wife and Margaret Cake my daughter.

Execs: Marion my wife and Robert Cake of Mendlesham ('Mendelesham').[2]

Proved at Fornham [*St Martin*], 29 July 1465. Admon to Robert Cake. Power reserved to Marion, executrix, when she comes &c[*sic*].

[1] Thomas Neve, tailor, feoffee to John Plante of Great Finborough, will pr. November 1450 (SROB, Baldwyne 115; Pt I, no. 538).

[2] Son of John Cake of Mendlesham. John's will pr. April 1459 (SROB Baldwyne 269; Pt I, no. 1315); Robert's will pr. June 1476 (SROB, Hervye 125, 128); executor of his brother John (no. 818 below).

276. AGNES HUKTON of CLARE, widow, 1 July 1465

Of Clare in the diocese of Norwich; in my pure widowhood; [*commendation*: to God &c]; to be buried in the churchyard of the parish church of Clare, next to the grave of my parents. In God's name (*ex parte dei*) I beg my execs to pay all my debts that I owe and that can be truly proved. To the high altar of the said church, for my tithes and offerings forgotten, withheld and underpaid, 20d; to the same altar a table-cloth of 'diaperwerk', 6½ yards long and 1¾ yards wide.

To Friar Walter Benygth, for saying a trental of St Gregory with the greatest haste possible after my death, 10s.

To the vicar of Clare church, to pray for my soul and for the soul of John Hucton my husband,[1] and for my parents', friends' and benefactors' [*souls*], in the pulpit, and also to celebrate for us one day in the week in the said church, for a whole year next after my decease, 4s 4d.[2]

To Joan Cagge, living in my house with me, to pray for my soul, my blue tunic furred (*penulatis*[*sic*]) with rabbit skin, a violet kirtle and a blue tabard, a blue hood, 2 smocks (*camis'*, *anglice* 'smokkes'), 2 kerchiefs of the largest and 20d in cash.

To Agnes, daughter of the late Ellis Porter, my goddaughter, living with Thomas Barkere of Hundon ('Honewden'), a table-cloth of 'pleynclothe holond',[3] 4 yards long and a yard wide, a kerchief, the smaller of two (*minor de ij*), a chest called a forcer (*cista'* *anglice* 'forsere'), a pair of jet beads with a silver ring hanging on them, a velvet purse (*loculu'*), 2 latten candlesticks, one larger and the other smaller, a pewter platter, a pewter dish and a pewter [*salt*]cellar ('saler'), to pray for my soul.

To Matilda, wife of John Clovyer of Cavendish ('Cavendyssh'), a sanguine and scarlet ('sangweyn' *cu'grano*) hood.

To Joan, wife of Walter Richere of the same place, my best brass pot, holding by estimation 3 gallons, and a sheet of old cloth.

To Agnes, wife of Clement Flowre of the same place, another brass pot of the same size, with short feet.

To Sir Richard Botilssham, chaplain,[4] to pray for my soul, a small deep basin (*parva' pelvi'profund'*) of latten.

To Richard Norman a brass chafer holding a pottle, a small brass pan with feet and a small iron spit for roasting fowl; to Joan, wife of the said Richard, a pair of my best sheets; [fol. 394v] to Richard their son an old latten ewer; to Avice their daughter a green bed-cover with yellow birds and a kerchief of 'pleyn clothe'.

To Katherine, widow of the late Richard Stecheford, an apron, an old sheet, a brass pan, an iron-bound gallon vessel (*lagene' ferr' ligat'*) with ears, and a bushel (*mod'*) of malt.

To Margaret my servant a sheet of brown cloth, an old blanket, an old red bed-cover with roses and a brass pan holding 3 gallons.

To John, son of Clement Caase, my late husband's godson, 2 latten candlesticks, one of the best and other of the least, and a small brass pan with a 'stele'.

To Rose, wife of Ed' Dytton, my best apron, a pewter platter and a pewter 'saler'.

To William Frede a chest with 'the middilwarde' in [*it*].[5]

To John, son of John Sadelere of Cavendish, monk of the house of Tilty ('Tyltey') [*Essex*],[6] my best basin with the best ewer of the same pattern (*de ead' factur'*), of latten, to pray for my soul.

Whereas John Hucton, my late husband, in his last will[7] left the reversion of all his lands and tenements in Clare, after my decease, to Richard our son,[8] he paying my husband's execs £20 to dispose in deeds of charity, as seemed to them best to please God and profit his soul, as appears more clearly in his last will, of the testament of which I am executrix, duly sworn, according to the form of law, before the ordinary of the lord bishop of the diocese, to implement everything specified in that testament in the best manner possible, as I should answer before the High Judge on the Day of Judgement; now, in exoneration of my soul and execution of that testament, I bequeath £10 of that £20 to the making of 'le roodeloftt' in Clare church, and 5 marks to the benches in the same church, to be newly made, and the stipend of a secular priest [*to be*] hired to celebrate in Clare church, and nowhere else, for the souls of John Hucton, my late husband, and myself, Agnes, and of our fathers and mothers, children and benefactors, for whom we are most bound, for a whole year. Residue of all the goods, both mine and John my late husband's, to the disposition of my execs, John Horold the younger of Clare,[9] Richard Norman of the same and John Portere of Castle Hedingham ('Hengham' *ad Castr'*), to dispose for the aforesaid souls of John my late husband and myself and for those for whom we are bound, in deeds of piety &c[*sic*]; to John Horold, for his diligent labour about these premises, 6s 8d, to be received of John Portere; to John Portere, for [*his*] counsel, a mazer, a silk girdle harnessed with silver and 5 silver spoons, he to pay John Horold the 6s 8d, as above; to Richard Norman, for [*his*] counsel, a brass cooking pot.

To Alice, daughter of John Clerk of Cavendish, a burnet-coloured hood.

Seal appended by my [*own*] hand, in the presence of Master Thomas Asty, vicar of Clare,[10] Richard Norman and Richard Clerk and others.

Proved at Clare, 24 July 1465. Admon to John Horold and Richard Norman, execs. Power reserved to John Portere, the other co-exec, when he comes.

1   John Hukton of Clare, probate only, July 1451 (SROB, Baldwyne 137; Pt I, no. 642).
2   A bequest for a sangred.
3   See Glossary.
4   Richard Bottysham, chaplain, witnessed the will of John Pryke the elder of Barrow (no. 531 below).
5   That is, a divided chest.
6   The Cistercian Abbey at Tilty, Essex, was founded in 1153. There were seven monks in 1377 and the same number at its dissolution (Knowles and Hadcock, *Medieval Religious Houses*, p.126). For a description and plan see Galpin, 'Abbey Church and Claustral Buildings of Tilty'.
7   As her husband's will has not survived, his bequests that she reiterates here are not recorded elsewhere.
8   Richard Hukton was one of the executors of John Hukton.

9   John Horold was another executor of John Hukton.
10   Thomas Asty was appointed vicar of Clare in 1462 (Tanner, p.1228); he also witnessed the will
     of Richard Barbore (no. 46 above).

[fol. 395]
277. JOHN GOLOFRE of SOHAM ('Saham') [Cambs], 25 November 1464

[*Year given as 1465*] [*Commendation*: to God &c]; my body to Christian burial in
the churchyard of St Andrew the Apostle of Soham; to the high altar of which 20d.
To Agnes my wife a house containing two chambers, with the stable, as it stands,
above and below (*sursum et insuper*), at the gate between my messuage and that of
Agnes Deye, for term of her life; and after her decease the house of two chambers
with the stable to remain to my said messuage.
My capital messuage to be sold by my execs and my debts to be paid with the money
from it and if anything remains beyond my debts, it to be disposed between my wife
and my sons (*fil' meos*).
To Agnes my wife all my implements (*implement' mea*).
Residue of all my goods, if any there be, to Agnes my wife and William Golofre,
execs.
Proved at Soham, 26 June 1465. Admon to execs.

278. THOMAS EVERARD of SOHAM ('Saham') [Cambs], 16 April 1465

[*Commendation*: to God &c]; to be buried in the churchyard of St Andrew of Soham;
to the high altar of which 6d; for 3 torches to the church, by the disposition of my
execs, 30s.
To Katherine Everard my daughter my messuage with 2 acres and 1 rood of arable
land, on condition that she pays my debts and pays for the aforementioned torches,
and keeps the anniversary of my father annually, and of my mother and of my wife;
whoever shall buy or have the said messuage with the 2 acres 1 rood of land, after
her, shall hold it on the same condition, for ever.
Residue of [*my*] goods to Katherine Everard my daughter and John Smyth 'at
Waleys Hyll',[1] execs.
Proved at Soham, 26 June 1465. Admon to execs[*sic*]. Power reserved to John
Smyth, when he comes.

1   Executor (as 'John Smyth at Hyll') of John Parys (no. 204).

279. THOMAS GOLDBOUR of SOHAM ('Saham') [Cambs],[1] 4 May 1465

[*Commendation*: to God &c]; my body to Christian burial; to the high altar 12d;
a candle (*cereus*) to be provided before the sepulchre for 10 years; to the fabric of
the church 6s 8d.
To Matilda my daughter a red mare.
To Alice my wife my messuage, newly built, with all the ground (*fundo*) belonging
to it, and 10 acres of arable land, for term of her life; if she should live into old age,
the messuage to be sold, with the 10 acres of arable land, to William Goldbour our
son, for 13 marks in money; if William dies, Joan our daughter to have it for the
same price; if Joan should die, Matilda our daughter to have it for the same price; if
William, Joan and Matilda [*all*] die, the messuage with the 10 acres of arable land

to be sold to the greatest value and the money from them to be disposed for my soul and the souls of all my benefactors.

To Thomas Pecche[2] a grey (*dosea'*) mare.

Residue of all my goods to Alice my wife and William Goldbour our son, execs. Seal appended.

Proved at Soham, 26 June 1465. Admon to execs. Seal of official appended.

[1] ?Related to William Goldbour the younger of Soham (no. 382). The Goldsboro family was prominent in Soham in the seventeenth century, several individuals being members of the parish élite.
[2] The Pechie family was also prominent in seventeenth-century Soham.

[fol. 395v]
280. WILLIAM HORSMAN of WETHERINGSETT ('Wetheryngset'),
10 February 1462/63

[*Commendation*: to God &c]; to be buried in the churchyard of the church of All Saints of Wetheringsett, aforesaid; to the high altar of the same church 3s 4d.

To Emote my wife all my land and tenements for term of her life, and after her decease, they to remain to Robert my son and his heirs, he providing a suitable priest to celebrate in Wetheringsett church for my soul and Emote's, and for the souls of all our friends &c[*sic*], for a year. Robert to provide a man to go on pilgrimage to St James in jubilee year.[1]

To John Lyse of Aspall ('Aspale') 6 marks, to be paid in 6 years after my wife Emote's death; if John troubles my execs about my will, he to have nothing of the 6 marks, and similarly if he wants more than I have given him in any way.[2]

To Emote my wife all my utensils and household (*domicil'*).

Residue of all my goods to the administration of my execs, Emote my wife and Robert Horsman my son.

Proved at Wetheringsett, 2 July 1465. Admon to Robert, exec. Power reserved to Emote, when she comes &c[*sic*].

[1] The Christian year of Jubilee was originally celebrated every 50 years but in the fifteenth century it was celebrated in 1423, 1450 and 1475. In these holy years the pope granted special indulgences to pilgrims and consequently the years were marked with great celebrations in Rome, attended by vast crowds of pilgrims ('Holy Year of Jubilee', in *Catholic Encyclopedia*). Presumably William Horsman wanted a pilgrim to go on his behalf to Compostella in 1475 (see note to no. 89).
[2] Perhaps John Lyse was a son of Emote Horsman by an earlier marriage.

281. JOHN TURNOUR the elder of KIRTLING ('Kertelynge') [*Cambs*],
8 June 1465 [*nuncupative*]

At the point of death; [*commendation*: to God &c]; his body to Christian burial; to the high altar of the same church, for tithes forgotten [*and*] underpaid, 12d.

To the convent of Friars Preachers of Cambridge (*Cantabr'*), to pray for his soul and the souls of his benefactors, 10s; to the convent of Friars Minor of Cambridge 10s; to the friars of Babwell 7s.[1]

To Alice his wife all his movable goods and chattels, of whatever kind and in whosoever's hands they are; Alice his wife to have all his lands and tenements for term of her life, and after her decease the lands and tenements to be equally shared between Thomas and John his sons, Thomas having the first choice.

167

Residue of all his goods to his execs, to dispose for his soul and the souls of all his benefactors, by the advice and discretion of his execs.

Execs: Alice his wife, John and Thomas Turnour his sons.

Witnesses: Sir Richard Frankelen, rector of Kirtling church,[2] Richard Deresle,[3] Richard Turnour, Thomas Pykchese[4] and others.

Proved at Woodditton ('Dytton'), 12 July 1465. Admon to Alice and Thomas, execs. Power reserved to John Turnour, son of the deceased, the other co-exec, when he comes, if he wishes to take up admon. Seal of official appended.

> [1] For the friars see notes to nos 1 (Babwell), 80 (Preachers of Cambridge) and 187 (Minor).
> [2] Richard Frankeleyn was appointed rector of Kirtling in 1462 (Tanner, p.1279).
> [3] Will no. 482 below.
> [4] Executor of wills of William Derysle (no. 461), Walter Derysle (no. 577) and Margaret Page (no. 609).

[fol. 396]

282. JOHN COTELERE of BARNHAM ('Bernham'), 3 September 1464

Dated 3 Nones September; [*commendation*: to God &c]; to be buried in the church-yard of the parish of St Martin of Barnham;[1] to the high altar of the said church 12d; to the emendation of the same church 20d; to the church of St Gregory in Barnham 12d; for a trental to be celebrated 10s.

To John Chambyr, monk, 40d.

To John Caten my godson a ewe with a lamb; to Margery my goddaughter a ewe with a lamb.

To the emendation of a bridge called 'Palmers Brygge' 6s 8d; to the emendation of a way called 'Holgate' 40d.

Residue of all my goods to William Cely, chaplain, and Robert Erlle *alias* Slaw, my execs.

Proved at Ixworth, 17 September 1465. Admon to execs.

Because of a deficiency of the deceased's goods, execs were dismissed from rendering any further accounts and were acquitted. And because the execs, being sworn, said and deposed that, besides what was contained in the testament, the testator willed that, out of the residue of all his goods, his son should have his provision and sustentation, they were charged accordingly (*secundum eorum instrumenta &c'*).[2]

> [1] The two parishes of Barnham, St Martin and St Gregory, were consolidated in 1693; the bells of St Martin's were sold in 1682 and today only a ruinous tower remains. See Blatchly and North-east, 'Lost and Ruined Churches', p.431.
> [2] An example of executors exceeding their legal obligation; no mention is made of the testator's son, nor of provision for him, in the will.

283. JOHN COLYERE of BURES ('Burys') ST MARY, 2 August 1465

[*nuncupative*]

[*Commendation*: to God &c; *no burial directions*]; to the high altar of the same church, for his tithes forgotten, 3s 4d; to the Friars Preachers of Sudbury 3s 4d;[1] to the gild of St Christopher of Bures 6s 8d;[2] to the use (*opus*) of the reparation of the same church 6s 8d; to each priest present at his obsequies 4d and to each clerk present at his obsequies and mass 2d, and to other boys 1d.

His tenement in which he lived he left to Margery his daughter for the whole term of her life and after her decease it to be sold by his execs [*and disposed*] in deeds of piety, according to their discretion.

Residue of all his goods to his execs, William Lovetopp and Richard Amerowce of Kersey.

Witnesses: Robert Newton, gentleman, Sir William Warner, vicar of Bures,[3] John Rosshey *alias* Barbour, John Hervy, Robert Wendon and others.

Proved at Bildeston ('Bylston'), 23 September 1465. Admon to execs.

[1] See note to no. 11.
[2] The gild of St Christopher at Bures was also mentioned in a will in 1479 (*PSIA*, xix, p.176).
[3] See note to no. 55 above.

284. WILLIAM HAWKEDON *alias* GLOVERE [of BILDESTON ('Bylston')], 16 April 1465

[*Commendation*: to God &c]; to be buried in the churchyard of Bildeston church; to the high altar of the same church 12d; to the fabric of the same church 6s 8d.

For a trental to be celebrated for the soul of Sir Alan Bangatt, 10s; for another trental to be celebrated for the souls of Simon Hawkedon and Joan his wife, Margaret Hawkedon and Simon Turnour, 10s;[1] for another trental to be celebrated for my soul and the souls of all my benefactors, 10s.

To Rose my wife a half-part of all my goods, [fol. 396v] after the sale of my tenement by my execs, except a brass pot of 3 gallons, which I bequeath to Sir John my son, with my best candlestick; the best brass pot to be sold to the use of my burial.

To each of my godsons and goddaughters, namely, Robert, Christian and Katherine, 6s 8d.

To Thomas Hawkedon the younger 6s 8d.

Residue of all my goods to my execs, to dispose for the health of my soul, as seems to them best.

Execs: Rose my wife, Sir John Hawkedon my son[2] and Hugh Wrygth[*sic*].

Witnesses: Sir Richard Swettock, rector of Bildeston,[3] Robert Wrygth and Ralph Smyth.

Proved at Bildeston, 23 September 1465. Admon to Sir John Hawkedon and Hugh Wrygth, execs. Power reserved to Rose the relict of the deceased, the other co-executrix, when she comes.

[1] Perhaps the testator was executor of those for whom trentals were to be celebrated.
[2] John Hawkedon was appointed rector of Nedging in 1462 (Tanner, p.1381); he acted as celebrant, executor, supervisor or witness for several parishioners of Nedging and neighbouring Bildeston and Chelsworth. See Pt I, nos 1458 and 1486 and this volume nos 303, 406, 431, 720 and 721.
[3] Richard Swettock was rector of Bildeston from 1442 to 1491 (Growse, *Bildeston*, p.8). See also nos 303, 431, 720 and 721.

285. THOMAS BLOWERE of BILDESTON ('Byldeston'), 1 March 1464/65

Sick of body; [*commendation*: to God &c; *no burial directions*]; to the high altar of the said church, for tithes forgotten, 6s 8d; to the fabric of the body (*corporis*) of the said church 6s 8d.

To John Blowere my son 20s and my best silvered leather girdle (*zona' mea' argent' de coreo*). To Joan Cowpere my daughter, living in Boxford ('Boxforth'), 20s.

To Thomas Blowere my brother a gown and a tunic, and 3s 4d.

To the emendation of the way of 'Newberystrete', where there is greatest need, 6s 8d.

To Rose my wife 40s and all the ostilments and movable necessaries belonging to my house, that is, of the hall and chamber, pantry or buttery and kitchen (*aule et camere panter' vel pincerne et coquine*).

To each of my execs implementing my testament 3s 4d.

Residue of all [*my*] goods &c[*sic*], after my debts have been paid, to the disposition of my execs, to be distributed where most appropriate.

Execs: John Boowstere and Thomas Selawys.

Supervisor: Rose my wife.

Proved at Bildeston ('Bylston'), 23 September 1465. Admon to execs.

[fol. 397]

286. THOMAS MOTTE of WICKHAMBROOK ('Wykhambrok'), 10 May 1464

Dated at Wickhambrook in the diocese of Norwich; [*commendation*: to God &c]; to be buried in the churchyard of the parish church of All Saints of Wickhambrook; to the high altar there, for tithes and other [*things*] forgotten, 6s 8d; to the poor present at my burial 3s 4d.

Robert Motte my son to have all my houses, lands and tenements in the street and fields of Aldersfield ('Alvyrsfeld'), except the pasture called 'Grenefeeld' and a meadow called 'Pekchys Medew', to hold to him and his heirs for ever.

Joan Motte my wife and John Motte my son to have all my houses, lands and tenements, and also all the goods and chattels and utensils, both within the houses and without, to hold to Joan for term of [*her*] life, and after her decease they wholly to remain to John my son, to hold to him and his heirs, in the towns and fields of Wickhambrook, Denston ('Denardyston'), Stradishall, Farley, Attleton ('Adylton'), Boyden ('Boyton') and Badmondisfield, with the aforesaid pasture called 'Grenefeld' and 'Pekcheis Medew', previously excepted, for ever, my debts and five hundred[1] of my sheep only being excepted (*debitis meis cum quingentis ovibus meis dumtaxat exceptis*).

And from those debts and five hundred sheep and their increase (*increment'*) being kept (*custodit' et conservatis*) for the space of 20 years, aided by divine grace (*gra' divina auxiliante*), my execs, Joan Motte my wife and John Motte my son, and Master John Nicol, rector of the parish church of Fornham [*St*] Martin,[2] supervisor, to give and pay in this form:

To the 4 orders of friars, for celebrating trentals, 53s 4d.[3]

To 7 churches, that is, Dalham 13s 4d, Ousden ('Ovisden') 10s, Lidgate 10s, Cowlinge 10s, Stradishall 10s, Denston ('Denardyston') 10s and Depden 10s.

To Wickhambrook church, for a new bell to be bought, £6 13s 4d.

To Katherine Motte my daughter, if she will be guided by, and marry with the agreement of, her mother and my execs, £13 6s 8d.

To Margery Motte my daughter 4 marks, provided she marries according to the wish and agreement of my execs.

To Robert my son 5 quarters of malt, 10 ewes, a cow and a heifer.

Residue of all my goods to the disposition of my execs to dispose according to what seems to them most pleasing to God and profit to my soul, especially in priests [*celebrating*] in Wickhambrook ('Wickham') church and other deeds of charity.

The residue produced over the period specified above to be disposed by my execs or their assigns in the most necessary [*things*] and priests celebrating in Wickhambrook church during the stated period, if the five hundred sheep last so long, otherwise not; if the five hundred sheep do last beyond the term of 20 years, then the sheep to be sold and the money received from them to be disposed by my execs as above. My will is that all persons (*Christiani*) having estate or feoffment, by right or inheritance, of and in all my lands and tenements, shall grant feoffment to, or enfeoff, my heirs and execs, or their assigns, when requested by them, to fulfil this will, [*and*] they to dispose for my soul and the souls of my parents, friends and all my benefactors, in the best way they know, to please God and profit our souls.

Seal appended.

Witnesses: Thomas Cranvyle, William Webbe, clerk,[4] and William Clynton of Bury St Edmunds.

Proved at Fornham [*St*] Martin, 7 January 1464/65. Admon to John Motte, exec. Power reserved to Joan Motte the relict of the deceased, the other co-exec, when she comes &c[*sic*].

1   Long hundreds, i.e. 120 in each, so 600 sheep in total.
2   John Nicoll was rector of Fornham St Martin from 1458 to January 1496/97 (Tanner, p.1434).
3   See note to no. 133.
4   William Webbe was the incumbent of Wickhambrook from 1461 to 1469 (Tanner, p.1256); he had formerly been chaplain at Cowlinge (Pt I, nos 549 and 561).

[fol. 397v]
287. JOHN BAKHOT of MILDENHALL, 20 December 1464

[*Same will as no. 229 above; the whole of no. 287 has been struck through and note added at head:* Registered in another place (*Reg' in alio loco*); *the date of proving is given as* 1 March 1464/65 *in no. 287, whereas no. 229 has* 4 March.]

288. ISABEL SPONERE of SAPISTON ('Sapston'), 14 October 1465 [*probate only*]

Proved at Fornham ('For') [*St Martin*]. Admon to John Sponere, son of the deceased,[1] exec.

1   Isabel Sponer and John Sponer were executors of Peter Sponer of Sapiston, probate November 1455 (SROB, Baldwyne 181; Pt I, no. 872). It seems likely that they were Peter's wife and son, since here, as executor to Isabel, John is described as 'son of the deceased'.

289. WILLIAM COO of BURWELL [*Cambs*],[1] 17 October 1465 [*probate only*]

Proved at Burwell. Admon to Isabel Coo, wife of the deceased, and Thomas Bonyfaunte, execs.

1   Executor of John Gelle of Burwell, will pr. November 1452 (SROB, Baldwyne 121; Pt I, no. 556).

[fol. 398]

290. THOMAS ALSTON of SUDBURY, 30 August 1469

Dated at Sudbury in the diocese of Norwich; to be buried in the churchyard of the church of St Gregory of Sudbury, next to the grave of Isabel my wife. My debts, for which I am in any way bound, to be paid first and foremost. To the high altar of the church of St Peter, in recompense of my tithes and offerings withheld or negligently omitted in any way, 13s 4d.

To the convent of the house of friars of Sudbury,[1] towards the reparation of the brick wall (*muri de* 'bryke'), they to celebrate for the souls of me, Thomas Alston, and Isabel my wife, 4 trentals of St Gregory, as quickly as they can after my decease, 40s; to the convent of the house of friars of Clare,[2] to celebrate 2 trentals among them for the souls of me and my wife 20s, as quickly as possible.

To Isabel my wife my capital messuage and a tenement with a piece of land adjacent to it, which was formerly John Suffeld's, in Sudbury, to hold to her and her assigns for ever, on condition that she pay George Prentys and John Alston, my execs, 10 marks in money in the five years after my decease, that is, each year of the five, 20s 8d [*sic*]; to Isabel 8 'sem'[3] of malt or 4 marks for it; the residue of the malt there to remain to my execs, to sell and dispose for my soul. To my wife, my best girdle ornamented with silver.

To Amee [*sic*] the wife of Adam Morawnt a charger, 3 platters, 3 dishes and 3 saucers of pewter and a brass pot of 2 gallons.

To Isabel at Hoo of [*Long*] Melford[4] a tenement in Melford, called 'Hammundes Crycke', to her and her assigns for ever.

To Isabel, the daughter of the late John Salter, a tenement in Sudbury, lying next to the messuage of Thomas Kerver, to hold to the same Isabel Salter and her heirs, for ever; to Isabel Salter a charger, 3 platters, 3 dishes and 3 saucers of pewter.

To the 6 sons of John Alston 40d each.

To William Alston, brother of the said Thomas Alston, 6s 8d.

To the reparation of the church of Belchamp Otten ('Belcham Otton') [*Essex*], that the parishioners pray for my soul, 40d; to the reparation of the church of Great Cornard ('Cornard Magna'), that the parishioners pray for my soul, 40d.

To the gild of St George of Sudbury[5] a brass pot, according to the discretion and wish of Isabel my wife.

My execs to provide a secular priest to celebrate divine service in the said church of St Peter for a whole year, for the souls of me and Isabel my wife and others for whom I am bound, he taking for his stipend 10 marks, which my wife shall pay him, as noticed above.

[fol. 398v] To John Alston my best basilard, ornamented with silver.

To Isabel my wife all the said utensils, ostilments and bedding of my house, not bequeathed above, to do with freely, as she will.

My execs to distribute, on the day of my death (*obitus*), among the poor in greatest need, 40d, and on [*my*] seven-day 100s, and on my thirty-day 100s, among the poor in greatest need, similarly.

To the parish priest of St Peter's church 4s; the curate of the said church to commend my soul and my wife's on the Sundays in his divine prayers (*precibus dominicalibus*) and in his mass, once a week, continuously during the 10 years after my death, and he to have for his labour 4s each year of the 10.

My execs to arrange for the obsequies for the souls of me and my wife to be celebrated and observed annually on my anniversary for the 12 years immediately following my decease, and to distribute among the poor in greatest need to the sum of 20s, as long as it can be conveniently done out of my goods, after my debts and legacies have first been paid.

Residue of all my valuables (*iocaliu'*) to my execs, to pay my debts and fulfil my legacies as noticed above, and to do as they see best to benefit the health of my soul. Execs: Isabel my wife, George Prentys and John Alston, to execute [*my will*] as above; to each of whom, for their labour, beyond their reasonable expenses, 13s 4d. In God's name (*parte dei*) I require all my feoffees in the said messuage, land and tenements, to deliver their estate that they have in them, in accordance with this testament, when duly requested by my execs.

Witnesses: John Risby[6] [*and*] John Potager, chaplains,[7] and others.

Proved at Sudbury, 25 September 1469. Admon to execs. Seal of official appended.

1   See note to no. 11.
2   See note to no. 1.
3   See Glossary.
4   ?Isabel the wife of Thomas Hoo of Melford. Will of Thomas Hoo, no. 464 below.
5   In 1464 John Russhford (no. 189) bequeathed his best iron spit to this gild. See note to that will.
6   John Rysby/Risby, chaplain, of Sudbury, also witnessed the wills of Stephen Barbour (no. 408) and Alice Turnour (no. 698).
7   See note to no. 271.

[fol. 399]

291. JOHN CLERK of NOWTON ('Newton *iuxta* Bury'),[1] 6 March 1468/69

[*Will*]

(*Hec est ultima voluntas*); [*so no commendation of soul or burial directions*]; to the friars of Babwell,[2] for a trental (*tricentali*), 10s; to the same friars, for 30 (*triginta*) masses,[3] 2s 6d.

I wish to have a 'certeyn' in the aforesaid church of Nowton; to the high altar of the aforesaid church of Nowton 20d; to the reparation of the church of St Edmund (*Sancti Ed'*) 20d;[4] I bequeath 2s for a cloth to be bought for the high altar of the said church of Nowton; to the rector of the said church, for his labour, 2s.

To William Clerk my cousin (*meo cognato*) 6s 8d.

The said rector and William to be execs, to implement this my last will.

Proved [*no more; see no. 296 for probate sentence*].

1   Legatee of his brother John Clerk the elder of Nowton (no. 812).
2   See note to no. 1.
3   The testator requested a trental, that is, a set of 30 masses that could be celebrated over a period of time or all on one day, and also 30 separate masses.
4   Perhaps the abbey church of Bury.

292. JOHN GOORE of BARNHAM ('Bernham *iux'* Thetford'), [*?*1458][1]

[Part of will]

(*Hec es' pars ultime voluntatis*); [*no date given*]; lately (*nuper*) of Barnham, lying on his death-bed (*iacentem in extremis*); he left his tenement, in which he lived in Barnham, to be divided equally between Edmund his son and Lucy his daughter. Furthermore, if Alice his wife should marry another man after his death, he wished that she should not live in his aforesaid tenement any longer, but should be put out and expelled [*from it*].

Witnesses: Sir John Twychyn, rector of Barnham,[2] Robert Kynge and others.

This codicil was proved as part of the last will of John Goore of [*the probate sentence breaks off here and the whole entry has been struck through; see no. 293 for another version*].

1   It is likely that both this fragment and no. 293 below relate to the probate sentence of John Goore of Barnham, dated 21 September 1458 (SROB, Baldwyne 267; Pt I, no. 1303); probate was granted to Alice, wife of the deceased, and John Fuller, execs.
2   John Twychyn was appointed rector of Barnham in 1447 (Tanner, p.1192); will of John Twechyng of Barnham St Gregory, clerk, dated 1488 (NRO, NCC 8 Typpes).

293. JOHN GOORE of BARNHAM ('Bernham *iux'* Thetford'), [*?*1458]

[Part of will]

(*Hec fuit pars ultime voluntatis*); [*no date given*]; lately (*nuper*) of Barnham, deceased; made when he was sick unto death (*fact' per eundem in extremis languent'*). If Alice his wife should marry another man, then she shall no longer remain in his tenement in which he lived, but shall leave it, and then his tenement in Barnham should be divided equally between Edmund his son and Lucy his daughter.

Witnesses: Sir John Twychyn, rector of Barnham,[1] Robert Kynge and others.

Codicil proved, as part of the will of John Goore, witnesses named in the codicil having been [*first*] examined by the official of the lord archdeacon of Sudbury, 13 March 1468/69, at Fornham [*St*] Martin. Seal of official appended.

1   See note to no. 292 above.

[fol. 399v]
294. RICHARD WALTER of CONEY WESTON ('Coneston'),[1] 17 June 1469

Dated the Sabbath before the feast of the Nativity of St John the Baptist, at Coney Weston; to be buried in the churchyard of the church of All Saints in Coney Weston. Before all else, my execs fully to pay, out of my goods, all my debts for which I am bound to others and which can be legally proved. To the high altar of Coney Weston, for tithes forgotten or unknown, 6s 8d; to the use (*proficuum*) of Coney Weston church 13s 4d, and to the walls about the churchyard 6s 8d.

To a man to go on pilgrimage to *Scala Celi* in Rome[2] and to St Peter there,[3] for half a salary (*pro di' celario*), 5 marks, and to a man to go on pilgrimage to St James[4] for half a salary, as my execs can agree with him.

To the Friars Minor of Babwell 5s;[5] to the friars of the Old House of Thetford 5s; to the friars of the New House there 5s; to the nuns of the same town 40d.[6]

To Robert Walter my nephew 40d; to Richard Walter my nephew 20d; to Thomas Walter their brother 20d;[7] to Alice Muryell their sister 20d; to John Walter her brother 20d.

To John Hawys of Walsham my nephew 20d; to John Hawys his brother, the younger, 20d; to Alice Hawys their sister 20d.

To each of my execs and supervisor 40d.

Residue of all my goods to my execs, Thomas Kynge and Andrew Ryngbell, [*and*] supervisor, Robert Walter, they to dispose for my soul and the souls of all my benefactors in the best manner, according to their discretion, as they will answer [*before*] God.

One of my nephews, sons of Geoffrey Walter my brother, to have all my lands and tenements in Coney Weston when they are sold by my execs, before all other people [*and*] at 5 marks within the price for which they could be sold to any others.[8]

Seal appended.

Proved at Fornham [*St*] Martin, 26 June 1469. Admon to execs.

1   Son of John Walter the elder of Hopton, will pr. July 1443 (SROB, Baldwyne 55; Pt I, no. 286).
2   See note to no. 244 above.
3   The Basilica of St Peter, also known as *Basilica Vaticana*.
4   See note to no. 89.
5   See note to no. 1.
6   See notes to nos 68 (Old House and nuns of Thetford) and 69 (New House).
7   Possibly the children of Walter Waltere of Coney Weston (no. 590).
8   In his will, John Walter the elder of Hopton recorded that his sons Richard and Geoffrey held land and tenements in Coney Weston (see note above).

[fol. 400]

295. JOHN WALSHAM of PAKENHAM, 27 September 1469

Dated at Bury St Edmunds; my body to Christian burial at Babwell;[1] to the high altar of Pakenham church, for my tithes and offerings underpaid, 12d; to the high altar of Norton 12d; to the high altar of Thurston church 12d.

To the fraternity of the Holy Trinity of Mottenden ('Modenden') [*Kent*] 6d;[2] to the monastery of St Edmund of Bury 10 quarters of malt; to each religious house in the town of Thetford, apart from the houses of monks and canons there, 5 quarters of malt.[3]

To Katherine my wife all her clothing (*vestimenta*), both linen and woollen, belonging to her body; to Katherine, out of my goods, from now on (*amodo*), for term of her life, 40s in money annually, for her sustentation.

To each of my godsons and goddaughters 4d.

To the emendation of the dangerous (*nocive*) ways, wherever they are, according to the discretion (*per visu*) of my execs, 6s 8d.

All those feoffees now enfeoffed in any of my lands and tenements in the towns of Pakenham, Norton and Thurston, or elsewhere in Suffolk, to enfeoff my execs in all my lands and tenements in those towns or elsewhere, without any withholding [*of them*], for the implementing of my will.

Residue of all my goods and chattels, and all my lands and tenements in the towns of Pakenham, Norton and Thurston, and elsewhere in the kingdom of England, to my execs to sell, receive and dispose for the health of my soul and the souls for whom I am bound, in the celebration of masses and other deeds of charity, as they see best to please God and profit the said souls.

Execs: Thomas Skelton, vicar of Thurston church,[4] Henry Hyrby, parson of Tostock ('Tostoke') church,[5] and John Clement of Stowlangtoft.

Supervisor: John Lopham of Ixworth, gentleman.

Seal appended.

Witnesses: Richard Batayle, gentleman, John Machon, John Reder and others.

Proved at Fornham St Martin, 23 October 1469. Admon to Sir Thomas Skelton, vicar of Thurston; Henry Irby, parson of Tostock church, and John Clement, co-execs, renouncing [*admon*].

1. That is, in the burial ground of the friary of Babwell, just outside Bury. See note to no. 1.
2. The house of Trinitarian Friars of Mottenden, in the parish of Headcorn, was founded by 1236. The friars of this house (strictly speaking, canons rather than friars) were sometimes described as of the 'Order of the Holy Cross', or *Cruciferi*, because the Trinitarian, or Maturine, Friars wore a blue and red cross on their habits. The friars of this house were first expressly called Trinitarians in 1254, when Henry III granted them the right to hold an annual fair on the vigil and feast of the Holy Trinity and 6 following days. Each house of Trinitarian Friars had originally 7 inmates (the minister, 3 clerks and 3 lay brethren) but the number later increased. The friars sometimes served chapels in different parts of the country. A third part of the income of the house from all sources had to be devoted to the redemption of captives imprisoned by the pagans for the faith of Christ. Lay men and women were admitted to the fraternity of the Order; for example, in 1477, John Prince, lord of the manors of Theydon Gernon and Theydon Bois, and Lucy, wife of William Margyte, having aided in an expedition against the Turks, were admitted as brother and sister of the order (*VCH Kent*, ii, pp.205–8). Perhaps John Walsham, the testator here, had aided the Order in the past. See also nos 634 and 636.
3. That is, the bequests were only to the houses of friars within Thetford, not those of monks or canons. See notes to nos 68 and 69.
4. Thomas Skelton was vicar of Thurston from 1460 to 1471 (Tanner, p.1444).
5. Henry Irby was rector of Tostock by 1467, when he was appointed executor by his brother, Master Nicholas Irby, rector of Norton (will pr. April 1467: NRO, NCC 121 Cobald); prior to that he had been chaplain at Tostock (will of Robert Wolman, rector of Tostock, pr. May 1464: NRO, NCC 318 Brosyard). In 1452 Robert Pykerell of Norton bequeathed Sir Henry Irby, chaplain, 4 sheep (SROB, Baldwyne 161; Pt I, no. 782) and in 1459 Isabel Bere of Norton made two bequests to Henry Irby, chaplain, for prayers of various souls (SROB, Baldwyne 268; Pt I, no. 1313), suggesting that he served both parishes. In 1474, he witnessed the will of William Mannyng of Norton (no. 743 below).

[fol. 400v]

296. JOHN CLERK of NOWTON ('Newton *iuxta* Bury'), 6 March 1468/69

[*Same will as no. 291, but with probate sentence*]

Proved at Fornham St Martin, 6 November 1469. Admon to execs.

297. THOMAS ANABLE of HARGRAVE ('Hardgrave'), 28 August 1469

Dated at Hargrave; my body to Christian burial; to the parish church of Hargrave 3s 4d.

To Rose (*Rosie*) my wife 20 marks.

To each of my sons and daughters 40s; if any of my children should die, the legacy of the deceased to be divided among the survivors.

Residue of all my goods and chattels to my execs to sell, receive, dispose and distribute for my soul and the souls for whom I am bound, in the celebration of masses, relief of the poor and doing other pious deeds, as seems best to please God and to profit the health of my soul.

Execs: Rose my wife, John Bateman, Robert Lye and Richard Motte.

Supervisors: Thomas Higham, esquire,[1] and Robert Harwell, gentleman.

Seal appended.

Witnesses: John Anable and John Froste.

Proved at Fornham St Martin, 20 November 1469. Admon to execs.

¹ See note to no. 243 above.

[fol. 401]

298. JOHN WEPSTED of BRETTENHAM ('Brethenham'),¹ 14 April 1469

['Whepsted' *in margin*] [*Commendation*: to God Almighty, the Blessed Virgin Mary]; to be buried in the churchyard of the Blessed Mary of Brettenham; to the church of the same town a cope, price 5 marks.

To Margery Ferthyng 2 bullocks; to my brother 4 sheep and 2 lambs; to Margaret Pelter² 8 sheep and 5 lambs, all the others being ?accounted (*omnibus aliis compotis*); to Margaret Whepsted the elder³ 2 sheep; to John Whepsted the younger⁴ a ewe.

To the light of the bachelors' tapers (*lumini de* 'Bachelers tapers')⁵ 12d, to be had ('resceyvyd') of John Steffe of Rattlesden.

Residue of all my goods to my execs, Hugh Whepsted⁶ and Robert Wryth of Brettenham, to dispose for my soul as shall best please God.

Seal appended.

Proved at Bildeston ('Bylston'), 6 July 1469. Admon to execs.

¹ Presumably related to the testator John Whepsted of Brettenham (no. 322); no. 298 was made nearly a year after no. 322, which would explain the lack of a bequest to 'John Whepsted the elder'.
² Legatee of John Whepsted (no. 322).
³ A Margaret Whepsted received a legacy in no. 322.
⁴ Probably John, son of John Whepsted (no. 322).
⁵ As he made a bequest to the bachelors' tapers, it is likely that this testator was a younger, unmarried man.
⁶ Son of John Whepsted (no. 322).

[OW 24/65]

299. WILLIAM DOWE of BARNHAM ('Bernham') [*ST*] MARTIN,¹ 8 July 1469 [*nuncupative*]

His body to Christian burial; to the high altar of the same church² 20d; to the emendation of the said church 12d.

He wished to have a trental celebrated for his soul according to the discretion of his execs.

Residue of all his goods to his execs to dispose for his soul, as they see best to please God.

Execs: Thomas Candelere and Robert Martyn; to each of whom, for [*their*] labour, 40d.

Witnesses: the rector of Barnham [*St*] Martin, Geoffrey Andrew, William Dowe and others.

Proved at Honington ('Honewton'), 13 July 1469. Admon to Thomas Candelere, exec. Power reserved to Robert Martyn when he comes.

¹ ?Son of John Dowe of Barnham, will pr. March 1444/45 (SROB, Baldwyne 53; Pt I, no. 281).
² See note to no. 282

[fol. 401v]

300. JOHN BAKOUN of BRENT ELEIGH ('Illy Conbusta'), 'smyth', 6 April 1469

Dated at Brent Eleigh; to be buried in the churchyard of the church of the said town; to the high altar there for tithes forgotten [*or*] in any way withheld, and for the health of my soul, 20d.

To the friars of the convent of Sudbury 10s, to celebrate masses immediately after my decease; to the friars of the convent of Clare 10s; to the friars of the convent of Babwell 10s.[1]

To Alice my wife all the ostilments, utensils and bedding (*supell'*), of whatever kind, belonging to my house, with all my malt.

To Joan my daughter 40s; to Alice my daughter 40s.

Alice my wife to have my whole tenement in which I live, for term of her life, [*she*] keeping up the reparations, rents and other dues required in that time; after her decease, it to be sold by her execs or attorneys and the money from it to be distributed in deeds of charity by their discretion. If Alice my wife should be reduced to indigence and poverty, the tenement to be sold by her in her lifetime and she to have her sustentation from it, and if there is anything left, it to be distributed in deeds of piety, that is, for the relief of the poor and prisoners, the repair of muddy ways (*viis lutosis*) and carrying out [*other*] such almsdeeds.

Alice my daughter to have my renter called 'Musteleres' and my grove called 'Wrenne Parke' after my decease, to hold to her and her heirs.

Residue of my goods and chattels to the disposition of my executrix, Alice my wife, to administer and implement my testament as quickly as she can, first paying my debts, as seems to her best to please God and profit my soul.

To the reparation and emendation of the way between the close called 'Parkfeld' and the meadow of '?Priestowe' (*prata de p'stowe*), 20s.

To a window in the said church 40s.

As to my last will concerning my tenements, I wish and in the name of God (*ex parte dei*) require my feoffees of the said tenements and grove to deliver estate to perform this will when so requested.

Seal appended.

Proved at Bildeston ('Bylston'), 6 July 1469. Admon to executrix.

[1] For the friars see notes to nos 1 (Babwell and Clare) and 11 (Sudbury).

[fol. 402]

301. THOMAS BARKER of HUNDON ('Honeden'),[1] 22 March 1468/69

[*nuncupative*]

[*Commendation*: to God &c]; his body to Christian burial; to the high altar of Hundon church, for tithes forgotten, 4d.

Residue of all his goods to Joan his wife, to pay his debts and dispose for the health of his soul as she sees [*best*] to please God.

Executrix: Joan his wife.

Witnesses: Sir William Passhbroke, chaplain, Katherine Gyles, Margaret Elsyng and others.

Proved at Stradishall ('Stradyshull'), 11 April 1469. Admon to executrix; vicar of Hundon commissioned to grant it to her.

¹ Executor of Robert Ufford of Hundon, will pr. September 1457 (SROB, Baldwyne 218; Pt I, no. 1083).

302. WILLIAM OLYVERE [of WANGFORD], 20 October 1448[*sic*]

Date given as *millesimo CCCC xl octavo* [*?*error for *lx octavo*]. [*Commendation includes* the Blessed Denis]; to be buried in the churchyard of the Blessed Denis of Wangford; to the high altar, for my tithes and offerings forgotten, 12d; to the sustentation of the church 6s 8d; to the reparation of Kennett [*Cambs*] church 6s 8d. To the friars of Babwell¹ 10s, to celebrate a trental as quickly as possible for the health of my soul.

Residue of my goods to Reginald Elyott and John Denton, execs, to dispose for the health of my soul.

Seal appended.

Witnesses: John Whetle, clerk, John Roo, John Schapman.

Proved at Mildenhall ('Myldenhale'), 13 April 1469. Admon to execs. Seal of official appended.

¹ See note to no. 1.

303. ALICE STRUT of BILDESTON ('Byldeston'), widow,¹ 9 April 1465

Dated at Bildeston in the diocese of Norwich; sick in body; [*commendation*: to God the Father Almighty *only*]; my body to the Christian burial of Bildeston; to the high altar of the same church 6s 8d; to the buying of a new thurible for the use of the said church 100s.

Residue of all my goods to my execs to dispose for my soul and the souls for whom I am bound, as seems to them best to please God and for the future health of my soul.

Execs: Sir Robert [*recte Richard*] Swettok, rector of Bildeston church,² and Robert Parle of Lavenham.

Supervisor: Sir John Hawkedon.³

Witnesses: John Haveell, Hugh Wryghte and William Hawkedon of Bildeston.

Proved at Bildeston ('Bilston'), 21 *?*February 1468/69. Admon to execs.

¹ Sister and executrix of John Parle of Hundon, will pr. July 1455 (SROB, Baldwyne 226; Pt I, no. 1125).
² See note to no. 284 above, and also nos 431, 720 and 721.
³ See note to no. 284, and also nos 406, 431, 720 and 721.

[fol. 402v]
304. JOHN TOFTYS of WEST STOW ('Westow'),¹ 5 July 1468

['Toftes' *in margin*]; to be buried in the churchyard of the church of West Stow; to the rector of the said church the best sheep that I have, in the name of a mortuary; all my other sheep, that is, 9, with 7 lambs, to be sold and the money from them to be fully disposed for my soul on the day of my burial.

To Joan my wife my messuage in the town of West Stow, to hold to her and her attorneys for term of her life; and after her decease the messuage to be sold and the money disposed for my soul and the soul of Joan my wife, and for the souls of our parents and benefactors.

To my son William Toftys 6s 8d; to my son Reginald Toftys 6s 8d.

Residue of all my goods I leave to the disposition of my execs, to dispose as seems to them most expedient for my soul.

Execs: Joan my wife and Roger Curray, to dispose as they will answer before the High Judge.

Proved 24 April 1469. Admon to execs.

1   ?Related to Reginald Toftes of Elveden (no. 185).

305. ELIZABETH TABERHAM of [GREAT WALDINGFIELD],
15 September 1468

Wife of John Taberham; dated at Great Waldingfield ('Waldyngfeld Magna') in the presence of many of the faithful (*pluriu' fideliu'*); to be buried in the churchyard of the parish church where I die.

To John Lovell my son 10s of his father's legacy; to Isabel Grey my daughter, also from her father's legacy, 10s; and of my own bequest, 6s 8d to each of them.

To the high altar of the parish church of Great Waldingfield 20d.

To John Taberham my husband half of my utensils, as arranged (*gubernetur*) according to the wishes (*secundum voluntate'*) of John Lovell, my exec.

I leave a trental to Friar Denis to celebrate for me and my friends.

To John Lovell my exec a brass pan (*patenam*) of 8 gallons; to Isabel Lovell a bed-cover (*unam superlectilem*).

Residue of all my goods to the disposition of the said John Lovell, exec, to dispose for the health of my soul as seems to him best to please God and profit my soul.

Proved at Newton, 16 May 1469. Admon to exec.

[fol. 403]
306. JOHN PONDERE of SUDBURY, fuller, 7 August 1467

Dated at Sudbury; [*commendation*: to God &c]; to be buried in the churchyard of St Gregory there; to the high altar of the church of St Peter of the same town, in recompense of my tithes, offerings or short-comings (*faltarum*) &c[*sic*] 4s 4d.

To Isabel my wife all the utensils, bedding (*supellect'*) and valuables (*iocalia*) of my house, and all the other movable goods that there are after my decease, to do with freely as she will; my debts for which I am in any way bound to be paid first and foremost.

The money owed by me for my messuage with the garden in Sudbury, lately bought by us, to be paid out of my goods, if they will stretch to it, and Isabel my wife to have the messuage with the garden to her for term of her life, she to meet all the dues for it in the meantime; after her decease the messuage and garden to be sold and out of the money from them I leave to Richard the son of Richard Gebelon[1] 5 marks, if he be alive then, and the residue from the messuage to be disposed for my soul and for the souls of Richard Gebelon[2] and Isabel my wife, and others for whom I am bound, that is, in the supporting of a secular priest in the church of St Peter for a whole year, and more if possible, he taking for his salary 8 marks 6s 8d.

Residue of all my goods and chattels to Isabel my wife with which to pay my debts and dispose as above, acting as she sees best to profit the health of my soul.

Execs: Isabel my wife and Simon Sparwe, to act as above, providing always that Isabel my wife, during the whole term of her life, disposes all my goods and chattels in implementing this testament only with the agreement of Simon Sparwe; to Simon Sparwe, for his labour, 40d.

Witnesses: John Rysby, John Potenger, chaplain,[3] and others.

Proved at Sudbury, 18 September 1467. Admon to execs.

[1] Legatee (as 'Gybelon') of his father, Richard (no. 84 above).
[2] Richard Gebelon of Sudbury (as 'Gybelon') had died by July 1462 (no. 84 above). The spelling of the surname might be 'Gebelou'. John Pondere was not mentioned in Gebelon's will; it is possible that he had married his widow, Isabel. Admittedly Isabel is not an uncommon name, but Richard Gebelon junior was bequeathed 5 marks out of his father's messauge and garden in Sudbury after the decease of his wife Isabel, and John Pondere made the same bequest here.
[3] See note to no. 271.

307. MATILDA STACE of SUDBURY, 16 May 1467

[*Commendation*: to God &c; *no burial directions*]; to the high altar of the church of St Peter of the said town, for tithes &c[*sic*] 12d.

An acre of my arable land lying by 'Bromhyll' to be sold and out of the money from it a trental to be celebrated by a friar of the order of Preachers,[1] and from the residue there to be distributed annually among churchmen (*inter ecclesiastic'*) in anniversary obsequies for me.

To Joan Sponere a best girdle, green in colour; to Margaret Shepperd a tunic called a 'frende',[2] sanguine in colour; to Geoffrey Cleypoll a pair of best sheets.

The feoffees in the said acre of land to deliver their estate in it to my execs when requested by them.

Residue of all my goods to my execs, John Pondere and Edmund Sponere; to each of them, for their labour, 20d, and if this appears small, it to be augmented according to their conscience.

Proved at Sudbury, 18 September 1467. Admon to execs.[3]

[1] A friar from the house of Dominicans at Sudbury; see note to no. 11.
[2] See Glossary.
[3] Perhaps the executor John Pondere was not the same man as the testator in no. 306 above, as both wills were proved on the same day and administration appears to have been granted to both of the executors named in this will.

[fol. 403v]

308. ISABEL CRANE [of REDGRAVE],[1] 12 February 1466/67

[*Commendation*: to God &c]; to be buried in the churchyard of the church of All Saints of Redgrave; to the said church 16 marks which Richard Crane of Rickinghall ('Rykynghale') Inferior owes me for the house and divers lands which I sold to him in my lifetime.

Residue of all my goods to Ed[*mund*] Subburne,[2] he to dispose for me and for the health of my soul as he sees most expedient, and him I make exec.

Proved at Eye, 25 November 1467. Admon to exec.

[1] Wife and executrix of John Crane of Botesdale in Redgrave, will pr. October 1461 (SROB, Baldwyne 280; Pt I, no. 1373).
[2] Will (as of Rickinghall) pr. April 1476 (SROB, Hervye 135); he was exectuor, supervisor or witness of several other wills in Baldwyne: see Part I, nos 726, 971, 1354 and 1371, and nos 327, 376 and 391 below.

309. WILLIAM MAYNERE of GROTON, 30 September 1467

[*Commendation*: to God &c]; to be buried in the churchyard of the parish church of St Margaret of Groton; to the high altar of the same church, for tithes forgotten &c[*sic*], 13s 4d; to the making of the tabernacle of St Margaret 20s; for a chalice 10 marks.

To the friars of Sudbury[1] 10s.

To my mother half a pack of wool (*sarcine lane*),[2] 26s 8d, a quarter of wheat, a quarter of malt and a quarter of barley.

To Phyllis (*Felicie*) my wife a pack of wool, 40s, a quarter of wheat, a quarter of malt, a quarter of barley and all the utensils belonging to the house, except a silver and gilt goblet (*cipho*).

To John Pryour [*my*] best gown.

Residue of all [*my*] goods to the disposition of my execs, to dispose &c[*sic*].

Execs: Thomas Writh and John Dogott of the same [*place*].

Proved at Preston, 1 December 1467. Admon to execs.

[1]   See note to no. 11.
[2]   See Glossary.

310. THOMAS FACON of BURES ST MARY, 6 April 1466

[*No commendation of soul or burial directions*]; to the high altar of the same church, for tithes forgotten, 12d; to each chaplain of the same church 4d, if present at my funeral offices; to each clerk 2d; to the beadle (*bedello*) 1d.

To Thomas Risshe my godson 8d.

To Alice Qwedwelle the younger 12d.

To Robert Nevereys 6d.

Residue of all my goods to Alice Facon my wife, executrix, with full power to execute this will.

Proved at [*Long*] Melford, 2 December 1467. Admon to executrix.

[fol. 404]
311. RICHARD MODY of NEWTON,[1] 28 July 1467

Of Newton in the diocese of Norwich; [*commendation*: to God &c]; to be buried in the churchyard of the church of St Gregory, Sudbury, if I happen to die there, and if not, wherever that occurs; to the high altar of the church of St Peter, Sudbury, for tithes negligently forgotten by me and not paid, 6s 8d; to the high altar of Newton church, for forgotten tithes, 6s 8d; to the reparation of the same church 20s; to the reparation of Acton ('Akton') church 20s; to the reparation of the church of St Gregory, Sudbury, 6s 8d; to the reparation of Chilton ('Chylton') church 3s 4d.

To a secular priest, honest and discreet, to celebrate in Newton church for a whole year, for my soul and all my parents' souls, 9 marks for his stipend.

To the common profit of the convent of Friars Preachers of Sudbury[2] 10s, to celebrate a trental of St Gregory for my soul and all my parents' souls.

To Margery, wife of Thomas Salman, my daughter, a brass pot, a pan, 12 'le plateris', 10 'le dischys', 6 'le sawcerys' and 2 chargers [*which*] she has in her keeping; to Margery a 'le materas', a pair of sheets and 40s in money of her husband Thomas Salman's debt.

To Agnes my daughter a brass pot holding 2 gallons which she [*already*] has, a pan holding 3 gallons, a basin with a laver, a pair of sheets and 20s in money.

To Margaret my daughter 6s 8d in money.

To Richard Salman, son of Thomas Salman, 6s 8d, to be delivered to him by my execs when he comes to the age of 21.

To Lettice (*Letitie*), daughter of Thomas Salman, a silvered girdle, green in colour, the best hanging laver and 6s 8d in money, to be delivered to her by my execs when she comes to the age of 16.

To Robert Mody of Polstead ('Polsted') 6s 8d.

To the reparation of the common way lying next to 'Cordewanerys' in Newton 20s.

To Thomas Salman my best furred (*penulata'*) gown.

To Richard Smyth, husband of Margaret my daughter, another furred gown.

To the common profit of the convent of friars of Clare 10s,[3] to celebrate a trental of St Gregory for my soul and all my parents' [*souls*].

To John Kendale of Sudbury, the younger, my godson, 6s 8d; to Alice his daughter 6s 8d; to Andrew Hallys of Acton, my godson, 6s 8d; to Robert Gosse of Assington ('Assyngton'), my godson, 6s 8d; to the sister of John Kendale, living in Acton, 6s 8d; to the daughter of John Copyng of Acton[4] 3s 4d.

For my obit to be kept for 10 years after my death, 5 marks, that is, each year 6s 8d.

To the youngest son of Thomas Salman 6s 8d.

To be distributed by my execs among the poor in greatest need in the town of Bury, 6s 8d.

To each priest present at my obsequies on the day of my death 2d,[5] and to each secular clerk 2d and to each boy 1d.

Residue of all my goods to my execs, to dispose as they know best in deeds of charity for the health of my soul and all my parents' [*souls*].

To be distributed among the poor of the town of Newton, 6s 8d; to be distributed among the poor of Acton, 6s 8d.

Execs: Alexander Cook, chaplain, and John Kendale the younger, they to implement all the above-written; 20s each for their labours.

Seal appended.

Proved at Lavenham, 20 December 1468.

1   Beneficiary of the will of Henry Pethyrton, pr. April 1442 (SROB, Baldwyne 16; Pt I, no. 91).
2   See note to no. 11.
3   See note to no. 1.
4   Will of John Copyn of Acton (no. 518 below); in this very brief will the testator did not mention any relatives.
5   Possibly 'to each priest … 7d': the '*v*' in the amount '*vij d*' may not have been deleted.

[fol. 404v]

312. JOHN PLAYFORD of MILDENHALL ('Mildenhale'), 10 December 1468

Dated 8 Edward IV; living in 'the Bekke Rowes';[1] [*commendation*: to God &c]; my body to Christian burial in the churchyard of Mildenhall church; to the high altar of the same church for forgotten tithes &c[*sic*] 20d; to the reparation of the same church 40d.

To John Playford my son 2 cows and 1½ quarters of barley; to Robert my son a cow and 1½ quarters of barley; to the aforesaid John my son a brass pot, a brass pan and a pewter platter; to the aforesaid Robert my son a brass pot, a brass pan and a pewter platter.

To John Playford my brother[2] my best gown and best doublet.

Residue of all my goods and chattels to my execs, to dispose for my soul and the soul of Matilda my wife and the souls &c[*sic*].

Execs: George Playford, John Playford, son of Thomas Playford,[3] and John Playford my brother.

Proved 16 January 1468/69. Admon to George and John, execs. Power reserved to John Playford the other co-exec when he comes, if &c[*sic*].

[1]   That is, Beck Row, one of the 'rows', outlying hamlets of Mildenhall, the other two being Holy-well Row and West Row.

[2]   As 'John Playford the elder of Mildenhall', will no. 754 below.

[3]   John Playford, son of Thomas, was one of the executors of John Playford 'the elder' (no. 754); from that will it is clear that Thomas was brother to the two testators named John Playford.

[fol. 405]

313. JOHN COK of HAUGHLEY ('Haughle'), 18 November 1468

[*Commendation*: to God &c]; my body to the Christian burial in Haughley; to the high altar of Haughley church, for tithes forgotten &c[*sic*], 12d.

To the friars of the order of St Francis of Babwell[1] 10s, for a trental to be celebrated for my soul and the souls of Marion and Avice my wives; to the said friars of Babwell, after the decease of Marion, now my wife, 10s, to celebrate a trental for my soul and the souls of the said Marion and Avice and Marion my wives.

To Anne my daughter a black cow and my blue gown.

To John Deye my gown of 'le russett' colour.

To Geoffrey Egmer my gown of 'le violett' colour.

To Marion my wife all the utensils of my house, for the whole term of her life, if she remains unmarried; but if she remarries, then I leave her half my utensils and the other half to be divided between Alice Deye and Anne my daughters. To Marion my messuage next to (*iux'*) the messuage of John Cotton in Haughley, for the whole term of her life; and after her decease it to be sold by my execs for the best price and the money from it distributed in this way: one part for our souls above-written, and the other part to be divided between my daughters.

Residue of all my goods and chattels to John Blogate, Henry Cole and Marion my wife, execs.

Witnesses: John Bettes, John Dey, John Spragg and others.

Proved at Stowmarket, 12 January 1468/69. Admon to execs.

[1]   See note to no. 1.

314. JOHN GARDENER of WHEPSTEAD ('Wepsted'), 1 October 1468

[*Commendation*: to God &c]; my body to Christian burial in Hawstead ('Hawsted'); to a priest, for a year after my decease, 8 marks; to a cross in the churchyard of the same town of Hawstead 8 marks; to a missal book (*missali libro*) for Hawstead church 33s 4d; to the emendation of the highway between William Dullyngham and John Clerk 33s 4d; to the reparation of Whepstead church 20s.

To William Dullyngham my best gown and my hood; to Margaret Dullyngham my biggest pot; to Rose, daughter of the same William, my best pan.

To my wife 5 marks and the ostilments and utensils belonging to my house; to my wife all my movable chattels; to my wife my tenement for a year after my decease, for her sustentation.

Residue of my goods to my execs, to dispose in deeds of charity &c[*sic*].

Execs: John Norman [*and*] John Grigge, they faithfully to implement my testament. Supervisor: the aforesaid William.

To John Norman, for his labour, 40d, and to John Grigge, for his labour, 40d.

Proved at Fornham [*St Martin*], 6 February 1468/69. Admon to execs.

[fol. 405v]
315. JOHN FRESSWATER of WETHERDEN,[1] 24 February 1468/69 [*probate only*]

['Fresshwater' *in margin*]; proved at Haughley ('Haghley'). Admon to Agnes, executrix.

> [1]   ?Executor of Thomas Hesset of Wetherden, will pr. May 1459 (SROB, Baldwyne 236; Pt I, no. 1182); executor of Margaret Marleton of Wetherden, will pr. November 1459 (SROB, Baldwyne 264; Pt I, no. 1295).

316. WILLIAM GOLDYNG of GLEMSFORD ('Glemesford),[1] 27 May 1468

Of Glemsford in the diocese of Norwich; [*commendation*: to God &c]; to be buried in the churchyard of St Mary of Glemsford; to the high altar there 6s 8d; to a priest, to celebrate for my soul in Glemsford church, £6; to the fabric of the same church £3 6s 8d; to my burial 40s; to 'le torches' 3s 4d.

To Joan, wife of John my son, 6s 8d; to Agnes, wife of Thomas my son, 10s; to Margery my daughter 6s 8d; to each of the children of John my son 3s 4d; to each of the children of Thomas my son 3s 4d; to each of the children of Margery my daughter 3s 4d; to Margery my daughter 4 silver spoons; to Thomas my son a 'le maser'; to the wife of Thomas all the utensils of my house.

Residue of all [*my*] goods to my execs, John and Thomas my sons, to dispose for my soul &c[*sic*].

Proved at Glemsford, 1 May 1468[*sic*] [*recte ?*March 1468/69]. Admon to execs.

> [1]   ?Related to Robert Goldyng of Glemsford (no. 564 below).

317. JOAN OLYFE of [GLEMSFORD], widow, 20 January 1468/69

Relict of John Olyffe; [*commendation*: to God &c]; to be buried in the churchyard of the church of the Blessed Mary of Glemsford; to the high altar, for my tithes badly paid (*malefactis*), 20d; to the gild of St Thomas 6s 8d;[1] to the use of the said church 6s 8d, to be disposed by the wardens of the church on what seems to them to be most necessary; to a suitable secular chaplain, to celebrate in the same church for my soul and the souls of all the faithful departed, for half a year, 5 marks.

To the convent of friars of Clare, to pray for my soul, 6s 8d; to the convent of friars of Sudbury 40d, in the same way; to the convent of friars of Babwell, to pray for my soul, 40d.[2]

Residue of my goods, after my debts have first been paid, to my sons Richard Gardener and Robert ?Heche.

Execs: the same Richard Gardener, and William Rogyll, they to have God before their eyes in the execution of this testament.

Proved at Glemsford, 1 March 1468/69. Admon to execs.

1. Thomas Roote (no. 508) asked for the mass-pence from the gild of St Thomas at Glemsford to be given to the four orders of frairs at Clare, Sudbury, Babwell and Cambridge, to pray for his soul. In his will, pr. February 1476/77 (SROB, Hervye 58), John Willyngham left 5 marks to Glemsford church provided that the churchwardens did not trouble his executors about the 'new building' of the gildhall.

2. For the friars see notes to nos 1 (Babwell and Clare) and 11 (Sudbury).

[fol. 406]

318. ALICE SARE of ELMSWELL ('Elmyswell'), widow, 24 November 1465

In my pure widowhood; sick in body; to be buried in the churchyard of the parish church of Elmswell, by the graves of my elders (*maiorum*); to the high altar of the said church 2s 2d.

To John Sare my godson a bed-cover (*supellectil'*), coloured red and yellow, a blanket and a pair of sheets of price 2s 8d, and a brass pot holding 2 gallons and more (*et ult'*).

All my other movable goods I leave to Master John Croftys, rector of Elmswell,[1] to pay my debts and dispose the residue, if any there be, for the health of my soul. The said John Sare, when he reaches the legal age of 21, to have my messuage in the town of Elmswell, together with the arable lands [*and*] closes of pasture (*past' clausur'*), free and bond, in the town of Elmswell; and in the meantime, before John is of legal age, Master John Croftes to have the messuage with the arable lands, pasture and feedings, as above, holding them to the use of John my godson, the rent to the lord of the fee being paid and reparations of the messuage seen to (*contentis*); if John should die before coming to the said age, or after that but without issue, Master John Croftys to sell the messuage, as described above, for a fair (*iusto*) price and dispose the money from it in pious uses, that is, to church and the poor.

Exec: Master John.

Witnesses, especially called: Robert Hotley and Robert Warde of Elmswell, with others.

Proved at Fornham [*St*] Martin, 14 April 1466. Admon to exec.

1. Probably the same man as John Crofftes, who was official to John Selot, archdeacon of Sudbury (see Introduction, under *Register 'Baldwyne'*). Crofftes was BCnL by 1470; appointed proctor at law for King's College in September 1470; presented as rector of Monxton (Hants) October 1468 (Emden, *BRUC*, pp.167–8); will pr. March 1478/79 (SROB, Hawlee 264).

319. ROBERT CHAPELEYN [of WANGFORD], 22 April 1467

[*Commendation*: to God &c]; my body to Christian burial in the churchyard of the parish church of St Denis of Wangford; to the high altar there 8d; to the reparations there 20d; to each of my godsons and goddaughters 4d; to the parish clerk 4d.

To John Hawle 4d.

To Thomas Heylott 4d; to Margery my daughter, after the decease of Anne my wife, a brass pot holding, by estimation, 3 gallons; to Robert Heylott a ewe (*ovem matric'*); to Christian, daughter of the same Robert, another ewe.

To the maintenance of the fraternity of St John (*subsidio sancti Johannis* 'de le

Frary') 8d;[1] to the hospital of St Thomas the Martyr in Rome 4d;[2] to the college of St Thomas Acre in London 4d;[3] to the college of St Anthony in London 4d.[4]

Residue of my goods to John Denton and Reginald Elyott, execs, to pay my debts, fulfil my legacies and [*dispose*] everything else (*omnia al'*) for my soul and the souls for whom I am bound, as seems to them best to please God; to each of my execs for executing this testament well, 20d.

[*Will, of same date*]

Anne my wife to have my messuage or dwelling house (*mans'*), lately Robert Santon's, to her and her assigns for ever; Anne to have 3 cows, a bullock and a mare, 6 ewes, 3 hoggets (*hoggastr'*), 3 lambs and a wether (*multon'*); Anne [*also*] to have 6s 8d and all the necessaries or utensils of my house (*hospicii'*).

Proved at Fornham [*St*] Martin, 22 June 1467. Admon to Reginald Elyot. Power reserved to John Denton when he comes.

[1] The fraternity of the Knights Hospitallers of St John, Clerkenwell, London (*VCH, Middlesex*, i, pp.193–200).

[2] The Hospice of St Thomas of Canterbury in Rome owed its foundation to the jubilees, which brought pilgrims to Rome from every country of Europe. See note to no. 280. Pilgrims arriving from England in 1350 found it difficult to obtain suitable accommodation and so an institution was founded where subsequent English pilgrims might receive shelter and hospitality. It appears that a gild of laymen was established and in 1362 it acquired certain property on the Via Monser-rato. The hospice declined from the time of Henry VII but during Elizabeth's reign some of the exiled English Catholic clergy who found their way to Rome were received into the hospice and formed a permanent community there. After William Allen's visit in 1576, the hospice formed the nucleus of the English College in Rome (Cronin, 'The English College, in Rome', in *Catholic Encyclopedia*, v).

[3] The order of St Thomas of Acre was established in the Holy Land at the time of the third crusade, when the cult of Becket was spreading rapidly throughout Europe. In the 1220s the order was re-established according to the military rule of the Teutonic knights and in 1227/28 it acquired as a site for a church the land in St Mary Colechurch parish, London, where Becket had been born. Over the next 40 years this site was enlarged and eventually, in the fourteenth century, this house became the headquarters of the order. The military role of the order was gradually abandoned. By the fifteenth century the brothers in London were living according to the rule of St Augustine (Keene and Harding (eds), *Historical Gazetteer of London before the Great Fire*, 'St Mary Colechurch').

[4] The brothers of St Anthony of Vienne established a cell before 1254 on some land given to them by Henry III, previously occupied by a synagogue. The house was founded for a master, two priests, a schoolmaster, and twelve poor men, but there appears to have been no endowment: in 1291 their whole property, which lay in the parish of St Benet Fink, was not worth more than 8s a year, suggesting that they depended entirely on alms. The college, or hospital, was appropriated to St George's Chapel, Windsor, in 1475 (*VCH, London*, pp.581–4). In 1460, Thomas Symond of Rougham made bequests to the same three London 'hospitals' (SROB, Baldwyne 302; Pt I, no. 1478).

[fol. 406v]

320. ROBERT KNYGTH of LITTLE SAXHAM ('Saxham Parva'), the elder, 10 July 1468

[*Commendation*: to God &c]; my body to Christian burial; to the high altar of Little Saxham church, for my tithes and offerings forgotten or underpaid and for the health of my soul, 6s 8d.

To Elizabeth my wife all my lands and tenements lying in the town of Little Saxham, to hold to her for term of her life, apart from two closes at 'le Hawe' and 5 acres of land lately belonging to the same closes, which are to go to Thomas Knygth my son and his heirs; but if it becomes necessary for Elizabeth to sell any part of the said lands in her lifetime to pay my debts, then that to be sold.

To the abovesaid Thomas Knygth 4 acres of land in the field called 'Westrycefeld', to hold to him and his heirs for ever.

After the decease of Elizabeth, all the said lands and tenements, except the fore-going bequests, to remain to Robert Knygth the younger, my son, and his heirs for ever.

To Elizabeth my wife all my movable goods, she to see my body honestly buried and my debts paid.

To Margaret my servant a bed and 2 coombs of barley.

Residue of all my goods to my execs to sell and dispose for my soul and the souls &c[*sic*].

Execs: Elizabeth my wife and Thomas Knygth my son; they faithfully to execute this testament.

Supervisor: Ralph Holdirnesse, clerk.[1]

Witnesses: Richard Oversouth, Walter Noble and others.

Proved at Fornham St Martin, 6 February 1468/69. Admon to execs.

[1] Ralph Holdernisse was rector of Little Saxham from 1446 to 1475 (Tanner, p.1422); he witnessed the will of John Fuller of Little Saxham (no. 507).

321. JOHN PYKERELL of THURSTON ('Thruston'),[1] 17 January 1468/69

Dated at Thurston; sick in body; [*commendation*: to God &c]; to be buried in the churchyard of the church of the Blessed Peter of Thurston; to the high altar of the same church for my tithes forgotten 12d, and I place myself wholly at God's mercy (*pono me tota' mercia dei*); to the use of the said church 40d.

To the Friars Preachers of Thetford,[2] for me and for those for whom I am bound, 40d; to the Friars Minor of Babwell 40d;[3] to the light of the Blessed Mary in Thurston church 2 ewes or 2 bushels (*mod'*) of barley.

Residue of all my goods and chattels to the disposition of John Pykerell, rector of Beyton ('Beketon') church[4] and Thomas Bullok of Thurston, they to pay my debts and fulfil my last will and see that all is done well.

Supervisor: John Pykerell, rector of Westhorpe church.[5]

Proved at Fornham [*St*] Martin, 6 February 1468/69. Admon to Thomas Bullok. Power reserved to the rector of Beyton, when he comes.

[1] Wills of other members of the Pykerell/Pekerell family of Thurston include John, pr. January 1461/62 (SROB, Baldwyne 293; Pt I, no. 1437); Roger, pr. October 1461 (SROB, Baldwyne 296; Pt I, no. 1451).

[2] See note to no. 68.

[3] See note to no. 1.

[4] As can be seen from the name of the supervisor below, there appear to have been two clerics named John Pykerell, but this first entry may have been a scribal error. The probate clause stated that power had been reserved to the rector of Beyton but did not refer to that cleric by name. In October 1439, John Smyth of Beyton had appointed Sir John *Parker* as his supervisor; this may have been the man appointed here as executor by John Pykerell, although admittedly there was a gap of 30 years (SROB, Baldwyne 9; Pt I, no. 52).

[5] John Pykerell was rector of Westhorpe by 1461 (Pt I, no. 1451); that John Pykerell, priest, was the son of John Pekerell the elder of Thurston was explicitly stated in the will of John Rose the younger of Thurston, pr. July 1448 (SROB, Baldwyne 119; Pt I, no. 552). His parents were John and Isabel (his father's will: SROB, Baldwyne 293; Pt I, no. 1437); he was the brother of Robert Pykerell of Norton, will pr. July 1453 (SROB, Baldwyne 161; Pt I, no. 782).

[fol. 407]

322. JOHN WHEPSTED of BRETTENHAM ('Brethenham'),[1] 9 May 1468

['Qwhepsted' *in margin*] [*Commendation*: to God &c; *no burial directions*]; to the high altar of the same church, for my tithes forgotten or underpaid, 20d; to the same church for buying a new chalice 26s 8d, to be received from Hugh Whepsted my son[2] for certain lands bought from me, that is, at the feast of St Etheldreda the Virgin [*23 June*] in the year 1469.

To the friars of Sudbury, to celebrate a trental of St Gregory for my soul there, 10s,[3] to be received from Hugh my son, as above, at the feast of St Michael next.

To Marion, daughter of the same Hugh, 20d, to be received from Hugh, as above.

To the friars of Babwell, to celebrate a trental of St Gregory for my soul.[4]

To Margaret Pelter[5] a quarter of barley of the great measure (*mag' mensura*); to Margaret Whepsted[6] 4 bushels of barley of the same measure; to William my son a quarter of barley of the same measure, and a calf.

To Marion my wife, for the whole of her life, my two messuages in Bury St Edmunds; and after her decease they to remain to William my son and his heirs for ever. To Marion a tenement called 'Goodales' in Brettenham, for all her life, except a chamber with the solar next to the street, in the use of my son Nicholas; and after Marion's decease, the whole tenement to remain to Nicholas my son and his heirs for ever.

To John my son[7] 5 acres of land, lying in two pieces, one contains 2 acres and lies in 'Rowlye', and the other 3 acres formerly John Folke's, [*to hold*] to him and his heirs for ever.

Marion my wife to have the use and occupation (*menuracionem*) of the whole tenement, formerly my father Walter Whepsted's, until the feast of St Michael next, for the removal and carting away of the corn growing there, and her other goods there. Any residue there may be of all my goods, after my debts have been completely paid, to Marion my wife, John Sennow of Thorpe Morieux ('Thorppmorieux') and Nicholas my son, execs.

Proved at Lavenham, 14 October 1468. Admon to Marion and Nicholas, execs. Power reserved to John Sennow, the other co-exec, when he comes.

1   Probably related to John Wepsted of Brettenham, no. 298 above.
2   Executor of no. 298.
3   See note to no. 11.
4   See note to no. 1.
5   Legatee of no. 298.
6   Margaret Whepsted the elder was a legatee of no. 298.
7   ?John Whepsted the younger, legatee of no. 298 above.

323. THOMAS KEBENHAM of WORTHAM,[1] 6 July 1468

['Kepenham' *in margin*] [*Commendation*: to God &c; *no burial directions*]; to the high altar of the said church for my tithes forgotten 2s; to the gild of the Holy Trinity in the said town[2] 3s 4d; to the said church of Wortham a quarter of malt; to Roydon ('Reydon') [*Norfolk*] church[3] 4 bushels of malt; to Palgrave church 4 bushels of malt; to Hinderclay ('Hyndircle') church 4 bushels of malt; to Garboldisham ('Garblysham') [*Norfolk*] church 4 bushels of malt.

To the Austin Friars of Thetford 10s; to the Friars Minor of Babwell 10s.[4]

I wish to have a 'le certeyn' in the church of Wortham, lasting for two years; to a suitable chaplain to celebrate in the church of Wortham for half a year, 4 marks.

To a man going to Rome for my soul and the souls of my benefactors 8 marks.[5]

To each of my godsons and goddaughters a bushel of malt.

To Richard my son all my lands and tenements in Wortham, on condition that he fulfils my will (*sub condicionem quod satisfac' voluntate'*), except, [*that is*], a tenement with a pightle and 5 roods of land belonging to it, which I wish Richard's mother to have, [*together with*] 20s for the term of her life, if Richard and his mother cannot agree under one roof (*in una domo*).

Residue of [*my*] goods to Richard my son and Walter Smalbergh, to dispose out of it &c[*sic*].

Execs: Richard my son and Walter Smalbergh.

Proved at Burgate, 5 October 1468. Admon to execs.

1   Executor (as 'Kepenham') of William Tubby of Wortham, will pr. November 1454 (SROB, Baldwyne 231; Pt I, no. 1164).
2   Walter Crane of Wortham (SROB, Baldwyne 280; Pt I, no. 1372) and Beatrice, widow of John Wrygh the elder, of Wortham (SROB, Baldwyne 291; Pt I, no. 1422) both made modest bequests to the gild of the Holy Trinity.
3   Dedicated to St Remigius. See note to no. 769 below.
4   For the friars see notes to nos 1 (Babwell) and 69 (Thetford).
5   A relatively generous bequest for a pilgrimage to Rome compared with other testators in Part II.

[fol. 407v]

324. HENRY MUSKETT of HAUGHLEY ('Haghley'),[1] 4 December 1466

[*Commendation*: to God &c; *no burial directions*]; to the high altar of the said church, for tithes forgotten, 3s 4d.

To the friars of Babwell for a trental of St Gregory 10s.[2]

To William Parker the younger a ewe.

To William Muskett a lamb; to John Muskett my son a large pan of 'le brazs' and a violet gown; to Ed' Muskett my son a green gown.

To Alice my wife all the utensils belonging to my house (*hospiciu'*) and all my goods and chattels, both live and dead, except one horse.

Residue of all my goods to my execs, Alice my wife, John Muskett my son and Thomas Muskett.

Supervisor: Roger Bell.

Proved at Haughley, 27 October 1468. Admon to execs.

1   Executor of Thomas Cobbe of Shelland, will pr. January 1457/58 (SROB, Baldwyne 199; Pt I, no. 977).
2   See note to no. 1.

325. JOHN WAREYN of STOWMARKET, 12 September 1468

[*No burial directions*]; to the high altar of the church of St Peter 12d; to the chaplain of the Blessed Mary there 6d.

Christian my wife to have one part of my tenement with my garden, next to the highway, for term of her life, with all my ostilments, apart from those relating to my craft; if Christian gets to the age when she can no longer work [*to obtain*] her food (*vict'*) then I wish that part of my tenement be sold [*to provide*] her [*with*] sustenance (*vict'*); Christian to have ingress and egress to [*and from*] the bakehouse as often as she pleases, without hindrance of anyone.

John my son to have the other part of my tenement, to him and his heirs.

Executrix: Christian my wife.

Supervisor: Robert Myles.

Proved at Stowmarket, 10 November 1468. Admon to executrix.

326. JOHN POTYER the elder of BURES ST MARY, 18 March 1467/68

Of Bures St Mary in Essex[*sic*]; dated 15 Kalends April; [*commendation*: to God &c; *no burial directions*]; to the high altar, for tithes forgotten, 3s 4d; to the fraternity of St John the Baptist called the gild 6s 8d;[1] to the use (*opus*) of the bells 6s 8d; to each chaplain of the same church, if present at my funeral offices, 4d; to each clerk 2d; to the beadle (*bedello*) 1d.

Residue of all my goods to John Potyer my son and Laurence my son, execs.

Proved at Sudbury, 16 November 1468. Admon to Laurence, exec. Power reserved to the other co-exec when he comes.

> [1]   The gild of St John the Baptist at Bures St Mary also received bequests from Robert Podeney (no. 55) and William Smyth (no. 658).

[fol. 408]
327. JOHN SMYTH the elder of BOTESDALE ('Botysdale') [in REDGRAVE], 1 June 1462

[*Will only*]

As for (*de*) my lands and tenements, John Smyth my son and Margaret his wife to have my messuage in which I live, in Botesdale, with 11 acres of land in three pieces, in the field called 'Botysdale Felde', and a large meadow called 'Breggemedew', to hold to them, John and Margaret, and their heirs, provided always that their heirs do not, in any way, sell or alienate the messuage with the lands and meadow, or any parcel of it; if John and Margaret should die without heirs, then the messuage, with the lands and meadow, to be sold by my execs and the money from the sale to be disposed in pious uses: firstly, to a suitable chaplain to celebrate in the chapel of St Botolph of Botesdale[1] for seven years; [*secondly*] to the reparation of the same chapel 20s; and the residue of the money from the sale to be disposed in the church and chancel of All Saints, Redgrave, in necessaries where most needed, and to the poor, according to the discretion of the execs doing the selling.

Matilda my wife to have my messuage called 'Randolffe', in Rickinghall ('Rykynghale') Inferior, with 16 acres of land in the field of the said Rickinghall, and an enclosure called 'Horsmere', to hold to her and her heirs for ever; Matilda to have of John my son and Margaret his wife 26s 8d annually during the term of her life, and 2 gallons of best ale and a gallon of small ale (*tenuis cervisie*) at each brewing, during the term of her life; should the said messuage be sold, then I wish John my son and Margaret his wife to have it before anyone else wishing to buy it, and for a sum £10 within the price.

Witnesses: John Martyn, Stephen Mersheoner, Ed[*mund*] Subborn,[2] Richard Crane and others.

Proved at Fornham St Martin, 9 May 1468. Admon to execs.

[*See no. 348 below for the testament relating to this will.*]

¹   See note to no. 15.
²   See note to no. 308.

328. JOAN FACON of EDWARDSTONE ('Edwardeston'), 11 July 1468

[*probate only*]

Proved at Fornham [*St Martin*]. Admon to William Facon, exec. Because of an insufficiency of goods, William was dismissed [*from taking further action*] and acquitted.

[fol. 408v]
329. PETER DROWGTH of FELSHAM, 16 May 1465

Dated at Felsham; [*commendation*: to God &c]; to be buried in the churchyard of Felsham church; to the high altar of the said church, for tithes forgotten, &c[*sic*] 12d.

To Margaret my daughter 26s 8d; to Alice my daughter 26s 8d.

A suitable priest to celebrate after my death in the church of St Peter of Felsham, for my soul and all my benefactors' souls, for a year.

After my death, Joan my wife¹ to have my tenement called 'Starlynges' in Felsham, [*to her and*] her heirs for ever; Joan also to have, after my death, all my ostilments in my house.

Joan my wife to be my faithful attorney.

Residue of all my goods to the disposition of my executrix, to dispose for me and all my benefactors in alms and deeds of charity, as she sees best &c[*sic*].

Proved at Felsham, 27 May 1468. Admon to executrix.

¹   Will (as 'Drowte'), no. 647 below.

330. WILLIAM JUSTICE of WITHERSFIELD ('Wetheresfeld'), 19 June 1468

[*Commendation*: to God &c]; to be buried in the churchyard of Withersfield church; to the high altar of the same church 12d.

4 acres of my arable land in 'Fermebetfeld', one head abutting on 'le Capels medewe', to be sold by my execs, and half of the money from it to be disposed for a 'le stok', that is, of cows, and with the income (*increment'*) from the same 'le stokke' a light of a wax candle to be provided before the image of the Blessed Mary in the chapel in the same church, for ever; and the other half of the money from the 4 acres to remain to Agnes my wife, during her lifetime, if possible (*si poterit fieri*), and after her decease that part of the money to remain to the sepulchre light of Withersfield church, [*in the same way*] as above (*supradict'*).

Agnes my wife to have my tenement in which I live, with a croft adjacent to it, during her lifetime; and after her decease the tenement with the croft to be sold by my execs and the money from them to be distributed among my children then living and in greatest need. If all my children should die, then the money from the sale to be disposed in pious uses for my soul and the souls of all my benefactors, and for those for whom I am most bound to pray.

To Agnes all the ostilments and utensils belonging to my house to her own use, doing with them freely as she wishes; to Agnes a cow.

To Eleanor my daughter a mattress [*and*] a blanket.

To John Justice my brother my best gown.

To John Pecok my blue gown.

To the torches of the said church 4d, and more if possible.

Residue of all my goods to my execs, to dispose for my soul and the souls of all my benefactors.

Execs: Robert Wiburgh and the above-mentioned John Justice, to see my will faithfully executed and implemented.

Agnes my wife to keep [*my*] anniversary day during her lifetime.

Proved at Haverhill, 20 June 1468. Admon to execs.

[fol. 409]

331. WILLIAM MAWDYON of BOXFORD,[1] 6 August 1468

[*Commendation*: to God &c; *no burial directions*]; to the high altar of the same church, for tithes forgotten, 20d; to the high altar of Polstead 12d; to each priest at my obsequies 4d; to each older clerk (*maiori clerico*) 2d; to each young clerk (*clericulo*) 1d; to the fabric of the new porch (*porticus*) of Boxford 6s 8d;[2] to the church of Polstead ('Polstede') 6s 8d; for a secular priest to celebrate in Boxford church for my soul and the souls of my parents, for a whole year, £6.

To Margaret Mawdyon my sister 5 marks; to Petronilla Ace my sister 40s; to Alice Hasylwode a lamb; to each of my godsons and goddaughters a lamb; to each of my servants, male and female, a lamb; to the aforesaid Margaret Mawdion my sister a heifer.

To John Ace my two-coloured (*bipartit' coloris*) gown; to Roger Nell my best hood; to John Benhale my best gown.

To Isabel my wife all the utensils of my house, for her own free use, and half my cattle (*catallorum*) and goods, such as grain, and the rest of the animals, after the above-recited legacies have been fully disposed; to Isabel, after my death, my capital tenement in 'Whigtstrete', for term of her life; and after her death the tenement to be sold by my execs then alive and disposed as follows: to a new aisle ('le ele') in Boxford church to be newly built, £6 13s 4d,[3] and the remainder, if any there be, to be disposed in the same church and town according to the decision (*arbitriu'*) of my execs.

To the fraternity of the gild of the Holy Trinity of Boxford[4] a parcel of arable land in the field called 'Sowthfeld', next to the land of John Fawkon and John Pratt, for ever.

To the sustentation and augmentation of a lamp burning before the crucifix in Boxford church, a parcel of arable land in the aforesaid field, next to the land of John Marchall, for ever.

To the sustentation and augmentation of the light before the image of the Blessed Mary on the north side, in Boxford church, a parcel of arable land in the same field, called 'Loverownys Wente', for ever.

Residue of all my goods to the disposition of my execs, they to have God before their eyes in the execution of this [*testament*].

Execs: Thomas Pursere, clerk,[5] Isabel Mawdyon my wife, John Bogays and Margaret Mawdyon my sister; to Thomas Pursere and John Bogays 10s each.

Seal appended.

Witnesses: Thomas Bullok, Thomas Baker, Robert Betrich and many others.

Proved at Sudbury, 27 September 1468. Admon to execs.

[*This whole testament and probate have been struck through and* Whether this testament has been registered within? (*quere istud test' infra regestratu'*) *entered in margin; no other version has survived.*]

1   Executor of Robert Dyster of Boxford, painter, will pr. February 1442/43 (SROB, Baldwyne 58; Pt I, no. 296).
2   See no. 247 for notes concerning the new porch; see also nos 332 and 440.
3   Robert Wasschsher also made a bequest to the work of 'le Ele' to be newly built there (no. 440).
4   John Cowper also beqeathed land to the gild of the Holy Trinity, Boxford (no. 247 above). This gild, together with those of St Peter, St John and St Christopher, was still in existence at Boxford in 1522 (*PSIA*, xxiii, p.52).
5   See note to no. 117 and also no. 247.

[fol. 409v]

332. THOMAS BOCKYNG the elder of BOXFORD, 12 March 1465/66

['Bokkyng' *in margin*] [*Commendation to* God &c; *no burial directions*]; to the high altar of the same church, for my tithes forgotten, 20d; to the fabric of the new porch of the said church 20d.[1]

Residue of all my goods and chattels to Joan my wife, after my legacies and debts have been fully paid.

Joan to have, after my decease, my tenement in the town of Boxford, in the street called 'Stonestrett', for term of her life; and after her death the tenement to be sold by my execs and co-feoffees then living, and the money from it to be distributed in this way: to William Bockyng my son 13s 4d; to Thomas Bockyng my son 13s 4d; to Margaret my daughter 13s 4d; to Joan Bockyng my daughter 13s 4d; if any of my sons and daughters should die before my wife, their legacies to be equally divided amongst my surviving children (*filios*).

My faithful execs: Joan my wife and William Karre of Boxted ('Boxstede').

Witnesses: Thomas Moore, William Bocher, John Bockyng and others.

Proved at Sudbury, 27 September 1468. Admon to execs.

1   See no. 247 for notes concerning the new porch; see also nos 331 and 440.

333. AGNES COO of STANTON, 4 October 1468 [*nuncupative*]

Lately (*nuper*) [*sic*] the wife of John Coo;[1] her body to burial in the churchyard of the church of All Saints of Stanton.

Her tenement, purchased by Thomas Yonge, her former husband and herself, to be sold and the money from it primarily [*to go*] to paying fully the debts of Thomas and herself.

For a trental to be celebrated by (*cu'*) the friars of the house of Babwell ('Badwell'), 10s.[2]

To Agnes her daughter 20s; to Agnes a copper (*erea'*) pot, a brass pan and jug (*urciolu'*), which were William Alsey's; to Agnes a sanguine-coloured gown and a complete bed.

To Joan Hornekek her daughter 6s 8d.

For a suitable priest to celebrate for a whole year in the church of All Saints, Stanton, 8 marks.

John Coo to have, for term of his life, a long house (*una' longa' domu'*)[3] with ?two chambers, by the churchyard of the church of All Saints.

Exec: John Coo her husband, to dispose for her soul, as he sees best to please God.

Witnesses: Sir Edmund Bene, rector of the same church,[4] and John Hervy and others. Proved at Fornham [*St*] Martin, 17 February 1468/69. Admon to exec.

[1]   Since she appointed her husband John Coo her executor, 'lately' presumably means that they had married recently; previously she had been married to Thomas Yonge.
[2]   See note to no. 1.
[3]   Probably not a 'long house' in the technical sense; perhaps a house that was longer than most.
[4]   Sir Edmund Bene was rector of both medieties (see Glossary) of the living of Stanton All Saints; he was appointed in 1460 in succession to John Rollecrosse and resigned the living in 1483 (Tanner, p.1215); will pr. November 1488 (NRO, NCC 13 Typpes); see also nos 566, 666 and 680.

[fol. 410]

[*Fol. 410 begins with an attempt at no. 334 which contains errors and omissions, the whole of which has been struck through; the corrected version then follows.*]

334. WILLIAM WESTBROME of WETHERDEN ('Wedyrden'), 1461

[*No day or month given in date*]; my body to be buried in the churchyard of the church of the Blessed Mary in Wetherden; to the high altar of the same church, for my tithes forgotten or underpaid, for the health of my soul, 12d; to the emendation of the same church 6s 8d.

To the friars of Babwell, for a trental, 10s.[1]

To John Westbrom my godson 12d; to William Westbrom my godson 12d; to John Purch my godson 12d; to William Marleton my godson 12d; to Thomas Yngham my godson 12d; to Anne Dyere of Rattlesden ('Ratyllysden') my goddaughter 12d; to Anne Westbrom my goddaughter 12d; to William Clerk my godson 12d.

To John Westbrom my son all those lands and tenements, rents and services, meadows, pastures and feedings, which I have at present in the towns of Wetherden and Ashfield ('Asschfeld'), together with all my goods and chattels, wherever they may be, except one piece of meadow, to hold to the said John and his heirs, for ever; except the previously mentioned meadow, which John Westbrom my son shall occupy for term of his life, on condition that he keeps the anniversary day of the said William and Joan his wife during the whole of his life, each year giving, on that day, 13d to 13 of the poor; after the decease of John Westbrom, the meadow to remain to the use of the church of Wetherden conditionally, according to a deed containing the condition, made the Thursday after the feast of the Purification of the Blessed Mary, 29 Henry VI [*4 February 1450/51*].

Exec: John Westbrom, my son.

Supervisors: John Bell and Thomas Moor, to whom 20d each, they to dispose for my soul as seems most expedient.

Proved at Bury, 20 June 1469. Admon to exec.

[1]   See note to no. 1.

[fol. 410v]

335. ADAM PYDENALE of OUSDEN ('Ovysden'), 7 November 1468

Dated at Ousden in the diocese of Norwich; [*commendation*: to God &c]; to be buried in the churchyard of the parish church of St Peter of Ousden; to the high altar there, for tithes and other [*dues*] (*al'*) forgotten, 6d.

Residue of all my goods to the disposition of Richard Spencer, Richard Denham and Richard Frost of Ousden, execs.

[*Will*]

I will that all faithful Christians and anyone who has estate or power, by gift and feoffment, by right or inheritance, of and in all my lands and tenements, meadows, pastures, feedings, woods and hedges (*sepibus*) in the town and fields of Ousden or elsewhere, grant feoffment to or enfeoff the said Richard Spenser, Richard Frost and Richard Denham; they, or one of them, to pay [*my*] debts and dispose for the health of my soul, my parents', friends' and benefactors' [*souls*] with the sum received for the lands and tenements sold, where most needed (*in magis necessar'*) in the said church and in the emendation of ways in the said town, in the best way they can to please God and profit our souls.

Proved at Fornham [*St*] Martin, on the penultimate [*27*] day of February 1468/69. Admon to execs. Power reserved to Richard Denham when he comes.

336. ALICE CLERK of DRINKSTONE ('Drynkston'), 25 July 1468

[*Will*]

Formerly the wife of John Paton;[1] dated Monday after the feast of St Margaret the Virgin.

Thomas Paton my son to have my whole tenement in Drinkstone, formerly my late husband John Paton's, to hold to him and his heirs, for ever, on condition that he pays out of it to John Clerk, the son of Richard Clerk of Preston, £13 in money, in the 13 years following a period of two years from this present date, by equal portions, at the feast of St Margaret the Virgin, and at the feast of St Margaret the Virgin next following that, 6s 8d.[2]

The same John Clerk to distribute the money in this way: to John Clerk 20s; to Joan my daughter 20s; to George my son 20s; to Margaret my daughter 20s; to John my son 20s; to Thomas my son 20s; to the two children (*pueris*) of Thomas my son 20s if they live, and if not, the said Thomas to have the 20s; to Drinkstone church 40s; to Preston church 6s 8d; to my godson in Preston 6s 8d; to my godson in Drinkstone 6s 8d; to Richard Clerk my husband 26s 8d, if need requires it (*si necessitas id deposcat*).

To Drinkstone church 10s which Robert Gerveys owes me, and wax to be got with it (*inde cereus habeatur*).

Also to John Clerk 6s 6d, which the same Robert Gerveys owes me.

Exec: John Clerk.

Proved at Cockfield ('Cokefeld'), 7 February 1468/69. Admon to exec.

1   Will, no. 95 above.
2   The timing of the payment of the £13 to John Clerk is unclear, to say the least.

[fol. 411]

337. THOMAS COLMAN of THORNDON,[1] 10 September 1469

My body to the Christian burial of Thorndon; to the high altar of Thorndon, for my tithes forgotten, 8d; to the reparation of the said church 4 bushels (*modios*) of malt; to the gild of the Holy Trinity of Thorndon 4 bushels of barley;[2] to the reparation of Eye church 4 bushels of malt.

To the Friars Minor of Ipswich (*Gippi'*) 2s;[3] to the nuns of Redlingfield 2s.[4]

To Juliana my wife my built-up (*edificat'*) tenement called 'Knollys' in Thorndon, for term of her life; and after her decease Richard my son to have it to him and his heirs; if he should die without heirs then the tenement to be sold by the disposition of my execs, or by Richard's execs, and the money from it to be disposed [*to the paying*] of all my debts and for the souls of my friends and all my benefactors now in purgatory.[5] To Juliana all my chattels and utensils, and ostilments of my house.

My execs to receive all my debts and fully implement this my last will.

Residue of all my goods to my execs to sell, receive and dispose for the health of my soul and all my friends' and benefactors' [*souls*], as they see best to please God and profit my soul.

Execs: Juliana my wife, William Bisshop and John Colman of Thorndon; to each of them for their labour 40d.

Seal appended.

Proved ?at Westhorpe,[6] 22 November 1469. Admon to execs.

1   Witness of the will of Alice London of Thorndon, pr. July 1457 (SROB, Baldwyne 219; Pt I, no. 1090).

2   For other bequests to the gild of the Holy Trinity in Thorndon, see: John Mundeford of Rishangles (Pt I, no. 648), William Loudon of Thorndon (Pt I, no. 742), Thomas Pyrty of Thorndon (Pt I, no. 817) and John Taylour of Thorndon (no. 126 above).

3   See note to no. 1.

4   See note to no. 83.

5   The purpose of such prayers is rarely stated so explicitly: for souls 'now in purgatory'.

6   'Westhorpe' written in margin next to probate clause.

[fol. 411v]

338. JOHN COLDHAM of BARNINGHAM ('Bernyngham'),[1] 15 November 1469

Dated at Barningham; my body to Christian burial; to the high altar of Barningham church, for my tithes and offerings forgotten or underpaid and for the health of my soul, 3s 4d; to the parish chaplain of the said church 12d, and to the parish clerk of the same church 6d.

To the Friars Austin of Thetford 5s; to the Friars Preacher of Thetford 5s; to the nuns of the same town 10s.[2]

To the gild of the Holy Name of Jesus, held in Stanton, 6s 8d.[3]

To William Coote, clerk, 20s.

To a suitable chaplain, to celebrate divine service for my soul and the souls for whom I am bound, in Barningham church for a whole year, 8 marks.

John Myllere, chaplain,[4] to distribute 20s of my goods and chattels, in the city of Rome, in pious uses, for my soul and the souls of all my benefactors.[5]

The tabernacle of the Blessed Virgin Mary in the chancel of Barningham church to be made and completed out of my goods, according to a covenant lately made between myself and a man of Cotton, carver and painter ('kerver et peyntour').[6]

To Katherine my wife all the ostilments or utensils belonging to my house. To Katherine certain lands and tenements in the town and fields of Barningham, that is: my tenement with the croft adjacent in the street called 'Westrete',[7] next to the pightle and croft of Isabel Agas, 2 acres of land at 'Ferthynges', 3 acres of land at 'Bastardeshill', 3 acres of land at 'Stanton Weye',[8] 1 acre of land at the end of the same, and 5 acres of enclosed land at 'Alderbreche', to hold for term of her life, together with the profit of all the corn of [*?to*] the last year of her life (*ultimi anni vite sue*). After her decease all the said lands and tenements to remain wholly to John my son and his heirs, for ever, if he survives Katherine my wife; if he should die before Katherine, then after Katherine's death, all the lands and tenements to be sold by my execs for the best price possible and the money received to be disposed for my soul, Katherine's soul and for the souls for whom I am bound, in the celebration of masses, the emendation of Barningham church, relief of the poor and needy, and the emendation of muddy and dangerous ways.

To Margaret my daughter £10.

To Roger Coldham my brother a cow, 2 quarters of malt and 2 quarters of barley.

To Agnes my sister[9] a messuage, in which she lives, in the town of Woolpit ('Wolpet'), and also an acre of land [fol. 412] in the town of Barningham, at 'Ryngoldyshe-flond',[10] between land of John Ayssfeld on one side and land of John Grymsyk on the other, to hold to her and her heirs, for ever; to Agnes a cow.

To Robert Fermour my servant 20 ewes.

To Robert Myllere my son (*filio meo*) a ewe and 4 bushels of barley.

Residue of all my goods and chattels, corn, grain and animals, and all my lands and tenements to my execs, to sell, receive, dispose and distribute for my soul and the souls for whom I am bound, in the fulfilling of the legacies in this testament, payment of my debts, the celebration of masses and other pious deeds, as seems best to please God and profit the health of my soul. If anything remains after my legacies have been fulfilled and my debts paid and all else done, I wish it to remain wholly to the said Katherine and John my son, their heirs and execs for ever.

I require all my feoffees enfeoffed to my use of and in the said lands and tenements, or in any part thereof, to deliver the estate that they have according to the effect of this my testament and will, when duly required by my execs and supervisor.

Execs: Katherine my wife, John Myllere, chaplain, and John Sutton of Thetford; to each of John Myllere and John Sutton, for their labour, 6s 8d.

Supervisor: William Coote, clerk.[11]

I require that none of my execs do anything or administer any of my goods and chattels without the agreement of the others or without the authority of my supervisor.

Seal appended.

Proved at Ixworth, 12 December 1469. Admon to execs. Execs dismissed and acquitted, 18 June 1470.

[1] Son of John Coldham the elder of Barningham, will pr. March 1453/54 (SROB, Baldwyne 168; Pt I, no. 807); ?executor of John Meller the elder of Barningham, will pr. July 1460 (SROB, Baldwyne 251; Pt I, no. 1248).

[2] See notes to nos 68 and 69.

[3] The gild of the Holy Name of Jesus was in the parish of Stanton St John. In 1461 Walter Rollecros of Stanton had requested burial in the churchyard of St John the Baptist and bequeathed to the friars of the old House of Thetford the mass-pence from 'the gild called Jesus gild', will pr. November 1461 (SROB, Baldwyne 284; Pt I, no.1395).

[4] Sir John Myller, chaplain, witnessed the will of Adam Berweham of Barningham (no. 452).

[5] This bequest suggests that the chaplain was expected to go on a pilgrimage to Rome.

[6] The testator had organised the mechanics of the provision of this bequest in advance.

[7] Perhaps the tenement called 'Coldhamys' with the adjacent croft, which he had purchased from his father (Pt I, no. 807).

[8] His father John had bequeathed 3 acres of land in 'Stantonweye' to Margaret his wife for term of her life, and after her death to be sold, and the money distributed in pious uses.

9   According to her father's will she was named Agnes Myggys.
10 John Coldham the elder had requested his feoffees to enfeoff Agnes of and in an acre of land called 'Ryngaldys', for term of her life; after her decease it was to remain to William her son and his heirs.
11 William Coote was appointed rector of Barningham in February 1446/47 (Tanner, p.1191); he was also rector of Fornham All Saints; will pr. May 1475 (SROB, Hawlee 196).

[fol. 412v]
339. WILLIAM SCHEDDE of LAVENHAM,[1] 7 June 1469

To be buried in the churchyard of Lavenham church; to the high altar of the same church, for my tithes and offerings underpaid, 20s; to a suitable secular chaplain, a reasonable stipend to celebrate divine service in the said church, for 4 years immediately after my death.

To be distributed among 12 persons 12d each week, for 6 years immediately after my death.[2]

To the fraternity of the gild of the Holy Trinity of Lavenham £20, on condition that they buy enough lands, tenements or rents, within 8 years, to provide a priest to celebrate divine service for ever in the said church, for the souls of the brothers and sisters of the fraternity; otherwise the £20 to be disposed by my execs in deeds of charity for my soul and the souls for whom I am bound.[3]

I wish the alderman ('aledruman'), with his fraternity of the gild of the Holy Trinity of Lavenham, to have the gift and disposition of 6 houses for the poor in the town of Lavenham, for time without end.[4]

£10, and more if necessary, to buy land, meadow or rents, for providing 5 lights to burn on festival days at the time of divine service, before the great image of the crucifix in the said church, for ever.

To John Scchedd[sic] 10 marks and my tabard; to Agnes Schedd, daughter of the said John Schedd, 10 marks.

To Thomas Spryng, son of William Spryng, 40s; to Agnes Spryng, daughter of the said William Spryng,[5] 20s.

I wish the last payment of my debts to be paid, that is, of my house.

To William Spryng 5 marks.

To the friars of Babwell, for a trental, 10s; to the friars of Sudbury, for a trental, 10s; to the friars of Clare, for a trental, 10s.[6]

To the emendation of the highway between the towns of Boxford and Lavenham, 4 marks.

To Thomas Koone 20s.

To the reparation of Lavenham church 20s.

I wish to have a stone of marble ('le marbyl') engraved ('le gravyd') with my image (*persona*) and that of Margery my wife.

To Thomas Spryng the elder 20s; to Robert Ditton 20s.

Residue of my movable goods to my exec to dispose in deeds of charity for my soul and for the souls for whom I am bound, as he sees [best] to please God and be healthful for my soul.

Exec: Robert Ditton.

Supervisor: Thomas Spryng of Lavenham.[7]

Proved at Lavenham, 19 December 1469. Admon to exec.

1   Executor (as 'Shedde') of Agnes, widow of John Helys of Lavenham, will pr. 14 October 1441 (SROB, Baldwyne 31(a); Pt I, no. 172).
2   A sizeable bequest to the poor of Lavenham.
3   There were several gilds in Lavenham. In a similarly worded bequest, John Harry (no. 681 below) bequeathed 10 marks to the gild of the Holy Trinity of Lavenham on condition that the fraternity of the gild bought as much livelihood ('lyfflode') as would provide a chaplain to celebrate divine service in Lavenham church for the souls of the fraternity time without end. In his will, pr. October 1476, Roger Cryott, a wealthy clothier, left £20 towards funding a priest for the Trinity gild (SROB, Hervye 52). Gilds always had difficulty financing permanent clergy and no doubt urged their members to consider this cause in their wills.
4   An example of a local gild running six almshouses for the poor.
5   Members of the famous Spring family of Lavenham.
6   For the friars see notes to nos 1 (Babwell and Clare) and 11 (Sudbury).
7   Thomas Spring II, who died in 1486; see note to no. 190.

[fol. 413]

340. JOHN SEGER of TUDDENHAM ('Tudynham'), 9 February 1468/69

[*Commendation*: to God &c]; my body to Christian burial; to the high altar of the church of the aforesaid Tuddenham, for my tithes and offerings forgotten, 6s 8d; to the reparation and emendation of an image of the Blessed Virgin Mary in Tuddenham chancel, 12d; to the reparation of the same church 40d; to the high altar of Cowlinge ('Cowlynge') church 40d; to the reparation of the same church 13s 4d.

To Rose my wife all my ostilments and utensils belonging to my house at the day of my death, to her and her assigns for ever.

Residue of all my goods and chattels to the disposition of my execs, Rose my wife, John Legatt of Tuddenham, clerk,[1] William Lamberd of Cowlinge and John Chapman of Tuddenham; they well and truly to implement and execute my testament; to each of them for their labour whatever they see to be just and right.

Witnesses: Ed' Hekedoun and John Gadircolde.

Proved at Fornham [*St*] Martin, 15 February 1468/69. Admon to execs.

1   John Legat was rector of Tuddenham from 1448 to 1492 (Tanner, p.1288).

341. MARGARET WARDE of HAVERHILL ('Haverill'), 31 July 1469

[*probate only*]

Proved. Admon to Master Nicholas Sylvestre, exec.[1] Because of an insufficiency of goods of the deceased, the exec was acquitted.

1   Nicholas Sylvester was the incumbent of Haverhill from February 1461/2 to 1464 (Tanner, p.1237); he was then appointed to the living of Withersfield St Mary (Tanner, p.1255).

[fol. 413v]

342. JOHN ERYSWELL of ERISWELL ('Erywell'), 3 September 1469

[*Testament begins with an invocation to the Trinity*]; parishioner (*paroichanus*) of Eriswell; to be buried in the churchyard of the church of St Lawrence of Eriswell; to the high altar of the same church of St Lawrence, for tithes and offerings forgotten and for the health of my soul and Alice my wife's, 2 wethers (*multones*).

To each godson and goddaughter of mine and Alice my wife's, a lamb.

The tenement in which I live to Thomas Eryswell my son, to him and his heirs, and also all the utensils of my house, on condition that he keeps (*servet*) two beds in my house in which to provide hospitality for the vagrant poor (*recipiet j hospicio pauperes vagantes*), for my soul and Alice my wife's, as long as Thomas lives;[1] and Thomas to have, for the upkeep of those two beds, an acre of land in divers places in the field of Eriswell, that is, half an acre in (*super*) 'le Wrogbrad Wey' between land of the lady on each side, and the other half acre of land in 'Bolnhowfeld', between land of the lady on the east and bond land of John Burgonye on the west.

Agnes my daughter, married to Robert Roo of Wangford, to have my tenement called 'Edryches' after my decease; Robert Roo to have my best green gown.

The rest of my goods to the disposition of my execs, John Symonde of Mildenhall and Thomas Eryswell my son; supervisor: Sir William Levy, chaplain; to each of them for [*their*] labour 40d.

Residue of all my goods to my execs, to dispose them for my soul and Alice my wife's, my parents' and benefactors' and all the faithful departeds' [*souls*], as they will answer on the Day of Judgement before the High Judge.

Witnesses: Sir John Clakston, rector of Eriswell,[2] Thomas Bette, subdeacon, John Chylderston, John Symond, Ralph Hay and others.

Proved at Fornham [*St Martin*]. [*No more legible.*]

1   This is a very unusual bequest for hospitality to the vagrant poor: to receive his inheritance, the son was required to maintain two beds within his house, not for the local poor but for vagrants, this work of mercy being for the benefit of his parents' souls.

2   The date of John Claxton's appointment as rector of Eriswell is unknown; he was succeeded by Thomas Hylling in 1480 (Tanner, p.1269).

[fol. 414]
343. JOHN COBBE of GISLINGHAM ('Gyslyngham'), 21 August 1468

[*Commendation*: to God &c]; to be buried in the churchyard of Gislingham church; to the high altar for my tithes forgotten 12d; to the reparation of the said church 6s 8d.

To the reparation of the way leading to the church of the said town, 20d; to the reparation of the way from 'Reedbregge' 20d.

To the gild of St John the Baptist in Gislingham 3s 4d.[1]

To each of my godsons and goddaughters 4d.

For a trental of St Gregory, 10s; I wish to have a suitable chaplain to celebrate in Gislingham church for a whole year.

To Margaret my wife and John my son all my lands and tenements in Gislingham for term of Margaret's life; and after her decease John to have full possession of all the lands and tenements, to him and his heirs; if John should die without heirs, then all the lands and tenements to be sold by my execs and disposed for my soul and the souls of my parents and benefactors.

If Margaret should take another man in marriage (*accipere aliu' viru' in thoro mari'*), then she to have £10 in money out of the lands and tenements, and half of my movable goods, as live 'catall', that is, sheep, oxen and cows, pigs and others, with half the utensils in the house.

Margaret and John to well and truly provide for (*inveniant*) Christian Cobbe my mother for the term of her life, as such a woman ought to be (*prout decet tal' muliere*), out of the said lands and tenements.

To Margery and Margaret my daughters 10 marks; if one of them dies, then the part

201

of the deceased to remain to the survivor; if both should die before marriage, then I wish to have another suitable chaplain for a whole year with part of the 10 marks, and the other part [*to go*] to the reparation of the said church.

Residue of all my goods to my execs, to dispose for me and for the health of my soul &c[*sic*].

Execs: John Godard the elder, Thomas Cobbe and Margaret my wife; to each of John and Thomas, my execs, 6s 8d.

Proved at Burgate, 5 October 1468. Admon to execs.

¹ Henry Mansere (no. 476) and John Hervy (no. 800) also made bequests to the gild of St John the Baptist at Gislingham.

344. JOHN JOURE of COMBS ('Combes'), 14 June 1462

Dated Monday after the feast of St Barnabas the Apostle; [*commendation*: to God &c]; to be buried in the churchyard of Combs church; to the high altar of the said church 3s 4d; to a new candlebeam ('candilben'), to be made in the same church, 20d.

To Isabel my daughter a cow; to Alice my daughter a cow; to Margaret my daughter a cow.

Residue of all my goods and chattels to my execs, to dispose for my soul and the souls of [*my*] parents &c[*sic*], as shall seem to them best to the praise of God.

Execs: Alice my wife, John Bakke the elder and Simon Turnour, to dispose &c[*sic*].

[fol. 414v] [*Will, of same date*]

I wish my feoffees in all my lands and tenements, rents and services, in the towns of Combs, Badley ('Badele') and Battisford ('Batesford') to make, within half a year after my decease, sufficient estate in all the said lands and tenements, rents and services, to Alice my wife, to hold for the term of her life of the chief lords of those fees by due service and custom; and I wish them, within half a year of Alice's decease, to make sufficient estate in all the said lands and tenements, rents and services, to John my son, to hold to him and his heirs similarly, for ever; if John my son should die in Alice's lifetime, then I wish my feoffees to sell all the lands and tenements, rents and services, quickly after Alice's decease and dispose the money from them for my soul and the souls of Alice and [*my*] parents &c[*sic*].

Proved at Wetherden, 6 October 1468. Admon to Alice and John, execs. Power reserved to Simon Turnour, the other co-exec, when he comes and if &c[*sic*].

345. RICHARD WORLICHE *alias* FLECCHERE of MILDENHALL ('Mildenhale'), 7 May 1468

[*Will; written in third person*]

[*Commendation*: to God &c]; his body to Christian burial; to the high altar of Mildenhall church, for tithes forgotten &c[*sic*], 12d; to the reparation of the said church 20d.

Margery his wife to have his whole messuage for term of her life, and after her death the messuage to be sold by his execs and the money from it to be disposed in pious uses and in deeds of charity, according to the discretion of Thomas Cullyng and William Wurliche of Wickhambrook ('Wekhambrok'), for his soul and for the souls of Isolde and Agnes and Margery, his wives, and the souls of all his benefactors.

To Simon his son a brass pot; to Agnes his daughter another brass pot.

Residue of all his goods he gives to Margery his wife and Thomas Cullyng, to dispose &c[*sic*].

Execs: Margery, and Thomas Cullyng.

Supervisor: William Wurliche his brother.

Proved at Mildenhall, 3 June 1468. Admon to execs.

[fol. 415]

346. THOMAS HILL the elder of [*LONG*] MELFORD, 21 March 1467/68

['Hyll' *in margin*] Sick unto death (*languens in extremis*); [*commendation*: to God &c]; to be buried in the churchyard of the Holy Trinity of Melford; to the high altar of the same church, for [*my*] tithes forgotten and less than well paid (*minus bene solutis*) 20d.

To Agnes my wife all my bedding and ostilments of my house, 4 heifers (*uvenculas*) and 10 piglets (*porcellos*), and £10 in money.

John my son to have my messuage in Melford, formerly John Slaughter's, to hold to him and his heirs for ever; if John my son should die under the age of 21, then the messuage to be sold by my execs and the money from it to be disposed by them for my soul.

All my other lands and tenements in Melford and elsewhere to be sold by my execs and the money from them to be disposed for my soul and the souls &c[*sic*].

Residue of all my goods and chattels I leave to John Hyll the younger, my brother, and John Barker the elder, son of John Barker the elder of Melford, execs, to pay my debts and legacies and dispose for my soul.

Proved at Melford, 21 June 1468. Admon to execs.

347. RICHARD LOTKYN *alias* ROPER of MILDENHALL ('Mildenhale'),[1] 20 March 1463/64

[*Commendation*: to God &c]; to be buried in the churchyard of the church of the Blessed Mary of Mildenhall; to the high altar of the same, for tithes forgotten, 12d; to the fabric of the same church 3s 4d.

After my decease I wish all my feoffees to enfeoff Alice my wife of and in all those my lands and tenements in the town and fields of Mildenhall, for term of her life; after her death, the lands and tenements to be sold by my execs, or by Alice's execs, and the money from them to be distributed in deeds of charity, where my execs or hers see best to please God and profit my soul and hers.

Residue of all [*my*] goods I leave to Alice my wife for her own use.

Execs: Richard Aleyn, 'kerver', of Bury St Edmunds and John Lotkyn of West Stow ('Westow'), they to dispose for the health of my soul.

Witnesses: Alexander Wymark, John Scott of Mildenhall and others.

Proved at Fornham [*St*] Martin, 30 November 1468. Admon to John Lotkyn, exec. Power reserved to Richard Aleyn when he comes, if &c[*sic*].

---

[1] Executor of Robert Hynge of Mildenhall, probate January 1457/58 (SROB, Baldwyne 199; Pt I, no. 980).

[fol. 415v]

348. JOHN SMITH the elder of BOTESDALE ('Botysdale') [in REDGRAVE],
1 June 1462

Dated at Botesdale; [*commendation*: to God &c]; to be buried in the church of All Saints of Redgrave; to the high altar there, for my tithes forgotten, 6s 8d; to each chaplain present at my obsequies 4d; to the reparation of the church of Rickinghall Superior ('Over Rykynghale') 6s 8d; to the reparation of the church of Rickinghall Inferior ('Nether Rykynghale') 6s 8d; to the reparation of the church of Brundish ('Brundyssh') 13s 4d.

To the Friars Minor of Babwell 6s 8d; to the Friars Preachers of Thetford 6s 8d; to the Austin Friars of the same town 6s 8d.[1]

A suitable chaplain to celebrate for a whole year, and to go on pilgrimage to the Court of Rome[2] for the health of my soul.

To John Jurden my best gown and my best leather belt harnessed with silver; to Thomas Jurden his brother a gown and a leather belt harnessed with silver.

To Matilda my wife 3 feather beds (*plumalia*), 6 bed-covers, 3 pairs of blankets, 12 pairs of sheets, with the 'testeres, curteyns and selours'; to John my son and Margaret his wife all the other goods at present in the chambers; to Matilda my wife half of all my utensils in the bakery, store-room and kitchen, and the other half I leave to John my son and Margaret his wife.

My feoffees to make estate sufficient in law to John my son and Margaret his wife, when required by my execs, of my tenement in which I now live, according to the effect of my will; my feoffees also to make estate sufficient in law to Matilda my wife, of my tenement called 'Randolffes', according to my will.

Residue of all my goods I leave to my execs, to sell, receive and dispose for my soul and the souls of all the faithful departed, in deeds of charity, as they see best to please God and profit my soul.

Execs: Matilda my wife and Master William Starlyng, clerk.[3]

[*See no. 327 for the will and probate relating to this testament.*]

---

[1] For the friars see notes to nos 1 (Babwell), 68 (Preachers of Thetford) and 69 (Austin Friars).
[2] The Papal Curia within the Basilica of St Peter, or *Basilica Vaticana*.
[3] A man named William Starlyng was vicar of Mendlesham from 1439 to 1449 (Tanner, p.1306), leaving to become rector of Eriswell (Tanner p.1269); perhaps this is a different man.

[fol. 416]

349. JOHN BREON of LITTLE WALDINGFIELD ('Waldyngfeld Parva'),
'bocher', 20 November 1466

[*Commendation*: to God &c; *no burial directions*]; to the high altar of the church of the aforesaid Waldingfield, for my tithes forgotten &c[*sic*], 6s 8d; to the gild of St Lawrence of the same town 20s;[1] to the reparation of the porch (*vestibuli*) of the same church 6s 8d; to the reparation of the font of the same church 6s 8d;[2] to the making of the new doors (*hostiorum*) of the said church 13s 4d.[3]

To Margery my wife all the ostilments or utensils of my house and 20s in money.

Residue of all my goods and chattels to my execs, to dispose for the health of my soul in deeds of charity, as in the reparation of the said church and other deeds of piety.

Execs: Stephen Colman and Thomas Breon.

Supervisor: Richard Ryseng the younger.

Witnesses: John Dalton, vicar of Little Waldingfield,[4] William Heyward the younger, Agnes Colman and others.

Proved at Lavenham, 20 December 1468. Admon to Stephen Colman, exec. Power reserved to the other [*exec*] when he comes, if &c[*sic*].

[1]   William Eve also bequeathed 20s to the gild of St Lawrence in Little Waldingfield (no. 83 above).
[2]   The late fourteenth-century font at Little Waldingfield is now much defaced but four of the bowl panels are very interesting, depicting seated monks studying (Cautley, pp.49 and 361).
[3]   The west doors of the tower are fifteenth-century (Cautley, p.361); perhaps these are the 'new doors' mentioned here.
[4]   John Dalton was appointed vicar of Little Waldingfield in March 1435/36 (Tanner, p.1395); it is possible that he was there until 1473.

350. THOMAS FORTHE of COCKFIELD ('Cokefeld'),[1] 8 December 1468

[*Commendation*: to God &c]; my body to Christian burial; to the high altar of Cockfield church, for tithes forgotten &c[*sic*], 3s 4d; to the rector of Cockfield church my harnessed belt and 'le baslard', and my hat (*galiru'*) with the liripipe (*liripipio*), in English, 'typett'.[2]

A suitable chaplain to celebrate divine service for a whole year in Cockfield church, as quickly as possible after my death, taking for his salary a reasonable stipend.

To the friars of Babwell for a trental 10s;[3] to the emendation of the highway in the said town 3s 4d.

I leave 'le melhows' at 'Croosgrene' to Cockfield church for 20 years for the reparation of the bells of the church; and after those 20 years I leave 'le melhows' to Cockfield church for ever.

I wish the porch (*vestibulu'*) of the said church to be built at my own cost, out of my goods, for the stone and 'menys', on condition that the parishioners of the town will provide 'le tymber' for the work.[4]

Joan my wife to provide a sufficient light before the image of the Blessed Mary in the said church, as long as she lives.

My execs well and sufficiently to make [*up*] the lane leading from 'Seven le Asshes' to the church of the said town, where there shall be most need, to the value of 26s 8d, that is, 'caste and graveled'.

To Joan my wife my tenement in which I live, as I hold it in my lifetime, that is, with the arable land, meadows and pastures, for term of her life; after her death, I leave the tenement to my child as yet unborn, and, if a boy, he to hold it to him and his heirs for ever; if a girl, [*she to hold it*] to her and her heirs for ever, on condition that she provides a suitable chaplain to celebrate divine service in Cockfield church for a year, sometime within two years after Joan her mother's decease; if the child, whether male or female, dies before Joan my wife, then I wish that, after Joan's decease, the tenement be sold to the next of my kin (*proximuri' generac' mee*), and the money from it be disposed by my execs for my soul and the souls for whom I am bound.

My new tenement to be sold and the money from it to be [*disposed*] for my soul and for the souls for whom I am bound.

To Joan my wife 2 horses, 4 cows and 12 sheep, and sufficient of my grain for food for her and her household for a year, and for sowing the arable land of the said tenement.

To Marion Forthe my niece a 'le matrasse', a pair of sheets and a blanket, and, if she wishes, she to live with Joan my wife until she, Joan, marries; [fol. 416v] to Marion a cow at Edward Brynglofe's, or the value, 6s 8d, 4 sheep and 2 quarters of malt.

To Thomas my nephew my tenement at 'Stowys Hyll', on condition that he pays Ralph his brother 40s in the next two years; to the said Ralph a cow at the rectory of the said town, a 'le matrasse', a pair of sheets and a blanket; to Katherine his wife a kettle ('le chetell') holding a gallon, and a quarter of malt. To Thomas my nephew a brass pot, the best bar one, and 4 sheep; to the said Marion a kettle ('le chetell'). All the other ostilments, and all else belonging to my house I leave to Joan my wife. To Richard my brother my green gown, my fustian doublet and my cap (*piliu'*); to Agnes my sister 2 bushels (*modios*) of wheat and a quarter of malt; to John Brown my black gown and my red cap (*piliu'*); to Thomas my nephew my blue gown; to the aforesaid Ralph, my next gown.

I wish to have another chaplain to celebrate divine service for a whole year in the said church, for my soul and the souls for whom I am bound, as quickly as my execs can provide one.

Residue of my goods to the disposition of my execs, Joan Forthe my wife, Thomas Forthe and John Brown of Cockfield, they faithfully to execute this testament; but my goods are in no way to be administered in respect of my will without the agreement of all three execs; and if any one of them should contravene (*frangere*) my last will, he is to be dismissed, especially if it adversely affects (*injuria' fecerit erga*) my wife.

Supervisor: Laurence Parker of Alpheton ('Alffleton').[5]

Witnesses: Sir Robert Forthe, rector of Cockfield,[6] John ?Bere and John Turnour. Seal appended.

Proved at Lavenham, 20 December 1468. Admon to execs.

[1]   Executor of Simon Foorth of Cockfield, probate November 1449 (SROB, Baldwyne 141; Pt I, no. 675); executor of Thomas Parker of Thorpe Morieux, probate September 1453 (SROB, Baldwyne 160; Pt I, no. 773).

[2]   See Glossary.

[3]   See note to no. 1.

[4]   The porch at Cockfield is a large fifteenth-century structure with three massive (empty) niches.

[5]   Possibly the Lawrence Cooke *alias* Parker who used lands in Thorpe Morieux and Preston to endow a chantry in Lavenham church (V. B. Redstone, 'Suffolk Chantry Certificates', *PSIA*, xii (1904), pp.30–71).

[6]   Robert Forthe had been rector of Great Whelnetham from 1451 to 1455 (Tanner, p.1450); he was appointed rector of Cockfield in October 1455 (Tanner, p.1359); the date of his successor's appointment is unknown, but Forthe was clearly still in office in 1468; perhaps he was related to the testator; he was one of the executors of John Chenery the elder of Cockfield, will pr. July 1460 (SROB, Baldwyne 255; Pt I, no. 1260).

351. WILLIAM GODMAN of THORPE MORIEUX ('Thorppmorieux'), 14 November 1468

Dated the morrow of St Brice; [*commendation*: to God &c]; my body to Christian burial; to the high altar of the aforesaid Thorpe a white horse, by way of [*a*] principal (*nomine principal'*).

To my mother a cow and 12 sheep; to Elizabeth my sister 6 sheep; to my mother all the utensils belonging to my house.

To John Carter a heifer; to Agnes, daughter of John Carter, a bed-cover (*coopertor'*) and a [*set of*] red bedding (*supellectil'*); to Joan, daughter of Richard Thurmod, a blue gown with fur lining (*furrura*), with a [*set of*] red bedding; to John Carter a green gown and a fustian 'le doblett'; to Richard Baron a bullock.

To the image of the Blessed Mary, in the chapel in the churchyard of Thorpe Morieux, a pair of beads with a silver ring.[1]

Residue of all [*my*] goods to Joan Godman my mother, executrix.

[*No probate recorded.*]

> 1   As at Long Melford, it appears that the original Lady Chapel at Thorpe Morieux was also in the churchyard, rather than inside the church. See note to no. 436 and also Paine, 'The Building of Long Melford Church', p.15. For donations of jewellery to shrines, see note to no. 142.

[fol. 417]

352. AGNES BOGAYS of EDWARDSTONE ('Edwardeston') *iuxta* Boxford, widow, 12 February 1465/66

Relict of Thomas Bogays;[1] dominical letter [*of the year*] E;[2] to be buried in the chapel of Edwardstone parish church, next to my husband; to the high altar of the same church, for my tithes forgotten, in the emendation (*emendac'*) of my soul, 3s 4d.

To the convent of friars of Sudbury, for a trental of masses, 10s; to the convent of friars of Colchester (*Colcestre*), for a trental of masses, 10s;[3] to the reparation of the way in 'Cheteburghstrete' of Edwardstone 16s 8d; to the footpath (*semite*) leading to Edwardstone church 40s.

To Edwardstone parish church, to the new arch to be made (*ad nova' archam fabric'*), 40s; to the making of the image of the new cross, and for the painting of that cross and image, 12s.

To each godson of mine now alive 12d.

Residue of my goods to my execs, John my son, of Boxford, and William my son,[4] of Edwardstone.

Seal appended.

Witnesses: William Cros, Alan Wrythe, Thomas Deelyng and others.

Proved at Boxford, 18 March 1465/66. Admon to execs.

> 1   Probate October 1461 (SROB, Baldwyne 296; Pt I, no. 1455).
> 2   To determine the date of Easter it is necessary to know the sequence of the days of the week following paschal full moon, and for this purpose special tables were devised in early Christian times. There are 7 possible relationships of the days of the week to the calendar of the year, and the letters A to G were used to indicate the cycle of 7 days beginning at 1 January. The dominical letter for the year is the letter allocated, according to this system, to the first Sunday of the year (Cheney, *Handbook of Dates*, pp.8, 9).
> 3   For the friars see notes to nos 11 (Sudbury) and 38 (Colchester).
> 4   Executor of the will of his father, Thomas (see note above); executor of John Cowper 'at the Stone' (no. 247 above).

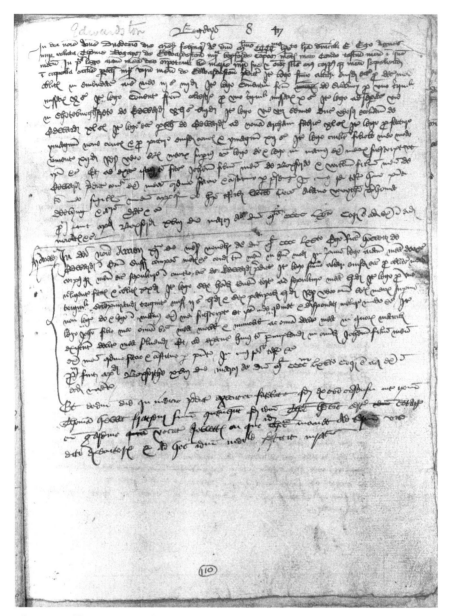

Plate 2. Wills nos 352 and 353 (fol. 417), the wills of Agnes Bogays of Edwardstone and Richard Howett of Edwardstone. *Photo: Geoff Cordy.*

208

353. RICHARD HOWETT of EDWARDSTONE ('Edwards'), 11 November 1465

[*Commendation*: to God &c]; to be buried in the churchyard of Edwardstone church; to the high altar of the same church, for my offerings negligently made and forgotten, 20d; to 6 men holding torches at my burial, 6d; for a trental of 30 masses to be celebrated, 2s 6d, and to 6 of the poor, 6d.

Residue of all my goods to my exec, to dispose in the best way &c[*sic*].

To John my son all my movable and unmovable goods and all my debts, in whosever hands they be, he to pay my debts and fulfil this testament in all ways (*in omnibus*). Exec: John my son.

Proved at Boxford ('Boxforthe'), 18 March 1465/66. Admon to exec.

[*Memorandum follows*]

On the same day, in the aforesaid judgement, the exec stated (*fatebat'*) that, by common consent between himself and Thomas Hewet his brother, Thomas should have a cottage, with a garden, called 'Howettes', in which Thomas lives, for the term of the said exec's life, and he swore on oath thereto.[1]

> 1   From the name of the cottage it is clear that this was a property that belonged to the family; here the brothers had had Thomas's occupation of it put on record.

[fol. 417v]

354. JOHN NEWRES the elder of BURES ('Burys') ST MARY, 26 February 1465/66

[*Commendation*: to God &c]; to be buried in the churchyard of All Saints of the aforesaid Bures.[1]

To Denise my wife 2 cows, such as she will choose; Denise to have 8 pieces of pewter (*electri*) and all the stock (*staur'*) that I have accumulated with her; Denise also to have a pair of sheets and a [*set of*] green bedding (*supellectil'*), and all the brewing vessels and the best trivet (*tripod'*); she to have 2 sows and a pig called 'le barwe'[2] and 2 piglets, and also all the geese and all the cocks and hens, capons, &c[*sic*]. Denise also to have 2 brass pots next to the best, a pair of shears (*forpic'*), in English, 'scheres', a turned chair (*una' cathedram versam*), a table and a pair of 'le trestells', a 'le fanne' and half the stock of 'le bacon' and a piece of beef (*pec' carn' bovinarum*), the rest being disposed to the poor; she also to have the grain growing on (*super*) the ground called 'le Ferthynghoke' and 2 cheese-moulds (*formulas*).

John my son to have a best brass pot, a large chest and a horse with the trappings (*phaleres*), in English, 'harneys', necessary for it; and he to have sufficient timber to repair his buildings (*domos*), and half the hay.

Robert my son to have the best pan, an old 'le materas' and a sanguine-coloured gown.

Joan my daughter to have a red hat (*piliu'*) which was her mother's, and a green gown.

Christine my daughter to have a [*set of*] white bedding (*supellectil'*) and a sheet.

Richard my son to have a red bullock (*boviculu'*), in English, 'a sterc'.

I wish John my son to have the boat (*navicula'*) with the leaps ('lepes')[3] belonging to the fishery.

Residue of all my goods to my execs, John Massangere of Bures and Richard Wareyn the younger of Halstead [*Essex*], to dispose for the health of my soul &c[*sic*].

Witnesses: Robert Wenden, John Barbour the elder, Thomas Facon, Richard Waspe, John Kyng, Geoffrey Lay and many others.
Proved at Sudbury, 19 March 1465/6. Admon to John Messangere, exec. Power reserved to Richard Wareyn when he comes &c[*sic*].

1   This reference to 'the church of All Saints' of the aforesaid Bures (St Mary) appears to be a
    scribal error: the parish church of Bures St Mary was dedicated to St Mary and the parish church
    of Mount Bures, over the river, in Essex, was dedicated to St John.
2   See Glossary.
3   See Glossary.

355. WILLIAM RAYSON [of ?KEDINGTON], 14 July 1465

['Reyson' *in margin*] [*No place given*; *year given as* Mccccxlv ?*in error for* Mcccclxv]; [*commendation*: to God &c; *no burial directions*]; to the high altar, for tithes forgotten and underpaid, 3 sheep (*biden'*); to the fabric of the church there, 3s 4d; to the emendation of the way in (*de*) Boyton Lane,[1] 3s 4d.
Residue of all my goods to Anne my wife, Thomas my son and Robert Reyson, execs.
Seal appended.
Proved at Kedington ('Kedyton'), 20 March 1465/66. Admon to execs.

1   Boyton Lane leading to Boyton End, 2 miles south-east of Kedington.

[fol. 418]
356. JOHN GODYNG of WITHERSFIELD ('Wetherysfeld'), 12 September 1468

['Goodyng' *in margin*] Dated at Withersfield in the diocese of Norwich; [*commendation*: to God &c]; to be buried in the churchyard of the church of the Blessed Mary of Withersfield.
To 40 of Christ's poor (*xlta Xi pauperibus*) on the day of my burial, 3s 4d, to be distributed among them.
To Joan my wife all my utensils.
Residue of all my goods to Joan my wife and John Barker of Withersfield, they to see to my funeral and pay my debts, and them I make execs.
Proved at Haverhill, 2 March 1468/69. Admon to execs.

357. JOHN BAYLE of Hanchet End ('Hanchache') in the parish of HAVERHILL,[1] 1 October 1468

['Bayly' *in margin*] [*Commendation*: to God &c]; to be buried in the churchyard of the upper (*superioris*) church of Haverhill;[2] to the high altar for tithes forgotten 8d; I bequeath a cow to provide a light, with the profits of the same, before the image of the crucifix in the same church for ever.
To the Friars Preachers of Sudbury 10s, to celebrate a trental for my soul.[3]
To John Bayle my son, all my lands and tenements, which I have in the town of Haverhill, in Suffolk, [*whether*] lying contiguously or diversely (*conti et dim iacen'*).
To Thomas Bayle, my ?next (*seq'*) son,[4] 3s 4d.
To Alice my wife all my other movable goods, for her upkeep (*exhibic'*).
Residue of all my goods to John Bayle and Thomas Bayle my sons, execs.

Proved at Haverhill, 2 March 1468/69. Admon to execs.

1   Hanchet End was a hamlet of Haverhill towards Withersfield. In his will, Thomas Baly, probably this testator's son, stated that Hanchet ('Hanchyche') was in the parish of Withersfield (no. 692).
2   See note to no. 14.
3   See note to no. 11.
4   ?Will no. 692 below. He appointed as his supervisor 'John Bayle the elder my brother': perhaps the other son of this testator here.

358. ROBERT GARLYNG of GREAT FINBOROUGH ('Fynberth Magna'), 12 January 1467/68

[*Commendation*: to God &c; *no burial directions*]; to the high altar of Finborough church, for my tithes forgotten, 6d.

To Joan my daughter a bed-cover, with a bed; to Joan all my ostilments and utensils; all my ostilments in the town of Eye to be equally divided between Joan my daughter and Robert Smyth, her son.

Whatever residue there be of all my goods I leave to the disposition of my execs, Joan, my beloved daughter, and Robert Smyth, to dispose for the health of my soul.
Proved at Stowmarket, 9 March 1468/69. Admon to execs.

[fol. 418v]
359. JOHN BROWSTER of BILDESTON,[1] 10 July 1468

Dated on the Feast of the Relics; [*commendation*: to God &c]; to be buried in the churchyard of the church of the Blessed Mary of Bildeston; my debts to be paid before all else; to the high altar of the said church, for omissions (*delictis*) and my offerings and tithes unpaid, 12d; to the emendation of the books of the said church 8d; to the emendation or reparation of 'le torchs', a pound of wax, price 6d.

To Ellen Braybeff my goddaughter, 20s in money; to Agnes my sister a cooking pot; to Robert Braybeff my blue gown; my best gown to John Braybeff, my brother-in-law (*fratri meo ex lege*).

My shop in the market to be sold and my wife to have 20s out of it, and the residue to be for paying my debts.
Executrix: Agnes my wife.[2]
Supervisor: John Screvener the elder.[3]
[*For probate, see no. 360.*]

1   In 1455, John Browster owed John Parle of Bildeston 5 marks for woollen cloth that he had purchased from the latter; this money was to be paid towards the new legend in Bildeston church (will of John Parle, SROB, Baldwyne 226; Pt I, no. 1125). John Browster was executor of Joan Aleyn of Bildeston, probate June 1455 (SROB, Baldwyne 228; Pt I, no. 1141).
2   See no. 360.
3   One of the executors of Agnes Browster (no. 360).

360. AGNES BROWSTER of BILDESTON, 12 December 1468 [*nuncupative*]

Late wife and executrix of the testament and last will of John Browster, late of Bildeston, deceased;[1] [*commendation*: to God &c]; her body to Christian burial; to Bildeston church a cloth [*for*] the housling towel (*una' ~~mappate~~* 'le huslyng towell').
John Screvener the elder[2] and Thomas Screvener of Bildeston, execs, to implement

and fulfil the testament and last will of John Browster, her deceased husband, and her own will.

Witnesses: Stephen Osmond, Thomas Cherche and others.

Proved, the testament of Agnes Browster of Bildeston, lately the wife and executrix of the testament of John Browster of the same, with the testament and last will of John Browster her deceased husband annexed, at Boxford, 14 March 1468/69. Admon of the goods of Agnes and John to John and Thomas the execs named in the testament of Agnes.

1. See no. 359 above.
2. Supervisor of the will of John Browster.

361. JOHN DOLETT [of WESTHORPE],[1] 18 January 1468/69

[*Commendation*: to God &c]; to be buried in the churchyard of the church of the Blessed Mary of Westhorpe; to the high altar of the said church, for my tithes and offerings underpaid, 40d; to the use of the said church 6s 8d.

To a suitable priest, to celebrate in Westhorpe church for a whole year, for my soul and my parents' [*souls*], 8 marks.

To the Austin Friars of Thetford 10s; to the friars of Babwell, 40d.[2]

To Finningham ('Fynyngham') church 40d and 4 bushels (*mod'*) of malt.

To the emendation of the 'sloughs' (*platerarum*) in the street of Westhorpe, 6s 8d.

To each of my godsons and goddaughters in the town of Westhorpe, 4d.

To Edward Dolet[*sic*] my son my tenement with all the land, pastures and leasows (*lesuris*), to him and his heirs for ever.

Residue of all my goods and chattels to the disposition of my execs, Edward Dolett my son and John Edgore of Stowmarket.

Proved at Botesdale, 22 March 1468/69. Admon to Edward Dolett, exec. Power reserved to John Edgore when he comes, if &c[*sic*].

1. Executor of Henry Coket of Westhorpe, probate February 1441/42 (SROB, Baldwyne 37; Pt I, no. 206).
2. For the friars see notes to nos 1 (Babwell) and 69 (Austin Friars of Thetford).

[fol. 419]

362. HENRY MONNYNGE of NORTON by WOOLPIT ('*iux*' Wolpet'), 3 February 1467/68

Of Norton by Woolpit in the diocese of Norwich; sick unto death (*languens in extremis*); to be buried in the churchyard of Norton church; to the high altar of the said church, for tithes and offerings underpaid, 6s 8d; to the light of the Blessed Virgin Mary in the same church, 13s 4d; to the fabric of the church of Great Ashfield ('Aisshfelde'), 6s 8d; to the fabric of Hunston ('Hustone') church, 6s 8d.

To the Friars Minor of Babwell ('Badwelle') 10s; to the Friars Preachers in Thetford ('Thetforthe') 10s;[1] to the prior and convent of the Blessed Virgin Mary of Ixworth, 20s.[2]

To the brethren and sisters of the gild of St Andrew the Apostle in Norton 2 bushels of wheat.[3]

To a cope, to be bought for celebrating the obsequies of the deceased (*exequira' martur'*[*sic*]) in Norton church, 6s 8d.

To the wives of John Cage and Nicholas Creme, 20s each.

To John Munyng my son, living in Hadleigh ('Hadley'), 5 marks.

To Christian my wife, for the term of her life, 6s 8d each year, to be received of Robert Munyng my son, or his attorneys; to Christian, [fol. 419v] for the term of her life, all my lands and tenements held according to the custom of the manors of 'Norton Hall' and 'Litilaugh';[4] after her decease, all the said lands and tenements to remain to Robert my son and his heirs, he providing Christian his mother with food and drink, woollen and linen, and all other necessaries of life during her lifetime, and then Robert to have the profit of all the said lands and tenements during her lifetime; to Christian my wife 2 cows and 20 ewes, kept (*sustent'*) for the use and profit of Christian for term of her life [*but*] at the cost and charge of Robert.

After the decease of Christian my wife, if they can gather (*recuperar'*) it from my debts, goods and chattels, there to be obtained a suitable chaplain to celebrate in Norton church for a year, for my soul and Christian's soul and the souls of all our benefactors, and all the faithful departed's [*souls*].

To each of [*my god*]sons and daughters, that is, John Cage, John Munyng of Hunston, John Monyngs of Hadleigh, Nicholas Creme and Robert Munyng and all the other children at whose baptism I have been present (*cum quibus interessem ad fontem baptismatis*) a ewe each.

To John Munynges the elder, of Norton, a sheep [*and*] a bushel of wheat.

To the emendation of the highway in 'Howstrete', if needed, 40s; to the emendation of the bridge called 'Nortonbrigge' one or two trees.[5]

To be distributed to each of the poor and poor children (*fil'*) present at my obsequies on my burial day, 1d.

To the aforesaid John Cage and John Edwarde of Norton, 6s 8d each, to execute and fulfil my last will.

Residue of all my goods to the disposition of John Cage and John Edwarde, my execs, firstly paying my debts, with full power of execution, according to their good discretion, in deeds of charity, as seems to them most expedient for my soul and all my benefactors' [*souls*] and to please God.

Seal appended.

Proved at Ixworth, 19 December 1468. Admon to execs.

1   For the friars see notes to nos 1 (Babwell) and 68 (Friars Preachers of Thetford).
2   See note to no. 69. In 1467, the prior of Ixworth was William Dense (*VCH Suffolk*, ii, pp.105–7).
3   There were also two gilds of St John and a gild of Corpus Christi in Norton at this time (see note to no. 743 below). The will of Walter Mannyng describes the collection of mass-pence on the death of a gild member (SROB, Baldwyne 80; Pt I, no. 373). He bequeathed 'to the rector of St Andrew, Norton, half of all the pence received from the brethren and sisters of the gilds of Corpus Christi and St Andrew in the church on the day of my burial, that is, of each brother and sister, according to the statutes of the said gilds, and the remaining half of the pence to the Friars Preachers in Thetford'. John Watyrnas of Norton bequeathed all the pence from the gild of St Andrew to the rector (SROB, Baldwyne 281; Pt I, no. 1379). In contrast to those bequests this testator, Henry Monnynge, bequeathed provisions to the gild's members.
4   See note to no. 209.
5   Norton Bridge was presuambly a wooden bridge.

[fol. 420]

363. JOHN BROKHOLE of [LONG] MELFORD,[1] 25 October 1467

[*nuncupative*]

Sick unto death; [*no commendation of soul or burial directions*]; to the new fabric of the said church, now begun,[2] 6s 8d; to the support (*exhibicionem*) of the annual chaplain (*cap' annual'*) celebrating the Jesus Mass (*missam de Jesu'*)[3] in the said church, 6s 8d.

To Rose his wife all his bedding and ostilments, and 10 marks which he had from Rose's friends with her marriage portion (*quas habuit de amicis dicte Rose cu' eius maritag'*).

Execs: Robert Hersete and John Smyth of Melford, to whom he bequeathed the residue of his goods and chattels, to pay his debts out of it and dispose in deeds of charity &c[*sic*].

Witnesses: Thomas Smyth, Lawrence Dowe, Roger Pondere and others.

Proved at Melford, 2 December 1467. Admon to execs.

1   ?Related to Thomas Brokhoole of Long Melford (no. 45); both men had an executor named John Smyth.
2   A significant bequest that marks the beginning of the dramatic rebuilding of Melford church. See Paine, 'The Building of Long Melford Church', p.10. Robert Sparow made two substantial bequests to the rebuilding; see nos 436 (testament) and 779 (testament and will).
3   See note to no. 45.

364. ROGER AGACE of BARDWELL ('Berdewell'), 10 October 1467

[*No commendation or burial directions*]; to the high altar of the said church 20d; to the high altar of Thurston ('Thruston') church 20d; to the fabric of the same church 6s 8d; a trental to be celebrated for my soul and the souls of my friends.

To Robert Agace my brother[1] a cloak and doublet, a pair of hose and a pair of shoes. To John my son all the utensils of my house, that is, the few small ones (*parva et pauca*) I left in my house at Thurston at the time of my leaving; to John 6s 8d at an appropriate time (*cum tempus oportunu' advenerit*).

Residue of all my goods to Roger Burden of Bardwell and Thomas Bullok of Thurston, execs.

Proved at Fornham [*St Martin*], 7 December 1467. Admon to execs.

1   Will, as Robert Agas of Thurston, no. 414 below.

[fol. 420v]

365. WILLIAM FOTOUR of RICKINGHALL INFERIOR ('Rykynghale Infer'),[1] 9 December 1468

Turning over in my mind that nothing is more certain [*than*] death and nothing is more uncertain [*than*] the hour of death; [*commendation*: to God &c]; to be buried in the churchyard of Rickinghall Inferior church; to the high altar of the said church, for tithes forgotten and not paid, 3s 4d; to the reparation of the same church 20s; to the reparation of Rickinghall Superior church 6s 8d.

To the common use of the gild of St Peter of Rickinghall Inferior 6s 8d;[2] to the gild of St Mary of Rickinghall Superior 3s 4d; to the gild of St John the Baptist of the said town 3s 4d.[3]

To the friars of Babwell 10s; to the Austin Friars of Thetford 10s; to the Friars Preachers of Thetford 10s.[4]

To Margaret my daughter, when she comes to marriage, 40s.

To Margaret Freyre my sister, of Coney Weston ('Conston'), 6s 8d and a coomb of malt and a bushel of rye.

To the reparation of a way called 'Pedderysweye' 20s, or the value of 20s in work on the said way.[5]

An honest chaplain to celebrate for my soul in the church of Rickinghall Inferior for a whole year, to whom 8 marks.

To Katherine my wife[6] my tenement lately purchased of William Olyver, with all the lands and tenements belonging to it, both free and bond and leased (*firm'*); also to Katherine a tenement in Rickinghall Superior, lately bought of John Bercher, to hold to her and her heirs for ever; to Katherine all the utensils of my house and all my chattels (*catalla*), on condition that she implements my will.

Residue of all my goods and all my debts to my execs, to pay my debts and dispose for my soul and the souls of my parents, as seems to them best to please God and profit the health of my soul.

Execs: Katherine Fotour my wife, John Osberne the elder and Thomas Ferdyng of the aforesaid Rickinghall; supervisor: Edmund Spark, clerk;[7] to each of them for their labour 6s 8d.

Proved at Fornham St Martin, 30 January 1468/69. Admon to execs. Seal of official appended.

[1] ?Executor (as 'Fotowr') of John Lane of Ixworth Thorpe, will pr. June 1442 (SROB, Baldwyne 18; Pt I, no. 101); executor of his father-in-law Henry Wroo of Rickinghall Superior, will pr. May 1461 (SROB, Baldwyne 273; Pt I, no. 1340).
[2] Henry Swanton of Botesdale also made a bequest to this gild (no. 376 below).
[3] The two gilds of St John the Baptist and the Blessed Mary of Rickinghall Superior are mentioned in the will of John Schepp, rector (SROB, Hervye 267; noted in *PSIA*, xxiii, p.70).
[4] For the friars see notes to nos 1 (Babwell), 68 (Friars Preachers of Thetford) and 69 (Austin Friars).
[5] 'Pedderysweye' is not necessarily the Peddars Way from Knettishall Heath to Holme-next-the-sea; other examples are known in East Anglia, as in Walsham le Willows.
[6] Daughter of Henry Wroo, who bequeathed her 3 acres of land in Rickinghall Superior, lying between the land of William Teroll and Thomas Hervy (see note above).
[7] See note to no. 194.

[fol. 421]

366. WILLIAM SWANTON of DEPDEN, 1468

[*No day or month given*] [*Commendation*: to God Almighty and the Blessed Virgin Mary]; to be buried in the said church.

To Walter my son 13s 4d; to John my son 13s 4d.

To the church of Depden, for its reparation, 13s 4d; to the friars of Babwell,[1] for a trental, 10s.

Residue of my goods to my execs, William Sparow of Chedburgh ('Chetbere') and Walter Swanton my son,[2] to dispose for the health of my soul; to each of whom, for their labour, 40d.

To Joan my wife[3] my whole tenement in Depden during her lifetime, if she does not take a husband, [*and after that*] my execs to sell it and dispose for the health of my soul; also to Joan my wife all [*my*] movable goods, with which to pay my debts.

Proved at Hawkeden ('Hawkdo'), 17 May 1469. Admon to execs.

1   See note to no. 1.
2   Executor of Joan Swanton (no. 685).
3   Will, no. 685.

367. NICHOLAS BASSE of RICKINGHALL INFERIOR ('Rykynghale Infer'), 1468

[*No day or month given*]; to be buried in the churchyard of the church of Ricking-hall Inferior; to the high altar of the same church, for [*my*] tithes not satisfactorily paid (*non satisfactis*) and forgotten, 6s 8d; to the reparation of the said church 20s. To Margaret Tynton my daughter 6s 8d.

To the friars of Babwell 5s; to the Austin Friars of Thetford 5s; to the Friars Preachers of Thetford 5s;[1] to the friars of the Blessed Mary of Ipswich ('Yeppyswych') 5s.[2]

To Agnes my wife all my utensils and all my goods, chattels and debts, on condition that she pays my debts and fulfils my will.

Execs: Agnes my wife and William Herte of Elmswell.[3]

Proved 6 June 1469. Admon to executrix.

1   For the friars see notes to nos 1 (Babwell), 68 (Friars Preachers of Thetford) and 69 (Austin Friars).
2   Probably the Dominican Friars of Ipswich, whose church and house were dedicated to St Mary (*VCH Suffolk*, ii, pp.122–3).
3   Will no. 519 below.

[fol. 421v]
368. MARGARET COKET of INGHAM, widow, 21 August 1467

Relict of Walter Coket, late of Ingham;[1] to be buried in Ingham church; to the high altar of Ingham 20s; my exec to dispose 20 marks about the church, tower or orna-ments of the same church, where seems to him best; to a suitable priest to celebrate for me in Ingham church for 6 years, 8 marks a year.

To each of [*my*] godsons and goddaughters, children of my brother John Parkyn of Ingham, 40d; to each of the daughters of Joan Coket of Timworth 6s 8d; to Agnes and Margaret Medue[2] all my sheep, of whatever kind or species they be; to each of my godsons or goddaughters, except those named above, 20d.

To Katherine my servant 40s and a black bed, except the celure and curtains.

To Isabel my sister 20s; to Isabel my daughter [*blank*].

My exec to dispose 20s to the church of Culford, where seems to him best.

Residue of all my goods to my exec, to sell and dispose for my soul and the soul of Walter Coket my late husband, and [*for*] the souls of all my deceased friends, in the celebration of masses and giving of alms, as he sees best to please God and profit my soul.

Exec: Walter Coket my son, to execute this my testament.

Seal appended.

Witnesses: Sir Walter Coket, rector of Ingham,[3] and others.

Proved at Fornham [*St Martin*], 13 June 1469. Admon to exec.

1   Will pr. April 1462 (SROB, Baldwyne 294; Pt I, no. 1441); it was later proved in the PCC in July 1464 (TNA, PCC 4 Godyn); Walter Coket described himself as a 'woolleman', that is, 'woolman', the 'middle man' between wool-producers and clothiers.

2   Daughters of Thomas Medwe of Great Livermere, goddaughters and legatees of Walter Coket (see note above).

3   ?Will of Walter Cokett, clerk of Ampton St Peter, pr. 1482 (NRO, NCC 124 A. Caston).

[fol. 422]

369. WILLIAM BRONDYSSH of FELSHAM,[1] 26 June 1469

Dated Monday after the feast of the Nativity of St John the Baptist; to be buried in the churchyard of the church of St Peter, Felsham.

All my goods to Thomas my son, to him and his assigns, for ever, he to pay all my funeral expenses; and he to pay 5 marks to Felsham church to buy a cover for the font, of the same form (*secundum formam*) [*as that*] of Rattlesden (*Ratlysden*) church;[2] otherwise Thomas to dispose [*it*] among the poor where there is greatest need, for my soul and my friends' [*souls*].

Exec: Thomas my son.

Seal appended.

Proved at Rattlesden, 18 July 1469. Admon to exec.

1   ?Executor (as 'Brundych') of John Rogyn of Rattlesden, will pr. January 1458/59 (SROB, Baldwyne 207; Pt I, no. 1031).

2   A good example of one parish deliberately copying another in the provision of ecclesiastical equipment. Neither of the font covers mentioned has survived but Cautley comments that at Felsham 'there is a fine and unusual 15C font' and at Rattlesden 'the font is a beautiful example of late 14C work' (Cautley, pp.284, 340).

370. WILLIAM AT LEE *alias* HURLEBATE of ASSINGTON, 14 June 1469

Dated at Assington, in the diocese of Norwich; sick in body; to be buried in Assington churchyard.

To John At Lee my son all my movables, to do with them freely as he wishes.

To the said John and Agnes his wife all those my lands and tenements, rents and services, in the town of Wissington ('Wyston'), to hold to them and their heirs male begotten between them (*de corporibus eorum ligittime inter eos procreatis*), for ever, of the chief lords of the fee, by due service and custom; if John should decease without heirs male, then all the lands and tenements, rents and services, to be sold, and the money from them to be distributed between the daughters of John and Agnes then alive, by equal portions; if they die without daughters, then the money received for the lands and tenements to be disposed on the highway from the heath (*bruer'*) called 'Levenheyheth' to the town of Nayland ('Neylonde') where most need is.

To Alice Prentys my daughter a sheep with a lamb.

Residue of all my goods and chattels to my execs, to pay my debts and dispose as above.

Execs: John At Lee *alias* Hurlebate and Agnes his wife.

Proved at Sudbury, 24 July 1469. Admon to execs.

[fol. 422v]

371. GEOFFREY COLCY of WOOLPIT ('Wolpet'), 7 July 1469

Dated Friday, the feast of the Translation of St Thomas the Martyr; my body to Christian burial; to the image of the Blessed Mary in the chapel there[1] a candle (*cereu'*) of wax weighing half a pound, to burn at the time of divine service.

To Christian my wife a messuage called 'Rychardys Place', in Woolpit, abutting on the highway to the west, and on the land of John Newman to the east, to hold to her and her heirs for ever; to Christian all my ostilments and utensils whatsoever (*quovismodo*) belonging to my house.

To John Colcy my son a tenement called 'Colcyes', at 'Wolpet Grene', to hold to him and his heirs for ever, provided that he behaves well and honestly towards his mother and my execs, and is willing to be governed by them; otherwise Christian to have the tenement for her whole lifetime.

To the said Christian a cow; to the said John my son another cow, if possible.

Residue of all my goods to my execs, to sell and dispose for my soul and the souls for whom I am bound, in celebrating masses and giving alms.

Execs: Christian my wife, John Reynold and John Colcy my son, they faithfully to implement this my testament.

Supervisors: John Berne and Thomas Berne.

Seal appended.

Witnesses: John Calfawe, William Waltere, Robert Steffe and others.

Proved at Fornham [*St Martin*], 7 August 1469. Admon to execs.

¹ See note to no. 142.

[fol. 423]

372. JOHN ELYS of STANTON,[1] 24 November 1469

['Elyis' *in margin*] To be buried in the churchyard of the church of All Saints, Stanton; to the high altar of the said church, for tithes forgotten and other defaults in offerings, 2s; to the emendation of the said church 20s.

To Friar John Lakenham of Babwell,[2] to celebrate divine service for a whole year, for my soul, the soul of Agnes my wife and for the souls of my benefactors, 6 marks.

To Robert my son and his heirs all those lands and tenements which were my father Thomas Elyis's, except that land previously sold by the said Thomas; to Robert my son and his heirs 3½ acres of land lying at 'Alyshege', which were Robert Aunger's; to the same Robert and his heirs a half-acre of land lying at 'Sowthhawe', 3 roods of land at 'Stonys', bought from John Clerke, an acre of land at 'Roschpath', bought from Simon Clerke, and 3 roods of land at 'Honecrofte', bought of divers men, that is, from Ralph Baldere and from the attorneys of Ed' Kechet.

To Margaret my daughter and her heirs a piece of land bought from Robert Bone-seriaunt and a piece of land bought from Nicholas Lystere, and an acre of land at 'Ryngolysmere', bought from Thomas Baldere.

To Isabel my daughter and her heirs 1½ acres of land at 'Ryngolysmere', bought of Nicholas Lyster.

An enclosure bought of Sir William Berdwell, knight,[3] an enclosure called 'Alecrofte' and 2 acres of land at 'Prowdysroode' to be sold, and the money from them to be disposed in paying my debts and legacies.

Residue of my goods to the disposition of Robert my son, John Taylyour and Simon Wyseman, execs, they to have God before their eyes and faithfully execute and fulfil this testament.

Seal appended.

Proved at Fornham St Martin, 2 December 1469. Admon to execs.

¹   Executor (as 'Helyis') of William Gardenere of Stanton, will pr. November 1449 (SROB, Bald-
     wyne 141; Pt I, no. 677).
²   See note to no. 1.
³   ?Sir William Berdwell, knight, of Bardwell, who made his will in 1434 (SROB, Osbern 211); see
     Copinger, *Manors of Suffolk*, i, p.264.

[fol. 423v]
373. JOHN DUKE of LITTLE SAXHAM ('Saxham Parva'), husbandman, 10 July 1469

Dated at Little Saxham; my body to Christian burial; to the high altar of the church of Little Saxham, for my tithes forgotten or underpaid, and for the health of my soul, 20d.

To Margaret my wife all my ostilments belonging to my house and my corn, grain (*blada, grana*) and animals of all kinds; to Margaret my tenement with a croft and an acre of land in the town of Little Saxham, to hold to her for term of her life; after her decease the tenement, croft and acre of land to be sold for the best price possible, and out of the money I leave to each of my sons, that is, Robert, John, Thomas, Richard and Ralph, 20d; the residue of the money from the sale to be disposed and distributed for my soul, Margaret's soul and the souls of all our benefactors, in deeds of charity.

Residue of all my goods and chattels to my execs, to sell, receive and dispose for my soul and the souls for whom I am bound, in the celebration of masses and other pious deeds, as seems best to please God and profit the health of my soul.

Execs: Margaret my wife and Ralph my son.

Seal appended.

Witnesses: Richard Oversooth, Walter Noble, Robert Ilger and others.

Proved at Fornham St Martin, 27 November 1469. Admon to execs.

[fol. 424]
374. ROBERT DUNCH the elder of MENDLESHAM ('Mendelesham'),¹ 14 July 1469

My body to Christian burial; to the high altar of Mendlesham church 3s 4d; to each priest there, present at my obsequies, 4d; to each clerk there, similarly present, 2d; to each boy, present there and surpliced, 1d; to each poor person present there 1d.

To Friar Lacy, my son, to celebrate a trental, 10s.

To each of my godsons a bushel of barley.

To Thwaite ('Thweyt') church 3s 4d; to Wetheringsett church 3s 4d; to Mickfield ('Mekefeld') church 3s 4d; to Stonham Parva church 3s 4d.

To the sons and daughters of William Dey 40s; to William Dey my best gown and my best doublet; to John, the son of the said William Dey, 40s; to the same John, and Thomas Thurston, my russet gown.

To Mendlesham church, for a vestment to be bought, with the advice (*per visum*) of my execs, with 20 marks which John Harlewyn owes for the tenement 'Bleantys'.

To the daughter of Robert Dunch of Ipswich (*Gippwic'*)² my second gown of violet.

To a suitable priest, to celebrate for my soul and the souls of my benefactors for a whole year in Mendlesham church, a competent stipend.

John my son to have all my lands and tenements, both free and bond, or extended (*aut per increment'*) land and tenements, in the town and fields of Mendlesham, to him and his heirs, except the tenements called 'Bramys' and 'Legates', and a close formerly Joan Benttysle's, which I assign to Margery my wife and her heirs, on condition that if John, or any of his heirs, wishes to sell the aforementioned lands and tenements, if any of the issue of Robert Dunch of Ipswich, brother of the said John, shall be able and willing to buy the lands and tenements, he to have preference before all others, if he is willing to pay what others are willing to pay.

To John my son all my carts and ploughs, with their harness and traces and all the necessaries belonging to the said carts and ploughs; to John 4 horses and also 'le choppe gere', with the appurtenances.³

Joan my daughter to have, at her marriage, 5 marks.

To Alice my daughter 5 quarters of barley.

To John my son a chest with the 'evidens'.⁴

[fol. 424v] My execs to have sufficient cheese for my thirty-day and obsequies, and the residue to be divided between my execs and my wife Margery.

I wish 2½ dozens of russet cloth (*ij docheyn et dimidiu' pannu' de russet*) to be divided by my execs between my sons and daughters and servants at their discretion (*per avisum dictorum executorum*).

To John my son an iron plate, a folding table, a 'coppebord', an almery, a hale, a hanging ewer and a pair of ?bowls ('bowgys').

Residue of all my utensils and ostilments to be divided by the discretion of Thomas Crowe, John Dunch my brother and Robert Smyth. And after they have divided them, my wife Margery to choose her part; the other part I leave to John my son, except that John shall have everything groundfast and nailfast (*fixa in argilla et clavis*); if any of the utensils and ostilments bequeathed to Margery remain after her death, I wish them to go to Alice and Joan my daughters after her death.

To Margery my wife 6 cows, 2 bullocks (*bovicul'*), 8 ewes, 3 pigs, a quarter of wheat, a quarter of malt, 4 jugers (*iuger'*) of wheat and as much of barley, and 2 jugers of peas and as much of oats, a 'doseyn de blanket' and 30lbs of wool, on condition that she does not, nor anyone in her name, trouble, vex or impede my execs after my decease in the execution of this my last will, nor claim any right in my lands and tenements assigned above, nor in any parcel of them; and then I wish her to have everything assigned to her above fully and peacefully; but if she in any way causes or produces dissension (*contrarium*) then she to have and enjoy nothing of all that is bequeathed to her above.

I wish Margery my wife to leave the place where I now live within 2 or 3 days at least (*ad minus*), immediately after my death.

Residue of all my goods and chattels, with my debts, to my execs, to sell, receive and dispose for the health of my soul and of all my friends' and benefactors' [*souls*], as they see best to please God and profit my soul; if my debts and chattels are not enough to implement this last will, then I wish John my son to fulfil it out of my goods assigned to him.

Execs: Thomas Crowe of Stonham Parva, John Dunch of Thornham Magna and John Dunch my son; to each of whom for their labour 13s 4d.

Seal appended.

Witnesses: Thomas Wylkeyns, vicar of Wickham [*Skeith*],⁵ Robert Smyth of Stoke [*Ash*], John ?Anty, John Maltyward, John Dunch, stainer ('steynour'),⁶ of Mendlesham and many others.

Proved at Mendlesham, *?*25 October 1469. Admon to execs.

1　Executor of Thomas Kynge of Mendlesham, will pr. September 1439 (SROB, Baldwyne 1; Pt I, no. 3); executor of Roger Metessharpp of Mendlesham, will pr. October 1457 (SROB, Baldwyne 191; Pt I, no. 932).
2　From a later bequest it is clear that Robert Dunch of Ipswich was the testator's son; the wording suggests that he had predeceased his father.
3　Given its context of carts, ploughs and horses, this bequest of the 'choppe gere' probably does not refer to the contents of a shop; perhaps it means 'head-gear' for the horses, that is, bits, bridles etc.
4　A chest in which records relating to the testator's properties were kept.
5　See note to no. 218 and also no. 715.
6　Witness of the will of Roger Metessharpp of Mendlesham (see note above).

[fol. 425]
375. ALICE WADE of WOOLPIT ('Wolpet'), 20 May 1469

Dated at Woolpit; to be buried in the Christian burial of Woolpit church; to the high altar of the same church, for my tithes forgotten or underpaid, 12d.

To Alice Thurmod, the wife of John Thurmod of Great Finborough ('Fymbergh Magna'), my best tabard, with the best hood.

To Rose, the wife of Peter Doo, a bed-cover.

To Alice Arnewey a tunic and a tabard, with a hood.

To John Wade my kinsman all my lands and tenements, meadows, pastures and feedings in the town[s] of Woolpit and Drinkstone ('Drynkestone'), to hold to him and his heirs for ever; to the same John Wade a brass pot with a plate and a trammel.

To Katherine Wade a posnet.

To John Wade 20d; and to Thomas Mellere 20d.

Whatever residue there shall be of all my goods I leave to the disposition of my execs.

Execs: John Wade and Thomas Mellere of Woolpit, they to have God before their eyes and faithfully execute my testament.

Seal appended.

Proved at Fornham St Martin, 13 November 1469. Admon to execs. Seal of official appended.

[fol. 425v]
376. HENRY SWANTON of BOTESDALE ('Botysdale') [in REDGRAVE], 1469

[*No day or month given*]; to be buried in the churchyard of the church of Rickinghall ('Rykynghale') Inferior; to the high altar of the church of Redgrave, for my tithes and offerings forgotten or underpaid, 3s 4d; to the reparation of the church of Rickinghall Inferior 3s 4d; to the gild of St Peter of Rickinghall Inferior 3s 4d.[1]

To Isabel my wife[2] my tenement in Botesdale, lately bought of the execs of William Gerrad,[3] to her and her heirs for ever.

To John Whytfote my brother 3s 4d.

Residue of all my goods to my execs, to sell and pay my debts therewith, and dispose for the health of my soul and the souls of my deceased friends, in the celebration of masses and the giving of alms, as they see best to please God and profit my soul.

Execs: Richard Crane and William Hochown, they faithfully to execute my testament; supervisor: Edmund Sparke, clerk;[4] to each of them for their labour 6s 8d.

Seal appended.

Witnesses: Edmund Subborn,[5] John Hoberd, glover, and others.

Proved at Fornham [St] Martin, 20 November 1469. Admon to execs.

1   William Fotour of Rickinghall Inferior also made a bequest to this gild (no. 365).
2   Will, no. 546.
3   Will (as 'Gerarde') pr. June 1461 (SROB, Baldwyne 276; Pt I, no. 1354). William Gerrard was
    Isabel Swanton's previous husband. In his will he had specified that if she remarried, his house or
    tenement was to be sold and she was to have half the money from it; it appears that she benefitted
    from this twice over since she would have received half of the sale price when Henry Swanton
    purchased the property and then Henry bequeathed the whole property to her.
4   See note to no. 194.
5   One of the executors of William Gerarde; his will (as of Rickinghall Inferior) pr. April 1476
    (SROB, Hervye 135); he gave instructions for a chaplain to celebrate for the soul of William
    Gerard for a year; see also note to no. 308.

[fol. 426]
377. JOHN PETYT of BRANDON FERRY ('Brandonfer'), 18 May 1470

['Petyett' *in margin*] To be buried in the churchyard of the church of Brandon Ferry; to the high altar for tithes forgotten 20d; to the fabric of Brandon Ferry church 6s 8d; to the fabric of Fincham [*Norfolk*] church 8d; to the fabric of Feltwell [*Norfolk*] church 8d; to the fabric of Barton Mills ('Berton') church 12d.

[*Will*]

Joan my wife to have my house in Brandon Ferry, with all the goods and utensils belonging to it, and after her death, John my son to have the house, to him and his assigns.

Joan my wife to have 40s from the sale (*pro vendacione*) of my house in Brandon Ferry; Margery my daughter to have 40s from the said house; James my son to have 40s from it; Agnes my daughter to have 40s from it; John my son to have 26s 8d from it; Robert my son to have 26s 8d from it; Richard my son to have 20s from the said house.

Cecily Bayly to have 12d and Joan Bateman to have 12d.

Agnes my daughter to have 2 sheets and a bed-cover.

Residue of my goods to Thomas Clavery and John Petyt my son, execs, to dispose for the health of [*my*] soul and the souls of all the faithful departed, to the laud of God Almighty.

Proved at Mildenhall ('Myldenhale'), 28 September 1470. Admon to execs.

378. RICHARD MORLE the elder of MILDENHALL ('Mildenhale'),[1]
7 March 1469/70

['Morlee' *in margin*] Dated 10 Edward IV; [*commendation*: to Almighty God my Creator and Saviour, the Blessed Virgin Mary his mother and all the saints]; to the high altar of the church of the Blessed Virgin Mary of Mildenhall, for my tithes and offerings forgotten and withheld, in exoneration of my soul, 40d; to the reparation of the said church 6s 8d.

To John Morle my son my messuage in which I live and 3 acres of arable land[2] [fol. 426v] in 'Thremowfeld' in one piece.

To Henry my son 1½ acres in 'Baggysholmefeld', between land of the charnel of Ralph de Walsham on the east,[3] and land of the manor of Mildenhall on the west; to

Henry another 3½ acres of land at 'Oxenhowepayth', between land of George Heth on the east, and land of the manor of Mildenhall [*on*] the west; to Henry 1½ roods of land lying at the gate of Robert Frere, and 3½ acres of meadow in 'le Breche'.

To each of my godsons 2 bushels (*modios*) of barley.

To the convent of Babwell 10s.[4]

To Henry my son my iron-shod cart (*bigam ferratam*).

To the gild of St Mary the Virgin of Mildenhall 20d.[5]

Residue of all my goods and chattels to my execs, to dispose for my soul, as they see best to please God and profit my soul.

Execs: Alice my wife,[6] principal executrix, and Robert Holme and Simon Place [*her*] helpers.

Seal appended.

Proved at Mildenhall, 28 September 1470. Admon to execs.

1   ?Related to John Morle the elder of Mildenhall (no. 545 below).
2   Or possibly '2 acres of arable land': the first '*i*' of '*iij*' is very feint.
3   In its churchyard, to the south of the church, Mildenhall had a charnel house with a chapel above dedicated to St Michael; it was endowed by Ralph de Walsham in 1387. The land mentioned here was part, if not all, of that endowment.
4   See note to no. 1.
5   For other bequests to the gild of St Mary the Virgin in Mildenhall see wills of Rose widow of Walter Place of Mildenhall (Pt I, no. 120) and Thomas Tydde of Mildenhall (no. 819 below).
6   An 'Alice Morle' received a bequest from John Morle the elder of Mildenhall (no. 545).

379. THOMAS GARDENER the elder of BARTON MILLS ('Berton'),[1] 7 July 1470

Dated at Barton; in the grip of sickness (*egretudine detentus*); my body to Christian burial; to the high altar of Barton church 40d; to the fabric of the said church 3s 4d. To Robert Gardener, son of John my son, a sheep; to John Gardener, son of the said John, a sheep; to Margaret Gardener, daughter of the said John, a sheep.

To the order of Friars Minor of Babwell 20d; to the Friars Preachers of Thetford 20d; to the friars of the order of St Augustine of Thetford 20d.[2]

Residue of all my goods wholly to Margaret my wife, John Gardener my son and Thomas Gardener my son, to pay my debts and to maintain Margaret my wife as long as she lives.

Execs: Margaret my wife, John Gardener and Thomas Gardener my son of Barton.

Seal appended.

Proved at Mildenhall, 26 September 1470. Admon to execs.

1   Witness of the original will of Robert Sopere of Barton Mills, pr. March 1439/40 (SROB, Baldwyne 7; Pt I, no. 46); ?executor of Robert Yonge of Barton Mills, probate October 1458 (SROB, Baldwyne 209; Pt I, no. 1037).
2   For the friars see notes to nos 1 (Babwell), 68 (Friars Preachers of Thetford) and 69 (Augustinians).

[fol. 427]

380. JOHN CURRAY of Chilton ('Chylton') hamlet in the parish of CLARE, 22 May 1470

(*De hamelett' voc' Chylton infra paroch' de Clare*); [*commendation*: to God Almighty]; to be buried in the churchyard of Clare parish church. I beg of my execs, in God's name (*ex parte dei*), that they pay all my debts which can be proved genuine. To the high altar of Clare, for my tithes and offerings forgotten and under-paid, 3s 4d.

To John and Robert, sons of Roger Marten, my godsons, 3s 4d between them; to Roger Marten my furred gown of a violet colour.

To the sustentation of the gild of St John the Baptist held in Chilton 10s.[1]

Isabel my wife to have my messuage in Chilton, in which I live, to hold to her for term of her life; after her death the messuage to be sold by my execs and disposed in deeds of charity, for the health of my soul and all the faithful departed's [*souls*]; but if Isabel is in need in her lifetime, then the messuage to be sold and Isabel sustained from the money from the sale.

Residue of all my goods to Isabel my wife and to the disposition of my execs.

Execs: Isabel my wife, Roger Marten and William Gerweys.

Supervisor: John Hengestman.

To each of my execs 6s 8d for their diligent labour about these premises, and to the supervisor 13s 4d, similarly.

Called as witnesses: Robert Colyngham, perpetual vicar of Clare,[2] Roger Marten, John Cowper the elder, John Norman the younger, Thomas Wheyt and others.

Proved at Clare, 7 November 1470. Admon to execs.

[1]   Robert Burwe of Hundon also made a bequest to the gild of St John the Baptist in Chilton (no. 79).

[2]   Robert Colyngham was vicar of Clare from February 1469/70 until 1476 (Tanner, p.1228); see also nos 456 and 687.

381. JOHN LEE the elder of STOWMARKET, 8 January 1469/70

Dated at Stowmarket; to be buried in the church of the Blessed Peter of the said town; to the high altar of the same church 6s 8d; to the church of the Blessed Mary of the same town 3s 4d.[1]

To each house and order of friars of Ipswich (*Gipp'c'*) 10s;[2] to the friars of Babwell 10s;[3] [fol. 427v] to Friar Thomas Lawshull of the same house 10s.[4]

To a suitable chaplain, to celebrate in the church of the Blessed Peter for my soul and the souls of my parents and benefactors for whom I am especially bound, for 3 years, 24 marks.

I wish to have marble paving (*pavimentu' marmoreu'*) about my burial place, as [*much as*] appears to be needed there.[5]

John Lee my son to have, to him and his heirs, a messuage in which he lives, called 'Bellys', with two closes by it, and 10 acres of land at 'Westmerheyth', and 3 acres of land at 'Thorneyschepecote'; to John a latten pot, a brass pot, a candlestick and 6 pieces of pewter ware (*vasarum electri*).

To Matilda Lee my servant 40s or its value, my worst feather bed, a brass pot and a candlestick.

To Margery my daughter the best feather bed, the best brass pot and a latten candlestick.

To John Lee, son of William Lee of Woodbridge ('Wodebregge'), 20s.

To Matilda my daughter 6 pieces of pewter ware.

To the servant of John Markys, draper, 6 pieces of pewter ware.

To the painting of the image of St Paul, in the chancel of the said church of St Peter, 6s 8d.

Residue of all my goods and debts, wherever and in whosoever hands they be, to my attorneys and execs, to distribute and dispose as seems to them best, to the laud and honour of God and the health of my soul and the souls of my parents, my wife Joan, and our benefactors and all the faithful departed.

Execs of this testament and last will: William Lee of Woodbridge, Roger Borugh and Robert Mylys of Stowmarket; to each of them, for their faithful labour, 20s. Seal appended.

[*No probate recorded.*]

1   In Domesday Book there were two churches in Stowmarket, one, SS Peter and Paul, the mother church of the huge vill of Thorney (encompassing Stowmarket, Stowupland, Newton, Gipping and Dagworth) and the other, St Mary, the town church of Stowmarket. The latter was rebuilt, according to the evidence of bequests, in 1473–78, but was demolished in about 1546. The remaining church, known today as SS Peter and Mary, took over the dedication and dropped St Paul (Blatchly and Northeast, 'Lost and Ruined Parish Churches of Suffolk', p.434).

2   There were houses of Carmelite, Dominican and Franciscan friars at Ipswich. See notes to nos 1 and 50.

3   See note to no. 1.

4   Probably the same man as Friar Lawshele of Babwell who was mentioned in the will of William Schelton of Stowmarket (no. 109).

5   That is, a 'marble' slab over his grave.

[fol. 428]

382. WILLIAM GOLDBOUR the younger of SOHAM ('Saham') [*Cambs*],[1]
1 January 1468/69

Of Soham in the county of Cambridge (*Cantebr'*); to be buried in the churchyard of the church of St Andrew, Soham; to the high altar of which, 12d; to the fabric of the same church a coomb of barley.

To the White Friars of Cambridge (*Cantebr'*) 2s 6d; to the Friars Preachers of Cambridge 2s 6d.[2]

To my mother a quarter of malt.

To Alice my wife 3 roods of arable land, for term of her life, and after her decease, the 3 roods of land to remain to William my son and his heirs; [*if William should die without heirs*] the 3 roods of land to be sold and the money from them to be given to priests, to celebrate for my soul and the souls of Alice my wife, my sons and our parents and friends.

To Alice my wife 1 acre of arable land in 'le Downefeld',[3] for the term of 12 years, and after that it to remain to William my son and his heirs; if William should decease without heirs, the acre of land to be sold and the money distributed for my soul, and the souls of Thomas Teype and William Goldbour and Joan his wife.

To Alice my wife 5 quarters of barley; the residue of my barley to be made into malt, to my profit and hers; also to Alice all my utensils apart from the lead vessel (*vas plumbeu'*).

To William my son a heifer with a calf, and 2 foals.

To William Dowe, for his labour, 40d and a bay mare (*equa' badea'*).

William Dowe to be exec and William Goldbour the elder, supervisor; they to dispose for my soul as they see best to please God, the Blessed Mary and all the saints. Seal appended.

Proved at Fornham St Martin, 2 December 1469. Admon to exec.

1   ?Related to Thomas Goldbour of Soham (no. 279). See note to that will concerning the Goldsboro family.
2   For the friars of Cambridge see notes to nos 42 (White Friars) and 80 (Friars Preachers).
3   'Downfield' appears on a map of Soham dated 1656 (see note to no. 232).

[fol. 428v]

383. JOHN FOOT of BUXHALL ('Buxhale'), 10 March 1455/56

To be buried in the churchyard of Buxhall church; to the emendation of the same church 4 bushels of malt.

A suitable chaplain to celebrate in the said church for my soul and for the souls of my parents and benefactors, and for the soul of John Tynton and Agnes his wife,[1] and of Stephen Tynton and Emme his wife, and of Henry Colyour, and of all at rest in Christ, for half a year.

To Joan my wife my whole messuage in Buxhall, which was formerly John Tynton the elder's,[2] together with a piece of land lying at 'le Combwall', to hold for the whole term of her life; after her decease the messuage with the piece of land to remain to John my son, to hold to him and his heirs for ever, on condition that out of them he provides the chaplain celebrating for my soul as stated above, and also that he pays to William my son 20s, and to Joan my daughter 20s. If John my son should die without heirs, then the messuage with the piece of land to remain to William my son, to hold to him and his heirs for ever, he providing the chaplain, as stated before, if John has not done so, and paying Joan my daughter 20s as aforesaid. If William dies without heirs, then after his decease, all the messuage with the piece of land to be sold for the best price possible, my will to be fully implemented out of it, if it has not been done already, and the residue to be spent faithfully in pious uses for the health of my soul, and the souls aforesaid.

To Isabel my daughter all my messuage in Buxhall, at 'Bretonstrete', to hold to her and her heirs for ever.

To the aid and relief of the poor of the town of Buxhall, that is, from the tax of the lord king when it falls, a piece of my land called 'Aldewerk', containing by estimation half an acre, to be held and peacefully occupied for ever in that way, for the health of my soul.[3]

If Isabel dies without heirs, then the messuage assigned to her to be sold and distributed in deeds of charity for the health of my soul.

Whatever residue there be of all my goods I leave to the disposition of my execs, in the execution of this testament and the faithful fulfilling of this my last will.

Execs: my beloved in Christ, Joan my wife, and William Saltere, to dispose for me and my soul where they see most expedient and to please God.

Seal appended.

Proved at Haughley ('Hawley'), [no date given].

1   Will, as 'John Tymton the elder of Great Finborough', pr. May 1461 (SROB, Baldwyne 273; Pt I, no. 1343); his wife's name was not mentioned in his will.
2   In his will, possibly dated 1440/41, but more likely 1460/61, John Tynton the elder bequeathed all his lands and tenements in the towns of Finborough and Buxhall to his son John; as John Foot's will was made in 1455/56, this messuage in Buxhall did not pass to John Tinton the younger but was sold by his father during his lifetime to Foot. The will of John Tynton (the younger) was pr. March 1476/77 (SROB, Hervye 46).

3   Another bequest to help a township pay lay taxes to the Crown but one that was aimed at helping poor taxpayers; see the Introduction, under *Charitable giving*, and also note to no. 240 for details of other bequests towards tax demands.

[fol. 429(a)]

384. JOHN BOTWRIGHT of LAKENHEATH ('Lakynghith'), 20 October 1469

[*The testament only of no. 399 below; this version struck through and at the head written:* Look for [*it*] registered in another place, with the will annexed (*Quer' reg' in alio loco cu' voluntate annex'*)]

385. ELLEN FULLER of WALSHAM LE WILLOWS ('Walsham'),[1] 28 November 1469

Dated at Walsham, in the diocese of Norwich; to be buried in the churchyard of Walsham church; to the high altar a heifer, for tithes forgotten or unknowingly withheld; I leave 3s 4d for candles burning about the sepulchre of the body of Christ on Easter Day.

To Elizabeth Fullere [*my*] niece the large chest and also a pair of beads.

Residue of all my goods to my execs to dispose for my soul and the souls of my friends and benefactors, as they see best to please God and profit my soul.

Execs: John Margeri my brother and Robert Fullere my son.

Seal appended.

Witnesses: John Bond, John Bay, Alice Bay, Katherine Bray, Alice Julian and others.

Proved 18 December 1469. Admon to execs.

1   Wife and executrix (as 'Helen') of John Fuller of Walsham le Willows, probate November 1458 (SROB, Baldwyne 209; Pt I, no. 1040).

[fol. 429(a)v]

386. ELIZABETH WYNEYEVE[1] of TROSTON, 8 August 1469

Dated at Troston; to be buried in the churchyard of the parish church of Troston.

To the Friars Preachers of Thetford 10s.[2]

To Edmund my son 6s 8d; to Nicholas my son 6s 8d; to John my son 6s 8d; to the said Edmund my son a brass pot; to the said Nicholas a brass pot with a 'le panne'; to the said John a 'le panne' and a brass pot; to Margaret my daughter a 'le panne'.

To Elizabeth Gilbert of Troston 4d; to Margery Rastall of the same 4d; to Agnes Man of the same 4d; to Elizabeth Hervy of Stanton 4d; to Constance Wynyeve of Troston 4d.

To Margaret my daughter a 'le cloke', with a blue coat ('le coote de blewe').

Residue of all my goods to William Wynyeve my son, exec.

Witnesses: William Smyth of the same, with others.

Proved at Fornham St Martin, 4 January 1469/70. Admon granted to exec.

1   The second 'y' in the surname is a yogh.
2   See note to no. 68.

[fol. 429(b)]

387. ROBERT MARHAM of MILDENHALL ('Myldenhale'), 7 December 1469

Dated at Mildenhall; to be buried in the churchyard of Mildenhall church; [*commendation*: to Almighty God my Creator and Saviour, the Blessed Virgin Mary his mother and all the saints]; my body to Christian burial in the churchyard of Mildenhall church; to the high altar of the church of the Blessed Mary of Mildenhall, for my tithes and offerings forgotten and in exoneration of my soul, 12d; to the reparation of the same church 20d.

To Robert Playford a mare of 'le grey' colour, a pair of sheets, a large brass pan and a green bed-cover.

To Agnes Parmenter 4 bushels of barley.

To Agnes Smyth my daughter 4 bushels of rye and 4 bushels of malt.

To Isabel my wife all [*my*] lands, tenements, meadows and pastures, a tenement called 'William Penne' being excepted, which I have sold to William Dokkynge, and, similarly, except a meadow at 'le Wyldestre',[1] which I have sold to Thomas Trewepeny; to Isabel all the utensils belonging to my house, except those before excepted.

To Thomas Smyth, son of John Smyth of 'Bekke',[2] a black calf.

Residue of all my goods and chattels to my execs, to pay all my debts which I am rightly due to pay to anyone, and to dispose for my soul in deeds of charity, according to their discretion and as they see most expedient.

Execs: Isabel my wife, principal executrix; Robert Morys and John Berton [*her*] helpers.

Seal appended.

Proved at Tuddenham ('Todenham'), 19 February 1469/70. Admon to Isabel Marham and John Berton, execs. Power reserved to Robert Morys, the other exec, if he wishes to take up admon.

1   Wild Street in Mildenhall.
2   That is, 'Beck Row', one of the 'rows', outlying hamlets of Mildenhall, the other two being Holywell Row and West Row.

388. RICHARD WODE of DRINKSTONE ('Drynkston'), 5 January 1468/69

Dated Thursday before the feast of the Epiphany, at Drinkstone; to be buried Christian burial in the churchyard of Drinkstone church; to the painting of the 'gawdes' ('le peyntyng le gawdes') before Our Lady, 10s.[1]

My attorneys, that is, Alexander Neve and John Myrton the elder, to provide (*adducerent*) a torch of price 10s [*to go*] with me to the church.

To the Friars Minor of Babwell, for a trental of St Gregory, 10s.[2]

To the poor 3s 4d; to the emendation of the way between 'Halkmerch' and 'Myllehyll', 3s 4d.

Seal appended.

Proved at Fornham St Martin, 16 March 1471/72. Admon to execs.

1   As 'gawdes' were the large beads of the rosary, representing a *paternoster*, presumably there was a set of such beads before the statue of Our Lady in Drinkstone church.
2   See note to no. 1.

[fol. 429(b)v]

389. THOMAS HUSKE of ICKWORTH ('Ikworth'), 16 May 1469

Dated at Ickworth ('Ikeworth'); my body to Christian burial; to the high altar of Ickworth church, for my tithes and offerings underpaid, 20d; to the reparation of a bridge there, called 'Bayardbregge', 3s 4d.

To John Huske my son, the elder, a brass pot, a salt-cellar ('saltesaler') of pewter and a cow.

To Beatrice Trowe my daughter, my great ark (*arcam*) and a cow.

To Thomas Huske my son a cow.

To Joan my wife all my ostilments [*and*] utensils belonging to my dwelling (*hospicio*); to Joan all my lands and tenements in the town and fields of Ickworth, to hold to her for term of her life; after her decease all the said lands and tenements to remain to John Huske my son, the younger, to hold to him and his heirs for ever; the same John to provide Joan his mother, for term of her life, with food, clothing, footwear, bedding and other necessaries of life, as she ought to be provided with, for the whole of the said term.

To the said John and John [*my sons*] all the grain on my said lands, and all my cart- and plough-horses (*equos carecta' et caruca' meos*), to pay my debts out of them, fulfil this testament and support (*sustendand'*) my wife.

Residue of all my goods to my execs, to sell, receive and dispose for my soul and the souls for whom I am bound in deeds of charity, as they see best to please God and profit my soul.

Execs: John and John my sons, truly to execute this testament.

Seal appended.

Proved at Fornham [*St*] Martin, 28 May 1470. Admon to execs.

[fol. 430]

390. MARGARET SYRE of GREAT ASHFIELD ('Asshfeld Magna'),
20 December 1469

To be buried in the churchyard of the church of the Blessed Mary of Ashfield ('Aysshfeld'); to the parish chaplain 2s; for a bell 4 marks.

To Robert my son a basin and ewer, a pair of the best sheets, a ?hand-towel (*mancipiu'*), 2 bed-covers, a 'donge', a pan, a brass pot and a cow.

To Isabel, wife of the said Robert, a red hood, a green tunic and a vessel called a ?mashing-vat ('maddyngfath'), a chest (*teca'*), a quilt ('qwylt') and a pair of cards ('cardys').

To William my son a cow, 2 bed-covers, 2 pairs of sheets, 2 pairs of blankets, a 'donge', 2 ?hand-towels (*mancip'*), a pot, a kettle ('qwatell'), a cauldron ('caudron'), a silver girdle of the best, a vessel called a 'maddyngfath' [*and*] a chest (*theca'*).

Residue of the goods belonging to me, of whatever kind, to the disposition of my exec.

Exec: William Syre my son, to receive and pay in my name and to do for my soul as he sees best.

Proved at Walsham [*le Willows*], 6 February 1469/70. Admon to exec.

391. JAMES DREWE of MELLIS ('Melles'),[1] 31 January 1466/67

To be buried in the churchyard of the Blessed Mary of Mellis; to the high altar of the said church 12d; to the reparation of the said church 40d; to the reparation of Stuston church 2 bushels of wheat and 2 bushels of barley.

To the gild of the Holy Trinity of Mellis[2] 40d.

To the Friars Minor of Babwell 2 bushels of barley; to the Austin Friars of Thetford 4 bushels of wheat.[3]

To Friar John Pecche 12d; to the parish clerk 2d.

To John Ponyard my son 40d.

To Thomas Harrald my godson[4] 12d.

To Margaret my wife all my lands and tenements, and all my goods, to her and her assigns; if Margaret should sell the said tenement and lands, Thomas Ponyard to have them within the price of any other man, if he wishes to buy them. My feoffees to deliver full and peaceful possession, when required, according to the wishes of the said Margaret.

Residue of all my goods to my execs to dispose for my soul, as seems to them best to please God and profit my soul.

Execs: Margaret my wife and Edmund Subborn of Botesdale.[5]

Seal appended.

Proved at Finningham ('Fynyngham'), 7 February 1469/70. Admon to execs. Because of an insufficiency of goods of the deceased, the execs are excused from rendering further accounts and are acquitted.

[1]   Legatee (as 'Drew') of James Drew the elder of Mellis, will pr. October 1461 (SROB, Baldwyne 280; Pt I, no. 1371).

[2]   For other bequests to the gild of the Holy Trinity in Mellis see the wills of: Rose Hunger of Mellis, widow (Pt I, no. 798), Thomas Punte of Occold (Pt I, no. 1165) and James Drew the elder of Mellis (Pt I, no. 1371). There was also a gild of St Peter, sometimes called SS Peter and Paul, there: Henry Pope of Mellis (Pt I, no. 369), Rose Hunger (as above) and James Drew the elder (as above).

[3]   For the friars see notes to nos 1 (Babwell) and 69 (Austin Friars of Thetford).

[4]   James Drew the elder made a bequest to William Harald; Roger Harald of Mellis was one of James's executors.

[5]   Supervisor (as 'Sudburne') of the will of James Drew the elder (as above); see also note to no. 308.

[fol. 430v]

392. JOHN REVE of HEPWORTH,[1] 9 February 1469/70 [*nuncupative*]

Made before John Scole of the same town, clerk,[2] and Isabel my wife; to be buried in the churchyard of the parish church of the same town. I exhort the execs of this my testament well and faithfully to pay the debts which I owe and to do this as quickly as they can [*and*] in the best way, thus: to the gild of St Peter of Thelnetham 6s;[3] to the townsmen (*villat'*) of Hepworth 6s and to the same townsmen, for farm of land, 4s; to John Inglond 2s; to Thomas Knyght 12d. To the high altar of the said church, for tithes forgotten and not duly tithed, 40d; to the use (*proficiu'*) of the light burning before the sepulchre of [*Our*] Lord 2 bushels of wheat and half a quarter of malt.

To the Friars Minor of Babwell for a half-trental 5s; to the friars of the New House of Thetford for a half-trental 5s.[4]

To a suitable chaplain to celebrate divine service in Hepworth parish church for half a year, 4 marks.

To Isabel my wife all the utensils of my house, with all the smaller necessaries (*omnibus necessariis minutis*) there, and all the beds and bedclothes of whatever [*kind*], together with the cart, plough and harrows and the harness belonging to them; also all my lands and tenements which I have in the town of Hepworth, except the half-part of a tenement with 5 acres of land called 'Crowys', and that part I wish Isabel to have, to her and her heirs, paying 5 marks to the implementing of my present testament and my legacies in it. Also to Isabel the half-part of all my goods not bequeathed above, of whatever [*kind*], which I have at the time of my death, and the residue of them to [*go to*] the implementing of my legacies; but if Isabel wishes to have [*them*] and to buy [*them*], I wish her to have [*them*] before [*all*] others and within the price of anyone else.

Any residue there should be of all my goods I leave to Isabel my wife and John Torald, execs, to execute this my testament and implement my legacies, with other deeds of piety, as seems to them best to please God, in exoneration of their conscience towards God in this matter.

Supervisor: John Scole.

Not sealed with my seal, but these were witnesses: John Scole and Isabel.

Proved at Fornham St Martin, 12 February 1469/70. Admon to execs.

[1] (As 'Rewe'), brother and executor of William Rewe of Thelnetham, will pr. October 1457 (SROB, Baldwyne 214; Pt I, no. 1063).

[2] Roger Drury of Hepworth, gentleman, described John Scole as rector of Hepworth (no. 402).

[3] There was also a gild of St John the Baptist in the parish in the fifteeth century, see John Barker of Thelnetham (SROB, Baldwyne 255; Pt I, no. 1262) and John Moyse of Hopton (no. 186 above). William Rewe of Thelnetham, the testator's brother, bequeathed the gild of St Peter 6s 8d for a banner cloth (see note above). The gild of St Peter was mentioned in a will of 1519 (*PSIA*, xii, p.85). Records also show that there was a gild of St Nicholas in the parish in 1524 (*PSIA*, xix, p.205).

[4] For the friars see notes to no. 1 (Babwell) and no. 69 (New House of Thetford).

[fol. 431]
393. NICHOLAS HARLYNG of HOPTON,[1] 28 April 1470

Of Hopton in the diocese of Norwich and deanery of Blackbourn ('Blakburne'); my body to Christian burial in the churchyard of the church of All Saints of Hopton; to the high altar of the said church for tithes underpaid 3s 4d.

To the Austin Friars of Thetford, for a trental, 10s; to the friars of the order of St Dominic of the same 2s.[2]

To the fabric of Hopton church 13s 4d.

To a suitable priest to celebrate divine service in Hopton church, for my soul and the souls of all my benefactors, 8 marks; to the rector of Hopton, for a 'certeyn' for a whole year, 4s 4d.

Agnes my wife to have my tenement called 'Scottys', which I lately purchased of Nicholas Scotte, clerk, with 2½ acres of land, for the time of her widowhood; if she should marry, then the tenement and 2½ acres of land to be sold by my execs and half the money from them to be paid to Agnes; if she does not marry, but keeps herself sole during her lifetime, then after her death the tenement and land to be sold by my execs and the money for them disposed for the health of my soul and the souls of all my benefactors.

To Matilda my daughter 40s.

All the utensils and household equipment (*demestia* [*sic*]) of my house to be distributed between Agnes my wife and Matilda my daughter.

To each of my execs 6s 8d.

Residue of all my goods to my execs, Thomas Harlyng of Hopton,[3] Thomas Reynoldes and Thomas Knyght of Walsham, to dispose for the health of my soul and the souls of all my benefactors, as seems to them best and to the most pleasure of God.

Supervisor: John Broun, clerk.

Seal appended.

Proved at Knettishall ('Gnatsale'), 8 May 1470. Admon to Thomas Reynoldes, exec, and power reserved to Thomas Harlyng of Hopton and Thomas Knight of Walsham, the other execs, by Sir John Broun, rector of Hopton,[4] commissary for this purpose, if they wish to take up admon.

1   Executor of John Walter the elder of Hopton, probate October 1446 (SROB, Baldwyne 66; Pt I, no. 323); executor of Richard Harlynge of Hopton, will pr. November 1452 (SROB, Baldwyne 132; Pt I, no. 622).
2   For the friars see notes to no. 68 (Dominicans of Thetford) and no. 69 (Austin Friars).
3   ?Will pr. May 1494 (SROB, Hervye 462).
4   John Broun had succeeded Sir John Worlych in the living of Hopton in 1460 (Tanner, p.1201); presumably this is the same man as the nominated supervisor 'John Broun, clerk'; see also nos 36 and 555.

394. WILLIAM BERARD of KNETTISHALL ('Gnatsale'), 8 May 1470

[*probate only*]

Proved. Admon to Matilda his wife and John his son.

[fol. 431v]

395. JOHN CARWENT of EYE, 20 January 1469/70

Seeing the perils of death approaching (*videns mortis pericula in dies eminer'*); to be buried in the churchyard of the parish church of St Peter of Eye; to the high altar of the same church, for my tithes forgotten, 20s; to the gild of the Blessed Mary of Eye 13s 4d;[1] to an honest chaplain, to celebrate divine office in Eye church for a whole year, 8 marks; to the reparation of the new tower of Eye church 40s.

Joan my wife to have my tenement in Gislingham ('Gyslyngham'), formerly Nicholas Bronde's, with the land belonging to it, for term of her life; after her decease the tenement, with the land, to be sold by my execs and the money from it to be disposed for the health of my soul.

My feoffees in a close of pasture, with a garden annexed, called 'Wylchones', in Gislingham, to deliver estate [*of them*] to my execs when so required by them.

Residue of all my goods to the disposition of Thomas Hervy, clerk,[2] and John Wyth, execs, to dispose for my soul and the souls of my benefactors, as they see best to please God and profit the health of my soul.

Seal appended.

Proved at Eye, 10 May 1470. Admon to execs.

1   For other bequests to the gild of the Blessed Mary, or of St Mary, at Eye see note to no. 2.
2   See note to no. 2.

396. THOMAS GARLYNG of EYE, [*c.1470*]

[*No date given*]; to be buried in the churchyard of Eye parish church; to the high altar of the said church 3s 4d; to the reparation of Oakley ('Ocelee') parish church 6s 8d; to a priest 8 marks, [*to celebrate*] in Eye church.

To Matilda my wife all my utensils of my house for her lifetime, and after her decease those utensils to remain with Thomas Torold.

To Thomas Torolde 5 marks, to provide all necessaries for my wife during her lifetime.

Residue of [*my*] goods to Matilda my wife and Thomas Torolde, my execs, to dispose for the health of my soul, as seems to them most expedient.

Proved at Eye, 10 May 1470. Admon to execs.

[fol. 432]
397. JOHN SMYTH of SOHAM ('Saham') [*Cambs*],[1] 15 October 1470

Of Soham in the county of Cambridge (*Cant'*); to be buried in the churchyard of St Andrew the Apostle of Soham, and my best animal in the name of a mortuary; to the high altar 12d; to the sepulchre 4lbs of wax; to each priest at my obsequies on the day of my burial (*aditus mei*) 4d, to each clerk 2d (*ijd clericus ijd*), and to each junior clerk (*clerico semit'*) there 1d.

To the gild of St John the Baptist of Soham 5s.[2]

To Alice Fraunceys 16s.

Residue of all my goods I wish to be sold, so that all my debts can be paid, and if anything is left over I wish it to be disposed for the health of my soul.

Execs: Andrew Buge[3] and John Salle, faithfully to execute my testament.

Seal appended.

Proved at Fornham St Martin, 10 December 1470. Admon to execs.

1   ?Executor of John Ode of Barway in Soham, will pr. September 1459 (SROB, Baldwyne 269; Pt I, no. 1319).
2   For the gilds of Cambridgeshire in general see Introduction, under *Gilds*, and note to no. 199 above. For gilds in Soham see note to no. 204 above.
3   The Bugge family was prominent in Soham in the seventeenth century, several individuals being members of the parish élite.

398. STEPHEN WYMBYSSH of BUXHALL ('Buxhale'), 3 January 1469/70

To be buried in the parish church of the said town; to the high altar of the same church, for my tithes underpaid, 2s.

To the canons of Ixworth, for two trentals of St Gregory to be celebrated by the convent there, for my soul, 20s.[1]

To Alice my wife my whole tenement in Buxhall called 'Jayes', for term of her life, and after her decease it to remain to Robert Bukden, the son of Robert Bukden, to him and his heirs; if Robert dies without heirs, then all the said tenement to be sold and [*the money*] spent purposefully in pious deeds of charity (*in pios usus caritatis finaliter*[sic]).

To Margaret my daughter my tenement in Buxhall called 'Hylles', for the whole term of her life, and after her decease it to remain to John Bukden her son and his heirs; if he dies without heirs, then the tenement called 'Hylles' to be sold and [*the money*] distributed in pious deeds of charity as aforesaid.

To Alice my wife all my land and tenements in Rattlesden ('Ratyllesden'), for the whole term of her life, on condition that she stays sole, without a husband; if she does marry, then I wish all my land and tenements, rents and services in Rattlesden assigned to her to be sold quickly, in the best way possible, by my execs, and of the money from them I assign 5 marks to Joan Bukden, the daughter of the abovesaid Margaret [fol. 432v] and 13s 4d to Agnes her sister; also I wish to have out of it a suitable and honest chaplain [*to celebrate*] for my soul and for the souls of my parents and benefactors and all those at rest in Christ.

To Alice my wife all my ostilments and utensils, wherever they be.

To Dame Margaret Chamberleyn[2] 20s; to Roger Saltere 6s 8d; to Alice Scarpe of Felsham 6s 8d.

To the reparation of Buxhall church a piece of land called 'Sohams' in Buxhall.

My whole tenement called 'Wymbyssh' in the town of Ingrave ('Yengeraf'), in Essex, to be sold in the best way possible by my execs, and of the money from it I assign 10 marks to a suitable and honest chaplain, to celebrate divine service for a whole year, for the souls of William Wymbyssh and Joan his wife, my soul and Alice my wife's, and for the souls of all at rest in Christ, and the residue of the money to be expended faithfully in deeds of charity by my execs.

Out of my fee (*feodo meo*) granted to me by Sir Roger Chambyrleyn, knight,[3] for 3 years after my decease, I give 5 marks to the reparation of the tower of Gedding church, for the souls of Sir Roger Chambyrleyn [*and*] his wife, of me, Stephen, and Alice my wife, and of all faithful Christians, to be prayed for; out of the same fee I assign 13s 4d to my master, Ralph Chambyrleyn.

To Richard Cook of Maldon 6s 8d.

To John Wymbyssh my brother a russet gown.

To John Sefowle of Rattlesden 20d.

Whatever residue there is of all my goods to the discretion of my execs.

Execs: Alice my wife, Robert Den of Newton by Sudbury ('*iuxta* Sudbur'), Sir John Powlyn, clerk, and John Nicoll of London, they to have God before their eyes and dispose for me and my soul where they see most expedient and best to please God. Seal appended.

Proved at Haughley ('Hawley'), 13 December 1470. Admon to Alice Wymbyssh, executrix. Power reserved to Robert Den of Newton by Sudbury, Sir John Powlyn, clerk, and John Nichole of London, the other execs, when they come, if they wish to take up admon.

[1] See note to no. 69.
[2] See note below.
[3] Sir Roger Chambyrleyn and his wife, Dame Margaret, of Gedding. Sir Roger succeeded to the estate in 1440 and was MP for Suffolk in 1450; he presented the rector of Gedding in 1448. See Olorenshaw, *Notes on Gedding*, pp.8, 10.

[fol. 433]

399. JOHN BOTWRYGHT of LAKENHEATH ('Lakynghithe'), 20 October 1469

Dated at Lakenheath; to be buried in the churchyard of the church of the Blessed Mary of Lakenheath; to the high altar of the same church, for my tithes forgotten and not well paid, 20d.

To each of my godsons and goddaughters a ewe.

To the convent of Friars Minor of Babwell 6s 8d; to the convent of Friars Preachers of Thetford 6s 8d.[1]

Residue of all my goods to Ellen my wife and John Mervyn, execs; they to see everything fulfilled and disposed, as they know best to please God and profit the health of my soul.

Seal appended.

Proved at Fornham St Martin, 28 December 1469. Admon to execs.

[*This probate sentence deleted and another substituted at the foot of the folio.*]

[*Will, of same date*]

All my legacies in my testament to be well and truly implemented; all my debts, which I justly and rightfully owe, to be well and truly paid.

Ellen my wife to have 3 cows and all the utensils of my house, except a large brass pan, and she to have the pan for her own use for term of her life; after her decease I wish the pan to remain to the 3 gilds in Lakenheath, for their use for ever.[2]

Ellen my wife to have an acre of meadow at 'Coppidmere' for term of her life, or to sell it if she wishes; she to have the whole messuage in which I live, for term of her life, and if she wishes to sell it in her lifetime, then she to have all the money from the sale for her support, if she is in need, and the residue, if any remain, to be disposed by my execs, as they know best for the health of my soul.

I wish to have a suitable chaplain to celebrate in Lakenheath church for half a year, for my soul and for the souls of my friends, and if it can be done from my goods I wish to have the chaplain [fol. 433v] for a whole year.

I wish all my neighbours (*proximi*) and the poor at my obsequies to have sufficient bread, cheese and ale, to pray for my soul.

Isabel my servant to have a basin and ewer of latten.

Ellen my wife to receive 7 marks from John Kykkele, to be paid in the next 7 years, for a tenement I lately sold to him, for her support if she is in need.

John Merveyn to have, for his labour at [*my*] obsequies and on the day of my burial, 6s 8d.

Proved at Mildenhall ('Myldenhale'), 30 January 1469/70. Admon to execs, with the supervision and advice of John Myllere and William Lacy, whom we, the Official, for various good reasons (*ex diversis causis veris*) ordained and assigned as supervisors.

[*This probate sentence, substituted for the one appearing after the testament, has been inserted within the text of the will, at the foot of fol. 433.*]

---

1   For the friars see notes to no. 1 (Babwell) and no. 68 (Preachers of Thetford).
2   This practical bequest suggests that the 3 gilds in Lakenheath shared facilities. Thomas Hyve made bequests to the gilds of St John the Baptist and of the Blessed Mary in Lakenheath (SROB, Baldwyne 263; Pt I, no. 1289). The dedication of the third gild is unknown; neither Morley nor Redstone identified any other gild there.

400. THOMAS POTTERE of REDE ('Reede'), 16 December 1469

Dated at Rede; my body to Christian burial; to the high altar of Rede church, for my tithes and offerings forgotten or underpaid, 3s 4d; to the high altar of Chedburgh ('Chetylber') church 3s 4d; to the curate (*curatori*) of Rede church, each year for the term of 20 years after my death, to celebrate a 'sangred' for my soul and the souls for whom I am bound, 4s 4d; to my execs, 2s annually, to keep my anniversary day during the said term, if it can be done that long out of [*my*] goods; to the making of a candlebeam ('candelbem') in Rede church, 20s; to the reparation of Depden church, 3s 4d.

To Agnes my wife, for her sustentation, 10 marks in money, 2 cows and all my ostilments and utensils belonging to my household (*hospicio*).

To John my son, Robert my son and Roger my son, 20s each; to Isabel my daughter 20s; to Nicholas Pottere 20s; to Matilda my servant 20s; to each of my godsons and goddaughters who have never married, 12d; to Joan Pottere a cow.

Residue of all my goods to my execs, to sell, receive and dispose for my soul and the souls of all my benefactors and all the faithful departed, in deeds of charity, as they see best to please God and be expedient (*expedire*) for the aforesaid souls.

Execs: Roger Pottere and John Sparwe of Chedburgh; to each of whom for their labour, 40d.

Seal appended.

Proved at Fornham St Martin, 5 February 1469/70. Admon to execs.

[fol. 434]

[*At the head of fol. 434, all struck through, are the last few lines and probate sentence of will no. 436. They have been put in their rightful place at the end of that will.*]

401. JOAN ROBHOOD of WALSHAM [LE WILLOWS], widow, 1 August 1468

Widow of John Robhood the elder of Walsham;[1] to be buried near (*fere iux'*) my husband in the churchyard of the church of the Blessed Mary of Walsham; to the high altar of the same church 2s.

To John Robhood my son my best brass pot; to John a tenement in the street called 'le Chyrchestret', and after his decease I leave it to Stephen my grandson (*nepoti*) if he survives his father;[2] otherwise it to be sold to the profit of Walsham church if Stephen dies without heirs. To John 10 acres of land, more or less, in 5 separate pieces (*divisim iac' in quinque pec'*) in the street called 'Westret', on condition that he pays 10 marks as part of the stipend of a priest crossing to Rome to visit the sepulchres of the Apostles Peter and Paul (*ad limina apostolorum Petri et Pauli*).[3] To John the accessories (*ornatu'*) of a bed, that is, the celure ('celowre') with a tester at the head (*ad cap'*), together with blue cloths going round it, with a bed-cover of 'ly say'.

To the sustentation of a lamp burning in honour of God in Walsham church, for me and my friends for ever, that is, a rood of meadow lying in the great meadow, lately of the tenement '?Prentys'.

To the same Stephen the best brass pot bar one, a pan holding 4 gallons and a cauldron, and a basin with the ewer and half a garnish of 'ly pewter' with a chafing dish, together with the spit and a 'lez droppyng panne' and a 'lez ladyll' of latten.

To Isabel Chapman my niece (*nepote*) a red bed-cover with a pair of sheets, together with a 'lez blankett' and a pan holding 4 gallons, and 6 pieces of pewter, that is, 2 'plateres', 2 'dysches' and 2 'sawceres'.

To Edmund Chapman my nephew (*nepoti*) a red bed-cover, with a 'lez par' of sheets.

To John Chapman my nephew (*nepoti*) 6s 8d.

To Sir Robert Vyncent[4] a chest.

To John and Thomas my sons[5] and my assigns (*assign' meis*) 1½ acres of meadow in [fol. 434v] the great meadow, to keep my obit day and my husband's, annually, both in the ringing of bells and in the celebration of masses.

Residue of all my goods to the disposition of Sir George Hawys, rector of Barrow ('Bargh'), clerk,[6] and John Robhood my son, execs, to dispose for me and the health of my soul and all my benefactors' [*souls*], as seems to them most expedient.

Seal appended.

To Elizabeth Robhood, wife of John Robhood, all those lands in the town and fields of Langham, in separate pieces (*in divers' pec'*).

Proved at Fornham St Martin, 15 December 1470. Admon to execs.

1   Will pr. December 1459 (SROB, Baldwyne 258; Pt I, no. 1272). He had bequeathed 11 marks for the new stonework to be done at the parish church, possibly the clerestory. See Blatchly and Northeast, *Decoding Flint Flushwork*, Walsham le Willows St Mary.

2   Perhaps 'grandson', rather than 'nephew': 'grandson' was the original meaning of *nepos* in Classical Latin. The wording seems to suggest that Stephen was the son of John Robhood, Joan's son.

3   '*Ad limina Apostolorum*' is an ecclesiastical term meaning 'a pilgrimage to the sepulchres of both St Peter and St Paul at Rome, that is, to the Basilica of the Prince of the Apostles and to the Basilica of St Paul "outside the walls"' ('*ad limina Apostolorum*', *Catholic Encyclopedia*, i).

4   Executor of Cecily Hamownde of Thorney hamlet in Stowmarket (no. 737).

5   John and Thomas, together with their mother Joan, were appointed executors of their father's will.

6   George Hawys (Hawes), obviously a member of the Walsham family of that name, was rector of Barrow from 1453 to 1474 (Tanner, p.1400); will pr. July 1474 (SROB, Hervye 40); he had been supervisor of the will of Joan Robhood's husband, John; he was also appointed supervisor by Agnes Meryll (no. 502 below).

[fol. 435]

402. ROGER DRURY of HEPWORTH ('Heppeworth'), 'gentylman', 19 May 1467

Dated at Hepworth; my body to Christian burial; to the high altar of Hepworth church, for my tithes and offerings forgotten and underpaid, 6s 8d; to the reparation of the said church 6s 8d.

To the reparation of the common way through the middle (*per mediu'*) of the said town 6s 8d. To a suitable chaplain to celebrate in the said church, for my soul and the souls for whom I am bound, 8 marks.

To William Purpylle my nephew a basin, a bronze ewer (*lavacru' auric'*), 2 platters, 2 dishes and 2 saucers of pewter, a ewe and a lamb; to Marion my niece a basin, a bronze ewer, 2 platters, 2 dishes and 2 saucers of pewter, a ewe, a lamb and a calf of a year old.

To John Scoule, rector of the said church,[1] a folding table (*mensam applicata'*).

To Isabel my servant a cow and a calf of a year old, and other of my goods to the value, with the cow and calf, of 20s.

To John Deye my servant as much of my barley and my other goods as [*come*] to the value of 6s 8d.

To Roger Alpe my godson 12d.

Residue of all my goods to my execs, to sell, receive and dispose for my soul and the souls of [*my*] parents and friends and all the faithful departed, in the celebration of masses and other deeds of charity, as they see best to please God and profit my soul.

Execs: Thomas Drury my son and William Drury my son, to execute this testament faithfully.

Seal appended.

Proved at Fornham St Martin, 22 June 1467. Admon to execs.

¹   Witness and supervisor of the will of John Reve of Hepworth (no. 392).

403. ANDREW att HERNE of ICKLINGHAM ('Iklyngham'), 'bochere', 12 January 1462/63

[*For a more complete version of this testament, with probate, see no. 72 above.*]

To be buried in the churchyard of St James the Apostle in Icklingham; to the high altar of the said church, for tithes forgotten and negligently detained, 3s 4d; to the use of the said church 20s; to the church of All Saints of Icklingham 3s 4d; to the parish church of Ixworth 3s 4d.

To each of my godsons and goddaughters a ewe; to each child of my 3 goddaughters (*triu' filialarum*) [*recte* daughters]¹ a ewe.

To Alice Northfolke my servant a brass pot and a brass pan, and 20s in money (*in argent'*).

To Isolde my wife all my goods and chattels, both live and dead, and all my utensils. Residue of all my goods to Isolde my wife and William Heryng and Thomas Symonde, execs, primarily to pay all my debts and legacies, as seems best to profit the health of my soul, of my parents' and of all the faithful departed's [*souls*].

Seal appended.

[*No probate recorded.*]

¹   See the equivalent bequest in no. 72.

[fol. 435v]

404. ED' RYSBY of BUXHALL ('Buxhale'), 1 March 1469/70

Dated at Buxhall; to be buried in the churchyard of Buxhall church; to the high altar of the same church, for my tithes forgotten or underpaid 20d; to the sustentation or reparation of the same church 20s; to the sustentation of the lights of the gild of Corpus Christi there 12d; to the sustentation of the light of the gild of the Holy Trinity there,¹ to celebrate for the health of my soul [*no sum*].

A trental of St Gregory be celebrated by the friars of Babwell for my soul; to the convent of friars of Sudbury 10s for a trental of St Gregory to be celebrated there for the health of my soul; to the convent of Clare, for a trental to be celebrated there for the health of my soul.²

To Alice Salter my daughter 40s; to Joan Cobbe my daughter 20s; to John Cobbe my son 6s 8d; to each of the daughters of Robert Cobbe 6s 8d.

To the emendation of the dangerous (*nocument'*) way leading from 'Paynys' tenement to 'Banyardes' 6s 8d.

To the parish clerk of the said church 6d.

To Anne my wife 4 cows, which she has, and all my ostilments and utensils.

Residue of my goods to the disposition of my execs.

Execs: Anne my wife, Robert Cobbe and Edmund Salter; they to implement everything as written above, having God before their eyes, in the execution and fulfilling of this testament.

Seal appended.

Proved at Fornham St Martin, 19 March 1469/70. Admon to Robert Cobbe and Edmund Salter, execs. Power reserved to Anne Rysby, the other co-executrix, when she comes, if she wishes to take up admon. Seal of official appended.

1 Redstone refers to an altar of St Margaret (1526) and a gild of St John (1546) but makes no mention of either the gild of Corpus Christi or the gild of the Holy Trinity at Buxhall (*PSIA*, xii, p.76; xix, p.177). The wills of John Copenger (Pt I, no. 90) and John Cryketot (Pt I, no. 1393) both mentioned 'mass-pence of the gilds of Buxhall' but did not specify the names of the gilds.
2 For the friars see notes to nos 1 (Babwell and Clare) and 11 (Sudbury).

[fol. 436]
405. ROBERT TURNOUR of EYE, 17 February 1469/70

To be buried in the churchyard of the church of St Peter of Eye; to the high altar of the same church, for my tithes forgotten, 6s 8d; to the making of the new tower of the same church 16s 8d.

To William Moour, chaplain, to celebrate divine service in the said church for the health of my soul for a whole year, 8 marks.

To the gild of St Peter of Eye half a quarter of wheat and a quarter of malt; to the gild of St Mary of Eye[1] half a quarter of malt.

To each of my godsons and goddaughters, [*being*] children, half a quarter of barley.

To Agnes my daughter 13s 4d and a cow.

To Margaret my wife all my other animals, utensils and necessaries, live or dead, except all my gold and silver.

Residue of all my goods to the disposition of John Fysk, Robert Saxcy and John Saxcy, to dispose for my soul as they see best to please God and profit the health of my soul.

Seal appended.

[*Will of same date; given at Eye*]

Whereas I have enfeoffed certain of my dearest friends in my tenement in the borough of Eye, opposite the market there, with 18 acres of bond land in Eye, that were lately John Jenewes' of the same,[2] [*now*] I beg all my aforesaid feoffees competently to execute and fulfil my will, underwritten, as follows:

Margaret my wife to have my said tenement with the bond land, as above, for term of her life, without impeachment of waste, on condition that she pays John Fyske and Robert Saxcy of Eye, as the co-execs of the will of Agnes Jenewe,[3] my late mother, 20 marks in money in this way, that is, 8 marks in the 8 years immediately following my decease and 12 marks in the 4 years after that, that is to say, 40s each year, of which 6s 8d is for the keeping of the anniversary of John Jenewe and Agnes herself, the payments to begin at the next feast of St Michael the Archangel; and after the decease of Margaret my wife the tenement with the bond land wholly to remain to Robert my son, to hold to him and his heirs for ever.

If Margaret my wife should die before the said 20 marks have been fully paid, then the tenement with the bond land to be let to farm by my execs and the rent from them to be used for completing the payment of the 20 marks. If Robert my son should die before reaching the age of 18 and my wife is still living, then the tenement and bond land to be sold by my execs, after Margaret's decease, and the money disposed thus: there to be 4 honest chaplains, one after the other, to celebrate divine service in Eye church; to Joan my daughter 10 marks, [fol. 436v] and to Agnes my daughter 10 marks; if Joan or Agnes should die, the survivor to have the other's 10 marks; if both die then the 20 marks to be disposed by my execs.

If Robert my son should enjoy the tenement, with the land, then he to pay Joan and Agnes his sisters 5 marks each; if Margaret my wife should be pregnant at the time of my death, and produces a boy or girl child, then Robert to pay that child 5 marks and another 5 marks to an honest chaplain to celebrate divine service in Eye church; if the tenement and lands should end up being sold by my execs, that child to have 10 marks from the sale.

Seal appended.

Proved at Eye, 10 May 1470. Admon to execs. Seal of official appended.

1   For both gilds see notes to no. 2.
2   John Jenewes was the testator's mother's husband (Pt I, no. 624).
3   Will (as 'Jenews'), no. 94 above. The executors of her will were named as Robert Jenews, Alice Turnore her daughter, Robert Saxcy and John Saxci. Robert Turnour's request here suggests that he was one of Agnes's executors. In her will she did not mention her son Robert Turnour; however, since she made bequests to Joan and Agnes, the daughters of Robert Jenews, and also made that Robert one of her executors it seems likely that she was referring to her own son. In his will, John Jenewes made a bequest to Robert Turnour, 'my wife's son' and there is no suggestion that John himself had a son named Robert. This is an illustration of how surnames might change, or be interchangeable, in an extended family.

406. HENRY STORY of WHATFIELD ('Wattesfeld'), 5 June 1470

Dated at Whatfield;[1] sensing the peril of death to be imminent (*senciens mortis periculum eminer'*); [*commendation*: to God Almighty and the Blessed Virgin Mary]; my body to Christian burial in the churchyard of Whatfield church; to the fabric of Naughton ('Nawton') church 20d; to the fabric of Elmsett ('Elmysset') church 20d; to the fabric of Offton church 20d; to the fabric of Aldham church 20d. Residue of all my goods, [*after*] my body has been buried [*and my*] seven-day and thirty-day (*septenario et tricenario*) celebrated, I leave to my exec, to dispose for the health of my soul [*and*] of my friends' and benefactors' [*souls*], in the works and essentials (*operibus et necessariis*) of the new tower of Whatfield.[2]

Exec: my faithful friend Richard Wareyn of Whatfield.

Seal appended.

Witnesses: Sir John Sadyngton, rector of Semer,[3] and Sir John Hawkdon, rector of Nedging ('Neddyng'),[4] and others.

Proved at Whatfield ('Wattesfeld'), 14 June 1470. Admon to exec. Seal of official appended.

1   'Wattesfeld' must mean Whatfield because of the associated parishes; Wattisfield was then usually 'Watlesfeld'.
2   Probably a restoration of Whatfield's tower, described by Pevsner as 'of the thirteenth century'.
3   John Sadyngton was appointed rector of Semer in 1454 (Tanner, p.1388); will pr. 1472 (NRO, NCC 151 Betyns).
4   See note to no. 284 and also nos 303, 431, 720 and 721.

[fol. 437]

407. ALICE PYE of ASSINGTON ('Assyngton'), widow, 2 May 1470

Dated at Assington, in the diocese of Norwich; to be buried in the burial [*place*] (*sepultura*) of Assington church, next to the grave (*sepultura*) of Thomas Pye, my late husband.[1]

To Agnes Forde my daughter all my goods and chattels, moveable and unmoveable, and all the ostilments, utensils and bedding (*suppellect'*) of my house, out of which to pay my debts and to do as she wishes with the residue. Agnes my daughter to have my tenement in which I live, formerly Thomas my husband's, called 'Sowdens', for her lifetime; after her death the tenement to be sold by her execs and the money to be disposed for my soul, for Thomas Pye's soul and for the souls of all our friends and the faithful departed according to Agnes's discretion and ordination.

Execs: John Forde and Agnes his wife, to whom I leave all my goods as above.

Seal appended.

Witnesses: Sir Robert, vicar of the same church,[2] John Baldewyn, Edward Underwode, John Jefferey.

Proved at Sudbury, 6 March 1470/71. Admon to execs.

1   Will pr. September 1443 (SROB, Baldwyne 40; Pt I, no. 215). Edmund, son of Alice and Thomas, had predeceased his mother, will pr. February 1457/58 (SROB, Baldwyne 213; Pt I, no. 1057).

2   Robert Cutte was vicar of Assington from 1469 to 1489 (Tanner, p.1346).

408. STEPHEN BARBOUR of SUDBURY,[1] 4 October 1470

Dated at Sudbury, in the diocese of Norwich; sick of body; all testaments made before this date being revoked; to be buried in the churchyard of St Gregory in Sudbury, on the north side; to the high altar of the chapel of St Peter in the same town for tithes forgotten 40d.

To Petronilla my wife all the utensils of my house with all my jewels, to do with them freely as she wishes; to Petronilla 20 marks (*xx marcas*) in ready money of the money coming from the messuages sold to John Barbour my son and Robert Lalford, that is, annually after my decease 40s until the said sum of £20 (*viginti librarum*) be fully paid to Petronilla.

The curate of St Peter's chapel to have my soul and the souls of my father and mother commended in his Sunday prayers for 2 years after my death; that curate to have for his labour 4d.

My execs [fol. 437v] to find annually for 12 years after my decease an anniversary for my soul and the souls of my father and mother in the chapel of St Peter, distributing to priests, clerks [*and*] the poor in greatest need to the sum of 20s, and in other charitable gifts, as they see best to profit my soul as long as can be done from my goods, my debts and legacies first being paid.

Residue of all my goods to my execs to do for my soul as they see best to please God most and profit my soul.

Execs: John Brook the elder and George Prentys; to each of them 6s 8d for their labour.

Witnesses: Sir John Rysby,[2] John Potager, chaplains,[3] and others.

Proved at Sudbury, 6 March 1470/71. Admon to execs.

1   Witness of the will of John Freot of Sudbury, mercer, will pr. April 1454 (SROB, Baldwyne 157; Pt I, no. 758); ?executor (as 'Barbere') of John Wombe of Great Cornard, will pr. March 1461/62 (SROB, Baldwyne 278; Pt I, no. 1365).

2   John Rysby/Risby, chaplain, of Sudbury, also witnessed the wills of Thomas Alston (no. 290) and Alice Turnour (no. 698).

3   See note to no. 271.

[fol. 438]

409. WILLIAM JAY of STOKE BY NAYLAND ('iuxta Neylond'), 6 November 1470

Dated at Stoke by Nayland; to be buried in the churchyard of the church of the Blessed Virgin Mary of Stoke by Nayland; to the high altar of the same church for my tithes forgotten 40d; to the emendation of the same church 6s 8d; to the gild of St John the Baptist in the same church 6s 8d;[1] to each of the 2 priests being present at my obsequies 4d; and to the parish clerk and the 2 other clerks 6d between them. To Margery my wife the house or cottage in which I live, with the garden and well adjacent with all the buildings (*domibus*) belonging to it.

Residue of all my goods to John Brame, esquire,[2] William Skett, chaplain,[3] and Margery my wife, execs, to pay all my debts and dispose for my soul as seems most expedient to them in the future and also to implement this my will.

Seal appended.

Witnesses: Master John Cranewys, vicar of the said church,[4] Robert Rodyng, gentleman, Robert Lunt and many others.

Proved at Lavenham, 18 December 1470. Admon to Margery the executrix. Power reserved to grant admon to John Brame, esquire, and William Skett, chaplain, the other co-execs, when they come, if they wish to take it up.

1   The wording of this bequest suggests that this gild met in the church. In 1521 a bequest was made to the gild of lands, a barn and garden, called Pondyard (*PSIA*, xii, p.84); in 1522 there were 3 gilds in the parish: St John the Baptist, Our Lady and St Peter (*PSIA*, xxiii, p.72).
2   Probably related to Sir John Braham of Braham Hall in Brantham (Copinger, *Manors of Suffolk*, vi, p.23).
3   Witness of the will of John Folke of Stoke by Nayland (no. 556).
4   See note to no. 150; Cranewyse also witnessed nos 150, 236 and 556.

410. JOHN HAWKYN of Attleton ('Attilton')[1] in WICKHAMBROOK ('Wykhambrook'), 6 April 1466

['Haukyn' *in margin*] Dated at Attleton in the parish of Wickhambrook; [*commendation*: to God Almighty my Creator and Saviour, the Blessed Virgin Mary his mother and all the saints]; to be buried in the churchyard of All Saints' church of the said parish; to the high altar of the same church for my tithes forgotten 12d.

To the friars of Clare 20d; to the friars of Babwell 20d.[2]

Residue of all my lands and tenements and of all my goods and chattels, live or dead, of whatever sort, [fol. 438v] after my legacies and debts have been paid, to Agnes my wife to dispose as she sees best to please God and most profit the health of my soul.

Executrix: Agnes my wife.

Seal appended.

Proved at Fornham St Martin, 14 January 1468/69. Admon to executrix.

1   Now Attleton Green.
2   See notes to no. 1.

411. ELIZABETH GATE of BARNINGHAM ('Bernyngham'), 8 July 1470

Dated on Relic Sunday, 1470; to be buried in the churchyard of Barningham church. I beg my execs well and truly to pay the debts which I owe, and this as soon as possible, in the best manner. To the high altar of the same church for tithes forgotten and not duly paid 12d; to the parish priest 6d; to the parish clerk 2d.

To Joan my daughter all the corn growing on my land and all my debts and any rents and farms belonging to my part of the manor in Barningham, both for arrears and for the term up to St Michael the Archangel next after the date of this testament; to Joan my daughter all the utensils of my house and all my goods and chattels, both moveable and unmoveable, wherever they may be; she to pay all my debts and the legacies of this testament well and truly, and meet all the costs and expenses of the day of my death (*obitus*).

Executrix: Joan my daughter, to dispose for me and the souls of all my benefactors as seems best to please [*God*] in exoneration of her conscience against God in this manner.

Proved at Wattisfield ('Watlesfeld'), 19 [*possibly 29*] January 1470/71. Admon to executrix.

[fol. 439]

412. THOMAS FLECCHER of WALSHAM [LE WILLOWS], 8 January 1469/70

Dated at Walsham, in the diocese of Norwich; to be buried in the churchyard of Walsham church. I wish my execs wholly to pay out of my goods all my debts for which I am bound to others and which can be legally proved. To the high altar for tithes forgotten or ignorantly paid 12d.

To Alice my daughter 20s, to be paid on the day of her marriage; to Joan my daughter 13s 4d, to be paid after the death of Isabel my wife; to Isabel my wife all the ostilments and utensils of my house and all my moveable chattels.

Residue of all my goods to my executrix for her disposition as she sees best to please God and profit my soul.

Executrix: Isabel my wife, faithfully to execute this testament.

Seal appended.

Proved 26 January 1469/70. Admon to executrix.

[fol. 439v]

413. THOMAS LADYMAN of LITTLE WHELNETHAM ('Parva Whelenetham'),[1] 23 April 1467

Dated at Little Whelnetham; to be buried in Christian burial; to the high altar of the church of Whelnetham aforesaid for my offerings forgotten and too little paid 12d; to the reparation of the same church 6s 8d.

To Agnes my wife all my lands and tenements for term of her life, and after her death all the said lands and tenements to remain to John my son and his heirs for ever, on condition that he be honestly governed by his mother, and also that he pays a suitable chaplain to celebrate divine service for half a year in the said church for my soul 4 marks, and also pays all my debts, and pays each of his brothers and sisters 6s 8d.

To the same John all the instruments whatsoever belonging to my trade.

To the friars of the convent of Sudbury to pray and intercede for my soul 3s 4d.[2]

Residue of all my goods and chattels to Agnes my wife and John my son on the above conditions; they to be execs to perform my testament well and truly.

Seal appended.

Witnesses: Edmund Dyx, Godfrey Ladyman, John Hachet and others.

Proved at Fornham St Martin, 29 January 1469/70. Admon to execs.

1. Executor of Isabel Bunne of Little Whelnetham, probate March 1450/51 (SROB, Baldwyne 112; Pt I, no. 525); executor of John Bunne (no. 93 above); executor of Simon Balley (no. 130 above); witness of both the testament and will of Robert Hunte of Rushbrooke (no. 191 above). Thomas Ladyman's daughter Isabel and his (unnamed) sons were beneficiaries of the will of Alan Godfrey of Little Whelnetham, pr. December 1450 (SROB, Baldwyne 114; Pt I, no. 533).
2. See note to no. 11.

[fol. 440]

414. ROBERT AGAS of THURSTON ('Thruston'),[1] 12 August 1469 [*English*]

To be buried in the churchyard of Thurston; to the high altar a mother sheep for my tithes and offerings forgotten; to the light of Our Lady a 'chephogge'.[2]

To Adam Agas my son my house, my land and all other chattels ('catell') and ostiments, with this condition, that he find meat, drink and all other necessaries to me 'longing during my life and honestly bring me the day of my burying to the earth and that the persons being present have bread and cheese and drink.

I will that Adam pays to the friars of Thetford, to the house where Master Pers Oldman is, 10s for a Gregory trental[3] and that Adam goes or 'do gone' 7 ('vij') pilgrimages: one to the Trinity at Norwich, another to St Leonard there,[4] another to St Nicholas at Tibenham ('Tybenham') [*Norfolk*],[5] another to Our Lady of Woolpit ('Wolpet'),[6] another to Our Lady of Sudbury,[7] another to St Theobald at Newmarket,[8] which pilgrimages have been long owing. [*Only these 6 are specified.*][9] Adam to pay Joan my daughter for the time she kept me [*when*] sick and all my other debts. When this writing is performed and fulfilled, then I require and pray my feoffees to deliver an estate to Adam Agas my son, or to such as he wills in his name, with God's blessing and mine.

Proved at Fornham St Martin, 15 January 1469/70. Admon to exec, Adam Agas the son.

1. The tenement of Robert Agas is mentioned in the will of John Rose the younger of Thurston, pr. July 1448 (SROB, Baldwyne 119; Pt I, no. 552); Robert was a beneficiary of the will of his brother, Roger Agace of Bardwell (no. 364 above).
2. See Glossary, under 'sheephog'.
3. This bequest was to the Dominican house at Thetford, for it is recorded that in 1475 Peter Oldman was prior of that house (*VCH Norfolk*, ii, pp.433–5). In 1474, Ed' Man of Rattlesden made a bequest to 'Doctor Oldman of the Thetford house' (no. 797 below). For the Dominican house at Thetford see note to no. 68.
4. That is, to the image of the Holy Trinity in Norwich cathedral and to the image in St Leonard's cell at Norwich. The *Valor Ecclesiasticus* recorded that in 1535 the three shrines in the hands of the cathedral priory received offerings from pilgrims totalling £3 13s 8½d: £2 19s 7d to the image of the Holy Trinity in the cathedral church; 13s 7d to St Robert at the cell of Holme; and 6½d to the image of St Leonard's cell, Norwich (*VCH Norfolk*, ii, pp.317–28).
5. Tibenham had a chapel of St Nicholas at the east end of the south aisle; it was a locally supported and recognised place of pilgrimage.
6. See note to no. 142.
7. A statue of Our Lady in the west wall of St Gregory's church (will of Joan Payne of Sudbury, 1472 (TNA, PCC 6 Wattys; now PROB11/6, image 67)).
8. The chapel of St Theobald in St Mary's church, Newmarket, which attracted pilgrims (May, *Newmarket: Medieval and Tudor*, p.24).
9. A particularly interesting list of minor pilgrimage centres in Norfolk and Suffolk.

[fol. 440v]

415. ROBERT MYNNYS of GREAT ASHFIELD ('Aysshffeld Magna'), 10 December 1469 [*nuncupative*]

Dated at Great Ashfield; to be buried in the churchyard of the church of St Mary of Ashfield aforesaid; to the high altar of the said church 12d.

To the friars of Babwell for a trental 10s.[1]

To Alice Hamyre of Stanton a coomb of barley.

All remaining goods to be to the use and discretion of my execs.

Execs: Alice Mynnys wife of the said John [*sic*; *recte* Robert], Robert Bret of Hunston ('Hunterstone').

Proved at Badwell, 16 January 1469/70. Admon to execs. Acquitted.

> [1] See note to no. 1.

416. ROBERT HUBERD [of REDGRAVE], 29 August 1469

To be buried in the churchyard of the church of All Saints of Redgrave.

To John my son[1] my house, but Isabel my wife is to have her dwelling in it for her lifetime, on condition that he pays all my debts; to John and Isabel all my moveable goods, to be shared between them, being indifferently valued.

The said John owes for wax for the sepulchre 11s; he owes to the gild of St Botolph 10s;[2] to Nicholas Base 13s 4d; to William Bryan 31s.

John Martyn owes the said Robert 6d; Terry of Burgate [*owes*] 6d; Fulchere of Burgate [*owes*] 4½d.

Residue of all my goods to my execs, John my son and Isabel my wife, to dispose for the health of my soul as they see most expedient.

Proved at Botesdale ('Botysdale'), 17 January 1469/70. Admon to execs.

> [1] ?Will no. 543 below.
> [2] The chapel of St Botolph was situated in Botesdale, a hamlet of Redgrave; perhaps the gild of St Botolph was attached to that chapel; no other testator in the Baldwyne register mentioned this gild. See note to no. 15 for the chapel and chapelry of Botesdale.

[fol. 441]

417. BALDEWIN COKSEDGE of FELSHAM, gentleman, 18 March 1467/8 [*testament*]; 5 July 1469 [*will*][1]

[*Testament*]

Dated 18 March 1467/8 at Felsham; to be buried in the churchyard of Felsham church, near the entrance to the chancel on the south side by my forefathers (*antecessores*); to the high altar of the said church 20d.

My execs to dispose for the soul of John Munnyng, former rector of the said church, 20d;[2] for the soul of John Sterre lately rector of the said church 20d.[3]

To Katherine Coksedge, nun of Redlingfield ('Redlyngfeld') 6s 8d;[4] to Margaret Coksedge my sister 5s.

Denise my wife[5] to have my new brass pot and my best brass pan for term of her life and after her decease the said pot and pan to remain to George my son and his assigns; my best old brass pot to be sold to the said Denise and the money from it I leave to Edmund my son.

To the same Edmund my large brass pitcher (*urciolu'*); he to have 2 silk belts harnessed with silver and gilt; he to give Denise his mother 6s 8d;[6] the residue of it [*the money*] to be distributed at her discretion among my daughters if they are in need; if they die, it to be distributed for our souls and for those for whom I am bound.

To Margaret my daughter 2 sheep, a brass pan, a cover and a pair of sheets; to Margery my daughter 2 sheep, a brass pan, a cover and a pair of sheets; to George my son a cover and a pair of sheets; to Robert son of John Coksedge a lamb and half a quarter of wheat.

I leave a cow sufficient for 2 candles burning for ever before the image of the Blessed Mary in the chancel of St Peter's church of Felsham.

To Denise my wife a small brass pot and a small brass pan for term of her life, and after her decease the said pot and pan to remain to Margery my daughter; to Denise half my chattels for her sustentation and to 'find' all her children;[7] to Alice Goderyche my goddaughter 20d; to each of my godsons and goddaughters surviving 12d.

Execs: Denise my wife, Edmund Coksedge my son and John Nune.

Supervisors: Henry Straunge, esquire,[8] and John Chapman of ?Shotley ('Sehotle'). Residue of all my goods to my execs to sell, receive and dispose for my soul and the souls for whom I am bound, in celebrating masses and distributing alms and other deeds of charity as seems best to them to please God and profit my soul.

Seal appended.

Witnesses: John Nune senior, William Ramsey, Robert Gentilman, John Moor and William Cotelere of Felsham.

[*Will; English*]

Dated 5 July 1469 at Felsham. I do own ('on") my testament before made; my debts to be 'plen'ly' paid.

Denise my wife to have 20s for her dower and my place called 'Upwode Hall', otherwise 'Coksedgys', in Felsham, during her lifetime. She to have the new house called a parlour ('parlure') with the kitchen ('kechyn') and the chambers [fol. 441v] pertaining to the said parlour and kitchen in my said place during her life, if she live sole without a husband; she to have the little garden on the east side of the said parlour, between the parlour and the chambers on that one 'party' and the quick hedge set from the gate unto the hall door on the other 'party', during her life; she to have all the garden on the west side of the said parlour and chambers with all the curtilage on the west side of my place, within the moat, from the kitchen door unto the pear tree and from the pear tree to the west end of the bakehouse ('bakhows') and so forth to the moat side, with all the commodities within the said garden and curtilage growing and being, as in herbages, fruits, feedings and fishings in the moat and the fruit of the said pear tree and of an apple tree standing in the same 'cours' falling within the said curtilage, and other profits, without destruction or cutting down of trees during her life as aforesaid. Denise to have her easement in the bakehouse in lawful time for brewing, for baking and for drying of malt, and a stable within the moat, and her easement in the malting house joined thereto, with this condition, that the occupier of my said place shall have his wetting of his barley in the vat ('fate') of Denise during malting time, that is, Denise one wetting and the occupier another wetting. Also the going of hens and fowls 'clovefotyd' as it pleases Denise reasonably, with twain hogs-going and free incoming and free outgoing in lawful time to and from the said parlour, kitchen, bakehouse, stable, malting house, gardens and curtilage, with her carriage of all manner of things such as she needs at both bridges ('breggis') well and in peace, without any impediment of the occupier of my said place during her life as above. Denise to have of the occupier of my place, for the said parlour, kitchen, chambers, bakehouse, stable, malting house, gardens and curtilage, if she will dwell with any of her daughters, or in any other place lawful, or to be married well at her friends' will, yearly 6s 8d, besides her dower aforesaid, during her life as abovesaid.

John my son to have my said place called 'Upwode Hall', otherwise called 'Coksedgys', in Felsham, with all the appurtenances, except all that is excepted in this will and upon that I will that my feoffees see that my will in all wise be fulfilled. If John will not pay the money that he owes for the farm of the said place, or shall owe according to the covenants of his indenture, or if he will not pay his mother the money for her dower aforesaid, or if he would let [*hinder*] any part of her easement as aforesaid, I will that my feoffees and my executors enter upon him and put him out and keep him out till he will find surety to be in peace and pay his duty. After the decease of Denise and after my will be fulfilled, I will that my execs and feoffees 'see the best mene that they can' in restoring again to the old entail of the said place. Denise to have my tenement called [fol. 442] 'Beeryns', with all the appurtenances, for the term of her life and after her decease the tenement to remain to my son Edmund and his \heirs and/ assigns for evermore. She to have all the lands, meadows, pastures and feedings called 'Southwode' and 'Walymerche' which I bought of Piers of Stonham, with all the appurtenances, during her life, and after her decease the said lands, meadows, pastures and feedings to remain to my son George and his heirs and assigns for evermore.

My daughter Agnes to [*have*] the farm of all the lands called 'Mekyll Southfyld' containing 8 acres by estimation, lying on the south 'party' of my land called 'Meryeakyr' and 'Brookhallende', and a croft with a piece of meadow containing 4 acres by estimation, which I bought of Sir John Gooderyche, priest, the said 8 acres with the said 4 acres abutting upon my lane towards the west; and a croft lying upon the west side of John Skottes, sometime called 'Dychehows', with a piece of pasture lying the nether end of the said croft containing 3 acres, more or less by estimation; and the land called 'Lytyll Southfeld' lying on the north side of 'Brokhallende' on one 'party' and the land of Robert Gentilman on the other 'partye', the which I bought of John of Dyche, Walter Moore and John of Moore of Felsham aforesaid; and another piece of land lying on the west side of the 'Otecrofte' otherwise called 'Coteleryscrofte', with a piece of meadow lying between the meadow of the said Robert Gentilman on the one 'partye' and the meadow of William Cotelere on the other 'parte', till the sum of 7 marks be levied for the said Agnes. My execs to keep the said 7 marks till the husband of Agnes will make a lawful estate and feoffment of his lands and tenements for the term of the life of Agnes unto such persons as be his friends and hers both, as of 3, 5, 7 or 9, as 2 of her kin and 1 of his. And if so be that he will not make such estate, then the sum to be kept till after his decease if it happen him to decease before her, and if he would make his will contrary to the covenant of the first feoffment that she should not have the said lands and tenements [*for*] term of her life, then my heirs and execs to make the best 'mene' of plea that they can for the recovery of the said lands and tenements according to the estate that should [*have*] been made at the time of the marriage-making, with the said 7

247

marks. If it happen her to decease before him, then she to dispose it as she and her friends think best.

The farm of the said lands, meadows and pasture before named, when the said 7 marks is levied for my daughter Agnes, go to my daughter Margaret/Margery ['*Margaret*' *deleted; '*Margery*' written above and then deleted*] till the sum of 10 marks be levied for the said Margaret/Margery [*deleted doubly as before*] and after the said 10 marks is so levied for the said Margery [*sic*] then I will that if it happen that any of my said ~~daughters do die unmarried~~ the said 10 marks be so levied for the said Margaret [*sic*] then the farm of the said lands, meadows, pastures before named go to my daughter Margery till the sum of 10 marks be levied for the said Margery. And after the said 10 marks is so levied for the said Margery, then if it happen [fol. 442v] that any of my said daughters to die unmarried, then the said farm of the said lands, meadows and pastures levied in the manner of form above said be evenly departed between all my ~~daughters~~ other children living. And the said 8 acres of land called 'Mekyll Southfeld', after the said money is so levied for my said daughters before named, to go to the said Denise my wife for term of her life, if she will live sole, or else not.

And after the decease of Denise, then the said 8 acres remain to my said place called 'Coksedgys' perpetually, without end. The said croft and meadow, late of the said Sir John Goderyche, priest, after the said money is levied for my said daughters, to go to Denise my wife during her life and after her decease the said croft and meadow to remain to my son Edmund and his \heirs and/ assigns for ever; 'without that' [*unless?*] George my son and his feoffees will make estate to the said Edmund of the said lands called 'Lytille Southfeld', to hold to him and his \heirs and/ assigns for ever, then the said croft and meadow be sold and the money thereof to be evenly departed between the said Edmund and George; or else the said Edmund to have the said croft and meadow as before said and the said George to have the said land called 'Lytill Southfeld', to him and his \heirs and/ assigns for ever.

The foresaid croft under 'Scottys' with the said piece of pasture at the nether end of the said croft, after my daughters be fully paid in the manner of form before rehearsed, to go to Denise my wife for the term of her life as before said, and after her decease the said croft and pasture to remain to my place called 'Coksegys' perpetually. After my daughters be paid in the manner and form above said, the said lands called 'Lytyll Southfeld' to go to Denise my wife for term of her life and after her decease the said lands to remain to my son Edmund and his \heirs and/ assigns, if the said George and the feoffees will deliver estate to him; or else be it as it is before said. After my daughters be so paid in the manner and form above said, the said piece of land lying on the west side of the 'Ote croft' together with the said piece of meadow thereto lying to remain to my son Edmund and his \heirs and/ assigns for evermore.

The said Edmund my son to have the 4 obligations that I took unto him to make thereof 'what that he can' in my name and that my execs 'avowe' him in his suit and make him a letter of attorney if need be. The 7d yearly rent which is not contained in my deed of entail to remain to my said place perpetually. John my son to have all the goods and 'catall' that be comprehended in his indenture without any claim of my execs.

Execs: Denise my wife, John Nune, and Edmund my son.

Supervisors: Henry Straunge, 'sqwyer', John Chapman of ?Shotley ('Shottele').

Seal appended.

Witnesses: John Nune the elder, William Ramsey, Robert Gentylman, John Moor and William Cotelere of Felsham.

Proved at Fornham St Martin, 2 April 1470. Admon to Denise; exec John Nonne renouncing.

[*A small piece of paper, sewn in between fols 441v and 442, records* (*in Latin*) *the examination of 2 of the witnesses concerning the* Reformac' (*?validation*) *of this will, dated 23 January 1480/81* (*in Roman numerals[9]*).]

John Nune of Felsham, aged 40 years and more, freeman, witness of the will, questioned about the making of the said Baldewin's will and about this clause 'to his heirs and assigns' (*heredibus & assignatis suis*) and he said that this was true.

Robert Jentilman of Felsham, aged 50, freeman, witness, questioned about the making of Baldewin's will, said that 'he bequeathed to him, his heirs and assigns' (*legavit sibi hered' & assig'is suis*).

[*As indicated in the text, in the register, the phrase* 'heirs and' *has been inserted between* 'his' *and* 'assigns' *at each occurrence.*]

[1]   This testament and will were published in Tymms, *Wills and Inventories*, pp.44–50.
[2]   John Munnyng had been rector of Felsham from 1431 to 1456 (Tanner, p.1433); will pr. July 1456 (NRO, NCC 17 Neve).
[3]   John Sterr had succeeded Munnyng in 1456; his successor, Ralph Wode, was appointed in 1466 (Tanner, p.1433).
[4]   See note to no. 83.
[5]   Daughter of John Rows of Pakenham, will pr. August 1460 (SROB, Baldwyne 253; Pt I, no. 1255).
[6]   The Latin is: *It' d'cus Ed's dabit Dionisie matri sue vj s viij d.* Tymms has rendered it: *It' dono Ed'e Davit Dionisie matri sue vj s viij d.*
[7]   The Latin is: *ad sustentacio'em suam & om'ib' pui's Invenis.* Tymms has rendered it: *ad sustentac'oem suam at om'ib' suis p'mis juvenis.*
[8]   Henry L'Estrange, lord of the manor of Felsham Hall (Copinger, *Manors of Suffolk*, vi, p.265) and lord of the manor of Thorpe Morieux (*Manors of Suffolk*, iii, p.205); he died in 1485 (IPM 1 Henry VII, 52) and was buried in the chancel of Hunstanton church; he had married Katherine, daughter of Roger Drury of Hawstead.
[9]   Possibly 1485/86 (there is a faint mark after '*lxxx*'); however, given the then ages of the witnesses, who had also witnessed the testament in 1467/8 and the will in 1469, the earlier date of 1480/81 seems more likely.

[fol. 443]

418. JOHN BARBOUR [of REDGRAVE], 4 December 1469

To be buried in the churchyard of the church of All Saints of Redgrave; to the reparation of the church of All Saints 3 marks; to the superior church of Rickinghall ('Rykynghale') 3s 4d; to the chapel of St Botolph 20d.[1]

To William Drynkston 3s 4d.

To my execs, Emme my daughter and William Drynkston, 2 cauldrons, a spit, a frying pan (*sartagine*), a spinning-wheel ('spynnyngwele') and a chest, to dispose as they see best to profit the health of my soul.

Proved at Botesdale ('Botisdale'), 17 January 1469/70. Admon to execs.

[1]   Regarding the chapel and chapelry of St Botolph, Botesdale, see notes to nos 15 and 416.

419. THOMAS COKE of WITHERSFIELD ('Wetherysfeld'),[1] 25 January 1468/69

['Cook' *in margin*] Dated at Withersfield; knowing the end of this present life of mine to be approaching (*sciens fine' mee presentis vite immuner'*[*sic*]); my body to Christian burial in the churchyard of the parish church of the Blessed Virgin Mary of Withersfield; to the high altar of the same church for tithes forgotten and offerings underpaid 6d; I bequeath a cow of price 8s, or the value of it, to find and sustain a light before the rood (*patibulo*) on the rood solar ('le rodesoler')[2] in the said church for ever.

To Isabel my wife 2 little groves (*grovetas*) in Withersfield for term of her life and after her decease the little groves to remain to John my son and his heirs for ever.

Residue of all my goods to Isabel my wife, Thomas Petyte and William Coke to see my funerals done, pay my debts and distribute for my soul and the souls of my friends as seems to them best to profit the health of my soul.

Execs: Isabel my wife, Thomas Petyte and William Coke, to implement my will as above.

Seal appended.

Proved at Clare, 25 January 1469/70. Admon to Thomas Petyte and William Coke, execs. Power reserved to the other co-executrix, when she comes, if she wishes to take up admon.

1 Executor (as 'Cok') of John Sare of Withersfield, probate June 1457 (SROB, Baldwyne 221; Pt I, no. 1107).
2 See Glossary.

[fol. 443v]

420. WILLIAM ADAM of WITHERSFIELD ('Wetherysfeld'), 1 May 1469

Dated at Withersfield; seeing the peril of death to be imminent (*videns me periculum mortis iminer'*); to be buried in the churchyard of the church of the Blessed Mary of Withersfield; to the high altar of the same church for tithes forgotten and offerings underpaid 4d; 40d to the buying of an alabaster panel (*tabule*) standing (*stant'*) in the said church; 20d to be distributed among the poor as quickly as it can be had of my goods.

After my decease, Alice my wife to find a light before the great cross in the said church, for term of her life, and after her decease, my execs to take a cow which she has of my legacy to maintain the light for ever.

40d to the reparation of the causeway (*calcet'*) between the church and my house.

To the friars of Clare 4d.[1]

To Eleanor my sister 40d, which she shall have at (*per*) divers times without the knowledge (*cognicione*) of her husband.[2]

To each priest present at my obsequies 4d and to each clerk of man's age (*etat'*) 2d. To Alice my wife all my moveable goods besides the foregoing legacies, she to implement everything in this will, pay all my debts and meet all the expenses relating to my funerals. My wife to have, for the term of her life, all my lands and tenements and, if she is in need, she to sell them for her sustentation; but if she is not in need, then my execs, after my wife's decease, to sell all the said lands and tenements and the money from them to be disposed in alms, that is, to the church, to the poor and to muddy (*turpis*) ways.

To Alice the daughter of John Heth 2 quarters of barley.

To each of my godsons 4d.

Residue of all of my goods to my execs: Alice my wife, John Shapman, John Barker. Seal appended.

Proved at Clare, 25 January 1469/70. Admon to John Shapman and John Barkere, execs. Power reserved to Alice my[*sic*] wife, the other exec, when she comes, if she wishes to take up admon.

¹   See note to no. 1.
²   ?an untrustworthy brother-in-law.

[fol. 444]

421. ALICE THYSTELDEN of STOWMARKET, 4 January 1462/63

['Thystylden' *in margin*] Dated at Stowmarket, 4 January 2 Edward IV; Alice Thystelden for long (*dudum*) the wife of Robert Kent of Stowmarket;¹ [*no commendation of soul or burial directions*].

I give notice by this present writing regarding the disposal of my goods for my soul and the soul of Robert Kent my late husband, after my decease, for disposing and distributing for the health of our souls and the souls of our benefactors and friends. My 2 best gowns, a green silvered belt, a green and blue cloak, a principal violet tunic, [*all*] to be sold and the money disposed thus: to the parish church of Mendlesham 6s 8d; to the poor 6s 8d, where there seems to be need.

An annual stipend to be disposed to an honest chaplain for a year from our goods.

All the ostilments and utensils of my house to be sold, and all other apparel (*apparatus*) of my body, by Thomas Cook of Cotton my brother, and the money to be disposed in honour of God and the health of our souls.

A pair of my best beads of 'geet' [*jet*] with silver paternosters to be given to the maintenance and reparation of the praise and ministration of the image of the Blessed Mary in the chapel of the Blessed Mary of St Peter's church of Stowmarket ('Stowe'), to serve there for ever, never to be removed (*sine alienacione*).² My 3 principal sheets to be sold and the money used for ministering (*ministrand'*) in the chapel of the Blessed Mary there. My best green and blue cover and a brass pot, a brass pan of 4 gallons and a dozen best pewter vessels to be sold similarly and disposed for our souls.

Thomas Cook my brother to have my 'fetherbed' as a remembrance of me.

Residue of all my goods to Thomas Cook my brother to dispose for our souls and our benefactors' and friends' [*souls*] for whom we are bound as he sees [*best*] to please God and for the health of our souls; he to be exec and attorney.

Seal appended.

A brass jug measuring a pottle and a brass pan of a quart similarly to be sold; 2 of my cows to be sold and the money to be disposed for the souls of Robert Kent and me [*and*] for whom they are bound.

Proved at Stowmarket, 31 January 1470/71. Admon to exec.

¹   Will pr. May 1443 (SROB, Baldwyne 56; Pt I, no. 288).
²   Since they were to remain in the Lady Chapel for ever, the jet and silver beads were to adorn the image of the Virgin and thus 'minister' to image by beautifying it; for donations of jewellery to shrines see note to no. 142.

[At the foot of fol. 444 is the beginning of a will, crossed through, which is apparently not entered elsewhere and so has been transcribed here.]

422. JOHN GRYGGE [of HARTEST?], [undated]

To be buried in the parish church of Hartest ('Hertest').

Ellen my wife to have and peacefully enjoy all [my] lands and tenements for term of her life and after her decease they to remain to my son John the elder and his heirs. If John should die without heirs, then the said lands and tenements to remain to John his brother and his heirs. And if he should die without heirs [nothing further]

[fol. 444v]

423. RICHARD DYKYS of CAVENDISH ('Cavndyssh'), 30 October 1469

Of Cavendish in the diocese of Norwich; sick in body; testament with last will; to be buried in the churchyard of Cavendish; to the new cross 20d; to the 'tabell' in the chapel (*basilic'*) of [St] John the Baptist 20d.[1]

To Marjory my wife all the utensils of my house, to do with them freely as she wishes.

To the reparation of the highway between Clare and Cavendish 6s 8d.

Residue of all my goods together with my debts to Richard Dykys my son, to pay my debts, see to my funerals and do other (*cetera*) works of piety for my soul, as he sees best to please God and profit my soul; he to be exec to see to the above.

Seal appended.

Proved at Sudbury, 6 March 1470/71. Admon to exec.

> [1] In 1459, John Glovere of Cavendish (no. 133) had bequeathed 10 marks to a suitable priest to celebrate for a year for his soul and the souls of his parents and benefactors in the chapel of St John the Baptist in Cavendish church.

424. JOHN RUSSELL the elder of GREAT WALDINGFIELD ('Waldyngfeld Magna'), churchwarden (*iconomus*), 1470

[No date or month.] In the presence of many of the great of the parish (*presencia ?plurium plurimum parochie*); to be buried in the churchyard [of Great Waldingfield] aforesaid; to the high altar 40d for tithes forgotten.

To the Friars Minor of Colchester (*Colcest'*) a trental to be celebrated for my soul; to the house of friars of Sudbury (*Sudbur'*) and to the house of friars of Clare in the same way.[1]

To William my son 13s 4d; to Robert my son 13s 4d.

Residue of all and singular my goods to the disposition of Agnes Russell my wife, Thomas Russell my son and Robert Smyth, execs, to dispose for me and for the health of my soul as seems best to them.

Proved at Sudbury, 6 March 1470/71. Admon to execs.

> [1] For the friars see notes to nos 1 (Clare), 11 (Sudbury) and 38 (Colchester).

[fol. 445]

425. WILLIAM DANON of SUDBURY, 10 February 1470/71

Dated at Sudbury, in the diocese of Norwich; sick in body; testament with last will; to be buried in the churchyard of St Gregory of the same town, that is, by the grave of Simon Danon my father;[1] to the high altar of the chapel of St Peter of Sudbury, for my tithes and offerings by me forgotten 12d.

To Isabel my wife all my utensils [*and*] bedding of my house and all my malt found in my house after my decease, to do with freely as she will; she to find a secular chaplain to celebrate divine service in the church of St Peter aforesaid for a whole year after my decease, for my soul and the souls of my father and mother.[2]

Residue of all my goods, with my debts, to Isabel to pay my debts, see to my funerals and do other (*cetera*) works of piety for my soul, as she sees best to please God most and profit my soul; Isabel my wife to support (*exhibeat*), annually after my decease, my anniversary, for my soul and the souls of my father and mother as long as it can conveniently be borne of my goods, my debts and legacies first having been paid.

Isabel my wife to be executrix; Sir John Potager[3] to oversee my wife in the execution of my testament.

Proved at Sudbury, 6 March 1470/71. Admon to executrix.

[1] Will (as 'Danown'), pr. February 1457/58 (SROB, Baldwyne 213; Pt I, no. 1058); his son William was executor.

[2] When he made his will Simon Danown's wife was named Agnes but she was not necessarily William's mother.

[3] See note to no. 271.

426. SIMON GALTE of WORLINGTON ('Wyrlyngton'), 6 February 1470/71

Dated 6 February 1470, 49 Henry VI from the first beginning of his reign and [*in*] the first year of his majesty's readeption (*nove depco'is regie sue magestatis*; literally 'of his newly taken-up royal majesty');[1] testament containing last will; [*commendation to*: Almighty God my Creator and Saviour, to the Blessed Mary his mother and all the saints]; my body to be buried in Christian burial; to the high altar of Worlington church for my tithes and offerings forgotten and withheld [*and*] in exoneration of my soul 40d; [fol. 445v] to the reparation of the said church of Worlington ('Wrydlyngton') 2s.

Residue of all my goods and chattels, both moveable and unmoveable, to Margaret my wife, she to pay all my debts which of right I owe to anyone. I request all my feoffees to deliver estate and seisin to Margaret my wife of all my lands and tenements when so required by her.

Margaret my wife to be executrix and Robert Kelyng co-exec.

Seal appended.

Proved at Newmarket (*Novum Mercat'*), 8 March 1470/71. Admon to execs.

[1] The register clerk clearly struggled with this phrase: first he wrote *adepco'is*, then crossed it out, then wrote it again, and then deleted the leading '*a*'. Henry VI had been re-crowned on 13 October 1470. *Readeptio* ('recovery') was first used in 1470 (Latham, *Revised Medieval Latin Word-List*, p.392). Letters patent and close in Henry VI's name are known from 9 October 1470 onwards, dated in his 49th year '*et readeptionis nostre regie potestatis anno primo*' (Cheney, *Handbook of Dates*, p.22). Although historians suggest that 'majesty' was not adopted as a title by kings before Henry VII, the word *magestatis* is used here to refer to Henry VI.

427. NICHOLAS QWYCHERCH ('Qwythcherch') of WICKEN ('Wykyn') [*Cambs*], 1 February 1470/71

['Qwhytcherche' *in margin*] Sick of body; [*commendation*: to Almighty God]; to be buried in the churchyard of the parish church of St Mary of Wicken; to the high altar of the same [*place*] for my tithes forgotten 20d; to the fabric of the church 2s. To the friars of the order of Preachers of Cambridge (*Cantebreg'*) 12d; to the Friars Minor of Cambridge (*Cantebr'*) 12d;[1] to the gild of All Saints 12d; to the gild of St Mary 12d.[2]

Residue of all my goods to my execs, John Balle of Exning ('Ixnynge') and Margaret my wife, to dispose it as seems best to them to profit the health of my soul.

Proved at Newmarket (*Novum Mercat'*), 8 March 1470/71. Admon to execs.

1   For the friars of Cambridge see notes to nos 80 (Preachers) and 187 (Friars Minor).
2   For the gilds of Cambridgeshire in general see Introduction, under *Gilds*, and note to will no. 199. It is possible that these two gilds were in Cambridge, rather than in Wicken; indeed, Palmer found no references to any gilds in Wicken (Palmer, 'Village Gilds of Cambridgeshire', p.401); however, in 1474 Willam Say of Wicken bequeathed his mass-pence of the gild of All Saints there to Sir Robert Wylton, parish priest of Wicken (no. 747).

428. ROBERT AVES of EXNING ('Ixnynge'), 13 February 1470/71

Of Exning in the diocese of Norwich; to be buried in the churchyard of the church of St Martin of Exning; to the high altar of the same church for my tithes forgotten 6d; to the roof (*ad coopertur'*) of the body of the same church 3s 4d.[1]

To the reparation and emendation of the church of the Blessed Mary of Swaffham Prior 6s 8d; to the gild of St Margaret of Needham ('Nedham') 3s 4d;[2] to the reparation and emendation of the chapel of St Etheldreda of Reach ('Reche') [*Cambs*] 3s 4d.[3]

To my son, a friar of the Augustinian order of Cambridge (*Cantebr'*),[4] to celebrate for my soul and my wife's soul and for the souls of my parents and benefactors in Reach ('Reche') chapel for a quarter of a year next following after my decease 20s. To Cecily my sister 3s 4d.

Residue of all my goods to my execs, Henry Mason[5] and John Dawe, to dispose as they see best to please God and profit my soul.

Seal appended.

Proved at Newmarket (*Novum Mercat'*), 8 March 1470/71. Admon to execs.

1   The almost exactly contemporary will of Henry Mason (no. 450), one of Robert Aves' executors, reveals that a final decision had not yet been made regarding the material to be used to the re-roofing of the nave of Exning church: either reed or lead.
2   Likely to be the gild of St Margaret in Gazeley: Needham Street was a hamlet of Gazeley. According to the returns of 1389, a gild of St Margaret was established in the parish church of All Saints, Gazeley, in 1359, to provide a chaplain to celebrate weekly, to provide a taper before St Margaret's image and to help towards church repairs; members offered at a funeral mass and gave 1d for a mass for the soul (TNA: C47/423).
3   St Etheldreda's chapel at Reach was in the parish of Swaffham Prior, on the west side of Fair Green; there are no remains today (RCHM, *Cambs*, ii, pp.85–6).
4   See note to no. 187.
5   Will, no. 450 below.

[fol. 446]

429. JOHN SYGO of WORLINGTON ('Wrydlyngton'), 12 March 1469/70

Dated at Worlington; my body to Christian burial in the churchyard of the church of All Saints of Worlington.

My wife to have my cottage for term of her life, and after her decease my daughter Alice to have the cottage, to her and her heirs. My wife to have the profit and increase (*increment'*) of 4 acres of arable land lying in divers pieces in the fields of Mildenhall ('Myldenhale'), for term of her life, and after her decease the said 4 acres of land to be sold by our executors and the money from them to be distributed in pious uses for the souls of my parents and benefactors; if my wife should be reduced to need or poverty, then the 4 acres to be sold by my execs in [*my*] wife's lifetime for her upkeep and relief, and what remains beyond her necessities [*and*] food to be distributed by our execs in pious uses according to the discretion of their (*eorum*) execs.

My wife to have all my goods, moveable and unmoveable, [*my*] debts first being paid and my funerals seen to.

My wife and my son Brother Thomas Mildenhale, canon of the house of Bromehill ('Bromhill') [*Norfolk*] in the diocese of Norwich[1] to be execs; they to dispose out of my goods as they see best to please God and profit my soul.

Proved at Kentford, 19 June 1470. Admon to execs.

1   Bromehill Priory, in the parish of Weeting and about a mile south-east of the village, was founded by Sir Hugh de Plaiz *c*.1200; this Austin house was dedicated to the Blessed Virgin and St Thomas the Martyr (*VCH Norfolk*, ii, pp.374–5). As a canon, the testator's son appears to have substituted a surname relating to his place of origin for his family name. See no. 776 for a bequest to the canons at Bromehill.

430. JOHN HALLE of WOOLPIT ('Wolpet'), 25 June 1470

Of Woolpit in the diocese of Norwich; dated the Monday on the morrow of the Holy Nativity of St John the Baptist 1470; to be buried in the churchyard of Blessed Mary of Woolpit.

To Simon Halle my father 11 yards of woollen cloth of price 11s; to the said Simon 13s 4d for payment of his tenement; the room next to the door (*porta'*) of the said tenement of my father's to be repaired with tiles and other necessaries well and sufficiently at my expense.

To the reparation of the bridge called 'Wolpetbregge' by the way leading to St Edmunds 26s 8d; to the common ways in the town of Woolpit where most needed 13s 4d.

Residue of all my goods to Elizabeth my wife, to be delivered to her by my execs William Hert of Elmswell ('Elmesswell')[1] and John Halle of East Bergholt ('Bergeholt'), they to dispose for [*my soul*] and for the souls of my benefactors as they see best to benefit [*them*] and please God.

Seal appended.

Proved at Fornham [*St Martin*], 16 July 1470. Admon to execs.

1   Will, no. 519.

[fol. 446v]

431. MARGARET NOCHE of BILDESTON ('Byldeston'), widow, 16 June 1467

Of Bildeston in the diocese of Norwich; sick of body; [*commendation*: to God Almighty and the Blessed Virgin Mary]; my body to Christian burial in the church-yard of Bildeston; to the high altar of Bildeston ('Bylston') church 12d; to the high altar of Lavenham 8d; to the emendation of Lavenham church 3s 4d; to the increase of the cattle (*incrementis catallarum*) of the gild of St Mary of Lavenham 3s 4d;[1] my obsequies to be celebrated annually in the church of Bildeston on the Sunday after my decease for the period of 10 years and at each anniversary to be spent 6s 8d.

To the poor of Lavenham 20d to be distributed among them on my seven-day (*septennario*) and similarly on my thirty-day 20d.

Because the three sons of John Holden my son,[2] that is, John, William and Edmund, have not received their legacies of Joan my daughter, because of [*their*] death, of which the whole sum is 10s, equally to be distributed among them, the said sum to be paid to John my son and also [*a further*] 3s 4d to the said John.

To James Eldhalle my brother 3s 4d.

To John Markeday a ewer with a basin and jug; to Richard Markeday a chest and a spit with the andiron (*ypopirgio*) and a table with the 'trestell'.

To Rose my daughter, Margaret and Joan her daughters [*no amount stated*]; to Margaret Markeday 6s 8d; to Joan Markeday 6s 8d; and the residue of all my ostil-ments to be divided between them.

Residue of all [*my*] goods to my execs to dispose as seems best to them to do for the health of my soul.

Execs: John Markeday and Richard his son, they having God before their eyes in the execution of this testament.

Seal appended.

Witnesses: Sir Richard Swettok, rector of Bildeston,[3] John Hawkedon, rector of Nedging ('Neddynge')[4] and Thomas Horold of Bildeston ('Bylston') and others.

Proved at Bildeston ('Bylston'), 19 July 1470. Admon to execs. Seal of official appended.

[1]   This is the only bequest in the Baldwyne register to the gild of St Mary of Lavenham. The other Lavenham gilds that are mentioned are: Corpus Christi (John Wareyn of Bildeston, Pt I, no. 415); Holy Trinity (Katherine Peretrych of Acton, Pt I, no. 289; William Schedde, no. 339 above); and SS Peter and Paul (Robert Taylour of Lavenham, Pt I, no. 416). William Curby of Lavenham simply mentioned 'the four gilds' (Pt I, no. 768).

[2]   ?Will, as John Holden the elder of Glemsford, no. 628 below.

[3]   See note to no. 284 above and also nos 303, 720 and 721.

[4]   See note to no. 284 above and also nos 303, 406, 720 and 721.

[fol. 447]

432. WALTER NOBLE of GREAT HORRINGER ('Magna Hornynghesherth'),[1] 12 December 1470

My body to Christian burial; to the high altar of the same church for my tithes and offerings underpaid 2s; to the reparation of the porch of the same church 20s; to the painting of the image of St Leonard[2] in the same church 2s; to the emendation of certain ways which lead from a pasture called 'Cowperisgrene' to the church of the said town 20s.

To the friars of Babwell[3] to celebrate a trental of [*St*] Gregory for my soul 5s and all the mass pence (*nu'mos missales*) due (*spectantes*) to me after my death from the gild of the Holy Trinity held in the said town; to the rector of the said church all the mass pence due to me after my death from the gild of St John the Baptist held in the same town;[4] to the reparation of the monastery of St Edmund of Bury 20d; to the reparation of the vessels belonging to the hall (*aule*) of the said gilds (*gyldarum*) 12d.[5]

To Katherine my daughter 6s 8d; to Thomas my son 10 marks. These to be paid to them by my execs out of my goods within 7 years after my death.

I remit to Walter Coppyng 2 marks of the purchase-money for my tenement in which I live that he lately bought from me; to each of his brothers 20d and his sister 20d.

To Stephen Noble, Henry Noble and Thomas Brycet 12d each; to Walter Fuller 8d; to Richard Noble of Westley ('Westle') 12d; to the sons of John Noble of Bury 12d between them.

To the poor of Horringer ('Horningsherth') aforesaid 12d between them.

To Thomas my son and Katherine my daughter all my hostilments and utensils of my house, to be divided equally between them.

To Agnes daughter of the said Walter Coppyng 2s; to Agnes servant of the same Walter 12d; to Seman 8d; to Margery Shedde and Alice Hunte 6d each.

Residue of my goods to my execs to sell, receive and dispose for my soul and the souls for which I am bound in pious works as they see best to please God and profit my soul.

Execs: Walter Noble of Little Saxham ('Parva Saxham') and John Noble of Bury St Edmunds, to execute this testament faithfully.

Supervisors: Adam Rodyng of Horringer ('Horningsherth')[6] and Katherine my daughter, to each of whom 2s for their labour.

Proved at Fornham [*St Martin*], 4 February 1470/71. Admon to execs.

1   Executor (as 'Nobyll') of John Nobyll of Great Horringer, probate October 1449 (SROB, Baldwyne 96; Pt I, no. 436).
2   The dedication of the church.
3   See note to no. 1.
4   Here Walter Noble bequeathed the mass-pence of the gild of the Holy Trinity to the friars of Babwell and the mass-pence of the gild of St John the Baptist to the rector of the parish church of Great Horringer, whereas Adam Rodyng (no. 654), one of Noble's supervisors, simply wished the mass-pence to be equally divided between the friars of Babwell and the 'parson' of Great Horringer.
5   As well as giving specific instructions regarding the mass-pence from the two gilds of Great Horringer (see note above), both Noble and Rodyng (no. 654) were concerned about the practicalities of gild membership: Noble made this bequest of 12d towards the repairs of the vessels belonging to the gildhall and Rodying bequeathed 20d towards the repairs of the gildhall itself, indicating that the gilds shared one hall. This hall at Horringer still survives on the east side of the village street.
6   Will no. 654.

[fol. 447v]

433. RICHARD SHERMAN of WATTISHAM ('Watesham'), 5 December 1470

Dated at Wattisham; [*commendation includes* St Nicholas[1]]; sick; to be buried in the churchyard of the parish church of Wattisham; to the high altar there for tithes forgotten 6d; a trental of St Gregory 10s; for a new image to be got (*h'end'*) in Wattisham church 3s 4d; to the sepulchre light 20d.

Residue of my goods to the discretion of my legal attorney and exec, George Swetman, to dispose everything (*omnia premiss'*) for my soul as best [*he can*] as he will answer before the High Judge.

[*Will, of same date*]

Dated at Wattisham.

After my decease, George Swetman of Wattisham to have my tenement situated in Wattisham called 'Shermans' with its appurtenances and commodities, and to this effect I have surrendered the said tenement into the hands of Robert Syre, bond tenant of the manor of Wattisham, to the use of the said George Swetman.

2 brass pots and a cauldron and an iron spit to be sold by the said George and the money from them to be disposed for me.

Proved, with the last will annexed, at Bildeston ('Bylston'), 5 February 1470/71. Admon to exec.

1   The dedication of the church.

[fol. 448]

434. JOHN HYLL of SUDBURY, 15 March 1470 [*new style*]

[*Will only*]

Dated at Sudbury, Thursday 15 March 1470, 10 Edward IV.

Denise my wife[1] to have the messuage formerly Robert Pryst's, to hold to her and her heirs for ever of the chief lords of the fee, by due service and custom; the feoffees of the said messuage to deliver estate of it to her when so required by her in the above form, without them imposing any conditions.

If there be any money remaining from the sale of the tenement lately called 'Melfordes' over and above the payment of my debts and of Denise's keep (*sustentac'*), it is to be disposed by Denise or her assigns in pious uses and alms, that is, to the poor in greatest need and in the celebration of masses for the souls of the said John Hyll and Denise and for the souls of our benefactors and wrongdoers (*malefactorum*).

Executrix: Denise my wife; William Rodland and John Brooke the elder to be her helpers; each of them to have 13s 4d for their labour, according to the discretion of Denise.

Seal appended by my own hand.

Witnesses: Sir John Wryght, parish chaplain there,[2] John Vyne, Thomas Howard and many others.

Proved at Sudbury, 20 July 1470. Admon to exec.

1   Will, no. 505.
2   Witness of the will of Thomas Lavenham of Sudbury (Pt I, no. 1273); see also nos 32 above and 596 below.

435. JOAN BONDE of TOSTOCK ('Tostoke'), 1460 [*nuncupative*]

To be buried in Christian burial; to the high altar of Tostock church 3s; to the church of Tostock 13s 4d; for 'sangredes' to be celebrated in Tostock church 13s 4d.

To John Peyton her husband[*sic*] 13s 4d; to Margaret Matthew her daughter 40d; to Agnes Brook 40d; to Alice Goldston 6s 8d; to the Abbot of Sibton ('Sypton') 7s, which she owed him for rent;[1] to John Asshfeld 6s 6d, which she owed him for rent; for burial expenses 6s 8d.

Residue of [*her*] goods to the disposition of her exec, Robert Bonde her son.

Supervisor: Master Robert Wolman, rector of the same [*place*].[2]

Proved at Fornham [*St Martin*], 30 October 1470. Admon to exec.

1 The Cistercian abbey of the Blessed Virgin of Sibton was founded before 1272 by William Cheney, and was colonised by an abbot and 12 monks from the abbey of Warden (Beds); the abbey owned land in more than 25 Suffolk parishes, of which Tostock was presumably one (*VCH Suffolk*, ii, pp.89–91). Description and plan in *PSIA*, viii, pt 1.

2 See note to no. 29. As Wolman's will was proved in 1464, he would not have been alive to carry out his duties as supervisor of this will.

[fol. 448v]

436. ROBERT SPAROWE of MELFORD, 6 March 1468/69

[*This entry is crossed through and has been entered again on fol. 576, no. 779 below*]

Of Melford in the diocese of Norwich; to be buried in the churchyard of the parish church of Melford, next to the grave of my late wife; to the high altar of the said church for my tithes and offerings forgotten and underpaid 6s 8d; to the new fabric of the same church £10;[1] to the reparation of the chapel of the Blessed Virgin Mary standing (*existens*) in the said churchyard 13s 4d;[2] to the emendation and reparation of the chapel of St James the Apostle in the said town of Melford, situated in 'Hellestret' 13s 4d.[3]

To each chaplain serving in the said church on the day of my death and being present at my first obsequies and at the mass of requiem on the day of my burial 12d; to each outside (*extranes*) priest present there at the same time 8d; to each of the 2 holy water clerks of Melford present then 8d; to the sacrist of the said church present there then ringing the bells and making my grave (*poliandri*) and other things relating to his office and done for me 2s; to each clerk of man's state being there to say *dirige* and mass 4d; and to each surpliced boy clerk singing and reading there 2d; to each of the needy poor coming to the church on my burial day, taking alms and praying for my soul, 1d.

To Joan who was lately the wife of John Hacche of Melford, my kinswoman, to pray for my soul 13s 4d; to each of Robert and John, the same Joan's sons and my godsons, 3s 4d; to Clemence daughter of the said Joan Hacche 3s 4d; to Marion also her daughter 20d, to pray for my soul; to each of the sons and daughters of Thomas Herberd of Melford 12d; to Agnes wife of Richard Thurkeld, to pray for my soul 3s 4d.

To the sustentation and profit of the gild of Jesus in Melford 6s 8d.[4]

To the convent of the house of friars of Sudbury, to pray for my soul, 10s; to the convent of the house of friars of Clare, to pray and celebrate masses for my soul, 20s; to Friar Osbert of the same house and convent of Clare, my brother, to pray for my soul 10s; to the convent of the house of friars at Babwell, to pray for my soul 10s; to the convent of Carmelite Friars of Cambridge (*Cantebrigge*), to do the same 10s.[5]

To be distributed to 13 poor of Melford for 2 continuous years next following after my death, each week on Friday, 13d.

To Helen my household servant 5 marks in money, 4 silver spoons with the round 'Acres' [*?acorns*] (*cum lez Acres rotund*'), a pair of jet ('gette') beads, a girdle studded with silver lately my wife's, a basin with a brazen (*auricalco*) laver of the best, a brass pot with long feet containing about 3 gallons, a brass pan containing about 4 gallons, 3 platters (*perapsides*), 3 dishes and 3 salts of pewter; also, a bed, that is, a blue-coloured cover next the best, 2 blankets and 2 linen sheets and a felted cover (*fultru'*)[6] of the best, of Helen's own choice.

Residue of all my goods and chattels to Roger Smyth and John Smyth of Melford, execs of this my testament and my last will, to distribute and dispose it forthwith*
... [*according to*] the discretion, counsel and ordering of John Clopton of Melford, esquire,[7] whom I make supervisor of my execs of my testament to see these premises executed and fulfilled; he to have 10 marks for his labour and each of my execs to have for their labour about these premises 40s.

Seal appended.

Witnesses: John Stannard, parish chaplain of Melford,[8] William Colman,[9] Thomas Wareyn and others at Melford.

Proved at Fornham St Martin, 30 July 1470. Admon to execs.

* Entry ends here on fol. 448v but is continued on fol. 434 which is the other folio of that biofolium. The leaf was obviously originally loose, or at the centre of gathering. It now has other material sewn in & has been reversed. The two sections have been put together here.

[*different hand*] See this testament below with the last will. [*i.e. fol. 576. no. 779*]

1   The first of two substantial bequests made by Robert Sparowe to the rebuilding of Melford church, the second bequest was in his will (see no. 779 and the note thereto); John Brokhole's bequest in October 1467 marked the beginning of the rebuilding programme (no. 363).

2   The Lady Chapel at the east end of Melford church was built by John Clopton in the years 1494–7 (Dymond and Paine, *Spoil of Melford Church*, p.5.). This chapel of the Blessed Virgin Mary mentioned by Sparowe was almost certainly not on the same site as the present Lady Chapel. The phrase 'standing in the churchyard' can either describe a separate building, or a chapel attached to the main structure of the church, but built on ground that was formerly used for burials. The will of Robert Barell (made in 1473) shows that the chapel was in the latter category, for he left ¾d 'to the emendation of the chapel of the Blessed Mary of the same church annexed ...' (SROB, Hervye 19). See Paine, 'The Building of Long Melford Church', p.15. At Thorpe Morieux there was also a Lady Chapel in the churchyard (see no. 351 above).

3   See note to no. 206.

4   For the Mass of Jesu and gilds of Jesus in general, see note to no. 45. For other bequests to the gild of Jesus in Melford see: Richard Wareyn (Pt I, no. 1329), William Rous (Pt I, no. 1363) and John Dow (Pt I, no. 1424). Henry Turnour *alias* Dyer of Long Melford (Pt I, no. 1369) bequeathed 'to Jesu there 20d': this may have been for the Mass of Jesu at Melford or it may have been for the gild of Jesus.

5   For the friars see note to no. 133.

6   The word *fultru[m]* might conceivably be a derivative of *fulcimen* (*fultura*) (bed [tenth century] or buttress (support) [after 1550]) but a derivative of *filtrum* (piece of felt, cover, cloak, horse-cloth) seems more likely (Latham, *Revised Medieval Latin Word-List*, pp.191, 203).

7   See note to no. 154 and also nos 181, 733 and 779.

8   John Stannard, 'parish chaplain of Melford', was supervisor of the will of Thomas Fraunceys (no. 446); and witnessed the wills of Isabel Grome (no. 728) and John Phelipe (no. 756).

9   In the other version of this testament (no. 779), William Colman is designated 'chaplain'.

[fol. 449]

437. JOHN AYLMER of THELNETHAM, 22 February 1469/70

Dated at Thelnetham in the deanery of Blackbourn ('Blakborn') [*and*] diocese of Norwich; to be buried in the churchyard of the parish church of Thelnetham; to the high altar of the said church for my tithes and offerings forgotten and negligently paid 12d.

A suitable man to go on pilgrimage to Canterbury (*Cantuar'*) to St Thomas the Martyr;[1] I wish to have a trental.

To Agnes my wife 2 cows, a piglet, 2 quarters of barley and the crop (*vestura'*) of an acre of land sown with wheat together with all the utensils and necessaries of whatever kind belonging to my house.

My messuage in which I live and half an acre and half a rood of land to be sold by my execs and of the money from them Agnes my wife to have 33s 4d.

To Joan Aylmer my mother 40d.

To a suitable chaplain to celebrate divine service for my soul and my parents' [*souls*] in Thelnetham church, or elsewhere, according to the discretion of my execs, for half a year.

Residue of all [*my*] goods to my execs to pay fully my debts and do other works of piety for my soul.

Execs: Valentine Stabyler, chaplain,[2] and William Symonde; they to ordain, do and dispose for my soul as they know best to please God, in exoneration of their consciences against God in this behalf (*in hac parte*).

Seal appended.

Proved at Botesdale ('Botyssdale'), 20 March 1469/70. Admon to execs.

1 One of the few testators in 'Baldwyne' to request a pilgrimage to the most important shrine in England; see also nos 508 and 604.
2 Executor of Robert Goche (no. 589); supervisor of John Shukford (no. 769); one of the witnesses of the will of John Coket of Ampton, will pr. October 1483 (TNA, PCC Logge 170–72; published in *Logge Register*, no. 301).

[fol. 449v]

438. JOAN NORMAN of Badlingham ('Badlyngham') [in CHIPPENHAM] [*Cambs*], widow,[1] 22 February 1469/70

[*Commendation*: my soul to the divine mercy (*divine misaracoi'*)]; my body to Christian burial in the churchyard of Blessed Margaret of Chippenham ('Chyp-pynham'); to the high altar of the said church for my tithes forgotten 40d; to the altar of St Mary there 40d; to the altar of the Holy Trinity there 40d; to the gild of St Margaret a coomb of barley.[2]

To each of my godsons and goddaughters a bushel of barley.

A trental of St Gregory to be celebrated for my soul and for the souls of my benefactors by some friar in the said church, he taking for his salary 10s.

All my debts to be paid well and truly.

Residue of [*all*] my goods, moveable and unmoveable, to go to John Norman my son, he to keep the anniversary day each year in Chippenham parish church for my soul and the soul of his father.[3]

Execs: the said John and William Norman;[4] supervisor: the vicar of Chippenham ('Cheppynham') parish church; they to dispose as they see best to please God and profit my soul.

Proved at Chippenham ('Chepynham'), 13 April 1470. Admon to execs.

1 Widow of Thomas Norman of Badlingham (no. 108).
2 For the gilds of Cambridgeshire in general and of Chippenham in particular see Introduction, under *Gilds*, and note to will no. 199.

³ Thomas Norman (see note above).

⁴ William Norman was also executor of Thomas Norman (see note above). He was probably Thomas's brother: Thomas's father, also Thomas, had made bequests to his two sons, Thomas and William, will pr. July 1448 (SROB, Baldwyne 97; Pt I, no. 440).

439. ELEANOR SMYTH of NAYLAND ('Neylond'), 1 September 1469.

Dated at Nayland; to be buried in the churchyard of the church of St James of Nayland; to the high altar of Nayland 12d; to the gild of the Holy Trinity 20d;¹ to the painting of the image of St Nicholas a brass pot and a pan.

To John my servant a brass pot and a bed in which I lie with the appurtenances; to Robert Karr a pair of sheets and two pillows; to the wife of Geoffrey Brown a sheet, a brass pan and a painted (*?dep'ctu'*) cloth; to Thomas Kynget a sheet and a *?*painted cloth; to Robert Campe my black cloak; to the wife of Thomas Kynget a brass pan.

Residue of my goods to my execs, Nicholas Hache of Nayland and Nicholas Lane of Nayland, they to execute my testament as they see best for the health of my soul. Proved at Lavenham, 8 November 1469. Admon to execs.

¹ At this time there was also a gild of St Thomas in Nayland. For other bequests to the gild of the Holy Trinity, see wills of: John Wareyn of Nayland (Pt I, no. 108), William Hamond of Nayland (Pt I, no. 142), John Facon the elder of Nayland (Pt I, no. 860), Joan widow of John Fakon of Nayland (Pt I, no. 1080), John Roos of Nayland (Pt I, no. 1479) and John Hyde of Nayland (no. 783 below).

[fol. 450]

440. ROBERT WASSHSCHER of BOXFORD, 4 April 1469

Dated at Boxford; to be buried in the churchyard of the parish church of Boxford, on the north side at the back of the wall (*retro parietem*) [*behind*] where the image of the Blessed Mary is worshipped there;¹ to the work of 'le Ele' to be newly built there 6s 8d;² to the high altar of the same church for my tithes forgotten and unpaid 6s 8d; to the new porch there 6s 8d;³ to each priest present at my obsequies 4d; to each major clerk 2d; to each lesser clerk 1d; to Richard Goldyng, chaplain,⁴ to celebrate in Boxford church for my soul and the souls of my parents for a whole year £6; for a trental 10s.

To Alice my wife all the utensils of my house, with all the other grain, all the cows and the other mares (*iumentis*), of whatever kind, belonging to me, for her own use and profit; my executors to provide for Alice if she suffers from any misfortune, as reason demands and according to her situation, from my other goods. To Alice my capital tenement in 'Whytstrett' in Boxford, with all the parcels of land, meadows and pastures lying divided in the same street for the term of her life, and after her decease the tenement with all the parcels belonging to it, as noted above, to remain to William Wasshscher my son and his heirs for ever. When William my son is seised of the premises, he to find at his own cost, for 20 years, our anniversary day and also our certain in Boxford church, for [*his*] legacy.

To Alice my other tenement called 'Dorys', with all its appurtenances, for the whole term of her life, and after her decease my execs then surviving to sell the tenement and appurtenances, together with my other tenement and its appurtenances of antiquity called 'Cotys' lying in the street called 'Alywade'⁵ in the town of Boxford, and distribute the money from them in the manner following: firstly, a secular priest to be provided (*exhibeatur*) to celebrate in Boxford church for our souls and the souls of all our parents for a whole year; and the residue of that received from the sale to be disposed for some ornament specially and most needed for that church at that time, expedient and most pleasing to God. If any of my execs wish to buy either of the 2 tenements, then he shall have it before any others under (*sub*) the sum and value for which it could well be sold.

To William Wasshscher my son, in money, 5 marks; to Joan his daughter 4d; to the same William my best pair of stoddles ('stodlys').[6]

[fol. 450v] To Robert Gauge of Groton, in money, 5 marks; to John his son 4d; to Alice his daughter 4d; to John Regnam of Hadleigh ('Hadleygh'), in money, 5 marks; to Robert his son, my godson, 12d; to Katherine his daughter 8d; to each of his sons and daughters, for themselves, 4d; to Joan Bronde, the wife of William Bronde of Boxford, the younger, in money 40s and it to be delivered to her according to what shall be to her greatest profit; to each of her sons and daughters, for themselves [*blank*]; to Robert Coupere my son 8d and a pair of old stoddles ('studelys'); to Agnes Heth my servant 8d; to John Wode 4d.

Residue of all my goods, if any there be, to the disposition of my execs that they dispose for the health of my soul and of my parents as seems to them most expedient in the sight of God.

Execs to well and truly execute this testament: Alice my wife, William Wasshscher my son, Robert Gauge and John Regnam.

Seal appended.

Witnesses: John Coupere, Robert Betryche, Walter Coupere and many others

Proved at Kersey, 22 November 1470. Admon to execs.

1   That is, in the churchyard by the wall of the Lady Chapel.
2   William Mawdyon also made a bequest to the new 'ele' in Boxford church to be newly built (no. 332 above).
3   See no. 247 for notes concerning the new porch; see also nos 331 and 332.
4   Beneficiary of the will of Alice Turnour of Sudbury (no. 698); ?will of Richard Goldyng of St Mary, Boxford, clerk, dated 1502 (NRO, NCC 227 Popy).
5   Olywade Street, now Stone Street.
6   See Glossary.

441. MATILDA GEGGE of KNETTISHALL ('Gnatsale'), 27 December 1470

[*probate only*]

[*Place where proved not given.*] Admon to Hugh Catton, exec.

[fol. 451]

442. JOHN WATYR of EYE, 3 April 1469

Dated at Eye; to be buried in the churchyard of the parish church of St Peter of Eye; to the high altar of the same church for my tithes forgotten 12d.

My wife to have my cottage in the borough (*burgum*) of Eye for term of her life and after the decease of the said Alice the cottage to be sold by my execs and of the money John my son to have 40s. Alice my wife to have for term of her life all the utensils of my house and after her decease, if possible, John my son to have all of them; if Alice should be reduced to poverty and need, she to sell all the said utensils and live on the proceeds.

Residue of all my goods to the disposition of my exec, Thomas Hervy, clerk,[1] to dispose for my soul as he sees best to please God and profit the health of my soul. Seal appended.

Proved at Eye, 9 May 1469. Admon to exec.

> [1] Thomas Hervy was vicar of Eye from 1452 to 1488 (Tanner, p.300); see also nos 2, 222, 395 and 457.

443. JOHN CLERKE the elder of OCCOLD ('Ocolt'), 6 January 1469/70

To be buried in the churchyard of the parish church of St Michael of Occold.
In the name of my principal, I leave my best animal [*deletion*].
[*No more. These lines have been struck through and the following added:* alio folio in fine reg'd. *But nothing has been found elsewhere.*]

444. JOHN BALLE of HITCHAM ('Hecham'), 16 May 1470 [*probate only*]

[*Place where proved not given.*] Admon to Katherine, executrix, by Master Henry Herdman,[1] deputed for the purpose.

> [1] Master Henry Herdman/Hardman was beneficiary and witness of the will of John Baret of Bury St Edmunds (Tymms, *Wills and Inventories*, pp.41, 44); he was also mentioned in the will of John Smyth of Bury (Tymms, pp.56, 58, 64); for his career see Emden, *BRUC*, p.286.

[fol. 451v]
445. ALICE LUTKYN of STOWLANGTOFT ('Stowlangtofte'),[1] 10 April 1470

Dated at Stowlangtoft; to be buried in the churchyard of the church of Stow aforesaid; to the high altar 12d; to Stowlangtoft church 6s 8d.
The last will of my husband, lately deceased, to be entirely fulfilled.
To Agnes my daughter all my brass and lead vessels and my bed and also sheets and the remainder of the necessaries, but each son and daughter of the said Agnes to have some part of those goods; if Agnes dies, then the aforesaid goods to be wholly divided among the said sons and daughters.
If my execs do not have sufficient money to fulfil my last will, then a certain part of the aforesaid goods to be sold, that is, 6 silver spoons and a silver belt and a horn goblet bound with silver and also a gown of 'vyolet' colour.
To the daughters of Thomas Lutkyn 3s 4d, that is, to Christine 20d and to Agnes 20d.
Residue of all my goods to my execs, they to do with them for my soul as it seems to them most expedient for the health of [*my*] soul.
Execs: John Lutkyn of West Stow and William Beylham of Stowlangtoft.
Proved 28 January 1470/71. Admon to execs.

> [1] Redstone (*PSIA*, xii, p.98) gives her status as *vidua* but this word is not in the register.

[fol. 452]
446. THOMAS FRAUNCEYS of MELFORD, 8 July 1469 [*nuncupative*]

His body to Christian burial; to the high altar 8d; to the reparation of Melford church 12d.
Residue of all his goods to Matilda his wife, to pay his debts and dispose for his soul as she sees best to please God and profit his soul.

Matilda to be executrix under the supervision and with the advice of John Stannard, parish chaplain of the same [*place*].[1]

Witnesses: John Ameot the elder, William Grome and Walter Fraunceys.

Proved at Melford, 14 February 1469/70. Admon to executrix.

[1] See note to no. 436.

447. HENRY BERNARDESTON of KEDINGTON ('Kedyngton'),[1]
6 November 1466 [*nuncupative*][2]

Dated at Kedington in the diocese of Norwich; sick unto death; my body to Christian burial in the churchyard of the parish church of St Peter the Apostle of Kedington.

To Edward my brother and Agnes my sister all those lands and tenements, with their appurtenances, which William Bernardeston my father left me in his testament, as they are in the town of Sturmer ('Sturmere') [*Essex*], called 'le Ovyrhell', to hold to them and their heirs for ever; to Edward and Agnes 6 calves.

Residue of all [*my*] goods to Walter Rys; he to see to my funerals, pay my debts and dispose for my soul and for the souls of all my benefactors as seems most expedient for the health of my soul; he to be exec, to implement all in my will as above.

Witnesses: Isabel Bernardeston my sister and Richard Sewale.

Proved at Clare, 16 February 1469/70. Admon to exec.

[1] A member of the Barnardiston family that owned the manor of Kedington.
[2] Although said to be nuncupative, the will is written in the first person.

[fol. 452v]
448. GEORGE LYNGE of FORNHAM ST GENEVIEVE ('Genevefe'),
31 March 1467

['Lenge' *in margin*] Dated at Fornham St Genevieve; my body to Christian burial; to the high altar of the church of Fornham aforesaid for my tithes forgotten and underpaid 6d; to the reparation of the same church half quarter of barley.

To the friars of Babwell, to pray for my soul, 10s.[1]

To Margery my wife all the hostilments and utensils of my house; to Margery 3 cows of her choice.

My children, if possible, to be supported (*relevant'r*) out of my goods.

Residue of all my goods and chattels to my execs to dispose for my soul and expend (*relevand'*) as they see best (*melior' modo*).

Execs: John Leynnge my brother and Margery my wife.

Proved 30 November 1470. Admon to Margery, executrix. Power reserved to John Lyenge when he comes if [*he wishes*] to take up admon.

[1] See note to no. 1.

449. JOHN KYRKEBY [of ICKLINGHAM], [*undated; English*]

[*Commendation*: to Almighty God of heaven]; my bones ('bonys') to Christian burial, to be buried in the churchyard of St James of Icklingham ('Ikelyngham'). It is my will to dispose 6d to the high altar for tithes forgotten; to the church 12d; to the 'hows of Rodys' 12d;[1] to the White Friars of Cambridge ('Cambrege') 12d.[2] Maud my wife to have all my house and lands, free and bond, during her life, but

265

[*if*] she have need, then to sell thereof a part to help herself; the other to be sold by my execs and disposed for the health of the souls of the said John Kyrkeby and Maud his wife, as they will answer before God.

Execs: Maud my wife and Thomas Dunwyche and John Chyrcheman; to each of them for their labour 12d.

Proved at Mildenhall ('Myldenhale'), 21 March 1471.³ Admon to execs.

1. It is most likely that 'Rodys' refers to Rhodes, and hence to the Hospitallers of St John of Jerusalem, who were known as the Knights of Rhodes from 1309 to 1522 ('Hospitallers of St John', in *Catholic Encyclopedia*, vii). There was a preceptory or hospital of the Knights at Battisford at least as early as the reign of Henry II; by 1338 the preceptory had two members or 'camerae' attached to it at Coddenham and Mellis (*VCH Suffolk*, ii, pp.120–1). For another instance of 'house of Ro[o]dys' see the will of John Bokenham of Pakefield, dated 31 August 1447 (SROI, Vol. I, 62v); for the 'pardon of Rodys' see the will of Thomas Smyth of Melford, dated 14 March 1481/82 (SROB, Hervye 259v).
2. See note to no. 42.
3. Date of probate originally given as *ultimo die mensis marcij Anno Domini Millesimo CCCC Lxxj* but *ultimo* has been crossed through and *xxjᵒ* written above; presumably, since the year has not been altered, probate was granted on 21 March 1471 (new style), rather than 1471/72.

[fol. 453]

450. HENRY MASON of EXNING ('Ixnyng'),¹ 14 February 1469/70

To be buried in the churchyard of the church of Exning; to the high altar of the same church for my tithes and offerings forgotten 12d.

To the roofing (*ad coopertura*') of the body of the said church 2 'fodirs' of lead lying against my gate, on condition that the men of the town begin to do the roofing of the body of the church with lead within 3 years following after my decease; and if they do not begin to do the roofing in lead within that time, then I leave to the roofing 700 (*Dcc*) 'reede' and not the aforesaid 2 'fodrys' of lead, but they then to be sold by my execs and the money disposed for the health of my soul in other charitable gifts.²

To the reparation of the church of Isleham ('Iselham') 3s 4d; to the reparation of the churches of Icklingham ('Ikelyngham') 4s, that is, to each church there 2s.³

My execs to find a suitable priest to celebrate in Exning church for a whole year next after my decease with the profit from the issues of my grain and from the next crop of my lands; my execs to pay the customary expenses at my obsequies on the day of my burial and at my seven-day and at my thirty-day, according to their discretion.

Thomas my son to have my messuage in which I live, with all the arable lands belonging to that messuage which I lately purchased of Robert Wyott and with 3 roods of land lying in 'Wyndmel Feld' which I lately purchased of Robert Gelle, with all the appurtenances, to hold to him and his heirs for ever. Thomas to help fulfil my last will and similarly to find Joan my wife food and drink, a chamber and easement to the fire for her lifetime; and Thomas also to pay Joan my wife 30s in money *per annum* during her lifetime.

To John Mason of Exning my son and Henry my son, 10 acres of my arable land to be divided equally between them, to hold to them and their heirs for ever; to the same John and Henry 40s, to be received of Robert Mason my son of the debts which he owes me, that is, 20s to each of them.

To Thomas my son all my horses and carts, and my large brass pot and my large pan after the decease of Joan my wife, and all my other utensils and household [*goods*]. Residue of all my goods to my execs, Joan my wife and John Mason my son, [fol.

453v] to dispose for the health of my soul as they see best to please God and profit [*my*] soul.

Seal appended.

Witnesses: Sir George, parish chaplain of Exning ('Ixnynge'), Thomas Qwhyttmowth, William Michell of the same and others.

Proved at Tuddenham St Mary ('Todenham'), 20 February 1469/70. Admon to Joan Mason and John Mason, execs.

[1] Executor of Thomas Brystowe of Exning, will pr. September 1458 (SROB, Baldwyne 201; Pt I, no. 995); and of Robert Aves of Exning (no. 428 above).
[2] Clearly there was a plan to re-roof the church but the final decision concerning the roofing material had yet to be made; Robert Aves had bequeathed 3s 4d to the roof of the nave.
[3] The churches of All Saints and St James.

451. MARGERY RODYNGE of WETHERDEN, 10 December 1470

Dated at Wetherden in the diocese of Norwich; to be buried next to the grave of John Rodynge my late husband, in the churchyard of the church of the Blessed Mary of the said town; to the high altar of the same church for my tithes and offerings underpaid 6s 8d; to the nave of the church 6s 8d.

To the gild of Jesus of the same town, for continuance (*continuac'*) of the service, 3s 4d;[1] to the gild of St John the Baptist 6s 8d;[2] to the church of Earl ('Erl') Stonham 6s 8d; to the friars of Babwell 10s;[3] 30d [*intention omitted*].

To John Cullynge my son 6s 8d.

I wish to have a secular priest to celebrate for a whole year for my soul and for the souls of my husbands (*animabus maritorum meorum*) and of our friends and he to have 8 marks for his salary.

Residue of all my goods to the disposition of my execs, Hugh, rector of the same church,[4] Thomas Moore and Robert Hersett, to dispose it as they see best for the health of my soul and my friends' [*souls*]; to Hugh the rector for his labour 6s 8d; to Thomas Moore 3s 4d; and to Ann Moore[*sic*] [*nothing further*].

Witnesses: John Parker, clerk,[5] and Agnes Turnour.

To Margery Herset 13s 4d.

Furthermore, notwithstanding that, for the sale by William Chapman and me, Margery, of 2 messuages belonging to me and Agnes [*my*] daughter, wife of the said William, I made him, for the trust I have in him, my seller and receiver of the money, or part of it, from the sale, as appears in a bill indented between us and Thomas Bettes, I now declare before God that William has received his due, the whole and entire payment of his part, for himself and his wife. From henceforth, from the making of my will, I wish that, as he will answer to God (*coram summo judice*) on the Day of Judgement, he does not involve himself in taking the whole of the sum received, but I wish my execs to take [*it*], in my name, and use [*it*] as is contained in my will.

Proved at Wetherden ('Wedyrden'), 14 February 1470/71. Admon to execs.

[1] The gild of the Holy Name of Jesus of Wetherden was mentioned in 1476 (*PSIA*, xix, p.209).
[2] John Baker of Wetherden (no. 573) bequeathed 20d to the gild of John[*sic*] in Wetherden.
[3] See note to no. 1.
[4] Master Hugh Leigh was rector of Wetherden from 1461 to 1497 (Tanner, p.1342).
[5] A John Parker had been rector of Wetherden before the appointment of John Pawlyn in November 1454 but this was probably not the same man (Tanner, p.1342).

[fol. 454]

452. ADAM BERWEHAM of BARNINGHAM ('Bernyngham'),[1] 4 October 1469

Dated at Barningham, the Wednesday on the feast of St Francis 1469; my body to Christian burial in the churchyard of St Andrew in Barningham. All my debts to be fully paid and the residue of all the money remaining, beyond the payment of my debts and legacies and other necessary expenses, to be disposed on the reparation of foul ways of the said town by my execs. To the high altar of the same church of tithes forgotten or not well paid 12d; to the parish chaplain 12d; to the parish clerk 2d.

To Margaret my wife the utensils of my house, that is, brass and wooden vessels, and my clothes both for body and for household necessity. To Margaret my wife, for term of her life, my messuage with a croft nearby, an enclosure called 'Daleclos'[2] and 7 roods of land at 'Stonhyll', and, after the decease of Margaret, the messuage with the croft and 7 roods of land to be sold by my execs and the money to be bestowed on the necessary reparations of the said church and necessary emendation of foul ways of the said town, according to the advice of my execs.

To Agnes my daughter and her heirs, 3 roods of land at 'Delacrys'; to Isabel my daughter and her heirs, 3 roods of land at 'Beltcrofte'.

3 acres of land at 'Alfatysmer'[3] to be sold to aid the making of the new beam called [*the*] 'Candlybem' in the said church; all my other lands to be sold by my execs and the money from them to be disposed in pious uses in the said town.

Residue of all my goods to be committed to the disposition of my execs, Geoffrey Berweham of Ixworth[4] and Robert Fuller of Barningham, to dispose for my soul, the souls of my parents[5] and benefactors and of all the faithful departed as seems best to please God and profit my soul and the souls above named.

Seal appended.

Witnesses: Sir John Myller, chaplain,[6] William Onge and others.

3 acres of land at 'Fystemer' to be sold for a trental to be celebrated for my soul.

Proved at Ixworth, 12 December 1469. Admon to execs.

[1] Beneficiary of the will of his mother, Agnes Berweham of Barningham, pr. July 1460 (SROB, Baldwyne 251; Pt I, no. 1247). Agnes made her will during her husband's lifetime and made many bequests of land to her/their children. She stated that 'I have been empowered to dispose of the above land by the licence of John Berweham, my husband, and by his special direction'.

[2] Bequeathed to him by his mother (see note above).

[3] In her will, Agnes had bequeathed 3 acres of arable land at 'Alferymere' to her son William, 'after the payment of the debts of his natural father'.

[4] Brother of testator, who was also a beneficiary of their mother's will.

[5] Probate granted for the will of his father, John Berweham, July 1460 (SROB, Baldwyne 244; Pt I, no. 1226); see note above for the will of his mother, Agnes.

[6] John Coldham of Barningham (no. 338 above) requested that John Myllere, chaplain, should distribute 20s in the city of Rome in pious uses for his soul.

[fol. 454v]

453. KATHERINE SKETH, relict of Thomas,[1] **of STANTON,** 21 August 1469

['Skeith' *in margin*] Dated at Stanton; to be buried in the churchyard of St John the Baptist of Stanton; to the high altar of the same church 12d; to the high altar of All Saints' church 12d; to the parish clerk of St John's church 2d; to the emendation of St John's church 13s 4d; to the emendation of All Saints' church 6s 8d.

To the friars of Babwell 40d;[2] to the Friars Preachers of Thetford 40d; to the friars of the New House of Thetford 40d; to the nuns of the same town 20d.[3]

To Elizabeth Edwyn 20d; to Roger Rollecrose 40d.

Residue of all my goods and chattels to Margaret Skeith my daughter,[4] beyond the expenses to do with my burial (*circa ?fimus meum sepellend'*) and on the principal day of my death (*in principali die obitus mei*).

Execs: Margaret Skeith and Roger Rollecros,[5] to well and truly execute this testament and dispose for my soul and the souls of all my benefactors as seems to them best to please God and profit my soul.

Seal appended.

Proved at Ixworth, 12 December 1469. Admon to execs.

1   Will (as 'Skeyth'), pr. January 1462/63, no. 817.
2   See note to no. 1.
3   See note to nos 68 (Friars Preachers and nuns of Thetford) and 69 (friars of the New House).
4   Will (as 'Sketh'), no. 711.
5   He was also executor of her husband Thomas (no. 817) and her daughter Margaret (no. 711).

[fol. 455]
454. WALTER PAGE of LAVENHAM, 18 November 1469

Dated at Lavenham; to be buried in the Christian burial place of Lavenham church. My whole tenement in the town of Lavenham, with all my goods and chattels, to be sold for the best possible price by my feoffees and execs as soon as possible, and from the proceeds: to the high altar of the said church for my tithes forgotten or underpaid 20s; I wish to have a suitable and honest chaplain to celebrate divine service for the health of my soul and of the soul of Cecily my wife and of the souls of all at rest with Christ, for a whole year.

To the friars of Sudbury for a trental of St Gregory to be celebrated there for my soul 10s; to the friars of Clare in the same way 10s; to the friars of Babwell in the same way 10s.[1]

To each chaplain coming to my obsequies 12d; to each adult clerk 2d; to the relief of the poor of the same town for a whole year 6d per week; to the emendation of the highway in 'le Heyestret' of the said town 20s.

To William my apprentice 10s.

I wish to have a suitable chaplain to go on a pilgrimage for the health of [*my*] soul to St Peter[2] if my goods will stretch to it, beyond my legacies and assignments.

Whatever the residue of all my goods to the disposition of my execs, my beloved in Christ, Henry Page my son and William Page of Barking ('Berkyng'); they to well and truly execute my will and, having God before their eyes, to dispose for me where they see most expedient for my soul and to please God.

Seal appended.

Proved at Fornham St Martin, 11 December 1469. Admon to exec Henry Page; power reserved to the other exec when he comes.

1   For the friars see notes to nos 1 (Babwell and Clare) and 11 (Sudbury).
2   That is, to the Basilica of St Peter in Rome.

[fol. 455v]

455. HENRY BALLARD of KETTLEBASTON ('Ketylberston'),[1]
15 December 1469

Dated at Kettlebaston, Friday 15 December 1469; to be buried in the churchyard of the Blessed Mary of Kettlebaston; to the high altar of the same church for my tithes and offerings underpaid 12d; to the sepulchre light of the same church 3s 4d, if it can be obtained from my goods.

To Joan my wife my whole tenement with a croft called 'Bellehowscroft', with their appurtenances, for term of her life, and after her death, the tenement and croft to be sold and disposed for the health of my soul, by the oversight of my execs; to Joan my wife all my ostilments and utensils of my house.

To Margaret my daughter the younger all those lands and tenements which I lately purchased of John Rowtt formerly of Kettlebaston, she to enter upon them on the feast of St Michael following the death of the said Henry Ballard her father.

To the sepulchre light of Preston church 12d and a bushel of wheat when it can be had of my goods.

Residue of my goods I leave in the hands of my execs, Joan my wife and John Schaftyng of Thorpe Morieux ('Thorpmeryous'), to dispose for my soul and for the souls of my parents and friends as best to please God and profit my soul.

Seal appended.

Witnesses: Thomas Havell, John Gardenere, Thomas Kegyll and others.

Proved at Fornham St Martin, 14 January 1469/70. Admon to execs.

[1] Witness of the will of William Sudbury of Kettlebaston, pr. July 1459 (SROB, Baldwyne 266; Pt I, no. 1300).

[fol. 456]

456. THOMAS CREK of CLARE, 6 July 1470

[*Surname written as* 'Clerke' *in margin*] Dated at Clare; my body to Christian burial, that is, in the churchyard of the parish church of the Apostles Peter and Paul of Clare. In God's name I beg my execs to pay all my debts, that is, those that can be truly proved. To the high altar of the said church for my tithes and offerings forgotten, withheld and underpaid 16d.

As to my lands and tenements, firstly, an enclosed meadow of mine called 'Barkeres Medewe', with its appurtenances, lying in the parish of Hundon ('Honyden'), to be sold by my execs for the best price possible, and with the money from it, as far as it will extend, I wish my execs to find an honest secular priest to celebrate divine service in Clare church, and not elsewhere, for a whole year immediately after my decease, praying for my soul and the souls of all my parents, friends and benefactors for whom I am most bound and all the faithful departed, taking for his stipend 9 marks for the year; but if the money from the sale is insufficient my execs to make up the amount for the priest from my other goods.

Alice my wife to have my messuage in which I now live in the town of Clare, with all its appurtenances, to hold to her and her heirs for ever, together with all the debts owed to me, on the following condition: that she pays all my debts which I owe and all my funeral expenses, and finds all the residue of the stipend of the priest; that she provides for Joan my daughter for her marriage, in money, 8 marks, and for James my son at the age of 16 years 4 marks, and for Agnes my daughter 40s at the age of 18, by the discretion of my execs, paying the 8 marks to Joan in the 8 years after the priest's year of service, that is, 13s 4d each year. If any of my said children dies, or if all die, before reaching the stated time, then that part or parts to go to my execs and be disposed at their discretion in deeds of charity for the health of my soul.

William my son to have all my leather, dressed and undressed (*corr' meum operat' & non operat'*), with shoes and leggings (*sotular' & ocri'*) made and to be made,[1] with all my instruments and tools, with all my shop stuff, as tallow (*sep'*) and other things, and all the other essentials belonging to my craft and now in my dwelling, with a 'Jakke' and 'salet'.

Joan my daughter to have a painted chest, with a lock and key, a brass pot late Peter Wykes's, and a brass pan holding 8 gallons, and 4 yards of white woollen cloth.

Alice my wife to have all my other utensils and ostilments, such as linen, woollen, [fol. 456v] pots, pans, cups, silver spoons and mazers, with all the other jewels and things, necessaries and utensils belonging to me, except above-bequeathed; she to have my 2 cows now in the keeping of Margaret Peyte, with the farm of the same [*cows*].

I beg and specially request my feoffees of and in the said messuage and meadow to deliver estate of them as above-stated and not otherwise when duly required.

Residue of all my goods to the disposition of my execs, Alice my wife, John Hadleigh and Richard Norman, to dispose for my soul in deeds of piety and mercy to the praise of God and as they see best to profit my soul; they to have 6s 8d each for their diligent labour about this matter.

Seal appended.

Witnesses: Sir Robert Colyngham, vicar of Clare church,[2] Christine Barbour, Richard Clerk and others.

Proved at Clare, 7 November 1470. Admon to execs.

<hr>

[1] Perhaps the testator was a cordwainer.
[2] See note to no. 380 and also no. 687.

[fol. 457]

457. ROBERT HARDYNG of EYE, 7 July 1470

Dated at Eye; to be buried in the churchyard of the parish church of St Peter of Eye. My tenement in Eye, with all the lands, meadows, pastures and feedings belonging to it, to be sold by my execs to pay my debts and implement my will. To the high altar of Eye church for my tithes forgotten and underpaid 10s; to an honest chaplain, to celebrate divine service in the said church for my soul and for the souls of my friends for a whole year, 7 marks; to the fabrication of the parish church of Eye 20s. To the gild of St Mary of Eye 3s 4d; to the gild of St Peter of Eye 3s 4d.[1]

To Margaret Gerard my servant 5 marks; to Robert Tame the younger 41s 8d; to Robert Radclyfe of Eye 10s; to Rose the daughter of the said Robert Radclyf 3s 4d. To the emendation of 'Lamset' way in Eye 30 cartloads of clay (*carect' argell'*);[2] to the emendation of 'Spetyll' way of the same town 30 cartloads of clay;[3] to the emendation of 'Kynggesstrete' way in Eye 30 cartloads of clay; to the emendation of Priory way in Eye 30 cartloads of clay.[4]

Residue of all my goods to the disposition of my execs, Thomas Hervy, clerk,[5] and John Botildes of Eye, together with William Harleston, esquire,[6] supervisor; they to dispose of it for my soul as they see best to please God and profit the health of my soul.

Seal appended.

Proved at Eye, 20 September 1470. Admon to execs.

¹   For other bequests to the gilds of the Blessed Mary, or St Mary, and of St Peter at Eye see notes to no. 2.
²   Agnes Jenews (no. 94) made a bequest to repairs of Lambseth bridge, which is to the north-west of the town of Eye, in Lambseth Street, the road leading out of the town to the north. William Goldyng (no. 2) owned a close with a garden at Lambseth Bridge.
³   A way leading to/from the hospital of St Mary Magdalene in Eye.
⁴   These four bequests of '30 cartloads of clay' represent major repairs to the roads in Eye; compare with the bequest 40 loads of stone by Walter Nicoll for the repair of 'Mellestrete' in Great Bradley (no. 642 below).
⁵   Thomas Hervy was vicar of Eye from 1452 to 1488 (Tanner, p.1300); see also nos 2, 222, 395 and 442.
⁶   Lord of the manor of Bludhall in Debenham, who died 1481 (Copinger, *Manors of Suffolk*, vii, p.136; IPM, 20 Edward IV, 100).

458. MARIOTA BALDWYN of ASSINGTON ('Assyngton'), widow, 10 May 1470

['Baldewyn' *in margin*] Of Assington in the diocese of Norwich; sick of body; to be buried in the churchyard of the parish church of Assyngton; to the high altar 3s 4d; to the fabric of the church 13s 4d.

Residue of my goods to my exec, John my son, to dispose freely as he pleases.

Proved at Sudbury, 26 September 1470. Admon to exec.

[fol. 457v] [OW 24/138 & 178]¹

459. JOHN OSMOND of ASSINGTON ('Assyngton'), 'husbandman', 18 August 1470

Dated at Assington in the diocese of Norwich; testament and last will; to be buried in the churchyard of the said parish church. I wish my debts to be paid, for which I am in any way bound, first of all. To the high altar of the said church 3s 4d; 46s 8d for the purchase of a chalice for the said church;² to the fabric of the said church 6s 8d.

To my wife a parcel of land called 'Cogmans', lying on the south side of the highway leading from Leavenheath ('Lavenheth') to Wissington ('Wiston'), and after her decease it to be given to Margaret my daughter and her heirs for ever.

Residue of all my goods, together with my debts, I give into the hand of my executrix, that is, Alice my wife.

Supervisors: John Kyng of Nayland ('Neylond') next Stoke and Robert Baldwyn of Assington.

Proved at Sudbury, 26 September 1470. Admon to executrix.

¹   OW has no probate sentence.
²   OW omits the purpose of the bequest of 46s 8d.

[*At the foot of the page, below this probate, is scribbled a note recording that a transaction (unspecified) has taken place before Thomas Byge in the presence of John Thyrlyng, A.M. and Master Christopher Bankes, notary public, in Fornham St Martin church on 19 September.*]

[fol. 458]

460. ROBERT QWYLTER (Qwylt') of BURES ('Burys') ST MARY,
16 December 1471

Dated at Bures St Mary; to be buried in the churchyard of the church of Bures aforesaid; to the high altar for tithes forgotten 12d; to the high altar of Alphamstone ('Alphamston') [*Essex*] 12d; to each of the chaplains of the same church 4d if they are present at my funeral offices; to each clerk 1d; to the beadle 1d; to the church of Bures aforesaid a cow to the sustentation of a light before the image of St Mary called Mother of Pity (*mater pietatis*).[1]

Residue of all my goods to my executrix, Christine Qwylter my wife, to dispose as seems best to her for the health of my soul.

Proved at Boxford, 13 May 1472. Admon to executrix.

[1] That is, the *Pietà*.

461. WILLIAM DERYSLE of KIRTLING ('Kertelyng') [*Cambs*],[1] 17 March 1471/72

Testament and last will; my body to Christian burial in the churchyard of the parish church of Kirtling ('Kertelynge'); to the high altar of the same church, in recompense of tithes forgotten and offerings underpaid, 6s 8d; to the high altar of Great Bradley ('Bradley Magna') 6s 8d.

To the friars of Babwell, to pray for my soul and for the souls of my parents and to celebrate a trental for us all, 10s;[2] to the Friars Augustinian, Preachers and Carmelite in Cambridge (*Cantebr'*), to celebrate 3 trentals for my soul and for the souls of my parents, 30s, to be divided in equal portions among them.[3]

10 marks to buy a vestment for Kirtling church.

To Constance my wife all my utensils and hostilments, 60 sheep, that is, 20 ewes (*oves matrices*), 20 lambs (*agnos*) and 20 hogs (*arietes*) of the best, 8 cows, 4 horses with the harness (*phaleribus*), the plough and cart, with all the equipment (*apparat'*) and their appurtenances; Constance my wife to have malt [*and*] wheat sufficient for keeping her household until she has the new (*faciet novum*); also Constance to have of the crop sown this year, of wheat, barley, peas, beans and oats, enough to sow next year and also, out of the same crop, as much as she shall need (*ocupabit*) in the year following for her house-keeping; the residue to be sold by my execs.

To Alice my daughter 20s; to each of my daughters Joan [*and*] Margaret 10 marks, 2 cows, 20 ewes and 10 lambs; to each of my daughters Agnes, Katherine and Flowr [*sic*] 10 marks, 2 cows, 10 ewes and 10 lambs; however, I wish my daughters to wait for their money until the time when it can be paid from my goods or when it can be raised from my lands let to farm as appears below. If one of them dies, then the part of the deceased to be divided among the rest of the sisters; if more than one should die, then the parts of those deceased to be disposed by my execs for my soul and for the souls of my deceased daughters; my daughters to have immediately after my decease [fol. 458v] the cattle and stock assigned to them.

[*Will, of same date*]

My wife to have for term of her life my whole tenement in which I dwell, with all its appurtenances and, after her decease, Walter my son to have it, to hold to him and his heirs of the chief lord of the fee by due service and custom.

The same Walter also to have 3 tenements, that is, 'Tuys', 'Vasys' and 'Bakers', when he comes to legal age, and not before; nor may he [*have*] the aforesaid tenement in the meantime even if his mother dies (*neque ten'tu' predcu' licet mat' sua obierit medio tempore*). If Walter should die during the lifetime of John his brother, then John shall have the lands and tenements that Walter should have had. If God so disposes that both die before reaching legal age, then all the said lands and tenements to be sold by my execs and the money disposed in works of charity.

John my son to have all [*my*] lands and tenements in Great Bradley ('Bradle Magna') when he reaches legal age; if he dies before that, then the said lands and tenements to be sold as above. If he survives Walter his brother and possesses the aforesaid lands in Kirtling, then he shall not have the lands in Bradley ('Bradle'), but they are to be sold by my execs to perform all my legacies and pay my debts. If a son of Richard Derysle my brother[4] wants to buy the said tenements and lands in Great Bradley when they are sold, then I wish him to have them before all others.

Residue of all my goods to my execs, Thomas Pykchese,[5] Walter Prat, Walter Derysle[6] and William Derysle, to dispose as seems to them most to please God and profit my soul.

Supervisors: my beloved wife Constance and my beloved Thomas Skryvyn[7] (*meos dil'cos*), to see everything well and faithfully carried out.

Seal appended.

Proved at Hawkedon, 14 May 1472. Admon to execs.

1   Brother of Richard Derysle of Kirtling (no. 482); probate was granted to both their wills on the same day. They may have been sons of Walter Derysle of Kirtling (no. 577): in December 1469 Walter appointed his sons Richard and William his executors.
2   See note to no. 1.
3   For the friars of Cambridge see notes to nos 42 (Carmelites), 80 (Preachers) and 187 (Augustinians).
4   Will, no. 482.
5   Executor of the wills of Walter Derysle (no. 577) and Margaret Page (no. 609); witness of the will of John Turnour the elder (no. 281).
6   This cannot be the same man as the Walter Derysle whose will is no. 577 below, as that will was proved on 30 June 1471 and this one was witnessed by 'Walter Derysle' on 17 March 1471/72.
7   According to the will of Richard Derysle (no. 482), Thomas Skryvyn was the brother of Richard's wife Alice.

462. JOAN MUNDSON of KIRTLING ('Kertelyng') [*Cambs*], 6 March 1471/72

To be buried in the churchyard of All Saints of Kirtling; to the high altar 12d; to the sepulchre light 12d; to the fabric of the church 12d; to the lights of the Blessed Mary in the chapel and in the church a cow.

Residue of all my goods to my exec, Thomas Mundson, to dispose as seems to him most to please God and profit my soul.

Seal appended.

Witnesses: John Suttun, Edmund Cowpere and others.

Proved at Hawkedon, 14 May 1472. Admon to exec.

[fol. 459]

463. JOHN MELLERE of STANSTEAD ('Stansted'), 12 December 1471

Dated at Stanstead in the diocese of Norwich; my body to Christian burial in the churchyard of Stanstead ('Stanstede') church; to the high altar of the same church for my tithes forgotten 12d; to the sustentation of the said church 20s to buy 2 cows and I wish that the wardens or guardians of the said church should see my anniversary kept annually, that is, in the ringing of bells and 1d offered at mass for ever, if it can be done.

To George Barell 6s 8d; to Avice his wife 6s 8d; to Joan Kok my sister 5s and to each of her sons 20d; to William Gallant son of Walter Gallant my godson 12d; to George the son of Henry Barell 12d; to Thomas Barell 12d; to Richard the son of John Smyth of Somerton 12d.

My exec to find a suitable and honest chaplain to celebrate divine service in the said church for a whole year for my soul and the aforesaid souls and [the souls] of my deceased friends.

Residue of all [my] goods and chattels to my execs, to dispose for the aforesaid souls in works of charity and alms as they see [best] to please God and profit the said souls.

Execs: Thomas Elyse of Melford and John Meriell of Glemsford; to each of them for their labour 6s 8d.

Seal appended.

Witnesses: George Barell, John Meriell of Stanstead and others.

Proved at Melford, 26 February 1471/72. Admon to execs.

464. THOMAS HOO of MELFORD, 10 January 1471/72

Dated at Melford; [commendation: to Almighty God and the Blessed Virgin Mary]; to be buried in the churchyard of the church of the Holy Trinity in Melford; I enjoin my execs to pay all my debts in which I am bound to others; to the high altar of the same church for my tithes forgotten and offerings withheld 8d; to a chaplain to celebrate divine service in the said church for half a year 4s 4d, for my soul and for all the souls for whom I am bound.

To Isabel my wife[1] 2 pieces of land called 'Duddescroftes' in the parish of Melford, as fully appears in a deed of feoffment, to have and to hold to [her] and her heirs, of the chief lords of the fee by due service and custom.

To Robert at Ho my son, John at Ho the younger [fol. 459v] and Roger at Ho, my sons, a pasture called 'le Waterhousyerde' in Melford, divided and enclosed by metes and bounds as is made clear in a deed, to have and to hold to them and their heirs for ever of the chief lords of the fee &c[sic].

Residue of all my goods to my execs, Isabel my wife and John Amyot, to fulfil my legacies and will and to dispose as seems to them most expedient; to John Amyot my exec for his labour 10s.

Seal appended.

Proved at Melford, 26 February 1471/72. Admon to execs.

[1] ?Isabel at Hoo of Melford to whom Thomas Alston of Sudbury bequeathed the tenement in Melford called 'Hammundes Crycke' (will of Thomas Alston, no. 290).

465. JOHN KENDALE the elder of SUDBURY, 2 March 1471/72

Dated at Sudbury, in the diocese of Norwich; to be buried in the churchyard of St Gregory; I beg my execs, in the name of God, to pay all the debts which I owe; to the high altar of St Peter of the same town for my tithes forgotten 13s 4d; to the church of Great Cornard ('Cornerth Magna') for the reparation to be done there 3s 4d.

To Joan my daughter 5 marks.

To John Kendale the younger 5 marks; to each of the daughters of the said John Kendale the younger 20s.

To the wife of William Halle 20s; to the wife of William Herde 20s.

To the convent of the friars of the Sudbury house, to the reparation of their church 10s.[1]

To the wife of William Sturnell 13s 4d.

All the utensils, hostilments [*and*] bedding of my house to be divided among my daughters and John Kendale the younger, by my execs, except the jewels, which I leave to my execs. All the apparel (*apparat'*) belonging to my body to be distributed among the poor in greatest need, similarly by my execs.

My execs, as soon as possible after my death, to find a secular priest to celebrate divine service in the said church of St Peter for my soul and for the souls of all the faithful departed for 2 years; to the reparation of St Peter's church of Sudbury 100s; my execs to keep my anniversary for 10 years after my decease in the said church of St Peter, distributing to priests, clerks and the poor up to the sum of 20s.

Residue of all my goods, together with my debts, to my execs, Sir John Potager[2] and George Prentis, to implement all the foregoing as they will answer before the High Judge on the Day of Judgement; to each of them for their labour 6s 8d.

Seal appended.

[*Will struck through and* Requir' alibi *added*] [*See fol. 506; no. 607 below.*]

[1]   See note to no. 11.
[2]   See note to no. 271.

[fol. 460]

466. AGNES PECAS of BRANDON, 6 March 1471/72

Dated at Brandon, in the diocese of Norwich; to be buried in the churchyard of the church of St Peter of Brandon; to the high altar of the same church for my tithes forgotten 12d; to the gild of the Holy Trinity of the said town 2 sheep; to the gild of St Mary the Virgin 2 sheep; to the gild of St Peter 2 sheep; to the gild of St Gregory 2 sheep;[1] to the painting of St Paul 6s 8d;[2] to the making of the image of St Michael the Archangel 6s 8d; for a trental of St Gregory 10s.

To William my brother[3] a red 'coverlyt' and a tabard; to Christian my[*sic*] wife[4] my tabard; to Isabel my sister a brass pot, a 'le coverlyte grene', a 'le blankett and a peyer schetys & iij le cluis yarne';[5] to Margery my goddaughter[6] a brass pan and a 'par bedys de gette'; to Agnes Paase a black tunic; to Lora (*Lore*) Barett a gown 'le vyolett'; to Margaret Ladde a tunic 'le vyolett'; to Alice Swastun a 'le rede kertyll'.

Residue of all my goods, after my debts and funeral expenses fully paid, to my execs, William Pecas [*and*] John Paase, faithfully to execute this my will, pay my debts and distribute [*my*] legacies and dispose for my soul as they see best faithfully to please God and all the saints.

Seal appended.

Proved at Fornham St Martin, 16 March 1471/72. Admon to execs.

[1]   These bequests of sheep to the four gilds at Brandon may indicate that they ran sheep-flocks to support themselves; Redstone could find no other mention of any of these Brandon gilds (*PSIA*, xxiii, p.52).
[2]   There appears to have been a movement in the middle years of the fifteenth century for churches

dedicated to St Peter to adopt the double dedication of 'Peter and Paul', and to add the extra image to the chancel.
3   ?Will (as 'William Pegays the elder'), no. 792.
4   Obviously 'my wife' is an error, but whether this should read 'his wife' or 'my sister' is unclear. The wife of William Pegays the elder (no. 792) was named Isabel; 'Christian' was not an unusual name for the Pecas/Pegays family: see probate of Christian Pegas of Brandon, January 1440/41 (SROB, Baldwyne 26; Pt I, no. 141).
5   See Glossary, under 'clue'. The first letter of 'yarne' is a yogh.
6   William Pegays the elder had a daughter named Margery.

467. THOMAS GOLDFYNCHE of BOTESDALE ('Botysdale') in REDGRAVE, 9 May 1471

Dated at Botesdale; my testament and last will; to be buried in the churchyard of the church of All Saints of Redgrave; to the high altar of which 3s 4d; to the fabric of the same church 5 marks; to the chapel of St Botolph in the same parish[1] 5s; to the church of Rickinghall ('Rykynghale') Superior 6s 8d; to the church of Rickinghall Inferior 3s 4d; to the church of Gislingham ('Gyslyngham') 3s 4d; to the church of Burgate 3s 4d; to the church of Wortham 3s 4d.

To the Friars Preachers of Thetford 3s 4d; to the Augustinian Friars of the same town 3s 4d[sic]; to the friars of Babwell 3s; to the Carmelite Friars of Ipswich ('Gyppewyc') 3s.[2]

To William my son[3] all my moveable goods to find (exhibeat) me a suitable man to [go to] the sepulchres of the Apostles Peter and Paul (ad limina Apostolorum Petri & Pauli),[4] and also a suitable priest to celebrate for a whole year in the parish [church] of Redgrave for the health of my soul, my parents' and my benefactors' [souls]; to my son William and his heirs all my lands and tenements, meadows, pastures [and] feedings, with all their appurtenances, towards implementing my testament [fol. 460v] and last will and fully paying my debts, the which well and truly done, he to enjoy the residue.

I beg all my feoffees to deliver full estate and seisin of and in all the said lands and tenements, meadows, pastures and feedings, with all their appurtenances, to my execs when so required, without any delay.

Execs: William Goldfynche and Alice his wife, to dispose for the health of my soul as they see best to please God and profit my soul.

Seal appended.

Witnesses: John Martyn, Robert Annour, Thomas Malverne, Thomas Hempman and others.

Proved at Finningham ('Fynyngham'), 18 March 1471/72. Admon to William Goldfynch, exec. Power reserved to Alice Goldfynch, wife of the said William Goldfynch, when she comes, if she wishes to take up admon.

1   See notes to nos 15 and 416.
2   For the friars see notes to nos 1 (Babwell and Carmelites of Ipswich), 68 (Friars Preachers of Thetford) and 69 (Augustinians of Thetford).
3   Executor of John Simond of Botesdale in Redgrave, probate October 1461 (SROB, Baldwyne 280; Pt I, no. 1374).
4   See note to no. 401 above.

468. SIMON KYY of STOWMARKET,[1] 21 February 1468/69

Dated at Stowmarket; my testament and last will; to be buried in the church of the Blessed Mary of the same town;[2] to the high altar of the same church 6s 8d.

My tenement called 'Coes' and my tenement called 'Cowperes' with a shop late John Byll's and land late William Brakstret's to be sold by my execs, but Marion my wife to have her dwelling in my tenement called 'Cowpers' for term of her life; Marion to have her daily needs (*?dietum*) honestly for term of her life from the money coming from the lands and tenements abovementioned; my meadow in Combs ('Combes') to be sold by my execs.

John Kyy my son to have all my lands and tenements in Saxham ('Saxton') to him and his assigns, he to find a suitable chaplain [*to celebrate*] for the health of my soul and for the souls of my parents and benefactors for a whole year in the church of the Blessed Mary aforesaid.

To Geoffrey Dowe and Katherine his wife and their heirs my messuage lying next to the messuage of the said Geoffrey.

Residue of all my goods to my execs, John Kyy my son and Geoffrey Dowe, [*to dispose*] as seems to them most to the laud and honour of God by the oversight of my supervisor, Robert Mylys.

Seal appended.

Proved at Stowmarket, 19 March 1471/72. Admon to execs.

[1] Son and executor of John Ky of Thorney hamlet in Stowmarket, will pr. January 1443/44 (SROB, Baldwyne 50; Pt I, no. 264).

[2] See note to no. 381.

[fol. 461]
469. MARGARET CRATERN of ICKLINGHAM ('Ikelyngham'), widow, 26 March 1472

Margaret Cratern, widow, late the wife of John Warde of Icklingham All Saints; to be buried in the churchyard of the same church; to a panel (*ad unam tabulam*) of alabaster at (*coram*) the high altar in the same church 6s 8d; to a chaplain to celebrate for my soul and the soul of John Warde my late husband, a certain stipend (*cert' stipen'*).

To William Cratern my husband 40s; to each of my sons 6s 8d.

Residue to the disposition of Sir William Ward priest, my son, exec,[1] to dispose for my soul as he sees best to please God and profit my soul.

Proved 13 April 1472. Admon to exec.

[1] John Chyrcheman of Icklingham requested William Ward, chaplain, to pray for his soul (no. 721).

470. KATHERINE HUNTE of RUSHBROOKE ('Rosshbrook'), 31 May 1470
[*English*]

[*Commendation*: to Almighty God]; to be buried in the Grey Friars at Babwell;[1] to the said friars 40s; to the high altar of the church of Rushbrooke 6s 8d; a secular priest of good conversation to have 8 marks for a whole year, to sing in the church of Dunmow ('Dunmowe') in the county of Essex for the souls of Robert Hunte,[2] me the said Katherine, Walter Bygwood and Isabel his wife[3] and for all Christian souls. To the Friars Minor in Ispwich ('Yppwych') 6s 8d;[4] to Friar Morall 13s 4d.

To Simon Lynsele my servant[5] my red bed with (*lectu' meu' cubin' cum*) the hangings, 3 pairs of sheets, a mattress, a feather bed, a pair of blankets; to the daughter of the same Simon my green bed; to John Lynsell, son of the same Simon, my dun cow; to Roger Drury of Hawstead ('Hausted')[6] my best mazer; to Katherine Strange my little mazer; to Agnes Manwod, my servant, 3s 4d; to Thomas Clerk[7] 6s 8d.

My chal' and my silver goblet to be sold and disposed by my execs, and the said Roger to have them afore any other person, giving therefor as another person will do; all my ostilments and utensils which sometime were Isabel Bygwode's, my mother, be sold and disposed by my execs.

All Cloptonnys obligations and all other obligations made to the said Robert Hunte, late my husband and testator[*sic*],[8] to be disposed and devised by the said Roger Drury and the said Simon Lynsell, whom I make execs.

Residue of all my goods to the disposition and discretion of my execs.

Proved at Fornham St Martin, 13 April 1472. Admon to execs.

1   See note to no. 1.
2   Will of Robert Hunte of Russbrooke, esquire, no. 191; Robert had requested burial within the chapel of the Blessed Mary of Rushbrooke.
3   Walter and Isabel Bygwood were Katherine's parents. (See later bequest of her mother's goods.)
4   See note to no. 1.
5   As 'Simon Lyndesell, yeoman', executor of Robert Hunte.
6   See note to no. 125.
7   Legatee of Robert Hunte.
8   There is no indication in Robert Hunte's will as to what these obligations might be.

[fol. 461v]

471. JOHN CHYRCHEMAN of ICKLINGHAM ('Ikelyngham'), 3 April 1472

Dated at Icklingham; my body to Christian burial; to the high altar of St James in Icklingham for my tithes and offerings forgotten or underpaid, 2 ewes; to the buying of a chalice in the same church 20d; to John Howys, parish chaplain of the same church, to pray for my soul, a sheep called 'a wederschepe'; to the high altar of All Saints in Icklingham, for my tithes and offerings there forgotten or underpaid and for the health of my soul, 2 ewes; to the buying of a panel (*tabul'*) called 'de Alebaster' to be put on (*super*) the altar in the same 13s 4d, to be paid in the next 4 years, that is, in each year 3s 4d.

To Margaret my wife[1] my tenement in the town of Icklingham, in the parish of All Saints, which I lately purchased of Thomas Bury, to her and her heirs for ever.

To Richard Chyrcheman my son all my tenement with its appurtenances in the same parish, which I lately purchased of Richard Chyrcheman my father,[2] together with the garden called 'Byrissyerd', in Icklingham, to him and his heirs for ever.

To John Chyrcheman my son all my tenement with its appurtenances in Icklingham, in the parish of St James, which I lately purchased of William Broom, to him and his heirs for ever, on condition that he pays William Warde, chaplain,[3] 6 marks, in a year to be agreed between them, for William Warde to pray for my soul.

To Ralph Chyrcheman my brother my best gown, my best doublet, a pair of the best hose and my straw hat ('strauen hate').

To Margaret my wife, Richard Chyrcheman my son and John Chyrcheman my son[4] 3 cows, that is, 1 cow each.

To William Helperby 6 sheep called 'wederschep'.

To William Steffe 2 sheep called 'wederschep'.

To Margery Otle my servant a green bed-cover.

To Margery [*sic*] my wife[5] all my hostilments and the utensils in any way belonging to my house.

Residue of all my goods and chattels to my execs to sell and dispose for my soul and the souls of my deceased friends in the celebration of masses and the distribution of alms as they shall see best to please God and profit my soul.

Execs: William Warde, chaplain, and William Steffe;[6] supervisor: William Helperby; to each of them for their labours 6s 8d.

Seal appended.

Witnesses: Thomas Cherecrofte, clerk,[7] John Howes, chaplain,[8] Ralph Chyrcheman, John Legat and others.

Proved at Fornham St Martin, 20 April 1472. Admon to execs.

1 Will, no. 479 below.
2 Will pr. September 1455 (SROB, Baldwyne 226; Pt I, no. 1129); John Chyrcheman was the executor.
3 Son and executor of Margaret Cratern of Icklingham (no. 469 above).
4 Richard and John were executors and legatees of their mother.
5 Testator's wife was *Margaret*, see her will, no. 479.
6 Witness of the will of Margaret Chyrcheman, no. 479.
7 Thomas Sherecroft was rector of Fornham All Saints from 1454 to 1456 (Tanner, p.1410) and of Icklingham All Saints from 1456 to 1474 (Tanner, p.1276); he witnessed the will of Robert Baghot (no. 683 below). Sherecroft's will was pr. April 1474 (SROB, Hervye 42); he requested burial in the chancel of Icklingham All Saints, on the north side of the grave of his predecessor, Richard Seynour.
8 Witness of no. 479 below.

[fol. 462]

472. THOMAS SWEYN of CREETING ST PETER ('Cretyng St Peter'),[1]
8 March 1471/72

Dated at Creeting, Mid-Lent Sunday (*die dominica medie xl^e*); my body to the burial of the church of St Peter aforesaid.

To Joan my daughter, to be paid from my goods by Marion my wife[2] after the term of 2 years following my death, in the 3 years after those 2 years, 40s in equal annual instalments.

For a trental of St Gregory to be celebrated for my soul, 10s.

To Anne my daughter and daughter of the said Marion, 26s 8d; to Alice [*sic*] a ewe and a lamb and a quarter of firewood.

To Marion [*my*] wife all my lands and tenements, meadows, pastures and feedings, with all their appurtenances, for term of her life, without committing any strip or waste in cutting down trees. After the decease of Marion, to Robert my son and his heirs all my said lands and tenements; if he dies without heirs, then my lands and tenements to go to Anne my daughter, his sister, and her heirs; if she dies without heirs, then the aforesaid lands and tenements, with their appurtenances, to remain and belong for ever to the use and profit of the said church of St Peter of Creeting for the health of my soul and [*of the souls*] of my parents and benefactors and of all the faithful departed.

Residue of all my goods to my execs, Marion my wife and William Chychele of

Creeting aforesaid, for paying my debts and arranging my burial and distributing as they see best to please God.

Supervisor and assistant for providing good counsel (*coadiutore' in bono consilio probendo*): Sir Robert Masham, rector of the said church.[3]

Proved at Stowmarket, 19 March 1471/72. Admon to Marion, wife of the deceased, co-executrix. Power reserved to William Chychele, the other co-exec, when he comes, if he wishes to take up admon.

[1] Son and executor of John Sweyn of Creeting St Peter, will pr. November 1452 (SROB, Baldwyne 139; Pt I, no. 665); John Sweyn's widow was possibly Alice (as 'Swan'), will pr. March 1458/59 (SROB, Baldwyne 211; Pt I, no. 1049).

[2] One of the beneficiaries of the will of John Sweyn was Thomas's wife, who was named there as Katherine. Given the wording of Thomas's bequest to Joan, it is likely that Joan was his daughter by his wife Katherine; his daughter Anne, mentioned later, is said to be his daughter by Marion.

[3] According to Tanner (p.1331), Robert Masham was rector of Creeting St Peter from March 1442/43 until he was succeeded by Alex Watteson in June 1446; however in 1459 he was executor of Alice Swan of Creeting St Peter (Pt I, no. 1049) and here, in 1472, Thomas Sweyn described him as rector.

[fol. 462v]

473. WILLIAM FLECHERE of BROCKLEY ('Brokley'), 20 March 1471/72

[*Commendation*: to God Almighty]; my body to Christian burial.

To Ada my wife all my hostilments and utensils whatsoever belonging to my house; [*to her*] 20s in money which John Flechere my son owes me for a tenement with its appurtenances in Brockley [*he*] lately bought of me.

To Margaret Flechere my daughter, out of the same tenement, 13s 4d.

Residue of all my goods to my execs, to sell and dispose for the health of my soul and of the souls of all [*my*] deceased friends, in the celebration of masses and in almsgiving as they see best to please God and benefit my soul.

Execs: Ada my wife, John Flechere my son and John Grygge.[1]

Seal appended.

Witnesses: Richard Gent, John Strut and others.

Proved at Fornham St Martin, 6 April 1472. Admon to execs.

[1] Beneficiary (as 'Gridge') of the will of John Cowper of Brockley (no. 75 above); see also note to that will.

474. EDMUND PORTE of HONINGTON ('Honewton'), 29 February 1471/72

Dated at Honington, the last day of February 1471; [*commendation*: to God Almighty &c]; to be buried in the churchyard of the parish church of All Saints of Honington; to the high altar of the same in the name of a mortuary, a bullock (*boviculu'*).

To Margaret my wife all my bedding and utensils and all my grain, both in the houses and in the fields, wherever it be; all my chattels and animals, of whatever sort and kind, with the plough, carts and harness (*phaler'*), with their appurtenances, and all my debts; to her and her heirs my right and title in all the lands, meadows and their appurtenances which I purchased from my father on two occasions, that is, at two separate times; she to pay all my debts.

Residue of all my goods, wherever they may be, to my executrix, the said Margaret, to administer and dispose as she sees best to please God and benefit the health of my soul.

Proved at Fornham St Martin, 6 April 1472. Admon to executrix. Seal of the official appended.

[fol. 463]

475. JAMES HAWYS of WALSHAM, 20 March 1472 [*new style*]

Dated 20 March 1472; to be buried in the churchyard of the church of the Blessed Mary of Walsham; to the high altar of Walsham 20d.

To the Friars Preachers of Thetford 5s; to the Augustinian Friars of Thetford 5s.[1]

To Walsham church 10s for the reparation of the aisle ('hele') of St Katherine.[2]

Residue of all my goods to execs Margery Hawys my wife and Richard Dei.

Seal appended.

Proved at Rickinghall Superior ('Rykynghale Superior'), 1 June 1472. Admon to execs.

[1] See notes to nos 68 (Friars Preachers of Thetford) and 69 (Augustinians).
[2] St Katherine's aisle was probably supported by a gild of St Katherine; the position of a panel depicting a Katherine wheel on the south side of the church may imply that St Katherine's aisle, or chapel, was on the south (Blatchly and Northeast, *Decoding Flint Flushwork*, Walsham le Willows St Mary).

476. HENRY MANSERE of GISLINGHAM ('Gyslyngham'), 6 March 1472 [*new style*]

Dated at Gislingham, 6 March 1472. Knowing myself to be surrounded by the vexations of death on all sides (*sciens mortis vexibus me undique esse involutu'*), I commend [*my*] soul to Jesus Christ my Saviour and my body to Christian burial. My debts for which I am indebted to creditors to be well and truly paid; to the high altar for my tithes forgotten 12d; to the gild of St John the Baptist 20d.[1]

To Katherine my daughter, wife of William Erle, a latten pot holding 3 gallons; to her my best cooking pot (*bacaliu'*[*sic*]) or 'cawdron' after the death of Joan my wife.

To Christian my daughter, wife of John Gerard, a pot, formerly bought of Thomas Funne now deceased, and holding 1½ gallons.

To Joan my wife all my goods moveable and unmoveable, with all their appurtenances, wherever they may be found, she to well and truly pay my debts and legacies with them.

Execs: Joan my wife, John Godard the elder, John Symes the elder.

Supervisor: Sir Simon Dryvere.[2]

To the said Simon Dryvere, John Godard and John Symes 6s 8d for their labour, equally divided between them; they to attend (*disponant*) to the premises that they may exonerate their conscience before God in this matter.

Seal appended.

My feoffees enfeoffed in all my lands and tenements with their appurtenances to grant sufficient estate, seisin and peaceful possession to my execs and supervisor when so required by them, without delay.

Proved at Finningham ('Fynyngham'), 3 June 1472. Admon to Sir Simon Dryvere, exec, and to the other execs by him acting on their behalf in this matter. Seal of official appended.

[1] John Cobbe (no. 343) and John Hervy (no. 800) also made bequests to the gild of St John the Baptist at Gislingham.

² A Master Simon Dryver was the incumbent of Rickinghall Superior before October 1465 (Tanner, p.1310); in 1465 William Metewyn of Wattisfield had made a substantial bequest for the 'finding' for a year of Sir Simon Dryvere and a stipend of 8 marks, 'he to have that service as far away as Cambridge' (no. 240); Master Simon Dryver was instituted at Gislingham in July 1485 (Tanner, p.1304) but, judging by this will, written in 1472, he was known to parishioners before then.

[fol. 463v]
477. JAMES TUNMAN of WESTHORPE ('Westhorp'), 16 May 1472

Dated at Westhorpe; to be buried in the churchyard of the Blessed Margaret of Westhorpe; to the high altar in the church of the Blessed Margaret of Westhorpe for my tithes underpaid 8d, and I put myself completely at the mercy of the Lord (*d'ni*); 10s for a trental to be celebrated for my soul, that is, to be divided between the friars of Babwell and Thetford.[1]

To Anne my wife all my goods, moveable and unmoveable, to pay my debts and fulfil my last will; she to be executrix.

Seal appended.

Proved at Westhorpe, 3 June 1472. Admon to executrix.

[1] For the friars see notes to nos 1 (Babwell), 68 (Friars Preachers of Thetford) and 69 (Austin Friars).

478. NICHOLAS RODYS of COMBS ('Combys'), 20 April 1472

Dated at Combs ('Combes'); my body to the Christian burial of Combs church; to the high altar of the same church for my tithes forgotten or underpaid 8d; to the east window of the south side (*partis*) of the same church 12d; to the making of the steps (*gradibus fiend'*) by which to get onto the beam of the candleloft (*per quos ascendetur super trabem candelebrum*)[1] in the said church 12d.

Whatever residue there shall be of all my goods to Joan my wife, to see to the execution of this testament.

Execs: my beloved in Christ, Joan my wife and Richard Scalpy, they to have God before their eyes in faithfully executing this testament.

Seal appended.

Proved at Buxhall ('Buxhale'), 4 June 1472. Admon to execs.

[1] An unusual reference to the inserting of twisting rood-stairs at the east end of the nave.

[fol. 464]
479. MARGARET CHYRCHEMAN of ICKLINGHAM ('Ikelyngham'), widow,[1] 8 April 1472

Dated at Icklingham; my body to Christian burial; to the high altar of the church of St James the Apostle of Icklingham for my tithes and offerings forgotten or underpaid and for the health of my soul 20d; to the high altar of the church of All Saints of Icklingham for my tithes and offerings 20d; to the buying of a painted cloth to hang before (*coram*) the high altar in the church of St James the Apostle of Icklingham 6s 8d; to the buying of a painted cloth to hang before the image of the Blessed Virgin Mary in the church of All Saints of Icklingham 3s 4d.

To Richard Chyrcheman and John Chyrcheman my sons[2] all my hostilments, utensils, chattels, lands and tenements, with all the appurtenances, to them and their heirs, they to pay all my debts and see me honestly buried.

To a suitable chaplain to celebrate for my soul and the souls for which I am bound, in the church of St James for a whole year, 8 marks.

Residue of all my goods to my execs to sell and dispose for my soul and the souls for which I am bound in the celebration of masses and the distribution of alms as they see best to please God and profit my soul.

Execs: Richard Chyrcheman and John Chyrcheman.

Seal appended.

Witnesses: John Howys, chaplain,[3] William Steffe,[4] Alexander Aspy and others.

Proved at Fornham St Martin, 3 May 1472. Admon to execs.

[1] Will of John Chyrcheman, her husband, no. 471 above.
[2] Also legatees of their father.
[3] Witness of her husband's will.
[4] Executor of her husband's will.

480. JOHN SHELDRAKE of STOKE by NAYLAND ('Stokeneylond'), 10 December 1468

To be interred (*tumuland' fore*) in the churchyard of the church of the Blessed Mary of Stoke aforesaid; to the high altar of the same church for my tithes and offerings forgotten and not remembered 8d.

To Matilda my wife all the utensils of my house; she to have my 2 messuages with their buildings (*suis edific'*) in the town of Stoke, of which one was formerly Katherine Warwell's, lying next to the messuage of Thomas Baker on the south, and the messuage formerly John Mannoke's, gentleman, on the north, one head abutting on the highway leading from Stoke church to 'Markellbrege' to the east and the other head abutting on Katherine Hache's field called 'Duffousfeld' to the west, and the other messuage was formerly the said John Mannoke's, and lies next to the said messuage which was formerly the said Katherine Warwell's on the south [fol. 464v] and the messuage of Robert Sergeaunt on the north, one head abutting on the said highway to the east, and the other head abutting on the said field of Katherine Hacche to the west, with the gardens adjacent and with half a well belonging to the same messuage, with all their appurtenances, for the whole term of her life.

After her decease, Thomas my son to have the said built-up messuage which was formerly Katherine Warewell's, with the said chamber and solar over it at the upper end (*insuperior' pariter*[*sic*]) of the same messuage with 2 chambers and half of an old house near the said messuage, the half of an old house containing in width 6ft 2ins and in length 10ft, with the garden adjacent being 4 perches long and 20ft wide at the east head and a little under 21½ft (*xxj ped' pauli & di'*) wide at the west end, and also a parcel of another piece of land at the west head of the aforesaid garden 28ft long and a little under 19½ft (*none deci' ped' pauli & di'*) wide, with part of the half well, for going to it and returning, without the gainsaying of anyone, to hold the said messuage with the buildings and garden adjacent and the half well, with all their appurtenances, as aforesaid, to the said Thomas my son and his heirs, for ever.

To Stephen my son, the other built-up messuage, formerly John Mannoke's, with the chamber and solar over it at each end of the messuage, with a bakehouse and with the other half of the old house, this half being 6ft 2ins in width and 10ft in length, with the garden adjacent, being 3 perches and a little under 11ft (*iij pertic' & xj ped' pauli*) in length and 25½ft in width at the east head and 2 perches in width at the west head, and also at the west head a piece of land, this part being a little under (*pauli*) 28ft in length and a little under 13ft in width, with half of the said well, to hold the messuage with the buildings and garden, with half the well, with all their appurtenances, as aforesaid, to the said Stephen and his heirs for ever.

[*The above two legacies*] on the following conditions: that Matilda shall be able to occupy or keep the 2 messuages with their appurtenances and have sufficient vict-uals and all her other necessaries, but if she does not and she is in need, then she [*to sell*] one of the messuages so that she can live on the money received for it, and if any of the money from the sale of the messuage is surplus beyond her keep, it is to be given and distributed for the health of our souls; and the other messuage, with its appurtenances, not sold, to be divided equally between Thomas and Stephen my sons. But if Thomas and Stephen 'find' and care (*foveant*) for Matilda, or one of them 'finds' and nourishes (*nutriat*) her well and sufficiently and honestly with all necessaries to her satisfaction (*ad bene placitu'*) and meets the rents and reparations and all the other dues (*onera*) relating to the messuages, then neither of messuages to be sold but remain to Thomas and Stephen as above.

Matilda to have all those parcels of land with the buildings which I lately purchased of the said John Mannock, gentleman, for the whole term of her life, and after her decease they are to be sold by the discretion of her execs and the money from them to be distributed and given in pious uses for the health of our souls, of our parents, friends and benefactors.

Residue of all my goods to my execs, Matilda, Thomas and Stephen, to be disposed by them for the health of my soul as seems most expedient.

Proved at Fornham, 29 April 1472. Admon to Stephen, exec; power reserved to the others when they come.

[fol. 465]

481. THOMAS FRAUNCEYS of WORLINGTON ('Wrydlyngton'), 4 May 1472

Dated at Worlington; to be buried in the churchyard of All Saints' church of Worlington; to the high altar for my tithes forgotten [*and*] not well paid 4d; to the fabric of the church 16d.

My wife to have my cottage with the appurtenances for term of her life and after her decease John my son to have the said cottage, paying 10 marks for it. Out of this 10 marks: to Margaret my daughter 20s; to Thomas my son 20s; 10s for a trental to be celebrated for my soul and for the souls of all my benefactors; the residue of the 10 marks to be disposed in pious uses, namely to the church and the poor according to the discretion of my executors.

Residue of all my goods to my wife, firstly to pay my debts.

Execs: my wife and John my son, to dispose for my soul as they see best to please God and profit my soul.

Proved at Herringswell ('Heryngeswell'), 15 May 1472. Admon to execs.

482. RICHARD DERYSLE of KIRTLING ('Kertelynge'), [*Cambs*],[1] 12 March 1471/2

Of Kirtling in the diocese of Norwich; my body to Christian burial in the churchyard of Kirtling parish church; to the high altar of the same church for tithes forgotten and offerings underpaid 6s 8d; 10 marks to the buying of a vestment for the said church to serve there in honour of God, the Blessed Mary and all the saints for the health of my soul and of the souls of my parents.

To the friars and convent of Babwell 10s to celebrate a trental for my soul and for the souls of my parents;[2] to the friars and convents of Carmelites, Preachers and Augustinians in Cambridge (*Cantebr'*), to each convent 10s, to celebrate a trental for my soul.[3]

To Alice my daughter 10 marks to be paid as soon as it can be received of my goods. 13s 4d to be distributed among the poor.

To the reparation of a lane called 'Tuftelane' 13s 4d.

To each of my godsons and goddaughters a bushel (*modium*) of malt.

To my wife all my utensils and ostilments and all my cows; she to have enough (*quosdam*) of my horses to keep up her husbandry, with plough and cart with their necessary [*equipment*] (*nec'ijs*); wheat and malt sufficient for her housekeeping this year, immediately after my decease, and part of my grain now growing for sowing next year and for her housekeeping.

[fol. 465v] [*Will, of same date*]

My wife to have, for term of her life, all my lands and tenements in 'Upheme',[4] she to keep up the reparation of all the buildings of the tenement sufficiently during her lifetime; after her decease, William my son to have my tenement in 'Uphem' with all the lands that I bought with the tenement when I first occupied it, and no others.

To Walter my son my tenement in Lidgate ('Lydgate'), 24 acres of land, all of which he is to have immediately after my decease; 5 acres of meadow lying at 'Cowlynge Brooke' on condition that my execs have the profit of those 5 acres for the term of 6 years immediately following my decease, to help pay my legacies, and after those 6 years the 5 acres of meadow to remain wholly to Walter and his heirs.

To Thomas my son 3 acres of land called 'Blakelonde' lying together in 'Cokes Felde', one acre [*sic*] and an acre of meadow lying next to the said land, and a croft called 'Aldercroft' and another croft called 'Hogemans Croft' and 4 acres of meadow lying at 'Cowlynge Broke' and 10 acres of land in 'Lydgate Feld', which my execs are to have for the term of 6 years after my decease with all the profits towards fulfilling all my legacies. If Thomas should, in the future, sell the said lands and meadow, then Walter to have them before all other men, paying his brother the true value for them.

To John my son my messuage called 'Potters' and the meadow which I bought of Agnes Parson and a 'le grove' at 'Cowlynge' and my part of a grove at Great Bradley ('Bradle Magna') and the lands and meadow formerly 'Cowpers', which [*lands and meadow (que & quas)*] my execs are to have to my use and for fulfilling my legacies for the term of 11 years after my decease.

To Richard my son 8 acres of land lying in (*super*) 'Kertelynge Hell' and the lands which I bought of John Berd and Joan Glover and a croft in Lidgate opposite the gate where William Catour formerly lived; my grove in Lidgate which my execs are to keep in their hands to my use and to perform my will for the term of 7 years immediately following my death.

My execs to keep the said Richard at grammar school (*ad scola' grammatical'*) for the term of 3 or 4 years after my decease until he has a reasonable knowledge of reading and writing (*quousque h'eat rac'onabilem intellectu' legend' & scribend'*). Residue of all my goods to my execs Walter Derysle [*and*] William Derysle my sons, Robert Motte and Thomas Fordham, to dispose as seems to them most to please God and profit my soul.

Supervisors: my dearly beloved in Christ, Alice my wife[5] and Thomas Skryvyn her brother,[6] to perform all of the above well and truly.

Proved at Hawkedon, 14 May 1472. Admon to execs.

1   Will of his brother, William Derysle, no. 461; probate was granted to both brothers' wills on the same day. They may have been sons of Walter Derysle of Kirtling (no. 577): in December 1469 Walter appointed his sons Richard and William his executors.
2   See note to no. 1.
3   For the friars of Cambridge see notes to nos 42 (Carmelites), 80 (Preachers) and 187 (Augustinians).
4   Now Upend, in the north of the parish; from Old English *upp-haeme*, 'up-dwellers' (Reaney, *Place-names of Cambridgeshire*, p.126).
5   Will (as 'Derysley'), no. 656.
6   Witness of his sister's will, no. 656.

[fol. 466]
483. ROBERT MYLLERE of NAUGHTON ('Nawton'), 3 July 1471

Dated 3 July 11 Edward IV; [*commendation*: to Almighty God my Creator who created and redeemed me, to the glorious Virgin Mary his mother and all the saints]; to be buried in the churchyard of the church of the Blessed Mary of Naughton ('Naueton'); to the high altar of the said church for my tithes and offerings under-paid 20d.

To Robert my son, Margaret and Margery my daughters, a ewe each.

Residue of all my goods and chattels, after my burial done and debts paid, to remain wholly to Margery my wife, to dispose of it of her [*own*] free will.

[*Executrix*] Margery my wife and supervisor Alexander Snellyng of Elmsett ('Elmes-sett'); they, having God before their eyes, faithfully to implement this my testament as they will answer before the High Judge.

[*Will, of the same date*] [*English*]

Margery my wife to have my house and my land, all whole together, to dwell there or to let it, term of her life, and after her decease, Robert Myllere my son to have it, to him and his heirs. If he dies without heirs, it to remain to Margaret and Margery my daughters.

Residue of my goods, if any there be, to Margery my wife, my executrix.

Seal appended.

Witnesses: William Braybrook, John Maschall, with others of Naughton ('Nauton') beforesaid.

Proved at Bildeston ('Bylston'), 24 September 1471. Admon to executrix.

[*Whole entry crossed through; see no. 563 below for a similar version of the testament but there the will is missing.*]

484. JOHN SALLE *alias* JOHN COOKE of BILDESTON ('Bylston') the elder, 18 February 1470/71

Dated at Bildeston, the first Tuesday after the feast of St Valentine the Martyr 1470; to be buried in the churchyard of the Blessed Mary of Bildeston; to the high altar of the same for my tithes underpaid 20d; to the choir of the same a surplice.

To each lesser friar, not a priest, of the town of Ipswich (*Gyppiwic'*) 4d.[1]

To Alice my wife all my utensils [*to be*] at her free will; she to have, after my decease, my capital messuage in Bildeston, with all its appurtenances belonging to it, to her and her assigns for ever; similarly, 3 acres of land which [fol. 466v] I have in Chelsworth called 'Chellesworth Crofte', alias 'Skypps', with its appurtenances.

To Margaret my daughter, in money or goods, 5 marks; to Joan the younger, my daughter, similarly, 5 marks; to each child of Simon my son 12d; to each child of Stephen Osmonde and Joan the elder, my daughter, 12d.

Residue of my goods to the disposition of my [*wife, my*] executrix, she to have God before her eyes and well and truly execute this testament.

Seal appended.

Witnesses: William Salle *alias* William Cook my brother, John my son, Stephen Osmond and others.

Proved at Bildeston ('Bylston'), 24 September 1471. Admon to executrix. Seal of official appended.

1   For the friars of Ipswich see notes to nos 1 (Franciscans and Carmelites) and 50 (Dominicans).

[fol. 466v]

485. WILLIAM BENSTY of HERRINGSWELL ('Heryngeswell'), 26 March 1472

Dated at Herringswell; to be buried in the churchyard of Herringswell parish church; to the high altar there 6s 8d; to the gild of St Ethelbert (*Alpelbert'*) 20d.[1]

To each of my sons 6 lambs and 6 wethers ('wederes').

To the friars of Babwell 5s and to each house of friars of Thetford 2s 6d.[2]

To my wife all my utensils and bedding belonging to my dwelling, and the house in which I live and the lands belonging as long as she keeps herself a widow; and if she takes herself another husband, then Richard my son to have the dwelling with the lands belonging and 2 horses.

Residue of all my goods to be left in the hands of my execs, John Bensty of Denston, Richard Balle of Freckenham ('Frekenham'), John Largaunt of Tuddenham ('Todenham'), they to dispose as they see best to please God and profit my soul.

Proved at Fornham St Martin, 30 March 1472. Admon to execs.

1   The dedication of Herringswell church is to St Ethelbert. The gild of St Ethelbert the King is recorded in the royal survey of gilds undertaken in 1388 and 1389. The certificate states that the gild was founded in 1349; its purposes being to provide a chaplain to celebrate weekly, to provide a taper before St Ethelbert's image, and to help towards church repairs; members were to offer at a funeral mass and give 1d for a mass for the soul (TNA, C47/424). The next certificate records that in 1375 a gild of St Peter had been founded in Herringswell with similar aims (TNA, C47/425).
2   For the friars see notes to nos 1 (Babwell), 68 (Dominicans of Thetford) and 69 (Augustinians).

[fol. 467]

486. HENRY NOBYLL of LITTLE SAXHAM ('Parva Saxham'),[1] 10 October 1471

Dated at Little Saxham; my body to Christian burial; to the high altar of the church of Saxham aforesaid, for my tithes and offerings underpaid 2s; to the friars of Babwell,[2] to celebrate a trental of [*St*] Gregory 10s; to the reparation of the church of Saxham aforesaid 3s 4d; to the reparation of Westley ('Westle') church 3s 4d; to the reparation of Great Horringer ('Magna Hornyngherth') church 3s 4d.

To Joan my wife 8 marks in money and all my hostilments and utensils belonging to my dwelling (*hospico'*).

My tenement in which I live to be sold by my execs, and of the money from the sale: Ralph my son to have 40s when he comes to the age of 20; Walter my son to have 40s when he comes to the age of 20. If either of the said Ralph and Walter dies under that age, he that survives to have the part of the deceased one; if both die under that age, Joan my wife to have my sons' legacies to her [*own*] sustentation.

Residue of all [*my*] goods to my execs, to sell, receive and dispose for my soul and for the souls for whom I am bound in the celebration of masses and the distribution of alms as they see best to please God and benefit my soul.

Execs: Walter Nobyll[3] and Richard Nobyll, to each of whom for their labour 2s. Seal appended.

Proved at Fornham St Martin, 28 December 1471. Admon to execs.

[1]   Executor of Adam Nobyll of Westley, will pr. June 1458 (SROB, Baldwyne 243; Pt I, no. 1220).
[2]   See note to no. 1.
[3]   Executor of Adam Nobyll. See note above.

487. RICHARD SMYTH of WESTLEY ('Westle'),[1] [*undated*] [*?1471*]

My body to Christian burial; to the high altar of Westley church for my tithes forgotten and underpaid 12d.

To Agnes my wife my tenement in which I live, with the appurtenances, to her and her assigns for term of her life [*and*] all [*my*] goods and chattels in the town of Westley and elsewhere, she to see me buried and pay my debts; whenever she wishes to sell my said tenement, she to sell it and live out of it, and of the money from it Margery my daughter to have 40s by the discretion of my execs.

Residue of all my goods to my execs, to sell, receive and dispose for my soul and for the souls for whom I am bound in the celebration of masses and distribution of alms and other deeds of charity, as they see best to please God and profit my soul.

Execs: Agnes my wife and John Stanton of Westley; to John for his labour 12d. Seal appended.

Proved at Fornham St Martin, 28 December 1471. Admon to execs.

[1]   Son and executor of Thomas Smyth of Westley, will pr. May 1442 (SROB, Baldwyne 18; Pt I, no. 98).

[fol. 467v]

488. HENRY HELLE of COCKFIELD ('Cokfeld'), 6 May 1469

Dated at Cockfield; seeing myself in peril of death; [*commendation*: to God Almighty]; to be buried in the churchyard of Cockfield church; to the reparation of the tabernacle of St Peter 20s; to the reparation of the said church 20s; to Friar Richard Lawshull and Friar Myldenhale 10s by equal portions for a trental of St Gregory; to the reparation of the 'perch' candlebeam (*pertice candelebru'*) 13s 4d. To Richard my son 40s; to William my godson (*confilio*) 6s 8d; to Anne Hode my goddaughter (*confilie mee*) 3s 4d.

Residue of all my goods to the disposition of my execs, Henry Helle my son and William Assy, they to implement my will in the way they know best to please God. Proved at Cockfield ('Cokfeld'), 10 January 1471/72. Admon to execs.

489. [*name omitted*] INGLOND[1] of ?TROSTON ('Thruston'),[2] 24 January 1471/72

[*Name omitted from will;* 'Inglond' *in margin*]; dated the Friday before the feast of the conversion of St Paul 1471; my body to Christian burial in the churchyard of Troston; to the high altar of the said church 6d; to the 4 men who shall carry my body to burial 4d; before all else, my debts to be paid; if the legacy assigned to me in my father's testament can be raised and received, I leave one part to Troston church, one part to Bardwell ('Berdwell') church where my parents are buried,[3] one part to Honington ('Henewton') church and one part to the house of Friars Preachers of Thetford,[4] according to the disposition of my execs.

Residue of all my goods to my exec, Stephen Purdy, clerk, rector of Honington ('Honewton'),[5] to administer (*exequ'*) for my soul as he sees best to profit it.

Seal appended.

Proved at Fornham, 24 February 1471/72. Admon to exec.

> 1   Probably either Robert or Henry Inglond, one of the sons of William Inglond of Bardwell; William's will pr. June 1460 (SROB, Baldwyne 245; Pt I, no. 1231).
> 2   'Thruston' would normally be 'Thurston' but the other villages named seem to point to Troston.
> 3   There were no burial directions in his father's will (Pt I, no. 1231).
> 4   See note to no. 68.
> 5   Sir Stephen Purdy was supervisor of the will of William Wellys of Bardwell (no. 16); see note to that will.

[fol. 468]

490. JOHN BARKERE of COWLINGE ('Cowlynge'), 28 December 1470
[*nuncupative*]

Dated at Cowlinge; to be buried in the churchyard of Cowlinge parish church; to the high altar there for my tithes forgotten and under paid 20d; to each priest present at my obsequies and on the day of my burial 4d and to each clerk 2d and to each boy 1d and to 4 poor 4d.

To the Friars Minor of Babwell for a trental 10s; to the Friars Minor of Cambridge (*Cantebr'*) for a trental 10s;[1] to a suitable priest a competent salary, to celebrate divine service in Cowlinge parish church for a whole year for the health of my soul, my father's and mother's and all our benefactors' [*souls*]; to a suitable priest a competent salary, to celebrate divine service in Helions Bumpstead ('Bumsted Helyon') [*Essex*] parish church for the health of my soul, Robert's and Alice's, [*my*] father's and mother's, and all our benefactors' [*souls*].

To Katherine my wife all that tenement called 'Femotes', with all its appurtenances, during her life and after her decease, [*it*] to be sold with all its appurtenances by my execs and the money from it to be disposed thus: to a suitable priest a competent salary to celebrate divine service in Cowlinge parish church for a whole year for the health of my soul, Joan's and Katherine's my wives, our fathers' and mothers' and all our benefactors' [*souls*]; the residue from the tenement to the emendation of the church of St Andrew of Cowlinge. If Katherine does not wish to live in the tenement called 'Femottes', then it, with all its appurtenances, to be sold with the oversight (*per visu'*) of my execs and by the discretion of Katherine, and she to have half its value, paid by my execs, and the rest to be disposed as above-stated.

All my tenement called 'Sowrall', with its appurtenances, to be sold by my execs and if Katherine wishes to buy it, she to have it at 13s 4d under its value, before all others; and the money from it for a competent salary to a pilgrim going on pilgrimage to Rome and there doing the circle of Rome three times (*ibidem circulum Rome eundo tria vice*) and to celebrate there, at *Scala Celi*, three masses[207] for the health of my soul, Katherine's and Joan's, my wives', our fathers' and mothers' and all our benefactors' [*souls*].

To Katherine all the years [*remaining*] of the 12 years farm of my land; she to have all her own utensils now in my dwelling and first choice of the utensils belonging to it, and they then to be divided strictly between us (*direct' separantur inter nos*), everything belonging to my dwelling, under the oversight of my execs.

[fol. 468v] A 'grovett' and a cart and a 'plate', with certain other chattels, to be sold to find a suitable priest to celebrate divine service in Cowlinge church, as above said, for a whole year.

Residue of all my goods to my faithful execs, John Alsey and Walter Cowper; supervisor: Edmund Meyner; they to dispose for the health of my soul, our fathers' and mothers' and all our benefactors' [*souls*] as seems most expedient to them.

Seal appended to nuncupative testament.

Witnesses: Sir Ed' Frankeleyn, chaplain of the parish church of Cowlinge, William Lombard, William More, John Barker and others.

Will [*of the same date*] annexed to my testament.

To Katherine my wife 8 of the best cows and 4 of the best bullocks and 3 of the best calves and the best bull of the 2 bulls and the best horse of the 4 horses and the little cart, 2 ploughs with their equipment (*pertin'*), all the sheep, pigs and piglets, geese, cocks and hens and all the grain, both inside and outside the buildings (*domos*) except that all the costs and expenses of my burial day, my seven-day and thirty-day shall be borne by (*conc'rant*) my own grain and chattels, with a mother cow and a pig. Katherine my wife to have the occupying of my 3 horses until the feast of the Invention of the Holy Cross next [*3 May*] for ploughing and carting for her own use (*suam propriam ocupacionem*).

To William Meyner my godson a bullock and to Christine Reve a bullock; to Edmund Barker my godson a bullock; to John Barker my godson a bullock; to John Reve my godson a bullock; to Eleanor Meyner a calf; to John Mychell my godson a calf and to Thomas Prat my servant a calf.

To John Barker aforesaid of Great Thurlow ('Thyrlow Magna') a gown, a 'dobelet' and a pair of hose, at present at Bury; he to have a 'chypex' [*?chipaxe*], a 'belte', a 'twbyll', a 'hatchett'.[3]

To Robert Wybour a 'fellyng belte'.

To John Goodyer a gown of 'musterdevelys' colour and a 'primer'.

To John Prat of Barnardiston ('Bernardeston') a gown of 'russett' colour and a 'dowblett' of 'blake fustyan' and a pair of black hose.

To Ed' Meyner the best brass pot.

My best gown and 'dublett' with the studded silver girdle, the purse with the silver ring (*bursa cum anulo argent'*) and all the other necessaries belonging to my body and all the tools (*instrument'*) and necessaries belonging to my craft, to be sold by my execs to go towards (*adiuvand'*) paying my debts.

Residue of all my goods to John Alsey and Walter Cowper, my faithful execs, to ordain as appears in [*my*] testament.

Proved at Fornham, 12 March 1470/71. Admon to execs. Seal of official appended.

1   For the friars see notes to nos 1 (Babwell) and 187 (Friars Minor of Cambridge).
2   'Doing the circle of Rome' meant completing the stations of the Holy City; however, as there were almost 400 stations, pilgrims were not expected to visit them all. This testator specifically requested masses at *Scala Celi*, thus ensuring that 'his' pilgrim visited that particular station. See Rossetti 'Notes on the Stacyons of Rome', pp. xxi–xxii.
3   'chypex', 'belte', 'twbyll' and 'hatchett' are all axes or wood chopping implements: see Glossary.

[fol. 469]

491. WILLIAM MELLE of STOKE BY NAYLAND ('Stokeneylond'),[1]
11 October 1470

Dated at Stoke by Nayland; to be buried in the churchyard of the parish church of Stoke by Nayland; to the high altar of the same church for my tithes and offerings forgotten and not remembered 22d[*sic*]; to the Christian work (*opus ecclesiasticum*) of the same church 22s; to each priest present at my obsequies on the day of my burial 4d; to each clerk present there then 2d.

To Margaret my wife my capital house in which I now live, with 2 fields and a grove belonging or annexed to the house, with their appurtenances, for term of her life; and after her decease, the capital house with the 2 fields and the grove, with their appurtenances, to remain to Thomas Melle my son, to hold to him and his heirs for ever in this manner: that Thomas or his heirs pay Robert Melle my son 40s and Matilda my daughter 40s. To Margaret my wife my 3 tenements called 'le Renteres' with the 3 gardens adjacent and belonging to the tenements, with their appurtenances, which 3 tenements and gardens and their appurtenances lie next to the said capital house in which I live, to hold to her and her heirs for ever. Margaret to have my whole tenement called 'Cokeres', with the garden adjacent and with all the appurtenances belonging to the same tenement, for term of her life; and after her decease, the tenement with all its appurtenances to remain to Joan my daughter, to hold to her and her heirs for ever.

Residue of all my goods to my executrix, Margaret my wife, to dispose in pious uses and in the name of charity as seems to her most expedient for the health of my soul and the souls of my parents and all my benefactors.

Seal appended.

Proved at Boxford, 20 June 1471. Admon to executrix.

1   Executor of John Berner the elder of Stoke by Nayland, will pr. September 1458 (SROB, Baldwyne 201; Pt I, no. 992).

[fol. 469v]

492. JOHN GARDYNER of ICKLINGHAM ('Ikelyngham'), 12 June 1471

Dated at Icklingham in the county of Suffolk; my testament and last will; to be buried in the churchyard of the church of St James the Apostle of Icklingham; to the fabric of the same church 3s 4d.

To Richard my son 20s.

To Matilda my wife all my bedding and utensils in my house.

My wife and William my son to have my dwelling house (*mansionem*) with all the lands belonging to it, they to pay my debts and legacies; they to have a cottage with 15 acres of land belonging to the abbot and convent of Bury held [*by me*] as shall plainly appear by a certain indenture of the said abbot and convent.

My execs, Matilda my wife and William my son, to execute this my testament and will as best they can to please God and profit my soul.

Proved at Icklingham All Saints, 25 June 1471. Admon to execs.

493. JOHN FULLERE of BARNHAM ('Bernham'),[1] 1471 [*exact date not given*]

To be buried in the churchyard of the church of St Martin of Barnham;[2] to the high altar of that church for tithes forgotten 12d; to the high altar of the church of St Gregory of the same [*place*] 4d.

To Alice my wife my messuage with all the lands belonging to it in Barnham, with the reparation as ?it [*?she*] requires (*cum reparacione ut dicet*).

[*Residue*] to execs, my wife and Edmund Caton, her brother, to dispose as they see most expedient for the health of my soul, my children's (*filiorum*) and my benefactors' [*souls*].

Seal appended.

Proved at Fornham St Martin, 8 July 1471. Admon to execs.

[1] Executor of John Goore of Barnham, probate September 1458 (SROB, Baldwyne 267; Pt I, no. 1303); executor of Alice Fullere of Barnham, probate April 1461 (SROB, Baldwyne 277; Pt I, no. 1362).

[2] See note to no. 282.

[fol. 470]

494. JOHN ESSEX of SHIMPLING ('Schymplyng'), 9 March 1476 [*recte ?1471 new style*]

Dated at Shimpling, in the diocese of Norwich, 9 March *Millesimo CCCCLxxvj*[to] [1476; *recte ?1471 new style*]; to be buried in the churchyard of the same town of Shimpling; to the reparation of the church of the same town 20s.

To the friars of the convents of Babwell and Sudbury 10s, to be shared between them, to celebrate and pray for my soul and the souls of my parents.[1]

To Margaret my wife all the utensils of my house and the bedding.

To John my son my place (*placeam*) with all the lands and tenements except that Margaret my wife is to have her dwelling with the solar and yard on the south side of the hall for term of her life; John my son to pay Margaret my wife 13s 4d annually during her lifetime.

Residue of all my goods I leave in the hands of my execs, John Germayn of Stanstead ('Stansted'), Margaret my wife and John my son, to pay my debts and see to my funeral and to do other deeds of piety for my soul as they see best to please God most and profit my soul.

Proved at Sudbury, 12 July 1471. Admon to co-execs John Germayn and John Essex. Power reserved to Margaret, co-executrix, when she comes if she wishes to take up [*admon*].

1   See notes to nos 1 (Babwell) and 11 (Sudbury).

495. WILLIAM TURNOUR of WALSHAM, 10 July 1471

Sick unto death; my body to Christian burial in the churchyard of Walsham church; all my debts to be fully paid; to the high altar of the said church for tithes forgotten or ignorantly done 40d; to the same church 10s.

To Agnes Bakon my daughter of Drinkstone ('Drynkston') 13s 4d.

To Joan Grocer my daughter of Walsham 6s 8d.

To William Reson my nephew 20s, to be received from the sale of the tenement lately John Howchon's, together with a horse, to be delivered to him at Michaelmas next coming.

[fol. 470v] To Bacton ('Bakton') church 40d.

I leave 40d for a mass at *Scala Celi* (*ad scalam le celi*) to be celebrated there in a circle (*cum circulo*)[1] for my soul and the souls of my friends or benefactors.

To Matilda my wife all my moveable goods and all my chattels, moveable and unmoveable, wherever they may be, over and above [*my*] legacies; to Matilda my wife my tenement in Bacton ('Baketon') lately William Turnowrs, to her and her heirs for ever.

My execs, Matilda my wife, John Robhood of Walsham[2] and John Bakon of Drinkstone,[3] to fulfil my legacies and dispose [*of the residue*] as by their discretion seems best for the health of my soul, as they will answer before God and men at the Last Judgement.

Proved on 17 July 1471. Admon to execs.

1   For 'a circle of Rome' see note to no. 490.
2   Legatee and executor of his mother, Joan Robhood of Walsham le Willows (no. 401).
3   ?His son-in-law.

496. ROBERT SARE of WALSHAM, 25 June 1471 [*nuncupative*]

His body to Christian burial in the churchyard of Walsham church.

To Marion his wife all his moveable goods, both quick and dead, to her own use for ever. To the same Marion his tenement with its appurtenances situated in Walsham for term of her life, and after her decease the tenement to be left to Thomas Sare his son, on condition that he pays Isabel his sister 10s, Joan his sister 10s and Joan his sister the younger 10s. If Thomas should die without heirs, then the tenement to be sold and from the money he wished to have a suitable priest [*celebrating*] for a whole year in the parish church of Walsham.

Residue to be disposed in pious uses; Marion his wife to be his executrix.

Witnesses: Sir William Potager[1] and James Hawys and others.

Proved at Walsham, 17 July 1471. Admon to executrix.

1   See note to no. 175, and also no. 258.

[fol. 471]

497. THOMAS WALLERE of FORNHAM ST MARTIN, 13 August 1471

Dated at Fornham St Martin; my body to Christian burial.

To Joan my wife all my hostilments and utensils whatsoever belonging to my house and also all my live cattle; to her my tenement with its appurtenances situated in Fornham aforesaid if she is able (*si ipsa valeat*) to pay the sum of 4 marks 6s 8d at present in arrears; otherwise, the tenement with its appurtenances to be sold by Joan to pay my debts and for her and her children's sustentation.

Residue of all my goods to Joan my wife, to dispose for my soul and the souls for whom I am bound, in the celebration of masses and the giving of alms as she sees best to please God and profit my soul; Joan to be my executrix, she to execute my testament faithfully.

Seal appended.

Proved at Fornham St Martin, 30 September 1471. Admon to executrix.

498. SIMON GODLARD of WICKHAM SKEITH ('Wykham'), 13 July 1471

['Godelard' *in margin*] Dated at Wickham Skeith, on the Saturday after the feast of Thomas, Bishop and Martyr, 1471; sick in body; my body to Christian burial; to the high altar [*of Wickham*] aforesaid for my tithes forgotten 8d.

My execs to sell enough of my grain and cattle (*cattall'*) to pay my debts out of the money received; they to sell a piece of land lying in the field at 'le Clynt' and the money received to be disposed in the said town by my execs in deeds of charity for my soul.

To Margaret my daughter my messuage with the garden and croft adjacent and 3 roods of land lying in 'Monsho[*damaged*]', which messuage, garden, croft and 3 roods of land I lately purchased from Edward Dale, which were John Gerard's, to hold for the whole term of her life; and after her decease, Margaret, daughter of the said Margaret, to have the said messuage with the garden and croft adjacent and the 3 roods of land to her and her heirs for ever. If Margaret the daughter of my daughter Margaret should die before her mother, then the said messuage with the garden and croft adjacent and the 3 roods of land to remain to the heirs of my daughter Margaret for ever. If she dies without heirs, they to be sold by my execs and the money received to be disposed by my execs in the said town in deeds [fol. 471v] of charity for my soul and the souls of Alice my wife, our friends and all our benefactors.

Alice my wife each year during her life to have easement within the said messuage to sow a peck of flax seed (*seminis lini*) and to pasture a calf there and a pig, and to go in and out (*transeund'*) without contradiction or impediment of Margaret. To Alice my wife my tenement in which I live and all the lands, meadows, pastures and feedings, both bond and free, except as bequeathed above, to hold to her for the whole term of her life; and after her decease, Margaret my daughter to have my meadow lying in the meadow called 'Holm Medew' and 3 roods of land lying at the end of the lane called 'Copynslane', next to the enclosure of John Deye on the west, to hold to her and Margaret her daughter under the form noted above. The said Margaret to have a piece of meadow lying in Thornham. This, my aforesaid tenement, with all my lands, meadows, pastures and feedings, except as above excepted, after the decease of Alice, to be sold by my execs and the money received from it to be spent by my execs in the town of Wickham in obsequies and the celebration of masses, or about the reparation of the church, the mending of roads or the relief of the poor or other deeds of charity as they see most to please God and profit my soul and the souls of Alice my wife and all of our benefactors.

John Bugge alias Gronge to enfeoff and make estate, sufficient in law, of and in a piece of land which I lately bought of the said John Bugge, to John Godlard of Thornham, Robert Clerk and Simon Bretlote, to hold to them and their heirs and to Alice my wife for the whole term of her life according to the form of my will above written.

Alice my wife, Robert Clerk and Simon Bertlote[*sic*] to be execs of this my last will and testament.

Proved at Palgrave, 2 October 1471. Admon to execs.

[fol. 472]

499. JOHN TYLBROK[1] of Upend ('Huphem')[2] in KIRTLING ('Kertelynge') [*Cambs*], 20 September 1470

['Tylbroke' *in margin*] Dated at Upend ('Upheme') in the parish of Kirtling; to be buried in the churchyard of the church of All Saints of Kirtling; to the high altar of the same church for my tithes forgotten 4d.

To the Friars Preachers of Cambridge (*Cantebr'*), for a trental, 10s.[3]

To the gild of St Mary's chapel of Kirtling (*gylde ste' marie capell' de Kertelynge*)[4] half a quarter of barley.

Residue of all my goods, my debts first being paid out of it, to Joan my wife to dispose as she sees best to please God and most profit the health of my soul.

The said Joan with John Whytyng of the same town to be my execs.

Seal appended.

Proved at Fornham, 4 June 1471. Admon to co-exec John Whytynge. Power reserved to Joan Tylbrok, co-executrix when she comes, if she wishes to undertake admon.

[1] Son of Peter Tilbrook of Kirtling, will pr. November 1445 (SROB, Baldwyne 69; Pt I, no. 337); brother of Thomas Tylbrook of Upend in Kirtling (no. 610 below).
[2] See note to no. 482.
[3] See note to no. 80.
[4] Or, 'to the chapel of the gild of St Mary's of Kirtling', or even 'to the chaplain of the gild of St Mary's of Kirtling'. For the gilds of Cambridgeshire in general see Introduction, under *Gilds*, and note to no. 199. In 1442, John Fortham of Kirtling made bequests to the gilds of All Saints and of the Blessed Mary of Kirtling (SROB, Baldwyne 37; Pt I, no. 203).

[fol. 472v]

500. ALICE HERVY of RICKINGHALL INFERIOR ('Rykynghale'), widow, 26 March 1471

Testament and last will; dated at Rickinghall; to be buried in the churchyard of the Blessed Mary of Rickinghall Inferior; to the high altar of the said church 12d; to the reparation of the said church 12d; to the rector of the said church to celebrate and pray for my soul and for the souls of all my benefactors 4s.

To Katherine Breon my niece all my tunics and my blue-coloured tabard.

To the Augustinian Friars of Thetford 12d.[1]

To the reparation of a way called 'Bussyscloth' 12d.

To Henry Breon my tenement called 'Lothysted', to hold to him and his heirs for ever; to Henry 2 acres of bond land lying in 'Redyng', to hold to him and his heirs according to the custom of the manor; to Henry all my hostilments and utensils on condition that he implements my will; he to be my exec, to dispose for my soul and the souls of my parents and benefactors as seems to him best to please God and profit my soul.

Supervisor: Sir Edmund Sparke, rector of the church of the aforesaid Rickinghall.[2]

Proved at Fornham St Martin, 11 June 1471. Admon to exec.

1   See note to no. 69.
2   See note to no. 194.

[fol. 473]

501. ROBERT LECHE of STOWMARKET ('Stowemarket'),[1] 20 April 1470 & 21 April 1471

[*Testament*]

Dated 20 April 1470; to be buried in the chapel of St Margaret of Stowmarket;[2] to the high altar of the church of the Blessed Mary of the same town for my tithes forgotten 3s 4d;[3] to the high altar of the church of St Peter of the same town for my tithes forgotten 6s 8d; a suitable secular priest to celebrate in the aforesaid chapel for my soul and the souls of all my benefactors immediately after my decease for a whole year.

Residue of all my goods moveable and unmoveable to Margaret my wife.

Margaret my wife and William Merche of 'Stroneton' to be my execs, they to dispose for the health of my soul as seems best to them to please God and profit my soul.

[*Will*]

Dated 21 April 1471.

Margaret my wife to have all my lands and tenements with their appurtenances in the town of Needham Market ('Nedhammarket') to her and her heirs for ever, on condition that she or her heirs pay Anne my daughter at her marriage 10 marks out of the abovesaid lands and tenements, so long as she is well-behaved according to the discretion of my execs until she reaches legal age. Margaret my wife to have my whole tenement with its appurtenances in 'Crowstret' in the town of Stowmarket aforesaid for term of her life; and after her death the said tenement with its appurtenances to be sold by my execs for fulfilling this my last will. Margaret my wife to have the tenement called 'Chylderhous' with the lands called 'Frostlond' with their appurtenances in the same town for term of her life; and after her decease the tenement called 'Chylderhous' with the lands called 'Frostlond' with their appurtenances to remain to John my son, to hold to him and his heirs for ever.

Robert my son [fol. 473v] to have 10 marks in cash after the decease of Margaret my wife, to be paid by Margaret's execs.

I require all my feoffees, in the name of Almighty God the Father, to deliver sufficient estate to my execs when requested by them, for which they will be required on the Day of Judgement to come before the Highest Judge.

Proved 11 July 1471. Admon to co-executrix Margaret. Power reserved to William Merche, the other co-exec, when he comes, if he wishes to take up [*admon*].

1   Executor of John Markys of Old Newton, will pr. March 1458/59 (SROB, Baldwyne 265; Pt I, no. 1296).
2   The chapel of St Margaret seems to have been a free-standing chapel in Chilton hamlet, on the

north-western edge of Stowmarket. John Kyng of Chilton also asked to be buried there (SROB, Baldwyne 227; Pt I, no. 1134); otherwise nothing is known of this chapel.

3   See note to no. 381.

[fol.473v]

502. AGNES MERYELL of BARROW ('Bargh'), 8 August 1471

Of Barrow in the diocese of Norwich; to be buried in the churchyard of Barrow church; to the high altar of the said church for tithes forgotten 3s 4d; to the mother church of Norwich 12d.[1]

To the convent of Babwell 6s 8d; to the Friars Preachers of Thetford 3s 4d;[2] for a priest to celebrate for the health of my soul and my friends' [*souls*] for a whole year 8 marks.

To Thomas my son my tenement in the street called 'Burthorp' with all its appurtenances together with an acre of arable land called 'Molond'.

To Margery my daughter, the wife of William Prate, a tenement next to 'Barghgrene', together with 1½ acres of land, for term of her life; and after her decease the tenement, with 1½ acres of land, to be sold by my exec or his execs and the money to be disposed in pious uses for the health of my soul and my benefactors' [*souls*].

To Thomas my son and Margery my daughter all my utensils to be equally divided between them by the discretion of my supervisor and two other trustworthy men.

Residue of all my goods to my exec, Thomas my son; Sir George Hawys, rector of Barrow,[3] to be supervisor; they to distribute for my soul and the souls for whom I am bound as they see best to please God and profit the health of my soul.

Proved at Fornham St Martin, 23 September 1471. Admon to exec.

1   See note to no. 193.
2   For the friars see notes to nos 1 (Babwell) and 68 (Friars Preachers of Thetford).
3   Sir George Hawys (Hawes) was executor of Joan Robhood (no. 401); see also note to that will.

[fol. 474]

503. JOHN LANE of NAYLAND ('Neylond'), 22 May 1471

Dated at Nayland; to be buried in the churchyard of the church of St James the Apostle of Nayland; to the high altar of the same church 12d.

To Katherine my wife all my utensils, both inside the house and outside. She to have my messuage at Stoke ('Stok') formerly called 'Grecys', with another messuage called 'Lokkes', with the garden adjacent and with all the rents and services of right belonging to the messuages, to her and her heirs for ever, after the decease of Thomas Chaterys, on condition that Katherine pays each of my three children, that is, Robert Lane my son £3 6s 8d, Thomas Lane my son £3 6s 8d and Katherine Lane my daughter £3 6s 8d. If one or all of them should depart this life, Katherine shall have the disposition of the legacies of the deceased. Katherine my wife to find (*exhibeat*) a priest to celebrate for a year for my soul, my mother's soul and for my friends' [*souls*].

All my co-feoffees to deliver to Katherine my wife, after the decease of Thomas Chaterys, full and peaceful seisin of and in the said 2 messuages with all their appurtenances, when so requested.

Katherine my wife and John Felyx to be my most faithful execs; they to pay all my debts for the health of my soul.

Seal appended.

Witnesses: Robert Reyman, John Balston, John Chapman, John Went and Nicholas Lane.

Proved at Stoke, 23 October 1471. Admon to co-executrix. Power reserved for admon to be granted by Master Stephen Boole, especially appointed for the purpose, to John Felix, the other co-exec, when he comes and if he wishes to take it up.

504. JOHN PETYWATE of GLEMSFORD ('Glemesford'), 23 April 1471

Of Glemsford in the diocese of Norwich; my body to Christian burial within the churchyard of Glemsford church. In God's name I require my execs to pay all of my debts that I owe, that is, those that can be truly proved. To the high altar of the said church for tithes and offerings withheld, forgotten and underpaid 12d; to the convents of the Augustinian Friars of Clare and of the Preachers of Sudbury[1] for certain masses to be said between them for my soul within 3 days next after my decease, to the sum of 5s; to the sustentation of the sepulchre light in the said church 3s 4d; to the reparation of the torches in the said church 3s 4d.

As for my lands and tenements, firstly, Margery my wife [fol. 474v] to have and enjoy for the whole term of her life all my lands and tenements, which I have at the date of making this, in the town of Glemsford, both free and copy, with their appurtenances. After the decease of Margery, William my son to have my enclosed garden, which I lately bought of John Bryce, in Glemsford, situated in the street called 'Podelstret', and an enclosed pightle adjacent to the said garden, lately William Goldyng's, and, by the lord's licence, an enclosed pasture called 'Monday-lond', lying on the other side of the same street, opposite the said garden, abutting with one head on 'Cattescrofte' and the other head on 'le Longemedewe', to hold to the same William and his heirs for ever. If William should die while Margery is living, then after her decease the said enclosed garden, pightle and pasture with their appurtenances to John my[sic] son of the same William, my godson, to hold to him and his heirs for ever.

After the decease of Margery, John my son the elder to have my tenement called 'Bryces' lying in 'Podelstret' with all its appurtenances, to hold to him and his heirs by licence of the lord. If William my son should have to sell, through necessity, anything belonging of antiquity to my tenement called 'Bryces', apart from the said pightle assigned to him, then I wish William to give up the pightle [*literally: be moved from*] (*ab eadem putello peniti' ammoveatur*) and it to remain to John for ever.

John my son the younger, after the decease of Margery, to have my tenement in Glemsford, lying in the street called 'Egremanstret', in which I now live, with the appurtenances, to hold to him and his heirs for ever by licence of the lord, reserving to the said William and John the elder, my sons, from the day of my death for term of their lives and of the longer liver of the two, free entrance and exit at all legitimate times through the said tenement to my wide tenter (*ad latam tenturam meam*)[2] situated in the croft of the same tenement for the hanging and working of their cloths (*pro eorum pann' desuper pendend' & operand'*), while saving harmless (*custodiend' indempn'*) the tenants of the tenement.

To Margery my wife £10 in cash and all my hostilments and utensils, as linen, wool, pots, pans, cups, spoons, with all the other essential utensils belonging to me.

To John my son the younger 40s when he shall be married; to Agnes, Katherine the elder, Joan and Katherine the younger, my daughters, 4 marks each when they shall be married; if any of these 5 of my children dies before being married, then the part or parts of those dying to remain to the survivors, equally divided among them. Residue of all my goods to Margery my wife to dispose at her own free will. Margery my wife, William and John the elder my sons to be my execs, to carry out everything in the best way they can or know to please God and profit my soul. William Rogyll and John Goldyng to be supervisors, to see that all above bequeathed be well and faithfully performed.

Witnesses: Sir John Smyth, chaplain,[3] John [*no more*].

Proved at Glemsford, 24 October 1471. Admon to executrix Margery; William and John the other execs renouncing.

1   For the friars see notes to nos 1 (Clare) and 11 (Sudbury).
2   The testator and his sons William and John the elder were probably fullers; see Glossary for 'tenter'.
3   Witness of the will of Thomas Roote (no. 508).

[fol. 475]

505. DENISE HYLL, lately the wife of John, of SUDBURY, 5 June 1471

Dated at Sudbury in the diocese of Norwich; Denise, lately the wife of John Hyll of Sudbury;[1] to be buried in the churchyard of the parish church of St Gregory of the same town; to the high altar of the same church for tithes and offerings and if [*anything*] remains [*unpaid*] of the bequests of the said John Hyll (*sique fuerint ex presept' & legac' Johannis Hyll prenominat'*) 13s 4d; to each chaplain coming to my obsequies 4d and to each clerk officiating in the said church [*sum omitted*].

To Julian my daughter 8 marks in sterling to be paid by my execs in the year 1474; to Julian, after my decease, all my utensils and hostilments and jewels in the messuage where I now live except the best 'federbed'.

To Robert Hyll, grocer of London, 40s in cash, to be paid to him in the year 1476.[2]

To Henry Maket 40s in cash, to be paid to him in that year 1476.

To the aforesaid Julian a horn harnessed with silver, with the silver belt going with the horn.

To Friar Nicholas Donewyche of the order of Preachers of the convent of Sudbury 18 marks sterling, to celebrate and pray for two whole years for the souls of the said John Hyll, Denise and all our friends, benefactors and malefactors.

To the convent of Friars Preachers of Sudbury[3] for reparations to their church 40s, to pray for the aforesaid souls.

Residue of all my goods I put at the disposition of my execs, William Gebelou the elder and John Buke of Sudbury, to dispose for the abovesaid souls as they see most expedient.

Witnesses: Thomas Goldyng and Richard Chester and John Barbour of Sudbury.

Proved at Sudbury, 26 November 1471. Admon to execs.

1   Will, no. 434.
2   Will of Robert Hyll, citizen and grocer of London (TNA, PCC 7 Holgrave; now PROB11/14, image 81). In this will, proved 30 March 1504, Robert Hyll bequeathed 40s to the master and brethren of the college of Sudbury in Suffolk to sing a *dirige* and a mass of requiem for him solemnly by note and to pray for the souls of him, his late wife and children, and of John Hill and

Denyse his late wife, and all Christian souls; he also bequeathed 3s 4d to be distributed among the poor inhabiting the parish of St Gregory in Sudbury.

³ See note to no. 11.

506. JOHN YONGE of RICKINGHALL SUPERIOR ('Rykynghale'),¹
25 October 1471

Dated at Rickinghall Superior, the Friday before the feast of the Apostles Simon and Jude 1471; to be buried in the churchyard of the Blessed Mary of Rickinghall Superior; to the high altar of the same church 12d; to the parish clerk of the same church 2d.

To Isabel my wife and Simon Yonge my son all my chattels (*catalla*) and goods, moveable and unmoveable, live or dead, wherever they may be and all the utensils and hostilments of my house.

Residue of all my goods to my faithful execs, Isabel my wife and Simon Yonge my son, they to dispose for the health of my soul and of all my benefactors' [*souls*].

Seal appended.

Proved at Eye, 4 December 1471. Admon to execs.

¹ Son and executor of Simon Yonge of Rickinghall Superior, probate November 1450 (SROB, Baldwyne 124; Pt I, no. 579). According to the will of John Egelyn of Rickinghall Superior, dated October 1450, John Yonge held land that abutted on Egelyn's (SROB, Baldwyne 257; Pt I, no. 1271).

[fol. 475v]
507. JOHN FULLERE of LITTLE SAXHAM ('Parva Saxham'),¹ 3 November 1471

Of Little Saxham in the county of Suffolk; to be buried in the churchyard of the church of Saxham aforesaid; to the high altar for my tithes and offerings forgotten or underpaid 3s 4d; for a banner ('Baner') for the gild of St Nicholas the Bishop to be bought and painted 10s;² to the said church for the sustentation of 2 lights before the image of the Blessed Mary 'in the Ilde[*sic*]' of the same church to be found there, a cow of the price [*blank*].

To the friars of Babwell to pray for my soul, my parents' and benefactors' [*souls*] 10s; to the friars of Thetford 10s.³

To a suitable chaplain, for his stipend, to celebrate in the church of Saxham aforesaid for a complete year for my soul, my parents' and benefactors', 8 marks.

To Margaret my wife all the ostilments and utensils of my house; to Margaret 2 horses, 3 cows and all the grain, both wheat and rye, and barley, peas and oats, now in my barns; to her in money from the tenement in which I live for her sustentation 10 marks.

To Margery my daughter from part of the price of the said tenement, on condition that Robert Ilger her husband and she deliver sufficient estate in law of and in 3 acres of land lying in the field called 'the Okys' to my execs when so required, 5 marks in cash.

To each child (*puero*) of the same Margery a sheep.

My tenement in Saxham aforesaid, with all its appurtenances, to be sold by my execs for the best price they know of to fulfil my testament. If John Simond of Barrow ('Barow') wishes to buy the tenement with its appurtenances, he to have preference before all others, and 20s within the price of others.

301

Residue of all my goods and chattels at the disposition of my execs, Margaret my wife and John Symonde of Barrow ('Barowe') and Richard Hermer; to John and Richard for their labour 6s 8d each.

All my co-feoffees to deliver sufficient estate in law, according to my will, of my lands and tenements to such persons as specified by my execs, when suitably (*congrue*) requested by my execs.

To Margaret my wife the residue of all my sheep, after delivering all my legacies, for her own use.

Witnesses: Ralph Holdernesse, parson of Little Saxham,[4] John Hyll, William Otle[5] and others.

Proved at Fornham St Martin, 14 December 1471. Admon to Margaret and John Symond, execs. Power reserved to Richard Hermer, the other co-exec when he comes and if he wishes to take up admon. Seal of official appended.

[1] ?Executor of William Ottley of Little Saxham, will pr. November 1439 (SROB, Baldwyne 4; Pt I, no. 34).
[2] A banner for the procession of the boy-bishop. See note to no. 247.
[3] For the friars see notes to nos 1 (Babwell), 68 (Dominicans of Thetford) and 69 (Augustinians of Thetford).
[4] Ralph Holdernisse was rector of Little Saxham from 1446 to 1475 (Tanner, p.1422); he supervised the will of Robert Knygth of Little Saxham (no. 320).
[5] ?Related to William Ottley (see note above).

[fol. 476]

508. THOMAS ROOTE of GLEMSFORD ('Glemesford'), 30 June 1471

Dated at Glemsford in the diocese of Norwich; my body to Christian burial in the churchyard of Glemsford church; in the name of God I ask my execs to pay all my debts; for a trental of St Gregory to be said for my soul according to the discretion of my execs 10s.

To the 4 orders of friars, that is, at Clare, Sudbury, Babwell and Cambridge (*Cantebr'*),[1] to pray for my soul, divided between them, all the mass pence arising and collected from the brethren and sisters of the gild of St Thomas held in Glemsford.[2] To John my brother for fulfilling certain vows made by me in going to the chapel of the Blessed Mary of Walsingham ('Walsyngham') and to St Thomas of Canterbury (*Cantuarien'*),[3] a reasonable stipend for his labour and expenses, if he is willing, and if not then to some other man of good disposition.

As for my lands and tenements: firstly, Margaret my wife to have my messuage called 'Crowche Hows' in Glemsford with its appurtenances, to hold to her and her heirs for ever; Margaret to have the newly built messuage, with part of the adjacent croft lately my father, Robert Roote's,[4] in Glemsford as it is divided by metes (*per metas*) with its appurtenances, to hold to her as long as she remains unmarried; and when she does remarry, then the newly built messuage with the part of the croft to be sold by my execs for the best price possible, and, out of the money from the sale, my execs to pay Margaret half and the other half to be equally divided between my three sons (*filios*).

After the decease of my aforesaid father, John my son to have a parcel of meadow of 1 rood lying in Stanstead ('Stansted'), with its appurtenances, to hold to him and his heirs for ever.

The 5 marks 6s 8d now in the hands of Thomas Gunse 'gentilman'[5] to be paid next Shrove Tuesday (*carnepriviu' proximi*) for certain lands and tenements called 'Jakes', in Glemsford, lately sold by me to Thomas Gunse, to remain for my part of the maintenance of my father [*and*] owed him for my part of the said croft according to the form and tenor of an indented deed made between us. John my brother to have that money is he if willing to keep and maintain my father and so discharge the newly built messuage against my father from being re-entered by him (*exonerar' dictum mesuagium de novo edificatum erga eundum patrem meum de reingress' eiusdem*). If John refuses to do this, Margaret my wife to have the money and provide for my father as aforesaid.[6]

All my utensils and ostilments, with all the tools and equipment (*artificial'*) of my craft and the debts owing to me, with my other goods in the said messuage to remain for paying my debts which I owe; but if Margaret is willing to pay all my debts, then she to have and enjoy all the said utensils and the rest of my goods.

My execs, Richard Roote my uncle[7] and John Roote my brother, [fol. 476v] to implement everything aforesaid in the best way possible to please God and profit my soul.

Seal appended.

Witnesses: Sir John Smyth,[8] John Panell the younger, William Gerrald and John Warde with others.

Proved at Melford, 13 November 1471. Admon to John Roote exec. Power reserved to Richard Roote the other co-exec when he comes, if he wishes to take up admon.

[1]   For the four orders of friars, see note to no. 133.
[2]   Joan Olyfe (no. 317) bequeathed 6s 8d to the gild of St Thomas in Glemsford. In his will, pr. February 1476/77 (SROB, Hervye 58), John Willyngham left 5 marks to Glemsford church, provided that the churchwardens did not trouble his executors about the 'new building' of the gildhall.
[3]   The two most important pilgrimage centres in medieval England; Nicholas Roberdson (no. 640) requested two pilgrimages to both shrines.
[4]   The testator's father, Robert Roote, was the son of that name of Christine and John Rote/Roote of Glemsford. Christine's will pr. September 1443 (SROB, Baldwyne 85; Pt I, no. 391); John's will pr. December 1454 (SROB, Baldwyne 175; Pt I, no. 838).
[5]   Thomas Gunse witnessed the will of Richard Roote, 20 June 1474 (SROB, Hervye 114).
[6]   Clearly, Thomas's father Robert was now aged and infirm. Christine Rote had bequeathed the tenement called 'Jakes' ('Jackes') firstly to her husband John, and then, after his death it was to be sold to her son Robert; Robert's son Thomas had now sold that property to provide for his father's needs.
[7]   The will of Christine Rote shows that she and her husband had a son named Richard; see note above regarding Richard's will.
[8]   Witness of the will of John Petywate (no. 504 above).

509. ROGER CALEW of BURWELL [*Cambs*], 22 October 1471

Of Burwell in the diocese of Norwich; to be buried in the churchyard of Burwell church;[1] to the high altar of the said church for tithes forgotten [*no more*] [*crossed through*]

[1]   The testator did not specify which church; see note to no. 234 concerning the two parish churches at Burwell.

510. THOMAS QWYLTER of NEWMARKET (*'Novo Mercato'*), 10 April 1471

Knowing the end of my present life to be approaching; my body to Christian burial in the churchyard of the parish church of the Blessed Mary of Newmarket in the diocese of Norwich;[1] to the high altar of the same 12d; to the reparation of the tower (*campanil'*) of the same church 4s.

My tenement in Newmarket to be sold by my execs and disposed in 3 parts, that is, one part for my soul and the souls of all my benefactors, the second part to Katherine my wife, and the third part to John my son.

Residue of all my goods to Katherine my wife and Thomas Poperyle of Newmarket, to see to my funeral and pay my debts and to distribute for my soul and for the souls of all [*my*] benefactors as seems most expedient to them for the health of my soul; they to be my faithful execs to implement my will in all things, as above.

Proved at Newmarket (*Novo Mercat'*), 15 November 1471. Admon to execs.

1 Technically this was a chapel, not a parish church; see note to no. 80.

[fol. 477]
511. LAURENCE SPRAGY of HAUGHLEY ('Haugle'),[1] 15 February 1469/70

Dated at Haughley in the diocese of Norwich; to be buried in the churchyard of the church of Blessed Mary of Haughley; to the high altar of the said church for tithes forgotten 4d; to a priest to celebrate for me and my friends in the chapel of Blessed Mary of Haughley 5s; to Rome for masses to be celebrated for me and my friends at *Scala Celi* 3s;[2] a cow to the church of Haughley aforesaid after the decease of Katherine my wife.

To Katherine my wife all my debts [*owing to me*] after my death, if she is still alive; to Katherine my wife all my utensils and necessaries belonging to my dwelling, wholly, without any hindrance.

The remainder of my debts coming in after the decease of Katherine my wife to remain to Haughley church.

To Eleanor Pynell 2s 2d; to Eleanor a 'bras' pan, holding 4 gallons.

Residue of all my goods to the disposition of my faithful execs, Katherine my wife, John Blogate, Roger Belle and Robert Goodhale, to dispose for me and the health of my soul and for all my benefactors as seems to them most expedient.

Seal appended.

[*No probate recorded; next probate dated 24 January 1471/72.*]

1 (As 'Spragge'), witness of the will of Rose Deneys of Haughley, pr. February 1453/54 (SROB, Baldwyne 164; Pt I, no. 795).
2 See note to no. 244.

512. THOMAS CALVYSBAN of 'Northestret' in BURWELL [*Cambs*],[1] 6 December 1471

Dated the day of the feast of St Nicholas the Bishop 1471; sick unto death; [*commendation of soul and burial directions omitted*]; to the high altar of the same church [*of Burwell*] for my tithes forgotten 12d; to the emendation of 'le torches' belonging to the same church 8d; to the reparation of the said church 12d.[2]

Agnes my wife to have my messuage in which I live to hold for term of her life;

and after her decease, the messuage with the appurtenances to remain to Thomas my son, to him and his heirs for ever.

2 acres and half a rood of my land lying in diverse fields in Burwell to be sold by my execs to pay my debts.

To Thomas Abry my godson my green gown.

To William Dene [?Deve] my godson the crop of 3 roods of wheat and my blue gown.

To Agnes my wife all my household and utensils and all my chattels (*catall'*).

Residue of all my goods to my executrix Agnes my wife, she to dispose as she sees best to please God and profit my soul.

Seal appended.

Proved at Soham ('Saham'), 24 January 1471/72. Admon to executrix.

1   Attorney (executor) of John Kempe of Burwell (no. 234); ?related to John Calvysbane of Burwell (no. 632).
2   The testator did not specify which church; see note to no. 234.

[fol. 477v]
513. THOMAS MADDY of WICKEN ('Wykyn') [*Cambs*], 18 December 1471

To be buried in the churchyard of the church of Blessed Mary of Wicken; to the high altar of the same church for my tithes forgotten 40d.

Residue of all my goods to my execs, Ellen my wife, Simon Maddy my brother and William Huberd of Stow cum Quy ('Stow Quay'), they to dispose for the health of my soul as seems most expedient to them.

Witnesses: Robert Wylton, curate there,[1] and William Mootte of the same and others.

Proved at Soham ('Saham'), 24 January [*1471/72*]

1   Also witnessed the will of William Say of Wicken (no. 747).

514. RICHARD ROOLE of BURWELL [*Cambs*], 17 January 1471/72

Sick unto death; [*commendation*: to Almighty God]; to be buried in the churchyard of Burwell church; to the high altar of the same church for my tithes forgotten 2 bushels of wheat; to the emendation and reparation of the benches (*stannorum*) of the said church 10s.[1]

To each of my children 4 bushels of wheat.

To each of my godchildren a bushel of barley.

Margaret my wife to have 5 acres 3 roods of my free [*land*] for term of her life; and after her decease, the 5 acres 3 roods of land to be divided among my children then living, by the discretion and the will of Margaret.

Residue of all my goods to my executrix, Margaret my wife, to pay my debts; she to dispose for the health of my soul as she sees best to please God and profit my soul.

Seal appended.

Proved at Soham ('Saham'), 24 January 1471/72. Admon to executrix.

1   The testator did not specify which church; see note to no. 234.

515. RICHARD PERSON of AMPTON, 31 December 1471, [*English*]

[*Whole entry crossed through; complete will appears on fol. 484v, no. 538.*][1]

Dated the last day of December 1471; to be buried in the churchyard of Ampton; to the high altar of the same town, the mass pence of the gild of St Peter of Ampton; to the reparation of the said church 3s 4d; to the reparation of Rougham ('Rowham') church 3s 4d.

To the friars of Babwell 10s for to pray for my soul and all my friends.

To Agnes my wife my messuage with all appurtenances in Rougham for term of her life [*no more*]

[1]   See notes to no. 538.

[fol. 478]

516. JOHN GOSSE of NEWTON, 5 March 1470/71

Dated Tuesday 5 March 1470; to be buried in the churchyard of the parish church of All Saints of Newton; to the high altar of the said church 3s 4d; to the fabric of the said church 6s 8d.

Agnes my wife to have two messuages with their appurtenances, that is, the messuage in which my wife lives called 'Hervye' and the other called 'Wyottes' during her lifetime; and after her death, Richard Gosse my son to have the messuage with appurtenances called 'Wyottes', to him and his heirs for ever, and John Gosse my son, after his mother's death, to have the messuage with appurtenances called 'Hervy' in which his mother [*now*] lives, to him and his heirs for ever.

Robert Gosse my son to have a messuage with its appurtenances lying in Great Cornard ('Cornerth Magna') called 'Whyttes' after my death, without any delay, to him and his heirs for ever.

To John my son my best gown; to Richard my son my second gown; to Robert my son my third gown with my best tunic.

For a trental, 10s.

Finally, to Agnes my wife all the utensils of my house, she to dispose them reasonably at her will.

To Robert Jordon and Agnes my wife all my debts, they to have full power to collect and pay them.

If anything remains unbequeathed, I leave it to my execs, Robert Jordon and Agnes Gosse, my wife, they, having God before their eyes, to dispose as seems most expedient for the health of my soul; Robert Dene [?Deve] to be my supervisor; they to execute faithfully this testament.

Seal appended.

Proved at Melford, 16 March 1470/71.

517. JOHN SWEYN the elder [of LAVENHAM],[1] 15 January 1470/71

Dated at Lavenham; to be buried in the churchyard of Lavenham church; to the high altar of the said church for tithes forgotten 6s 8d; to the reparation of the said church 13s 4d; for my soul and for the souls for which I am bound, 19 marks to be distributed among the poor of Lavenham, that is, 3s 4d each week immediately after my death until the sum of 19 marks has been fully distributed.

To John Saxy, clerk, serving in Lavenham church,[2] 13s 4d in part payment of his stipend for 7 years after my death, if he remains in service there that long, that is, each year 2s; otherwise it to be disposed by my execs among the poor of Lavenham in that same form as above.

To Agnes my wife my tenement with its appurtenances in the burgh of Lavenham, [fol. 478v] lying in 'le Prentystrett'[3] between the tenement of Thomas Bernryve the younger on one side and the tenement lately John Dyer's on the other side, for term of her life, she to repair the tenement sufficiently during that term; and after her decease, the tenement to be divided between my sons by equal portions, that is, between Robert Sweyn my son and William Sweyn my son and their heirs for ever. To Agnes my wife a garden lying between 'Pykkys Pett' on one side and the tenement of John Drewe on the other side, [to her] and her heirs for ever. To Agnes my wife £10 in money from the debt which Thomas Bernryve owes me for his tenement that he bought from me, as appears fully in the court rolls of the lord. To Agnes my wife all my ostilments, bedding, jewels and all other things necessary to her belonging to my house and all the 'barkfattes' or leather.[4]

To John Sweyn my son 10s.

To John Kembold my servant 10s and my best gown.

To John Newman my exec[5] for his labour 10s.

Residue of all my goods to my execs, they to receive and pay my debts and dispose of the residue as they see most expedient to profit the health of my soul. I grant to my execs Agnes Sweyn my wife and John Newman full power to administer [my] debts as above.

Seal appended.

Witnesses: William Jacob and Thomas Bernryve the younger and many others.

Proved at Lavenham, 3 April 1471. Admon to execs.

1   Witness and legatee (as 'John Sweyn the younger') of the will of his father, John Swayn of Lavenham, will pr. May 1441 (SROB, Baldwyne 30; Pt I, no. 164).

2   This man may have been one of the sons of John Saxsy of Stanningfield, will pr. September 1441 (SROB, Baldwyne 44; Pt I, no. 233); that testator instructed his son John to make annual payments to 'Dan (*domino*) John, monk, his brother'.

3   Prentice Street still survives in Lavenham. John Swayn (Pt I, no. 164) had bequeathed his principal tenement in 'Prentystrete' to his wife Margaret, after whose death it was to be sold by his executor, John Newman elder; his son John Sweyn had since acquired it.

4   Given this bequest of bark vats and leather, the testator was obviously a tanner; indeed, his father had bequeathed him 'all the bark, bark-vats and barkwose that are left after the leather [*now*] ready to be tanned has all been tanned' (Pt I, no. 164).

5   John Swayn, this testator's father, had appointed John Newman the elder as his executor and John Newman the younger had witnessed that will (Pt I, no. 164).

518. JOHN COPYN of ACTON ('Aketon'), 20 March 1468/69

Of Acton in the diocese of Norwich; sick in body; to be buried in the churchyard of the same town; to the mother church of Norwich 4d;[1] to the high altar of Acton church 12d; to the fabric of Acton church 40d.

Residue of all my goods and chattels to my execs to pay therewith my debts and dispose as above, and furthermore, to do as they see most expedient for the health of my soul.

Execs: Sir Thomas Webbe, perpetual vicar of Acton,[2] and Robert Colett of Melford, to act as above, but Sir Thomas Webbe principally to dispose all my goods in the execution of my testament, with the assistance of Robert Colett.

Proved at Lawshall ('Lawshull'), the last day of April [*30*] 1471. Admon to execs.

1   See note to no. 193.
2   Thomas Webb was vicar of Acton from 1466 to 1475 (Tanner, p.1345); he witnessed the will of
    James Thurgor (no. 651).

[fol. 479]

519. WILLIAM HERT of ELMSWELL ('Elmeswell'),[1] 8 March 1471 [*new style*]

Dated at Elmswell, 8 March 1421(*Millesimo cccc xxj*);[2] [*commendation includes*: to St John the Evangelist];[3] to be buried in the churchyard of Elmswell parish church; to the high altar for tithes and offerings not well paid 6s 8d; for a tabernacle of the most Blessed (*Batissime*) Virgin Mary to be situated at the right end (*in dextr' fine*) of the high altar, sufficient money; for 'le selyng' to be made in the said church, sufficient money; to a priest to celebrate for one year in the said church for my soul and the souls of John Brende and Joan his wife, Robert my father and my benefactors, 8 marks; to the reparation of the aisle ('le elee') of St John the Baptist, 20s; for 'le sangrede' to be observed for ever in the said church, 'le Terellecrofte';[4] for a light to be kept before the image of the Blessed Mary in the said church for ever, a 'pytyll' called 'Nunbregge Pytyll', and from the said 'pytyll' to be received [*money*] for a pound of wax to burn before the sepulchre on Easter Day for ever; to the Blessed Mary in the chapel of Woolpit ('Wolpett') my silver girdle.[5]

To the reparation of the way against (*versus*) the tenement of Elmswell ('Emmeswell') rectory and of the lane leading into the field, 40s; to the reparation of the bridge by my tenement, formerly John Brende's, and the lane called 'Becones lane' 40s.

To the friars of Babwell for 'le trentall' to be celebrated, 10s;[6] to the friars of the Old House of Thetford for a trental or 'trentell' to be celebrated, 10s;[7] for 'the glasyng' to be done in the refectory of the monastery of St Edmund, 13s 4d.[8]

To my wife [*Margery*]:[9] my tenement with 'le Maggescrofte', for term of her life; a close or a 'crofte' with 2 'pytyll' called 'Mundes of Halle', for term of her life; a 'crofte' called 'Gerveyss Crofte', for term of her life; 2 pightles called 'le Gerveyss'; a 'crofte' called 'le Harwe', with 'le Owthren' under the wood; 2 acres with a rood called 'le Flaxlonde', for term of her life; a small 'pytyll' lying under 'Turtyll', for term of her life; half an acre of land lying in 'le Wongefeld', for term of her life; half an acre lying at 'Blakfen' next to the land of Richard Ballard, for term of her life; a meadow lying in 'le Hardwyk', for term of her life; a small 'pytell' lying in 'le Halke', with 'le grovett', for term of her life; a close or 'closs' called 'le Dotthorness' with 'le pytyll' leading to 'le Dotthorness', to give, sell [*or*] dispose freely at her will. To my wife the 3 best cows which she will choose with 2 calves [*but*] the rest of my animals and chattels to be sold by my execs; all the utensils of my house with the appurtenances of my chamber (*cum pertin' camere mee*). Finally, all the legacies left to my wife for term of her life to be divided between Nicholas and William my sons by equal portions by the discretion of my execs. If one of my sons should die, then the survivor to have the deceased's part; if both die in their mother's lifetime, then all the said legacies to be sold and out of the money from them my wife to have 20 marks to dispose at her will. If my wife should depart this world in the lifetime of my sons then the legacies to remain at the discretion of my execs until the said sons come to legal age. To my wife 20 coombs of malt, with all the grain [fol. 479v] in the barns and newly growing.

To my mother her chamber in which she now lives, for term of her life, or a similar value.

To John my brother[10] a 'crofte' or close lying next to my close; to Margery my sister 10s.

To Dom John my son 5 marks; to Nicholas my son 10 marks and to William my son as much, when they come to legal age.

To Elizabeth my daughter 5 marks with a close called 'Nunbregge closs'.

To Joan my daughter[11] a tenement called 'le ad Leess', with 'le Teynrowe crofte', at her marriage; to Joan an acre of arable land called 'Cressmedewe', with half an acre of land lying by the land of John Bettes to the west.[12]

To John Elsegood my servant 6s 8d; to William Elsegood 6s 8d.

To each of my [god]sons (*filiorum*) 4d and as much to my goddaughters (*filiolarum*). Residue of all my goods, moveable and unmoveable, to my execs, to sell, give [and] dispose for my soul and the souls of my benefactors as they see best to please God and profit the health of my soul.

Margery my wife, John Hert my brother and Robert Otelee to be my execs; to each of them for their labour 6s 8d.

Proved at Fornham St Martin, 8 April 1471. Admon to execs.

1   Executor of Henry Palmere of Elmswell, probate March 1449/50 (SROB, Baldwyne 99; Pt I, no. 445); of John Scateron of Elmswell, will pr. July 1458 (SROB, Baldwyne 202; Pt I, no. 1001); of John Bokyll of Elmswell, probate May 1461 (SROB, Baldwyne 272; Pt I, no. 1338); of John Wedyr of Elmswell, will pr. May 1461 (SROB, Baldwyne 307; Pt I, no. 1495); of John Halle of Woolpit (no. 430 above).

2   Probably a mistake for *Mcccclxxj*, that is March 1471, but not March 1471/72, since probate was granted on 8 April 1471.

3   The dedication of Elmswell church was to St John the Evangelist, sometimes known as St John the Divine.

4   Presumably 'the Terellecrofte' was a piece of land that the testator was giving to support this perpetual sangred.

5   See note to no. 142.

6   See note to no. 1.

7   See note to no. 68.

8   See note to no. 88 and also no. 772.

9   The testator's widow, Margery, subsequently married Edmund Walter, who had been co-executor of John Wedyr with William Hert (see note above). Margery Walter bequeathed 40s to the building of the new tower at Elmswell and it appears that either she or her executors planned the whole decorative scheme that not only includes religious symbolism but also commemorates her two husbands; her will pr. April 1479 (SROB, Hawlee 266). See Blatchly and Northeast, *Decoding Flint Flushwork*, Elmswell St John the Evangelist.

10   Will of John Hert of Elmswell, no. 660.

11   Ada Welde bequeathed 12d to 'Joan Hert, daughter of William Hert' but this may have been another Joan Hert as here in her father's will, dated 1471, Joan was as yet unmarried and Ada's will was proved in April 1453 (SROB, Baldwyne 161; Pt I, no. 777).

12   Margery Walter made bequests to all five of her children surnamed Hert (see note above). She left: to Dom John, 40s, a cover of white and green, a brazen candlestick, a chair of green wood and a brazen hanging ewer; to Nicholas, 6s 8d, a similar cover, a mattress, a pair of blankets, a brass pot, a basin, a brazen candlestick and four pieces of pewter, a bowl holding 8 gallons, a 'warre' mazer and two silver spoons; to William, the same as to his brother Nicholas; to Joan and Elizabeth as clothes and household possessions.

520. JOHN WETHER of HONINGTON ('Honewton'), 29 April 1471 [*probate only*]

Proved the penultimate day of April [*29*] 1471. Admon to Alice the wife of the said John the deceased and John Wether of Honington, execs.

521. JOHN SEGBROOK of STOWMARKET ('Stowemarket'),[1] 2 November 1469

Dated on Thursday the commemoration of all the faithful departed [*All Souls' Day*] 1469; my testament and last will; to be buried in the churchyard of the town's church of St Peter the Apostle; to the high altar of the said church 6s[*sic*]; to the maintenance of books and of a cupboard for vestments in the same church (*refect' librorum & vestiment' capan' eiusdem ecc'*), 13s 4d; to the poor of the same town, 6s 8d; to the emendation of the highway before (*penes*) the entrance (*ostium*) of my messuage in the said town, 40d.

Residue of all my goods to Joan my wife to dispose and distribute well for my soul and all my benefactors' [*souls*] as she sees to please God and for the health of my soul and those of all the faithful departed.

Seal appended.

Proved 2 September 1471. Admon to Joan the executrix.

> [1] ?Executor (as 'Segbroke') of Joan Elyne of Haughley, probate February 1452/53 (SROB, Baldwyne 156; Pt I, no. 746).

[fol. 480]

522. JOHN CHAPMAN the elder of RICKINGHALL INFERIOR ('Rykynghale'), 11 April 1471

Dated at Rickinghall Inferior, on Tuesday 11 April 1471; to be buried in the churchyard or in the church of the Blessed Mary of Rickinghall aforesaid; to the high altar of the said church 6s 8d; to the fabric (*fabricacionem*) of the said church 6s 8d.

I wish to have a suitable priest to go on a pilgrimage and visit the sepulchres of the Apostles [*and*] the Court of Rome (*ad limina Apostolorum Cur' Romanam*).[1]

To the Augustinian Friars of Thetford 10s; to the Friars Preachers of the same town 10s.[2]

To Hepworth church 20d; to the church of All Saints, Stanton, 20d; to the church of St John the Baptist, Stanton, 20d; to Weston church 20d; to Knettishall ('Gnatsale') church 20d; to Hopton church 20d; to Ixworth Thorpe ('Thorp Ixworth') church 20s; to Riddlesworth ('Rydlysworth') church, [*Norfolk*], 20d; to Gasthorpe church, [*Norfolk*], 20s; to Brettenham ('Brethenham') church, [*Norfolk*], 20d; to Kilverstone ('Kylwareston') church, [*Norfolk*], 20d; to Euston church 20d; to Blo' Norton ('Blonorton') church, [*Norfolk*], 20d; to Thelnetham church 20d; to Hinderclay ('Hyndrcle') church 20d; to Redgrave church 20d; to Burgate church 20d.

To Anne Chapman my wife my tenement in Rickinghall aforesaid, with all the free lands, meadows, pastures and feedings and closes, except one close called 'Costynys Clos' lying in Rickinghall aforesaid and a meadow lying in 'le Holme', to hold to her, with all the appurtenances, except as excepted, for term of her life. If she [*re*] marries, then she to have 20s out of the tenements[*sic*] and lands, for term of her life, from John Chapman my son, and then John to have the tenement with all the lands, meadows, pastures and feedings, with all the closes, exceptions excepted, to hold to him and his heirs. If Anne does not marry, then John my son to have the tenement with all its appurtenances, exceptions excepted, after Anne's decease, to hold to him and his heirs.

To Ed' my son a close called 'Costynys Clos' lying in Rickinghall aforesaid, after the decease of the said Anne; she to have the close for term of her life.

To Isabel my daughter, wife of John Balery of Knettishall ('Knatsale'), a meadow in Rickinghall in 'Holm Medue', containing by estimation 9 roods of meadow, lying between the close lately John Slawe's, now Robert Dyer's of Botesdale ('Botysdale') on the south; to Isabel my daughter 5 marks or their worth.

To Anne Cole 40s, or their worth, according to the discretion of my execs.

To John [*or,* Anne] [*overwritten*] Fytte 40s, or their worth, according to the discretion of my execs.

To Thomas Fytt 26s 8d, according to the discretion of my execs.

[fol. 480v] To Anne my wife all the utensils and hostilments belonging to my house. Residue of all my goods to my execs, Anne Chapman my wife and Thomas Robhod, to sell and dispose for my soul and the souls of all my benefactors in the celebration of masses or in other deeds of piety as seems most profit to the health of my soul.

Supervisor: Sir Edmund Spark, rector of the church of Rickinghall aforesaid.[3]

Seal appended.

Proved at Hopton, 8 May 1471. Admon to execs.

1   For *ad limina Apostolorum* see note to no. 401.
2   See notes to nos 68 (Friars Preachers of Thetford) and 69 (Augustinian Friars).
3   See note to no. 194.

[OW24/82]

523. JOAN BREDSTRET of LITTLE WHELNETHAM ('Qwelnetham Parva'),[1] 4 March 1470/71

To be buried in the churchyard of the church of the aforesaid town. I wish to have a trental of St Gregory the Pope celebrated once for the health of my soul.

To John Bredstret my nephew a folding table (*tabulam plicatam*) and to Joan Bredstret my niece a pair of beads of jet ('gagate').[2]

Residue of all my goods to Roger Bredstret my son,[3] to pay my debts and to faithfully implement this my will; he to be my faithful exec to dispose for me and my soul as seems to him most expedient and to please God.

Proved at Fornham St Martin, 10 June 1471. Admon to exec.

1   Redstone transcribed the name as '*Johannes* Bredstret' but the register definitely says '*Joh'na* Bredstret' (*PSIA*, xii, p.100). She was the widow of William Bradstrete of Little Whelnetham (no. 825), who appointed as his executors his wife Joan and his son Roger. Joan appointed her son Roger as her executor.
2   Or perhaps, 'grandson' and 'granddaughter'; see note to no. 401.
3   Executor of his father William.

[fol. 481]

524. JOHN WRYGHT of SOHAM ('Saham') [*Cambs*], 13 July 1471 [*English*]

To be buried in the churchyard of the church of St Andrew the Apostle in Soham; to the sepulchre light in the said town 12d.

Agnes my wife to have my tenement 'oole lykke' for term of her life; and after her decease, it to be sold and part the money betwixt my 2 children and if the one decease then the other child to have it for term of life; and after they both decease, it to be sold and do for me and Agnes my wife and all my good doers. Agnes my wife to have my 2 kine and a calf and a 'howyd sterkyn'.

Residue of my goods to Agnes my wife 'lytll mekyll lesse and moore'.[1]

Robert Wryght my father and Agnes my wife to be my true attorneys.

Supervisor: Robert ?Faverell.

Proved at Soham ('Saham'), 23 January 1471/72. Admon to execs.

1   'Little, much, less and more', i.e. however much there is remaining. See Glossary.

525. RICHARD WYNTER of SOHAM ('Saham') [*Cambs*], 22 October 1471 [*English*]

To be buried in the churchyard of St Andrew the Apostle in Soham; to the high altar of the said church a bushel of barley; to the sepulchre light 6d.

Agnes my wife to have my tenement 'oole lyk' as it lieth for term of her life; and after her decease, it to be sold and do for me and my wife and all our good doers to the church, highways and poor people.

My 4 mares ('meeres') and the cart be sold to pay my mother with for the said tenement.

William my brother to have my best gown.

Residue of my goods to Agnes my wife, she to pay my debts. Agnes my wife and Thomas ?Goore to be my attorneys.

Proved at Soham ('Saham'), 24 [?23] January 1471/72. Admon to execs.

526. THOMAS WARNERE of BARDWELL ('Berdwell'), 9 January 1471/72 [*nuncupative*]

Dated at Bardwell; his body to Christian burial; to the high altar of Bardwell church 4d.

To his wife a messuage with all the lands belonging to it to pay all his debts and provide for his children; if she should die without heirs, then after the decease of the said Isabel, the messuage with all the lands to be sold and disposed for the soul of the said Thomas and all his benefactors.

Executrix: Isabel his wife.

Witnesses: the vicar of Bardwell, Robert Wellys and John Wellys and others.

Proved at Walsham, 28 January 1471/72. Admon to executrix.

[fol. 481v]
527. ALICE BETTES of BADWELL ASH ('Badwell Asshfeld'),[1] 4 April 1471

Dated at Badwell, the Thursday after Passion Sunday 1471; to be buried in the churchyard of All Saints of Badwell Ash; to the high altar of Badwell 3s 4d; to the church of Badwell 3s 4d.

To Isabel Masham my stepdaughter (*filiastr'*) a cow.

To Joan Carpenter of Langham, my stepdaughter, a cow.

To a suitable priest, to celebrate for my soul, my father's, my mother's and my friends' [*souls*], 8 marks.

Residue of all my goods to my execs, John Dounham, canon of Ixworth,[2] William Smyth and Joan Cook of Badwell.

Seal appended.

Proved at Walsham, 28 January 1471/72. Admon to execs.

[1] In the medieval period the rectory of Badwell was sometimes known as the rectory of Badwell with Ashfield; it had been appropriated to the priory of Ixworth before 1291 (*VCH Suffolk*, ii, pp.105–7).

[2] See note to no. 69.

528. ALICE GELDERE of GLEMSFORD ('Glemesford'), widow,[1] 20 April 1471

Dated at Glemsford in the diocese of Norwich; my body to Christian burial in the churchyard of the parish church of the Blessed Mary of Glemsford, by the graves of my parents, according to the discretion of my exec. I beseech my exec and request in God's name that he pays all my debts that can be shown genuine.

To the 4 orders of friars, namely, at Clare, Sudbury, Babwell and Cambridge (*Cantebr'*) 20s, that is, 5s to each house, to pray for my soul.[2]

To each child of William Skott my son, a cow.

William Skott my son to be my exec; he to perform all the above-written in the best way he knows to please God and profit my soul. Residue of all my goods, moveable and unmoveable, live and dead, over and above the payment of my debts and the expenses of my funeral, to William Skott my son to do with as he will.

Seal appended.

Witnesses: James Breustre,[3] William Hawe, Richard Clerk and others.

Proved at Fornham St Martin, 3 February 1471/72. Admon to exec.

[1] ?Widow of Robert Foster *alias* Geldere, will pr. 28 January 1441/42 (SROB, Baldwyne 20; Pt I, no. 109).

[2] See note to no. 133.

[3] One James Browster had witnessed the will of Robert Foster *alias* Geldere (see note above).

[fol. 482]

529. JOAN CARTERE of OLD NEWTON ('Newton Veteri'),[1] 15 January 1468/69

Dated at Old Newton; to be buried in the churchyard of the church of the Blessed Mary of Newton aforesaid; to the emendation and sustentation of the holy mother church of Norwich diocese 6s 8d;[2] to the reparation and emendation of the church of St Mary of Old Newton 10 marks, on condition that my execs have the disposition of the 10 marks; to the high altar of Newton aforesaid 12d; to the high altar of Mellis ('Melles') church for my tithes underpaid 12d; to the emendation of Mellis church 13s 4d;[3] to the emendation of Burgate church 3s 4d.

To the Friars Minor of Babwell 6s 8d;[4] to the emendation of Thwaite ('Thweyte') church 13s 4d; to the sisters of the convent (*senob'*) of Thetford 3s 4d.[5]

To Thomas Sagor, otherwise called Rede, 4 marks; to Margaret Sagor, otherwise called (*al' vocat'*) Rede, 4 marks and a cooking pot (*cacabu'*) and a brass pot; to Helen Sagor, otherwise called Rede, 4 marks and a basin and an ewer and an iron spit (*verutum*).

To Agnes Jentre 13s 4d; to John Jentre 6 [*damaged*].

313

To Robert Cotyngham the elder 6s 8d; to Margaret Cotyngham, daughter of Robert Cotyngham, 13s 4d and a red cow.

To Joan Puls[*damaged; ?Pulsham*] my goddaughter 3s 4d; to Joan Newman my goddaughter 3s 4d; to Margaret Pulsham, daughter of Richard Pulsham, 3s 4d; to Clemence (*Cleme't'*), daughter of William Cross, 3s 4d; to Agnes Endrys 6s 8d.

To Joan Sagor, otherwise called Rede, all my utensils.

All of my above legacies be paid out of the payments and obligations paid to me [*and*] my execs in the future.

Residue of all my goods to my execs, Robert Dobbys, chaplain,[6] and Joan Sagor, otherwise called Rede, they to ordain and dispose in the best manner for my soul and for the souls of my friends as they see most pleasing to God and profit to my soul.

Witnesses: William Pulsham, John Deye, Henry Caryngton and others.

To Hawley church 3s 4d.

Proved at Hawley, 25 October 1470. Admon to Sir Robert Dobbes, exec. Power reserved to Joan Saguor, otherwise Rede, co-executrix, when she comes and if she wishes to take up [*admon*].

1   Wife and executrix of John Carteer of Mellis, will pr. May 1457 (SROB, Baldwyne 221; Pt I, no. 1097).
2   See note to no. 193.
3   Two bequests to her former parish church.
4   See note to no. 1.
5   See note to no. 68.
6   From 1473 to 1479 Robert Dobbys was the incumbent of Old Newton (Tanner, p. 337); from this will it is clear that prior to his appointment he was a chaplain in the parish.

530. JOHN LONDEN [*or*, LOUDEN] of BARROW ('Barugh'), 10 October 1470 [*English*]

Dated 10 October *MCCCCLx & x*; to be buried in the churchyard of Barrow; to the high altar of the said church 20d.

To Margaret my wife my place for term of her life and, if she have need thereof by her life, to take part thereof of the said place.

To Sir Thomas of Barrow 6s 8d.

To my cousin Thomas [fol. 482v] Bowes of Ware [?*Herts*] 6s 8d.

Such gear as I have beside forth ('sweche gere as I have be syd forth') to be sold and done for me.

To John Fryet of Barrow and William Meller of the same town[1] [*bequest not stated*]. They shall be my execs and my assigners ('asygneres'), to ordain and dispose for the health of my soul; to each of them for their[*sic*] labour of the said execs, 3s 4d.

Proved at Fornham St Martin, 29 October 1470. Admon to execs.

1   Witness of the will of John Pryke (no. 531).

531. JOHN PRYKE the elder of BARROW ('Barugh'), 10 September 1470

Of Barrow in the diocese of Norwich; [*commendation*: to God the Father Almighty]; to be buried in the churchyard of Barrow parish church; to the high altar of the said church for my tithes forgotten 12d; to Barrow parish church 3s 4d.

To John Pryke my son the elder 3s 4d; to John Pryke my son the younger 3s 4d; to William Pryke my son 3s 4d.

To Margery Pryke my wife all my utensils and all my moveable goods unbequeathed, on condition she pays all my debts and legacies and funeral expenses.

Residue of my goods to my execs, Margery Pryke my wife and John Leyston of Barrow.

Witnesses: Richard Bottysham, chaplain,[1] William Pye, William Meller of Barrow[2] and many others.

Proved at Fornham St Martin, 29 October 1470. Admon to execs.

[1] Agnes Hukton of Clare requested Sir Richard Botilssham, chaplain, to pray for her soul (no. 276).
[2] Executor of John Londen/Louden (no. 530).

532. WILLIAM SCARPE of FELSHAM, 17 August 1470 [*English*]

To be buried in Felsham churchyard; to the high altar for tithes forgotten 6s 8d; for a sangred [*for*] a year 4s 4d; I will have after my decease a priest [*for*] a year as soon as my goods may bear it.

Cecily my wife to have, term of her life, all my lands and tenements in Felsham and Gedding ('Geddyng'), except mine inheritance ('herytans'), which I will Walter my son to have and to go forth as an inheritance after his decease. After my wife's decease, Walter my son to have all my lands and tenements in Felsham and Gedding, if he will pay for them 40 marks in years, that is 5 marks every year until the 40 marks be [fol. 483] fully paid. If Walter will not buy them, then they to be sold by the will of my execs to the most value, and Walter my son to have thereof 10 marks to his marriage.

My wife or Walter my son or my execs to pay to Alison my daughter[1] 5 marks within 3 years of my decease, or else my feoffees to give estate in a piece of land lying in Gedding called 'Bregges Crofte' to Alison my daughter.

If he buys my lands, Walter my son to pay William my son 5 marks after my wife's decease and Thomas my son 5 marks, to be paid in 2 years. If one of them dies, the other to have 10 marks; if they both decease before the time, it to be disposed for me and them by the will of my execs. If Walter does not buy my lands, then they to be sold and my execs to pay for them as aforesaid.

All other goods I give to the will of my execs, Cecily my wife [*and*] William Malty-warde of Felsham [*and of my*] supervisor, Robert Storur, clerk, parson of Felsham;[2] they to pay my debts and do for me as they would I should do for them.

Seal appended.

Witnesses: William Ramsey, William Coteler, Thomas Parle and others more.

Also, Cecily my wife to repair that place, term of her life, and make neither strip nor waste but as she needs.

Proved at Fornham, 26 November 1470. Admon to execs.

[1] Walter and Alison (Alice) Scarp were beneficiaries of the will of Rose Goddrych (no. 533).
[2] Robert Storrur was appointed rector of Felsham in November 1469 (Tanner, p.1433); he was supervisor of the will of Rose Goddrych (no. 533) and executor of Joan Drowte (no. 647).

533. ROSE GODDRYCH of FELSHAM, widow, 2 August 1470

['Godryche' *in margin*] To be buried in the churchyard of the church of St Peter of Felsham; for my tithes forgotten 3s 4d; for a trental of St Gregory 10s; for a sangred for 7 years, for each year 3s 4d[*sic*];[1] I wish to pay for an offering to (*p' oblacoe' de*) 'ley porche' of the same church [*no sum*]; I wish to pay for the glass and work of a window of the same 'ley porche' [*no sum*].

To John Wyborth, the son of Elizabeth Hawe my daughter, 6s 8d.

To Walter Scarp, son of William Scarp,[2] 3s 4d; to Alice Scarp, daughter of the same William, 3s 4d.

Residue of all my goods to my execs, William Ramsey and Isabel his wife, and to my supervisor, Robert Storrur, clerk;[3] they to dispose for the health of my soul as seems most expedient to them.

Proved at Fornham St Martin, 27 November 1470. Admon to execs.

1   Usually 4s 4d, that is, 1d per week.
2   Will, no. 532.
3   See note to no. 532.

[fol. 483v]
534. ROBERT PAGE of GREAT SAXHAM ('Magna Saxham'), 8 February 1469/70

Dated at Saxham; my body to Christian burial; to the high altar of Saxham aforesaid for my tithes forgotten or underpaid 2s; to a suitable chaplain to celebrate for my soul and the souls of those for whom I am bound for a whole year after my death, 8 marks.

To Joan my daughter 3s 4d and 4 ewes; to Rose my daughter 20d, 2 bushels (*mod'*) of wheat and 2 ewes.

To Anne Werden half a quarter of barley.

To Margaret my wife all the hostilments and utensils of my dwelling (*hospicii*) and all forms of my grain wherever it is found, she to bear all the costs concerning (*circa*) my funeral, that is to say, my burial day, and seven-day and thirty-day after my death. To Margaret all my cows and horses and all my carts, ploughs and harrows, with all the harness belonging to them, to have for term of her life for her maintenance, and anything remaining after her decease to be sold by my execs [*and*] disposed for my soul and her soul in deeds of charity. To Margaret my wife all my lands and tenements, rents and services with all their appurtenances in the towns of Great Saxham, Barrow ('Barwe') and Little Saxham ('Parva Saxham') in the county of Suffolk, to hold to her for term of her life, meanwhile bearing all my dues for them both to the lords of those fees and [*for*] the reparations of the buildings and closes there.

After the decease of Margaret, all the said lands and tenements, rents and services, with all their appurtenances, wholly to remain to Roger Page my son, to hold to him and his heirs for ever, except for a tenement called 'Mellers' and another tenement lately Joan Bery's and 2 acres of arable land lying in the field called 'Polyngden-feld', with all their appurtenances in the town of Great Saxham, which 2 tenements and 2 acres of land, with all their appurtenances, I leave to Isabel my daughter, to hold to her and her heirs for ever.

Residue of all my goods and chattels to my execs, to sell and receive and dispose for my soul and for the souls for whom I am bound in deeds of charity, as they see most pleasing to God and profit to the said souls.

Execs: Roger my son and Richard Hermer; to each of them for their labour, 12d.

[*Probate not recorded: previous probate dated 27 November 1470, next 3 February 1471/72.*]

[fol. 484]

535. RICHARD ROBYN of RUSHBROOKE ('Rosschebroke'), 5 September 1471

Dated at Rushbrooke; my body to Christian burial; to the high altar of Rushbrooke church for my tithes forgotten or underpaid 6d.

To Agnes my wife all my goods and chattels, both moveable and unmoveable, live and dead, and of whatever kind or nature (*generis sive specie*) and wherever and in whosoever possession (*penes*) they may be in the town of Rushbrooke and elsewhere in the county of Suffolk, for her maintenance and my children's and hers and for paying all my debts.

Residue of all my goods to my executrix, Agnes my wife, to sell, receive [*and dispose*] for the health of my soul and the souls for whom I am bound in deeds of charity.

Seal appended.

Witnesses: John Hoog of Rougham, William Cros of the same, George Dounham of the same, and others.

Proved on 3 February 1471/72. Admon to executrix.

536. WILLIAM COMAYAN of RATTLESDEN ('Ratlesden'),[1] 19 August 1468

['Comayen' *in margin*] Dated at Rattlesden; to be buried in the churchyard of Rattlesden parish church; to the high altar for tithes forgotten 12d; I bequeath a cow to find a light before the image of the Blessed Mary; I bequeath another cow to find another light before the cross in the said church.

To Thomas my son the younger 6s 8d; to William my son 6s 8d.

To the gild of St Margaret 12d;[2] to the gild of St John the Baptist 10s.[3]

To the Friars Minor of Babwell for a trental of St Gregory 10s.[4]

To Alice my wife the residue of my goods, except I give the tenement with the croft for term of her life if she is willing to pay my debts; if not, it can be sold and the residue of my debts (*residuum debitorum meorum*) disposed for me and my benefactors.

William Camayen[*sic*] my son and Alice my wife to be my execs; they to dispose for my soul as seems most expedient to them.

Proved at Brent Eleigh ('Illygh ?comp[*damaged*]'), 4 February 1471/72. Admon to execs.

[1]   Executor (as 'Comayn') of Richard Blome of Rattlesden, probate February 1452/53 (SROB, Baldwyne 156; Pt I, no. 747).
[2]   John Rogyn of Rattlesden (Pt I, no. 1031) also made a bequest to the gild of St Margaret, as did Thomas Martham (no. 615 below).
[3]   As well as a gild of St Margaret and this gild of St John the Baptist, there was also a gild of the Holy Trinity in Rattlesden at this time (see no. 615).
[4]   See note to no. 1.

[fol. 484v]

537. ROBERT RUDLONDE of GREAT WALDINGFIELD ('Waldyngfeld Magna'),[1] 3 July 1468

Of Great Waldingfield in the county of Suffolk; dated the Sunday before the Translation of St Thomas the Martyr, Bishop of Canterbury (*Epi' Cantuarien'*) 1468; in the presence of many of the faithful; [*commendation*: to God Almighty, the Blessed Virgin Mary]; to be buried in the churchyard of the aforesaid town; to the high altar for tithes forgotten 20d; I bequeath 3 trentals to the friars of Sudbury, Colchester (*Cocestria*) and Clare;[2] I leave a priestly stipend to a priest (*unum stipendiu' sacerdotale uni sacerdoti*) to celebrate in the church of the said town for my soul; to the fabric of the church of the same town 40s and more if it can be spared from my goods at the will of my execs.

Residue of all my goods I put to the disposition of my execs, John[3] and Richard Rudlond, to dispose for me and for the health of my soul, as they will answer before God as the Great Judge (*coram deo in summo judicio*).

Proved at Sudbury, 5 February 1471/72. Admon to execs.

1 Related to William Rodeland of Great Waldingfield, will pr. July 1451 (SROB, Baldwyne 137; Pt I, no. 643).
2 For the friars see notes to no. 1 (Clare), 11 (Sudbury) and 38 (Colchester); William Rodeland had also made bequests to the friars of Sudbury, Colchester and Clare.
3 ?Executor of William Rodeland (see note above).

538. RICHARD PERSON of AMPTON, 31 December 1471 [*English*]

[*Commendation*: to God Almighty, Our Lady St Mary &c; *burial directions omitted, but see the beginning of the same will, no. 515 above, where these directions are given*]; to the altar of the same town in recompense of tithes and other duties forgotten, the mass pence of the gild of St Peter of Ampton;[1] to the reparation of the said church 3s 4d; to Rougham ('Rowham') church 3s 4d.

To the friars of Babwell 10s, to pray for my soul and all my friends.[2]

To Agnes my wife all my household and all my cattle ('catell'); to Agnes my messuage with all the appurtenances in Rougham, term of her life, and after her decease, it to be sold by her execs to dispose in good deeds for us and the friends that it came of.

Residue of my goods to my executrix, Agnes my wife, to dispose in good deeds.

Seal appended.

Witnesses: John Coket[3] and the parson of Ampton.

Proved 10 February 1471/72. Admon to executrix.

1 Richard Person was the only testator in the whole Baldwyne register to mention this gild in Ampton; nor was it mentioned in the very long will of John Coket of Ampton (see note below).
2 See note to no. 1.
3 Will pr. 2 October 1483 (TNA, PCC 22 Logge, published in *Logge Register*, no. 301).

539. MARGARET HERWARD of WORDWELL ('Wordewell'), 1 August 1471

['Herverd' *in margin*] Dated the feast of St Peter *ad vincula* 1471; my body to the Christian burial of the parish; to the reparation of the ways 5s if my goods are sufficient.

To Margaret Crose of Bury a 'bras pott & a panne of a galonn and my best cote'.

To Matilda Hurry of Wordwell 'all myn bede & 1 cote & 1 kertyll'.

Five ewes to the sustentation of the light of the Blessed Mary.

Residue of all [*my*] goods to my exec, Thomas Shyllyng *alias* Bakere of Flempton, to dispose for the greatest benefit (*utilitate*) of my soul.

Proved at Fornham St Martin, 10 February 1471/72. Admon to exec.

[fol. 485]

540. STEPHEN BLOME of COCKFIELD ('Cokfeld'), 20 February 1470/71

To be buried in the churchyard of Cockfield church; to the high altar for my tithes and offerings forgotten 12d; to Cockfield church for surplices a quarter of malt.

To Agnes my wife my messuage with its appurtenances for the whole term of her life; and after her decease the messuage to be sold preferably (*principaliter*) to my brothers, before all others, if any of them wishes to buy it, for the price and conditions (*consideracionem*) of my execs, and the money received to be disposed for the health of my soul and the souls of all my benefactors. To Agnes my wife all my hostilments and chattels, moveable and unmoveable.

To the friars of Babwell 10s.[1]

To Robert Barell my household servant (*famulo*) my tenement called 'Anderwys' at the feast of St Michael next and then Robert to bear all the charges relating to it; to Robert Barell 'my jakke'.

To Margery my servant (*servient'*) a cow.

To Thomas Felyp my green gown.

I leave 'myn maspens' [*my mass pence*] to the Trinity[2] and to the poor.

Residue of all my goods to my execs, to sell and dispose in charity, for my soul and the souls of all my benefactors as seems best to please God and profit our souls. Agnes my wife, Peter Blome and Robert Lely to be my execs to implement my will. Seal appended.

Proved at Lawshall ('Lawshull'), 30 April 1471. Admon to execs.

1   See note to no. 1.
2   This bequest suggests that there was a gild of the Trinity at Cockfield; Redstone found one reference to a gild of St Trinity there and also several to a gild of St Peter (*PSIA*, xxiii, p.56).

541. THOMAS PEEK the elder of LAWSHALL ('Lawshull'), 6 March 1470/71

Seeing and fearing the peril of death approaching me (*videns timensque periculum mortis m' iminer'*); to be buried in the churchyard of Lawshall; to the high altar for my tithes forgotten 2s; to the purchase of a new missal 3s 4d; to the purchase of a new bell [*or,* of the new bell] 3s 4d, if it is bought within a short time, but otherwise I wish my execs to dispose it on other necessary uses of my parish church.

Margery my wife to have my dwelling for her lifetime, with the appurtenances, and all my goods, moveable and unmoveable; after her decease, all those goods to be sold and disposed for the health of my soul and the souls of my parents by my execs. If Thomas Moore wishes to buy my goods or any part of them, he to have them before all others and to purchase [*them*] under the price.

Residue of all my goods to my execs, Margery my wife, John Moore of Stanstead and Simon Brygthyew[1] of Lawshall, to dispose for the health of my soul as seems to them most expedient.

Witnesses: John Revell, John Byrd the younger, Simon Cowper

Proved at Lawshall, 29 [*or,* 30] (*?p'ltimo*) April 1471. Admon to execs.

1   The second 'y' in this name is a yogh.

[fol. 485v]

542. WILLIAM PYTT of WATTISFIELD ('Watlesfeld'),[1] 20 April 1471

Dated at Wattisfield, to be buried in the churchyard of the church of Blessed Margaret in Wattisfield; my debts due (*levari*) to be paid; to the high altar of the said church 12d; to the parish clerk 2d.

To Alice my wife all the hostilments and utensils of my house, and after her decease, they to remain to Robert my son. To Alice my wife all my lands and tenements in Wattisfield, with all their appurtenances, for term of her life; and after her decease, they to remain to Robert my son and his heirs. If Robert should die without heirs, all the said lands and tenements to remain to Alice Pytte, wife of the said Robert, for term of her life; and if she [*re*]marries after Robert's decease, then all the lands and tenements to be sold and the money from them disposed in the church of Blessed Margaret of Wattisfield, except I wish Alice, wife to Robert, to have of the money 100s.

Residue of all my goods to my faithful execs, Alice Pytt my wife and John Molows of Wattisfield,[2] to dispose for me and for the health of my soul and for the souls of all my friends as seems most expedient.

Proved at Hopton, 8 May 1471. Admon to execs.

[1] ?Related to John Pytt the elder of Wattisfield, will pr. January 1458/59 (SROB, Baldwyne 197; Pt I, no. 964).

[2] Also executor of no. 561 below; will of his father, Almeric Molows, written 10 February 1461/62 (SROB, Baldwyne 287; Pt I, no. 1409).

543. JOHN HUBERD [of REDGRAVE],[1] 20 January 1470/71

['Hubert' *in margin*] To be buried in the churchyard of the church of All Saints of Redgrave. I will there to be made, at my expense, a new window in the chapel of St Mary in the said church following the form of the adjacent window (*secundum formam fenestre immediate sequentis*), so that I shall have the old (*antiquam*) material of the window of the said chapel.

All my goods, moveable and unmoveable, to my wife and my son jointly, and after my wife's death, to Robert my son.

Execs: Margery my wife and Robert my son.

Proved at Gislingham ('Gyslyngham'), 15 May 1471. Admon to execs.

[1] ?Son of Robert Huberd of Redgrave, no. 416 above.

[fol. 486]

544. PETER KYNG of SAPISTON ('Sppeston'),[1] 25 & 26 January 1470/71

[*Testament, dated 25 January 1470/71*]

Dated, at Sapiston ('Sappeston'), the day of the conversion of St Paul the Apostle 1470; [*commendation includes*: to St Andrew the Apostle[2]]; my body to Christian burial in the churchyard of my parish church of Sapiston ('Sapston'); to Thomas Waldyngfeld, canon, to celebrate there 4s; to Sapiston parish church 20s.

To the Augustinian friars of the New House of Thetford[3] a coomb of wheat and a coomb of malt.

To Thorpe ('Thorp') church 40d; to Troston church 40d; to Little Livermere ('Lyvermer parva') church 40d.

To my older (*sen'*) children, that is, Thomas, Margaret, Margery, Agnes and John, 4 marks each in cash, if my goods will stretch to it.

To Thomas my son a 'paksadyll', a 'wantayll' and a 'pakecloth', the best.

To John my son, the elder, 40s in goods (*cattall'*), with his malt, a whole bed, a 'paksadyll', a 'wangtayll', a 'pakcloth', the worst.

To Margaret my wife all my other utensils and bedding, with the horses, cows, carts and ploughs, harness (*phalibus*), grain [*and*] hay, both in the barn and in the fields, with 40 ewes and 40 lambs (*xl agnis tui'*). The residue of my sheep to be sold.

To a suitable, good and honest priest to celebrate for a year for the souls of me, my parents and my benefactors and also going to the Court of Rome, staying there for the whole of Lent [*and*] completing to all the stations and circles customarily done by good pilgrims, 18 marks.[4]

Margaret my wife, John Purpyll, Robert Breton and John Myller alias Vyell to be execs of my testament and last will; Roger Rookbode[*sic*] to be supervisor; to each of whom 6s 8d for their labour.

Residue of all my goods not bequeathed in this testament or in my last will to my execs to dispose and execute for my soul and the souls of all for whom I am bound and of all the faithful; but if my goods are not sufficient for the legacies, then the execs with the supervisor to moderate them and dispose according to the extent of the goods.

Seal appended.

[fol. 486v] [*Will, dated 26 January 1470/71*]

Dated at Sapiston, the morrow of the conversion of Paul the Apostle.

Margaret my wife to have my tenement called 'Davyes' in Sapiston, with the appurtenances, to hold to her and her children (*filiis*) born of our bodies, for term of their lives, or of any of them, who happens to live the longest, and if the children happen to die but Margaret lives, then the tenement to remain to her and her heirs for ever. If Margaret should die and the children or any one of them outlive her, then the tenement with its appurtenances to remain to them for term of [*their*] lives, according to the assignment and apportionment (*distribucionem*) of Margaret; [*and*] after their deaths, the tenement with its appurtenances to be sold and distributed for our souls. My tenement called 'Lottes' in Bardwell, with its appurtenances, to be sold by my execs to perform and implement my testament with all appropriate (*accomoda*) haste.

To Thomas my son after my decease my 2 acres of land called 'Ingham Bussh' lying in Ingham which came to me by right of marriage (*iur' nupciarum*), to hold to him and his heirs of the chief lords of the fee for ever.

Residue of all my [*goods*] to be sold to pay my debts and to fulfil my stated legacies. My legacies and gifts (*assignat'*) in my above testament to be respited and delayed (*ponantur in respect' & dilatione*) until my goods can be realized (*levari*) sufficiently to implement them, especially the legacies and gifts to my children, and if those children or any of them ungratefully worry my execs by importuning and impetuously claiming their legacies or gifts, or obstruct or result in obstructing my testament or this will, then it shall be at the disposition and will of my execs to limit and reduce the legacies and gifts, and if in their view the demand is made maliciously, to withhold and deny them totally.

One seal for testament and will.

[*Probate not recorded; the previous probate was granted in May 1471 and the next in April 1471.*]

¹ Executor of Thomas Clere of Little Livermere (no. 118 above); witness of the unproven will of John Betys of Sapiston, dated December 1450 (SROB, Baldwyne 104; Pt I, no. 464).
² The dedication of Sapiston parish church.
³ See note to no. 69.
⁴ See notes to nos 89 (stations of Rome) and 490 (circles of Rome); Lent was a time of particular austerity and penitence.

[fol. 487]

545. JOHN MORLE the elder of MILDENHALL ('Myldenhale'),¹ 17 March 1471 [*new style*]

Dated at Mildenhall, 17 March 1471; my testament containing my last will; [*commendation*: to the divine mercy of Almighty God, and to the Blessed Mary his mother and all the saints]; my body to Christian burial; to the high altar of the church of the Blessed Virgin Mary of Mildenhall for my tithes and offerings forgotten and withheld, in exoneration of my soul, 40d; to the reparation of Mildenhall church 6s 8d. Margaret my wife to have all the utensils of my house.

To Alice Morle² a 'posnet'; to Simon Aleyn 40d.

Residue of all my goods and chattels to the discretion of my execs Margaret my wife and the said Simon Aleyn, they to dispose for my soul as seems to them most to please God and profit my soul.

Seal appended.

Proved at Icklingham St James ('Iklyngham Jacobi'), 5 April 1471. Admon to Simon Morle[*sic*], co-exec. Power reserved to Margaret Morle, co-executrix, when she comes, if she wishes to take up admon.

¹ ?Executor of John Tyd of Mildenhall, will pr. April 1454 (SROB, Baldwyne 152; Pt I, no. 727); ?related to Richard Morle the elder of Mildenhall (no. 378 above).
² ?Widow of Richard Morle the elder (no. 378).

546. ISABEL SWANTON of BOTESDALE ('Botysdale') [in REDGRAVE],¹ 3 March 1470/71

To be buried in the churchyard of the church of All Saints of Redgrave; to the high altar of which 12d; a suitable priest to celebrate in the chapel there for half a year, for his stipend 4 marks.

My tenement in which I live to be divided equally and by equal portions between Robert Gerard my son² and Richard Taylour, according to the good advice of William Mordok and other trustworthy persons asked to do it. If either of them should intend selling his share awarded him, the other brother to buy it if he wishes, and not a stranger.

The rest of my moveable goods to be divided in two, equally, between the said Robert and Richard, similarly according to the advice of William Mordok and Alice his wife, whom I make execs; Master John Pynswale, rector of Redgrave church³ to be supervisor; they to dispose everything as they know will please God and profit my soul and ensure peace and agreement between my sons.

Proved at Botesdale, 26 April 1471. Admon to execs.

1   Will of Henry Swanton, her husband, no. 376.

2   Isabel Swanton was formerly the wife of William Gerarde, will pr. June 1461 (SROB, Baldwyne 276; Pt I, no. 1354). William had bequeathed Robert a small sum of money from the sale of his tenement, after Isabel's remarriage or death. Following her remarriage, the tenement was purchased by her new husband, Henry Swanton, and subsequently bequeathed to her in his will. Thus, the half share of a tenement bequeathed here to Robert Gerard was half of the tenement formerly owned by his father William.

3   John Pynkeswall was rector of Redgrave from 1463 to 1476 (Tanner, p.1312).

[fol. 487v]

547. THOMAS WAREYN of HAUGHLEY ('Hawley'), 22 April 1471

Dated at Haughley in the diocese of Norwich; to be buried in the churchyard of the church of Blessed Mary of Haughley; to the high altar of the same church 6d; to the use (*proficium*) of the said church the trunk of an oak (*stub querc'*);[1] I bequeath 5 marks 6s 8d for an anniversary to be observed annually there in Hawley church, that is, 4s annually until the sum is fully paid in divers years, being done for the health of my soul and all my benefactors' [*souls*].

To John Wareyn my son a 'bras' pan; to Richard Wareyn, son of John Wareyn, a 'bras' pan holding 2 gallons, a 'jake' with the 'salett'; to Thomas Wareyn, son of John Wareyn, a 'bras' pan holding 1 gallon; to Alice Wareyn, daughter of John Wareyn, a 'posnet'.

To Rose Wareyn, my daughter, a 'bras' pot holding 2 gallons.

To William Stannard a 'bras' pan holding 4 gallons; to Anne, daughter of William Stannard, a 'shett' [*and*] a 'blankett'.

To John Elys my blue gown.

To John Wareyn my son for his labour 12d [*and*] to William Stannard for his labour 12d [*as execs*].

Residue of my goods to be disposed for me and my friends as seems best to them. Seal appended.

Proved at Haughley, 27 April 1471. Admon to execs.

1   This unusual bequest of the trunk of an oak was probably to replace a roof timber.

548. JOHN ABELL of THURSTON,[1] 15 April 1471 [*nuncupative*]

Dated Monday in Easter week 1471; his body to Christian burial in Thurston parish church.

All his goods to the satisfying of all his creditors and his moveable and unmoveable [*goods*] to the disposition of Alice Abell his wife, to the pleasure of God and exoneration of his conscience.

Alice his wife and John Shyllyston [*?*Shyllynston] to be his execs.

Witnesses: Thomas Bullok and many others.

Proved at Fornham St Martin, 6 May 1471. Admon to execs.

1   Anne, daughter of John Abell, was a beneficiary of the will of John Pekerell of Thurston, pr. January 1461/62 (SROB, Baldwyne 293; Pt I, no. 1437).

[fol. 488]
549. THOMAS BRYAN [of NAYLAND], 20 December 1471

To be buried in the churchyard of the church of St James of Nayland ('Neylond'); to the fabric of the said church 3s 4d.

To John Bryan my father a chest and a candlestick.

To Richard Wayte of Sudbury a sanguine robe.

To Richard my brother a pair of sheets; to Matilda my sister 2 candlesticks.

Residue of all my goods to my execs to dispose, and especially pay my debts, for the health of my soul and of all my benefactors' [souls] as they see most expedient. John Bryon my father and Stephen Bryon my brother to be my faithful execs.

Seal appended.

Witnesses: Robert Terry, Richard Fyssher, Peter Fryth and others.

Proved at Kersey, 8 January 1471/72. Admon to execs. Seal of official appended.

550. WILLIAM GOODWYN of BURWELL [*Cambs*],[1] 20 November 1471

Sick unto death; [*commendation*: to Almighty God, the Blessed Mary &c]; to be buried in the churchyard of the church of St Andrew of Burwell; to the high altar of the said church for my tithes forgotten 6d; to the reparation and emendation of the same church 4 bushels of barley.

To Thomas Goodwyn my brother a bushel of barley; to John Goodwyn my brother a bushel of barley; to Alice my sister a bushel of barley.

The reversion of 20 acres of arable land which Nicholas at Hyll my grandfather[2] gave me in his last will, after the decease of Joan my mother, to remain to Margaret my wife and my children for ever.

Residue of all my goods to Margaret my wife to maintain and provide for Margaret and for my children; she to be my executrix.

Seal appended.

Proved at Kentford, 11 January 1471/72. Admon to executrix.

1   ?Related to William Goodewyn of Burwell (no. 12).
2   ?Executor (as 'att Hyll') of John Kent of Burwell, will pr. September 1447 (SROB, Baldwyne 63; Pt I, no. 313).

551. JOHN BRYGGEMAN of BURWELL [*Cambs*],[1] 14 November 1471

Dated at Burwell; sick unto death; [*commendation*: to Almighty God, the Blessed Virgin Mary &c]; to be buried in the churchyard of the church of the Blessed Mary of Burwell; to the high altar of the said church for my tithes forgotten 12d; to the high altar of the church of Snailwell ('Sneylwell') [*Cambs*] 12d; to the reparation of the church of the Blessed Mary of Burwell 6s 8d; to the reparation of Snailwell ('Sneyllwell') church 6s 8d; for a trental of masses to be celebrated for the health of my soul, 10s.

Margaret my wife to have my messuage lying in the town of Snailwell with 5 acres of land belonging to it, lying dispersedly (*particularit'*) in the fields of Snailwell, to hold for term of her life; and after her decease, [fol. 488v] the messuage and land to be sold my execs, and of the money from them, half to be disposed for the health of my soul and of my wife's soul and the residue to be divided by equal portions among my children then living.

Residue of all my goods to my wife and Richard Breggeman my brother, my execs, to dispose for the health of my soul as they see best to please God and profit my soul. Seal appended.

Witnesses: Thomas Catelyn, chaplain,[2] Nicholas Wylkyn and others.

Proved at Kentford, 11 January 1471/72. Admon to execs.

1   ?Related to Richard Brygman of Snailwell, probate only, April 1452 (SROB, Baldwyne 110; Pt I, no. 505).

2   A chaplain of Burwell St Mary's; he had witnessed the will of Sir John Andrew, a fellow chaplain there, will pr. October 1465 (NRO, NCC 105 Betyns). Catelyn was supervisor of the will of Thomas Walleys (no. 631 below).

552. JOHN BRID [*recte* BIRD] the elder [of LAVENHAM],[1] 20 January 1471/72

['Bryd' *in margin*] Dated at Lavenham, the Monday after the feast of St Wulfstan ('Wulstoon') the Bishop 1471; to be buried in the churchyard of the said church; to the high altar of the said church for tithes forgotten and underpaid 20d; a friar to celebrate for a whole year, in his house or wherever he pleases, for my soul and for the souls for whom I am bound, he to have a reasonable stipend for his salary.

To Katherine Byrd my wife all my ostilments, bedding and household utensils and all other necessaries belonging to my house; to Katherine my wife my tenement in which I live with all its appurtenances lying in the borough (*burgo*) of Lavenham in 'le Nethir strete', between the tenement of Thomas Spring,[2] lately John Cobold, on one side and the tenement of Thomas Beryle the elder on the other side, to hold the tenement and appurtenances [*to her and*] her heirs for ever.

Residue of my goods to Katherine my wife, executrix, to receive and render my debts and from the residue to dispose for my soul and for the souls for whom I am bound, as she sees most expedient for the health of my soul and [*those*] souls and to satisfy God.

Katherine Bird my wife to be my executrix, to whom I give full power to execute and fulfil the premises due above in the form stated.

Seal appended.

Witnesses: Robert Hervi, chaplain,[3] Robert Dytton and William Joli of Lavenham.

Proved at Lavenham, 4 February 1471/72. Admon to executrix.

1   According to the will of John Archer of Lavenham, in 1452 'John Byrd the elder' held a tenement in 'Lyestrete'[*sic*] (*?the High Street*), Lavenham, next to Archer's tenement called 'Parych', will pr. October 1452 (SROB, Baldwyne 100; Pt I, no. 446); Byrd was executor of Joan Cogman of Lavenham, probate September 1452 (SROB, Baldwyne 111; Pt I, no. 510).

2   See note to no. 190.

3   Roberty Hervy, parish chaplain of Lavenham, was a beneficiary of the wills of several parishioners (Pt I, nos 263, 446 and 1002) and witnessed this and at least two others (Pt I, no. 1048 and no. 681 below). In his own will he left money to the repair and 'keeping' of the organs in the parish church, and for the schooling of his bastard son to be a priest 'if the law will allow', will pr. June 1479 (NRO, NCC 238 Gelour).

[fol. 489]

553. SIMON FULLER of MILDENHALL ('Mildenhale'),[1] 28 October 1471
[*probate only*]

Proved at Fornham St Martin. Admon to Alice his wife, named in the testament.

554. ROBERT MOROWHYLL of MENDLESHAM ('Mendelesham'),
7 October 1471

My testament and last will; my body to Christian burial.

To Joan my wife all my moveable goods; to Joan my whole tenement with all the lands except a piece of land called 'Whynnys' which I leave to Thomas my son when he reaches legal age.

To Alice my daughter when she comes to legal age, 13s 4d; to Robert my son when he comes to the same age, 13s 4d; to William my son when he comes to legal age, 13s 4d. If any of those children die before reaching legal age, then I wish their legacy to be disposed by my execs.

Joan my wife to have my said tenement with all the lands, except the piece of land excepted, for term of her life; and after her decease, the tenement with all its appurtenances to remain to John my son and his heirs.

Residue of all my goods to my execs to sell and dispose for the health of my soul as they see best to please God and profit my soul.

Execs: Thomas Morwhyll and Joan my wife, to each of whom for [*their*] labour 2s.

Witnesses: William Baret, John Maunger and others.

Proved at Cotton, penultimate day [*30*] of October 1471. Admon to execs.

555. SIMON PERKYN of HOPTON,¹ 20 June 1471

Dated at Hopton; [*commendation*: to Almighty God and the Blessed Virgin Mary]; to be buried in the churchyard of All Saints of Hopton ('Hoopton'); to the high altar of the same church for my tithes forgotten and underpaid 12d; to the fabric of Hopton church 6s 8d; to Barningham ('Bernyngham') church 6s 8d; to Weston church 3s 4d; to Garboldisham ('Garbelysham') [*Norfolk*] church 6s 8d.

To Robert Seman 6d.

To each of my sons 5 marks.

To my godson John Hamelyn 4d; to [*my*] godson the son of Richard Lathery 4d; to my godson the son of Thomas Harlynge 4d; to my godsons the sons of Thomas Perkyn of Coney Weston ('Conston')² 8d.

To the abbot and convent of Langley ('Langle') [*?Norfolk*] 6s 8d;³ to the high altar of Barningham church 12d.

To John Hamelyn 6s 8d.

A priest to have a competent stipend [fol. 489v] to celebrate for my soul for a year in Hopton church.

Margaret my wife to hold for the whole term of her life all [*my*] lands and tenements, rents and services, with all their appurtenances belonging to the same lands and tenements whatsoever, which I have of right in the town of Hopton or elsewhere in the county of Suffolk; and after her decease, they are to be sold and the money received to be disposed for the health of my soul and for the soul of Margaret my wife and all our benefactors in pious uses, that is, in the giving of alms, the celebration of masses and other works of piety as seems best to my execs to please God most [*and*] in exoneration of their conscience against (*erga*) God in this matter. But if Margaret has need at any time during her life to sell any of the said lands and tenements to pay my debts that I owe for my lands and tenements that I lately bought of Stephen Fen,[4] or to fulfil my legacies, then I wish her to sell what is necessary and I wish my execs to act in keeping with this testament.

Finally I beg my feoffees to diligently grant full and peaceful seisin to those persons purchasing any parcel of the said lands and tenements as required by my execs.

Residue of all my goods to Margaret my wife during her life and after her death to be sold by my execs.

Execs: John Hamelyn and Margaret my wife.

Supervisor: John Broun, rector of Hopton church.[5]

Seal appended.

Witnesses: Sir Thomas Hunte, priest,[6] Sir John Henn, Richard Laderer, Joan Swan and Matilda Fen.[7]

Proved at Fakenham Magna, 28 October 1471. Admon to execs.

1 ?Son of John Perkyn the elder of Barningham, will pr. September 1457 (SROB, Baldwyne 195; Pt I, no. 954).
2 Son and executor of John Perkyn the elder of Barningham (see note above).
3 Although there are several places named Langley in England, it seems likely that the abbey of Langley near Loddon is being referred to here. The founder of this Premonstratensian abbey, dedicated to the honour of the Blessed Virgin in 1195, was Sir Robert FitzRoger Helke who was lord of Langley by marriage. The house was colonized by brethren from Alnwick, the abbot of Alnwick thus becoming the father abbot to Langley (*VCH Norfolk*, ii, pp.418–21).
4 Testament and will, no. 661.
5 For John Broun's career see note to no. 36; see also no. 393.
6 Thomas Hunte was rector of Gasthorpe from 1459 to ?1482 (Tanner, p.698).
7 Wife of Stephen Fen of Hopton; his will, no. 661.

556. JOHN FOLKE the elder of STOKE by NAYLAND ('Stokeylond'), ?3 August 1471[1]

Dated at Stoke by Nayland; my body to Christian burial; to the high altar 12d.

To Christian my wife my 2 tenements for term of [*her*] life, that is, 'Boymans' and 'Hydis', with all the appurtenances, and if it happens that she comes to be in need I wish her to sell whichever she wishes of the tenements and live on the money from the sale; and after her death the other tenement to be sold and distributed between my 3 sons and daughter in equal portions. If any of the sons or daughter should depart this life, then after my wife's decease, the money from the tenement to be divided among the survivors in equal portions; if all should depart from this life before their mother, then the money to be disposed by the discretion of my execs for the health of my soul and of my parents in the best way they know to please God. To Christian my wife all the ostilments of my house and all my other goods, moveable and unmoveable, on condition that she pays all my debts clearly and completely.

Execs: Christian my wife and John Hyde of Nayland ('Neylond') the younger.

Witnesses: Master John Cranewys,[2] Sir William Skeat, chaplain,[3] with others.

Seal appended.

Proved at Boxford, 12 November 1471. Admon to execs.

1 The figure of the date in August is unclear. It might be 3°, but it could be 2°, or even *p* with an abbreviation mark meaning *primo*. Redstone transcribed it as 3 August (*PSIA*, xii, p.101).
2 See note to no. 150; Cranewyse also witnessed nos 150, 236 and 409.
3 Executor of William Jay of Stoke by Nayland (no. 409).

[fol. 490]

557. ISABEL MACHON of FELSHAM, 1 April 1471

To be buried in the churchyard of the church of St Peter of Felsham; to the high altar of the said church for tithes forgotten 20d; I bequeath a cow to the finding of 2 lights in the said church, one before the image of Corpus Christi and the other before the image of St Katherine; I wish to pay for the glass of a window of 'ly porche' of the same church.

The rest of all my goods I leave to the disposition of William Moore and Joan his wife, whom I make execs, to dispose for the health of my soul as seems to them most expedient.

Seal appended.

Witnesses: Robert Brone, Thomas Bykby, John Goodryche the younger and others. The said William and Joan to have all my lands and tenements in Felsham after my decease and all my other goods, moveable and unmoveable, to dispose for my soul as above.

Proved at Fornham St Martin, 16 December 1471. Admon to execs.

558. JOHN ALYESAWNDRE of RUSHBROOKE ('Rooshebroke'), 21 April 1471

['Alysaundre' *in margin*] Dated at Rushbrooke; to be buried in the churchyard of the church of St Nicholas of Rushbrooke ('Rooshebrook'); to the high altar of the said church for my tithes forgotten and offerings underpaid 3s 4d; to the reparation of the said church 3s 4d.

To Robert my son 2 brass pots, a brass pan, a brass cauldron, a basin and ewer and 2 latten candlesticks.

To each of my godsons and goddaughters 6d.

To the indulgence of *Maison Dieu* ('Massendewe') 12d.[1]

Residue of all my goods and chattels to my execs to sell and receive, dispose and distribute for my soul and the souls of all for whom I am bound, in the payment of my debts, the celebration of masses and doing other pious works as seems best to satisfy God and profit the health of my soul.

Execs: Robert my son and Thomas Chyrche of Rushbrooke ('Roshebroke'), to each of whom for their labour 3s 4d.

Seal appended.

Witnesses: Thomas Helpston, John Yermyn, John Skultoke and others.

Proved at Fornham St Martin, 16 December 1471. Admon to execs.

[1] '*Maison Dieu*' is French for 'God's House'. This bequest probably refers to one of the hospitals in nearby Bury St Edmunds. The hospital of St John, more usually known as the *Domus Dei* or 'God's House', was founded by Abbot Edmund sometime between 1248 and 1256 to supply hospitality and refreshment to Christ's poor. Under Abbot Simon the house was enlarged and a chapel and altar were provided for the inmates, and there was also a graveyard attached for the burial of any who died there. In 1425 it was described as being outside the south gate of the town of St Edmunds, and under the governorship of the prior of the monastery (*VCH Suffolk*, ii, pp.133–4).

[fol. 490v]

559. ROBERT BRWNWYN of WETHERINGSETT ('Wetheryngset'),[1]

9 November 1471

['Brunwyn' *in margin*] Dated at Wetheringsett; to be buried in the churchyard of the church of All Saints of Wetheringsett; to the high altar of the same church 4s 2d [*sic*]; for a silver chalice 5 marks for the particular use of the same church; for 4 trentals to be celebrated for my soul and the soul of my wife and for the souls of our fathers and mothers and of all our benefactors 40s; to the particular light of the crucifix and of the Blessed Mary, 2 cows; to Winston ('Wynston') church 13s 4d; to the reparation of the path to the church 20d.

To Rose my household servant 2 heifers.

If my substance (*facultates*) will extend so far, I wish a priest to celebrate for a year for my soul and my wife's soul and our parents' and benefactors' [*souls*] in Wetheringsett church and in Winston church.

My execs to receive all my debts for fulfilling this my last will and paying my debts. Residue of all my goods to my execs to dispose for the health of my wife's soul and our friends' [*souls*] as they see to please God most and profit our souls.

Execs: William Annes of Wetheringsett and John Lynge of Winston, to each of whom for their labour 6s 8d.

Seal appended.

Witnesses: John Kempe, chaplain,[2] Edmund Crakenell and others.

Proved at Finningham ('Fynyngham'), 18 December 1471. Admon to execs.

1   Son and under-age legatee of Thomas Brounewyn of Wetheringsett, will made August 1457 (SROB, Baldwyne 206; Pt I, no. 1023); related to Robert Brunwyn of Mendlesham (no. 788 below).

2   Also witness of the wills of two other Wetheringsett parishioners, nos 796 and 810.

560. JOHN FULLER of THURSTON, 5 December 1471

Dated at Thurston; to be buried in the churchyard of Thurston parish church; to the high altar of the same church 8d; to the sustentation of the light of St Mary in the same church 8d.

To Thomas Taylour of Beyton ('Bekton') 2 bushels of malt.

Residue of all my goods I give into the hands of my executrix, Alice my relict, to dispose them all for my soul and the souls of all my benefactors and to pay my debts without delay.

Supervisor: John Lynge the elder.

Proved at Fornham St Martin, 24 December 1471. Admon to executrix.

[fol. 491]

561. JOHN SHUKFORD of THELNETHAM,[1] 25 August 1471

To be buried in the churchyard of Thelnetham church; I wish my debts to be fully paid; to the high altar of the said church for my tithes forgotten 2s; I wish to have a suitable priest to celebrate in the said church for a whole year for the health of my soul and of my benefactors' [*souls*].

Katherine my wife to have a tenement called 'Joys' with the adjacent croft and with other lands, both free and bond, belonging to the said tenement for term of her life; and after her decease, Thomas my son to have the tenement with the croft and other lands, both free and bond, belonging to it, and then he, Thomas, to pay Joan my daughter 13s 4d. Katherine my wife to have 4 acres and 3 roods of land lying in 'le Wodebotome' for term of her life; and after her decease, Richard my son to have the said 4 acres 3 roods of land, and he, Richard, to pay Joan my daughter 13s 4d. To John my son 4 horses and a cart shod with iron (*de ferro calciat'*).

All the utensils and ostilments of my house to Katherine my wife.

Residue of all my goods to Katherine my wife and John Molows of Wattisfield ('Watlesfeld'),[2] my faithful execs, to dispose for the health of my soul and of all my friends' [*souls*], and John Bole of Garboldisham ('Garbelysham') to be my supervisor, as seems to them most expedient.

Seal appended.

Proved at Hopton, 15 October 1471. Admon to execs.

1 ?Related to John Shukford of Thelnetham (no. 769).
2 Executor of William Pytt (no. 542); see note to that will.

562. JOHN BONDE of WALSHAM, 4 August 1471

Dated at Walsham; my body to Christian burial in the churchyard of Walsham church; I wish all my debts to be paid; to the high altar 12d; to the painting of the image of the Blessed Mary 3s 4d.

To John[*sic*] an acre of pasture lying in the fields of Stanton between the land of the said John on both sides.

To John Snell the younger my stepson (*filiastro*) 6s 8d.

Execs: Agnes Bonde my wife and Thomas Knygth[*sic*].

Supervisor: Thomas Smyth.

Proved at Hopton, 15 October 1471. Admon to execs.

[fol. 491v]
563. ROBERT MELLERE of NAUGHTON ('Nawton'), 3 July 1471

['Myllere' *in margin*] Dated at Naughton; to be buried in the churchyard of the church of the Blessed Mary of Naughton; to the high altar of the same church for my tithes forgotten and underpaid 20d.

To Robert my son, Margaret and Margery my daughters, a ewe each.

Residue of all my goods and chattels, after my burial done and paid for and my debts paid, to remain wholly to Margery my wife to dispose at her free will.

Margery my wife to be my executrix and Alexander Snellyng of Elmsett ('Elmesset') to be supervisor, they to have God before their eyes in fulfilling faithfully this my present testament.

Seal appended.

Proved at Kersey, 22 October 1471. Admon to executrix.

[*Largely a repeat of the testament on fol. 466, no. 463 above; there the will has also survived.*]

564. ROBERT GOLDYNG of GLEMSFORD ('Glemesford'),[1] 8 September 1471

Of Glemsford in the diocese of Norwich; to be buried in the churchyard of the church of the Blessed Mary of Glemsford.

To Katherine my wife 5 marks and all my hostilments and utensils.

To a priest to celebrate for me and all my benefactors in the church of the blessed Mary of Glemsford £3.

Residue of all [*my*] goods I place in the disposition of William my son and John my son of Glemsford, whom I make execs; to each for their labour 6s 8d; my execs to pay all my debts.

Seal appended.

Proved at Glemsford, 24 October 1470[*sic*]. Admon to execs.

> 1   ?Related to William Goldyng of Glemsford (no. 316).

565. JOHN SCHAPMAN of WITHERSFIELD ('Wederysfeld'), 1 June 1471

Dated at Withersfield; knowing the end of my life to be near (*presentis*); my body to Christian burial in the churchyard of the parish church of the Blessed Virgin Mary of Withersfield; to the high altar 20d.

To the order of friars of Clare,[1] to pray for [*remainder deleted*].

Residue of all my goods to John my son, the same John to keep and support his mother for term of [*her*] life; and after his decease I leave [*it*] to the friary of Clare, to pray for our souls and for the souls of all my benefactors as seems to them most expedient for the health of my soul.

John my son to be my true attorney to implement my testament and will in all things.

Seal appended.

[*No probate recorded: previous probate dated 24 October 147[1]; next one, on new folio, dated 9 July 1471.*]

> 1   See note to no. 1.

[fol. 492]

566. JOHN SMYTH of STANTON [ALL SAINTS], 6 April 1471 [*nuncupative*]

Dated at Stanton in the diocese of Norwich; being near to death; his body to be buried in the churchyard of the church of All Saints of Stanton; to the high altar for tithes forgotten 6d.

To Anne his sister 12d.

To the said church for the new sepulchre to be made 5 marks.[1]

To Joan Dunham, wife of William Dunham, his best gown; to John Dunham a small brass pan.

He assigned his messuage and all his land to be sold by his execs for the execution of his testament and to pay all his debts.

Residue of all his goods he placed in the hands of Thomas Robhod of Walsham and Adam Mundys of Stanton, whom he made his faithful execs to dispose for the health of his soul and the souls of all his benefactors as seems best to please God and profit the souls abovesaid.

Seal appended.

Witnesses: Edmund Bene, rector of the church of All Saints,[2] John Dunham and William Dunham.

Proved at Thelnetham, 9 July 1471. Admon to execs.

1 A bequest for a new Easter Sepulchre, which could have been of wood or stone. See Glossary.
2 See note to no. 333 regarding Edmund Bene's career; see also nos 666 and 680.

567. JOHN NEWMAN of WOOLPIT ('Wolpett'), 6 February 1469/70

Dated at Woolpit; to be buried in the churchyard of Woolpit church.
To the friars of Babwell for a trental 10s.[1]
To John and Thomas sons of Richard Neweman, 20d each, on condition that the said Richard pays my attorneys 13s 4d withheld for a long time.
To Joan my wife my tenement, to hold to her and her assigns, and all the bedding on condition that she pays all my debts and legacies.
Seal appended.
Executrix: Joan my wife, to dispose for my soul where she sees most expedient.
Proved at Fornham St Martin, 23 September 1471. Admon to executrix.

1 See note to no. 1.

[fol. 492v]
568. ROGER COVE of MENDLESHAM ('Mendelesham'), 8 October 1470

[*Commendation incomplete*: to Almighty God, Blessed]; to be buried in the church-yard of the said church; to the gild of the Holy Trinity 12d;[1] to the gild of the Blessed Mary 2s.[2]
To the friars of Babwell for a trental 10s.[3]
To Katherine my wife for term of her life all my goods, moveable and unmoveable, without any hindrance (*interrupcione*).
Residue of all my goods to Katherine my wife and Robert Cake [*and*] Richard Rowt, whom I make execs.
After the decease of Katherine, my execs to sell my tenement and out of it to pay Joan Cove my daughter 10 marks; also to pay out of the tenement Olive Qwhytyng 6 marks within 2 years after my wife's decease. The residue I wish my execs to dispose to please God and [*to*] the most profit of my soul.
Witnesses: Richard Pytman, John Awty and Thomas Water and others.
Proved at Mendlesham, 11 July 1471. Admon to execs.

1 Several testators made bequests to the gild of the Holy Trinity of Mendlesham: Geoffrey Chapman of Haughley (Pt I, no. 775), Roger Metessharpp of Mendlesham (Pt I, no. 932), Olive widow of John Kyng of Mendlesham (Pt I, no. 1035), John Cake of Mendlesham (Pt I, no. 1315), Robert Yestas of Mendlesham (no. 774 below) and Robert Brunwyn of Mendlesham (no. 788 below).
2 Robert Yestas (no. 774) and Robert Brunwyn (no. 788) also made bequests to the gild of St Mary.
3 See note to no. 1.

569. JOHN GLAUNVYLL of HAUGHLEY ('Hawley'), 20 April 1471

To be buried in the churchyard of the church of St Mary of Haughley; to the high altar of the same church for my tithes and[*sic*] underpaid 3s 4d.
To the friars of Babwell 3s 4d.[1]
To Thomas my son a blue gown of mine; to the said Thomas and Alice his wife 40s in money to be paid in 6 years after this present date, in each year 6s 8d.
Residue of all my goods to my exec, Peter Glaunvyle my son, to dispose as he sees best to please God and profit my soul.
Seal appended.

Proved at Stowmarket ('Stowemarket'), 11 July 1471. Admon to exec.

[fol. 493]
570. JOHN REGNOLD of WOOLPIT ('Wolpett'), 20 February 1470/71

Dated at Woolpit; my body to the Christian burial [*place*] of Woolpit; to the high altar of that church for my tithes forgotten or underpaid 40d; to the emendation of the said church for the health of my soul 40d.

To the convent of friars of Babwell to pray there for the health of my soul 4 bushels of barley; to the convent of friars of Sudbury 4 bushels of barley; to the convent of Clare to pray there for the health of my soul 2 bushels of barley.[1]

I wish to have a suitable and honest chaplain to celebrate divine service in the said church for a whole year for my soul and the souls of my parents and benefactors and all those at rest in Christ.

To Margaret my wife[2] all my tenement in which I now live with the appurtenances, to hold to her and her attorneys, for 10 years immediately after my decease; and after that the whole tenement with the appurtenances to remain to Richard my son, to hold to him and his heirs for ever, paying out of it to Margaret his mother 20s a year if Margaret remains unmarried, but if she marries 10s. If Richard dies under age or without legal heirs, then the tenement to remain to William my son in the same way, to him and his heirs for ever. If William dies under age or without legal heirs, then the tenement with appurtenances to remain to John my son in the same way, to him and his heirs for ever. If John dies under age or without legal heirs, then the tenement with appurtenances to be sold by my execs and all the proceeds to be faithfully distributed for the health of my soul and of the souls aforesaid in pious uses.

To John my son 2 closes called 'Jaksmethis', 3 acres of land lying in a field called 'Eytheokes' [*?Eight Oaks*] and a piece of land called 'in le Wente' called 'le Reycroft'[*sic*], to hold to him and his heirs for ever, on condition that if Richard my son ever has the said closes and lands [*he shall pay*] 20 marks.

To William my son 8 marks.

To Margery, Joan, Isabel, Agnes and Alice my daughters 40s each.

To Richard, William and John my sons a bullock of 1 year; and to Margery, Joan and Isabel, Agnes and Alice a bullock of 1 year each.

To Margaret my wife and Richard my son all the hostilments and utensils of my house.

To Simon Coket my best green gown.

To Thomas Pertryche my blue gown; and the son of William Smyth a gown; and Thomas Abell a tunic; and Margery Puske my servant 4 bushels of malt.

Whatever the residue of all my goods after my debts have been paid, I leave to Margaret my wife and Richard my son.

[fol. 493v] My beloved in Christ, Margaret my wife, John Belle, John Calfawe and John Deynys[3] to be my faithful execs of this my testament and last will, they having God before their eyes to put this testament into effect; to John, John and John 6s 8d each for their labour.

Seal appended.

Proved at Fornham St Martin, 8 April 1471. Admon to John Belle and John Calfaw, co-execs. Power reserved to John Deynys the other exec when he comes, if he wishes to take up admon.

1   For the friars see notes to nos 1 (Babwell and Clare) and 11 (Sudbury).
2   Will of Margaret Regnold, no. 571.
3   Will of John Deynys, no. 579; Margaret Regnold also appointed him one of her executors (no. 571).

571. MARGARET REGNOLD of WOOLPIT ('Wolpett'), 1 March 1470/71

Margaret late the wife of John Regnold;[1] dated 1 March 1471;[2] my body to the Christian burial [*place*] of Woolpit church; to the high altar of that church for my tithes forgotten or underpaid 20d. I wish to have a suitable and honest chaplain to celebrate divine service in the same church for a whole year for my soul and the soul of John my late husband and for the souls of my parents and benefactors and all faithful Christians, having for his stipend 8 marks, to be had of my goods and chattels.

My tenement called 'Puskes' in Woolpit to remain in my feoffees' hands for 10 years after my decease and all the proceeds coming from it in the meantime to be at the disposition of my execs; and after the 10 years, the tenement called 'Puskes' with its appurtenances to remain to John my son, to hold to him and his heirs for ever. If John should die under age or without legal heirs, then I wish the tenement with its appurtenances to be sold for the best possible price, and half the money arising from it to be divided equally between William my son and Margaret, Isabel, Agnes, Joan and Alice my daughters, and the other half to be distributed by my execs in pious uses of charity for my soul and the souls above stated.

The whole tenement that John my late husband left me for 10 years to be let by my execs for 3 years and all the proceeds coming from it in the meantime to be at their disposition for faithfully paying my debts and effectively implementing my legacies and those of John my late husband; and after the 3 years, the tenement to pass to Richard my son.

To Margery my daughter a brass pan holding 10 gallons; to Alice my daughter a pan holding 4 gallons.

Residue of all my goods to the disposition of my faithful execs, beloved in Christ, Richard my son, John Belle, John Calfawe and John Deynys[3] to dispose for me and my soul where they see most expedient and to please God and to put my testament into effect.

Proved at Fornham St Martin, 8 April 1471. Admon to Richard Regnold, John Belle, John Calfaw & John Deynys[*sic*], execs. Power reserved to John Deynys, the other exec, when he comes, if he wishes to take up admon.

1   Will of John Regnold, no. 570. Both this will and her husband's were proved on 8 April 1471, but John must have died by 1 March when this will was written.
2   An attempt has been made to erase the final 'j', to make it 1470.
3   Will, no. 579; John Regnold also appointed him one of his executors.

[fol. 494]

572. JOHN RECHARD of BEYTON ('Beketon'), 13 August 1471

[*nuncupative*]

His body to Christian burial.

To his father, William Rechard of Lawshall ('Lawshull'), his best gown; to his mother a pair of 'lomys' or 'wevyng lomes'; to his sister Joan Rechard a cover; to his mother a sheet; to John Rechard his brother his bow and arrows (*satiggat*) and a 'daggard'; to his other sisters 3 'dysshes'; to his sister, the wife of Nicholas Arlond, 4 'yerdys' of 'bankes'.[1]

He wishes all his debts to be faithfully paid.

Residue of his goods to the disposition of his execs, John Cok of Whelnetham ('Qwelnetham') and William Crocham of Icklingham ('Ikelyngham').

Witnesses: Marion Rechard, Agnes Rechard, Richard Sterne, James Legge and many others.

[*Probate not recorded. Next probate dated 19 September 1471; previous probate (on a different leaf) dated 8 April 1471.*]

   [1]   See Glossary; the first 'y' of 'yerdys' is a yogh.

573. JOHN BAKERE of WETHERDEN ('Wederden'), 11 May 1471

To be buried in the churchyard of Wetherden church; to the high altar of the same church for my tithes underpaid 20d.

To the friars of Babwell 5s [*and*] to the friars of Sudbury 5s for the relief and sustentation of the said houses.[1]

I wish there to be distributed after my decease, for my soul, to the poor in alms, 12d; to the gild of John[*sic*] in Wetherden 20d.[2]

To Margery my wife my messuage in Wetherden with all the lands and appurtenances; to Margery my wife all the utensils of my house.

Residue of all my goods to Margery, my wife and executrix, specifically and generally, and to Master Hugh Lye, rector of Wetherden church,[3] and to Robert Barkere my godson, whom I make execs, they to pay all my debts and implement my last will and dispose as they see best to please God and profit my soul; to the said Robert Barkere for his labour 6s 8d in money.

Supervisor: Richard Barkere of Wetherden.

Seal appended.

Proved at Stowmarket ('Stowemarket'), 19 September 1471. Admon to Margery Barkere, one of the execs. Power reserved to Master Hugh Lye, rector of Wetherden, and Robert Barkere, the other co-execs, when they come, if they wish to take up admon.

   [1]   For the friars see notes to nos 1 (Babwell) and 11 (Sudbury).
   [2]   Margery Rodynge of Wetherden (no. 451) bequeathed 6s 8d to this gild.
   [3]   Hugh Leigh was rector of Wetherden from 1461 to 1497 (Tanner, p.1342).

[fol. 494v]

574. RICHARD CAGGE of CAVENDISH ('Cavendyssh'), 20 June 1471

Of Cavendish in the diocese of Norwich; my body to Christian burial, that is, in the churchyard of Cavendish parish church. In God's name, I beg my execs to pay all my debts that I owe, that is, those that can be truly proved. To the high altar of the said church for my tithes forgotten and offerings retained and underpaid, 3s 4d; to the fabric of the new aisle to be made on the south side of the said church, 5 marks;[1] to the reparation and emendation of the stone walls around the churchyard where most need is, 26s 8d.

To the six children of William Olyve and Agnes his wife, my daughter, to pray for my soul 40s, that is, 6s 8d each; and if any of them die, the share of the deceased to remain to the survivors, right down to (*limaliter usque*) the last.

To the children of Thomas Wagge and Alice his wife, my daughter, to intercede for my soul 20s, that is, 6s 8d each.

To William Curteys to intercede for my soul 6s 8d.

To John de Foxherde my kinsman to pray for my soul 6s 8d.

William Olyve and Thomas Clerk to be my execs to perform all the above legacies; to each of them for their diligent labour, 6s 8d.

I beseech John Stysted, clerk, that he will be pleased to be supervisor of all the premises and I leave to him for his good friendship (*amicitio*) and counsel in this matter 6s 8d.

Residue of all my goods to the disposition of my execs, that they, with the advice and supervision of my supervisor, dispose of those goods in works of charity for the health of my soul and of the souls of my parents [*and*] friends for whom I am most bound and of all the faithful departed as seems best to them to please God and profit my soul.

Seal appended.

Witnesses: Friar John Heyward, Richard[*sic*] Clerk the aforesaid exec and others being there.

Proved at Sudbury, 24 September 1471. Admon to execs.

[1] The south aisle of Cavendish church is said to be 'fully Decorated' (Pevsner), so 'the fabric of the new aisle' in 1471 was probably repair work.

575. JOHN CHATTYSLEY of IXWORTH, 12 August 1471

['Chatysley'*in margin*] Dated at Ixworth; my body to Christian burial; to the high altar of the said church 12d; to the building of the tower of the same church of the said town 26s 8d.

Sir Robert Chattysley, my brother,[1] to be my exec.

Proved at Fornham St Martin, 14 October 1471. Admon to exec.

[1] The testator was probably the brother of William Chatysle of Ixworth (no. 219 above) as both John and William stated that Sir Robert Chatysle/Chattysley was their brother and appointed him their executor.

[fol. 495]
576. WILLIAM KEBYLL of OLD NEWTON ('Eldenewton'),[1] 27 May 1471

To be buried in the churchyard of the church of Newton aforesaid; to the high altar of the same church for my tithes [*forgotten*] and underpaid 12d; to the reparation of a buttress ('le boteras') on the north side of the same church 3s 4d.

To the Carmelite Friars of Ipswich (*Gypwice*) 10s, to celebrate a trental for my soul.[2]

I wish to have a suitable priest to celebrate in Old Newton ('Eldnewton') church for my soul [*and*] the souls of [*my*] parents, friends and benefactors for a whole year.

To Robert, Richard [*and*] John my sons, each of them a bed sufficient for him (*sibi sufficient'*).

Anne my wife to have [*my*] capital messuage in Newton ('Neweton'), with all the profits and appurtenances without strip or waste, for 2 years after my decease; and after the 2 years I bequeath to her annually for the whole term of her life 40s, to come from my said capital messuage. Anne to have all the utensils and ostilments of my house except before bequeathed.

To Robert my son and his heirs, when he comes to the age of 24 years, my said capital messuage with all the lands belonging to it and with 4 horses and 4 cows with the cart and plough and with all the equipment (*ornamentis*) belonging to them. I beg Robert, after the decease of Anne my wife, to keep my obit and the obit of Anne in Old Newton church for the whole term of his life.

To Richard my son my tenement called 'Paynys' in Newton aforesaid and Dagworth. To the said Richard and John my sons the tenement called 'Blakys', with all the lands, meadows [*and*] pastures belonging to it, as they lie in a close in Newton, to be divided between Richard and John when they come to the age of 24.

If Robert my son should die without heirs, then I wish Richard to have my capital messuage under the same conditions and form as Robert should have it, and then I wish John my son to have the whole tenement called 'Blakys'. If Richard should die without heirs, then I wish John to have my capital messuage [fol. 495v] in the way that Robert should have it. If John should die without heirs, then I wish Anne my daughter to have my capital messuage in the way that Robert should have it. If Anne my daughter should die without heirs, then I wish Anne my wife to have my capital messuage for term of her life; and after her decease I wish it to be sold by my execs, or theirs, and the money from it to be distributed for our souls in pious uses and in works of charity.

To Anne my daughter 20 marks in money, to be paid in the years following as it can be had from my chattels and from the profits of the said capital messuage.

To each of my execs for their labour 6s 8d.

Residue of all my goods to Anne my wife, William Mansere of Ipswich, Thomas Kebyll of Gipping Newton ('Gyppynge Newton') [*and*] John Kebyll the younger of Stowmarket ('Stowemarket'),[3] execs, they to fulfil my last will and dispose as they see best to please God and profit my soul.

Seal appended.

Witnesses: Ralph Bonnell, Richard Banyard, Thomas Cowpere and others.

Proved at Stowmarket, 11 July 1471. Admon to execs.

---

1   Executor of John Jenowr of Old Newton, will pr. October 1457 (SROB, Baldwyne 187; Pt I, no. 908).

2   See note to no. 1.

3   For the complicated genealogy of the families of Keble (etc.) in the Stowmarket area, see Muskett, *Manorial Families*, ii, pp.269–80.

[fol. 496]

577. WALTER DERYSLE of KIRTLING ('Ketelynge') [*Cambs*],[1] 20 December 1469

My body to be buried in Christian burial in the churchyard of Kirtling ('Kerte-lynge') parish church. I wish, for the health of my soul, that if any man or any woman can truly prove, with reliable witnesses or legal evidence, that I Walter Deresle have obtained or detained anything from them unjustly, then I beg my execs to make restitution for what was taken or detained first of all. To the high altar for my tithes forgotten and offerings not paid 3s 4d; 6s 8d to be distributed on the day of my burial in equal portions among 20 poor folk of my neighbourhood; to each priest present at my obsequies 4d and to each clerk 2d; 10s to be distributed among the poor present at my obsequies and at mass on my burial day.

To each child of Richard Deresle[2] and of my sons (*filiorum meorum*) 6s 8d.

William my son to find 3 lights in Kirtling church, for the term of 40 years, before the great cross [?the rood] and the images of St John the Baptist and St James the Apostle.

Residue of all my goods to Richard and William my sons, Thomas Pykchese[3] and Walter Prate, execs, they to ordain as seems best to them to please God and profit my soul.

Proved at Fornham St Martin, 30 June (*ultimo die*) 1471. Admon to execs.

1   Supervisor of the will of Ralph Hancok, pr. October 1447 (SROB, Baldwyne 82; Pt I, no. 379).
2   Will, no. 482 above.
3   Executor of William Derysle (no. 461) and Margaret Page (no. 609).

[fol. 496v]

578. NICHOLAS GERARD of BARNHAM ('Bernham St Martin'), 2 July 1471

To be buried in the churchyard of St Martin aforesaid;[1] to the high altar of the same church for my tithes negligently forgotten 12d; to the sustentation and reparation of the said church 20d; to the high altar of the church of St Gregory 8d.

To Margaret my wife all my utensils, to have [*them*] for herself (*habend' sibi*).

To Margaret my daughter a brass pot holding a gallon.

To Margaret my wife my tenement for her own use for term of her life; and after her decease I wish it to be sold by my execs and disposed in pious uses for the health of my soul.

Residue of my goods I leave in the hands of my execs, Margaret my wife and Edmund Madam, they to dispose for the health of my soul to please God and profit my soul.

Proved at Fornham St Martin, 8 July 1471. Admon to execs.

1   See note to no. 282.

[fol. 497]

579. JOHN DEYNYS of WOOLPIT ('Wolpett'),[1] 24 June 1471 [*English*]

Dated at Woolpit on the Monday within the feast of St John the Baptist 1471; my body in the sepulture of the holy Church; to the high altar of the said church of Woolpit for my tithes and offerings forgotten or else not paid and for my soul's 'hele'

338

20s; to the amending and reparation of the said church a place clepyd 'Bekatys' with all the land that belongs thereto, if it so be that my bequeath word may be borne out, and if it may not, I will that the church shall have 10 marks; to the highway before my door 20s; to the town of Ashfield ('Aysshffeld') to their steeple ('stepyll') 40d.

To a priest £10 to go to Rome and to sing there or to have sung ('do synge') three masses at *Scala Celi*[2] and two masses at Fabian and Sebastian,[3] and, when he is come [*here*] again, he to sing or to 'do synge' the residue of the year in Woolpit church for me and my wife and my good doers.

To the house of religion of Babwell 10s and a coomb of barley to sing and pray for me and those for whom I am bound;[4] to the house of religion of Sudbury 10s and a coomb of barley to sing and pray for me and my good doers.[5]

To John my son my head place, to give and sell, with all the land that belongs thereto; to the said John a close clepyd 'Watersslade' and half an acre of arable land lying by a piece of land of Edmund Serian and an acre of land lying in 'Inham' and 2 acres of land lying on the 'Bromehyll' of three 'parsonell'; to John a feather bed with 2 transoms and the best donge; the best brass pot save one and the best of the second sort and the best of the third sort; the best brass pan and the best of the second sort and the best of the third sort; to John 3 of the best kettles ('chetelys') and 3 'stelyd' pans; 12 pewter platters and 12 pewter dishes and 12 pewter saucers and 2 saltcellars and 2 candlesticks of the best; to John 2 of the best trivets ('treffdys') and 2 griddles and a dropping pan and the best spit save one with an andiron; the best mazer with half a dozen silver spoons; 3 of the best coverlets and 3 blankets and 3 pairs of the best sheets; to John a pair of coral beads and a pair of jet beads; the best blue coarse girdle and a crimson girdle.

Every godchild of mine and of my wife to have 6d.

To the said John the best basin and a ?ewer ('hevour') and a falt table and the best next [*to*] that and the best hanging ?ewer ('hevour');[6] to John a quern.

To Joan [fol. 497v] Nedham 6s 8d.

My tenement clepyd 'Cooys' to be sold to find John to school until he be of lawful age. My place to be let to the behoof of John till he be of lawful age to enter 'the good' [*i.e. the place*] and to the reparation of the place. If John decease within age, the good to be sold and I put it to the disposition of my execs to dispose in singing masses and in alms giving.

Residue of all my goods to the disposition of my execs, my well beloved in Christ, Thomas Deynys, William Bekon and William Awbry,[7] for the true execution of this present testament; to each of them for their labour 6s 8d.

Seal appended.

Proved at Fornham St Martin, 15 July 1471. Admon to execs.

1   Executor of both John and Margaret Regnold (nos 570 and 571).
2   See note to no. 244.
3   The Basilica of SS Fabian and Sebastian marked the site of early Christian catacombs just outside Rome. The church stood about two miles beyond the gate of St Sebastian on the Appian Way (Rossetti, 'Notes on the Stacyons of Rome', p.xxviii).
4   The Franciscan friary of Babwell; see note to no. 1.
5   The Dominican friary of Sudbury; see note to no. 11.
6   A 'hevour' cannot be identified in any glossary or dictionary, but Robert Dunch (no. 374) bequeathed his son John a hanging ewer.
7   Executor (as 'Aubry') of [*unknown*] Aubry of Woolpit (no. 786).

580. THOMAS ASTON of WOODDITTON ('Camoys Dytton')[1] [*Cambs*], 1472

Dated 1472 [*date and month not given*]; of Woodditton in the diocese of Norwich; [*commendation includes*: to SS Peter and Paul];[2] to be buried in the churchyard of All Saints of Ditton; to the panel (*tabule*) of the high altar[3] 2 measures (*mensuras*) of barley and [*sic*] 2 bushels; to the torches (*torturis*) of the said church a churchale (*potationem ecclesiasticam*).

Residue of my goods to Katherine my wife and John my son, under the supervision of John Ray, they to dispose for me and my soul in the manner seeming best to them. Seal appended.

Witnesses: John Payn, Simon Cobberte and others.

Proved at Herringswell ('Heryngeswell'), 15 May 1472. Admon to execs.

1   In the Middle Ages the manors in Woodditton were Ditton Camoys, Ditton Valence, Saxton, the rectory, and Ditton Priory (the latter two being relatively small). Ditton Camoys and Ditton Valence manors acquired their names in the later thirteenth century from the surnames of the families which had owned them from *c.*1200 (*VCH Cambs*, x, pp.86–9).

2   Both Thomas Aston and John Avbre of Woodditton (no. 630) included SS Peter and Paul in the commendation of their souls. There is no obvious connection between the parish and those saints: the church was dedicated to All Saints from the twelfth century to the early nineteenth, its modern name of St Mary being first recorded in 1852; three of the four Woodditton wills in Part II (nos 630, 646 and 762) mention only a gild of the Holy Trinity there. Perhaps there was an altar or lights to Peter and Paul. From architectural evidence it is clear that the late medieval church had altars in both the north and south aisles and a number of statue niches (*VCH Cambs*, x, pp.95–7).

3   During the 1890s numerous fragments from an apparently large alabaster reredos were discovered; these have been reset in the north aisle (*VCH Cambs*, x, p.97).

[fol. 498]

581. JOHN NOREYS of BROCKFORD ('Brokford') in WETHERINGSETT,[1]
10 November 1471

['Noreyce' *in margin*] Dated at Brockford in the diocese of Norwich; my testament and last will; my body to the Christian burial of Wetheringsett ('Wetheryngsett'); to the high altar of Wetheringsett church 12d.

To each of my godsons 4d.

If Ellen my wife has a child by me, then our child to have my tenement with all the lands, formerly belonging to Walter Noryce my father, to him and his heirs; if the child should die, then the tenement, with all its lands and appurtenances in Brockford or elsewhere, to be sold for the best price by my execs and disposed in priests and works of piety and alms.

Residue of all my goods to the administration of my execs, to sell, receive and dispose for the health of my soul and the souls of all my friends and benefactors as they see best to please God and profit my soul.

Execs: Robert Bronde of Gislingham ('Gyslyngham'), Robert Saham of Wetheringsett and Neville ('Newell') Dookyll; to each of whom for his labour 20s.

Seal appended.

Witnesses: John Man, John Andrew, John Dunkon and many others.

Proved at Fornham St Martin, 4 May 1472. Admon to Robert Bronde and Robert Saham, execs. Power reserved to Neville Dookyll, the other exec, when he comes, if he wishes to take up admon.

1   See note to no. 5 regarding Brockford in Wetheringsett.

582. JOHN ROWNTON of LAWSHALL ('Lawshull'), 28 March 1482

Seeing and fearing the peril of death; to be buried in the churchyard of Lawshall; to the high altar there for my tithes forgotten or underpaid 12d; to Lawshall church for a chalice to be bought 20s, if my goods will stretch to it after my debts have been paid.

Execs: Margaret my wife, William Hamon and Andrew Gyppys of Bury St Edmunds (*Sancti Edi*').

Residue of all my goods to my execs, they to dispose for the health of my soul as seems to them most expedient.

Proved at Fornham St Martin, the penultimate day [*30*] of May 1472. Admon to Margaret Rownton, lately the wife of the deceased, executrix. Power reserved to William Hamonde and Andrew Gippys, the other execs, when they come, if they wish to take up admon.

[fol. 498v]

583. ISABEL SMALWODE of BRADFIELD ST GEORGE ('Bradfeld Monachorum'),[1] 6 December 1471

Dated at Bradfield St George; to be buried in the churchyard of the church of St George of Bradfield aforesaid; to the high altar of the said church [*blank*]; to the reparation of the said church 16d.

George Smalwode to have all my lands called 'Ballysdenhill' and 'Bakonnys croft' and 'Newecroft Morepytyll', 'Gylden Acre' and 3 acres of land lying within 7½ acres of land in 'Magna Rawhawfeld', with all their appurtenances, to find a suitable priest to celebrate for my soul and the souls of all my benefactors for the space of one year in the church of St George of Bradfield aforesaid; the said George Smalewod to have all my lands within named within the reckoning time (*spaciu' conpotens*) 6s 8d.[2]

Benedict Smalwode my husband to have my tenements called 'Harnessys' and 'Templeres' with all their appurtenances after my decease for the space of 4 years; after 4 years, Joan my daughter to have the 2 tenements called 'Harneyssys' and 'Templerys' to her and her heirs.

Residue of all my goods and chattels to my execs, to sell, receive, dispose and distribute for my soul and the souls for whom I am bound in paying my debts, celebrating masses and doing other pious works as seems best to please God and most healthily (*saluberimus*) profit my soul.

Execs: George Smalwode and Thomas Byrde of Bradfield St George.

Seal appended.

Witnesses: John Cowpere, John Hynard, John Hachet and others.

Proved at Fornham St Martin, 8 June 1472. Admon to execs.

[1] There is a place called 'Smallwood Green' at Bradfield St George.
[2] This bequest does not make sense as it stands and so it seems likely that the registry clerk has omitted a line or phrase that was in the original will.

584. MARGERY POWERE of ?GREAT BARTON ('Berton'), *c.* 4 October
1471 [*nuncupative*]

Dated about the feast of St Francis 1470; late the wife of Henry Powere of Barton;[1]
her body to Christian burial.

She left all her goods belonging to her to Philip Bokenham and John Weykes, execs
of Henry Powere her husband, deceased, to dispose for the souls of Henry and
Margery as they see best to please God and profit their souls; and them she made
her execs.

Witnesses: Nicholas Powere, Alice Powere and divers others.

Proved 15 June 1472. Admon to execs.

> 1   Probate only, March 1459/60 (SROB, Baldwyne 246; Pt I, no. 1236).

[fol. 499]
585. WILLIAM LARDYNERE of KENNETT ('Kenett') [*Cambs*], 24 July
1471

Dated at Kennett; to be buried in the churchyard of Kennett parish church; to the
said parish church 20s; to the high altar of the said parish church for my tithes
forgotten 3s 4d; to the gild of the Holy Trinity of the said church 3s 4d;[1] to Kentford
parish church 3s 4d; to the gild of St John of the said church 3s 4d.[2]

To Joan my wife the messuage in which I live with all its appurtenances; and after
her decease, the messuage with its appurtenances to be sold for the highest price
and the money to be disposed for our souls and the souls of all the faithful departed.
To each of my daughters an acre of land.

Residue of all my goods to Joan my wife and John Cartere, execs, to dispose and
distribute as they see best to benefit the health of my soul.

Supervisor: John Hadenam of Kentford.

Proved at Fornham St Martin, 14 October 1471. Admon to execs.

> 1   For the gilds of Cambridgeshire in general see Introduction, under *Gilds*, and note to no. 199.
>   Palmer could find no record of a gild in Kennett (Palmer, 'Village Gilds of Cambridgeshire',
>   p.381) but this bequest of William Lardynere clearly refers to the gild of the Holy Trinity of the
>   parish church of Kennett.
> 2   The gild of St John the Baptist of Kentford was recorded in the gild survey of 1389. It was
>   founded in 1349 by certain men and women who, out of devotion to St John the Baptist, gathered
>   from their corn to provide a chaplain to celebrate once a week and to provide three lights before St
>   John's image; each member was to cause a mass to be celebrated for the soul of a dead member;
>   all were to offer at mass for the dead (TNA, C47/428). John Hadynham the elder made bequests
>   to both the gild of St John the Baptist and the gild of the Blessed Mary in Kentford (Pt I, no.
>   762). In 1457, John Whyte had left 10s to the building of the new hall of the gild (*gilde*) of the
>   Blessed Mary and St John the Baptist of the church of Kentford (Pt I, no. 894). It is likely that
>   there were two separate gilds but that there was one communal hall.

586. WILLIAM KYNG of WICKHAMBROOK ('Wykhambrook'),
20 September 1471

Of the parish of Wickhambrook, in the diocese of Norwich; [*commendation includes:*
to the court of Heaven]; my body to Christian burial in the churchyard of the parish
church of All Saints of Wickhambrook; to the high altar there for tithes and other
[*things*] forgotten 2s; to the fabric of the church there 20d; to the annual (*annual'*)

service of a priest celebrating divine service there, all the gild mass pence belonging (*pertinent'*) to me.[1]

To John Hawkyn my servant a gown.

Residue of all my goods to the disposition of my execs, Thomas Kyng of Bury St Edmunds and Robert Kyng, my brothers, that they jointly and separately (*coniunctim & divisim*) arrange for my burial and pay my debts and keep, or see to the keeping of, my children and distribute for my soul and Agnes my wife's (*consortis*) and all my parents', friends' and benefactors' souls as they see best to please God and profit our souls.

Proved at Fornham St Martin, 14 October 1471. Admon to execs.

[1] William Kyng did not specify of which gild in Wickhambrook he was a member; John Frost of Wickhambrook (Pt I, no. 302) was a member of the gild of the Holy Trinity and John Ray of Wickhambrook (Pt I, no. 696) was a member of the gild of St John.

[fol. 499v]

587. WILLIAM ORDERYCH of HITCHAM ('Hecham'),[1] 8 March 1471/72

Dated at Hitcham; my body to Christian burial; to the high altar of Hitcham church for my tithes and offerings forgotten or underpaid and for the health of my soul 20d. My small house next to the manor to remain to the use and accommodation (*habitacionem*) of the poor, for ever, for interceding (*ad intercedend'*) for my soul and the souls of my friends.[2]

My house newly built by the gate of the churchyard of Hitcham church to be sold and the money from it distributed by my execs in works of charity for my soul and the souls of my parents and benefactors, as seems best to them to please God.

My dwelling house (*mansu'*) in which I live to remain to Alice my wife for term of her life, she paying and rendering all rents and services due for it and maintaining all kinds of reparations for that term; and after her death, the brewing lead[3] and malt mill to be retained in the said dwelling house (*reservent' predicto manso plumbum pandosatorum & mola pro brasio*); and after Alice's death, the dwelling house to be sold and the money to be distributed in works of charity for my soul and [*the souls*] of my wife, my parents and all the faithful departed.

To Alice my wife in ready money, or its worth, £6 13s 4d, the £3 6s 8d already received from [*her*] husband in her life[*time*] being counted (*tribus li sex solid' viij d a marito in vita sua premitus receptis computatis*); to Alice all my utensils and ostilments, that is, brass and pewter together with the bedding (*superlictilibus an[gli]ce* 'beddyng'), except that belonging to my body which I have given away (*donavi*); to Alice 4 'le flychys de bakoun' and half my cheese, wherever it may be, a quarter of wheat, a quarter of malt and 13lbs of blue-coloured wool, £3 in cash (*iij denariorum libra*), with all the firewood, timber and boards excepted.

To John Bole, at the time of the celebration of the marriage between him and my daughter, 5 marks, on condition that John purchases a tenement to the value of 10 marks, John to enfeoff me, the said William Orderych, or my daughter, or some other of my daughter's friends and one of John Bole's friends, with the condition that if John Bole dies before my daughter, the tenement should remain to Joan my daughter, his wife; that condition being fulfilled, I wish him to have the 5 marks, otherwise not – the price of a cow of the value of 7s, which John Bole has received from me, being included in the said sum of 5 marks.

To Isabel my daughter, at her marriage, 26s 8d.

Residue of all my goods, my debts being paid, to the disposition of my execs, to sell, receive, dispose and distribute for my soul and the souls for whom I am bound as seems best to please God.

Execs: John Orderych my son, Thomas Brome and Henry Colman; to each of them for [*their*] labour 20s.

Witnesses[*sic*]: John Bemys

Proved at Fornham St Martin, 24 March 1472 [*?new style*]. Admon to execs.

   1   Executor (as 'Ordrych') of John Gronger [of ?Hitcham], probate January 1458/59 (Pt I, no. 1047).

   2   The foundation of an almshouse at Hitcham.

   3   See Glossary.

[fol. 500]

588. JOHN EWSTASSE of ROUGHAM ('Rowham'), 27 April 1472

Dated at Rougham; to the buried in the churchyard of the church of St John the Baptist of Rougham; to the new tower of Rougham church £10.[1]

To my father and mother if they are alive 40s.

To the friars of Babwell for a trental 10s.[2]

To Matilda Walleworth a ewe and a lamb; to Robert Nunne the elder a ewe and a lamb; to John Kervere a ewe and a lamb; to Thomas Thakere a ewe and a lamb.

Thomas Maltywade and Roger Stanton to be my faithful execs; the residue of all my goods and chattels I put to their discretion to dispose, sell, receive and distribute for my soul and the souls for whom I am bound, to pay my debts, celebrate masses and do other works of charity as seems best to please God and profit the health of my soul.

Witnesses: George Downham, John Hachett.

Proved at Fornham St Martin, 25 May 1472. Admon to execs.

   1   Another substantial bequest to Rougham tower; see note to no. 184, and also no. 634 below.

   2   See note to no. 1.

589. ROBERT GOCHE of THELNETHAM, 20 March 1471/72

Of Thelnetham in the deanery of Blackbourn ('Blakburn'), in the diocese of Norwich; to be buried in the churchyard of Thelnetham parish church; for my tithes and offerings forgotten and negligently paid 3s 4d.

To Margery my wife 3 yards (*verg'*) of 'blanket'.

To John my son a black gown, a tunic and a small tunic.

To Thomas my son 6 yards of 'blankyt'.

To Thomas Ocle a blue gown.

I wish to have a trental at the Friars Preachers of Thetford;[1] I wish to have a suitable chaplain to celebrate after my decease for a whole year in Thelnetham church for my soul and my parents' and my friends' [*souls*].

Residue of all my goods to my execs, Valentine Stabilere, clerk,[2] and Thomas Hardy of Thelnetham, to pay my debts and legacies fully and do other deeds of piety for my soul.

Proved at Rickinghall ('Rykynghale'), 1 June 1472. Admon to execs.

   1   See note to no. 68.

   2   See note to no. 437.

[fol. 500v]

590. WALTER WALTERE of CONEY WESTON ('Conston'),[1] 9 January 1471/72

To be buried in the churchyard of Coney Weston church; to the high altar of which for tithes and offerings forgotten and not duly paid 6s 8d; to the fabric or emendation of the said church 5 marks; to Hopton church 6s 8d; to Fakenham Magna church 13s 4d; to the high altar of the church of the said Fakenham 2s.

To the convent of Augustinian Friars of Thetford 20s; to the Old Friars of the same town 6s 8d; to the nuns of Thetford, that is, to each sister of the house, 4d; to the Prioress of the same 8d; to the reparation of that house 3s 4d; to the friars of Babwell 6s 8d.[2]

To the emendation of the way leading through the middle of the town of Coney Weston 6s 8d; I wish to have a suitable priest celebrating in the parish [*church*] of Coney Weston for a whole year for my soul and my friends' [*souls*].

Isabel my wife to have all the utensils of my house.

Robert my son to have the tenement called 'Walterys' with all its appurtenances, paying Isabel 20s per annum during her life[*time*].

Thomas my son to have the tenement called 'Reynoldys' containing 24 acres of land with the messuage, paying to his mother 6s 8d [*per annum*] during her life[*time*].

Richard my son[3] to have the tenement in Fakenham Magna with all its appurtenances, paying to his mother 20s [*per annum*] during her life[*time*].

Isabel to have annually for term of her life the pasturing of 20 wethers (*arietes*) with Richard, at Richard's cost.

Richard to pay, after my decease, 25 marks to my execs; Robert my son, after my decease, to pay my execs £10.

Residue of all my goods, after my debts have been paid and my legacies fulfilled, I put to the disposition of my execs, John Walter of Hepworth, Robert Walter my son and Thomas Waltere, they to dispose it for my soul and the souls of all my friends as seems best to them to do. John Waltere to have 6s 8d for his labour; to each of the others 3s 4d.

Proved at Rickinghall ('Rykynghale'), 1 June 1472. Admon to execs.

[1] ?Related to Richard Walter of Coney Weston (no. 294 above).
[2] See notes to nos 1 (friars of Babwell), 68 (Dominicans of the Old House of Thetford and the Benedictine nuns of Thetford) and 69 (Augustinians of Thetford).
[3] Richard Walter (no. 294) bequeathed to 'Robert Walter my nephew 40d; to Richard Walter my nephew 20d; to Thomas Walter their brother 20d'. These sons of Walter Waltere of Coney Weston may have been those legatees. Richard Walter also made bequests to 'Alice Muryell their sister' and 'John Walter her brother'. This testator does not mention a daughter Alice or a son John, but both of them may have been older children who had already been provided for, indeed Richard's bequest indicates that Alice was married.

[fol. 501]

591. HENRY SALTER of BUXHALL ('Buxhale'), 11 March 1471/72

['Saltere' *in margin*] To be buried in the churchyard of Buxhall; to the high altar of the said church 12d.

To the house of Babwell 10s.[1]

To the ways from the house of Roger Saltere my father to the cross in 'Cherchestret' 20d; to the ways from the house 'Rysbyes' to 'Terrent' 20d.

To Ed' my brother my best bed.

To John Saltere my best hat and 20d; to Edward Saltere my white tunic and 20d.

To my godmother (*commatri*) 4 bushels (*modios*) of wheat.

To Katherine Barkere 4d and to Petronilla Chapeleyn 4d and to Agnes Hendy 4d.

To Walter my brother my tenement next to 'Fenstrett' called 'Rysbyes' with all its appurtenances lying in the town and fields of Buxhall, to hold to him and his heirs for ever, of the chief lords of the fee by due service and by customary right.

To Marion Saltere my sister 13s 4d; if it should happen that Marion dies within the year after my death, then I wish the said sum of 26s 8d[*sic*] to remain to the sustentation and reparation of the aforesaid church.[2]

Residue of all my goods to my execs, Edmund Saltere my brother and John Saltere the younger, to dispose for my soul as seems best to them to do; they, having God before their eyes, to execute my testament faithfully.

Proved at Creeting St Peter ('Cretynge *sancti Petri*'), 29 April 1472. Admon to execs.

[408] See note to no. 1.
[409] The first sum mentioned is definitely 13s 4d and the second 26s 8d.

592. RALPH SHERLYNGE of STOWMARKET, 10 April 1472

Dated at Stowmarket, on Friday 10 April 1472; my testament and last will; to be buried in the churchyard of the church of the blessed Apostles Peter and Paul of the said town;[1] to the high altar of the same church for tithes underpaid and forgotten 3s 4d; to the common sepulchre light in the same church at Easter time 3s 4d; to the maintenance and reparation of vestments and ornaments in the same church 3s 4d; to be disposed and distributed at the office of my burial 20s.

To be expended on the highway leading from Stow to Haughley ('Hawley') 6s 8d.

To Alice my wife all my hostilments and utensils of my house for her own profit and use.

The messuage with the appurtenances, which I hold of the feoffees of the property (*bonorum*) of the chapel of the Blessed Virgin Mary in the said church, to remain in the hands of their feoffees to dispose as they see best to please God and to the best profit of the said mass (*misse*), for its upkeep.[2]

My whole messuage, formerly Elizabeth Harpowre's, with all its appurtenances, rents and services, to remain to Alice my wife [fol. 501v] to provide for her and for her dwelling for her lifetime; and if she is in need in her old age, to sell it while she still lives as need demands.

Residue of all my goods, chattels and debts of whatsoever sort to the disposition of my execs and attorneys, John Wareyn, Robert Nekton and John Peyntour of Stow-market, they to be rewarded for their faithful labour as they deserve.

Proved at Stowmarket, 29 April 1472. Admon to John Wareyn and Robert Neketon, execs. Power reserved to John Peyntour, the other exec, when he comes.

[1] See note to no. 381.
[2] Possibly property previously bequeathed to the parish for the maintenance of the Lady Chapel.

593. WILLIAM WHYTE [of WETHERINGSETT], 20 February 1471/72

To be buried in the churchyard of the church of All Saints of Wetheringsett ('Wetheryngset'); to the high altar of the same church 12d.

To Joan my wife all my household (*domicil'*); to Joan my tenement with all my lands for term of her life, and after her decease, the tenement with all the lands to be sold by my execs and from the money received I leave to the emendation of the ways of the town of Wetheringsett, where there is greatest need, 5 marks.

To Henry my son 10s.

To each of my other [*omitted*] 6s 8d.

To the said church to the buying of an 'awter cloth' 3s 4d.

Residue of all my goods to my execs to sell and dispose for the health of my soul as they see best to please God and profit my soul.

Execs: Robert Godewyn and John Saham, to whom 3s 4d each.

Proved at Wyverstone ('Wyverston'), 30 April 1472. Admon to execs. Seal of official appended.

[fol. 502]

594. SIMON TURNOUR of COMBS ('Combes'), 26 March 1472

[*Commendation*: to Almighty God and the Blessed Mary]; my body [*to be buried*] in the churchyard of the same church; to the high altar of the same church for my tithes forgotten or underpaid 12d; to the east window of the south side of the said church 8s.

To the friars of Ipswich (*Gippewyc'*) to pray for my soul and for the souls of my friends 2s.[1]

To Agnes my wife all my moveable goods of whatever kind or type they be; Agnes my wife to have my tenement [*in which*] I now reside, to her and her heirs for ever; to Agnes my other tenement for her whole life, and after her decease it to be sold and the money from it to be disposed in masses, alms and other pious works for my soul and the soul of Agnes and for the souls of our parents and friends; and if any of my sons or daughters wishes to buy my tenement [*when*] being sold, they to have it at a lower price than any outsider (*extraneus*).

Executrix: my beloved in Christ, Agnes my wife.

Seal appended.

Proved at Buxhall ('Buxhale'), 4 June 1472. Admon to executrix.

[1] The testator did not specify which friars of Ipswich; see notes to nos 1 (Franciscans and Carmelites of Ipswich) and 50 (Dominicans).

595. STEPHEN BYRD of KERSEY, 'husbundeman', 10 April 1472

Of Kersey, in the diocese of Norwich; my testament containing my last will; [*commendation*: to Almighty God my Creator and Saviour, the Blessed Mary his mother and all the saints]; to be buried in the churchyard of the church of St Mary of Kersey, next to the bodies of my children buried there; to the high altar of the same church for my tithes and offerings forgotten and withheld, in exoneration of my soul, 20d; the expenses of my funeral to be duly and honestly done by the good order and discretion of my execs.

All my debts which I owe of right to anyone to be paid and satisfied immediately after my decease; after that, to the convent of the Friars Minor of Colchester (*Colcestre*) 10s for a trental.[1]

To Bryghtena my wife my tenements called 'Smertes' and 'Dowys', with all their appurtenances, to hold to her and her assigns for term of her life of the chief lords of the fees by the services relating to the said tenements; and after her decease, the tenements to revert to Rose my daughter and her heirs if she is then alive, and if not, the tenements to be sold by my feoffees, or by theirs, and the money from them to be disposed in works of charity for my soul and the souls of our parents and benefactors and of all the faithful departed as seems best to them to please Almighty God and profit our souls.

Residue of all my goods, chattels and debts, of whatever sort and wherever they be, after the payment of my debts and my funerals done and my legacies fulfilled, I leave wholly to Bryghtena my wife to do with and to dispose at her free will for ever, without contradiction of anyone, and of it to dispose for my soul and the souls for whom I am most bound and the souls of all the faithful departed as seems to her best to please God and profit the health of my soul.

Execs: Bryghtena my wife and John Marshall her brother, labourer.

Seal appended.

Proved at Kersey, 5 June 1472. Admon to execs.

1   See note to no. 38.

[fol. 502v]
596. ALICE BROOK of SUDBURY, widow, 12 February 1466/7

Dated at Sudbury, in the diocese of Norwich; infirm of body; to be buried in the churchyard of the church of St Gregory of Sudbury; to the high altar of the same church for tithes and offerings forgotten 10s; to Sir John Wryght, parish chaplain of the same church,[1] 3s 4d; for 3 trentals of St Gregory to be celebrated in the said church, that is, for my soul and the souls of John my late husband[2] and Robert our son,[3] immediately after my decease, one after the other in succession, 30s; to each priest present at my obsequies [*and*] on my thirty-day, both religious and secular, to be distributed to them at the discretion of my execs, and to the clerks and boys present there, according to the discretion of my execs [*no sum*]; my execs to find a secular priest to celebrate divine service in the said church of St Gregory for our souls aforesaid, for a whole year, as quickly as it can conveniently be done.

To the 6 children of John Brook the elder, my son,[4] and the 2 children of John Brook the younger,[5] my other son, each of them, for themselves, 20d.

To Sir John Baas, chaplain, my son, 6s 8d.

To John Brook the elder, my son, a cow, he to pay John Brook the younger, my son, in money, 6s.

Residue of all my goods to my execs, they to pay my debts out of it and dispose as they see best to please God and most profit the health of my soul.

Execs: John Brook the younger and John Brook the elder, my sons; to each of them for their labour 13s 4d.

Seal appended.

Proved at Sudbury, 6 June 1472. Admon to execs.

1   Witness of the will of Thomas Lavenham of Sudbury (SROB, Baldwyne 258; Pt I, no. 1273); see also nos 32 and 434 above.

2   Will of John Brook the elder of Sudbury, 'wever', pr. January 1454/55 (SROB, Baldwyne 232;
     Pt I, no. 1168); although designated a weaver, he was obviously not a lowly tradesman since he
     possessed a capital messuage and at least one other tenement.
3   Legatee of his father but obviously dead by the time his mother made her will; he was under age
     when his father made his will, and at that time there was a possibility that he would take holy
     orders.
4   Executor of his father; his father had bequeathed him his weaving loom.
5   Legatee of his father.

597. PATRICK KEDLOWE of NEWTON, 5 April 1472

Dated at Newton, in the diocese of Norwich; sick in body; my testament containing my last will; to be buried in the churchyard of the church of All Saints of Newton; to the high altar of which for my tithes forgotten 12d; to the painting of the image of the Blessed Mary there my best sanguine-coloured gown; a cow to the sustentation of the light of a lamp burning before the image of St Saviour[1] in Newton church at the time of divine service on feast days.

Residue of all my goods together with my debts to David my son and Marion his wife to be at their own will, they to pray especially for my soul; they to be my execs to fulfil the above legacies.

Witnesses: Sir Thomas Hollond, chaplain there, Robert Jordan and Ed' Waspe of Newton.

Proved at Sudbury, 6 June 1472. Admon to execs.

1   An 'image of St Saviour' was an image of Christ that depicted an aspect of his Passion.

[fol. 503]
598. JOHN DOWE of BARNARDISTON ('Barnardeston'),[1] 3 April 1472

Of Barnardiston, in the diocese of Norwich; knowing the end of my present life [*to be near*]; my body to Christian burial in the churchyard of the parish church of All Saints of Barnardiston ('Bernardeston'), with my due mortuary; to the Augustinian Friars of Clare for celebrating a trental for my soul and the souls of all my benefactors 10s.[2]

To Alice my daughter a tenement lying in Colchester, in the parish of St Mary the Virgin, for her marriage, or, for (*pro*) the said tenement 4 marks in money, that is, after the decease of Agnes my wife.

To Rose my daughter another tenement, lying next to the aforesaid tenement, that is, after the decease of the said Agnes my wife, for her marriage, or 4 marks in money.

To Simon Jonson a gown of 'musterdelere'.

To Thomas Dowe my uncle (*avunculo*) a blue gown.

Residue of all my goods to Agnes my wife to see to my funerals and pay my debts and distribute for my soul and for the souls of all my benefactors as seems most expedient to her; she to be my faithful executrix, to implement my will in all things as above-written.

Seal appended.

Witnesses: Sir Richard Simpson, rector of the church of Barnardiston,[3] John Heyward, John Cukkoo and others.

Proved at Hundon ('Hunden'), 16 April 1472. Admon to executrix.

1   In 1441, one John Dowe owed money to William Hay of Barnardiston, will pr. May 1441 (SROB, Baldwyne 13; Pt I, no. 85).
2   See note to no. 1.
3   Richard Simpson was rector of Barnardiston from June 1471 until April 1483 (Tanner, p.1224); he was executor of John Smyth of Barnardiston (no. 655).

599. JOHN WARNERE [of GREAT LIVERMERE], 10 April 1472

To be buried in the churchyard of the church of St Peter the Apostle of Great Livermere ('Livermere Magna'); to the high altar of the same church for my tithes forgotten and underpaid 3s 4d; to the emendation of the same church 3s 4d.

To the friars of Babwell for a trental 10s; to the Friars Preachers of Thetford 6s 8d.[1] To John Dantre 6s 8d.

To Katherine my wife,[2] out of the money received from the sale of my tenement in Livermere ('Lyvermere') aforesaid, 6 marks; further, to Katherine the cows, sheep and all the cattle (*catall'*) and all my hostilments.

Residue of all my goods and chattels, moveable and unmoveable, to my execs to dispose and distribute according to their discretion in the best way they see to profit the health of my soul, of [*my*] parents, benefactors and all the faithful departed and faithfully to execute all the premises in this testament as specified above.

Execs: Katherine my wife and John Hawe.

Proved at Fornham St Martin, 11 May 1472. Admon to execs.

1   For the friars see notes to nos 1 (Babwell) and 68 (Thetford).
2   Katherine, the wife of John Warner of Great Livermere, was a beneficiary of the will of Thomas Gatle of Great Livermere, pr. January 1440/41 (SROB, Baldwyne 32; Pt I, no. 180). Her will is no. 760 below.

[fol. 503v]
600. THOMAS FRYOT of BARROW ('Barowe'),[1] 4 December 1471 [*English*]

Of Barrow, in the county of Suffolk; my body to be buried in the churchyard afore-written; to the altar for tithes forgotten 3s 4d.

My wife Margery to have the place on the green between 'Stevys' and 'Harwellys' and the land called 'Py Rowe'; Margery to have all my household and a horse, a cow and an acre of barley.

The friars of Thetford to have 5s;[2] the church of Barrow to have 6s 8d; 6s 8d to the poor people.

John Fryot my son to have the place at 'Holmys', save he shall pay in 4 years 4 marks, if it may be borne.

Thomas and Herry[*sic*] my sons each to have 8 marks, if it may be borne; Margaret, Joan and Agnes my daughters to have 4 marks each, if it will be borne.

My house and my land to be sold and my 'qwethe word' be fulfilled with it; if any of my sons will buy my house or land, they to be preferred before any other man.

My execs to be John my son and Thomas my son.

Witnesses: John Symond, John Hardgrey,[3] John Jekeman and others.

Proved at Fornham St Martin, 8 June 1472. Admon to Thomas Fryot exec. Power reserved to John Fryot, the other exec, when he comes, if he wishes to take up admon.

1   Executor (as 'Fryote') of John Warner of Barrow, will pr. October 1452 (SROB, Baldwyne 109; Pt I, no. 494).

2   For the friars of Thetford, see notes to nos 68 (Dominicans) and 69 (Augustinians).

3   ?(As 'Harlegrey'), son and executor of Henry Harlegrey of Mildenhall, will pr. June 1458 (SROB, Baldwyne 243; Pt I, no. 1219); in his will, dated 1472, John Hardgrey mentioned the gild of St Mary of Icklingham (*PSIA*, xxiii, p.62).

[fol. 504]

601. ED' MAYNERE of GREAT THURLOW ('Magna Thyrlowe'), 20 October 1471

My body to Christian burial in Thurlow ('Thyrlow') aforesaid; to the vicar of the same church 4s which I owe him for celebrating for the souls of my parents; 10s to be distributed and given to the poor to pray for my soul.

To John Valentyn 12d to pray for my soul.

To Thomas my son 2 cows, a brass pot [*and*] a pan, and to William my son 2 cows, a brass pot and a pan.

To the reparation of the torches in the same town 3s 4d.

To the sustentation of the sepulchre light 3s 4d.

To Eleanor my wife all my goods and chattels, moveable and unmoveable, wherever they may be found, to pay my debts and legacies and fulfil my last will; Eleanor to have all my lands and tenements, with all their appurtenances, for term of her life, she to keep the house and close of the said tenement in good repair all the time of her life, [*holding them*] of the chief lords of the fee by due service and by customary right for ever.

After the decease of Eleanor, William my son to have all the said lands and tenements, with all their appurtenances, to him and his heirs, he to pay to Thomas his brother £20 in 3 years, by equal portions, after the decease of his mother. If William should die during the lifetime (*vivente*) of Thomas his brother, then Thomas to have all the said lands and tenements, he to give the child with which his mother is now pregnant £20. If William, Thomas and the child now in my wife's womb should go the way of all flesh (*viam carnis universe ingredi*) before having the said lands and tenements, then my execs to sell all of them, with all of their appurtenances, wholly and undivided, and the money received from them to be distributed by my execs in works of charity for the health of my soul and of the souls of all my benefactors as seems to them best to please God and profit my soul.

Execs: Eleanor my wife, William Hoberd and Thomas Smyth *alias* Barkere.

Seal appended.

I leave 6s 8d and 6 silver spoons to providing a new chalice for the church of Thurlow aforesaid.

Proved at Stoke Clare, 14 November 1471. Admon to Eleanor and Thomas Smyth *alias* Barkere, co-execs. Power reserved to William Hoberd, the other exec, when he comes, if he wishes to take up admon.

[fol. 504v]

602. WILLIAM NEEL of FORDHAM [*Cambs*], 24 October 1471

Dated the Thursday after the feast of St Luke the Evangelist 1471; to be buried in the churchyard of the church of the Blessed Mary of Fordham; to the high altar of the said church for my tithes forgotten 3 bushels of barley; to the work of the reparation of the said church an acre of land lying in the field of Fordham, which I lately purchased of the exec of John Rous.

3 roods of land, which I lately purchased of my father, to be sold straightaway after my decease by my execs and the money raised to be bestowed in the celebration of prayers and masses in Fordham parish church in this way: that is, on the principal feasts of the Nativity of our Lord, Easter and Pentecost, a friar chaplain of Cambridge (*Cantebr'*) to celebrate divine service in the said church for my soul and the souls of my benefactors and of all the faithful departed.[1]

To Margaret my wife my principal tenement for term of her life, she to repair it as often as necessary, and after her decease, it to remain to Andrew our son; if he should die in his mother's lifetime, the tenement to be sold after Margaret's decease and disposed for our souls in pious works.

To Andrew our son the whole tenement that I purchased of William Berhors, that is, I wish it to remain to the use of my wife, with the duty of repairing it, until Andrew reaches legal age; if he should die in the lifetime of his mother, the tenement to remain to his mother for term of her life, and after her decease, in the same way as my principal tenement, above, to be sold and disposed.

To John Turfyge an acre of bond land lying in (*sub*) 'West fen' and to William Turfyge another acre lying diversely in the same field, a 3 rood [*strip*] and 1 rood lying in the same furlong (*quarentena*).

To John Cok an acre of bond land lying in 'Gosecrofte'.

To Margaret my wife and her assigns another acre of bond land lying in 'le Halys'; to Margaret for term of her life my other lands not bequeathed, together with my other goods and debts, she to pay my debts and fulfil my will. After the decease of Margaret, the land not bequeathed, with the said tenements, to be sold in the best way by my execs and feoffees, and all the money from them to go to finding a suitable chaplain to celebrate divine service for our souls and [*the souls of*] all the faithful and in other works of mercy.

Execs: Margaret my wife, John Thebade and William Cheswryth, to execute my testament as they would wish it were performed for me and as they know best to please God and profit my soul; and to each of my execs undertaking the execution of my testament 5s.

Supervisor: Andrew Cheswryth, chaplain,[2] faithfully to execute it to the greatest health of my soul.

Proved at Newmarket (*Novum Mercat'*), 15 November 1471. Admon to execs.

[1]   Fordham parish church belonged to the priory of the order of Gilbertines that was situated in Fordham. In 1307 the priory had appropriated the vicarage and the church probably remained incorporated with it until the priory's surrender in 1538 (*VCH Cambs*, x, pp.412–17). This bequest for a 'friar chaplain of Cambridge' to celebrate in the church might have caused tension with the regular clergy in the priory.

[2]   See note to no. 60.

[fol. 505]
[*No. 603 and the beginning of no. 604 have been written in the same hand, which is different from the rest of Baldwyne. '1461' occurs 3 times in the part so written: possibly an error for 1471.*]

603. JOHN WEBBE of ELMSWELL ('Elmeswell'), 20 January 1461/62[*sic*]

Dated at Elmswell; to be buried in the manner of all faithful Christians in the churchyard of Elmswell parish church; to the high altar of the same church for my tithes forgotten 12d; for a chalice to be newly bought 12d.

To some friars to celebrate a trental 10s.

To Alice my wife all my goods, moveable and unmoveable, provided that she honestly feeds and maintains my father during his lifetime, as far as she is able, out of those goods; he being dead, the goods remaining, if any, after the decease of Alice my wife, to be disposed according to her will for my soul and the souls of my benefactors.

Executrix: Alice my wife.

Seal appended.

Proved at Ixworth, 18 February 1461/62[*sic*]. Admon to executrix.

604. THOMAS SPENCERE of BARDWELL ('Berdwell'), 4 November 1461[*sic*]

My testament and last will; my body to Christian burial in the churchyard of Bard-well parish church; to the high altar of the said church 12d; to Bardwell church 13s 4d, to be paid when my execs can conveniently do so; to Langham church 6s 8d, to be paid in the same way.

To Agnes my daughter 3 acres of my land, of which 1½ acres lie in the furlong (*quarentener'*) called 'le Croftes' and the other 1½ acres lie in 'le Bowrys', for term of her life.

To Elizabeth my daughter 2 acres of land lying between the gates (*portas*) for term of her life.

To each of my godsons and goddaughters a bushel (*modiu'*) of barley.

To the convent of the Friars Minor of Babwell a coomb of barley; to the convent of the Friars Minor[*sic*] of Thetford a coomb of barley; to the convent of the Augustinian Friars of Thetford a coomb of barley; to the convent of the Friars Minor of Babwell 10s for a trental to be celebrated there.[1]

To John my son 7 acres of my land which he now possesses, to hold to him and his heirs for ever of the chief lord &c[*sic*]; to John my messuage with the adjacent croft and a croft called 'Welhowsyerd', with their appurtenances, in the second year after the decease of his mother, if he behaves himself in due manner towards his mother in the eyes of God and the world (*secundum deum mundum*), and provided that he heeds (*pendeat in*) the will and disposition of his mother; to John the profit of an acre of meadow each year during the life of his mother, and if it is sold during that time, or after, I wish him to have preference in the buying of it before others if he is willing and able to buy.

To Isabel my wife all my lands and tenements, meadows, pasture and feedings, with all their appurtenances, not bequeathed, to her heirs for ever, she to pay all my debts and implement my testament and will; to Isabel all my utensils and bedding and animals.

After their deaths, I wish the land above assigned to my daughters to be sold by my execs and disposed for my soul.

I wish the said acre of meadow, the crop and profit from which is assigned to John my son, [fol. 505v] to be sold after my wife's death and if John wishes to buy that land and meadow when they are sold, he to have preference over others.

Residue of all my goods to Isabel my wife, William Mannynge and Thomas Goore, execs; to William and Thomas 12d each; they to execute for my soul as they see best to please God and profit my soul.

Proved 18 February 1471/72. Admon to Isabel, executrix. Power reserved to the other execs when they come, if they wish to take up admon.

<hr>

¹ For the friars see notes to nos 1 (Babwell), and 69 (Augustinians of Thetford); as there was no house of Friars Minor (Franciscans) at Thetford it seems likely that this is an error for Friars Preachers (see note to no. 68).

605. AGNES HAWKERE of ELMSWELL ('Elmeswell'), December 1471
[*nuncupative*]

['Hawken' *in margin*] Dated in the week of the Nativity of our Lord 1471 [*22–28 December*]; [*commendation*: to God Almighty]; her body to the Christian burial of Hunston; she left 3lbs of wax to the sepulchre light (*in stipite sepulchro*) of Hunston church; she left 30s to provide (*ad exhibend'*) the anniversary of Ralph Hawkere her husband and of herself for as long as the 30s will last.

Exec: Robert Palmer of Elmswell ('Elmysswell').

Proved at Ixworth, [*no date*]. Admon to exec.

606. WILLIAM BERNARD of THURSTON ('Thruston'), 7 March 1471/72

Dated at Thurston; to be buried in the churchyard of the church of St Peter of Thurston; to the high altar of the same church 12d; to the friars of the order of St Dominic of Thetford ('Thedford') 20d;¹ to the friars of the order of St Francis of Babwell ('Babwelle') 20d;² to the sustentation of the light of the Blessed Mary burning in the same church 10d.

To Richard Bernard my son 12d; to *Dido* [*or, Dide*] Bernard my son 12d; to Margaret my daughter 12d.

Residue of all my goods to John Man of Thurston to do with them as seems best, that is, to dispose for my soul and the souls of all my friends, and to pay my debts; he to be my faithful exec.

Seal appended.

Proved at Fornham, 21 March 1471/72. Admon to exec.

<hr>

¹ See note to no. 68.
² See note to no. 1.

[fol. 506]
607. JOHN KENDALE the elder of SUDBURY, 2 March 1471/72

Dated at Sudbury, in the diocese of Norwich; [*commendation includes*: to the most Blessed Mary his mother]; my body to Christian burial in the churchyard of St Gregory of Sudbury; I beg my execs, in God's name, to pay all my debts that I owe; to the high altar of the church of St Peter of Sudbury for my tithes and offerings forgotten and underpaid 13s 4d; to the reparation of the said church of St Peter 100s. To Joan Cook my daughter 5 marks.

To the wife of William Halle of Sudbury 20s; to the wife of William Herd of Sudbury 20s.

To John Kendale of Sudbury, butcher, 5 marks in good (*mera*) money; to each of the daughters of the said John Kendale, butcher, 20s

All the utensils or hostilments and bedding of my house to be divided among my daughters and the said John Kendale by my execs, except the jewels, which I leave to my execs for the performance of my testament.

All the apparel (*apparat'*) belonging to my body to be distributed among the poor of Sudbury in greatest need by my execs.

To the convent of the friars of the Sudbury house, for carrying out the reparation of the church there 10s.[1]

To the wife of William Sternrell ('St'nrell') of Sudbury 13s 4d.

To the reparation of the church of Great Cornard ('Cornerd Magna') 40d.

My execs, as quickly after my death as they can, to find a secular priest to celebrate divine service in the said church of St Peter for my soul and for the souls of all the faithful departed for 2 years and more if it can be done, he taking for his salary 8 marks 6s 8d; my execs to provide my anniversary for 10 years after my decease in the said chapel of St Peter, distributing to priests, clerks and the poor in greatest need to the sum of 20s; I bequeath a shop opposite the church of St Peter, that is, on the north side of the church, for the poor to live in for ever.[2]

Residue of all my goods, together with my debts, I leave in the hands of my execs, Sir John Potager[3] and George Prentis of Sudbury, to implement all the above, as they will answer before the High Judge on the Day of Judgement.

In God's name, I require all my feoffees and co-feoffees in all my lands and tenements to deliver their estate in them in accordance with this my testament when so required by my execs.

To each of my execs for their labour beyond their reasonable expenses in this business 6s 8d.

Seal appended.

Proved at Lavenham, 24 March 1471/2. Admon to execs.

[*See fol. 459, no. 465 above, a version of this will that was struck through.*]

1 See note to no. 11.
2 A bequest to found an almshouse in the market place on the north side of St Peter's, Sudbury.
3 See note to no. 271.

[fol. 506v]

608. JOHN TURNOUR of GREAT THURLOW ('Thyrlowe Magna'), gentleman,[1] 28 October 1471

['Turnewe' *in margin*] Dated at Great Thurlow ('Thillowe Magna'), in the diocese of Norwich; sick unto death, knowing the end of my present life to be near; my body to Christian burial in the chancel of the parish church of All Saints of the said Thurlow; to the high altar there 6s 8d; to the reparation of the same church 20s; to the making of torches in the same church 3s 4d; to the reparation of the lower church of the Blessed Mary in Haverhill 10s.[2]

To each of my brothers and sisters a quarter of barley.

To each of my servants 2 bushels (*modios*) of barley.

My execs to provide for a suitable chaplain to celebrate for my soul and for the souls of all [*my*] benefactors for a whole year.

Residue of all my goods to Thomasine my wife to see to my funerals and to pay all my debts and to distribute for my soul and for the souls of all my benefactors as seems best to her to profit the health of my soul.

My faithful execs to be Thomasine my wife and Henry Turnour, esquire;[3] they to fulfil all in my will as above.

Seal appended.

Proved at Stradishall ('Stradeshull'), 12 March 1471/72. Admon to Thomasine, wife of the deceased and executrix. Power reserved to Henry Turnowr, the other exec, when he comes, if he wishes to take up admon.

1 Perhaps the John Turnour of Haverhill, son of Henry, who had married Thomasine, daughter and co-heir of Henry Caldebeck and his wife Cecily; John and Thomasine had sons named Henry and John (Hervy, *Visitation of Suffolk 1561*, vol. I, pp.77–8). According to Weever, in 1464 Henry Turnour senior, his two wives and his son John lay buried in the choir of Haverhill church (Hervy, p.78). Given Weever's observations and the coincidence here of the executors' names with the names of the wife and son of the John Turnour identified by Hervy in the *Visitation*, it seems likely that this testator was another son of Henry senior also named John.

2 See note to no. 13 concerning the churches in Haverhill.

3 Probably the son of the testator; see note above. Perhaps he was also the Henry Turnour of Haverhill esquire who, in March 1465/66, was executor of Joan Deynys of Sudbury, widow (no. 259); Henry's will pr. 1498 (TNA, PCC 20 Horne; now PROB11/11, image 250).

[fol. 507]

609. MARGARET PAGE of KIRTLING ('Kertelynge') [Cambs], 29 February 1471/72

Dated the last day of February 1471/72; to be buried in the churchyard of All Saints of Kirtling; to the high altar of Kirtling a half part of 5 roods of wheat and the other part to the fabric of the same church; to the convent and friars of Babwell[1] 10s to celebrate a trental for my soul; to the lights of the Blessed Mary in the chapel and in the church, a cow.

I wish my messuage to be sold.

Residue of all my goods to Thomas Pychese[2] and Thomas Mundson, my execs, to dispose for the health of [*my*] soul as seems to them best to please God and profit my soul.

Seal appended.

Witnesses: John Sutton, Thomas Pychese the younger and many others.

Proved at Hawkedon, 14 May 1472. Admon to execs.

1 See note to no. 1.
2 Thomas Pychese was executor of Walter Derysle (no. 577).

610. THOMAS TYLBROOK[1] of UPEND ('Hupem Hamelett')[2] in KIRTLING ('Kertelynge') [Cambs], 1472

Dated at Upend hamlet in the parish of Kirtling; [*only the year given*]; to be buried in the churchyard of the church of All Saints of Kirtling; to the high altar of the same church for tithes forgotten 20d.

To Agnes my wife all my grain, my debts having been paid from it first; to Agnes all my utensils and ostilments, except a brass pot that I wish to be sold for the health of my soul.

2s to be paid equally among 12 poor [*folk*] to pray for the soul of John Mayn, formerly rector of Kirtling church[3] and of Richard Coke of the same.

Residue to the disposition of my execs, Agnes my wife and Walter Derysle and Thomas Kreke, they to dispose as seems to them best to please God and profit my soul.

Seal appended.

Proved at Hawkedon, 14 May 1472. Admon to Agnes Tylbrok and Walter Derysle, execs. Power reserved to Thomas Kreke, the other co-exec, when he comes, if he wishes to undertake admon.

> [1]   Executor of his father Peter Tilbrook of Kirtling, will pr. November 1445 (SROB, Baldwyne 69; Pt I, no. 337); brother of John Tylbrok of Upend in Kirtling (no. 499 above).
> [2]   See note to no. 482.
> [3]   John Mayn must have been rector of Kirtling some time before August 1462, when Richard Frankeleyn was appointed rector there (Tanner, p.1279).

[fol. 507v]

611. JOHN COWERN of MILDENHALL ('Myldenhale'), 23 April 1472

Dated at Mildenhall; my testament and last will; [*commendation*: to Almighty God my Redeemer and Saviour and to the Blessed Mary his mother [*and*] all the saints]; my body to Christian burial; to the high altar of Mildenhall church, for tithes and offerings underpaid, 6d.

To Margaret Taylour, my household servant, a brass pot and a pair of sheets.

To Katherine Sterre, daughter of William Sterre of Worlington ('Wrydlyngton'), another brass pot.

To Isabel Sterre a table (*mensam*) and a cupboard.

Residue of all my goods to the sound discretion of my execs to dispose for my soul as seems best to them to please God and profit the health of my soul.

Execs: John Grene of Mildenhall, chaplain,[1] John Dobyn and William Sterre of Worlington.

Seal appended.

Proved at Herringswell ('Heryngeswell'), 15 May 1472. Admon to execs.

> [1]   Two other Mildenhall parishioners, Thomas Dokkyng (no. 635) and John Wareyn (no. 638), also appointed John Grene as their executor.

612. JOHN PAGE of WORLINGTON ('Wrydlyngton'), 1 May 1472

Dated the Kalends of May 1472; my body to Christian burial in the churchyard of the church of All Saints of Worlington; to the high altar for my tithes forgotten [*and*] not well paid 12d; to the fabric of the church for my soul and my father's soul 13s 4d.

Margaret my wife to have my messuage with 2 acres of land and half an acre of meadow, lying in divers pieces in the fields of Worlington and Freckenham ('Frekenham') for term of her life. After her decease, Thomas my son to have the said tenement[*sic*] with 2 acres of land and half an acre of meadow, to him and his heirs. If Thomas decease, the messuage, with the 2 acres of land and half-acre of meadow, to be divided between my two daughters [*if*] alive (*viventibus*); if all my daughters decease, the messuage, with the 2 acres of land and half-acre of meadow to revert to the legitimate heirs of my father.

Residue of all my goods, moveable and unmoveable, to my wife, my funerals done and debts [*paid*].

My faithful execs: Sir Simon Bakhot, rector of Worlington church,[1] and John Eton of Freckenham; they to dispose for my soul as they see best to please God and profit my soul.

Proved at Herringswell ('Heryngeswell'), 15 May 1472. Admon to execs.

1   Simon Bakhot was rector of Worlington from 1447 to 1474 (Tanner, p.1289); it is likely that he was a member of the Bakhot family of Mildenhall (see note to no. 229); in 1434 Simon witnessed the will of Richard Bakhot of Mildenhall (NRO, NCC 181 Surflete) as 'chaplain'.

[fol. 508]
613. MARION NUNE of THORPE MORIEUX ('Thorpmeryus'), widow, 20 August 1474

Dated at Thorpe Morieux, the Saturday after the feast of the Assumption of the Blessed Mary 1474; [*commendation*: to God Almighty, the Blessed Mary &c]; to be buried in the churchyard of the parish church of the Blessed Mary of Thorpe Morieux ('Thorpmerux'); I wish my debts to be paid before all else; to the high altar of the said church for my tithes and offerings forgotten 3s 4d; to the reparation and sustentation of the said church 20s.

To the convent of friars of Babwell to celebrate for my soul and the souls of my friends a trental of St Gregory 10s.[1]

I wish to have a suitable priest to celebrate for my soul and the souls of my friends for half a year in Thorpe Morieux ('Thorpm") church.

To Alice my daughter my largest brass pot, my best lined (*penulata'*) gown, a mattress (*materas*) called 'a donge', a cloth (*vestem*) called 'a blanket' and a coverlet (*coopertoriu'*) called 'a coverlyght', a silvered silk girdle and a chest.

To Agnes my daughter another brass pot, a 'blanket' and a 'coverlyth', my lined tunic, a pair of beads with the silver ring.

To William [*my*] son the third brass pot, a 'blanket'.

To Henry my son a brass pan holding 3 gallons, a 'blanket'.

To Robert my son a spit and an andiron ('aunderne'), a 'blanket'.

To William, Henry and Robert my sons 16 pieces of pewter, equally between them; to my aforesaid daughters my basins with a ewer (*uno lavour'*) and my candlesticks, to be divided equally between them; to my sons and daughters aforesaid all my sheets, equally between them.

To Joan, wife of Richard Clerk of Preston, 6s 8d in money.

My execs to fulfil the last will of John Nune my late husband,[2] in the following words: firstly, he left 10s to the convent of friars of Babwell to celebrate for his soul and all his friends' souls a trental of St Gregory; to the convent of friars of Sudbury similarly 10s;[3] to the said Marion he left all the money coming from the legacy of George Nune [*relationship omitted*] of John Nune, my late husband, to descend equally to my sons and daughters then alive, according to the tenor of the testament of the said George, when they come to the age of 18; and if any of them dies before that age, then that part to remain among those living, down to the last child.

Residue of all my goods to my execs to dispose for my soul and my friends' souls to please God for the health of my soul and my friends' [*souls*].

Execs: John Nune of Felsham[4] and Robert Bekysby of Thorpe aforesaid.

Seal appended.

Witnesses: Sir Robert Chapman, rector of Thorpe,[5] Hugh Wryght of Bildeston ('Bylston') and William Cooke of the same.

Proved at Cockfield ('Cokefeld'), 3 November 1474. Admon to execs.

1   See note to no. 1.
2   The will of her husband has not survived. The wife of John Nune the elder of Rougham (no. 634) was named Isabel.
3   For the friars see notes to nos 1 (Babwell) and 11 (Sudbury).
4   John Nunne the elder of Felsham was executor of Baldewin Coksedge (no. 417) and executor of John Nune the elder of Rougham (no. 634).
5   See note to no. 131.

[fol. 508v]

614. THOMAS AUNCELL the younger of STANSTEAD ('Stansted'), 23 June 1474 [*English*]

Dated at Stanstead; [*commendation to* God Almighty, to our Lady Saint Mary &c]; to be buried in the churchyard of Stanstead.

To my father my best bullock and my mother a cow; to my father half my corn in the field, that is, 2½ acres of wheat, 3 acres of barley, 3 roods of peas ('pesyn') and oats.

To my wife my other half of my grains.

Residue of all my goods to my father to dispose for my soul and pay my debts.

Exec: Thomas Auncell my father, he to fulfil my last will.

Witnesses: John Lensere[?], fuller, and others.

Proved at Cockfield ('Cokefeld'), 3 November 1474. Admon to exec.

[fol. 509]

615. THOMAS MARTHAM of RATTLESDEN ('Ratlesden'), 30 August 1474

Dated at Rattlesden, the penultimate day of August 1474; [*commendation*: to Almughty God, the Blessed Mary &c]; to be buried in the churchyard of the said church; to the high altar of the same church for my tithes forgotten 3s 4d.

To Alice my wife all my lands and tenements in Rattlesden, to hold to her and her heirs for the whole term of her life; and after her decease, all the said lands and tenements with their appurtenances to be sold by my execs for the best price that they can, and from the money arising from them, I assign [*the following*]: one part, to the making (*enfectionem*) of a canopy ('canepe') over the altar in the said church, 40s; to the emendation of the way next to my gate 40s; to Joan my daughter 40s; to Peter my son 10 marks in money; to the sustentation of the gild of the Holy Trinity there 12d and to the sustentation of the gild of St Margaret 12d;[1] to the convent of friars of Babwell[2] for a trental of St Gregory to be celebrated there for the health of my soul and for the souls of all my benefactors 10s.

Residue of all my goods to the disposition of all my execs, my beloved in Christ, Peter Rednale, John Abell and Robert Rogyn, to dispose as seems best to them to profit the health of my soul and please God.

Seal appended.

Proved at Ixworth, 10 January 1474/75. Admon to execs.

1   No other testator in the Baldwyne register made a bequest to the gild of the Holy Trinity in Rattlesden. John Rogyn also made a bequest to the gild of St Margaret (SROB, Baldwyne 207;

Pt I, no. 1031); as did William Comayan (no. 536 above). There was a gild of St John the Baptist there at this time as well (see no. 536).

2   See note to no. 1.

616. JOHN ROBERD of LAWSHALL ('Lawshull'), 18 January 1474/75
[*probate only*]

Proved at Cockfield ('Cokefeld'). Admon to execs.

[fol. 509v]
617. THOMAS LEWYN of STUSTON, 13 April 1473

Dated at Stuston; [*commendation*: to God Almighty, the Blessed Mary &c]; to be buried in the churchyard of the church of All Saints in the same town; to the high altar of the same town for my tithes forgotten 4d.

Margaret my wife to have my built-up messuage, with all its appurtenances, during her life. If it happens that Margaret is unable to live well by her own means (*per se*), then the messuage to be sold by my execs and the money received from it, as it arises (*cresc'*), to be given (*deliber'*) annually by my execs to Margaret for her maintenance during her life; if any money from said messuage remains after Margaret's decease, that money to be spent in pious uses for my soul and Margaret's soul and the souls of my friends and benefactors by my execs. To Margaret all my utensils with all my moveable chattels.

If Henry Harald wishes to buy the said messuage, he to have [*it*] before others and he to give as good a price as others are willing [*to give*].

Residue of all my goods to the disposition of my execs, John Wareyn of Stuston and the said Henry Harald of the same, they to dispose as they see best to please God and profit my soul.

Seal appended.

Proved at Eye, 11 January 1474/75. Admon to execs.

618. ED' NORIS of PALGRAVE, 20 November 1474

[*Commendation*: to God Almighty &c]; to be buried in the churchyard of Palgrave church; to the high altar of the said church 12d; to the gild of St Peter 40d;[1] to the making of a cross in the churchyard of St Peter of Palgrave 13s 4d; to the bells 12d; to the reparation of the walls 12d; to the emendation of the ways 12d; I wish a trental to be celebrated in Palgrave church for the health of my soul and the souls of all my benefactors

To William my son a close at the mill and a pair of millstones (*unum per' molare*) and the third brass pot.

To Margery my daughter 3s 4d and the largest brass pot and the largest dish (*patena'*).

To John my son 3s 4d and the second brass pot and a pewter dish (*stanu' patena'*).

Residue of all the utensils (*ustiliamentorum*) to be shared among the said William, Margery and John.

Furthermore, I wish my place called 'Payns' to be sold by William Smyth [*and*] Adam Smyth, whom I make my execs.

Proved at Eye, 11 January 1474/75. Admon to execs.

1   Roger Ropkyn of Thrandeston also made a bequest to the gild of St Peter (SROB, Baldwyne 108; Pt I, no. 492), as did John Cotelyn of Palgrave (no. 688 below). This gild was still in existence in 1517 (*PSIA*, xxiii, p.69).

[fol. 510]

619. GEOFFREY ROGERE of GREAT FINBOROUGH ('Fynbergh Magna'), 4 January 1474/75

Dated at Great Finborough; [*commendation to* God Almighty, the Blessed Mary &c]; to be buried in the churchyard of Great Finborough; to the high altar of the same church for tithes and offerings forgotten 4d; to the reparation of the church there 12d; to the new bell there 6s 8d.

All my utensils and hostilments to be divided equally between Cecily my wife and Thomas my son.

To Thomas my son the whole tenement in which I now live, with its appurtenances, to hold to him and his heirs for ever, he to pay Cecily my wife 5 marks in money, paying it in 5 years immediately following, and to pay also each of my daughters 6s 8d and John my son 13s 4d, and all my debts to be paid by him, the said Thomas.

Any residue there might be of all my goods I leave to the disposition of my execs, my beloved in Christ, Cecily my wife and Thomas my son, to fulfil this testament and dispose where they see best to profit the health of my soul and please God.

Seal appended.

Proved at Stowmarket ('Stowe'), 26 January 1474/75. Admon to Thomas Roger, exec. Power reserved to Cecily the wife, when she comes.

[fol. 510v]

620. THOMAS POPE of REDGRAVE, 27 August 1474

[*Commendation*: to God Almighty, the Blessed Mary &c]; to be buried in the churchyard of the church of All Saints of Redgrave; to the high altar for tithes forgotten 12d.

To Margery my wife and Thomas my son the house in which I dwell for term of their lives, if they can agree together; otherwise, Thomas my son to make my wife a chamber in the house called 'Aschman' with half an acre of land, so that she may live there and have it to sell; and if she sells it, then I wish Thomas my son to have it under the price to anyone else by 6s 8d.

My wife to have annually 2 coombs of malt and a coomb of wheat so long as she remains in widowhood; she to have all the utensils of my house except a brass pot and a brass pan and a brazen candlestick, which I give to Thomas.

To my wife one cow and the other to my son, to whom I leave all the acres of land that I have, both bond and free.

Execs: my wife and my son and William Hactre, to dispose as they see best to profit the health of my soul.

Proved at Mendlesham ('Mendelesham'), 22 February 1474/75. Admon to execs.

[fol. 511]

621. THOMAS DENEYS of COMBS ('Combes'), 12 November 1471

[*probably an earlier version of no. 694, on fol. 542*][1]

Dated at Combs; [*commendation*: to God Almighty &c]; my body to Christian burial; to the high altar of Combs church 6s 8d; to the said church 5 marks to buy a chalice; I wish the image of St Thomas of Judea[2] to be painted totally with my goods; I wish to have a suitable priest to celebrate for my soul and the souls of my parents[3] and the soul of Ed' Turnour and for the soul of [*Alice*] my wife and for

361

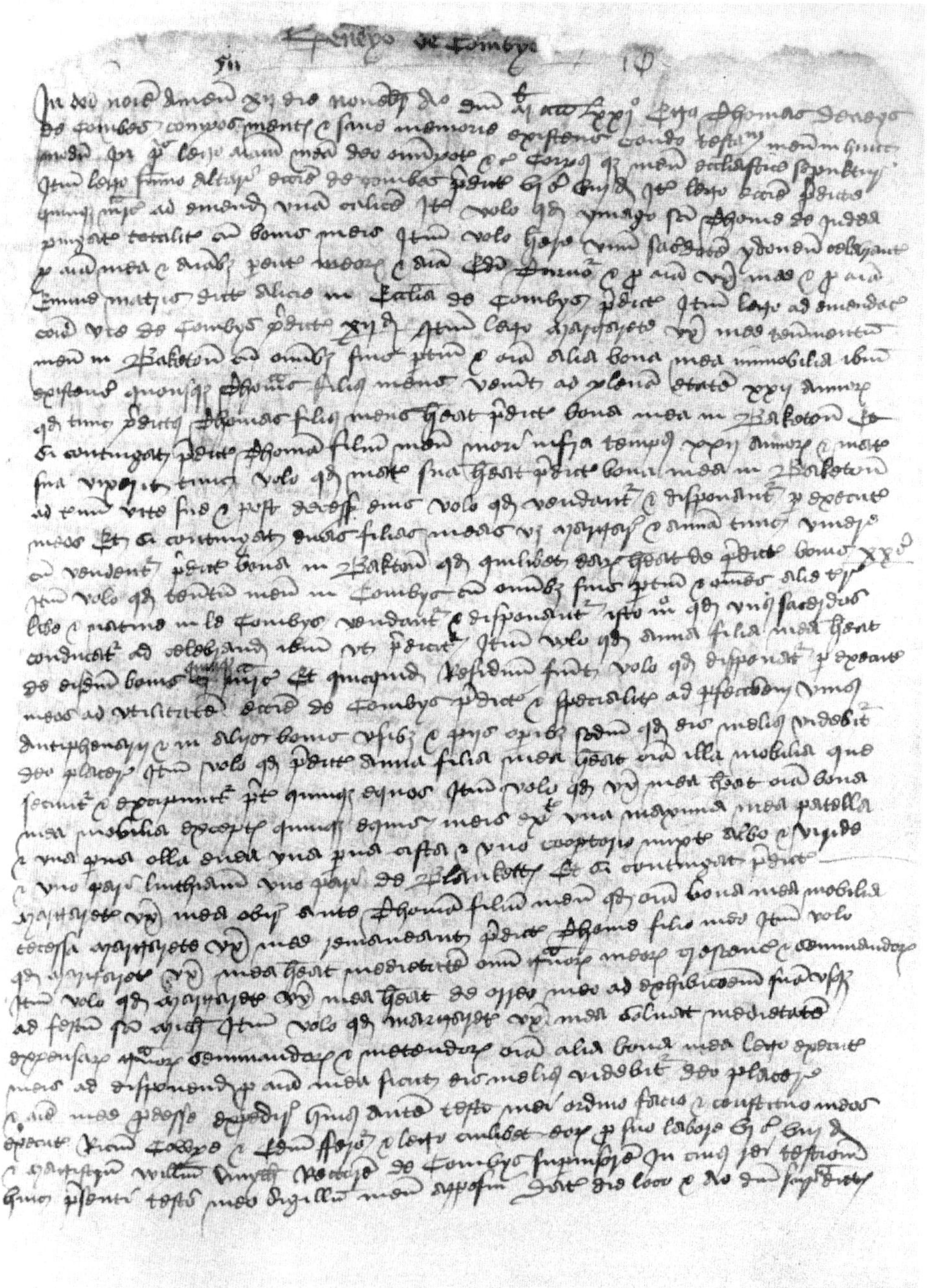

Plate 3. Will no. 621 (fol. 511), the will of Thomas Deneys of Combs.
Photo: Geoff Cordy.

the soul of Emma, mother of the said Alice, in Combs ('Combys') church; to the emendation of the common way in (*de*) Combs 12d.

To Margaret my wife my tenement in Bacton ('Baketon') with all its appurtenances and all my other non-moveable goods there, until Thomas my son comes to the full age of 22[*sic*] years and then he to have my goods in Bacton. If Thomas should die under the age of 22, while his mother is still living, then his mother to have my said goods in Bacton for term of her life; and after her decease, they to be sold and disposed by my execs. If my 2 daughters, Margaret and Anne, are still living when the goods in Bacton are sold, then each of them to have 20s from them.

My tenement in Combs with all its appurtenances and all the other lands, bond and free, in 'le Combys' to be sold and disposed in this way: a priest to be hired (*conducatur*) to celebrate there, as aforesaid; Anne my daughter to have from those goods 5 marks; any residue there may be to be disposed by my execs to the use (*utilitate'*) of Combs church, and especially to the completion (*perfectionem*) of an antiphoner and in other good uses and pious works as seems best to them to please God.

Anne my daughter to have all those moveables excepted below, apart from the 5 horses.

My wife to have all my moveable goods, except my 5 horses [*and*] except my largest pan and a small brass pot, a small chest and a cover of mixed white and green, and a pair of sheets and a pair of 'blanketts'. If Margaret my wife dies before Thomas my son, then all my moveable goods given to Margaret to remain to Thomas. Margaret my wife to have a half-part of all my grain growing and sown; she to have out of my barn [*enough*] for her maintenance until the feast of St Michael; she to pay a half-part of the expenses of sowing and reaping the grain.

All my other goods I leave to my execs to dispose for my soul as seems best to them to please God and profit my soul.

Execs: Richard Cowpere and Edmund Ferour, to each of whom for his labour, 6s 8d.
Supervisor: Master William Smyth, rector of Combs.[4]
Seal appended.

[*No probate recorded: previous probate (fol. 510v) dated 22 February 1474/75, next one (fol. 511v) dated 8 March 1474/75. However, if no. 694 is a later version of this will, probate was granted to the executors of Thomas Deneys on 18 February 1472/3.*]

1   See no. 694, will of Thomas Deynes of Combs, which appears to be a less detailed will by the same man, made exactly one year later. In no. 694 the testator also had a current wife Margaret, an under-age son Thomas and a daughter Anne; the same executors were appointed. The most conclusive evidence is the fact that no grant of probate to no. 621 was recorded in the register but a grant to no. 694 was recorded.
2   'St Thomas of Judea' was St Thomas the Apostle, as distinct from St Thomas à Becket.
3   The testator's mother may have been Rose Deneys of Haughley, will pr. February 1453/54 (SROB, Baldwyne 164; Pt I, no. 795).
4   Master William Smith was rector of Combs from 1468 to 1476 (Tanner, p.1330).

[fol. 511v]
622. HERRY ERDRYCHE of FINNINGHAM ('Fynyngham'), 18 November 1473 [*English*]

['Edryche' *in margin*] To be buried in the churchyard of Finningham; to the high altar of the said church for my tithes forgotten 20d; to Finningham church 15s.

To Denise my wife 2 kine and the keeping of them for term of her life; to Denise 12 mother sheep with all the profits coming from them; she to have the 'fyndyng' of the said kine and sheep from the feast of Easter till the feast of Hallowmass [*1 November*] and the keeping of the calves ('calfryn') till they are weaned; Denise to have her 'fydyng', both meat and drink, in the same place of Finningham; she to have all the 'rewle' of my ostilments.

William my son to have all my lands and tenements, both free and bond, that I have in Gislingham ('Gyslyngham'), Finningham and Westhorpe ('Westhorpp'), with all other 'cattall' not bequeathed, moveable and unmoveable, on condition that he pays my debts. If William dies without issue, the said lands and tenements to be sold by my execs for the souls of all my friends and for all Christian souls.

To Walter Pette 6 sheep.

Residue of all my goods to William my son and John Elyon, execs.

Seal appended.

Witnesses: Sir William Clare, priest, John Hervy and Thomas Hoberd, with others.

To John Elyon for his labour 3s 4d.

Proved at Finningham, 8 March 1474/75. Admon to execs.

[fol. 512]
623. JOHN SAWNDYR the younger of CHEVELEY ('Chevely') [*Cambs*], 6 December 1474

[*Testament; Latin*]

To be buried in the churchyard of Cheveley parish church; to the high altar of the said town for tithes forgotten 2s; to [*?the gild of*] St John the Baptist a coomb of barley;[1] to the torches of the said church 20d.

[*Will; of the same date; English.*]

After the death of my mother, the place at the little green to be sold and John my son to have thereof 40s and all the remnant of the money to be done for my father and my mother and me.

Alice my wife to have all my ?chattels ('catel') and ostilments that she brought to me and 5 marks in money to the keeping of the child.

To Edmund my brother an acre of wheat, neither with the best nor with the worst, and 3 coombs of barley.

Marg' my sister to have my least ('lest') black horse when harvest is done.

To every godchild that I have 2 bushels of barley.

To William Cage a sheep; to Thomas Cage a sheep.

Residue of all my goods I give to my true attorneys, John Colet of Ashley ('Ayschele') [*Cambs*] and Edmund Mayow of Cheveley, to each of whom for their labour and to be true to me 6s 8d.

To Alice my sister a ewe with a lamb.

[*No probate recorded: previous probate (fol. 511v) dated 8 March 1474/75; next probate (fol. 512) dated 24 January 1474/75.*]

---

1   For the gilds of Cambridgeshire in general see Introduction, under *Gilds*, and note to no. 199. In 1457 John Sybly of Cheveley made bequests to the gilds of St John the Baptist and St Mary in Cheveley (SROB Baldwyne, 218; Pt I, no. 1082); in 1474, John Gateward of Cheveley also made bequests to these two gilds (no. 649 below). There was also a gild of St Anne there in 1491 and a gild of the Holy Trinity in 1500 (Palmer, 'Village Gilds in Cambridgeshire', p.387).

624. ROBERT WEBBE [of WOOLPIT], clerk, 8 July *?*1474 [*English*]

Dated at Woolpit ('Wulpett'), in the diocese of Norwich, 8 July M^l v xiiij;[1] my testament and last will; to be buried in the churchyard of Woolpit.

To the friars of Babwell 10s; to the friars of the New House of Thetford 6s 8d; to the friars of the Old House in Thetford 10s.[2]

To the parish church of Kentford ('Kenford') 6s 8d; to the parish church of Elmswell ('Emswell') 6s 8d if it may be borne; to every poor man and poor woman in the parish of Woolpit 1d, by the advice of my exec.

Residue of all my goods I remit to the disposition of Edmund Webb of Risby ('Rysby'), exec.

Witnesses: Master Lane, parson of Woolpit,[3] James Lane, George Fen and others.

[*No probate recorded: previous probate (fol. 511v) dated 8 March 1474/75; next probate (fol. 512) dated 24 January 1474/75.*]

[1] *M^l v xiiij* could be interpreted (loosely) as 1514, which is clearly wrong; as the will has been recorded amongst wills made in 1474 and proved in 1474/75, perhaps 1474 should be understood.

[2] For the friars, see notes to nos 1 (Babwell), 68 (Old House of Thetford) and 69 (New House).

[3] The rector of Woolpit from January 1442/43 to January 1474/75 was Master Robert *Lynton* (Tanner, p.1449); perhaps 'Lane' is a scribal error for 'Lynton', especially as the second witness was named James Lane. In his will, dated 1474, Lynton bequeathed £20 for five statues to fill the niches in the fine new porch of Woolpit church (NRO, NCC 93 Gelour).

[fol. 512v]

625. THOMAS DANBY of MARKET WESTON, 10 December 1474

Dated at Weston Market; [*commendation: to* God Almighty and the Blessed Mary &c]; to be buried in the churchyard of the church of the Blessed Mary of Weston; to the high altar of the same church for my tithes and offerings forgotten 12d; to the emendation of the said church 2 bushels of wheat and 4 bushels of malt.

To the friars of Babwell for a trental 10s.[1]

My wife to have for term of her life all my lands and tenements in Weston, with all their appurtenances, and all my chattels, live and dead, and all my necessaries, on and off (*infra & extra*) my tenements, she to pay all my debts.

To John my son 6s 8d; to Robert my son 6s 8d; to Thomas my son 6s 8d; to Katherine my daughter 6s 8d; to Margaret my daughter 6s 8d; to Isabel my daughter 6s 8d; to Joan my daughter 6s 8d.

After the decease of Alice my wife, William my son the elder to have my said lands and tenements, with their appurtenances, to hold to him and his heirs male for ever. If William should die without heirs male, then all my lands and tenements, with their appurtenances, to remain to John my son and his heirs male for ever. If John should die without heirs male, then all of my lands and tenements to remain to Robert my son and his heirs male for ever. If Robert should die without heirs male, then all of my lands and tenements to remain to Thomas my son and his heirs male for ever. If Thomas should die without heirs male, then all my lands and tenements, with their appurtenances, to be sold by my feoffees and execs, or by their execs, and the money from them to be distributed in pious uses for my soul and the soul of Alice my wife, as in priests celebrating divine service in Weston church for our souls, in ornaments for the said church, in ways and the poor, for our souls, [*our*] parents' and friends' [*souls*] and all the faithful departed.

Residue of all my goods I leave in the hands of William Fulverston, Alice my wife and John my son, execs, to dispose and pay my debts as they know best to please God.

Seal appended.

Proved at 'Badwell', 24 January 1474/75. Admon to execs.

¹ See note to no. 1.

[fol. 513]

626. WILLIAM WYLKYN of BURWELL [*Cambs*], 8 July 1474

Dated at Burwell, in the diocese of Norwich; [*commendation*: to God Almighty, the Blessed Mary &c]; to be buried in the churchyard of the church of St Andrew the Apostle of Burwell; to the high altar of the same church for my tithes forgotten 16d; to an honest priest to celebrate for my soul and for souls of my parents, wives and all our benefactors in the said church for a whole year 106s 8d (*Cvj s viij d*).

Margaret my wife to have 2 chambers within my dwelling house for term of her life, of which one is called 'le Bowre', at (*in*) the west end of the hall and the other annexed to it, on its west side, with free entrance and exit at convenient times, if she wishes to live there; to Margaret each year during her life 13s 4d, to be paid annually from my lands and tenements; to Margaret 16 wethers (*arietes*).

If the wardens of St Andrew's church, with the consent of the parishioners, wish to sell the small bell now in the tower and buy a larger one, so that it shall be the biggest and tenor to the other 2 bells (*ita quod sit maior & tenor aliis duabus campanis*), then they shall have 40s; if they [*do not*] want to buy (*voluerunt* for *noluerunt?*) the new bell, the said 40s to be disposed in the said church, according to the discretion and will of my execs.

To the reparation of the church of St Mary [*of Burwell*] 3s 4d.¹

John my son to have my tenement in which I live, to him and his heirs, he to pay for the tenement 106s 8d as follows: to Margaret my wife for 8 years, each year, 13s 4d as above; and if in the meantime Margaret dies, then the residue of the money not received by her to be expended by my execs in pious works for my soul.

Margaret to have for term of her life all those lands, which were sometime William Fabbe's,² of which I have purchased the reversion after the death of Margaret; and if she is reduced to such need and poverty that she is incapable of supporting herself, then I wish my execs to sell one or 2 acres of the said land and she to have the money from them; and if there be any residue of the lands after her death that has not been sold, I wish it to be sold by my execs and the money from it disposed in works of charity for my soul and the souls of the said William Fabbe, Margaret, our parents, friends and all our benefactors.

To John my son and his heirs 2 acres of land lying in the field called 'le Breche'; to John and his heirs, for ever, half an acre of land lying in 'Estfeld' at 'Belamyes Cornere', a rood of land lying at 'Woodlaneshend' and another lying in 'Larkedene', to observe and keep my anniversary day for ever; he and all his successors to give each year to the parish chaplain of St Andrew's parish church, for the time being, in the way of offerings for the said obsequies and mass 4d, and to the sacrist ringing the bells 2d, and to the reparation of the church 2d.

To Thomas my son the elder 3 roods of land lying in the field [fol. 513v] called 'Dyschfeld' at 'Dyschegate' and a rood lying in 'Estefeld' called 'Rawlynesrode'.

366

To Thomas my son the younger half an acre of land lying in the field called 'North-efeld' at the end of the town.

To Alice my daughter half an acre of land lying in 'Estefeld' at 'Foxleweye'.

Residue of all my lands to be sold by my execs and, of the money received for them, my last will to be performed, together with the last will of John Wylkyn my father,[3] as entered in the missal of the said church.[4] If John my son wants to buy any parcel of, or all of, the said lands, I wish him to have them before all others.

Residue of all my goods to my execs to sell and dispose for my soul and for the souls of [*my*] parents, wives and all our benefactors as they see best to please God and profit our souls.

Execs: my beloved in Christ, John my son and John Taylour the younger.

Supervisor: Thomas Wylkyn my brother.

Proved at Fornham St Martin, 24 October 1474. Admon to execs.

1   See note to no. 234 regarding the two parish churches at Burwell.
2   Will, no. 215.
3   ?Probate of John Wylkyn of Burwell, dated March 1452/53 (SROB, Baldwyne 147; Pt I, no. 697).
4   One method of recording bequests made to the parish. At Bassingbourn (Cambs) unpaid bequests were recorded in the churchwardens' book as debts owed to the parish. See Dymond, *Church-wardens' Book of Bassingbourn*, pp.13–24.

627. JOHN CRYSPYN of THORNEY in STOWMARKET ('Stowemarket'),
4 October 1474 [*nuncupative*]

John Cryspyn of Thorney hamlet of Stowmarket, son of Hugh Crispyn of Creeting ('Cretynge'); dated Tuesday, the feast of St Francis the Confessor 1474; to be buried in the churchyard of the church of the Blessed Peter and Paul in Stow.[1] He said that he wished to bequeath, out of his goods, to the high altar of the said church for tithes forgotten 20d; to the painting of the image of St Paul in the chancel of the said church 12d.

He wished to have out of his goods and the debts owed to him, if they could be recovered, a chaplain to celebrate for his soul and all the faithful departed for half a year.

He wished Hugh his father and Richard his brother to dispose all his goods, and he made them execs to receive his debts and dispose for his soul, so as to please God and profit his soul.

Proved at Fornham, 5 November 1474. Admon to execs.

1   See note to no. 381.

[fol. 514]
628. JOHN HOLDEN the elder of GLEMSFORD,[1] 21 March 1472/73

Dated at Glemsford, in the diocese of Norwich, 21 March 1472, 13 Edward IV; afflicted by a divine visitation of illness and, by his special grace, in sound mind; [*commendation*: to Almighty God, Jesus my Saviour, the Blessed Mary his mother and the celestial company (*societati superiorum*)]; to be buried in holy burial in the churchyard of Glemsford ('Glemsforde') parish church. I require my execs and my supervisor, because he knows all my debts, to pay all my debts that can be truly proved. To the high altar of the said church for tithes forgotten and offerings due 3s

4d; to the same church 100s, so that the rector, with my execs, dispose of it for the health of my soul as seems best to them.

To the 4 orders of friars, that is, Clare, Sudbury ('Sudbery'), Babwell and Cambridge (*Cant'*), 40s, to be divided by equal portions.[2]

To Anne my wife £11 to be paid in 10 years, and 2 cows and 2 pigs and an acre of wheat and another of barley.

To a suitable priest to celebrate for the health of my soul and of all my parents (*p'emptu'*) and benefactors for a whole year £6 13s 4d; to the emendation of the way before my gate 10s.

To Margaret my daughter £7, to be paid in 5 years; to John my son £5 and a croft called 'Turpyttis';[3] to Richard my son £2; to Thomas my son £2 13s 4d.

To Thomas Hervy 13s 4d.

To Thomas my son the elder my tenement called 'Caustons', with all its rightful appurtenances.

To each of the children to whom I am godfather 3s 4d; to Alice Holden 6s 8d; to John Holden to whom I am godfather 6s 8d.

For the expenses on my burial day 40s.

To Anne Heywarde 6s 8d; to Agnes Wolffe 13s 4d; to John Wolffe 13s 4d; to Richard Franco 6s 8d; to William Rogul 20s.

To Sir Richard Fenrother 20s; to Sir Philip, the chaplain, 3s 4d.

My tenement in which I live to be sold, with all the appurtenances, to pay my debts and fulfil all my legacies.

To Anne my wife all my ostilments and utensils as linen and woollen, cups, spoons, pots, pans and all the other necessaries of the house.

Sir Richard Fenrother, chaplain, to be supervisor[4] and Anne my wife and William Rogul to be my execs, to dispose all my goods in works of charity as seems to them best for the health of my soul, all my parents (*p'emptu'*) and benefactors for whom I am most bound, as they will answer before God on the Day of Judgement. And this is my last will: I beg my execs, with my agreement, to implement all the above with every effort.

Seal appended.

Witnesses: Thomas Holden, Robert Robynson, John Holden and many others.

Proved at Lavenham, 13 April 1473. Admon to execs.

1   ?Witness (as 'Holdeyn') of the will of Thomas Fryotthe of Glemsford, pr. December 1447 (SROB, Baldwyne 77; Pt I, no. 362); probably the father of John Holden the younger of Glemsford (no. 742 below).
2   For the four orders of friars see note to no. 133.
3   John Holden the younger of Glemsford (no. 742) bequeathed to Agnes his wife a croft called 'Tonpites'.
4   Also supervisor of the will of John Holden the younger (no. 742).

[fol. 514v]

629. JOHN SCHILDYRSTON the elder of MILDENHALL ('Mildenhale'),[1]
4 March 1472/73

['Childirston' *in margin*] Dated at Mildenhall; my testament and last will; [*commendation*: to the divine mercy of Almighty God, the Blessed Mary his mother and all the saints]; to be buried in Christian burial in the churchyard of the church of the Blessed Mary of Mildenhall; to the high altar of the said church of Mildenhall for my tithes and offerings forgotten and withheld, in exoneration of my soul, 3s 4d; to the reparation of the same church 6s 8d.

[*Will; of the same date*]

Henry my son to have the fishery (*piscaria*) in 'Berewey', with its appurtenances, after the decease of Margaret my wife, to him and his heirs. If he dies without heirs, then I wish it to go to the next heir. To Henry all [*my*] lands and meadows in 'Westyn dyche', after the decease of Margaret my wife, except half an acre of land lying next to the land of John Playforde, which half acre I leave to Alice my daughter, after the decease of Margaret.

I wish 5 roods of land lying together in 'Westyndych' to be sold and disposed in pious uses according to the discretion of my execs as seems to them best to please God.

To Matilda Tyde, wife of Thomas Tydde of Bury St Edmunds (*Sancti Edmundi*)[2] and Matilda Schyldyrston, my daughter, living with the said Thomas Tydde, 1½ acres of land at 'Havydlonde', after the decease of Margaret my wife.

To Margaret my daughter half an acre of land at 'Pollardes', after the death of Margaret my wife.

After the death of Margaret my wife, to Joan my daughter 3 roods of land at 'Berehyle'.[3]

To Agnes my daughter half an acre of land at 'Mundes', after my wife's decease.

After Margaret's decease, Thomas my son to have 3 acres of land lying together in one piece at 'Fenhowcrose' and my messuage in which I live; to Thomas a meadow called 'Wedmerisholme', [*possibly* 'Tedmerisholme'] after Margaret's death.

To the aforesaid Henry, another meadow called 'Fenhowyerd', after Margaret's death.

To John Childerston, son of William Schilderston, a foal.

To William ?Shakyntyn a 'grey' coloured horse.

To John Fairwater a 'bay' horse.

To Simon Schilderston, son of William Childerston, 4 bushels of barley.

To William Childerston, my brother,[4] and Richard Childerston, his son, a red horse.

To the said Thomas my son 2 acres of arable land and 3 acres of meadow in 'Holmesey', to hold to him and his heirs after the decease of Margaret my wife.

To Margaret my wife all the utensils belonging to my house.

Residue of all my goods and chattels to my faithful execs to do with them and dispose for my soul and for the souls of my parents (*peremptu'*) and of all the faithful departed as they see most expedient.

My faithful execs: Margaret my wife, principal executrix, and Thomas Tydde of Bury St Edmunds, tanner.

Seal appended.

Proved at Fornham, 15 April 1473. Admon to execs. Seal of official appended.

[1] ?Executor (as 'Chyldyriston') of testator surnamed Marham, probate September 1452 (SROB, Baldwyne 109; Pt I, no. 498); son and executor (as 'Chylderston') of Richard Chylderston of Mildenhall, will pr. September 1457 (SROB Baldwyne 218; Pt I, no. 1084); son and executor of Matilda Chylderston (no. 239 above).

[2] The children of Thomas Tydde were legatees of Matilda Chylderston (no. 239).

[3] His mother Matilda had bequeathed him these 3 roods of land abutting on 'Berehylle'.

[4] ?Will pr. March 1479/80 (SROB, Hervye 186).

[fol. 515]

630. JOHN AVBRE of WOODDITTON ('Woddytton') [*Cambs*],[1] 1472

['Avbree' *in margin*] Of Woodditton, in the diocese of Norwich; [*commendation includes*: to Peter and Paul];[2] to be buried in the churchyard of Woodditton church; to the high altar for tithes forgotten by me and my wife 2s; to the gild of the Holy Trinity[3] and the torches 10s and a gown; to the panel (*tabule*) of the high altar[4] 3s 4d.
To Isabel Blaunteyn 2 sheep (*oves*) with 2 small lambs (*agniculis*), a cover, a sheet, a tunic.
To John Bakere, his wife and children 5 sheep.
To John Vancy and Thomas Teell[5] 4 sheep.
To William Clerk my stepson (*filiestri*) a sheep and to Thomas Howlot a sheep.
To Isabel and Margaret Colyn 2 sheep.
To Joan Colyn my stepdaughter (*filiastr'*) a sheep.
Residue of my goods to John Folkes and Walter Colyn, my execs, to dispose for me and my wife as seems to them best.
Seal appended.
Witnesses: the vicar of Woodditton,[6] John Vancy of the same, John Bakere of the same and many others.
Proved at Newmarket (*Novu' Mercatu'*), 9 June 1472. Admon to execs.

1 Although the surname 'Aubre' (Aubry) might seem more likely the second letter is definitely 'v'.
2 See note to no. 580.
3 For the gilds of Cambridgeshire in general see Introduction, under *Gilds*, and note to no. 199. Also in 1472, Agnes Glovere of Woodditton made a bequest to the gild of the Holy Trinity there (no. 762), as did John Clerk *alias* Webbe in 1475 (no. 646). In 1528, according to the will of Agnes Raye, this gild was still in existence; there was also a gild of St Agnes in the parish at that time; in 1564 the gildhall at Woodditton was sold to Grice and Foster (Palmer, 'Village Gilds of Cambridgeshire', p.402).
4 See note to no. 580.
5 John Vancy and Thomas Teell witnesses of the will of John Clerk alias Webb (no. 646).
6 Robert Draper was vicar of Woodditton at this time. See note to no. 646.

631. THOMAS WALLEYS of BURWELL [*Cambs*], 14 February 1471/72

['Waleys' *in margin*] To be buried in the churchyard of the church of St Mary of Burwell; to the high altar for my tithes forgotten 4 bushels of wheat.
To Elizabeth my wife, after my decease, my unshod (*nudum*) cart with 3 mother horses (*cum tribus equiis matru'*) and all the equipment belonging to them; to Elizabeth 3 bullocks and all the utensils of my house, of whatever kind they be; to Elizabeth all my stock (*stauru'*) growing on my land, on condition that she pays the rent (*firma'*) of the said lands and then the remainder of those stocks to remain to her use. To Elizabeth 3 acres of arable land lying diversely in the fields of Burwell during her life, and after her decease, I wish John Waleys my son to have the 3 acres of land when he wishes to buy them at 20s the acre. If he cannot buy them, then I wish Nicholas Walleys his brother to have the 3 acres in the same way. If Nicholas cannot buy them, then I wish my execs to sell them to him who will give the most for them, and the money to be divided thus: to each of my children 6s 8d; if any of my children should die during the lifetime of Elizabeth my wife, then the part of the deceased to remain to St Mary's church of Burwell; the rest of the money from the 3 acres to remain to the performance of my will and to the use of Elizabeth my wife.

To Thomas, son of Thomas Worwold, after my decease, 4 bushels of barley; to Alice, daughter of the said Thomas, 4 bushels of barley.

To Elizabeth my wife [fol. 515v] my messuage with the croft adjacent, late William Paxman's,[1] for term of her life; and after her decease, I wish John Waleys my son to have the messuage with the croft to him and his assigns for 6 marks in cash, paying for them each year for 6 years 13s 4d to Thomas Catelyn, chaplain,[2] and John Fabbe, to the use of the said church.

Residue of all my goods to Elizabeth my wife, John Waleys my son and John Fabbe, execs, they to well and truly execute this testament.

Supervisor: Thomas Catelyn, chaplain.

Proved at Burwell, 10 June 1472. Admon to execs.

[1]   Will of William Paxman of Burwell, pr. October 1449 (SROB, Baldwyne 143; Pt I, no. 682).
[2]   See note to no. 551 above.

632. JOHN CALVYSBANE of BURWELL [*Cambs*],[1] 14 March 1471/72

['Calvysban' *in margin*] To be buried in the churchyard of the church of the Blessed Mary of Burwell; to the high altar of the same church for my tithes and offerings forgotten 6d.

Agnes my wife to have my 3 half-acres of freehold arable land, of which 3 roods are lying in the field called 'Estbreche', next to the land late John Powle's on one side, and 3 roods are lying in the field called 'Northefeld' in 3 furlongs (*quarentenis*), one head abutting on 'Northefenne' and the other head on 'Nessewey', to hold for term of her life; and after Agnes's decease, the 3 half-acres of land to be sold and the money from thence to be disposed to the use of the said church for the health of my soul and for the souls of my parents and all my benefactors. To Agnes, all my chattels, household and utensils.

Residue of all my goods to Agnes my wife and Thomas Kyrkeby, execs, to dispose for the health of my soul as they see best to please God and profit my soul.

Seal appended.

Proved at Burwell, 10 June 1472. Admon to execs.

[1]   ?Related to Thomas Calvysban of 'Northestret' in Burwell (no. 512).

633. JOHN MARTYN of LAKENHEATH ('Lakyngheth'), 20 May 1472

Sick unto death; to be buried in the churchyard of the Blessed Mary of Lakenheath; to the high altar there for my tithes forgotten 8d.

To Katherine my wife all the utensils with all my cows and my house for term of her life; afterwards, John my son to have my house with all the lands, at the price of 26s 8d, and 2 horses and a cart.

All my goods not bequeathed to be at the disposition of my wife.

Proved at Mildenhall ('Myldenhale'), 11 June 1472. Admon to executrix.

[fol. 516]

634. JOHN NUNNE the elder of ROUGHAM,[1] 25 June 1472

['Nonne' *in margin*] Dated at Rougham, in the county of Suffolk; my body to Christian burial; to the high altar of Rougham church for my tithes and offerings forgotten or underpaid and for the health of my soul 20d; to the parish chaplain of the same church 8d and to my parish clerk 4d; to the new fabric of the tower of the said church 40s;[2] to the light of the Blessed Virgin Mary burning in the same church 3 wethers (*arietes*) and 3 ewes (*oves matrices*); to the light of St Nicholas of the same church 3 ewes; I wish a suitable chaplain to be supported out of my goods and chattels to celebrate divine service in the said church for a whole year for my soul and the souls for whom I am bound.

To the friars of Babwell to celebrate a trental (*trentale*) of St Gregory for my soul, 10s; to the friars of Clare to celebrate a trental (*trigintale*) of St Gregory for my soul 10s;[3] to the nuns of Thetford ('Thetforde') to pray for my soul 6s 8d;[4] to the friars of the order of the Holy Trinity 12d.[5]

To Isabel my wife all the ostilments and utensils belonging to my house for term of her life; and immediately after her decease, I wish the sons and daughters of Agnes and Margaret, my daughters, to have all the said hostilments and utensils for ever, equally divided between them, but if Agnes does not have any children alive after my decease, then I wish her to have 13s 4d from the said ostilments and utensils. To Isabel my wife 5 horses, 6 cows, 40 wethers, 40 ewes, my carts and ploughs with all their equipment.

To Isabel the rest of the lands and a tenement (*cetera terras & ten'*), with their appurtenances, in the town of Rougham, that is, my tenement, with the lands, pastures and their appurtenances, in which I live, 2 closes, one of which is called 'Bakownis' and the other 'Dokettesland', a piece of land called 'Flaxmere' and all the parcels of my land which were lately Thomas Boldiroo's, to hold the tenement, lands, pastures and closes, with all their appurtenances, to Isabel and her assigns, if she remains sole and unmarried for her whole life, without waste. If she should remarry after my death, then I wish her to have to her and her assigns, similarly, a half part of the lands and tenement, with the appurtenances, for term of her life; and my execs to receive the issues and profits of the other half part and to dispose the value of the issues and profits annually for my soul and for the souls for whom I am bound, for the life[*time*] of Isabel, in pious works, without delay.

After Isabel's decease, all the aforesaid lands and tenement, with their appurtenances, to be sold by my execs for the best price possible, and 16 marks of the money to be disposed thus: 40s of it to the sons and daughters of Agnes Tynton, my daughter, divided equally between them; 13 marks residue to the sons and daughter of Thomas Tyllott, 'husbondman',[6] that is, 5 marks to Thomas, 5 marks to Edmund, 20s to Roger, the sons, and the 20s residue to Katherine, the daughter of Thomas Tillot, 'husbondman'. [fol. 516v] But if any of the sons and daughter of Thomas Thyllott, 'husbondman', should die before receiving their part, [*then*] all the money assigned above to those deceased to remain to those surviving, or to other sons and daughters subsequently born of the body of Margaret, wife of Thomas Thillott, 'husbondman', equally divided between them by the discretion of my execs. The residue of the money from the sale to be disposed for my soul and the souls for whom I am bound in works of charity.

To the said Agnes Tynton, my daughter, a tenement with a croft, 2 pieces of land and their appurtenances in Rougham, called 'Betryches', to hold to her and hers heirs for ever.

To John Tyllott my godson (*filio meo sp'uali'*), son of the said Thomas Tillott, 'husbondman', certain lands and tenements with their appurtenances in the town of Rougham, that is, a tenement with 2 pieces of land called 'Cowperes', a piece of land containing 1½ acres lying at 'le Mellehill' and which was lately John Godriche's, a grove containing by estimation an acre of wood lying at 'le Netherstrette', and a parcel [*or*, pightle] (*piella*) of wood and pasture abutting on 'le Netherstret', to hold to the same John Tillott and his heirs for ever.

To each of my godsons and goddaughters 4d.

I wish that certain persons be named or chosen by the discretion of my execs to be enfeoffed of and in 3 pieces of land with their appurtenances in the town of Rougham lying in 'le Cherchefeld', lately John Goodrich's, abutting on the west on conventual land of the monastery of Bury St Edmunds (*sc'i Ed*'), of which 3 pieces of land one contains 2½ acres, the second half an acre and the third half an acre, to hold to the persons so chosen and their heirs for ever, to be given to the use of the town of Rougham and to the acquittance of the poor and most needy of the town of the fifteenths or taxes of the lord king imposed [*on them*].[7]

To Robert Nune 4 bushels of malt.

To the poor and needy of the town of Rougham 2 quarters of malt to be distributed among them.

To Thomas Nune, my servant, a cow, 5 wethers and 5 ewes; to John Wynchestere, my servant, a cow, 4 wethers and 4 ewes; to John Nune, my servant, 6s 8d; to John Brygth, my servant, a ewe; to John Kempe, my servant, 2 ewes and a cow.

I wish Isabel my wife to have sufficient of my grain to use in her house from the day of my death to the feast of St Michael the Archangel next following; to Isabel all my corn growing on my lands in the town of Rougham, on condition that she pays at the feast of St Michael the Archangel following my decease all the rents and services and other dues for the said lands and also the salaries of my servants, except 5 coombs of wheat and 5 coombs of barley to be taken out of it by my execs and disposed for the health of my soul in works of charity.

Residue of all my lands and tenements with their appurtenances, and all my goods and chattels, grain and animals, to my execs to sell, receive, dispose and distribute for my soul and the souls for whom I am bound in celebrating masses, relieving the poor and needy, amending foul and ruinous ways and doing other pious works as seems best to please God and profit the health of my soul.

I renounce and annul [fol. 517] all other testaments, notices and last wills made before this present time.

I beg and require all my feoffees of and in all the aforesaid lands, with their appurtenances, to make and deliver the seisin which they have in them according to the tenor and effect of this my testament and last will as they shall be duly requested by my execs.

Execs: John Nune of Felsham,[8] Thomas Tillott, 'husbondman', and John Tynton of Finborough ('Fynberowe'); to each of whom for their labour 8s.

Seal appended.

Witnesses: Henry Creme, John Hoge, Roger Stanton and others.

Proved at Fornham, 21 June 1473. Admon to execs. Seal of official appended.

1   Several men named John Nunne (etc.) were mentioned in the Baldwyne register and it is not possible to identify which of those entries refer to this testator. He was probably related to John Nunne the younger of Rougham, will pr. August 1459 (SROB, Baldwyne 265; Pt I, no. 1297).

2   Another bequest to the new tower of Rougham church; see note to no. 184, and also no. 588.

3   For the friars of Babwell and Clare see notes to no. 1.

4   See note to no. 68.

5   See note to no. 295, and also no. 636.

6   Son of Roger Tyllot, the first major benefactor of Rougham's church tower, Roger's will pr. July 1459 (SROB, Baldwyne 247; Pt I, no. 1240). Roger is commemorated in the main inscription of the south face of the tower: 'Pray for The Sowle of roger Tillot'. See Blatchly and Northeast, *Decoding Flint Flushwork*, Rougham St John.

7   In 1456 John Foot of Buxhall (no. 383) bequeathed half an acre of land for the relief of the poor from the tax of the king. In 1465 William Metewyn of Wattisfield (no. 240) bequeathed 11 acres of pasture towards paying the fifteenths of the lord king. See note to no. 240 for details of earlier bequests to cover tax assessments.

8   John Nune the elder of Felsham was executor of Baldewin Coksedge (no. 417); executor of Marion Nune of Thorpe Morieux (no. 613); and executor of Joan Drowte of Felsham (no. 647).

635. THOMAS DOKKYNG the elder of MILDENHALL ('Mildynhale'), 21 February 1472/73

Dated at Mildenhall; my testament containing my last will; [*commendation*: to Almighty God my Creator and Saviour and the Blessed Mary his mother and all the saints]; my body to Christian burial; to the high altar of the church of the Blessed Mary of Mildenhall ('Mildenhale') for my tithes and offerings underpaid 8d; to the reparation of the same church 20d.

Joan my daughter to have my whole messuage for term of her life, on condition that if she should marry and her husband (*maritus*) nurtures, keeps and treats her as a husband (*sponsus*) should keep his wife (*sponsa*), she to have it, but if not, it to be sold by my execs; to Joan all the utensils belonging to my house; to her, 2 cows, 2 horses and a young horse and the cart with the harness (*fallere*).

To William my son 2 horses.

To William Weyng a heifer (*juvenca'*), a collar (*coler'*) and a pair of trappings (*p' allere*) for a horse; to Agnes, daughter of William Weyng, 4 bushels of barley and a 'posnet'; to each of the children of the said William Weyng a bushel of barley.

To Thomas Dokkyng, son of the said William Dokkyng [*my son*], 4 bushels of barley; to each of the other children of the same William Dokkyng a bushel of barley.

Residue of all my goods to my execs to do of them for the health of my soul as seems best to them to please God and profit my soul.

Execs: William Dokkyng my son, Joan Dokkyng my daughter and John Grene, chaplain,[1] to whom 20d for his labour about this testament.

Seal appended.

[fol. 517v] Proved at Fornham, 10 March 1473/74. Admon to execs.

[*rest of fol. 517v blank*]

1   Two other Mildenhall parishioners, John Cowern (no. 611) and John Wareyn (no. 638), also appointed John Grene as their executor.

[fol. 518]

636. SIMON GARDENER of MILDENHALL ('Myldenhale'), 25 February 1471/72

Dated at Mildenhall; my body to Christian burial; to the high altar of the church of the Blessed Mary in Mildenhall for my tithes and offerings forgotten or underpaid and for the health (*in sal'm*) of my soul 6s 8d; to the reparation of the same church to be done (*eiusdem ecclesie faciend'*) 20s.

To each monk of the monastery in Bury St Edmunds (*sci' Edi'*) 12d;[1] to the friars of Babwell to intercede and pray for my soul and the souls for whom I am bound 6s 8d; to the friars of the house of Preachers in Thetford, similarly, 6s 8d; to the Augustinian friars of the same town to pray 6s 8d;[2] to the friars of Mottenden ('Motynden') [*Kent*] of the order of the Holy Trinity and for the redemption of the captives of the Holy Land who are imprisoned for the faith of our Lord Jesus Christ by the pagans 4s.[3]

To Margaret my wife all the ostilments and utensils belonging to my house at my death; to the same Margaret 2 cows, 2 horses, 20 ewes, 20 'sheephoges', 60 quarters of barley and 4 score sheep (*bidentes*).

To William my son 20 marks to be paid to him in one [*sum*] in the year when he takes sacred orders (*sibi solvend' in una anno cum cepit' sacros ordines*), always provided that he celebrates divine service for my soul and the souls for which I am bound for that year immediately following his receiving sacred orders.

To John my son 20s and 10 sheep; to Robert my son 20s and 10 sheep; to Margaret my daughter 20s and 12 sheep; to Christine my daughter 20s; to Agnes my daughter 20s; to Thomas my son 6 ewes and 12 lambs.

To John Clerk my servant 6 ewes.

Residue of all my goods and chattels to my execs to sell, receive and dispose for my soul and the souls for whom I am bound, in celebrating masses, relieving the poor and needy and doing other pious works as seems best to please God and profit the health of my soul.

Execs: Margaret my wife, Thomas Redere, Henry Barnard and Nicholas Gardener; to Thomas Redere 20 'wedyrhogges' and to Henry 5 quarters of barley and to Nicholas Gardener 10 ewes for their labour.

Seal appended.

Witnesses: Robert Morys, John Galte, John Vyncent and others.

Proved at Mildenhall, 11 June 1472. Admon to execs.

1 A rare bequest to the monks of Bury.
2 For the friars see notes to nos 1 (Babwell), 68 (Preachers of Thetford) and 69 (Augustinians).
3 See note to no. 295 and also no. 634. This bequest spells out one of the primary functions of the Trinitarian Friars: one third of their income was devoted to freeing captive Christians. The friars involved at first-hand must have been guaranteed safe-passage by both sides. One wonders what prompted this bequest, and that in no. 634; perhaps an itinerant Trinitarian preacher had recently passed through Suffolk. For Christian slaves in later centuries see Davis, *Christian Slaves*.

637. NICHOLAS STROUDE alias TAYLOUR of STOKE BY CLARE ('Stok *iuxta* Clare),[1] 12 May 1472

Dated at Stoke by Clare; to be buried in the churchyard of Stoke aforesaid, next to the graves of my parents; to the high altar there 3s 4d; to the reparation of the said church 3s 4d; to the gild of the Holy Trinity in the same town 12d;[2] to the reparation of the highway in 'Mooreende' 12d.

Residue of all my goods to the disposition of Joan my wife, Robert Stroude and Richard Stroude, chaplain, my sons, they to dispose as seems to them most expedient for my soul.

Seal appended.

Witnesses: William Man, vicar of the college (*colgate*) of Stoke aforesaid,[3] John Everard and John Algere.

Proved at Stoke, 17 June 1472. Admon to execs.

1   Supervisor of John Melkesop of Stoke by Clare, will pr. May 1462 (SROB, Baldwyne 291; Pt I, no. 1423).
2   Agnes Dyke (no. 803 below) bequeathed her best brass pan to this gild. There was also a gild of Jesus in the parish (*PSIA*, xii, p.84).
3   In 1415 Edmund Mortimer, earl of March, founded the college of St John of Stoke by Clare. Records of its detailed statutes have survived. The college was to consist of a dean and six canons, eight vicars choral, two upper clerks and five choristers, as well as two under-clerks and various laymen. The statutes were amended occasionally and as benefactions increased so did the number of prebends. The college received many endowments, including the Suffolk rectories of Gazeley, Cavenham, Hundon and Stoke (*VCH Suffolk*, ii, pp.145–50).

[fol. 518v]

638. JOHN WAREYN of MILDENHALL ('Myldenhale'),[1] 27 March 1472

Dated at Mildenhall; my testament containing my last will; [*commendation*: to God Almighty my Creator and Saviour and the Blessed Mary his mother and all the saints]; my body to Christian burial; to the high altar of Mildenhall ('Mildenhale') church for tithes and offerings underpaid 4d; to the reparation of the same church 4d.

Alice my wife to have that messuage of mine in which John Akworth now lives, with all the adjacent garden extending (*limaliter*) to the wall to the south, for term of her life; and after her decease, the whole messuage with the garden and its appurtenances to remain wholly to my other messuage in which I now live. To Alice 40s of the money received from my said messuages when they have been sold.

To each of my children 6s 8d of the money from the same messuages if my legacies and debts can be met, and if not, each of them to have only 3s 4d.

To each of my godsons and goddaughters 4d.

To Alice my wife a cow and all the utensils belonging to my house.

Residue of all the money coming from my two messuages, after my debts paid, my burial done and my legacies fulfilled, to my faithful execs to dispose for my soul as seems best to them to please God and profit the health of my soul.

Execs: John Wareyn *alias* Barkere of Stoke by Clare ('Stoke Clare'),[2] Robert Wareyn of Worlington ('Wyrlyngton'), my brothers,[3] and John Grene, chaplain.[4]

Seal appended.

Proved at Tuddenham ('Todynham'), 13 July 1472. Admon to Robert Wareyn of Worlington and John Grene, chaplain, execs. Power reserved to John Wareyn of Stoke by Clare, the other exec, when he comes, if he wishes to take up [*admon*].

1   Son of John Wareyn the elder of Mildenhall, will pr. August 1461 (SROB, Baldwyne 300; (Pt I, no. 1471).
2   John Wareyn *alias* Barkere died in 1482; his will: SROB, Hervye 262. In their father's will, John

the elder distinguished between 'John Wareyn the younger, my son, of Mildenhall' and 'John Wareyn my son, living at Clare'. The designation '*alias* Barkere' suggests that John Wareyn of Stoke by Clare may have been a barker, that is, someone engaged in peeling bark for tanning.

3   The sons of John the elder were widely dispersed: when he made his will he noted that his son William was 'of Ely'. That there were sons in Clare, Ely and Worlington shows the family was spreading away from the ancestral home.

4   Two other Mildenhall parishioners, John Cowern (no. 611) and Thomas Dokkyng (no. 635), also appointed John Grene as their executor.

[fol. 519]

639. ROBERT SYRE of ASHFIELD ('Ayssheffeld'), 4 January 1473 [*new style*] [*English*]

Lying *in extremis*; [*commendation*: to Almighty God, to our Blessed Lady &c]; to be buried on the south side under the wall of the church of Ashfield ('Aysshfeld').

I assign the land of the tenement of 'Berardes' to Elizabeth my wife and all my moveable goods, and as for my tenement and lands, the term of her life, and after her decease to return to Thomas my son and his heirs male. And if it fortune Thomas decease without any heirs male, the lands and tenements to return to William my son and to his heirs male and his issue. And if William decease without any heirs male, the lands and tenements to return to John my son and his heirs male and his issue. And if it fortune that there come no heirs male of the foresaid Thomas, William and John, then the lands and tenements to be sold and disposed by the advice ('be the vyce') of Elizabeth my wife, Thomas my son and John Hardyman, the which I ordain to be my attorneys.

Proved at Fornham St Martin, 26 April 1473. Admon to execs.

640. NICHOLAS ROBERDSON of GLEMSFORD ('Glemesford'), 22 February 1471/72

['Robertson' *in margin*] Of Glemsford; dated at Stradishall ('Stradeshull'), on the feast of St Peter *in cathedra* 1471; [*commendation*: to God Almighty and the Blessed Virgin Mary &c]; to be buried in the church of St Margaret of Stradishall; to the high altar for my tithes forgotten 12d; to each priest present at my obsequies and mass on [*my*] burial day, seven-day and thirty-day 4d and to surpliced clerks 1d; I leave 30s for 3 trentals to be celebrated for my soul and those for whom I am bound. To John Wareyn of Hartest ('Hertest') a striped gown.

To Katherine my wife and my stepsons (*filiis meis legis*) all my lands and tenements and ostilments and the utensils of my house, after my debts have been paid and my last will fulfilled, to hold to them and their heirs.

To a pilgrim [fol. 519v] a reasonable stipend to go twice to St Thomas of Canterbury (*Cantuar'*) and to the Blessed Virgin Mary of the town of Walsingham ('Walsyngham') [*Norfolk*] to make holy offering.[1]

Residue of all my goods and chattels to Thomas Cranevyle and Isabel his wife, my execs, to dispose for the health of my soul and those souls for whom I am bound as seems to them best to please God and do for the health of my soul.

Witness: John Brown.

Seal appended.

Proved at Stradishall, 27 April 1473. Admon to execs.

1   One of the few testators in 'Baldwyne II' to request pilgrimages to the two most important shrines in medieval England; Thomas Roote of Glemsford (no. 508) requested one pilgrimage to each.

641. JOHN SPERLYNG of STOKE BY NAYLAND ('Stokeneylond'),[1]
1 March 1472/73

Dated at Stoke; [*commendation*: to God Almighty, the Blessed Mary &c]; to be buried in the churchyard of the church of St Mary of Stoke aforesaid; to the high altar of the said church for my tithes and offerings forgotten 12d.

Rose my wife to have my messuage called 'Leveneys' with a field called 'Honeleys', with all the appurtenances, for term of her life, and if it happens that Rose should come to such need of money that she cannot live decently, then I wish it to be perfectly possible (*bene licebit*) for her to sell the tenement with its appurtenances. If she does not [*sell it*], I wish the one of my sons who can first (*qui prius potest*) fulfil my legacies to buy and have the messuage with the field, after the decease of Rose my wife, and then immediately I wish that son or my execs to pay to the fabric of Stoke by Nayland church 10s.

To Rose my wife all my utensils, both within the house and without.

To John my son 13s 4d; to Thomas my son 13s 4d.

To Julian my daughter 13s 4d; to Isabel my daughter 13s 4d.

To Robert Sperlyng my godson 6s 8d; to John Sperlyng my godson 6s 8d.

If any of my sons or daughters decease, I wish the part bequeathed to them to pass into the hands of my execs.

My faithful execs: Rose my wife and John my son.

Seal appended.

Witnesses: Hugh Smyth, Robert Lunte, Thomas Bulsmyth and others.

Proved at Bures ('Burys'), 6 May 1473. Admon to execs.

[1]   Executor of John Sperlyng, probate May 1458 (SROB, Baldwyne 262; Pt I, no. 1238).

[fol. 520]
642. WALTER NICOLL of GREAT BRADLEY ('Bradle Magna'), 1 July 1474

['Nycoll *Al*' Clerk' *in margin*] Dated at Great Bradley; [*commendation*: to God Almighty, the Blessed Mary &c]; my body to Christian burial in the churchyard of the church of the Blessed Virgin Mary of Great Bradfield ('Bradfeld Magna')[*sic*] aforesaid;[1] to the high altar of the same church for tithes forgotten and offerings 3s 4d.

To each of my godsons 12d.

I leave 40s for providing an antiphoner to the honour of the Blessed Virgin Mary.

I wish my execs to arrange, as quickly as possible after my decease, for a suitable priest to celebrate for a whole year in the said church for my soul and the soul of my wife and the souls of my parents.

To my wife for term of her life my tenement in which I now live and 6 acres of land, with the appurtenances; and after her decease, I wish the tenement and 6 acres to be sold to Peter, the son of John Nicoll my son, before all others if he is able and willing, and he to have them 40s within the price, and the money received to be disposed in alms and other works of charity for my soul and the soul of my wife.

To John my son all my other lands and tenements, except 2 acres of land which Peter my son shall have by the handing over of John, and the same John to pay the stipend of the priest who celebrates for me for a whole year and the 40s for the aforesaid book out of his own goods and to have carried 40 loads of stone for the reparation of 'Mellestrete'[2] and to pay to his mother annually during her lifetime 40s.

To my wife all the other goods to pay my debts beyond those which my son pays.

To John Syngewell my blue gown.

Residue of all my goods to my wife and John my son, to the use of my wife; they to be my execs.

Seal appended.

Proved at Clare, 20 October 1474. Admon to John Nicoll, exec. Power reserved to Isabel, wife of the deceased, when she comes, if she wishes to take up [*admon*].

1. Clearly a scribal error for Great Bradley, the parish church of which was dedicated to St Mary; none of the three Bradfield villages/parishes had a church dedicated to the Virgin.
2. '40 loads of stone' represents a major repair to one of the roads in Great Bradley. Robert Hardyng made four bequests of 30 cartloads of stone for the repair of different roads in Eye (no. 457); John Gateward bequeathed 20 cartloads of stone to the highway in Cheveley (no. 649).

[fol. 520v]

643. THOMAS PAXMAN of BURWELL [*Cambs*],[1] 26 April 1473

[*Commendation*: to God Almighty, the Blessed Mary &c]; to be buried in the churchyard of the church of St Andrew the Apostle of Burwell; to the high altar of the said church for my tithes and offerings forgotten 12d; to the sustentation of the said church an acre of arable land lying in the fields of Burwell, that is, next to 'Seint Tomers', one head of which is on 'le Nesse Wey'.

Alice Paxman my mother[2] to have her dwelling with Margaret Paxman my wife for her lifetime.

Margaret my wife to have my tenement in which I live, together with all the lands belonging to it, for her lifetime; and after her decease, Thomas Paxman my son to have the tenement similarly for his lifetime; and after his decease his heir to have it for his lifetime; and if Thomas Paxman my son should die without an heir, then the tenement with all the lands pertaining to it wholly to remain to Robert Paxman my brother[3] for his lifetime and no more; and after his decease the tenement with all the lands to be sold and distributed for the health of my soul and [*the souls*] of all my benefactors.

Margaret my wife to pay all my debts.

Residue of all my goods, moveable and unmoveable, to Margaret, executrix, together with John Resam,[4] they to fulfil (*disponant*) my present testament as seems to them best to please God for the health of my soul.

Seal appended.

Witnesses: Thomas at Hylle, William Kempe and Thomas Fraunceys.

Proved at Newmarket (*Novu' M'cat'*), 21 October 1474. Admon to execs.

1. ?Son of Thomas Paxman of Burwell, will pr. October 1457 (SROB, Baldwyne 187; Pt I, no. 911). The bequests made in the will of Thomas the elder to 'Thomas Paxman' were made to his grandson Thomas, son of his son John; the passage of only 16 years between the two wills make it unlikely that this testator was that legatee.
2. The wife of Thomas Paxman (Pt I, no. 911) was named Alice; however, so was the wife of that testator's son John, who had a son named Thomas.
3. Robert Paxman was not mentioned in the will of Thomas Paxman the elder (Pt I, no. 911).
4. ?Executor (as 'Reefham') of William Paxman of Burwell, will pr. October 1449 (Pt I, no. 682).

Plate 4. Fol. 521, line drawing of Miles Crosby. *Photo: Geoff Cordy.*

[fol. 521]

644. ALICE MARKAUNTE of BADWELL, 6 May 1474

['Markante' *in margin*] Dated at Badwell; my testament and last will; [*commendation*: to God Almighty, the Blessed Mary &c]; my body to Christian burial in the churchyard of the parish church of Badwell; to the high altar of the said church 2s; to the reparation of the above church 3s 4d.[1]

I wish my close called 'Jestys' to be sold for the provision (*sustentacionem*) of a priest for a whole year to celebrate for me and John Markaunte my husband[2] and our friends in the said church, and in the sale of the close I wish John Markawnt to have preference (*preponatur*).

My beads of 'le corall' to be sold to implement my will.

To Alice Markaunt my daughter my green girdle of 'le corse'.[3]

To each of my godchildren living in Badwell 4d.

Residue of all my goods to Daniel Gate and John Markaunt, execs, they to pay my debts before all else.

Witnesses called here: Ralph Pundyre, clerk, John Masham,[4] Robert Berdwell and many others.

Proved at Badwell, 24 January 1474/75. Admon to execs.

1   Much building work was done on the parish church of Badwell Ash in the late fourteenth and early fifteenth centuries. See Blatchly and Northeast, *Decoding Flint Flushwork*, Badwell Ash St Mary.
2   ?Son and executor of Alice Markaunt of Badwell Ash, will pr. October 1449 (SROB, Baldwyne 141; Pt I, no. 674).
3   See Glossary.
4   In his will made in 1476, John Masham bequeathed 10 marks to the building of Badwell church tower (SROB, IC/1/2/36). See *Decoding Flint Flushwork*, Badwell Ash St Mary.

[*Down the right hand margin, at 90° to no. 644, is written the beginning of the will of John Sawndyr the younger of Cheveley, dated 6 December [1474], see no. 623, fol. 512.*]

[*On the bottom half of the page is a contemporary line drawing of a man with curly hair, wearing a hat, a (very) short doublet and hose. Above it is written* M' Crosby Mylys at the *in a later ?sixteenth-century hand.*[1] *The drawing has been reproduced opposite.*]

1   The M' might be a symbol of some kind; there is no word after '*at the*'. See the Introduction, under *The assembling of register 'Baldwyne'*, for various references to Miles Crosby.

[fol. 521v]

645. ROBERT BYRD of STOWMARKET, 19 October 1474

['Byrde' *in margin*] Dated the Wednesday after the feast of St Luke the Evangelist 1474; [*commendation*: to God Almighty &c]; to be buried in the churchyard of the church of St Peter in the said town.

Joan my wife to have for term of her life my messuage in 'Stowemarye',[1] and after her decease, it to remain to my children if they survive; if they die, then after the death of Joan, the messuage to be sold and the money arising to be disposed in the best way which seems to please God.

To the high altar of the church of the Blessed Mary [*of Stowmarket*] 20d.

I wish that my messuage called 'Smethes' in Thorney be sold and Joan my wife to have the money arising to pay the costs of [*my*] burial and 5 marks for her maintenance and that of our children.

To the emendation of the highway in Thorney 6s 8d.

Residue of all my goods to the disposition and ordering of the said Joan and Isabel my mother, they to give John my son 13s 4d and Isabel my daughter 13s 4d and to dispose all the other goods; they to be my executrixes, together with Thomas Gowle and Edmund Draper as helpers, in the best way they, of their charity, see (*optimo in quo viderint caritat'*).

Proved at Stowmarket, 26 January 1474/75. Admon to execs.

¹   That is, in the parish of St Mary, Stowmarket; see note to no. 381.

[fol. 522]

646. JOHN CLERK *alias* WEBBE [of WOODDITTON] [*Cambs*],¹ 6 February 1474/75

[*Commendation*: to God Almighty, the Blessed Mary &c]; to be buried in the church of All Saints of Woodditton ('Woddytton'); to the high altar 3s 4d; to the gild of the Holy Trinity a quarter of wheat;² to the panel (*tabule*) of St Nicholas 13s 4d.

To Walter Hancok my brother my hooded (*galeru'*) gown and a pair of hose.

To Isabel my wife my tenement in [*the manor of*] Ditton Valence ('Dytton Valens'),³ lying between the croft of Ed' Oldhalle on the east and the croft of the prioress and convent of nuns ('nunys') in Swaffham Bulbeck ('Sofham') on the west,⁴ for term of her life, if she does not need to sell it to pay my debts; and after her decease, to Robert my son and his heirs, with my copy (*cum copia mea*) called 'Taylours Crofte', with all their appurtenances.

To Thomas my son 2 of my best horses, 2 acres of wheat, 2 acres of barley, 2 acres of oats (*venarum*) and an iron-shod cart (*biga' ferrata'*).

To the church of All Saints of Woodditton ('Wooddytton') a cow called a church cow (*una' vacca' vocat' ecclesiastica'*)⁵ to keep an obit and anniversary annually, and for ever, for me and my wives Margaret and Isabel and all my friends, to the high altar 6d, and the remainder (*remanens*) to bell-ringing and praying for me and my aforenamed friends.

To each of my godsons and goddaughters 4d.

Residue of all my goods to Isabel my wife, John Ray,⁶ John Clerk and William Breton of Dullingham ('Dullyngham'), execs, they to dispose for me and my wife, my young son and daughter,⁷ and duly paying all my debts as seems to them most expedient.

Seal appended.

Witnesses: Master Robert Drapere,⁸ Walter Hancok, John Vauncy and Thomas Teele⁹ and others.

Proved at Ditton ('Dytton'), 3 March 1474/75. Admon to Isabel, John Ray and John Clerk, execs. Power reserved to William Breton when he comes, if he wishes to take up [*admon*].

¹   ?Executor of John Ray of Woodditton, probate September 1459 (SROB, Baldwyne 269; Pt I, no. 1320).
²   For gilds in Woodditton, see note to the will of John Avbre of Woodditton (no. 630).
³   For the manors in Woodditton, see note to no. 580.

4   The Benedictine priory at Swaffham Bulbeck was probably founded in the second half of the twelfth century. In 1242/43 Robert de Valoignes made the substantial gift of a carucate of land in Ditton Valence on condition that he was remembered in the prayers of the nuns (*VCH Cambs*, ii, pp.226–9). This is probably the land referred to here.

5   'A church cow' would have been part of a herd kept for the profit of the church.

6   Executor of John Ray of Woodditton (see note above); ?his will pr. June 1481 (SROB, Hervye 209).

7   The residue was to be disposed for the souls of the testator, his former wife Margaret and a son and daughter who had died young.

8   Robert Draper was vicar of Woodditton, probably appointed during the 1460s; he was succeeded in 1479 (Tanner, p.1266); see also Emden, *BRUC*, p.193.

9   John Vauncy and Thomas Teele were beneficiaries of the will of John Avbre of Woodditton (no. 630).

647. JOAN DROWTE, relict of Peter Drowte, of FELSHAM, 2 August 1474

Joan Drowte of Felsham, relict of Peter Drowte[1] of the same; dated at Felsham; [*commendation*: to God Almighty, the Blessed Mary &c]; to be buried in the church-yard of St Peter of Felsham; to the high altar of the said church for my tithes forgotten 12d.

To the friars of Babwell for a trental 10s.[2]

All my ostilments that are in my house to be divided equally between my 2 daughters.[3]

Residue of all my goods to Sir Robert Storure, rector of Felsham,[4] and John Nune of the same town,[5] execs, to dispose for my soul and the souls of my benefactors in alms and works of charity as they see best to please God.

Seal appended.

Proved the penultimate day of February [*27*] 1474/75. Admon to execs.

1   Will (as 'Drowgth') no. 329.

2   See note to no. 1.

3   The two daughters of Peter Drowgth were called Margaret and Alice (see no. 329).

4   See note to no. 532 and also no. 533.

5   John Nune the elder of Felsham was executor of Baldewin Coksedge (no. 417); executor of Marion Nune of Thorpe Morieux (no. 613); and executor of Thomas Dokkyng of Mildenhall (no. 635).

[fol. 522v]

648. JOAN MYNTON of STOWMARKET ('Stowmarkett'), 20 October 1474
[*nuncupative*]

Her testament and last will; [*commendation*: to God Almighty, the Blessed Mary &c]; her body to the burial [*place*] of St Peter of the same [*town*], to the north, near her kin.

She stated that distribution should be made, with the advice of Robert Cake her brother,[1] at her obsequies to priests and clerks as Robert thinks fit, taking into consideration the amount done in other things. She left an annual stipend to the support of a chaplain (*uni' capellani perimpleatur*) with whom she had made an agreement for a year, immediately.

She left [*some*] clothes to her poor neighbours [*to be delivered*] by certain hands (*proximis suis manibus certis vesturas pauperibus*).

To Marion her sister she left all her other clothes, utensils, vessels of pewter and brass, tables and stools for term of her life, according to the view and discretion of the said Robert her brother, she to live decorously and behave discretely and honestly, protecting her honour (*ad bene vivend' & ipsam gubernand' discrete & honeste salvo honore suo*); and after her decease, that which remains to be distributed in equal parts to the children of the same Robert when they come to legal age.[2] Residue of all her goods and chattels she bequeathed to the said Robert, whom she made exec.

Proved at Stowmarket, 9 March 1474/75. Admon to exec.

[1] ?Husband and executor of Elizabeth Cake of Stowmarket (no. 689).
[2] Perhaps Elizabeth Cake was Joan Mynton's sister-in-law: two years earlier, in 1472, when Elizabeth made her will, her five children were all under legal age.

649. JOHN GATEWARD of CHEVELEY ('Chevele') [*Cambs*], 2 November 1474

Dated at Cheveley, the day of [*All*] Souls (*die animarum*) 1474; [*commendation*: to God Almighty &c]; to be buried in the churchyard of Cheveley parish church; to the high altar of the said [*church*] for tithes and offerings forgotten 2s.

To the highway between 'Broode Grene' and 'Lyttll Grene' 20 cart[*load*]s of stone.[1] To each of my godsons 8d.

To the gild of St John the Baptist of the same town 2 bushels of wheat and a coomb of barley; to the gild of St Mary of the same 2 bushels of wheat and a coomb of barley.[2]

Sir Henry Sybly to have 4 marks to celebrate half [*a year*] for my soul.

Residue of all my goods to John Gateward my son, to sell and dispose as he sees best to please God and profit my soul.

Proved at Cheveley ('Cheleley'), 17 March 1474/75. Admon to exec.

[1] See nos 457 and 642 for other substantial bequests of stones for road repairs.
[2] For gilds in Cheveley see note to the will of John Sawndyr the younger (no. 623).

[fol. 523]
650. WILLIAM SUTTON of MILDENHALL ('Myldenhale'), 17 January 1473/74

Dated at Mildenhall; my testament containing my last will; [*commendation*: to God Almighty, the Blessed Mary &c]; my body to Christian burial, that is, in the church of the Blessed Mary of Mildenhall; to the high altar of Mildenhall church for my tithes and offerings forgotten and withheld, in exoneration of my soul, 10s; to the reparation of the same church 10s.

To the house and convent of friars of Thetford called the Old House ('Olows') 13s 4d.[1]

I wish a suitable priest to celebrate in Mildenhall church for a whole year, if possible, according to the discretion of Isabel my wife; I wish John Sutton my son to be preferred in the said service if he has reached the state of priesthood when he has attained the age of 20 years.

To Isabel my wife all the utensils of my house, with horse and cart and everything belonging to them.

I leave all the merchandise at the sign of the Bell (*ad signum campane*) to Isabel my wife, together with my debts, to pay all my debts and legacies.

I wish my feoffees to make William Cappe of Mildenhall, barber, and Edith his wife, and their heirs, full and peaceful seisin of and in a messuage with its appurtenances in Mildenhall, that is, in which John Maryott lives.

I wish my feoffees to make Isabel my wife sufficient and legal estate of and in a messuage, with its appurtenances, called 'le Swan' in the town of Mildenhall, she to hold it for term of her life; and the reversion of it after her decease to be sold by her, with the consent and will of my said feoffees, and the money from it to be disposed in pious uses for my soul and for the souls of my father and mother and of Richard Sutton,[2] always providing that, if any of my children should be in position (*in potestate*) and in good estate to buy the reversion of the messuage, they should be preferred in the purchase of the messuage before [*all*] others at 10 marks [*less*], with the agreement of Isabel and my feoffees; and if any of my children be in such good condition [*as to buy*] the reversion of Isabel and my feoffees [*they to pay at least*] £20.

My messuage called the 'Tabbard' in the town of Mildenhall,[3] with all the lands belonging to it, to be sold by Isabel my wife and my feoffees, for the best price and, from the money received, I wish John Coket to be paid and satisfied what I owe him, and the remainder to be disposed by Isabel and my execs for my soul and the souls of my parents, friends and benefactors and of all the faithful departed [fol. 523v] in pious uses and charitable alms, according to their sound discretion, as they see most expedient.

To Isabel my daughter 10 marks in money, if she will be ruled by Isabel my wife, and if she behaves better, she shall have better, according to the discretion and will of my wife.

To the wife of William Alyngton, esquire,[4] my best horse.

Residue of all my goods, debts and chattels, whatever and wherever they be, after my debts have been paid, my funeral done and my legacies fulfilled, I leave wholly to Isabel my wife to dispose for my soul as seems best to her to please God and profit my soul.

Execs: Isabel my wife, my principal executrix; Master Robert Bakhotte of Mildenhall[5] and Robert Wyse of Barton Mills ('Berton *iuxta* Myld').

Supervisor: William Alyngton of Bottisham ('Botylsham'), esquire.

Seal appended.

Proved at Mildenhall, 14 February 1474/75. Admon to Isabel Sutton, executrix. Power reserved to Robert Wyse, the other exec, when he comes, if he wishes to take up [*admon*]. Seal of official appended.

1   See note to no. 68.
2   Richard Suttone of Oxborough (Norfolk) will pr. March 1451/52 (SROB, Baldwyne 107; Pt I, no. 489). William Sutton was executor and 'attorney' of Richard, who was clearly of high status, having bequeathed a thousand pennies for a thousand masses for his soul.
3   William Sutton apparently owned three inns at Mildenhall: the Bell, the Swan and the Tabard.
4   William Allyngton was probably a member of the family that held the manors of Halesworth in Blythling Hundred (Copinger, *Manors of Suffolk*, ii, pp.75–6) and of Newmarket Argentine's in Newmarket (*Manors of Suffolk*, iv, p.189).
5   Presumably a cleric who was a member of the family of wealthy Mildenhall mercers; possibly Robert, son of Thomas Bakhot, who was a legatee of Margaret Boole of Timworth, will pr. February 1452/53 (SROB, Baldwyne 156; Pt I, no. 749).

[fol. 524]

651. JAMES THURGOR of ACTON ('Aketon'),[1] 6 August 1474

Dated at Acton, in the diocese of Norwich; [*commendation*: to God Almighty &c]; to be buried (*tradend'*) in the churchyard of Acton church; to the high altar of Acton church, for my tithes by me forgotten, 40d.

To the reparation of the church of the friars of Sudbury 5s, to plead (*rogand'*) for my soul;[2] to the reparation of the church of Babwell 5s, to plead for my soul.[3]

To Ann my wife all my moveables to do freely with them as she wishes, in paying all my debts and fulfilling all my legacies.

To Christian, my wife's daughter, 5 marks in money and goods (*cattall'*).

I wish all my lands and tenements, with the appurtenances as they lie together and diversely (*conti' & di'm*) in the town of Acton, to be sold by my execs and theirs, after the death of Ann my wife, and out of the money coming from them I wish to have a secular priest celebrating divine service in Acton church for a whole year for the souls of my father and mother[4] and the souls of all our benefactors.

To Alice Wareyn my sister a 'seem' of barley and half a 'seem' of wheat.

Residue of all my goods, together with my debts, I leave in the hands of my execs to pay my debts, see to my funerals and do other works of piety for my soul as they see best to please God most and profit my soul.

My execs to be Ann my wife and John Bryan of Acton, and James Rodland of Sudbury to be supervisor; [*and*] for executing as has been written, for term of her life, Ann my wife to dispose for the health [*of my soul*], principally paying all my legacies with the advice of the said John Bryan, and after her decease, my exec abovenamed to have full power of executorship over my lands and tenements then ?remaining (*viventis*); to each of them for their labour 10s.

Made in the presence of: Thomas Webbe, vicar there,[5] John Potagere, chaplain[6] and others.

Proved at Sudbury, 15 December 1474. Admon to execs.

1   Will of his father, Robert Thurgore of Acton, no. 20 above.
2   See note to no. 11.
3   That is, of the church of the Franciscan friary of Babwell (see note to no. 1).
4   In his will, James's father Robert did not mention the Christian name of his wife, even though he appointed her joint executrix with his son William.
5   Thomas Webb was vicar of Acton from 1466 to 1475 (Tanner, p.1345); he was executor of John Copyn (no. 518).
6   See note to no. 271.

[fol. 524v]

652. MARGARET SHEPHERD of SUDBURY, widow, 30 October 1472

Dated at Sudbury, in the diocese of Norwich, on the penultimate day of October; in my pure widowhood; [*commendation*: to God Almighty &c]; to be buried in the churchyard of St Gregory of the same town; to the high altar of St Peter there for my tithes forgotten 8d.

To Alice, wife to Thomas Tropynell of Sudbury, 8s.

To Alice Coteras 13s 4d, a 'coverlyght' of 'ruby' colour, a 'materas', a 'shete', a gown of 'Musturdeler', a blue-coloured girdle ornamented with silver, a 'laten' candlestick, a chest and 3 pewter platters.

To Margaret Thedam a 'sangweyn' tunic.

I wish to have a secular priest to celebrate divine service in the church of St Peter of Sudbury for a whole year after my decease out of the money from the sale of the messuage to John Elyngham of Sudbury.

To Robert Coteras 30s in money in recompense for the repairs done by him on the said messuage.

I wish my execs, or theirs, to keep an anniversary annually after my decease, for my soul and the souls of my husbands as long as can be satisfactorily done out of my goods, my debts and legacies first being paid.

Residue of all my goods to the said Alice Coteras, my servant, to do with it freely as she wishes.

Execs: Simon Sparwe and George Prentys, to execute as above; to each of them 6s 8d for their labour.

Made in the presence of: Sir John Potagere,[1] John Elyngham and others.

[Probate not recorded. Previous one [fol. 524] dated 15 December 1474; next one [fol. 525] dated 5 December 1474.]

1   See note to no. 271.

[fol. 525]
653. JOHN CLERYS of LITTLE LIVERMERE ('Lyvermere Parva'),
27 September 1474

[*Commendation*: to God Almighty &c]; to be buried in the churchyard of the parish church of Livermere aforesaid; to the high altar of the said church for tithes and offerings 3s 4d; to the reparation of the same church 10s; I wish to have a secular priest to celebrate in the parish church of Little Livermere for a year for my soul and my parents'[1] and all my friends' [*souls*].

To Agnes my wife a messuage with 1 acre called 'Bowyers' for term of her life, and after her decease, it to be sold and disposed for my soul and hers and all our friends' [*souls*]; to Agnes 20 ewes and 20 lambs with their wool (*cum lana*) to be delivered before the feast of St John the Baptist, with 3 cows and 12 calves [*and*] 4 pigs, with all the utensils and necessaries belonging to my house; she to have of wheat, rye and malt sufficient for her for a year.

To my 4 sons 6s 8d each and if any of them dies, their part to be distributed among those alive by equal portions; if all die, then it to be disposed for them and for me. Of the residue of my goods, after all debts and legacies have been paid, my wife to have one penny (*unu' denariu'*) and I the other.

Execs: Agnes my wife, Edmund Cleres and Thomas Cleres, my brothers, to each of whom 6s 8d.

Proved at Fornham St Martin, 5 December 1474. Admon to execs.

1   Will of his ?father, Thomas Clere of Little Livermere, no. 118 above.

654. ADAM RODYNG of GREAT HORRINGER ('Mekyll Hornyngesherth'),[1]
4 May 1474 [*English*]

[*Commendation*: to God Almighty and to his mother St Mary &c]; to be buried in the churchyard of St Leonard of Horringer aforesaid; to the high altar for tithes and offerings forgotten 40d; to the reparation of the porch 6s 8d; to the reparation of the guildhall 20d.[2]

~~I bequeath 15 marks for a friar of Babwell for to sing for me~~; to the friars of Babwell a trental [*sic*]; I will that the mass-pence of both of the gilds of the Trinity and St John the Baptist in Horringer be parted equally,[3] half to be sung for in the parish church of Horringer by the parson and the residue [fol. 525v] to the friars of Babwell.

To my wife my dwelling-place, with all the lands belonging thereto, for term of her life; and after her decease to remain to Thomas her son, to give and sell.[4]

To William my son 5 marks and Thomas his brother to pay it as soon as he enters the said place.

To Thomas my son 1 bullock.

Thomas to pay to a friar 5 marks to sing for my soul after the decease of his mother.

To Joan Hendy 2 sheep.

To Margaret Rodyng a lamb.

My lands in 'Ikeworth Feelde' and 'Stubbyng feeld' to be sold to pay my debts.

Joan my wife to be my principal executrix; and William Edward[5] and John Bryset the younger overseers; to Joan my wife, as principal executrix, all the residue of all my other goods; to William Edward for his labour 40d; to John Brysett the younger for his labour 40d.

Witnesses of the testament making: Joan my wife and Thomas my son.

Proved at Fornham St Martin, 2 February 1474/75. Admon to executrix.

1   Executor of John Edward of Fornham St Martin, will pr. November 1459 (SROB, Baldwyne 246; Pt I, no. 1233); executor of William Godfrey of Great Horringer (no. 773 below).
2   As well as giving specific instructions regarding the mass-pence from the two gilds of Great Horringer (see note below), both Adam Rodyng and Walter Noble (no. 432) were concerned about the practicalities of gild membership: Rodying made this bequest of 20d towards the repairs of the gildhall and Noble bequeathed 12d towards the repairs of the vessels belonging to 'the hall of the said gilds', indicating that the gilds shared one hall.
3   Adam Rodyng wished the mass-pence to be equally divided between the friars of Babwell and the 'parson' of Great Horringer, whereas Walter Noble (no. 432) bequeathed the mass-pence of the gild of the Holy Trinity to the friars of Babwell and the mass-pence of the gild of St John the Baptist to the rector of the parish church of Great Horringer.
4   There are a number of deletions and insertions in the registered copy of this will regarding the disposal of the testator's house and land; perhaps the original had been amended.
5   Son and executor of John Edward of Fornham St Martin (see note above).

[fol. 526]
655. JOHN SMYTH of BARNARDISTON ('Bernston'),[1] 1 June 1472

Of Barnardiston, in the diocese of Norwich; [*commendation*: to God Almighty, the Blessed Virgin Mary]; my body to Christian burial in the churchyard of Barnardiston parish church; to the rector of the same church, in the name of his mortuary, the best animal; to the high altar of the same church for my tithes forgotten and offerings underpaid 12d.

To each of my sons and daughters who are married 20s, which my execs are to pay to my children only when they are married, and not otherwise, and not before.

To the wife of Thomas Davy 10s; to the wife of John Bayle 10s; to the wife of Stephen Melche 10s; which 30s my execs are not to pay unless it can be raised of my goods without harming them or my execs (*sine lesiones bonorum meorum & gravamines ex' meorum*).

Each of my sons to have, after my wife's decease, a piece of land, to be effected (*fieri*) by the assignment of my wife before her decease.

The friars of Babwell to celebrate a trental for my soul and the souls of my parents and all our benefactors.[2]

To the reparation of Barnardiston church 6s, to be paid in the 6 years immediately following my decease.

Residue of all my goods to Isabel my wife and Sir Richard Sympson, rector of Barnardiston church,[3] to the use of Isabel, on condition that all my debts are paid; they to be my execs, to dispose as seems to them best to please God and profit my soul.

Proved at Clare, 22 October 1472. Admon to execs.

1   ?Son and executor of John Smyth the elder of Barnardiston, will pr. May 1460 (SROB, Baldwyne 245; Pt I, no. 1229).
2   See note to no. 1.
3   Richard Simpson was rector of Barnardiston from June 1471 until April 1483 (Tanner, p.1224). He witnessed the will of John Dowe of Barnardiston (no. 598).

656. ALICE DERYSLEY late the wife of Richard Derysley[1] of KIRTLING ('Kertlenge') [*Cambs*], 15 September 1472 [*nuncupative*]

['Deryslee' *in margin*] To be buried in the churchyard of the same church.

For a cross to be bought for Lidgate ('Lydgate') church 6s 8d.

To Alice her daughter of her goods to the value of 5 marks, or 5 marks in money.

Residue of all her goods to Walter Derysley and William Derysley,[2] execs, to dispose for her soul and for the souls of her mother and all her friends and for those for whom she was bound.

Witnesses: Thomas Skreven,[3] Walter Pond, Alice Derysley, Thomas Derysley and others.

Proved at Newmarket (*nov' mercat'*), 23 October 1472. Admon to execs.

1   Will (as 'Derysle') no. 428.
2   William and Walter Derysle, sons of Richard, were executors to their father; they may have been Alice's sons.
3   According to the will of Richard Derysle, Thomas Screven (as 'Scryvyn') was Alice's brother.

[fol. 526v]
657. JOHN DUNCHE of WORDWELL ('Wrydwell'),[1] 16 June 1472

Dated at Wordwell, the Tuesday after the feast of St Barnabas the Apostle 1472; to be buried in Wordwell church before the great cross;[2] to the high altar there 6s 8d; to the fabric of the said church, for the breaking of the ground there, 6s 8d.

To the friars of Babwell 10s; to the friars of Thetford called 'the new freres' 6s 8d; to the friars there called 'le Olde freres' 3s 4d.[3]

To the church of Spinney ('Spynney') priory [*Cambs*], to the reparations there 20s.[4]

To the fabric of Culford ('Colford'), to the reparations there 3s 4d.

To each of my execs 6s 8d.

I wish to have a priest to celebrate in the said church of Worlington ('Wrydlyngton') [*sic*] [?*recte* Wordwell ('Wrydwell')] for me and for my friends for a whole year.

To Alice my wife all my hostilments and utensils whatsoever belonging to my house and all my other goods and chattels, both live and dead; to Alice all my lands and tenements with their appurtenances to hold for term of her life, and, after her decease, all the lands and tenements to be sold and disposed for our souls by my execs.

Residue of all my goods to Alice my wife, Thomas Dunch of Culford and Edmund Perkyn of West Stowe ('Westowe'), to dispose for me as they see most expedient and best to please God; they to be my execs to perform and faithfully execute my testament.

Seal appended.

Witnesses: Richard Burdews, John Plesauntes and others.

Proved at Fornham St Martin, 14 October 1472. Admon to Alice, executrix, and Edmund Perkyn, exec. Power reserved to Thomas Dunche, the other exec, when he comes, if he wishes to take up [admon].

1　Executor of William Palmere of Wordwell, probate February 1457/58 (SROB, Baldwyne 213; Pt I, no. 1060).

2　Perhaps, before the rood.

3　For the friars, see notes to nos 1 (Babwell), 68 (the Old House of Thetford) and 69 (the New House).

4　Sometime before 1228 the Augustinian priory of St Mary and the Holy Cross was founded at Spinney in Wicken for three canons. It was endowed with the rectory of Wicken and had property in Cambridge, Ely, and Wisbech. By 1401 the house appears to have consisted of a prior and five canons. In the 1450s it became a cell of the Benedictine priory of Ely, but it continued as an Augustinian house until its dissolution, with Ely's, in 1539. Most of the canons' house survived until 1774 and parts are incorporated in the building presently on the site (*VCH Cambs*, ii, pp.249–54).

[fol. 527]

658. WILLIAM SMYTH of BURES ST MARY ('Burys Sce Marie'),
11 February 1472/73

Dated at Bures St Mary; to be buried in the churchyard of the parish church of Bures aforesaid; to the high altar of the same church for my tithes underpaid 20d; to the high altar of Assington ('Assyngton') 12d; to the parish church of Little Cornard ('Crowherth parva') 5s.

To the gild of the Assumption of the Blessed Mary of Bures aforesaid, 4 bushels (*modios*) of wheat;[1] to the gild of St John the Baptist, 4 bushels of wheat.[2]

For a panel (*tabula*) to be bought for the altar of St Peter, 20d. I bequeath a cow for the sustentation of a candle weighing 4lbs burning at the sepulchre of our Lord for ever on the feast of Easter.[3] To each chaplain of the same church 4d, if involved in my funeral offices; to each clerk 1d; to the beadle (*bedello*) [*sum omitted*].

Residue of all my goods to Alice Smyth my wife and William Lynch, execs, to dispose for the health of my soul as seems best to them.

Proved at Bures ('Buris'), 6 May 1473. Admon to execs.

1　The gild of the Assumption of the Blessed Mary at Bures St Mary also received a bequest (as the gild of St Mary) from Thomas Gybloue (no. 51); the gild is mentioned in a will of 1471 (*PSIA*, xxiii, p.53).

2　The gild of St John the Baptist at Bures St Mary also received bequests from Robert Podeney (no. 55) and John Potyer (no. 326).

3　Provision of a paschal candle for the church of Bures St Mary.

659. JOHN BUGE[1] of Hall Street ('Hallestrete')[2] in SOHAM ('Saham') [*Cambs*], 18 July 1472 [*English*]

[*Commendation*: to God Almighty &c]; my body to be buried in the churchyard of St Andrew the Apostle in Soham; to the high altar in the said church a coomb of barley; to the common ('comown') light 2 bushels of barley or the price of the same. Joan my wife shall have my tenement next to the highway, with all the 'prevayles' for term of her life, with 4 half-acres of land 'as the Evydens specyfyeth moore pleynere' if so be she keeps herself sole from marriage; if she be married, then John my son to enter the said tenement and Thomas my son the land, or else likewise to enter after her decease.

John my son to enter the 'nedyre hows' with half the barn, as soon as I am deceased, for his own, and after John's decease, if Thomas my son lives, he to enter the said tenement whole, like as it lies, for term of his life, and after his decease, Robert my son to enter; and whichever of them that 'menowr'[3] to keep my year-day and my wife's year-day; and after all their deceases, it to be sold and done for me and my wife and all our good-doers.

Joan my wife to choose 4 of the best kine to her own proper use; [*she to have*] 4 calves of this year of age and a grey mare, a bay, a sorrel 'sterryd' and a dun 'sterryd' with their foals, my black horse, also half my crop clearly, she to pay for the 'Innynge' thereof.

Whichever of them 'menour' the tenement aforesaid to repair it.

All the residue of my goods [fol. 527v] to Joan my wife, to her own proper use, to do with all as she will.

To Friar Meryell place of Cambridge ('Cambrege') a coomb of barley;[4] to the White Friars a coomb of barley.[5]

To William Peche[6] and Robert my son, to be my attorneys and if they will buy anything of my part, I will that they have it before any man.

Proved at Soham, 12 May 1473. Admon to execs.

1   Legatee (as 'Bugge') and executor of William Bugge of Soham (no. 823). The Bugge family was prominent in Soham in the seventeenth century, several individuals being members of the parish élite.
2   Hall Street is still the main street in the north part of Soham.
3   See Glossary.
4   Perhaps 'to Friar Meryell's place of Cambridge', that is, to the friary to which he belongs.
5   For the Carmelites (White Friars) of Cambridge see note to no. 42.
6   Legatee and executor (as 'Petche') of William Bugge (no. 823). The Pechie family was also prominent in the seventeenth century.

660. JOHN HERT of ELMSWELL ('Elmeswell'),[1] 18 April 1473

To be buried in the churchyard of the same [*place*]; to the high altar for my tithes forgotten or underpaid 3s 4d; to the reparation of Elmswell church 6s 8d.

To Joan my wife[2] my tenement called 'le Dethes', with 6 acres of land, and with all the utensils belonging to my house and my chamber, and with all my chattels, to sell and hold and dispose as best pleases her.

To Joan my daughter, after the decease of her mother, my tenement called 'le Browness', with a close called 'Wranggylyerd',[3] to her and her heirs, on condition that she pays Robert her brother[4] 26s 8d; if Joan my daughter should die without heirs, then the tenement to be sold and disposed for my soul and the souls of my benefactors.

Residue of all my goods to my execs, to sell, pay and dispose as they see best to please God and profit my soul.

Execs: Joan my wife, Thomas Edon, Edmund Walter.

Seal appended.

Proved at Elmswell, 16 May 1473. Admon to execs.

1   ?Beneficiary of the will of Ada Welde, widow of John, of Woolpit (SROB, Baldwyne 161; Pt I, no. 777); brother, legatee and executor of William Hert of Elmswell (no. 519 above).

2   Joan Hert, wife of John, was the daughter of Alice Bakere, will pr. May 1447 (SROB, Baldwyne 86; Pt I, no. 397).

3   The second 'y' is a yogh.

4   Beneficiary of the will of his grandmother, Alice Bakere (see note above).

[fol. 528]

661. STEPHEN FEN of HOPTON,[1] 7 January 1472/73

Dated at Hopton; to be buried in the churchyard of Hopton church; I wish my debts that I owe to be well and truly paid, quickly and in the best way possible; to the high altar of Hopton church for tithes forgotten and not duly paid 40d.

I wish all coming to my burial to have refreshment (*repastum*) according to the discretion of my execs.

To the friars of the New House of Thetford for a trental 10s.[2]

I wish to have a suitable chaplain to celebrate divine service for my soul and the souls of all my benefactors in Hopton parish church for a quarter of a year, he to have 26s 8d for his salary, out of the money owed me by Robert Fen my son, that is, from the two payments from Robert to my execs next after my death.

To the emendation of Hopton church 13s 4d; to the emendation of the gild of St Peter of 'Nethyrgate' 12d.[3]

To each of my children, that is, Robert, William, John, John[4] and Katherine 10s, in total 50s between them; if any of them should die before the money is paid to them, then I wish my execs to dispose that money for the health of my soul and of my benefactors' [*souls*] as seems to them to please God best.

To each of my godchildren, children of Robert my son, 2s; to Robert Partrich and Isabel Partrich my godchildren, 2s each; to Robert Catton my godson and Isabel Catton 2s each; to Stephen Goole my godson 4d; to the son of William Fen my godson 2s; to each of my godchildren not named above 4d. If any should decease before receiving their money, then I wish that money be disposed in pious uses by my execs.

To each of my execs for their labour 5s.

I wish to have another suitable chaplain to celebrate divine service for my soul and the souls of all my benefactors in Hopton parish church for another quarter of a year or more if my money will stretch to it beyond my legacies above-mentioned.

To Matilda my wife all the utensils of my house and all my necessaries in my chamber, of whatever kind to give, sell or bequeath to whomsoever she wishes.

To Matilda all the covenants specified in certain deeds indented made between me and my feoffees on the one part and Hugh Catton[5] and his co-feoffees on the other, except the money owed me by the said Hugh, of which money I bequeath to my wife Matilda to the end of her life, 10s annually, as long as the sum owed lasts. If Matilda dies, then I wish all the money still owed by Hugh to be disposed in pious uses according to the discretion of my execs. If Hugh should default in his bargain and surrenders all his lands and tenements into the hands of my execs or of my feoffees, then I wish them to be sold by my execs, reserving a chamber for my wife and free entrance and exit for term of her life, and from the money raised I wish Matilda to have annually during her life[*time*] whatever can be found (*unde inveniri poterit*) for her maintenance as long as it lasts.

Residue of all my goods to my execs, Matilda my wife, Richard Partrich of Lopham [*Norfolk*] and John *?*Lows of Hopton, to dispose in pious uses, that is, in the giving of alms, celebration of masses and other works of piety as seems best to them to please God, in exoneration of their consciences.

Seal appended.

[*noted at the bottom*] Fen: see last will on the next folio

[fol. 528v] [*Will; of the same date*]

Dated at Hopton, 7 January 12 Edward IV.

By a deed, dated 20 July 3 Edward IV [*1463*], made at Knettishall ('Gnatissale') I, Stephen Fen, and Matilda my wife, with the agreement of John Poleyn and Alice his wife, sister to Matilda my wife and late the wife of Henry Horn, John Baldry the elder, John Gent of the same and Robert Poleyn of Ixworth Thorpe, granted all those lands lying in the fields of Knettishall ('Gnateshale'), with a parcel of a messuage in the town of Knettishall late Robert Pope's, father to Matilda my wife, and lying between the messuage of John Gent late John Wallere's on the west side, and another parcel of the same messuage late John Baxtere's formerly Matilda Baxtere's on the east side, of which the south head abuts on the highway leading from Knettishall ('Gnateshalle') to Rushworth ('Rosshworth'), which came to me in the right of Matilda my wife [*as of*] her right and entailed to her by right and inheritance according to a deed to John Baxtere and Margaret his wife and their heirs, of whom Joan was daughter and heir and was formerly wife of Robert Pope, of whom Matilda and Alice were daughters and heirs, the tenor of which deed was thus: "We, Reginald Millere of Martham [*?Norfolk*] and Isabel my wife, granted by this deed to John Baxtere of Knettishall and Margaret his wife all my lands and tenements in the town of Knettishall ('Gnatsshale') in the county of Suffolk with all the appurtenances, to hold all the said lands and tenements with the appurtenances to them and their heirs freely and peacefully for ever. Should John and Margaret have no heirs, then after their death the said lands and tenements with the appurtenances to the heirs of John for ever. Dated at Knettishall the Sunday after the feast of St Michael the Archangel 48 Edward IIII [*recte* Edward III]".

I the said Hugh[*sic; recte* Stephen], not knowing the tenor and effect of this deed, effected an alienation of the said lands and messuage to the said John Poleyn and Alice his wife and the others named above, for the benefit of myself and my wife contrary to conscience and contrary to the will of the former grantor, [*and now*] in recompense, restitution and full satisfaction of the value of my part of the said messuage and lands, I leave to Robert Fen my son 2 pieces of land containing 2 acres of land lying in divers places in the fields of Hopton, of which one piece containing half an acre lies in 'Fenfeld' in (*super*) 'Medilferlong' between the land of John Swan on the north and the land of Isabel Moyse on the south [*and*] of which the west head abuts on the land of the said Robert Fen, and the second piece of land containing 1½ acres lies in the same field in (*super*) 'Lampettes Furlong' between the land of the lord of the manor of Hopton on the west and the land late Simon

Parkyn's the younger, now William Frorre's, on the east, the south head abutting on 'Portwey', to hold to him and his heirs of the chief lords of the fee by due service and custom. Should Robert die without heirs, then I wish the 2 pieces of land with the appurtenances to remain to William Fen my son and his heirs; if William should die without heirs, then I wish the land to remain to John Fen my son and his heirs; if John should die without heirs, then I wish the land to remain to John Fen my son the younger and his heirs; if he should die without heirs, then I wish the land to remain to Katherine Catton my daughter and her heirs; should she die without heirs, then I wish the 2 pieces of land to remain to the right heirs of the said Stephen Fen for ever. For the performing of this will I beg my feoffees to deliver estate and seisin of and in the said 2 pieces of land to my children according to the form and effect of this will. Seal appended.

Proved at Hopton, 22 May 1473. Admon to execs. Seal of official appended.

[*On fol. 548, no. 707 below, the testament of this will is largely repeated and struck through.*]

1. Executor of Richard Pope of Knettishall, will pr. January 1457/58 (SROB, Baldwyne 199; Pt I, no. 975).
2. See note to no. 69.
3. This may have been a gild which served a hamlet rather than the entire parish of Hopton. John Broun of Hopton had bequeathed 20s to the gild of St Peter in 'Northgate' (SROB, Baldwyne 151; Pt 1, no. 723); Broun's widow, Marion, bequeathed 2s to the gild of St Peter in 'Northgat-estrete' (SROB, Baldwyne 207; Pt I, no. 1026). Gilds of St Peter and of All Saints at Hopton were mentioned in a will of 1525 (*PSIA*, xii, p.80 and xix, p.190). In Norton at this time there were two gilds of St John. One was gild of St John the Baptist in 'Upstrete', the other the gild of St John in 'Townestrete' or 'Tunstret'. These two gilds each served a particular area of the parish (see no. 743 below).
4. From this and subsequent bequests it is clear that Stephen Fen did have two sons named John.
5. Probably Stephen Fen's son-in-law; in his will proper Fen made a bequest to 'Katherine Catton my daughter'.

[fol. 529]
662. MARIOTA SPRUNTE of CLARE, widow, 16 October 1466

Dated at Clare, in the diocese of Norwich; my body to Christian burial in the church-yard of Clare parish church, next to the grave of Richard Sprunte late my husband.[1] I beg my execs in God's name to pay all my debts which I owe, that is, which can be truly proved. To the high altar of Clare church for my tithes and offerings forgotten, detained and underpaid, 20d.

To a good honest secular priest to celebrate divine office, for my soul and the souls of Richard Frede and Richard Sprunte, late my husbands, and of my father and mother and of all my parents, friends and benefactors for whom I am most bound and of all the faithful departed, in Clare church and not elsewhere for half a year, serving it in two parts, that is, a quarter of a year in the year following my decease and the other quarter in the year after that, taking for his stipend what he and my execs can agree upon.

To the reparation and emendation of Chilton causey ('Chylton Cawse') and the footbridges (*pontium pedestr'*) of the same 6s 8d.

To John, the son of William Frede my son, 40s, one half of the money to be paid him at the age of 16 and the other half at 21, and my mazer to be given him after the death of William his father. To Margaret, the daughter of the said William my son,

40s, to be paid her at the same ages as John her brother, and 6 silver spoons to be delivered to her when she marries. If John dies before reaching the said ages, then his share to remain to Margaret his sister; in the same way, if Margaret dies before the stated ages, her part to remain to John her brother; if both die before that age, both parts, both money and jewels, to remain to William my son.

To Matilda the wife of Thomas at Hyll of Glemsford ('Glemesford'), my sister, to pray for my soul, my coloured gown of 'musterdevelers', a 'petycote', a 'smoke' and a 'kercheffe'.

To Katherine the wife of John Coupere of Clare, to pray for my soul, my best blue furred gown.

To Joan the wife of William Hell of Clare, to pray for my soul, my 'vyolett' tunic.

To Joan the wife of the said William my son my best blue and green tabard.

I beg all my feoffees to deliver all their estate and possession which they have in my messuage in the town of Clare to William my son and others named by him, to hold to him and his heirs for ever according to an indenture made between me and him and written in this present paper as appears below.[2]

Residue of all my goods to the disposition of my execs, they to dispose of my goods in works of charity as seems best to please God and profit my soul.

Execs: Christian Barbour and William my son.

[fol. 529v] To the same Christian for her diligent labour about these presents a 'kercheeffe' priced 20d and an 'aperon' of 'braboncloth'; to William for his labour my black silk belt ornamented with silver.

Seal appended.

Witnesses: the said Christian and William, Richard Clerk and others.

Proved at Clare, 22 December 1472. Admon to execs.

[1] Will no. 155 above; in her husband's will she is called 'Marion'.
[2] The indenture has not been copied into the register.

663. JOHN SAWYER *alias* GYLLY of BRADFIELD ST GEORGE ('Bradfeld Monachorum'), 3 May 1472

John Sawyer otherwise called John Gylly; testament and last will; to be buried in the churchyard of St George of Bradfield aforesaid; to the high altar of the said church in recompense for my dues and tithes 12d.

To Isabel my wife all my lands and tenements for the whole term of her life; and after her decease all my lands and tenements in Bradfield St George to be sold to George my son and his heirs, if he shall be sufficient in goods and chattels to buy them, 40s within a competent price; if not, I wish all my lands and tenements with their appurtenances to be sold to one of my sons who is able to buy them at 40s within a competent price.

To Isabel my wife all my goods and chattels and all the utensils belonging to my house.

My faithful execs: Isabel my wife, George Sawyer my son, John Sawyer my son and William Sawyer my son.

I beg all my feoffees to deliver full estate and seisin to Isabel my wife of and in my lands and tenements in which they stand, according to the tenor of my deed of gift, when so required.

I will that Isabel my executrix be not answerable to my other execs but only to God,

Holy Church and its ministers (*eius ministris*) but all the other execs to be answer-able at all times to Isabel and her attorneys; and if any of my said sons and execs violate, impede or obstruct this my will and testament, he shall forgo the legacy [*assigned*] to him.

Residue of all my goods I put to the discretion of my execs to dispose for my soul and for all my benefactors for whom I am bound in alms and all works of charity as they see best to please God and profit my soul.

Seal appended.

Witnesses: Walter Humfrey and William Bryght.

Proved at Fornham St Martin, 14 August 1472. Admon to execs.

[fol. 530]
664. ROBERT CHYLDERSTON the elder of MILDENHALL ('Myldenhale'),[1] 25 August 1472

['Chyldyrston' *in margin*] Dated at Mildenhall; my testament containing my last will; [*commendation*: to Almighty God my Creator and Saviour, the Blessed Mary his mother and all the saints]; my body to Christian burial, that is, in the church-yard of the church of the Blessed Mary of Mildenhall; to the high altar of the said church for my tithes and offerings underpaid 40d; to the reparation of the same church 13s 4d.

Robert my son to have 1½ quarters of barley; to Simon my son 3 coombs of barley; to William my son 3 coombs of barley; to Thomas my son 3 coombs of barley; to John my son 3 coombs of barley.

To each of my godsons and goddaughters a chorus[2] of barley.

To the convent of friars of the conventual house of friars at Thetford called 'le Oldhows' 2s.[3]

Alice my wife[4] to have all the utensils belonging to my house; she to have my whole messuage with its appurtenances for term of her life; and after her decease I wish one of my sons, who is of good and honest behaviour [*and*] discretion and of competent authority (*vigencie*) by the judgement of John Sygo my exec, to have preference in the having of the messuage with its appurtenances, to him and his heirs in fee simple, paying John Sygo my exec 4 marks in money; John Sygo to dispose those 4 marks according to his discretion in pious uses, alms and works of charity as he sees most expedient.

Residue of all my goods and chattels to my faithful execs to dispose for my soul and the souls of my parents, friends and all my benefactors as seems best to them to please God and profit my soul.

Execs: Alice my wife and John Sygo.

Seal appended.

Proved at Cavenham, 8 December 1472. Admon to execs.

1 ?Executor (as 'Chylderyston') of Henry Morle of Mildenhall, probate October 1443 (SROB, Baldwyne 40; Pt I, no. 220); ?witness (as 'Chyldreston') of the will of Emma Curteys of Milden-hall, pr. November 1455 (SROB, Baldwyne 224; Pt I, no. 1117). The testator does not appear to be directly related to Richard Chylderston (Pt I, no. 1084), Matilda Chylderston (no. 239 above) or John Schildryston (no. 629 above).

2 See Glossary.

3 See note to no. 68. This bequest to the friary is repeated and underlined the second time.

4 Alice Chylderston was the daughter of John Tyd of Mildenhall, will pr. April 1454 (Pt I, no. 727).

665. ED' DIL HOO of STOWMARKET ('Stowemarkett'), 3 July 1470

Dated at Stowmarket; my body to Christian burial in the church of St Peter of Stow ('Stowe') aforesaid; to the high altar of the same church for my tithes forgotten 3s 4d; to the high altar of the church of the Blessed Mary of the same town 3s 4d; to the reparation of the same church 3s 4d.[1]

To be expended and distributed about my obsequies and on my burial day, as to chaplains, clerks and the poor and in refreshment for my friends and neighbours and in other necessary expenditure done at that time 40s; [fol. 530v] to the reparation of the candles burning about my body 2s.

I wish to have 3 trentals of St Gregory celebrated for my soul, one by the convent of Friars Minor of Ipswich (*Gippwici*), another by the convent of Carmelite Friars there and the third by the convent of friars of Babwell.[2]

To a suitable and honest chaplain for celebrating divine service in the church of St Peter aforesaid for a whole year for my soul and the souls of my parents and benefactors and for all those at rest in Christ 8 marks.

To the reparation of Onehouse ('Onhows') church 6s 8d.

To the emendation of the highway called 'Haghlestrette' 6s 8d.

To Friar William Levynge to pray for my soul 3s 4d.

To the chapel of St Mary in St Peter's church, for the emendation of a beam there, 3s 4d.

To Margaret Ledgate my servant a basin with a ewer and 3s 4d; to Joan Lethenard 3s 4d; to John Wareyn 2s.

To Robert Hotott my son 2s.

To Joan my wife all my hostilments and utensils not otherwise assigned. Also to her my whole tenement in Stow called 'Bogays' with the appurtenances, that is, with a renter (*redditual i '*) called 'Seynte Marie Rentere' situated next to the tenement, with its gate, and 2 pieces of land formerly 'Bogays', one of which is called 'Spadeakere' and the other 'Crosselaneland', a pightle called 'Brostretys Pictyll', and a piece of land lying at 'le Whitecros', to hold them for the whole term of her life; after her decease the tenement with all the foregoing to be sold for the best price possible. And from the money I assign: to a suitable and honest chaplain to celebrate divine service for my soul and the souls aforesaid in St Peter's church for a whole year, 8 marks; and to the chapel of St Mary in St Peter's church a vestment for a single chaplain from the same money; and to the church of Onehouse another vestment similarly; the residue of all the money from the tenement to be disposed in pious uses for the health of my soul.

I wish all my other lands, tenements and renters (*reddutualia*) with their appurtenances to be sold to pay my debts and fulfil my will.

Whatever residue there may be of all my goods I leave to the disposition of my faithful execs, my beloved in Christ, Joan my wife, Ralph Scherlynge and John Wareyn; they, having God before their eyes, faithfully to execute this testament and implement my will.

Seal appended.

Proved at Stow, 16 December 1470. Admon to Joan, executrix; power reserved to Ralph Scherlynge and John Wareyn, the other execs, when they come.

[1] See note to no. 381.
[2] For the friars see notes to no. 1.

[fol. 531]

666. WILLIAM BAXSTERE of STANTON, 1 August 1472

Dated at Stanton, in the diocese of Norwich; to be buried in the churchyard of the church of All Saints of Stanton; to the high altar of the said church for [*my*] tithes forgotten and other defaults in [*my*] offerings 12d; to the emendation of the said church of All Saints 8d.

To the convent of Friars Minor of Babwell 12d.[1]

To Margery my wife all my goods not bequeathed and the utensils of my house.

Residue of all my goods I put in the hands of Margery my wife, John Taylour and Robert Elys, execs, to ordain and do for my soul and the souls of all the faithful departed as they see best to please God.

Seal appended.

Witnesses: Edmund Been, clerk,[2] John Calffe, Ralph Bakere and others.

Proved at Stanton, 15 Otober 1472. Admon to execs.

1   See note to no. 1.
2   See note to no. 333; see also nos 566 and 680.

667. AGNES MARTYN of LITTLE ASHFIELD ('Aysshffeld parva'),
25 March 1471

Dated at Little Ashfield; to be buried in the churchyard of the church of All Saints of Ashfield aforesaid; to the high altar of the said Ashfield 3s 4d; to the church of Great Ashfield ('Aysshffeld magna') 3s 4d; to the high altar of the same 3s 4d.[1]

To Ralph Pundyr, clerk, 10s; to John Drynkmelk 5s; to William Syre 20s; to William Caly 20s.

To Ellen Hundyrwod 3 covers, 2 'dongys', 2 blankets, 1½ pairs of sheets, 2 featherbeds (*pulvinar'*), a pair of 'gette' beads, a brass pot, a brass pan.

To Rose Brustall a tunic and a 'kertyll'.

I wish my messuage in which I live to be sold by my execs and the money from it to be disposed thus: to the church of Great Ashfield 8 marks to buy a bell; to the said church 2 marks to keep my anniversary annually in the said church and that of Robert Martyn my former husband and to find a candle before the image of the Blessed Mary in the same church.

[*Residue*] to William Syre and William Caly, execs.

Seal appended.

Proved at Wattisfield ('Watlesfeld'), 26 May 1471. Admon to execs.

1   The parish of Little Ashfield is now known as Badwell Ash. The dedication of the parish church of Little Ashfield was to St Mary; it was the dedication of the church of Great Ashfield that was to All Saints. Although the testatrix asked to be buried in the churchyard of the church of All Saints of 'Aysshffeld *predict'*', having previously mentioned 'Aysshffeld *parva*', further bequests to the church of All Saints later in the will suggest that she wished to be buried in the churchyard of Great Ashfield.

[fol. 531v]

668. JOHN TYMBYRMAN the elder of MILDENHALL ('Myldenhale'),
26 July 1472

Dated at Mildenhall 26 July 1472 and 12 Edward IV; my testament containing my last will; [*commendation*: to God Almighty my Creator and Saviour, and the Blessed

Mary his mother, and all the saints]; to be buried in the churchyard of the church of the Blessed Mary of Mildenhall; to the high altar of Mildenhall church for my tithes and offerings forgotten and withheld, in exoneration of my soul, 40d; to the reparation of the said church 3s 4d.

To the convent of friars of Babwell to celebrate a trental for my soul 10s; to the convent of friars of the house of Thetford called 'le Newhows' 10s.[1]

To John my son all the tools belonging to my workshop.

Joan my wife to have my whole messuage for term of her life; and after her decease, John my son to have the messuage with all its appurtenances in fee simple; to Joan my wife all the bedding and utensils belonging to my house.

Residue of all my goods to my faithful execs to dispose for my soul as seems best to them to please God and profit the health of my soul.

Execs: Joan my wife, John Tymbyrman my son and John Blythe my brother.

Seal appended.

Proved at Mildenhall, 24 October 1472. Admon to execs. Seal of official appended.

[1]   For the friars see notes to nos 1 (Babwell) and 69 (New House of Thetford).

[fol. 532]
669. MARGARET WETHERARD of STOWMARKET, 5 March 1457/58

Dated at Stowmarket; [*commendation*: to Almighty God, the Blessed Mary &c]; to be buried in the churchyard of the church of St Peter of Stow ('Stowe') aforesaid; to the high altar of the said church 6s 8d; to the reparation of the same church 20s; to the church of the Blessed Mary of the same [*town*] 20s;[1] to Combs ('Combes') church 6s 8d; to Newton church 6s 8d; to Haughley ('Hawley') church 13s 4d; to Finborough ('Fynbrgh') Magna church 6s 8d; to Finborough ('Fynbergh') Parva church 6s 8d; to Buxhall ('Buxhale') church 6s 8d.

I wish to have a chaplain for 3 years to celebrate for the soul of John Wetherard[2] and for my soul, [*and the souls*] of our parents and benefactors, he to have for his stipend 24 marks.

To each chaplain present at my obsequies 4d; to each clerk of the higher state (*de superior' gradu*) 2d; and to the other, minor, clerks 1d each.

To the friars of Ipswich (*Gippewic'*), that is, the Preachers 20s, the Carmelite Friars 10s, and the Friars Minor 10s.[3]

To Marion Bradwater my daughter £20.

To the emendation of the highways to 'Hawle markett' 20s.[4]

I wish to have a parclose ('parclos') made by the discretion of my execs next to the altar of the Holy Cross to the value of 5 marks; for a tabernacle of the Blessed Mary in the church of St Peter of Stow to be made similar to (*ad similitudine*) the tabernacle of the Holy Trinity there £10; for a book called an antiphoner ('antiphonare') 10 marks; for 2 copes (*capis*) for the choirmasters (*rectoribus choris*)[5] in the said church 7 marks.

To each of my godchildren 3s 4d.

To Adam/Ada (*Ade*) Parmentere 46s 8d, to be paid to him/her at divers times, according to his/her need.[6]

To Richard Schelton[7] a piece of woollen cloth of sanguine (*sang'*) colour; to Katherine Baldewen a piece of cloth of sanguine colour.

To 5 chaplains 5 silver spoons, one each.

Marion Bradwater my daughter to have the tenement in 'Breggestrett'[8] if [*my*] will can be fulfilled.

I assign a pasture called 'Bernardyerd' with all its appurtenances[9] to the provision (*pronunciand'*) of the obit of John Wetherard my husband and my obit and to the reparation of the common hall (*reparacionem co'e aule*) called 'le gyldehalle'[10] for ever, that is to say, the farm or profit to be divided by the discretion of my execs and other good men and apportioned as above.

John Schalforth and Margaret Lyster my household servants to have my tenement in 'Cowystrette'[*sic*].[11]

My pasture in Thorney ('Thorneye') to be sold by my execs to fulfil my will.

Residue of all my goods to my execs, Edward Edgore,[12] John Gowle, Richard Bradwater and Robert Mylys; they to faithfully execute this testament.

[*Will, of the same date*]

Margaret Wetherard, lately the wife of John Wetherard of Stowmarket.

I wish the anniversary day of John Wetherard my late husband and [fol. 532v] my anniversary to be kept always on one day, that is to say, on 5 Kalends September [*28 August*]; and for that day of our anniversaries to be kept for ever, annually serving God, I give my piece of pasture in Stow called 'Bernardesyerd', with the appurtenances, to remain for ever in the hands of feoffees, trustworthy and faithful, it to be let to farm by them for the best price possible and out of the money arising annually from the said farm, I assign in offerings on the said anniversary day 2d, and to the vicars of St Peter and of the Blessed Mary 4d, in obsequies and *placebo* and *dirige* and mass of requiem for the health of our souls and for the health of the souls of our parents and benefactors and all those at rest in Christ, by note if it can legally be done, in the church of St Peter of Stow, saying [*them*] in person (*personaliter*), and to 4 clerks ministering to them 4d. If the said vicars at any time default in this duty, then 2 other chaplains to take their turn for the same pay. And to the sacrist of the said church for his office of bell-ringing 6d; and in charity to the poor 6d. I wish the chaplain of the Blessed Mary celebrating in St Peter's church to have annually from the profits of the said pasture 20d, for ever.

Seal appended.

Witnesses: Edward Egore, John Dowe, Robert Mylis, Richard Shelton, Sir Robert Ferour, vicar of the church of the Blessed Mary,[13] and others.

Proved in the church of St Peter of Stowmarket, 3 May 1458. Admon to execs.

[*This is the same testament as that crossed out on fol. 193v (Pt I, no. 943). The only difference in the wording is the name 'Cowystrette', given as 'Crowystrete' on 193v. The will was not entered previously. The year of the testament, will and probate is 1458.*]

1   See note to no. 381.
2   Her late husband; will of John Wetherard the elder of Stowmarket, pr. September 1453 (SROB, Baldwyne 149; Pt I, no. 714).
3   For the friars of Ipswich see notes to nos 1 (Carmelites and Friars Minor) and 50 (Preachers).
4   The market at Haughley was chartered in 1231.
5   Or 'directors of music'.
6   Margaret Wetherard's husband had requested prayers for the souls of John Parmenter and Alice his wife.
7   One of the executors of John Wetherard; brother and executor of William Schelton (no. 109).
8   John Wetherard had bequeathed his messuage in 'Breggester'[*sic*] to Margaret for the term of her life.

9   John Wetherard had bequeathed the enclosed pasture called 'Bernardesyerd' to his wife.

10 In 1460, two years later, John Gowle of Stowmarket bequeathed 6s 8d to the repairing of the community hall (*commune aule*) of Stow called 'le gylde halle' (SROB, Baldwyne 297; Pt I, no. 1462). In 1462, William Schelton of Stowmarket (no. 109 above) bequeathed 6s 8d to the emendation of 'le gylde hall' there. The hall evidently served more than one gild and was in need of maintenance. See note to no. 109 above for further details. John Welham of Hitcham referred to the gildhall there as the community hall (*aule communit'*) implying that the hall was used for a range of public and private purposes, rather than by one group or gild (SROB, Baldwyne 160; Pt I, no. 772). Roger Charite of Hitcham used the same expression (no. 75 above).

11 John Wetherard had bequeathed the messuage in 'Crowestrete' to Margaret (although the wording of his will is somewhat ambiguous).

12 Another of the executors of John Wetherard.

13 Robert Ferour was vicar of the church of St Mary, Stowmarket, from 1461 to 1478 (Tanner, p.1341); will pr. June 1478 (NRO, NCC 195 Gelour); he was executor of William Schelton (no. 109).

670. JOHN TYLLE of SUDBURY ('Sudbur'), 15 September 1472

[*nuncupative*]

[*Commendation*: to Almighty God, the Blessed Mary &c]; to be buried in the churchyard &c [*sic*].

He bequeathed to Friar Thomas Langham and Friar William Bury 10s, to celebrate a trental.

He bequeathed to Agnes my[*sic*] wife all the utensils of my[*sic*] house and £10 which John Tylle my father bequeathed to me, as appears in my father's will, on condition that Agnes pays my debts.[1]

Residue of my goods I commit to the disposition of Agnes my wife, executrix, to dispose as she sees best to please God &c[*sic*]

Witnesses: Sir Robert Hynderwell[2] and Margaret Tylle.

Proved at Fornham, 1 March 1472/73. Admon to executrix.

1 ?Will of John Tille of Sudbury, dyer, pr. December 1460 (SROB, Baldwyne 305; Pt I, no. 1489). This may not be the testator's father: one 'John Tille the younger' witnessed that will but there was no bequest of £10 to a John Tylle/Tille. See also the will of John Tylle of Boxford, in which there were bequests to 'John Tylle the elder, my son, of Sudbury', pr. February 1442/43 (SROB, Baldwyne 39; Pt I, no. 214). Tylle was not an uncommon surname: a man named John Tylle was mayor of Sudbury in 1454 (Sperling, *Sudbury*, p.76).

2 Robert Hinderwelle became the incumbent of All Saints', Sudbury, in January 1465/66; the date that he was succeeded is unknown (Tanner, p.1390).

[fol. 533]

671. WILLIAM JURDON of NEWMARKET (*Novo Mercato*), 9 February 1472/73

Dated at Newmarket, in the diocese of Norwich; to be buried in the churchyard of the church of All Saints of Newmarket;[1] to the high altar of the same church for my tithes and offerings negligently forgotten 6d.

I wish Margaret Jurdon my wife to have the tenement in which I dwell during her life[*time*], but if necessary I wish the tenement to be sold by Margaret and from the proceeds Thomas Jurdon my son to have £10. From the same tenement: to Henry Jurdon my son 13s 4d; to John Jurdon my son 13s 4d; to Margery my daughter 13s 4d; to Isabel Jurdon my daughter 13s 4d. If Margaret is able to live without selling the tenement, then I wish that after her decease Thomas Jurdon has the tenement, on condition that he pays [*the bequests*] as directed above to his mother.

My faithful execs: Robert Berton and Margaret my wife, together with Thomas Jurdon.

Residue of all my goods to Margaret my wife [*to dispose*] as she wishes.

Seal appended.

Proved at Newmarket, 12 February 1472/73. Admon to execs.

[1] See note to no. 80.

672. ALICE TAYLOUR of BRADFIELD ST GEORGE ('Bradfeld Monachorum'), 2 February 1471/72

Dated at Bradfield aforesaid; to be buried in the churchyard of the church of St George of Bradfield aforesaid; to the parish chaplain of the same [*place*] 12d; to the light of the Blessed Mary burning (*lucent'*) in the same church, a hive of bees. To the friars of Babwell 10s for a trental.[1]

To Benedict the son of Margaret Dey of Stowlangtoft ('Stowelangtofte') 2 posnets and a pan holding half a gallon and a small pan called a 'stelpanne'.

To Isabel daughter of the said Alice[*sic*] [*?the testatrix*] a garment (*tunicam*) called 'a petycoote', white, and a blue kirtle and a russet lined tunic (*rucet' tunic' penulat'*). Residue of all [*my*] goods to Thomas Dey of Stowlangtoft, my faithful exec, to dispose for my soul and all my friends' [*souls*] where he sees most effective.

Proved at Norton, 16 February 1472/73. Admon to exec.

[1] See note to no. 1.

[fol. 533v]

673. RICHARD BALDRE of THORNEY in STOWMARKET ('Stowe Petri'), 16 January 1471/72

['Baldree' *in margin*] Dated at Thorney ('Thorneye') the Thursday after the feast of St Hilary 1471; of Thorney in the parish of St Peter, Stow; I make my testament and dispose my last will; [*commendation*: to God Almighty, the Blessed Mary &c]; to be buried in the churchyard of the said parish church. Firstly I wish my debts to be paid. To the church of St Peter 3s 4d; to the use (*opus*) of the said church 10s; to the use of Old Newton ('Eldnewton') church 10s.

To the convent of Friars Minor of Ipswich (*Gypwic'*) 2s; to the convent of Friars Preachers in the same town 2s; to the convent of White Friars of the same 2s; to the convent of Augustinian Friars of Clare 20d.[1]

Margaret my wife to have all my lands and tenements, both free and bond, for her maintenance (*sustentacionem*), or their value (*valencia'*), yearly, in rents and farms, for the whole term of her life. And after her decease, I wish John the elder my son, if he is obedient and well-disposed to Margaret his mother, and not awkward (*sine rigore*) or disobedient, and wants to buy the said lands and tenements, both free and bond, to have them under the price and before any other man when they are sold after my decease. Similarly, if John remains obedient and well-disposed to his mother, he is to have my meadow called 'Reves' of the said Margaret. If John is not obedient and well-disposed to his mother, as a son should be, then all the said lands and tenements, both free and bond, are to be disposed according to the last will of John Baldree my father[2] after Margaret's decease.

I wish Thomas the elder my son to have of my goods, when it can be paid from them, 5 marks; Robert my son [*to have*] 40s; John the younger my son 40s; Thomas the younger my son 40s;³ my 3 daughters, each of them, 40s.

I leave to be distributed among the poor of the town of Stow and Thorney 5s; in recompensing for the soul of Matthew Heccham 10s.⁴

Residue of my goods to the disposition of my attorneys and execs, Margaret my wife, Robert Symondes and John Kebyll of Thorney ('Thorneye') the heir.⁵

Supervisor: Master Thomas Hyll, clerk.

Seal appended.

Witnesses: Richard Warnere, Henry Bayle, William Baldre, John Baldre, William Goslyn, William Scheppard and others.

Proved at Stowmarket ('Stowemarkett'), 18 February 1472/73. Admon to Margaret Baldre, executrix. Power reserved to Robert Symond and John Kebyll, the other co-execs, when they come, if they wish to take up [*admon*].

¹   For the friars see notes to nos 1 (Friars Minor and White Friars of Ipswich, and Augustinians of Clare) and 50 (Friars Preachers of Ipswich).

²   Will of John Baldre of Thorney in the parish of St Peter, Stowmarket, pr. March 1449/50 (SROB, Baldwyne 99; Pt I, no. 444).

³   One of the sons of Richard Baldre named Thomas was Lord Mayor of London in 1524–25 (d.1534).

⁴   Perhaps Richard Baldre was an executor of Matthew Heccham.

⁵   There was a family in Stow called 'Keeble the heir'.

[fol. 534]

674. JOHN KYMBOLD of HITCHAM ('Heccham'),¹ 16 March 1472/73
[*probate only*]

Proved at Bildeston ('Bylston'). Admon to execs.

¹   Executor (as 'Kembold') of Thomas Kembold the elder of Hitcham, will dated and pr. November 1452 (SROB, Baldwyne 121 and 148; Pt I, nos 560 and 712); executor (as 'John Kembold the younger') of John Gronger, probate January 1458/59 (SROB, Baldwyne 211; Pt I, no. 1047); executor (as 'Kembold') of Isabel Carter of Hitcham, probate November 1457 (SROB, Baldwyne 214; Pt I, no. 1066).

675. JOHN GLASWRYGTH the elder of GREAT WALDINGFIELD ('Waldyngfeld Magna'), 29 April 1471

Dated at Great Waldingfield, the penultimate day of April 1471; in the presence of many of the faithful; [*commendation*: to Almighty God and the glorious Virgin and all the saints of heaven]; to be buried in the churchyard of the said town; to the high altar of the said church for my tithes by me forgotten 12d; to the fabric of the said church 20s; to a secular priest to celebrate divine service in the said church for a whole year after my decease, 8 marks sterling 6s 8d.

Residue of all my goods, both moveable and unmoveable, to John Glaswrygth my son, he to pay all my debts, bury me and dispose for the health of my soul, with the help of Robert Clerk of Little Waldingfield ('Waldyngfeld parva'), whom I make execs.

Seal appended.

Proved at Sudbury, 17 March 1472/73. Admon to execs.

676. THOMAS HOWTON of HAWKEDON, 29 December 1472

To be buried in the churchyard of Hawkedon church; to the crucifix and Mary [*and*] John (*crucifixio Marieque Johanne*) of Hawkedon 6s 8d;[1] to the panel ('tabell') on the high altar 6s 8d; to the emendation of the candles, especially for torches (*cerorum sp'lit' torchis*) 6s 8d; to the reparation of the chapel of the Blessed Mary of Somerton 6s 8d.[2]

I leave 8 marks for a priest to celebrate for my soul in Hawkedon church for a year. Margaret my wife to have my principal house, that is, the hall with all the chambers belonging to it; she shall use the bakehouse (*faciat in pistrino*) as she needs [*it*] and she shall see to (*administrabit*) the repairs of the houses [*i.e. the bakehouse and principal house*] which she occupies, with straw and clay (*glice*); she to have the barn called 'Nedyre bern' with the byre (*bostar'*); she to have the yard (*ortu'*) called 'Grene Yerd' with the gardens, [*and*] with 3 crofts, one called 'the Medylcrofte', another called 'the Nedyr crofte', and the other 'the iiij Acres croft', with the ditches and fences (*cepibus*) for cropping and shredding (*ad croppand' & schredand'*); she to have the pasture called 'the Den pasture' with the meadow called 'the Lytyll Medewe', with all their profits.

Margaret to have all my ostilments and bedding, except John my son the elder to have my brass pot and 6 pieces of pewter.

John my son the younger to have 5 marks in money; to Joan my daughter 40s; to Isabel my daughter 40s; if any of those children, that is, John the younger, Joan and Isabel, die in the meantime, their part of remain to the others.

John my son the elder to have 40s if he is well satisfied (*si bonus placebil' sit*).

Margaret my wife to have 5 of my best cows and one of the best horses and 4 of the best pigs.

To Isabel Ayschdon the best animal that she will choose, next to her mother.

Residue of all my goods to my execs, Margaret my wife and John Fyrmyn of Hawkedon and Walter my son, to dispose for my soul as seems best to them; they to be [fol. 534v] my execs to perform my will and each of them to have for [*their*] labour 6s 8d out of my goods.

I wish each of those children (*filiorum*) whose godfather I am to have 4d.

And the goods that Thomas Howton has on the day of his death shall remain in the hands of my execs until the feast of St Michael following and if it can be spared (*haber'*) from his things, Thomas Howton wishes Margaret his wife to have 20s in money.

Proved at Haverhill ('Haveryll'), 18 March 1472/73. Admon to Margaret Howton and Walter Howton, execs. Power reserved to John Fyrmyn, the other co-exec, when he comes.

[1] That is, to the rood.
[2] Situated in the south aisle of the parish church, the Lady Chapel is almost as big as the chancel; there is a large squint between the two.

677. MARGERY the wife of John HUNTE of BARNARDISTON ('Bernardeston'), 20 June 1472

[*Commendation*: to God Almighty, the Blessed Virgin Mary]; to be buried in the churchyard of the church of All Saints of Barnardiston, beside John Borgayne my first husband; to the high altar of the same church 12d for my tithes forgotten and offerings underpaid.

To Alice Rasure my 'violet' gown; to Katherine Prate my 'burnett' tunic and my sanguine 'kertyll'; to Agnes Hunte my best gown and best girdle; to the wife of John Hervye of Great Wratting ('Wrattynge Magna') my everyday clothes (*cotidiana vestiment'*).

To Parnell Maryott my household servant, at her marriage, 40s, if she lives so long, and if she happens to depart this life before she is married, then I wish the 40s to be disposed in works of charity for my soul and all my benefactors' [*souls*] and for the soul of the same Parnell.

I bequeath 9 marks to find a priest to celebrate in Barnardiston church for a whole year for the souls of John Borgayn my late husband and for my soul and all our parents' and our benefactors' [*souls*].

Residue of all my goods to John Hunte my husband, he to implement well and faithfully the will of John Burgeyn my late husband and mine; and he, John Hunte my husband, to be my exec.

William Ayloth of Hunden to be supervisor of my exec.

Proved at Haverhill ('Haveryll'), 18 March 1472/73. Admon to exec.

[fol. 535]
678. RICHARD BROWNYNG of HAVERHILL ('Haveryll'), 9 September 1472

[*Commendation*: to Almighty God, the Blessed Mary &c]; my body to Christian burial in the churchyard of the upper parish church of Haverhill; to the reparation of the lower church of the Blessed Mary in the same town, 6s 8d, and more according to the discretion of my execs.[1]

To a suitable chaplain to celebrate for my soul and for the souls of all my benefactors for the term of half a year, 56s 8d.

Margaret my wife to have for the whole term of her life my meadow called 'Sweynnesmede'; and after her decease, I wish the meadow with the appurtenances to remain to my execs and feoffees for the keeping of my anniversary once in the year in the upper parish church aforesaid for my soul and for the souls of all my benefactors for ever, and also for the finding of a lamp burning in the upper church on Sundays and double festivals (*festiviis dupplic'*)[2] each year for ever. In default of my anniversary being kept and the lamp being found as above, I wish my feoffees [*to sell*] the meadow with the appurtenances and dispose the money from it in the reparation and sustentation of the upper church for my soul and the souls of all my benefactors.

To Margaret my wife 2 acres of land lying in the field called 'Overeyfeld', to give and to sell as she wishes.

To Margaret a croft of land called 'Londoncroft' with its appurtenances for the whole term of her life; and after her decease, I wish the croft with its appurtenances to be sold at the hands of my execs and out of the money from it 10s to be disposed for the celebration of a trental for my soul and for the soul of Alice my late wife and the souls of our benefactors; of the residue, I leave to the reparation of the lower church of Haverhill 13s 4d.

Residue of all my goods to Margaret my wife and Thomas Mayster, to see to my

funerals and pay my debts and distribute for my soul and for the souls of my benefactors as seems best to profit the health of my soul; they to be my faithful execs to
fulfil my will in all respects.

Seal appended.

Proved at Haverhill, 18 March 1472/73. Admon to execs.

1   See note to no. 14 regarding the parish churches in Haverhill.
2   See Glossary.

[fol. 535v]

679. THOMAS SKYNNERE of ROUGHAM ('Rowham'), 28 January 1472/73

Dated the Thursday after the conversion of St Paul 1472; [*commendation*: to
Almighty God, the Blessed Mary &c]; my body to Christian burial; to the high
altar of Rougham church, for my tithes and offerings forgotten, for the health of
my soul 40d.

To Isabel my wife all my lands and tenements, with their appurtenances, which I
have in the town and fields of Rougham, for term of her life.

To Margery my daughter 40s; to Christian my daughter 40s.

Residue of all my goods to my execs, Isabel my wife, Roger Stanton and John Sken-
nere, to dispose for me and for the souls of my benefactors as they see best to please
God and to answer [*no more*]

Seal appended.

Proved at Fornham St Martin, 22 March 1472/73. Admon to execs.

680. JOHN LARGE of STANTON, 24 April 1472

Of Stanton in the county of Suffolk; [*commendation*: to God Almighty, the Blessed
Mary &c]; to be buried in the churchyard of All Saints; to the high altar of the said
church 10d; to the emendation of the said church 6s 8d; to the emendation of the
church of St John the Baptist 40d.

To my mother for her maintenance 20s.

To Margery Mayster, wife of Adam Mayster, 20d.

To my sister living with Roger Rollecross 40d.

Residue of all my goods to the disposition of Roger Rollecros, Adam Mayster and
Adam Mundys, execs, to dispose for my soul and the souls of my benefactors as
seems best to them to please God and profit the health of my soul.

Seal appended.

Witnesses: Edmund Been, clerk,[1] Robert Mayster the younger, Ed' Trekere and
others.

Proved at Ixworth, 22 March 1472/3. Admon to Roger Rollecross, exec. Power
reserved to Adam Mayster and Adam Mundes, the other co-execs, when they come,
if [*they wish to take up admon*].

1   See note to no. 333; see also nos 566 and 666.

[fol. 536]

681. JOHN HARRY of LAVENHAM, 28 March 1473

Dated at Lavenham; [*commendation*: to God Almighty and all his saints]; my body
to Christian burial; to the high altar of the said church for my tithes underpaid 20s.

I wish to have a suitable secular chaplain to celebrate divine service in the said church for 2 years, having for his stipend 18 marks; I leave 10 marks to be distributed among the poor of Lavenham, that is to say, each week 3s 4d until the full amount has been disposed.

To Olive my wife my tenement in which I live lying in the borough (*burgo*) of Lavenham in 'lee Heystrette', between the tenement of John Nevman[*sic*] on one side and the tenement of Robert Parson on the other side, for term of her life, she to keep it in repair so long as she lives; and if [*she does*] not, it is to be sold by my execs, and out of the proceeds I leave £20 to purchase a vestment for the deacon and subdeacon and a black cope to the honour of God in Lavenham church, and to be there as long as it lasts; also from the same money I wish to have a secular chaplain to celebrate divine service in Lavenham church for 2 years, having for his salary 18 marks, [*being*] for my soul and the soul of my wife and the souls for whom I am bound; the residue of the proceeds to be disposed in alms and the emendation of the highways about the town of Lavenham.

To Olive my wife all the hostilments, utensils and jewels and everything else belonging to my house, and the wheat and malt in my house, but I wish to have for the keeping of my funeral day and seven-day and thirty-day sufficient of the malt to make ale for those 3 days. Also to my wife all my wool, except the wool for 4 cloths of 30 cloths (*pro quat'* 'clothys' *de triginta* 'clothys'), and her fuel; to Olive 5 quarters of wheat and 2 cows; to her £20 in money.

To John Harry my son a tenement situated in the borough (*burgo*) of Lavenham in 'le Master John strete', between the tenement of John Fyppe on one side and the tenement of Geoffrey Hermere on the other side, to hold to him and his heirs. If he should die without heirs, then the tenement to be sold by my execs or theirs, and the money from it to be disposed in works of charity for my soul and the souls for whom I am bound. My execs to newly build the said tenement according to their discretion. To the said John Harry my son £20 as it may be had of my debts.

To Joan Harry my daughter a tenement in the borough (*burgo*) of Lavenham in the 'lee Heystrette', lying between the tenement lately Thomas Wylymot's on one side and the lane leading to the park,[1] with the stable, to hold to her and her heirs. If she should die without heirs, then the said tenement to be sold by my execs or theirs, and the proceeds to be disposed in charitable gifts for my soul and the souls for whom I am bound. To Joan £20, [fol. 536v] as it may be had of my debts.

To Elizabeth my daughter 'lee croftes' called 'Bramstonys croftes' and 'Borythys croft' and 'lee Teyntour yerd', to hold to her and her heirs. If she should die without heirs, then the 'croft[*s*]' and 'Teyntour yerd' to be sold and disposed as above. To Elizabeth £20 as it may be had of my debts.

To the gild of the Holy Trinity of Lavenham 10 marks, on condition that the fraternity of the gild shall buy as much livelihood ('lyfflode') as will provide a chaplain to celebrate divine service in Lavenham church for the souls of the said fraternity time without end (*sine fine durat'*), or if not, the said 10 marks to be disposed according to the discretion of my execs or theirs.[2]

I leave 10 marks to the emendation of the highway to Brent Eleigh ('Illigh Combust').

To Thomas Harry my father 6d per week, for term of his life.

To the friars of Babwell ('Babewell') 10s; to the friars of Sudbury 10s.[3]

To Thomas Punder and Alice Punder his wife 20s; to Thomas Punder the elder 3s 4d.

To Matilda Taylour 3s 4d; to Richard Greneleff 6s 8d

To each of my sons at Thomas Punder's the elder (*cuilibet filio meo apud Th' Punder sen'*) 12d.

To John Trewe 3s 4d; to Laurence Trewe 3s 4d; to Thomas Trewe 20d; to Alice Trewe 20d.

Simon Trewe and John Newman of Lavenham to be my execs to fulfil my last will; to each of whom for his labour 20s. Residue of all my goods to my execs to dispose in charitable gifts as they see best to please God.

Witnesses: Sir Robert Hervy, parish chaplain,[4] Roger Crytott, William Sayyer, Thomas Herry and many others.

Proved at Lavenham, 13 April 1473. Admon to execs.

[1] The earl of Oxford's park lay to the north-west of the town of Lavenham. Today the lane to it is Park Road.
[2] In a similarly worded bequest William Schedde (no. 339) bequeathed £20 to the gild of the Holy Trinity, on condition that they buy enough lands, tenements or rents, within eight years, to provide a priest to celebrate divine service for ever in the church, for the souls of the brothers and sisters of the fraternity. See note to no. 339 regarding yet another similar bequest.
[3] For the friars see notes to nos 1 (Babwell) and 11 (Sudbury).
[4] See note to no. 552.

[*Folios 537 and 538 comprise one piece of paper (?inserted), all entries are in a completely different and better formed hand, akin to that used in the Norwich Consistory Court register.*]

[fol. 537]

682. EDMUND MAYOWE of REDE, 16 January 1471/72

['Mayhewe' *in margin*] Dated 16 January 1471 and 11 Edward IV; in the parish of Rede in the county of Suffolk, sick in body and seeing the peril of death approaching, in the presence of my acquaintances (*notis*) and friends, I make my testament and last will; [*commendation to* God Almighty my Creator and Saviour, and the Blessed Virgin Mary his mother, and all the saints of the celestial host]; to be buried in the churchyard of the parish church of All Saints of Rede; to the high altar of the same church for my tithes and offerings forgotten or negligently withheld, in exoneration of my soul, 3s 4d; to the high altar of Brockley ('Brokle') parish church 3s 4d; to the rector of ?Chedburgh ('Chetbury') parish church 3s 4d, especially to pray for my soul.

To Isabel my niece (*nepti*) a cow.

To the friars of Babwell, to celebrate a trental for my soul, 10s; to the friars of Sudbury ('Sudbery'), similarly, 10s; to the friars of Clare, in the same way, 10s.[1]

I wish to have a suitable priest to celebrate [*blank*] sangred[*s*] ('sancrych') in Rede church.

To the buying of a silver chalice for Rede church 26s 8d.

Residue of all my goods, chattels and debts, wherever they are, after my debts have been paid first and foremost, my burying done and my testament fulfilled, I leave wholly to Isabel my wife, to do with and dispose as her own goods, debts and chattels.

Isabel my wife to be my principal executrix, with co-execs John Mayowe and William Mayow my sons; they to faithfully execute and fulfil everything contained in this testament.

Seal appended.

[*headed in a different hand:* Mayhew]

[*Will, of the same date*]

As to the disposition of my whole tenement with the houses built [*upon it*] (*cum domibus edificiis*), lands, crofts, feedings, pastures, gardens and their appurtenances lying in the parish of Rede and in the parish of Brockley:

First, William Mayow my son to have and enjoy, for ever, my tenement called 'Turnours House', with the croft and its appurtenances, lying in the fields and town of Rede.

Henry Mayowe my son to have and enjoy, for ever, a croft called 'Millars Crofte', with its appurtenances, lying in the fields of Rede.

A croft called 'Millars Crofte' lying in the fields of Brockley to be sold in the best way possible and, out of the money for it, I wish Agnes my daughter, the elder, to have 13s 4d, Sibyl my daughter 13s 4d, and Agnes my daughter, the younger, 13s 4d, and the residue, if any remains, Henry my son to have.

John my son has bought of me a tenement and he owes me 6 marks in money from it; of the said 6 marks, John to have 26s 8d [*and*] Katherine my daughter to have 4 marks of it.

Isabel my wife to have all the profit from my tenement in which I live during her whole lifetime; and, immediately after her decease, the tenement to be sold by my feoffees and I wish John Mayowe my son to buy and have it, with its appurtenances, before anyone else; and out of the money from it, I wish a suitable honest and secular chaplain to celebrate [fol. 537v] for my soul and [*the souls*] of Isabel my wife, [*my*] friends and all the faithful departed for 2 whole years after Isabel's decease, taking for his stipend and salary 8 marks a year during that time.

But if my goods are insufficient to stretch to the fulfilling of this testament, then I wish the money from the tenement to go to the fulfilling of the will and then the chaplain should not celebrate divine service beyond the rate of the portion remaining clear after the fulfilling of this testament.

Proved at Fornham, 24 January 1471/72. Admon to Isabel and John, execs. Power reserved to William, the other co-exec, when he comes and if he wishes to take up admon. Seal of official appended.

[1]   For the friars see notes to nos 1 (Babwell and Clare) and 11 (Sudbury).

683. ROBERT BAGHOT of ICKLINGHAM ('Ikelyngham'), 26 January 1471/72

['Bacott' *in margin*] Dated at Icklingham, in the county of Suffolk and diocese of Norwich, on 26 January 1471 and 11 Edward IV; [*commendation*: to God the Father Almighty, the Blessed Virgin Mary and all the saints of God]; to be buried in the churchyard of the church of St James the Apostle of Icklingham; to the high altar of which 12d for my tithes and offerings forgotten or underpaid; to the reparation, or the reparation of the ornaments, of the same church, where greatest need, 13s 4d. I wish all my customary tenement in which I live at present, with all the lands belonging to it, to remain in the possession and occupation of John Sponere of Icklingham, to the sustentation and provision of Alice my wife for term of her life; and after Alice's decease, the tenement and customary lands, with all the appurtenances, to be sold by the same John Sponere and the money coming from it to be distributed in pious uses by him for the health of my soul and all my benefactors' [*souls*].

To the same Alice all the utensils and ostilments of my house according to the discretion of John Sponere, except those assigned below; to Alice a horse to give and sell at her pleasure.

John Baghot my son to have my free tenement in which he now lives, and a barn with the customary croft situated in Icklingham, as it lies near the said free tenement on the east and a common lane on the west, the south head abutting on the highway and the head of the croft abutting on 'Birrwey' to the north, to hold to him and his heirs for ever. To the same John a horse of 'grey' colour and 3s 4d in money, to be paid by John Sponere.

To each male child of the said John Sponere 20d in money and 4 bushels of barley, to be divided equally; to Agnes Sponere, wife of the said John, 6s 8d.

To Isabel, wife of Thomas Holden of Icklingham, 10s, to be paid at divers times (*divers' vices*); to Agnes, daughter of Thomas Holden and Isabel, when she reaches the age of 15 years, 13s 4d in money, and when she marries, she to have an honest bed (*unum lectum honestum*) and a brass pot of mine.

To Thomas Sponere, son of the said John, 6s 8d.

As to the residue of all my other lands and tenements, both bond and free, [fol. 538] I wish my exec, with all possible haste after my death, to sell them through (*per*) the said John Sponere to fulfil this my present testament and will.[1] Should John Sponere be able and willing to buy all those my lands and tenements, both free and bond, or any parcel of them, I wish him to be preferred before others in the sale and within the price of any other.

I wish my iron-bound cart to be sold and divided between the said John Sponere and John Baghot.

Residue of all my goods and chattels I leave to the distribution of John Sponere, my true and faithful exec, to dispose for the health of the souls of me and of Alice my wife and all my benefactors as he sees best to please God and profit our souls. Seal appended.

Witnesses: Thomas Sherecroft, clerk,[2] and Richard Nedeham.

Proved at Fornham St Martin, 24 January 1471/72[*sic*]. Admon to exec. Seal of official appended.

1   A little confusing, since John Sponere *was* the executor.
2   See note to no. 471.

684. PETER JAFEREY of BARNHAM ('Bernham'),[1] 20 April 1471

['Jaffrey' *in margin*] To be buried in the churchyard of St Gregory of Barnham; to the high altar of the same church 12d; to the fabric (*fabricand'*) of the same church 6s 8d.

To each of the orders of friars of Thetford 3s 4d, to be divided equally among them.[2] I leave a tenement with its appurtenances in Barnham high street (*in alto vico de Bernham*) to Isabel my wife, to have her dwelling in it all her life[*time*]; and after her decease, the whole tenement with its appurtenances to be sold by my execs and the money raised from it to be disposed wholly in pious uses for the health of my soul by my execs.[3]

Residue of my goods to Isabel my wife, to pay my debts.

Execs: Isabel my wife and Thomas Alysaundere of Little Livermere ('Lyvermere Parva'); they, having God before their eyes, faithfully to execute and fulfil my testament.

Seal appended.

Proved at Fornham St Martin, 2 March 1471/72. Admon to execs. Seal of official appended.

1   Son and executor of William Jaffrey of Barnham, will pr. December 1450 (SROB, Baldwyne 114; Pt I, no. 534); son and executor of Marion Jaffrey of Barnham, probate only, dated January 1457/58 (SROB, Baldwyne 199; Pt I, no. 974).
2   For the orders of friars at Thetford see notes to nos 68 (Friars Preachers) and 69 (Austin Friars).
3   This property was bequeathed to the testator by his father, William: it was to pass in turn to Peter's son, also Peter, if he lived; if not it was to be sold and disposed for the health of William's soul and various others' souls. Peter's son must have predeceased him.

[fol. 538v]

685. JOAN SWANTON of DEPDEN, widow, 18 January 1471/72

Widow and relict, lately the wife of William Swanton, deceased;[1] sick in body and seeing the peril of death approaching me; in the presence of my acquaintances (*notis*) and friends; [*commendation*: to Almighty God my Creator, the Blessed Mary his mother and all the saints of the celestial host]; to be buried in the churchyard of the church of the Blessed Mary in the parish of Depden; to the high altar of the same church one of my best tablecloths (*mappam*); to the work of the same church a 'violet' gown.

To John Swanton[2] a red [*bed*]cover and a blanket.

To the fabric of the parish church of Polstead ('Polstede') in the county of Suffolk 3s 4d, especially to pray for my soul.

Residue of all my goods, after my debts have been paid before all else and my burial seen to, wholly to Walter Swanton, my exec,[3] to dispose for the health of my soul as he sees most expedient to please God.

Proved at Fornham St Martin, 2 March 1471/72. Admon to exec. Seal of official appended.

1   Will, no. 366 above.
2   John Swanton of Rede, will no. 686 below. In his will William Swanton mentioned two sons, John and Walter. He did not state specifically that they were also the sons of his wife Joan. Here, Joan does not identify John and Walter Swanton her sons but she makes a bequest to the former and appoints the latter her executor; if they were not her sons, they were her step-sons. There are striking similarities between the wills of Joan and John: they were made within a day of each other and proved on the same day; both testators were sick and 'seeing the peril of death approaching'; both appointed Walter Swanton as their executor. Perhaps mother and son/stepson were suffering from the same mortal illness. Depden and Rede are, of course, neighbouring villages.
3   Son of William Swanton (no. 366 above).

686. JOHN SWANTON of REDE,[1] 19 January 1471/72

Of the parish church of the parish[*sic*] of All Saints of Rede in the county of Suffolk; sick in body and seeing the peril of death approaching me; in the presence of my acquaintances (*notis*) and friends; [*commendation*: to Almighty God my Creator and Saviour, the Blessed Mary his mother and all the saints of the celestial host]; to be buried in the churchyard of the parish church of All Saints of Rede; to the high altar of the same church for my tithes and offerings forgotten or by negligence withheld 3s 4d; for a trental 10s.

To John Thomas of Lawshall ('Lawsill') a blue gown and to his wife a green gown. To Alice Wiseman my wife's best gown and tunic.

To the said church to the divers lights burning in the church 2 beehives with the bees (*duo apiaria cum apibus*), as long as they last; to the light burning before the image of the Holy Trinity 6s 8d.

My feoffees and execs to sell my tenement lying in the town of Rede in the best manner they know and are able; the money from it to be distributed for my soul [*and the souls*] of my friends and of all the faithful departed in divers 'sangriches' [*and*] masses to be celebrated in Rede church as long as it [*i.e. the money*] lasts.

Residue of [*my*] utensils and all my goods to Walter Swanton[2] and William Wyseman, my execs, to dispose for the health of my soul as they see most expedient to please God.

Proved at Fornham St Martin, 2 March 1471/72. Admon to execs. Seal of official appended.

¹ See note to the will of his mother/step-mother, Joan (no. 685).
² His brother; executor of both William Swanton (no. 366) and Joan Swanton (no. 685).

[fol. 539]
687. JOHN MYLON of CLARE, 10 December 1472

Dated at Clare, in the diocese of Norwich; seeing the peril [*approaching*] me &c; [*commendation*: to Almighty God, the Blessed Mary &c]; to be buried in the churchyard of Clare parish church, next to the grave of my mother there. Firstly, in God's name, I beg and require my execs to pay all my debts that can be truly proved I justly owe; to the high altar of the said church for my tithes and offerings detained, forgotten and underpaid 6s 8d.

To the priests, clerks and other ministers present at my obsequies on the day of my death and administering divine service there 6s 8d; for distribution to the poor on my burial day 20s; to my acquaintances (*notis*) and friends present at my funeral on the day of my burial, to be spent and distributed in victuals 20s.

To the provision of an honest secular priest to celebrate divine service in Clare church for my soul and the soul of Helen my wife and the souls of my father and mother and of all my benefactors for whom I am most bound, for a whole year with the greatest haste possible after my death, a competent stipend such as my execs can agree with the said chaplain.

Residue of all my goods, wherever and whatever they are and in whosoever hands they are, to Rose my wife, Henry Bakere and John Neve, my execs, to distribute and dispose in alms out of those goods as they see most to the laud and honour of God and most expedient for the salvation (*salvacionem*) of my soul and theirs; to Henry and John, for their diligent labour about the premises, 6s 8d each, beyond their expenses.

Seal appended.

Witnesses: Master Robert Colyngham, vicar of Clare,¹ Richard Clerk, John Feen and others.

[*Will; of the same date*]

Dated 10 December 1472 and 12 Edward IV; all the legacies and bequests in my testament to be fulfilled.

Rose my wife to have my tenement in which I now live in the town of Clare, in the street called 'le Nethyrgate', and a messuage with the garden adjoining called 'Cherchys' lying in the same street opposite the said tenement, and an enclosed croft called 'Tylkeulncroft'[2] also lying in the same street next to the highway there leading to Stoke, with all its appurtenances, to hold to her for term of her life of the chief lords of the fee by due service and custom, she to keep up the reparations of the tenement and messuage; and after her decease, the tenement, messuage and croft, with appurtenances, to be sold by my execs and the money from them to be disposed by the discretion of my execs for the health of my soul and of my benefactors' [*souls*] as seems to them most expedient; provided always that if Rose shall be in sickness or need, and scarcely able to live by her own means, then I wish that [fol. 539v] she, with the agreement of my execs, and not otherwise, may sell the said messuage or croft, or both if necessary, to support her sufficiently for her degree.

Ann my daughter to have my tenement situated in the market place of Clare, late William Barkere's, with the cottage lately William Fydyan's adjacent to the same tenement, with a garden belonging to the tenement, with all the appurtenances, to hold to her and her heirs for ever of the chief lords &c[*sic*], on condition that she behaves well, in accordance with the counsel of Rose her mother and my execs, and obeys their instructions; but if she does not behave well and honestly as aforesaid, then I wish her to have nothing, but my execs to sell the tenement with the cottage and garden in the best way they can and dispose the money for the health of my soul and all the faithful in pious works and alms.

Rose to have all my jewels, ostilments and utensils belonging to my house, and also all the store of my house, as wheat, malt and woollen and linen cloths.

My execs to pay to[*wards*] the fabric of Clare church 33s 4d, being the amount unpaid of the 100s given to the church by me under my obligation, and of which 5 marks have been paid.[3]

Everything else I commit to the disposition and discretion of my execs.

Proved at Clare, 2 April 1473. Admon to execs.

[1] See note to no. 380 and also no. 456.
[2] Tile Kiln Croft.
[3] That is, John Mylon of Clare had promised £5 to Clare church; 5 marks (66s 8d) had already been paid and in his will he left the remaining 33s 4d.

[fol. 540]

688. JOHN COTELYN of PALGRAVE,[1] 6 January 1471/72

[*No invocation or statement concerning state of mind; opens with* This is the last will of me, John Cotelyn]; [*commendation*: to God Almighty, the Blessed Mary &c]; to be buried in the churchyard of the church of St Peter of Palgrave; to the high altar for tithes forgotten 12d; to the mother church of Norwich 4d;[2] I leave for a trental of St Gregory to be celebrated for me and the souls of my friends, 10s; to the gild of St Peter of Palgrave 2 bushels of barley;[3] to the sepulchre light a bushel of barley. Margaret my wife to have my capital dwelling house with all the lands, meadows and pastures belonging to it, with all the appurtenances, for term of her life except

413

the exceptions below; and after her decease, the dwelling house, with its appurtenances, to remain to John my son; and after their decease, if he dies without heirs,
then it to be sold by my execs to fulfil this will. The tenement called 'Puntys', with
all its appurtenances, to remain to Margaret my wife and John my son similarly,
except the excepted. Margaret my wife to have a tenement called 'Jamys Cranys' for
her life[*time*], similarly. Margaret my wife to have all my utensils and my moveable
goods, except a pan (*patell'*) late my mother's, which I wish Margery my daughter
to have.

I wish that when the said tenements and lands come into the hands of John my son,
he to pay the child that my wife is now with, if it survives, 40s.

Margery my daughter to have 40s, to be paid by my execs when she reaches the age
of marriage, or sooner if she has need of it; if she dies, the money to remain to her
sister, if she survives; if Margery survives to the time when John enters the lands
and tenements, and her sister is dead, then she to have the other money from John.
I wish certain parcels of my land to be sold by my execs, that is to say: a parcel of
land lying in 'Westbrook'; 2½ acres 1½ roods; a pightle containing 1 acre 1½ roods
at 'Lagmer wey'; 1 acre lying among the lands of St John the Baptist;[4] 4 acres of
land at Palgrave mill. The money from these to be expended by my execs in pious
uses and in implementing this will.

To each of my godchildren 1d

To each of my surviving sisters 40d.

Residue of all my goods to the disposition of my execs, Thomas Fulchere of Palgrave
and Robert Fulchere of Roydon ('Reydon') [*Norfolk*], son of the same Thomas, to
dispose as they see best to profit my soul and please God.

Seal appended.

Witnesses: John Crayles, Robert Smyth, William Smyth, John Payn, Valentine
Cotelyn and others.

Proved at Wortham, 24 March 1472/73. Admon to execs.

1   ?Executor (as 'Coteler') of Thomas Broun of Palgrave, probate October 1460 (SROB, Baldwyne
    275; Pt I, no. 1350).
2   See note to no. 193.
3   For other bequests to the gild of St Peter of Palgrave see note to no. 618.
4   That is, an acre lying between pieces of land belonging to the (now lost) chapel of St John the
    Baptist of Palgrave. The chapel, which was served by five secular priests from Bury Abbey, was
    taken down in the middle of the sixteenth century (Blatchly and Northeast, 'Lost and Ruined
    Parish Churches', p.434).

[fol. 540v]

689. ELIZABETH CAKE, wife of Robert Cake, of STOWMARKET,
21 September 1472

Dated the Monday after the Exaltation of the Holy Cross 1472; my testament and
last will; to be buried in the churchyard of the Apostles Peter and Paul of the said
town.[1]

I wish the 20 marks that were bequeathed me by Robert Gavell my father, if they can
be recovered by my husband Robert Cake, to remain in his hands to be distributed
thus: 5 marks for my soul; the residue to be divided equally among my 5 children
when they reach legal age; if the 20 marks cannot be recovered by Robert Cake, then
Robert not to undertake their distribution.

I wish all my goods that I have to be distributed according to the will and discretion of Robert my husband between my children as he sees best to please God; if any of them die under legal age, the survivors to have the deceased's part; if all should die under legal age, then all or any of the 20 marks to be recovered to be disposed in the church of Kirby Cane ('Kyrkebycam') [*Norfolk*] where I was born and [*my*] other goods [*to be disposed*] by the discretion of the said Robert in Great Waldingfield ('Mekyll Waldingfeld') for the health of my soul and of my benefactors' [*souls*]. Proved at Stowmarket, 30 March 1472[*sic*]. Admon to exec.

1   See note to no. 381.

690. WILLIAM FROST of HARTEST ('Hertest'),[1] 3 February 1472/73

['Froste' *in margin*] [*Commendation*: to God, the Blessed Mary &c]; my body to the Christian burial [*place*] of Hartest; to the high altar of Hartest church for tithes and offerings 12d; to [*Our*] Lord's sepulchre of the same church 6d.
To the friars of Sudbury 5s.[2]
To Isabel my wife all my lands and tenements as long as she remains a widow, but if she cannot or does not wish to keep them, then I wish Isabel to have the house formerly Thomas Frost's with a croft, with the keeping of a cow and a pig and 6 hens with a cock. If Isabel remarries, then Henry my son to have all my lands and tenements; but if Isabel should become destitute, then I wish her to revert to having what she had before (*volo reverti & habere sicut prius habuit*).
To Richard my son 40s; to Helen my daughter a mark.
I wish Henry my son to pay annually 3s to Richard his brother, and similarly to Helen his sister 40d, beginning to pay them in the quarter year that he is in possession; if either Richard or Helen should die during the time of the payments, then I wish their part to be paid to Hartest church. If Henry should die without children, then I wish Richard my son to have all due to him (*totum ius suum*) and pay the 3 marks to those that Henry was assigned [*to pay*]; if Richard should die without children, then I wish John my son to have all due to him and pay the 3 marks as Richard should have done.
To Isabel my wife all my goods, moveable and unmoveable, to do with freely, subject to the conditions above.
Residue of all my goods to the said Isabel.
Execs: Ralph Mason, James Spede and John Gryge, to dispose for the health of my soul as they see best to please God.
Proved at Melford, 1 April 1473. Admon to Ralph Mason exec. Power reserved to James Sped and John Grygge when they come.

1   ?Related to John Frost of Hartest (no. 807).
2   See note to no. 11.

[fol. 541]
691. JOHN YOWDE the elder of HAVERHILL ('Haveryll'), 9 March 1472/73

Of Haverhill, in the diocese of Norwich; [*commendation*: to God Almighty, the Blessed Mary his mother &c]; my body to Christian burial in the churchyard of the upper parish church of the Blessed Mary of Haverhill;[1] to the high altar there for my tithes forgotten 20d.

To Agnes my wife all my lands and tenements with their appurtenances which I have in Haverhill in the county of Suffolk for the whole term of her life, for the provision and upkeep of all our children during her lifetime; [*and afterwards*] I wish the lands and tenements to remain wholly to John my son, to hold to him and his heirs for ever of the chief lords of the fee, and he, John, to give Thomas my son 13s 4d. To the same Thomas a bullock when he finishes serving his apprenticeship.

I bequeath 12d to be distributed to poor Christian people on the day of my burial.

Residue of all my goods to Agnes my wife, Thomas Resoun and John Catelen, the son of Eleanor Catelen, to see to my funeral and pay my debts and distribute for my soul and the souls of our benefactors as seems to them most expedient for the health of my soul.

My faithful execs: Agnes my wife, Thomas Resoun and John Catelen, to implement my will in all things as above.

Proved at Haverill, 18 March 1472/73. Admon to execs.

[1] See note to no. 14 concerning the parish churches in Haverhill.

692. THOMAS BALY of Hanchet End ('Hanchyche') in the parish of WITHERSFIELD ('Wetherysfeld'),[1] 31 December 1472

[*Commendation*: to Almighty God]; my body to Christian burial in the churchyard of Withersfield church; to the high altar there for my tithes forgotten 3s 4d.

I leave 40s to be distributed in works of charity for my soul and the souls of all our benefactors by the discretion of my execs.

To John my son all the lands and tenements with their appurtenances which I recently bought from John Stobyn and Thomas Sare, with a croft lately Thomas Gernoun's in Hanchet ('Hanchiche'), when he reaches the age of 20 years; and until then I wish Ann my wife to have all the lands and tenements with their appurtenances, she committing no waste or strip and leaving them in as good a state as she receives them. If John should die before reaching 20, then all the lands and tenements to remain to Ann my wife for the term of her life; and then, after her decease, I wish them all to be sold by my execs and the money from them disposed by my execs for my soul and the souls of our benefactors as seems to them most expedient for the health of my soul.

To William my son, when he reaches the legal age of marriage, 40s.

To God and the parishioners of Withersfield [fol. 541v] a cow, with the profits of which to find a candle of wax burning in Withersfield church before the image of the crucifix on every Sunday and on double feast days[2] each year for ever.

Residue of all my goods to Ann my wife and Robert Wyburgh of Withersfield to see to my funeral and pay my debts and distribute for my soul and the souls of all my benefactors as seems to them most expedient for the health of my soul.

Ann my wife and Robert Wyburgh[3] to be my faithful execs to implement my will in all things as above, with the supervision of John Bayle the elder my brother.

Proved at Haverhill ('Haveryll'), 18 March 1472/73. Admon to execs.

[1] Hanchet End was a hamlet in the parish of Haverhill, towards Withersfield; see nos 357 and 693.
[2] See Glossary.
[3] Also executor of no. 693.

693. WILLIAM BREGGE of Hanchet End ('Hanchiche') in the parish of HAVERHILL ('Haveryll'),[1] 16 December 1472

['Brygge' *in margin*] Dated at Haverhill; [*commendation*: to God Almighty &c]; my body to Christian burial in the churchyard of the upper church of Haverhill; to the high altar there for my tithes forgotten 2s; to the reparation of the lower church in the same town 3s 4d.[2]

To Alice my wife, with an obligation for £10 to Alice and her assigns made and sealed by me as more clearly appears in it, 20 marks in money or in goods to be delivered to her by the discretion of my execs; to Alice 3 quarters of wheat and 4 bushels (*modios*), 3 quarters of barley and 4 bushels, 3 quarters of malt and 4 bushels.

To John Marchall and Joan his wife a bushel of wheat and a bushel of malt.

To John Wysbeche and Margaret his wife a bushel of wheat and a bushel of malt.

To John Drory and Alice his wife a bushel of wheat and a bushel of malt.

To William Drory and Eleanor his wife a bushel of wheat and a bushel of malt.

Residue of all my goods to Robert Bregge of Withersfield ('Wetherysfeld') my brother and Robert Wyburgh of the same to see to my funeral and pay my debts and distribute for my soul and for the souls of my benefactors as seems to them most expedient for the health of my soul.

My faithful execs: Robert Bregge and Robert Wyburgh,[3] to implement my will in all things as above.

Seal appended.

Proved at Haverhill ('Haveryll'), 18 March 1472/73. Admon to execs.

1   In no. 692, Hanchet End in Haverhill was said to be in the parish of Withersfield.
2   See note to no. 14 concerning the parish churches in Haverhill.
3   Also executor of no. 692.

[fol. 542]

694. THOMAS DEYNES of COMBS ('Combys'), 12 November 1472

[*Probably a later version of no. 621, on fol. 511.*][1]

Dated at Combs; my testament and last will; [*commendation*: to Almighty God, the Blessed Mary &c]; to be buried in the churchyard of the church of the Blessed Mary of Combs; to the high altar of the same church 6s 8d; to a suitable priest to celebrate in the said church for a whole year for my soul and my benefactors' [*souls*] [*blank*]; for a chalice for the said church [*blank*].

To Thomas my son my tenement in Bacton ('Baketon') with all the appurtenances when he comes to full age (*ad maturam etatem*), and I wish Margaret my wife meanwhile to have the tenement in her own hands for his finding (*ad inveniendu' ip'm*); if Thomas should die within that time, then I wish the tenement to remain to my execs to sell and dispose for the health of my soul.

To Ann my daughter my largest brass pot with a pan and my best bed-cover with 2 'blankettes' and a gown that was her mother's.

To Margaret my wife all the utensils of my house.

Residue of all my goods to my execs, Richard Cowpere and Edmund Ferrour, to sell and dispose for the health of my soul and my benefactors' [*souls*].

Seal appended.

Proved at Stowmarket, 18 February 1472/73. Admon to execs.

¹ This appears to be a less detailed version of no. 621, made exactly one year later. In no. 621 the testator, Thomas Deneys of Combs, also had a current wife Margaret, an under-age son Thomas and a daughter Anne; the same executors were appointed. The most conclusive evidence is the fact that no grant of probate to no. 621 was recorded in the register but a grant is recorded here.

695. THOMAS PAGE of ICKWORTH ('Ikworth'),¹ 10 February 1472/73

Dated at Ickworth ('Ikeworth'); [*commendation*: to Almighty God]; my body to Christian burial; to the high altar of Ickworth church for my tithes and offerings forgotten 12d.

John Page my brother² to have, to him and his heirs for ever, all my lands and tenements with their appurtenances in the town of Ickworth.

To Thomas the son of Thomas Kynge my godson (*filio meo sp'uali*) 2d.³

Residue of all my goods and chattels to the said John Page to sell, receive and dispose for my soul and the souls for whom I am bound, in the payment of my debts, in the celebration of masses and in other pious works as seems best to please God and profit my soul.

Execs: the said John Page and William Gylle.

Seal appended.

Witnesses: William Langlee, Thomas Kynge and others.

Proved at Fornham St Martin, 1 March 1472/73. Admon to execs.

¹ Executor of his father, Walter Page, will pr. November 1440 (SROB, Baldwyne 26; Pt I, no. 139); will of his sister, Alice, no. 709 below.
² Will, no. 708 below.
³ Thomas Kynge (the father) was executor of John Page, no. 708 below.

[fol. 542v]
696. JOHN ANDREW of OUSDEN ('Ouesden'), 6 August 1472

Dated at Ousden; [*commendation omitted – possibly a scribal error as the committal phrase was omitted and then inserted above the relevant line*]; to be buried in the churchyard of Ousden church; to the high altar of the said church for tithes and offerings 2d; to the bells (*campan'*) of the said church 2s.

Residue of all my goods to William Baldewyn of Moulton ('Multon'), Thomas Smyth of the same and Thomas Taylour of Ousden, my execs, to dispose as they see most expedient for my soul.

Seal appended.

Proved at Fornham St Martin, 8 March 1472/73. Admon to execs.

[*The rest of fol. 542v is blank.*]

[fol. 543]
697. HENRY BOTHE of SHELLAND ('Shellond'), 13 January 1472/73

[*Commendation*: to God the Father Almighty &c]; to be buried in the churchyard of the parish church of St Nicholas of Ipswich (*Gippewic'*); to the same church 40d; to Shelland church 20s for a cope.

To the Friars Minor of Ipswich 6s 8d.¹

Agnes my wife to have my tenement, with all the utensils of my house and all my chattels, moveable and unmoveable, and with all the lands, pastures, woods and fences with all their appurtenances, called 'Aylstonys', for term of her life; after her decease I wish Robert my son to have [*them*]. If Robert should die without children, then I wish John my son to have [*them*]; if John should die, then I wish Katherine my daughter to have [*them*]; if Katherine should die, then I wish Alice my daughter to have [*them*]; if all my daughters should die without children, then I wish my tenement called 'Aylstonys', with all the lands, pastures and appurtenances as above, to be sold by my execs, or by the execs of Agnes my wife, for the best possible price and the money received to be disposed by the discretion of my execs for the health of my soul. I request all my feoffees enfeoffed in the tenement with the lands and appurtenances to release full seisin to Agnes my wife.

To Shelland church my tapestry of 'sarcenet' to the honour of the sacrament of the altar.

After the decease of Agnes my wife, I wish that Robert my son have my cloths (*vestes*) that hang in the hall and a hanging board (*mensa'penulu'*) or 'a coppebord', panelling (*tabulatoriu'*) or 'a skrene', a chest (*sistula'*) or 'a spruce huche'[2] which stands in the chamber and my sword and my new saddle (*assella'*), my javelin, my tapet (*tapetu'*)[3] and my bow, my shield or defence [*?archer's bracer*] (*scutu' meu' vel defensoriu'*) and 'a bokelere' and my defensive tunic and my helm.

After the death of Agnes my wife, Joan my daughter to have 2 cows and Katherine my daughter to have 1 cow and Alice my daughter to have 1 cow.

After my wife's death, Robert my son to have my great cauldron and half 'le garnyssh' of 'pewter fessell' and my covering (*tectoriu'*) or 'a selowre for a beed'.

Execs: Agnes my wife and Thomas Norwold.

Residue of all my goods [fol. 543v] to the disposition of my execs, to dispose as seems to them best to please God and profit my soul and the souls of all my friends. Seal appended.

Proved at Fornham, 5 March 1472/73. Admon to Agnes, executrix. Admon remained to be granted to Thomas Norwold, the other exec. Seal of official appended.

1   See note to no. 1.
2   See Glossary.
3   A 'tapet' was a piece of figured cloth, used as a hanging, which does not fit with the sequence of of arms and protective clothing listed; perhaps here it refers to a decorated cover for the bow (translation and information supplied by Dr Ralph Moffat).

[*The rest of fol. 543v is blank.*]

[fol. 544]
698. ALICE TURNOUR of SUDBURY, widow, 25 March 1456

Dated on Thursday the feast of the Annunciation of the Blessed Virgin Mary 1456, at Sudbury, in the diocese of Norwich; [*commendation*: to God Almighty, the Blessed Mary &c]; to be buried in the churchyard of the church of St Gregory of Sudbury, nearest (*maxime prope*) to the grave of John Turnour my late consort and spouse (*nuper consortis et spons' mei*); to the high altar of the same church 20s; to each priest present in the said church on the day of my death (*die obitus mei*), if they participate in the obsequies and mass in order to pray sincerely and devoutly for my soul and for the souls of all the faithful for whom I am in any way bound, 12d. To Richard Crysale, parish chaplain, 12d; to John Rysby, chaplain, 12d.[1]

To Margery Qwyntyn the holy woman (*casti mulieri*) 2s.[2]

419

To Katherine Crudde my household servant[3] 2s.

To the reparation of the house of the Friars Preachers of Sudbury 6s 8d;[4] to the nuns of Hedingham ('Hethyngham') [*Essex*] 6s 8d.[5]

To Richard Goldyng chaplain[6] the best basin and ewer, with 2 curtains for a bed.

To Joan Turnour, wife of Henry Turnour my son, a pair of silver beads with gilt paternosters.[7]

To Joan (*Joh'i*) Myst of Melford, my kinswoman (*consanguinee mee*),[8] a 'violet' gown lined with 'grey' fur[9] and a black silk girdle ornamented with silver.

To Agnes Kynge, my household servant, my best tabard.

To Annabel ('Anabyll') Revell, wife of William Revell, a pair of sheets and a cover.

To Katherine Turnour, daughter of Henry Turnour, a silver bowl (*cratera'*) with a cover.

I wish John Turnour the elder, son of Henry Turnour, to have the meadow formerly purchased of Thomas Buste after my decease, to him and his heirs; if he should die without heirs, I wish the meadow to remain to John Turnour, his brother, and his heirs; and if John Turnour the younger should die without heirs, then the meadow to remain to Thomas Turnour his brother and his heirs; and so to each of the children (*puer'*) of Henry Turnour my son [*then*] living.

To Margaret Kendale, wife of John Kendale the younger, lately my household servant, a 'medly' gown with fur inside (*unam togam de Medly cum penula infra*).

To Agnes Cok, my household servant, one of the best lined tunics; to Agnes Barkere, my household servant, one of the worst lined tunics; to Alice Barbour, lately my household servant, a black gown.

To John Turnour the elder my best mazer with two large candlesticks.

To Joan Myst, my kinswoman,[10] 3 silver spoons.

To Thomazine, daughter of Henry my son, a silver bowl (*cratera'*) and a small mazer ornamented with silver and gilt.

To John Turnour the elder 6 of the best silver spoons and a bed 'federbed' with the 'wyth & transom' (*unum lectum* federbed *cum* wyth & transom).[11]

Residue of all my goods to Henry Turnour my son and John Vyne of Sudbury, my execs, to dispose of them for the health of my soul as seems to them best to please God and most profit my soul.

I leave 6 silver spoons and a girdle with silver ornamentation to the making of a pair of censers for St Gregory's church, Sudbury.[12]

To the said John Vyne 6s 8d for his labour.

[*Probate not recorded: the previous probate (fol. 543v) is dated 5 March 1472/73 at Fornham, the next (fol. 544v) 15 November 1472 at Fornham.*]

---

1   John Rysby/Risby, chaplain, of Sudbury, also witnessed the wills of Thomas Alston (no. 290) and Stephen Barbour (no. 408).

2   This reference is very likely to be to a female anchorite. There is both written and architectural evidence for the presence of male and female anchorites at St Gregory's, Sudbury, in the Middle Ages. See Clay, *Hermits and Anchorites*, p.12. (Thanks are due to Dr Elizabeth McAvoy for this information.) Although not described by them as a holy woman, three other testators from Sudbury also made bequests to Margery Qwyntyn: Henry Pethyrton (SROB, Baldwyne 16; Pt I, no. 91); William Herward the elder (SROB, Baldwyne 217; Pt I, no. 1077); and John Brook the elder (SROB, Baldwyne 232; Pt I, no. 1168).

3   The other three testators who made bequests to Margery Qwyntyn also made bequests to Katherine Crudde. See note above.

4   See note to no. 11.

5   The nunnery (priory) of Castle Hedingham was founded some time in the latter half of the twelfth century by Aubrey de Vere, first earl of Oxford, and Lucy his wife. The advowson of the priory belonged always to the de Veres. It was dedicated to St Mary, St James and the Holy Cross (*VCH, Essex*, ii, pp.122–3).

6   Robert Wasschsher of Boxford (no. 440) requested Richard Goldyng, chaplain, to celebrate in Boxford church for his soul and the souls of his parents.

7   See Glossary.

8   John Flegge the elder of Sudbury (no. 727) had a daughter named Joan Myste.

9   See Glossary.

10 See note above. This may have been the same woman, or 'of Melford' may have been used to distinguish between two women of the same name.

11 No suitable defintion for the noun 'wyth' (or 'with') has been found. In the text of this bequest, the Latin words are immediately followed by their English translation and it seems likely that the writer (or the registry clerk) became confused with his 'withs': perhaps the translation should simply read 'a featherbed with a transom'.

12 These items might have been sold to provide the censers or even used in the making of them.

[fol. 544v]

699. ALICE BRAY, relict of John Bray, of BARNHAM ('Bernham'), 24 October 1472

Lately the relict of John Bray; seeing the peril of death [*approaching*]; sick unto death; dated the Sunday before the feast of the Apostles Simon and Jude 1472; my testament and will; [*commendation*: to God Almighty, the Blessed Mary &c]; my body to Christian burial in the churchyard of the church of St Martin in Barnham;[1] to the high altar of the same church in recompense of my tithes not fully paid 12d; to the emendation of the same church 6s 8d.

I wish a wax candle to be found to burn on feast days in the chapel of St Mary, before the image of the Blessed Mary there, for the term of 7 years following my decease; to the sustentation of the sepulchre light in the said church 12d; I wish to have a certain celebrated for my soul and for the souls of all my benefactors for a whole year in the said church of St Martin, that is to say, every Sunday 1d; I wish to have a trental celebrated for me and for the souls of all my benefactors as soon as it can be done after my death; to the emendation of the church of St Gregory in the said town 20d.

To Alice the daughter of Robert Wylde a black heifer and a brass pot; to Ed' the son of the said Robert a brass pot.

The largest pan and a horse and 2 cows to be sold by my execs.

The said Robert and Isabel his wife to have their dwelling in my messuage in which I live for the term of 3 years after my decease without paying any farm for it, on condition that they repair and keep up all the houses there well and competently and so hand them over (*sic eos dimittent*); and after the term of the said 3 years, I wish Robert and Isabel to have my messuage with the appurtenances, and to have the purchase [*of it*], to hold to them and their heirs for ever, on condition that they pay my execs for the said messuage with the appurtenances £10 within the next 10 years, that is to say, every year on the feast of St Michael the Archangel 20s, without any default during that time. I wish that the money arising from it be disposed in the celebration of masses and in other alms and pious uses by my execs.

Residue of all my goods to the disposition of William Bray and John Palmere, my execs, to fulfil this my testament as they see best to please God and profit the health of my soul and of the souls of all my friends.

I require my co-feoffees to deliver full seisin and possession to my execs of and in my said messuage with the appurtenances whenever they shall be required by my said execs that this my testament be perfectly fulfilled.

Proved at Fornham, 15 November 1472. Admon to execs.

¹ See note to no. 282.

[fol. 545]

700. THOMAS COOK of COTTON,[1] 9 October 1471

To be buried in the churchyard of the church of St Andrew of Cotton; to the high altar of the same church for my tithes underpaid 10s; to the high altar of Bacton ('Baketon') church 3s 4d; to the reparation and building of the new roof of Cotton church, a close called 'Garlekis' in Cotton, on condition that no man of Cotton makes any unjust claim or causes trouble about my close called 'Clarys close' in Cotton.

To the friars of the order of St Francis of Babwell ('Babbewele') 20s; to the friars of Orford ('Orforde') 20s to celebrate 2 trentals for my soul and the souls of Matilda my wife, my parents and all my benefactors; to the Carmelite Friars of Ipswich (*Gypwico*) 6s 8d; to the Friars Preachers of Dunwich (*Denewic'*) 6s 8d; to the friars of the order of St Augustine of Thetford (*Thetfoedia*) 6s 8d.[2]

To Mendlesham ('Mendylsham') church 6s 8d; to Wyverstone ('Wyverston') church 6s 8d; to Haughley ('Haule') church 6s 8d; to Ixworth church 6s 8d; to Rickinghall Inferior ('Nether Rykelynghale') church 3s 4d.

I wish to have 4 suitable priests to celebrate for a whole year in Cotton church for my soul and for the souls of Matilda my wife, of my children, my parents and benefactors.

To Margaret my wife all my lands and tenements, meadows, pasture and feedings in the towns of Cotton and Bacton, both free and bond, except 2 closes called 'Clarys close' and 'Garlekes', for term of her life, if she remains unmarried; to Margaret my 4 cows, my 4 horses and my 20 sheep and all the utensils of my house, and my grain and crops (*segetes*), if she remains unmarried; if she remarries, then I leave her only the cows, the horses, the sheep, the household utensils and the grain [*out*] of my crops and £10 in money.

After Margaret's decease, all the said lands and tenements, meadows, pasture and feedings in the said towns to be sold by my execs in the best way possible and the money received to be distributed in repairs to the churches [*and*] ways and in masses and pious uses. If John Coke my son wishes to buy all my lands and tenements, meadows, pasture and feeding, I wish him to have them £10 below (*infra*) the price, by the oversight of Richard Thurburne, Thomas Kyrre, William Stebbyng of Cotton and Nicholas Garnham of Bacton.

To the reparation of the lane leading from Bacton to Cotton church 40s; to the reparation of the way on the north side of 'le Pynfold' in Bacton ('Bakton') 3s 4d.

I wish to have a certain ('serteyne') celebrated in Cotton church for my soul and the souls of Matilda and Margaret my wives, my children, my parents and my benefactors, and our obit to be kept, sustained with a piece of meadow called 'Denseys medowe' in Bacton, for ever.

To each child of John Coke and Robert Goche 20d.

To each of my execs for their labour 6s 8d outright, and beyond that to have for their expenses as right and conscience require.

Residue [fol. 545v] of all [*my*] goods to John Cocke my son and Robert Goche of Bacton, my execs, to fulfil my will and dispose as they see best to please God and profit my soul.

Seal appended.

Witnesses: Richard Thurberne, John Blake, Thomas Kyrre and others.

Proved on 28 December 1472, [*place not given*]. Admon to execs. Seal of official appended.

> 1   Executor of Thomas Holm of Cotton, will pr. December 1445 (SROB, Baldwyne 87; Pt I, no. 400).
> 2   For the friars see notes to nos 1 (Franciscans of Babwell and Carmelites of Ipswich), 6 (Orford), 65 (Friars Preachers of Dunwich) and 69 (Augustinians of Thetford).

701. BRITANA HUM[M]YS of KERSEY, widow, 22 September 1472

Of Kersey in the diocese of Norwich; my testament and last will; [*commendation*: to God Almighty]; to be buried in the churchyard of St Mary of Kersey; to the high altar of the same church for my tithes and offerings forgotten 8d. I wish my funeral expenses to be met (*fiant*) in due manner and honestly by the good office and discretion of my execs; also I wish all my debts which I of right owe anyone to be paid and satisfied immediately after my decease; and after that I leave to the reparation of Kersey church 3s 4d.

To the convent of Friars Minor of Ipswich (*Gypwici*) 2 trentals,[1] that is, one for the soul of Gregory Cayle[2] and the other for the soul of John Cayle and for the souls of all his benefactors.

To Joan my daughter my best furred gown, my best hood, my silver girdle, a pair of amber beads ('hambyr bedes') with all its rings; to her a cauldron, a large pan, a brass pot and a pitcher (*urciolum*).

To Joan the daughter of my son a pitcher and a small pan.

To Joan my said daughter all my goods that she now has in her possession, unconditionally; to each of her children a small pan.

The rest of my goods I leave to John my son, my faithful exec, to dispose as seems best to him to please God and profit my soul.

Seal appended.

Witnesses: John Frawce, Robert Cook, William Okyre and others.

Proved at Fornham, 8 January 1472/73. Admon to exec.

> 1   See note to no. 1.
> 2   ?Sir Gregory Cayle, rector of Somerton church from at least 1440 (Morley, 'Suffolk Clergy', p.43).

[fol. 546]

702. WALTER OLDHALLE of SUDBURY,[1] 10 May 1472

Dated at Sudbury, in the diocese of Norwich; to be buried in the church of St Gregory of the same town, opposite the window which I had made in that church;[2] to the high altar of the same church for tithes and offerings forgotten 6s 8d; to the reparation of the same church 6s 8d.

I wish my execs to support a secular priest to celebrate divine service in the said church for 2 years out of the sale of my goods, as soon as it can conveniently be done.

Christine my wife to have my tenement in Sudbury, in the parish of St Gregory, situated on the corner opposite the wall of the Friars Preachers there,[3] to her and her assigns for ever; and also £10 in money, to be paid out of the sale of my capital messuage, as it can be raised from it.

To Joan my daughter 5 marks, to be raised similarly from my capital messuage.

My capital messuage, with the tenement annexed to it and my other tenement in the lane to the house of the Preachers and all [*my*] other goods, moveable and unmoveable, to be sold by my execs to implement this my testament and last will and to pay my debts from [*the proceeds*].

I will and require my cofeoffees in all my said messuages and tenements to deliver their estate in them when reasonably required by my execs for implementing my last will.

John Brooke of Sudbury, the elder, and William Gebelon the elder of the same [*place*] to be my execs; to each of whom 20s for their labour; to them the residue of all my goods to dispose of them as they see best to please God and most profit the health of my soul.

Seal appended.

Proved at Sudbury; [*date not given*].

[*Previous probate (fol. 545v) 8 January 1472/73; next (fol. 546v) 25 June 1472.*]

1   ?Executor and former husband of Ann, 'wife of Walter Oldale of Sudbury', probate only, January 1461/62 (SROB, Baldwyne 295; Pt I, no. 1447).
2   To have paid for a part of the church fabric gave the testator a good claim to be buried in the church, adjacent to that part.
3   See note to no. 11.

703. JOHN CALDEWELL the elder of THELNETHAM, turner, 1 March 1471/72

Dated at Thelnetham; to be buried in the churchyard of Thelnetham parish church; to the high altar of the said church 4d.

To Isabel, daughter of Robert Caldewell, a chafing-dish ('a chafowr'); to Margaret, daughter of the said Robert Caldewell, a pan holding the measure of a gallon and 8d; to John, son of the said Robert, 8d; to William, son of the said Robert, 8d; to Thomas, [*son*] of the said Robert, 8d.

To Agnes, daughter of John Caldewell living at 'Fenstret', 4d.

Thomas Caldewell my son to have, after the decease of Katherine my wife, a large cauldron.

To the four daughters of the said Thomas Caldewell 4s, that is, 12d each.

After my decease, Katherine my wife to have all the utensils of my house not bequeathed above; she to have all the future payments for a messuage lying in Thelnetham, at 'Fenstret' and elsewhere, sold to John Caldewell my son, for the term of the life of Katherine my wife; and if any [fol. 546v] of the payments of money, as [*specified*] in certain indentures made of it between me, John Caldewell, turner, and John Caldewell my son, remain after the decease of Katherine, then I wish that I shall have the money so remaining. And with the residue of all my goods, to be sold by my execs,[1] a suitable priest to celebrate in Thelnetham parish church for my soul and for all my benefactors for the space of three quarters of a year, that is, half a year and a quarter of a year, or for a trental to be celebrated in the said church, as it can be done by my execs.

Residue of all my goods to my execs to dispose for the health of my soul and of all my benefactors' [*souls*].

Execs: Robert Caldewell of Thelnetham and Thomas Caldewell of the same [*place*].

Proved at Langham, 25 June 1472. Admon to execs.

1   The 'And' (*Et*) appears to start a new sentence, but as the testator did not specify for what the money remaining from his son's payments should be used, perhaps he wanted that money put with the proceeds of the residue.

704. WILLIAM HOTON of WOOLPIT ('Wolpet'), 5 July 1471

Dated at Woolpit; [*commendation*: to Almighty God &c]; my body to Christian burial; to the high altar of Woolpit ('Wolpett') church for my tithes forgotten &c[*sic*] 6d.

To Alice my wife all my goods and chattels, moveable and unmoveable, both live and dead, of whatever kind and wherever they are in Woolpit, for her upkeep and to pay my debts.

Residue of all my goods to my execs, to sell, receive and dispose for the health of my soul and for all those for whom I am bound in works of charity, as they see best to please God.

Execs: Alice my wife, William Crystemess and Thomas Badewyn[*sic*] of Woolpit; to each of them for their labour 12d.

Supervisor: Richard Hoton.

Seal appended.

Witnesses: John Coppyng, John Baude [*or*, Bande], John Leneys [*or*, Leveys], William Aubry and others.

Proved 4 December 1471, [*place not given*]. Admon to Alice Hoton, late wife of the deceased, and William Crystemesse, execs. Power reserved to Thomas Baldewyn, the other co-exec, when he comes and if he wishes to take up [*admon*].

[fol. 547]
705. WILLIAM BRON of FORNHAM [ST] MARTIN, 13 April 1473

Dated at Fornham aforesaid; my body to Christian burial.

To the friars of Babwell 10s to celebrate a Gregorian trental (*unum trigintale gregorianu'*), if the value of my goods will stretch to it.[1]

To Robert Bron of Felsham, my father, 5½ yards (*virgatas*) of woollen cloth of violet colour (*coloris de* 'vyolett').

To Thomas Bron of Barton ('Berton'), my brother, a russet-coloured gown.

To George Bron of Felsham, my brother, a russet-coloured tabard (*collobiu'*), a doublet, a pair of shoes, a pair of hose and two pairs of smocks (*paria camisiarum*).[2]

To Joan Bron my wife my tenement, with its appurtenances, situated in the town of Fornham aforesaid; to her all the utensils and hostilments in any way belonging to my house; to her all my live cattle.

Residue of all my goods to Joan, my wife, my faithful executrix, to dispose in works of charity for the health of my soul and of my friends' [*souls*] as seems best to her to most please God and profit my soul.

Proved at Fornham St Martin, 7 June 1473. Admon to executrix.

¹ See note to no. 1.
² Possibly 'two sets of underwear'.

[fol. 547v]

706. WILLIAM LAMBE of HAUGHLEY ('Hawle'),¹ 20 April 1473

Dated at Haughley; to be buried in the churchyard of Haughley ('Hawley') church; to the high altar of the same church for tithes underpaid 4s; to the said church for a vestment 4 marks.

To the Carmelite Friars of Ipswich (*Gippewic'*) 10s; to the friars of Babwell 3s 4d.² To Wetherden church 2s.

To be distributed among the poor in Haughley 20d.

To my godsons and goddaughters in Haughley ('Hawhle') 4d each, up to the number of 16 persons.

To Margaret my wife all the utensils and hostilments of my house; to her my whole messuage with my lands, meadows and pastures in Haughley ('Hawhley') for the whole term of her life; and after Margaret's decease, I leave to Robert my son my pasture called 'le Fen'.

After Margaret's decease, my said messuage, with the lands and meadows, to be sold by my execs for the best price possible; however if Robert my son wants, and is able, to buy it, then I wish him to have it under the price to any other.

I wish to have a suitable priest for a whole year, after the decease of Margaret my wife, out of the money coming from the said messuage, to celebrate divine service for our souls.

To the reparation of the way leading from the market to 'Fysshpond' 13s 4d.

To Robert my son 4 yards of white cloth and a blue gown.

To the two children of the said Robert my son 6s 8d each.

Residue of all my goods to Margaret my wife, Henry Coke and Robert my son, execs, to fulfil my last will and dispose as they see best to please God and profit my soul.

Seal appended.

Witnesses: Thomas Schepey, John Bette, William Turnour and others.

Proved at Stowmarket, 6 October 1474. Admon to execs.

¹ Witness of the will of Rose Deneys of Haughley, pr. February 1453/54 (SROB, Baldwyne 164; Pt I, no. 795).
² For the friars see notes to no. 1.

[fol. 548]

[*All of this testament has been struck through. It is a repeat of the major portion of that on fol. 528 (no. 661). See the notes to no. 661 as they have not been repeated here.*]

707. STEPHEN FEN of HOPTON, 7 January 1472/73

To be buried in the churchyard of Hopton church; I wish all my debts that I owe to be well and truly paid, quickly and in the best way possible; to the high altar of Hopton church for tithes forgotten and not well paid 40d.

I wish all coming to my burial to have refreshment (*repastum*) according to the discretion of my execs.

To the friars of the new house of Thetford for a trental 10s.

I wish to have a suitable chaplain to celebrate divine service for my soul and the souls of all my benefactors in Hopton parish church for a quarter of a year, he to have 26s 8d for his salary, out of the money owed me by Robert Fen my son, that is, from the two payments from Robert to my execs next after my death.

To the emendation of Hopton church 13s 4d; to the emendation of the gild of St Peter of 'Nethergate' 12d.

To each of my children, that is, Robert, William, John, John [*sic*] and Katherine 10s, in total 50s between them. If any of them should die before the money is paid to them, then I wish my execs to dispose that money for the health of my soul and of my benefactors' [*souls*] as seems to them best to please God.

To each of my godchildren, children of Robert my son, 2s; to Robert Partryche and Isabel Partrych my godchildren, 2s each; to Robert Catton my godson and Isabel Catton 2s each; to Stephen Goold my godson 4d; to the son of William Fen my godson 2s; to each of my godchildren not named above 4d. If any should decease before receiving their money, then I wish that money be disposed in pious uses by my execs.

To each of my execs for their labour 5s.

I wish to have another suitable chaplain to celebrate divine service for my soul and the souls of all my benefactors in Hopton church for another quarter of a year or more if my money will stretch to it beyond my legacies above-mentioned.

To Matilda my wife all the utensils of my house and all my necessaries in my chamber, of whatever kind to give, sell or bequeath to whomsoever she wishes. To Matilda all the covenants specified in certain deeds indented made between me and my feoffees on the one part and Hugh Catton and his co-feoffees on the other, except the money owed me by the said Hugh, of which money I bequeath to my wife Matilda to the end of her life, 10s annually, as long as the sum owed lasts. If Matilda dies, then I wish all the money still owed by Hugh be disposed in pious uses according to the discretion of my execs. If Hugh should default in his bargain [*and surrenders*] all his lands and tenements into the hands of my execs or of my feoffees, then I wish them to be sold by my execs, reserving a chamber for my wife and free entrance and exit for term of her life. I wish Matilda to have annually during her life[*time*] whatever can be found (*unde inveniri poterit*) for sustentation [*breaks off here*]

[fol. 548v]

708. JOHN PAGE of ICKWORTH ('Ikeworth'),[1] 7 May 1473 [*nuncupative*]

To be buried in the churchyard of Ickworth church; to the high altar of Ickworth church for his tithes and offerings underpaid 12d.

He wished all his debts to be paid faithfully.

He wished Alice Page[2] and Joan, his sisters, to be provided for (*exhibeantur*) out of his goods for term of their lives.

To Alice Skott[3] 2 bushels (*mod'*) of oats.

Residue of all my[*sic*] goods, moveable and unmoveable, he committed to the disposition of Thomas Traylys, Thomas Kyng[4] and William Edward,[5] whom he made his execs, especially to dispose for his soul as they see best to please God and profit his soul.

Witnesses: the rector of Ickworth church, Henry Godhay, John Barkar, Joan Huske and Thomas Huske.

Proved at Fornham, 14 June 1473. Admon to execs. Seal of official appended.

1   Executor of his father Walter, will pr. November 1440 (SROB, Baldwyne 26; Pt I, no. 138); executor of his brother Thomas (no. 695 above).
2   Will, no. 709 below.
3   A beneficiary of, and witness to, the will of Alice Page.
4   Witness of the will of Thomas Page (no. 695).
5   Also executor of Alice Page.

709. ALICE PAGE of ICKWORTH ('Ikeworth'), 12 May 1473

Dated at Ickworth; 'in my pure virginity'; my body to Christian burial; to the high altar of Ickworth church for my tithes and offerings unpaid and for the health of my soul [no sum].

To the friars of Babwell ('Babwel')[1] to celebrate a trental of St Gregory and a half for the soul of my lady, lately the Lady of Ickworth, the souls of Dame Katherine Cokerell and Eleanor her servant,[2] the souls of Walter Page[3] and Agnes his wife, and my soul, 15s.

To Alice Skott[4] a sheet.

To Margaret Kyng a sheet.

To Joan my sister[5] a featherbed ('federbet'), a pair of sheets, a pair of blankets and a bedcover.

Residue of all my goods and chattels to my execs, to sell, receive and dispose for my soul and the souls for whom I am bound in celebrating masses, relieving the poor and needy and doing other pious works as seems [best] to please God and profit my soul.

Execs: William Langle of Ickworth[6] and William Edward of Great Horringer[7] ('Magna Horningherth').

Seal appended.

Witnesses: Alice Skott, widow ('wedow'), Joan Langle, widow ('wydowe') and others.

Proved at Fornham, 14 June 1473.[8] Admon to execs. Seal of official appended.

1   See note to no.1.
2   Dame Katherine Cokerell, wife of Sir John Cokerell, was the daughter of Thomas de Ickworth (third of that name), lord of the manor of Ickworth in the late fourteenth century. Both her brother, Thomas (the fourth), and his only son, Ralph, predeceased her and so she became entitled to the reversion of the manor upon the death of Ralph's wife (Copinger, *Manors of Suffolk*, vii, p.70); Katherine died on 2 October 1428 (IPM, 6 Henry VI 63). By 1438 the manor was in the hands of Henry Drury, escheator for Suffolk, who was married to Elizabeth; they had a son Henry, who died while an infant, and a daughter Jane. Henry the elder had died by 1455; Elizabeth Drury was tenant for life of the manor of Ickworth; she made her will in March 1475/76. Jane, sole heir of Henry Drury, married Thomas Hervey (died *c.*1470), whose family originated in Bedfordshire; she had died by the time her mother made her will. Copinger, *Manors of Suffolk*, vii, p.72; Hervy, *Visitation of Suffolk 1561*, vol. I, p.69. Perhaps 'my lady, lately the Lady of Ickworth' was Jane Hervey since Elizabeth Drury was still alive.
3   Will pr. November 1440 (SROB, Baldwyne 26; Pt I, no. 139); Walter Page was the father of Agnes, the testatrix, of John (no. 708 above) and of Thomas (no. 695 above).
4   Also a beneficary of the will of John Page (no. 708).
5   Also a beneficiary of the will of her brother, John Page.
6   Witness (as 'Langlee') of the will of Thomas Page (no. 695).
7   Also an executor of John Page.
8   Perhaps Alice and her brother John died from the same illness: their wills, which were made within five days of each other, were proved on the same day.

[fol. 549]

710. JOHN KYNG of BRADFIELD COMBUST ('Bradfeld Combust'),
27 May 1472

Dated at Bradfield Combust; my body to Christian burial.

To Margaret my wife all the utensils belonging to my house in Bradfield aforesaid.

I wish Margaret my wife to have celebrated for my soul and my parents' [*souls*] in the church of All Saints of Bradfield aforesaid a trental, [*the celebrant*] taking for his salary 10s.

To Margaret my tenement called 'Wysys' in Bradfield aforesaid, with all its appurtenances, for term of her life; and after her decease, it to remain to my daughter Grace, to hold to her and her heirs for ever; if Grace should die during the lifetime of Margaret my wife, then Margaret to have the tenement to her and her heirs for ever, to sell and dispose for all our friends.

I beg all my feoffees enfeoffed to my use of and in my tenement called 'Wysys', with its appurtenances, to deliver their estate and title in it according to the tenor of this last will.

Execs: William Clerk and Margaret my wife.

Seal appended.

Proved at Fornham St Martin, 26 October 1472. Admon to execs.

[fol. 549v]

711. MARGARET SKETH of STANTON, daughter of Thomas Sketh,[1] 20 July 1472

Dated at Stanton; to be buried in the churchyard of the church of All Saints of Stanton; to the high altar of the said church for tithes forgotten and other defaults in offerings 12d; to the adornment (*ad ornatu'*) of the high altar of the said church a sanguine-coloured cover with white and blue roses interwoven [*or*, embroidered] (*intextis*); to the said church a towel of diaper (*unum* 'le towale de le dyapere'); to the same church [*my*] best sheet for use in making a cope (*pro capa involvenda*); to the church of St John the Baptist for the adornment of the high altar a green-coloured cover; to the emendation of the said church of St John a towel ('le towayle') of plain-work.[2]

To Agnes Calfe a table-cloth (*mappam*) of plain-work.

To Adam Fyzce[3] 2 yards of white woollen cloth; to John Fyzce 2 yards of white woollen cloth.

I wish all my utensils, my messuage and my land, with all the crops (*vestura*) to be sold and with the money from them I wish a suitable priest to be supported, to celebrate divine service for my soul and the souls of my parents.

To Cecily Burnell a blue gown.

To Joan Eglyn a violet-coloured tunic that was formerly my mother's[4] and an under-garment called a smock ('le smoke').

To Cassandra Tolsent an old cloak.

To the emendation of the gild of All Saints 6 wooden dishes, 6 wooden platters, 6 wooden vessels (*vasa*) called 'le sawseres', 6 goblets (*ciphos*), a pewter salt (*salsariu'*) and 6 trenchers (*scissoria*).[5]

Residue of all my goods I place in the hands of Roger Rollecros,[6] John Taylour and

John Edwyn, my execs, to dispose for my soul and the souls of my parents as seems to them most to please God and profit the health of my soul.
Seal appended.
Witnesses: John Fyzce, Thomas Rudham, Peter Spark and others.
Proved at Fornham St Martin, 26 October 1472. Admon to execs.

1 Will, pr. January 1462/63 (no. 817 below).
2 This testatrix donated several pieces of fabric of various colours and qualities to the two parish churches of Stanton. See Glossary for definitions.
3 The third letter in this surname is a yogh.
4 Katherine Sketh of Stanton, relict of Thomas; her will is no. 453.
5 Either these eating and drinking vessels could be sold for the benefit of the gild, or they could be used by gild members at communal celebrations. Walter Noble (no. 432) bequeathed 12d to the gilds of Great Horringer for the reparation (repair) of the vessels belonging to the gildhall, indicating that testators made practical as well spiritual bequests to gilds.
6 Executor of both her father (no. 817) and mother (no. 453).

[fol. 550]
712. JOHN MAN of THORPE MORIEUX ('Thorppmoryus'),[1] 30 August 1474

Dated at Thorpe Morieux, the penultimate day of August 1474; [*commendation*: to Almighty God, the Blessed Mary &c]; my body to Christian burial; to the high altar of the church of Thorpe Morieux ('Thorppmeryus') for my tithes forgotten 12d.
To the convent of the friars of Babwell 10s for a trental to be interceded (*deprecand'*) for my soul.[2]
To Margaret my wife all my utensils and household hostilments for the whole of her life; and after her decease I wish the utensils or hostilments to be shared equally between Thomas and John my sons.
To Thomas my son my whole tenement lately John Man's, deceased, with all its appurtenances or rents lying in Thorpe Morieux and Felsham, reserving to Margaret my wife a chamber at the lower end of the hall (*unam cameram inferior parte aule*), with free entry and exit for the whole of her life[*time*]; also he to provide his mother with food and clothing and all other necessaries for her life[*time*]; and when she forsakes this world, Thomas to pay her funeral and burial expenses out of his own pocket (*sumptibus*). And afterwards, Thomas to pay John my son 20 marks in money in the next 7 years, if he does not die under age, and pay to Margaret my daughter 10 marks in money if she marries and similarly she to have a wedding dress (*vestem nupsialem*) decently prepared for her. If Thomas should decease without heirs, then I wish John my son to have the messuage with all the appurtenances and rents under the above conditions (*oneribus*). If John should decease without heirs, then I wish the messuage with all its appurtenances to be sold by my exec for the best price possible and the money from it to be disposed in pious uses by my exec. If Margaret [*my wife*] should be in need or poverty, she to be relieved with the goods of the said messuage during her life[*time*].
I wish my feofees to grant full and peaceful seisin to Thomas my son and Robert Hardhed of Buxhall ('Buxhale') in all those lands, tenements and rents with all their appurtenances.
Whatever residue there shall be of all my goods, I leave to the disposition of my exec, Thomas my son, to see to the faithful execution of this my testament and last

will; he, having God before his eyes, to dispose as seems to him most to profit me and my soul and to please God.

Seal appended.

Proved at Bildeston ('Bylston'), 24 September 1474. Admon to exec.

1   Although this testator and the next, William Man (no. 713), both had the same surname and both lived in Thorpe Morieux, there is no other obvious connection between the two men.
2   See note to no. 1.

[fol. 550v]

713. WILLIAM MAN of THORPE MORIEUX ('Thorppmeryus'), 11 August 1474

Dated at Thorpe Morieux in the diocese of Norwich, the Thursday after the feast of St Lawrence the Martyr 1474; somewhat sick in body and in peril of death; [*commendation*: to Almighty God, the Blessed Mary &c]; to be buried in the churchyard of the church of the Blessed Virgin Mary of Thorpe aforesaid; to the high altar of which I leave, for forgotten tithes and offerings, 3s 4d; I wish all my debts to be paid before all else; to the sustentation and reparation of Thorpe church 20s in money.

To a suitable priest 9 marks to celebrate for a year in the said church for my soul and the souls of my friends.

To Alice my wife all my hostilments and bedding.

To Alice Chenerey a cow and 13s 4d, when or before she marries, to use it as she pleases.

Residue of all my goods I place in the hands of my execs to dispose for the health of my soul as they will answer before God.

Execs: Richard Man of Hadleigh ('Hadley'), my brother, and Robert Bochere of Thorpe.

Supervisor: Hugh Wryght of Bildeston ('Bylston').

Seal appended.

Witnesses: John Skarpp of Felsham, Hugh Wryght of Bildeston, William Cooke of the same town and others.

Proved at Bildeston, 24 September 1474. Admon to execs.

[fol. 551]

714. ROGER CLERK of EDWARDSTONE ('Edwardeston'), 17 October 1474 [*nuncupative*]

['Clerke' *in margin*] In the presence of us, Sir John Howse, rector of Groton,[1] Thomas Cowell, John Spenser of Edwardstone and John Wychham of Sudbury ('Sudbr'), Roger Clerk our neighbour expressed his last will nuncupative thus:

Of Edwardstone in the diocese of Norwich; sick unto death, before you my good friends, this is my last will; my body to Christian burial in the churchyard of Edwardstone church; to the high altar of the same church for my tithes forgotten 12d.

To the reparation of the church of the friars of Clare for pleading (*rogand'*) for my soul 40d.[2]

To John Clerk my son all my lands and tenements with all their appurtenances as they lie in the town of Edwardstone, to him and his heirs for ever; to him all my moveables, live and dead, freely to do with as he wishes, on condition that he finds

431

a priest to celebrate divine office in Edwardstone church for a whole year after my decease for the souls of me, Margery and Isabel my wives.

Residue of all my goods together with my debts I leave to John Clerk my son, to perform this will; he to be my exec to implement everything above.

I beg in God's name all my feoffees in the said lands and tenements to deliver estate according to my will when duly required by John my exec.

Proved at Fornham St Martin, ultimate day [*31*] of October 1474. Admon to exec. Seal of official appended.

1   John Hows was rector of Groton from 1462 to January 1484/85 (Tanner, p.1365).
2   See note to no. 1.

715. JOHN SPORLE of BURGATE, 9 November 1474 [*probate only*]

Proved at Westhorpe ('Westhorpp'). Admon to Sir Thomas Wylkyn, vicar of Wickham ('Wykham'), exec.[1] Power reserved to William Wyghteman the other [*exec*] when he comes.

1   See note to no. 218 and also no. 374.

[fol. 551v]
716. JOHN CLERK of PRESTON, 23 October 1474

['Clerke' *in margin*] Dated at Preston; [*commendation*: to Almighty God, the Blessed Mary &c]; to be buried in the churchyard of the Blessed Mary of Preston; to the high altar of the said church 20d.

To my father's wife a cow, a heifer and bedcover.

To Richard Crakoll my best gown; to George Patown my green gown.

To John Bryan my exec 20s.

My tenement called 'Ingoldes', with all its appurtenances as they lie in the town of Preston, to be sold and disposed by the hands of my execs, that is, out of it to pay my debts and make [*up*] (*faciant*) a way called 'Cherchewey' lying between the lord's land on one side and Thomas Machoun's land on the other.

The tenement called 'Damessell' in the said town to be sold after my father's decease and disposed by my execs as they see best to profit my soul.

Execs: John Bryan and Richard Crakell

Supervisor: Sir Robert Warnere, vicar of the said church.[1]

Seal appended.

Proved at Brent Eleigh ('Illy Combust'), 15 November 1474. Admon to execs.

1   Robert Warner was vicar of Preston from 1472 to January 1476/77 (Tanner, p.1382).

[fol. 552]
717. THOMAS BLAKE of BARTON MILLS ('Berton Myllys'), 19 August 1474

Dated at Barton Mills; my testament containing my last will; [*commendation*: to Almighty God, the Blessed Mary &c]; my body to Christian burial in the churchyard of the church of Barton aforesaid; to the high altar of the same church of Barton for my tithes and offerings forgotten 6s 8d.

To the gild of Corpus Christi of Mildenhall ('Myldenhale') 6s 8d;[1] to the gild of St John the Baptist of the said town of Mildenhall 40d.[2]

To Joan my daughter a black cow and 1½ quarters of barley.

To Margaret my daughter another cow, red, and 1½ quarters of barley.

To Joan my wife all my goods, moveable and unmoveable, of whatever kind and wherever they are; to her my messuage in which I live, with the garden on the north side which extends as far as (*usque*) the private water way (*separalem aqua' vie*) for term of her life, [*and then*] I wish John my son to have [*it*] for term of his life; and after the decease of John my son, I wish that William my son have it; and if William should die without heirs, then I wish the messuage with the garden to be sold by the execs of Joan my wife or by her assigns, and of the money received from it, I wish two parts to be divided equally between Joan and Margaret my daughters and the third part to remain to the church of Barton aforesaid.

Residue of all [*my*] goods [*and*] chattels to Joan my wife and John Spencere of Mildenhall, execs, to pay all my debts which I rightly owe anyone and to do out of it for my soul as seems best to please God and profit the health of my soul.

Seal appended.

Proved at Mildenhall ('Mildenhale'), 8 November 1474. Admon to Joan Blake, relict of the deceased, executrix. Power reserved to John Spencer the other exec, when he comes.

[1]   See note to no. 230.
[2]   See note to no. 107.

718. WILLIAM UNDERWOODE of BURGATE, [*undated*] ?1474

['Undyrwod' *in margin*] [*Commendation*: to God Almighty &c]; [*burial directions omitted*]; in the name of a mortuary a cow; I wish a certain to be celebrated in Burgate parish church for a year, 4s 4d; to the fabric of the 'Roode lofte' of Burgate 6s 8d.

To Margaret my daughter 2s.

To Roger my son 4 bushels of wheat.

To William my son 4 bushels of wheat.

Residue of all my goods to my execs, Emma and John my children.

Proved at Westhorpe ('Westhorpp'), 10 November 1474. Admon to execs.

[fol. 552v]

719. JOHN KENTE the elder of HERRINGSWELL ('Eryngeswell'), 5 March 1473/74

Dated at Herringswell; my testament containing my last will; [*commendation*: to God Almighty, the Blessed Mary &c]; my body to Christian burial in the churchyard of Herringswell church; to the high altar of the said church of Herringswell for my tithes and offerings forgotten 2s; to the reparation of the same church 10s.

To the house of friars of Babwell for a 'le trentele' 5s; to the Old House of Thetford 5s.[1]

To each of my sons and daughters, each for themselves, 6s 8d, if it is possible after the full payment of my messuage, which I have sold to John Kente my son.

To each of my sons and daughters [*?recte* godsons and goddaughters] 4d if they are living after the payment days of my said messuage.

433

Residue of all my goods to Margaret my wife and Robert Kente of Mildenhall ('Myldenhale') my son, execs, to dispose for my soul as seems to them most expedient.

Seal appended.

Proved at Mildenhall, 8 November 1474. Admon to Robert Kente exec. Power reserved [*to executrix*] if she wishes to take up [*admon*].

> 1   For the friars see notes to nos 1 (Babwell) and 68 (Old House of Thetford).

[fol. 553]

720. RALPH SMYTH of BILDESTON ('Bylston'),[1] 30 October 1472

Dated the penultimate day of October 1472; of Bildeston in the diocese of Norwich; my body to be buried in the churchyard of Bildeston aforesaid; to the high altar of the same church for my tithes forgotten 3s 4d; to the reparation of the said church of Bildeston 3 quarters of barley.

To Hitcham ('Hecham') church 2 quarters of barley; to Kettlebaston ('Ketylberston') church 4 bushels (*modios*) of barley; to Nedging ('Neddyng') church 4 bushels of barley; to the chapel of the Blessed Mary of Nedging ('Neddynge') aforesaid 4 bushels of barley and 3s 4d.[2]

To a suitable chaplain 9 marks to celebrate for my soul and the souls of my parents and friends in Bildeston church for a whole year.

To Joan my wife all my ostilments belonging to my house.

To Thomas my son all the expenses for grammar school (*ad scolas gramaticales*) for a whole year; to Thomas 40s.

To John my son 40s; to Alice my daughter 40s.

To Agnes Walkfare my niece 4 bushels (*modios*) of barley.

Residue of all my goods to Joan my wife and Sir John Hawkedon, rector of Nedging,[3] execs of this my testament and last will, to dispose those goods in works of charity and alms for my soul and the souls of my parents and benefactors as they see best to please God, under the supervision of Sir Richard Swettock, rector of Bildeston church,[4] and Hugh Wryght of the same place.

Witnesses: the rector, Sir Richard Swetto[*sic*], William Cook, Rose the wife of John Markeday of the same [*place*], John Huwett, John Frost.

[*Will; of the same date; English*]

Last will of me Ralph Smyth of Bildeston in the diocese of Norwich; made in the presence of Sir Richard Swettok, parson of the town of Bildeston, with others; dated the last day save one of October 12 Edward IV.

As for the disposition of my lands and tenements with their appurtenances that I have or any other man has unto my use in the county of Suffolk:

Joan my wife to have my two tenements as they lie in the town of Hitcham, with all my lands lying in the towns of Bildeston and Chelsworth ('Chelysworth'), except the lands that I have assigned to be sold as appears afterwards, so that she repairs the tenements sufficiently when need shall fall till the time that Thomas my son comes to the age of 26 'wynters and yeres'. And then my tenement lying on the west 'party' of that street in Hitcham, with all the appurtenances, [fol. 553v] with a croft called 'Wattys croft' also lying in Hitcham and a meadow lying in Chelsworth under a grove called 'Edwardyshey', to remain to Thomas and his heirs for evermore. When

John my son comes to the age of 26 years, my tenement lying on the east 'party' of the said street in Hitcham, with all the appurtenances, with lands called 'Frelond' and 'Lokyn croft' lying in Bildeston and the land called 'Calstok', to remain to John and his heirs for evermore. If any of them, Thomas or John, decease before the other within their age of 26 years, then all the part of tenement, lands or meadow of him that is deceased to remain to him that his living and his heirs for evermore 'so that' he comes to the age of 26 years; and if both Thomas and John decease within the age of 26, then Joan my wife to have and keep still both tenements and all the appurtenances [*for*] term of her life; and if she decease also, the tenements, lands, meadows, with all the appurtenances, to be sold and the money thereof be spent in deeds of charity.

If Alice my daughter live, then I will that she be 'wyll seyn and do to' unto the value of 10 marks.

All my other parcels of land lying in Chelsworth ('Chelysworthe') to be sold, except 'Bollyslond'.

Joan my wife to have 'Parkers' tenement to [*her and*] her heirs.

Alice my daughter to have 'Gangeys' tenement or the money that is paid there for. Joan my wife to have 'Bollys lond' to [*her and*] her heirs for evermore with the garden pertaining to 'Parkers'.

I will that all my feoffees both of and in my free lands and also copylands give up all their estate to the fulfilling of my will whenso[*ever*] my execs pray you and desire you, as in the conscience of you I trust verily that you will do, and I specially pray you in the charity of God and also charge you in God's behalf that none of you contrary this my last will.

Thomas my son and John my son to pay Joan my wife, their mother, yearly, each of them, 6s 8d.

Seal appended.

[*Witnesses:*] Sir Richard Swettock, parson, John Huwett, Rose Markeday and John Frost and others.

Proved at Bildeston, 3 December 1472. Admon to execs.

1   For a different version of this will see the next entry.
2   The other version of this will (no. 721) reveals that the chapel of the Blessed Mary of Nedging was a separate chapel situated 'by Semer bridge', that is, by the bridge on the road leading to the neighbouring village of Semer.
3   See note to no. 284 and also nos 303, 406, 431 and 721.
4   See note to no. 284 and also nos 303, 431 and 721.

[fol. 554]
[*at the head*] *Quere infra istud test'*
[*whole entry written in two different hands and struck through*]
721. RALPH SMYTH of BILDESTON ('Bylston'),[1] 30 October 1472

Dated the penultimate day of October 1472; of Bildeston in the diocese of Norwich; my body to Christian burial in the churchyard of the parish church of Bildeston aforesaid; to the high altar of the same church for my tithes forgotten 3s 4d; to the reparation of the said church of Bildeston 3 quarters of barley.

To Hitcham ('Heccham') church 2 quarters of barley; to Kettlebaston ('Ketyl-berston') church 4 bushels (*modios*) of barley; to Nedging ('Neddyng') church 4 bushels of barley; to the chapel of the Blessed Mary of Nedging ('Neddynge'), by Semer bridge, 4 bushels of barley and 3s 4d.

To a suitable chaplain to celebrate for my soul and my parents' and friends' [*souls*] for a whole year 9 marks.

To Agnes Walkfare my niece 4 bushels of barley.

To Joan my wife all my hostilments belonging to my house; to Joan all my tenement lying in the town of Hitcham during her life[*time*], so that she keeps up reparation sufficiently of the said tenements; and after her decease, the tenement on the west side to remain to Thomas my son, with all its appurtenances, with the meadow lying under the wood called 'Edwardsely' in Chelsworth.

To Thomas a croft called 'Wattes crofte' in the town of Hitcham, after the decease of Joan my wife; I wish Thomas my son to be found to grammar school (*inveniatur ad scolas gramaticales*) for the space of a year; to Thomas, according to the discretion of my execs, 40s if he behaves well.

To John my son 40s on the same condition; John my son to have a tenement lying on the east side of the way in the town of Hitcham, with all its appurtenances, after the decease of Joan my wife; to John a piece of land called 'Frelonde', after the decease of my wife; to John a croft called 'Loke crofte' and another croft called 'Calst...' [*damaged*] and a piece of land called 'Bretoneslond'.

If Thomas should decease and John should live, then I wish John to have all those lands and tenements bequeathed to Thomas; in the same way, if John decease and Thomas live, then I wish Thomas his brother to have all the lands and tenements bequeathed to John above; if both Thomas and John decease, then I wish all the said lands bequeathed to them above to be sold by my execs or theirs and disposed for my soul and the souls for whom I am bound.

Alice my daughter to have my tenement called 'Gawgys' or 40s at the time of her marriage.

Joan my wife to have my tenement called 'Parkeres' in Bildeston, with a close lying in Chelsworth ('Cheslworth') under the wood called 'Haverynggale', lately John Bolle's, to her and her heirs.

I wish my tenement in Chelsworth, lying next to 'Sawyere', with the lands belonging to it and the other lands not above bequeathed, to be sold by my execs to fulfil my testament and last will.

Residue of all my goods to Joan my wife and Sir John Hawkedon, rector of Nedging ('Neddyng') church,[2] execs, to dispose for my soul and the souls of all our friends, under the supervision of the rector of Bildeston church[3] and Hugh Wryth.

Witnesses: William Cook, Rose Markeday and John Huwet and John Noreys.

[fol. 554v] Proved at Bildeston, 3 December 1472. Admon to execs.

1   Another version of this will is no. 720 above. This version is a testament and will proper combined, whereas the previous one comprises a separate testament and will proper.
2   See note to no. 284, and also nos 303, 406, 431 and 720.
3   That is, Richard Swettock; see note to no. 284 and also nos 303, 431 and 720.

722. THOMAS SHEPPARD of MELFORD, 13 October 1470

[*Commendation*: to Almighty God, the glorious Blessed Mary &c]; to be buried in the churchyard of Melford parish church; to the high altar of the said church for tithes forgotten 20d; to the chapel of the Blessed Mary of Melford 3s 4d;[1] to the

Mass of Jesu (*Misse Jh'u*) celebrated in Melford 3s 4d;[2] to the painting (*ad pictura'*) or to 'le payntyng' of the image of St Leonard in Melford 20d.[3]

To the friars of Sudbury for a trental 5s; to the friars of the town of Clare 5s.[4]

To an honest priest to celebrate divine service for my soul in Melford church 8 marks for a whole year.

To Alice my wife my new house with the half part of a croft adjacent, with the appurtenances, in Melford, situated in the street called 'le Heyghstret', to hold for term of her life on [*condition*] that she keeps and maintains sufficient reparations of it at her own cost. If it should happen that Alice, during that time, suffers poverty while remaining unmarried, then I wish the house with the half part of the croft to be sold by my execs to support her with the money from it as long as she lives (*perduraverit*). And if she should marry, then after her decease I wish the house and the half part of the croft to be sold by my execs and the money from it to be disposed in the celebration of masses and other pious uses for the souls of me and Alice my wife. To Alice all my hostilments belonging to my house and 2 cows.

To Thomas Prentyse my godson 12d; to Marit' Grome my goddaughter 12d; to Thomas the son of Richard Grome 12d; to Thomas the son of John Cryke 12d.

To each of my execs 6s 8d.

Residue of all my goods to the disposition of my execs, to dispose them for the souls of me and my wife as seems, according to their discretion, to be most healthy (*saluberius*) for the future.

Execs: Robert Sherman and Alice my wife, to execute this testament faithfully. Proved at Melford, 3 December 1472. Admon to execs.

1 See note to no. 436 regarding the chapel of the Blessed Mary that stood in the churchyard at Melford.
2 See note to no. 45.
3 In 1529 there was still an image of St Leonard in Melford church, before which was laid a white cloth (Dymond and Paine, *Spoil of Melford Church*, p.24).
4 For the friars see notes to nos 1 (Clare) and 11 (Sudbury).

[fol. 555]

723. THOMAS VYELL the elder of IXWORTH,[1] 11 October 1472 [*English*]

Dated at Ixworth; 'of very sad & hoole mynde & good avysemente'; to be buried in the parish church of Ixworth before the altar of St James; to the high altar there 3s; to the 'stepyll' of the same church 6 marks.[2]

To the prior of Ixworth 2s; to the sub-prior 20d; to Sir Edmund Stowe 20d; to every canon, priest, there 12d and to each novice 6d.[3]

To the new friars of Thetford, to a trental, 10s; to the same house 2 bushels of wheat and a coomb of malt; to the Old House of the same town, to a trental, 10s; to the friars of Babwell, to a trental, 10s.[4]

My mashing vat ('masshyng fatte') to the gild of St Thomas,[5] so that my wife and John my brother have the keeping thereof [*during*] their lives.

To my wife all the ostilments of my household.

To Thomas my son[6] my 'splytyng sawe', my 'brod exe', a 'luggyng belte', a 'fellyng belte', a 'twybyll', a 'sqwyer', a 'morteys wymbyll', a 'foote wymbyll', a 'drawte wymbyll', a 'compas', a 'hande sawe', a 'kyttyng sawe'.[7]

To Thomas my son the place that I dwell in, with all the appurtenances, and to his heirs without end; if he dies without heirs, the place to remain to John my son and his heirs without end, so that my wife have the place, with the appurtenances, unto the time my heir be of age to maintain it by himself.

To Christian my wife[8] my place with the appurtenances that was John Knottes' for term of her life; and after her decease to remain to John my son and his heirs without end. If John happen to inherit my other abovesaid place, then I will the place which John Knottes had be sold and disposed for mine and my friends' souls, to the execution of this my last will and testament.

Execs: my wife and John Vyell my brother, to whom I bequeath the residue of all my goods to do therewith as they 'open' best to please God and most to profit my soul and all Christian [*souls*].

Seal appended.

Proved at Ixworth, 9 December 1472. Admon to execs.

1 ?Executor (as 'Wyell') of Joan Worlych of Ixworth, probate September 1457 (SROB, Baldwyne 187; Pt I, no. 905).
2 Vyell's bequest of £4 to the building of the steeple (that is, the tower) of Ixworth church is recorded on a tile in the tower. For a description and drawing see Colman, 'Inscribed Tiles', pp.13–17; see also Blatchly and Northeast, *Decoding Flint Flushwork*, Ixworth St Mary.
3 For the priory of Ixworth see note to no. 69. William Dense was prior of Ixworth in 1472, having been appointed in 1467 (*VCH Suffolk*, ii, pp.105–7).
4 For the friars see notes to nos 1 (Babwell), 68 (Old House at Thetford) and 69 (New House).
5 See note to no. 219 regarding gilds in Ixworth.
6 Will, no. 804 below.
7 The testator was a craftsman as these are obviously specialist woodworking tools. See Glossary.
8 Executrix of her son Thomas (no. 804).

[fol. 555v]
724. JOHN DERMAN of DENSTON ('Dernardeston'), 18 August 1472

Of Denston in the diocese of Norwich; [*commendation*: to God Almighty &c]; to be buried in the churchyard of Denston church; to the high altar of the same church for my tithes forgotten 2s; to Stradishall ('Stradeshull') church, for the reparation of ornaments, 2s.

To each priest of Denston 8d out of my mass-pence of the gild of St John the Baptist held in Denston and the remainder of the pence to the needy poor.[1]

My tenement with its appurtenances in Denston to be sold by my execs and with the money from it I wish an honest secular chaplain to have a competent stipend to celebrate for my soul and the souls of my benefactors in Denston church for half a year. Denston church to have, out of the same money from the sale of my tenement, 20s, to be disposed by the discretion of my execs. Matilda my wife to have all the residue of the money from the sale, my debts being paid and all my legacies and funeral expenses met.

The rest of all my goods and chattels, with all my debts owed to me, I leave to Matilda my wife.

My faithful execs: William Jerold, clerk, and Matilda my wife, they to pay and dispose for the health of my soul as seems to them most expedient.

To John my son 26s 8d.

Seal appended.

Proved at Hundon ('Hunden'), 18 December 1472. Admon to Matilda, co-executrix. Power reserved to William Jerold, clerk, when he comes.

¹ In November 1472, William Wyburgh of Denston (no. 785) bequeathed his mass-pence of the gild
of St John the Baptist in Denston to two chaplains to pray for his soul; he also made a bequest to
the gild's torches that would burn 'about my body' on his burial day.

725. THOMAS CHAPMAN of GAZELEY ('Gaysley'), 13 January 1472/73
[*nuncupative*]

Dated the Wednesday after the feast of the Epiphany 1472; his body to Christian burial; to the high altar 12d.

To the friars of Babwell 10s for a trental; to the friars of Thetford 10s for a trental.¹

To Andrew his son 4 horses, 8 coombs of wheat, 6 coombs of barley; to Andrew his hostilments for term of his life and after his decease he bequeathed the hostilments to Thomas, Andrew's son.

To John his son a quarter of wheat, a quarter of barley and 3 coombs of oats, 6 bushels of peas, a 'bullok', a pot, 2 brass pans.

He wished Andrew to keep his wife, Andrew's mother, for term of her life.

Residue of all his goods to Andrew, whom he made exec.

Witnesses: John Chapman, Rose Chapman and others.

Proved at Dalham, 21 January 1472/73. Admon to exec.

¹ For the friars see notes to nos 1 (Babwell), 68 (Dominicans of Thetford) and 69 (Augustinians of Thetford).

[fol. 556]
726. WILLIAM KENDALE of OCCOLD ('Ocolt'), 24 July 1471

Dated at Occold; my body to Christian burial in the churchyard of Occold ('Ocolte') church; to the high altar of the same church 6d.

To the nuns of Redlingfield ('Redlyngfeld'), each of them 20d; to the prioress of the same place 40d.¹

To the reparation of Rysangles ('Rishangles') church 6s 8d; to the reparation of the chancel of Stoke [*Ash*] 6s 8d; to the reparation of Occold church 6s 8d; to the reparation of Stoke [*Ash*] church 6s 8d; to the reparation of Eye church 6s 8d.

To Isabel my wife my tenement in which I live, with all its appurtenances, to her and her heirs for ever; to her all my hostilments and my utensils of my house; to her £10 in money, to be paid in the year 1477.

To Friar John of St Augustine of Orford 8 marks; to Friar William of St Augustine of Orford 8 marks; to be paid to John and William my sons in the year 1478. If John and William should die before the age of 20, then I wish that the 16 marks be given to the prior and convent of Orford to the reparation of that place by my execs.² If Friar John should die before Friar William, I wish the 16 marks to remain to William his brother; and if Friar William should die before John, then I wish the 16 marks to remain to John his brother.

To Friar Ralph of Orford 4 marks, to be paid in the year 1479.

Residue of all my goods to the disposition of my execs, Sir Walter Qwyntyn, rector of Stoke,³ Thomas Clerke, Robert Mayhew and John Mayhew; to each of whom for their labour 6s 8d.

Seal appended.

Proved at Westhorpe, 22 November 1471. Admon to execs.

439

1   See note to no. 83.
2   For the Austin Friars of Orford, see note to no. 6.
3   Walter Qwyntyn became rector of Stoke on 23 August 1461; he was succeeded by Thomas Goldyng on 5 May 1497 (Tanner, p.1315).

727. JOHN FLEGGE the elder of SUDBURY, fuller, 24 September 1471

Dated at Sudbury, in the diocese of Norwich; to be buried in the churchyard of the parish church of All Saints of Sudbury; to the high altar of the said church for tithes and offerings forgotten, if any there be, 12d.

Residue of all my goods, moveable and unmoveable, my debts first being paid, to the [fol. 556v] disposition of my execs, to dispose for the health of my soul and for the health of the souls of all my benefactors as they see best to please God.

Execs: Joan my wife, John Chapman and Robert Flegge my son; to each of whom for their labour in fulfilling my last will [*no sum*].

Seal appended.

[*Will; of same date*]

Dated 24 September 11 Edward IV, at Sudbury in the county of Suffolk.

As to the disposition of all my lands and tenements, with all their appurtenances, in Sudbury and Middleton ('Mydelton') [*Essex*]:

Joan my wife to have and enjoy immediately after my decease my capital messuage called, of antiquity, 'Hydes', with its appurtenances, and with the rest of the lands lying in the town of Middleton, in the fields called 'Apton' [*preceded by* &] and 'le Peke', to hold for term of her life; I wish her to have and enjoy my tenement called 'le Cornereschope', in which she now lives, with 2 renters and 'le garryte' annexed, and with the garden adjacent, lately Thomas Tylere's, formerly the vicar of the church of All Saints there,[1] to hold for term of her life in the same way. After the decease of Joan my wife, all the said lands and tenements to be sold by my execs or theirs, and out of the money from the sale I wish a suitable priest to celebrate for a whole year in the church of All Saints in the town of Sudbury, for my soul and for the souls of all my benefactors.

William my son to have 10 marks in money from the sale of the said lands and tenements.

Robert my son to have 10 marks similarly from the sale.

John my son to have and enjoy my tenement in which William Myllere lives, to hold to him and his heirs for ever, on condition that he obeys (*placuerit*) his mother while she lives.

If William Flegge my son dies before the sale of the lands and tenements, then I wish the 10 marks to remain to John his brother and his assigns.

Thomas Myste, son of Joan Myste my daughter,[2] to have of the sale of the said lands and tenements, if he survives, 6s 8d; John Myste and William Myste to have 6s 8d each of the sale in the same way, if they survive.

To the buying of the bell, if it goes ahead (*si contingat'*), for All Saints' church 6s 8d.

If the parishioners of the said church wish to complete (*facere finem*) the paving in the said church with marble (*cum mariona*), then I wish my execs to pay the church 6s 8d.[3]

In God's name I require all my feoffees in all my lands and tenements, with all their appurtenances, [fol. 557] that they deliver their estate when reasonably required by my execs.

Seal appended.

Witnesses: John Buste, William Jacob, Richard Meryell, chaplain.

Proved at Sudbury, 26 November 1471. Admon to execs.

1   Previously rector of Alby, Norfolk, Thomas Tyler had been vicar of All Saints' Sudbury from 1454 to 1465 (Tanner, p.1390); see also no. 166.
2   Alice Turnour of Sudbury, widow, made bequests to 'Joan Myst of Melford, my kinswoman' and to 'Joan Myst, my kinswoman' (no. 698).
3   There had been a great deal of rebuilding work at All Saints during the preceding years. By December 1456 the south aisle had been rebuilt and fitted with seating and the parish was preparing to rebuild the north aisle (will of Thomas Schorthose, pr. January 1459/60; SROB, Baldwyne 235; Pt I, no. 1181). Now, in April 1471, the whole church is about to be paved and a new bell purchased.

728. ISABEL GROME, wife of John Grome the elder, of MELFORD, 30 April 1471

Dated the last day of April; my body to Christian burial; to the high altar of Melford church, for my tithes forgotten, 6s 8d; to the sustentation and keeping of the Mass of Jesu (*Jhu*) of the same church[1] 40s in 20 years, that is, each year 2s; to the reparation of the said church 6s 8d and a diaper table-cloth (*mappam de* 'dyapyre'); to the reparation of the bells in the tower of the same church 12d; to the chapel of the Blessed Mary in the churchyard of the said church 12d.[2]

To each of my godsons and goddaughters 12d.

To John Grome my husband 9 marks and 6 silver spoons.

I wish that my messuage, with the appurtenances, in Melford, which was John Bakere's my late husband,[3] be sold by my execs and from the money arising all my legacies to be paid.

My execs to support a suitable and honest chaplain to celebrate divine service in the said church for a whole year for my soul and the souls of the said John Bakere and John Bullyngton[4] and of our deceased friends.

Residue of all my goods to my execs to dispose it for the souls aforesaid in works of charity and alms as they see [*best*] to please God and profit my soul.

Execs of my testament and last will: Henry Bullyngton and Robert German; to each of whom for their labour 13s 4d.

Seal appended.

Witnesses: John Stannard, parish chaplain of Melford,[5] William Grome and others.

Proved at Sudbury, 26 November 1471. Admon to execs.

1   See note to no. 45.
2   See note to no. 436.
3   John Baker(e) was a common name so it has not been possible to identify the probate records of the testatrix's husband. There are six testators of that name to be found in the Baldwyne Register: John Baker of Badwell Ash (Pt I, no. 339); John Bakere of Stowmarket St Peter (no. 201 above); John Bakere of Cavendish (no. 224 above); John Bakere of Culford (no. 227 above); John Baker of Wetherden (no. 573 above); and John Bakere of Glemsford (no. 751 below).
4   Pesumably John Bullyngton was another former husband of Isabel Grome: the probate of John Bullyngton of Long Melford, dated 9 April 1458, states that admon was granted to Isabel, wife of the deceased, and John Deye, execs (SROB, Baldwyne 212; Pt I, no. 1051).
5   See note to no. 436.

[fol. 557v]

729. WILLIAM MOORE of [GREAT CORNARD], 20 November 1471

Dated at Great Cornard ('Cornerth Magna'); to be buried in the churchyard of the church of St Andrew of Great Cornard ('Cornerd Magna'); to the same church a 'howyd' cow and a quarter of wheat; to the high altar for tithes unpaid 6s 8d; to the church of Little Cornard ('Cornerth Parva') a black cow and a quarter of wheat; to the rector of the same church 6s 8d.

To Phyllis (*Felice*) Moore, the daughter of my brother, a black cow and a quarter of wheat and all the hostilments of my house.

To Thomas Moore a heifer (*iuvencam*); to John Moore a calf (*vitulum*).

To Selina Venour a sheep; to John Bakere the younger a sheep; to John Tylere a sheep.

To Alice Lay 2 bushels (*modios*) of mixtlin ('mystlon').

To Walter Tylere 4d; to William Tylere 4d.

To William Kendale half a quarter of mixtlin ('mystelen').

To the friars of Sudbury 2s; to the friars of Clare 2s; to the friars of Colchester (*Colcestr'*) 2s.[1]

My house to be sold with the lands and pastures according to the discretion of my execs and supervisor, and the money arising I leave to the churches of Great and Little Cornard and to the church of Mount Bures ('Monte Bures') [*Essex*], according to the discretion and will of my execs and supervisor, costs and expenses deducted. Residue of all my goods to John Moore my brother and John Bakere, my execs, and John Frankeleyn, rector of Little Cornard, supervisor.[2] The execs not to do anything in the executing of my will without the agreement of my supervisor, but to dispose for the health of my soul as seems most expedient to them.

Witnesses: Richard Waspe, William Kendale, Robert Goselyn and others.

Proved 11 December 1471. Admon to execs.

[1] For the friars see notes to nos 1 (Clare), 11 (Sudbury) and 38 (Colchester).
[2] John Frankleyn was rector of Little Cornard from 1464 to 1475 (Tanner, p.1357).

730. [   ] ASPY, 26 October 1471 [*probate only*]

[*Surname (only) of testator in margin only; no place of residence given.*] Proved at Woodditton ('Dytton') [*Cambs*], 26 October 1471. Admon to executrix.

[fol. 558]

731. JOHN FLEMYNG of ELVEDEN, 18 November 1472

Dated 18 November in the year from the incarnation of the Lord, according to the reckoning and computation of the church of England, 1472, and in the twelfth year of the reign of King Edward IV after the conquest of England; of Elveden in the diocese of Norwich.

I commend my soul to Almighty God, who has redeemed it with his precious blood, to the Blessed Virgin Mary his glorious mother, to blessed Andrew the Apostle, my advower (*advocanti meo*) and all the saints. To be buried in the churchyard of Elveden; to the high altar of the same church for my tithes negligently forgotten 3s 4d; to the aid (*subsidio*) of the reparations of the same church 13s 4d; to the gild of St Andrew of which I am a brother (*confrat'*) 3s 4d;[1] to the gild of St John the

Evangelist of Rushworth ('Russheworth') [*Norfolk*] 3s 4d;[2] to the church of St John [*the Baptist*] of Rushworth 13s 4d.

To the Friars Preachers of Thetford 3s 4d; to the Augustinian Friars of Thetford 3s 4d.[3]

Isabel my wife to have her dwelling in my messuage for term of her life; and after her decease, my messuage to be sold by my execs in the best manner possible and the money arising to be disposed in pious uses for the health of my soul and of the souls of my benefactors. To Isabel all the utensils of my house.

To each of my daughters 20 ewes.

To each of my godsons a ewe with a lamb.

To John Halsted a complete bed.

Residue of all my goods to Isabel my wife, John Webbere, Laurence Gotche and John Estmore, my execs; they to have God before their eyes and faithfully execute my testament and fully pay my debts and legacies, fulfil my will and do other deeds of piety for my soul and for the souls for whom I am bound and of all the faithful departed; and to them I give 3s 4d.

Supervisor: John Cokett, he to have God before his eyes, to please God and profit my soul.

Seal appended.

Proved at Fornham St Martin, 10 December 1472. Admon to execs.

1   Simon Wattys of Downham (no. 826) also made a bequest to the gild of St Andrew of Elveden; the gild is mentioned in the 1524 Lay Subsidy returns (*PSIA*, xix, p.183).

2   Now Rushford. The gild of St John at Rushworth was actually the gild of St John the Baptist, not the Evangelist (Farnhill, *Guilds and the Parish Community*, p.200). However, it is not surprising that the testator was confused with his St Johns: although the parish church and the gild were dedicated to St John the Baptist, there was also a college of St John the Evangelist in Rushworth. In 1492, William Halliday, the senior fellow of the college of St John the Evangelist of Rushworth, bequeathed a 'good stone house' in Rushworth to the college to be used as a gild hall (for the gild of St John Baptist) or as a hostelry for guests when there was not room for them at any time in the college (*VCH Norfolk*, ii, pp.458–60).

3   For the friars of Thetford see notes to no. 68 (Friars Preachers) and 69 (Augustinians).

[fol. 558v]

732. WILLIAM JAY of BURWELL [*Cambs*],[1] 12 August 1472

[*Commendation*: to Almighty God, the Blessed Mary &c]; to be buried in the churchyard of St Mary of Burwell; to the high altar of the said church for tithes forgotten 12d; to the reparation of the said church 10s.

To the Friars Preachers in Cambridge (*Cantebr'*) 4 bushels of wheat and 4 bushels of barley; to the Friars Minor of the said town 4 bushels of wheat and 4 bushels of barley.[2]

To John Borwe one quarter of wheat and one quarter of malt.

To William Jonson 4 quarters of wheat and 4 quarters of malt.

To Cecily my wife all the utensils of [*my*] house and all my moveable goods of whatever kind to fulfil my will and pay all my debts; Cecily to have an acre of land lying in 'Estfeld' to dispose at her own will.

Margaret Rolfe my daughter to have 3 roods of land lying together in the North Field (*in campo borialis*), after the death of my wife.

Cecily my wife to have my messuage and 7 roods of land lying in the fields of

443

Burwell for term of her life; and after her death, if Margaret my daughter wishes to buy the messuage, I wish her to have it under the price by 6 marks; and if she does not wish to buy it, it is to be sold to the one willing to give most for it and then Margaret to have of the money 6 marks.

Marion Bonyfaunte, daughter of the said Margaret, to have out of the said money from the messuage 6s 8d; Matilda Bonyfaunte, daughter of the said Margaret, to have of the said money 6s 8d.

Residue of the money to be distributed in pious uses by my execs, that is, to the church of St Mary of Burwell in the celebration of masses.

Execution of my will to Cecily my wife, Thomas Canforth and William Role, my faithful execs, to dispose for the health of my soul and of all my friends' [souls] as seems to them most expedient.

Proved at Fornham St Martin, 25 January 1472/73. Admon to execs.

1 ?Brother and executor of John Jay of Burwell, probate October 1440 (SROB, Baldwyne 11; Pt I, no. 66).
2 For the friars of Cambridge see notes to nos 80 (Preachers) and 187 (Minor).

[fol. 559]

733. THOMAS GERMAYN of MELFORD, 26 March 1472

Dated at Melford in the diocese of Norwich; to be buried in the churchyard of Melford church; to the high altar of the same church for my tithes and offerings forgotten and not well paid 12d; to the emendation of the chapel of the Blessed Mary in the said churchyard 12d.[1]

To the house and convent of friars of Babwell to pray for my soul 12d; to the house and convent of Carmelite Friars of Cambridge (*Cantebr'*) 12d.[2]

To the emendation of the highway opposite my tenement in which I now live 12d.

To Rose my wife all my bedding and the hostilments and utensils of my house, and also 3 cows, 5 ewes and 4 lambs.

Residue of all my goods and chattels to John Germayn of Stanstead ('Stansted') and John Amyot the elder of Melford, execs of this testament and my last will, to pay my funeral expenses and to dispose what then remains in works of charity and alms for my soul, and for the souls of my parents and friends deceased, as they see best to please God and profit the said souls; to each of my execs for their labour 6s 8d. Seal appended.

Witnesses: John Smyth, Robert Germayn of Melford and others.

[*Will, of same date; English*]

Dated 26 March 12 Edward IV; made in the presence of John Clopton, esquire,[3] and William Colman, priest. As for the disposition of all my lands and tenements with their appurtenances that I have, or any other man has to my use in the county of Suffolk:

I will that my tenement in Melford called sometime 'Stevenes Hichen', with other lands and their appurtenances in Melford, which Walter my son now has of me in farm, that the said Walter, after my decease, have the said tenement and lands with their appurtenances, to him and his heirs, on condition that he pays to Rose my wife, his mother, term of her life, a yearly annuity of 20s out of the said tenement and lands, at Easter and Michaelmas by even portions, in recompense for her dower; and I will that yearly annuity be made to her as sure as John Clopton can think reasonable during her life. And if it happens that Walter my son dies without heirs, then I will the tenement and lands, with their appurtenances, wholly remain to John my son, brother of Walter, and to his issue. For default of such issue of the said John, to remain to Alice my daughter, wife to Thomas Jobesson of Colchester, term of her life, and after her decease, the remainder thereof to Thomas my godson, the second son of Thomas Jobesson and Alice, and to his heirs. For default of such issue of the said Thomas, the remainder thereof to the issue of the [*damaged: corner torn off*] [*?heirs*] of the said Alice lawfully begotten. And for default of such issue [*damaged*] [*?of the said*] Alice, the said tenement and lands with their appurtenances to be sold by [*damaged*] [fol. 559v] and feoffees or by their assigns and the money thereof coming to be disposed to Melford church, to the poor people of the said town and to the highways. I pray and require my feoffees in the said tenement and lands that they execute thereof this my last will.

As for my tenement which I bought of Adam Mason, with the appurtenances, in Melford, I will that Rose my wife have it term of her life; and after her decease, if John my son live, then I will that John have it in fee to give and sell, except a croft called 'Crukkes Crofte', lying by the new cross that William Clopton did make in Melford, which croft, after the death of Rose my wife and of John my son, I would that it remain to the owners of the tenement called 'Stevenes Hichen', as the same tenement shall do.

If John my son be a priest, I would he sing for my soul by a year in Melford church. And in case John my son die, leaving Rose his mother, then I would the said tenement which I bought of Adam Mason, with the appurtenances, except the croft, after the decease of Rose my wife, be sold and the money thereof coming be disposed by my execs, finding a priest [*for*] a year in Melford church for my soul and her soul and the souls of our friends and in other alms. Provided always that if Rose my wife overlives my son John and falls into poverty, then I will it be sold in her life[*time*] and she to have a part thereof to live thereby.

Also I will that John my son [*has*] yearly, during 3 years next after Michaelmas that now next comes after the date aforesaid, 20s out of the said tenement called 'Steven Hichen', to find him therewith to school.

Also I will that Alice my daughter have 10 marks of the 'catell' that Walter my son has of mine, to be paid to Alice by Walter her brother the 10 marks.

Also I will that Rose my wife have, during her life, the third part of [*the*] pigeons in the dovehouse ('Duffehous') at the tenement called 'Stevenes Hichen' and yearly the third part of the fruit growing there in the garden.[4]

I will that, as long as Rose my wife dwells in Melford, she has the pasture by Roger Genytas in Melford, if she will allow the owner of the tenement called 'Steven Hichen' yearly thereof 4s of her annuity of 20s aforesaid.

Seal appended.

Proved at Glemsford ('Glemesford'), 15 November 1472. Admon to execs. Seal of official appended.

[1] This repair clearly relates to the earlier Lady Chapel at Melford; see note to no. 436.
[2] For the friars see notes to nos 1 (Babwell) and 42 (Carmelites of Cambridge).
[3] See note to no. 154 above; see also nos 181, 436 and 779.
[4] To own a dovecote was a sign of high status.

[fol. 560]

734. THOMAS CROPLEY of DALHAM, 5 December 1472

Dated at Dalham, in the diocese of Norwich; to be buried in the churchyard of Dalham church; to the high altar for my tithes negligently forgotten 6d; to the sustentation of the said church 6s 8d.

To the friars of Babwell for a trental 10s.[1]

To Margaret my wife all the grain of 18 acres; to Margaret a black cow; to her a brass pot; to her a pig of the best, to be delivered to her by the feast of St Michael the Archangel next coming; to her a brass pan; to her 3 bushels of wheat, 3 bushels of rye ('reye') and 6 bushels of barley.

Residue of all my goods to John my son, my exec, to dispose as seems best to him for the health of my soul.

To the said John a cart and 4 horses with 'le harneys' and a cow.

Seal appended.

Proved at Dalham, 20 January 1472/73. Admon to exec.

> [1] See note to no. 1.

735. JOHN TREWPENY of MILDENHALL ('Mildenhale'), 9 January 1472/73

Dated at Mildenhall ('Myldenhale'); my testament containing my last will; [*commendation*: to God Almighty &c]; my body to Christian burial; to the high altar of Mildenhall church for tithes and offerings underpaid 12d; to the reparation of the same church 6d.

To Joan my wife my messuage in which I live, with the appurtenances, for term of her life; and after her decease, I wish Roger Whithed to have it, paying 40s.

To Thomas Trewpeny my son the messuage in which he lives, except the meadow adjacent, which I wish Joan my wife to have for term of her life. If she happens to be in need, I wish it to be sold to find her food and clothing; but if she is not needy, then I wish Thomas my son to have the meadow, with the barn excepted [*in*] which Robert Trewpeny my son has, for term of his life, easement at the end (*in fine*) of the barn, with free ingress and egress whenever he wishes.

To the reparation of the ways of 'Wyld stret' 7s, that is, 12d each year, until the whole 7s are expended.[1]

To Joan my wife all the utensils belonging to my house.

Residue of all my goods to my execs to dispose for the health of my soul as seems best to them to please God and profit my soul.

Execs: Joan my wife, principal exec, Roger Whithed and Robert Trewpeny.

Proved at Mildenhall ('Mylden'), 22 January 1472/73. Admon to execs.

> [1] Wilde Street is an outlying hamlet of Mildenhall.

[fol. 560v]

736. JOHN HOWARD of GREAT BARTON ('Berton *iuxta* Bury Sancti Edmundi'), 5 December 1472

Dated at Barton; my body to Christian burial in the churchyard of the church of Barton aforesaid; to the high altar there in recompense of my tithes 4d; to the making of the new banner-cloth (*vexelli*) for the cross 6s 8d.

I require my feoffees to deliver full estate and legal seisin of my tenement containing, by estimation, 5 roods of land more or less, to Margaret my wife for term of her life; and after her decease, my execs to sell the tenement for the best price possible, if they are not in accord regarding to whom to sell it.

Residue of all my goods to the disposition of my execs, to pay all my debts and fulfil this my last will as they will please God and discharge their conscience.

Execs: William Bradfeld and John Fyston of Barton aforesaid.

Proved at Fornham St Martin, 15 January 1472/73. Admon to execs.

737. CECILY HAMOWND of THORNEY ('Thorney hamelet') in STOWMARKET, 7 September 1470

My testament and last will; [*commendation*: to God Almighty, the Blessed Mary &c]; to be buried in the churchyard of the church of the Blessed Peter of Stow; to the high altar of the same church 12d; to the edification (*edificacionem*) of the church of the Blessed Mary of Stow ('Stowe') half a quarter of wheat and half a quarter of barley.[1]

To Agnes Wode my best blue gown with a hood and also my lined tunic with a 'kertyll'.

Residue of all my goods to my execs to dispose for the health of my soul and all my benefactors' [*souls*].

Execs: Sir Robert Vyncent[2] and John Kebyll the younger.

Supervisor: Robert Milys.

Proved at Stowmarket ('Stowemarket'), 28 January 1472/73. Admon to execs.

[1] See note to no. 381.
[2] Legatee of Joan Robhood of Walsham le Willows (no. 401).

[fol. 561]

738. THOMAS SAMPSON of BARDWELL ('Berdwell'),[1] 21 September 1474

[*Register heading:* Sampson *alias* Goore]

Dated at Bardwell, in the diocese of Norwich; [*commendation*: to God Almighty, the Blessed Mary &c]; to be buried in the churchyard of Bardwell church; to the high altar of the said church for my tithes forgotten 12d; to Barningham ('Bernyngham') church 40d; to the finding and sustentation of the sepulchre light of Bardwell a pightle adjacent (*pigtellu' adiac'*) in the town of Bardwell in the meadow called 'Caldwellemedewe', between the meadow of John Seefrey on the west and the meadow of Bardwell church on the east, the south head abutting on the common way.

To the friars of Babwell 6s 8d; to the Friars Preachers of Thetford 6s 8d; to the Augustinian Friars there 6s 8d; to the Carmelite Friars of Norwich 6s 8d; to the canons of Ixworth 6s 8d.[2]

To John my son the elder 10 marks, of which 50s has already been paid.

To William my son 10 marks; to the same William a messuage with the adjacent croft, lying next to the messuage called 'Gorys', for term of his life, after the decease of John Barbour; and after William's decease, I wish the messuage and croft to revert to the messuage called 'Gorys'.[3]

To John my son the younger 10 marks.

To Robert my son a messuage, built up, and half an acre of land in the croft adjacent in the street called ?'Netherfonton', between the tenement and land formerly William Julyon's on the south side and the bondland of John Wareyn, parcel of the tenement called 'Gunneldeys', on the north side, to hold to him and his heirs, or, otherwise, 10 marks, whichever he will choose.

To Beatrice Smyth of Ixworth 12d; to William Smyth of the same 12d; to Alice Syre of the same 12d.

To Thomas Rascald a russet (*rusceter*) gown.

To each of my [*god*]sons 12d.

To Thomas Sampson my nephew an acre of land called 'Dolys', lying between the land of William Mannyng on the east side and the land of the said Thomas on the west side, to hold to him and his heirs &c[*sic*].

To Walter Clerk 40d; to Agnes Caldwell a heifer.

To John my son the elder 2 horses, 1 bay (*badiu'*) and another.

To Margaret my wife all my ostilments and utensils, together with all my cows; to Margaret all my lands and tenements, both free and bond, not previously bequeathed, to hold to her and her heirs of the chief lords &c[*sic*]; when Margaret alienates or sells the said lands and tenements, or any parcel of them, I wish John my son the elder to have preference before any others and at a lower price.

Residue of all my goods to my execs to sell [fol. 561v] and dispose for my soul and for the souls of my friends or benefactors, deceased, in the celebration of masses and the distribution of alms, as they see best to please God and profit my soul.

Execs: Margaret my wife and John Seman the elder of Bury St Edmunds, faithfully to execute this testament. William Mannyng to be supervisor, to whom 6s 8d; and to John Seman for [*his*] labour 6s 8d.

Seal appended.

Proved 18 October 1474. Admon to execs. [*noted in margin:* Account received]

1   Executor of William Ingold, will pr. June 1460 (SROB, Baldwyne 245; Pt I, no. 1231); executor of Alice Goore, probate December 1459 (SROB, Baldwyne 258; Pt I, no. 1275).
2   See notes to nos 1 (friars of Babwell), 68 (Friars Preachers of Thetford), 69 (Augustinians of Thetford and canons of Ixworth) and 269 (Carmelites of Norwich).
3   Presumably the name of the messuage 'Gorys' refers to the Goore family; the register heading 'Sampson *alias* Goore' suggests that the testator was part of that family, as does the fact that he was executor of Alice Goore (see note above).

739. ROBERT BAKERE of STANTON, 4 July 1474

Dated at Stanton, the Monday after the feast of the Blessed Peter and Paul 1474; [*commendation*: to God Almighty, the Blessed Mary &c]; to be buried in the church-yard of the church of All Saints of Stanton; to the high altar of the said church for tithes forgotten 4d; to the emendation of the said church 8d.

To Joan my wife all my goods and chattels, both dead and alive; to Joan and her heirs all my lands and tenements which were formerly John Furbusshere's, except the tenement called 'Persysben'.

To John my son that tenement called 'Perysbene'[*sic*], on condition that he is bound to pay all my debts and legacies and all other dues whatsoever relating to me.

I wish the said John to pay Margery my daughter 40d; to Margery a calf.

Residue of all my goods I place in the hands of Joan my wife and John my son, my execs, to ordain and dispose for my soul and the souls of all my benefactors as seems best to them to please God and profit the health of my soul.

Seal appended.

Witnesses: Thomas Clerk, John Hervy, Thomas Lorens and others.

Proved at Hopton, 25 October 1474. Admon to execs.

[fol. 562]

740. THOMAS LEFELD the elder of HAVERHILL ('Haveryll'), 1 September 1474

Dated at Haverhill; [*commendation*: to God Almighty, the Blessed Mary &c]; my body to Christian burial in the churchyard of the lower parish church of the Blessed Mary of Haverhill;[1] to each priest present at my obsequies and at mass 4d; to each clerk 2d; to the reparation of the bridge called 'Belyngesbregge' 6s 8d; to the sepulchre light in the said church an acre of land lying in two pieces in the field called 'Closemedowe' near the land of the chapel of 'Alwarton',[2] except that I wish that Agnes my wife shall have the said acre for the whole term of her life, paying annually from it 12d to the sepulchre light.

To Agnes all my lands and tenements which I have in the town of Haverhill, in the counties of Suffolk and Essex, to hold for the whole term of her life from the chief lords of the fee by the accustomed service due for them, provided always that if my wife has necessity, she shall sell the lands and live on the proceeds to the end of her life. After Agnes's decease, Thomas my son to have the lands and tenements with their appurtenances under the price of any others and before all others, if he behaves himself well towards Agnes his mother.

I wish Thomas my son to have my ?shop (*venda'*) for the space of a year after my death, if his mother agrees (*si placebit matri sue*); to Thomas all my necessaries relating to my craft.

To Thomas 20s; to William my son 20s; to Agnes my daughter 20s; to be paid to them by my execs after the decease of my wife.

Residue of all my goods to Agnes my wife and William Umfrey of Withersfield ('Wethyresfeld') to see to my funeral, pay my debts and dispose for my soul and for the souls of all my benefactors as seems to them most expedient for the health of my soul; they to be my faithful execs, to implement my will in all things as above. Seal appended.

Proved at Haverhill, 17 November 1474. Admon to execs.

1   See note to no. 14 concerning the parish churches of Haverhill.
2   Some of the land in the field called Close Meadow in Haverhill belonged to the chapel of 'Alwarton'. Presumably there was a chapel belonging to the manor of that name near Haverhill that had been endowed with lands in the fields of Haverhill. The manor is mentioned in the Close Rolls of Edward III (*Calendar of Close Rolls of Edward III*, vol. 13).

[fol. 562v]

741. THOMAS WALLOURE of WATTISFIELD ('Watelsfeld'), 17 November 1474

Dated at Wattisfield ('Watelesfeld'), the Thursday before the feast of St Ed', King and Martyr, 1474;[1] [*commendation*: to God Almighty, the Blessed Mary &c]; to be buried in the churchyard of the Blessed Margaret of Wattisfield; to the high altar of the said church 3s 4d; to the parish clerk of the said town 4d; to the emendation of the said church a quarter of barley; to the emendation of the gild of St Margaret of Wattisfield 4 bushels of barley and a tablecloth (*mappa'*).[2]

To Friar Robert Brown of Babwell, for a trental, 10s.[3]

I wish to have a suitable priest to celebrate in the church of the Blessed Margaret of Wattisfield for a whole year, so that (*quatinus*) the money of divers obligations [*or, bonds*] shall be spent by my execs.

To Katherine Scrappe my daughter 3s 4d; to John Walloure my son 3s 4d; to Margaret my daughter 3s 4d.

To the said Katherine my daughter a 'yelew'-coloured cover and a pair of sheets.

Residue of all my goods to my execs to sell and dispose for my soul and the souls of all my benefactors in celebrating masses or in other works of piety as seems most expedient and healthful for my soul.

Execs: John Qwynte and John Molows of Wattisfield;[4] they to faithfully execute my testament; to each of them for their labour 3s 4d.

Seal appended.

Proved at Wattisfield, 1 December 1474. Admon to execs.

1 If Ed' means Edmund, the date of this testament is 17 November, the feast of St Edmund, King and Martyr, being on 20 November. The feast of St Edward, King and Martyr, was on 18 March.

2 William Metewyn of Wattisfield (no. 240) made a substantial bequest to this gild of his tenement called 'Leparys' and the adjacent croft.

3 In 1462 Almeric Molows of Wattisfield had bequeathed Friar Robert Brown his best bed (SROB, Baldwyne 287; Pt I, no. 1409); in 1465 William Metewyn (no. 240) had requested that the friar celebrate divine service for a year for his soul and others. For the friars of Babwell see note to no. 1.

4 Either the son of Almeric Molows, or John Molows, smith, a legatee of Almeric Molows (Pt I, no. 1409).

[fol. 563]

742. JOHN HOLDEN the younger of GLEMSFORD ('Glemesford'),[1] 20 June 1474

Of Glemsford, in the diocese of Norwich; smitten by a divine visitation of sickness and being, by His special grace, sound in mind; [*commendation*: to God Almighty my Saviour and the Blessed Mary his mother and all the company above]; to be buried in the churchyard of Glemsford parish church. I require my execs and supervisor to pay all those debts that can be genuinely proved. To the high altar of the said church for my tithes forgotten, and offerings, 12d; to the fabric of the body of the said church (*fabrice corporis ecclesie predict'*) 6s 8d, to be disposed by the wardens of the church for the health of my soul, as they trust (*sperent*) to please God; to the parish priest 6d and to each of the other priests present at my obsequies 4d and to each of the clerks 2d; to a suitable chaplain to celebrate for my soul and the souls of my parents and benefactors for whom I am most bound, for a quarter of a year, 33s 4d, and, if it pleases my supervisor to do it, he to celebrate where he pleases.

To Agnes my wife a croft called 'Tonpites' with all the due appurtenances, together with Alice my daughter, and the survivor of them to enjoy it for term of her life; and after their decease, it to be sold and the money from thence to be disposed for the health of my soul and my parents' and benefactors' [*souls*].[2]

I wish my sheep to be sold to pay for all the necessaries on my burial day.

Residue of all my goods to Agnes my wife and Alice my daughter.

Supervisor: Sir Richard Fenrothere, chaplain.[3]

Execs: Agnes my wife and John Holden the elder; they to dispose for the health of my soul as they see most expedient; to each of whom for their diligent labour 20d. This is my last will, which I beg my execs, with the agreement of my supervisor, to implement wholeheartedly (*conanime*).

Witnesses: Sir Maurice (*?Moricio*), chaplain, John Holden ~~the elder~~ the younger[4] and many others.

Proved at Clare, 22 September 1474. Admon to execs.

1 Son of John Holden the elder of Glemsford (no. 628 above).
2 John Holden the elder had bequeathed to John his son a croft called 'Turpyttis' (no. 628).
3 Supervisor of the will of John Holden the elder (no. 628).
4 The scribe has crossed out *sen'* and put *jun'*. It is hardly surprising that he had made an error: the testator was identified as John Holden the younger; John Holden the elder was one of the named executors; and it seems that *another* John Holden the younger was a witness. Alternatively, the scribe's initial entry would have been correct if the executor John Holden the elder had also witnessed the will. The executor John Holden the elder is not the same man as the testator of no. 628, who had died by April 1473 and was this testator's father.

[fol. 563v]
743. WILLIAM MANNYNG of NORTON, 30 July 1474

Of Norton by Woolpit (*iuxta* 'Wolpet'); dated at Norton, the Saturday after the feast of St James the Apostle 1474; [*commendation*: to God Almighty, the Blessed Mary &c]; to be buried in the churchyard of the church of St Andrew of Norton aforesaid. Alice my wife to have, for term of her life, my messuage in which I dwell, with the croft adjacent with all their appurtenances; and after her decease, I wish my messuage with the adjacent croft and all their appurtenances to be sold to Richard my son for 8 marks, to be paid as he is able.

I wish my tenement at 'le Heth', with the lands, meadows and pastures belonging to it, to be sold by my execs. I wish one piece of my land containing 9 acres lying in the field called 'Brettysfeld' to be sold also by my execs to pay my debts and fulfil my legacies.

To the gild of St John the Baptist, called 'le towngylde', my best brass pot.[1]

To the high altar for my tithes forgotten 2s.

To Richard my son my best gown, 6s 8d and the best brass pot next to the one bequeathed to the gild of St John the Baptist.

To John Mellere my second gown and 6s 8d.

To Thomas Ketyll my third gown and 6s 8d.

To Henry my son my fourth gown and 6s 8d.

To Alice my wife an acre of wheat and an acre of barley and all my utensils of my house, apart from those already bequeathed.

I bequeath a piece of meadow reckoned at 1½ roods, lying in the town of Norton in the meadow called 'Broomhylmedewe', to the finding of a light in Norton church before the crucifix there, for ever.

Residue of all my goods to my execs to dispose for my soul and the souls of my parents, friends and benefactors as they see best to please God and profit my soul.

Execs: William Rowe of Tostock ('Tostoke'), Richard Mannyng my son and John Mellere.

Supervisor: John Lapham of Ixworth.

Witnesses: Sir Henry Irby, rector of Tostock,[2] John Mannyng of Norton, John Goche, 'smyth', of the same and others.

Proved at Fornham St Martin, 3 October 1474. Admon to execs.

[1] As well as a gild of St Andrew and a gild of Corpus Christi there were two gilds of St John in Norton at this time: the gild of St John the Baptist in 'Upstrete' in Norton and the gild of St John of 'Townestrete' or 'Tunstret'. These two gilds each served a particular area of the parish. (This compares with a similar situation at Hopton: see no. 661.) As William Mannyng made his bequest to the gild of St John the Baptist called 'le townegylde', it seems likely that he was referring to the gild of 'Townestrete'. For the gilds of St John in Norton see: John Caly of Great Ashfield, the gild of St John the Baptist in 'Upstrete' (Pt I, no. 1249); William Spetyllman of Norton, the fraternity of St John of 'Townestrete' (Pt I, no. 1333); Thomas Coke of Norton, the fraternity of St John of 'Tunstret' (Pt I, no. 1381).

[2] See note to no. 295 above.

[fol. 564]

744. THOMAS GOORE of SOHAM ('Saham') [*Cambs*], 16 August 1473, [*English*]

To be buried in the churchyard of St Andrew the Apostle in Soham; to the high altar 2 bushels of barley; to the rood loft light a coomb of malt; to the altar in the chapel of Our Lady by the highway ('heye way') a sheet.[1]

Alice my wife to have my tenement, whole as it lies, with an acre of land on 'the dyche Furlong' for term of her life; and after her decease, William my son to have it likewise; and after his decease, it to be sold by my attorneys to 'my most avayle' and the money to be done 'ther the most nede is' for me and Alice my wife and all our good-doers; if William my son will buy the said tenement after the decease of his mother, he to have it for 10 marks, to be paid in 10 years.

If Alice be married again, then all my goods, that is, the household and 'cattell' to be evenly parted, and Alice my wife to choose the one part and William my son the other part.

I will that my attorneys shall 'dele' to the convent of Black Friars at Cambridge ('Cambrygge') 10s.[2]

To the high ways 'ther most neyd ys' 6s 8d.

To every godchild of mine a bushel of barley.

I will that Alice my wife shall repair the said tenement sufficiently, or else my attorneys to put them out thereof and let them not dwell therein.

If my wife have the child that she is withal at my passing, and it live till the tenement be sold, [*it*] to have of the money 40s.

Residue of my goods to the disposition of my attorneys.

Alice my wife and Simon Gore to be my attorneys and John Wilke supervisor; each of them to have for their labour 3s 4d.

Proved at Soham, 1 July 1474. Admon to execs.

[1] The site of the wayside chapel of 'Our Lady in the Highway' in Soham is unknown. References to it occur in wills dating from the 1470s to the 1520s. By 1552 a chapel, perhaps this one, with its chapel house, perhaps Our Lady's almshouse, and yard, was in lay ownership. It is possible that the chapel was connected to the parish's gild of St Mary (*VCH Cambs*, x, pp.533–42; Olorenshaw, *Notes on the Church of St Andrew*, p.19).

[2] For the Black Friars (Dominicans) of Cambridge see note to no. 80.

[fol. 564v]

745. ELIZABETH HUNGYRE of THWAITE ('Thweytes'), 20 June 1474

Dated at Thwaite; [*commendation*: to God Almighty &c]; to be buried in the parish church of St Gregory[*sic*; *recte* George] of Thwaite; to the high altar of the same church for my tithes forgotten 3s 4d; to the perpetual use of Thwaite church a cover and a sheet; to the new image of St ~~Gregory~~ George to be bought, with the tabernacle for it, 53s 4d.

To Katherine, wife of Roger Qwyntyn, a piece of land lying in the fields of Thwaite for the whole term of her life; and after her decease, I wish it to be divided between the sons of John Schaftyng.

To John Sowthgate 3s 4d, a sheet and a kettle ('chetyll').

To Margaret, daughter of John Shaftyng, 3s 4d, a pan and a sheet.

To Simon, son of Robert Brastret, 6s 8d; to William Brastrete a sheet; to Thomas Brastret, my godson, 3s 4d.

To Margaret, daughter of Richard Turnour, 3s 4d; to Elizabeth Turnour a candlestick; to Margaret Turnour a 'stertepane';[1] to Alice Turnour a tabard.

To Katherine, wife of Roger Qwyntyn, 10s and a gown.

If there is any residue of my goods or debts unbequeathed, I leave it to my execs to dispose for my soul and the soul of John Hungyre my husband[2] and for the souls of [*my*] parents and friends and of all our benefactors.

Execs: to faithfully implement this testament, Richard Turnour, William Brastret and Nicholas Chevelere; to each of whom for their labour 6s 8d.

To each of the rest of (*reliquorum*) my godsons 12d.

To Nicholas Chevelere a sheet and a 'le donge'; to the wife and children of the same Nicholas 3s 4d.

Proved at Wetheringsett ('Wetheryngset'), 7 July 1474. Admon to execs.

1   See Glossary.
2   Probate only (as 'Hungyr'), October 1458 (SROB, Baldwyne 201; Pt I, no. 996).

746. JOHN HEYWARD of HESSETT ('Heggessett'),[1] 4 May 1473

To be buried in the churchyard of the aforesaid church; to the high altar aforesaid for my tithes and offerings unpaid 12d; to the fabric of the church 20s; for a suitable priest to celebrate for my soul and my parents' [*souls*] 8 marks; I leave 10s for a trental of St Gregory; to the sacristan of the said church 6d.

Residue of all my goods to my execs to dispose for the health of my soul and of the souls of my parents and benefactors in the celebration of masses and works of charity as they see best to please God and profit the health of my soul.

Execs: John Hoo, Roger Heyward my son and Katherine my wife.

Seal appended.

Proved at Drinkstone ('Drenkston'), 29 September 1474. Admon to Roger and Katherine, execs; power reserved to John Hoo when he comes.

1   Executor of John Kyng, probate March 1453/54 (SROB, Baldwyne 171; Pt I, no. 825).

[fol. 565]

747. WILLIAM SAY of WICKEN ('Wykyn') [*Cambs*], 25 February 1473/74

[*Commendation*: to God Almighty &c]; to be buried in the churchyard of the church of the Blessed Mary of Wicken; to the high altar of the same church for my tithes forgotten 6d; to Sir Robert Wylton, priest of Wicken parish church, my mass pence of the gild of All Saints.[1]

Residue of all my goods to Katherine my wife and John Barown of Reach ('Reche'), my execs, to dispose for the health of my soul as seems to them most expedient.

Witnesses: Sir Robert Wylton, curate there,[2] and William Dullyngham of the same, and others.

Proved at Soham ('Saham'), 1 July 1474. Admon to execs.

[1]   For gilds in Wicken see note to no. 427.
[2]   Also witnessed the will of Thomas Maddy of Wicken (no. 513).

748. THOMAS SALYSBERY of SOHAM ('Saham') [*Cambs*],[1] 28 January 1473/4 [*English*]

[*Commendation*: to God Almighty, our Lady Saint Mary &c]; to be buried in the churchyard of St Andrew the Apostle in Soham; to the high altar in the said church a bushel of barley ('barly'); to the common light half a bushel of barley (*ordij*).

Marion my wife to have my tenement as it lies in 'Pratte strete'[2] for term of her life and she to repair [*it*] wind-tight and water-tight ('wynde thyte and water thyte'); and after her decease, it to be sold to the most avail by my attorneys and of the money to be bought a jewel most necessary to the church 'avayle' of 20s [*and to be*] dealt among poor folks and to repair highways [*where*] there [*is*] most need in the said town of Soham.

Richard my son to have my close called ('clepyd') 'the Herpe' with all 'prewayll' thereto belonging as the ?copies ('copes') thereof appear more plainly, to give and to sell; and Richard to pay 10s for a trental for me and all my good-doers. If Richard will buy any of my goods, he shall have it before any man, so that he will pay there for [*what*] another man will.

Residue of all my goods I put in the disposition of my attorneys, Richard Salysbery my son and Marion my wife; they to do for the weal of my soul.

Proved at Soham ('Saham'), 1 July 1474. Admon to execs.

[1]   ?Related to Richard Salysbery of Soham, will pr. November 1455 (SROB, Baldwyne 181; Pt I, no. 871).
[2]   'Prattstreete closes' appear on a map of Soham dated 1656 (see note to no. 232).

749. JOHN ALBON of SOHAM ('Saham') [*Cambs*], 1 July 1474 [*probate only*]

Proved at Soham, 1 July 1474. Admon to execs.

[fol. 565v]

750. ROBERT COSYN of STOWMARKET, 19 March 1473/74

Dated at Stowmarket, the Saturday before mid-Lent Sunday (*die Sabbati prox' ante mediam dominicam xl^{ine}*) 1474; to be buried in the church of the Blessed Apostles Peter and Paul of the said town, in the aisle beyond the font near the position of the torches (*in Ecclesia … in alura ultra fontem penes stacionem* 'le torchis'); to the new-making and repairing of the paving similar (*de novo reficiend' & reparand' secundum similitudine*) to the other paving of the church, 20s;[1] to the work of the church of the Blessed Mary in the same town, to be newly built, 20s;[2] to the chapel of St Nicholas of Gipping ('Gyppyng'), for rebuilding and repairing, 20s.[3]

To a suitable chaplain to celebrate in the said church of the Blessed Peter and Paul at the altar of St John the Baptist an annual stipend, as soon as possible after my decease, for my soul and my benefactors' [*souls*].

Thomas my son to have, to him and his heirs, my messuage in 'Breggestrett', after the decease of Marion my wife, reserving to Marion the occupation of the messuage during the term of her life; and if Thomas dies before his mother, then the messuage to remain to Geoffrey my son after Marion; if Geoffrey dies before Marion, then the messuage to be sold by Marion and her attorneys and the money to be disposed in the best way she knows for the health of our souls.

When Thomas my son reaches the age of 18, he to have 40s in value out of my goods and chattels; when Geoffrey my son reaches the age of 18, he to have 40s in value out of my goods and chattels; if either of my sons die under 18, the other to have both parts; if both die, then [*the money*] to remain to Marion to dispose in the best way as she will.

I wish that, if she is able by recovering my debts and realizing my goods and chattels, Marion is to have newly paved the whole aisle (*alura*) called 'le Seynt Johannis heele', from the area (*spacione*) by the south door of the church as far as the other area near the west door, with marble similar to the other paving.[4]

Residue of all my goods, chattels and debts, moveable and unmoveable, to Marion my wife and Thomas my son to benefit, dispose and distribute in alms and works of charity for my soul and our benefactors' [*souls*] as they see [*best*] to please God and profit the health of my soul; they to be my execs and attorneys.

Seal appended.

Proved before William Wood. Admon to Marion the executrix; power reserved to Thomas Cosyn when he comes. [*Place and date not given; previous 2 probates dated 1 July 1474.*]

1   This testator clearly had an interest in church building works. This initial bequest to the church of SS Peter and Paul contributing to the provision of new paving and to the on-going repairs to existing paving over and around his grave is supplemented below by a much larger bequest for provision of paving for the whole of St John's aisle.

2   Provision for new building work at St Mary's, Stowmarket; see note to no. 381.

3   Pevsner suggested that the chapel at Gipping was built *c.*1483 but here it is being repaired in 1474.

4   This bequest states clearly the location of St John's chapel within the church of SS Peter and Paul, Stowmarket.

[fol. 566]

751. JOHN BAKERE of GLEMSFORD ('Glemesford'), 13 January 1471/72

Of Glemsford, in the diocese of Norwich; my body to Christian burial in the churchyard of Glemsford parish church; in God's name, I beg my execs to pay and fulfil all my debts that can be genuinely proved that I owe; to the high altar of the said church, for my tithes and offerings withheld, forgotten and underpaid, 6d.

To the convent of Friars Preachers of the Sudbury house, my brethren (*confratribus*), to pray for my soul 5s; to the convent of Friars Minor of the Babwell house, my brethren (*confratribus*), to pray for my soul 5s; to the convent of the Friars Carmelite of the Cambridge (*Cantebr'*) house to pray for my soul 5s, similarly my brethren.[1] As for my lands and tenements, firstly I wish Alice my wife, with the licence of the lord, to have all my lands and tenements which I hold in the town of Glemsford by copy of court roll of the lord of the same town, with all their appurtenances, and a piece of meadow of free tenure in the same town lying at 'lez Sloholes', containing by estimation about half an acre, more or less, with all its appurtenances, to hold to her and her heirs for ever of the chief lords of the fee by due services, under the condition that she pays Christian my daughter 5 marks in money in 5 years after my decease, that is, 13s 4d annually, and also pays all my bequests and funeral expenses and the debts that I owe. The same Alice to have all my ostilments and utensils, as in linen and woollen, pots, pans, cups, spoons and all the other necessaries belonging to my house.

Residue of all my goods to Alice to dispose at her own free will for my soul.

Execs: Alice and John Jakes, to implement all the above and [*pay my*] legacies in the best way they know to please God and profit my soul.

Seal appended.

Witnesses: John Mellere, John Jakes, William Cross, Richard Clerk and others.

Proved at Glemsford, 17 November 1472. Admon to execs.

[1]   For the friars see notes to nos 1 (Babwell), 11 (Sudbury) and 42 (Carmelites of Cambridge). For fraternities of friars see Introduction, under *Religious houses*.

752. JOHN HARPOUR of GLEMSFORD ('Glemesford'), 21 August 1472

[*nuncupative*]

Dated the Friday before the feast of St Bartholomew the Apostle 1472; [*commendation*: to God Almighty, the Blessed Mary &c; *no burial directions*].

He left all his goods, moveable and unmoveable, his lands and tenements to Juliana his wife for her sustentation and the sustentation of his children (*filiorum*).

Witnesses: John Hawngere, Sir Henry Rynggold, parish chaplain of Glemsford, Robert Jakes.

Proved at Glemsford, 17 November 1472. Admon to Juliana, wife of the deceased, executrix.

[fol. 566v]

753. JOHN TURNOUR of CHIPPENHAM ('Chepynham') [*Cambs*], 23 November 1472 [*probate only*]

Proved at Herringswell ('Eryngeswell'), 23 November 1472. Admon to [*execs*].

754. JOHN PLAYFORD the elder of MILDENHALL ('Myldenhale'), 15 June 1474

Dated at Mildenhall; John Playford the elder, living in the street called 'le Westrow-stret';[1] my testament containing my last will; [*commendation to*: God Almighty &c]; to be buried in Christian burial in Mildenhall church; to the said church for my tithes and offerings forgotten 6s 8d; to the reparation of the same church 40s; I wish a suitable priest to celebrate in the said church for a whole year, taking for his stipend 8 marks.

I wish George Playford my son[2] and John Playford, my execs, to buy an ornament for Mildenhall church, to the value of 8 marks, as seems most suitable to them, according to their discretion.

To the house of friars of Babwell 10s; to each house of friars of Thetford 10s; to the friars of Cambridge (*Cantebr'*) 10s;[3] to the gild of Corpus Christi of Mildenhall 6s 8d.[4]

Margaret my wife to have my tenement in which I live, with 20 acres of land and meadow, for term of her life, reserving to George my son his dwelling for himself and his family, with free ingress and egress whenever and as often as he wishes for him and his. After the decease of Margaret, the whole tenement with the 20 acres of land to remain to George my son and his heirs in fee simple. To Margaret my wife 1 acre of land, to sell if she wishes; to her 6 cows of the best and of her choice, 6 calves, 6 heifers of the best, 40 ewes and 20 wethers (*bidentes*).

To Alice Jerveys, the daughter of Robert Jerveys, a calf.

To Alice Playford, the daughter of George Playford, 1 acre of land called 'Sowteres Acre' and a calf.

To Robert Jerveys, the son of Robert Jerveys of Barton Mills ('Berton Mellys'), 2 sheep.

To John Playford, the son of the said George Playford, 4 sheep; to Thomas Playford, the son of George Playford, 4 sheep; to each of the children of George Playford, 2 sheep.

To Robert Mey the elder a mare of the best and I remit to him all the debts he owes me; to Thomas Mey a mare and a calf.

To Robert Symonde a mare with the foal; to Henry Clyffe a mare; to Richard Shene a calf and a sheep; to Joan Wareyn 2 sheep.

To each of [*my*] godsons and goddaughters a bushel of barley.

To Joan Playford, the wife of John Playford, a good calf.

To Joan Lambe a cow with the calf and 6 sheep.

To each of the children of John Playford of the town of [*left blank*] 4 bushels of barley.

To Margaret Playford, the wife of George Playford, a cow.

To John Playford, my cousin and my exec, 20s for his labour in this cause.

[fol. 567] To the said George Playford all my lands and tenements, messuages, pastures and feedings, rents and services with all their appurtenances, to him and his heirs in fee simple.

Residue of all my goods and chattels to the said George my son to pay all my debts which of right I owe.

Execs: George Playford my son and John Playford, the son of Thomas Playford my brother.[5]

Seal appended.

Proved at Herringswell ('Heryngeswell'), 12 July 1474. Admon to execs.

---

1   West Row is one of the outlying hamlets of Mildenhall, the other two being Holywell Row and Beck Row.
2   Executor of Katherine Bowne of Mildenhall (no. 768).
3   For the friars see notes to nos 1 (Franciscans of Babwell), 68 (Dominicans of Thetford), 69 (Augustinians of Thetford), 42 (Carmelites of Cambridge), 80 (Dominicans of Cambridge) and 187 (Augustinians and Franciscans of Cambridge). The testator may have intended a bequest only to the Carmelites of Cambridge, thus remembering all four orders of friars once only (see note to no. 133).

⁴ For the gild of Corpus Christi at Mildenhall see note to no. 230.

⁵ John Playford, executor of this will of John Playford the elder of Mildenhall, is described variously by the testator as 'my cousin' and 'the son of Thomas Playford my brother' thus indicating
the flexibilty of the term 'cousin' at this time: he was in fact the testator's nephew. He was also
executor of 'John Playford of Mildenhall', this testator's brother (no. 312).

755. WILLIAM GENTE the younger of EUSTON,¹ 26 May 1474

Dated at Euston; mindful of the end of my days and knowing nothing is more certain
(*n'l certior*) than the hour of death; my sinful (*peccat'cem*) soul to Almighty God,
the Blessed Mary &c[*sic*]; to be buried in the churchyard of Euston parish church;
to the rector there, for his labour, 3s 4d.

To the White Friars of Norwich, for celebrating a trental, 10s.²

To Euston church 6s 8d.

I wish that an honest priest be hired to celebrate for half a year for my soul and the
souls of my friends, to whom I leave for that half year 4 marks.

To Margaret my wife 'ly parlour' with the other house (*domo*) newly erected, for
term of her life; to Margaret 8 acres of arable land during her life[*time*] and all my
utensils belonging to my house.

To Thomas my son a tenement called 'Wyltonys', with 2 acres of land.

The rest of [*my*] goods to my execs, Margaret my wife and Thomas Rucwoode, to
dispose for my soul as seems best to please God and profit my soul.

Seal appended.

Proved 18 July 1474, [*place not given*]. Admon to Thomas Rucwoode, exec. Power
reserved to Margaret, when she comes and if she wishes to take up [*admon*].

¹ ?Related to John Gent of Euston, will pr. December 1450 (SROB, Baldwyne 114; Pt I, no. 535).

² For the White Friars (Carmelites) of Norwich see note to no. 269.

[fol. 567v]

756. JOHN PHELIPE of MELFORD, 18 August 1473 [*English*]

To be buried in the churchyard of [*the Holy*] Trinity in Melford; to the said ('sede')
altar of the said church for tithes and offerings forgotten 12d.

My place which I dwell in, with all my lands, goods and chattels, be sold by my
execs, and therewith my debts to be paid as far as it may stretch; and if any part of
my goods may be spared, besides my debts, I will it be disposed by the best offices
('offeyse') of my execs.

If William Preen my 'sone lawe' desires to buy the said place, with all the appurtenances, I will that he shall have it before any other man.

And whoever buys that place, I will that Rose my wife shall have her dwelling in
a chamber assigned to her within the said place [*for*] term of her life, if it may be.

Execs: William Preen of London ('Loondon') and Rose my wife; they to sell and
pay according to my will.

Witnesses: Sir ('Seere') John Stannard,¹ William Meriel, Nicholas Rokelle, Robert
Yowng and others.

Proved at Fornham, 17 September 1474. Admon to William Preen, exec. Power
reserved to Rose, relict of the deceased, co-executrix, when she comes, if she wishes
to take it up. Seal of official appended.

¹ See note to no. 436.

[fol. 568]
757. WILLIAM GYLBERD of TROSTON ('Trostunn'), 28 May 1474

Dated at Troston, the Saturday before the feast of Pentecost 1474; to be buried in the churchyard of the church of the Blessed Mary of Troston; to the high altar for my omissions (*transgressionibus*) 12d; to the fabric of Troston church 40d.

To Margaret Bussche a ewe with a lamb; to William Hannyngton another ewe and lamb.

All my other goods and chattels, besides those bequeathed above, to Margaret my wife to fulfil my last will; she to be my executrix, to dispose them as she sees best to profit my soul.

Proved at Fornham St Martin, 11 July 1474. Admon to executrix.

758. WILLIAM MAKRO of 'the Meere Strete' in SOHAM [*Cambs*], 10 February 1472/73 [*English*]

Dated at Soham; to be buried in the churchyard of St Andrew the Apostle in Soham; to the high altar in the said church 2 bushels of barley; to the sepulchre light 3s.

Agnes my wife shall have my capital ('hedde') tenement whole, like as it lies, with all the land that belongs thereto, term of her life and Thomas my son's life. And if she will sell any of the land during her life ('be her lyve'), I will that she and Thomas my son sell it to one of my children, which of them has readiest money; and if they have no money ready, to sell it to whom they like best for ready money; and my wife to receive the money and she to 'do parte' where she likes best for me and her and our 'alderes' good-doers. If it so be that Thomas my son will buy any of my land, though he be my attorney, he shall have it as soon as any man so [*long*] that he pays therefor as it is worth.

Agnes my wife shall have 'the Toppe of the lake' for term of her life; and after her decease, Thomas my son shall have the said tenement with 6 acres of land to him and his heirs, on condition that he repairs the tenement wind-tight and water-tight ('wynde thyte and water thyte').

Agnes my wife to have all the residue of my goods, small, great, less and more ('lytyll mekyll lesse & moore') to her own proper use.

Whosoever occupies my capital tenement ('menour myn heed tenement') to keep my year day and Agnes my wife's, perpetually, yearly.

Execs: Agnes my wife and Thomas Makro my son.

Proved at Soham, 1 July 1474. Admon to execs.

[fol. 568v]
759. MARGARET GLOVERE, of STANTON, widow, 10 June 1474

[*Commendation*: to God Almighty, the Blessed Mary &c]; my body to Christian burial; to the high altar of the church of St Petronilla in the town of Stanton, for my tithes and offerings forgotten, 3s 4d;[1] to the reparation of the same church 3s 4d;[2] to the high altar of Great Livermere ('Lyvermere Magna') church 3s 4d; to the reparation of the same church 20d; to the reparation of the lower (*inferior'*) church of Stanton 3s 4d.[3]

Residue of all my goods to my execs to sell and dispose for my soul and the souls of those to whom I am bound in the celebration of masses and the distribution of alms as they see best to please God and profit my soul.

459

Execs: Edmund Cleres of Great Livermere, John Glovere my son and Robert Tyllott of Rougham ('Rowham') to faithfully execute this testament; to each of whom for their labour 2s.
Seal appended.
Witnesses: William Coket, clerk,[4] Thomas Alysaundre and others.
Proved at Fornham, 13 July 1474. Admon to execs. Power reserved to Robert Tyllot, when he comes.

1   The chapel of St Petronilla was in the parish church of All Saints, Stanton; the image of this saint within that chapel was said to have attracted many pilgrims in medieval times (Dymond, *Parish Churches of Stanton*, pp.8–9).
2   Possibly meaning the chapel of St Petronilla, but more likely the church of All Saints.
3   The 'lower church' refers to the church of St John the Baptist, the other parish church in Stanton.
4   Incumbent of Great Livermere (see note to no. 241).

760. KATHERINE WARNERE of GREAT LIVERMERE ('Lyvermere Magna'),[1] 25 May 1474

[*Commendation*: to God Almighty, the Blessed Mary &c]; to be buried in the churchyard of the parish church of St Peter of Livermere aforesaid; to the high altar of the same church for offerings forgotten 6s 8d; to the emendation of the same church 6s 8d.
To the Friars Minor of Babwell 3s 4d;[2] to Friar John Habyngton of Babwell for a trental 10s.
Residue of all my goods to my execs to dispose and distribute in the best manner, according to their discretion, for the health of the soul of John Warnere[3] and mine, [*the souls of our*] parents, benefactors and all the faithful departed as seems to them most expedient.
Execs: Henry Bryon of Troston and Richard Redgrave of Livermere; they to faithfully execute everything specified in this testament.
[*No probate recorded; previous probate, on same folio, dated 13 July 1474*]

1   As 'Katherine, the wife of John Warnere of Great Livermere', legatee of Thomas Gatle of Great Livermere, will pr. January 1440/41 (SROB, Baldwyne 32; Pt I, no. 180).
2   See note to no. 1.
3   Will no. 599 above, of which Katherine was executrix.

[fol. 569]
761. JOHN BRAY of NAYLAND ('Neylond'), 8 January 1472/73

To be buried in the churchyard of St James of Nayland aforesaid; to the high altar 6d; to the fabric of the church 12d.
To Isabel Byndere a pair of sheets.
My cow to be sold to pay my debts with the money from it.
Faithful execs: John Blakpayn and John Balle.
Seal appended.
Witnesses: William Profete, John Mendham, John Barkere, William Moryell and others.
Proved at Cockfield ('Cokefeld'), 9 February 1472/73. Admon to execs.

762. AGNES GLOVERE [of WOODDITTON] [*Cambs*], widow, 1472

[*Day and month not given*] In my widowhood; [*commendation*: to God Almighty, the Blessed Mary]; to be buried in the churchyard of the church of All Saints of Woodditton ('Woddytton'); to the high altar 4d; to the image of All Saints 6d; to the gild of the Holy Trinity 12d.[1]

To John the younger my son a messuage in the town of Saxon ('Saxton') in the county of Cambridge, with all its appurtenances, lying between the messuage of Robert Vys on the south side and the tenement lately the lord earl of Oxford's on the north, one head abutting on the same earl's land to the west and the other on the highway to the east, to hold to him and his heirs.[2] If John dies without heirs, then the messuage to be sold and disposed on the church and highways for the health of his father's [*soul*] and mine and the souls of all our benefactors.

Residue of all my goods, moveable and unmoveable, to John the younger to dispose for his father and me as seems best to him.

Seal appended.

Witnesses: William Prat, John Vaucy and many others.

Proved at Newmarket (*Novu' Mercat'*), 12 February 1472/73. Admon to exec.

1   For gilds in Woodditton see note to no. 630.
2   The manor of Saxton, or Saxton Hall, was one of the three main early manors at Woodditton, the other two being Ditton Camoys and Ditton Valence. In 1086 the manor of Saxton was held by Aubrey de Vere, and thence for over 400 years by Aubrey's descendants, the de Vere earls of Oxford. The medieval manor house stood on a moated site immediately east of the modern Saxon Hall. Saxton developed into the settlements of Saxon Green and Saxon Street, the former disappearing at enclosure (*VCH Cambs*, x, pp.86–90).

[fol. 569v]

763. JOHN KYNG[1] of BROCKFORD ('Brokeford') in WETHERINGSETT,[2] 14 March 1452[*sic*]

['Kynge' *in margin*] Dated at Brockford, the Tuesday after the feast of St Gregory 1452; my body to Christian burial in the churchyard of the church of All Saints of Wetheringsett; to the high altar 12d; to each parish clerk 2d; to the parish priest 12d; to the emendation of the church 6s 8d.

To each exec [*of mine*] 12d.

For a trental to be celebrated, on one day among the friars, for my soul and the soul of Margaret my wife and [*the souls*] of all my benefactors, 10s; to each order of friars a coomb of malt.[3]

Olive my mother to have my tenement and all my lands for term of her life; and after her decease, Robert my son to have them, on condition he pays to Wetheringsett church 14 marks, and to Alice his sister on [*her*] marriage 5 marks, and if she dies before marriage, the 5 marks to remain to Robert my son. If Robert dies under legal age and Alice before marriage, I wish the said goods (*bona*) to be disposed by [*my*] execs.

Residue of all my goods to the disposition of my execs, Robert Kynge my son and John Palmer, to dispose for my soul and the souls of my friends as seems best to please God and profit my soul.

Seal appended.

Proved at Wetheringsett, 12 April 1452[*sic*].[4] Admon to John Palmer, exec. Power reserved to Robert Kynge when he comes, if he wishes to take it up. Seal of official appended.

1   ?Executor (as John Kyng the younger) of John Kyng the elder of Wetheringsett, will pr. July 1443 (SROB, Baldwyne 47; Pt I, no. 248); John the elder's will mentions both his son John and 'John Kyng the younger'. This testator was not the son of John Kyng the elder since the wife of the latter, named Elizabeth, was still alive when he made his testament and will in 1442 and 1443, and this testator's mother, named Olive, was still alive when he made his will in ?1452.

2   See note to no. 5 regarding Brockford in Wetheringsett.

3   Although this testator did not specify which friars were to receive bequests, bequests made to 'each order of friars' were often to one of the houses of each of the four orders of friars (see note to no. 133).

4   All other probates in this part – and on this leaf – of Baldwyne are dated 1472.

[fol. 570]
764. PETER STONHAM of THORNDON,[1] 20 August 1471

My testament and last will; [*commendation*: to God Almighty, the Blessed Mary]; to be buried within the churchyard of Thorndon parish church, next to my parents. I wish to have a certain recited in Thorndon church each Sunday and celebrated there for a year, according to the custom followed there (*secundum consuetudinem ibidem celebrat'*), for my soul, the souls of my parents and benefactors.

To the reparation of the said church 4 bushels (*modios*) of malt and 2 bushels (*modios*) of wheat for an ale[2] to be made there (*ad unam potacionem ibidem faciend'*).

To each of my godsons and goddaughters 4d.

To Agnes my wife all the utensils of my house for term of her life; and after her decease, what remains of the utensils to be distributed among my children, according to the discretion of my execs. Agnes my wife to have 40s in cash, to be paid to her half yearly each year of her life, by way of dower, to be received from all the lands, meadows, pastures and other appurtenances in the towns of Thorndon, Thwaite ('Thweytes'), Wetheringsett ('Wedersett') and Stoke ('Stok'); if the 40s should remain unpaid, in part or in whole, for any whole year during her life, then my execs shall legally enter the lands, meadows, pastures and others in those towns, which I can legally sell on this day, and distrain the 40s for the benefit of Agnes.

Matilda my daughter to have a close called 'Lesser (*minus*) Bradhege'; if William my son is willing to pay Matilda 10 marks in money within a year after my decease, then I wish him to have the said close to him and his assigns for ever; otherwise Matilda to have it freely to her and her assigns for ever.

Katherine my daughter to have 5 acres of land lying together in the field called 'Langemedewefeld'; if William my son is willing to pay Katherine 40s in cash within a year after my decease, then I wish him to have the 5 acres of land; or otherwise Katherine to have them freely to her and her assigns for ever.

Agnes my wife to have 4 cart[*load*]s of timber annually for term of her life.

I oblige William my son to pay all my debts, legacies and assignments; and if he will not do so, then I wish my execs to occupy all the lands, meadows, pastures and all the other appurtenances until all the debts, legacies and assignments in this my last will be fully paid.

The residue &c[*sic*].

Execs: Agnes my wife, John Bedyngfeld, Richard Turnour of Thwaite ('Thweyte') and Ralph Eustasse.

James Lampytte to be supervisor of this my testament and last will.

Each of my execs to have for [*their*] labour 3s 4d.

I beg and require my feoffees to deliver legal estate to my assigns, as they will answer before the High Judge, according to this will when legally required by my assigns.

Proved at Botesdale, 18 February 1472/73. Admon to Richard Turnour and Ralph Eustas. Power reserved to Agnes Stonham and John Bedyngfeld, co-execs, when they come and if [*they wish*] to take up admon.

1   ?Executor of John Elmyswell of Thwaite, will pr. December 1449 (SROB, Baldwyne 138; Pt I, no. 658).
2   See Glossary.

[fol. 570v]

765. JOHN COOK of THRANDESTON, 12 June 1472

My last will; dated at Thrandeston; to be buried in the churchyard of the church of the same town; to the high altar of the same for tithes forgotten 6d.

To Margaret my wife all my utensils and all my live cattle.

To the said Margaret and Thomas my son all my messuages, lands and tenements with their appurtenances to be divided equally between Margaret and Thomas during the life of Margaret; and after her decease, all the messuages, lands and tenements to remain to Thomas and his heirs; [*if*] Thomas dies, then all the messuages, lands and tenements to remain to John my son. If both die, then all the messuages, lands and tenements, after the decease of Margaret, to be sold by my execs and the money from them expended for me and the souls of my friends in pious works, except 4 acres of land lying in 2 pieces. Of these, the first piece of land lies in Thrandeston in the field called 'le Mellefeld', containing 3 acres, between the land of Thomas Mavesen, chaplain,[1] on the west, and the land of divers men on the east, one head abutting on the land of the said Thomas Mavsen to the north; which piece I leave to John my son; and if he dies, then it to remain to Margaret my wife and Thomas my son, as above. The second piece contains 1 acre and lies in the said town in the field called 'le Langgesyk' between land of Thrandeston church on the north and bond-land of the Prior of Hoxne ('Hoxon')[2] in the tenure of Thomas Ropkyn on the south, one head abutting on the land of Matilda Paternoster to the west; which piece I wish my execs to sell and pay my debts out of it.

To John my son a quarter of barley.

I beg my feoffees to deliver, when required, to Margaret and Thomas and John my sons full and peaceful seisin of and in all those messuages, lands and tenements bequeathed above according to the effect of this my last will and not otherwise, as they will answer before the High Judge on the Day of Judgement.

Residue of all my goods to the disposition of my execs, Margaret my wife and Thomas my son, and my supervisor William Styward of Dunwich ('Donewyche'), to dispose as they see best to please God and profit my soul and the souls of my friends. Seal appended.

Witnesses: Roger Wryghte, John Byrd, John Carman the elder, William Lely, John Peyine and others.

Proved at Eye, 3 October 1472. Admon to execs.

1   Executor of John Mavesyn of Thrandeston, probate only, September 1452 (SROB, Baldwyne 111; Pt I, no. 509).

2   In 1101 the bishop of Norwich founded at Hoxne a cell of the great Benedictine cathedral priory. By 1267 the house consisted of a prior, and seven or eight monks. The monks kept a school for the children of the parish, and supported or boarded two of the scholars (*VCH Suffolk*, ii, pp.76–7).

[fol. 571]

766. SIMON FAYERWARE of MILDENHALL ('Mildenhale'), 16 April 1472

Dated at Mildenhall; my testament containing my last will; [*commendation*: to God Almighty my Creator and Saviour, the Blessed Mary his mother, and all the saints]; my body to Christian burial in the churchyard of the church of the Blessed Mary of Mildenhall ('Myldenhale'); to the high altar of Mildenhall church for my tithes and offerings underpaid 12d; to the reparation of the same church 40d.

Margery my wife to have my whole messuage and all the utensils and bedding belonging to my house and all the beasts of whatever kind, on this condition, that she pays all my debts which of right I owe anyone.

Margery my wife to be my principal executrix, and Richard Coole[1] and Simon Aleyn to be co-execs and helpers with her to see my last will faithfully executed.

Seal appended.

Proved at Tuddenham ('Todynham'), 15 July 1472. Admon to Margery Fayerware and Richard Coole, execs. Power reserved to Simon Aleyn, when he comes.

1   Executor of Katherine Bowne of Mildenhall (no. 768).

[fol. 571v]

767. WILLIAM LOVETOP of KERSEY,[1] 20 June 1472

Dated at Kersey, in the diocese of Norwich; my testament containing my last will; [*commendation*: to God Almighty my Creator and Saviour, the Blessed Mary his mother, and all the saints]; to be buried in the churchyard of the parish church of St Mary of Kersey; to the high altar of the same church for my tithes and offerings forgotten and retained, in exoneration of my soul, 3s 4d. I wish my funeral expenses to be met duly and honestly by the good ordering and discretion of my exec. I also wish that all my debts, which of right I owe anyone, are paid and satisfied immediately after my decease. To Kersey parish church 6 marks towards the purchasing of a chalice, if my goods and chattels will stretch to it; to the sustentation of the fraternity of the Blessed Mary of Kersey 3s 4d.[2]

To the Friars Preachers of Sudbury, to celebrate 30 masses for my soul and the souls of my benefactors, 10s.[3]

To Kersey church, 5s for the purchasing of linen cloth for 'Rochetes'.[4]

Joan my wife to have her reasonable maintenance by the discretion of my exec during the term of her life.

The rest of my goods I leave in the hands of William Sturnell of Sudbury to dispose of them as he will answer on the Day of Judgement before the High Judge.

Seal appended.

Proved at Preston, 21 July 1472. Admon to exec.

1   Witness of the will of John Gybbe, pr. November 1445 (SROB, Baldwyne 70; Pt I, no. 342); supervisor of the will of Rose Waryn, pr. 28 March 1447 (SROB, Baldwyne 84; Pt I, no. 390); executor of John Perye, will pr. January 1453/54 (SROB, Baldwyne 150; Pt I, no. 719).

2   In 1445, as well as bequeathing 3s 4d to the gild of the Blessed Mary in Kersey, John Gybbe
    also made bequests to the gilds of the Holy Ghost and of St Peter the Apostle in Kersey (SROB,
    Baldwyne 70; Pt I, no. 342).
3   See note to no. 11.
4   See Glossary.

768. KATHERINE BOWNE late the relict of Thomas Bowne[1] of MILDENHALL ('Mildenhale'), 17 March 1471/72

Dated at Mildenhall; my testament containing my last will; [*commendation*: to Almighty God Creator &c]; my body to Christian burial in the churchyard of the church of Blessed Virgin Mary of Mildenhall; to the high altar of Mildenhall church for tithes and offerings 4d; to the reparation of the same church 8d.

I wish the priest of Mildenhall to celebrate a trental for my soul and the souls of my parents and friends and all my benefactors.

Thomas Bowne my son and Margaret Sygo my daughter[2] to divide equally between them all my utensils.

Thomas Bowne my son to have 3 roods of land; he to have a house called 'the Newhows' for term of his life.

The third part of the money arising from my messuage to be equally divided between Thomas my son and Margaret my daughter; the remainder of the money from the messuage to be disposed for my soul and the souls of my friends by my execs.

Margaret my daughter to have, to her and her heirs, 2 acres of arable land which Henry Berton demised to my mother to keep his anniversary; Margaret to have them under the same form, to her and her heirs; and if she dies without heirs, then I wish Thomas my son to have them to him and his heirs; and if he dies without heirs, then I wish the land to remain to the next heir.

Residue of all my goods to my execs to dispose for my soul as they see best to please God and profit my soul.

Thomas my son to be my principal exec and Richard Coole[3] and George Playford[4] to be his co-execs.

Proved at Tuddenham, 15 July 1472. Admon to Thomas Bowne, exec. [*Power reserved*] to Richard Coole and George Playford, the other execs, when they come, if they wish to take up [*admon*].

1   Witness of the will of John Frere, pr. July 1448 (SROB, Baldwyne 144; Pt I, no. 683).
2   ?Wife of John Sygo of Worlington; his will no. 429 above, proved June 1470. John Sygo
    bequeathed his wife his cottage and the profit of 4 acres of land lying in the fields of Mildenhall
    for her lifetime but he did not identify her by name.
3   Executor of Simon Fayerware of Mildenhall (no. 766).
4   Legatee and executor of John Playford the elder of Mildenhall (no. 754).

[fol. 572]

769. JOHN SHUKFORD of THELNETHAM,[1] 27 May 1472

['Shukforth' *in margin*] Dated at Thelnetham, in the deanery of Blackbourn ('Blakborn'), diocese of Norwich; to be buried in the churchyard of Thelnetham parish church. I wish my debts to be fully paid. To the high altar of the said church for my tithes and offerings forgotten 3s 4d; to the emendation of the said church 3s 4d; I wish to have a trental 10s; to the reparation of the said church, in respect of my father's legacy, 3s 4d.[2]

I wish to have a suitable pilgrim to go on pilgrimage to the image of the Blessed Mary of Woolpit ('Wolpet').³ I wish to have a suitable pilgrim to go on pilgrimage to the image of St Remigius (*Remicii*) of Roydon ('Reydon') [*Norfolk*].⁴

I bequeath all the utensils and hostilments whatsoever belonging to my house and all my moveable chattels, with 1½ acres of free land in the town of Thelnetham to Marion my wife; she to pay all my debts and see to my burial and all the expenses and also pay all my legacies as above.

Marion to have a messuage with the croft adjacent in which I live in Thelnetham for term of her life; and after her decease, the messuage with the croft to be sold for the best price and, of the money coming from it, I wish to have a secular priest celebrating in Thelnetham church for a whole year for my soul and my parents'⁵ and all my benefactors' [*souls*], to whose stipend I leave 8 marks. Residue of the money coming from the messuage and croft to be divided between my 2 sons and my 2 daughters by equal portions; if one of them should die, the deceased's part to be divided among those living; if all die except one, then he or she should have their own part and the part of one of the deceased, and I wish the residue of those deceased to be disposed for my soul.

Residue of all my goods to Marion my wife, my faithful executrix, to pay my debts and implement my legacies according to the form of this testament as above and to do other works of charity for my soul.

Supervisor: Valentine Stabelere, clerk.⁶

Seal appended.

Proved at Langham, 25 June 1472. Admon to executrix.

¹   Son of Robert Schucford of Thelnetham, will pr. April 1452 (SROB, Baldwyne 110; Pt I, no. 506); ?related to John Shukford of Thelnetham (no. 561 above).

²   In his will, Robert Schucford of Thelnetham had bequeathed 40d to the church of St Nicholas, Thelnetham, and also 40d to the sepulchre light there, both sums of money to be paid from the proceeds of the sale of an acre of arable land called 'Haweboschakyr' (Pt I, no. 506).

³   See note to no. 142.

⁴   St Remigius or Remi, Bishop of Rheims, was known for his learning, sanctity and miracles, which, in his episcopacy of over 70 years, made his name famous in the Church. In 459, when only 22 (too young to fill a priest, much less a bishop) he was chosen to fill the vacant see of Rheims; he was ordained and consecrated in spite of his youth, and was said to have amply made up for lack of experience with his fervour and energy. Under the protection of King Clovis, whom he baptized, Remigius spread the Gospel among the Franks, in which work God was said to have endowed him with an extraordinary gift of miracles. He died *c*.530. His feast day is 1 October (www.Catholic.org).

⁵   John's parents were Robert and Agnes (Pt I, no. 506).

⁶   See note to no. 437.

[fol. 572v]

770. WILLIAM FULLERE of HUNSTON ('Hunterston'), 4 June 1472

I leave my body to the disposition of God, to be buried in the churchyard of the church of St Michael the Archangel of Hunston.

Execs: Marion my wife and with her, Roger, [*my/her*] son, and John.

To the high altar 20d; to the making of the tower of Hunston 6s 8d, in this form, that they begin in the aforesaid year,¹ otherwise I leave the 6s 8d to the common way where there is need (*ubi opus est*).

My execs to dispose for me, on my burial day, 6 bushels of wheat and a quarter of malt.

To the Augustinian Friars of Thetford[2] [*for*] a trental 10s; to the friars of Babwell[3] 12d [*out*] of the mass pence.[4]

I bequeath all my goods, moveable and unmoveable, wherever they may be, both live and dead, to Marion my wife; to Marion all my lands and tenements with all their appurtenances lying in Hunston and Norton for term of her life; and after her decease, they are to be sold and disposed by her execs or by her heirs for my soul and for our benefactors.

Residue of all [*my*] goods to Marion my wife with the said execs to dispose for my soul and the souls of all my friends.

Proved at Langham, 25 June 1472. Admon to executrix.

¹ This suggests that in 1472 work on the tower of Hunston church was planned but possibly not implemented.
² See note to no. 69.
³ See note to no. 1.
⁴ The bequest of mass-pence suggests that William Fullere belonged to a gild at Hunston. In 1446 John Barough of Bardwell had bequeathed 4 bushels of barley to the gild of the Holy Trinity of Hunston (SROB, Baldwyne 125; Pt I, no. 583).

771. ROBERT JUDY of TOSTOCK ('Tostok'), barker, 30 July 1472

['Barkere *alias* Judy' *in margin*]¹ Dated at Tostock; to be buried in the churchyard of the parish church of St Andrew of Tostock; to the mother church of Norwich 6d;[2] to the high altar of St Andrew's church aforesaid 20d.

To Katherine my wife 5 marks in money to be delivered by Walter Judy, my father.

To the light of St Mary in Tostock church 40d; for an antiphoner to be got (*h'end'*) for the same church 6s 8d.

My wife to have my house with the arable and non-arable land and all the chattels, with all the moveables and unmoveables belonging to me, those pertaining to my craft only excepted.

Execs: Walter Judy of Walsham, my father, and Katherine my wife, doing everything for the health of my soul.

Witnesses: John Smyth of Norton, John Baldry of Barningham ('Bernyngham') and Thomas Judy of Thetford.

Proved at Fornham St Martin, 13 July 1472. Admon to execs.

¹ This marginal note demonstrates how *alias* surnames might arise: in the body of the will 'barker' is given as the occupation of the deceased.
² See note to no. 193.

[fol. 573]

772. BENEDICT OTHOO the elder of BRADFIELD ST GEORGE ('Bradfeld Monachorum'), 20 August 1471

['Benyth Athoo' *in margin*] Dated at Bradfield aforesaid; my body to Christian burial; to the high altar of the church of Bradfield aforesaid for my tithes and offerings forgotten or underpaid and for the health of my soul 20d; for the expenses of burying my body and of paying the chaplains, clerks [*and*] the poor and needy present at my obsequies, for my soul, 10s; to the reparation of the said church 40s; to the rector of the same church for celebrating a certain called 'a sangred' in the said church for my soul 4s 4d.

To the friars of Babwell, for celebrating a trental of St Gregory for my soul and for the souls of those for whom I am bound, 10s.[1]

To the new fabric of the monastery of Bury St Edmunds (*Sci' Edmundi*) 20s.[2]

To a suitable and honest chaplain to celebrate divine service for my soul, the soul of Margaret my late wife, the souls of my father and mother and all the souls for whom I am bound, for a whole year in the church of Bradfield aforesaid, 8 marks.

To Katherine my wife all my bedding and vessels of latten, brass and pewter belonging to my house, except the best brass pot and a brass cauldron.

Benedict my son to have to him and his heirs for ever all the lands and tenements, rents and services, meadows, pastures, feedings and woods, with their appurtenances, which I have at this date in the towns of Bradfield St George and Bradfield St Clare ('Bradfeld Seynclere') or elsewhere in Suffolk, and all my goods and chattels, moveable and unmoveable, corn, grain and animals of whatever kind and wherever they may be, except those bequeathed in this will, provided always that he, Benedict my son, shall be bound by a certain written obligation for 40 marks (*xl marcarum*) to my execs, to pay those execs £20 (*xx li'*) in money in 4 years immediately following my death.[3]

I pray and require all my feoffees of and in the said lands and tenements, rents and services, meadows, pastures, feedings and woods, with their appurtenances, to deliver their estate, which they have of them, according to the tenor of this testament and will, when duly required by my execs and supervisor to do so.

To Joan Bryght my sister 20s.

To Isabel Othoo my goddaughter 6s 8d.

To Alice my daughter my best gown and 20s, to be paid to her in 6 years next after my decease, that is, each year of the six 3s 4d.

Residue of all my goods and chattels to my execs, to receive and dispose for my soul and for the souls for whom I am bound, in the payments of my debts, the celebration of masses and the doing of other pious works as seems best to please God [fol. 573v] and profit the healthfulness of my soul.

Execs: William Clerk of Bradfield aforesaid and Walter Dorcetre of the same; John Derlyng of Bury St Edmunds to be supervisor of the execution of this my testament and my last will; to each of William, Walter and John for their labour 6s 8d.

Seal appended.

Witnesses: Edmund Tylney, rector of the church of Bradfield St Clare,[4] William Bryght, John Kempe and others.

Proved at Fornham, 14 October 1471. Admon to execs.

[1] See note to no. 1.
[2] See note to no. 88 and also no. 519.
[3] That is, Benedict the son was to pay his father's executors £20 within four years; if he failed to do so he would forfeit to them 40 marks (£26 13s 4d).
[4] See note to no. 130 and also no. 184.

773. WILLIAM GODFREY of GREAT HORRINGER ('Magna Hornyngesherth'), 25 September 1471

Dated at Great Horringer; my body to Christian burial; to the high altar of the church of Great Horringer for my tithes and offerings forgotten and underpaid 2s; to the reparation of the same church 6s 8d.

To the friars of Babwell 10s.[1]

I wish a suitable chaplain to be sustained to celebrate for half a year in the said church for my soul and the souls for whom I am bound, receiving for his salary 4 marks.

To my execs 4 marks to dispose in works of piety for the health of my soul as follows: to the blind, lame and imprisoned, and especially in the emendation of the highway called 'Clenewallstrete'.

To Margaret my wife all my hostilments and utensils, with all my grain and live cattle of whatever sort, except my sheep, of which one part I leave to Margaret my wife, another part to John my son and the third part to Thomas my son, to be equally divided. To Margaret a pightle called 'Lytylmedewe' and a piece of land lying in 'Hakferescroft' with its appurtenances in Horringer aforesaid, to hold to her for ever.

To John my son a croft called 'Fynstoft' with its appurtenances, to hold to him and his heirs for ever.

To Ed' Ussheere a piece of land with the appurtenances containing 2 acres in 'Hopleyfeld', to hold to him and his heirs for ever.

To Margaret my wife my tenement in which I live with the adjacent croft, a pightle called 'Gooses' lying opposite the tenement, and a croft lying opposite 'le Cundewyte', with 7 pieces of land lying diversely in the field called 'Beryfeld', with all their appurtenances, to hold for term of her life; and after her decease, the tenement with the adjacent croft, pightle, croft and 7 pieces of land with their appurtenances [fol. 574] wholly to remain to John my son, to hold to him and his heirs for ever, on condition that he pays Thomas my son 10 marks in money with the advice of (*per visum*) my execs and feoffees. If John should die in the lifetime of his mother, then the said tenement with the adjacent croft, pightle, croft and 7 pieces of land [*etc*] after the decease of Margaret, are to remain wholly to Thomas my son, to hold to him and his heirs for ever of the chief lords of the fee.

Residue of all my goods and chattels, after my debts have been paid, to my execs to sell, receive and dispose for my soul and the souls for whom I am bound and in pious works as my execs see best to please God and profit my soul.

Execs of this my testament and last will: Margaret my wife, Adam Rodyng[2] and John Welham the elder;[3] to each of the said Adam and John for their labour 40d. Seal appended.

Witnesses: John Goose, William Rodynge, Thomas Redere and others.

Proved at Fornham St Martin, 14 October 1471. Admon to execs.

[1]   See note to no. 1.
[2]   Will no. 654, proved in February 1474/75.
[3]   Legatee of his father, William Welham of Great Horringer (no. 10).

774. ROBERT YESTAS of MENDLESHAM ('Mendelesham'), 20 September 1471

Of Mendlesham, in the diocese of Norwich; I make my testament and dispose my last will; my body to Christian burial; to the high altar of the same church of Mendlesham 2s; to the reparation of the same church 6s 8d; to the gild of the Holy Trinity there 4s; to the gild of St Mary of the same [*place*] 2s;[1] for a trental to be celebrated for my soul and for the souls of all my friends 10s.

469

To John Thurston my household servant 6s 8d; to Katherine Yestas my household servant 6s 8d.

To Katherine my wife all my moveable goods; to her my whole tenement with all the lands, both free and bond, for term of her life; and after her decease, the tenement with all the lands to be sold by my execs.

I wish to have a priest to celebrate in Mendlesham church for my soul and I leave for his stipend 8 marks.

If Katherine [*my wife*] should marry, I wish the tenement with all the lands to be sold and disposed in works of piety.

Residue of all my goods to the administration of my execs to sell, receive and dispose for the health of my soul as they see best to please God and profit my soul.

Execs: Katherine my wife, John Yestas of Brockford ('Brokford') and John Morgan of Earl Stonham ('Stonham Comitis'); to each of them for their labour 6s 8d.

Proved at Westhorpe 'Westhorp', 22 November 1471. Admon to execs.

1   For the gilds of the Holy Trinity and St Mary of Mendlesham see notes to no. 568 and also no. 788.

[fol. 574v]

775. RICHARD CALFFE of WESTHORPE ('Westhorp'), 10 May 1471

Dated at Westhorpe; to be buried in the churchyard of the church of the Blessed Margaret of Westhorpe; to the high altar of the said church 12d.

To Agnes my wife my whole tenement with all its appurtenances during her life[*time*]; and after her decease, it is to go to Stephen my son, to him and his heirs; if Stephen should die without heirs, then I wish the tenement to be sold with its appurtenances and disposed for my soul and my wife's, my father's and my mother's [*souls*], except that Agnes my wife have an acre (*unam cram*) of land lying at '[*?the*] Welle' to her and her heirs for ever.

I wish Stephen my son to pay the friars of Babwell ('Babwelle') for a trental 10s;[1] he to pay for another trental wherever his mother wishes.

Stephen to pay his sister Isabel 40s; he to pay his sister Cecily 20s.

Residue of all my goods and chattels to my execs, Agnes my wife and John Lynge, to dispose and have God before their eyes and to see all done well.

Supervisor: John Pykerell, clerk.[2]

Proved at Westhorpe, 22 November 1471. Admon to execs.

1   See note to no. 1.
2   John Pykerell was rector of Westhorpe (see note to no. 321).

[fol. 575]

776. THOMAS LEEM the elder of BRANDON FERRY ('Brandonfery'), 20 February 1471/72

Of Brandon Ferry, in the county of Suffolk; to be buried in the church of the Apostles Peter and Paul of Brandon; to the high altar of Brandon for tithes forgotten 6s 8d; to the fabric of Brandon church 6s 8d; to the painting of St Paul in Brandon church 3s 4d; I bequeath 2 latten candlesticks to the altar of the Blessed Mary of Brandon; I wish that a piece of land called 'Ferowres Yard' be put to the sustentation of 2 lights in the above candlesticks on feast days; I bequeath 20s to the buying of an ornament for Brandon church.

To the church of the Blessed Mary of Weeting ('Wetyng') [*Norfolk*] 3s 4d; to the church of St John of Weeting [*Norfolk*] 3s 4d; to the church of St George of Methwold ('Methewold') [*Norfolk*] 3s 4d; to the church of Feltwell ('Feltewell') St Mary [*Norfolk*] 20d; to the church of St Nicholas of Feltwell [*Norfolk*] 20d.

To the canons of Bromehill ('Bromehyll') [*Norfolk*] 10s, to celebrate faithfully a trental for my soul soon after my death.[1]

[*Will; undated*]

My house in Brandon Ferry to be sold and, if he wants to buy it, I wish William my son to have the house £10 under the price; otherwise it is to be sold to others and William is to have £10 from the money from it.

Isabel my wife to have all her goods in my house without exception, and 10 marks from my goods.

William Lem[*sic*] my son to have all the hostilments in my house, and each of his children 3s 4d.

Thomas Leem my son to have 10 marks.

Katherine my daughter to have 5 marks, a cow and a heifer.

Joan my daughter to have 6s 8d, and each of her children 3s 4d.

My house lying in the town of Brandon called 'Archeres' [*or*, 'Artheres'] to be sold and the money from it to provide the sustentation of a priest for 8 years, celebrating in Brandon church for my soul and the souls of my parents and the souls of my benefactors and the souls of my children and for the soul of Thomas Dokkyng.[2]

Sir Thomas Cowell, parish chaplain of Brandon, to have 6s 8d.

Robert Talbot to have 20s as it accrues to my execs from all my goods.

My house lying in the town of Brandon called 'Bolterys' to be sold, otherwise Thomas my son to have it in place of the 10 marks left him already.

Each of my execs to have for his labour 10s.

Residue of my goods to my execs, William Lem my son, Thomas Claveryng and John Elyngham, to dispose for the health of my soul and the souls of all the faithful departed.

Seal appended.

Witnesses: William Edward the elder, Thomas Swaston and William Helseden and many others.

Proved at Tuddenham ('Todenham'), 15 July 1472. Admon to execs.

[1] See note to no. 429.
[2] ?Relative of Thomas Dokkyng the elder of Mildenhall, will pr. March 1473/74 (no. 635).

777. THOMAS HERNYNGE of SANTON DOWNHAM ('Downham'), ?13 May 1472

Dated at Downham, the Wednesday after the feast of St John before the Latin Gate 1472;[1] to be buried in the churchyard of the church of the Blessed Mary of Downham; to the high altar of Downham 20d.

To Isabel my wife all my grain, all my hostilments and 10 ewes; to Isabel my wife my tenement as long as she remains a widow and, if she remarries, I assign the tenement to John my son the younger.

To Alice my daughter 26s 8d, to be received from John my son the younger for the tenement.

To John my son the elder 6s 8d, to be received from his brother [fol. 575v]; to John my son the elder, after the death of his mother, my best brass pot; to him a close called 'Bolysyerd'.

To John my son the younger, after the death of his mother, 2 brass pots.

To the prior and convent of Ixworth 12 ewes.[2]

To the church of Downham 6s 8d.

To the gild of the Holy Trinity of Downham 3s 4d.[3]

My execs to dispose for me and my friends 20s.

To John my son the elder my best gown; to John my son the younger my second gown.

To Margaret Tram 20d.

To each of my execs 2s.

Residue of all my goods to Sir John Downham, Isabel my wife, Geoffrey Skyte and Geoffrey Nors of Downham, execs.

Seal appended.

Proved at Badwell, 16 July 1472. Admon to Sir John Downham, exec. Power reserved to Isabel Hernyng, Geoffrey Skyte and Geoffrey Nors of Downham, the other co-execs, when they come and if they wish to take up [admon].

[1]   The feast of St John before the Latin Gate was always on 6 May and in 1472 fell on a Wednesday, therefore the Wednesday after the feast would be 13 May. The dating of this will is a little strange since Ascension Day 1472 fell on 7 May.

[2]   See note to no. 69.

[3]   The gild of the Trinity at Downham is mentioned in the 1524 Lay Subsidy list (*PSIA*, xix, p.181); Simon Wattys also made a bequest to the gild (no. 826 below).

778. WILLIAM COBBE of WETHERINGSETT ('Wetheryngset'), 2 May 1472

[*Commendation*: to God Almighty]; to be buried in the churchyard of the church of All Saints of Wetheringsett; to the high altar of the same church 20d; to the gild of St Thomas of Canterbury ('Cant') in the same church 6s 8d;[1] to the said church of Wetheringsett an oak for making a chest (*pro cista componend'*).

To Joan Wedden the younger (*Joh'e Wedden jun'*) 6s 8d.

After [*my*] decease, my wife to have my whole tenement with all the appurtenances and cattle (*catall'*) and all the household (*domicilium*), grain and peas, and all the other goods for as long as she remains a widow; if she should take a husband, then my execs to sell my tenement, with all the appurtenances and cattle and all the other goods, and she to have out of them 5 marks, or the value of 5 marks, with all the cows and utensils in the house, except the mill and the clock (*orligeo*) and the utensils within the smith's shop,[2] which are to be sold by my execs. If my wife should contest or in any way impede my will, then she shall have nothing of her legacies.

I wish to have a secular priest to celebrate for my soul and my friends' [*souls*] in the said church for a whole year.

To Sir John Kempe 40d to pray for me.

To each of my execs 20d for his labour.

Residue of all my goods I leave to the most needful uses of the said church according to the disposition of my execs, Alice Cobe my wife, Thomas Cobe my brother, John Medew of Wetheringsett.

Seal appended.

Witnesses: Master William Heisham, rector of the same church,[3] Robert Wedden and others.

I wish my wife to receive all the debts that I am owed and to pay my debts that I owe. Proved at Eye, 17 July 1472. Admon to execs.

[1] The gild of St Thomas of Canterbury at Wetheringsett was mentioned in 1439 (*PSIA*, xix, p.209). In 1445, Richard Aniys of Wetheringsett bequeathed 20d to the repairing of the image of St Thomas of Canterbury in the parish church (SROB, Baldwyne 72; Pt I, no. 345).

[2] The testator was a wealthy smith.

[3] William Heissham was rector of Wetheringsett from 1460 to 1490 (Tanner, p.1323); he also witnessed the will of William Sheryngton of Wetheringsett (no. 796).

[fol. 576]

779. ROBERT SPAROW of MELFORD, 6 March 1468/69

[*The testament entered here was originally recorded on fol. 448v, no. 436, and then crossed through. The will, dated 8 March, does not appear in the earlier entry.*][1]

Dated 6 March 1468/69 at Melford, in the diocese of Norwich; [*commendation includes* the Blessed Mary glorious Virgin]; to be buried in the churchyard of Melford parish church next to the grave of Marion my late wife; to the high altar of the said church for my tithes and offerings forgotten and underpaid 6s 8d; to the new fabric of the same church £10; to the reparation of the chapel of the Blessed Virgin Mary standing in the said churchyard 13s 4d; to the reparation and emendation of the chapel of St James within the town of Melford in 'Hallestret' 13s 4d; to each chaplain serving in the said church on the day of my death and being present at my first obsequies and at the mass of requiem on the day of my burial 12d; to each outside (*extraneo*) priest present there at the same time 8d; to each of the two holy-water clerks of Melford then present there 8d; to the sacrist of the said church then present there for ringing the bells and for digging (*fover'*) my grave (*poliandri*) and for doing for me other things relating to his office 2s; to each adult clerk being there to say *dirige* and mass 4d; and to each surpliced boy clerk then present there, singing and reading, 2d; to each of the needy and poor coming to the church on [*my*] burial day, taking in alms and praying for my soul, 1d.

To Joan, who was lately the wife of John Hacche of Melford, my kinswoman, to pray for my soul 13s 4d; to each of Robert and John, the same Joan's (*Joh'e*) sons and my godsons, 3s 4d; to Clemence, daughter of the said John (*Joh'is*) Hacche, 3s 4d; to Marion, also the same Joan's (*Joh'e*) daughter, 20d, to pray for my soul.

To each of the sons and daughters of Thomas Herberd of Melford 12d.

To Agnes, wife of Richard Thurkeld, to pray for my soul, 3s 4d.

To the sustentation and profit of the gild of Jesu in Melford 6s 8d.

To the convent of the house of friars of Sudbury, to pray for my soul, 10s; to the convent of the house of friars of Clare, to pray and celebrate masses for my soul, 20s; to Friar Osbert of the same house and convent of Clare, my brother, to pray for my soul, 10s; to the convent of the house of friars of Babwell, to pray for my soul, 10s; to the convent of Carmelite Friars of Cambridge (*Cantebr'*), to do in the same way, 10s.

To be distributed to 13 poor folk of Melford for 2 continuous years straight after my death, weekly on a Friday, 13d.

To Helen my household servant 5 marks in money, 4 silver spoons with the round 'Acres' [*?acorns*] (*cum lez Acres rotund'*), a pair of jet ('gett') beads, a girdle studded with silver lately my wife's, a basin with a brazen (*auricalco*) laver of the best, a brass pot with long feet containing about 3 gallons, a brass pan containing about 4 gallons, 3 platters (*perapsides*), 3 dishes and 3 salts of pewter; also, a bed, that is, a blue-coloured cover next the best, 2 blankets and 2 linen sheets and a felted cover (*fultru'*) of the best, of Helen's own choice.

Residue of all my goods and chattels to Roger Smyth [fol. 576v] and John Smyth of Melford, execs of my testament and last will, to distribute and dispose it according to the discretion, advice and ordering of John Clopton of Melford, esquire, whom I make supervisor of my testament and of my execs in the execution of all these premises and doing other things for me. John Clopton having for his labour 10 marks; and each of my said execs for his labour about these presents 40s.

Seal appended.

Witnesses: John Stannard, parish chaplain of Melford, William Colman, chaplain, Thomas Wareyn and others.

[*Will; 8 March 1468/69*]

Last will made 8 March 1468 [1468/69], in addition to what is contained in my testament of the 6 March that year:

All my lands and tenements with their appurtenances in Melford, except the land called 'Coppyinges' and the adjacent lands which I recently bought of Richard Cheppard, to be sold by John Clopton esquire and my execs for the best price they can, and of the money arising there from and from my other goods and chattels not bequeathed by me in my testament, I wish all my debts which I rightly owe to be paid and all my legacies contained in my testament and in this will to be duly performed.

The said land called 'Coppynges' with the lands which I bought of Richard Shepperd[*sic*], which are excepted above, to be sold by John Clopton and my execs and the money arising there from to be wholly spent on the fabric and reparation of Melford church according to their discretion.[2]

A secular honest chaplain to be maintained (*exhibeat*) in Melford church for 5 whole, continuous years as soon after my death as can be had, to celebrate divine service for my soul and for the souls of Marion my wife, Osbert Sparowe my father, Agnes my mother, Robert Clerk and Joan his wife, and all our friends and benefactors and all the faithful departed, taking annually for his stipend or salary 9 marks, or under if possible.

Osbert Shepperd of Earls Colne ('Colne Comitis') to have 6s 8d and John Shepperd, brother of the said Osbert, to have 3s 4d to pray for the aforesaid souls.

Thomas Herberd of Melford to have my large closing table (*magnam tabulam inclus'*) with the bench and cushion (*bancar'* & 'cusshon') in my parlour, my largest brass pot, a large brass pan of 14 gallons and 2 'le rakkes' of iron.[3]

I wish there to be spent annually for 10 years immediately following my decease on keeping my anniversary in Melford church, that is, each year 6s 8d, singing a *dirige* and mass of requiem.

Master Osbert, my brother, of Clare, to have as a legacy my mazer bound with silver and 6 silver spoons; after his death these to remain to Master John Bery, friar, of

Clare, for term of his life; and after his death, they to remain to the convent of friars of Clare to pray for the souls aforesaid.[4]

John Plandon of Melford to have my lead weights containing about 2½ hundreds in weight (*circa CC & di' ponder'*)[5] with the iron beam, paying me, the said Robert, for them.

Alice Clopton my mistress[6] to have my book of the lives of SS Margaret and Katherine (*librum meum de vita s'tarum Margarete & Katerine*).[7]

Seal appended.

Proved 30 July 1470. Admon to execs.

1   For notes to Robert Sparow's testament, see the other version (no. 436).
2   Sparow's generosity is recorded in the very building itself. The inscription over the north clerestory reads: '(Pra)y for the sowlis of Roberd Spar(o)we and Maryon his wife, and for (T)homas Cowper, and Mabel his wife of qwos [whose] good is Mast(er) Giles Dent, Jon Clopton, Jon Smyth and (R)oger Smyth wyth ye help of the weel disposyd me(n) of this (Tow)n ded these sevi archis new repare anno domini milesimo CCCC(LXXXI)'. See Paine, 'Building of Long Melford Church', p.10.
3   Or possibly, 3 'rakkes' of iron: the number could be '*iij*' but it looks as though the first '*i*' has been deleted.
4   For the Austin friars of Clare see note to no. 1.
5   Or perhaps, 'containing about 2½ hundredweight'.
6   The wife of John Clopton. John and Alice lie in a place of great honour, to the left of the high altar in Melford church. Their table-tomb, which is set in the wall between the chancel and John's chantry chapel, under an ogee arch, served as an Easter Sepulchre. The tomb has no effigy, but in the arch are fresco paintings of John and Alice facing the risen Lord Jesus (Dymond and Paine, *Spoil of Melford Church*, pp.4–5; Paine, 'Building of Long Melford Church', p.14).
7   The early Roman virgin martyrs Katherine and Margaret, and to a lesser extent Barbara, attracted enormous devotion throughout the Middle Ages, and prayers addressed to them were included in almost all Books of Hours. The privileged place of Katherine and Margaret in late medieval piety is attested by the fact that their statues stood either side of the shrine image of Our Lady at Walsingham (Duffy, *Stripping of the Altars*, p.171).

[fol. 577]

780. JOHN ANDREW of HAWKEDON, 20 October 1471

['Andrewe' *in margin*] Dated at Hawkedon, in the diocese of Norwich; my body to Christian burial in the churchyard of the parish church of Hawkedon, next to the graves of my parents; in God's name I beg my execs to pay all my debts that I owe; to the high altar of the same church of Hawkedon for my tithes and offerings withheld, forgotten and underpaid, 12d; to the rector of the same church all my masspence coming from the brethren and sisters of the gild of the Holy Trinity held in Hawkedon, to celebrate for my soul in Hawkedon church for as long as the money will last;[1] to a suitable secular priest to pray and celebrate in Hawkedon church, and nowhere else, for my soul for such time as 13s 4d will last; to the purchase of the new panel (*tabule*) of alabaster now standing and present (*iam stant' & existent'*) at the high altar of the said church 13s 4d; to the purchase of the new bell for the same church 13s 4d.

As for my lands and tenements: firstly I wish Joan my wife to have all the lands and tenements that I have on the day of making this in the towns of Hawkedon and Stanningfield ('Stanfeld')[2] with all their appurtenances, 3 roods of meadow, a rood of wood and half an acre of arable land, lying diversely in the town of Hawkedon with their appurtenances only being excepted, to hold them, with the exceptions, to her, Joan, for term of her life, without doing [*any*] waste or strip (*estripiamento*), of the chief lords of the fee by due service and custom. And after her decease, all the said lands and tenements in the town of Hawkedon, with all their appurtenances, except before excepted, to remain wholly to Richard my son, to hold to him and his heirs for ever, on these conditions: that he will pay the above said 40s to the secular chaplain, the panel and the bell assigned above to be paid; Richard to pay William my son £4 and Margaret my daughter 4 marks in cash, paying them in 5 years next following the death of Joan my wife, if they live so long. And if they die, or if one of them dies, while Joan their mother is living, then I wish that half of the portion of the one, or of them, so dying remain to my execs to dispose for my soul and their souls in masses and other works of piety as they see most expedient, and the other half to remain to my surviving children, to be divided between them equally.

Richard my son to have, immediately after my decease, the said 3 roods of meadow, rood of wood and half-acre of arable land above excepted, so that he pays and bears the funeral expenses necessary for my burial.

Thomas my son to have, after the decease of Joan my wife, all the said lands and tenements that I have in the town of Stanningfield, to hold to him and his heirs [fol. 577v] for ever of the chief lords of the fee by the service due of right for it.

Residue of all my goods to the disposition of all my execs that they may order and dispose them in works of charity, mercy and piety for my soul and for the souls of my father[3] and mother,[4] my children, parents, friends and benefactors for whom I am most bound, and of all the faithful departed, as seems to them best to please God and profit the aforesaid souls.

Execs of this my testament and last will: Joan my wife, Richard and Thomas my sons, to execute and perform all the foregoing bequests in the best way they can.
Seal appended.

Witnesses: Sir William [*recte* Ed'] Frere, rector of Hawkedon,[5] Richard Andrew, Thomas Hucton, Thomas Gamelyn and others.
Proved at Clare, 16 June 1472. Admon to execs.

[1] Neither Redstone nor Morley found any other reference to the gild of the Holy Trinity at Hawkedon.
[2] 'Stanfeld' (no 's' before the 'f') nearly always refers to Stanningfield and 'Stansfeld' to Stansfield, but there are exceptions.
[3] Will (as Richard Andru) pr. April 1459 (SROB, Baldwyne 240; Pt I, no. 1203); John Andru was a legatee and executor of his father.
[4] His father's will shows that John's mother's name was Matilda.
[5] Ed' Frere was rector of Hawkedon from 1463 to 1488 (Tanner, p.1236); while a chaplain in Long Melford, Frere witnessed the wills of Robert Coteras, dated October 1450 (Pt I, no. 1387), and of Henry Turnour *alias* Dyer, dated September 1461 (Pt I, no. 1369).

781. GEOFFREY SMETH of BURES ST MARY, 5 February 1471/72

Dated at Bures St Mary; to be buried in the churchyard of the parish church of Bures aforesaid; to the high altar of the same church for my tithes forgotten 12d; to each chaplain of the same church 12d, if present at my funeral; to each clerk 1d; to the beadle (*bedello*) 1d; to the said church a cow for the sustentation of a light before the image of St Saviour (*s'ti salvatoris*).[1]

To each of my sons and daughters a calf of 2 years old by estimation.

Residue of all my goods to Margaret my wife, executrix, to dispose as seems best to her for the health of my soul.

Proved at Bures, 14 June 1472. Admon to executrix.

¹   See note to no. 597.

[fol. 578]

782. JOHN DERBY of SUDBURY,[1] 4 January 1472/73

[*Commendation*: to God Almighty, the Blessed Mary &c]; to be buried in the churchyard of the parish church of St Gregory of Sudbury; to the said church for my tithes and offerings forgotten 12d and a ?colander (*collenoriu'*).

To Joan my sister my best gown and a pair of silver beads; to Joan my sister's daughter my next gown; to Christian my said sister's daughter my next gown.

To Joan my sister another gown and all my debts in Walden [*Essex*],[2] to dispose as she will (*ad libitum suum*), that is: 27s 8d that Thomas Batell owes me; 40s that John Kyng owes; 26s 8d that Raymond Dyere the elder owes; 6s 8d that Dom (*Do'pnus*) John Walden, monk, owes; £4 that the abbot (*abbas*) of Walden owes.[3] Also [*to Joan*] one of the painted cloths hanging in my chamber, a pair of sheets, a pair of blankets ('blankettes'), 2 bedcovers and the mattress ('le materas').

My messuage in Walden[4] to be sold by my execs and the money from it to be disposed for my soul and the souls of my parents, except 5 marks of it that I leave to Joan my sister.

To the library of the college of Sudbury a book of grammar (*librum gramaticalem*).[5]

To Henry son of the said Joan a silver spoon.

I wish my 3 girdles and 6 silver spoons to be sold and disposed for my soul &c[*sic*].

Residue of all my goods to the disposition of my execs, Joan my sister, Sir John Wate and William Horarld, they to dispose as they see best to please God and profit my soul.

To William Horald for his labour 20s.

Seal appended.

Proved at Melford, 3 February 1472/73. Admon to execs.

¹   Executor of Richard Cheryaunt, will pr. November 1444 (SROB, Baldwyne 52; Pt I, no. 276).
²   Now Saffron Walden.
³   Walden was founded as a priory by Geoffrey de Mandeville, earl of Essex. Its site was on the west of the town at the confluence of two streams and at the meeting of four roads, for the convenience of the poor and of travellers. In 1190 the priory was made into an abbey and the patronage came to the crown. In 1473 the abbot was John Halstede (d.1484) (*VCH Essex*, ii, pp.110–15).
⁴   Technically this will should not have been proved in the court of the archdeaconry of Sudbury since the property was situated in Essex.
⁵   See note to no. 32.

[fol. 578v; OW24/161[1]]

783. JOHN HYDE the elder of NAYLAND ('Neylond'), 20 August 1472

To be buried in the churchyard of St James of Nayland ('Neylonde'); to the high altar of the said church for my tithes forgotten 3s 4d; to the gild of the Holy Trinity 3s 4d;[2] to the gild of St Thomas 3s 4d.[3]

To John Wymere my gown; to John Galyot[4] a pair of sheets; to John Clampe a brass pot; to Isabel Brewere 2 candlesticks.

To Eleanor Tebald my tenement at 'le Horswatryng' for term of her life.

Residue of all my goods to John Hyde my son and John Danon of Horkesley

('Harkesle') [*Essex*], my faithful execs, to pay all my debts and dispose the rest of my goods in pious uses for the health of my soul and of the souls of my friends as seems best to them.

Seal appended.

Witnesses: John Prentyse, Nicholas Hache, John Brewer, John Clampe and others.

Proved at Cockfield ('Cokfeld'), 9 February 1472/73. Admon to execs.

¹ The 'original will' is actually a copy.
² For other bequests to the gild of the Holy Trinity see note to no. 439.
³ Joan, widow of John Fakon of Nayland, also made a bequest to the gild of St Thomas (SROB, Baldwyne 218; Pt I, no. 1080).
⁴ In the 'original will' the name 'John Malyot' is given for the second legatee.

784. WILLIAM BRETT of NAYLAND ('Neylonde'), 20 December 1472

To be buried in the churchyard of St James of Nayland; to the high altar 6d.

Christian my wife to have all my utensils and my messuage and my large garden with the house at the gate for term of her life; Richard my son to have, after the death of his mother, the said messuage and the large garden with the house to him and his assigns.

I leave my 3 small gardens next to 'Newlondelane' to the church of St James, to be sold and the money from them to be spent on the building (*edficacionem*) of the said church.

To Robert my son my house with the garden next to the garden of George Harvy, to him and his assigns.

To Joan Smyth my daughter 20s; to Alice Frende my daughter 20s; to Agnes Brett my daughter 20s. Richard my son to provide security (*satisfaciat*) to his 3 sisters or their attorneys for each 20s and if he cannot pay [*them*] out of [*his*] own goods, then I wish such part of my large garden to be sold as will meet (*satisfacere*) the cost.

Faithful execs: Christian Brett my wife and Richard Brett my son.

Seal appended.

Witnesses: Nicholas Lane, Thomas Ros, William Spore and others.

Proved at Cockfield ('Cokefeld'), 9 February 1472/73. Admon to execs.

[fol. 579]

785. WILLIAM WYBURGH of DENSTON ('Dernardeston'), 19 November 1472

[*Date written as* 19 November 1402]; dated at Denston, in the diocese of Norwich; [*commendation*: to God Almighty &c]; to be buried in Christian burial in the parish church of Denston, next to the grave of Margaret his (*sue*) late wife. In God's name I beg and require my execs to pay all my debts that I owe, that is, those which can be truly proved. To the high altar of the said church for tithes and offerings withheld 2s; to the buying and preparation of a new image of St Nicholas for the said church 20s.¹

To the convent of Friars ~~Preachers~~ Minor of Babwell, my brethren, for a similar reason 3s 4d.²

To the Augustinian Friars of the house of Clare, to pray for [*my*] soul, half of all the mass pence coming from my brethren and sisters of the gild of St Mary the Virgin held in Stanningfield ('Stanfeld');³ to the Carmelite Friars of Cambridge (*Cantebr'*), to pray for my soul, the other half of the mass pence collected from my aforesaid brethren and sisters of the said gild.

To Sir John Sendrell and Sir John Mayhew, chaplain, to pray for my soul, all the mass pence coming from my brethren and sisters of the gild of St John the Baptist held in Denston, equally divided between them.[4]

To each priest present at my obsequies and at mass on the day of my burial, celebrating divine service, 4d; to each clerk present at the same time and ministering at divine service, of man's age 2d and of boy's age 1d.

To Agnes, the wife of William Mayhew the elder, my goddaughter, to pray for my soul 12d.

To John Flechere of Denston, needy poor man, as alms for my soul, half a bushel of wheat and half a bushel of malt. To Robert Pyngyll of the same [place] half a bushel of malt, to John Preston half a bushel of malt, to Agnes Chapman of Stanningfield half a bushel of malt and to William Bradbrook of Stradishall ('Stradeshull') a bushel of wheat, to pray for my soul.[5]

To the reparation of [the] 4 torches of the said gild burning about my body at the time of the celebration of divine service on my burial day 4 bushels of malt.[6]

To the reparation and emendation of a worn and dangerous (*debil' & noc'*) way called 'Cokestrete lane' in Denston for the length of 4 perches, 4 days' work with a cart for carting sand (*arena*) and putting it in place (*ponend'*) there, begging Master Denston for the said sand.[7]

As to my lands and tenements, first I wish John my son to have all the lands and tenements, rents and services, which I have in the towns and fields of Denston, Stanningfield and Chipley ('Chyppley') in the county of Suffolk, with all their appurtenances, to John and his assigns for ever, [to hold] of the chief lords of the fee by the service due of right for them, but on this condition: that John pays and performs all the above-mentioned legacies and bears the necessary costs and expenses of my burial and pays Robert [my] son 5 marks in money in the 10 years immediately following my decease, provided that Robert is of good behaviour and disposition towards his brother John, by the discretion of my supervisor and execs.

I beg all my feoffees of and in all my aforesaid lands and tenements, rents and services, with their appurtenances, to deliver to the aforesaid John, and others he [fol. 579v] may wish to name, the full estate and possession that they have of and in my lands and tenements when duly required, for the true performance of this will.

John my son to have all my other goods, chattels, grain and stock and debts, moveable and unmoveable, live and dead, of whatever kind, with all the ostilments and utensils of my house.

Residue of all my goods to John my son to dispose in works of charity for my soul and the soul of Margaret my late wife and for the souls of our fathers and our mothers, our parents, friends and benefactors and of all the faithful departed to the praise of God and our salvation as seems most expedient to him.

Execs: John my son and John Brown of Denston, to implement all the afore-written and afore-bequeathed in the best way they know to please God and profit my soul; to John Brown, for his diligent labour about these premises, 6s 8d.

I humbly beseech my honourable and especially good master, John Browgton, esquire,[8] to be pleased, to the honour of God and in the way of charity, to supervise the performance of all of these premises well and truly as aforesaid, to see them paid and executed.

Seal appended.

Witnesses: Sir John Sendrell, Sir John Mayhew, chaplain, John Brown, John Wyburgh, Richard Clerk and others.

Proved at Fornham St Martin, 13 July 1473. Admon to execs.

1   The church was dedicated to St Nicholas.
2   It seems that the bequest that preceded this one in the original has been omitted from the regis-
    tered version. Given the deletion in the register and the recorded bequests to the Friars Minor of
    Babwell, the Augustinians of Clare and the Carmelites of Cambridge, the missing bequest was
    probably to the convent of Friars Preachers at Sudbury. See note to no. 133 concerning bequests
    to the four orders of friars.
3   Both Redstone and Morley assumed that this gild was in Stansfield (*PSIA*, xii, p.84; xix, p.203;
    xxiii, p.72).
4   John Derman of Denston bequeathed his mass-pence from the gild of St John the Baptist at
    Denston to the parish priests and the poor (no. 724).
5   Unlike the more usual general bequests of alms to the poor, this testator was very specific
    regarding the identities of the deserving poor whom he wanted to pray for his soul and the food-
    stuffs that he wanted them to be given; hence we have a very rare record of the names of some
    late fifteenth-century poor.
6   Presumably the torches of the gild of St John the Baptist at Denston, since that was where William
    Wyburgh requested burial.
7   Another road repair, this time involving the spreading of sand. See nos 457 and 642 above where
    cartloads of stone were bequeathed for road repairs.
8   John Broughton was lord of the manor of Denston. When he died in 1479 the manor passed to his
    widow Anne; when she died in 1481 it passed to John's brother and heir Robert (IPM, 21 Edward
    IV 44 cited in Copinger, *Manors of Suffolk*, v, p.228).

[fol. 580]

786. [unknown] AUBRY of WOOLPIT ('Wolpet'), ?1473, [English]

['Aubry' *written in margin but not in body of will*][1] [*Undated; commendation*: to God Almighty and Our Lady St Mary]; to the high altar of Woolpit, for tithes forgotten or any other duties, 20s; the parish church of Shelland ('Shellonde') to have 6s 8d; the parish church of Tostock ('Tostok') to have 6s 8d.

I will that 6s 8d go to amend 'an heywey betwex the cross at the towyns ende and the brygge ledying to bury warde'.

I will that the town of Woolpit have 13s 4d to 'put forth to cres [*increase*] and the cres therof to helpe to pay the taske qwan it fallyth but I wolnat that the stoke be broken'.

I will that the gild of the Trinity in Woolpit have a cow to 'be put forth to cres of the same gylde'.[2]

Of the money that shall come from my tenement called 'Wadys', half to Woolpit church and the other half to the mending of highways, at the disposition of my execs, as the money is taken.

Each of my godchildren to have 6d.

Each of [*my*] brother's [*or*, brothers'] ('Broderes') children to have 20d.

My wife to have my tenement called 'the Pels', with all the appurtenances, with a parcel of ground late James Lane's to the said tenement, with all the household hostilments; she to have a bargain of wood ('wode') that I bought of Master Bothe in Shelland ('Chellond').

My son to have the tenement called 'the Herte'; my daughter to have my tenement called 'Colsys' and my tenement called 'Skenners'; if either child dies within the age of 20, then the one to be the other's heir.

I will have a priest to sing for me for half a year.

My wife to have the keeping of my children and she to have for their keeping as they are worth of their goods bequeathed ('be sett') them.

The friars of Babwell to have 10s for a trental.[3]

If my children die within age, I will that all that 'be sett' them be sold at the disposition of my execs and done for me and my friends.

I will that my son have my tenement in Buxhall ('Buxhale') if it comes into my hands; and if it comes not into my hands, 6s 8d of the money from it to go to Shelland ('Shellond') church and 6s 8d to Buxhall church, and the other 26s 8d my son to have; if it be less, then all 3 parcels to be 'abatyd' evenly.

I will that 40 coombs of wheat be sold and done for me and [*used to*] pay my debts; 100 coombs of malt be sold and used similarly; 40 coombs of peas and oats be sold and used similarly.

My wife to have all my cloth and my wool that is 'withynne the place'.

I will that 5 of my kine be sold as soon as I am dead.

My wife to have 4 kine and each of my children 4 kine; I will that my wife have [fol. 580v] them all at her disposition if she keep my children well; but if she does not, I will that my execs 'take a rewle therin' and see that they are kept.

My wife to have 30 coombs of malt and 10 coombs of wheat for sure ('in serteyn') besides what may be spared 'more overe' in rye.

I will that the places I bequeath ('be sett') my children be kept in due reparation as now.

When my children be of age to earn their living, I will that the profit of the said goods be put forth to increase ('in cres') and profit of the said children, at the disposition of my execs.

Agnes Goose of Horringer ('Hornyngesherth') to have 2 kine.

Margaret the daughter of my wife to have a cow.

All other goods that 'cometh over' besides my tenement I put to the disposition of my execs, William Aubry, my brother,[4] Simon Gelgett and Thomas Baldewyn, to do for me in alms to poor folk weekly 12d, if it may be gathered; each of my execs to have 6s 8d for their labour.

Proved at Fornham St Martin, 14 June 1473. Admon to execs.

1   The second letter of the surname is definitely '*u*', giving 'Aubry', unlike no. 630, where the second letter is '*v*', giving 'Avbre'.

2   Margery Koo of Woolpit, widow, bequeathed a pound of wax to the gild of the Holy Trinity (SROB, Baldwyne 132; Pt I, no. 619); Ada, widow of John Welde of Woolpit, bequeathed 3s 4d to the gild (SROB, Baldwyne 161; Pt I, no. 777). In 1451 there was also a gild of the Nativity of the Blessed Mary in the parish: John Stevynesson stated that certain of his bequests would be null and void if the fraternity of that gild troubled his executors in any way (SROB, Baldwyne 105; Pt I, no. 469).

3   See note to no. 1.

4   Executor (as 'Awbry') of John Denys of Woolpit (no. 579 above).

787. JOHN MELON of STRADISHALL ('Stradesshul'),[1] 31 May 1473

Dated at Stradishall ('Stradeshul'); to be buried in the churchyard of Stradishall church; to the high altar of the same church, for my tithes and offerings forgotten and underpaid, 12d; to Sir Nicholas, parish priest of Stradishall ('Stradeshull'), 8d.

To Thomas my son my tenement with the croft called 'Percy croft', with their appurtenances, and I wish Helen my wife, as long as she remains unmarried, to live
together with Thomas my son in that tenement and they to enjoy the profits of the
tenement and croft equally, each of them.

Residue of all my goods to Helen my wife.

Faithful execs: Helen my wife and Thomas Melon my son; they to pay my debts and
dispose for my soul and my benefactors' [*souls*].

Seal appended.

Proved 3 July 1473. Admon to execs.

₁ ?Executor (as 'Melown') of John Wode of Cowlinge, will pr. July 1461 (SROB, Baldwyne 282;
Pt I, no. 1386); executor of John Ballard *alias* Canown of Wickhambrook, probate only 8 March
1461/62 (SROB, Baldwyne 295; Pt I, no. 1450).

[fol. 581]

788. ROBERT BRUNWYN of MENDLESHAM,[1] 13 April 1472

Dated at Mendlesham, in the diocese of Norwich; I make my testament and dispose
my last will; my body to the Christian burial of Mendlesham; to the high altar of
the same church 3s 4d; to the gild of the Holy Trinity of the same town 3s 4d;[2] to
the gild of the Blessed Mary there 3s 4d;[3] to the reparation of the said church 13s
4d, as my wife can recover it; to the altar of the Blessed Mary of Wetheringsett
('Wetheryngset') a cloth 'steyned' with a picture (*figura*) of the Blessed Mary.

To Joan my wife all my household and all my tenement, with all my lands, both
free and bond, in the towns of Mendlesham and Brockford ('Brokeford'), for term
of her life, as long as she remains unmarried; and after her decease, all my said
household to be distributed among my surviving sons and daughters, according to
the advice of my execs.

Joan my wife to pay Margaret my daughter £10 in money, that is, at her marriage 5
marks and annually thereafter 13s 4d until the £10 be fully paid.

To Robert my son all my aforesaid tenement with all my lands, after Joan's decease,
on the condition that he pays his brother John 20 marks in money, that is, when he
enters [*the property*] 5 marks that year, and annually thereafter 13s 4d until the 20
marks are paid to John, his heirs or execs. If Robert should die without heirs, then
John to have my tenement, with all the aforesaid lands, to him and his heirs, and he
to pay 16 marks for 2 priests to celebrate in Mendlesham church for my soul and
the souls of all my friends. If Robert is unwilling to abide by my will, then John to
have the said tenement with all the lands as aforesaid, according to the advice of my
execs, and to pay Robert 20 marks as he [*Robert*] should have paid him. If Robert
and John should both decease without heirs, then the tenement with all its lands and
appurtenances to be sold by my execs, and Margaret my daughter to have it at 10
marks within the price of any other.

If any of my aforesaid children (*siquis predictorum filiorum meorum*) have the tenement as above, then they are to find a priest in Mendlesham church to celebrate for
my soul and all [*my*] friends' [*souls*]. If the tenement is sold by my execs, then I
wish it to be disposed in works of piety in Mendlesham and Wetheringsett where
most need is.

Residue of all my goods to the administration of my execs, to sell, receive and
dispose for the health of my soul as they see best to please God and profit my soul.

Execs: Joan my wife, Thomas Berd of Cotton and John Bronewyn the elder, 'mercer';[4] to each of whom for their labour 20d.

Supervisor: Master John Solyard; to whom 10s.

Witnesses: Sir Thomas Saham, chaplain, Robert Percy, Robert Teryton and others.

Proved at Finningham ('Fynyngham'), 29 October 1472. Admon to execs.

[1] ?Related to Thomas Brounewyn of Wetheringsett, will made August 1457 (SROB, Baldwyne 206; Pt I, no. 1023). Although this testator was 'of Mendlesham', a relationship seems likely since he made several references to Wetheringsett in his will. The will of Thomas's son Robert, who died about a year before this testator, is no. 559 above.

[2] For other bequests to the gild of the Holy Trinity of Mendlesham see note to no. 568.

[3] For other bequests to the gild of St Mary of Mendlesham see nos 568 and 774.

[4] Another of the sons of Thomas Brounewyn of Wetheringsett (see note above). Perhaps Thomas had also been a mercer: he bequeathed to his son William 'my stall in Eye market, and my stall at the gate of Wetheringsett churchyard'.

[fol. 581v]

789. AGNES PLAYFORD of TROSTON, 26 September 1472

Dated at Troston, 6 Kalends October 1472; my body to Christian burial; to the high altar of Troston's church of St Mary, for my tithes forgotten or underpaid, 6d; to the fabric of the said church 12d.

To the friars of Babwell for half a trental 5s; to the Augustinian Friars of Thetford for half a trental 5s; to the Dominican Friars of Thetford 12d.[1]

To John my son 2s 6d; to Margaret my daughter a cloak (*clocam*).

To Agnes Wagard my best tunic.

I wish to have a suitable secular or regular chaplain out of my goods to celebrate for the health of my soul, [*and the souls of*] John Playford, my husband, my benefactors and all the faithful departed, if it can be done and done as quickly as possible. Residue of all my goods to my execs to sell, receive and dispose in paying my debts and in works of piety as my execs see suitable (*ydm'*) to please God and profit my soul.

Execs: Robert Playford and John Playford my sons.

Seal appended.

Witnesses: John Apylthorp, esquire,[2] Thomas Drury, gentleman,[3] and others of Troston.

Proved at Fornham St Martin, 9 November 1472. Admon to execs. [*?different hand*] Acquitted.

[1] For the friars see notes to nos 1 (Babwell), 68 (Dominicans of Thetford) and 69 (Augustinians of Thetford).

[2] The Apylthorp family held the manor of Althorpe's or Applethorpe *alias* Bovill's in Troston from 1315 to 1499 (the name has several variations); John 'Alwthorpe' died seised of the manor in 1499, when it passed to his daughters and coheirs (Copinger, *Manors of Suffolk*, v, p.238).

[3] Perhaps the Thomas Drury of Troston who was executor of his mother-in-law, Matilda Roungtun of Troston (SROB, Baldwyne 234; Pt I, no. 1174).

790. ADAM DUN of YAXLEY ('Yaxlee'), 16 October 1472

Dated at Yaxley; [*commendation*: to God Almighty, the Blessed Mary &c]; to be buried in the churchyard of Yaxley church; to the high altar of the same church, for [*my*] tithes underpaid, 12d; to the reparation of the same church 6s 8d, if the sum of 6s 8d can be had of my debts.

To Master Slolee, friar of the order of St Augustine, for celebrating a trental 10s.
To Robert my son 10s; to Joan my daughter 10s.
To Margaret my wife 10s and a quarter of barley.
To Thomas Dun, son of Richard Dun, a ewe.
To Margaret my wife a sheep, and to Margaret Dun, wife of Richard Dun, a sheep.
Residue of all my goods to the disposition of my execs, Richard Dun, my son, and
Thomas Carman, vicar of the said church,[1] to dispose for my soul as they see best
to please God and profit my soul.
Proved before the Commissary, the venerable Master John Bonewell,[2] visitor for
the chapter of Norwich Cathedral, in the vacancy of the episcopal see, at Eye, 11
November 1472. Admon to execs.

[1]   Thomas Carman was vicar of Yaxley from 1467 to 1490 (Tanner, p.1327); will pr. October 1491
      (NRO, NCC 49 Typpes); he witnessed the will of Joan Herberd of Yaxley (SROB, Baldwyne 259;
      Pt I, no. 1276).
[2]   Bonewell was a monk of Norwich; he became prior in 1480 until his death in 1488 (Emden).

791. RICHARD STALEY of THORNDON,[1] 11 November 1472 [*probate only*]

Proved at Eye ('Eyee'), 11 November 1472. Admon to executrix.

[1]   Executor (as 'Stale') of Alice, daughter of William London, will pr. July 1457 (SROB, Baldwyne
      219; Pt I, no. 1090). As well as being her executor, Alice had required Richard Staley to go on
      various pilgrimages and to have two trentals celebrated for her and her friends.

[fol. 582]
792. WILLIAM PEGAYS the elder of BRANDON,[1] 23 August 1468

To be buried in the churchyard of St Peter of Brandon; to the high altar there 3s 4d;
to the reparation or emendation of the same church 20s.
To the Friars Preachers of Thetford 3s 4d; to the Augustinian Friars of Thetford 3s
4d; to the nuns of Thetford 20d; to the friars of Babwell ('Badvell') 3s 4d.[2]
To Isabel my wife and John my son a cart with 3 horses with all the equipment.
To Isabel all my utensils and necessaries of my house (*hospicii*).
To Joan my daughter 20s; to Margery my daughter[3] 5 marks and brass pot.
Residue of all my goods to the disposition of my execs, William, Robert the elder
and Robert the younger, my sons, to dispose my goods and legacies for my soul as
they see best to please God and profit my soul.
Seal appended.
Proved 23 November 1474. Admon to execs.
[*This testament and probate, written carelessly in the same hand, have been crossed
through. At the head of the folio are two notes: "quere alio loco cu'ult'voluntat'" &
"No^{tt} quere alibi cu'ult'volunt'". The will appears again, in the form of a testament
and will, in SROB, Hervye fol. 357. This later version indicates that the 'Baldwyne'
version omitted various words.*]

[1]   ?Brother of Agnes Pecas (no. 466).
[2]   See notes to nos 1 (friars of Babwell), 68 (Friars Preachers and Benedictine nuns of Thetford)
      and 69 (Augustinians of Thetford).
[3]   ?Legatee of Agnes Pecas (no. 466).

[fol. 582v]

793. JOHN FROSTE of WICKEN ('Wykyn') [*Cambs*], 1 July 1474, [*probate only*]

Proved 1 July 1474. Admon to execs.

794. ROBERT STACY of BARWAY ('Berwey') [*in Soham, Cambs*], 1 July 1474, [*probate only*]

Proved at Soham ('Saham'), 1 July 1474. Admon to execs.

795. JOHN SAMPSON of HINDERCLAY ('Hyndercle'), 30 March 1474

Dated at Hinderclay; sick unto death; [*commendation*: to God Almighty &c]; to be buried in the churchyard of Hinderclay parish church; I wish my debts to be fully paid; to the said high altar 20d; to the reparation of the said church 6s 8d.

To the new friars of Thetford for celebrate a trental for the health of my soul [*and*] my friends' [*souls*] 10s.[1]

To Robert Sampson my son 10s; to Joan Sampson my daughter 10s; to Eleanor my daughter 10s; if the aforesaid [*children*], or any of them, should die before marriage, then I wish their portion be given to the reparation of the said church.

Residue of all my goods to my execs, to dispose for the health of my soul and of all my benefactors' [*souls*] as seems to them most expedient.

Execs: Margaret my wife, William Moordok, William Londe and Thomas Dooke of Hinderclay; they to execute faithfully this testament.

Seal appended.

Proved before William Woode &c[*sic*], at Norton, 19 July 1474. Admon to Margaret, executrix. Power reserved to William Mordok, William Londe and Thomas Dooke, the other execs, when they come.

[1] For the new friars of Thetford see note to no. 69.

[fol. 583] [*right hand margin damaged*]

796. WILLIAM SHERYNGTON of WETHERINGSETT ('Wetheryngset'), 25 January 1473/74

Of Wetheringsett in the diocese of Norwich; my testament and last will; [*commendation*: to God &c]; to be buried in the church of All Saints of Wetheringsett; to the high altar 2s.

To each of the houses of mendicant friars in Norwich 6s 8d.[1]

For a trental to be celebrated 10s.

Residue of all my goods to Joan my wife, executrix.

Witnesses: William Heissham, rector of Wetheringsett church,[2] John Braham the elder, Geoffrey Braham, Sir John Kempe[3] and others.

Proved at Wetheringsett, 7 July 1474. Admon to executrix.

[1] For the Carmelite Friars of Norwich see note to no. 269. Early in the reign of Edward I, Austin friars were established in Norwich. In 1348 they obtained the grant of the church of St Michael Conisford; they were permitted to include the church within their precincts on undertaking to have there a chapel in honour of St Michael. The friars further undertook only to use the churchyard for preaching, for burials and for the building of a church. On their much enlarged site the friars built a fine church, with cloisters on the south side (*VCH Norfolk*, ii, pp.428–33). The Norwich house of the Dominicans was founded in 1226 next to the old parish church of

'St John Baptist over-the-Water', on the north side of Black Boy Street. In 1310 they began to erect a large church, dedicated to the honour of St John Baptist, and conventual buildings for the accommodation of 60 religious. In the late fourteenth century they built another even larger church on the other side of the river but in May 1413 the serious fire that broke out at Norwich destroyed, amongst many other buildings, the new house and church of the Dominicans. They returned to their old house and church across the water, known as the Black Hall, until 1449, when they returned to their newly built convent. The church was restored on a magnificent scale between 1440 and 1470, mayors and other leading citizens giving generously (*VCH Norfolk*, ii, pp.428–33). In 1226 the Franciscans were established in Norwich on a site between the churches of St Cuthbert and St Vedast in Conisford. As they had gradually increased in numbers, 60 years later they decided to build a large church with suitable conventual buildings. The new church was built on a grand scale, the nave being 105 feet in length, and the cloister on the north side of the nave being a square of its full length (*VCH Norfolk*, ii, pp.428–33).

2   See note to no. 778.

3   Also witness of the wills of two other Wetheringsett parishoners, nos 559 and 810.

797. [*damaged*] [?ED'] MAN of RATTLESDEN ('Ratlesden'),[1] 24 July 1474

Dated at Rattlesden ('Ratelesden'); to be buried in the chapel of the [*damaged*] church, before the image there; to the high altar of the same church, for my tithes forgotten or underpaid, 10s.

To the convent of friars of Babwell, for a trental of St Gregory to be celebrated there for the health of my soul, 10s;[2] to the convent of friars of Sudbury, for a trental to be interceded there, 10s;[3] and to Doctor Oldman of the Thetford house 10s.[4]

I wish to have a suitable honest chaplain celebrate divine service for a whole year for my soul and the souls of my benefactors in the said church.

To each of my sons and daughters 10 marks in silver, if they do not die underage.

To Alice my wife my whole tenement in which I now live, to hold to her and her heirs, with the appurtenances, for ever; she to have all my ostilments and utensils, together with all my chattels, live and dead, moveable and unmoveable.

I assign to a window of the church there, for glazing, 20s.

My manor in Rattlesden, with its appurtenances,[5] to be sold by my execs for the best price possible, and out of it all my debts to be paid and to be disposed in pious uses, to priests, and the poor, for me and my soul and for the souls of my parents [*and*] benefactors, and for the souls of all the faithful in Christ and of all others for whom I am bound.

Residue of all my goods to the disposition of my execs, to dispose for the health of my soul as seems to them most expedient.

Faithful execs: Alice, my beloved wife, Robert Sergeawnt of Stoke and Robert Cage of Rattlesden; they faithfully to execute and fulfil my testament and will.

Seal appended.

Proved at Fornham 16 September 147[*damaged; ?1474*]. Admon to Alice and Robert Cage of Rattlesden, execs. Power reserved to Robert Sergeawnt, the other exec, when he comes and if he wishes to take up admon. Seal of official appended.

1   Relative of Joan Man of Rattlesden, probate dated August 1453 (SROB, Baldwyne 161; Pt I, no. 784).

2   See note to no. 1.

3   See note to no. 11.

4   'Doctor Oldman of Thetford' was a Dominican, who was later prior of the 'Old House' of Thetford (Emden). In 1469, Robert Agas of Thurston made a bequest to 'the friars of Thetford, to the house where Master Pers Oldman is' (no. 414 above).

5   For the minor manor in Rattlesden held by the Man family see Copinger, *Manors of Suffolk*, vi, 319.

[fol. 583v]

798. ROBERT DONEWYCH of FORNHAM ALL SAINTS ('Fornham Sanctorum'), 20 March 1469/70, [*nuncupative*]

His body to Christian burial; to the high altar of the same church 20d.

To Laurence Prynce of the same the debt which Thomas Spaldynge owed Robert, that is, 26s 8d, to pay the debts he owes and to dispose to the said church and to repair ways and give alms (*vijs emendand' & elem' faciend'*) as he sees best to please God and profit his soul; which Laurence he made exec.

Witnesses: Sir Thomas Cox, chaplain, and others.

Proved at Fornham, 23 March 1469/70. Admon to exec.

[*Concerning folios 584 to 591. Folios 584 & 591, 585 & 590 are two similar sheets, containing wills of approximately the same dates; folios 586 & 589, 587 & 588 are two dissimilar sheets, which have been sewn one into the other, and which together have been sewn into the two previously mentioned sheets. Folios 586 to 589 actually belong to the next register 'Hervye' but have 'strayed' into 'Baldwyne'. Consequently wills nos 799 to 808 are not in any logical date sequence.*]

[fol. 584]

799. THOMAS THEWYTES of BILDESTON ('Bylston'), 18 March 1473/74

To be buried in the churchyard of Bildeston ('Bilston') parish church; to the high altar of the same church for my tithes forgotten 40d; to a canon [*a*] stipend to celebrate for my soul and the souls of [*my*] parents and friends and those for whom I am bound, for half a year, £3.

Agnes my daughter to have 5 marks at her marriage and [*a*] chamber at the will of her mother.

To William Hamond 5 marks and a cow.

To Simon Cook and his wife 6s 8d, and to each of their sons and daughters 20d, by the discretion of my wife.

To each of my godsons and goddaughters 4d.

To Friar Bokenham of Dunwich ('Donewic')[1] to celebrate for my soul and the souls for whom I am bound a trental of St Gregory, 10s, and more if it can be done, according to the discretion of my wife and supervisor.

To each priest present at my obsequies 4d, and to each clerk 2d, and to the other clerks 1d, according to the discretion of my executrix.

To the reparation of the torches in Bildeston church 40d; to the reparation of the church and to the ornaments of the same, in Bildeston, 6s 8d.

To Robert Ofwade a gown.

To Alice my wife all my lands and tenements and meadows held by the rod at the will of the lord of the manor of Bildeston, to hold to her and her heirs, except a barn lying against the tenement of Richard Cowpere, which I leave to William my son, and all my other lands and tenements lying in Bildeston which are held by charter as free land, after the decease of Alice, my wife and William's mother. If my said son should die in the lifetime of his mother, then, after Alice's decease, I wish all

487

the lands and tenements to be sold and disposed by my wife[*sic*] and my supervisor in deeds of charity for the souls of me, my wife and all [*my*] benefactors [fol. 584v] and the faithful departed.

Residue of all my goods to the disposition of Alice my wife, my executrix, with the supervision and advice of Master W[*illiam*] Thweytes, my supervisor;[2] and I wish my wife to be governed by the discretion and advice of [*my*] supervisor regarding all my legacies and goods.

Witnesses: Hugh Wryth, William Qwytop, Richard Cowpere, Thomas Ofwode, William Carter, William Cook and John Cook &c[*sic*].

Proved at Bildeston, before William Woode, *Dec. Lic.*, [*Commissary*] of James, Bishop of Norwich, on his ordinary visitation, 19 April 1474. Admon to executrix, with the supervision and advice of the supervisor. Seal of official appended.

1   For the Dominican and Franciscan friars of Dunwich see note to no. 65.
2   Probably William Thweytes the elder, notary and registrar, of Bury St Edmunds. See Introduction, under *Register 'Baldwyne'*.

800. JOHN HERVY of GISLINGHAM ('Gyslyngham'), 24 March 1473/74

[*Commendation*: to God Almighty, the Blessed Mary &c]; my body to Christian burial in the churchyard of Gislingham church; to the profit of the same church a coomb of malt and a bushel of wheat; to the gild of St John the Baptist 6 bushels of malt.[1]

To Joan Hervy my wife my tenement in which I dwell, with all the lands belonging to it, for term of her life; and after her decease, the tenement with all the land to remain to Thomas Oxne and Christian, wife of the said Thomas Hoxne[*sic*], daughter of John Hervy, for ever.

Joan my wife to have the making (*fa'i'cionem*) of 10 coombs of malt and 4 sheep and a cow feeding (*vaccam pasturen'*).

Residue of all my goods to Joan Hervy and Thomas Oxne, my execs.

Proved before William Woode &c[*sic*], at Finningham ('Fynyngham'), 26 April 1474. Admon to execs.

1   John Cobbe (no. 343) and Henry Mansere (no. 476) also made bequests to the gild of St John the Baptist at Gislingham.

[fol. 585]
801. THOMAS HOVELL [of COWLINGE],[1] 16 March 1473/74

[*Will; dated 16 March 1473/74*]

Written in addition to my testament (*prescript' ultra testamentum meum*) [*the testament is missing*].

Alice my wife[2] to have the whole tenement called 'Hovelles' with all the lands, meadows, pastures [*and*] feedings, with all their appurtenances, together with 'Farwelles crofte' and the other land which I purchased from Copsye,[3] until William my son is of the age of 18. If William should die under that age, then my wife to have the tenement with all the premises for term of her life; and after her decease, they to be sold immediately and the money received from them to be disposed according to the discretion of my execs to Cowlinge ('Cowlyng') church and in other works of charity for the health of my soul and the souls of my parents.[4] If

William lives to the age of 18 and beyond, then immediately he shall possess and hold the said tenement with all the premises, as above, to him and his heirs for ever without the impediment or contradiction of any man of any sort. And I require all my feoffees to deliver to William and his heirs their full estate and possession when so required by William or any other in his name. And when William is of the age of 18, then I wish his mother and he to divide all my goods and chattels, moveable and unmoveable, equally between them, by the view of Walter Cowper and William Moore, my execs, his mother to choose first and they to divide only such goods and chattels as were mine on the day of making this present [*will*].

Alice my wife to keep and maintain the anniversary of my parents together (*invisem*) on the day of the Assumption of the Blessed Mary [*15 August*] only as long as she possesses the said tenement, and after that time it to be incumbent on William my son to keep the said anniversary for ever; and in the same manner, he shall keep my anniversary and my [*recte: his*] mother's anniversary as the days of our death dictate (*cum dies & obitus nostri postulent*); in the same way I wish that William's successors will keep the aforesaid anniversaries.

Alice my wife to pay for 'Farwelys crofte' and 'Copsyes' with part of those goods that I have assigned to her.

I wish 'Knappynges' and 'Cokkes' to be sold immediately after my decease by my execs, as quickly as they can, and with the money from them to pay a priest for celebrating for my soul his stipend and [*also*] to pay out of that money 5 marks for a vestment. The residue of the money from 'Knappynges' and 'Cokkes' to be disposed for my soul and the souls of my parents to the honour of God and for the health of my soul.

Furthermore, my wife and William my son to live together in the tenement called 'Hovelles' for term of her life, if they can agree sufficiently; [*if not*], my wife to have for her dwelling that messuage called 'Wodgate' and an acre of land in 'Mellefeld' and William to pay and give his mother annually after entering the said tenement, with all the appurtenances [*and*] premises, as aforesaid, 26s 8d. And William shall sow during his mother's lifetime, for her use (*ad suu' opus*), with his own seed, an acre of wheat, an acre of barley, an acre of 'bolymong',[5] with all the tillage (*tellur'*), at his cost, and shall reap, mow and bind in the autumn, and after that carry the grain to his mother's dwelling house; and all this to be done at his own proper cost during his mother's life. And William shall find his mother, during her life, sufficient fuel [*but written 'jocale'*] and make and carry the fuel (*focale*) in faggots at his own cost to his mother's dwelling [fol. 585v] if she remains in Cowlinge.

When he comes to the age of 18, William my son to have my plough with the horses and all the equipment, as they are at the time of the making of this present [*will*].

My execs to pay the expenses of my burial day about my funeral and other monies with part of the money which they receive for the tenements called 'Knappynges' and 'Cokkes'.

Seal appended.

Proved before William Woode, *Dec. Lic. Cn. L. &c*[*sic*], 7 June 1474. Admon to execs.

---

1   The family seems to have spelt its name variously as Hovyle, Hovell and Howell.
2   The will of her father-in-law shows that Alice, wife of Thomas Hovell, was the daughter of John More of Whepstead (see note below).

³ There was a family called Copsy/Copcy in Cowlinge; see, for example, the will of John Copcy of Cowlinge (no. 91 above).
⁴ Will of Richard Hovyle of Cowlinge, the testator's father, pr. November 1452 (SROB, Baldwyne 118; Pt I, no. 549).
⁵ See Glossary.

802. JOHN WAYSBORN of HINDERCLAY ('Hyndercle'), 8 March 1473/74

Dated at Hinderclay; [*commendation*: to God Almighty, the Blessed Mary &c]; to be buried in the churchyard of Hinderclay parish church; to the high altar for tithes forgotten 6s 8d; to the said church for the buying of a new book 6s 8d.
To Agnes Cooke my daughter 10s; to Ellen (*Elwyne*) Caldewell my daughter 6s 8d. To Robert Cooke the younger 12d.
To Thomas Caldewell, son of John Caldewell of Thelnetham, 12d.
The aforesaid Agnes to have 20s in her own hands, on condition that she sees my anniversary kept (*ipsa observari faciat ... anniversarium meum*) in the said church for the whole of her lifetime.
To each of my execs for their labour 6s 8d.
To the friars of the New House of Thetford 3s 4d.¹
Residue of all my goods to my execs to dispose for the health of my soul as seems to them most expedient.
Execs: Robert Cooke and John Lynge of Hinderclay.
Proved before William Woode, *Dec. Lic. &c*[*sic*], 27 June 1474. Admon to execs.

¹ See note to no. 69.

[fol. 586]
803. AGNES DYKE of STOKE BY CLARE ('Stoke *iuxta* Clare'), widow, 2 December 1477

Of Stoke by Clare, in the diocese of Norwich; my testament and last will; [*commendation*: to God Almighty my Creator and the most Blessed Mary &c]; my body to Christian burial in the parish church of St Augustine the Bishop of Stoke aforesaid,¹ next to the grave of John Dyke my late husband. In God's name, I beg my execs to pay all my debts that I owe, that is, those that can be truly proved. To the high altar of the said church, for my tithes and offerings withheld, forgotten and underpaid, 2s; to the purchase of a canopy for the pyx to hang in over the high altar of the said church where the Lord's body may rest (*requiescit*)² and a new and precious container (*loc'li*) to be prepared and adorned, suitable for placing the body of Our Lord Jesus Christ in, for carrying from the church into the town there when necessary,³ 26s 8d; to the making of a new solar (*solari*) in the same church, called 'le Rodlofte', to be newly made, 13s 4d;⁴ to the provision of new stools (*ad scabelland de novo*) in the same church 13s 4d; to the paving (*pavac'*) of the same church 6s 8d; to the maintenance of the sepulchre light of the said church 6s 8d; to the maintenance of a light burning before the image of the Blessed Virgin Mary in the same church, to endure for ever, my best cow.
To the reparation and emendation of the highway at 'Babthernbregge' leading to 'le Four (*iiij^{or}*) Asshes', where there is most need, 20s; to the reparation of the bridges at 'Babthernbregge' aforesaid and the way between the said bridge there, on the riverbank, 13s 4d.⁵

To Friar James Exsale, to celebrate a trental of St Gregory for my soul with all possible haste after my decease, 10s, if James can do the service;[6] if not, it all to go to Friar John Colson to do it, according to the discretion of my execs.

To John my son 20s; to William my son 20s; to Thomas my son 26s 8d; to Reginald my son 20s; and to Joan my daughter, the wife of Thomas Throsshere, 20s and 4 yards of woollen cloth for making a 'kertyll'; [*to all of them*] to pray especially for my soul, between them all and each of them separately.

To Agnes, the daughter of John my son, my goddaughter, to pray (*erogend'*) for my soul 13s 4d; to Agnes, the daughter of Reginald my son, my goddaughter, to pray for my soul, 20s, 4 pieces of pewter and a 'forcer'.

To Margaret Mellere, my household servant, to pray for my soul 6s 8d in money and my cow called 'le Northen Cowe', black-coloured, a quarter of malt, a platter and 2 dishes of pewterware (*de vas lectrum*).

To each of my godsons and goddaughters to pray for my soul 6s 8d.

To the gild of the Blessed Trinity held in Stoke aforesaid, my best brass pan.[7]

To Reginald my son my mill (*molam*) and my lead[8] now lying in my tenement called 'Wyndeowtes' and a kneading trough ('knedyngtrowe') [586v], to pray for my soul.

To Joan my daughter, wife of Thomas Throsshere, to pray for my soul, a 'materas', a cover of 'yelew' colour, 2 blankets and 3 sheets, the width of each a yard, of my own making.

To each of my aforesaid 4 sons, to pray for my soul, a blanket [*and*] a pair of sheets.

To Thomas my son a mattress [*and*] a cover of 'yelew' colour.

To Agnes, daughter of Thomas my son, my goddaughter, to pray for my soul, 13s 4d.

To the buying of a new chrismatory of brass (*arucalco*), to be bought for the said church, 6s 8d.

To each priest present at my obsequies and at mass on the day of my burial 3d; and to each adult clerk 2d; and to each needy poor person there, to pray for my soul, 1d.

To Reginald my son my 6 silver spoons of one pattern (*de una factione*); and to Margaret his wife my best furred (*penulat'*) blue gown.

To be sold, another 5 of my best silver spoons, with lions and crowns, decorated (*ornat'*) with gold, and the money from them I leave to all the children of my children afore-named, who have had nothing bequeathed by me above, equally divided between them.

I will there be offered to the Blessed Virgin Mary of Walsingham ('Walsyngham') my best pair of beads with my ring with which I was married, to be placed about the image in her honour and there to remain as long as God wills.[9]

To John my son my featherbed with the transom (*meum* 'federbed' *cum* 'le tranzom'); and to Agnes his daughter, my goddaughter, my pair of jet ('geett') beads.

To Margery, wife of William Dyke my son, my lined tabard.

To Alice, wife of Thomas my son, my furred green tunic and a brass pot holding almost (*fere*) 2 gallons.

To Joan Throsshere, my daughter, a brass pot holding, by estimation, about 4 gallons, a spit, 2 andirons ('aundernes') and my lined violet gown.

To Agnes, daughter of Reginald my son, my goddaughter, a brass posnet ('possenett').

To Margaret Mellere, my household servant, provided she behaves herself well and marries someone on the good advice and agreement of my execs, my basin and ewer of brass.

To a good and honest secular priest to celebrate for the soul of John my late husband,

and for my soul, and for the souls of all our parents, friends and benefactors for whom I am most bound, in the said church and nowhere else, for a whole year, a reasonable stipend [*such*] as the priest and my execs can agree.

To the making and emendation of the timber cross standing on the green called 'Stoke Grene' 20d.[10]

To John, the son of the late John and Alice his wife, my daughter, to pray for my soul a 'blake howed' [*?black coloured*] bullock of the age of [fol. 589 – *see note at end of will*] 2 years and more, and a pair of sheets.

To Ellen, sister of the said Margaret my household servant, to pray for my soul, 20s and a pair of sheets.

To Isabel Semper, to pray for my soul, my best red-coloured 'kertyll'.

I leave all of my linen yarn ('lyneneyern') now within (*infra*) my messuage to be worked up (*operatur*) with all haste after my decease and distributed among the needy poor of the town of Stoke, where it is known there is greatest need; to be distributed among the same poor all my fuel with the taleshides and faggots (*cum* 'talsshyd' & 'fagett')[11] now within my dwelling house, for the health of my soul.

To each of the children of William my son, to pray for my soul, a bushel (*modium*) of wheat, a bushel (*bz*) of barley and 6d in money.

To the buying of a new vestment to be bought for the said church, by the good discretion of my execs, according to how much (*tantum quantum*) remains of my goods beyond my foregoing legacies (*ultra prelegat'*).

As to my lands and tenements, first I wish my messuage in Stoke aforesaid, in which I now live, with 4 parcels of land in the same town belonging to that messuage, to be sold by my execs immediately after my decease to implement, fulfil and pay all the foregoing directions and legacies (*omnia prescriptis & prelegatis*) in the best way (*precio*) possible. Residue of the money from the sale, if any there be, to be disposed in works of charity, that is, on the anniversary of us, the said John and Agnes, the testatrix, to be held for 5, 6 or 7 years following my decease; and if the money will stretch to it, in other good works as seems most expedient to the glory of God and our salvation (*salvac'*). If Reginald my son wishes to purchase one of the 4 pieces of land called 'le Dedwoman', I wish him to have it before all others, paying for it as much as another man will give, fraud and deceit apart (*fraude & dolo po'itis*). If Thomas, son of John my son, now an apprentice at Bury St Edmunds (*sancti Edmundi*) wishes to buy my said messuage with the other 3 pieces of land, and their appurtenances, immediately after my decease, I wish him to have it before all others and 20s within the price. If he is unwilling to do this, then I wish him to have 20s in money out of the sale, to pray for my soul.

I wish my execs to provide and purchase a marble stone to place over the bodies of John my late husband and me, Agnes.

Residue of all my goods to the disposition of my execs, John, William and Reginald my sons, and John Algere, to fulfil all the foregoing as they see best to please God and profit all the aforementioned souls. To each of my 3 sons, for their diligent labour about the premises, 3s 4d; to John Algere for the same [*or,* for [*his*] counsel] (*per consil'o*) 3s 4d.

Seal appended in the presence of my 4 execs and Richard Clerk.

Proved at Clare, 3 October 1478. Admon to execs.

[*This will is written on folios 586 and 589, which comprise one bifolium, but it has had another bifolium, now folios 587 and 588, sewn into it.*]

1   The original dedication of the church, which is now dedicated to St John the Baptist.
2   A very rare example of a pyx canopy survives at Dennington: see Cautley, pp.187–8 and photo-
    graph on p.198. This is the first of many bequests by the wealthy widow Agnes Dyke to the
    fabric and religious accoutrements of the church of St Augustine at Stoke by Clare. Her bequests
    illuminate many of the ways in which God and the saints were worshipped and venerated during
    the late medieval period.
3   That is, a viaticum, a container for the sacrament carried by a priest when visiting the sick and
    dying.
4   The testatrix refers to the new roodloft as a 'solar' in the church. Although the word may derive
    from *sol* (Latin for 'sun') and hence a room open to the sun, a more convincing derivation is from
    Old French *sol* ('floor') and *solive* 'beam', that is a room on a beam, the upper floor (Yaxley,
    Researcher's Glossary, p.193).
5   'Babthern' is now 'Baythorn End'; perhaps 'the Four Ashes' is the place now known as 'Ashen';
    the river is, of course, the River Stour.
6   Both Robert Belamy of Boxted (SROB, Baldwyne 204; Pt I, no. 1006) and John Glovyere of
    Cavendish (no. 133 above) also requested Friar James Exsale to say a trental of St Gregory for
    their souls.
7   Nicholas Stroude (no. 637) bequeathed 12d to this gild; there was also a gild of Jesus in the parish
    (*PSIA*, xii, p.84).
8   See Glossary.
9   For donations of jewellery to shrines see note to no. 142.
10 A rare reference to an open-air cross being of 'timber'.
11 See Glossary.

[fol. 587]

804. THOMAS VYELL of IXWORTH,[1] 10 October 1479

[*Commendation*: to God Almighty, the Blessed Mary &c]; to be buried in the churchyard of the parish church of the Blessed Mary of Ixworth; to the high altar of the said church 12d; to the reparation of the said church 3 bushels of wheat.

To Christian my mother[2] a half part of my grain, wheat and barley.

To Isabel my sister[3] a 'vyolett' gown.

Residue of all my goods to Christian my mother and Roger Godrych, execs, to dispose as they see best to please God and profit the health of my soul.

Seal appended.

Proved before William Duffeld, *Dec. Lic.*, Commissary General in the archdeaconry of Sudbury to Bishop James of Norwich, on his ordinary visitation. And because of an insufficiency of the deceased's goods, the execs were absolved from rendering further accounts and dismissed.

[*no probate date; next will on this folio proved 17 November 1479*]

1   Will of his father, also Thomas Vyell of Ixworth, no. 723 above.
2   Executrix of her husband Thomas (no. 723).
3   Not mentioned in the will of Thomas Vyell the elder.

805. THOMAS GYNOWS of MENDLESHAM, 13 October 1479 [*Latin and English*]

To be buried in the Christian burial of Mendlesham church; to the high altar for my tithes forgotten, for the health of my soul, 12d; to the high altar of Mickfield ('Medylfeld') church 8d; to the making of an antiphoner for the same church 6s 8d. To the friars of Ipswich (*Gyppewici*) 10s, to celebrate a trental of St Gregory for my soul and those for whom I am bound.[1]

[English from this point forward.]

To Alice my wife all my moveable goods and all my cattle ('catell'), with all my grain, as well sown and unsown. Alice to have my tenement with the appurtenances lying in Mendlesham ('Mendelysham') term of her life. If she fortune to come to necessity and need and such poverty, then she to sell the tenement with the appurtenances; if it fortune her not to come to such poverty and need, then I will the tenement with the appurtenances remain to John my son and his heirs [fol. 587v: *blank*] [fol. 588] after the decease of Alice my wife. And then I will John, having possession of the tenement with the appurtenances, pay to George his brother 5 marks in money. If John should die ere he come to lawful age and have possession of the tenement, as above, then I will the tenement remain to George my son and his heirs, that is, after the decease of Alice my wife, under this condition, that he shall find a priest to sing for my soul and Alice my wife and for our good friends that we are bound to, by the space of half a year. If it fortune that John and George my sons both die within lawful age and afore they be possessed of the tenement as above, and after the decease of Alice, then I will that the tenement with the appurtenances be sold and of the money thereof received I will have a priest to sing for the souls of me and Alice my wife and our benefactors by a whole year; and the residue of the money received of the tenement, besides the stipend of the priest, to be divided betwixt my daughters by even portions. I will that each of my children have 20s, when they come to lawful age, of the said residue. If it happen Alice die afore John and George my sons come to the age of 20, then I will the tenement be governed and kept by my execs and feoffees till John and George come to the age of 20, keeping the reparations and charges of the same, and what comes over thereof to be disposed by the discretion of my execs.

Residue of all my goods to the good disposition of Alice my wife, whom I make my true executrix, with John Dunche of Mendlesham[2] and Gilbert Blomevyle of Little Stonham ('Lytylle Stonham'), this my last will truly to perform and fulfil; to John Dunche and Gilbert Blomevyle, each of them for their labour, 3s 4d.

Proved before William Duffeld, Commissary General, 17 November 1479. Admon to Alice and John Dunche, execs. Power reserved to Gilbert Blomevyle, when he comes.

1   For the friars of Ipswich see notes to nos 1 (Carmelites and Franciscans) and 50 (Dominicans).
2   There were at least two men named 'John Dunche of Mendlesham', one of whom was a stainer ('steynour'): see will of Robert Dunch the elder of Mendlesham (no. 374 above).

[fol. 589: *see no. 803 above*]
[fol. 589v]

806. THOMAS CABOWE of HITCHAM ('Hecham'),[1] 5 August 1478

Dated at Hitcham; to be buried in the churchyard of Hitcham church; to the high altar of the same church for my tithes underpaid or forgotten 2s.

To William Welham a brass pot.

To Hugh Chapman a brass pan.

To Robert Bantofth a stone 'morter'.

Residue of all my goods to the disposition of my exec, my dearly beloved in Christ, Henry Boule,[2] to dispose for the health of my soul as seems to him best to please God.

Seal appended.

Proved at Fornham, 2 November 1478. Admon to exec.

1 Executor (as 'Cabow') of Thomas Hardhed, probate dated January 1457/58 (SROB, Baldwyne 199; Pt I, no. 979). Related to Thomas Cabow and his wife Margaret, perhaps their son, although neither of them made any bequests to him: will of Thomas Cabaw of Hitcham pr. February 1440/41 (SROB, Baldwyne 31; Pt I, no. 177); a slightly different version that was not proved (Baldwyne 20; Pt I, no. 110); will of Margaret Cabow of Hitcham pr. January 1459/60 (SROB, Baldwyne 246; Pt I, no. 1234).

2 Henry Boule (as 'Bawle', 'Boule' and 'Bowle') was married to Marion, perhaps the daughter of Margaret and Thomas Cabow senior. Margaret bequeathed Henry and Marion her tenement provided that they took care of her while she lived. Henry was one of Margaret's executors and was mentioned in the will of Thomas senior.

807. JOHN FROST of HARTEST ('Hertest'),[1] 22 March 1478/79 [*nuncupative*]

His body to Christian burial; to the high altar of the same church 20d; to the parish chaplain 8d.

To John his son 6s 8d.

To Sir Richard Frost 10s, for celebrating a trental.

Residue of all his goods to Marion his wife to her own use.

Execs: Marion his wife and William Frost his son.

Witnesses: Sir Richard Frost, chaplain, Marion Frost and Joan Frost.

Proved at Fornham, 30 March 1479. Admon to William Frost, exec. Power reserved to Marion, when she comes.

1 ?Executor of Thomas Struth, will pr. November 1449 (SROB, Baldwyne 101; Pt I, no. 456); ?related to William Frost of Hartest (no. 690 above).

[fol. 590]

808. ROBERT PARMAN of ALDERSFIELD ('Alverisfeld') in WICKHAMBROOK, 18 September 1463

Dated the Sunday before the feast of St Matthew the Apostle 1463; my body to Christian burial in the churchyard of the parish church of All Saints of Wick-hambrook ('Wykhambrok'); to the high altar there, for tithes and other [*things*] forgotten, 6s 8d.

Katherine Parman my wife to have all my goods and chattels, both live and dead, a cow only excepted, which I leave to Thomas Parman my son after my decease.

Katherine to have all my houses and lands and tenements with the meadows, pastures, fences and ditches, with all their appurtenances, for term of her life. And after her decease, I wish all the said houses, lands and tenements, with their appur-tenances, to be sold, from the total receipts of which I bequeath: to Thomas Parman my son 20s; to Joan my daughter the elder £3 6s 8d; to John my son 20s; to Agnes my daughter 20s; to Margaret my daughter 20s; to Joan my daughter the younger 20s; to a suitable priest to celebrate in the said church for the space of half a year 53s 4d; and to the fabric and sustentation of the said church 53s 4d.

Residue of all my goods to the disposition of my execs, Simon Dalham of Hundon ('Honden') and Katherine Parman my wife, to dispose for my soul and for the souls of my parents, friends and all my benefactors in the best way they see to please God and profit our souls.

Witnesses: Simon Dalham, Joan Reve, wife of Richard Reve, Agnes Batman, wife of John Bateman, and others.

Proved at Clare, 28 September 1463. Admon to Simon Dalham, exec. Power reserved to Katherine, the other co-exec, when she comes and if she wishes to take up [*admon*].

[*See no. 99 above [fol. 339], where a shortened version of this will has been written out and then struck through. In the margin beside that version is written: Cancelled because written below at end of register, with witnesses examined* (cu' testibus examinatis).]

[fol. 590v: *blank*] [fol. 591]

809. JOHN LYNCOLNE of STONHAM ASPAL ('Aspale'), 4 March 1473/74

[*Commendation*: to God Almighty &c]; to be buried in the churchyard of Stonham Aspal church; to the high altar of the same 3s 4d; to the emendation of the said church 6s 8d.

To Margaret my wife 8 cows.

To Marion my daughter 4 cows, 4 ewes and 2 'blankettes' and a quarter of malt.

To Robert my son the elder, Robert the younger, Thomas my son, Joan and Audrey my daughters (*Joh'e & Audre filiabus meis*), a cow each.

Residue of all my goods to Margaret my wife and Robert my son the elder, execs, to dispose for the health of my soul as they hope to please God and profit my soul.

[*Will, of same date*]

My last will, annexed to my testament and made 4 March 1473 [1473/74].

Margaret my wife to have all my lands and tenements with their appurtenances in the towns of Bedingfield ('Bedyngfeld') and Debenham ('Debynham') for term of her life, but if she remarries, not so. If she does remarry, then Robert my son the elder to have my said lands and tenements in Bedingfield to him and his heirs, on condition that he pays Margaret my wife annually, for term of her life, 13s 4d in money, at Easter and St Michael the Archangel in equal portions. Also, if Margaret remarries, then Robert my son the younger to have all [*my*] lands and tenements in Debenham to him and his heirs, on condition that he pays Margaret annually, for term of her life, 6s 8d, at the said feasts in equal portions. If Robert the elder should die during the lifetime of Margaret my wife, then I wish Thomas my son to have the said lands and tenements to him and his heirs, paying as Robert the elder should pay. If Robert the younger should die during the lifetime of Margaret my wife and she remarries, I wish Marion my daughter to have all my lands and tenements in Debenham during Margaret's lifetime and remarriage, on condition that Marion pays Margaret my wife annually, term of Margaret's life, 6s 8d, as my younger son [*Robert*] should pay, and also [*on condition*] that Marion pays Joan my daughter 13s 4d and Audrey her sister 13s 4d. If Robert the elder and Robert the younger, Thomas and Marion should die in Margaret's lifetime, and she should remarry, then I wish all the said lands and tenements in the said towns to be sold and the money arising to be disposed for the health of my soul and for the souls of my wife and all our benefactors.

Proved before William Woode, at Wetheringsett ('Wetheryngset'), 27 April 1474. Admon to execs.

[fol. 591v]

810. ROBERT SPRYNG *alias* WEDERDEYN of BROCKFORD ('Brokeford') [in WETHERINGSETT],[1] 13 March 1473/74

My testament and my last will; [*commendation*: to God Almighty, the Blessed Mary &c]; to be buried in the churchyard of the church of All Saints of Wetheringsett ('Wedyryngset'); to the high altar of the same church for tithes forgotten 12d.

To Joan my daughter the younger 26s 8d and a cow with a calf and all my vessels, utensils and bedding with all the ornaments within the house and without.

To a chalice 30s.

I wish to have a priest [*to celebrate*] for a whole year and a half for my soul and [*the souls of*] all my benefactors; I wish to have a trental celebrated for my soul, price 10s.

To each of my execs 20d for his labour.

Residue of all my goods to be disposed by my execs as seems to them best and [*for the*] health of my soul.

Execs: Robert Horsman and John Eustas.

Witnesses: Sir John Kemp,[2] John Eustac and Robert Horsman, Richard Cobbe and John Spring and others.

Seal appended.

Proved before William Woode, 27 April 1473 [*recte* 1474]. Admon to execs.

1   See note to no. 5, regarding Brockford in Wetheringsett.
2   Also witnessed the wills of two other Wetheringsett parishoners, nos 559 and 796.

This will on fol. 591v is the last one in the existing 'Baldwyne' register. At the end of it is written, in large letters, liber proximus (*next book*).

The final 17 wills transcribed in this volume were originally part of 'Baldwyne' but are now to be found in a later register known as 'Fuller' (SROB reference IC500/2/12). See Introduction, The assembling of register 'Baldwyne', for details.

811. [Fuller fol. 11] **RICHARD REDER of REDGRAVE,** 8 March 1462/63 [*probate only*]

Proved at Hopton, 8 March 1462/63. Admon to William Londe, exec.

812. [Fuller fol. 11] **JOHN CLERK the elder of NOWTON,** 22 January 1462/63

Dated at Nowton; [*commendation*: to God &c; *burial directions omitted*]; to the high altar of Nowton church for my tithes and offerings forgotten or underpaid 6s 8d.

To the friars of Babwell, to celebrate a Gregorian trental for my soul, 10s.[1]

To John Clerk, my brother,[2] 4 horses, an iron-bound cart and the other things belonging to it, and a chamber in the messuage in which I live, to hold to him and his assigns for term of his life and 8 days after his death.

Residue of all my goods and chattels, both live and dead, to Agnes my wife for her maintenance; she to be executrix.

Seal appended.

Proved at Fornham [*St*] Martin, 13 March 1462/63. Admon to executrix.

813. [Fuller fol. 11] **AGNES DEKENYS of STOKE BY CLARE ('Stoke *iuxta* Clare'),** 17 March 1462/63 [*probate only*]

Proved at Clare, 17 March 1462/63. Admon to Richard Gawge and William Howton, execs.

814. [Fuller fol. 11] **JOHN NORMAN of STANSFIELD ('Stansfeld'),**
17 March 1462/63 [*probate only*]

Proved at Clare, 17 March 1462/63. Admon to John Eylmyn[*sic*] and Peter Grey, execs.

815. [Fuller fol. 11] **JOHN SMYTH of CLARE,** 16 January 1462/63

Of Clare, in the diocese of Norwich; [*commendation*: to God &c; *burial directions omitted*]. In God's name I request my execs to pay all my debts which I owe, that is, those that can be proved. To the high altar of the said church for my tithes and offerings withheld, forgotten and underpaid, 3s 4d; to each priest present at my obsequies and at mass on the day of my burial 4d; to each clerk there at the same time 2d; to 4 needy poor [*folk*] holding 4 torches around my body on that day 4d.

To Marion my wife all my household things and utensils, that is, linen, woollen, pots, pans, cups, spoons and all of the essential utensils belonging to me.

To Katherine my daughter an annuity of 46s 8d and 300 'faggetes' annually for term of her life.

To a suitable priest to celebrate for my soul and the souls of my father and my mother and all my parents and friends for whom I am most bound, for a whole year in Clare parish church, 9 marks.

To Hugh my son 40s.

To Joan my daughter, the wife of Thomas Ede, 40s.

To Anne my daughter, the wife of John Kegyll, 5 marks.

To each of the children of the said Thomas Ede 3s 4d.

To Margery Flowre 3s 4d.

To John my son my best anvil (*imcuden*) and 3 hammers (*malleas*), 3 pairs of tongs (*forcip'*) and the blacksmith's tools (*instrument' fabril'*) for making door nails ('dorenall') and plank nails ('planchernall'), a pair of bellows ('beloes'), a toyere ('tovere') and a wheel (*rota*) with all its fittings (*apparata*).[1]

To Agnes Poteer to pray for my soul 3s 4d.

Residue of all my goods to the disposition of my execs, [fol. 11v] Hugh my son, Thomas Ede and John Gylmyn, to perform all the premises in the best way possible that they know, to the pleasure of God and the profit of my soul.

I entreat John Hengessman, if he will, to be my supervisor.

To each of my execs and supervisor 6s 8d for their labour.

Seal appended.

Proved at Clare, 17 March 1442/43 [*sic*; *recte* 1462/63]. Admon to Thomas Ede and John Gylmyn, execs. Power reserved to Hugh, son of the deceased, when he comes, if he wishes to take up [*admon*].

¹   So John Smyth really was a smith. It is likely the wheel was a waterwheel to power the bellows.

816. [Fuller fol. 11v] **JOHN HEPSTON of ROUGHAM ('Rowgham'),** 1 March
1461/62

['Helpston' *in margin*]. Of Rougham in the diocese of Norwich; [*commendation*: to
God Almighty &c; *burial directions omitted*]; to the high altar of the church aforesaid, for my tithes and offerings forgotten or underpaid and for the health of my
soul, 2s; to the high altar of Rushbrooke ('Roschbrook') church 2s.
To the friars of Babwell, for a trental, 10s; to the friars of Sudbury 5s.¹
To Isabel my wife all my ostilments and utensils of my house. Isabel to have all
my other lands and tenements, with all their appurtenances, in the towns and fields
of Rougham, Rushbrooke and Little Whelnetham ('Qwhelnetham Parva') which
I purchased of John Bowyere of Bury St Edmunds, and another tenement called
'Stambornes', for term of her life; after her decease, I wish all the lands and tenements, with all their appurtenances, to remain to Nicholas Helpston my son and his
heirs for ever; if Nicholas should die under legal age, I wish all the lands and tenements, with their appurtenances, to remain to Thomas Hepston my son and his heirs
for ever; if Thomas should die under legal age, then I wish all the lands and tenements, with their appurtenances, to remain to Roger Hepston my son and his heirs
for ever; if Roger should die under age, I wish all the lands and tenements, with their
appurtenances, to be sold by my execs and my co-feoffees and the money disposed
for my soul and the soul of the said Isabel and the souls of all my departed friends.
Residue of all my goods to my execs, to sell and dispose for my soul and the souls
of those for whom I am bound, in the celebration of masses and distribution of alms
as they see best to please God and profit my soul.
Execs: Isabel my wife and Nicholas Hepston and Edmund Tyllote,² faithfully to
execute this testament.
Seal appended.
To Isabel my wife 4 score wethers (*ariet'*), 20 ewes, 5 horses, 5 cows and 3 bullocks
(*bovicula'*).
To the fabric of the new tower of Rougham 5 marks.³
Proved at Fornham [*St*] Martin, 23 March 1462/63. Admon to Nicholas Hepston,
exec. Power reserved to Isabel and Edmund, the other execs, when they come, if
they wish to take up [*admon*].

¹   For the friars see notes to nos 1 (Babwell) and 11 (Sudbury).
²   Son of Roger Tyllot of Rougham; Roger's will pr. July 1459 (SROB Baldwyne 247; Pt I, no.
    1240).
³   Roger Tyllot had made the first and largest bequest to the new tower of Rougham church (see note
    to no. 184 above).

817. [Fuller fol. 12] **THOMAS SKEYTH of STANTON,** 25 April 1462

[*Commendation*: to God Almighty &c; *burial directions omitted*]; to the high altar
of the church of St John the Baptist of Stanton for tithes and other defaulted offerings 6d; to the high altar of the church of All Saints [*of Stanton*], for tithes forgotten,
6d; to the emendation of the said church of St John 20d.
To Margaret my daughter¹ 10 marks; to Richard my son 40s.

To the friars of Babwell 20d; to the friars of the Old House of Thetford 20d.[2]
Residue of all my goods I put into the hands of Katherine my wife[3] and Roger Rolle-crosse[4] for the payment of my debts and legacies and the rest done in pious works; and them I make execs, to dispose for my soul and the souls of my benefactors as they know best to please God and profit the health of my soul.
Proved at Ixworth, 21 January 1462/63. Admon to Katherine the wife. Power reserved to Roger Rollecrosse, the other co-exec, when he comes.

1   Will (as 'Sketh'), dated 20 July 1472, no. 711.
2   For the friars see notes to nos 1 (Babwell) and 68 (Old House of Thetford).
3   Will (as 'Sketh'), dated 21 August 1469, no. 453.
4   Executor of Thomas Skeyth's wife Katherine (no. 453) and daughter Margaret (no. 711).

818. [Fuller fol. 12] **JOHN CAKE of MENDLESHAM,**[1] 29 October 1462

Dated at Mendlesham, the Friday before the feast of All Saints 1462; [*commendation*: to God &c; *burial directions omitted*]; to the high altar of Mendlesham church 3s 4d; to the reparation of the said church, as seems best to my execs, 40s; for the stipend of 2 chaplains, for them to celebrate for a whole year in Mendlesham church, or for one chaplain for 2 years, 16 marks.
To Katherine my wife 20 marks, 2 cows with their upkeep (*cum stipendio earundem*); to Katherine a half part of all the bedding and all the other utensils and household, except a plate of iron,[2] and her dwelling in my messuage until the feast of St Michael the Archangel next to come; to Katherine a half part of the firewood at present on the said messuage.
Residue of all my goods to the administration of my execs, to sell, receive and dispose for the health of my soul and the souls of all the faithful departed in works of piety as, according to their discretion, they see [*best*] to please God and profit my soul.
Execs: Sir William Mason and Robert Cake of Mendlesham.[3]
[*Will, of same date*]
Katherine my wife to have my bargain of a messuage, with all its appurtenances, in Brockford ('Brokford') called 'le Swanne', of which I have paid 6 marks before my death, which 6 marks I wish to be parcel of the 20 marks which I have bequeathed to Katherine in my testament.
John and William my sons to have all my messuage in Mendlesham, formerly Robert Lord's, and a close call 'Dentonys' [fol. 12v] to them and their heirs. If John should die without heirs, then my messuage, with the appurtenances, to remain wholly to William and his heirs. If William should die without heirs, then the messuage to remain wholly to John. If both should die without heirs, then the messuage, with all the lands and pasture and other appurtenances, to remain wholly to my execs, to sell and dispose for my soul and for the souls of all my benefactors.
John my son to have my stall (*stallagium*) in the town of Debenham with all the tools belonging to my craft (*artem*).
Proved, with the last will annexed, at Westhorpe ('Westhorp'), 22 January 1462/63. Admon to execs.

1   Son and executor of John Cake of Mendlesham, will pr. April 1459 (SROB, Baldwyne 269; Pt I, no. 1315).
2   See Glossary.

³   Brother of the testator; see note to no. 275.

819. [Fuller fol. 12v] **THOMAS TYDDE of MILDENHALL ('Myldenhale'),**
5 May 1463

My testament containing my last will; [*commendation*: to divine mercy &c; *burial directions omitted*]; to the high altar of Mildenhall church for my tithes and offerings forgotten and withheld, in exoneration of my soul, 5s; to the reparation of the same church 13s 4d.

To John Wetewelle my servant 40d.

To Isabel Sabelotte my servant a cow price 6s 8d or the price.

To the gild of St Mary of Mildenhall ('Mildenhale') 5s.[1]

To Alice Skonyng, the wife of Richard Skonyng, a heifer of 2 years.

I wish a suitable priest to celebrate in Mildenhall church for a whole year for my soul and the soul of Alice my wife and for the souls of our parents[2] and friends and all our benefactors and all the faithful departed, having for his stipend 8 marks.

Residue of all my goods and chattels whatever and wherever they be, after my debts have been paid and my burial done and my legacies fulfilled as above, to my faithful execs to dispose of it for our souls in works of charity according to their discretion as they see most expedient, and to keep, support and maintain all my children, whom I put in the care and control of my execs until they come to legal age.

Execs: William Chylderston[3] and John Halstede;[4] to each of them for their faithful labour in this matter, 5s.

Proved at Fornham St Martin, 16 May 1463. Admon to execs. Seal of official appended.

¹   For other bequests to the gild of St Mary the Virgin in Mildenhall see note to no. 378.
²   It is difficult to determine the identity of this testator's father: Robert Tyd of Mildenhall had a son named Thomas, Robert's will pr. September 1452 (SROB, Baldwyne 128; Pt I, no. 598); John Tyd of Mildenhall also had a son named Thomas, John's will pr. April 1454 (SROB, Baldwyne 152; Pt I, no. 727). Thomas, the testator here, had an executor in common with both Robert and John.
³   Executor of John Tyd (Pt I, no. 727); ?William's will pr. May 1479 (SROB, Hervye 186).
⁴   Executor of Robert Tyd (Pt I, no. 598); ?John's will pr. March 1477/78 (SROB, Hervye 181).

820. [Fuller fol. 15] **THOMAS BARKERE of THELNETHAM
('Thelwetham'),**[1] 6 October 1461

Knowing death to be inevitable, and the certainty of death but the uncertainty of the time, and now desirous of God that that time should come; my testament or last will; [*commendation*: to God Almighty &c; *burial directions omitted*]; to the high altar of Thelnetham church, for tithes forgotten, 6s 8d; to Thelnetham church, towards the buying of another book or another ornament to serve in the church for ever, according to the discretion of my execs.

I wish to have a chaplain to celebrate for my soul and the soul of Agnes my wife, our parents and all our benefactors, to whom I bequeath 8 marks for the year, he to celebrate in Thelnetham church or elsewhere according to the discretion of Master Thomas Bretown, rector of that church,[2] and William Barkere, my son, chaplain.[3]

To each of the sons and daughters of Robert Barkere, John Barkere and Margery Lerlyng 2s.

To the friars of Babwell 5s; to the friars of Thetford 5s; to the Augustinian Friars there 5s; to the nuns there 5s.[4]

To William Barkere my son, chaplain, 2 acres of arable land.

Robert my son to have my tenement with the appurtenances, the tenement 'Mormanys' with the appurtenances, the tenement 'Moyses' with the appurtenances, [*and*] the tenement 'Drurys' with the appurtenances.

Richard my son to have the tenement 'Goodwyns' with the appurtenances and 6 acres of land. I wish him to have all the tenement and land, with the pasture, feeding and 'foldage', before all buyers and for a price lower (*leviori*) by £13 6s 8d, if he is willing to give as much as it can be sold for to others; and if he is not willing to give as much, then I wish him to have £13 6s 8d of the price.

I wish John Martyn to buy, before all other purchasers, the tenement and land that I bought of Robert Glinkford.

My goods to my execs to dispose for the souls of all my benefactors, as they see best to please God and profit my soul.

Execs: Master Thomas Breton, rector of Thelnetham, William Barkere my son, chaplain, Robert Barkere my son.[5]

Seal appended.

Witnesses: William Bretoun,[6] Richard Barkere, John Symond and many others.

To each chaplain serving in Thelnetham church on the day of my death and obsequies, 12d, and to William Barkere my son, chaplain, on the same day, 3s 4d.

[*no probate recorded; fol. 15v blank*]

1   Father of John Barker of Thelnetham, will pr. July 1460 (SROB, Baldwyne 255; Pt I, no. 1262).
2   Thomas Breton was rector of Thelnetham by 1442, when Thomas Seman of Thelnetham appointed him supervisor of his will (SROB, Baldwyne 39; Pt I, no. 213); he was still alive when his brother Sir William made his will in March 1475/76 (see note below). Thomas and William were two of the executors of their father, Richard Breton of Rickinghall Inferior, will pr. June 1457 (SROB, Baldwyne 186; Pt 1, no. 900).
3   Legatee and executor of his brother John (see note above); Master William Barker *A.M.* was rector of Rushbrooke from 1439 to his death in 1470 (Tanner, p.1442); he witnessed both the testament and will of Robert Hunte of Rushbrooke, esquire (no. 191).
4   See notes to nos 1 (friars of Babwell), 68 (Dominican friars and Benedictine nuns of Thetford) and 69 (Augustinian friars of Thetford).
5   Robert and William were also executors of their brother John, together with his wife Joan (see note above).
6   Probably the brother of Master Thomas Breton. William was rector of Euston from 1466 he until he died in 1476 (Tanner, p.1196); will pr. August 1476 (NRO, NCC 45 Gilberd). He wished to be buried in the chancel of Euston parish church before the newly painted image of the Blessed Virgin Mary on the south side, and left 6s 8d to Thelnetham church for the rector there, that is, his brother Thomas, to say obsequies for him.

821. [Fuller fol. 18] **RICHARD BUNTYNG of TOSTOCK ('Tostok'),**[1]
7 January 1461/62

Dated the Thursday after the feast of the Epiphany 1461; in peril of death; [*commendation*: to God &c; *burial directions omitted*]; to the high altar of Tostock ('Tostoke') church 6s 8d; to the said church 10 marks for the buying of a cope and vestment according to the discretion of [*my*] execs.

To the cellarer of Bury[2] 26s 8d, humbly beseeching that obsequies will be solemnly done once by the convent for me and my benefactors.

To the high altar of Pakenham 20d, and to the fabric of the same church 13s 4d; to the high altar of Beyton ('Beketon') 20d, and to the fabric of the same church 6s 8d; to the high altar of Thurston 20d, and to the fabric of the same church 13s 4d; to the high altar of Drinkstone ('Drenkston') 20d, and to the fabric of the same church 6s 8d.

To the friars of Babwell 6s 8d; to the Friars Preachers of Thetford 6s 8d.[3]

To Thomas Creme 6s 8d; to Richard Creme 6s 8d; to Nicholas Creme 6s 8d.

To Richard Barkere 6s 8d.

To John Gebown 6s 8d; to Robert Gebon 6s 8d; to Joan Gebon 6s 8d; to Katherine Gebon 6s 8d.

To Richard Creme, son of Thomas Creme, 6s 8d; to Richard Creme, son of Nicholas Creme, 6s 8d; to Richard Creme, son of Richard Creme, 6s 8d.

To each of my godsons 6d.

To the house of Ixworth 6s 8d;[4] to the house of Sibton ('Sybton') 3s 4d.[5]

I assign my tenement called 'Baxsters', and the tenement 'Caschys', and the tenement 'Carletones', and the tenement 'Cokes', after the decease of Joan my wife, to John Gebon and Isabel his wife for term of his life; and after the decease of the said John and Isabel, to the oldest son of the same John and Isabel and his heirs, the oldest son paying his brothers and sisters certain sums of money to be divided among them, according to the discretion of my execs. If the sons of John and Isabel should die without heirs, then I wish the oldest daughter to have the tenements, to her and her heirs, paying to her sisters then alive certain sums of money, according to the discretion and advice of my execs.

My tenement called 'Wethereldes', except a close at the rectory gate [in] Tostock and the meadow called 'Closmedwe' by 'le Brook', to be sold to fulfil and pay all my legacies and debts.

All my utensils and chattels of my house belonging to 'Baxsterys' to remain to John and Isabel after Joan's decease.

I assign the aforesaid meadow called 'Closmedwe' to John and Isabel and their heirs, on condition that they provide, one day each week, a special commemoration, that is, a 'sangred' for my soul, my parents and benefactors and all the faithful departed, for ever. If they refuse to keep this 'sangrede' as above, then the rector of Tostock church for the time being shall assign the said meadow to him or them who are willing to see it done. If the sons and daughters of John and Isabel should [all] die without heirs, then I wish the lands and tenements to be sold and disposed for my soul, my parents', friends' and all my benefactors' [souls].

Residue [fol. 18v] of all my goods to the discretion of my execs, Isabel Gebon my daughter and Thomas Creme of Thurston, to dispose in pious uses as they know best to please God and profit my soul.

Proved at Ixworth ('Ixworthe'), 26 August 1462. Admon to execs.

[1] Son and executor of John Buntyng of Tostock, will pr. June 1440 (SROB, Baldwyne 26; Pt I, no. 133).
[2] The cellarer was one of the principal obedientiaries of Bury abbey.
[3] For the friars see notes to nos 1 (Babwell) and 68 (Friars Preachers of Thetford).
[4] See note to no. 69.
[5] See note to no. 435.

822. [Fuller fol. 18v] **ISABEL BAKERE of MARKET WESTON, widow,** 20 September 1462

[*Commendation*: to God &c; *burial directions omitted*]; to the high altar of Weston 3s 4d; to the reparation of the same church 2s.

To the friars of the Minors order of Babwell 10s,[1] to celebrate a trental for my soul and for the soul of John Baker, once my husband.

To Margaret my daughter 6s 8d; to Agnes my daughter 10s; to Isabel my daughter 6s 8d; to Helen my daughter 6s 8d; to Alice my daughter 6s 8d, together with a chest of fir ('fyr') and with a red bedcover.

To Agnes the daughter of Thomas Chapman 3s 4d.

I wish Master Robert my son to have the 5 marks that I borrowed from him; to him for the reparation of 'le Insette' 7s.

Residue of all my goods to Master Robert Bakere my son of Cambridge (*Cantabri'*), exec, to dispose for my soul as he sees best to please God and profit my soul.

Supervisor: Master Thomas Meryell, rector of Weston ('Wiston').[2]

If the legacies cannot be fully met with the things left, then I wish them to be met after the sale of the tenement with the appurtenances, as the payments grow and come to my exec.

Witnesses: John Debenham, Thomas Crask and Thomas Honge of Weston and others.

Proved at Fornham 8 October 1462. Admon to exec.

[1] See note to no. 1.
[2] Thomas Meryell (Muryell) was rector of Market Weston from March 1457/58 until 1465 (Tanner, p.1221); will pr. 1465/66 (NRO, NCC 83 Cobald). In his will, pr. April 1491, William Howys bequeathed an acre of land to Market Weston church to have his, his wife's and his parents' souls remembered annually at the obit of Master Thomas Moryell, rector there (SROB, Fuller 25). Not to be confused with Thomas Muryell (Maryell), the rector of Chelsworth, who died in 1495 (see note to no. 154 above).

823. [Fuller fol. 21] **WILLIAM BUGGE of SOHAM [*Cambs*],**[1] 16 September 1462

Of Soham in the county of Cambridge (*Cantabrig'*); [*commendation*: to God &c; *burial directions omitted*]; to the high altar of Soham a coomb of wheat and a quarter of barley; to the buying of a pyx for the sacrament 20s.

To each of my children 12 lambs.

To John Goodale my servant 3s 4d and 2 sheep.

To Ellen Overmede a lamb.

To Alice Styward 4 sheep and 2 bushels (*modios*) of barley.

To Alice Bugge my wife 2 acres of arable land lying diversely in 'Reedlond'[2] and abutting on 'Cley Causy' for term of her life for the keeping of my anniversary and the anniversary of my father and mother annually for ever; and I wish that anyone who has the 2 acres after Alice's decease should have them on the same conditions.

To Alice my wife my messuage with all the lands, meadows and appurtenances for term of her life; and after her decease, I wish Richard Bugge my son to have the messuage with 20 acres of arable land and meadow to him and his heirs. If he should decease without heirs, then I wish each of my children to be heir to the other.

Residue of all my arable lands unbequeathed, after the decease of Alice my wife, I wish to be divided between all my other children.

To William Petche 6s 8d;[3] to John Bugge of 'Halle strete' 6s 8d.[4]

Residue of all my goods to Alice Bugge my wife, executrix, William Petche and John Bugge, co-executors with her, to dispose for my soul and the souls of all my benefactors as seems best to please God &c[*sic*].

Proved at Fornham St Martin, 8 January 1462/63. Admon to execs.

[1] Executor (as 'Bugg') of [*unknown*] Herne of Soham, will pr. June 1461 (SROB, Baldwyne 303; Pt I, no. 1483); see note to no. 659 regarding the Bugge family.

[2] 'Redlands' appears on a map of Soham dated 1656. See note to no. 232.

[3] Executor (as 'Peche') of no. 659. The Pechie family were prominent in Soham in the seventeenth century.

[4] Will (as Buge), no. 659; Hall Street is still the main street in the north part of Soham.

824. [Fuller fol. 21v] JOHN DRAWSWERD of SNAILWELL ('Snaylwell') [*Cambs*], 6 November 1462

[*Commendation*: to God &c; *burial directions omitted*]; to the high altar of Snailwell half a quarter of barley; to the same church, for its reparation, the same.

To Thomas my son 6s 8d; to Richard my son the same.

To John Coole and Margaret his sister 13s 4d.

To John Drawswerd the usufruct[1] of 1½ acres of arable land for term of his life; and I wish my son Richard and his heirs to enjoy the possession of them; to the said John a small pan.

To each of my godchildren 2 bushels (*modios*) of barley.

Margaret my wife to have my messuage, together with the croft adjacent, so long as she lives; and after her death, it to be sold to provide a priest to celebrate for the faithful departed for a year if it can be done; and if not, for as long as the value of the same will stretch to, according to the discretion of the rector, William Brigeman, Richard Drawswerd, Richard Brigemen and 3 parishioners chosen by them. Richard my son to be given preference in the purchase of that messuage and within the price, before others, if he wants to buy it.

To my wife an acre of arable land, on condition that she, or whoever possesses the acre, keeps or sees kept in the future my anniversary [*and the anniversaries of*] my parents John and Marion, my brother Richard and his wife Emmot, on 14 November each year in the future, according to the custom of the said parish.

Residue of [*my*] goods, if any there be, to my execs, Margaret my wife and Richard my son.

Witnesses: John ?Lode, rector there, Richard Brigeman, John Coole and John Mason and others.

Proved at Fordham, 19 January 1462/63. Admon to execs.

[1] See Glossary.

825. [Fuller fol. 22] WILLIAM BRADSTRETE of LITTLE WHELNETHAM ('Qwelnetham Parva'),[1] 10 March 1462 [*?new style*][2]

['Bradstret' *in margin*] [*Commendation*: to God &c; *burial directions omitted*]; to the high altar of Whelnetham aforesaid 20d; to the fabric of the said church 3s 4d. To Joan my wife all my hostilments and utensils belonging to my house; also to her all my lands and tenements in the towns and fields of Whelnetham aforesaid, Great Whelnetham ('Welnetham Magna'), Rushbrooke ('Ruschbroke'), Bradfield St

George ('Bradfeld Monachorum') and Nowton, to hold to her and her heirs for term of her life; and after her death, I wish them to remain to Roger my son[3] and his heirs.
To a suitable chaplain 8 marks in money to celebrate for my soul and for the soul of Joan my wife and for all our benefactors for a whole year after my decease.
Residue of all my goods to Joan my wife, to receive, sell and dispose and pay my debts.
I beg all my feoffees to deliver full estate and seisin of and in all my lands and tenements as soon as requested, according to this will.
Execs: Joan my wife and Roger my son, to implement my will and pay all my debts as quickly as they can.
Supervisor: Thomas Drury of Rougham ('Rowgham').[4]
Proved at Fornham [St] Martin, 28 March 1462[sic]

[1]   Husband of Joan Bredstret of Little Whelnetham (no. 523); Redstone had transcribed her name as '*Johannes* Bredstret' but the register definitely says '*Joh'na* Bredstret' (Redstone, *PSIA*, xii, p.100).
[2]   The will is said to have been proved on 28 March 1462, so presumably the date of the will is 10 March 1462 in the new style, that is, not 1462/63.
[3]   Executor of his mother Joan (no. 523).
[4]   Lived *c*.1430–1486, son of Sir William Drury (Campling, *Drury Family*, p.96).

826. [Fuller fol. 22] SIMON WATTYS of SANTON DOWNHAM ('Downham'), 20 March 1463[sic] [?recte 1462, new style][1]

Of Downham by Brandon Ferry ('Brandonferi'); [*commendation*: to God &c; *burial directions omitted*]; to the high altar there 20d; to the profit of the parish church there 40d; to the gild of the Holy Trinity 2s 6d.[2]
To the sacrist of the monks of the monastery of St Edmund of Bury ('Buri') 6 wethers (*arietes*) to dispose according to his will.
To the gild of St Mary of Icklingham ('Ikelyngham') 4 wethers, to pray for the health of my soul;[3] to the gild of St Andrew of Elveden ('Helveden') 2 wethers.[4]
To the wife of Robert Turnour of Bury a ewe with her lamb.
To the wife of William Turnour of Bury a mother hogget (*unam hoggast' matrice'*).[5]
To each of my godsons and goddaughters a hogget, to pray for me.
To Isabel my wife the tenement in Elveden, standing between the tenement of John Colyng and the tenement of Laurence Gotche, for her whole life; after her death, the tenement to be sold for the best price that my execs can get, unless one of my sons wants to buy it.
Rest of my goods to the disposition of Isabel my wife and Gregory Skete, execs, to dispose for the health of my soul, my parents' and all my benefactors' [*souls*] as they see best to please God.
Proved at Fornham, 18 April 1462 [*sic*]. Admon to execs.

[1]   This will is said to have been proved on 18 April 1462, so presumably the year of the will should be 20 March 1461/62.
[2]   For the gild of the Trinity at Downham, see note to no. 777.
[3]   The gild of St Mary of Icklingham was also mentioned in the will of John Hardgrey, dated 1472 (*PSIA*, xxiii, p.62). For Icklingham the gild certificates of 1389 record the gild of the Holy Cross, founded in 1364, and the gild of St James, founded *c*.1362 (TNA, C47/426 and 427). A gild of St John at Icklingham was mentioned in 1504 (*PSIA*, xix, p.191).

⁴ John Flemyng of Elveden also made a bequest to the gild of St Andrew (no. 731). The gild is mentioned in the 1524 Lay Subsidy returns (*PSIA*, xix, p.183). Simon Wattys provides a good example of an individual supporting three gilds in three different parishes.

⁵ A contradiction in terms, since a hoggett was a castrated male sheep; perhaps 'a mother sheep'.

827. [Fuller fol. 22v] **HUGH BEDWELL of MILDENHALL ('Myldenhale'),** 15 April 1462

My testament containing my last will; [*commendation*: to God &c; *burial directions omitted*]; to the high altar of the said church of Mildenhall, for my tithes and offerings forgotten and withheld 2s; to the fabric of the said church 6d.

To Alice Bedwell my wife all my messuage with its appurtenances for term of her life; and after her death, the messuage with all its appurtenances to be sold by William Paget, or according to the discretion of his execs, as he or they see most expedient; if John Bedwell my son wishes to buy the messuage with its appurtenances, I wish him to be preferred at 20s under everyone else.

Residue of all my goods and chattels to William Pachet, exec, to dispose for my soul as seems to him best to please God and to profit the health of my soul.

Proved at Fornham, 10 May 1462. Admon to exec.

Bibliography

Badham, C., *The History and Antiquities of All Saints Church, Sudbury* (1852)

Bailey, M., 'The Sheep Accounts of Norwich Cathedral Priory, 1484 to 1534', in M. Bailey, M. Jurkowski and C. Rawcliffe (eds), *Poverty and Wealth: Sheep, Taxation and Charity in Late Medieval Norfolk* (Norfolk Record Society, lxxi, 2007)

Bailey, M., Jurkowski, M., and Rawcliffe, C. (eds), *Poverty and Wealth: Sheep, Taxation and Charity in Late Medieval Norfolk* (Norfolk Record Society, lxxi, 2007)

Bainbridge, V. R., *Gilds in the Medieval Countryside: Social and Religious Change in Cambridgeshire c.1350–1558* (1996)

Barber, P., 'What is a Peculiar?', *Ecclesiastical Law Journal*, 3, no. 16 (1995), pp.299–312

Bean, J. M. W., *The Decline of English Feudalism 1215–1540* (1968)

Beck, S. W., *The Draper's Dictionary* (n.d.)

Bell, P. L. (ed.), *Bedfordshire Wills 1484–1533* (Bedfordshire Historical Records Society, 76, 1997)

Betterton, A., and Dymond, D., *Lavenham: Industrial Town* (1989)

Blatchly, J., and Northeast, P., *Decoding Flint Flushwork on Suffolk and Norfolk Churches: A Survey of more than 90 Churches in the Two Counties where Devices and Inscriptions Challenge Interpretation* (SIAH, 2005)

Blatchly, J., and Northeast, P., 'The Lost and Ruined Parish Churches of Suffolk', in H. M. Cautley, *Suffolk Churches and their Treasures* (5th edn, 1982)

Blomefield, F., *An Essay towards a Topographical History of the County of Norfolk, continued by C. Parkin* (2nd edn, 11 vols, 1805–10)

Boatwright, L., Habberjam, M., and Hammond, P. (eds), *The Logge Register of PCC Wills, 1479 to 1486* (2 vols, Richard III Society, 2008)

Boccaccio, G., *see* Pognon, E.

Britnell R., and Hatcher, J. (eds), *Progress and Problems in Medieval England: Essays in Honour of Edward Miller* (1996)

Brown, R. D., *A Village Heritage: The History of England as Experienced by a Small Suffolk Community (Stoke-by-Clare, Clare and Neighbourhood)* (1993)

Bryant, T. H., *County Churches: Suffolk* (2 vols, 1912)

Burgess, C., '"A Fond Thing Vainly Invented": an Essay on Purgatory', in S. J. Wright (ed.), *Parish, Church and People* (1985)

Burkholder, K. M., 'Threads Bared: Dress and Textiles in Late Medieval English Wills', in R. Netherton and G. R. Owen-Crocker (eds), *Medieval Clothing and Textiles*, i (2005)

Butler, H. E. (ed.), *The Chronicle of Jocelin of Brakelond* (1949)

Caley, J., and Hunter, J. (eds), *Calendarium Inquisitionum Post Mortem sive Escaetarum* (4 vols, 1806–28)

Caley, J., and Hunter, J. (eds), *Valor Ecclesiasticus temp. Hen. VIII* (6 vols, 1810–34)

Camp, A. J., *Wills and their Whereabouts* (1963)

Campling, A., *The History of the Family of Drury* (1937)

Catholic Encyclopedia (8 vols, 1905–1914) (online version)

Cautley, H. M., *Suffolk Churches and their Treasures* (5th edn, 1982)

Cheney, C. R., *Handbook of Dates for Students of English History* (1981 edn)

Clay, J. W. (ed.), *The Visitations of Cambridge* (Harleian Society, xli, 1897)

Clay, R. M., *The Hermits and Anchorites of England* (1914)

Colman, S., 'Inscribed Tiles in the Church of St Mary, Ickworth', *PSIA*, xxxvii (1989), pp.13–17

Cooper, T. (ed.), *The Journal of William Dowsing: Iconoclasm in East Anglia during the English Civil War* (Ecclesiological Society, 2001)

Copinger, W. A., *The Manors of Suffolk* (7 vols, 1905–11)

Cowen, P., *A Guide to Stained Glass in Britain* (1985)

Cox, N. C., and Cox, J. J., 'Probate 1500–1800: a System in Transition', in T. Arkell, N. Evans and N. Goose, *When Death Do Us Part: Understanding and Interpreting the Probate Records of Early Modern England* (2000)

Cox, N. C., and Cox, J. J., 'Probate Inventories: the Legal Background', *The Local Historian*, 16 (1984)

Crawford, A. (ed.), *The Household Books of John Howard, Duke of Norfolk, 1462–1471, 1481–1483* (1992)

Crosby, A., *A History of Thetford* (1986)

Cross, F. L., *The Oxford Dictionary of the Christian Church* (1974)

Dalton, O. M., 'The Five Wounds of Our Lord', *Proceedings of the Society of Antiquaries*, xxiii (1911), pp.340–44

Davis, R. C., *Christian Slaves, Muslim Masters: White Slavery in the Mediterranean, the Barbary Coast, and Italy, 1500–1800* (2003)

Descriptive Catalogue of Ancient Deeds in the Public Record Office, 6 vols (1890–1915)

Duffy, E., *The Stripping of the Altars: Traditional Religion in England, c.1400–c.1580* (1992)

Duncan, L. L., *Index of Wills Proved in the Rochester Consistory Court between 1440 and 1561* (Kent Archaeological Society, Records Branch, ix, 1924)

Dyer, C., 'Taxation and Communities in Late Medieval England', in R. Britnell and J. Hatcher (eds), *Progress and Problems in Medieval England: Essays in Honour of Edward Miller* (1996)

Dyer, C., 'The English Medieval Village Community and its Decline', *Journal of British Studies*, 33 (1994), pp.407–29

Dymond, D., 'Chapels-of-Ease and the Case of Botesdale', in A. Longcroft and R. Joby (eds), *East Anglian Studies* (1995)

Dymond, D., 'God's Disputed Acre', *Journal of Ecclesiastical History*, 50 (1999), pp.464–97

Dymond, D., *The Churchwardens' Book of Bassingbourn, Cambridgeshire, 1496–c.1540* (Cambridgeshire Records Society, 17, 2004)

Dymond, D., *The Parish Churches of Stanton, Suffolk* (1977)

Dymond, D., and Martin, E. (eds), *An Historical Atlas of Suffolk* (1999)

Dymond, D., and Payne, C., *The Spoil of Melford Church: The Reformation in a Suffolk Parish* (1992)

Edwards, A. C., *Essex Monasteries* (Essex Record Office publications, 41, 1964)

Emden, A. B., *Biographical Register of the University of Cambridge* (1963)

Emden, A. B., *Biographical Register of the University of Oxford* (3 vols, 1957–59)

Evans, J. (ed.), *The Flowering of the Middle Ages* (1985)

Evans, N. (ed.), *Wills of the Archdeaconry of Sudbury 1630–1635* (SRS, xxix, 1987)

Farnhill, K., *Guilds and the Parish Community in Late Medieval East Anglia, c.1470–1550* (2001)

Farrow, M. A., *Index to Wills Proved in the Consistory Court of Norwich, 1370–1550* (3 vols, Norfolk Record Society, London, 1943–45)

Fisher, J. L., *Medieval Farming Glossary of Latin and English Words* (2nd edn, revised A. and R. Powell, Essex Record Office, 1997)

Fryde, E. B., *et al.* (eds), *Handbook of British Chronology* (1986)

Furnivall, F. J. (ed.), *Political, Religious and Love Poems* (EETS, original series, xv, 1866)

Furnivall, F. J., *The Fifty Earliest English Wills in the Court of Probate, London* (EETS, original series, lxxviii, 1882)

Galpin, F. W., 'The Abbey Church and Claustral Buildings of Tilty', *TEAS*, new series, 18 (1928), pp.89–95

Gibbons, A., *Early Lincoln Wills* (1888)

Grimwood, C. G., and Kay, S. A., *History of Sudbury, Suffolk* (1952)

Growse, F. S., *Collections for a History of the Parish of Bildeston* (1892)

Halliwell, J. O., *A Dictionary of Archaic and Provincial Words* (2 vols, 1847)

Hamilton-Thompson, A., 'Diocesan Organization in the Middle Ages: Archdeacons and Rural Deans', *Proceedings of the British Academy*, xxix (1943), pp.153–94

Hanawalt, B. A., 'Keepers of the Lights: Late Medieval English Parish Gilds', *Journal of Medieval and Renaissance Studies*, 14 (1984), pp.21–37

Hasted, E., *The History and Topographical Survey of the County of Kent* (2nd edn, 7 vols, 1798)

Hervy, W., *The Visitation of Suffolk, 1561*, transcribed and ed. J. Corder (Harleian Society, n.s. ii, iii, 1981, 1984)

Hey, D., *The Oxford Companion to Local and Family History* (1996)

Hindle, S., *The State and Social Change in Early Modern England, c.1550–1640* (2000)

Horrox, R., *Richard III: A Study in Service* (1989)

Hutchins, J., *History and Antiquities of the County of Dorset* (3rd edn, Westminster, 1873)

Hutton, R., *The Rise and Fall of Merry England: The Ritual Year 1400–1700* (1994)

Jacob, E. F. (ed.), *The Register of Henry Chichele*, ii: *Wills Proved before the Archbishop or his Commissaries* (1938)

Jocelin: *see* Butler, H. E.

Jurkowski, M., 'Income Tax Assessments of Norwich, 1472 and 1489', in M. Bailey, M. Jurkowski and C. Rawcliffe (eds), *Poverty and Wealth: Sheep, Taxation and Charity in Late Medieval Norfolk* (Norfolk Record Society, lxxi, 2007)

Jurkowski, M., Smith, C. L., and Crook, D., *Lay Taxes in England and Wales 1188–1688* (1998)

Keene, D. J., and Harding, V. (eds), *Historical Gazetteer of London before the Great Fire: Cheapside; Parishes of All Hallows Honey Lane, St Martin Pomary, St Mary le Bow, St Mary Colechurch and St Pancras Soper Lane* (1987)

Kendall, H. P., *The Story of Whitby Jet* (1936)

Knowland, L. (ed.), *Samuel Dove's Debenham* (1986)

Knowles, D., and Hadcock, R. N., *Medieval Religious Houses: England and Wales* (1971)

Latham, R. E. (ed.), *Revised Medieval Latin Word-List* (1965)

Le Goff, J., *The Birth of Purgatory* (trans. A. Goldhammer, 1984)

Lepine, D., and Orme, N. (eds), *Death and Memory in Medieval Exeter* (Devon and Cornwall Record Society, 46, 2003)

Letters and Papers, Foreign and Domestic, of the reign of Henry VIII, 1509–1547, 21 vols (1864–1920)

Lock, R. (ed.), *The Court Rolls of Walsham le Willows 1303–1350*, SRS, xli (1998)

Longcroft, A., and Joby, R. (eds), *East Anglian Studies* (1995)

Martin, J., 'Ecclesiastical Jurisdictions', in D. Dymond and E. Martin (eds), *An Historical Atlas of Suffolk* (1999)

May, P., *Newmarket: Medieval and Tudor* (1982)

McCann, J., *The Dovecotes of Suffolk* (SIAH, 1998)

Middle English Dictionary (in progress, 1956–)

Middleton-Stewart, J., *Inward Purity and Outward Splendour: Death and Remembrance in the Deanery of Dunwich, Suffolk, 1370–1547* (2001)

Milward, R., *A Glossary of Household, Farming and Trade Terms from Probate Inventories* (Derbyshire Record Society, 3rd edn, 1986)

Morley, C., 'Catalogue of Beneficed Clergy of Suffolk, 1086–1550', *PSIA*, xxii (1936), pp.29–85

Morley, C., 'Check-list of the Sacred Buildings of Suffolk to which are added Gilds', *PSIA*, xix (1926), pp.168–211

Muskett, J. J., *Suffolk Manorial Families* (3 vols, 1900–14)

Netherton, R., and Owen-Crocker, G. R. (eds), *Medieval Clothing and Textiles*, i (2005)

Nicolas, N. H., *Testamenta Vetusta* (2 vols, 1826)

Northeast, P. (ed.), *Boxford Churchwardens' Accounts, 1530–1561*, SRS, xxiii (1982)

Northeast, P., 'Moving the Signposts: Changes in the Dedication of Suffolk Churches after the Reformation', in A. Longcroft and R. Joby (eds), *East Anglian Studies* (1995)

Northeast, P., 'Parish Gilds', in D. Dymond and E. Martin (eds), *An Historical Atlas of Suffolk* (1999)

Northeast, P., 'Religious Houses', in D. Dymond and E. Martin (eds), *An Historical Atlas of Suffolk* (1999)

Northeast, P., *Wills of the Archdeaconry of Sudbury, 1439–1474. Wills from the Register 'Baldwyne', part I: 1439–1461,* SRS xliv (2001)

O'Day, R., 'The Role of the Registrar in Diocesan Administration', in R. O'Day and F. Heal (eds), *Continuity and Change* (1976), pp.77–94

O'Day, R., and Heal, F. (eds), *Continuity and Change* (1976)

Olorenshaw, J. R., *Notes on Gedding, County Suffolk* (1905)

Olorenshaw, J. R., *Notes on the Church of St Andrew, Soham, Cambridgeshire* (1905)

Orme, N. (ed.), *Cornish Wills 1342–1540* (Devon and Cornwall Record Society, 50, 2007)

Orme, N., *Education and Society in Medieval and Renaissance England* (1989)

Orme, N., *English Church Dedications, with a Survey of Cornwall and Devon* (1996)

Owen, A. E. B., 'A Scrivener's Notebook from Bury St Edmunds', *Archives*, xiv (1979), pp.16–22

Owen, D., *Church and Society in Medieval Lincolnshire* (1971)

Oxford Dictionary of National Biography (2004, online version)

Oxford English Dictionary (2nd edn, online version)

Paine, C., 'The Building of Long Melford Church', in C. Sansbury (ed.), *A Sermon in Stone: The 500th Anniversary Book of Long Melford Church* (1983)

Paine, C., 'The Chapel and Well of Our Lady of Woolpit', *PSIA*, xxxviii (1996), pp.8–11

Palmer, W. M., 'The Village Gilds of Cambridgeshire', *PCHAS*, i (1902), pp.330–402

Peacock, E., *English Church Furniture, Ornaments and Decorations at the Period of the Reformation* (1866)

Pevsner, N. (rev. E. Radcliffe), *The Buildings of England: Suffolk* (1974)

Pfaff, R. W., *New Liturgical Feasts in Later Medieval England* (1970)

Pfaff, R. W., 'The English Devotion of St Gregory's Trental', *Speculum*, xlix (1974), pp.75–90

Platt, C., *The Parish Churches of Medieval England* (1981)

Pognon, E. (trans. J. P. Tallon), *Boccaccio's Decameron* (1978)

Purvis, J. S., *Dictionary of Ecclesiastical Terms* (1962)

Purvis, J. S., *Notarial Signs* (1957)

Raine, J. (ed.), *Testamenta Eboracensia*, Pt I (Surtees Society, iv, 1836)

Rawcliffe, C., *Leprosy in Medieval England* (2006)

Rawcliffe, C., *Medicine for the Soul: The Life, Death and Resurrection of an English Medieval Hospital, St Giles's, Norwich, c.1249–1550* (1999)

Raymond, S. A., *Words from Wills and Other Probate Records* (2004)

Reaney, P. H., *The Place-names of Cambridgeshire* (1943)

Redstone, V. B. (ed.), *Calendar of Pre-Reformation Wills, Testaments, Administrations Registered at the Probate Office, Bury St Edmunds* (1907); also bound in with *PSIA*, xii (1906)

Redstone, V. B., 'Chapels, Chantries and Gilds in Suffolk', *PSIA*, xii (1904), pp.1–87 and xxiii (1937), pp.50–78

Richardson, J., *Local Historian's Encyclopedia* (1986)

Rickett, R., and Rose, E., 'Monastic Houses', in P. Wade-Martins (ed.), *An Historical Atlas of Norfolk* (1993)

Roberts, E., and Parker, K. (eds), *Southampton Probate Inventories, 1447–1575* (2 vols, Southampton Records Series, xxxiv, 1992)

Robinson, J., *Boxford: A Miscellany* (1998)

Rock, D. (ed. G. W. Hart and W. H. Frere), *Church of Our Fathers* (4 vols, 1903–4)

Rossetti, W. M., 'Notes on the Stacyons of Rome', in F. J. Furnival (ed.), *Political, Religious and Love Poems* (EETS, original series, xv, 1866), pp.xxi–xlv

Rye, W., *Norfolk Families* (1913)

Salzman, L. F., *Building in England down to 1540* (1952)

Sansbury, C. (ed.), *A Sermon in Stone: The 500th Anniversary Book of Long Melford Church* (1983)

Slack, P., *Poverty and Policy in Tudor and Stuart England* (1988)

Sperling, C. F. D., *A Short History of the Borough of Sudbury, in the County of Suffolk, compiled from materials collected by W. W. Hodson* (1896)

Storrs, C. M., *Jacobean Pilgrims from England to St James of Compostella from the Early Twelfth to the Late Fifteenth Century* (1994)

Swanson, R. N., *Catholic England: Faith, Religion and Observance before the Reformation* (1993)

Tate, W. E., *The Parish Chest: A Study of the Records of Parochial Administration in England* (1969)

Taylor, R. C., *Index Monasticus; or The Abbeys* [etc] *Established in the Diocese of Norwich* (1821)

Thomas, G., 'Local Government since 1872', in D. Dymond and E. Martin (eds), *An Historical Atlas of Suffolk* (1999)

Thurston, H., 'A Mediaeval Mortuary-Card', *The Month*, lxxxviii (1896), pp.473–93

Thurston, H., 'Benediction of the Blessed Sacrament: The Benediction', *The Month*, xcviii (1901), pp.186–93

Torlesse, C. M., *Some Account of Stoke by Nayland* (1877)

Tymms, S., *Wills and Inventories from the Registers of the Commissary of Bury St Edmunds and the Archdeacon of Sudbury* (Camden Society, xlix, 1850)

Victoria County History, Cambridgeshire, ii (1948), x (2002) (online version)

Victoria County History, Essex, ii (1907) (online version)

Victoria County History, Kent, ii (1926) (online version)

Victoria County History, London (1909) (online version)

Victoria County History, Middlesex, i (1969) (online version)

Victoria County History, Norfolk, ii (1906) (online version)

Victoria County History, Suffolk, ii (1975) (online version)

Virgoe, R., 'The Will of Hugh atte Fenne', in *A Miscellany* (Norfolk Record Society, lvi, 1993)

Wade-Martins, P. (ed.), *An Historical Atlas of Norfolk* (1993)

Walcott, M. E. C., 'Parish Churches before the Reformation', in *Reports and Papers of Associated Architectural Societies*, xv (1879), pp.79–120

Watkin, A. (ed.), 'Objects Recorded in the Inventories', in *Inventory of Church Goods temp. Edward III*, Pt II (Norfolk Record Society, 1948)

Way, A. (ed.), *Promptorium Parvulorum sive Clericorum* (3 vols, Camden Society, 1843–65)

Weever, J., *Antient Funeral Monuments* (2nd edn, 1767)

Whittingham, A. B., *Bury St Edmunds Abbey, Suffolk* (1971)

Wright, S. J. (ed.), *Parish, Church and People* (1985)

Yaxley, D. (ed.), *A Researcher's Glossary of Words Found in Historical Documents of East Anglia* (2003)

Yaxley, D., *The Prior's Manor-Houses* (1988)

Zell, M. L., 'Fifteenth- and Sixteenth-century Wills as Historical Sources', *Archives*, xiv (1979), pp.67–74

Wills of the Archdeaconry of Suffolk
'Baldwyne' Parts I and II

Although full indexes are necessary for readers to make best use of volumes such as this, it should be noted that it has not been possible to supply detailed indexes here. However, we are including two indexes to Parts I and II: firstly, an index of testators, including their place of residence; secondly, an index of the place of residence of testators. Full indexes to Part I, which Peter constructed after that book was published, are available on the Suffolk Records Society's website, in the Publications section, under Volume 44, *Wills of the Archdeaconry of Sudbury, Part I*. It is hoped that a full index to Part II will also be available, eventually, on the same website. There are plans to publish the indexes as a supplementary SRS volume, as and when funds permit.

Index of Testators

All numbers refer to entries, not pages, in the two Suffolk Records Society volumes (44 and 53). Those numbers in Normal Font refer entries that are testaments and/or wills together with the probate sentence, where it has been added; those in *Italic Font* refer to entries that are solely probate sentences. The Roman numerals I and II denote the two volumes; both begin at number 1.

Abbot (Abbott): Nicholas, of Chelsworth, II, 267
    Ralph, of Thorpe, I, 1328
Abell: John, of Thurston, II, 548
    Richard, of Stowmarket, II, 103
    William, of Elmswell, I, *1199*; of Pakenham, I, *514*
Abthorp: *see* Clare *alias* Abthorp
Adam: John, of Haverhill, II, 14
    William, of Withersfield, II, 420
Adgor: John, of Old Newton, I, 340; the elder, of Combs, I, 609
Agace (Agas): John, of Barningham, I, 159
    Robert, of Barningham, I, 889; of Thurston, II, 414
    Roger, of Bardwell, II, 364
Albon: John, of Soham (Cambs), II, *749*
Albred: John, of Fornham, I, *1099*
Aleyn: Joan, of Bildeston, I, *1141*
    John, of Groton, I, 1388
    William, of Sudbury, I, 717
Alfey: John, of Cavendish, I, 83
Alger: Robert, of Lavenham, I, *1114*
    William, of Stoke by Clare, I, *1185*
Allote: John, of Occold, I, *250*
Almere: William, of Silverley (Cambs), I, *1029*
Alston: Richard, of Fornham All Saints, I, *994*
    Thomas, of Sudbury, II, *290*
Alunday: William, of Kedington, I, 1094
Alyesawndre: John, of Rushbrooke, II, 558
Anable: Thomas, of Hargrave, II, 297

Andrew (Andru, Andrw): John, of Hawkedon, II, 780; John, of Ousden, II, 696; the elder, of Eye, I, 58
    Richard, of Bures, I, *1335*; of Hawkedon, I, 1203
    Simon, of Brockford in Wetheringsett, I, 721
Angold: John, of Fornham All Saints, II, 58
    William, of Hengrave, I, 61
Aniys: Richard, of Wetheringsett, I, 345
Anows *alias* Smyth: Thomas, of Botesdale in Redgrave, I, *442*
Appylthorp: Isabel, of Troston, I, *1019*
Apylthweyt (Apylweyt): Henry, of Stoke Ash, I, *223*; I, 285
Archer: John, of Lavenham, I, 446; I, 661
Arford: Mary, of Hawstead, I, *100*
Arnold: Thomas, of Old Newton, I, 1419
Artur: Geoffrey, of Wattisham, I, 1346
Aspy: [*not given*], of [*not given*], II, 730
Astlot: John, of Sudbury, I, 127
Aston: Thomas, of Woodditton (Cambs), II, 580
Asty: Peter, of Market Weston, I, 295
At Fen (Atte Fen): William, of Glemsford, I, *644*
At Herne (Atherne, Att Herne): Andrew, 'bocher', of Icklingham St James, II, 72; 'bochere', of Icklingham, II, 403
    William, of Bardwell, I, 858
At Hyll: Joan, of Long Melford, I, *1004*
At Lee *alias* Hurlebate: William, of Assington, II, 370

515

At Mere (At the Mere, Atte Mere): Isabel,
widow, of Sudbury, I, 539
William, of Cavenham, I, 387
At Wood (Attewoode): Adam, of Great
Waldingfield, I, 186
Aubry: [not given], of Woolpit, II, 786
see also Avbre
Auncell: Thomas, the younger, of Stanstead, II,
614
Austyn: John, of Fornham St Martin, I, 849; I,
1152
William, of Thorney in Stowmarket, I, 408
Avbre: John, of Woodditton, II, 630
Avelyn: Robert, of Thrandeston, I, 973
Avenant: Thomas, of Thrandeston, I, 1317
Aves: Robert, of Exning, II, 428
Awnselme: Henry, of Wyverstone, I, 1402; I,
1408
Aylmer: John, of Thelnetham, II, 437
Aylnoth: John, of Burwell, I, 237
Aynoth: John, of Hundon, II, 160

Bacon (Bacown, Bakoun): John, of Haughley, I,
1406; smith, of Brent Eleigh, II, 300
Stephen, of Hessett, I, 232
Bacot: Ed', of Sudbury, I, 593
see also Baghot and Bakhot
Baculer: John, of Thorndon, I, 242
Badey: [not given], of [not given], I, 635
Baff: Stephen, of Thelnetham, I, 1186
Baghot: Robert, of Icklingham, II, 683
see also Bacot and Bakhot
Baker (Bakere): Alice, widow, of Elmswell, I,
397
Geoffrey, of Stradishall, I, 571
Isabel, widow, of Weston Market, II, 822
John, of Badwell Ash, I, 339; of Cavendish,
II, 224; of Culford, II, 227; of Glemsford,
II, 751; of Stowmarket St Peter, II, 201; of
Wetherden, II, 573
Robert, of Stanton, II, 739
William, of Clare, I, 149
Bakhot: John, of Mildenhall, II, 229; II, 287
William, mercer, of Mildenhall, I, 1481
see also Bacot and Baghot
Bakke: Margaret, wife of John & heir of Andrew
Pakenham, of Combs, I, 877
Baldewyn: John, of Thrandeston, I, 71; I, 199
Baldre: Geoffrey, of Barningham, I, 1225
John, of Thorney in Stowmarket, I, 444; I, 577
Richard, of Thorney in Stowmarket, II, 673
William, of [not given], I, 230; of Creeting All
Saints, I, 309; of Thornham Parva, I, 811
Baldwyn: Mariota, widow, of Assington, II, 458
Ballard: Henry, of Kettlebaston, II, 455
Ballard alias Canown: John, of Wickhambrook,
I, 1450
Balle: John, of Hitcham, II, 444

Balley: Simon, of Little Whelnetham, II, 130
Balsham: Thomas, of Little Thurlow, I, 1490
Baly: Thomas, of Hanchyche in Withersfield, II,
692
see also Bayle and Tregegold alias Baly
Barbour (Barbore): Agnes, of Ixworth, I, 1072
Alan, of Lavenham, I, 73
John, of Redgrave, II, 418
Richard, of Clare, II, 46
Stephen, of Sudbury, II, 408
Walter, of Boxford, I, 144
see also Smyth alias Barbour
Baret: Nicholas, of Fornham All Saints, I, 222
Barker (Barkare, Barkere): Agnes, widow of
John, of Clare, I, 64
Beatrice, of Long Melford, I, 1208
John, of Brent Eleigh, I, 375; of Clare, I, 43;
of Cowlinge, II, 490; of Thelnetham, I,
1262; the elder, fuller, of Long Melford, I,
1064
Nicholas, of Ickworth, II, 138
Robert, of Eye, I, 105
Rose, of Lavenham, I, 570
Thomas, of Little Horringer, I, 422; of,
Hundon, II, 301; of, Thelnetham, II, 820
Walter, of Bildeston, I, 592
see also Mychill alias Barker
Barleston: John, of Hepworth, I, 353
Barnard: John, of [not given], I, 1151
Baron (Barown): John, of Bildeston, I, 744
Thomas, of Hitcham, I, 820; I, 1013
William, of Newmarket, I, 28
Barough: John, gentleman, of Bardwell, I, 583
Basse: Nicholas, of Rickinghall Inferior, II, 367
Baxster (Baxstere): John, of Eye, I, 972
Peter, of Hundon, II, 42
William, of Stanton, II, 666
Bayle: John, of Hanchet in Haverhill, II, 357
see also Baly
Beche: John, of Soham (Cambs), I, 691
Bedwell: Hugh, of Mildenhall, II, 827
Beere: Margaret, of Lavenham, II, 237
Bekysby: Walter, of Thorpe Morieux, I, 1244
Belamy: Robert, of Boxted, I, 1006
William, of Tuddenham, I, 1460
Belcham: John, of Kersey, I, 1212
Belcher: John, of Rickinghall, I, 989
Belle: Thomas, of Haughley, I, 174
Belman: Isabel, of Hitcham, I, 791
Bemay: William, of Combs, I, 145
Beneyt: John, of Thornham Magna, I, 1; I, 338
Benne: John, of Troston, I, 694
Bensele: [not given], of [not given], I, 486
Bensty: William, of Herringswell, II, 485
Berard: William, of Knettishall, II, 394
Berde: John, of Dalham, I, 850
Bere: Isabel, of Norton, I, 1313
Thomas, of Norton, I, 438; I, 441

Berehors: Richard, of Fordham (Cambs), I, *94*
Bernard: William, of Thurston, II, 606
Bernardeston: Henry, of Kedington, II, 447
Berne: Thomas, of Felsham, I, 613
Berner (Bernere): John, of Long Melford, I,
      1160; of Stoke by Nayland, II, 197; the
      elder, of Stoke by Nayland, I, 992
Bertlot: John, of Wickham Skeith, I, 24
Berweham: Adam, of Barningham, II, 452
   Agnes, wife of John, of Barningham, I, 1247
   John, of Barningham, I, *1226*
Bete (Betty): John, of Harleston, I, 497
   Margaret, of Sapiston, I, *1137*
Bettes (Bettis, Betes, Betys): Alice, of Badwell
      Ash, II, 527
   Amice, of Pakenham, I, *956*
   John, of Sapiston, I, 464
   Marion, of Harleston, I, *862*
   Robert, of Burgate, I, 787
   William, of Pakenham, I, 821
Bevereche: John, of Sudbury, I, 805
Bird: John, the elder, of Lavenham, II, 552
Blak: Robert, of Fornham St Martin, I, 45
Blake: Thomas, of Barton Mills, II, 717
Blakgroom: John, of Sudbury, I, *26*
Blaksale: Alan, of Bures, I, *477*
   John, of Naughton, I, *745*
Blome (Bloome): Richard, of Ixworth, II, 174; of
      Rattlesden, I, *747*
   Stephen, of Cockfield, II, 540
Blowere: Thomas, of Bildeston, II, 285
Blunte: Alexander, of Wiston, I, *685*
Blyawnt: Simon, of Thornham Magna, I, 1169
Blythe: Alexander, of Stowmarket, I, *999*
Boc: John, of Wetheringsett, I, 641
Bochard: John, of Barnardiston, I, *536*
Bocher (Bochere): Joan, of Stansfield, I, *835*
   John, of Haughley, I, 741
   William, of Chelsworth, I, *559*
   see also Hecham *alias* Bochere
Bocher *alias* Grondysborgh: Thomas, of
      Stansfield, I, 507
Bockyng: Thomas, the elder, of Boxford, II, 332
Bode: John, of Tostock, I, 836
Bogays: Agnes, widow, of Edwardstone, II, 352
   Thomas, of Edwardstone, I, *1455*
Bokeham: Alice, widow of John, gentleman, of
      Hawstead, I, 493
Bokenham: John, of Fornham All Saints, I, *950*
Bokyll: John, of Elmswell, I, *1338*
Boldiroo (Boldyroo): Ed', of Rougham, I, *584*
   Joan, of Hessett, I, *364*
   Richard, of Hessett, II, 113
Bole: John, of Little Livermere, I, 684; of
      Wetherden, I, 394
   Stephen, of Combs, I, 601
Boleman: Joan, of Rattlesden, I, 146
Bolowre: John, of Thwaite, II, 218

Bolton: John, of Lavenham, I, 298
Bolyngton: William, of Glemsford, I, 319
Bonde: Joan, of Tostock, II, 435
   John, of Fornham St Martin, I, 359; of
      Walsham, II, 562
   Simon, of Walsham le Willows, I, *1042*
Boner *alias* Jerweys: Ralph, of Barton Mills, I,
      131
Bonsergeaunt: Adam, of Pakenham, II, *167*
Bonyffaunte: Thomas, the elder, of Burwell
      (Cambs), I, 389
Boole: Edmund, of Great Livermere, II, 134
   Henry, of Little Livermere, I, 304
   Isabel, of Little Livermere, II, 129
   Margaret, widow of Richard, of Timworth, I,
      749
   Richard, of Timworth, I, 305
   William, of Timworth, I, 594
Bootre: Isabel, of [*not given*], I, *262*
Borle: John, of Sudbury, I, 800
Boteld: John, of Sudbury, I, 667
Botelere: John, of Palgrave, II, 221
Boter: William of Tuddenham, I, *1470*
Bothe: Henry, of Shelland, II, 697
Boton: William, of Little Waldingfield, I, 582
Botwright (Botwryght): John, of Lakenheath, II,
      384; II, 399
Bowe: John, of Nayland, I, *909*
Bownde: John, of Lavenham, I, 511
Bowne: Katherine, relict of Thomas, of
      Mildenhall, II, 768
   Margaret, of [*not given*], II, 15; widow of
      William, of Ixworth, I, *280*
Bowre: William, of Barnham, I, *1235*
Bowyere: John, of [*not given*], II, *249*
Box: William, of Hitcham, I, *978*
Boxsted: John, of Sudbury, I, 62
Boyes (Boys): John, of Sudbury, I, *602*
   William, of Tuddenham, II, 243
Braby: Margaret, of Elmsett, II, *71*
Bradstrete (Bredstret): Joan, of Little
      Whelnetham, II, 523
   William, of Little Whelnetham, II, 825
Brakstret: John, of Wickham Skeith, I, 1273
Bray: Alice, relict of John, of Barnham, II, 699
   John, of Gazeley, II, 82; of Nayland, II, 761;
      of Rougham, I, 1345
Braybrook: William, of Poslingford, I, 1190
Bredge: Agnes, of Bottisham (Cambs), I, 1398
Bregge: William, of Hanchet in Haverhill, II,
      693; of Stoke by Clare, I, 1382
Brende: Simon, of Felsham, I, *1452*
Brendwod: John, of Thorndon, I, 962
Breon: John, 'bocher', of Little Waldingfield, II,
      349; the elder, of Sudbury, I, 398
Breton: Richard, of Rickinghall Inferior, I, 900
Brett (Bret, Brette): John, of Preston, I, *1124*
   Richard, of Stanningfield, I, 531

William, of Nayland, II, 784
Brightewell: Richard, of Gazeley, I, 303
Brock (Brok, Broke): John, of Walsham le
    Willows, I, 169
  Margaret, wife of John, of Langham, I, 8
  Reginald, of Rickinghall Superior, II, 253
  see also Brook
Brodok: Stephen, of, Ousden, I, 449
Brokhole (Brokhoole): John, of Long Melford,
    II, 363
  Thomas, of Long Melford, II, 45
Bron: William, of Fornham St Martin, II, 705
Brond (Broond): John, elder, of Groton, II, 117
  Richard, of Kedington, I, *528*
Brondyssh: William, of Felsham, II, 369
Brook: Alice, of Sudbury, II, 596
  John, the elder, weaver, of Sudbury, I, 1168
  see also Brock
Brounewyn: Thomas, of Wetheringsett, I, 1023
Brouston: Isabel, of Stanton, I, *1130*
Brown (Broun): John, of Hopton, I, 723; of
    Pakenham, I, *1378*; of Wortham, II, 170;
    carpenter, of Sudbury I, 1132
  Marion, of Hopton, I, 1026
  Thomas, of Palgrave, I, *1350*
Brownyng: Richard, of Haverhill, II, 678
Browster (Brouuster): Agnes, of Bildeston, II,
    360
  John, of Bildeston, II, 359, *360*; of Somerton,
    I, 216
  Robert, of Lavenham, I, 329
Brunwyn (Brwnwyn): Robert, of Mendlesham,
    II, 788; of Wetheringsett, II, 559
Bryan (Bryon): John, of Long Melford, I, *668*
  Richard, of Preston, I, *761*
  Thomas, of Nayland, II, 549
Bryche: Geoffrey, of Haughley, I, 1307
Bryggeman (Brygman): John, of Burwell
    (Cambs), II, 551
  Richard, of Snailwell (Cambs), I, *505*
Brygh: [*not given*], of [*not given*], I, *500*
Brygth (Bryth): John, of Long Melford, II, 52
  Robert, of Alpheton, I, *1106*
Brynkely: Thomas, husbandman, of Kedington,
    I, 681
Brystowe: Thomas, of Exning, I, 995
Bug (Buge, Bugge): John, of Soham (Cambs),
    II, 659
  Thomas, of Soham (Cambs), I, 1325
  William, of Soham (Cambs), II, 823
Bullebrook: Edith, of Whepstead, II, 135
Bullok: John, of Risby, I, 1210; of Woolpit, I,
    757
Bullyngton: John, of Long Melford, I, *1051*
Bulney: Roger, of Long Melford, I, 195
Bunne: Isabel, of Little Whelnetham, I, *525*
  John, of Little Whelnetham, II, 93
  William, of Elmsett, I, 1427

Buntyng: John, of Tostock, I, 133
  Richard, of Tostock, II, 821
Burteyn: Richard, of Soham (Cambs), I, 1298
Burwe (Borwe): Robert, of Hundon, II, 79
Burwell: John, of Kirtling (Cambs), I, 881
Bury: John, of Kersey, I, *1184*
Bussh: Geoffrey, of Mendlesham, II, 202
  Richard, of Mendlesham, I, *1482*
Bygge: John, of Mildenhall, I, 569
Bynd: John, of Little Thurlow, I, *567*
Byrd: Robert, of Stowmarket, II, 645
  Stephen, husbandman, of Kersey, II, 595
Byrlyngham: John, of Botesdale, II, 257
Bysse: Walter, of Assington, I, 176
Byssop: Geoffrey, of Nayland, I, *666*

Cabaw (Cabow, Cabowe): John, of Woolpit, I,
    823
  Margaret, of Hitcham, I, 1234; of Woolpit, I,
    508
  Thomas, of Hitcham, I, 110; I, 177; II, 806
Cade: Agnes, of Stuston, I, *1163*
Cage (Cagge): John, of Rickinghall Superior, I,
    1334
  Peter, of Wattisfield, I, *1377*
  Richard, of Cavendish, II, 574
  William, of Whepstead, I, 160
Cake: Elizabeth, wife of Robert, of Stowmarket,
    II, 689
  John, of Mendlesham, I, 1315; II, 818
  Thomas, of Mildenhall, I, 1009
Cake *alias* Reve: Isabel, of Mildenhall, II, 172;
    II, 177
Cakestrete: John, of Poslingford, I, *524*
Calabyr: John, of Pakenham, I, 1287
Caldewell: John, the elder, turner, of Thelnetham,
    II, 703
Calew (Calwe): Roger, of Burwell (Cambs), II,
    509
  William, of Barrow, I, 187
Calffe (Calve): John, of Little Waldingfield, I, 92
  Richard, of Westhorpe, II, 775
Calle: Simon, of Little Waldingfield, II, 30
Calvysban (Calvysbane): John, of Burwell
    (Cambs), II, 632
  Thomas, of Burwell (Cambs), II, 512
Caly: John, of Great Ashfield, I, 1249; of Kersey,
    I, 1227; of Norton, I, 1465
Camplyon *alias* Wryght: John, of Stowmarket,
    I, 711
Campyon: William, of Icklingham, I, 603
Candeler: Robert, of Botesdale in Redgrave, I,
    971
Canown: *see* Ballard *alias* Canown
Cansoham: John, of Cheveley (Cambs), I, *625*
Capell: Agnes, of Brockford in Wetheringsett,
    I, 764
  John, of Stoke by Nayland, I, 365

Cappe: Thomas, of Eye, I, *1316*
Carles: John, of Sudbury, II, 212
Carter (Carteer, Cartere, Kartere): Henry, of
Sudbury, I, 326
Isabel, of Hitcham, I, *1066*
Joan, of Old Newton, II, 529
John, of Mellis, I, 1097
Katherine, of Acton, I, 1385
Roger, of Long Melford, II, 206
William, of Long Melford, I, *202*
Carwent: John, of Eye, II, 395
Casse: John, of Great Bradley, I, *1196*; the
younger, of Great Bradley, I, *736*
Cate: Walter, of Stuston, I, *156*
Catelyn (Catelyne, Katelyn, Kattelyng):
John, of Haverhill, I, *523*; son of the late
Thomas, of Burwell (Cambs), I, 1133
Robert, of Snailwell (Cambs), I, 702
Thomas, of Burwell (Cambs), I, 284
Catour *alias* Neve: Anne, of Ixworth, I, 321
Catton: John, skepmaker, of Mildenhall, I, 119
Cavenham: Henry, of Westley, I, *4*
John, of Sudbury, I, *1267*
Richard, of Fordham (Cambs), II, 60
William, of Acton, I, 1312
Chaas: Andrew, of Withersfield, I, *396*
Chambyr (Chawmbre): John, of Nayland, I,
32; esquire, of Stratford (Middx), I, 863
(*possibly* Brown 'of the chamber')
Chambyrlayn (Chawmberleyn): [*not given*], of
Redlingfield, I, 756
Alice, of Poslingford, I, 113
Chapeleyn: Robert, of Wangford, II, 319
Chapman: Adam, of Barrow, II, 152
Christian, widow of John, of Rattlesden, I, *123*
Euphemia, of Hopton, I, 331
Geoffrey, of Haughley, I, 775
Joan, of Livermere, I, *483*; of Thorndon, I,
1102
John, of Burgate, I, *1477*; of Oakley, I, *1476*;
the elder, of Rickinghall Inferior, II, 522
Nicholas, of Coney Weston, I, 957
Richard, of Mildenhall, I, 1155; of Rickinghall
Inferior, I, 393
Thomas, of Gazeley, II, 725; of Little Thurlow,
I, *866*; of Livermere, I, *656*
William, the elder, of Mildenhall, II, 230
see also Schapman
Charite: Roger, of Hitcham, II, 75
Chaterle: Thomas, of Hinderclay, I, *268*
Chattysley (Chatysle): John, of Ixworth, II, 575
William, of Ixworth, II, 219
Chaundlere: Simon, of Semer, I, *1454*
Chenery: Ellen, of Cockfield, II, 115
John, the elder, of Cockfield, I, 1260
Cheryaunt (*or* Seriaunt): Richard, of Sudbury,
I, 276
Chetelerth: Adam, of Drinkstone, I, *115*

Child (Chyld): John, of Badwell Ash, I, 96; of
Higham in Gazeley, I, 1439
Chylderston (Chyldriston, Chyldryston,
Schildyrston): John, of Mildenhall, I, 865; I,
870; the elder, of Mildenhall, II, 629
Matilda, of Mildenhall, II, 239
Richard, of Mildenhall, I, 1084
Robert, the elder, of Mildenhall, II, 664
Simon, of Mildenhall, I, 1156
Chyrche (Chirche): Elizabeth, widow of John, of
Barnham, I, 1206
John, of Barnham, I, *1007*; of Hopton, I, *1178*
Margaret, of Herringswell, I, *704*
Robert, of Eye, II, *3*
Chyrcheman: John, of Icklingham, II, 471
Margaret, widow, of Icklingham, II, 479
Richard, of Icklingham All Saints, I, 1129
Clare *alias* Abthorp: Richard, of Troston, I, 599
Claydon: John, of Haverhill, I, 106; of Haverhill,
I, 210
William, of Haverhill, I, 50
Clere: John, of Felsham, II, 137
Thomas, of Little Livermere, II, 118
Clerk (Clerke): Alice, of Bardwell, II, 168; of
Drinkstone, II, 336
Ed', of Edwardstone, II, 274
Edmund, of Lavenham, I, 130
James, of Ixworth, I, 372, p
John, of [*not given*], I, *1415*; of Ashfield, I,
136; of Boxford, I, *403*; of Chelsworth, I,
629; of Nowton, II, 291; II, 296; of Preston,
II, 716; the elder, of Clare, I, 1448; the
elder, of Nowton, II, 812; the elder, of
Occold, II, 443
Robert, of Wetheringsett, I, 1438
Roger, of Edwardstone, II, 714; of Stuston,
I, *170*
Simon, of Stanton, I, 457
Thomas, of Boxford, II, 70
William, of Great Ashfield, I, *218*; of Sudbury,
I, 554
see also Nicoll *alias* Clerk, *and* Crek
Clerk *alias* Webbe: John, of Woodditton (Cambs),
II, 646
Clerys: John, of Little Livermere, II, 653
Cletyr: Richard, of Hundon, I, 448
Clopton: Stephen, of Woolpit, I, *107*
Cobbe: John, of Edwardstone, I, 1446; of
Gislingham, II, 343; of Glemsford, I, 1353;
of Soham (Cambs), I, 254
Thomas, of Shelland, I, 977
Walter, of Long Melford, I, 88
William, of Wetheringsett, II, 778
Cobbold (Cobold): Henry, of Preston, I, *1111*
John, of Lavenham, I, 618
Codman: John, of Cockfield, I, 179
Coggeshall: John, the elder, of Hundon, I, 1216
Cogman: Joan, of Lavenham, I, *510*

Cok (Coke, Cokke): John, of Chevington, I, 1410; of Haughley, II, 313; of Stowmarket, II, 139
Margaret, of Stoke by Clare, I, *437*
Thomas, of Norton, I, 1381; of Withersfield, II, 419
Walter, of Haverhill, I, 633
Coket: Henry, of Westhorpe, I, *206*
John, of Hitcham, I, *273*; of Stoke by Clare, I, *1187*
Margaret, widow, of Ampton, I, 1400; of Ingham, II, 368
Walter, 'wolleman', of Ingham, I, 1441
Cokkow: John, of Little Wratting, I, *1146*
Coksedge: Baldwin, gentleman, of Felsham, II, 417
Colberd: John, of Wickhambrook, I, 846
Colcy: Geoffrey, of Woolpit, II, 371
Coldham: John, of Barningham, I, 807; II, 338
Margaret, of Barningham, I, *955*
Cole: Margaret, widow of John, of Stoke by Nayland, II, 150
Colman: Nicholas, of Stowmarket, I, 1126
Richard, of Little Waldingfield, I, 1024; of Mildenhall, I, 1403
Thomas, of Thorndon, II, 337; of Wortham, I, 1076
Colyere: John, of Bures St Mary, II, 283
Comayan: William, of Rattlesden, II, 536
Comber: William, of Stradishall, I, 1142
Combes: Thomas, of Wyverstone, I, *841*
Conyn: Geoffrey, of Buxhall, I, 1065
Coo (Koo): Agnes, of Stanton, II, 333
John, 'barbour', of Boxford, I, 548
Margery, of Woolpit, I, 619
William, of Burwell (Cambs), II, *289*
Cook (Cooke): John, of Combs, I, *410*; of Creeting St Peter, I, *998*; of Thrandeston, II, 765
Thomas, of Cotton, II, 700
Walter, 'bocher', of Nayland, I, 192
William, of Occold, I, *104*
see also Fermere *alias* Cook
see also Salle *alias* Cooke
Cook *alias* Parker: John, of Lavenham, I, 454
Coole: John, of Snailwell (Cambs), I, *239*
Copcy (Copsy): John, of Cowlinge, II, 91
Roger, of Brockley, I, 1390
Copenger: John, of Buxhall, I, 90
Richard, of Rattlesden, I, *1144*
Coppyng (Copyn): John, of Acton, II, 518
William, of Somerton, II, 125
Cordy: John, of Thelnetham, I, *132*
Corray: John, of Little Livermere, I, 138
Cosyn: John, the elder, of Cavenham, II, 77; the younger, of Cavenham, I, *987*
Robert, of Stowmarket, II, 750
Thomas, of Cavenham, I, 95

Cotelere: John, of Barnham, II, 282
Cotelyn: John, of Palgrave, II, 688
Coteras: Nicholas, of Sudbury, I, *651*
Robert, of Long Melford, I, 1387
Seman, of Long Melford, I, *272*
Coupere (Cowper, Cowpere): Joan, of Badwell Ash, I, 944
John, at the Stone, of Boxford, II, 247; of Bardwell, I, 97; of Boxford, I, 316; of Bradfield St George, I, 611; of Brockley, II, 76; of Walsham le Willows, I, 672
Nicholas, of Knettishall, I, *1321*
Roger, of Long Melford, I, *1167*
Stephen, of Stowmarket, I, 53
Thomas, of Boxford, I, 458
William, of Boxford, I, 547
Cove: Roger, of Mendlesham, II, 568
Cowdon: Richard, of Dalham, II, 28
Cowe: John, of Wickham Skeith, II, 22
Cowelle: John, of Sudbury, I, 1364
Cowerde: John, of Cheveley (Cambs), II, 182
Cowern: John, of Mildenhall, II, 611
Crane: Adam, of Redgrave, I, *1015*
Ed', of Palgrave, I, *997*
George, of Redgrave, I, 341
Isabel, of Redgrave, II, 308
John, of Botesdale in Redgrave, I, 1373; of Wortham, I, 6
Thomas, of Wortham, II, 269
Walter, of Wortham, I, 1372
Crask: Matilda, of Market Weston, I, 1250
Cratern: Margaret, widow, of Icklingham, II, 469
Crek (*written as* Clerke *in margin*): Thomas, of Clare, II, 456
Crenche (Krenche): John, of Kedington, I, 572
Richard, of Polstead, II, 33
Cressent: John, of Harleston, I, 1306
Cristian: Robert, of Ixworth Thorpe, I, *1396*
Cropley: Thomas, of Dalham, II, 734
Cros: Thomas, of Edwardstone, II, 96
Crouch (Crowche): Geoffrey, of Fornham St Genevieve, I, 443
John, of Fornham St Genevieve, I, 729
Crowe: Cecily, of Hitcham, II, 211; widow of Thomas, of Hitcham, II, 196
Thomas, of Hitcham, I, 1116; of, Soham (Cambs), I, 903
Cryketot: John, of Buxhall, I, 1393
Crymbyll: John, of Worlington, I, 1119
Cryspyn (Cryspyng): John, of Gislingham, I, *970*; of Thorney in Stowmarket, II, 627
Crystemesse: John, of Stoke by Nayland, I, 36
Cullum: Walter, of Thorndon, I, 785
Cullyng: Richard, of Cookley, hamlet of Eye, I, 479
Curby: William, of Lavenham, I, *766*; I, 768
Curpayle: John, of Haverhill, II, *250*

Curray: John, of Ampton, II, *114*; of Chilton in Clare, II, 380

Curtes (Curteys): Emma, of Mildenhall, I, 1117
John, of Brockford in Wetheringsett, I, 1417; of Snailwell (Cambs), I, *703*
Thomas, of Wetherden, I, *557*
William, of Tostock, II, 29; the elder, of Mildenhall, I, 219

Cusset: William, of Newmarket, I, *732*

Custe: Simon, of Great Horringer, II, 88

Dacrys: Reginald, of Woolpit, I, 655

Dag: Katherine, of Acton, I, 1384

Dale: Simon, of Wickham Skeith, I, 879
see also Dele

Dalham: Stephen, of Cowlinge, I, *730*

Damok: Thomas, of Elveden, I, *1211*

Damport: Roger, of Eye, I, 367

Danby: Thomas, of Market Weston, II, 625

Danon (Danown): Simon, of Sudbury, I, 1058
William, of Sudbury, II, 425

Darry: Richard, of Sudbury, I, 49

Dassh: Walter, of Botesdale in Redgrave, I, *596*

Davy: Michael, of Honington, I, 690; I, *783*
Thomas, of Sudbury, I, 165; of Wratting, I, *919*

Debenham (Debynham): John, of Shimpling, I, 184
Stephen, of Rickinghall, I, *1070*
Thomas, of Stradishall, I, 426

Deere (Dere): John, of Exning, I, 435
Thomas, of Exning, I, 429

Dekenys: Agnes, of Stoke by Clare, II, *813*

Dekys: Joan, of Whelnetham, I, 824

Dele: Stephen, of Oakley, I, 1005
see also Dale

Deneys (Denysy, Deynes, Deynis, Deynys): Joan, widow, of Sudbury, II, 259
John, of Ixworth Thorpe, I, *1323*; of Woolpit, II, 579
Robert, dyer, of Sudbury, I, 740
Rose, of Haughley, I, 795
Thomas, of Combs, II, 621; II, 694
William, of Mildenhall, II, 260

Denham: John, of Ousden, I, *926*
Robert, of Wickhambrook, II, 263

Denton: [*not given*], of [*not given*], I, *515*

Derby: John, of Sudbury, II, 782; of Thrandeston, I, *1304*; mercer, of Sudbury, I, 803

Derlyng: John, of Snailwell (Cambs), II, 24

Derman: John, of Denston, II, 724

Derysle (Derysley): Alice, wife of Richard, of Kirtling (Cambs), II, 656
Richard, of Kirtling (Cambs), II, 482
Walter, of Kirtling (Cambs), II, 577
William, of Kirtling (Cambs), II, 461

Deve: Agnes, of Burwell (Cambs), I, *555*

Dexster: John, of Wetherden, I, *1215*

Dey (Deye): John, of Creeting, I, *1161*; of Hawstead, I, 411; the elder, cordwainer, of Long Melford, I, 517
Ralph, of West Stow, I, 1361
Sybil, of Eye, I, *886*
[*not given*], of [*not given*], I, *224*

Dil Hoo: Ed', of Stowmarket, II, 665

Dobbys: Thomas, of Sudbury, I, 188

Dobyll: John, of Layham, I, 639

Doffouus (Doffows): John, of Bardwell, I, 212

Dokkyng: Thomas, the elder, of Mildenhall, II, 635

Dolett: John, of Westhorpe, II, 361

Donewych: John, of Rushbrooke, I, *1205*
Robert, of Fornham All Saints, II, 798

Dorant (Doraunt, Dorawnt): John, of Dalham, I, *450*; of Nayland, I, *1222*
Richard, of Brettenham, I, *1324*
William, of Thornham Magna, II, 193

Dormowr: William, of Wickham Skeith, I, 87; I, 705; I, 706

Dow (Dowe): Gilbert, of Lakenheath, I, 388
John, of Barnardiston, II, 598; of Barnham, I, 281; of Kirtling (Cambs), I, 1348; tailor, of Long Melford, I, 1424
Thomas, of Haverhill, I, 1383
William, of Barnham St Martin, II, 299

Dowres: Robert, of Combs, I, *952*

Draper: John, of Great Wratting, I, *447*

Drawswerd: Alice, widow, of Finningham, I, 385
John, of Snailwell (Cambs), II, 824

Drew (Drewe): James, of Mellis, II, 391; the elder, of Mellis, I, 1371

Drowgth (Drowte): Joan, relict of Peter, of Felsham, II, 647
Peter, of Felsham, II, 329

Drury: Roger, gentleman, of Hepworth, II, 402
Thomas, esquire, of Hessett, I, 231

Dryver: Ed', of Combs, I, 660

Ducheman: John, of Haverhill, II, *13*

Duke: John, husbandman, of Little Saxham, II, 373

Dun: Adam, of Yaxley, II, 790
Gilbert, of Finningham, I, *75*; I, 178
Sarah, of [*not given*], I, *476*

Dunch (Dunche): John, of Kennett (Cambs), I, *12*; of Wordwell, II, 657
Robert, the elder, of Mendlesham, II, 374
see also Knyth *alias* Dunch

Dunkon: Robert, of Mendlesham, I, 333

Dyer: *see* Turnour *alias* Dyer

Dyke: Agnes, widow, of Stoke by Clare, II, 803

Dykys: Richard, of Cavendish, II, 423

Dymbyll: Robert, of Groton, I, *1157*

Dymerssh: Robert, of Sudbury, I, *1311*

Dyster (Dister): Robert, of Boxford, I, *414*; of Long Melford, I, 1104; painter ('pegntor'), of Boxford, I, 296
see also Lorkyn *alias* Dyster

Dyxster: Joan, of Long Melford, I, 181

Edgor: Robert, of Thorndon, I, 117
Edward: John, of Fornham St Martin, I, 1233;
    of Great Horringer, I, *826*; of Haverhill, I,
    1147
  Thomas, of Fornham All Saints, I, 297
Edwyn: William, of Occold, I, *74*
Egeleyn (Egelyn): John, of Rickinghall Superior,
    I, 1271
  Thomas, of, Redgrave, I, 726
Egelot: John, of Clare, I, *646*
Elmyswell: John, of Thwaite, I, 658
Elsegood: John, the elder, of Elmswell, II, 116
Elsyng: Robert, of Hundon, I, *1189*
Elyne: Agnes, of Hitcham, I, *265*
  Joan, of Haughley, I, *746*
Elyot: Nicholas, of Wangford, I, *1266*
Elys: John, of Stanton, II, 372
Erdryche: Herry, of Finningham, II, 622
Erle: Thomas, of Haughley, I, *966*
Ernald: John, of Polstead, II, 104
Eryswell: John, of Eriswell, II, 342
Essex: John, of Shimpling, II, 494
Eton: John, of Haughley, I, 18
Eve: William, of Little Waldingfield, II, 83
  see also Ive
Everard: John, the elder, of Stoke by Clare, I, 631
  Thomas, of Soham (Cambs), II, 278
  William, of Lawshall, I, 293
Ewstasse: John, of Rougham, II, 588
Eyre: Edith, of Glemsford, I, *1087*
  William, of Glemsford, I, 251
Eyres: John, the elder, of Sudbury, I, 718

Fabbe: John, the elder, of Burwell (Cambs),
    I, 1265
  William, of Burwell (Cambs), II, 215
Fabyan: John, of Exning, I, 1480
Facon (Facoun, Fakon): Joan, of [*not given*], II,
    328; widow of John, of Nayland, I, 1080
  John, of Nayland, I, 860; the elder, of
    Boxford, I, 380
  Regnold, of Groton, I, 843
  Thomas, of Bures St Mary, II, 310
  William, of Cavenham, I, *1145*
  see also Nelynnge *alias* Facon
Farewell (Farwell): Alice, of Silverley (Cambs),
    I, 1473
  Ralph, of Ashley (Cambs), I, 381
  William, of Newmarket, I, 54
Fayerware: Simon, of Mildenhall, II, 766
Feltewell (Feltwell): John, of Santon Downham,
    I, *371*
  Margery, of Santon Downham, I, *1069*
  William, of Culford, II, 208
Femnale: John, of Ashley in Silverley (Cambs),
    II, 80

Fen (Fenn, Fenne): John, of Semer, I, *728*;
    of Soham (Cambs), I, *953*; the elder, of
    Boxford, I, 235
  Katherine, of Glemsford, I, 1068
  Richard, of Kersey, I, *720*
  Robert, of Withersfield, I, *1456*
  Stephen, of Hopton, II, 661; II, 707
  Thomas, of Groton, I, 529
Fenforth: John, of Cheveley (Cambs), I, *739*
Fenkele: Marion, of Gipping, I, 346
Fermere *alias* Cook: Richard, of Badwell Ash,
    I, 1397
Fleccher (Flechere, Fletcher): Robert, of
    Botesdale in Redgrave, I, 325
  Thomas, of Stradishall, I, *669*; of Walsham le
    Willows, II, 412
  William, of Brockley, II, 473
Flecchere, *see* Worliche *alias* Flecchere
Flegge: John, the elder, fuller, of Sudbury, II, 727
Flemyng: John, of Elveden, II, 731; of Wortham,
    I, *1239*
Fodryngay: Gerard, of Brockley, II, 35
Folke (Folkes, Folkys): Herry, of Kedington, I,
    1213
  John, the elder, of Stoke by Nayland, II, 556
  Margaret, of Eye, II, 252
Foorth (Forthe): John, of Cockfield, I, *1108*
  Simon, of Cockfield, I, *675*
  Thomas, of Cockfield, II, 350
Foot: John, of Buxhall, II, 383; of Long Melford,
    I, *1301*
Fordham: George, of Bradfield St George, I, 662
Fortham: John, of Kirtling (Cambs), I, 203
Foster: Peter, of Sudbury, I, 157
  Richard, of Stoke by Nayland, I, 42
Foster *alias* Geldere: Robert, of Glemsford, I,
    109
Fotour: William, of Rickinghall Inferior, II, 365
Fowre: Robert, of Cavendish, I, 1375
Fraunceys (Frawnceys): Robert, of Ixworth, I,
    357; I, 366
  Thomas, of Melford, II, 446; of Mendlesham,
    II, 203; of Worlington, II, 481
Frebern: John, of Soham (Cambs), I, *1443*
Freman: John, of Ixworth, I, 335; of Redgrave,
    I, *1270*; of Stoke by Nayland, I, 1088
Freot (Fryot, Fryotthe): John, mercer, of Sudbury,
    I, 758
  Katherine, of [*not given*], I, 831
  Thomas, of Barrow, II, 600; of Glemsford, I,
    362
Frere: Henry, of Burwell (Cambs), II, 226
  John, of Fordham (Cambs), I, *551*; of
    Mildenhall, I, 683
Fresswater: John, of Wetherden, II, *315*
Frost (Froste): John, of Hartest, II, 807; of
    Ousden, I, 1285; of Wicken (Cambs), II,
    793; of Wickhambrook, I, 302

William, of Hartest, II, 690

Frynge: John, of Eriswell, I, *1101*

Frythe: John, of Nayland, II, 48; II, 86

Fuller (Fullere): Alice, of Barnham, I, *1362*
Ellen, of Walsham le Willows, II, 385
John, of Barnham, II, 493; of Glemsford,
II, 262; of Little Saxham, II, 507; of
Mildenhall, I, 1259; of Thurston, II, 560;
of Walsham le Willows, I, *1040*; mercer, of
Sudbury, I, 864
Simon, of Mildenhall, II, *553*
William, of Hunston, II, 770

Fyn: William, of Rattlesden, I, *699*

Fynche: Richard, of Tostock, I, *605*

Fyrmin: William, of Boxted, I, 205

Fysch (Fysche, Fyshe): Ed', of Westhorpe, II,
102
Isabel, widow of William, of Worlington, I,
311
Thomas, of Soham (Cambs), II, *8*

Fysher (Fysscher): John, of Redgrave, I, 1238
Peter, of Hepworth, I, 17

Fyshyve: John, of Stoke by Nayland, II, 236

Fyston: Thomas, of Pakenham, I, *1017*; I, 1046

Fytzkeys: Robert, of Brandon, I, 1008

Fyzstevene: Roger, of Hitcham, I, 51

Galey: John, of Soham (Cambs), I, 1327

Galfawe: William, of Woolpit, I, 1172

Galte: Simon, of Worlington, II, 426

Galyon: Thomas, of Fornham All Saints, I, 229

Gambon: William, of Pakenham, I, 343

Gamelyn: John, of Polstead, II, 97

Gardener (Gardenere, Gardyner): John, of
Icklingham, II, 492; of Lidgate, I, 190; of
Whepstead, II, 314
Margery, of Stanton All Saints, I, 802
Simon, of Mildenhall, II, 636
Thomas, of Haverhill, I, *834*; the elder, of
Barton Mills, II, 379
William, of Stanton, I, 677

Garlyng: Robert, of Great Finborough, II, 358
Thomas, of Eye, II, 396

Garnenere: John, the elder, of Beyton, I, 1394

Gate: Elizabeth, of Barningham, II, 411

Gateward: John, of Cheveley (Cambs), II, 649

Gatle: Alice, widow of Thomas, of Great
Livermere, I, 116
Thomas, of Great Livermere, I, 180

Gebon: William, of Euston, I, *30*

Gegenere: Robert, of Worlington, I, 1389

Gegge: Matilda, of Knettishall, II, *441*

Geldere: Alice, widow, of Glemsford, II, 528
see also Foster *alias* Geldere

Gelham: William, of Mildenhall, I, 1404

Gelle: John, of Burwell (Cambs), I, 556

Gent (Gente): John, of Euston, I, 535
William, the younger, of Euston, II, 755

Gentylman: John, of Norton, II, 209

Gerard (Gerarde): Nicholas, of Barnham, II, 578
William, of Botesdale in Redgrave, I, 1354

Germayn: Thomas, of Melford, II, 733

Gernays: John, of Long Melford, I, *201*

Gervys: John, of Denston, II, 242
see also Jervys

Gesyer: William, of Redgrave, I, *1016*

Glamvyle (Glaunvyll): John, of Drinkstone, II,
18; of Haughley, II, 569

Glaswrygh (Glaswrygth): John, the elder, of
Great Waldingfield, II, 675
William, of Pakenham, I, *887*

Glemsford: Robert, of Somerton, I, 789

Glovere (Glovyere): Agnes, widow, of
Woodditton (Cambs), II, 762
John, of Cavendish, II, 133; of Kersey, I, 1067
Margaret, widow, of Stanton, II, 759
Stephen, of Clare, I, 833
see also Hawkedon *alias* Glovere

Goche: Robert, of Thelnetham, II, 589

Godard (Goddard): John, of Rattlesden, I, 868
Robert, of Bradfield Combust, I, 1367
Thomas, of Bradfield Combust, I, 412

Goday: Thomas, carpenter, of Sudbury, I, 310

Goddrych: Rose, widow, of Felsham, II, 533

Godewyne: Richard, of Thornham Magna, I,
1096

Godfrey (Godferey): Alan, of Little Whelnetham,
I, 533
George, of Hessett, I, 933
William, of Great Horringer, II, 773

Godlard: Simon, of Wickham Skeith, II, 498

Godman: William, of Thorpe Morieux, II, 351

Godyng (Godynge): John, of Withersfield, II, 356
Thomas, of Groton, I, 816
William, of Pakenham, I, *10*

Gojon: Thomas, of Lakenheath, I, *1018*

Goldbour: Thomas, of Soham (Cambs), II, 279
William, the younger, of Soham (Cambs), II,
382

Goldfynche: Thomas, of Botesdale, II, 467

Goldyng: John, of Cavendish, I, 80
Robert, of Glemsford, II, 564
Thomas, of Preston, I, *814*
William, of Eye, II, 2; of Glemsford, II, 316

Golofre: John, of Soham (Cambs), II, 277
Thomas, of Little Thurlow, I, *1197*
William, of Eye, I, 354

Gonevyn: Henry, of Kirtling (Cambs), I, 1432

Gooch (Gooche): Adam, of Rushbrooke, II, 127
Nicholas, of Sudbury, I, 48
see also Reede *alias* Gooch

Goodwyn (Goodewyn): William, of Burwell
(Cambs), II, 12; II, 550

Goore (Gore): Alice, of Bardwell, I, *1275*
John, of Bardwell, I, 55; of Barnham, I, *1303*;
II, 292; II, 293; the elder, I, 377

Thomas, of Barnham St Martin, I, 1302; of
  Soham (Cambs), II, 744
William, of Elveden, I, 891
Gorldston: Thomas, of Old Newton, I, 1411
Gosse: Agnes, of Fordham (Cambs), I, 1131
Henry, of Fordham (Cambs), I, 986
John, of Newton, II, 516
Thomas, of Hawkedon, I, *1251*
Goule (Gowle): John, of Mendlesham, I, 799; of
  Stowmarket, I, 1462
Grace: John, of Stoke by Nayland, I, *154*
Gregory: Thomas, of Thrandeston, I, *575*
Grene: Andrew, of Fornham All Saints, I, 1279
John, of Chelsworth, I, *1428*; of Newmarket,
  I, 716; I, 724; I, 793; of Rattlesden, I, *455*;
  the younger, of Bardwell, I, *453*
Nicholas, of Thurston, I, 760
Robert, of Thorney in Stowmarket, I, 882
Thomas, of Creeting St Peter, I, 20
Walter, of Withersfield, I, 893
William, of Creeting St Peter, II, 44; II, 89; of
  Lindsey, I, 1429; of Nayland, I, *318*
Grenegres: Ralph, of Great Fakenham, I, 69
Grenhell: John, of Layham, II, 54
Grome: Isabel, wife of John the elder, of
  Melford, II, 728
Grondysborgh: *see* Bocher *alias* Grondysborgh
Gronger: Hugh, of Wickham Skeith, I, 228
John, of Hitcham, I, *1047*; of Hopton, I, 1179
Grugeman (Gruggeman): John, of Barnham, I,
  1078; of Ixworth, I, *859*
Robert, of Euston, I, *985*
Gryffyn: Thomas, of [*not given*], I, *1098*
Grygge (Grygges): Andrew, of Lavenham, II, 11
John, of Hartest, II, 422; of Lavenham, I, 350
Grymsyk: John, of Hepworth, I, 854
Gybbe: John, of Kersey, I, 342
Gybelon (Gybloue): Richard, of Sudbury, II, 84
Thomas, of Bures St Mary, II, 51
Gylberd (Gylbertt): Thomas, of Ixworth Thorpe,
  II, 69
William, of Troston, II, 757
Gylly: *see* Sawyer *alias* Gylly
Gynows: Thomas, of Mendlesham, II, 805

Hache: William, of Stradishall, II, 264
Hadynham: John, the elder, of Kentford, I, 762
Hale: John, of Great Bradley, II, 56
Hall (Halle): John, of Semer, I, *990*; of Thurston,
  I, *1407*; of Woolpit, II, 430
Thomas, of Withersfield, I, *914*
Hammyle (Hamvyll): Rose, of Little Bradley, I,
  1430
Thomas, of Little Bradley, I, 876
Hamond (Hamownd, Hamownde): Cecily, of
  Thorney in Stowmarket, II, 737
John, of Lawshall, I, *140*; of Thrandeston, I,
  1062; of Tuddenham, I, *427*

Richard, of Barrow, II, 62
Thomas, of Lawshall, II, 151
William, of Nayland, I, 142; of Timworth, I,
  1288
Hamond *alias* Pedder: Robert, of Ixworth, I,
  1033
Hancok: Ralph, of Newmarket, I, 379; the elder,
  of Newmarket, I, 399
Hardhed: Thomas, of Hitcham, I, *979*
Hardy: Alice, widow of Matthew, of Rattlesden,
  I, *1032*
Hardyng: Robert, of Eye, II, 457
Hare: William, of Pakenham, II, 101
Harlegrey: Henry, of Mildenhall, I, 1219
Harleston: Henry, of Stanton, II, 183
Harlyng (Harlynge): Nicholas, of Hopton, II, 393
Richard, of Hopton, I, 622
Thomas, of Hopton, I, *68*
Harpour: John, of Glemsford, II, 752
Harry: John, of Lavenham, II, 681
Hasylwode: Thomas, of Haverhill, I, *781*
Hawe: Nicholas, of Cavendish, I, *946*
Hawkedon *alias* Glovere: William, of Bildeston,
  II, 284
Hawkere: Agnes, of Elmswell, II, 605
Hawkyn: John, of Attilton in Wickhambrook, II,
  410
Hawys: James, of Walsham, II, 475
Hay: William, of Barnardiston, I, 85
Haydyff: Thomas, of Rattlesden, I, 1143
Hecham *alias* Bochere: Stephen, of Haughley,
  II, 180
Hedgeman (Heggeman): Joan, of Glemsford, II,
  100
John, the elder, of Glemsford, I, 1246
Hegge: John, of Ingham, I, 227
Margaret, widow, of Ingham, I, 963
Ralph, of Icklingham St James, I, 585
Hekedon: John, of Timworth, I, *225*
John, of Tuddenham, I, *363*
Hell (Helle): Alice, of Stowmarket, I, *386*
Henry, of Cockfield, II, 488
Helys: Agnes, widow of John, of Lavenham, I, 172
Henman: John, of Occold, I, *659*
Hepston: John, of Rougham, II, 816
Herberd: Joan, widow of John, of Yaxley, I, 1276
Hergiswell: Ed', of, Westley *iuxta* Bury, I, *542*
Herman: William, of Rickinghall Superior, I, 194
Hermer: John, of Great Saxham, I, 77
Richard, of Little Horringer, I, 1291
Herne: [*not given*], of Soham (Cambs), I, 1483
Hernynge: Thomas, of Santon Downham, II, 777
Herry: Geoffrey, of Fornham All Saints, I, 271
Hersent: Stephen, of Edwardstone, I, 1223; I,
  1281
Herset (Hersete): Isabel, of Long Melford, I, *217*
John, of Sudbury, I, *31*

Hert: John, of Bardwell, I, *1232*; of Cowlinge, I, 897; of Elmswell, II, 660; of Haverhill, I, 306; of Worlington, I, 89
Thomas, of Wixoe, I, 580
William, of Elmswell, II, 519

Hervy: Alice, widow, of Rickinghall Inferior, II, 500
John, of Gislingham, II, 800; of Layham, I, *1336*
Richard, of Barnardiston, I, *1488*
Thomas, the younger, of Wortham, I, 595

Herward: Alice, widow of William the elder, of Sudbury, I, *993*
John, of Sudbury, I, *606*; I, *645*
Margaret, of Wordwell, II, 539
Thomas, of Sudbury, I, *947*
William, the elder, of Sudbury, I, 1077

Heryot: Thomas, of Bures, I, *384*; I, *657*

Hesset (Hessete): John, of Wetherden, II, 149
Thomas, of Wetherden, I, 1182

Hethe: John, of Long Melford, I, 221
Marion, of Rattlesden, II, 57
Thomas, esquire, of Hengrave, I, 41

Hetheman: John, of Bures, I, *274*

Heylok: John, of Barnardiston, I, 249

Heynes: John, of Thorpe Morieux, II, 17

Heyward (Heyvard, Heywode): John, of Barnardiston, I, *84*; of Hessett, II, 746; of Saxon Street in Woodditton (Cambs), I, 553; of Woodditton (Cambs), I, 678
Marg', of [*not given*], I, *852*
Robert, of Wattisham, II, 111
[*not given*], of [*not given*], I, *503*

Hill (Hille, Hyll, Hylle): Agnes, of Little Saxham, I, 1044
Alice, of Stoke by Nayland, II, 38
Denise, of Sudbury, II, 505
Henry, of Cockfield, I, *615*
John, of Elmswell, I, 1337; of Little Saxham, I, 1123; of Rickinghall, I, *878*; of Sudbury, II, 434; the elder, of Whepstead, I, 965
Margaret, of Westhorpe, II, 4
Thomas, the elder, of Long Melford, II, 346

Hobbes (Hobbys): Alice, of Timworth, I, 1201
William, of Acton, II, 261

Hoberd: Adam, of Wattisfield, II, 273
John, of Oakley, I, *16*
Katherine, of Burwell (Cambs), I, *67*
Richard, of Thrandeston, I, 543

Hog (Hogge): Margaret, widow of James, of Clare, I, *915*
Robert, of Rougham, II, 184

Hoker (Hokyr): John, of Edwardstone, I, 1209; the younger, of Edwardstone, I, 931

Hoket: John, the elder, of Long Melford, I, 122

Holden: John, the elder, of Glemsford, II, 628; the younger, of Glemsford, II, 742

Holm: Alice, of Brent Eleigh, I, *167*

John, of Barrow, I, 290; of Long Melford, I, *540*
Thomas, of Cotton, I, 400

Holond: Agnes, of Icklingham St James, I, 853

Hont: Richard, of Buxhall, I, *465*
see also Hunt

Hoo: Thomas, of Melford, II, 464

Hoode (Hod): Thomas, of Felsham, I, 901; II, 173

Horn: John, of Cheveley (Cambs), I, 792; I, 822
Thomas, of Snailwell (Cambs), I, 183

Horold: John, of Lakenheath, I, 861; the elder, of Mellis, II, 235

Horsman: William, of Wetheringsett, II, 280

Hose: Robert, of Botesdale in Redgrave, I, 981

Hoton: William, of Woolpit, II, 704

Hovell (Hovyle): Richard, of Cowlinge, I, 549
Thomas, of Cowlinge, II, 801

Howard: John, of Great Barton, II, 736

Howchon (Howchyn): Cecily, of Ixworth Thorpe, I, 828
Marion, of Livermere, I, *1086*
see also Huchon

Howett: Richard, of Edwardstone, II, 353

Howlot (Howlote): John, of Barnham, I, 1139; of Mendlesham, I, 2

Howton: John, of Great Livermere, I, *405*
Thomas, of Hawkedon, II, 676

Howys: Katherine, of Market Weston, I, *935*

Hoy: John, of Icklingham St James, II, 119

Hubberd (Huberd): John, of Redgrave, II, 543
Robert, of Finningham, II, 65; of Redgrave, II, 416

Huchon: John, of Ixworth Thorpe, I, 827
see also Howchon

Hucton (Hukton): Agnes, widow, of Clare, II, 276
John, of Clare, I, *642*; of Hawkedon, I, 735

Hummys: Britana, of Kersey, II, 701

Hunger (Hungyr, Hungyre): Elizabeth, of Thwaite, II, 745
John, of Thwaite, I, *996*
Rose, widow, of Mellis, I, 798

Hunt (Hunte, Huntt): Alice, of Withersfield, II, 171
John, of Whatfield, I, 162
Katherine, of Rushbrooke, II, 470
Margery, of Barrow, II, 136; wife of John, of Barnardiston, II, 677
Robert, esquire, of Rushbrooke, II, 191
Roger, of Barrow, I, 1191
William, of Hopton, I, 1332
see also Hont

Hurlebate: *see* At Lee *alias* Hurlebate

Hurt: William, of Fordham (Cambs), I, 550

Hurton: John, of Icklingham, I, 1221

Huske: Thomas, of Ickworth, II, 389

Hyde: John, the elder, of Nayland, II, 783

Hyndebest (Hyndebeste): Adam, of Thurston, I, *1440*; II, 74
Hyne: Matilda, widow, of Sudbury, I, 421
Hynge: Robert, of Mildenhall, I, *980*
Hynton: Katherine, wife of John, of Great Bradley, I, 368
Hyon: Godwin, of Occold, I, 537
Hyve: Thomas, of Lakenheath, I, 1289

Ide: Agnes, of Glemsford, I, 137
Ingham: Robert, of Newmarket, I, 574
Inglond: William, of Bardwell, I, 1231
  [*not given*], of Troston, II, 489
Ingold: Thomas, of Brandon, I, *928*
  [*not given*], of [*not given*], I, *485*
Instans: Robert, of Rattlesden, I, *1436*
Ive (Yve): Henry, of Little Waldingfield, I, *1487*
  John, the elder, of Great Finborough, I, 348
  see also Eve

Jacob: John, of Sudbury, II, *98*
  Thomas, of Stowmarket, I, *1420*
  William, the elder, of Sudbury, I, 578
Jaferey (Jaffery, Jeffrey): Marion, of Barnham, I, *974*
  Peter, of Barnham, II, 684
  William, of Barnham, I, 534
Jakeman: John, of Ousden, I, *883*
Jakys: Lawrence, of Depden, I, 125
Jamys: William, of Milden, I, 81
Jay: John, of Burwell (Cambs), I, *66*
  William, of Burwell (Cambs), II, 732; of Stoke by Nayland, II, 409
Jegnere: Thomas, of Undley, Lakenheath, II, 246
Jenewes (Jenews): Agnes, of Eye, II, 94
  John, of Eye, I, 624
Jenowr: John, of Old Newton, I, 908
Jervys: Joan, of Bildeston, I, 982
  see also Gervys
Jerweys: *see* Boner *alias* Jerweys
Jorge: John, of Exning, I, *590*
Joure: John, of Combs, II, 344
Judy: Robert, of Badwell Ash, I, 1342; barker, of Tostock, II, 771
Julian: William, of Bardwell, I, 1368
Jurdon: William, of Newmarket, II, 671
Justice: William, of Withersfield, II, 330

Kartere: *see* Carter
Katelyn: *see* Catelyn
Kattelyng: *see* Catelyn
Kebenham: Thomas, of Wortham, II, 323
Kebyll: Richard, the elder, of Stowmarket, I, 797
  William, of Old Newton, II, 576
Kedlowe: Patrick, of Newton, II, 597
Kedyngton: John, of Chippenham (Cambs), I, *1100*
Keggyll: John, of Bildeston, I, 520

Kelyng: John, of Haverhill, I, 968
Kembold (Kymbold): John, of Hitcham, II, *674*
  Thomas, of Hitcham, I, *560*; I, 712
Kempe: John, of Burwell (Cambs), II, 234
  Katherine, of Burwell (Cambs), II, 233
  Richard, of Cockfield, II, *49*; II, 85
Kendale: John, of Sudbury, II, 465; II, 607
  Simon, of Chelsworth, II, 50
  William, of Occold, II, 726; of Stansfield, I, *382*
Kengeth: John, of Nayland, I, *763*
Kenman: John, of Barningham, II, *63*
Kent (Kente): John, of Burwell (Cambs), I, 313; the elder, of Herringswell, II, 719
  Robert, of Stowmarket, I, 288
  Thomas, of Withersfield, I, *709*
Keppyng: William, of Ixworth, I, *829*
Ketyll: William, of Preston, I, 929
Knotyng: William, of Stowmarket, I, 103
Knygth (Knyth): Robert, the elder, of Little Saxham, II, 320
  Simon, of Barningham, I, *1359*
Knyth *alias* Dunch: William, of Creeting, I, *1294*
Koo: *see* Coo
Krenche: *see* Crenche
Ky (Kyy): John, of Thorney in Stowmarket, I, 264
  Simon, of Stowmarket, II, 468
Kymys: William, of Combs, I, *743*
Kyng (Kynge): Agnes, of Soham (Cambs), I, *904*
  John, of Bradfield Combust, II, 710; of Brockford in Wetheringsett, I, 763; of Chilton in Stowmarket, I, 1134; of Hessett, I, *825*; of Mendlesham, I, *361*; I, *786*; the elder, of Wetheringsett, I, 248
  Nicholas, of Brettenham, I, 1036
  Olive, widow of John, of Mendlesham, I, 1035
  Peter, of Sapiston, II, 544
  Richard, of Wetheringsett, I, 15
  Robert, of Wickhambrook, I, *737*
  Thomas, of Mendlesham, I, 3; of Wattisfield, I, *936*
  William, of Thorney in Stowmarket, I, 600; of Wickhambrook, II, 586
Kyngesbery: Thomas, of Cornard, I, *1177*
Kyrkeby: John, of Icklingham, II, 449
Kyrtelynge: *see* Tew *alias* Kyrtelynge

Ladyman (Ladysman): John, of Great Finborough, I, 129
  Thomas, of Little Whelnetham, II, 413
Laggard: John, of Lavenham, I, 86
Lakke: Thomas, of Snailwell (Cambs), II, 214
Lambe: William, of Haughley, II, 706
Lamberd (Lanberd): Richard, of Lavenham, I, *769*
  Robert, of Whepstead, I, 417

Landlond (Langlond): Isabel, of Eye, I, *707*
John, of Eye, I, 1293
Lane: Isabel, of West Stow, I, 56
John, of Ixworth [Thorpe], I, 101; of Nayland,
I, *815*; II, 503
Peter, of Nayland, I, *383*
Langham: Alice, of Snailwell (Cambs), I, 588
Langley: William, of Ickworth, II, 112
Lardynere: William, of Kennett, II, 585
Large: John, of Stanton, II, 680
Largeawnt: John, of Elveden, I, 111
Larke: Ralph, of Stanton, I, *1261*
Lauerauns: Margaret, of Eye, I, *752*
Lavenham: Thomas, cutler, of Sudbury, I, 1274
Laverok: Joan, of Cockfield, I, *1175*
Lay: John, of Bures, I, *1188*
Leche: Laurence, barker, of Stoke by Nayland,
I, 324
Robert, of Stowmarket, II, 501
Walter, of Botesdale in Redgrave, I, 344
Lee: John, of Stowmarket, II, 381
Leem: Thomas, the elder, of Brandon Ferry, II,
776
Lefeld: Thomas, the elder, of Haverhill, II, 740
Leff: John, of Woodditton (Cambs), I, *135*
Legat: Alan, of Hawstead, II, 39
Robert, of Rattlesden, II, 90
Leman: John, of Wetheringsett, I, *1202*
Lenad: William, of Thelnetham, I, *349*
Lenge: John, of Thurston, I, 287
Lenys: Matilda, of Tostock, I, *614*
Nicholas, of [*not given*], I, *467*
Lerlyng: William, of Hopton, I, *1214*
Leventhorp: John, of, Snailwell (Cambs), I, *240*
Leverich: John, of Felsham, I, 185
Levote: Ralph, of Little Saxham, I, *501*
Lewyn (Lowyn): Thomas, of Stuston, II, 617; of
Wicken (Cambs), I, 1121
Lokwode: Joan, widow of John, of Sudbury,
I, *898*
London (Londen, Louden): Alice, daughter of
William, of Thorndon, I, 1090
John, of Barrow, II, 530
William, of Thorndon, I, 742
Longe: John, the elder, of Acton, I, 259; smith, of
Acton, I, 404
Margery, of Wickham Skeith, I, *880*
Lord: Walter, of Cockfield, I, 899
Lorkyn *alias* Dyster: John, weaver, of Long
Melford, I, 300
Lotkyn *alias* Roper: Richard, of Mildenhall, II,
347
Loudon: *see* London
Lovetop: William, of Kersey, II, 767
Lowyn: *see* Lewyn
Lunt: John, of Stoke by Nayland, I, 638
Lutkyn: Alice, of Stowlangtoft, II, 445
Luton: John, of Lindsey, I, 942

Lylye: John, of Barrow, I, *23*
Lynch: John, of Great Cornard, I, 1149
Lyncolne: John, of Stonham Aspal, II, 809
Lyne (Lynne): Richard, of Poslingford, I, *70*
Robert, of Burwell (Cambs), I, *482*
Lynge: George, of Fornham St Genevieve, II, 448
[*not given*], of [*not given*], I, *617*
Lys: Katherine, of Edwardstone, I, *196*
Walter, of Edwardstone, I, *76*
Lythman: Thomas, of Long Melford, I, 837
Lytyll: Richard, of Stowmarket, I, 1050; the
younger, 'bocher', of Bures St Mary, I, 317
[*not given*], of [*not given*], I, *502*

Machon: Isabel, of Felsham, II, 557
Maddy: Thomas, of Wicken (Cambs), II, 513
Makell: John, of Long Melford, II, 162
Makemere: John, of ?Rattlesden, I, *148*
Makro: William, of Soham (Cambs), II, 758
Malcher: Thomas, of Great Waldingfield, I, 1280
Maltyward: Ann, of Bradfield St George, II, 270
Man (Manne): Ed', of Rattlesden, II, 797
Isabel, widow, of Brettenham, I, 1466
Joan, of Rattlesden, I, *784*
John, of Brettenham, I, *917*; of Thorpe
Morieux, II, 712; the elder, of Lakenheath,
II, 245
Katherine, wife of John the elder, of Kersey,
I, 521
Stephen, of Stowlangtoft, I, *1322*; of Troston,
I, *255*
William, of Clare, I, *948*; of Thorpe Morieux,
II, 713; of Wetheringsett, I, *913*
Mannok: William, tawer (*alutarii*), of Stoke by
Nayland, I, 546
Mannyng: Helen, of Bardwell, I, *1230*
John, of Badwell Ash, I, 1039; of Norton, I,
671
Walter, of Norton *iuxta* Woolpit, I, 373
William, of Bradfield Combust, I, 407; of
Norton, II, 743
see also Munnyng
Mansere: Henry, of Gislingham, II, 476
Manwode: Isabel, of Shimpling, I, 1154; widow
of Robert, of Shimpling, I, 830
Marant: Robert, of Stowmarket, I, *754*
Marcaunt (Marchaunt, Markaunt, Markaunte):
Alice, of Badwell, II, 644; of Badwell Ash,
I, 674
John, of Ixworth, I, 1176
Robert, of Bradfield St Clare, I, 1045
Marchall: Matilda, of Stoke by Nayland, I, *153*
Mardon: William, of Fordham (Cambs), I, 1277
Marham: Robert, of Mildenhall, II, 387
[*not given*], of [*not given*], I, *498*
Markys: John, of Old Newton, I, 1296
Richard, of Old Newton, I, 1192
Marleton: Margaret, of Wetherden, I, 1295

Rose, of Bardwell, I, *519*
Martham: Thomas, of Rattlesden, II, 615
Martyn: Agnes, of Drinkstone, I, 1253; of Little
    Ashfield, II, 667
  Augustine, of Semer, I, 143
  John, of Lakenheath, II, 633; of Soham
    (Cambs), I, 207; of Sudbury, I, *322*; of
    Troston, I, *1401*
  Margaret, of Honington, II, 157
  Roger, of Drinkstone, I, *778*
Mason: Edmund, the younger, of Rickinghall
    Inferior, II, 194
  Henry, of Exning, II, 450
  Richard, of Eye, I, *480*
  Robert, of Eye, I, 433
  Thomas, of Hartest, I, *1136*
Mathew: Robert, of Mildenhall, I, *1434*
Mavesyn: John, of Thrandeston, I, *509*
Mawdyon: William, of Boxford, II, 331
May (Mey): Agnes, of Lavenham, II, 122
  John, of Lavenham, I, 263; of Thornham
    Magna, I, 63
Maydegoode: John, of Great Bradley, I, 193
Mayhew (Mayowe): Edmund, of Rede, II, 682
  John, of Boxford, I, 208
Maynere: Ed', of Great Thurlow, II, 601
  William, of Groton, II, 309
Mayster: Peter, of Kedington, I, 236
Mekylwoode: John, of [*not given*], II, *140*
Melkesop: John, of Stoke by Clare, I, 1423
Melle: Thomas, of Polstead, II, 161
  William, of Stoke by Nayland, II, 491
Meller (Mellere): John, of Stanstead, II, 463; the
    elder, of Barningham, I, 1248
  Robert, of Hinderclay, I, *1198*; of Naughton,
    II, 563
  Thomas, of Withersfield, II, 123
  see also Mondessone *alias* Meller
Melon: John, of Stradishall, II, 787
Melton: John, of [*not given*], I, *845*
  William, of Soham (Cambs), I, 1256
Mersche: Isabel, of Creeting All Saints, I, *283*
Meryell: Agnes, of Barrow, II, 502
  Richard, of Long Melford, I, 1091
  see also Moriell *and* Muriell
Metessharpp (Metscherpe): Roger, of
    Mendlesham, I, 932
  Thomas, of Mendlesham, II, 41
Metewyn (Mettewynd): John, of Wattisfield, I,
    945
  Katherine, of Wattisfield, II, *7*
  William, of Wattisfield, II, 240
Meyn: John, of Barnardiston, I, *39*
Mody: Richard, of Newton, II, 311
  Robert, of Great Finborough, I, 810
Molows: Almeric, of Wattisfield, I, 1409
Mondessone *alias* Meller: Thomas, of Long
    Melford, I, *1105*

Mone: John, the elder, miller, of Fornham St
    Genevieve, I, 924
  Margaret, of Fornham St Genevieve, II, 110
Monnynge: Henry, of Norton, II, 362
  see also Mannynge
Moor (Moore, More): John, of Haughley, I, *710*;
    of Stanstead, I, 132
  Simon, of Boxford, I, 586
  Thomas, of Fornham St Martin, I, 1356
  Walter, of Stowmarket, I, *1305*
  William, of Great Cornard, II, 729
Moriell (Morowhyll, Moryell): Clarissa, widow
    of John, of Barrow, I, 488
  Joan, of Burwell (Cambs), I, *1030*
  Nicholas, mercer, of Stanton, I, 1352
  Robert, of Mendlesham, II, 554
  see also Meryell *and* Muriell
Morle: Henry, of Mildenhall, I, *220*
  John, of Mildenhall, II, 545
  Richard, the elder, of Mildenhall, II, 378
Mortemer: John, of Haverhill, I, *1011*
Motte: Thomas, of Wickhambrook, II, 286
Mowe: Richard, of Bradfield St Clare, I, 848
Mows: William, of Chelsworth, I, 1458
Moyse: John, of Hopton, II, 186
Multon: John, of Little Thurlow, I, *1093*
Mumforte: William, of Polstead, II, 248
Mundeford: John, of Rishangles, I, 648
Mundson: Joan, of Kirtling (Cambs), II, 462
Munnyng: Richard, of Badwell Ash, I, 842
  see also Mannyng
Muriell (Muryell): John, of Barrow, I, 471; of
    Hopton, I, 347
  Margery, widow, of Hawstead, I, 640
  see also Meryell *and* Moriell
Muschat (Musket, Muskett): Henry, of Haughley,
    II, 324
  John, of Drinkstone, I, 1079
  William, of Sudbury, I, 632
Mychill *alias* Barker: John, of [*not given*], I, *910*
Mylde: Thomas, of Clare, II, 148
Myller (Myllere): John, the elder, of Lakenheath,
    I, 779
  Robert, of Naughton, II, 483
  Thomas, of Mildenhall, I, *1286*
Mylon: John, of Clare, II, 687
Mynnys: Robert, of Great Ashfield, II, 415
Mynton: Joan, of Stowmarket, II, 648
  John, of Mendlesham, I, 413

Neel (Neell): Dennis, of Landwade (Cambs), I,
    627
  Roger, of Long Melford, I, *545*
  Thomas, of Haverhill, I, *312*
  William, of Fordham, II, 602
Nelyngge *alias* Facon: John, of Boxford, I, 257
Neve: Thomas, of Great Finborough, II, 275
  see also Catour *alias* Neve

Newelond: John, of Bildeston, I, *1103*
Newhawe: John, of Great Horringer, II, 81
Newman: John, of Lavenham, II, 87; of Woolpit, II, 567; baker, of Sudbury, I, 818
Newres: John, the elder, of Bures St Mary, II, 354
Nicole: Roger, of Chevington, I, 589
Nicoll *alias* Clerk: Walter, of Great Bradley, II, 642
Noble (Nobyll): Adam, of Westley, I, 1220
   Henry, of Little Saxham, II, 486
   John, of Great Horringer, I, *436*; of Nayland, II, 141
   Walter, of Great Horringer, II, 432
Noche: Margaret, widow, of Bildeston, II, 431
Nooke: Robert, executor of Robert Pury, of Kersey, II, 153
Norbowr: William, of Elveden, I, *780*
Noreys (Noris): Ed', of Palgrave, II, 618
   John, of Brockford in Wetheringsett, II, 581
   William, of Brockford in Wetheringsett, II, 5
Norfokk: [*not given*], of [*not given*], I, *1118*
Norman: Alice, of Barrow, I, 890
   Joan, of Badlingham in Chippenham (Cambs), II, 438
   John, of Little Finborough, I, 1180; of Stansfield, II, *814*; the elder, of Barrow, I, 291; mercer, of Barrow, I, 693
   Thomas, of Badlingham in Chippenham (Cambs), I, 440; II, 108; of Chippenham (Cambs), I, *93*
   William, of Great Thurlow, I, *134*
North: John, of Bardwell, I, 78
Northaghe: Adam, of Thorndon, II, 146
Norwold: Matilda, of Icklingham, I, 940
Note (Noote, Notte): John, of Norton *iuxta* Woolpit, I, *307*; of Thurston, I, 358; and Margaret his wife, of West Stow, I, *1022*
   Robert, of Groton, I, 812
   Thomas, of Groton, II, *254*
   William, of Langham, I, 7; of Thurston, II, 265
Nune, Nunne: Marion, widow, of Thorpe Morieux, II, 613
   Nicholas, of Hessett, I, 370
   John, the elder, of Rougham, II, 634; the younger, of Rougham, I, 1297
Nydyll: John, of Lavenham, I, 299

Ode: John, of Barway in Soham (Cambs), I, 1319
Odelyn (Odlyn): Agnes, of Wortham, II, 34
   Ed', of Wortham, I, *733*
Oky: John, of Mellis, I, *734*
Oldhalle (Oldale): Anne, wife of Walter, of Sudbury, I, *1447*
   Walter, of Sudbury, II, 702
Oldman: John, of Chippenham (Cambs), II, *143*
Olyfe (Olyve): Joan, of Glemsford, II, 317
   John, of Haughley, I, 461; of Mendlesham, I, 29

William, the elder, of Cavendish, I, 776
Olyvere: William, of Wangford, II, 302
Omfrey: John, the elder, of Combs, I, 1392
Onge: Adam, of Barningham, I, 59; I, 124
Orderych: William, of Hitcham, II, 587
Orger: Thomas, of Mendlesham, I, *1159*
Osbern: Geoffrey, of Stowmarket, I, *1000*
   William, of Cotton, II, 6
Osmond: John, husbandman, of Assington, II, 459
Osteler: Roger, of Shelland, I, 21
Othoo: Benedict, the elder, of Bradfield St George, II, 772
Ottley (Ottele): John, of Little Saxham, I, 246
   William, of Little Saxham, I, 34
Oversouth: William, of Westley by Bury St Edmunds, I, 226

Page: Alice, of Ickworth, II, 709
   John, of Ickworth, II, 708; of Ixworth, I, *452*; of Stanstead, II, 22; of Worlington, II, 612
   Margaret, of Kirtling (Cambs), II, 609
   Robert, of Great Saxham, II, 534
   Thomas, of Ickworth, II, 695
   Walter, of Eye, II, 178; of Ickworth, I, 139; of Lavenham, II, 454
Pakenham: John, of Cockfield, I, *607*
Pakke: William, of Eye, I, *1318*
Paleyser: John, of Culford, I, 315
Palgrave: William, of Newmarket, I, 499
Palmere: Henry, of Elmswell, I, *445*
   John, of Soham (Cambs), I, 478
   Thomas, of Layham, I, 197
   William, of Wordwell, I, *1060*
Pap': Walter, of Glemsford, I, *576*
Parker (Parkere): Henry, of Semer, I, 1416
   John, of Stowmarket, I, 19
   Robert, of Lidgate, I, 114
   Thomas, of Thorpe Morieux, I, *773*
   see also Cook *alias* Parker
Parkyn: John, of Great Livermere, I, 182; the elder, of Barningham, I, 1278
   Margaret, of Culford, I, *1464*
   see also Perkyn
Parle (Perle): John, of Bildeston, I, 1125; of Lavenham, I, 1073; barker, of Lavenham, I, 402
Parman (Perman): Robert, of Aldersfield in Wickhambrook, II, 99; II, 808
Parmenter: John, of Great Finborough, II, 1
   William, of Hitcham, I, *27*
Parys: John, of Soham (Cambs), II, 204
Paton: John, of Drinkstone, II, 95
Patyll: William, of Badwell Ash, I, *1491*
Paxman: Thomas, of Burwell (Cambs), I, 911; II, 643
   William, of Burwell (Cambs), I, 682

Payn: Geoffrey, of Wortham, I, 873
  John, of Wortham, I, *424*
  Margaret, of Wortham, I, *1140*; widow of
    John, of Haverhill, I, 211
  Robert, of Sudbury, I, 1492; of Thelnetham,
    I, 1494
  William, of Sudbury, I, 1493
Payntour: John, the elder, husbandman, of
  Burwell (Cambs), I, 150
Peak (Peek): Thomas, of Lawshall, I, *587*; II, 541
Pecas (Pegas, Pegays): Agnes, of Brandon, II,
  466
  Christian, of Brandon, I, *141*
  William, the elder, of Brandon, II, 792
Peddere (Pedder): Alice, widow, of Ixworth, II,
  228
  William, of Stoke by Clare, II, *106*
  see also Hamond alias Pedder
Peers: Philip, of Sudbury, II, 271
Pekerell (Pekyrell): John, of Thurston, I, 1437; of
  Wetherden, I, 33
  Roger, of Thurston, I, 1451
  Thomas, of Rickinghall Superior, I, 1207
Pellycan: John, of Sudbury, I, 277
Peltyr: John, of Clare, II, 26
Penteney alias Sporyere: Ralph, of Ixworth, II,
  220
Peper (Pepyr): Robert, the elder, of Eye, I, 481
  Sarah, of Palgrave, I, *432*
Peretrych: Katherine, of Acton, I, 289
Perkyn (Perken): John, the elder, of Barningham,
  I, 954
  Simon, of Hopton, II, 36; II, 555
  see also Parkyn
Perpontes (Perpount): John, the younger, of
  Denston, I, *715*
  Margaret, of Westhorpe, I, 5
Person: Richard, of Ampton, II, 515; II, 538
Pery (Perye, Pury): John, of Great Whelnetham,
  II, 66; of Haverhill, I, *1148*; of Kersey, I,
  719
  Robert, of Kersey, I, 1115
Pethyrton: Henry, of Sudbury, I, 91
  John, of Brandon Ferry, II, 377
Petywate: John, of Glemsford, II, 504
Peykot: John, of Withersfield, I, *504*
Phelipe: John, of Melford, II, 756
Picher: Meliora, widow, of Kentford, I, *1020*
Place: John, of Lavenham, I, 126
  Rose, widow of Walter, of Mildenhall, I, 120
  Thomas, of Mildenhall, I, 938
Plante: John, of Great Finborough, I, 538
Playford: Agnes, of Troston, II, 789
  John, of Mildenhall, II, 312; the elder, of
    Mildenhall, II, 754
Podeney: Robert, of Bures St Mary, II, 55
Polle: Adam, of Barnham, I, 1268
Polych: William, of Oakley, I, *1166*

Ponder (Pondere): John, of Great Ashfield, II,
  192; of Waldingfield, I, 1469; fuller, of
  Sudbury, II, 306
Ponge: Agnes, of Poslingford, I, *332*
Poole: William, of Fordham (Cambs), I, *1351*
Pope: Henry, of Mellis, I, 369
  John, of Eye, II, 222; of Wattisfield, I, *591*
  Richard, of Knettishall, I, 975
  Thomas, of Redgrave, II, 620
  Walter, of Thrandeston, I, *649*
Port (Porte): Edmund, of Honington, II, 474
  John, of Barningham, I, *121*
Porter: John, of Chelsworth, I, 1194
Potter (Poteer, Pottere, Potyer): John, the elder, of
  Bures St Mary, II, 326
  Marion, of Clare, I, 1218
  Thomas, of Rede, II, 400
  William, of Bures, I, *1135*
Pouncy: Thomas, of Wickhambrook, II, 213
Power (Powere): Henry, of ?Great Barton, I, *1236*
  Margery, of Great Barton, II, 584
Powlyn: John, of Timworth, I, 892
  Katherine, of Timworth, II, *1109*
Poye: Peter, of Walsham, I, *518*
Prath: Richard, of Ashley (Cambs), I, 247
Prentys (Prentyzys, Preyntese): John, of Clare, I,
  1010; of Kersey, I, 566
  Katherine, of Sudbury, I, 420
Prom: John, of Brockford in Wetheringsett, I, 801
Pryke: John, the elder, of Barrow, II, 531
Pryme: James, of Thrandeston, I, *604*
Prynchet: John, of Chelsworth, I, 204
Pryor: William, of Great Cornard, I, 941
Pulkoo: John, of Lavenham, I, 355
Punge: Richard, of Poslingford, I, 173
Punte: John, of Palgrave, I, *1349*
  Thomas, of Occold, I, 1165
Purpyll: Henry, of Denham by Bury, I, 269
Pursere: John, of Stoke by Nayland, I, 610
Pusk (Puske): James, of Kersey, I, 392
  John, of Kersey, II, 92
Puttok: Thomas, barker, of Mildenhall, II, 147
Pydenale: Adam, of Ousden, II, 335
Pye: Alice, of Assington, II, 407
  Edmund, of Assington, I, 1057
  Thomas, of Assington, I, 215
Pyke: John, of Stanton, I, 634
Pykerell: John, of Thurston, II, 321
  Robert, of Norton, I, 782
Pypere: John, of Thorpe Morieux, II, 131
  Thomas, of Thorpe Morieux, II, 238
Pyrty: Thomas, of Thorndon, I, 817
Pytt: John, the elder, of Wattisfield, I, 964
  William, of Wattisfield, II, 542

Qwarry: Henry, of Hitcham, I, 1459
Qwhelmere: John, of Hundon, II, 78
  Nicholas, of Wicken (Cambs), II, 427

Qwyk: William, of Edwardstone, I, 1496
Qwylter: Robert, of Bures St Mary, II, 460
    Thomas, of Newmarket, II, 510
Qwyn: Marion, of Thrandeston, I, *906*
    Thomas, of Eye, I, *808*
Qwyntyn: Peter, of Hitcham, II, 43
Qwyythand: Sarah, of Icklingham, I, *581*

Rampoly: John, of Rickinghall Superior, I, 679
    Thomas, of Rickinghall, I, *1376*
Raunde: Joan, of Little Wratting, I, *266*
    John, of Great Waldingfield, I, *513*
Rawlyn: Isabel, of Chippenham (Cambs), II, 199
    Robert, of Chippenham (Cambs), II, *124*
    William, of Barnham St Gregory, II, *73*
Ray: John, of Newmarket, I, 1463; of
    Wickhambrook, I, 696; of Woodditton
    (Cambs), I, *1320*
Rayner: Andrew, of Soham (Cambs), I, 1041
Rayson: William, of Kedington, II, 355
Rechard: John, of Beyton, II, 572
Reche: Margaret, widow, of Boxford, I, 1089
Recheford: Margery, of Worlington, I, *1053*
Rede: John, of Thornham, I, *1445*
Redelysworth: William, of Badwell Ash, I, 1399
Reder: John, of Timworth, I, *856*
    Richard, of Redgrave, II, *811*
Redgrave: Clement, of Great Livermere, I, *35*
Reede *alias* Gooch: John, of Wickhambrook, I,
    473
Regewyn: John, of Sudbury, I, 258
    Margaret, of Woolpit, II, 571
Rekedon: Margery, widow of John, of Gazeley,
    I, 759
Resshebrook: John, of Combs, I, 47
Reve: Isabel, of Wickham Skeith, I, *1264*
    John, of Cowlinge, I, 896; of Hepworth, II,
    392; of Wickham Skeith, I, 1252
    see also Cake *alias* Reve
Rewe: John, of Whepstead, I, 351
    William, of Thelnetham, I, 1063
Reyffham: William, the elder, of Fordham
    (Cambs), I, *839*
Reygham: Thomas, of Waldingfield, I, *647*
Reynold (Regnold): John, of Woolpit, II, 570
    William, of Woolpit, I, *563*
Reynoldysson: Edward, of Great Thurlow, I, *527*
Roberd: Alan, of Sudbury, I, 128
    Alice, of Sudbury, I, *686*
    Cecily, of Sudbury, I, *770*
    John, of Lawshall, II, *616*
Robertson: Nicholas, of Glemsford, II, 640
Robhod (Robhood): Joan, widow, of Walsham le
    Willows, II, 401
    John, of Walsham le Willows, I, 1272
    Robert, of Walsham le Willows, I, 767
Robyn: Richard, of Rushbrooke, II, 535
    William, of Exning, I, 984

Rodelond: Joan, widow of John, of Kersey, I,
    1228
    John, the elder, of Kersey, I, 1245
    William, of Great Waldingfield, I, 643
    see also Rudlonde
Rodyng (Rodynge): Adam, of Great Horringer,
    II, 654
    Margery, of Wetherden, II, 451
Rodys: Nicholas, of Combs, II, 478
Roger (Rogere): Geoffrey, of Great Finborough,
    II, 619
    John, of Barrow, I, 495
    Thomas, of Snailwell (Cambs), I, *1414*
Rogere *alias* Wever: Andrew, of Eye, I, 460
Rogyll: Thomas, of Glemsford, II, 164
Rogyn: John, of Rattlesden, I, 1031
Rokeby: William, of Fordham, I, *1442*
Rokell: John, of Lavenham, I, *804*; of Melford
    Tye, II, 59
    Thomas, of Lavenham, I, 376
Rolf (Rolff): John, of Burwell (Cambs), I, 1162
    Thomas, of Burwell (Cambs), I, 927
    William, of Snailwell (Cambs), I, *243*
Rollecros: Thomas, of Stanton, I, 796
    Walter, of Stanton, I, 1395
Rongnyng: William, of Little Bradley, I, *664*
Roodese: John, glover, of Ixworth, II, 37
Roole: Richard, of Burwell (Cambs), II, 514
Roos: John, of Nayland, I, 1479
Roote (Rote): Christine, wife of John, of
    Glemsford, I, 391
    John, of Glemsford, I, 838; I, *1021*
    Matilda, of Glemsford, I, *688*
    Richard, of Mildenhall, II, 347
    Thomas, of Glemsford, II, 508
Ropere (Roper): John, of Nayland, I, *1290*
    Thomas, of Hopton, I, 794
    see also, Lotkyn *alias* Roper
Ropkyn: Roger, of Thrandeston, I, 492
Rose: John, the younger, of Thurston, I, 552
Roungtun: Matilda, of Troston, I, 1174
Rous (Rows): John, of Brockley, I, 191; of
    Pakenham, I, 1255
    William, of Long Melford, I, 1363
Rowhed: William, of Thorndon, I, *907*
Rowhey: William, of Little Thurlow, II, 23
Rownton: John, of Lawshall, II, 582
Rowt: John, of Rattlesden, II, 231
Rudham: William, of Great Barton, I, 40
Rudlonde: Robert, of Great Waldingfield, II, 537
    see also Rodelond
Rukke: John, of Wetheringsett, I, 1034
Rumbylowe John, of Gazeley, I, 1344
Runneye: William, of Preston, I, *1282*
Rus: John, of Woolpit, II, 27
Russch: John, of Wetherden, I, 608
Russell: John, the elder, churchwarden, of Great
    Waldingfield, II, 424

Russhford: Joan, wife of Richard, of Hitcham,
I, 1461
John, of Sudbury, II, 189
Rygge: John, of Combs, II, 169
Rynglage: John, of Fornham St Genevieve, I,
1153
Rysby: Ed', of Buxhall, II, 404
Rysyng: William, of Mellis, I, *875*

Sad: Matilda, of Clare, I, *1127*
Salle *alias* Cooke: John, the elder, of Bildeston,
II, 484
Salter: Henry, of Buxhall, II, 591
Salysbery (Salysbure, Salysbury): Joan, wife of
Richard, of Soham (Cambs), I, *819*
Richard, of Soham (Cambs), I, 871
Thomas, of Soham (Cambs), II, 748
Sampson (Sawmpson): John, of Hinderclay, II,
795
Thomas, of Bardwell, II, 738; of Stansfield,
I, *695*
Sansom (Sawnsum): Laurence, of Great Cornard,
I, 630
Santon: Robert, of Wangford, II, 47
William, of Wangford, I, *1254*
Sare: Alice, widow, of Elmswell, II, 318
John, of Withersfield, I, *1107*
Robert, of Walsham, II, 496
Sawndyr: John, the younger, of Cheveley
(Cambs), II, 623
Sawyer (Sawer, Sawere): John, of Lavenham, I,
462; of [*not given*], I, *434*
Thomas, of Thelnetham, I, 969
Sawyer *alias* Gylly: John, of Bradfield St George,
II, 663
Saxsy (Saxi, Saxsi): Clement, of Eye, I, 623
John, of Cookley, hamlet of Eye, I, *425*; of
Stanningfield, I, 233
Say: William, of Wicken (Cambs), II, 747
Scarpe: William, of Felsham, II, 532
Scateron: John, of Elmswell, I, 1001
Schapman: John, of Withersfield, II, 565
see also Chapman
Schedde: William, of Lavenham, II, 339
Schelton: William, of Stowmarket, II, 109
Schep: John, of Woolpit, I, 11
Schildyrston: *see* Chylderston
Schorthose: Thomas, weaver, of Sudbury, I, 1181
Schouthar: Geoffrey, of Mellis, I, *484*
Schyrlok: [*not given*], of [*not given*], I, 738
Scoot: John, of Hopton, I, 1292
Screvener: John, of Wickhambrook, I, 1418
Scut: Thomas, of Soham (Cambs), I, 238
Segbrook: John, of Stowmarket, II, 521
Seger (Segore): John, of Tuddenham, II, 340
William, of Stradishall, II, 272
Seman: John, the elder, of Drinkstone, II, 19
Thomas, of Thelnetham, I, 213

William, of Little Cornard, I, 356
Semancrofth: John, of [Regrave], II, 195
Sephar: Alice, of Barnham, I, *885*
Seriaunt: *see* Cheryaunt
Serjawnt: William, of Stoke by Nayland, I, 189
Serle: John, of Great Wratting, I, *1284*; of
Hundon, I, 967; of Stanton, I, 663
Sewale: John, of Stowmarket, I, *1138*
Robert, of Great Barton, II, 266
Seymour: John, the elder, of Stanningfield, I, 431
Sheldrake: John, lettered man, of Little
Waldingfield, I, 1193; of Stoke by Nayland,
II, 480
Margaret, of Waldingfield, I, *1360*
William, of Little Waldingfield, I, 171
Sheperde (Shepherd, Sheppard): Margaret,
widow, of Sudbury, II, 652
Thomas, of Botesdale in Redgrave, I, 1341; of
Melford, II, 722
Sherlynge: Ralph, of Stowmarket, II, 592
Sherman: John, of Yaxley, II, 244
Richard, of Wattisham, II, 433
Sheryngton: William, of Wetheringsett, II, 796
Shomere (Schomer): John, of Layham, I, 334
Katherine, of Layham, I, *1071*
Shukford (Schucford): John, of Thelnetham, II,
561; II, 769
Robert, of Langham, II, 207; of Thelnetham,
I, 506
Simond: John, of ?Berans, II, *144*; of Botesdale
in Redgrave, I, *1374*
Skeete: Alice, widow, of Great Livermere, II, 241
Skeppere: John, the elder, of Woolpit, II, 40
Sketh (Skeyth): Katherine, relict of Thomas, of
Stanton, II, 453
Margaret, of Stanton, II, 711
Thomas, of Stanton, II, 817
Skoyle: John, of Brockley, I, 472
Skynall (Skynale): Richard, of Snailwell
(Cambs), II, 9
Skynner (Skynnere): John, of Stoke by Nayland,
I, 1347
Thomas, of Rougham, II, 679
Walter, of Rickinghall Inferior, I, 1170
William, of Kedington, I, *38*
Skyppyng: Robert, of Haverhill, I, *1012*
Slade: Ed', of Stoke by Nayland, I, 1331
Slaw (Sclawe): John, of Botesdale in Redgrave,
I, 252
Matilda, of Botesdale in Redgrave, I, *925*
Walter, of Botesdale in Redgrave, I, *401*
Smalwode: Isabel, of Bradfield St George, II, 583
Smith (Smeth, Smethe, Smyth): Cecily, of
Burwell (Cambs), I, *79*
Denise, of Eriswell, I, *166*
Eleanor, of Nayland, II, 439
Geoffrey, of Bures St Mary, II, 781

Henry, of Rattlesden, I, 1310; of West Stow,
I, *698*
Isabel, of Great Finborough, II, 142
James, of Eriswell, I, 352
John, of Barnardiston, II, 655; of Beyton, I,
52; of Clare, II, 815; of Exning, I, *1308*;
of Hundon, I, *847*; of Kersey, I, 923; of
Kirtling (Cambs), I, 1468; of Lindsey, I,
292; of Polstead, I, *650*; of Soham (Cambs),
II, 397; of Stansfield, II, 255; of Stanton
All Saints, II, 566; of Stoke by Nayland, I,
1120; of Wickhambrook, I, 459; I, *653*; the
elder, of Barnardiston, I, 1229; the elder, of
Botesdale, II, 327; II, 348; limeburner, of
Ballingdon, I, *147*
Margaret, widow, of Boxford, I, 308
Nicholas, of Walsham le Willows, I, 1370
Ralph, of Bildeston, II, 720; II, 721
Richard, of Great Livermere, I, 1003; of
Shimpling, I, *168*; of Tuddenham, I, *14*; of
Westley, II, 487
Robert, of Wyverstone, I, *72*
Roger, of Barnardiston, I, 654
Seman, of Great Finborough, II, 156
Simon, of Worlington, I, 1241
Thomas, of Hessett, I, 857; I, 1113; of
Stansfield, II, 121; of Westley, I, 98
William, of Bures St Mary, II, 658; of
Cowlinge, I, *561*; the elder, of Clare, I, 832
see also Anows *alias* Smyth, Watlok *alias*
Smyth
Smyth *alias* Barbour: Marion, of Stowmarket,
I, 152
Snawe: John, of Nayland, I, *874*
Snode: Richard, of Westley, I, *360*; I, 692
Robert, of Westley, I, 616
Somerton: Robert, of Chevington, I, 314
Sopere: Robert, of Barton Mills, I, 46
Sorell: John, of Chelsworth, I, 516
Spaldyng: John, of Wortham, I, 1224
Sparham: John, of Eye, II, *176*
Spark: John, of Wetheringsett, I, *918*
Sparman: Philip, of Groton, I, 1150
Sparow (Sparowe): Robert, of Melford, II, 436;
II, 779
Sparwe: John, of Bury St Edmunds, I, 279
Walter, of Boxford, I, *378*
Speed: William, of Little Saxham, I, 245
Spencer (Spencere, Spenser): John, of Dalham,
I, *1204*
Thomas, of Bardwell, II, 604
Walter, of Ousden, I, *163*
Sperlyng (Sperlynge): John, of Stoke by Nayland,
I, *1283*; II, 641
Katherine, of Combs, II, *200*
Spetyllman (Spetylman): William, of Glemsford,
I, 158; of Norton, I, 1333
Sponer (Sponere): Isabel, of Sapiston, II, *288*

Peter, of Sapiston, I, *872*
[*not given*], of [*not given*], I, *620*
Sporle: John, of Burgate, II, *715*
Sporyere: *see* Penteney *alias* Sporyere
Spragy: Laurence, of Haughley, II, 511
Spring (Spryng, Sprynge): Thomas, of Lavenham,
I, 102
William, of Soham (Cambs), I, 902
Spring (Spryng) *alias* Wederdeyn: Robert, of
Brockford in Wetheringsett, II, 810
Spront (Sprunte): Mariota, widow, of Clare, II,
662
Richard, of Clare, II, 155
Sprot: John, of Sudbury, I, *748*
Spycere (Spyser): John, of Bildeston, I, 895; of
Walsham le Willows, II, 175
Stace (Stacy): John, of Thurston, I, 430
Matilda, of Sudbury, II, 307
Robert, of Barway in Soham (Cambs), II, *794*
Staley: Richard, of Thorndon, II, *791*
Stalman (Staloun): John, the elder, of Mildenhall,
II, 107; the younger, of Mildenhall, I, 708
Stanbowe: John, of Great Livermere, I, 1195
Stanton: James, of Brome, I, 920
John, of Clare, I, *670*; of Rougham, I, 1183
Starchant: John, of Boxford, I, 155
Steff: Robert, of Barrow, I, *25*
Sterlond: William, of Icklingham, I, 1472
Stevenes: John, of Ixworth, I, 961
Stevynesson: John, of Woolpit, I, 469
Stiward: John, of Nayland, I, 573
Stonham: Peter, of Thorndon, II, 764
Story: Henry, of Whatfield, II, 406
Stroude *alias* Taylour: Nicholas, of Stoke by
Clare, II, 637
Strut (Struth): Alice, widow, of Bildeston, II, 303
Robert, of Acton, I, 813
Thomas, of Hartest, I, 456
Sturdy: John, of Kedington, II, *105*
Sturmyn: Christian, of Lavenham, I, 1002; I,
1048
Stuston: Thomas, of Oakley, I, 636
William, of Oakley, I, 949
Sudbury: William, of Kettlebaston, I, 1300
Sugge: Annabel, widow of Seman, of
Edwardstone, I, 234
Surych: John, of Nayland, I, *755*
Susan: Alice, of Cockfield, I, *9*
Sutton (Suttone): Clemencia, of Bradfield St
Clare, I, 867
Margaret, of Tuddenham, I, *1061*
Richard, of Oxborough (Norfolk), I, 489
William, of Mildenhall, II, 650
Swan: Thomas, of Thorndon, I, *241*
see also Swayn
Swanton: Henry, of Botesdale, II, 376
Isabel, of Botesdale, II, 546
Joan, widow, of Depden, II, 685

John, of Rede, II, 686
William, of Denston, I, *731*; of Depden, II, 366
Swayn (Sweyn): Alice, widow, of Creeting St Peter, I, 1049
James, of Glemsford, II, 163
John, of Creeting St Peter, I, 665; of Lavenham, I, 164; of Rattlesden, I, *558*; the elder, of Lavenham, II, 517
Thomas, of Creeting St Peter, II, 472; of Mildenhall, II, 216
see also Swan
Swyfte (Swyftt): John, of Walsham le Willows, II, 258
Thomas, of Long Melford, I, 1237
Sybbys: Alice, of Coney Weston, I, 1497
Sybly: John, of Cheveley (Cambs), I, *1081*; I, 1082
Syday (Sydey): John, fuller, of Great Waldingfield, II, 225; weaver, of Great Waldingfield, I, 541
Sygo (Sygoo): John, of Worlington, II, 429
Robert, of Mildenhall, I, 65
Symond: Thomas, of Cheveley (Cambs), I, *1426*; of Rougham, I, 1478; of Thelnetham, I, 1355
William, of Mildenhall, I, *1435*
Synton: William, of Sudbury, II, 31
Syre: Margaret, of Great Ashfield, II, 390
Robert, of Ashfield, II, 639

Tabbard: John, of West Stow, I, 1309
Taberham: Elizabeth, of Great Waldingfield, II, 305
Talworth: John, of [*not given*], I, *844*
Taylor (Taillour, Talyour, Taylore, Taylour Taylowr): Alice, of Bradfield St George, II, 672
Cecily, of [*not given*], I, *327*
Henry, of Brockford in Wetheringsett, I, 1453
John, of Bradfield St George, I, *466*; of Buxhall, I, *1366*; of Thorndon, I, 809; II, 126
Robert, of Lavenham, I, 416
Thomas, of Hitcham, I, 921; of Lavenham, II, 223
William, of Eriswell, I, *751*; of Preston, I, *1173*; of Sudbury, I, 198
see also Stroude *alias* Taylour
Taylour *alias* Wyllyamsone: John, of Mildenhall, I, 1263
Tebawde: John, of Fordham (Cambs), II, 187
Tew *alias* Kyrtelynge: John, of Stoke by Clare, I, 522
Therlyng: William, of Little Thurlow, I, *1413*
Thewytes (Thweyt): Matthew, of Wetheringsett, I, 869
Thomas, of Bildeston, II, 799

Thomson: Alexander, of Brandon, I, *884*
Threchere: John, of Clare, I, 260
Thurgor (Thurgore, Thurgur): James, of Acton, II, 651
John, of Waldingfield, I, *1038*
Robert, of Acton, II, 20
William, of Great Waldingfield, II, 158
Thurmod: John, of Bildeston, I, 1486; of Thorpe Morieux, I, *774*
Richard, of Thorpe Morieux, I, *1122*
Thyknesse: John, of Newmarket, I, 1358
Thystelden: Alice, long time wife of Robert Kent, of Stowmarket, II, 421
Tilbrook: *see* Tylbrook
Tille: *see* Tylle
Toffay: Thomas, of Bardwell, II, 159
Toftes (Toftys): John, of West Stow, II, 304
Reginald, of Elveden, II, 185
Tollere: Robert, of Wangford, II, 120
Toly: Margaret, of Barnham, I, *1171*
William, of Barnham, I, 983
Tomson: Alice, widow, of Haverhill, I, 1457
Tone: John, of Little Whelnetham, I, *1025*
Torald: Joan, of Thornham, I, *1095*
Tornore: John, of Depden, II, 53
see also Turnour
Trapet (Trapett): Margery, of Market Weston, II, 268
Ralph, of Hepworth, II, 68
Thomas, of Hepworth, I, 1257
Tregegold *alias* Baly: Henry, of Exning, I, 1128
Trewpeny: John, of Mildenhall, II, 735
Treylys: William, of Palgrave, II, *217*
Trooll: Stephen, of Wickhambrook, I, 1055
Tubby: William, of Wortham, I, 1164
Tuffeld: Alice, of Whepstead, I, *267*
John, the elder, of Whepstead, II, 179
Tunman: James, of Westhorpe, II, 477
Turnour: Alice, of Sudbury, II, 698
Beatrice, of Woolpit, I, 806
Isabel, widow of John Bachbrook, of Sudbury, I, 175
James, of Drinkstone, I, 439
John, of Chippenham (Cambs), II, *753*; of Norton, I, *1380*; of Whepstead, I, *888*; of Woolpit, I, 60; of [*not given*], I, *328*; the elder, of Kirtling (Cambs), II, 281; gentleman, of Great Thurlow, II, 608
Robert, of Eye, II, 405
Simon, of Combs, II, 594
Thomas, of Sudbury, I, 374
William, of Walsham, II, 495
see also Tornore
Turnour *alias* Dyer: Henry, of Long Melford, I, 1369
Tyd (Tydde): John, of Mildenhall, I, 727
Robert, of Mildenhall, I, 598
Thomas, of Mildenhall, II, 819

Tye: John, of Poslingford, I, *988*
  Margaret, of, Sudbury All Saints, II, 166
  Robert, of Lavenham, I, 1243
Tyell: William, of Boyton End in Stoke by Clare,
  I, *526*
  see also Tylle
Tylbrok (Tilbrook, Tylbrook): John, of Kirtling
  (Cambs), II, 499
  Peter, of Kirtling (Cambs), I, 337
  Thomas, of Upend in Kirtling (Cambs), II, 610
Tyler (Tylere): Alice, of Wetheringsett, I, *912*
  John, of Westley, II, 128
  Thomas, of Westley, I, *1391*
  William, of Creeting St Peter, I, 209
Tylkys: John, of Glemsford, II, 21
Tylle (Tille): Agnes, of Preston, II, 145
  John, of Boxford, I, 214; of Rattlesden, I,
  765; of Sudbury, II, 670; dyer, of Sudbury,
  I, 1489
  see also Tyell
Tyllot (Tyllott): Margaret, of Great Barton, I, 294
  Roger, of Rougham, I, 1240
Tymbyrman: John, the elder, of Mildenhall, II,
  668
Tymtewell: William, of Stowmarket, I, 1421
Tymton: John, of Great Finborough, I, 1343
Tymworth: John, of Timworth, I, 468
Tyso: John, formerly of Drinkstone, of
  Stowmarket, II, 205
  Margaret, of Drinkstone, I, *922*
  Thomas, of Drinkstone, I, 1054; I, *1056*

Ufford: Robert, of Hundon, I, 1083
Umfrey: Isabel, of Sapiston, I, 1242
Underwoode: William, of Burgate, II, 718

Vale: John, of Long Melford, I, 82
Venour: George, of Cornard, I, *1027*
Vyell: Thomas, of Ixworth, II, 804; the elder, of
  Ixworth, II, 723
Vypownd: Stephen, of Lidgate, II, 188

Wade: Alice, of Woolpit, II, 375
  James, of Woolpit, I, 564
  John, of Creeting, I, *851*
Wadsell: John, of Stradishall, II, 198
Waggard: Davy, of Sapiston, I, *1059*
Wagge: John, of Haverhill, I, 1092
Wagon: John, of Timworth, I, 1074
Wale: John, of Thornham Parva, I, 1014; the
  elder, of Thornham Magna, I, 788
Walenger: Nicholas, of Nayland, I, *200*
Waleys (Walleys): Alice, of Soham (Cambs), I,
  1085
  John, of Hundon, I, *689*
  Thomas, of Burwell, II, 631
  Walter, of Thorndon, I, *597*
Walkefar: Richard, of Hitcham, I, 487

Wall: John, of Boxford, I, 612
Wallere (Walloure, Walour): Nicholas, of Market
  Weston, I, *951*
  Thomas, of Fornham St Martin, II, 497; of
  Wattisfield, II, 741
Walsham (Walsom): John, of Pakenham, II, 295;
  of Woolpit, I, 282
Walter (Waltere): John, the elder, of Hopton, I,
  286; I, *323*
  Richard, of Coney Weston, II, 294
  Walter, of Coney Weston, II, 590
  see also Watyr
Wanton: Robert, of Stanton, I, 1299
Warde: Alice, of Fornham All Saints, I, 12
  John, of Saxon Street in Woodditton (Cambs),
  I, *428*
  Margaret, of Haverhill, II, *341*
  Robert, of Walsham le Willows, I, *1043*
Wareyn (Waryn): Amfritha, of Sudbury, II, 32
  Henry, of Combs, I, *753*
  John, of Bildeston, I, 415; of Brettenham, I,
  840; of Mildenhall, II, 638; of Stoke by
  Nayland, I, 301; of Stowmarket, II, 325;
  barker, of Nayland, I, 108; the elder, fuller,
  of Long Melford, I, 474; the elder, of
  Mildenhall, I, 1471; the younger, of Long
  Melford, I, 790;
  Margaret, daughter of John the younger, of
  Long Melford, I, 916
  Richard, of Long Melford, I, 1329
  Robert, of Great Ashfield, I, 1258; of Kirtling
  (Cambs), I, 1467
  Rose, of Kersey, I, 390
  Thomas, of Haughley, II, 547
Warner (Warnere): Alice, of Elmswell, I, *855*
  John, of Barrow, I, 494; of Great Livermere,
  II, 599
  Katherine, of Great Livermere, II, 760
  Margaret, of Barrow, I, 57
  Thomas, of Bardwell, II, 526
  William, of Bradfield St George, II, 61; of
  Soham (Cambs), II, 232
Warton: John, of Milden, I, *512*
Warwell: William, of Polstead, I, 1484
Waschepoke: Eleanor, of Haverhill, I, 491
  William, of Haverhill, I, 490
Wasshscher: Robert, of Boxford, II, 440
Watlock: John, of Clare, I, 112
Watlok *alias* Smyth: John, of Rede, I, 960
Wattys: Simon, of Santon Downham, II, 826
Watyr: John, of Eye, II, 442
  see also Walter
Watyrnas: John, of Norton, I, 1379
Waysborn: John, of Hinderclay, II, 802
Webbe: Alice, of Palgrave, II, 251
  John, of Elmswell, II, 603; the elder, of
  Palgrave, I, *1330*

Robert, of Great Thurlow, I, *395*; clerk, of
Woolpit, II, 624
Thomas, of Lidgate, I, *1028*; of [*not given*],
I, *673*
William, of Long Melford, I, *532*
see also Clerk *alias* Webbe
Webster: Richard, of Ixworth, I, *628*
Wederdeyn: *see* Spryng *alias* Wederdeyn
Wederton: Richard, of Hitcham, II, 181
Wedyr: John, of Elmswell, I, 1495
Wedyrdene: Mariola, of Bildeston, I, 680
see also Spryng *alias* Wederdeyn
Welde: Ada, widow of John, of Woolpit, I, 777
John, of Woolpit, I, 261
Welham: William, of Great Horringer, II, 10
Well (Welles, Wellis, Wellys): Margaret, wife of
John Well, of Hartest, I, 1075
Matilda, of Bardwell, I, *451*
Robert, of Coney Weston, I, *330*; of Hartest, I,
687; of Newton Green, I, 463
Simon, of Woolpit, I, 713
Thomas, of Stoke by Nayland, I, *1412*; of,
Walsham, I, *562*
William, of Bardwell, II, 16
Wellam: John, of Hitcham, I, 772
Welton: John, of Cheveley (Cambs), I, 676
Wenden: Emma, of Bures, I, *275*
Wepsted (Whepsted): John, of Brettenham, II,
298; II, 322
Westbrome: William, of Wetherden, II, 334
Wether (Wethere, Wethyr): Ed', of Elmswell, I,
700
John, of Honington, II, *520*; the elder, of
Elmswell, I, 725
Robert, of Elmswell, I, *1112*; of Norton, I, *336*
William, of Stanton All Saints, II, 256
Wetherard (Wetherhard): John, of Stowmarket, I,
934; the elder, of Stowmarket, I, 714
Margaret, of Stowmarket, I, 943; II, 669
Wever: *see* Rogere *alias* Wever
Wevour: Richard, of Little Cornard, I, *565*
Weyneyld: Simon, of Chelsworth, II, 154
Whasshman: Katherine, of Lavenham, I, 161
Whytbred: Agnes, of Eye, I, 320
Whyte: John, of Kentford, I, 894
Thomas, of Haughley, II, 25
William, of Wetheringsett, II, 593
Whythcde: Margaret, of Soham (Cambs), I, 626
Wodeman: John, of Sudbury, I, 937
Woderys: Robert, of Mildenhall, I, *750*
Wodesey (Wodsey): Stephen, of Nayland, I, *1314*
Thomas, of Stoke by Nayland, I, 930
Wombe: John, of Great Cornard, I, 1365
Wood (Wode, Woode): John, of Cowlinge, I,
1386; of Elmswell, I, *496*
Matilda, of Ixworth, I, *1405*
Nicholas, of Thornham Magna, I, 771

Richard, of Drinkstone, II, 388; smith, of
Drinkstone, I, *1339*
Worliche *alias* Flecchere: Richard, of Mildenhall,
II, 345
Worlych: Joan, of Ixworth, I, *905*
Wrangyll: Katherine, widow of William, of
Drinkstone, I, 423
Wrenche: Walter, of Long Melford, I, *1425*
Wrethe: Thomas, of Soham (Cambs), I, *1444*
Wroo: Henry, of Rickinghall Superior, I, 1340
Wrygh (Wryght, Wryghte, Wrygth, Wryht,
Wryth): Agnes, of Brome, I, 1158
Beatrice, widow of John the elder, of
Wortham, I, 1422
John, of Barway in Soham (Cambs), I, 253;
of Soham, II, 524; of Wickham Skeith, I,
1200; II, 210; the younger, of Barway in
Soham, I, 256;
Richard, of Bures St Mary, II, 67; of
Glemsford, I, *991*; of Hitcham, I, 151
Robert, of Sudbury, I, *652*
Simon, of Cotton, I, 409
Thomas, of Stuston, II, *165*
William, of Great Bradley, I, *568*
see also Camplyon *alias* Wryght
Wyat (Wyot, Wyott): John, of Burwell (Cambs),
I, *244*
Robert, of Exning, I, 278
William, of Preston, II, 190
Wybbyll: Joan, of Hunston, I, 1217
Wyburgh: William, of Denston, II, 785
Wyff: John, of Cockfield, I, *470*
Wygenale: Roger, of Boxford, I, 118
Wykham: John, of Great Horringer, I, 722; of
Wickhambrook, I, *1431*
Wylchyn: William, of Gislingham, I, 958
Wylkyn: John, of Burwell (Cambs), I, *697*
Robert, of Burwell (Cambs), I, 1052
William, of Burwell (Cambs), II, 626
Wyllyamsone: *see* Taylour *alias* Wyllyamsone
Wyllyham: Beatrice, of Brandon, I, 99
Wyllymot: Thomas, of Lavenham, I, 1485
Wymbush (Wymbych, Wymbysch, Wymbyssh):
John, the elder, of Kentford, I, 270
Margery, widow, of Kentford, I, 1110
Stephen, of Buxhall, II, 398
William, of Kentford, I, 44
Wymer (Wymere): John, of Honington, I, 1269
Margaret, of Honington, I, 530
Rose, of Honington, I, *959*
Wynd: Margaret, widow of John, of Pakenham,
I, *1449*
Wyneyeve: Elizabeth, of Troston, II, 386
Wynter: Richard, of Soham (Cambs), II, 525
Wysbyche: John, of Brandon, I, 1433
Wyskyn: Thomas, of Hundon, I, 939

Yakesley: Richard, of Soham (Cambs), I, *1326*
Yardley: John, of Lidgate, I, 1474
Ydeyne: Cecily, of Burwell (Cambs), I, 1357; I, 1475
Yebyswych (Yepisswich): John, of Burgate, I, *976*
    Nicholas, of Burgate, I, 406
Yestas: John, of Thorndon, II, *64*
    Robert, of Mendlesham, II, 774
Yngeram: William, of Stoke by Nayland, I, 544
Yonge (Young): John, of Rickinghall Inferior, II, 506; of Santon Downham, I, 419
    Robert, of Barton Mills, I, *1037*
    Simon, of Rickinghall Superior, I, *579*

You': John, of Lawshall, I, *701*
Yowde: John, the elder, of Haverhill, II, 691
Yungman: Nicholas, of Hopton, I, *621*
Yve: *see* Ive

[*name not given*]: of Feltwell, I, *418*
    of Hecham, I, *475*
    of [*not given*], I, 37; I, *637*

Wills of the Archdeaconry of Suffolk
'Baldwyne' Parts I and II

Index of Place of Residence of Testators

All numbers refer to entries, not pages, in the two Suffolk Records Society volumes (44 and 53). Those numbers in Normal Font refer entries that are testaments and/or wills together with the probate sentence, where it has been added; those in *Italic Font* refer to entries that are solely probate sentences. The Roman numerals I and II denote the two volumes; both begin at number 1.

Acton, I: 259, 289, 404, 813, 1312, 1384, 1385; II: 20, 261, 518, 651
Aldersfield, *see* Wickhambrook
Alpheton, I: *1106*
Ampton, I: 1400; II: *114*, 515, 538
Ashfield, I: *136*; II: 639
Ashfield, Great, I: *218*, 1249, 1258; II: 192, 390, 415
Ashfield, Little, II: 667,
    see also Badwell Ash
Ashley (Cambs), *see* Silverley
Assington, I: 176, 215, 1057; II: 370, 407, 458, 459
Attleton, *see* Wickhambrook

Badlingham (Cambs), *see* Chippenham
Badwell, II: 644
Badwell Ash, I: 96, *339*, 674, 842, 944, 1039, 1342, 1397, 1399, *1491*; II: 527
    see also Ashfield, Little
Ballingdon, I: *147*
Bardwell, I: 55, 78, 97, 212, *451*, *453*, *519*, 583, 858, *1230*, 1231, *1232*, *1275*, 1368; II: 16, 159, 168, 364, 526, 604, 738
Barnardiston, I: *39*, *84*, 85, 249, *536*, 654, 1229, *1488*; II: 598, 655, 677
Barnham, I: 281, 377, 534, *885*, *974*, 983, *1007*, 1078, 1139, *1171*, 1206, *1235*, 1268, *1303*, *1362*; II: 282, 292, 293, 493, 578, 684, 699
Barnham St Gregory, II: *73*
Barnham St Martin, I: 1302; II: 299
Barningham, I: 59, *121*, 124, 159, 807, 889, 954, *955*, 1225, *1226*, 1247, 1248, 1278, *1359*; II: *63*, 338, 411, 452
Barrow, I: *23*, *25*, 57, 187, 290, 291, 471, 488, 495, 693, 890, 1191; II: 62, 136, 152, 502, 530, 531, 600
Barton, Great, I: 40, 294, *1236*; II: 266, 584, 736
Barton Mills, I: 46, 131, *1037*; II: 379, 717
Barway (Cambs), *see* Soham
?Berans, II: *144*

Beyton, I: 52, 1394; II: 572
Bildeston, I: 415, 520, *592*, 680, 744, 895, 982, *1103*, 1125, *1141*, 1486; II: 284, 285, 303, 359, 360, 431, 484, 720, 721, 799
Botesdale, *see* Redgrave
Bottisham (Cambs), I: 1398
Boxford, I: 118, 144, 155, 208, 214, 235, 257, 296, 308, 316, *378*, 380, *403*, *414*, 458, 547, 548, 586, 612, 1089; II: 70, 331, 332, 440
    at the Stone, II: 247
Boxted, I: 205, 1006
Bradfield Combust, I: 407, 412, 1367; II: 710
Bradfield St Clare, I: 848, 867, 1045
Bradfield St George, I: *466*, 611, 662; II: 61, 270, 583, 663, 672, 772
Bradley, Great, I: 193, 368, *568*, *736*, *1196*; II: 56, 642
Bradley, Little, I: *664*, 876, *1430*
Brandon, I: *99*, *141*, *884*, *928*, 1008, 1433; II: 466, 792
Brandon Ferry, II: 377, 776
Brent Eleigh, I: *167*, 375; II: 300
Brettenham, I: *840*, *917*, 1036, *1324*, 1466; II: 298, 322
Brockford, *see* Wetheringsett
Brockley, I: 191, 472, 1390; II: 35, 76, 473
Brome, I: 920, 1158
Bures, I: *274*, *275*, *384*, *477*, *657*, *1135*, *1188*, *1335*
Bures St Mary, I: 317; II: 51, 55, 67, 283, 310, 326, 354, 460, 658, 781
Burgate, I: 406, 787, *976*, *1477*; II: *715*, 718
Burwell (Cambs), I: *66*, *67*, *79*, 150, 237, *244*, 284, 313, 389, *482*, *555*, 556, 682, *697*, 911, 927, *1030*, 1052, 1133, 1162, 1265, 1357, 1475; II: 12, 215, 226, 233, 234, *289*, 509, 512, 514, 550, 551, 626, 631, 632, 643, 732
Bury St Edmunds, I: 279

Buxhall, I: 90, *465*, 1065, *1366*, 1393; II: 383, 398, 404, 591

Cavendish, I: 80, 83, 776, *946*, 1375; II: 133, 224, 423, 574
Cavenham, I: 95, 387, *987*, *1145*; II: 77
Chelsworth, I: 204, 516, *559*, 629, 1194, *1428*, 1458; II: 50, 154, 267
Cheveley (Cambs), I: *625*, 676, *739*, 792, 822, *1081*, 1082, *1426*; II: 182, 623, 649
Chevington, I: 314, 589, 1410
Chilton, *see* Clare *and* Stowmarket
Chippenham (Cambs), I: *93*, *1100*; II: *124*, *143*, 199, *753*
   Badlingham, I: 440; II: 108, 438
Clare, I: 43, *64*, 112, 149, 260, *642*, *646*, *670*, 832, 833, *915*, *948*, 1010, *1127*, 1218, 1448; II: 26, 46, 148, 155, 276, 456, 662, 687, 815
   Chilton, II: 380
Cockfield, I: *9*, 179, *470*, *607*, *615*, *675*, 899, *1108*, *1175*, 1260; II: *49*, 85, 115, 350, 488, 540
Cookley, *see* Eye
Combs, I: 47, 145, *410*, 601, 609, 660, *743*, *753*, 877, *952*, 1392; II: 169, *200*, 344, 478, 594, 621, 694
Coney Weston, I: *330*, 957, 1497; II: 294, 590
Cornard, I: *1027*, *1177*
Cornard, Great, I: 630, 941, 1149, 1365; II: 729
Cornard, Little, I: 356, *565*
Cotton, I: 400, 409; II: 6, 700
Cowlinge, I: 549, *561*, *730*, 896, 897, 1386; II: 91, 490, 801
Creeting, I: *851*, *1161*, *1294*
Creeting All Saints, I: *283*, 309
Creeting St Peter, I: 20, 209, 665, *998*, 1049; II: 44, 89, 472
Culford, I: 315, *1464*; II: 208, 227

Dalham, I: *450*, 850, *1204*; II: 28, 734
Denham, by Bury St Edmunds, I: 269
Denston, I: *715*, *731*; II: 242, 724, 785
Depden, I: 125; II: 53, 366, 685
Drinkstone, I: *115*, 423, 439, *778*, *922*, 1054, *1056*, 1079, 1253, *1339*; II: 18, 19, 95, 336, 388
   see also Stowmarket

Edwardstone, I: *76*, *196*, 234, 931, 1209, 1223, 1281, 1446, *1455*, 1496; II: 96, 274, 352, 353, 714
Elmsett, I: 1427; II: *71*
Elmswell, I: 397, *445*, *496*, *700*, 725, *855*, 1001, *1112*, *1199*, 1337, *1338*, 1495; II: 116, 318, 519, 603, 605, 660
Elveden, I: 111, *780*, 891, *1211*; II: 185, 731
Eriswell, I: *166*, 352, *751*, *1101*; II: 342

Euston, I: *30*, 535, *985*; II: 755,
Exning, I: 278, 429, 435, *590*, 984, 995, 1128, *1308*, 1480; II: 428, 450
Eye, I: 58, 105, 320, 354, 367, 433, 460, *480*, 481, 623, 624, *707*, *752*, *808*, *886*, *972*, 1293, *1316*, *1318*; II: 2, *3*, 94, *176*, 178, 222, 252, 395, 396, 405, 442, 457
   Cookley, I: *425*, 479

Fakenham, Great, I: 69
Felsham, I: 185, 613, 901, *1452*; II: 137, 173, 329, 369, 417, 532, 533, 557, 647
Feltwell, I: *418*
Finborough, Great, I: 129, 348, 538, 810, 1343; II: 1, 142, 156, 275, 358, 619
Finborough, Little, I: 1180
Finningham, I: *75*, 178, 385; II: 65, 622
Fordham (Cambs), I: *94*, 550, *551*, *839*, 986, 1131, 1277, *1351*, *1442*; II: 60, 187, 602
Fornham, I: *1099*
Fornham All Saints, I: 12, 222, 229, 271, 297, *950*, *994*, 1279; II: 58, 798
Fornham St Genevieve, I: 443, 729, 924, 1153; II: 110, 448
Fornham St Martin, I: 45, 359, 849, 1152, 1233, 1356; II: 497, 705

Gazeley, I: 303, 759, 1344; II: 82, 725
   Higham, I: 1439
Gislingham, I: 958, *970*; II: 343, 476, 800
Glemsford, I: 109, 137, 158, 251, 319, 362, 391, *576*, *644*, *688*, 838, *991*, *1021*, 1068, *1087*, 1246, 1353; II: 21, 100, 163, 164, 262, 316, 317, 504, 508, 528, 564, 628, 640, 742, 751, 752
Great Ashfield, *see* Ashfield, Great
Great Barton, *see* Barton, Great
Great Bradley, *see* Bradley, Great
Great Cornard, *see* Cornard, Great
Great Fakenham, *see* Fakenham, Great
Great Finborough, *see* Finborough, Great
Great Horringer, *see* Horringer, Great
Great Livermere, *see* Livermere, Great
Great Saxham, *see* Saxham, Great
Great Thurlow, *see* Thurlow, Great
Great Waldingfield, *see* Waldingfield, Great
Great Whelnetham, *see* Whelnetham, Great
Great Wratting, *see* Wratting, Great
Groton, I: 529, 812, 816, 843, 1150, *1157*, 1388; II: 117, *254*, 309

Hanchet End, *see* Haverhill *and* Withersfield
Hargrave, I: 297
Harleston, I: 497, *862*, 1306
Hartest, I: 456, 687, 1075, *1136*; II: 422, 690, 807
Haughley, I: 18, 174, 461, *710*, 741, *746*, 775,

795, *966*, 1307, *1406*; II: 25, 180, 313, 324, 511, 547, 569, 706
Haverhill, I: 50, 106, 210, 211, 306, *312*, 490, 491, *523*, 633, *781*, *834*, 968, *1011*, *1012*, 1092, *1147*, *1148*, 1383, 1457; II: *13*, 14, *250*, *341*, 678, 691, 740
  Hanchet End, II: 357, 693
  see also Withersfield
Hawkedon, I: 735, 1203, *1251*; II: 676, 780
Hawstead, I: *100*, 411, 493, 640; II: 39
Hengrave, I: 41, 61
Hepworth, I: 17, 353, 854, 1257; II: 68, 392, 402
Herringswell, I: *704*; II: 485, 719
Hessett, I: 231, 232, *364*, 370, *825*, 857, 933, 1113; II: 113, 746
Higham, *see* Gazeley
Hinderclay, I: *268*, *1198*; II: 795, 802
Hitcham, I: *27*, 51, 110, 151, 177, *265*, *273*, 487, *560*, 712, 772, *791*, 820, 921, *978*, *979*, *1013*, *1047*, *1066*, 1116, 1234, 1459, 1461; II: 43, 75, 181, 196, 211, 444, 587, *674*, 806
Honington, I: 530, 690, 783, *959*, 1269; II: 157, 474, *520*
Hopton, I: *68*, 286, *323*, 331, 347, *621*, 622, 723, 794, 1026, *1178*, 1179, *1214*, 1292, 1332; II: 36, 186, 393, 555, 661, 707
Horringer, Great, I: *436*, 722, *826*; II: 10, 81, 88, 432, 654, 773
Horringer, Little, I: 422, 1291
Hundon, I: 448, *689*, *847*, 939, 967, 1083, *1189*, 1216; II: 42, 78, 79, 160, 301
Hunston, I: 1217; II: 770

Icklingham, I: *581*, 603, 940, 1221, 1472; II: 403, 449, 469, 471, 479, 492, 683,
Icklingham All Saints, I: 1129
Icklingham St James, I: 585, 853; II: 72, 119
Ickworth, I: 139; II: 112, 138, 389, 695, 708, 709
Ingham, I: 227, 963, 1441; II: 368
Ixworth, I: *280*, 321, 335, 357, 366, *372*, *452*, *628*, *829*, *859*, *905*, 961, 1033, *1072*, 1176, *1405*; II: 37, 174, 219, 220, 228, 575, 723, 804
Ixworth Thorpe, I: 101, 827, 828, *1323*, *1396*; II: 69

Kedington, I: *38*, 236, *528*, 572, 681, 1094, 1213; II: *105*, 355, 447
Kennett (Cambs), I: *12*; II: 585
Kentford, I: 44, 270, 762, 894, *1020*, 1110
Kersey, I: 342, 390, 392, 521, 566, 719, *720*, 923, 1067, 1115, *1184*, 1212, 1227, 1228, 1245; II: 92, 153, 595, 701, 767
Kettlebaston, I: 1300; II: 455
Kirtling (Cambs), I: 203, 337, 881, 1348, 1432, 1467, 1468; II: 281, 461, 462, 482, 499, 577, 609, 656

Upend, II: 610
Knettishall, I: 975, *1321*; II: *394*, *441*

Lakenheath, I: 388, 779, 861, *1018*, 1289; II: 245, 384, 399, 633
Undley, II: 246
Landwade (Cambs), I: *627*
Langham, I: 7, 8; II: 207
Lavenham, I: *73*, 86, 102, 126, 130, 161, 164, 172, 263, 298, 299, 329, 350, 355, 376, 402, 416, 446, 454, 462, *510*, 511, 570, 618, 661, *766*, 768, *769*, *804*, 1002, 1048, 1073, *1114*, 1243, 1485; II: 11, 87, 122, 223, 237, 339, 454, 517, 552, 681
Lawshall, I: *140*, 293, *587*, *701*; II: 151, 541, 582, *616*
Layham, I: 197, 334, 639, *1071*, *1336*; II: 54
Lidgate, I: 114, 190, *1028*, 1474; II: 188
Lindsey, I: *292*, 942, 1429
Little Ashfield, *see* Ashfield, Little
Little Bradley, *see* Bradley, Little
Little Cornard, *see* Cornard, Little
Little Finborough, *see* Finborough, Little
Little Horringer, *see* Horringer, Little
Little Livermere, *see* Livermere, Little
Little Saxham, *see* Saxham, Little
Little Thurlow, *see* Thurlow, Little
Little Waldingfield, *see* Waldingfield, Little
Little Whelnetham, *see* Whelnetham, Little
Little Wratting, *see* Wratting, Little
Livermere, I: *483*, *656*, *1086*
Livermere, Great, I: *35*, 116, 180, 182, *405*, 1003, 1195; II: *134*, 241, 599, 760
Livermere, Little, I: 138, 304, 684; II: 118, 129, 653
Long Melford, I: 82, 88, 122, 181, 195, *201*, *202*, *217*, 221, *272*, 300, 474, 517, *532*, *540*, *545*, *668*, 790, 837, 916, *1004*, *1051*, 1064, 1091, 1104, *1105*, 1160, *1167*, *1208*, 1237, *1301*, 1329, 1363, 1369, 1387, 1424, *1425*; II: 45, 52, 162, 206, 346, 363
  see also Melford *and* Melford Tye

Market Weston, I: 295, *935*, *951*, 1250; II: 268, 625, 822
Melford, II: 436, 446, 464, 722, 728, 733, 756, 779
Melford Tye, II: 59
Mellis, I: 369, *484*, *734*, 798, *875*, 1097, 1371; II: 235, 391
Mendlesham, I: 2, 3, 29, 333, *361*, 413, *786*, 799, 932, 1035, *1159*, 1315, *1482*; II: 41, 202, 203, 374, 554, 568, 774, 788, 805, 818
Milden, I: 81, *512*
Mildenhall, I: 65, 119, 120, 219, *220*, 569, 598, 683, 708, 727, *750*, 865, 870, 938, *980*, 1009, 1084, 1117, 1155, 1156, 1219, 1259, 1263, *1286*, 1403, 1404, *1434*, *1435*, 1471,

1481; II: 107, 147, 172, 177, 216, 229, 230, 239, 260, 287, 312, 345, 347, 378, 387, 545, *553*, 611, 629, 635, 636, 638, 650, 664, 668, 735, 754, 766, 768, 819, 827

Naughton, I: *745*; II: 483, 563
Nayland, I: *32*, 108, 142, 192, *200*, *318*, *383*, 573, *666*, *755*, *763*, *815*, 860, *874*, *909*, 1080, *1222*, *1290*, *1314*, 1479; II: 48, 86, 141, 439, 503, 549, 761, 783, 784
Newmarket, I: 28, 54, 379, 399, 499, 574, 716, 724, *732*, 793, 1358, 1463; II: 510, 671
Newton, II: 311, 516, 597
   see also Old Newton
Newton Green, I: 463
Norton, I: *336*, 438, 441, 671, 782, 1313, 1333, 1379, *1380*, 1381, 1465; II: 209, 362, 743
Norton *iuxta* Woolpit, I: *307*, 373
Nowton, II: 291, 296, 812

Oakley, I: *16*, 636, 949, 1005, *1166*, *1476*
Occold, I: *74*, *104*, *250*, 537, *659*, 1165; II: 443, 726
Old Newton, I: 340, 908, 1192, 1296, 1411, 1419; II: 529, 576
   see also Newton
Ousden, I: *163*, 449, *883*, *926*, 1285; II: 335, 696
Oxborough (Norfolk), I: 489

Pakenham, I: *10*, 343, *514*, 821, *887*, *956*, *1017*, 1046, 1255, 1287, *1378*, *1449*; II: 101, *167*, 295
Palgrave, I: *432*, *997*, *1330*, *1349*, *1350*; II: *217*, 221, 251, 618, 688
Polstead, I: *650*, 1484; II: 33, 97, 104, 161, 248
Poslingford, I: *70*, 113, 173, *332*, *524*, *988*, 1190
Preston, I: *761*, *814*, 929, *1111*, *1124*, *1173*, *1282*; II: 145, 190, 716

Rattlesden, I: *123*, 146, *148*, *455*, *558*, *699*, *747*, *765*, *784*, 868, 1031, 1032, *1143*, *1144*, 1310, *1436*; II: 57, 90, 231, 536, 615, 797
Rede, I: 960; II: 400, 682, 686
Redgrave, I: 341, 726, *1015*, *1016*, 1238, *1270*; II: 195, 308, 416, 418, 543, 620, *811*
   Botesdale, I: 252, 325, 344, *401*, *442*, *596*, *925*, 971, 981, 1341, 1354, 1373, *1374*; II: 257, 327, 348, 376, 467, 546
Redlingfield, I: 756
Rickinghall, I: *878*, *989*, *1070*, *1376*
Rickinghall Inferior, I: 393, 900, 1170; II: 194, 365, 367, 500, 506, 522
Rickinghall Superior, I: 194, *579*, 679, 1207, 1271, 1334, 1340; II: 253
Risby, I: 1210
Rishangles, I: 648
Rougham, I: *584*, 1183, 1240, 1297, 1345, 1478; II: 184, 588, 634, 679, 816

Rushbrooke, I: *1205*; II: 127, 191, 470, 535, 558

Santon Downham, I: *371*, 419, *1069*; II: 777, 826
Sapiston, I: 464, *872*, *1059*, *1137*, 1242; II: *288*, 544
Saxham, Great, I: 77; II: 534
Saxham, Little, I: 34, 245, 246, *501*, 1044, 1123; II: 320, 373, 486, 507
Semer, I: 143, *728*, *990*, 1416, *1454*
Shelland, I: 21, 977; II: 697
Shimpling, I: *168*, 184, 830, 1154; II: 494
Silverley (Cambs), I: *1029*, 1473
   Ashley, I: 247, 381; II: 80
Snailwell (Cambs), I: 183, *239*, *240*, *243*, *505*, 588, 702, *703*, *1414*; II: 9, 24, 214, 824
Soham (Cambs), I: 207, 238, 254, 478, 626, 691, *819*, 871, 902, 903, *904*, *953*, 1041, *1085*, 1256, 1298, 1325, *1326*, 1327, *1443*, *1444*, 1483; II: *8*, 204, 232, 277, 278, 279, 382, 397, 524, 525, 744, 748, *749*, 758, 823
   Barway, I: 253, 256, 1319; II: *794*
   Hall Street, II: 659
Somerton, I: 216, 789; II: 125
Stanningfield, I: 233, 431, 531
Stansfield, I: *382*, 507, *695*, *835*; II: 121, 255, *814*
Stanstead, I: 132; II: 22, 463, 614
Stanton, I: 457, 634, 663, 677, 796, *1130*, *1261*, 1299, 1352, 1395; II: 183, 333, 372, 453, 666, 680, 711, 739, 759, 817
Stanton All Saints, I: 802; II: 256, 566
Stoke Ash, I: *223*, 285
Stoke by Clare, I: *437*, *522*, 631, *1185*, *1187*, 1382, 1423; II: *106*, 637, 803, *813*
   Boyton End, I: *526*
Stoke by Nayland, I: 36, 42, *153*, *154*, 189, 301, 324, 365, 544, 546, 610, 638, 930, 992, 1088, 1120, *1283*, 1331, 1347, *1412*; II: 38, 150, 197, 236, 409, 480, 491, 556, 641
Stonham Aspal, II: 809
Stowlangtoft, I: *1322*; II: 445
Stowmarket, I: 19, 53, 103, 152, 288, *386*, 711, 714, *754*, 797, *934*, 943, *999*, *1000*, 1050, 1126, *1138*, *1305*, *1420*, 1421, 1462; II: 103, 109, 139, 325, 381, 421, 468, 501, 521, 592, 645, 648, 665, 669, 689, 750
   Chilton, I: 1134
   formerly of Drinkstone, II: 205
   Gipping, in the parish of St Peter, I: 346,
   St Peter, II: *201*
   Thorney, I: 264, 408, 444, 577, 600, 882; II: 627, 673, 737
Stradishall, I: 426, 571, *669*, 1142; II: 198, 264, 272, 787
Stratford (Middlesex), I: 863
Stuston, I: *156*, *170*, *1163*; II: *165*, 617
Sudbury, I: 26, *31*, 48, 49, 62, 91, 127, 128, 157, 165, 175, 188, 198, 258, 276, 277, 310,

322, 326, 374, 398, 420, 421, 539, 554, 578, *593, 602, 606*, 632, *645, 651, 652*, 667, *686*, 717, 718, 740, *748*, 758, *770*, 800, 803, 805, 818, 864, *898*, 937, *947, 993*, 1058, 1077, 1132, 1168, 1181, *1267*, 1274, *1311*, 1364, *1447*, 1489, 1492, 1493; II: 31, 32, 84, *98*, 189, 212, 259, 271, 290, 306, 307, 408, 425, 434, 465, 505, 596, 607, 652, 670, 698, 702, 727, 782
All Saints, II: 166

Thelnetham, I: 213, *349*, 506, 969, 1063, 1186, 1262, 1355, 1494; II: *132*, 437, 561, 589, 703, 769, 820
Thorndon, I: 117, *241, 242*, 597, 742, 785, 809, 817, *907*, 962, 1090, *1102*; II: *64*, 126, 146, 337, 764, *791*
Thornham, I: *1095, 1445*
Thornham Magna, I: 1, 63, *338*, 771, 788, 1096, 1169; II: 193
Thornham Parva, I: *811*, 1014
Thorpe, I: 1328
Thorpe Morieux, I: *773, 774, 1122*, 1244; II: 17, 131, 238, 351, 613, 712, 713
Thrandeston, I: *71, 199*, 492, *509*, 543, *575, 604, 649, 906, 973, 1062, 1304, 1317*; II: 765
Thurlow, Great, I: *134, 395, 527*; II: 601, 608
Thurlow, Little, I: *567, 866, 1093, 1197, 1413, 1490*; II: 23
Thurston, I: 287, 358, 430, 552, 760, *1407*, 1437, 1440, 1451; II: 74, 265, 321, 414, 548, 560, 606
Thwaite, I: 658, *996*; II: 218, 745
Timworth, I: *225*, 305, 468, 594, 749, *856*, 892, 1074, *1109*, 1201, 1288
Tostock, I: 133, *605, 614*, 836; II: 29, 435, 771, 821
Troston, I: *255*, 599, *694, 1019*, 1174, *1401*; II: 386, 489, 757, 789
Tuddenham, I: *14, 363, 427, 1061, 1460, 1470*; II: 243, 340

Undley, *see* Lakenheath
Upend, *see* Kirtling (Cambs)

Waldingfield, I: *647, 1038, 1360*, 1469
Waldingfield, Great, I: 186, *513*, 541, 643, 1280; II: 158, 225, 305, 424, 537, 675
Waldingfield, Little, I: 92, 171, 582, 1024, 1193, *1487*; II: 30, 83, 349
Walsham, I: *518, 562*; II: 475, 495, 496, 562
Walsham le Willows, I: 169, 672, 767, *1040, 1042, 1043*, 1272, 1370; II: 175, 258, 385, 401, 412
Wangford, I: *1254, 1266*; II: 47, 120, 302, 319
Wattisfield, I: *591, 936*, 945, 964, *1377*, 1409; II: *7*, 240, 273, 542, 741
Wattisham, I: 1346; II: 111, 433
West Stow, I: 56, *698, 1022*, 1309, 1361; II: 304

Westhorpe, I: 5, *206*; II: 4, 102, 361, 477, 775
Westley, I: *4*, 98, *360*, 616, 692, 1220, *1391*; II: 128, 487
Westley *iuxta* Bury St Edmunds, I: 226, *542*
Wetherden, I: 33, 394, *557*, 608, 1182, *1215*, 1295; II: 149, *315*, 334, 451, 573
Wetheringsett, I: 15, 248, 345, 641, 869, *912, 913, 918*, 1023, 1034, *1202*, 1438; II: 280, 559, 593, 778, 796, 810
  Brockford, I: 721, 764, 801, 1417, 1453; II: 5, 581, 763, 810
Whatfield, I: 162; II: 406
Whelnetham, I: 824
Whelnetham, Great, II: 66
Whelnetham, Little, I: *525*, 533, *1025*; II: 93, 130, 413, 523, 825
Whepstead, I: 160, *267*, 351, 417, *888*, 965; II: 135, 179, 314
Wicken (Cambs), I: 1121; II: 427, 513, 747, *793*
Wickham Skeith, I: 22, 24, 87, 228, 705, 706, 879, *880*, 1200, 1252, *1264*, 1273; II: 210, 498
Wickhambrook, I: 302, 459, *473, 653*, 696, 846, 1055, 1418, *1431*, 1450; II: 213, 263, 286, 586
  Aldersfield, I: *737*; II: 99, 808
  Attleton Green, II: 410
Wiston, I: *685*
Withersfield, I: *396, 504, 709*, 893, *914, 1107, 1456*; II: 123, 171, 330, 356, 419, 420, 565
  Hanchet End, II: 692
  see also Haverhill
Wixoe, I: 580
Woodditton (Cambs), I: *135*, 678, *1320*; II: 580, 630, 646, 762
  Saxon Street, I: *428*, 553
Woolpit, I: 11, 60, *107*, 261, 282, 469, *508, 563*, 564, 619, 655, 713, 757, 777, 806, 823, 1172; II: 27, 40, 371, 375, 430, 567, 570, 571, 579, 624, 704, 786
Wordwell, I: *1060*; II: 539, 657
Worlington, I: 89, 311, *1053*, 1119, 1241, 1389; II: 426, 429, 481, 612
Wortham, I: 6, *424*, 595, *733*, 873, 1076, *1140*, 1164, 1224, *1239*, 1372, 1422; II: 34, 170, 269, 323
Wratting, I: *919*
Wratting, Great, I: *447, 1284*
Wratting, Little, I: *266, 1146*
Wyverstone, I: *72, 841*, 1402, *1408*

Yaxley, I: 1276; II: 244, 790

[*place not given*], I: 37, *224*, 230, *262, 327, 328, 434, 467, 475, 476, 485, 486, 498, 500, 502, 503, 515, 617, 620, 635, 637, 673, 738*, 831, *844, 845, 852, 910, 1098, 1118, 1151, 1415*; II: *15, 140, 249, 328*

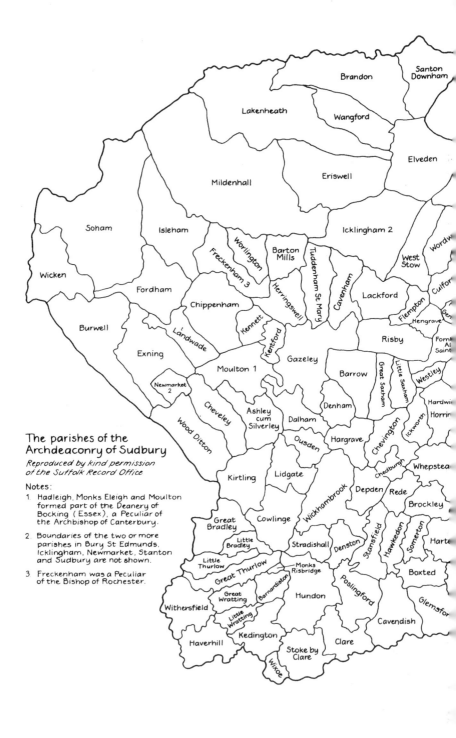

The parishes of the Archdeaconry of Sudbury

Reproduced by kind permission of the Suffolk Record Office

Notes:

1. Hadleigh, Monks Eleigh and Moulton formed part of the Deanery of Bocking (Essex), a Peculiar of the Archbishop of Canterbury.

2. Boundaries of the two or more parishes in Bury St Edmunds, Icklingham, Newmarket, Stanton and Sudbury are not shown.

3. Freckenham was a Peculiar of the Bishop of Rochester.